WORLD AT RISK

WORLD AT RISK

A Global Issues Sourcebook

Second Edition

CQ PRESS

A Division of SAGE
Washington, D.C.

CQ Press
2300 N Street, NW, Suite 800
Washington, DC 20037

Phone: 202-729-1900; toll-free, 1-866-4CQ-PRESS (1-866-427-7737)

Web: www.cqpress.com

Editorial Development by MTM Publishing, Inc.
  Publisher: Valerie Tomaselli
  Associate Editor/Project Manager: Zach Gajewski
  Editorial Coordinator: Ingrid Wenzler
  Illustrator: Richard Garratt

CQ Press
  Acquisitions Editor: January Layman-Wood
  Development Editor: Andrew Boney
  Production Editor: Sarah Fell

Cover design: Anne C. Kerns, Anne Likes Red, Inc.
Cover photograph: 2001 Hurricane Erin, GeoEye Satellite Image
Spine photograph: The Blue Marble courtesy NASA, http://visibleearth.nasa.gov/
Composition: C&M Digitals (P) Ltd.

Data on pp. 2, 3, 16, 133–135 © International Bank for Reconstruction and Development

♾ The paper used in this publication exceeds the requirements of the American National Standard for Information Sciences—Permanence of Paper for Printed Library Materials, ANSI Z39.48-1992.

Printed and bound in the United States of America

13 12 11 10 09   1 2 3 4 5

Library of Congress Cataloging-in-Publication Data

World at risk : a global issues sourcebook. — 2nd ed.
    p. cm.
Includes index.
  ISBN 978-0-87289-919-3 (cloth : alk. paper) 1. International relations. 2. World politics—21st century. 3. Security, International. 4. Environmental policy. 5. Emigration and immigration. 6. Economic history—21st century. 7. Social history—21st century. I. CQ Press.

  JZ1242.W67 2010
  300—dc22

                           2009040270

CONTENTS

ALPHABETICAL LIST
OF CHAPTERS

TABLES, MAPS, AND FIGURES

TABLES

MAPS

FIGURES

CONTRIBUTORS

Tim Allman, Freelance writer, Nottingham, United Kingdom

Suresh C. Babu, Program leader and senior research fellow, International Food Policy Research Institute

David E. Bloom, Chair, Department of Global Health and Population, Clarence James Gamble Professor of Economics and Demography, Harvard School of Public Health

Daan Bronkhorst, Staff writer, Amnesty International, Netherlands

David Canning, Professor of economics and international health, Department of Global Health and Population, Harvard School of Public Health

Bruce Cronin, Associate professor of political science, City College of New York

Melanie Jarman, Freelance writer, Buckfastleigh, Devon, United Kingdom

Edward Kissi, Associate professor, Africana Studies Department, University of South Florida

Ulla Larsen, Fellowship director, Ibis Reproductive Health, Cambridge, Massachusetts

Stephen C. Lubkemann, Associate professor of anthropology and international affairs, George Washington University

Tara Magner, Senior counsel to Senator Patrick Leahy (chairman, U.S. Senate Committee on the Judiciary). The views contained in this chapter do not necessarily reflect the views of Senator Leahy or the U.S. Senate Committee on the Judiciary.

Scott B. Martin, Consultant and lecturer on international affairs, Columbia University and The New School

Erin McCandless, Co-executive editor of the *Journal of Peacebuilding and Development,* adjunct faculty at The New School, and peacebuilding and development consultant

Timothy L. H. McCormack, Australian Red Cross Professor of International Humanitarian Law, University of Melbourne

Richard B. Norgaard, Energy and Resources Group, University of California, Berkeley

Jennifer O'Brien, Researcher, Department of Global Health and Population, Harvard School of Public Health

Clint Peinhardt, Assistant professor of political science, School of Economic, Political, and Policy Sciences, University of Texas at Dallas

Ann E. Robertson, Freelance writer, Robertson Writing, Gaithersburg, Maryland

Mary Hope Schwoebel, Program officer, United States Institute of Peace

J. Peter Scoblic, Executive editor, *The New Republic* and author of *U.S. vs. Them: Conservatism in the Age of Nuclear Terror*

Rachel Shigekane, Director of programs at the Human Rights Center and lecturer in Peace and Conflicts Studies, University of California, Berkeley

Mary Sisson, Freelance writer, Bothell, Washington

Murat Somer, Associate professor of international relations, Koç University, Istanbul

Eric Stover, Faculty director of the Human Rights Center and adjunct professor of law and public health, University of California, Berkeley

Bob Sutcliffe, Independent writer and editor; former professor of development and international economics, most recently for University of Massachusetts, Amherst, and Universidad del Pais Vasco (Euskal Herriko Unibersitatea), Spain

Aili Tripp, Professor of political science and gender & women's studies and director, Center for Research on Gender and Women, University of Wisconsin, Madison

Catherine E. Weaver, Assistant professor of public affairs, Lyndon B. Johnson School of Public Affairs, University of Texas at Austin

Kar-yiu Wong, Professor of economics, University of Washington

PREFACE

Since the publication of the first edition of *World at Risk: A Global Issues Sourcebook,* much has changed on the world stage. In 2009, as the world reels from the effects of a massive economic crisis, the effects of the September 11, 2001, terrorist attacks are still being felt throughout the world. Those attacks, along with the wars in Afghanistan and Iraq, have changed how we think about global issues—not just about international terrorism but about international relations, the global balance of power, and the usefulness of institutions of transnational governance. In addition, issues of environmental protection loom large. In fact, the growing consensus about the threat of climate change surges to the foreground of global security issues, even as planet-wide terrorism and a worldwide economic meltdown are now such urgent concerns in our daily life.

The second edition of *World at Risk: A Global Issues Sourcebook* takes its cue from the expanding complexity and severity of the global crises that we face. In efforts to increase the reader's ability to engage with these complex issues, we have restructured the book, reformulating the first edition's A-to-Z organization to one based on six subject categories: Demographics and Settlement; Economics; Environment; Education, Health, and Welfare; Politics and Governance; and Security. The coverage in these six areas has been enhanced by five completely new chapters to ensure coverage of trends that have become more pressing in recent years: Immigration, International Finance, Transnational Governance, Human Trafficking, and Drug Trafficking.

In addition to its new organization and expanded coverage, the original chapters have been updated, with each issue being analyzed afresh, with new events, trends, research models, and policy paradigms. This enhancement has resulted in substantive revisions, such as analysis throughout the International Criminal Justice chapter of the initial efficacy of the work of the International Criminal Court (ICC), which was officially established in July 2002, and of the "hybrid" tribunals that meld the efforts of the ICC (and other international organs) with domestic legal mechanisms.

The structure of each chapter has remained the same as in the first edition. Each chapter follows a similar sequence, allowing readers to compare the different issues and their components with ease. The discussions move from general analysis to detailed assessments on regional and national levels. After a brief opening introduction describing the importance of that particular issue to the world community, the Historical Background and Development section provides readers with an understanding of the historical context in which the contemporary issue has developed. Next, in the Current Status section, authors review the state of research on the issue and discuss how this research defines the topic; they also address the policies and programs being undertaken in response to the issue's impact. These discussions explore a wide range of thoughts and practices, some of which are controversial. In revised articles, new research and policy trends are fully explored.

The next section, Regional Summaries, which includes a map to supplement the analysis presented, ranges from general assessments to specific examples of how the issue plays out in different areas of the world. The regional categories differ from chapter to chapter because of variations in how researchers approach their subjects. For example, researchers studying environmental issues divide the world into regions that differ from those devised by researchers analyzing economic issues or arms control. The regional summaries and maps have all been updated with new analysis and details.

Next, the Data section provides up-to-date tabulated information to further illustrate the topic under discussion. In most cases, the statistics and other material in this section derive from respected sources; the nomenclature and presentation have been standardized when appropriate. Sources are provided for each table so that readers can refer to the data sets in their entirety. In a few instances, however, the data presented are complete, having been researched and compiled by the author.

The Case Study section brings the issue into sharper focus, with new cases being introduced in many chapters. Here the authors illustrate how the general research and policy parameters being discussed have manifested in specific situations and countries, instructing the reader through example.

Helpful reference sections, fully updated, follow the case studies: short biographies of researchers, policymakers, political leaders, and activists who have had an impact on current research and policymaking; a directory of government agencies, nongovernmental and multinational organizations, and research institutions that includes a mission statement and contact information for each group; and a bibliography of books, articles, reports, and Web sites to guide the reader to the sources used and to augment further investigation. Each chapter closes with extracts from treaties, conventions, and reports crucial to the development of the international community's understanding of and response to the issue at hand. Sources for accessing the full texts are provided in this section or, occasionally, in the bibliography.

A detailed index concludes the volume, offering various points of entry to the issues to assist researchers who approach the book from assorted angles and with different questions in mind. For instance, in researching AIDS, a reader might go directly to the chapter on AIDS or, alternatively, approach the topic through index entries on specific regions or countries, manifestations of the disease, or the economic or social consequences of the pandemic.

The statistical sources are incorporated in the text, and citations for these sources, if written reports, articles, or books, appear in the bibliography. In-text sources for widely accepted data and those that are considered part of the historical record have not been included. Occasionally, authors cite statistics from the tables in the Data section; in these cases, they omit in-text citations. The authors have made every effort to present the most up-to-date information and analysis possible.

Because of the interconnectedness of today's world, some overlap among the issues featured here is necessary. For instance, the chapter Pollution discusses air, water, and terrestrial pollution, while Climate Change explores one particularly troublesome aspect of pollution on a global scale. Some of the issues covered in Health, which offers an overview of the range of concerns arising from health conditions throughout the world, overlap with those in AIDS. Also, each topic lends itself to a cross-disciplinary approach. For example, issues categorized under Education, Health, and Welfare, such as Hunger and Food Security, also relate to issues in Economics, such as Income Inequality and Development Aid, and to issues in Security, such as Ethnic and Regional Conflict and Peacemaking and Peacebuilding. Cross-references help readers navigate these interconnected pathways.

PART I

Demographics and Settlement

IMMIGRATION

Tara Magner

Immigration poses vexing problems for nations around the globe. Every government strives to balance a desire to welcome foreigners, especially those who will contribute to the society and economy, with national security considerations and the protection of native workers. Globalization both helps and hinders in this process. On the one hand, governments can better track the immigrants who cross borders, and businesses can more easily recruit talented foreign labor. Yet, on the other hand, the integration of economies and societies worldwide greatly aids syndicates of smugglers and traffickers who move migrants through irregular channels. Not surprisingly, the dramatic rise of immigration and large-scale population transfers in recent years has become a politically volatile issue in both the destination and source countries.

Historical Background and Development

The movement and migration of peoples is a common feature of human history and far predates our contemporary system of governments. Immigration often followed conquest, as exemplified by Romans' settling in Great Britain in 55 BC and the influx of Turkic tribes into formerly Byzantine lands. Immigration also occurred in response to natural disasters, a dearth of arable land, famine, major economic upheavals, political repression, or the lack of religious freedom.

Governments have alternatively welcomed immigrants with few restrictions and tried with all their might to prevent the newcomers' arrival. National policies on immigration generally reflect the economic conditions in the receiving states and are rooted in labor needs, abundance of resources, and other economic considerations. Social and humanitarian issues are also taken into account by governments that wish to assist refugees and other vulnerable groups.

According to the Library of Congress's Web page, "Immigration/Migration: Today and during the Great Depression," since 1600, over 60 million people have immigrated to the United States. Following the first forays by explorers in the fifteenth and sixteenth centuries, immigration to the New World from Europe began early in the seventeenth century. Settlers and those seeking religious freedom sailed across the Atlantic Ocean to take advantage of vast territory and abundant resources in the New World. The lands that became Canada and the United States were settled by Europeans, who pushed westward until they reached the Pacific Ocean.

Because of its vast territory, the United States became a destination for immigrants from European nations that suffered from a lack of available land or jobs. From the seventeenth through the early nineteenth century, immigrants from the British Isles—English, Welsh, Scottish, and Irish—dominated the flows to the New World. Germans, French, and Dutch were also early migrants. Northern Europeans also emigrated to Australia, New Zealand, South Africa, and to other lands, which they settled as colonies.

A mass influx of migration to the United States occurred from the 1820s to the 1880s, with approximately 15 million immigrants entering the young nation. These immigrants came to work in the developing port cities of New York, Philadelphia, Boston, and Baltimore. Settlements in the Midwest of the United States also grew, especially after the opening of the Erie Canal in 1825, which linked Lake Erie to the Hudson River. Immigrant labor, especially Irish and Chinese, contributed significantly to the building of the transcontinental railroad in the 1850s and 1860s.

The large number of Irish and German Catholics that came to the United States in the early 1800s alarmed nativist segments of the Protestant population, a reaction that reached a peak with the rise of the anti-immigrant and anti-Catholic political party, the Know Nothings, in the 1840s. Nativism and a post–Civil War economic depression contributed to the first restriction on free immigration to the United States, the Chinese Exclusion Act of 1882 (which was not repealed until 1943). The act prohibited the entry of Chinese workers, both skilled and unskilled, to the United States. It also barred Chinese who were already present on U.S. soil from becoming naturalized. The Immigration Act of 1924 further limited immigration by prohibiting the entry of other Asians.

Immigration of non-Asians to the United States was not limited during this time, however, and another surge of European immigrants came to the United States in the late 1800s and early 1900s. Nearly 25 million immigrants from southern and central Europe, primarily from Italy, Greece, Hungary, and Poland, arrived during this period. The Department of State estimates that, of the 25 million total immigrants, between 2.5 and 3 million European Jews also immigrated to the United States during this era. During this wave of migration, the federal government established the first immigration agency, in 1891, and the first inspection centers, including Ellis Island, New York, in 1892.

Restrictive legislation followed World War I, with a 1921 law that set quotas for immigrants from various countries. In 1952, Congress set a cap on total immigration to the United States at just over 150,000 people per year. In later years, country quotas were replaced with preference categories that favored skills in certain industries and family ties to those already in the United States. Due to a complicated calculation scheme, the total number of lawful permanent resident visas (commonly referred to as green cards) available per year in the United States is now between 416,000 and 675,000.

In 1986, Congress passed the Immigration Reform and Control Act, a law regularizing the status of many immigrants who had entered the United States without authorization prior to 1982. The law led to more than 2.5 million undocumented immigrants' gaining legal status. Opponents of increased immigration point to the 1986 law as an offer of amnesty to immigrants who were living in the country unlawfully. In 1996, Congress enacted a restrictive immigration reform bill, increasing border security and refusing immigration status to immigrants who had committed certain crimes, including many minor infractions. The 1996 law also severely restricted access to protections for refugees and asylum seekers.

The terrorist attacks of September 11, 2001, triggered a host of anti-immigrant laws and policies. The nationals of special-interest countries, which were almost exclusively in the Middle East or of majority Muslim population, were required to register with the federal government. In addition, over 5,000 foreign nationals of Arab descent or the Muslim faith were rounded up and held in detention until they were cleared by the Federal Bureau of Investigation, a process that typically took weeks or months. In the end, not one of those arrested in the sweeps was convicted of a terrorism-related charge.

Through the 2000s, with the U.S. government's lawful immigration program backlogged, and with the undocumented immigrant population growing by as many as 800,000 people per year, pressure built among the immigrant and business communities to pursue a comprehensive reform of the immigration laws. In both 2006 and 2007, Congress attempted to pass broad-based immigration reform legislation, including the regularization of the status of the undocumented population, increased availability of temporary worker visas, the expansion of border security, and the elimination of green card–processing backlogs. Political divisions prevented the enactment of a bill in both 2006 and 2007. In the 2008 presidential election, both major party candidates spoke of the need for reform. Since taking office in January 2009, President Barack Obama has reiterated his support for Congress to enact a comprehensive immigration reform package.

Europe has also been a primary destination region for migration and, like the United States, has traditionally struggled with how to manage lawful and unlawful migration. Countries such as the United Kingdom and France have been destination countries for many but especially for the nationals of their former colonies. Spain, Italy, and Malta have attracted tens of thousands of migrants who venture across the Mediterranean Sea from Africa to reach southern Europe's long coastline. Leading European destination states, such as France and the United Kingdom, have tended to favor highly skilled immigrants and students in their lawful immigration programs, while other states have sought a wider array of skilled and unskilled workers for health care, domestic services, agriculture, and construction.

The integration of these immigrants, whether lawfully admitted or not, has posed significant challenges to receiving states. In France, the egalitarian national ethos calls for all people, immigrant and native-born, to be considered French. Despite these well-intentioned policies, immigrants have strained to integrate fully into French society. Social policies initiated in the 1960s and 1970s place immigrants in public housing in the suburbs of major cities, which have the unintended effect of isolating the immigrants from other segments of French society. The projects now primarily house poor immigrants from North Africa, sub-Saharan Africa, and Turkey. Residents of French immigrant public housing are characterized as young in age, with approximately 40 percent under the age of twenty, and experience unemployment rates reaching as high as 20–30 percent.

Tensions mounted in 2004 when France passed a law that banned students from wearing religious symbols in the public schools. Although the law extended also to Jewish yarmulkes and Christian crosses, the law was widely viewed as a ban on Muslim girls' wearing headscarves in school. Then in 2005, riots broke out in the Paris suburbs that lasted three weeks. These protests consisted primarily of second-generation immigrant youth who alleged they were subjected to harassment by the police, racial discrimination, and socioeconomic repression. The French government responded by reaching out to suburban residents, but riots broke out again in 2006.

The United Kingdom also has faced policy and cultural challenges with its immigrant population. Those accused of perpetrating the London train bombings of 2005 were mainly raised in immigrant communities in the United Kingdom. Some were native-born, while others were naturalized British citizens who originally entered the United Kingdom as asylum seekers. Even before the July 2005 bombings, however, the government of Prime Minister Tony Blair had introduced legislation restricting immigration and limiting the rights of asylum seekers. Since the middle of the decade, both France and the United Kingdom have enacted new laws enforcing tighter border security, calling for the full integration of lawful immigrants, and explicitly favoring new immigrants in highly skilled visa categories. Whether these new laws will effectively redress past failures of integration in France and the United Kingdom remains to be seen.

Current Status

The world's population is approximately 6.7 billion. In 2004, one-sixth of that population—over a billion people—lived in thirty countries with high levels of per capita income. Those thirty counties hold approximately 80 percent of the world's wealth. The remaining five-sixths of the world's population—about 5.5 billion people—live in nations with a small share of the wealth. Not surprisingly, much of the world's migration consists of people from poorer countries trying to reach wealthier ones (see POPULATION; map, p. 12).

Research

The International Organization for Migration (IOM) estimated the total number of migrants worldwide at 191 million in 2005, with approximately one-third of these moving from southern countries to northern ones. Although many migrate to a foreign land to join family, to study, or to flee violence or persecution, most immigration is rooted in economic considerations. Individuals, regardless of skill level, generally migrate to obtain a higher standard of living than that available in their home country or to raise their children in a nation with opportunities for the future. For the most part, migrants are evenly split between men and women.

Where individuals choose to migrate depends on a number of factors. Immigrants tend to move from less-developed to more-developed nations, frequently following employment or economic opportunities. Language, cultural similarities, shared history, or colonial ties also play a significant role.

The governments of the destination countries strongly favor highly skilled immigrants, inviting them to enter as students or professionals and often offering long-term visas with the chance to eventually settle permanently. Of the pool of people living outside their country of origin who have a college education or higher, Asians make up 35 percent, with Europeans a close second at 34 percent; 23 percent of these immigrants are from the Western hemisphere, and 7 percent are from Africa. Low-skilled workers are critical to certain countries' labor requirements, but such workers who immigrate lawfully are often limited to short-term visas and expected to return home at the end of the work contract.

Irregular migration is the movement of people across borders without authorization, such as with those who cross the Mexican-U.S. border through the desert, escaping the notice of Border Patrol agents. This term also applies to those who previously held a valid immigration status, such as a visa, that expired. Irregular migration is common worldwide, with undocumented immigrants working mainly in industries with lower skill requirements, such as construction, hospitality, and agriculture.

Although exact data are difficult to obtain for this population, the International Labour Organisation (ILO) estimates that 10–15 percent of all migrants have an irregular or undocumented status. These migrants move not only from south to north but also within regions. For example, Africans from throughout the continent have migrated south to work in the mining industries in South Africa. In Asia, Thailand and Malaysia are the destination counties for undocumented migrants working in manufacturing and other low-skill industries.

Irregular migration presents unique challenges for governments, which strive to control the entry and exit of non-nationals. Borders are frequently porous and difficult to patrol. Smugglers and traffickers respond to increased border security by devising new schemes to evade inspection, often putting their human cargo at grave risk. In the United States, as security has increased on the southern border with Mexico, immigrants and smugglers have developed new routes, crossing through remote areas of the desert. All too often, immigrants trying to reach industrialized nations are hidden in containers on ships or in trucks, frequently without adequate air, food, or water. Irregular migration at sea frequently ends in tragedy as unseaworthy boats operated by smugglers sail overloaded with no room for safety equipment or life vests. Despite the dangers, immigrants continue to migrate in search of better economic, political, or personal conditions (see HUMAN TRAFFICKING).

The developing world is a quickly growing source of well-educated people. However, many of these professionals choose to leave and settle elsewhere. With so many immigrants seeking to settle in comparatively wealthy industrialized nations, an inevitable "brain drain" occurs in their countries of origin. Ten percent of the highly skilled individuals from the developing world live in Europe, North America, or Australia; between 30 and 50 percent of those trained in science and technology who are originally from nations in the developing world now live in the developed world. Globalization and the ease of recruiting through modern technology has created a professional class whose credentials open doors around the world (see LABOR AND EMPLOYMENT).

Remittances, the funds sent by immigrants to family members in their home countries, have emerged as a major force in the economies of those native lands, with a global impact of $300 billion per year. This amount is equal to three times the amount donated to developing nations through foreign aid programs (see DEVELOPMENT AID). Approximately 80 percent of those funds are quickly spent by the recipients, adding to family budgets for basic needs, consumer goods, and longer-term investments in home improvements. Remittance funds help reduce poverty in the recipient countries, influencing the actions of governments in planning for domestic spending. They can also diminish the amount of funds lost to government corruption because the transfer of funds is direct from person to person. India, China, and Mexico each received over $24 billion in remittances in 2006. The Philippines, a much smaller country by population, received $15 billion, explaining in part why its government heavily promotes the emigration of overseas workers. In several countries, remittances now equal a sizable share of the national gross domestic product (GDP), including Moldova (32 percent), Haiti (23 percent), and Lebanon (22 percent). The global economic downturn is expected to reduce remittances to some degree. Mexico saw remittances climb each year of the 2000s until 2007, when the rate rose just 1 percent over the year before. In 2008, for the first time, remittances to Mexico fell. However, a decrease of 3.6 percent from 2007 still left Mexico with $25 billion in remittances.

The integration of immigrants into the destination countries poses a challenge as the governments of the receiving countries struggle with competing goals. These governments want to recruit permanent residents from a highly educated immigrant population and invite those individuals to eventually naturalize. At the same time, governments typically want lower-skilled immigrants to come and go in an orderly manner. Even so, governments often extend the time periods of temporary worker programs, indirectly encouraging immigrants to put down roots in the host country. Employers come to rely on good workers who have mastered a trade, even in what are generally described as lower-skilled industries such as agriculture or manufacturing. Inevitably, many of these immigrants build ties to the host nation, purchasing property, opening businesses, marrying, and having children. The undocumented population poses its own unique problems, with immigrants' increasingly integrating into the host communities without gaining any broad legal rights.

Policies and Programs

Immigration policies are devised to protect national security and to manage the flow of citizens, visitors, and workers entering a country. All nations strive to control their borders and closely regulate immigration. Negotiating immigration policies at the national and regional levels poses vexing challenges, however, with debates over which categories of immigrants to allow entry, how many per year, and for what period of time. Economics and politics both influence these debates. Certain industries seek increased immigrant labor, typically arguing that native workers are not available in adequate supply or that the wages demanded by native workers are too high for the market to bear. Some assert that immigrants contribute to economic growth, buying homes and establishing businesses. Other segments of society argue that native workers must be protected from the downward pressure on wages created by a supply of immigrant labor willing to work for lower pay.

Destination countries frequently establish caps and quotas on the number of immigrants, with those limits set through a political process. U.S. policy is rooted in family-based immigration, with separate programs for temporary worker visas and employment-based permanent residency. Some argue that a focus on family immigration, and not on skill-based immigration, has diluted the quality of the immigrant pool. Canada, in contrast, devised a point system that favors highly skilled immigrants. Other nations, including Australia, Hong Kong, the United Kingdom, and New Zealand, have followed suit.

Debates over national immigration policy can become highly politicized and sometimes affect the outcome of elections. For example, in fall 2001, after several boats carrying asylum seekers from Afghanistan and other nations tried to reach Australia, the conservative majority party in that country severely restricted migration and limited protections for asylum seekers. Soon after, in December 2001, the Australian conservative leadership won reelection.

Debates over immigration policy in the United States are heated and highly complex. Positions do not break down along clear party lines, and parochial interests carry significant influence. One politician's constituency may depend on immigrant labor for local industries, such as agriculture, hospitality, tourism, and manufacturing. Another's constituency may fear that immigrant labor will take jobs from American workers or drive down wages.

The political debates over immigration in the United States raged from 2005 through 2008, and the impact on elections was mixed. Polling suggests that pro-immigrant candidates generally did not lose elections based on their immigration positions; at the same time, anti-immigration candidates often lost their races. Both presidential candidates in 2008 had previously supported increased immigration and a program to regularize the status of undocumented immigrants. Both pledged to work for immigration reform if elected. Because Latinos are the fastest growing demographic group in the United States, the two leading political parties in the United States vied for these votes. In 2008, Latino voters, who represented 9 percent of the electorate and approximately 11 million votes, flocked to the Democratic candidate Barack Obama over the Republican John McCain 67 to 31 percent. Despite McCain's prior support for immigration reform, the Republican Party was generally viewed by Latinos as responsible for blocking immigration reform legislation in the mid-2000s. This voting trend has been noted by politicians of all stripes and may influence the positions of both parties in the future.

Increasingly, sending and receiving countries have established bilateral or multilateral agreements to regulate migration, generally focused on labor but occasionally based on historical ties or geographic proximity. The harmonization of migration policy across the European Union is the most expansive such agreement. Citizens of EU member states are able to cross borders freely and work lawfully in other member states. As part of an effort to establish a free-trade zone, the Association of Southeast Asian Nations (ASEAN) has committed to protecting migrant workers, a recognition of the very large numbers of Asians who migrate within the region to seek employment.

Enforcement is a challenge at every level of immigration policy implementation. Governments strive to maintain open trade routes and ease of travel for businesspeople and law-abiding citizens. Yet they must simultaneously protect their borders from smuggling and trafficking networks, criminal syndicates, and terrorists. After the September 11, 2001, attacks in the United States and subsequent train bombings in Europe, the prevention of terrorism became a major influence on immigration policy in the early 2000s.

Nations struggle to prevent migration through their unprotected borders. The United States responded to the unauthorized crossings of its southern border by ordering the construction of a seven-hundred-mile fence in 2006. The project faced intense criticism from immigrant advocates, local landowners, and environmentalists. Other nations have struggled to prevent migrants from reaching their shores by sea. Irregular migration by sea continues across the Mediterranean from West and North Africa to Spain, Italy, and Malta. The use of such dangerous routes has been curtailed by increased enforcement at sea, but approximately 200,000 people still seek to enter Europe in this manner each year.

To address the persistent problem of undocumented immigration, destination countries occasionally allow unauthorized migrants to regularize, or legalize, their status. Although controversial among politicians and the public, regularization undermines the informal economies that support irregular migration and leave workers vulnerable to low wages and often lead to the abuse of workers. Destination countries such as Greece, Italy, Spain, and Portugal have all engaged in regularization as their undocumented populations have grown. With its 2008 population of approximately 12 million undocumented people, the United States has tried repeatedly to enact laws that would regularize a sizable percentage of that population but has failed. Critics of regularization argue that offering legal status to an undocumented population will only encourage more irregular migration.

Given the broad scope and impact of global migration, one might assume that international laws and treaties exist to govern mass movements. An international regime for migration, however, is far from well established. International law gives individuals the right to leave their native lands and to seek asylum in others, but it does not necessarily give them the right to reside in foreign countries. No governing body has enforcement authority for migration akin, for example, to the World Trade Organization.

The majority of international conventions that address migration are protection-based, focusing on refugees or trafficking victims, or labor-based, focusing on protecting the rights of migrant workers. Most leading destination countries for immigrants have not ratified migrant worker conventions and no major developed nation has ratified the International Convention on the Protection of the Rights of All Migrant Workers and Members of Their Families, a convention adopted by the United Nations in 1990 to bring migrant workers under the protection of an international human rights regime (see Document 1). In 2005, the Global Commission on International Migration, an ad hoc body charged with proposing a framework for global migration, recommended the creation of a global agency charged with "economic migration," which would encompass economic motivations for migration that are broader than migrant labor, including family migration and other considerations. Until such an agency is created, however, most efforts to globally regulate migration will be left to regional entities or bilateral agreements that focus on temporary workers.

Regional Summaries

The Americas

North and South America together host over 51 million immigrants. More than 44 million of these are in North America, with over 38 million in the United States. Immigration to North America has long been dominated by both regular and irregular flows into the United States. South America, on the other hand, experiences intraregional migration, as well as increasing emigration to Western Europe.

The United States imposes strict annual limits on the number of permanent resident visas available for lawful entry. As a result, many immigrants enter with an undocumented status or overstay a visa in order to work primarily in lower-skilled jobs in construction, agriculture, and the service industries. From 2000 to 2004, approximately 800,000 undocumented immigrants entered the United States each year, but that number appears to have declined, with roughly 500,000 per year entering between 2005 and 2008. Whether this decrease is due to the weak U.S. economy, which reduced the number of jobs available in immigrant-heavy industries, or to heightened enforcement is subject to debate.

Canada remains a destination country for immigration, with approximately 6 million immigrants representing nearly 19 percent of its population. Canada relies on a point system for lawful migration, assigning values to certain equities and then granting visas to qualified applicants. Canada is also a country of emigration, primarily to the United States.

Mexico is a major source of U.S. immigrants, with nearly 11 million Mexican nationals living in the United States; 90 percent of Mexicans who emigrate go to the United States. Mexico also serves as a transit country for Central Americans, Asians, and Africans attempting to reach the United States.

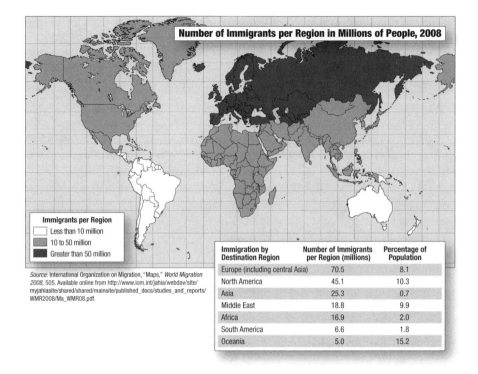

Number of Immigrants per Region in Millions of People, 2008

Immigrants per Region
- [ ] Less than 10 million
- 10 to 50 million
- Greater than 50 million

Source: International Organization on Migration, "Maps," *World Migration 2008*, 505. Available online from http://www.iom.int/jahia/webdav/site/myjahiasite/shared/shared/mainsite/published_docs/studies_and_reports/WMR2008/Ma_WMR08.pdf.

Immigration by Destination Region	Number of Immigrants per Region (millions)	Percentage of Population
Europe (including central Asia)	70.5	8.1
North America	45.1	10.3
Asia	25.3	0.7
Middle East	18.8	9.9
Africa	16.9	2.0
South America	6.6	1.8
Oceania	5.0	15.2

South America experiences a good deal of intraregional migration, with most immigrants entering Argentina, Venezuela, and Brazil. South Americans also emigrate outside the continent to destination countries such as Spain and Portugal.

Europe

As of 2005, Europe hosted over 44 million immigrants. With an aging population and shrinking population growth, Europe is increasingly dependent on immigrant labor. It is also a destination region for highly educated immigrants and students.

The expansion of the European Union, now with twenty-seven member countries, led to considerable intraregional immigration in the 2000s, with large flows from new EU members in central and Eastern Europe migrating to Western Europe. Germany, France, and the United Kingdom are the leading destination countries in terms of the number of immigrants. Spain and Italy show the highest rates of growth in their immigrant populations. The majority of immigrants to Western Europe are Poles, followed by Slovaks, Lithuanians, and Latvians. However, as the global economy began to suffer, many migrants returned to their home countries. By late 2008, approximately half of the EU nationals that had emigrated within the region had returned home.

Russia is both a source and a destination country for immigrants. Russians most often emigrate to central and Western Europe, while central Asians commonly migrate to Russia. The Russian government has experienced a significant influx of migration since the breakup of the Soviet Union. Russia has enacted laws to regularize the status of its immigrant population, and estimates of how many are currently present vary widely, ranging from 5 to 10 million. In 2008, an estimated 2.5 million Uzbeks, 1 million Tajiks, and 800,000 Kyrgyz nationals immigrated to Russia, some with lawful and some with unlawful status. Abuse of the lower-skilled immigrant population is rampant, especially as economic conditions worsen and the jobs that these immigrants originally came to fill are no longer available.

Europe is also a leading destination for irregular migration. Smuggling routes carry economic migrants and asylum seekers overland from East to West or through North Africa and then overseas to Spain and Italy.

Middle East and North Africa

The Middle East and North Africa represent the widest array of immigration characteristics, serving as source, destination, and transit countries. The Gulf States are now the third most common destination region in the world, after North America and Europe.

The Middle East and Gulf States have emerged as major destination countries for temporary contract migrant laborers. In 2005, the Middle East hosted 19 million migrants, with more than 9 million in the Gulf States. In the United Arab Emirates, 85 percent of the workforce is made up of immigrants. Many of the workers in the Gulf States come from other parts of the Middle East and Asia, such as India, Pakistan, Egypt, and Yemen, but they also include nationals from Nepal, Bangladesh, and the Philippines. These contract workers typically have no right to permanent residence, have no ability to bring family members with them, and must return home at the end of the work period. Nonetheless, many return multiple times on subsequent contracts. The Gulf States attract highly skilled workers, such as engineers, doctors, lawyers, and academics, as well as lower-skilled immigrants in construction, hospitality, and domestic services. Women represent approximately 30 percent of the guestworkers in the Gulf States.

Other areas of the Middle East also host sizable immigrant populations. The Iraq War displaced millions, with over 1 million refugees fleeing to Syria and half that number fleeing to Jordan. Meanwhile, 45 percent of the population of the Palestinian Territories and 18 percent of the population of Lebanon are non-natives. Israel invited foreign-born Jews to emigrate, resulting in the relocation of Ethiopian and Soviet Jews. Israel also hosts Asian migrant workers from the Philippines, Thailand, and China, who work in home health, agriculture, and construction, respectively (see REFUGEES AND FORCED MIGRANTS).

The North African nations of Libya and Tunisia have long served as transit countries for African immigrants making their way to Europe. Asians from Bangladesh, China, India, and Pakistan have increasingly joined Africans in seeking passage from North Africa to Europe. Meanwhile, immigrants in transit, numbering in the tens of thousands in certain port cities, become de facto residents as they wait for an opportunity to cross the Mediterranean.

Sub-Saharan Africa

Africa is a source of emigrants, but with the exception of South Africa, it is less often a destination for immigrant flows. Of all the world's regions and continents, Africa has the lowest rate of immigrant growth. It also receives the lowest rates of remittances from immigrants working abroad.

Immigration in Africa is mainly intracontinental, with migrants spread across regions. The most significant destination country on the continent is South Africa, which hosts approximately 1 million immigrants. Many of these enter with irregular status seeking employment or fleeing unrest in their countries of origin.

Immigrants in Africa also move to regional centers or to relatively peaceful and prosperous countries. Côte d'Ivoire is the leading destination country in West Africa, followed by Ghana and Nigeria.

Political and ethnic strife continue to dominate many parts of Africa, producing the highest concentration of internally displaced persons (IDPs) in the world, 13 million as of the end of 2007. Somalia, Ethiopia, and Kenya are the leading African sources of people seeking asylum outside the continent.

The brain drain is a serious problem across Africa because highly educated people frequently emigrate to Europe or the United States. However, South Africa is a magnet for certain skilled workers on the continent, with doctors and nurses from other countries emigrating to South Africa in increasing numbers.

Central and South Asia

The nations of central and South Asia are dominated by emigration to both the West and East; considerable intraregional migration also occurs. Nearly 9 million Asian workers reside in the Middle East, with Bangladesh, India, and Pakistan supplying the majority of laborers for infrastructure projects in the Gulf States.

India's vast population includes approximately 5.7 million migrants, representing only 0.5 percent of its total population. India is also a country of emigration, with large numbers leaving for Australia, Canada, and the United States. India sent approximately 80,000 students to the United States in the mid-2000s.

Similarly, Nepal is both a country of immigration and emigration. Over 800,000 international migrants live in Nepal, and approximately 465,000 Nepalese live in the Gulf States and more than 200,000 live in other parts of Asia, Europe, and the United States. One out of every eleven Nepalese adult males works abroad, sending home remittances that have helped decrease Nepal's poverty rate.

Central Asians have migrated in large numbers to Russia, as already described. Kazakhstan is a magnet for migration because of its relative wealth compared to other central Asian states. Yet migrants there complain of violent attacks, substandard working conditions, limited freedom of movement, and uncertain compensation.

Far East and Pacific Rim

Asia has long been a source of immigrants, but is also emerging as a destination for intraregional migration. An estimated 25 million Asian migrants live and work outside their countries of origin. They are spread around the world, with approximately 7.5 million of the 25 million residing in foreign lands without lawful status. The city-state of Singapore boasts the highest number of immigrants per capita, at forty-three migrants per one hundred inhabitants. China experienced a massive internal movement of migrants—with estimates ranging from 130 to 200 million—from rural villages to industrial centers in the mid-2000s as the demand for factory workers surged. With the economic downturn in 2009, 20 million of those workers were let go and returned to their villages.

Asia sends many of its highly skilled immigrants to the United States, Canada, Australia, and Europe, but certain countries have enticed their nationals to return home in a "reverse brain drain." Hong Kong and Singapore, in particular, have attracted highly skilled workers to high-tech and other professional centers.

Middle- and lower-skilled workers often leave the region to work in the Middle East or Gulf States in health care, construction, domestic and hospitality industries (see the Middle East and North Africa regional summary). Irregular workers often move within the region, such as the majority of the millions of Myanmar nationals working in Malaysia and Thailand.

Data

Table 1 Immigration by Destination Country

Destination country	Number of immigrants per country (millions)	Immigrants as percentage of population
United States	38.3	12.9
Russia	12.0	8.4
Germany	10.1	12.3*
Ukraine	6.8	14.7
France	6.5	10.1*
Canada	6.1	18.9
India	5.7	0.5
United Kingdom	5.4	8.8*
Spain	4.8	11.8*
Australia	4.1	20.3
Pakistan	3.3	2.1
Hong Kong	3.0	42.6
Italy	2.5	4.3*
Kazakhstan	2.5	16.9
Côte d'Ivoire	2.3	13.1
Jordan	2.2	39.0
Japan	2.0	1.6
Iran	1.9	2.8
Singapore	1.8	42.6
Palestinian Territories	1.7	45.4

Source: International Organization on Migration, "Regional Overviews," *World Migration 2008,* available at: http://www.iom.int/jahia/webdav/site/myjahiasite/shared/shared/mainsite/published_docs/studies_and_reports/WMR2008/Ro_WMR08.pdf. Percentages marked by * were calculated by using population numbers "CIA Factbook 2008," available at: https://www.cia.gov/library/publications/the-world-factbook/.

Table 2   Remittances to Developing Nations by Region, 2006–2008

Region	2006 (in billions of US$)	2007 (in billions of US$)	2008 (in billions of US$)
East Asia and Pacific Rim	53	58	62
Europe and central Asia	39	51	54
Latin America	57	61	61
Middle East and North Africa	27	32	35
Asia (South)	40	44	51
Sub-Saharan Africa	13	19	20
Total	228	265	283
Percentage of GDP	2.1	2.0	1.8

Source: Dilip Ratha et al., "Outlook for Remittance Flows 2008–2010," Migration and Development Brief, World Bank, November 2008, available at: http://siteresources.worldbank.org/INTPROSPECTS/Resources/334934-1110315015165/MD_Brief8.pdf.

Note: GDP, gross domestic product.

Table 3   Leading Remittance-Recipient Countries, 2008 (billions of US$)

Receiving country	Amount of remittances
India	30.0
China	27.0
Mexico	23.8
Philippines	18.7
Poland	11.0
Nigeria	10.0
Egypt	9.5
Romania	9.0
Bangladesh	8.9
Pakistan	7.1

Source: Dilip Ratha et al., "Outlook for Remittance Flows 2008–2010," Migration and Development Brief, World Bank, November 2008, available at: http://siteresources.worldbank.org/INTPROSPECTS/Resources/334934-1110315015165/MD_Brief8.pdf.

Case Study—The Philippines
Encouraging Citizens to Work Abroad

In the nineteenth and twentieth centuries, governments commonly encouraged their citizens to migrate to foreign lands in an attempt either to expand colonial interests or to overcome shortages of land and resources at home. Such official policies are less common today. Many nations quietly depend on remittances from abroad to offset official expenditures on social programs, but few governments aggressively promote emigration as a mechanism for increasing development and reducing poverty.

The Philippines, however, actively encourages its citizens to work overseas and send remittances home. This program was initiated in the 1970s and was expanded in subsequent years. In 2007, approximately 10 percent of Filipinos lived abroad; one in seven Filipino workers is employed overseas. The Philippines offers a provocative example of emigration policy that has transformed the nation and its culture in extraordinary ways.

With over 6 million Filipino citizens working overseas and at least 3 million permanent émigrés, the Philippines has a larger portion of its population living overseas than any other nation. These emigrants, who live in 170 different countries, send home $18 billion per year in remittances. The Philippines has a population of approximately 90 million people and a per capita income in 2007 of $1,620. The remittances sent home by Filipino overseas workers amount to over $18 billion per year, boosting the income of family members who remain in the Philippines.

The majority of Filipinos working overseas are in the Middle East and Asia, with large numbers of Filipinos in Saudi Arabia, United Arab Emirates, Japan, Hong Kong, and Taiwan. Male workers predominate in construction and hospitality. Women workers (60 percent of the overseas workers) are commonly nurses or work in domestic service; in Asia, many women work in "entertainment," a euphemism for the sex industry. Overseas workers generally cannot bring family with them. In the Gulf States, they are often monitored closely to prevent any fraternization with locals or even other immigrant workers.

The government of the Philippines enthusiastically supports the émigré workers, calling them "heroes." Recognizing that the abuse of temporary immigrant workers is rampant in many destination countries, the Filipino government established the Overseas Worker Welfare Administration, an agency charged with protecting the rights of Filipinos working overseas. The Philippines also enacted a law specifically addressing overseas-worker safety. Still, some argue that the government is not doing all it can. For example, female workers, in both domestic services and the "entertainment" industry, continue to be highly vulnerable to exploitation or virtual slavery.

The Philippines' experience of promoting emigration to serve national goals is somewhat analogous to a policy that has been promoted on a much broader scale by one economist. Lant Pritchett proposes that immigrant guest-worker programs be expanded greatly, placing up to 16 million workers from the world's poorest nations in jobs in the world's wealthiest. The workers would take temporary positions without the ability to bring family to the destination country. They would not be offered a path to permanent immigration status or citizenship in the host country. They would, in effect, do what so many Filipinos do: work on a time-limited contract, send remittances home, eventually return home, and then possibly leave again on a new contract.

Critics charge that Pritchett's proposal would reduce wages in the destination countries, encourage the brain drain from developing nations, and erode the ties that bind families together by promoting separation. Recognizing the social costs, Pritchett argues that individuals from poor countries should be able to decide for themselves whether they are willing to make sacrifices for the financial benefits that would accrue. He believes this expansion of guest-workers worldwide could produce annual gains of $300 billion to the citizens of poor countries. In 2005, the World Bank estimated that if wealthy nations increased incoming immigration by 3 percent, those nations would generate $51 billion in growth worldwide in capital returns and lower costs of production.

Whatever one thinks of such proposals, the cultural shift in the Philippines is undeniable. Recipients of immigrant remittances benefit from increased income, yet families are shaped by the absence of parents, siblings, and spouses who are working overseas for long stretches of time. Overseas workers commonly accept one contract after another, so they are effectively away for years with only occasional short visits home. The costs and benefits are tangible to all, yet economic motivations continue to drive Filipinos overseas.

Biographical Sketches

Aderanti Adepoju is an eminent scholar of African migration currently serving as the chief executive of the Human Resources Development Center at the University of Lagos. A Nigerian economist and demographer, Adepoju has assisted several African nations in the development and implementation of population and development programs. Adepoju was a pioneer in developing population and labor policy in Africa for the International Labour Organisation and was previously president of the Union for African Population Studies.

Manuel Orozco is senior associate and director of remittances and development at the Inter-American Dialogue, a research institute in Washington, D.C. He focuses his research, policy analysis, and advocacy efforts on global flows of remittances sent home by immigrants to family in their home countries. He also studies migration and development worldwide. Orozco encourages the use of remittances as a development tool and is studying new modes of remittance, such as through hometown associations in countries of origin.

Demetrios G. Papademetriou is the president of the Migration Policy Institute, a research institute focused on international migration. He is the convener of the Transatlantic Council on Migration and the Athens Migration Policy Initiative, a task force that advises EU member states on immigration issues. Papademetriou advises officials in the United States, Canada, Mexico, and Europe. His nonpartisan institute has released numerous influential studies and recommendations for immigration policy reform in the United States and other leading destination countries.

Lant Pritchett is professor of the Practice of International Development at the Kennedy School of Government at Harvard University. Pritchett is a consultant to Google.org, a fellow of the Center for Global Development, and co-editor of the *Journal of Development Economics,* among other positions. He is the co-author of numerous World Bank reports on development, poverty, and foreign aid. In 2006, Pritchett published *Let Their People Come,* which argues for vastly expanded programs for temporary migrant workers.

Dilip Ratha is a senior economist at the World Bank who in 2003 produced the first major study on the size and impact of remittances. His work stunned the immigration and development communities, which had not previously studied remittances as a major force in international finance. He continues to research and publish on remittances as well as on development and poverty alleviation. A native of a small hamlet in the state of Orissa, India, Ratha has seen the effect of remittances on his own family and his village.

Directory

Centre on Migration, Policy and Society (COMPAS), University of Oxford, 58 Banbury Road, Oxford, United Kingdom OX2 6QS. Telephone: +44 (0) 1865 274711; email: info@compas.ox.ac.uk; Web: http://www.compas.ox.ac.uk.
Research and policy assessment organization that aims to provide a "strategic, integrated approach to understanding contemporary and future migration dynamics"; focused on the United Kingdom and European Union.

Global Commission on International Migration, Rue Richard-Wagner 1, 1202 Geneva, Switzerland. Telephone: +41 22 748 48 50; email: http://www.gcim.org/en/contact.html; Web: http://www.gcim.org/en.
Independent organization launched by the UN and various national governments and charged with establishing the foundation and framework through which a coherent global policy on international migration can be formulated.

Institute for Migration and Ethnic Studies, University of Amsterdam, Het Binnen Gasthuis, Room 0.25, Oudezijds Achterburgwal 237, 1012 DL. Amsterdam, Netherlands. Telephone: +31 20 525 3627; email: t.zijlstra@uva.nl; Web: http://www.imes.uva.nl/index.html.
Interdisciplinary research institute that considers migration and integration within an international and comparative context.

International Organization for Migration (IOM), 17 Route des Morillons, CH-1211 Geneva 19, Switzerland. Telephone: +41 22 717 9111; email: hq@iom.int; Web: http://www.iom.int/jahia/jsp/index.jsp.
Intergovernmental organization with a broad international reach, focused on supporting humane and orderly migration for the benefit of all through services and advice to governments and migrants.

Migration Policy Institute, 1400 16th Street NW, Suite 300, Washington, D.C. 20036. Telephone: (202) 266-1940; Web: http://www.migrationpolicy.org.
Independent think tank committed to the evaluation and analysis of the movement of people across the world and development of migration and refugee policies at all levels of government: local, national, and international.

Further Research

Books

Castles, Stephen, and Mark J. Miller. *The Age of Migration, International Population Movements in the Modern World.* 3d ed. New York: Guilford Press, 2003.

Cornelius, Wayne A., et al., eds. *Controlling Immigration: A Global Perspective.* Stanford, Calif.: Stanford University Press, 2004.

Ghosh, Bimal, ed. *Managing Migration, Time for a New International Regime?* Oxford: Oxford University Press, 2000.

Martin, Philip L., et al. *Managing Labor Migration in the Twenty-First Century.* New Haven: Yale University Press, 2006.

Özden, Calgar, and Maurice W. Schiff, eds. *International Migration, Remittances, and the Brain Drain.* London: Palgrave-Macmillan, 2006.

Pritchett, Lant. *Let Their People Come: Breaking the Gridlock on Global Labor Mobility.* Washington, D.C.: Center for Global Development, 2006.

Ratha, Dilip, and Zhimei Xu. *Migration and Remittances Factbook 2008.* Washington, D.C.: World Bank Publications, 2008.

Sassen, Saskia. *Territory, Authority, Rights: From Medieval to Global Assemblages.* Princeton, N.J.: Princeton University Press, 2006.

Tamas, Kristof, and Joakim Palme. *How Migration Can Aid Development.* Stockholm: Institute for Future Studies, 2006.

Articles and Reports

Adepojou, Aderanti. "Migration in West Africa." Policy Analysis and Research Programme, Global Commission on International Migration, Geneva, September 2005.

Chishti, Muzaffar. "The Rise in Remittances to India: A Closer Look." Migration Information Source, Migration Policy Institute, Washington, D.C., February 2007.

Choe, Julie. "African Migration to Europe." Council on Foreign Relations, July 10, 2007. Available at: http://www.cfr.org/publication/13726/african_migration_to_europe.html.

European Commission. "Policy Plan on Legal Migration." Commission on Migration, Brussels, December 21, 2005.

de Hass, Hein. "The Myth of Invasion: Irregular Migration from West Africa to the Mahgreb and the European Union." International Migration Institute (IMI) Research Report, Oxford, October 2007.

Docquier, Frédéric. "Brain Drain and Inequality Across Nations." IZA Discussion Paper no. 2440, Institute for the Study of Labour, Bonn, November 2006.

Global Commission on International Migration. "Migration in an Interconnected World: New Directions for Action." Report, Geneva, October 2005.

Hasenau, Michael. "ILO Standards on Migrant Workers: The Fundamentals of the UN Convention and Their Genesis." *International Migration* 25, no. 4 (1991): 687–697.

Hugo, Graeme. "Migration in the Asia Pacific Region." Policy Analysis and Research Program, Global Commission on International Migration, Geneva, 2005.

Institute for the Study of International Migration. "Facilitating High-Skilled Migration to Advanced Industrial Countries: Comparative Policies." Working Paper, Georgetown University, Washington, D.C., 2000.

Inter-American Development Bank Multilateral Investment Fund. "Sending Money Home: Leveraging the Development Impact of Remittances." Washington, D.C., October 2006.

International Labour Organisation. "Preventing Discrimination, Exploitation and Abuse of Women Migrant Workers." Gender Promotion Programme, International Labour Office, Geneva, 2003.

———. "Towards a Fair Deal for Migrant Workers in the Global Economy." International Labour Office, Geneva, 2004.

International Organization for Migration. "World Migration 2008: Managing Labour Mobility in the Evolving Global Economy." Geneva, February 2008.

Kastoryano, Riva. "Territories of Identities in France." Social Science Research Council, June 11, 2006. Available at: http://riotsfrance.ssrc.org/Kastoryano.

"Key Facts: Africa to Europe Migration." July 2, 2007. Available at: http://news.bbc.co.uk/2/hi/europe/6228236.stm.

Library of Congress. "Immigration/Migration: Today and during the Great Depression." Washington, D.C., 2003. Available at: http://memory.loc.gov/learn/lessons/98/migrate/essay.html.

Murphy, Kara. "France's New Law: Control Immigration Flows, Court the Highly Skilled." Migration Policy Institute, November 2006. Available at: http://www.migrationpolicy.org/pubs/Backgrounder2_France.php.

National Public Radio. "Understanding the Paris Riots." November 6, 2005. Available at: http://www.npr.org/templates/story/story.php?storyId=4991726.

Organisation for Economic Cooperation and Development. "International Migration Outlook." OECD, Paris, 2006.

Orrenius, Piam. "Do Amnesty Programs Reduce Undocumented Immigration?: Evidence from IRCA." *Demography* 40, no. 3 (2003): 437–450.

Passel, Jeffrey S., and DeVera Cohn. "Trends in Unauthorized Immigration: Undocumented Inflow Now Trails Legal Inflow." Pew Hispanic Center, Washington, D.C., October 2, 2008.

Ruhs, Martin. "The Potential of Temporary Migration Programmes in Future International Migration Policy." Policy Analysis and Research Program, Global Commission on International Migration, Geneva, September 2005.

Shah, Nasra M. "Restrictive Labor Immigration Policies in the Oil-Rich Gulf: Implications for Sending Asian Countries." Paper presented at the XXV International Union for the Scientific Study of Population, July 2005.

United Nations. "Report of the Secretary-General on International Migration and Development." UN General Assembly, 60th Session, UN Doc A/60/871, May 18, 2006.

World Bank. "Global Economic Prospects 2006: Economic Implications of Remittances and Migration." Washington, D.C., 2006.

———. "Revisions to Remittance Trends 2007." Washington, D.C., 2008.

Web Sites

Center for Migration and Refugee Studies, American University of Cairo
http://www.aucegypt.edu/ResearchatAUC/rc/cmrs/Pages/default.aspx

European Union, Migration Policy
http://ec.europa.eu/justice_home/fsj/intro/fsj_intro_en.htm

Global Commission on International Migration
http://www.gcim.org/en

International Migration, Integration, and Social Cohesion
http://www.imiscoe.org

The International Organization for Migration
http://www.iom.int/jahia/jsp/index.jsp

Institute for the Study of International Migration, Georgetown University
http://isim.georgetown.edu

Migration Policy Institute
http://www.migrationpolicy.org

Pew Hispanic Center
http://pewhispanic.org

U.S. Department of Homeland Security
http://www.dhs.gov/index.shtm

World Bank, Migration and Development
http://web.worldbank.org/WBSITE/EXTERNAL/TOPICS/EXTPOVERTY/
EXTMIGDEV/0,,menuPK:2838383~pagePK:149018~piPK:149093~theSite
PK:2838223,00.html

Document

1. International Convention on the Protection of the Rights of all Migrant Workers and Members of Their Families

Entered into force July 1, 2003

Full text available at http://www.un.org/documents/ga/res/45/a45r158.htm.

Extracts

PART III
HUMAN RIGHTS OF ALL MIGRANT WORKERS AND MEMBERS OF THEIR FAMILIES

Article 8

1. Migrant workers and members of their families shall be free to leave any State, including their State of origin. This right shall not be subject to any restrictions except those that are provided by law, are necessary to protect national security, public order (ordre public), public health or morals or the rights and freedoms of others and are consistent with the other rights recognized in the present part of the Convention.

2. Migrant workers and members of their families shall have the right at any time to enter and remain in their State of origin.

Article 11

1. No migrant worker or member of his or her family shall be held in slavery or servitude.

2. No migrant worker or member of his or her family shall be required to perform forced or compulsory labour.

Article 12

1. Migrant workers and members of their families shall have the right to freedom of thought, conscience and religion. This right shall include freedom to have or to adopt a religion or belief of their choice and freedom either individually or in community with others and in public or private to manifest their religion or belief in worship, observance, practice and teaching.

2. Migrant workers and members of their families shall not be subject to coercion that would impair their freedom to have or to adopt a religion or belief of their choice.

3. Freedom to manifest one's religion or belief may be subject only to such limitations as are prescribed by law and are necessary to protect public safety, order, health or morals or the fundamental rights and freedom of others.

4. States Parties to the present convention undertake to have respect for the liberty of parents, at least one of whom is a migrant worker, and, when applicable, legal guardians to ensure the religious and moral education of their children in conformity with their own convictions.

Article 13

1. Migrant workers and members of their families shall have the right to hold opinions without interference.

2. Migrant workers and members of their families shall have the right to freedom of expression; this right shall include freedom to seek, receive and impart information and ideas of all kinds, regardless of frontiers, either orally, in writing or in print, in the form of art or through any other media of their choice.

POPULATION

Ulla Larsen

The population of the world is at an all time high of 6.7 billion humans. Nonetheless, in recent years the rate of global population growth has declined. The populations of several European countries are declining because of fewer annual births than deaths and little net migration, whereas in some African countries the acquired immunodeficiency syndrome (AIDS) epidemic has caused severe population and development concerns. In fact, for the most part, the dire predictions of the *Population Bomb,* written in 1968 by Paul Ehrlich, have not occurred. Despite about forty years of research since Ehrlich's publication, the precise relationship among population growth, economic development, and consequent effects on the environment has proven to be complex and situation dependent. In some circumstances, increases in population appear coupled with economic growth because the generation of new knowledge has been able to overcome environmental deterioration; in other instances, however, rapid population growth has led to economic and environmental decline. Thus, although population growth has not caused insurmountable problems to date, a consensus has been reached among population researchers that a finite limit to population growth exists and that a better understanding of the balance among population, development, and the environment is essential.

Historical Background and Development

Population growth did not achieve its current rates until around 1800, when the world's population reached 1 billion people for the first time. According to the Population Division of the United Nations Department of Economic and Social Affairs, the subsequent two hundred years witnessed such unprecedented growth that the next 5 billion people were born in increments of 1 billion in 1927, 1960, 1974, 1987, and 1999. The source of this accelerated growth was a decline in death rates, later followed by a reduction in birthrates. The decline in mortality was due to medical innovations (such as the vaccination against smallpox), improved hygiene (such as new provisions for clean water and sewage systems and better personal hygiene), and better social and economic conditions (such as more dependable food supplies). After World War II, improved medical technologies played the biggest role in further reducing mortality rates.

The highest reliably recorded level of fertility in a population is about ten births per woman among seventeenth- and eighteenth-century French Canadians and mid-twentieth-century North American Hutterites (a religious sect that prohibits all forms of fertility control). Below-maximum fertility in historical populations has been rendered by such customs as late entry into marriage and permanent abstinence from sexual intercourse. For instance, in Western Europe before its fertility decline in the modern era, the mean age of marriage was twenty-five years or more; only 10–15 percent of women remained unmarried at age fifty.

At the end of the eighteenth and the beginning of the nineteenth centuries, economist and population scientist Thomas Robert Malthus expressed concern that the world's population would eventually exceed Earth's capacity for subsistence, so he recommended fertility control through "moral constraint." That is, people should delay marriage so that the number of children born would keep population growth within the limits of the planet's natural resources. (Malthus was a Protestant clergyman who explicitly rejected contraception.) In Europe and North America, fertility began to decline in the mid- to late nineteenth century. Reduced fertility was achieved largely by male withdrawal before ejaculation, or *coitus interruptus.* Modern contraceptives, including the birth control pill and other hormonal methods, became available in the 1960s. Subsequently, the development of new birth control methods and the spread of knowledge about and use of contraception have been foci for government and nongovernment agencies concerned with population control.

In the 1950s, demographers noted that many low-income countries were experiencing a drop in mortality, while fertility remained the same or only declined slightly. This demographic pattern led to concerns that increased population growth in these less-developed countries would impede their economic development. The relationship between population and economic development soon became a popular subject for scientific inquiry. An example of this research is the 1958 case study of India and Mexico by U.S. demographer Ansley Coale and U.S. economist Edgar Hoover at Princeton University. In the case of Mexico, they made projections of future population size using the following assumptions: that mortality would decline gradually and, by 1985, life expectancy at birth would be seventy years; and that fertility would remain unchanged or would be reduced by 50 percent from 1955 to 1980 or would decline by 50 percent from 1965 to 1980. They then analyzed the differential effects on economic growth. The study concluded that the projected income per adult consumer would be about 40 percent higher if fertility were reduced by half. (Coale reevaluated the situation in Mexico in the late 1970s and in the 1980s and drew largely the same conclusions as the original study.) Mexico ultimately experienced a multistage response to population growth: (1) the economy expanded to meet the needs of the increasing population; (2) internal migration from rural to urban areas (especially to Mexico

City) increased; and (3) outmigration became prevalent (especially to the United States). Coale and Hoover's study was an important influence on scientific research and public policy on population and development in the 1960s and 1970s.

Popular and scientific concerns about a population crisis were heightened by the 1968 publication of Ehrlich's *Population Bomb,* in which he used such phrases as "too many people," "too little food," and "environmental degradation." In 1990, Ehrlich, with his wife Anne Ehrlich, published a followup, *The Population Explosion,* in which they argue that the destruction of the environment, including the depletion of nonrenewable resources, climate change, and increasing international tensions, had become much worse since 1968. The negative consequences of population growth were also the primary focus of international debates, including at the United Nations World Population Conferences in 1974 (in Bucharest) and 1984 (in Mexico City), but less so at the International Conference on Population and Development (ICPD) in 1994 (in Cairo).

The debate at the 1974 conference was polarized between the perspective of developing countries and that of the United States and other developed countries. The latter argued that developing countries should establish growth-rate targets and that these targets should be met through family planning programs. The developing countries, however, wanted to discuss and implement new ways of integrating population programs with economic development programs. This disagreement aside, all the delegates agreed to a World Population Plan of Action, which was largely an international program for promoting family planning (see Document 1). The phrase "development is the best contraceptive"— meaning that increased schooling and labor force participation of women and men, industrialization, and urbanization would automatically result in fewer births per woman—originated at this conference. At the 1984 conference, the United States proposed that population growth is a neutral factor, that is, that population growth does not have an effect on economic development. (This position was inspired by the late professor Julian Simon's influence in the administration of Ronald Reagan and its support by groups opposed to abortion. Simon's main thesis was that population growth does not hinder economic progress and eventually raises standards of living.) The Recommendations for the Further Implementation of the World Population Plan of Action, passed at Mexico City, raised concerns about the environment, the role and status of women, and meeting the need for family planning, but the overall consensus was that the 1974 World Population Plan of Action was still valid.

The 1994 ICPD resulted in the Programme of Action, which covered a wide range of topics. The conference was preceded by several meetings sponsored by the United Nation; gatherings called by nongovernmental organizations; and numerous books, articles, newspaper columns, and radio and television segments assuring the world that a broad section of people had input in the development and formulation of the Programme of Action. Of importance, at these preliminary meetings women's organizations had a chance to participate and to make women's voices and concerns part of the final program, which had not been the case at the 1974 and 1984 meetings. A strong commitment to improving women's reproductive health and securing their reproductive rights (see Document 2) is evident throughout the Programme of Action. Women's concerns about fertility control were broadened to include all aspects of reproductive health (see WOMEN). The first five-year review of the implementation of the Programme of Action demonstrated that the ICPD goals were still relevant and that much progress had been made advancing them. In 2004, ten years after the 1994 ICPD conference in Cairo, several activities took place at the national, regional, and global levels. Country-by-country analyses of achievements, constraints, lessons learned, and the way to full implementation of ICPD were conducted.

Current Status

The welfare of individuals is affected by and has an effect on population growth and the environment. Recent research on this topic has aimed to enhance the understanding of interrelations among population, development (especially economic development), and the environment and to ascertain whether population trends are sustainable (see map, p. 33). Since the 1990s, women's organizations and their supporters shifted the values and priorities of the population and development debate away from demographic target setting by placing equity, gender, and human rights at the center of the discussion and by proposing a more holistic agenda for action. Thus, the recent population policy debate emphasized the role of women's health and women's empowerment and how these affect population growth, development, and the environment.

Research

The twentieth century experienced an unprecedented rate of population growth and economic improvement. The economic performance of individual countries bore a modest relation to the intensity of its population growth. According to the World Bank, world gross domestic product (GDP) per capita—based on international U.S. dollars using purchasing power parity (PPP) conversion rates, or GDP per capita in PPP—increased eightfold between 1950 and 2000. The World Bank, in *Beyond Economic Development: Meeting the Challenges of Global Development,* defines *GDP per capita in PPP* as "the number of units of a country's currency required to buy the same amount of goods and services in the domestic market as one dollar would buy in the United States." During the same period, world population grew from 2.5 billion to 6.7 billion, meaning that the world's population in aggregate terms became more productive. The tripling of the number of people increased the world's economic output by a factor of eight.

Economic growth was uneven, and disparities in income widened between countries (see INCOME INEQUALITY). From 1990 to 2007, gross national income (GNI) showed almost no change in industrial countries and increased in developing countries, although it declined in Africa. The World Bank estimates that GNI per capita in PPP in 2006 ranged from $44,260 in the United

States to $710 in Burundi. (GNI PPP is GNI converted to international dollars using a PPP conversion factor. International dollars indicate the amount of goods and services one can buy in the United States with a given amount of money.) Further evidence suggests that income inequalities widened within many countries, raising concerns about the effects of this growing disparity.

The relationship between population growth and economic development is complicated by the presence of other factors, such as the availability of natural resources, institutional conditions, and the timing of the start of the population growth process. Edward Crenshaw and his colleagues, in a 1997 study published in *American Sociological Review*, show that in developing countries an increase in the child population hinders economic progress, while an increase in the adult population fosters economic development. They suggest that a decline in the average number of children per woman results in an increase in economic development because rapid labor force growth occurs in the presence of a growing adult population and reduced youth dependency. This pattern is illustrated by the population and economic trends in Japan after World War II, where steep declines in mortality and fertility were followed by an economic boom.

It is well known that a host of environmental problems are linked to population and economic growth, as described so vividly by Ehrlich in *Population Bomb*. These include global warming, resulting from increases in carbon dioxide emissions and greenhouse effects; deforestation, resulting from the expansion of cropland and the harvesting of wood for fuel; and water shortages, resulting from increased pressure on watersheds (see DEFORESTATION, FRESHWATER and CLIMATE CHANGE). The challenge remains to determine the complex and sometimes harmful effects that population and economic growth have on the environment. Esther Boserup documented that increased population pressure has traditionally led to new technologies aimed at intensifying agriculture production and increasing agricultural yields. Julian Simon advanced this school of thought, suggesting that in the long run societies adjust to additional people. The debate remains about whether possible limits exist on how intensive food production can become before resources are degraded.

In October 1993 at the Population Summit of the World's Scientific Academies in New Delhi, Samuel Preston presented the results of an in-depth study on population and the environment. Among his findings, published in 1994 as "Population and the Environment: The Scientific Evidence," he concluded, "Population growth is not the only factor capable of affecting the extent of resource degradation. Depending on time, place and criterion, it may not be the most important factor. Because they have multiple origins, it would be foolhardy to think that problems of food production and resource maintenance can or should be solved by population policy alone."

Preston's statements about the relationships between population and environment were substantiated later in the 1990s and 2000s by additional empirical data and research generated and reported by, among others, the National Research Council's Board on Sustainable Development and Policy and the National Research Council's Forum on Biodiversity Committee, as well as in the United Nations Development Programme's annual *Human Development Report* and the World Bank's annual *World Development Report.*

Although annual global population growth rates have declined steadily since the late 1960s, the total number of people continues to grow (see Tables 1, 2, and 3). For instance, the annual growth rate of 1.3 percent between 1995 and 2000 added about 80 million people to the population each year. At the core of the population problem lies the concern about how many people Earth can support, called its human carrying capacity. In a 1995 study, Joel Cohen showed that estimates of Earth's carrying capacity varied widely, from fewer than 1 billion to more than 1,000 billion people; about two-thirds of the estimates fell in the range of 4–16 billion people, and the median value was 12 billion. In 2006, the United Nations projected that the global population would reach 9.2 billion in 2050; its projected estimate in 2000 was 9.3 billion. This decreased projection was based on the assumption that fertility is trending downward— the 2000 estimate was derived using a fertility rate of 2.1 children per woman over the fifty-year period, but because the current fertility rate of 2.1 (measured in 2000–2005) is not likely to hold given the generally declining trend in fertility rates, UN analysts lowered their 2050 projection.

Future population size, indeed, is sensitive to small deviations in annual population growth rates, and the global population projection in 2050 would be 7.9 billion or 10.9 billion if the assumption about the fertility rate were half a child lower or half a child higher than 2.1 children per woman. Cohen did not attempt to estimate the carrying capacity of Earth, but he stressed that it depends on natural constraints and human choices about everything from food and the environment to lifestyles. The National Research Council's Board on Sustainable Development echoed Cohen's concerns about the validity of measures of carrying capacity and requested that more work be done on this concept, in terms of either a scientific foundation supporting the idea of safe limits for world population size or alternative concepts for efforts to attain sustainability. The general consensus at the beginning of the 2000s was that the prevailing level of population growth was not sustainable and that trends toward zero population growth were desirable and should be promoted.

Policies and Programs

According to the general consensus of the international population community, the 1994 ICPD represents a paradigm shift in the population and development discourse. Ruth Dixon-Mueller and Adrienne Germain described eloquently the strides made in population policies and programs following the conference by contrasting a more traditional, narrow demographic approach— illustrated by John Bongaarts's recommendations for achieving the highest demographic impact—to the Programme of Action signed by the delegates. Shortly before the ICPD, Bongaarts proposed in *Science* that governments pursue three policy options for reducing population growth: reduce unwanted pregnancies by strengthening family planning programs and addressing unmet contraception needs; reduce the need or demand for large families by investing in human development, such as education, improvements in women's status, and infant and child survival; and slow the momentum of population growth by raising the average age of childbearing. In contrast, the ICPD Programme of Action emphasized, with respect to childbearing decisions, that the manipulation of the decision-making process, whether concerning a person's decision to use contraception or addressing broader socioeconomic issues, should be guided not by demographic objectives but by the primacy of health, empowerment, and human rights (see HEALTH and HUMAN RIGHTS). It is in this sense, argues Dixon-Mueller and Germain, that ICPD moved beyond family planning and even beyond demography to encompass a broader range of political, developmental, and ethical concerns. In general, the post-Cairo perspective shifted population policies away from slowing population growth and toward improving the lives of individuals, in particular, women, and providing family planning in the broader context of reproductive health. Underlying this new perspective was a belief that enhancing individual health and rights would ultimately lower fertility and slow population growth.

The Cairo consensus was supported by the 1995 World Summit for Social Development in Copenhagen and the 1995 Fourth World Conference on Women in Beijing, where many women's organizations were active and helped to ensure that similar policies were adopted. In 1999 and 2004, five and ten years after Cairo, the United Nations held several meetings to discuss population and development policies, to review progress made since 1994, and to develop new approaches aimed at fully implementing the ICPD. The 1994 review, ICPD+5, resulted in *Key Actions for the Further Implementation of the Programme of Action of the International Conference on Population and Development,* which included new benchmarks for 2015 and sharpened the goals of the 1994 Programme of Action. Three of the pivotal benchmarks involved family planning, maternal mortality, and prevention of sexually transmitted diseases (STDs). In 2005, a compendium was published of the affected outcomes of the ICPD, "The World Reaffirms Cairo: Official Outcomes of the ICPD at Ten Review" (ICPD at 10).

ICPD+5 and ICPD at 10 concluded that the use of contraception was up. For instance, in India the use of contraception among women in a union increased from 42 to 49 to 58 percent from 1992–1993 to 1998–1999 to 2005–2006, and in Cameroon (also among women in a union) from 15 to 27 to 39 percent from 1991 to 1998 to 2004. Concerns were raised about whether adequate supplies of affordable contraceptives were available and whether prevailing levels of aid could keep pace with the growing demand for them. Price discounts and donations of contraceptives had been made possible by funding from the World Bank and developed countries, but this was deemed inadequate.

The 1994 ICPD called for a reduction in maternal death rates to below 60 per 100,000 births. The level of maternal mortality in developing countries is not well documented, but estimates developed by the World Health Organization (WHO), United Nations International Children's Emergency Fund (UNICEF), United Nations Population Fund (UNFPA), and World Bank suggest that in 2005 maternal mortality ratios per 100,000 births were about

820 in Africa, 330 in Asia, 130 in Latin America and the Caribbean, 9 in developed countries, and 400 worldwide. The World Bank has exhibited a long-term and ongoing commitment to safe motherhood, but progress has been slow, partly because of insufficient funding, lack of political support, and weak health-care systems in many developing countries.

Concerns about STDs, including human immunodeficiency virus (HIV/AIDS), increased during the 1990s and 2000s (see AIDS). The United Nations estimated that 33.2 million (30.6–36.1 million) people were living with HIV/AIDS in 2007. The potentially destabilizing effects of the HIV/AIDS epidemic led the Security Council to declare in 2000 that AIDS was a global security concern.

According to the World Bank, more than one adult in ten worldwide acquires an STD each year, and some 333 million new infections occur annually. Gonorrhea and chlamydia are two common STDs that often do not show any symptoms. In women, they can spread and cause scarring and blockage of the fallopian tubes, leading to infertility. Syphilis is another prevalent STD that can cause miscarriages in women and, at an advanced stage, mental illness in both sexes. HIV prevention strategies and programs often include all STDs. It has been difficult to evaluate the effectiveness of such programs because population-based data about STDs and HIV are rare and generally of poor quality, even though since 2001 nationally representative HIV data have been collected from numerous countries by the Demographic and Health Surveys. The MEASURE DHS (Demographic and Health Surveys) Project has earned a worldwide reputation for collecting and disseminating accurate, nationally representative data on health and population in developing countries. The project is implemented by Macro International, Inc., and is funded by the U.S. Agency for International Development (USAID) with contributions from other donors such as UNICEF, UNFPA, WHO, and the Joint United Nations Programme on HIV/AIDS (UNAIDS).

At the time of ICPD at 10 in 2004, many developing countries still had high rates of unwanted childbearing, maternal mortality, and STD and HIV infection, suggesting that the agenda of the 1994 Programme of Action had not yet been realized, despite recorded progress. The shortcomings in the implementation of the program were partly due to insufficient funding; during the 1990s and 2000s, overall funding from governments and multilateral organizations, such as the World Bank, declined. The United States is the largest single contributor to population and reproductive health programs and is an important influence on the availability of assistance. After the Republican Party won a majority in Congress in 1994, the United States shifted away from supporting international family planning programs, so funds for family planning were cut. In the 2000 U.S. budget, the global "gag rule" was enacted, denying U.S. funding to private organizations overseas if they provided abortion services or counseling or lobbied for changes in abortion laws in their country. In January 2001, after taking office, President George W. Bush reinstated the so-called Mexico City policy imposed by the Reagan administration, forcing overseas organizations to steer clear of abortion issues or forgo U.S. funding. As of 2008, the last year of the Bush administration, the policy had not changed. Despite funding shortages, progress had been made and nongovernmental organizations, religious and community leaders, and the private sector were instrumental in implementing the ICPD agenda. Many countries had modified their laws in favor of women's empowerment and health, and the international debate on population and development led to national debates. For instance, many European countries extended maternity leave and increased the monetary benefits provided to couples with children. Brazil made reproductive health care a part of primary health care, to which all its citizens have free access.

Some environmental scientists, including Paul Ehrlich, expressed concern that the post-Cairo policy debate had lost sight of the links among population growth, pollution, and natural resource depletion. Bongaarts and his colleagues commented in *Environment* in 1997 that the 1995 assessment of the Intergovernmental Panel on Climate Change had paid almost no attention to the role of population growth in global warming and that by not addressing population growth the debate missed the opportunity to simultaneously promote developmental and environmental benefits. In 2008, in *Demography and Policy: A View from outside the Discipline,* Paul Erlich pointed out that population scientists had had little impact on the political debate about environmental issues. To promote population scientists' or demographers' expertise and interests, Erlich suggested strengthening the collaborative efforts among ecologists, demographers, and other environmental scientists.

Regional Summaries

Although the problems of population growth, development, and possible depletion of Earth's natural resources are global, they have taken significantly different forms in different regions of the world. The data reported in these summaries are from John Week's *Population: An Introduction to Concepts and Issues,* the United Nations Population Division's *World Population Prospects: The 2006 Revision,* and the Population Reference Bureau's "2007 World Population Data Sheet."

North America

In mid-2007, the United States and Canada had a population of about 335 million people, or 5 percent of the world's total. Women had on average 2.1 children each in the United States and 1.5 in Canada; these children could expect to live until the age of 78 and 80, respectively (see Tables 2 and 3). Thus, in both countries fertility and mortality were low, but even so the annual growth rate was about 0.9 percent because of immigration (see IMMIGRATION). In the United States, the majority of immigrants came from Latin America. Many settled in urban areas, where in some situations they essentially remained segregated from native-born Americans. In 2007, the World Bank documented that residents of the United States had the world's highest purchasing power, that the purchasing power ratio of Canada to the United States was 0.78, and that the purchasing power ratio worldwide to the United States was 0.22.

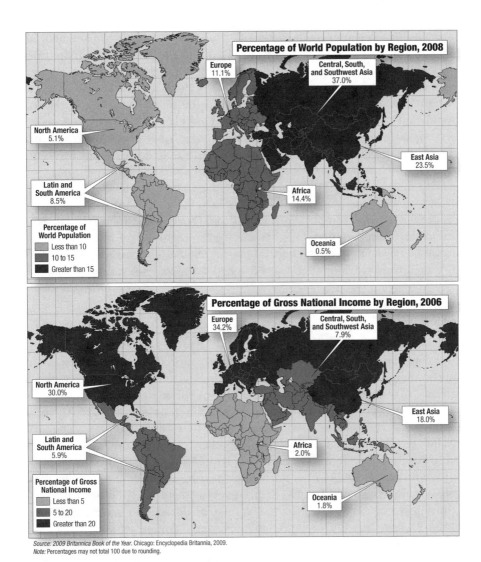

Percentage of World Population by Region, 2008

Europe 11.1%

Central, South, and Southwest Asia 37.0%

North America 5.1%

East Asia 23.5%

Latin and South America 8.5%

Africa 14.4%

Oceania 0.5%

Percentage of World Population
Less than 10
10 to 15
Greater than 15

Percentage of Gross National Income by Region, 2006

Europe 34.2%

Central, South, and Southwest Asia 7.9%

North America 30.0%

East Asia 18.0%

Latin and South America 5.9%

Africa 2.0%

Oceania 1.8%

Percentage of Gross National Income
Less than 5
5 to 20
Greater than 20

Source: 2009 Britannica Book of the Year. Chicago: Encyclopedia Britannia, 2009.
Note: Percentages may not total 100 due to rounding.

The U.S. population increase of 32.7 million people between 1990 and 2000 is the largest ten-year population increase in U.S. history. Increasing population and economic growth rates in North America, however, took their toll on the environment. For instance, in 2002 carbon dioxide emission per capita (metric tons) was 19.6 in North America, the highest in the world outside selected countries in western Asia (for example, Qatar, Kuwait, United Arab Emirates, and Bahrain).

Latin America and the Caribbean

In mid-2007, Latin America and the Caribbean had 569 million people, or 9 percent of the world's population. At the beginning of the twenty-first century, mortality had declined significantly; life expectancy at birth had reached the age of 73 in 2007, up from 69 in 2001; the average number of children per woman had declined from 2.7 in 2001 to 2.5; and the population was growing at an annual rate of 1.5 percent. The decline in mortality was steeper than the decline in fertility and had started earlier, so the relatively young age of the population contributed to the region's rapid population increase.

Mitigating the effects of rapid population growth, Mexico and several other countries experienced substantial rural-to-urban migration, as well as outmigration, which reduced under- and unemployment. The rapid and unplanned growth of the urban population is one of the gravest problems in this region because it has led to huge slums. In 2006, Latin America contributed 8.7 percent of the world's GNI per capita in PPP, and Trinidad and Tobago and Argentina ranked numbers one and two among the region's largest economies as measured by GNI per capita in PPP. In terms of environmental impact, in 2002 carbon dioxide emissions per capita reached 2.5 metric tons.

Europe

In mid-2007, Europe's population reached 733 million, or 11 percent of the world's population. Mortality was low, although some Eastern European countries, including Russia, experienced increasing mortality with the dissolution of communist rule and the breakup of the Soviet Union. For a couple of decades, many European countries had below-replacement fertility, with couples having fewer than the approximately two children needed to keep the next generation at the same level (see Case Study—Low Fertility in Italy). The total fertility was 2.1 in Iceland in 2007, but all other European countries had lower rates. For instance, Germany and Russia had fertility rates of 1.3. (In populations with low mortality rates for prechildbearing ages, each woman needs to produce about two children to reach the replacement rate.) Thus, fertility was below replacement during the last couple of decades in several European countries, and the population growth rate hovered around zero, except in Eastern Europe, where it was negative.

Several European governments encouraged higher fertility by reducing the length of the workday and by offering childcare services. For instance, the Scandinavian countries provided support or incentives aimed at helping the employment of mothers. Thus, today's labor market is characterized by families with two full-time workers and institutional childcare. In 2007, the fertility rate was 1.9 in Sweden, Norway, and Denmark. Women in other countries faced greater challenges in balancing family and work obligations. In southern Europe, for example, services facilitating the full-time employment of mothers were lacking and public childcare facilities were limited. Today, mothers are typically employed part-time, and fathers are often the sole provider for the family. The total fertility rate is 1.3 in Greece and 1.4 in Italy and Spain. Further, in the 1960 cohort as many as 15 percent of women were childless in Italy compared to 11 percent in Norway in 2002, probably reflecting the varying difficulties in combining work and family roles.

In the 1980s and early 1990s, West Germany became the home of a large number of immigrant guestworkers from Greece, Italy, Turkey, and Yugoslavia, while England, France, and the Netherlands received migrant laborers mainly from their former colonies. These new arrivals proved difficult to integrate, however, and in the late 1990s and 2000s, the European Union restricted legal immigration while encouraging internal migration within EU member countries. In 2006, the GNI PPP per capita was $22,690 in Europe, documenting that having high economic productivity in times of stagnant or negative population growth is possible. Europe was confronted with an increasingly aging population and a declining proportion of people in the productive age range of 15 to 64. Simultaneously, Europe was confronted with issues related to limited resources; for instance, in 2005 the European Parliament discussed a report showing that Europe used 20 percent of the biosphere's services to serve 7 percent of the world's population—a resource demand that had risen nearly 70 percent since 1961.

North Africa and Western Asia

The area often referred to as the *Middle East* includes Egypt and western Asia; the remaining countries of North Africa west of Egypt are considered part of the Maghreb. In mid-2007, North Africa had about 195 million people and western Asia had 223 million people, or 2.9 and 3.4 percent of the world's total, respectively. Egypt was the most populous country in North Africa, with 73 million Egyptians and an annual growth rate of 2.1 percent. Mortality dropped significantly in Egypt after World War II, while fertility remained high until recently. The second most populous country in North Africa was the Sudan. The most populous country in western Asia was Turkey, with 74 million people and an annual growth rate of 1.2 percent.

Total fertility was 3.1 in 2007 in the Middle East and North Africa. Similar trends of mortality and fertility have prevailed throughout North Africa and western Asia, resulting in a youthful population. Exceptions to this pattern are Yemen, with a total fertility rate of 6.2 and infant mortality rate of 94 per 1,000 births, and Iraq, with a total fertility rate of 4.9 and an infant mortality rate of 75 per 1,000 births. Economic development, however, has not followed rapid population growth. Today, youth unemployment is high, and the political situation in many parts of the region is unstable. Large numbers of young people have left the area in search of work in Europe and in North and South America.

Sub-Saharan Africa

In mid-2007, 11 percent of the world's population, or 750 million people, lived in sub-Saharan Africa. This region had the highest levels of mortality and fertility, as well as the highest annual population growth rate. In most African countries, mortality declined gradually from the 1960s to the 1980s, but fertility remained unchanged until around 1985, resulting in an unprecedented growth rate. The onset of the decline in the fertility rate was earliest and most pronounced in southern Africa, where in mid-2007 women had on average 2.8 children, compared to 6.3 children in central Africa, 5.7 in western Africa, and

5.5 in eastern Africa. Today, most sub-Saharan African countries have experienced a fertility decline, albeit a modest one. The HIV/AIDS epidemic has halted or reversed downward mortality trends throughout the region. In 2008, UNAIDS/WHO estimated that 33 million people lived with HIV and that 22 million of these people lived in sub-Saharan Africa. As many as 2 million had died from AIDS, and 75 percent of these people were from sub-Saharan Africa. Further, the HIV/AIDS epidemic has resulted in 15 million orphans (ages zero to seventeen years), of which 11.6 million live in sub-Saharan Africa.

Internal labor migration was prevalent in sub-Saharan Africa in the 1990s and early 2000s, with rural-to-rural and male migration being dominant (except where marriage migration was common). In contrast, international migration appeared to be modest, but the evidence is poor. For many sub-Saharan African countries in 2006, the ratio of GNI PPP per capita to that of the United States was 0.05 or lower. At this time, pollution was also low, as seen by the finding that carbon dioxide emissions were only 0.8 metric tons per capita. The region, however, suffered from other environmental problems, including deforestation and water shortages.

Asia

In mid-2007, Asia was the most populous region, with 4 billion people, or 61 percent of the world's population. The people of China constituted 20 percent and the people of India 17 percent of the world's total. Asia is diverse in terms of population, development, and environmental impact. Japan had 9 deaths per 1,000 people, below-replacement fertility, and 0 percent population growth. China had the world's largest population, more than 1.3 billion people, relatively low mortality, below-replacement fertility (partly the result of a coercive government population policy, in place since about 1970), and a growth rate of 0.5 percent. India, the second most populous country, with slightly more than 1.1 billion people, had higher mortality and fertility rates than China but a similarly high growth rate of 1.6 percent. The Asian countries with the most rapid declines in fertility, such as Japan and Taiwan with rates of natural increase close to zero (0.0 and 0.3, respectively), are currently experiencing problems caring and providing for the elderly because state services and institutional supports are not yet available to replace the care previously provided by children and relatives.

In mid-2007, Japan had one of the world's largest economies, and the ratio of its GNI PPP per capita to the United States was 0.76; the ratio for China was 0.17 and that for India was 0.09. The carbon dioxide emissions per capita were 9.5 tons in Japan, 2.9 tons in China, and 1.1 tons in India in 2002, reflecting the gravity of pollution problems in this region.

Oceania

The population of Oceania was 35 million in mid-2007. Mortality and fertility were low in countries with peoples of mainly European origin. For example, women in Australia and New Zealand had, on average, 1.8 children, and these children could expect to live until the age of 81. In contrast, countries with people primarily of largely indigenous origin had high mortality and fertility rates. For example, in Papua New Guinea and the Solomon Islands each woman had an average of 4.1 and 4.5 children, respectively, and the children could expect to live fifty-seven years in Papua New Guinea and sixty-two years in the Solomon Islands. Similarly, economic development was also higher in countries with mainly European populations. These states had no shortage of land; in fact, they possessed large surpluses of underused cropland. Pollution, including levels of carbon dioxide emissions, however, was high in Australia and New Zealand but minor in Papua New Guinea and the Solomon Islands.

Data

Table 1   Total Population and Annual Growth Rate in Selected Countries

Country	Total mid-2007 (millions)	Rate of natural increase (%)
Algeria	34.1	1.7
Argentina	39.4	1.2
Australia	21.0	0.6
Brazil	189.3	1.4
Canada	32.9	0.3
China	1,318.0	0.5
Colombia	46.2	1.5
DRC	62.6	2.7
Egypt	73.4	2.1
France	61.7	0.4
Georgia	4.5	0.1
Germany	82.3	−0.2
Guatemala	13.4	1.0
India	1,131.9	1.6
Indonesia	231.6	1.4
Israel	7.3	1.5
Japan	127.7	0.0
Russian Federation	141.7	−0.5
Saudi Arabia	27.6	0.0
Spain	45.3	0.3
Sweden	9.1	0.2
Switzerland	7.5	0.2
Tajikistan	7.1	1.9
Thailand	65.7	0.7
Turkey	74.0	1.2
Uganda	28.5	3.1
United Kingdom	61.0	0.3
United States	302.2	0.6
More-developed countries	1,221.0	0.1
Less-developed countries	5,404.0	1.5
World	6,625.0	1.2

Source: Population Reference Bureau, *2007 World Population Data Sheet,* 2007, available at: www.prb.org.

Note: DRC, Democratic Republic of Congo.

Table 2   Life Expectancy at Birth in Selected Countries, 1970–1975 and 2007 (years)

Country	1970–1975			2007		
	Male	Female	Both sexes	Male	Female	Both sexes
Algeria	54	56	55	71	74	72
Argentina	64	71	67	71	79	75
Australia and New Zealand	69	75	72	79	83	81
Brazil	58	62	60	68	76	72
Canada	70	77	73	78	83	80
China[a]	63	64	63	71	74	72
Colombia	60	64	62	69	76	72
DRC	44	48	46	51	53	52
Egypt	51	53	52	68	73	71
France	69	76	72	77	84	81
Georgia	65	73	69	69	77	73
Germany	68	74	71	76	82	79
Guatemala	52	55	54	66	73	69
India	51	49	50	63	64	64
Indonesia	48	51	49	67	71	69
Israel	70	73	72	78	82	80
Japan	71	76	73	79	86	82
Russian Federation[b]	63	74	68	59	72	65
Saudi Arabia	52	56	54	73	77	75
Spain	70	76	73	77	83	80
Sweden	72	78	75	79	83	81
Switzerland	71	77	74	79	84	81
Tajikistan	60	66	63	61	66	64
Thailand	58	62	60	68	75	71
Turkey	56	60	58	69	74	72
Uganda	45	48	47	47	47	47
United Kingdom	69	75	72	77	81	79
United States	68	75	71	75	80	78
Uzbekistan	61	67	64	63	70	67
More-developed regions[c]	68	75	71	73	80	77
Less-developed regions[d]	54	56	55	64	67	66
World	57	59	58	66	70	68

Source: United Nations, Department of Economic and Social Affairs, Population Division, *World Population Prospects: The 1998 Revision, vol. 1, Comprehensive Tables* (New York: United Nations, 1999); Population Reference Bureau, *2007 World Population Data Sheet,* 2007, available at: www.prb.org.

Note: DRC, Democratic Republic of Congo.

[a]Data do not include Hong Kong for 1970–1975.

[b]The 1970–1975 data refer to the USSR. The 2007 data refer to the Russian Federation.

[c]Comprising Australia, Europe, Japan, New Zealand, and North America.

[d]Comprising Africa; Asia (excluding Japan); Latin America and the Caribbean; and Melanesia, Micronesia, and Polynesia (all other regions and countries not listed in more-developed regions).

Table 3 Fertility Rate per Woman in Selected Countries, 1970–1975 and 2007 (%)

Country	1970–1975	2007
Algeria	7.4	2.4
Argentina	3.2	2.5
Australia and New Zealand	2.6	1.8
Brazil	4.7	2.3
Canada	2.0	1.5
China[a]	4.9	1.6
Colombia	5.0	2.4
DRC	6.3	5.3
Egypt	5.5	3.1
France	2.3	2.0
Georgia	2.6	1.3
Germany	1.6	1.3
Guatemala	6.5	4.4
India	5.4	2.9
Indonesia	5.1	2.4
Israel	3.8	2.8
Japan	2.1	1.3
Russian Federation[b]	2.0	1.3
Saudi Arabia	7.3	4.1
Spain	2.9	1.4
Sweden	1.9	1.9
Switzerland	1.8	1.4
Tajikistan	6.8	3.4
Thailand	5.0	1.7
Turkey	5.1	2.2
Uganda	6.9	6.7
United Kingdom	2.1	1.8
United States	2.0	2.1
Uzbekistan	6.0	2.7
More-developed regions[c]	2.1	1.6
Less-developed regions[d]	5.4	2.9
World	4.5	2.7

Source: United Nations, Department of Economic and Social Affairs, Population Division, *World Population Prospects: The 1998 Revision, vol. 1, Comprehensive Tables* (New York: United Nations, 1999); Population Reference Bureau, *2007 World Population Data Sheet,* 2007, available at: www.prb.org.

Note: DRC, Democratic Republic of the Congo.

[a] Data do not include Hong Kong for 1970–1975.

[b] The 1970–1975 data refer to the USSR. The 2007 data refer to the Russian Federation.

[c] Comprising Australia, Europe, Japan, New Zealand, and North America.

[d] Comprising Africa; Asia (excluding Japan); Latin America and the Caribbean; Melanesia, Micronesia, and Polynesia (all regions and countries not listed for most-developed regions).

Case Study—Low Fertility in Italy

Sustained below-replacement fertility leads to population decline and eventual extinction. To prevent this bleak prospect, European policymakers and researchers are attempting to understand the social and economic forces behind low fertility to implement policies aimed at encouraging people to have more children. In 2007, the rate of natural increase (mortality − fertility) was −0.1 percent in Europe, and it ranged from 0.2 percent in northern Europe to 0.1 percent in Western and southern Europe to −0.4 percent in Eastern Europe.

Italy offers a compelling illustration of these patterns of low fertility prevalent in Europe. By European standards, it had a relatively high fertility rate until around 1970–1975, when the rate was 2.3. From 1995 through 1999, the fertility rate declined to 1.2 and then, in 2007, increased to 1.4. The rate of natural population growth was zero in 2007. This trend resulted in a population at the beginning of the twenty-first century with almost no large families (defined as containing four or more children), with two-child families being the norm and one-child and childless families rapidly becoming more common. As many as 15 percent of women born in 1960 remained childless in their early forties. Northern Italy has traditionally had lower fertility rates than the rest of Italy and has in the past been a harbinger of future trends for the whole of Italy. Within this context, demographer Antonio Golini has speculated about the existence of a fertility threshold below which a population does not go and about whether the fertility recorded in some northern Italian regions can be considered to have reached this minimum.

Several factors have contributed to Italy's low fertility rate. More than 90 percent of women use contraception, and abortion is legal and available. Thus, unwanted fertility is low. Almost all children are born within marriage, the age of marriage is going up, and childbearing is being postponed, resulting in some cases in a reduction of the number of children per couple. The postponement of marriage can be explained, in part, by the facts that people are waiting to marry until they finish their education, youth unemployment is high, and housing is expensive. Finally, Italians' desired fertility—the number of children that people say they would like to have—is low, about two children per couple.

It is difficult to fully explain the factors behind Italians' low fertility. An opinion poll from 1991 suggests that Italians believed that they had very low fertility because of women's needing to work, the high cost of rearing children, and the increased appreciation for individual fulfillment and freedom. Italian gender roles had not kept pace with women's entry into the workforce. Women continued to be the primary caretakers of children, and access to quality day care was limited. Furthermore, the business sector had not adjusted to women's increasing participation in the workforce, so the opening hours of retail stores and public offices remained generally limited to standard business hours, making it difficult for all working people (including women) to find time to shop and do other errands, such as going to the post office and the doctor.

The main demographic consequences of low fertility are an aging and declining population. In the case of Italy, the medium variant, as reported by the United Nations in 2007, suggests that the population of Italy will be 54.6 million people in 2050. Changes in Italy's age distribution will include a fall of 11.3 percent of people ages 15 to 49 and an increase of 13.3 percent of people ages 60-plus, with the average age increasing from 42 to 50 years. Further, the working-age population will fall to about the same number of people as that above age 60, with 2.6 times more people over age 80 compared to those in 2005 and 3.1 times more people above age 80 than below age 5.

Given these circumstances, we may question whether Italy will be able to maintain its current standard of living if the working-age population is out-numbered by the dependents. Changes in the social security system will be needed as the proportion of retired people grows. Also, children will grow up surrounded mainly by adults and old people, providing for very different inter-personal relations. So far, however, welfare remains high and is increasing in Italy, as suggested by the human development indexes of 0.85, 0.87, 0.91, and 0.94 in 1975, 1985, 1995, and 2005, respectively.

Italy's demographic problems resulting from low fertility probably cannot be solved by increased immigration in light of the fact that Italy has historically had difficulties integrating immigrants. Furthermore, a level of immigration higher than that experienced in the past would be needed to prevent the total population from declining. Thus, the current situation is unsustainable, and the Italian population risks disappearing if fertility stays at the low levels recorded in the last couple of decades. The Italian government and other institutions in Italian society have not taken measures to correct this critical problem, although recently signs are evident of an increased awareness of the current and future problems that the state is facing. As already mentioned, the total fertility rate went up to 1.4 in 2007 from 1.2 in the years prior to 2000.

In conclusion, a low level of fertility prevails throughout Europe, which had a total fertility of 1.5 in 2007. Net migration is 2 per 1,000 people in 2007, and migration into Europe is difficult and discouraged in many countries. Low mortality is considered a common good, and fertility must go up or Europe will move toward depopulation.

Biographical Sketches

John Bongaarts is a Population Council vice president and Distinguished Scholar, Research Division. His research focuses on a variety of population issues, including the determinants of fertility, population-environment relationships, the demographic impact of the HIV/AIDS epidemic, and population policy options in the developing world. He is a member of the U.S. National Academy of Sciences and the Royal Dutch Academy of Sciences and is a fellow of the American Association for the Advancement of Science.

John Caldwell is professor emeritus at the Australian National University. His research focuses on understanding declining fertility, childbearing decisions, intergenerational relationships, sexual behavior, and other issues critical to population conditions in developing countries, particularly in Bangladesh, India, and Nigeria. He is a fellow of the Academy of Social Sciences, and from 1993 to 1997, he was president of the International Union for the Scientific Study of Population.

Ansley Coale was a professor at Princeton University; he died in 2002. His research included methods of indirect estimation, demographic transitions in Europe and elsewhere, and the demography of China. He taught and was a mentor to an entire generation of demographers. He was a member of the U.S. National Academy of Sciences and the American Academy of Arts and Sciences. From 1977 to 1981, he was president of the International Union for the Scientific Study of Population.

Paul Ehrlich is a population biologist and ecologist with a distinguished research record on population and the environment. He is a professor of biology at Stanford University, and his work on overpopulation has been widely debated in the scientific and popular press. Ehrlich is the author of the influential *Population Bomb* (1968) and co-author of *Population Explosion* (1990). He is a fellow of the American Association for the Advancement of Science, American Academy of Arts and Sciences, and American Philosophical Society.

Jane Menken is a professor of sociology and demography at the University of Colorado, Boulder. Her research focuses on mathematical modeling, microsimulation and empirical analyses of child survival, and the determinants of fertility. She authored the influential "Demographic-Economic Relationships and Development" (1994). Menken is a member of the U.S. National Academy of Sciences and a fellow of American Academy of Arts and Sciences and the Institute of Medicine.

Samuel H. Preston is the Frederick J. Warren Professor of Demography at the University of Pennsylvania. He has written on mortality patterns, world urbanization, and the history of child health, among other subjects. He advises the U.S. government on the reform of the social security system and is an authority on the methodologies applied in the U.S. census. He is a member of the U.S. National Academy of Sciences and the Institute of Medicine and a fellow of American Academy of Arts and Sciences, American Association for the Advancement of Science, and the American Statistical Association.

Directory

Alan Guttmacher Institute, 125 Maiden Lane, 7th Floor, New York, N.Y. 10038. Telephone: (212) 248-1111; email: info@guttmacher.org; Web: http://www.guttmacher.org. *Organization that conducts research on contraceptive use, fertility, and other reproductive health issues.*

European Association for Population Studies, EAPS Secretariat, P.O. Box 11676, 2502 AR The Hague, Lange Houtstraat 19, 2511 CV, The Hague, the Netherlands. Telephone: 31 70 35 65 200; email: contact@eaps.nl; Web: http://www.eaps.nl/. *Association of European population scientists; publishes the* European Journal of Population.

International Union for the Scientific Study of Population, 3-5 Rue Nicolas, F-75890 Paris cedex 20, France. Telephone: (33) 1 56 06 21 73; email: iussp@iussp.org; Web: http://www.iussp.org.

Association of population scientists that organizes meetings and working groups on topics of interest to the population field.

MEASURE DHS, Macro International Inc., 11785 Beltsville Drive, Suite 300, Calverton, Md. 20705. Telephone: (301) 572-0456; email: info@measuredhs.com; Web: http://www.measuredhs.com.
A project funded by the U.S. Agency for International Development that assists developing countries in collecting and using data to monitor and evaluate population, health, and nutrition programs.

Population Association of America, 8630 Fenton Street, Suite 722, Silver Spring, Md. 20910. Telephone: (301) 565-6710; email: membersvc@popassoc.org; Web: http://www.popassoc.org.
Association of population scientists; publishes Demography.

Population Council, One Dag Hammarskjold Plaza, New York, N.Y. 10017. Telephone: (212) 339-0500; email: pubinfo@popcouncil.org; Web: http://www.popcouncil.org.
Research organization that focuses on population and social policy, reproductive health, and family planning and other areas.

Population Reference Bureau, 1875 Connecticut Avenue NW, Suite 520, Washington, D.C. 20009-5728. Telephone: (800) 877-9881, (202) 483-1100; email: popref@prb.org; Web: http://www.prb.org.
Research organization that focuses on population trends, the environment, reproductive health, and HIV/AIDS.

United Nations Department of Economic and Social Affairs, Population Division, 2 United Nations Plaza, Room DC2-1950, New York, N.Y. 10017. Telephone: (212) 963-3179; Web: http://www.un.org/esa/population.
Section that houses the Population Division and gathers population-related data and research.

U.S. Census Bureau, 4600 Silver Hill Road, Washington, D.C. 20233. Telephone: (301) 763-4636; email: pop@census.gov; Web: http://www.census.gov.
U.S. government agency that conducts a census every ten years, distributes information about population trends, and provides data for administrative planning and policy.

Further Research

Books

Boserup, Esther. *Population and Technological Change.* Chicago: University of Chicago Press, 1981.

Chopra, Kanchan, and C. H. Hanumantha Rao, eds. *Growth, Equity, Environment, and Population: Economic and Sociological Perspectives.* New Delhi: SAGE, 2007.

Coale, Ansley J., and Edgar M. Hoover. *Population Growth and Economic Development in Low-Income Countries.* Princeton, N.J.: Princeton University Press, 1958.

Cohen, Joel. *How Many People Can the Earth Support?* New York: W. W. Norton, 1995.

Eberstadt, Nicholas. *Prosperous Paupers and Other Population Problems.* New Brunswick, N.J., and London: Transaction Publishers, 2000.

Ehrlich, Paul R. *One with Nineveh: Politics, Consumption, and the Human Future.* Washington, D.C.: Island Press/Shearwater Books, 2004.

———. *The Population Bomb.* New York: Ballantine Books, 1968.

Ehrlich, Paul R., and Anne Ehrlich. *The Population Explosion.* New York: Simon and Schuster, 1990.

Kwaak, Anke van der, and Madeleen Wegelin-Schuringa, eds. *Gender and Health, Policy and Practice: A Global Sourcebook.* Amsterdam: KIT (Royal Tropical Institute) and Oxford: Oxfam GB, 2006.

Lee, Ronald Demos. *Global Population Aging and Its Economic Consequences.* Washington, D.C.: AEI Press, 2007.

Livi Bacci, Massimo. *A Concise History of World Population.* 3d ed. Oxford: Blackwell Publishers, 2001.

National Research Council, Board on Sustainable Development Policy Division. *Our Common Journey: A Transition toward Sustainability.* Washington, D.C.: National Academy Press, 1999.

National Research Council, Committee on the Human Dimensions of Global Change. *Population, Land Use, and Environment: Research Directions.* Washington, D.C.: National Academic Press, 2005.

National Research Council, Forum on Biodiversity Committee. *Nature and Human Society: The Quest for a Sustainable World.* Washington, D.C.: National Academy Press, 2000.

Newbold, K. Bruce. *Six Billion Plus: World Population in the Twenty-first Century.* 2d ed. Lanham, Md.: Rowman & Littlefield, 2007.

Presser, Harriet B., and Gita Sen, eds. *Women's Empowerment and Demographic Processes: Moving beyond Cairo.* Oxford: Oxford University Press, 2000.

Robinson, Warren C., and John A. Ross, eds. *The Global Family Planning Revolution: Three Decades of Population Policies and Programs.* Washington, D.C.: World Bank, 2007.

Simon, Julian L., ed. *The Economics of Population: Classic Writings.* New Brunswick, N.J.: Transaction Publishers, 1998.

———, ed. *The Economics of Population: Key Modern Writings.* Cheltenham, UK: Edward Elgar, 1997.

———. *Population and Development in Poor Countries: Selected Essays.* Princeton, N.J.: Princeton University Press, 1992.

Weeks, John R. *Population: An Introduction to Concepts and Issues.* 9th ed. Belmont, Calif.: Wadsworth Publishing, 2005.

Articles and Reports

Ashford, Lori S. "New Population Policies: Advancing Women's Health and Rights." *Population Bulletin* 56, no. 1 (March 2001).

Bernstein, Stan. "The Changing Discourse on Population and Development: Toward a New Political Demography." *Studies in Family Planning* 36, no. 2 (2005): 127–132.

Bongaarts, John. "Late Marriage and the HIV Epidemic in sub-Saharan Africa." *Population Studies* 61, no. 1 (2007): 73–83.

Bongaarts, John, Brian C. O'Neill, and Stuart R. Gaffin. "Global Warming Policy: Population Left Out in the Cold." *Environment* 39, no. 9 (1997): 40–41.

Corrêa, Sonia, Adrienne Germain, and Rosalind P. Petchesky. "Thinking beyond ICPD+10: Where Should Our Movement Be Going?" *Reproductive Health Matters* 13, no. 25 (2005): 109–119.

Crenshaw, Edward M., Ansari Z. Ameen, and Matthew Christenson. "Population Dynamics and Economic Development: Age-Specific Population Growth Rates and Economic Growth in Developing Countries, 1965 to 1990." *American Sociological Review* 62 (December 1997): 974–984.

Dixon-Mueller, Ruth, and Adrienne Germain. "Reproductive Health and the Demographic Imagination." In *Women's Empowerment and Demographic Processes: Moving beyond Cairo*, ed. Harriet B. Presser and Gita Sen, 69–94. Oxford: Oxford University Press, 2000.

Ehrlich, Paul R. "Demography and Policy: A View from outside the Discipline." *Population and Development Review* 34, no. 1 (2008): 103–113.

Foster, Caroline. "The Limits to Low Fertility: A Biosocial Approach." *Population and Development Review* 26, no. 2 (2000).

Frumkin, Howard, Jeremy Hess, George Luber, Josephine Malilay, and Michael McGeehin. "Climate Change: The Public Health Response." *American Journal of Public Health* 98, no. 3 (2008): 435–445.

Haslegrave, Marianne. "Implementing the ICPD Programme of Action: What a Difference a Decade Makes." *Reproductive Health Matters* 12, no. 23 (2004): 12–18.

Kohler, Hans-Peter, ed. *Special Issue on Low Fertility. European Journal of Population* 17, no. 1 (2001).

Malthus, Thomas Robert. "An Essay on Population," 1798. Available at: http://www.ecn.bris.ac.uk/het/malthus/popu.txt.

Menken, Jane. "Demographic-Economic Relationships and Development." In *Population: The Complex Reality*, ed. Francis Graham-Smith, 59–70. Cambridge, UK: Cambridge University Press, 1994.

Population Reference Bureau. *2007 World Population Data Sheet*, 2007. Available at: www.prb.org.

Preston, Samuel. "Population and the Environment: The Scientific Evidence." In *Population: The Complex Reality*, ed. Francis Graham-Smith, 85–92. Cambridge, UK: Cambridge University Press, 1994.

United Nations, Department of Economic and Social Affairs, Population Division. "Below Replacement Fertility." *Population Bulletin of the United Nations*, no. 40–41 (1999).

———. *Demographic Yearbook, 2007*. New York: United Nations, 2008.

———. *Population, Development and HIV/AIDS with Particular Emphasis on Poverty: The Concise Report*. New York: United Nations, 2005.

———. *Population, Environment and Development: The Concise Report*. New York: United Nations, 2001.

———. "Recommendations for the Further Implementation of the World Population Plan of Action, Mexico City 6–14 August 1984." UN document E/CONF.76/19, 1984. Reprinted in *Population and Development Review* 10, no. 4 (1984): 758.

———. *World Population Prospects: The 2006 Revision*. New York: United Nations, 2007.

———. *World Urbanization Prospects: The 2007 Revision*. New York: United Nations, 2008.

United Nations Population Fund (UNFPA). "World Reaffirms Cairo: Official Outcomes of the ICPD at Ten Review." New York, 2005.

U.S. Congress, House Committee on Foreign Affairs. "The Mexico City Policy/Global Gag Rule: Its Impact on Family Planning and Reproductive Health." Hearing before the Committee on Foreign Affairs, House of Representatives, One Hundred Tenth Congress, first session, October 31, 2007.

World Bank. *Healthy Development: The World Bank Strategy for Health, Nutrition, & Population Results.* Washington, D.C.: World Bank, 2007.

———. *World Development Report, 2007–2008.* New York: Oxford University Press, 2008.

World Resources Institute et al. *World Resources, 2000–2001.* New York: Oxford University Press, 2001.

Web Sites

Horizons
http://www.popcouncil.org/horizons/

Population and Development Review
http://www.popcouncil.org/publications/pdr/default.htm

U.S. Census Bureau, International Data Base
http://www.census.gov/ipc/www/idb

Population Connection
http://www.zpg.org

Documents

1. World Population Plan of Action

United Nations World Population Conference, Bucharest, Romania, 1974

The full text is reprinted in Population and Development Review *1, no. 1 (1975): 163 and is available at http://www.un.org/popin/icpd/conference/bkg/wppa.html.*

Extracts

17. Countries which consider that their present or expected rates of population growth hamper their goals of promoting human welfare are invited, if they have not yet done so, to consider adopting population policies, within the framework of socio-economic development, which are consistent with basic human rights and national goals and values. . . .

37. In light of the principles of this Plan of Action, countries which consider their birth rates detrimental to their national purposes are invited to consider setting quantitative goals and implementing policies that may lead to the attainment of such goals by 1985. Nothing herein should interfere with the sovereignty of any Government to adopt or not to adopt such quantitative goals. . . .

97. This Plan of Action recognizes the responsibility of each Government to decide on its own policies and devise its own programmes of action for dealing with the problems of population and economic and social progress.

2. Programme of Action

International Conference on Population and Development, Cairo, Egypt, 1994

The full text is reprinted in Population and Development Review *21, no. 1 (1995): 187; 21, no. 2 (1995): 437 and is available at http://www.un.org/popin/icpd/conference/offeng/poa.html.*

Extracts

3.4 The objectives are to fully integrate population concerns into:

(a) Development strategies, planning, decision-making and resource allocation at all levels and in all regions, with the goal of meeting the needs, and improving the quality of life, of present and future generations;

(b) All aspects of development planning in order to promote social justice and to eradicate poverty through sustained economic growth in the context of sustainable development....

4.3 The objectives are:

(a) To achieve equality and equity based on harmonious partnership between men and women and enable women to realize their full potential;

(b) To ensure the enhancement of women's contributions to sustainable development through their full involvement in policy- and decision-making processes at all stages and participation in all aspects of production, employment, income-generating activities, education, health, science and technology, sports, culture and population-related activities and other areas, as active decision makers, participants and beneficiaries;

(c) To ensure that all women, as well as men, are provided with the education necessary for them to meet their basic human needs and to exercise their human rights....

6.3 Recognizing that the ultimate goal is the improvement of the quality of life of present and future generations, the objective is to facilitate the demographic transition as soon as possible in countries where there is an imbalance between demographic rates and social, economic and environmental goals, while fully respecting human rights. This process will contribute to the stabilization of the world population, and, together with changes in unsustainable patterns of production and consumption, to sustainable development and economic growth....

15.1 As the contribution, real and potential, of nongovernmental organizations gains clearer recognition in many countries and at regional and international levels, it is important to affirm its relevance in the context of the preparation and implementation of the present Programme of Action. To address the challenges of population and development effectively, broad and effective partnership is essential between Governments and non-governmental organizations (comprising not-for-profit groups and organizations at the local, national and international levels) to assist in the formulation, implementation, monitoring and evaluation of population and development objectives and activities.

REFUGEES AND FORCED MIGRANTS

Stephen C. Lubkemann

Almost a decade into the twenty-first century, displacement remains a significant global phenomenon and a prominent international policy concern. While 16 million people have an official status as refugees that is recognized by the United Nations, the number of those who have been forced to leave their homes to avoid violence, persecution, or natural calamity is dramatically higher and has grown substantially since the turn of the millennium. Since 2000, significant new conflicts in Sudan, Iraq, and Afghanistan, along with dramatic natural calamities (felt in places as diverse as Burma, Sri Lanka, China, and Pakistan) have generated tens of millions of new forced migrants. The persistence of long-standing civil wars (such as those in Colombia; Uganda; Somalia; and the Democratic Republic of the Congo, DRC) have also continued to produce forced migrants in significant numbers. By the beginning of 2008, the Office of the United Nations High Commissioner for Refugees (UNHCR) estimated that the total number of forced migrants worldwide was 67 million.

However, this number excludes an estimated 12 million stateless persons as well as a large number of people who are displaced but have not been officially registered as refugees. Some leading experts believe this unregistered population significantly outnumbers the registered refugees. Ultimately, a very conservative estimate that includes stateless persons and those who remain unregistered places the total number of the world's displaced at no less than 85 million, while recognizing that this number could actually be considerably higher.

Since World War II, a growing number of international humanitarian organizations have been developed to assist and protect refugees and other displaced people. Long recognized as a humanitarian problem because of its traumatizing and dehumanizing effects, forced migration has also become a core

I would like to acknowledge the contributions of my student research assistant Ally Pregulman, whose background research proved invaluable in updating this chapter and expanding its scope.

consideration in global debates about the limits of sovereignty and international intervention, in conflict resolution and peacebuilding, and in postconflict development. Over the last decade, the displacement of millions as a result of natural disasters has also generated greater awareness of environmental displacement, which is likely to become an even more prominent concern as sea levels rise, weather patterns change, and desertification intensifies because of global climate change. Displacement is thus likely to continue to pose pressing practical and moral challenges to the international community for the foreseeable future.

Historical Background and Development

Although attempts to assist uprooted people have been constant throughout history, only in the twentieth century were attempts made to create international standards and institutions for protecting displaced people. The first international effort to assist refugees occurred when the newly formed League of Nations appointed its first high commissioner for refugees in 1921. Although initially limited to assisting stateless refugees fleeing the Russian Revolution, the office of the commissioner eventually also assisted millions of ethnic minorities expelled from countries in Eastern Europe. The political weakness of the League of Nations, however, limited its ability to prevail on nations to receive asylum seekers. Most notably, it failed to assist European Jews, millions of whom perished in the Holocaust.

In the wake of World War II, the Allies, through the recently established United Nations, organized several efforts to assist the estimated 30–45 million people displaced by the war. In 1950, as postwar reconstruction in Europe progressed, the UNHCR was created to assist those who had not been resettled under previous UN programs. In 1951, the United Nations Convention Relating to the Status of Refugees established the basic definition of *refugees* recognized by international law today and specified the rights of this population and the obligations of states to uphold those rights (see INTERNATIONAL LAW). These include freedom of thought, freedom of movement, freedom from torture or degrading treatment, freedom from *refoulement* (repatriation against one's will), and the right to safe asylum and to education and medical care. The convention also requires that refugees uphold the laws of their host countries and be civilians.

The UNHCR and the 1951 convention were initially limited in scope to Europe. Prior to the late 1950s, displacement outside of Europe was addressed only on an ad hoc basis through the creation of specialized UN agencies. For example, the United Nations Relief and Works Agency for Palestine Refugees in the Near East (UNRWA) was created in 1948 to assist the more than 700,000 Palestinians displaced during the first Arab-Israeli war, and the United Nations Korean Reconstruction Agency (UNKRA) was created to assist civilians displaced by the Korean War. However, the displacement of more than 14 million people during the violent partition of India and creation of Pakistan in 1947 was never addressed by a largely Eurocentric international community that felt few of its geostrategic interests were at stake.

By the late 1950s, the emergence of new nations in the third world and the growing displacement of people during anticolonial struggles shifted the focus of international assistance to refugees outside Europe. The UNHCR undertook its first activities outside Europe in 1958 when it assisted more than 150,000 Algerian refugees who had fled to Morocco and Tunisia during the war against French colonialism. But only in 1967 did an international protocol make the UNHCR's mandate and the terms of the 1951 convention applicable worldwide (see Document 1).

In 1969, the Organization of African Unity (OAU) drafted its own regional refugee convention that broadened the UN convention's definition of *refugees* to include all people fleeing the general conditions of war, violence, or danger resulting from public disorder. Most of these refugees were self-settled and received assistance from sympathetic populations, often of the same ethnic group, or by governments in neighboring countries that had recently fought anticolonial wars. Throughout the 1970s, the UNHCR worked with host governments in Africa to create more than one hundred planned settlement schemes for refugees that were integrated into national rural development projects.

The end of several major anticolonial struggles in Africa and the conclusion of the Pakistani civil war (which led to the creation of Bangladesh) allowed significant repatriations to take place. These positive developments, however, were offset in the 1970s and 1980s by the intensification of the cold war. Proxy wars fought with superpower backing produced massive new refugee flows in Afghanistan, Angola, Cambodia, El Salvador, Ethiopia, Mozambique, and Nicaragua. External interference also contributed to the displacements produced by ethnic conflicts in Burundi, Iran, Iraq, Lebanon, Rwanda, Sri Lanka, Sudan, and Uganda.

The massive scale of refugee flows significantly affected international policies toward the displaced. Policies of humane deterrence, in which refugees were refused entry, became more commonplace. Large-scale displacements were increasingly dealt with through the creation and management of huge refugee camps. Many refugees were forced into a semidetained status in which they were dependent on aid, sometimes for decades. Refugees in such conditions became particularly susceptible to the appeals of political factions organizing armed resistance movements, sometimes with superpower support, as in the cases of Afghans and Palestinians. Consequently, refugee camps increasingly became military targets during conflicts, endangering the lives of civilians.

The end of the cold war raised hopes that such conflicts would end and that large-scale refugee repatriations might be possible. The end of apartheid in South Africa contributed to the resolution of conflicts in Mozambique and Namibia and, indeed, led in the early 1990s to successful large-scale repatriations. Lacking Soviet support, Vietnam withdrew its forces from Cambodia, paving the way for a peace settlement in 1991 and the largely successful repatriation of more than 360,000 refugees. In Central America, the negotiated settlement of long-standing civil wars in El Salvador, Guatemala, and Nicaragua and the military defeat of an insurgency in Peru resulted in the largely self-organized repatriation and resettlement of displaced populations.

Elsewhere, however, expectations that the end of the cold war would reduce the level of armed conflict and result in a dramatic decrease in displacement proved unfounded. Throughout the 1990s, major displacement-producing conflicts in Afghanistan, Angola, Eritrea, Ethiopia, Palestine, Sri Lanka, Somalia, and Sudan persisted and even intensified, driven by agendas other than those of cold war rivalry. In addition, new waves of massive displacement resulted from the first Persian Gulf War; the disintegration of the former Yugoslavia; the Rwandan genocide; and civil wars in Burundi, Colombia, East Timor, Haiti, the DRC, Liberia, Sierra Leone, and several of the former Soviet republics in central Asia. By 2001, more than 35 million people were estimated to be displaced worldwide (see ETHNIC AND REGIONAL CONFLICT and GENOCIDE).

Since 2001, several displacement-producing conflicts either were fully resolved (Angola, Liberia, Rwanda, Sierra Leone, and southern Sudan) or diminished in intensity (Haiti). However, at the same time new conflicts in Iraq, Afghanistan, and western Sudan have generated massive new forced-migration flows. Thus, as of the beginning of 2008 an estimated one in every five Iraqis (approximately 5 million people) had fled their homes, and between 3.6 and 5 million Afghans also remained displaced. Estimates of those displaced in the Darfur (western Sudan) range from 2 to 5.5 million. Moreover, seemingly intractable civil wars have persisted in northern Uganda, Colombia, Sri Lanka, the DRC, and Somalia, maintaining—and in some cases dramatically increasing—the number of those displaced in these countries and their surrounding regions. A complexly intertwined political, economic, and ecological crisis in Zimbabwe has generated a brand-new wave of displacement since 2003, estimated to number between 1.5 and 3.8 million people.

During the first decade of the new millennium, dramatic natural calamities have also displaced millions more in Pakistan, Burma, China, the southern United States, and countries along the Indian Ocean rim. In fact, at the end of 2007 the UNHCR estimated that the number of internally displaced persons (IDPs) resulting from natural calamities (25 million) almost equaled the number of IDPs created by violent conflict (26 million). While refugees with an official status recognized by the United Nations number only 16 million (11.4 under UNHCR's mandate and 4.6 million under UNRWA's), the number of individuals who are displaced worldwide—including IDPs, stateless persons, and those who have been forcibly resettled but not registered—can be conservatively estimated to number no less than 85 million (approximately one in every eighty people living on the planet).

Current Status

As defined by the 1951 UN convention, *refugees* are "individuals who are outside their own country and are unable to return as a result of a well-founded fear of persecution on grounds of race, religion, nationality, political opinion, or membership of a social group." The majority of people forcibly uprooted from their homes, however, do not fit the legal definition of a "convention refugee," either because they have been forced to move for reasons other than those specified in the convention or they are displaced internally (IDPs). Displacement is thus a process that includes but is not limited to refugees.

Moreover, individuals and groups adversely affected by displacement often include people other than those who are forced to move, such as the host populations in the impoverished nations where most uprooted people are resettled or those whose social networks are destroyed because of the outmigration of others when they are left behind in war zones. The causes of displacement today are related to the global historical trends of the past century, such as the changing structure of global geopolitics during the cold war; the rise of ethnonationalism and xenophobic sentiments in many regions of the world since the September 11, 2001, terrorist attacks in the United States; global environmental degradation; and international development policies (such as structural adjustment).

Research

During the last three decades of the twentieth century, refugees have attracted the attention of various disciplines as the relationship between displacement and a wider variety of processes—for example, conflict resolution, development, demographic change, immigration, ethnonationalism, public health, and the environment—was increasingly recognized. The development of refugee and humanitarian studies as specialized interdisciplinary subfields in their own right is a response to the heightened international visibility of complex emergencies and growing concern about how to prevent and solve displacement. Current research examines the different types of displacement and their causes; the psychological, social, and public health effects of displacement on refugees; the broader political and economic effects of displacement; how to assist and protect the uprooted; and how these challenges are changing as a result of worldwide political and economic developments and trends.

Typically, people fleeing wars and political violence have been regarded as involuntary migrants and distinguished from voluntary migrants, who move to improve their economic situation (see IMMIGRATION). Increasingly, however, researchers have questioned this distinction, pointing out that political conflict and economic well-being are often closely related. Many researchers argue that people are still displaced if they migrate because their economies have been devastated by warfare or political instability, even if they have not been the targets of violence. Cases such as Sudan and Ethiopia—where governments have forbidden the distribution of food aid within insurgent areas in an effort to starve populations thought to be harboring enemy troops—demonstrate how economic and political processes are often interrelated.

Wars can also produce forced migration by limiting people's options in the face of adverse environmental conditions. During the Mozambican civil war (1977–1992), the inability of IDPs to move from rural areas held by one warring faction to urban areas held by the other made implementing the mechanisms for coping with drought that had worked in peacetime impossible. The massive exodus across international borders that resulted was thus not caused solely by environmental hardship but also by political conditions that constrained and hampered traditional coping mechanisms.

Forced-migration researchers have also increasingly focused on the relationship between the environment and displacement. Researchers working in Bangladesh and throughout Africa coined the term *environmental refugees,* arguing that environmental insecurity can also be a cause of displacement. Work in this area considers the potential effects of worldwide environmental trends, such as global warming, on possible future displacement (see CLIMATE CHANGE and DEFORESTATION).

A related body of research that focuses on how natural disasters also produce displacement has been energized by recent natural calamities that have resulted in particularly massive population displacements. At the end of 2007, the UNHCR estimated that 25 million people remained internally displaced worldwide as a result of natural calamities. These natural disasters include the 2004 tsunami in the Indian Ocean that displaced between 1 and 2 million people, including 450,000 in Sri Lanka and 533,000 in Aceh, Indonesia, alone; Cyclone Nargis that displaced an estimated 800,000 Burmese in 2008; Hurricane Katrina that devastated Gulf Coast communities in the United States and displaced over 600,000 from the greater New Orleans metro region (over a third of which are estimated to have not yet returned); and massive earthquakes in Pakistan (2005) and in China (2008) that each left millions homeless.

Efforts such as those organized over the last several years by the National Research Council have also worked to improve data collection and estimation methods for populations affected by natural disasters. A growing body of research has shown that the effects of these natural disasters are often related to broader social, political, and economic factors because people who are economically and politically marginalized are more likely to live in areas that are more vulnerable to catastrophic events; this is still an emerging line of research that requires much more empirical work. Early estimates by Nicholas Stern suggest that as many as 200 million people may be displaced by 2050 because of the effects of climate change (including desertification and the rising sea level). The relationship between environmental degradation and displacement is likely to gain even greater research attention in the future.

Another important subfield of research examines development-induced displacement. The construction of the Three Gorges Dam on China's Yangtze River has already displaced over 1.3 million people, and as many as 4 million may ultimately be forced to relocate (see FRESHWATER). Policy researchers have also begun to investigate the relationship between natural conservation efforts and displacement. Pioneering studies conducted over the last few years in the Congo basin have focused on the socioeconomic effects of the displacement of 120,000–150,000 people that has resulted from the creation of natural parks and on the reciprocal effects on conservation efforts when these displaced communities reacted.

Researchers and policymakers have also become increasingly concerned with categories of displaced people other than those who have official status as convention refugees. At the end of 2007, UNHCR estimated that IDPs were almost three times as numerous as convention refugees. The fact that wars are increasingly internal rather than between states has also placed this population at the center of broader conflict resolution, peacebuilding, and human rights agendas (see HUMAN RIGHTS and PEACEMAKING AND PEACEBUILDING). However, research on IDPs is harder to conduct because, unlike refugees, IDPs remain in war zones and are thus much less accessible. Much as is the case with the displaced who flee across international borders but never register, reliably estimating the number of IDPs is often difficult.

Researchers have also examined how displacement affects other populations, such as those in host nations. The rapid arrival of large numbers of destitute and desperate refugees can have far-reaching and often negative economic effects on host populations. This is especially true in developing countries, which bear the brunt of the world's refugee burden and where poverty may already be widespread. Social scientists working with refugees in countries as varied as Burundi, the DRC, Guinea, Kenya, Germany, Russia, Macedonia, Rwanda, Pakistan, Turkey, Venezuela, Tanzania, and Uganda have also examined how national political stability and regional political dynamics can be affected when population movements influence ethnic composition, balances of power, and socioeconomic conditions and relations.

The political effects of displacement on the refugees themselves have also been studied, particularly cases in which refugee status has become especially prolonged. Thus, for example, millions of Palestinians have been living in camps or other forms of exile for decades, with multiple generations born and reaching adulthood as refugees. In these cases, social identities can come to be tied to political objectives that paradoxically contribute to perpetuating the very conflicts that produced displacement in the first place. Not surprisingly, refugee camps in Palestine, Jordan, and Lebanon have proved to be fertile grounds for recruitment by military groups fighting against Israeli occupation. Similarly, the Taliban traces its origins to the long-standing Afghan refugee communities that first emerged in Pakistan immediately after the 1979 Soviet occupation of Afghanistan.

Considerable research has been conducted on how displacement affects social organization, personal identities, and psychological well-being. In many refugee situations, women and children make up over 80 percent of the population, and evidence shows that wartime violence and displacement often have more negative economic and social effects on women than on men. For example, refugee women are usually more vulnerable to predatory sexual violence than refugee men, even when ostensibly under the protection of international humanitarians—in UN surveys conducted in the DRC, over 70 percent of all women reported having been raped within some internal displacement camps (see INTERNATIONAL CRIMINAL JUSTICE, WAR CRIMES, and WOMEN). A great deal of policy research has attempted to identify the most vulnerable groups within displaced populations, such as women-headed households, children, the elderly, and people with disabilities, in order to devise ways to provide them with greater assistance and protection. Some nongovernmental organizations (NGOs) and UN organizations focus exclusively on assisting vulnerable populations. The United Nations International Children's Emergency Fund (UNICEF), for example, focuses on children and their mothers. The challenges of ensuring the safety of those assisted and those who assist them have also led to more research, not only on how to protect refugees but also on how to promote their human rights.

The psychological effects of exposure to violence and displacement are attracting increased attention from mental health experts. The trauma of displacement can make adaptation to unfamiliar social and cultural environments particularly difficult. Differences between refugee cultural norms and those of the host societies often create further tensions within refugee families and between refugees and their neighboring hosts. The challenges of adaptation may be exacerbated by the uncertainty and insecurity of refugee status or by a sense of being highly constrained in a refugee camp environment. Prolonged reliance on aid while in refugee camps can also lead to diminished self-esteem and a sense of dependency and disempowerment.

One of the most fruitful recent areas of collaboration between researchers and organizations assisting refugees has been in understanding and improving humanitarian reactions to the health problems faced by refugees in complex emergencies. The catastrophic mortality rates in the Rwandan refugee camps in former Zaire (now the DRC) sounded a wake-up call within the humanitarian community that has since sparked greater collaboration with the U.S. Centers for Disease Control and Prevention and research and training programs on refugee health at leading schools of public health (see Case Study—Rwandans in Zaire 1994–1996 and Internal Displacement in the Democratic Republic of Congo 1996–2008). Note that Africa is the continent with the greatest number of IDPs and the world's highest rates of fertility, urban growth, and human immunodeficiency virus (HIV) (see AIDS, HEALTH, and POPULATION), yet the relationship between forced migration and these demographic processes has scarcely been examined.

With the growing reluctance of governments worldwide to take in immigrants, legal research has increasingly examined the relationship between refugees and immigration policies. In North America, considerable debate has revolved around the question of how *social groups* are defined and, in particular, whether women who face gender discrimination in their home countries qualify as refugees on the basis of their gender—that is, can women be considered a social group. To date, court rulings have been inconsistent regarding this matter, even in cases in which women face considerable physical danger, such as the possibility of genital mutilation.

A growing number of refugee researchers are also focusing on the active political and economic role that some refugees play as diaspora populations when they remain involved and influential in their countries of origin. Diasporas may represent an important source of direct revenue, grassroots investment, and entrepreneurship that can help kick-start the economy of war-torn societies while also providing vital human capital to societies whose educational systems have been devastated by prolonged conflict. Diasporas may also serve as the repositories and/or incubators of an independent civil society that has otherwise been crushed by wartime violence. However, research has also shown that diasporas may be highly politicized and often contain elements that avail themselves of international borders to perpetuate conflict or pursue predatory economic interests with impunity. Moreover, even though the wealth and power of diasporas may be a boon to postconflict societies, they may also be the source of significant social tension between returning diaspora groups and those in their homelands who resent the economic and educational advantages and political influence that have been afforded to their compatriots living abroad.

Another area in which research continues to develop is the field of humanitarian studies, which examines the activities of organizations that provide assistance. Some researchers have criticized humanitarian organizations because their activities are often observed to be more responsive to external pressures, such as funding, and to interorganizational rivalry and competition than to the needs of refugees themselves. Similarly, researchers have shown that humanitarian assistance that does not create sustainable solutions or use local capacities often causes considerable harm instead of helping refugee populations.

Over the last decade, research on refugees, displacement, and complex humanitarian action has grown immensely and benefited from increased institutionalization. Well-known peer-reviewed journals that focus on forced migrants now include the *Forced Migration Review, Refuge, International Migration Review,* and *Disasters,* in addition to the long-established *Journal of Refugee Studies.* A growing number of institutions of higher education also offer graduate programs in refugee and/or humanitarian studies.

Policies and Programs

The UNHCR plays a leading role in international efforts to assist and protect refugees and displaced people worldwide. The number of persons of concern to the UNHCR at the beginning of 2008 was 31.7 million, according to the UNHCR's *2007 Global Trends,* although it recognized the total number of displaced worldwide to be far higher (67 million) (see map, p. 62).

Of the 31.7 million people considered to be persons of concern to the UNHCR, approximately two-thirds were IDPs or others who did not qualify as convention refugees. The appointment in 1992 of the first UN special representative on IDPs represented a critical step in institutionalizing international concern about this group of people. The UNHCR's mandate technically has not extended to IDPs, although in practice starting in the 1990s the agency was increasingly authorized on a case-by-case basis to extend its "good offices" to assist IDPs. Other international organizations, such as the International Organization for Migration (IOM), also came to play a major role in assisting IDPs, often in conjunction with or with support from the UNHCR. In 2005, the UN Inter-Agency Standing Committee endorsed the Cluster Approach arrangement, by which UNHCR was recognized as the lead UN agency for dealing with the protection, shelter, and camp coordination in situations of internal displacement.

Assisting and protecting IDPs pose particularly thorny challenges for the international community because these populations tend to be in areas where wars are still actively being fought. National governments, often parties in these conflicts, are sometimes reluctant to allow food or other aid to be provided to civilians whom they believe to be harboring or supporting rebel factions. Conversely, insurgent groups may see receiving assistance as tacitly supporting the regimes that they are trying to overthrow when such aid is provided only to government-controlled areas or through government-approved channels.

Regional international bodies such as the OAU and the Organization of American States (OAS) have extended the definition of *refugees* to include individuals and groups forced to flee their countries because of conditions of generalized violence and insecurity rather than because of individual, specific persecution. However, at best these criteria have been applied only within these regions. In practice, countries throughout the world increasingly follow the lead of Western European and North American governments in trying to limit the number of refugees allowed to settle within their borders.

Such policies are a reaction by industrialized nations to over a quarter century of rapid growth in migration to developed countries as people flee deteriorating political and economic conditions in developing and/or war-torn nations such as Armenia, Haiti, Mexico, Nigeria, North Korea, Colombia, Iraq, Zimbabwe, and Afghanistan. These immigrants relocate in search of greater opportunity, usually settling in immediately neighboring countries, with a minority (under 15 percent) moving to the industrialized West. Flows from the developing to the developed world, in particular, have been encouraged by the globalization of mass communication, which has increased people's awareness of and aspirations for the opportunities available in many industrialized nations, and by international transportation systems that facilitate transcontinental travel.

Because the UNHCR can only advise individual states on how to interpret the refugee convention's criteria on individuals seeking asylum within their borders, governments have been able to restrict whom they accept as refugees in ways that serve their political and economic interests. Fears of the negative economic effects of excessive immigration have led industrialized nations to interpret the convention's criteria in ever more restrictive terms. Thus, for example, starting in the 1990s, some North American courts recognized that asylum seekers had fled their homes because of a legitimate fear of violence and yet still denied them refugee status because the courts determined that they were being persecuted for "nonpolitical" reasons, such as sexual orientation or gender.

Governments have also developed ways to provide temporary relief for people fleeing insecurity without incurring the legal obligations implied in granting convention refugee status. Throughout Europe and North America, different forms of temporary protection status (TPS) have been created that provide havens for displaced people fleeing generalized violence until they can safely return to their home countries. During their stay, people under TPS are usually not afforded the social benefits to which refugees are entitled, such as education and employment or the possibility of seeking asylum or permanent resettlement. Although such policies were put forth initially as short-term measures, prolonged insecurity and challenging conditions, as in, for example, Liberia and Guatemala, led to annual renewals of TPS for some displaced populations in the United States for over a decade.

In the most extreme cases, industrialized nations have resorted to more severe measures to prevent immigrant flows due to forced migration. EU states have refused entry to some asylum seekers on the grounds that they had already passed through safe countries en route from their countries of origin. Heavy fines have been imposed on airlines that transport asylum seekers who do not already have visas. Even more draconian and legally dubious measures involve intercepting refugees before they arrive on host country shores and turning them back without asylum hearings. This has been the U.S. government's policy toward the thousands of Haitian boat people who sought to land on U.S. shores since the mid-1990s. These increasingly restrictive measures represent a policy of containment, often seen as an attempt to create fortress regions with highly restricted access for forced and other migrants. Since the September 11, 2001, terrorist attacks in New York and Washington, particularly restrictive policies have at times been applied in particularly ironic ways. Thus, for example, despite being centrally involved in the conflicts in Iraq and Afghanistan that have produced millions of new forced migrants, as of the end of 2007 the United States hosted fewer than 6,000 Iraqi and fewer than 8,900 Afghan refugees.

Notably, such policies have not stemmed the rising tide of forced migrants but, instead, have tended to encourage greater levels of clandestine immigration into industrialized nations while deferring the major economic burden of displacement to less-industrialized countries, which are even more adversely affected by massive refugee influxes. In addition, the level of financial assistance that industrialized nations provide to international organizations and third world nations to assist refugees has diminished. The socioeconomic burden of hosting refugees has increasingly fallen on the countries that are the immediate neighbors of the countries that generate forced migrants. Thus, among the countries that host the largest numbers of displaced people are Jordan, Iran, Syria, Pakistan, Tanzania, and South Africa. This can be an overwhelming burden for countries that are developing nations in their own right. For example, between 1999 and 2004, Botswana, a country whose total native population numbers just over 1.8 million, became the host to an estimated 800,000 Zimbabweans fleeing mounting political and economic turmoil in their homeland.

With the unwillingness of governments everywhere to host refugees, the violence and hostility from host populations and governments toward refugees has grown. Even governments that historically were very generous hosts (such as Tanzania and Iran) started to carry out large-scale forced repatriations during the late 1990s and have continued to do so periodically since. Thus, in 2007 Iran deported over 360,000 unregistered Afghans displaced by the ongoing war in that country, while South Africa and Botswana are reported to have deported over 150,000 and 60,000 Zimbabweans, respectively.

Restrictions on asylum also reduce the options for the displaced in ways that subject them to greater risks. An example is the creation of so-called safe zones or safe havens within areas of conflict as an alternative to allowing refugees to cross international borders. In the mid-1990s, EU countries—already overwhelmed by the massive population influxes that resulted from the fall of the Berlin Wall—were reluctant to receive refugees from the former Yugoslavia and so urged the creation of safe zones in Bosnia-Herzegovina. However, insufficient military provision for ensuring the refugees' safety led to the notorious massacre of thousands of Bosnian civilians when the safe zones in Srebrenica and Zepa were overrun in 1995.

The increase in the number of IDPs and the failure of fortress policies to successfully contain forced migration flows encouraged the international community in the 1990s to begin considering how to prevent displacement in the first place. In that decade, the international community took the unprecedented step of intervening in the internal affairs of countries (for example, in Iraq and Serbia) to protect IDPs and to prevent forced migration flows across international borders. However, interest in this option has arguably waned since the turn of the millennium. The fact that the United Nations is an organization premised on the sovereignty of its members, along with the requirement that the UNHCR act at the request and with the permission of sovereign governments, has made it particularly difficult for the UNHCR to provide assistance in many cases with large numbers of IDPs (such as the Sudan). Moreover, international intervention on behalf of those internally displaced by the violent actions of their own governments—even when these acts are officially labeled genocidal—has proven particularly problematic in cases in which global powers are competing for resources and influence. Thus, in the case of Darfur, international efforts over the last five years to assist displaced populations and to pressure the Sudanese government to cease its support for the militants causing that displacement have been stymied by Chinese support for the Khartoum regime (which has become one of China's most significant sources of oil). Also, difficult and prolonged wars in Iraq and Afghanistan have channeled the bulk of U.S. (and, in the latter case, European and other U.S. allies') resources, attention, and energy and severely undermined any interest in addressing the plight of the displaced in other places (such as Myanmar, Zimbabwe, and the DRC) through direct forms of intervention.

The international community of NGOs remains divided on this issue, although some groups have taken positions that clearly prioritize assistance at the expense of considerations of national sovereignty. Note that over the last forty years, NGOs such as CARE (Cooperative for Assistance and Relief Everywhere), Catholic Relief Services, Doctors Without Borders, the International Rescue Committee, Oxfam International, and Save the Children have come to play a pivotal role in organizing and providing assistance to displaced and war-affected people worldwide. Many of these organizations work with the UNHCR, sometimes doing much of the operational work on the ground. Often these and other advocacy organizations (such as Refugees International and the U.S. Committee for Refugees International) have also influenced policymakers and national governments by bringing the plight of displaced people to the attention of the media, as in the cases of Rwanda, Kosovo, Afghanistan, and Darfur.

The nature of current conflicts presents considerable new challenges to organizations that want to assist the displaced. Many civil wars—such as those that occurred in the former Yugoslavia and Rwanda and the ongoing civil conflicts in Darfur and the eastern DRC—have been driven by ethnonationalist sentiments in which military forces have directly targeted civilian populations in an effort to eliminate or uproot minorities, a process called ethnic cleansing. In these cases, humanitarian efforts to assist the displaced do not serve the interests of the warring parties and therefore are often hindered. Long-term solutions to the displacement produced by ethnically driven violence may be particularly difficult to find. Repatriation efforts that bring ethnic groups back into the area often spark renewed violence, "revenge killings," and new displacement, as was witnessed in Kosovo.

In other situations, warring parties have an interest in the persistence of conflict. The blood diamond trade during the Sierra Leonean conflict of the 1990s and narcotrafficking in Colombia's still ongoing civil war are cases in which the targeting of populations and the creation of displacement helped perpetuate the conditions of violence, instability, and insecurity on which illegal profitable activities thrive. In some places, as has long been the case in Somalia, humanitarian aid itself has been appropriated by combatants, transforming assistance intended for refugees into a means of supporting the violent activities that produced the displacement in the first place.

Finally, in some of the major conflicts that have erupted since the September 11, 2001, terrorist attacks in the United States, armed factions have tended to treat international humanitarians as partisans in the conflict itself and have thus turned humanitarian organizations and agents into preferred targets. This has been particularly the case in the conflicts in Afghanistan and Iraq. In the first seven months of 2008 alone, twenty-three humanitarian actors were killed in Afghanistan. Among the most notable humanitarian casualties: in August 2003, the UN main office in Iraq was bombed, resulting in the death of the UN secretary-general's special representative Sergio Viera de Mello; and in August of 2006, fifteen humanitarian workers for the NGO Action Against Hunger were summarily executed by combatants in the town of Muttur in Sri Lanka.

As policymakers and humanitarian organizations have struggled with the challenges of assisting people who remain in harm's way, some organizations have shifted away from providing only basic assistance to giving greater emphasis to protecting the displaced and promoting their human rights. Thus, Doctors Without Borders (recipient of the 2000 Nobel Peace Prize) has often publicly denounced human rights violations, even if doing so insults governments or political factions and prevents them from carrying out assistance activities. In some situations in which assistance has been diverted to serve the interests of combatants (such as in the Rwandan refugee camps in eastern Zaire) or where human rights violations have been particularly grave (such as the Taliban's mistreatment of women in Afghanistan), some organizations have ceased their assistance activity. Other groups, such as the International Committee of the Red Cross/Red Crescent, have chosen not to comment on human rights violations and to remain politically neutral in order to continue to provide assistance, even if it is diverted or has unintended and undesired consequences. In extreme situations in which the climate for humanitarian action has grown dramatically insecure—such as in Iraq—a majority of international humanitarian organizations have chosen to simply forgo any presence altogether.

Important recent collaborative attempts have been made to improve humanitarian action and advocacy despite the considerable range of positions within the humanitarian community and the problems of coordination among independent and often competing organizations. Important developments in this direction include the establishment in the mid-1990s of Interaction, a coalition of more than 165 U.S.-based associations involved in voluntary international humanitarian relief, development, and advocacy work, and the Sphere initiative, a project to draft a voluntary charter with standards and ethical principles for humanitarian action. Although international humanitarian assistance efforts continue to gradually expand in scope to provide aid to all populations affected by displacement—including IDPs, hosts, and even those left behind in devastated war zones (the "displaced in place")—it has become increasingly evident that humanitarian action can be effective only if the more fundamental political and economic roots of displacement and conflict are also addressed.

Regional Summaries

North America

In contrast to other regions of the world, North America has historically been a receiver of refugees rather than a producer of displacement. In the 1990s, Canada and the United States introduced TPS to assist asylum seekers without granting them refugee status on the assumption that they would eventually return home. The unforeseen prolongation of insecurity in some refugees' countries of origin has created problems for them. Many have lived in the United States for almost a decade, during which time their social ties back home have eroded and their attachment to their host society has grown.

In the aftermath of the terrorist attacks against the United States on September 11, 2001, restrictive immigration measures diminished the rate at which the United States accepted refugees, although in 2007 the United States (followed by Canada) still accepted the largest numbers of any country for purposes of permanent resettlement (48,300 and 11,200, respectively, out of a total of 75,300 worldwide). Notably, the exact percentage of the large numbers of legal and illegal immigrants in the United States—particularly those from Haiti, Colombia, and Guatemala—that have been displaced by violence or natural calamity and yet did not enter the country as refugees is uncertain.

Convention refugees hosted in region: 281,000 (this UNHCR figure excludes 820,000 refugees who have been permanently resettled in the United States and Canada over the last decade)

IDPs: not applicable

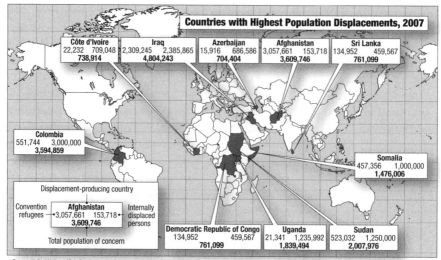

Countries with Highest Population Displacements, 2007

	Convention refugees	Internally displaced persons	Total population of concern
Côte d'Ivoire	22,232	709,048	**738,914**
Iraq	2,309,245	2,385,865	**4,804,243**
Azerbaijan	15,916	686,586	**704,404**
Afghanistan	3,057,661	153,718	**3,609,746**
Sri Lanka	134,952	459,567	**761,099**
Colombia	551,744	3,000,000	**3,594,859**
Somalia	457,356	1,000,000	**1,476,006**
Democratic Republic of Congo	134,952	459,567	**761,099**
Uganda	21,341	1,235,992	**1,839,494**
Sudan	523,032	1,250,000	**2,007,976**

Displacement-producing country

Convention refugees → **Afghanistan** 3,057,661   153,718 ← Internally displaced persons
3,609,746
Total population of concern

Source: United Nations High Commissioner for Human Rights, "Refugees, Asylum-Seekers, Internally Displaced Persons (IDPs), Returnees (Refugees and IDPs), Stateless Persons, and Others of Concern to UNHCR by Origin, End–2007," *2007 UNHCR Statistical Yearbook*, 2008. Available online from http://www.unhcr.org/cgi-bin/texis/vtx/home/opendoc.pdf?id=4981c3dc2&tbl=STATISTICS.
Note: "Convention refugees" includes all persons recognized as refugees under the 1951 UN Convention/1967 Protocol and the 1969 OAU Convention, as well as those persons in refugee-like situations; "internally displaced persons" includes persons who are displaced within their country who have received protection or assistance from the UNHCR, as well as persons in IDP-like situations; the total of these two categories does not equal the "total population of concern" figure, which also includes other categories that the UNHCR tracks, such as pending cases of asylum seekers.

Latin America and the Caribbean

During the 1990s, after three decades of widespread political violence that produced massive displacements, Latin America crafted political or military resolutions for a number of conflicts that allowed most of its displaced populations to return home. The most alarming exception to this trend remains the ever-escalating civil war in Colombia. Whereas in 2001 approximately 2.1 million people were estimated to be internally displaced within the country, by 2007 that number was estimated by Refugees International to have increased to over 3.8 million, and the UNHCR estimated that another 550,000 Colombians have fled abroad. The U.S. government's controversial decision to provide billions of dollars in mostly military aid to the Colombian government and its armed forces has contributed to the escalation of this decades-old civil war involving left-wing guerrillas, right-wing paramilitary groups, and narcotraffickers. The intensification of the civil war has increased displacement, in particular from rural to urban areas, where IDPs live in conditions of worsening poverty in shantytowns. Growing displacement across Colombia's border remains a threat to the stability of neighboring countries hosting growing numbers of forced migrants—particularly Ecuador and Venezuela, where UNHCR assists 250,000 and 200,000 Colombians, respectively, in refugee-like situations. The aftereffects of prior conflicts in Peru, Guatemala, and Mexico account for at least another 170,000 IDPs.

Convention refugees hosted in region: 487,000 (primarily the 450,000 Colombians in Venezuela and Ecuador officially recognized by UNHCR as being in "refugee-like situations")

IDPs: 3–4.2 million (including an estimated 1.4 million unregistered Colombian IDPs)

Europe

The last decade of the twentieth century witnessed massive displacement within Europe, primarily resulting from the disintegration of the former Yugoslavia in successive waves of ethnonationalist strife. Beginning in 1991, ethnic conflict in Croatia, one of the former constituent states of Yugoslavia, produced more than 200,000 refugees and 350,000 IDPs; this was followed by civil war in Bosnia-Herzegovina, which produced almost 1.2 million refugees and 1.3 IDPs between 1992 and 1995. Starting in 1998, the conflict in Kosovo produced more than 1 million refugees and 300,000 IDPs and sparked further ethnonationalist tensions in neighboring Macedonia. The apparent resolution of these conflicts has led to significant repatriations, although an estimated 132,000 IDPs remain in Bosnia-Herzegovina and 247,000 IDPs remain in Serbia.

Over the last decade Western European governments have responded to their diminishing need for immigrant labor, the rising xenophobia among their citizens, and the massive immigration from former Eastern bloc countries by instituting policies making obtaining asylum and entering EU countries in the first place more difficult. EU states have continued the efforts they began in the 1990s to harmonize their asylum and border-control policies through a series of agreements, including the Dublin and Schengen Conventions. The overall trend has been toward narrower interpretations of the 1951 refugee convention and a barrage of measures that hinder refugees from resettling in what is now often described as Fortress Europe.

Convention refugees hosted in region: 1,585,000
Conflict-induced IDPs: 350,000

Africa

At the beginning of 2008, Africa was estimated to host approximately 20 percent of the world's refugees and just under 50 percent of the world's IDPs, despite making up only 12 percent of the world's total population and remaining the most impoverished region of world. Displacement on the continent is concentrated in five subregions that have experienced political violence for more than a decade: (1) in West Africa, the end of protracted civil wars in Liberia and Sierra Leone has been counterbalanced by civil war in Côte d'Ivoire that has generated over 700,000 IDPs; (2) in the Great Lakes region in the central part of the continent, complexly intertwined civil and interstate conflicts in Burundi, the DRC (1.7–3.4 million IDPs), and Uganda (1.25 million IDPs) have produced massive forced migration flows; (3) the negotiation of an end to a long civil war and large-scale returns in southern Sudan has been eclipsed by the genocidal conflict in Darfur, the western region of Sudan, such that this country alone has an estimated 5.5–5.8 million IDPs; (4) chronic conflict in Somalia has internally displaced over 1 million people and pushed hundreds of thousands more into neighboring countries; and (5) the deterioration of political, ecological, and economic conditions in Zimbabwe has led an estimated 1.5–3.5 million Zimbabweans to flee abroad (primarily to South Africa and Botswana) and by the most reliable estimates has internally displaced at least 500,000 more. (This last contrasts with conditions a decade ago when southern

Africa was the bright spot of the continent with the resolution of conflicts in Mozambique, Namibia, and South Africa that led to largely successful repatriation efforts.) Confronting the deterioration of economic conditions throughout the continent, African governments are increasingly reluctant to host refugees, who are seen as a growing threat to national security and economic development. In 2007, South Africa alone deported over 150,000 Zimbabweans. Smaller pockets of displacement have resulted from civil wars in Algeria and in the Western Sahara, from recent violent political strife in Kenya (200,000 IDPs), and from intrastate conflicts between Eritrea and Ethiopia.

Convention refugees hosted in region: 2,271,000
Conflict-induced IDPs: 12.7–14 million

Middle East and Central Asia (including Turkey, Azerbaijan, Afghanistan, and Georgia)

The Middle East and central Asia have the world's largest number of convention refugees—more than 8 million—and three of the world's three largest producers of displacement: Afghanistan (an estimated 5–6 million abroad and 160,000 IDPs), Iraq (estimated 2 million abroad and 2.5 million IDPs), and Palestine (over 4.5 million). The Iraq and Afghan wars have been the most important causes of new displacement in the region—and globally—since the turn of the millennium. Pakistan hosts the largest number of the world's refugees, including at least 2.6 million registered Afghan refugees and possibly over 2 million more that are unregistered, while also hosting up to 500,000 people internally displaced by government action against Taliban supporters in the country's northeast provinces. Neighboring Iran hosts over 1 million registered Afghans and claims to host 1.5 million more that remain unregistered. At the end of 2007, 2.8 million Iraqis were internally displaced, with another 2 million displaced abroad (1.3 million resettled in Syria and 450,000 in Jordan alone). Significant numbers of IDPs remain in Azerbaijan (over 650,000) and Georgia (over 225,000 before the recent war with Russia), in Lebanon as a result of the recent war with Israel (over 100,000), and in Turkey (1 million). The 4.6 million Palestinians assisted by UNRWA remain the world's longest-standing refugee population, dating back to the creation of Israel and the 1948 Arab-Israeli war. This ethnoreligious and political conflict has proven to be one of the most intractable problems of the last half century and has continually produced displacement throughout the region. In another of the world's longest displacements, hundreds of thousands of Kurds remain displaced primarily in Iran, Iraq, Syria, and Turkey; at least 300,000 stateless Kurds live in Syria alone.

Convention refugees hosted in region: 2,700,000 (excluding 4,600,000 Palestinians administered by UNRWA)
Conflict-induced IDPs: more than 4,750,000

South Asia, East Asia, and the Pacific

The resolution of several major conflicts in Indochina during the early 1990s led to major repatriations that significantly reduced the number of conflict-induced refugees in this region. China continues to host over 300,000 refugees from the Sino-Vietnamese war of the early 1980s, and approximately 400,000 Burmese have sought refuge from the Myanmar regime in Thailand. Approximately 100,000 IDPs remain in East Timor in the aftermath of the conflict associated with its independence from Indonesia.

The major source of conflict-induced IDPs continues to be the persistent Sri Lankan civil conflict, where approximately 500,000 IDPs remain. Less-certain figures exist for the number of conflict-induced IDPs resulting from a variety of civil conflicts and state counterinsurgency actions in Myanmar and Bangladesh (up to 500,000 each), the Philippines (up to 140,000–300,000), Indonesia (100,000–200,000), Nepal (over 70,000), and India (up to 600,000).

Meanwhile, natural disasters have produced dramatic new waves of internal displacement in this region during the last decade, including over 1 million Sri Lankans estimated to have been displaced by the 2004 tsunami, over 800,000 Burmese believed to have been left homeless by Cyclone Nargis in 2008, and an as yet undetermined number of Chinese displaced by the massive 2008 earthquake in the southern part of that country.

Convention refugees hosted in region: 800,000
Conflict-induced IDPs: 1.5–2 million

Data

Table 1   Forced Migrant Populations in Selected Host Countries, 2001

Host country	Registered refugees	Estimated unregistered forced migration from other countries	IDPs
Botswana	3,000	up to 800,000	
Colombia			2.5–4 million
Germany	579,000		
Iran	963,000	1.5 million	500,000
Pakistan	2,160,000	2 million	
South Africa	144,000	1.5–3 million	
Somalia	2,000		1.1 million
Sudan	310,000		5.5–6 million
Syria	1,850,000	300,000 stateless Kurds	
Tanzania	435,000	Unkown but significant	
Venezuela	250,000		
Uganda	230,000		1.2 million
United States	281,000		

Source: United Nations High Commissioner for Human Rights (UNHCR), *The State of the World's Refugees: Fifty Years of Humanitarian Action* (New York: Oxford University Press, 2000); UNHCR, *2007 Global Trends Report* (Geneva: Field Information and Coordination Support Section); U.S. Committee on Refugees, *World Refugee Survey* (Washington, D.C.: USCR, 2008); Norwegian Refugee Council, "Internal Displacement: Global Overview of Trends and Developments 2007," Internal Displacement Monitoring Centre-Norwegian Refugee Council, Geneva, Switzerland.

Note: IDPs, internally displaced persons.

Case Study—Rwandans in Zaire 1994–1996 and Internal Displacement in the Democratic Republic of Congo 1996–2008

Throughout late 1994 and into 1995, the world was captivated by the media spectacle of the deplorable living conditions and appalling death rates experienced by hundreds of thousands of Rwandan Hutu refugees who had fled into Zaire (now the DRC). The media and even the international organizations assisting this population failed, however, to sufficiently examine the root causes of this displacement, which eventually led to disastrous consequences for the political stability of central Africa as a whole.

In early 1994, the Hutu-led government of Rwanda incited the Hutu majority to engage in the genocidal killing of more than 800,000 members of the Tutsi ethnic minority; this led in turn to the intensification of a Tutsi-led insurgency against the government. The eventual success of this insurgency resulted in the flight of more than 2 million Hutus into neighboring countries, including a large number of the extremists who had incited and perpetrated the genocide. Throughout eastern Zaire, the extremists quickly gained power in the largest refugee camps, leading to their militarization and use as bases for continued aggression against Rwanda in direct violation of the 1951 refugee and 1969 OAU conventions as well as to numerous human rights violations within the camps. No government was willing to take the military action necessary to separate the combatants from the civilians being used as human shields.

Humanitarian organizations were thus forced to choose between withdrawing assistance critical for civilians' survival and continuing to provide assistance, knowing that they were also supporting war criminals who continued to fight and were actually controlling the flow of aid to civilians to control these noncombatants. Eventually the use of these camps as bases led to the camps' being attacked by Rwandan government troops in alliance with insurgents in Zaire, leading in turn to that country's degeneration in 1996 into a devastating civil war that has since spilled over into or involved in some way most of the neighboring countries. Since 1996, the civil war in the DRC has claimed an estimated 4 million lives and displaced over 3.5 million people (over 1 million of whom remained uprooted as of 2008).

This case demonstrates how the resolution of refugee problems is implicated in broader political issues that require resolution before protection of and assistance to the displaced can be provided effectively. The intentional targeting and strategic manipulation of civilian populations by combatants in contemporary warfare create dilemmas for humanitarian efforts, often forcing zero-sum game choices among equally important goals, such as assistance, protection, ensuring justice, and upholding human rights. The Rwandan-DRC case also provides an example of how displacement increasingly factors as a key *cause* of conflict rather than simply being a by-product.

Biographical Sketches

Barbara Harrell-Bond founded the first and largest contemporary refugee studies program at Oxford University in the early 1980s and continues to play a key role in the institutionalization and intellectual direction of refugee studies as an interdisciplinary subfield. While director of the refugee program at Oxford, Harrell-Bond founded the *Journal of Refugee Studies* and conducted anthropological research with refugees throughout Africa. She was influential in the establishment of new refugee studies programs in Kenya, Egypt, and South Africa and in the development of the International Association for the Study of Forced Migration.

Francis Deng, a career Sudanese diplomat and scholar, was appointed by UN Secretary-General Ban Ki-moon as the special adviser for the prevention of genocide in 2007. At the time of his appointment, Deng was serving as a Wilhelm Fellow at the Center for International Studies of the Massachusetts Institute of Technology (MIT) and a research professor of international politics, law, and society at the Johns Hopkins University Paul H. Nitze School of Advanced International Studies. Deng has been the most important scholarly and policy voice focusing international attention on the growing phenomenon of internal displacement. He is co-author of the landmark volumes *Masses in Flight: The Global Crisis of Internal Displacement* (1998) and *The Forsaken People: Case Studies of the Internally Displaced* (1998).

Larry Minear is the director of the Humanitarianism and War Project, currently based at Tufts University. He organized and co-directed the project in 1990, after working more than two decades as a humanitarian aid practitioner. The project has produced arguably the most thorough critical assessment of humanitarian action through a series of more than forty case-based studies drawing on more than one hundred of the top specialists and leading practitioners and policymakers in the field. The Humanitarianism and War Project has played a significant role in stimulating reflection among humanitarian aid organizations and in the way humanitarian assistance is provided to refugees and other populations affected by complex emergencies.

Sadako Ogata is a scholar and former chair of the UNICEF executive board. In 1990, she became the first academic and female UN high commissioner for refugees, an office she held until 2000. Her tenure was marked by an expansion of the UNCHR's activities to encompass the growing number of displaced and war-affected people who are not recognized as convention refugees, in particular IDPs. In part through her efforts, the link between international security and refugees was increasingly recognized.

Directory

CARE, 151 Ellis Street NE, Atlanta, Ga. 30303. Telephone: (800) 521-CARE; email: info@care.org; Web: http://www.care.org.
Organization that provides assistance in complex emergencies worldwide.

Catholic Relief Services, 228 West Lexington Street, Baltimore, Md. 21201-3413. Telephone: (888) 277-7575; email: infi@crs.org; Web: http://crs.org.
Faith-based organization that assists displaced and disadvantaged people worldwide.

Center for Migration and Refugee Studies, American University in Cairo, P.O. Box 74, New Cairo 11835, Egypt. Telephone: 20 2 2615 1000; Web: http://www .aucegypt.edu/ResearchatAUC/rc/cmrs.
An academic center for the study of refugee issues.

Center for Refugee and Disaster Response, Johns Hopkins Bloomberg School of Public Health, 615 N. Wolfe Street, Room E8646, Baltimore Md. 21205. Telephone: (410) 502-2632; Web: http://www.jhsph.edu/refugee.
Academic research center for the study of disaster and humanitarian relief.

Centre for Humanitarian Dialogue, 114, Rue de Lausanne, CH-1202 Geneva, Switzerland. Telephone: +41 (0)22 908 11 30; Web: http://www.hdcentre.org.
Conflict-mediation organization that publishes an influential policy paper series on humanitarian issues.

Centre for Refugee Studies, 4700 Keele Street, York University, York Lanes, Room 321, Toronto, Ont. M3J1P3, Canada. Telephone: (416) 736-5663; email: crs@yorku.ca; Web: http://www.yorku.ca/crs.
Academic-based policy and research institute for refugee issues.

Doctors Without Borders, 333 7th Avenue, 2nd Floor, New York, N.Y. 10001-5004. Telephone: (212) 679-6800; Web: http://www.doctorswithoutborders.org.
International organization dedicated to providing medical assistance in complex emergencies.

European Council on Refugees and Exiles, 153-157 Commercial Road, 4th Floor, London E1 2DA, United Kingdom. Telephone: (44) 171 729 5252; email: ecre@ ecre.org; Web: http://www.ecre.org.
Umbrella organization of seventy refugee-assisting agencies in twenty-five European countries.

Forced Migration Studies Programme, School of Social Science, University of Witwatersrand, P.O. Box 76, Wits 2050, Johannesburg, South Africa. Telephone: 27 11 7174033; email: info@migration.org.za; Web: http://migration.org.za.
Academic research and training program focused on forced migration.

Human Rights Watch, 350 Fifth Avenue, 34th Floor, New York, N.Y. 10118-3299. Telephone: (212) 216-1221; email: hrwnyc@hrw.org; Web: http://www.hrw.org.
Organization that advocates for human rights worldwide, including those of refugees, asylum seekers, migrants, and IDPs.

Interaction—American Council for Voluntary International Action, 1400 16th Street NW, Suite 210, Washington, D.C. 20036. Telephone: (202) 667-8227; email: ia@ interaction.org; Web: http://www.interaction.org.
Umbrella organization of 165 voluntary agencies involved in humanitarian action and relief.

Internal Displacement Monitoring Centre—Norwegian Refugee Council, Chemin de Balexert 7-9, 1219 Châtelaine, Geneva, Switzerland. Telephone: +41 22 799 07 00; Web: http://www.internal-displacement.org.
Premier international initiative that monitors internal displacement trends and developments worldwide.

International Association for the Study of Forced Migration (IASFM), c/o Institute for the Study of International Migration, Georgetown University, 3300

Whitehaven Street NW, Suite 3100, Washington, D.C. 20007. Telephone: (202) 687-2258; email: secretariat@iasfm.org; Web: http://www.iasfm.org.
Organization that every two years brings together researchers, academics, and policymakers for a major international conference to assess the state of the art of forced migration research and discuss prominent refugee and related policy trends and issues.

International Federation of the Red Cross and Red Crescent Societies, P.O. Box 372, CH-1211, Geneva 19, Switzerland. Telephone: (41) 22 730 4242. Web: http://www.ifrc.org.
World's largest humanitarian organization dedicated to improving the lives of vulnerable people.

International Organization for Migration (IOM), 17 Route des Morillons, CH-1211 Geneva 19, Switzerland. Telephone: (41) 22 717 9111; email: hq@iom.int; Web: http://www.iom.int.
Intergovernmental organization working to provide humane responses to migration and displacement worldwide.

International Rescue Committee, 122 East 42nd Street, New York, N.Y. 10168-1289. Telephone: (212) 551-3000; Web: http://www.theirc.org/.
International organization dedicated to assisting people fleeing persecution or uprooted by violence.

Jesuit Refugee Services, 1016 16th Street NW, Suite 500, Washington, D.C. 20036. Telephone: (202) 462-0400; email: jrsusa@jesuit.org; Web: http://www.jrsusa.org.
Faith-based organization that assists, accompanies, and defends the rights of people forcibly displaced worldwide.

Oxfam International, 226 Causeway Street, 5th Floor, Boston, Mass. 02114-2206. Telephone: (800) 77-OXFAM; email: info@oxfamamerica.org; Web: http://www.oxfam.org.
Confederation of twelve NGOs that provides emergency relief in developing countries.

Refugee Studies Centre, Oxford Department of International Development (QEH), University of Oxford, 3 Mansfield Road, Oxford OX1 3TB, United Kingdom. Telephone: (44) 1865 281 720; Web: http://www.rsc.ox.ac.uk.
Academic research center focusing on the interdisciplinary study of forced migration and related issues.

Refugees International, 2001 S Street NW, Suite 700, Washington, D.C. 20009. Telephone: (202) 828-0110; email: ri@refintl.org; Web: http://www.refugeesinternational.org.
NGO responding to the needs of refugees and displaced and dispossessed people.

United Nations High Commissioner for Refugees (UNHCR). Case Postale 2500, CH-1211 Geneva 2, Switzerland. Telephone: (41) 22 739 8111; Web: http://www.unhcr.org.
UN agency involved in refugee assistance and protection worldwide.

U.S. Committee for Refugees and Immigrants, 2231 Crystal Drive, Suite 350, Arlington, Va. 22202-3711. Telephone: (703) 310-1130; Web: http://www.refugees.org.
Organization dedicated to defending the rights of uprooted people.

Women's Commission for Refugee Women and Children, 122 East 42nd Street, New York, N.Y. 10168. Telephone: (212) 551-3089; Web: http://www.womens commission.org.
Organization that advocates for the protection and well-being of displaced women, children, and adolescents.

Further Research

Books

Ahearn, Frederick L., Jr., ed. *Psychosocial Wellness of Refugees: Issues in Qualitative and Quantitative Research.* New York: Berghahn, 2000.

Black, Richard. *Refugees, Environment, and Development.* New York: Longman, 1998.

Black, Richard, and Khalid Koser, eds. *The End of the Refugee Cycle?: Refugee Repatriation and Reconstruction.* New York: Berghahn, 1999.

Cernea, Michael, and C. McDowell, eds. *Risks and Reconstruction: Experiences of Resettlers and Refugees.* Washington, D.C.: World Bank Press, 2000.

Chimni, B. S., ed. *International Refugee Law: A Reader.* New Delhi: Sage Publications, 2000.

Cohen, Roberta, and Francis Deng. *Masses in Flight: The Global Crisis of Internal Displacement.* Washington, D.C.: Brookings Institution, 1998.

Crepeau, François, et al. *Forced Migration and Global Processes: A View from Forced Migration Studies.* Lanham, Md.: Lexington Books, 2006.

Essed, Philomena, G. Frerks, and J. Schrijvers, eds. *Refugees and the Transformation of Societies: Agency, Policies, Ethics and Politics.* New York: Berghahn, 2004.

Harrell-Bond, Barbara. *Imposing Aid: Emergency Assistance to Refugees.* Oxford: Oxford University Press, 1986.

Indra, Doreen, ed. *Engendering Forced Migration: Theory and Practice.* New York: Berghahn, 1999.

Kemp, Charles, and Lance Rasbridge. *Refugee and Immigrant Health: A Handbook for Health Professionals.* Cambridge, UK: Cambridge University Press, 2004.

Koslowski, Rey, ed. *International Migration and the Globalization of Domestic Politics.* New York: Routledge, 2000.

Long, Lynellyn, and E. Oxfeld, eds. *Coming Home: Refugees, Migrants, and Those Who Stayed Behind.* Philadelphia: University of Pennsylvania Press, 2004.

Malkki, Liisa H. *Purity and Exile: Violence, Memory, and National Cosmology among Hutu Refugees in Tanzania.* Chicago: University of Chicago Press, 1995.

Minear, Larry. *The Humanitarian Enterprise: Dilemmas and Discoveries.* Bloomfield, Conn.: Kumarian Press, 2002.

National Research Council Committee on the Effective Use of Data, Methodologies, and Technologies to Estimate Subnational Populations at Risk. *Tools and Methods for Estimating Populations at Risk from Natural Disasters and Complex Humanitarian Crises.* Washington, D.C.: National Academies Press, 2007.

Ohta, Itaru, and Y. D. Gebre, eds. *Displacement Risks in Africa: Refugees, Resettlers and Their Host Population.* Kyoto: Kyoto University Press, 2005.

Van Hear, Nicholas. *New Diasporas: The Mass Exodus, Dispersal and Regrouping of Migrant Communities.* London: University College London Press, 1998.

Van Hear, Nicholas, and C. McDowell, eds. *Catching Fire: Containing Forced Migration in a Volatile World.* Lanham, Md.: Lexington Books, 2006.

Verdirame, Guglielmo, and B. Harrell-Bond. *Rights in Exile: Janus-Faced Humanitarianism.* New York: Berghahn, 2005.

Vincent, Mark, and B. R. Sorenson, eds. *Caught between Borders: Response Strategies of the Internally Displaced.* London: Pluto Press, 2001.

de Wet, Chris, ed. *Development-Induced Displacement: Problems, Programs and People.* New York: Berghahn, 2006.

Articles and Reports

Black, R. "Environmental Refugees: Myth or Reality?" UNHCR, Geneva, 2001. Available at: http://www.unhcr.ch/refworld/pubs/pubon.htm.

Black, R., et al. "Demographics and Climate Change: Future Trends and Their Policy Implications for Migration." Brighton, Development Centre on Migration, Globalisation and Poverty, 2008. Available at: http://www.migrationdrc.org/publications/working_papers/WP-T27.pdf.

Cernea, Michael, and K. Scmidt-Soltau. "Poverty Risks and National Parks: Policy Issues in Conservation and Resettlement." *World Development* 34, no. 10 (2006): 1808–1830.

Lubkemann, Stephen. "Involuntary Immobility: On a Theoretical Invisibility in Forced Migration Studies." *Journal of Refugee Studies* 21, no. 3 (2008): 1–22.

Malkki, Liisa. "National Geographic: The Rooting of Peoples and the Territorialization of National Identity among Scholars and Refugees." *Cultural Anthropology* 7, no. 1 (1992): 24–43.

Myers, N. "Environmental Refugees: A Growing Phenomenon of the 21st Century." *Philosophical Transactions: Biological Sciences* 357 (2001): 609–613.

United Nations High Commissioner for Human Rights (UNHCR). *The State of the World's Refugees: Fifty Years of Humanitarian Action.* New York: Oxford University Press, 2000.

———. *2008 Global Trends Report.* Geneva: Field Information and Coordination Support Section, 2008.

U.S. Committee on Refugees. *World Refugee Survey.* Washington, D.C.: USCR, 2008.

Web Sites

Global IDP Survey
http://www.idpproject.org

International Association for Study of Forced Migration
http://www.iasfm.org

Document

1. Protocol Relating to the Status of Refugees of 31 January 1967

United Nations General Assembly, October 4, 1967

The full text is available at http://www.unhcr.org/cgi-bin/texis/vtx/protect/opendoc.pdf?tbl= PROTECTION&id=3b66c2aa10.

Extract

Considering that the Convention relating to the Status of Refugees done at Geneva on 28 July 1951 (hereinafter referred to as the Convention) covers only those persons who have become refugees as a result of events occurring before 1 January, 1951,

Considering that new refugee situations have arisen since the Convention was adopted and that the refugees concerned may therefore not fall within the scope of the Convention,

Considering that it is desirable that equal status should be enjoyed by all refugees covered by the definition in the Convention irrespective of the dateline 1 January 1951,

Have agreed as follows:

Article 1

General provision

3. The present Protocol shall be applied by the States Parties hereto without any geographic limitation, save that existing declarations made by States already Parties to the Convention in accordance with Article 1 B (1)(a) of the Convention, shall, unless extended under Article 1 B (2) thereof, apply also under the present Protocol.

URBANIZATION

Melanie Jarman

More than half the world's population lives in urban areas. In the foreword to the United Nations report *State of the World's Cities 2008/2009,* UN Secretary-General Ban Ki-moon described the twenty-first century as "the urban century," a time when "harmonious urbanization" has never been more important. Within two decades, nearly 60 percent of the world's people are predicted to be urban dwellers. Urban growth is taking place most quickly in the developing world, where, according to the UN's report, cities gain an average of 5 million residents a month. Although urbanization is a potent force for economic, social, and cultural development, these benefits are sometimes won only at considerable environmental and social costs that frequently have international and sometimes global implications.

Historical Background and Development

The urban environment may seem a quintessential feature of the modern world, but even ancient civilizations had cities. Mohenjo-Daro in the Indus Valley (ca. 3000 BC), Kahun in Egypt (ca. 2000 BC), and Miletus in Greece (ca. 500 BC) were methodically laid out in what were probably the earliest examples of urban planning. By the time of the ancient Greeks, theories of urban planning had been formalized by Plato, Hippocrates, and Aristotle. Centuries later, the Roman writer Vitruvius wrote the first major treatise on architecture, *De architectura,* which greatly influenced urban planning in the centuries that followed.

Cities span centuries, yet the process of urbanization is a much more recent phenomenon, closely tied to the spread of industrial development from the middle of the nineteenth century to the present. Urbanization brought such problems as pollution, high infant mortality rates, and a massive increase in slum dwellings. It also brought responses in the form of public health legislation, such as England's Health of the Towns Act (1868), which allowed local government authorities to set standards for sewage disposal and the general condition of housing. In addition, it led to theories of how to build better

This chapter is based on the original, written by Chris Woodford, that appeared in the first edition of *World at Risk.*

settlements, where people could live and work at high population densities without suffering the usual problems created by urbanization.

Nineteenth- and twentieth-century architects proposed numerous solutions to these problems. The Chicago School of architects pioneered skyscrapers during the mid-nineteenth century. Sir Ebeneezer Howard (in Britain) and his disciples Clarence Stein and Henry Radburn (in the United States) offered a new vision of the "garden city," a small urban settlement permanently surrounded by countryside. Modernist architects, notably Le Corbusier (from Switzerland), sketched visions that replaced existing cities with massive tower blocks separated by roads and surrounded by parkland.

Nevertheless, architectural utopias have little to offer in solving the most fundamental urban problem of all: satisfying the basic human right to shelter as enshrined in the 1948 Universal Declaration of Human Rights. During the second half of the twentieth century, informal shantytowns became defining features of most cities in developing countries, housing an estimated 30–60 percent of the urban population. Since the 1987 World Commission on Environment and Development's Brundtland Report, *Our Common Future,* popularized the term *sustainable development,* the idea of sustainable cities has become fashionable as the solution to the urban crisis. A major advance toward urban sustainability was made when 171 governments adopted the Istanbul Declaration and the Habitat Agenda at the Second United Nations Conference on Human Settlements (Habitat II) in June 1996. The Habitat Agenda, which emphasizes the importance of citizen participation and local work to achieve sustainable habitation, contains over one hundred commitments and six hundred recommendations on human settlements issues, although commentators have suggested that it is not specific enough in its targets and time scale. The Habitat Agenda has been supported by the World Urban Forum. This first met in 2002 and was heralded by Anna Kajumulo, executive director of the United Nations Human Settlements Programme (UN-Habitat), as a path-breaking global initiative.

Current Status

Urbanization itself is not a bad thing. As the World Bank report *Cities in Transition* argued, "The urban transition offers significant opportunities to improve the quality of life for all individuals, but whether this potential is realized depends critically on how cities are managed and on the national and local policies affecting their development." In other words, whether urbanization results in benefits or problems depends on whether it is managed through effective policies and programs or simply allowed to proceed in a laissez-faire manner, unplanned and unchecked.

Research

In February 2001, the American Association for the Advancement of Science published a series of satellite maps, called the *Atlas of Population and Environment,* that revealed the extent of humankind's influence on the natural environment. According to the association's data, around half of Earth's surface has been transformed for humankind's use. Although just 2–3 percent has been urbanized for industry, housing, services, and transportation, a much greater area has been transformed by the farming, commercial forestry, and pastures needed to support an increasingly urban population (see POPULATION). Megacities (areas with 10 million inhabitants or more) cover vast amounts of territory; yet any megacity's ecological footprint (the area of land needed to feed the people of an area, provide energy, and dispose of their waste) may be vastly greater. For example, London's ecological footprint is estimated to be as much as 125 times greater than the area occupied by the city itself.

Because different regions are in different stages of development, urbanization presents different problems in different parts of the world. In the developed countries of Western Europe and North America, for example, a net movement away from many urban areas is found. Here, one of the main problems of urbanization is reconciling the progressive deterioration of urban areas with the gradual suburbanization of the rural areas that surround them. In rapidly industrializing nations such as China and India, urbanization may bring other problems, such as pollution or excessive stress on natural resources, including the water supplies needed to support a growing urban population (see FRESHWATER and POLLUTION). The worst effects of urbanization, however, often fall on developing nations, those least equipped to cope with them, and, within these nations, they fall disproportionately on the growing underclass of urban poor (see INCOME INEQUALITY). The highest levels of urban poverty in the world are found in sub-Saharan Africa. In the poorest countries there, more than 50 percent of the urban population lives below the poverty line, according to the UN report *State of the World's Cities 2008/2009*. Urbanization therefore involves not only the extension of cities but also the growth of the urban poor within them, people who are disproportionately affected by problems such as pollution, poor sanitation, and natural disasters. According to the United Nations Environment Programme, the slums and squatter camps in large cities in some developing nations are growing twice as fast annually as the cities themselves are growing.

The adverse social and environmental impacts have saddled the term *urbanization* with a negative connotation. The frequent pairing of the word *urban* with terms such as *decay, renewal*, and *regeneration* insinuates that the urban dream has condemned millions of people to lives of poverty and degradation. Chapter 2 of the UN report *State of World Population 2007* estimated that one out of every three city dwellers lives in slums or shantytowns. This adds up to approximately 1 billion people—one-sixth of the world's population—living on the fringes of megacities often with little or no access to safe water and sanitation, let alone electricity. The report said that South Asia has the largest share of slum dwellers, followed by Eastern Asia, sub-Saharan Africa, and Latin America. Over 90 percent of slum dwellers are in the developing world. Often the first urban living environment for rural migrants, shanty settlements provide a significant proportion of the accommodations for poor people in many large cities of the developing world.

Shantytowns, usually constructed illegally by the people who live there, are perhaps the most obvious example of unplanned urbanization, yet even in developed countries, cities continue to evolve in a largely inefficient and haphazard way. Pioneers of modernist architecture, such as Le Corbusier, may have sketched gleaming urban dream cities as "machines for living in," but they invariably started with blank sheets of paper. The reality of the modern metropolis is more likely to be unplanned sprawl, reinvented over many decades or even centuries, using land and environmental resources in an inefficient and therefore unsustainable manner and often lacking overall cohesiveness.

In developing countries, a lack of financial support for urban planning and development is partly to blame. In 2008 in Doha, world leaders reiterated their commitment to financing development as laid out in the Monterrey Consensus of 2002. This consensus included commitments to development aid, but, at the time of the Doha meeting, it was criticized by the European Network on Debt and Development for not bringing about necessary policy changes.

Cities in developed countries are older and more constrained and therefore evolve with more difficulty. Developing greenfield areas bordering suburbs is often cheaper and easier than recycling "brownfield" sites in city centers, so market incentives tend to favor urban sprawl over urban regeneration. Despite sound environmental reasons for coordinating housing, office developments, and transportation links in an approach known as integrated land-use planning, economic imperatives may favor large out-of-town developments accessible only by automobile. Multiple-use cities that mix housing, urban developments, and open space may gradually be replaced by concentric circles of ghettoization, with the business district at the center surrounded by the downtown "no-go" ghettos and high-security residential suburbs on the periphery. Without effective policies and programs to control urbanization, the social and environmental problems associated with human settlements become self-perpetuating and mutually reinforcing.

What of the future? According to the 2007 UN report on the state of the world's population, almost 5 billion people will be living in urban areas by 2030. This will include an unprecedented growth in urban dwellers in the developing world. The urban population in Asia is expected to increase from 1.36 billion to 2.64 billion between 2000 and 2030, in Africa from 294 million to 742 million, and in Latin America and the Caribbean from 394 million to 609 million. Towns and cities of the developing world are expected to make up 81 percent of urban humanity by 2030. Rural-urban migration, the urbanization of rural settlements, and natural increase are all contributing factors to this trend. Although megacities such as New York and Beijing, with their 10 million or more inhabitants, attract more attention than smaller towns and cities, they are not expected to account for the bulk of urban population growth. Many of the largest cities, including Buenos Aires, Calcutta, Mexico City, São Paulo, and Seoul actually have more people moving out than in, and few are close to the size predicted in the 1970s. Smaller cities are expected to account for about half of urban population growth between 2005 and 2015. The 2007 UN population report said that this trend toward smaller cities "offers both comfort and concern." Smaller cities may have more flexibility in terms of territorial expansion, attracting investment, but, according to the UN report, they generally have more unaddressed problems; have fewer human, financial, and technical resources at their disposal; and are underserved in housing, transportation, piped water, waste disposal, and other services.

Policies and Programs

Urbanization first made a noticeable appearance on the international policy agenda in 1976, when the UN held an event in Vancouver titled "Habitat: United Nations Conference on Human Settlements." This landmark event released a declaration noting that "the condition of human settlements largely determines the quality of life." It called on the international community to develop policies to address problems stemming from massive urban growth, particularly in the developing world. Given the task to "promote socially and environmentally sustainable towns and cities with the goal of providing adequate shelter for all," the United Nations Human Settlements Programme (UN-Habitat) spent the next two decades struggling to address the problems stemming from massive urban growth, particularly in the developing world.

In 1996, the United Nations held a second conference on cities, Habitat II in Istanbul, to assess the progress since Vancouver and set fresh goals for the new millennium. The document that came out of this summit is known as the Habitat Agenda and has been adopted by 171 countries (see Document 3). As previously mentioned, it contains over one hundred commitments and six hundred recommendations on human settlements issues. The Habitat agenda was reaffirmed in 2001 with the release of the "Declaration on Cities and Other Human Settlements in the New Millennium," known as the Millennium Declaration (see Document 2). This recognized that the world was facing the unprecedented growth of urban population and also "widespread poverty" as a "core obstacle." The declaration also included the goal of improving the lives of at least 100 million slum dwellers by the year 2020.

Alongside these significant declarations on urbanization issues, the early years of the new millennium also saw the establishment of the World Urban Forum. This is a biennial gathering whose attendees include representatives from governments, local authorities, and national and international associations of local governments along with nongovernmental organizations, community-based organizations, urban professionals, and academics. The World Urban Forum gives this wide range of participants a common platform to discuss— and make proposals on—rapid urbanization and its impact on governments, local authorities, and national and international associations of local governments. Speaking after the first World Urban Forum in 2002, Anna Tibaijuka, executive director of UN-Habitat, said, "the high turn out shows how concerned the world is about the state of their cities." Approximately 1,200 people attended this first forum in Nairobi and the number of attendees rose sharply— to 4,400—at the second World Urban Forum in Barcelona in 2004.

The third session of the World Urban Forum took place in Vancouver in 2006 and had as its main theme "Our Future: Sustainable Cities—Turning Ideas into Action" (see Document 1). Participants at the forum took the view that sustainability and its link to poverty were a major challenge facing all cities. Although the World Urban Forum has no legislative powers and does not follow the formal rules of procedure that usually govern official UN meetings, the sessions can feed into UN processes. For example, UN-Habitat committed to take the outcomes of the third session of the World Urban Forum to its Governing Council and, through it, to the UN General Assembly, with a call for a strengthened role of the United Nation system and international agencies in meeting the urban sustainability challenge.

UN-Habitat runs programs and projects in sixty-one countries around the world, most of them in the least-developed countries. These include major projects in postwar societies such as Afghanistan, Kosovo, Somalia, Iraq, Rwanda, and the Democratic Republic of Congo. Current UN-Habitat projects also include a slum-upgrading initiative that is run jointly with the World Bank. This initiative, the Cities Alliance, is a global coalition committed to addressing poverty. Its work includes promoting effective housing development policies and strategies, helping to develop and campaign for housing rights, and promoting sustainable cities and urban environmental planning and management.

UN-Habitat publications that support the development of policies and programs on urbanization issues include the *State of the World's Cities*. This report is published every two years and is intended as a tool to connect monitoring information to policy. Each report takes a different focus. The 2008–2009 report focused on strategies to develop harmony among the spatial, social, and environmental aspects of a city and among its inhabitants in the face of significant growth in urban populations. The 2006–2007 report looked at urban and slum trends in the twenty-first century, recognizing that 2007 saw the number of slum dwellers cross the 1 billion mark. Other useful monitors on urbanization issues include annual reports produced by the UN Population Division, which include latest estimates of global urban population.

The World Health Organization (WHO) has also initiated a notable program on urbanization issues—the Healthy Cities Program. The term *healthy cities* was coined in 1985 in the title of a speech given at an international meeting in Canada. The thinking behind it is that people are healthy when they live in nurturing environments and are involved in the life of their community. After opening a Healthy Cities Project office in Europe, the WHO invited interested parties to come together and share strategies, resources, and success stories. The Healthy Cities movement now includes projects in more than 1,000 cities.

Regional Summaries

Patterns of urbanization vary dramatically around the world. In Europe and the Americas, roughly 80 percent of the population live in urban areas. Elsewhere in the world, notably in East Africa, levels of urbanization are as low as 6 percent.

North America

In North America during the early part of the twentieth century, immigration, population growth, and the development of transportation systems such as railroads and highways spurred considerable urban and suburban development; by 1980 around three-fourths of the population in the United States and in

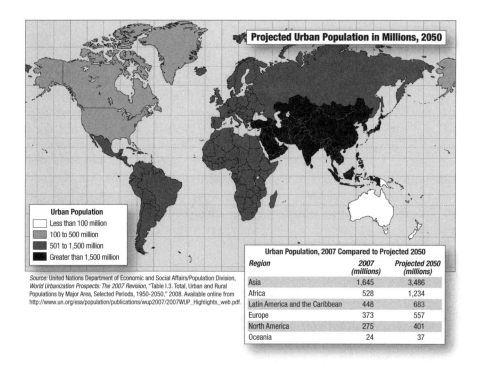

Projected Urban Population in Millions, 2050

Urban Population
- Less than 100 million
- 100 to 500 million
- 501 to 1,500 million
- Greater than 1,500 million

Source: United Nations Department of Economic and Social Affairs/Population Division, *World Urbanization Prospects: The 2007 Revision,* "Table I.3. Total, Urban and Rural Populations by Major Area, Selected Periods, 1950-2050," 2008. Available online from http://www.un.org/esa/population/publications/wup2007/2007WUP_Highlights_web.pdf.

Urban Population, 2007 Compared to Projected 2050		
Region	2007 (millions)	Projected 2050 (millions)
Asia	1,645	3,486
Africa	528	1,234
Latin America and the Caribbean	448	683
Europe	373	557
North America	275	401
Oceania	24	37

Canada lived in urban areas. Although this rapid growth slowed substantially toward the end of the century, a trend towards urbanization continues. The Statistics Canada Web site has reported that in 2006 80 percent of all Canadians lived in an area classified as urban, up from 78 percent in 1996.

Cities in the United States with major urban problems include Los Angeles and New York, which rank among the world's most heavily polluted cities. Los Angeles is also notable for the way its neighborhoods have become increasingly segregated in recent decades.

Latin America

Latin America and the Caribbean is the most urbanized region in the developing world. Overall, the region experienced dramatic urbanization during the second half of the twentieth century, with the urban population growing from 41.4 percent in 1950, to 73.4 percent in 1995, and to 77.5 percent in 2005, according to UN population figures. This population is expected to reach approximately 83 percent by 2030. Spectacular urban growth occurred in a number of mega-cities; some of the world's largest cities are in this region, including Bogotá, Buenos Aires, Mexico City, Rio de Janeiro, and São Paulo. Substantial population growth is now occurring in small and medium-size cities too. The small Brazilian city of São José dos Pinhais, in the Paraná region, has grown at an annual rate of over 9 percent, partly due to its hosting of an international airport.

Bogotá, Mexico City, Rio de Janeiro, and São Paulo are cities suffering the strains of urbanization, including chronic air pollution. Caracas, La Paz, Lima, Rio de Janeiro, and São Paulo, among other cities, have severe urban sanitation problems.

Europe

Roughly three-fourths of the population of Europe currently live in urban areas. Despite massive urban and suburban growth throughout the twentieth century, current rates of urbanization have slowed virtually to zero except in Eastern Europe, where urban growth is now negative. According to UN population figures, the urban annual growth rate for Europe in 2005–2010 is estimated to be 0.17 percent, compared to 1.18 percent in 1975–1980. For Eastern Europe alone, the urban annual growth rate in 2005–2010 is estimated to be −0.43 percent, compared to 1.66 percent in 1975–1980. Nevertheless, some 77.8 percent of all Europeans and 73.1 percent of Eastern Europeans will live in urban areas in 2030, compared to just 65.7 and 60.6 percent, respectively, in 1975. London typifies cities in the region that are trying to deal with gridlocked roads, expensive real estate, huge economic disparities, crime, and health problems associated with pollution.

North Africa and the Middle East

Urbanization is, at present, much greater in North Africa (where roughly half the people live in urban areas) than in sub-Saharan Africa (where urbanization stands at roughly 40 percent). In the Middle East, urbanization has occurred partly through a gradual drift of the population from rural to urban regions and, in the Arabian Peninsula, partly because of the sudden industrialization prompted by the postwar oil boom. In a November 2008 interview on the World Bank Web site, Anna Bjerde, sector manager for urban and social development in the World Bank's Middle East and North Africa region, identified a rapid urbanization rate that, according to UN projections, by 2020 will see an urban population increase of over 65 percent, compared to a projected rural population increase of 8.5 percent.

Sub-Saharan Africa

The twentieth century marked a period of substantial change for sub-Saharan Africa. At the start of the century, just 5 percent of Africans lived in towns and cities. In 1970–1995, however, Africa as a whole had the world's highest rate of growth of urbanization—roughly 4 percent per annum. UN population figures predict that half of Africa's population—approximately 1.2 billion people—will be urban by 2050 (see map, p. 79). Yet this figure disguises dramatic variations in the level of urbanization from country to country. For example, UN population figures state that 86.1 percent of the population in Djibouti was urban in 2005 and 59.3 percent of the South African population was urban, whereas elsewhere, particularly in the east, figures for urban population are considerably lower: 17.5 percent for Rwanda in 2005 and 9.5 percent for Burundi.

Sub-Saharan African countries have the highest levels of urban poverty in the world. According to *State of the World's Cities 2008/2009,* six out of every ten urban residents are slum dwellers. This figure is nearly four times the rate in North Africa, where slum growth is slowing.

Asia and the Pacific

Between 2000 and 2030, Asia's urban population is expected to increase from 1.36 billion to 2.64 billion. As a region, Asia and the Pacific has a pattern of urbanization quite different from other regions. It has the largest rural population (and will continue to do so until around 2030), and the proportion of the population living in urban areas is less than half that of most other regions. Only slightly more than one-third of the people in Asia and the Pacific live in urban areas, yet the region contains a significant proportion of the world's major cities. In a speech to an Asia-Pacific Economic Summit, a vice president of the Asian Development Bank noted that in 1995 Asia had nine of the world's megacities and that by 2025 it will have eleven more. In other words, the region has more dramatic concentrations of population than the other regions. Many cities in China are growing at staggeringly high rates of more than 10 percent per year, and according to UN population figures, the country is expected to be 72.9 percent urban by 2050 (see map, p. 79).

Many countries in the region are grappling with income disparities between rural and urban areas. China, in particular, has one of the widest income gaps between rural and urban areas of any country in the world.

Data

Table 1 Environmental Infrastructure in Rural and Urban Areas in Selected Countries, 2004 (%)

Country	Improved drinking water coverage		Household connection to improved drinking water		Improved sanitation coverage	
	Urban	Rural	Urban	Rural	Urban	Rural
Algeria	88	80	74	58	99	82
Argentina	98	80	83	45	92	83
Brazil	96	57	91	17	83	37
Canada	100	99	100	38	100	99
Colombia	99	71	96	51	96	54
France	100	100	100	100	n/a	n/a
Germany	100	100	100	97	100	100
Guatemala	99	92	89	65	90	82
India	95	83	47	8	59	22
Indonesia	87	69	30	6	73	40
Japan	100	100	98	91	100	100
Mexico	100	87	96	72	91	41
Russian Federation	100	88	93	52	93	70
Spain	100	100	99	99	100	100
Switzerland	100	100	100	99	100	100
Thailand	98	100	85	16	98	99
Ukraine	99	91	89	48	98	93
United Kingdom	100	100	100	98	n/a	n/a
United States	100	100	100	100	100	100
Venezuela	85	70	84	61	71	48

Source: United Nations Human Settlements Programme (UN-Habitat), *Enhancing Urban Safety and Security: Global Report on Human Settlements 2007,* 2007, Table B.5, available at: http://www.unhabitat.org/pmss/getpage.asp?page=download&alt=1&publicationID=2432.

Note: n/a, not available.

Table 2   Urban Population Distribution, 1950–2050

Region	Urban population (millions)			Percentage urban			Total population (millions)		
	1950	2000	2050	1950	2000	2050	1950	2000	2050
North America	110	250	401	63.9	79.1	90.2	172	316	445
Latin America and the Caribbean	69	394	683	41.4	75.3	88.7	168	523	769
Europe	281	520	557	51.2	71.4	83.8	548	729	664
Africa	33	295	1,234	14.5	35.9	61.8	224	821	1,998
Asia	237	1,373	3,486	16.8	37.1	66.2	1,411	3,705	5,266

Source: Population Division of the Department of Economic and Social Affairs of the United Nations Secretariat, *World Population Prospects: The 2006 Revision and World Urbanization Prospects: The 2007 Revision* (New York: United Nations, 2008).

Table 3   Urban and Rural Population Changes in Selected Countries (%)

Country	Population distribution, 2005		Average annual rate of change in population, 2000–2005	
	Urban	Rural	Urban	Rural
Algeria	63	37	1	−2
Argentina	91	9	0	−3
Australia	88	12	0	−2
Brazil	84	16	1	−4
Canada	80	20	0	−1
China[a]	40	60	2	−2
Colombia	74	26	0	−1
DRC[b]	31	68	1	−1
Egypt	43	57	0	0
France	77	23	0	−1
Georgia	53	47	0	0
Germany	73	27	0	0
Guatemala	47	53	1	−1
India	29	71	1	0
Indonesia	48	52	3	−2
Israel	92	8	0	0
Japan	66	34	0	0
Russian Federation	73	27	0	0
Saudi Arabia	81	19	0	−1
Spain	77	23	0	0
Sweden	84	16	0	0
Switzerland	73	27	0	0
Tajikistan	26	74	0	0
Thailand	32	68	1	0
Turkey	67	33	1	−2
Uganda	13	87	1	0
United Kingdom	90	10	0	−1
United States	81	19	0	−2

Source: Population Division of the Department of Economic and Social Affairs of the United Nations Secretariat, *World Population Prospects: The 2006 Revision and World Urbanization Prospects: The 2007 Revision* (New York: United Nations, 2008).

[a] The data for China do not include Hong Kong, Macao, or Taiwan.

[b] DRC, Democratic Republic of Congo.

Case Study—Urban Dreams: Brasília versus Curitiba

The Brazilian cities of Brasília and Curitiba offer contrasting approaches to real-izing urban dreams—through a grand overarching design in one and through active citizen participation in the other. In 1956 in an attempt to relieve pressure on the burgeoning capital of Rio de Janeiro, Brazil began to build a new and more central capital inland, Brasília. Constructed over the following two decades according to the design of urban planner Lucío Costa, Brasília became a monu-ment to grand urban ideals. While architects Le Corbusier and Albert Speer had sketched similarly ambitious designs for the reinvention of Paris and Berlin, respectively, but never actually built them, Costa and Brazilian architect Oscar Niemeyer realized every architect's dream with their commission to construct an entire city from scratch. Monumental and sculptural, Brasília is breathtaking in its ambition, with heroic government and public buildings constructed along massive avenues resembling the shape of a bird. The United Nations Educa-tional, Scientific, and Cultural Organization (UNESCO) recognized Brasília's unique contribution to urban architecture by designating it a World Heritage Site in 1987, "a landmark in the history of town planning."

Yet Brasília has been notably less successful as a "machine for living in" than its designers intended. It proved so expensive to construct that it led indirectly to the 1964 military coup and the downfall of the administration that created it. Once constructed, the city was hard to populate and generally unpopular, not least because it was perceived to isolate the government in a city of its own far from the people it was meant to serve. Today, climate has taken its toll on Nie-meyer's buildings. The city, designed around the automobile, is now frequently gridlocked, and many poorer people have to live in satellite towns and shanties miles from the center, a situation that was never part of Costa's original vision.

Grand designs are not the only way to make cities into popular vibrant places for their inhabitants, however. Another Brazilian city, Curitiba, has been held up as a model of how rapidly expanding cities can become more sustain-able through the active participation of their citizens. Unlike Brasília, Curitiba has expanded over the last quarter century around an innovative public trans-portation system featuring subway buses that operate like a ground-level sub-way system (the city could not afford to excavate an underground subway). Regarded as one of the best models of public transportation in the world, the Curitiba system has reduced fuel consumption by 30 percent and can transport up to 1.8 million passengers per day. One reason for the system's popularity is a government initiative that offered shantytown dwellers travel tokens in exchange for bags of garbage. Another example of the citizen-government partnership involved schemes by which the unemployed urban poor can work in exchange for health care, education, or rent. A major expansion of open space was undertaken to make the city a more pleasant place to live, and a cultural center was constructed in the city's abandoned quarries.

Case Study—Indonesia's Kampung Improvement Program

Striving for utopia in a third-world megacity is less about realizing some ideal-ized state of urban perfection than about generally improving the lot of the urban poor. One of the most celebrated urban improvement initiatives along these lines is the Kampung Improvement Program (KIP) in Indonesia.

Kampungs are "do-it-yourself" shantytowns on the fringes of Indonesian cities that house a large percentage of the urban population, including 60 percent in Jakarta and 63 percent in Surabaya. More than half of all Kampung dwellings are constructed by their occupants, and unlike squatters, Kampung dwellers have a legal right to occupy their land and construct dwellings of a variety of types and sizes according to their needs. Typically, these settlements also provide employment through their own industrial areas. The Kampungs grew quickly and suffered a variety of problems, such as construction of dwellings on land possibly prone to flooding, large households, open sewage, and poor access to public transportation.

With so many people living in Kampungs, mass relocation was not a practical or affordable option. Therefore, beginning in Jakarta in 1968, KIP was devised to regenerate the Kampungs and improve the lives of their occupants through a systematic program of urban renewal based on a high degree of community participation. With help from the United Nations Development Programme (UNDP) and the World Bank, the program built schools, roads, footpaths, and health-care facilities; upgraded water supplies and sanitation; and introduced garbage collection.

KIP is held up as an example of best practice in urban improvement for developing countries. The secret of KIP's success can be found in three features of its design. First, it targeted resources through neighborhood organizations, which were able to generate considerable community support for improvements and ensure that projects were truly effective and relevant to the lives of local people. Second, despite limited funds, it managed to improve the lives of an estimated 15 million people and an urban area of around 50,000 acres in its first thirty years. In Jakarta, the per capita cost of KIP was around $118; in smaller cities, the per capita cost was as low as $23. Building new dwellings or a major new settlement would have helped only a fraction of this many people and probably at a greater overall cost. Third, the program was not conceived as a means of simply improving the urban infrastructure of the Kampungs but as a way of also improving the lives of their occupants. Separate areas of KIP concentrate on physical development (improving basic facilities, such as roads and sanitation facilities), economic development (supporting community businesses to provide employment), and social development (strengthening local communities and empowering people to improve their own lives).

Since 1969 KIP has been so successful that it has now spread to hundreds of cities and towns in Indonesia. Other countries have modified the program for their needs.

Biographical Sketches

Shigeru Ban is an architect and engineer noted for building structures from low-tech materials, such as cardboard tubes and recycled paper. Fashionable with the architectural avant-garde, Ban's no-nonsense designs have also found an immensely practical application in easily constructed emergency relief shelters for disaster victims and refugees; one of Ban's four-person emergency houses can be erected in just six hours.

Jaime Lerner pioneered some of the key principles of the late-twentieth-century sustainable city during three terms as mayor of Curitiba, Brazil. These principles include expanding cities around well-used public transportation links, ensuring the active participation of citizens, and improving lives through social and cultural activities, as well as improving basic urban infrastructure. Lerner also served as governor of Parana.

Richard Rogers is an architect with a keen interest in developing sustainable cities. He has designed urban master plans for a number of cities, including Berlin, London, and Shanghai. Most recently, he has advised the British government on ways of using urban regeneration to prevent ongoing suburbanization of the countryside.

David Satterthwaite is a senior fellow with the Human Settlements Program at the International Institute of Environment and Development and has advised numerous organizations on urban environmental issues, including the United Nations Centre for Human Settlements, the United Nations International Children's Emergency Fund (UNICEF), the *World Commission on Environment and Development* (WCED), and the Intergovernmental Panel on Climate Change. He has written and edited numerous publications on the subject, including *Environmental Problems in an Urbanizing World* (2000) and *The Earthscan Reader on Sustainable Cities* (1999).

Anna Tibaijuka is an under-secretary-general of the United Nations and is executive director of the United Nations Human Settlements Programme. She is an agricultural economist who has worked with numerous organizations, including the United Nations Conference on Trade and Development (UNCTAD), UNESCO, and UNICEF. She has also worked to encourage educational and local economic development initiatives in Tanzania, her home country.

Directory

International Institute for Environment and Development, 3 Endsleigh Street, London WC1H 0DD, United Kingdom. Telephone: (44) 20 7388 2117; email: info@iied.org; Web: http://www.iied.org.
Organization researching environmental and development policy issues, including those concerning human settlements.

Local Governments for Sustainability, ICLEI World Secretariat, City Hall, West Tower, 16th Floor, Toronto, ONT M5H 2N2, Canada. Telephone: (416) 392-1462; email: iclei@iclei.org; Web: http://www.iclei.org.
Environmental organization linking local governments around the world.

United Nations Human Settlements Programme (UN-Habitat; formerly the United Nations Centre for Human Settlements, UNHCS), P.O. Box 30030, Nairobi, 00100 Kenya. Telephone: (254 20) 7621234; email: infohabitat@unhabitat.org; Web: http://www.unhabitat.org.
Agency concerned with urban sustainability and overseeing the Habitat Agenda and the World Urban Forum.

WaterAid, Supporter Services, 47-49 Durham Street, London SE11 5JD, United Kingdom. Telephone: +44 (0)845 6000 433; email: via Web site; Web: http://www .wateraid.org.uk.
Organization attempting to relieve problems in developing countries.

World Bank, Urban Development Division, 1818 H Street NW, Washington, D.C. 20433. Telephone: (202) 473-1000; email: urbanhelp@worldbank.org; Web: http://web.worldbank.org/WBSITE/EXTERNAL/TOPICS/EXTURBAN DEVELOPMENT/0,,menuPK:337184~pagePK:149018~piPK:149093~theSite PK:337178,00.html.
International organization focusing on relieving poverty by financing development projects.

Further Research

Books

American Association for the Advancement of Science. *AAAS Atlas of Population and the Environment.* Berkeley: University of California Press, 2001.
Ashton, John, ed. *Healthy Cities.* Buckingham, UK, and Bristol, Pa.: Open University, 1992.
Barton, Hugh. *Sustainable Cities.* London: Earthscan, 2000.
Black, Maggie. *Mega-Slums: The Coming Sanitary Crisis.* London: WaterAid. Available at: http://www.wateraid.org.uk/research/slums.html.
Drakakis-Smith, David. *Third World Cities.* London and New York: Routledge, 2000.
Girardet, Herbert. *The Gaia Atlas of Cities.* New York: Anchor Books, 1993.
Hall, Peter. *Cities of Tomorrow: An Intellectual History of Urban Planning and Design in the Twentieth Century.* Oxford and New York: Blackwell, 1996.
Jacobs, Jane. *The Death and Life of Great American Cities: The Future of Town Planning.* London and New York: Penguin, 1961.
Lynch, Kevin. *The Image of the City.* Cambridge, Mass.: MIT Press, 1968.
Mitchell, William J. *E-topia.* Cambridge, Mass., and London: MIT Press, 1999.
Mumford, Lewis. *The City in History.* New York: Harcourt Brace, 1961.
Rogers, Richard. *Cities for a Small Planet.* London: Faber and Faber, 1997.
Satterthwaite, David, ed. *The Earthscan Reader in Sustainable Cities.* London: Earthscan, 1999.
Sherlock, Harley. *Cities Are Good for Us.* London: Paladin, 1991.

Articles and Reports

Kenworthy, Jeff. "Urban Ecology in Indonesia: The Kampung Improvement Program (KIP)." Available at: http://www.istp.murdoch.edu.au/ISTP/casestudies/Case_ Studies_Asia/kip/kip.html.
"Report from the Fourth Global Forum of Parliamentarians on Habitat." Berlin, 28 May 2003. Available at: http://ww2.unhabitat.org/documents/declaration.pdf.
Swerdlow, Joel. "A Tale of Three Cities." *National Geographic,* August 1999, 34.
United Nations Department of Economic and Social Affairs, Population Division. *World Urbanization Prospects: The 2007 Revision.* New York: United Nations, 2008. Available at: www.un.org/esa/population/publications/wup2007/2007WUP_High lights_web.pdf.

United Nations Human Settlements Programme (UN-Habitat). *Enhancing Urban Safety and Security: Global Report on Human Settlements 2007.* Available at: http://www .unhabitat.org/pmss/getpage.asp?page=download&alt=1&publicationID=2432.

———. *State of the World's Cities 2008/2009: Harmonious Cities.* London: Earthscan, 2008.

United Nations Population Fund. *State of World Population 2007: Unleashing the Potential of Urban Growth.* New York: United Nations Population Fund, 2007. Available at: http://www.unfpa.org/swp/2007/english/introduction.html.

World Bank, Infrastructure Development Group. *Cities in Transition: A Strategic View of Urban and Local Government Issues.* Washington, D.C.: World Bank, 2000. Available at: http://www-wds.worldbank.org/external/default/WDSContentServer/WDSP/ IB/2000/05/25/000094946_00051005302084/Rendered/PDF/multi_page.pdf.

World Commission on Environment and Development. *Our Common Future.* Oxford and New York: Oxford University Press, 1987.

Web Sites

Brasília, UNESCO World Heritage Site
http://www.worldheritagesite.org/sites/brasilia.html

Global Environment Outlook, 2000 (GEO-2000), Urban Areas
http://www.grida.no/ge02000/english/0049.htm

The Mega-Cities Project: Global Network
www.megacitiesproject.org/network.asp

UN-Habitat, Best Practices Database
http://www.bestpractices.org

Documents

1. World Urban Forum

Report of the Third Session of the World Urban Forum, June 19–23, 2006

The full text is available at http://www.unhabitat.org/downloads/docs/4077_70142_WUF3-Report-final%20%20dm1%2023%20june.REV.1.pdf.

Extracts

Overview

It was promising that participants, in such large numbers and from all walks of society, began to converge towards an outline for the way forward:

• They agreed on the need for all urban players—citizens, local governments, state and provincial governments, national governments, the private sector and civil society organizations—to work harder to solve urban problems and challenges. There was widespread agreement that they all must do their part, rather than simply transfer responsibility to others.

• They agreed that risk-taking and the pursuit of innovation must characterize municipal leadership if cities are to achieve sustainable development. Vancouver's example in taking the lead in such areas as air and water quality, public transit and planning was mentioned often in this context.

- They agreed that appropriate engagements, partnerships and relationships need to be built in an inclusive manner to better understand challenges and develop practical solutions. Participants from many parts of the world presented examples that can serve as guideposts for these strategies.
- They agreed on the importance of transparency and accountability. Citizens need to be informed of challenges and steps taken by governments to address them. Transparency goes hand-in-hand with accountability, which speeds up the process of enhancing actions that work and curtailing those that do not work. . . .

The spirit and enthusiasm evinced at the Forum in formal sessions and in the interstices are difficult to capture in words. But it was very clear that every participant was committed to the basic theme of the Forum on turning Ideas into Action. Hundreds of actionable ideas were proposed, described and exchanged. No doubt they will provide the basis for renewed vigour and commitment to a sustainable urban development that is inclusive.

2. Declaration on Cities and Other Human Settlements in the New Millennium

Resolution adopted by the United Nations General Assembly, June 9, 2001

The full text is available at http://www.unhabitat.org/content.asp?cid=2071&catid=1&typei d=25&subMenuId=0.

Extracts

We, the representatives of Governments, being guided by the purposes and principles of the Charter of the United Nations, meeting at the special session of the General Assembly to review the implementation of the Habitat Agenda, to recognize progress and to identify obstacles and emerging issues, reaffirm our will and commitment to implement fully the Istanbul Declaration on Human Settlements and the Habitat Agenda and decide on further initiatives, in the spirit of the United Nations Millennium Declaration. The Istanbul Declaration and the Habitat Agenda will remain the basic framework for sustainable human settlements development in the years to come.

Therefore, we:

9. Also take note with satisfaction of the growing awareness of the need to address, in an integrated manner, poverty, homelessness, unemployment, lack of basic services, exclusion of women and children and of marginalized groups, including indigenous communities, and social fragmentation, in order to achieve better, more liveable and inclusive human settlements worldwide. Governments, international organizations and members of civil society have made continuous efforts to address those problems;

17. Take note with great concern of the current conditions of human settlements worldwide . . . widespread poverty remains the core obstacle, and environmental conditions need significant improvement in many countries. Critically, the majority of people living in poverty still lack legal security of tenure for their dwellings, while others lack even basic shelter. Thus, serious impediments to sustainable human settlements development still persist;

28. Recognize that . . . for the first time in human history a majority of the world's 6 billion people will live in cities. Many people have experienced a deterioration in their

living environment, not an improvement. The gaps and obstacles encountered in the past five years have slowed down global progress towards sustainable human settlements development. It is essential that actions are taken to ensure that the Habitat Agenda is now translated into policy and practice in every country;

29. . . . At the start of the new millennium, aware of our responsibilities towards future generations, we are strongly committed to adequate shelter for all and sustainable human settlements development in an urbanizing world. We invite people from all countries and all walks of life, as well as the international community, to join in renewed dedication to our shared vision for a more just and equitable world. . . .

3. The Habitat Agenda

Second United Nations Conference on Human Settlements (Habitat II), Istanbul, June 3–14, 1996

The full text is available at http://staging.unchs.org/declarations/ch-1a.htm.

Extracts

1. We recognize the imperative need to improve the quality of human settlements, which profoundly affects the daily lives and well-being of our peoples. There is a sense of great opportunity and hope that a new world can be built, in which economic development, social development and environmental protection as interdependent and mutually reinforcing components of sustainable development can be realized through solidarity and cooperation within and between countries and through effective partnerships at all levels. International cooperation and universal solidarity, guided by the purposes and principles of the Charter of the United Nations, and in a spirit of partnership, are crucial to improving the quality of life of the peoples of the world. . . .

7. During the course of history, urbanization has been associated with economic and social progress, the promotion of literacy and education, the improvement of the general state of health, greater access to social services, and cultural, political and religious participation. Democratization has enhanced such access and meaningful participation and involvement for civil society actors, for public-private partnerships, and for decentralized, participatory planning and management, which are important features of a successful urban future. Cities and towns have been engines of growth and incubators of civilization and have facilitated the evolution of knowledge, culture and tradition, as well as of industry and commerce. Urban settlements, properly planned and managed, hold the promise for human development and the protection of the world's natural resources through their ability to support large numbers of people while limiting their impact on the natural environment. The growth of cities and towns causes social, economic and environmental changes that go beyond city boundaries. Habitat II deals with all settlements—large, medium and small—and reaffirms the need for universal improvements in living and working conditions.

8. To overcome current problems and to ensure future progress in the improvement of economic, social and environmental conditions in human settlements, we must begin with recognition of the challenges facing cities and towns. According to current projections, by the turn of the century, more than three billion people—one half of the world's population—will live and work in urban areas. The most serious problems confronting cities and towns and their inhabitants include inadequate financial

resources, lack of employment opportunities, spreading homelessness and expansion of squatter settlements, increased poverty and a widening gap between rich and poor, growing insecurity and rising crime rates, inadequate and deteriorating building stock, services and infrastructure, lack of health and educational facilities, improper land use, insecure land tenure, rising traffic congestion, increasing pollution, lack of green spaces, inadequate water supply and sanitation, uncoordinated urban development and an increasing vulnerability to disaster. All of these have seriously challenged the capacities of Governments, particularly those of developing countries, at all levels to realize economic development, social development and environmental protection, which are interdependent and mutually reinforcing components of sustainable development—the framework for our efforts to achieve a higher quality of life for all people. Rapid rates of international and internal migration, as well as population growth in cities and towns, and unsustainable patterns of production and consumption raise these problems in especially acute forms. In these cities and towns, large sections of the world's urban population live in inadequate conditions and are confronted with serious problems, including environmental problems, that are exacerbated by inadequate planning and managerial capacities, lack of investment and technology, and insufficient mobilization and inappropriate allocation of financial resources, as well as by a lack of social and economic opportunities. In the case of international migration, migrants have needs for housing and basic services, education, employment and social integration without a loss of cultural identity, and they are to be given adequate protection and attention within host countries.

PART II

Economics

DEVELOPMENT AID

Catherine E. Weaver

Behind the facade of the globalized, integrated world economy lies the stark reality of the growing disparities between the wealthier countries of the North and the struggling nations of the South. According to the 2007 *Human Development Report,* issued by the United Nations Development Programme (UNDP), just over 1 billion people in the developing world live on less than the equivalent of $1 per day, and nearly 3 billion live on less than $2 per day. More than 1.1 billion people are illiterate, and an equal number do not have access to improved water sources. Of the 33.2 million people in the world with human immunodeficiency virus (HIV)/acquired immunodeficiency syndrome (AIDs) in 2007, two-thirds (22.5 million) lived in sub-Saharan Africa. Absolute poverty, the spread of epidemic diseases, and the high prevalence of conflict and failed states have together contributed to declining life expectancy in the least-developed countries of the world. In 2000, the United Nations adopted the Millennium Development Goals (MDGs) to reinvigorate and refocus international aid efforts on the goals of poverty alleviation and socioeconomic development (see Document 2). The MDGs set distinct targets for 2015 and include a commitment by donors to double all official development aid. Yet amid the excitement surrounding the MDGs is a growing cynicism. Despite persuasive evidence of progress toward development in many of the world's regions over the last seventy years, experts today increasingly question the purpose, form, and effectiveness of development aid.

Historical Background and Development

International development aid is largely a post–World War II phenomenon driven by political, economic, and philanthropic concerns. In June 1947, U.S. Secretary of State George C. Marshall called for massive U.S. assistance to help rebuild European economies through the European Recovery Program. The Marshall Plan was supported by an earlier declaration by President Harry S. Truman in a speech to a joint session of Congress in March 1947. The Truman Doctrine called for U.S. development aid to be a key component in the U.S. strategy of containment, with the belief that economically stable countries would "choose freedom" over communism. U.S. foreign aid soon spilled over into the developing world through multilateral institutions, such as the newly established World Bank, and bilateral institutions, such as the U.S. Agency for International Development (USAID). As European countries recovered, they too became donors, providing assistance to developing regions through numerous multilateral and bilateral channels. Most often, the direction of aid was dictated by political motives. European bilateral assistance targeted the economic recovery of the former colonies, and U.S. bilateral aid focused on regions deemed susceptible to Soviet influence. In 1961, President John F. Kennedy made a plea to the United Nations General Assembly for a "decade of development." The speech ushered in a golden age of international development aid and the peak of U.S. development aid in 1964, when the United States contributed nearly two-thirds of all global official development assistance (ODA).

In the 1970s, development aid underwent a gradual transformation: from a model emphasizing economic growth to an approach incorporating social and human development. This was triggered by the 1974 World Bank report *Redistribution with Growth,* which argued that traditional development strategies were leading to a "development gap" in the third world. Although economic growth projects funding industrial infrastructure and promoting foreign investment did lead to higher economic growth rates in terms of gross domestic product (GDP), growing national incomes were not being distributed equally within and between developing countries (see INCOME INEQUALITY). The report further showed that nearly half the population in the developing world was living in a state of *absolute poverty,* defined in 1979 by former World Bank president Robert McNamara (in *The McNamara Years at the World Bank: Major Policy Addresses of Robert S. McNamara, 1968–1981*) as "a condition of life so limited by malnutrition, illiteracy, disease, high infant mortality, and low life-expectancy as to be below any rational definition of human decency."

The recognition and definition of *absolute poverty* quickly led to the basic human needs approach to development assistance. Although this new strategy by no means replaced the economic growth strategy, it shifted aid donors' attention to the provision of basic social services and the necessities of life, including increased numbers of grants and loans for improvements in agriculture, rural employment, education, sanitation, and health. During the 1970s, the World Bank firmly established itself as the preeminent international development aid institution amid a growing number of regional development banks such as the Inter-American Development Bank (established 1959) and the Asian Development Bank (established 1966). Under McNamara's leadership, the World Bank quadrupled in size, and its lending for development projects increased by six times. Nearly seventy years after its inception, the World Bank continues in this role, disbursing in 2007 over $24 billion for development aid projects and programs, producing the most widely read research on development, and publishing the most influential and cited reports and statistical resources, including the annual *World Development Report* and *World Development Indicators.*

In the 1980s, however, the World Bank and its sister institution, the International Monetary Fund (IMF), came under attack. Oil crises in the 1970s and deterioration in the international prices of export commodities caused developing countries to run out of the currency reserves necessary to make payments on their international loans. As a result, the developing world suffered a series of severe debt crises, beginning with Mexico's default on commercial bank and development aid loans in 1982. The World Bank and IMF responded by initiating structural adjustment lending, issuing loans designed to bail out countries suffering from unsustainable balance of payment deficits caused by the value of imports exceeding the revenues derived from exports. These loans, however, came with strict conditions obligating recipient countries to institute massive macroeconomic reforms, including wide-scale deregulation, removal of state-controlled pricing, decentralization, and privatization of the economy. Later called the Washington Consensus by renowned economist John Williamson, this set of orthodox economic reforms did improve economic growth rates. However, the improved growth rates came at a high social cost, resulting from the severe cutbacks in welfare, health-care, and education spending forced on developing-country governments. The tension between the economic growth strategies and the basic human needs approach did not go unnoticed by critics.

As the adverse effects of structural adjustment were realized in the late 1980s and 1990s, the ideologies informing development aid began to shift away from poverty alleviation through economic growth to older notions of basic human needs, finding new life within the framework of sustainable development, good governance, and empowerment of marginalized groups, especially women. The paradigm shift was most vividly reflected in the 1990 launch of the UNDP's annual *Human Development Report* and the accompanying new statistical database, the Human Development Indicators. Today, aid discourses and practices embrace a broad conception of socioeconomic and human development and tackle the daunting challenges of corruption, the spread of HIV/AIDS, populations affected by natural disasters related to changing global climate patterns, and problems associated with refugees and societies recovering from ethnic conflict and civil war (see AIDS, CLIMATE CHANGE, and ETHNIC AND REGIONAL CONFLICT).

Current Status

Development seeks to improve the welfare of people living in conditions of economic and social poverty (see Tables 1 and 2). How the alleviation of poverty is achieved, however, is contentiously debated. Nonetheless, today a widely held consensus in international development discourse holds that the focus should go beyond economic growth to also address the role of women, ecologically friendly and sustainable economic growth, and the link between the political problems of corruption and conflict in relation to social and economic development. The result is a rich understanding that drives a diverse and expanding field of research. Yet, at the same time, this growth in theory has in practice contributed to the increasingly unwieldy agendas of international aid organizations, which now face the complex task of translating these new views of development into manageable policies and programs.

Research

Development aid research is devoted to understanding the causes and consequences of poverty in the third world. Although economic growth is still deemed essential, purely economic conditions are no longer the primary variables in discussions of underdevelopment. The experience of the past century reveals that social, environmental, and political variables are equally, if not more, important. Economic growth gauged through increases in gross national product (GNP) and per capita incomes does not result in real and equitable development absent human progress, which is measured in terms of the ability of individuals to meet their most basic needs in health and personal safety and to acquire the skills and education necessary to improve their lives and those of their children. Likewise, increases in the productive industrial and agriculture capacity of developing nations can actually pose a catch-22 if economic advancement is won at the price of the environment, thereby sacrificing the long-term supply of natural resources and endangering human health through pollution, deforestation, and human-made disasters caused by, for example, oil spills, soil erosion, and excessive irrigation. Finally, globalization has incited controversial discussions concerning the relationships between development and widespread corruption, ethnic conflict, civil war, and terrorism, thus adding a fourth dimension to development (see TERRORISM).

Four topics stand out as illustrative of current trends in development research. The first concerns the link between socioeconomic development and the environment. The relationship is symbiotic—changes in the environment, such as global warming, rising pollution levels, and increasing occurrences of droughts or floods, can affect the health, livelihood, and security of populations. Likewise, economic growth associated with industrialization, urbanization, and growing populations can place enormous stresses on the environment by increasing the demand for finite natural resources, causing the deterioration of land, contamination of water sources, and threats to biodiversity. In 1987, the UN-sponsored World Commission on Environment and Development, or the Brundtland Commission, published a report that articulates this relationship using the concept *sustainable development,* which is defined as the ability to meet "the needs of the present without compromising the ability of future generations to meet their own needs" (see Document 1). The report asserts that environmental degradation constitutes a cause and consequence of perpetual poverty, so to achieve development for future generations environmental considerations must be fully integrated into development aid. Today, ensuring environmental sustainability is the seventh of the eight MDGs (see Document 2).

A second significant dimension of development research, closely following the work of Nobel Prize–winner Amartya Sen, focuses on the twin notions of participatory development and empowerment of the poor. Here, the key to poverty alleviation is to target opportunities directly to the most impoverished, thereby allowing those most in need to identify the priorities of development and the chance to lift themselves out of poverty. Likewise, participatory development builds on this bottom-up approach by asserting that the people toward whom development assistance is aimed should participate fully in the decision-making process surrounding development and that as many people as possible should enjoy the benefits of economic growth. Both concepts point to the need to include groups previously neglected in development discourses and groups that have not received their fair share of development aid benefits under past development strategies.

Central in this inclusive approach is a third focus on the role of women in development, which has been spurred by concern that women have traditionally benefited far less from economic growth than men. In the past decade, the UNDP's *Human Development Report* has included statistics derived from a gender empowerment measure (GEM) and a Gender-Related Development Index (GDI). Each of these composite indexes is designed to gauge levels of equality between men and women along economic and political lines, such as access to economic resources and political participation, as well as along social and human lines, such as life expectancy, literacy rates, and access to health care and higher levels of education. A consensus among researchers now holds that progress in women's development feeds into the broader goals of development: decreased fertility rates contribute to lower population growth rates, increased participation of women in the workforce raises overall levels of economic growth, and an awareness of health issues decreases levels of malnutrition and helps stem the spread of infectious diseases, such as HIV/AIDS. Moreover, research indicates that the development and empowerment of women also have a powerful and direct effect on the welfare of children. Women who have greater access to employment and health care can take better care of their children, and those who enjoy a higher level of education tend to encourage their children to pursue the same. Especially since the 1995 Fourth World Conference on Women in Beijing, the centrality of gender in development debates has prompted increased lending for women's programs and efforts to mainstream gender in the institutional policies and practices of the international development agencies. Like the environment, women's socioeconomic development is highlighted in the third and fifth MDGs, to "promote gender equality and empower women" and "improve maternal health," as well as being the central feature of the second MDG, to achieve universal primary education for both boys and girls.

A fourth prominent feature of research is the political nature of development in the third world, a topic that is a response to the failure of past development aid policies and programs. This research agenda recognizes that progress in social and economic development has been repeatedly set back, and sometimes reversed, by state failures, rampant corruption, ethnic conflict, and civil war. This has prompted greater attention to public administration infrastructures in developing nations and their institutional capacity—as evident in the public accessibility, transparency, and predictability of the legal, financial, and regulatory systems—to successfully implement and sustain development programs. The underlying logic of research on the role of good governance reflects the belief that strong stable democracies, the rule of law, and vibrant market economies are the springboards for sustainable and participatory development. In the late 1990s, United Nations Secretary-General Kofi Annan declared that good governance was the most critical factor in the promotion of development and the eradication of poverty. Moreover, good governance is directly tied to aid effectiveness. In 1998, a team of leading economists at the World Bank published a study, entitled *Assessing Aid*, that found the effect of aid on economic growth to be neutral or even negative in countries that had poor governance. On the other hand, countries with good governance, as measured by the World Bank's newly constructed governance indicators, enjoyed a 0.5 percent growth in per capital income and a 1 percent reduction in poverty for every additional 1 percent of GDP in aid. Today, promoting good governance and tackling corruption are widely considered to be essential to development goals, prompting vibrant debates on when and how international agencies may condition or direct aid to achieve such ends.

Policies and Programs

Development aid can be funded through governments, private voluntary organizations and charities, private commercial agencies, and nongovernmental organizations (NGOs). The focus here is on ODA, defined as the funds provided by governments for the purpose of promoting economic growth and human welfare in the developing world. Such assistance can take the form of grants, project loans, financial credits, and technical assistance offered through bilateral agencies of individual donor countries, such as USAID, and multilateral governmental organizations, such as the World Bank, the various regional development banks, and the specialized agencies of the United Nations (such as the UNDP). The amount, direction, content, and effectiveness of ODA is carefully tracked each year by the Development Assistance Committee (DAC) of the Organisation for Economic Cooperation and Development (OECD). The committee comprises the European Commission and the twenty-two industrialized countries that constitute the major donors in international development aid (see Table 3; map, p. 101). The $104 billion in ODA in 2007 was devoted to social development, such as education and health; economic infrastructure of developing nations, including loans disbursed for road building, telecommunication networks, and large-scale agricultural reform; and debt relief and emergency aid (see Table 4).

The development aid industry faces several challenges today. The first is a growing debate over the relevance of aid. Critics of development aid argue that official aid is no longer needed due to the abundance of private capital flows and emergence of new sources of aid monies from the sovereign wealth funds (state-owned investment funds) owned by rapidly growing economies such as China. At the same time, defenders of development aid argue that reliance on these alternatives is precarious. Private capital flows to the developing world are approximately six times the amount of ODA. However, such private flows are highly volatile and tend to flow to a select set of rapidly growing emerging market economies concentrated in East Asia, as opposed to the least-developed countries. To the extent that private capital flows, including foreign direct investment, largely bypass the least-developed countries, proponents claim that aid is still needed to reach those in absolute poverty.

A related problem of aid dependency exists for those least-developed countries that cannot attract private capital flows. These countries, largely located in sub-Saharan Africa, rely very heavily on official development aid. In fact, in the ten least-developed countries (as measured by their Human Development Index scores)—Democratic Republic of the Congo, Ethiopia, Chad, Central African Republic, Mozambique, Mali, Niger, Guinea-Bissau, Burkina Faso, and Sierra Leone—the average life expectancy is 48.2 years, the average adult literacy rate is 36.4 percent, and the average annual GDP per capita is $952. On average, ODA accounts for nearly 17 percent of the gross national income (GNI) in these ten countries (perhaps offsetting the average $85.8 million outflow of private capital each year). In many cases, such aid dependency (when it comes in the form of loans) coupled with an inability to attract foreign investment has led to severe debt crises. In the mid-1990s, demands for debt relief led to the establishment of the Heavily Indebted Poor Countries (HIPC) Initiative. As shown in Table 4, debt relief now accounts for a very large portion of official development aid, nearing $22 billion in 2006.

The second major challenge to development aid concerns its effectiveness. Numerous studies have revealed weak statistical support for the relationship among aid, economic growth, and poverty reduction. Based on anecdotal evidence, critics quickly point out that sub-Saharan Africa is less developed today than it was in the 1970s, despite heavy flows of aid. Likewise, other critics charge that aid has often fueled corruption and lined the pockets of political leaders. Paul Collier, former World Bank economist and now a professor at Oxford University argues in his recent book, *The Bottom Billion,* that ODA adds only about 1 percent to the annual growth rate of the least-developed countries. Problematically, aid suffers from diminishing returns; when aid exceeds 16 percent of annual GDP, it ceases to be effective. In the context of the discussion of aid dependency, this is particularly disconcerting for the ten least-developed countries that, as noted, receive aid equivalent to 17 percent of their GNI.

These two complex challenges are compounded by a final concern relating to the legitimacy of the current international development aid architecture. Disenchantment with the aid system—which many feel is structured to reflect the interests of the powerful industrialized nation with little attention paid to the voices of the poor countries themselves—has been growing and deepening. Most of the multilateral institutions are governed by a system of weighted voting among the member countries, giving the most votes to the richest countries who contribute the most to the institution. Likewise, leadership selection is an issue—the process of choosing the heads of the World Bank and IMF remains driven by a gentleman's agreement struck in 1944 that the president of the Bank would be an American and the managing director of the IMF would be a European. The democratic deficit in the structure of these institutions—or at least the appearance of one—has taken a toll and led to many recent efforts to reform the fundamental rules of the institutions. Disenchanted borrowing countries, particularly those middle-income nations able to attract private capital, have turned away from multilateral and bilateral aid and, in some cases, have created their own regional development banks and monetary funds, such as the Bank of the South led by Venezuelan President Hugo Chavez, that are independent from the post–World War II Bretton Woods system.

Regional Summaries

Organisation for Economic Cooperation and Development Countries

The Development Assistance Committee (DAC) of the OECD, which comprises twenty-two nations (Australia, Austria, Belgium, Canada, Denmark, Finland, France, Germany, Greece, Ireland, Italy, Japan, Luxembourg, the Netherlands, New Zealand, Norway, Portugal, Spain, Sweden, Switzerland, the United Kingdom, and the United States) and the Commission of the European Communities, offers official development aid. Since 1990, the top contributors in terms of total dollars have been the United States, Japan, Germany, the United Kingdom, France, and the Netherlands (see Table 3). These numbers do not, however, accurately represent each country's devotion to development aid. The largest donors in absolute terms are among the lowest contributors in terms of aid expenditures as a percentage of GNP. The United States is currently one of the lowest contributors in terms of ODA as a percentage of GNP, a remarkable drop since the country's initiation of development aid in the 1940s. Only five countries—Denmark, Luxembourg, the Netherlands, Norway, and Sweden—actually meet the assistance target of 0.7 percent of GNP established by the United Nations.

A significant portion of development assistance is given via the multilateral development agencies (the World Bank, IMF, and specialized UN agencies) as well as the regional development banks (the African Development Bank, Asian Development Bank, European Bank for Reconstruction and Development, and the Inter-American Development Bank). Member states' influence over the policies and programs of these organizations varies and is often a matter of great debate. Political control over the majority of ODA is exercised through bilateral aid, coordinated through domestic organizations. A majority of aid, however, is given through bilateral agencies due to donors' ability to more directly control and channel aid in line with national interests. European countries, for example, tend to direct aid to former colonies in Africa, Latin America, and South Asia. U.S. aid allocations likewise are largely determined by geopolitical imperatives. Historically, Egypt and Israel have topped the U.S. aid recipient list. However, since 2003 U.S. aid has been redirected toward Iraq and Afghanistan to support U.S. military efforts in these countries; in 2006, Iraq and Afghanistan received nearly $10 billion out of the total $23.5 billion in U.S. aid. Moreover, bilateral aid funds are usually allocated for specific purposes, with certain amounts earmarked to require aid recipients to purchase

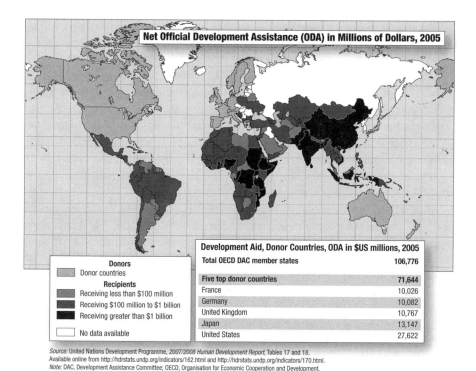

Net Official Development Assistance (ODA) in Millions of Dollars, 2005

Donors
- Donor countries

Recipients
- Receiving less than $100 million
- Receiving $100 million to $1 billion
- Receiving greater than $1 billion
- No data available

Development Aid, Donor Countries, ODA in $US millions, 2005	
Total OECD DAC member states	106,776
Five top donor countries	**71,644**
France	10,026
Germany	10,082
United Kingdom	10,767
Japan	13,147
United States	27,622

Source: United Nations Development Programme, *2007/2008 Human Development Report,* Tables 17 and 18.
Available online from http://hdrstats.undp.org/indicators/162.html and http://hdrstats.undp.org/indicators/170.html.
Note: DAC, Development Assistance Committee; OECD, Organisation for Economic Cooperation and Development.

equipment or hire consultants from donor countries. The prevalence of such tied aid undermines the altruistic image of development aid. In the past ten years, the OECD has been tracking and strategically targeting the reduction of tied aid.

The development aid practices of the OECD member countries have, since 2000, been strongly focused on the MDGs (see Document 2). As mentioned, the launch of the MDGs in 2000 embodied a commitment by major donor countries to double the amount of ODA they provide each year. However, to date, donors are not on track to meet their stated commitments to increase aid. Despite renewed pledges in 2005 at the Gleneagles Summit and in the Paris Declaration, overall ODA fell by 8.4 percent between 2006 and 2007. This decline is explained in part by the artificially high ODA numbers in 2005 due to debt relief programs in Iraq and Nigeria. Nonetheless, the OECD projects that donors will need to dramatically increase overall ODA by 2010 if the MDGs are to be met by 2015.

Latin America and the Caribbean

As a whole, the countries in Latin America and the Caribbean have made considerable progress in human development. Despite negative economic growth in 2001–2002 due to several financial crises, since 2003 the region has enjoyed GDP per capita growth rates of around 4 percent per year. Reliance on ODA has gradually declined as many countries have graduated from developing to middle-income status. In 2006, the region received $6.9 billion in ODA, or approximately 6.6 percent of all ODA in the world. On a per capita basis, this translates into $12.45 of aid to each citizen.

Latin American and Caribbean nations have made steady progress on most of the MDGs. Nonetheless, several development challenges persist and demand global attention. One issue is the problem of absolute poverty even in the face of growth because the growth has not been evenly distributed. Income inequality, as captured in the Gini coefficient, remains high. For example, according to UNDP's *Human Development Report 2007/2008,* in Bolivia the poorest 10 percent of the population earns less than 0.3 percent of the national income, while the richest 10 percent earns more than 47 percent.

Another key development challenge is the urbanization of the region. Today, nearly 77 percent of people in the region live in densely populated urban areas, increasing the risk of infectious diseases through overcrowding, lack of clean water, and other unsanitary conditions. Moreover, continued fear of political instability leading to economic instability has steered development aid toward rule of law, governance, anticorruption efforts, and civil society–building projects. Sustainable development is also a concern in relation to the increasing deforestation in the Amazon rainforest, soil erosion due to poor agricultural practices, and industrial pollution in the major cities.

Eastern Europe and the Former Soviet Union

The flow of development assistance to Eastern Europe and the former republics of the Soviet Union peaked in the mid-1990s during the region's transition from communism to market-oriented democracy. According to the *World Development Indicators 2007,* the region received approximately 1 percent of total ODA in the 1960s through the 1980s but nearly 20 percent of total ODA in the 1990s. In 1995, the region received aid equivalent to 1.16 percent of GNI, or nearly $25 in aid per person. Russia, due to its sheer size and political importance, was one of the largest recipients of development aid, receiving nearly $2 billion in 1999 alone. By 2008, the picture had changed dramatically. Due to strong economic growth in Russia from commodity (oil and gas) exports, the region as a whole received aid equivalent to just 0.26 percent of GNI, or approximately $13 per person. Russia recently transitioned from a net recipient to a net donor of ODA.

Although the region as a whole enjoys levels of social development on par with OECD countries, including highly educated societies with an average literacy rate of close to 99 percent, on a subregional level the progress toward development is mixed. The central Asian and Balkan countries continue to make slow and uneven progress toward the MDGs and remain highly dependent on ODA. Kyrgyzstan, for example, receives aid equal to 11 percent of its GDP. The region as a whole is also suffering from serious health epidemics, including the spread of HIV/AIDs and tuberculosis. It also continues to face serious challenges in sustainable development due to the legacy of the highly polluting Soviet industrial infrastructure.

North Africa and the Middle East

The countries of North Africa and the Middle East have, on average, higher rates of GDP per capita and lower levels of poverty than other developing regions, yet the geopolitical importance of the region ensures that it receives a disproportionate share of ODA. As previously mentioned, Israel was historically the top recipient of U.S. assistance despite the fact that the UNDP places it in the high human development category. Today, Iraq is the central focus; it received nearly 10 percent of all ODA in the world in 2006. Aid statistics are somewhat misleading because of the Iraq factor. Aggregate numbers indicate that the region as a whole received aid equal to over 2 percent of GNI in 2006, or nearly $54 per person, despite growth rates averaging 3.5 percent in 2004–2006. The West Bank and Gaza remain highly dependent on aid, which in 2006 reached the equivalent of 35 percent of GNI.

The social and environmental dimensions of the MDGs are the primary areas of concern for international development agencies involved in the region. Inequality in the development status of men and women remains a significant challenge. In 2005, the literacy rate for adult women reached 65 percent, compared to 85 percent for adult men. Sustainable development is endangered by scarce water resources, which in turn fuels resource-related conflicts throughout the region. Several billion dollars in development aid from multiple organizations is devoted each year to agricultural and infrastructure projects addressing overirrigation and the improper treatment of wastewater.

Sub-Saharan Africa

Today the central focus of international development aid is sub-Saharan Africa. The region as a whole, despite recent positive economic growth rates near 3 percent (reversing a long run of negative growth rates), has made the slowest progress toward the MDGs and is not on track for meeting any of the development goals by 2015. Over 40 percent of the population lives on less than $1 per day. Many countries suffer from severe and unsustainable external debt burdens that detract from critical social and human welfare expenditures. According to the African Development Bank and OECD's *African Economic Outlook 2008,* the region's average total debt, outstanding from ODA aid sources, equals $286 billion, of which 23 percent is debt to multilateral aid agencies and 58 percent is debt to bilateral aid agencies. This total is equivalent to 26.2 percent of GDP of the region. Burundi, for example, shoulders a debt service equal to 49 percent of its export revenues. As a result, since the mid-1990s, aid has included large debt relief programs, facilitated by the enhanced HIPC Initiative administered by the World Bank and IMF. Moreover, to help sub-Saharan Africa meet the MDGs, donor countries have dramatically increased aid in the past few years. Aid to the region increased from $16.4 billion in 2001 to over $43 billion (nearly 40 percent of global ODA) in 2006. Today the average aid per capita in the region is over $45.

Despite these efforts, the development challenges are daunting. The effectiveness of development aid programs has been hindered by ongoing political instability and widespread corruption that contribute to the misuse of funds and the difficulties in attracting private capital and foreign direct investment. Yet perhaps the most serious development challenge in sub-Saharan Africa today is the spread of HIV/AIDS. According to "AIDS Epidemic Update, 2007," a product of the Joint United Nations Programme on HIV/AIDS (UNAIDS), the region accounts for nearly 59 percent of the world's population living with HIV/AIDS. Life expectancy rapidly declined to only 49.6 years in 2005. Poor health-care infrastructure, the absence of doctors, weaknesses in education on prevention and treatment, and cultural and political factors have impeded efforts to stem the epidemic's spread. Many reports indicate that the spread of AIDS has actually reversed progress in human development, leading the aid community to focus strongly on AIDS prevention and treatment alongside the region's other development goals in education, agricultural reform, and infrastructural development.

South Asia

South Asia has experienced strong economic growth compared to the rest of the developing world. Between 2003 and 2006, annual economic growth averaged 6.5 percent. However, as in Latin America and the Caribbean, this growth has not effectively translated into poverty reduction. The average GDP per capita remains under $2,300. Despite progress since the MDGs were launched in 2000, South Asia is still home to 47 percent of the world's poor, living on less than $1 per day. As a result, the region still receives close to 1 percent of its GNI in aid, although the high population translates this number into $6.19 in aid to each citizen. In 2006, the region enjoyed a growth rate of 7.0 percent, but still received nearly $9.3 billion in foreign aid.

Widespread malnutrition, maternal and infant mortality rates, and the spread of HIV/AIDS in the region top the list of development aid concerns. Nearly half of all children in Bangladesh and Nepal are malnourished, and maternal mortality rates remain high (nearing 600 maternal deaths per 100,000 live births). As a result, aid is strongly focused on family planning, health-care facilities, and provisioning of health education. Women's economic and political empowerment, the third goal of the MDGs, is also at risk. In Pakistan, for example, the adult literacy rate for women is only 35.4 percent, compared to 64.1 percent for men. Many leading aid loans are dedicated to educational opportunities for young girls. Microlending programs, modeled on the Grameen Bank in Bangladesh, have made some progress in creating economic opportunities for the poor, especially women (see Case Study—Microlending in Bangladesh and Document 3). Finally, environmental degradation due to rapid population growth, industrialization, and urbanization has threatened sustainable development. Several natural disasters in the past few years, including the tsunami of December 2004 and the recent cyclone in Myanmar, have increased demand for disaster relief. This, in turn, has revealed numerous problems in coordinating and delivering such aid, particularly in the face of sometimes staunch domestic political resistance to external assistance.

East Asia and the Pacific

The countries of East Asia and the Pacific are relatively well off compared to the rest of the developing world. Led by the four tigers—Hong Kong, South Korea, Taiwan, and Singapore—the region experienced tremendous economic growth in the last three decades, which the World Bank in the early 1990s labeled the East Asian Miracle. The Asian financial crisis of 1997 reversed this trend briefly, but the average annual growth rate per capita since has increased steadily from 5.16 percent in 1999 to 8.60 percent in 2006. Aid per capita is relatively small, about $4 per person, compared to other regions. Overall, like Latin America, the countries of East Asia and the Pacific, with only a few exceptions, are no longer widely considered to be developing economies. The region has made significant progress toward the MDGs, and extreme poverty has fallen from 29.6 percent in 1990 to less than 10 percent today. Health care remains a concern, particularly in light of limited progress in reversing the HIV/AIDS epidemic.

The most dramatic development progress has been in China. In 2005 and 2006, China's annual GDP grew by an average of 10.5 percent, reaching an average GDP per capita of $4,644. China's remarkable growth has propelled it from the status of low- to middle-income country in a very short period of time. Recently, due to a strong balance-of-payments surplus, China has started to act as a net lender to other developing countries, primarily through its sovereign wealth funds. However, China still struggles with core development challenges in areas such as education, health policy, and sustainable development. The 2008 Olympic Games starkly revealed China's horrific pollution levels and raised questions about systemic corruption. Today, despite the fact that China holds nearly half of the U.S. foreign dollar reserves, it still receives levels of official development aid that, in absolute terms, make it one of the largest aid recipients in the world. In 2006, China received nearly $1.25 billion in official aid; most of this was in the form of bilateral aid from Japan. However, in per capita terms this translated into less than $1 per person, and official aid was dwarfed by the $12.8 billion in new private capital that flowed into China's rapidly growing productive sectors in 2006.

Data

Table 1   Key Indicators of Social and Economic Development for Selected Aid-Receiving Countries

Country	GNI per capita (PPP), 2006 (US$)	GDP per capita percentage growth, 2005–2006	Population living on less than $1 per day (%)	Life expectancy at birth, 2005, male/female (years)	Under-five mortality rate per 1,000, 2005	Adult literacy rate, 2000–2005 (% age 15 and older)
Algeria	6,900	1.5	< 2	70/73	39	70
Argentina	15,390	7.4	6.6	71/79	18	97
Brazil	8,800	2.4	7.5	67/75	33	89
China	7,740	10.1	9.9	70/74	27	91
Colombia	7,620	5.4	7.0	70/76	21	93
DRC	720	1.9	n/a	43/45	205	67
Egypt	4,690	4.9	3.1	68/73	33	71
Georgia	3,690	10.3	6.5	68/75	45	n/a
Guatemala	4,800	2.1	13.5	64/72	43	69
India	3,800	7.7	34.3	63/64	74	61
Indonesia	3,950	4.3	7.5	66/70	36	90
Mali	1,130	2.5	36.1	48/49	218	24
Pakistan	2,500	4.1	17.0	64/65	99	50
Romania	9,820	8.2	< 2	68/75	19	97
Tajikistan	1,410	5.6	7.4	61/67	71	99
Thailand	9,140	4.2	< 2	68/74	21	93
Turkey	9,060	4.8	3.4	69/74	29	87
Uganda	1,490	1.5	n/a	49/51	136	67
East Asia and the Pacific	6,821	8.6	n/a	69/73	33	91
Europe and central Asia	9,662	6.8	n/a	64/74	33	98
Latin America and the Caribbean	8,789	4.2	n/a	69/76	31	90
Middle East and North Africa	6,447	3.6	n/a	68/72	52	73
South Asia	3,444	6.9	n/a	63/64	83	58
Sub-Saharan Africa	2,032	3.2	n/a	47/48	163	59
High-income countries (OECD)	34,701	2.6	n/a	76/82	7	99
World	10,218	2.8	n/a	n/a	n/a	82

Source: World Bank, *World Development Indicators 2008* (Washington, D.C.: World Bank, 2008).

Notes: DRC, Democratic Republic of the Congo; GDP, gross domestic product; GNI, gross national income; n/a, not available; OECD, Organisation for Economic Cooperation and Development; PPP, purchasing power parity.

Table 2   Trends in Official Development Aid: Recipient Countries

	Net ODA (millions of US$)		Bilateral share of ODA (%)		Net ODA/GNI (%)		Net private flows (millions of US$)	
	2004	2006	2004	2006	2004	2006	2004	2006
Algeria	314	209	77	81	0.4	0.2	−101	297
Argentina	93	114	76	69	0.1	0.1	−1,575	5,084
Brazil	157	82	89	89	0	0	2,735	27,498
China	1,685	1,245	91	90	0.1	0.0	1,5845	12,835
Colombia	519	988	90	91	0.6	0.8	889	4,171
DRC	1824	2,056	64	72	29.1	25.2	−19	−189
Egypt	1,456	873	8	73	1.8	0.8	2,193	4,174
Georgia	314	361	62	58	6.1	4.9	32	176
Guatemala	220	487	86	88	0.8	0.8	−78	628
India	694	1,379	59	53	0.1	0.2	3,958	10,185
Indonesia	130	1,405	82	77	0.1	0.4	1,292	2,371
Mali	568	825	58	17	12.1	13.4	−25	14
Pakistan	1,424	2,147	23	50	1.5	1.7	160	1,519
Romania	n/a	n/a	n/a	n/a	n/a	n/a	n/a	n/a
Tajikistan	243	240	41	41	12.2	8.8	−1	0
Thailand	46	−216	94	86	0.0	−0.1	3,489	3,108
Turkey	286	570	55	57	0.1	0.1	1,410	15,051
Uganda	1,194	1,551	55	19	17.9	16.9	−8	23

Source: OECD Development Cooperation Directorate, Recipient Aid Charts, available at: http://www.oecd.org/dac/stats/donorcharts (accessed May 4, 2008).

Notes: DRC, Democratic Republic of Congo; GNI, gross national income; n/a, not available; ODA, official development assistance.

Table 3   Trends in Official Development Aid: Contributions of OECD DAC Member Countries since 1990 (in millions of US$)

	France		Germany		Japan		Netherlands		United Kingdom		United States		Total OECD DAC	
	Total ODA	ODA (% of GNI)	Total ODA	ODA (% of GNI)	Total ODA	ODA (% of GNI)	Total ODA	ODA (% of GNI)	Total ODA	ODA (% of GNI)	Total ODA	ODA (% of GNI)	Total ODA	ODA (% of GNI)
1990	7.2	0.60	6.3	0.42	9.1	0.31	2.5	0.92	2.6	0.27	11.4	0.21	53.0	0.33
1991	7.4	0.62	6.9	0.40	11.0	0.32	2.5	0.88	3.2	0.32	11.3	0.20	56.7	0.33
1992	8.3	0.63	7.6	0.39	11.2	0.30	2.8	0.86	3.2	0.31	11.7	0.20	60.9	0.33
1993	7.9	0.63	7.0	0.37	11.3	0.26	2.5	0.82	2.9	0.31	10.1	0.15	56.5	0.30
1994	8.5	0.64	6.8	0.33	13.2	0.29	2.5	0.76	3.2	0.31	9.9	0.14	59.2	0.30
1995	8.4	0.55	7.5	0.31	14.5	0.28	3.2	0.81	3.2	0.29	7.4	0.10	58.9	0.27
1996	7.4	0.48	7.5	0.32	9.4	0.20	3.2	0.81	3.2	0.27	9.1	0.12	55.1	0.25
1997	6.3	0.45	5.9	0.28	9.4	0.22	2.9	0.81	3.4	0.26	6.9	0.09	48.3	0.22
1998	5.7	0.40	5.6	0.26	10.6	0.28	3.0	0.80	3.9	0.27	8.8	0.10	52.1	0.23
1999	5.6	0.38	5.5	0.26	15.3	0.35	3.1	0.79	3.4	0.23	9.1	0.10	56.4	0.24
2000	4.1	0.30	5.0	0.27	13.1	0.28	3.1	0.84	4.5	0.32	10.0	0.10	53.7	0.22
2001	4.2	0.31	4.9	0.27	9.8	0.23	3.2	0.82	4.6	0.32	11.4	0.11	52.4	0.23
2002	5.4	0.37	5.3	0.27	9.2	0.23	3.3	0.81	4.9	0.31	13.2	0.13	58.3	0.25
2003	7.2	0.40	6.7	0.28	8.8	0.20	3.9	0.80	6.2	0.34	16.3	0.15	69.0	0.26
2004	8.4	0.41	7.5	0.28	8.9	0.19	4.2	0.73	7.9	0.36	19.7	0.17	79.4	0.33
2005	10.0	0.47	10.0	0.36	13.1	0.28	5.1	0.82	10.7	0.47	27.9	0.23	107.1	0.31
2006	10.6	0.47	10.4	0.36	11.1	0.25	5.4	0.81	12.4	0.51	23.5	0.18	104.4	0.28

Source: OECD StatExtracts, available at: http://stats.oecd.org (accessed May 4, 2008).

Notes: The members of the Development Assistance Committee of the OECD are Australia, Austria, Belgium, Canada, Denmark, Finland, France, Germany, Greece, Ireland, Italy, Japan, Luxembourg, Netherlands, New Zealand, Norway, Portugal, Spain, Sweden, Switzerland, United Kingdom, United States, and the European Commission. DAC, Development Assistance Committee; GNI, gross national income; ODA, official development assistance; OECD, Organisation for Economic Cooperation and Development.

**Table 4 Official Development Aid by Selected Sectors, 2000–2006
(in millions of US$)**

	2000	2001	2002	2003	2004	2005	2006
Social infrastructure and services[a]	14,331	13,707	16,999	21,560	27,765	29,515	32,744
Economic infrastructure and services[b]	7,432	6,293	6,171	6,428	12,450	10,458	11,087
Production sectors[c]	3,151	3,701	3,364	3,714	4,639	5,140	4,625
Commodity aid/general program assistance	3,178	2,907	2,495	3,631	2,334	2,575	3,574
Action relating to debt	3,504	4,156	6,449	15,969	8,071	25,903	21,889
Humanitarian aid	2,086	1,932	2,941	4,425	5,339	7,973	6,688
Total ODA (all sectors)	43,587	41,263	48,955	68,473	72,364	94,407	96,709

Source: OECD StatExtracts, available at: http://stats.oecd.org (accessed May 20, 2008).

Notes: ODA, official development assistance; OECD, Organisation for Economic Cooperation and Development.

[a]Social infrastructure and services include education, health, population planning and programming, water supply and sanitation, government and civil society, and conflict, peace and security.

[b]Economic infrastructure includes transportation, communications, energy, banking, and business services.

[c]Production sectors include agriculture, forestry, industry, mining, and construction.

Case Study—AIDS in Swaziland

The HIV/AIDS epidemic is one of the most serious challenges to development in sub-Saharan Africa today. According to the UNAIDS *2007 AIDS Epidemic Update,* of the approximate 34 million people living with HIV/AIDS in the world today, over 60 percent (nearly 22.4 million) reside in sub-Saharan Africa. In the entire region, over 5 percent of the adult population is infected with the disease, compared to 0.6 percent in North America. AIDS is the leading cause of death in the region, producing severe consequences for human development, including declining life expectancies, declining economic growth rates (due to loss of labor), and the orphaning of an estimated 11.4 million children because of the death of one or both parents to AIDS. The MDGs seek to halt and reverse the spread of AIDS by 2015. To date, some progress has been made in slowing the spread of the disease, but the outlook remains bleak. In response, the global community has dramatically increased aid to promote greater education about, prevention of, and treatment of HIV/AIDS. The United Nations created UNAIDS, a joint effort of ten specialized agencies including the UNDP, the World Bank, and World Health Organization to coordinate funds and activities. Bilateral aid has also increased significantly. In 2003, the United States announced the largest single-country contribution to the global fight against AIDS—a five-year, $15 billion bilateral initiative entitled President's Emergency Plan for AIDS Relief (PEPFAR).

Swaziland currently has the highest rate of HIV/AIDS in the world. Between 34 and 39 percent of its population is infected with the disease. A tiny country of just over 1 million people nestled between South Africa and Mozambique,

Swaziland actually enjoys a middle-income and medium human development status. Its annual GDP is well above the average for the region at close to $4,825 (adjusted for purchasing power parity, PPP). Yet the AIDS epidemic has taken a severe toll. It has actually set the country back in terms of socioeconomic and human development and put it behind schedule for reaching the MDGs. The annual economic growth rate between 1990 and 2005 was only 0.2 percent, and population growth has slowed dramatically, from over 3 percent annual growth in 1996 to 0 percent growth in 2006. More shocking is the decline in life expectancy from nearly fifty-eight years in 1997 to forty years in 2006. Health-care expenditures have skyrocketed from less than $70 per person in 2001 to $146 per person in 2006 (equal to nearly 6.4 percent of GDP).

According to the UNAIDS Global Report from 2006, the key drivers of HIV/AIDS in Swaziland include a lack of public awareness about the causes and prevention of the disease, cultural beliefs and practices regarding intergenerational sex, denial of the disease, low condom use, and the spread of the infection through migrant labor. The AIDS epidemic is compounded by more systemic problems, including the poor health-care infrastructure. Swaziland has only 16 doctors per 100,000 people and generally poor service delivery and provision of antiretroviral drugs (only 31 percent of HIV-infected adults receive antiretroviral therapy, which is used to reduce the effects of the disease on individuals and makes living with AIDS possible).

Women are disproportionately affected by the AIDS epidemic. In sub-Saharan Africa as a whole, almost 61 percent of adults living with HIV in 2007 were women, and the rate is similar in Swaziland. Beyond the higher infection rate, attributed to the polygamous culture and biological reasons, women bear the burden of the AIDS epidemic more directly in terms of caring for family members affected by the disease and the risk of transmitting the disease during childbirth. According to the United Nations General Assembly Special Session (UNGASS) 2008 Swaziland country report, 42.9 percent of pregnant women in 2004 had HIV, yet only 12 percent of pregnant women received treatment to reduce mother-to-child transmission. As of 2006, an estimated 15,000 children ages zero to fourteen were living with HIV, and an estimated 63,000 were AIDS orphans. Experts estimate that the number of AIDS orphans will reach 120,000—approximately 15 percent of the projected total population—by 2010. Swaziland is also expected to lose momentum on the other MDG goal of universal primary education due to the deaths of teachers and the increased poverty of families that will be unable to send their children to school. Primary school enrollment is expected to decrease from 96.5 percent in 1999 to 70 percent by 2015.

Swaziland currently receives over $30 per person in ODA, much of which addresses the AIDS epidemic. The response to the AIDS epidemic has been aggressive and exhibits the concerted collaboration between domestic and international actors. In 1999, Mswati III, the king of Swaziland, declared HIV/AIDS a national disaster and initiated a National Strategic Action Plan to address the crisis. UNAIDS has worked closely with the Swaziland government, including providing technical and financial support for the National

Strategic Plan. In 2006, UNAIDS launched the Joint UN Implementation Support Plan to the Second Multisectoral National HIV and AIDS Strategic Plan, as well as an Action Plan for 2006–2008, focusing on enhancing national efforts to provide universal access to prevention and treatment.

Case Study—Microlending in Bangladesh

Bangladesh is one of the most densely populated and impoverished countries in South Asia. Nearly 42 percent of the population lives on less than $1 per day, only 74 percent has access to improved water sources, and 48 percent of children under five are underweight. The extreme poverty of Bangladesh has most affected women and children. Child and maternal mortality rates are high, and 41 percent of women over the age of fifteen are literate, compared to 54 percent of men. ODA to Bangladesh has focused on the most basic needs, including aid directed at education, health care, sanitation, and agriculture. Floods and famines have also created a demand for disaster relief funds. Overall, however, poverty alleviation through traditional means of ODA has made only modest progress.

In 1976, Muhammad Yunus, economics professor from the University of Chittagong, conducted a research project exploring the possibilities of a program that would provide small loans to the rural poor without the need for the assets normally required for bank lending. The goal was to enable the poorest sections of the society—most often women and the illiterate, who have difficulty qualifying for commercial bank loans—to gain access to credit and create opportunities for self-employment. The underlying belief was that the poor can lift themselves out of poverty if provided with the education and financial means to do so.

After the resounding success of the pilot project in the small village of Jobra, the program was extended to several other villages. In 1983, the Grameen Bank project (as it was later called) was turned into an independent bank, and today over 90 percent of its shares are owned by the rural poor who are the bank's borrowers. Small amounts of money are lent on a weekly basis to groups of five people who, through peer pressure and commitment to the Grameen Bank's sixteen decisions (see Document 3), ensure that the loans are repaid and the profits are reinvested. Women make up more than 97 percent of the borrowers; most use their funds for small entrepreneurial ventures, such as pottery making, weaving, and other retail services.

The program also has an educational purpose in teaching the participants not only how to handle money but also how to take care of their families and how to build and maintain safe housing and sanitary conditions. Among the sixteen decisions are pledges by borrowers to become more self-sufficient in food production, become more involved in the education of their children, and practice family planning. The Grameen Bank has expanded rapidly in the last thirty-five years and now has more than 2,500 branch offices in over 81,000 villages throughout Bangladesh; it has an astonishing repayment rate of 98 percent—far above that of conventional commercial banks. Overall, since its inception, the Grameen Bank has lent over $372 billion.

The Grameen Bank, a private commercial organization, has been held up as an example of the power of NGOs in global development. It is also heralded as a model for multilateral and bilateral development aid strategies targeting grassroots assistance and the empowerment of women. Most remarkably, the microlending model has been integrated into the development agendas of major institutions, including the World Bank. More important, the Grameen Bank's emphasis on enabling the poor to improve their own conditions through financial and educational opportunities reflects a shift in development aid thinking based on poverty alleviation through simple macroeconomic growth to a more equitable, participatory, and grassroots approach capturing the social and human aspects of development. In 2006, Muhammed Yunus and the Grameen Bank received the Nobel Peace Prize.

Biographical Sketches

Robert S. McNamara served as U.S. secretary of defense under Presidents John F. Kennedy and Lyndon B. Johnson. He was president of the World Bank from 1968 to 1981. During his tenure at the bank, McNamara fundamentally changed the focus of international development aid by defining the concept absolute poverty. In doing so, he shifted the focus of the bank from building basic economic infrastructure to broader development goals based on the fulfillment of basic human needs, including the alleviation of malnutrition, illiteracy, disease, infant mortality, and low life expectancy. During McNamara's presidency, the World Bank became the premier global development aid institution.

Jeffrey Sachs is an economics professor and director of the Earth Institute at Columbia University in New York. He is one of the most widely recognized economists of the 1980s and 1990s, having served as an adviser to governments in Eastern Europe, Latin America, and the former Soviet Union. Sachs was the primary author of the shock therapy method of transition from command to market economies in Poland and Russia. More recently, Sachs led the Millennium Development Project and serves as a special advisor to United Nations Secretary-General Ban Ki-moon. In 2005, he wrote the best-selling book, *The End of Poverty.*

Amartya Sen won the 1998 Nobel Prize in Economics and has promoted a theory of development based on the empowerment of the poor through opportunities in education and work. He argues that improvement in per capita income is not enough absent real progress in the social aspects of development. In 1990, Sen was one of the authors of the first *Human Development Report,* in which he formulated a new measure of development—the Human Development Index—based on the three variables of life expectancy, adult literacy, and income. His 1999 book, *Development as Freedom,* is one of the most widely read works on global development.

George Soros is a Hungarian investment banker and philanthropist and one of the leading individuals in development aid. During the past two decades, he established a network of initiatives—through his Open Society Institute—in Eastern Europe, Guatemala, Haiti, southern Africa, the nations of the former Soviet Union, and the United States dedicated to building the infrastructure and institutions of a free market economy and democracy.

Joseph Stiglitz is a prize-winning economist and former senior vice president and chief economist of the World Bank. As an academic, Stiglitz helped to create the new and influential theory of the economics of information. As a policymaker, Stiglitz has become well known for his opposition to the Washington Consensus, the set of policies favoring free-market principles that have informed the development agendas of the World Bank and the IMF since the 1980s. Stiglitz was pushed out of the World Bank after publicly criticizing the IMF's response to the Asian financial crisis in 1997. In October 2001, Stiglitz received the Nobel Prize in Economics and has since become a vocal advocate for reform of Washington's international financial institutions.

Directory

African Development Bank, 15 Avenue du Ghana, P.O. Box 323-1002, Tunis-Belvedère, Tunisia. Telephone: (216) 71 103 450; email: afdb@afdb.org; Web: http://www.afdb.org.
Institution that targets social and economic development in Africa by facilitating partnerships between African and non-African countries.

Asian Development Bank, 6 ADB Avenue, Mandaluyong City 1550, Philippines. Telephone: (632) 632 4444; Web: http://www.adb.org.
Institution that promotes economic and social development in the Asia-Pacific region.

Bretton Woods Project, c/o Action Aid, Hamlyn House, Macdonald Road, London N19 5PG, United Kingdom. Telephone: +44 (0)20 7561 7610; email: info@brettonwoodsproject.org; Web: http://www.brettonwoodsproject.org.
Nongovernmental watchdog organization that monitors the activities of the multilateral development banks.

CARE International, 151 Ellis Street NE, Atlanta, Ga. 30303-2439. Telephone: (800) 521-CARE; email: info@care.org; Web: http://www.care.org.
One of the largest private international relief and development organizations.

Center for Global Development, 1800 Massachusetts Avenue NW, Third Floor, Washington D.C. 20036. Telephone: (202) 416-0700; email: cgd@cgdev.org; Web: http://www.cgdev.org.
Think tank devoted to policy-related research on global development practice.

Development Assistance Committee (DAC) of the OECD, 2 Rue André Pascal, 75775 Paris Cedex 16, France. Telephone: (33) 1 4524 8200; email: doc.contact@oecd.org; Web: http://www.oecd.org/dac.
Specialized committee of the OECD that provides a forum for consultation, development research, and aid coordination among the organization's major donor countries and the European Commission.

European Bank for Reconstruction and Development, One Exchange Square, London EC2A 2JN, United Kingdom. Telephone: (44) 20 7338 6000; Web: http://www.ebrd.com.
Institution promoting economic reform and the emergence of democracies in the former Soviet Union and Eastern Europe.

Food and Agricultural Organization, Viale delle Terme di Caracalla, 00153 Rome, Italy. Telephone: (39) 06 5705 1; email: fao-hq@fao.org; Web: http://www.fao.org.
UN agency devoted to alleviating poverty and hunger through food security.

Grameen Bank, Mirpur - 2, Dhaka - 1216, Bangladesh. Telephone: (88) 02 8011138; email: grameen.bank@grameen.net; Web: http://www.grameen-info.org.
Microlending institution established in Bangladesh in 1977.

Inter-American Development Bank, 1300 New York Avenue NW, Washington, D.C. 20577. Telephone: (202) 623-1000; email: pic@iadb.org; Web: http://www.iadb.org.
Institution providing development assistance to Latin American and Caribbean countries through the provision of low-interest loans and technical assistance.

International Monetary Fund (IMF), 700 19th Street NW, Washington, D.C. 20431. Telephone: (202) 623-7000; email: publicaffairs@imf.org; Web: http://www.imf.org.
Institution promoting international monetary cooperation and the growth of world trade by stabilizing foreign exchange rates, promoting an open trading system by deterring protectionist policies, and serving as a lender of last resort.

Joint United Nations Programme on HIV/AIDS (UNAIDS), 20 Avenue Appia, 1211 Geneva 27, Switzerland. Telephone: (41) 22 791 3666; email: unaids@unaids.org; Web: http://www.unaids.org.
UN agency advocating worldwide action against HIV/AIDS.

Oxfam International, 226 Causeway Street, 5th Floor, Boston, Mass. 02114-2206. Telephone: (617) 482-1211; email: info@oxfamamerica.org; Web: http://www.oxfam.org.
Coalition of international NGOs devoted to development issues, advocacy, and relief.

United Nations Conference on Trade and Development (UNCTAD), Palais des Nations, 8-14 Avenue de la Paix, 1211 Geneva 10, Switzerland. Telephone: (41) 22 917 1234; email: info@unctad.org; Web: http://www.unctad.org.
UN agency responsible for trade and development issues.

United Nations Development Fund for Women (UNIFEM), 304 East 45th Street, 15th Floor, New York, NY 10017. Telephone: (212) 906-6400; Web: http://www.unifem.org.
UN agency devoted to promoting women's empowerment and gender equality.

United Nations Development Programme (UNDP), One United Nations Plaza, New York, N.Y. 10017. Telephone: (212) 906-5000; Web: http://www.undp.org.
UN agency addressing the causes of poverty and promoting development, the protection of human rights, and the empowerment of women; publishes the Human Development Report.

United Nations Environment Programme (UNEP), United Nations Avenue, Gigiri, P.O. Box 30552, 00100, Nairobi, Kenya. Telephone: (254-20) 762 1234; email: unepinfo@unep.org; Web: http://www.unep.org.
UN agency tackling a range of environmental issues on an international basis, including the study and promotion of sustainable development.

United Nations International Children's Emergency Fund (UNICEF), 3 United Nations Plaza, New York, N.Y. 10017. Telephone: (212) 326-7000; Web: http://www.unicef.org.
UN agency working to resolve problems related to the poverty and rights of children around the world.

U.S. Agency for International Development (USAID), Information Center, U.S. Agency for International Development, Ronald Reagan Building, Washington, D.C. 20523-1000. Telephone: (202) 712-4810; Web: http://www.usaid.gov.
Primary U.S. government agency through which U.S. development assistance is channeled.

World Bank, 1818 H Street NW, Washington, D.C. 20433. Telephone: (202) 473-1000; Web: http://www.worldbank.org.
World's largest and most influential multilateral development bank.

World Health Organization (WHO), 20 Avenue Appia, 1211 Geneva 27, Switzerland. Telephone: (41) 22 791 2111; email: info@who.int; Web: http://www.who.int.
UN agency advocating health for all people.

Further Research

Books

Collier, Paul. *The Bottom Billion: Why the Poorest Countries Are Failing and What Can Be Done about It.* New York: Oxford University Press, 2007.

Easterly, William. *The White Man's Burden: Why the West's Efforts to Aid the Rest Have Done So Much Ill and So Little Good.* New York: Penguin, 2006.

Lancaster, Carol. *Foreign Aid: Diplomacy, Development, Domestic Politics.* Chicago: University of Chicago Press, 2006.

Moss, Todd J. *African Development: Making Sense of the Issues and Actors.* Boulder, Colo.: Lynne Rienner, 2007.

Narayan, Deepa, et al. *Crying Out for Change: Voices of the Poor.* Washington, D.C.: World Bank, 2000.

Rapley, John. *Understanding Development: Theory and Practice in the Third World.* Boulder, Colo.: Lynne Rienner, 2007.

Riddell, Roger. *Does Foreign Aid Really Work?* New York: Oxford University Press, 2007.

Sachs, Jeffrey. *The End of Poverty: Economic Possibilities for Our Time.* New York: Penguin, 2005.

Sen, Amartya. *Development as Freedom.* London: Anchor, 2000.

World Bank. *Assessing Aid: What Works, What Doesn't, and Why.* Washington, D.C.: World Bank, 1998.

World Commission on Environment and Development. *Our Common Future.* Oxford and New York: Oxford University Press, 1987.

Yunus, Muhammad. *Banker to the Poor: Micro-Lending and the Battle against World Poverty.* New York: Public Affairs, 2003.

Articles and Reports

African Development Bank and Organization for Economic Cooperation and Development. *African Economic Outlook 2008.* Paris: OECD, 2007.

Development Assistance Committee of the Organization for Economic Cooperation and Development. *Development Cooperation Report.* Paris: OECD, various years.

Joint United Nations Programme on HIV/AIDS (UNAIDS). *AIDS Epidemic Update 2007.* Geneva: UNAIDS, 2007.

United Nations. "Millennium Development Goals Report 2007." Available at: http://www.un.org/millenniumgoals/documents.html.

United Nations Development Programme (UNDP). *Human Development Report.* New York and Oxford: Oxford University Press for the UNDP, various years.

United Nations General Assembly Special Session (UNGASS). *Monitoring the Declaration of Commitment on HIV/AIDS: Swaziland Country Report 2008.* Available at: http://www.unaidsrstesa.org/Documents/ungass_report.html (accessed May 21, 2008).

World Bank. *World Development Indicators.* Washington, D.C.: World Bank, various years.

———. *World Development Report.* Washington, D.C.: World Bank, various years.

Web Sites

Electronic Development and Environment Information System (ELDIS)
http://www.ids.ac.uk/eldis

Global Development Network, World Bank
http://www.gdnet.org

Highly Indebted Poor Countries Initiative, World Bank
http://www.worldbank.org/hipc

Millennium Development Goals
http://www.un.org/millenniumgoals

One World Online
http://us.oneworld.net

ReliefNet
http://www.reliefnet.org

Women Watch
http://www.un.org/womenwatch

World Directory of Development Organizations and Programs
http://ospiti.peacelink.it/zumbi/org/wddop.html

Documents

1. Our Common Future (The Brundtland Report)

World Commission on Environment and Development, 1987

Extract

Sustainable Development

Humanity has the ability to make development sustainable—to ensure that it meets the needs of the present without compromising the ability of future generations to meet their own needs. The concept of sustainable development does imply limits—not absolute limits but limitations imposed by the present state of technology and social organization on environmental resources and by the ability of the biosphere to absorb the effects of human activities. But technology and social organization can be both managed and improved to make way for a new era of economic growth. The Commission believes that widespread poverty is no longer inevitable. Poverty is not only an evil in itself, but sustainable development requires meeting the basic needs of all and extending to all the opportunity to fulfill their aspirations for a better life. A world in which poverty is endemic will always be prone to ecological and other catastrophes.

2. Millennium Development Goals

Available at http://www.un.org/special-rep/ohrlls/ldc/Workshop/MDG%20indicators.pdf.

Goal 1: Eradicate Extreme Poverty and Hunger

Target 1: Halve, between 1990 and 2015, the proportion of people whose income is less than one dollar per day.

Target 2: Halve, between 1990 and 2015, the proportion of people who suffer from hunger.

Goal 2: Achieve Universal Primary Education

Target 3: Ensure that, by 2015, children everywhere, boys and girls alike, will be able to complete a full course of primary schooling.

Goal 3: Promote Gender Equality and Empower Women

Target 4: Eliminate gender disparity in primary and secondary education, preferably by 2005, and in all levels of education no later than 2015.

Goal 4: Reduce Child Mortality

Target 5: Reduce by two-thirds, between 1990 and 2015, the under-five mortality ratio.

Goal 5: Improve Maternal Health

Target 6: Reduce by three-quarters, between 1990 and 2015, the maternal mortality ratio.

Goal 6: Combat HIV/AIDS, Malaria and Other Diseases

Target 7: Have halted by 2015 and begun to reverse the spread of HIV/AIDS.

Target 8: Have halted by 2015 and begun to reverse the incidence of malaria and other major diseases.

Goal 7: Ensure Environmental Sustainability

Target 9: Integrate the principles of sustainable development into country policies and programmes and reverse the loss of environmental resources.

Target 10: Halve, by 2015, the proportion of people without sustainable access to safe drinking water and basic sanitation.

Target 11: By 2020, to have achieved a significant improvement in the lives of at least 100 million slum dwellers.

Goal 8: Develop a Global Partnership for Development

Target 12: Develop further an open, rule-based, predictable, non-discriminatory trading and financial system.

Target 13: Address the special needs of the least developed countries.

Target 14: Address the special needs of landlocked developing countries and small island developing states.

Target 15: Deal comprehensively with the debt problems of developing countries through national and international measures in order to make debt sustainable in the long term.

Target 16: In co-operation with developing countries, develop and implement strategies for decent and productive work for Youth.

Target 17: In co-operation with pharmaceutical companies, provide access to affordable essential drugs in developing countries.

Target 18: In co-operation with the private sector, make available the benefits of new technologies, especially information and communications.

3. The Sixteen Decisions of the Grameen Bank

Available at http://www.grameen-info.org/index.php?option=com_content&task=view&id=2 2&Itemid=109.

1. We shall follow and advance the four principles of Grameen Bank—discipline, unity, courage and hard work—in all walks of our lives.

2. Prosperity we shall bring to our families.

3. We shall not live in dilapidated houses. We shall repair our houses and work towards constructing new houses at the earliest.

4. We shall grow vegetables all the year round. We shall eat plenty of them and sell the surplus.

5. During the plantation seasons, we shall plant as many seedlings as possible.

6. We shall plan to keep our families small. We shall minimize our expenditures. We shall look after our health.

7. We shall educate our children and ensure that they can earn to pay for their education.

8. We shall always keep our children and the environment clean.

9. We shall build and use pit-latrines.

10. We shall drink water from tubewells. If it is not available, we shall boil water or use alum.

11. We shall not take any dowry at our sons' weddings, neither shall we give any dowry at our daughter's wedding. We shall keep our centre free from the curse of dowry. We shall not practice child marriage.

12. We shall not inflict any injustice on anyone, neither shall we allow anyone to do so.

13. We shall collectively undertake bigger investments for higher incomes.

14. We shall always be ready to help each other. If anyone is in difficulty, we shall all help him or her.

15. If we come to know of any breach of discipline in any centre, we shall all go there and help restore discipline.

16. We shall take part in all social activities collectively.

INCOME INEQUALITY

Bob Sutcliffe

Income in the world is distributed more unequally than it was in South Africa during apartheid, a system universally condemned as intolerably unequal. As well as being an indicator of social injustice, income inequality is a cause and a consequence of major problems facing human society, including poverty, crime, ill health, waste of resources, climate change, and threats to democracy. Welfare states can attenuate the extremes of inequality inside countries, although they are now under pressure to reduce spending. However, most world inequality exists not within countries but among them, and the absence of any global equivalent of the welfare state is a glaring issue.

Historical Background

Early humans, practicing hunting and gathering or subsistence agriculture, did not produce the surplus of production necessary to sustain economically privileged groups or classes. Once settled agriculture allowed a higher level of production, urbanization and exchange produced new divisions of labor, and economic privileges and hierarchies became entrenched. Unequal societies based on agriculture lasted for thousands of years, but inequality gained new momentum with the development of urban, industrial, capitalist society from the eighteenth century onward and from the associated spread of imperialism. With more inequality came new egalitarian critiques of society, which both pervaded the literature of the nineteenth century and formed an essential part of emerging socialist and liberal ideologies.

The economic historian Simon Kuznets suggested that rising inequality would be a temporary feature of industrial economies. As more people moved from agriculture to new higher-productivity manufacturing activities, inequality would fall again as the old low-productivity activities were superseded (the famous inverted-U-shaped Kuznets curve). Some evidence exists that this change has often occurred, but many other factors still influence inequality. Also, some see a recent small reduction of intercountry inequality as evidence that the curve now exists at a global level.

This chapter is based on the original, written by James Heintz, that appeared in the first edition of *World at Risk*.

Data on inequality in preindustrial societies are scarce; despite this, recent research uses the same tools for analyzing both current data on inequality and distant historical data. For example, using contemporary methods, Branko Milanovic, Peter Lindert, and Jeffrey Williamson have concluded that the level of intracountry inequality in preindustrial countries or empires was not dissimilar to levels encountered today, thus casting doubt on an alternative hypothesis to the Kuznets curve that inequality has a tendency to rise over the long term. Most historical information on inequality, however, refers to intercountry rather than intracountry differences in income.

The most common tool used to examine contemporary and historical data is the Gini coefficient. The Gini coefficient is an overall measure of inequality among individuals, geographical regions, or countries that takes on a value in the range 0 to 1 (the alternative Gini index is just the coefficient multiplied by 100). A value of 0 means complete equality (each person or country has the same income) and a value of 1 means maximum inequality (one person or country receives all the income and the others nothing). So, the higher the value of the Gini coefficient, the greater the inequality.

The incomes of different countries can be made comparable by using purchasing power parity (PPP), a method of converting incomes in all currencies into a common standard that reflects purchasing power (known as the "international dollar"). Various sources of PPP data are available; here those produced by Angus Maddison are used for historical comparisons (Table 3) and those produced by the World Bank are used for recent comparisons (as in Tables 1 and 2). These data can be used to calculate the degree of global inequality, using one of three concepts (as characterized by Branko Milanovic):

1. Inequality among countries' average income, each having equal weight, meaning that population differences are not taken into account;
2. Inequality among countries weighted by their populations but assuming that all the inhabitants receive the average income of the country in which they live;
3. Inequality among countries that takes into account differences among average incomes, differences in the sizes of their populations, and income inequalities within each country.

The Gini coefficient for the world based on concept 2 was 0.155 in 1820, and it rose more or less continuously until 1990; since then (largely because of the growth of China and a few other Asian countries), it has been slightly reduced (B in Table 3). The gap between the North (Western Europe, North America, and Japan) and virtually all other regions has widened during the past two centuries (A in Table 3). The exceptions are Latin America and the USSR. These areas partially caught up with the North in 1870–1950 and 1913–1960, respectively—periods when these countries were relatively isolated from the capitalist world market. The gap between the North and Africa has continuously grown since 1820. This ever-widening gap provides strong support for the hypotheses put forward by the once-influential dependency theorists that capitalism and imperialism have led to a radical and hard-to-reverse polarization of the world into center and periphery countries.

François Bourguignon and Christian Morrisson have integrated Maddison's figures with historical estimates of intracountry inequality drawn from a variety of sources to calculate the concept 3 Gini coefficient for the world as a whole (see C1 in Table 3). This shows global inequality rising continuously from 1820 to 1980 and then leveling off to a point at which the Gini coefficient is approximately the same as that estimated by completely different methods (C2 in Table 3). The difference between the concept 2 and concept 3 calculation of the historical Gini coefficients (B and C1/C2) implies that during the past two centuries the nature of global inequality has shifted in an important way; in 1820, the largest component of global inequality came from differences within countries, but today, the largest component comes from the differences among countries.

Current Status

Research

The question posed by economic research on this theme is whether equality has an economic cost. In other words, does a trade-off exist between equality on the one hand and efficiency or growth on the other? The growing discussion of those questions has been fueled by improvements in the available statistics regarding national income and its distribution that make possible increasingly sophisticated studies of inequality both among and within countries.

Measuring Inequality. The accumulation of data about income distribution since the 1980s shows that all countries are unequal but some are more unequal than others. National Gini coefficients range from 0.610 to 0.165 (see Table 1). Another commonly used measure of inequality is the ratio of the income earned by the top decile of income receivers to the bottom decile (the 10/10 ratio). Again, the higher this measure is, the greater the inequality is. The range is astonishingly wide: from 93.91 (Bolivia) to 2.86 (Azerbaijan).

On the basis of the World Bank figures that lie behind Table 1, the whole world Gini coefficient (concept 3) is 0.665 and the 10/10 ratio is (by a curious fluke) exactly 100. Hence, according to both these measures, the world is considerably more unequal than any single country.

Researchers generally believe that better data would reveal an increase in the amount of inequality because people in richer classes respond less to surveys. Ascertaining how much these measures of inequality have changed in recent years also is problematic because household surveys of income and consumption exist only in a minority of countries. World figures exclude (through lack of comparable data) a number of countries that are likely to be at the extremes of the distributions (for instance, most of the oil-producing countries of the Arabian/Persian Gulf and some of the poorest countries in Africa).

For countries where a comparison over time is possible, two recent reports from the International Labour Organisation (ILO) and the Organisation for

Economic Cooperation and Development (OECD) show that in the majority of countries studied Gini coefficients have risen since 1980. In other words, in the majority of countries for which data exist inequality has grown.

One intriguing feature of the data about the distribution of income in different countries reflects a law first discovered by Gabriel Palma: although the ratio of the top decile to the four bottom deciles (that is, the poorest 40 percent of the population) varies a great deal among countries, the total percentage of income received by these five deciles varies very little from country to country. In other words, the middle groups (deciles 5–9) receive a roughly constant percentage of national income, while the rest is shared in very different ways between the top decile and bottom four deciles. Whether this also applies to a single country over time is not clear yet.

Some important elements of inequality, however, are missed by these data. Very little information is included about the distribution of nonmonetary objectives, which contribute in part to the concept of "human development." Human development, as explained by Amartya Sen and others, stresses that the ultimate goal for society should be human capacity and freedom, although monetary income can improve such opportunities through access to education and life-prolonging health services. In addition, most inequality data come from household surveys, which do not capture important aspects of inequality that affect women. By definition, these data cannot reveal anything about the inequalities inside the family or household. This important limitation has been stressed by Nancy Folbre and other feminist economists. Despite these shortcomings, the data used to measure inequality have greatly improved over time.

Income Inequality and Growth. Taking advantage of increases in the amount and quality of relevant data, most scientific studies of this subject are attempts in various contexts to answer questions of whether inequality is good or bad for other aspects of the economy. In the field of economics, perhaps the most studied question has been the relationship between income inequality and economic growth. This relationship is closely linked to the classic conundrum of how to eliminate poverty: Will the poor benefit most by receiving a bigger share of a cake of constant or falling size (redistribution) or by receiving a possibly smaller share of a cake that is growing (growth)? Since the dawn of economics, many thinkers have supported the idea that inequalities are necessary for economic growth. According to this theory, profits are the reward that investors receive for the sacrifices they make and the risks they incur. Productive investments, however, require a prior accumulation of wealth and are only made by asset-owning classes. Efforts to redistribute income throughout a population weaken the incentive to invest and therefore reduce growth. This reasoning is consistent with the idea of an efficiency/equity trade-off, that is, that the price of greater equality is a loss of efficiency. This idea, always present in economics, gained new popularity with the rise of neoliberal thinking in some governments and in international organizations during the 1980s. The argument came to be commonly known as trickle-down economics.

In the 1990s, however, many economists began to reassess the relationship between distribution and growth. Statistically significant relationships were discovered between lower inequality and growth. Countries with less inequality tend to grow faster, according to a study by Alberto Alesina and Dani Rodrik and to another by Torsten Persson and Guido Tabellini. Such findings contradict the earlier idea of an efficiency/equity trade-off and could help explain differences in the growth experiences of developing countries. For example, in 1960 Argentina had a higher per capita income than Japan, but income inequality was much higher in Argentina. During the past forty years, however, the Japanese economy has consistently outperformed the Argentine economy. The same comparison has been made more generally between the Latin American and East Asian economies. Such patterns of growth support the argument that less inequality contributes to relative success. Other contributors to the debate have slightly modified these conclusions. Robert Barro has concluded that inequality impedes growth in lower-income countries (but not in high-income ones), and Giovanni Andrea Cornia and Julius Court conclude that Gini coefficients of over 0.400 impede growth (although Gini coefficients of less than 0.250, they argue, can also be harmful to growth).

Others have also concluded that, in general, inequality is negatively correlated with growth. For instance, Lorenzo Kristov, Peter Lindert, and Robert McClelland argue that in a situation of highly unequal income distribution, growth is negatively affected by the lack of social concern for the poor. Such a situation could lead to fewer public investments in services that would benefit low-income households, such as health care and education. This lack of basic services for a large segment of the population could reduce growth because pervasive health problems or a poorly educated workforce could reduce overall productivity.

Another explanation of how inequality negatively affects growth focuses on access to credit. Low-income households generally have restricted access to credit because they are deemed to be high-risk borrowers. When income is unequally distributed, a large fraction of the population is unable to invest in educational or economic opportunities because of unequal access to credit markets. Such underinvestment can constrain growth, according to Oded Galor and Joseph Zeira and to Ben Bernanke and Mark Gertler.

Another widely accepted argument is that unequal income distributions violate norms of fairness or justice to the extent that a high level of social and political conflict results. Such conflict makes coordinating productive activities such as minimizing workplace disruptions and maintaining stable supplies of materials more difficult; these conflicts can also increase uncertainty about the production process and profitability, and destabilize important institutions, such as property rights, all of which could impede increased economic activity, according to Alesina, Roberto Perotti, and Jakob Svensson.

Income Inequality in a Social and Environmental Context. In addition to growth, economists have studied the relationship between inequality and many other social and economic phenomena. Researchers have concluded that higher inequality is associated with increased crime (especially homicide), increased economic waste (due to higher unemployment or to public and private spending on security and the protection of property), lower levels of public health, and less democratic forms of government. All these associations are indirect arguments for the redistribution of income to encourage efficiency, social peace, and democracy, as well as growth.

Interesting as this increasingly complex debate has become, some may think that it fails to ask, let alone answer, a more fundamental set of questions, such as: Why is growth always the goal? Why do we not make the search for equality the goal and ask if it is helped or hindered by growth? The assumption that equality and growth can be achieved together may be convenient, but this is an empirical question. Answers may change with new data or new analytical methods. What if growth and equality cannot be achieved together? Which of them will we sacrifice, and why? The debates have tended to regard equality as an instrument to reach some other goal rather than as a goal in itself. Can equality not be defended intrinsically rather than instrumentally? To answer these questions, economic theorists have turned to political philosophy to gain insight.

Economist John Harsanyi and philosopher John Rawls have proposed similar ideas about fair income distribution. Suppose everyone, from the richest to the poorest, were faced with the prospect of swapping positions with another person in the world and that the probability of selecting any particular person was the same across the population. Under these circumstances, what distribution of income would people freely choose? Rawls, in *A Theory of Justice,* argues that if people were unaware of the position they would occupy in society, and they could freely choose a set of rules governing income distribution, they would choose the principal of justice that maximized the welfare of the least advantaged. Very few egalitarian arguments in the last forty years have not been based partly on Rawls's analysis. His ideas have been used not only to argue for the justice of more equality in developed democratic countries (those he mostly had in mind) but also have been applied (for instance, by Thomas Pogge) to inequality between rich and poor nations. It therefore came as an unwelcome surprise to many when Rawls himself (in *The Law of Peoples,* 1999) rejected the idea that his arguments could be relevantly applied to international inequality. Another prominent philosopher, Peter Singer, in his 2009 *The Life You Can Save,* strongly argued that individuals as well as institutions in richer countries can and should make a significant contribution to a more equal world.

The environmental context of economic growth and income inequality—particularly climate change—has begun to get more attention from researchers (see CLIMATE CHANGE). Inequality relates to climate change in complex ways. Different nations emit very different quantities of CO_2 and other greenhouse gases both in total and per head. The problem can be solved only by reducing total emissions, but a worldwide bargaining process is under way to decide who will reduce emissions most. All countries wish to minimize their reductions because reducing emissions is costly. A clear relationship exists between levels of income per head and the emission of CO_2 per head. The United States, however, is an outlier and emits even more per head than other developed countries at similar income levels. The United States and China are the two largest emitters, being responsible in 2008 for about the same total quantity of CO_2. If either one of them does not agree to major restrictions, disastrous global warming appears to be inevitable regardless of what all other countries do. China will agree only to reduce emissions as long as the United States agrees to reduce its emissions more than China, on the grounds that the final criterion of international justice should be that all countries have equal emissions per head. To get China to agree to some limited action before reaching higher levels of income per head, the United States would have to agree to give considerably more priority to reducing emissions than to its own economic growth. This would involve a decline in its income relative to China's and would thus promote greater world economic equality. Some argue that the United States will not have to face such a reduction because new fuel technology will solve the emissions problem in time, although this theory is likely to be wrong. Others have proposed a zero-growth policy for the world; this is unacceptable because it would freeze inequality at its current level and would not solve the problem of reducing emissions.

Policies and Programs

The redistribution of income is one of the key mechanisms used to address income inequality, and virtually every country—no matter where it stands on the capitalist-socialist-communist spectrum—uses some form of income redistribution to reapportion resources and welfare among its population. The redistributive process takes place in four stages: (1) people receive pay from their employment; (2) they pay taxes, higher incomes incurring higher tax rates (a progressive system); (3) they receive income from the state that is not the result of their work (such as pensions, unemployment pay, and family welfare benefits); and (4) when they spend the net result of the first three stages (the family's or individual's disposable income), they pay extra (hidden) taxes because the price of goods and services includes indirect taxes (such as sales tax, value-added tax, excise duties, and tariffs). A critical question in analyzing policies aimed at reducing, or at least controlling, income inequality is: How effective is this system at reducing inequality?

A detailed 2008 OECD report, *Growing Unequal,* found, not surprisingly, that the pay structure in all countries is very unequal. On average, in the twenty-four richest OECD countries (countries that roughly make up the North) direct taxes equal 31.1 percent of disposable income and cash benefits (such as pensions) equal 15.8 percent. If we look at direct taxes alone, the United States (surprisingly to some) has the most progressive tax system and, in the words of the report, "collects the largest share of taxes from the richest 10 percent." This richest 10 percent, however, has also been rapidly increasing its share of pretax income. The least progressive direct taxes are in the Scandinavian countries (also a surprise to some), but this is partly because wages and salaries are more equally distributed to begin with. In the United States, the richest 10 percent receives 33.5 percent of the market income and pays 45.1 percent of the direct taxes, while in Sweden the figures are 26.6 and

26.7 percent, respectively. Because cash benefits are less generous in the United States than elsewhere, it (along with Japan, France, and Canada) reduces inequality least through the combination of direct taxes and benefits. Countries that reduce inequality most through the combination of direct taxes and benefits are Denmark, Sweden, Australia, and the United Kingdom. In Latin America and East Asia, a few countries carry out significant redistributions on the pattern of the welfare state, but hardly any do so in Africa. In general, countries that have the most progressive tax structures do not have the most progressive benefit structures—and benefits seem to be most effective in redistributing income, especially when they are targeted.

Other policies and programs also contribute to the narrowing of inequalities: public health care, public education, and public housing are among the most important. These are, to a great extent, components of human capital that have a strong effect on earnings. Strong evidence is available showing that health spending decreases real inequality, as does primary and secondary education spending. In most countries of the North, however, tertiary education in general perpetuates or increases inequality, an effect even more marked in developing countries.

Because reducing inequality is hardly ever the overriding objective of government policies, policies that are designed to redistribute income may be offset by others. Although income taxes and national insurance contributions tend to be progressive, indirect taxes (such as sales taxes, value-added taxes, excise taxes, and tariffs) tend to be regressive and to affect the consumption of the poor more than that of the rich. So, a significant proportion of what is redistributed by welfare state policies is, as far as inequality is concerned, reversed.

Redistribution policies are not sufficient to eliminate poverty. In developed countries, poverty is often measured not in relation to an absolute poverty line, as it is in developing countries, but in relation to the median income of the country. The most common definition of *poverty* in developed nations is having an income less than 50 or 60 percent of the median. If we apply the absolute definition, less poverty does not necessarily mean more equality; if we apply the relative criterion, it does. According to the 2008 OECD report, relative poverty (people who earn below 50 percent of the median income) varies in developed countries from 5 percent of the population in Denmark and Sweden to over 15 percent in the United States, Japan, and Ireland.

The U.S. government uses a (periodically adjusted) absolute measure of poverty. During the administration of Bill Clinton (1993–2000), the officially estimated overall poverty rate in the United States fell from 14.8 to 11.3 percent. During the administration of George W. Bush (2001–2008), the rate rose slowly to 12.7 percent in 2004; since then it has been virtually unchanged, but it is almost certain to rise as a result of the economic downturn that began in 2007. As with other statistics, this is an average figure, and the rate is different for different groups of people. In most developed countries, people under the age of eighteen have a higher poverty rate than older age groups; and those over sixty-five, the age group that until the mid-1960s experienced the most poverty, now, according to the OECD, have the lowest rate of poverty. In the

United States, according to the 2007 U.S. Census, black people were more likely to be poor (24.5 percent in 2007) than white non-Hispanic people (8.2 percent); Hispanic people had an intermediate level of poverty (21.5 percent).

Other factors, such as the number of people in the household and gender, also affect poverty levels. For instance, in the United States, black households headed by women with no husband present had a poverty rate of 39 percent in 2007 (compared with 18 percent for similar white households).

In addition to their taxation and spending policies, many governments also have antipoverty programs. Such campaigns may include measures to increase the number of jobs, to improve access to jobs, and to make working hours flexible to accommodate working parents; other measures include special education programs, publicly provided child care, minimum wage statutes, and campaigns against low pay. One program that has received much attention in recent years (especially in the 1990s in the United States and the United Kingdom) has been "welfare to work"—attempts to ease (or, as many of its critics argue, to force) people out of welfare dependence and into the labor market. However, whether these programs are really designed to combat poverty or just to eliminate the public responsibility for the costs resulting from poverty is difficult to ascertain.

On a world scale, as on the national level, eliminating poverty is given much more importance as an objective than reducing inequality. The first target of the millennium development goals (MDGs), and the one that has attracted most discussion, is to "halve, between 1990 and 2015, the proportion of people whose income is less than $1 a day" (now revised to $1.25 per day at 2005 PPP prices). The World Bank estimates that 1,400 million people in the world (almost one-quarter of the population) live below the $1.25 per day threshold. The antipoverty objective, however, has become less ambitious over time; the baseline year used as a starting point has been moved back from 2000 to 1990, when the incidence of poverty was greater, and the goal has been changed from halving the absolute *number* of people in poverty to halving the *proportion* of the (growing) population in poverty.

The MDGs, however, had the effect of shifting poverty—and, indirectly, inequality—into a more central place in the discussion of development. International organizations have given great prominence to pro-poor growth, which is designed to focus development programs more on future growth rather than on the redistribution of existing income, concentrating on profitable investments to create a solid economic base rather than first focusing on instituting the benefits of a welfare state.

International economic aid has always been seen as part of the struggle against poverty, partly by providing resources for short-term humanitarian aid, and partly by investing in infrastructure to assist longer-term development. The problem with aid, aside from the fact that it often becomes a tool in foreign policy, is that it is usually underfunded; since the late 1990s, humanitarian needs have grown and the amount of aid has relatively declined.

As discussed, the largest proportion of global inequality is the result of inter-country, not intracountry, inequality (see map, p. 128). Yet mechanisms for intercountry transfers to mitigate inequality are far less developed than those to reduce inequality within countries. In 2007, international development and humanitarian aid amounted to merely 0.22 percent of the national income of the countries of the North (ranging from more than 0.9 percent from Norway and Sweden to under 0.2 percent from the United States) and targeted poverty intervention much more than inequality per se.

Regional Summaries

North America

North America contains 4.6 percent of the world's population and produces 21.1 percent of the world's gross domestic product (GDP). The GDP per head therefore is a little over four times the world average. It remains relatively the world's richest region.

The United States has a Gini coefficient of disposable income of 0.392, markedly higher than any country of the European Union, higher than its northern neighbor Canada (0.317), and about the same as that of Chad. The top 10 percent of the population receives 16.84 times as much as the bottom 10 percent (about the same ratio as Rwanda).

Inequality in the United States arouses a great amount of critical interest, not only because it is particularly high but also because the United States, as the world's largest economy, has disproportionate influence in the world economy. The top 10 percent of U.S. income receivers (after tax and benefits) get 30 percent of the national income, three times their proportion of the population. Their average income was approximately $140,000 per head in 2005. The concentration of income increases the smaller the group being considered. In 2002, the top 1 percent received 14.67 percent of income, while the top 0.01 percent received 2.25 percent of taxable income—225 times its proportion of the population and approximating an annual income of over $9 million. These astronomic shares of the top fractions have emerged in the United States, Canada, the United Kingdom, and Australia since around 1980, during the beginning of the era of deregulation, tax cuts, and freer trade. These statistics are not visible via household surveys and were discovered by Anthony B. Atkinson, Thomas Piketty, and others in researching top income receivers using data from tax returns.

High U.S. inequality is especially influenced by two features of the country. First, a widening of extremes in income from work is apparent. Between 2003 and 2007, for instance, the minimum wage in real terms stayed virtually the same, the wages of average employees increased by 0.7 percent a year, the pay of corporation executives rose by 3.5 percent, and the income of chief executive officers (CEOs) rose by 9.7 percent. CEO compensation has risen to over five hundred times the average wages of employees. The trend toward such high pay has been especially pronounced in the fast-growing financial-services industry. At the high extreme, in 2007 three hedge fund managers, John Paulson, James Simon, and George Soros, each were paid a sum said to be in the region of $3 billion.

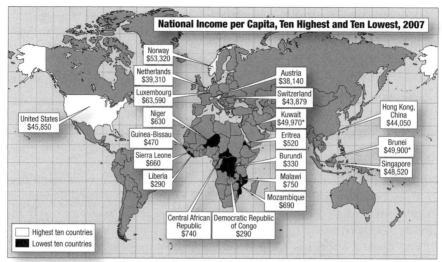

Source: World Bank, *World Bank Development Indicators, 2007*. Washington D.C.: World Bank, 2007. Available online from http://sitesources.worldbank.org/DATASTATISTICS/Resources/GNIPC.pdf.
Note: Income figures are in U.S. dollars, based on the purchasing power parity (PPP) method of calculating comparable international income figures. Asterisk denotes a country's income per capita from 2005 or 2006.

A second particularly powerful influence on inequality is ethnicity. African Americans are much more likely to be found in poverty than whites. In 2007, 28.5 percent of African Americans had incomes below the poverty line, whereas only 8.2 percent of (non-Hispanic) whites were in this category. This ethnicity-based inequality is the result of both direct economic discrimination and of indirect factors influencing family income levels. For instance, African Americans receive less education than whites, and education is a major determinant of income. Not only is black unemployment higher than white unemployment, but another significant brake on family income is the fact that 2.3 percent of African Americans (nearly 12 percent for the 25–29 age group) are incarcerated, while many others are under judicial supervision (probation). States with higher proportions of black residents also tend to spend less on redistributive policies.

Western Europe

The average national Gini coefficient for Western European countries is about 0.305. On this measure it is the world's most equal region. But around the average is a wide range—the most unequal countries of the region are the United Kingdom (0.368) and Portugal (0.363); the most equal are Denmark (0.235) and France (0.240).

According to the OECD, developed countries experienced an average 0.02 increase in the Gini coefficient from the mid-80s to the mid-2000s (an increase of approximately 7 percent in the level of inequality). The countries with more than twice this amount of increase in inequality were Finland, Germany, Italy, the Netherlands, Norway, Portugal, and Sweden. Those that registered less inequality during the same period were France, Greece, Ireland, and Spain. These figures, however, were based on a questionnaire in which the super-rich were underrepresented due to their lack of response. Inclusion of a more representative sample of the highest-income groups usually tends to show an increase in income inequality.

In almost all Western European countries, the composition of the lowest-income groups has changed. In the majority of countries, young adults between eighteen and twenty-five years old experienced a relatively deteriorating economic situation during the twenty-year period covered by the OECD study, while individuals between fifty-one and seventy-five experienced the most improved economic situation. In most countries, retired people relatively improved their position, while the position of single-parent families significantly declined.

Rising inequality has largely resulted from a rising dispersion of wages and salaries, usually attributed to changes in technology, the growth of the service industries (which often depend on very low wages), and the growth of part-time employment. Wage dispersion between men and women has declined in most European countries, especially in the United Kingdom. A continued rise in the participation of women in the paid labor force has tended to compensate for the growing overall dispersion of wages so that interhousehold inequality has grown less than interwage earner inequality.

As to its position in the world distribution of income, Western Europe (twenty-nine countries, more or less corresponding to the European Union) contains 6.1 percent of the world's population and receives 17.8 percent of the world's income. In other words, the average national income or product per head is about three times the world average.

Eastern Europe and Former USSR

The sudden death of communism in Eastern Europe and Soviet Asia after 1990 and the subsequent policies of transition to capitalism led to a huge increase in inequality. Even though inequality still existed through privileged access to goods and services, communist regimes had maintained very low levels of inequality in the structure of wages and monetary incomes. During the transition, wage control was weakened, if not abolished; internal labor markets were established; and many people in uncompetitive activities lost their jobs. The quantity and quality of state medical and educational services fell, creating problems particularly for the poor. And in some places, notably Russia, a new business elite gained the positions previously occupied by the top communist bureaucrats (and were sometimes the same people).

The effects on inequality were sudden and drastic. According to the World Bank, the Gini coefficient of the Russian Federation rose from 0.238 in 1988 to 0.483 in 1993. By later in the 1990s, it had declined again as recovery from the shock of transition began. By 1999, the Gini had fallen to 0.375 and, as of 2005, had not changed substantially since then. A similar rise and fall in inequality occurred in most other former Soviet-bloc countries, such as Ukraine, Poland, and Azerbaijan.

Notably, inequality in these countries did not rise even higher. The levels of inequality in these countries remain below those of Latin America and Africa despite much talk of the "Latin Americanization" of Russia and Eastern Europe (that is, the development of unequal oligarchic regimes with high levels of foreign debt). The fact that inequality did not increase even more shows how important the legacy of a country is in explaining international differences in inequality. In Eastern Europe, the legacy of communism influenced customary relative wages and customary redistributive institutions, which, despite the wholesale political transformation, did not completely collapse.

Latin America and the Caribbean

According to Maddison, average incomes in Latin America and the Caribbean in 1820 were about two-thirds of those in Western Europe and the United States. This ratio fell sharply during the nineteenth century to approximately one-third the levels in Western Europe and the United States. By 1950, after undergoing some industrialization in isolation from the world market, average incomes climbed back to 62 percent of the level of the North. The percentage then fell every year of the next twenty years, stabilized for a few years while Latin American countries accumulated vast debts, fell again through the 1980s (the lost decade following the debt crisis of 1982), and has remained roughly static at about 40 percent ever since (see Table 2).

One of the important causes of Latin America's declining historical position in the world economic hierarchy may be its exceptional level of intracountry inequality. Statistics show that Latin America's ill fame as the most unequal part of the world is fully justified. In 2005, the Gini coefficient (concept 3) for South America was almost 0.547, compared with 0.32 for South Asia and, most pertinently, the newly industrializing countries (NICs) of East Asia with 0.398. In Latin America, the ratio of the share of income going to the top decile and the share going to the bottom 10 percent ranged from the internationally high figure of 16.2 (close to the U.S. figure) in Uruguay to the internationally unequaled figure of 93.9 in Bolivia.

After 1950, high inequality, according to many observers, condemned Latin American countries to small internal markets for the kind of industrial goods that East Asia began producing for itself and then exported. Setting up industry in Latin America required high tariffs on imports, and the result was the disastrous program of import substitution. State economic policies were biased toward the landowning elite, who had no interest in the development of industrial economies.

Since 2000, however, poverty and income inequality have been lessening. In several countries, the poverty headcount rate has been falling; these include Brazil (see Case Study—Brazil), Chile, Mexico, Costa Rica, the Dominican Republic, Ecuador, El Salvador, Guatemala, Nicaragua, and Venezuela. Gini coefficients have improved less but have nonetheless fallen in Brazil, Mexico, and Chile.

Inequality in the continent, however, remains very high. The average Gini coefficient is 0.490, higher than that of any other major grouping of countries (see Table 2). The continental Gini for the whole of Latin America taken together is also high but not as high as sub-Saharan Africa or, more surprisingly, developing East Asia.

Sub-Saharan Africa

The 14 percent of the world's population in sub-Saharan Africa receives only a little over 3 percent of total world income. The region's GDP per capita fell from 38 percent of the level of the North in 1820 to 20 percent in 1913 and recovered a little to 22 percent by 1950. Africa's GDP per head fell relative to the North in every year from 1950 to 1991; since then, it has remained stable at 8 percent (see A in Table 3).

The countries of Africa show a huge range in Gini coefficients—from over 0.6 in Comoros and Namibia (the world's most unequal countries based on this criterion) to under 0.3 in Ethiopia. The intraregional Gini is higher than for any other region, showing that huge differences exist among, as well as within, the countries of Africa (see Table 2). General trends are hard to find, and both headcount poverty rates and Gini coefficients have fluctuated erratically, the shifts being partly due to internal political instability. Nonetheless, improvements in the poverty rate are reported for a number of countries, including Botswana, Cameroon, Central African Republic, Ethiopia, Ghana, Kenya, Lesotho, Mali, Mauritania, Senegal, and Uganda. But in a number of countries more than half the population is below the $1.25 per day poverty line, including Central African Republic, Madagascar, Mali, Mozambique, Niger, Nigeria, Rwanda, Sierra Leone, Swaziland, Tanzania, Uganda, and Zambia (with the almost certain addition of Zimbabwe, if figures were available). A few countries report slight declines in the Gini coefficient, but no strong tendency toward increasing equality is apparent, even in countries where poverty has fallen.

South Africa's history makes it a world emblem of inequality. At 0.563, its Gini coefficient means it is still one of the most unequal countries in the world. Inequality has fallen a little since the end of apartheid, but the headcount poverty rate has risen.

West Asia and North Africa

As is seen in the Middle East, immigrant status is a frequent source of discrimination and, therefore, inequality. As a result of the oil industry, oil-producing countries of the Gulf are characterized by a number of fabulously rich individuals. Oil and related income is quite widely redistributed to the countries' citizens, but the large majority of the population and labor force are immigrant workers, not citizens. These workers, from countries in South and East Asia and especially the South Asian subcontinent, are almost universally without rights. They are often paid poorly and live in segregated conditions. They may not practice their religion or vote. They are also forbidden to organize themselves into trade unions or other organizations. Yet these workers come voluntarily because wages are still higher in the Middle East than in their home countries, and they can send remittances back to their families. In the world as a whole in 2007, the remittances of migrant workers from developing countries were $240 billion a year, about two and a half times the amount of official development aid; remittances from the Middle East were at least $9 billion. Ironically, working and living in conditions of extreme inequality enable poor workers to lift their families out of poverty, causing them to be relatively well-off. So, inequality can increase in both the countries of origin and countries of destination; yet, at the same time, international inequality is reduced.

Since at least 2000, figures have shown very low headcount poverty levels in Egypt, Jordan, Morocco, Tunisia, and Turkey. The average Gini coefficient for these countries is 0.381 and shows no clear upward or downward trend. The intraregional Gini is 0.459, but would almost certainly be much higher if figures were available for the Gulf oil-producing countries.

East Asia

Starting in 1820 at 48 percent of the level of the North, East Asia's relative income per head fell to 14 percent by 1950. At the end of the 1950s, it started to fall even further, and by 1970, it was a little over 9 percent. Then, in the mid-1970s, it began to rise—first due to the growth of a few, relatively small NICs and then due to China's economic advance, which has been the most spectacular of the whole capitalist epoch. In 2006, East Asia's income was 26 percent that of the North and is still rising fast. This development has done more than any other in recent decades to reduce the level of inequality among the countries of the world. In the process, however, inequality is growing within the successfully industrializing states, especially in China. Three major trends lie behind the recent overall increase in China's inequality: the inequality of urban incomes is rising, the inequality of rural incomes is rising, and the gap between urban and rural incomes is growing.

Nearly all the countries of the region report major falls in the headcount poverty rate and, at the same time, a rise in inequality (except Malaysia, which has a falling Gini coefficient). The poor, therefore, have benefited in absolute but not relative terms from the region's strong economic growth. Whether this should be counted as pro-poor growth is, therefore, debatable. If these countries were to count poverty in the same way as is done in developed countries (that is, as the percentage of the population with incomes below half the median), poverty rates would probably be seen to be rising.

South Asia

South Asia (India, Pakistan, Bangladesh, Nepal, Bhutan, and Sri Lanka) contains a little under 22 percent of the world's population and receives a little over 7 percent of its income. This region's income per head in 1820 was 48 percent of the North's and then fell to 14 percent by 1950, to 9 percent by 1966, and to 7 percent by 1974. In the mid-1990s, this figure started to rise with India's new economic dynamism, and by 2006, it had reached 12 percent.

During the last fifty years, estimates of India's internal income distribution have shown noticeably less inequality than that of Latin America or Africa. But many studies show that as India's economic growth rate has increased so has its level of inequality. Gini coefficients have risen during the last two decades in all countries of the region except for Pakistan. In India, rural inequality has fallen slightly in recent years, but urban inequality has risen. Given the fact that urbanization continues unabated, the urban increase has predominated a rise in overall inequality, although so far not nearly as fast as in China. The World Bank reports significant recent declines in the poverty level in all countries except for Bangladesh. This conclusion, however, is controversial in India itself, where some critics argue that the $1.25 per day poverty threshold is too low and should be increased to $2.50. Critics also argue that the national PPP conversions of local income levels into international dollars exaggerate the incomes of the poor and that migrant workers, who are often especially poor, tend to be missed by local poverty surveys.

Data

Table 1   Measures of Inequality by Countries

	Gini coefficient	10/10 ratio	Headcount poverty rate (%)
Albania	0.306	7.98	0.85
Algeria	0.346	9.62	6.79
Angola	0.569	74.57	54.31
Argentina	0.510	38.90	4.5 (urban)
Armenia	0.327	7.93	10.63
Australia	0.326	8.74	
Austria	0.287	6.99	
Azerbaijan	0.165	2.86	0.03
Bangladesh	0.323	7.07	49.64
Belarus	0.274	6.12	0.00
Belgium	0.315	8.32	
Benin	0.375	10.80	47.33
Bhutan	0.454	16.33	26.23
Bolivia	0.563	93.91	19.62
Bosnia and Herzegovina	0.350	9.90	0.16
Botswana	0.580	39.99	31.23
Brazil	0.530	40.59	5.21
Bulgaria	0.285	6.87	0.00
Burkina Faso	0.384	10.77	56.54
Burundi	0.325	6.77	81.32
Cambodia	0.404	11.36	48.55
Cameroon	0.432	14.98	32.81
Canada	0.318	9.43	
Cape Verde	0.487	23.05	20.56
Central African Republic	0.426	15.73	62.43
Chad	0.388	11.80	61.94
Chile	0.500	26.23	0.19
China	0.432	17.44	26.11 (rural) 1.71 (urban)
Colombia	0.563	60.36	16.01
Comoros	0.610	60.65	46.11
Congo, Democratic Republic of	0.432	15.15	59.22
Congo, Republic of	0.460	17.81	54.10
Costa Rica	0.459	23.38	2.37
Côte d'Ivoire	0.466	20.18	23.34
Croatia	0.284	6.41	

Table 1 (Continued)

	Gini coefficient	10/10 ratio	Headcount poverty rate (%)
Czech Republic	0.251	5.25	
Denmark	0.235	4.84	
Djibouti	0.358	11.75	18.84
Ecuador	0.523	35.20	4.69
Egypt	0.311	7.17	1.99
El Salvador	0.483	38.55	10.97
Estonia	0.351	10.39	0.00
Ethiopia	0.289	6.28	39.04
Finland	0.262	5.62	
France	0.240	4.92	
Gabon	0.402	13.29	4.84
Gambia	0.459	18.94	34.34
Georgia	0.398	15.94	13.44
Germany	0.285	6.85	
Ghana	0.416	16.77	29.99
Greece	0.340	10.56	
Guatemala	0.517	33.93	12.65
Guinea	0.421	14.38	70.13
Guinea-Bissau	0.346	9.54	48.83
Guyana	0.432	25.54	7.68
Haiti	0.571	54.35	
Honduras	0.535	59.42	18.19
Hong Kong, China	0.486	26.96	
Hungary	0.294	6.84	0.00
India	0.329	7.68	43.83 (rural)
			36.16 (urban)
Indonesia	0.339	8.33	24.01 (rural)
			18.67 (urban)
Iran	0.373	11.59	1.45
Ireland	0.334	9.39	
Israel	0.383	13.42	
Italy	0.350	13.07	
Jamaica	0.441	16.96	0.24
Japan	0.243	4.52	
Jordan	0.366	10.19	0.38
Kazakhstan	0.332	8.48	3.12
Kenya	0.412	13.48	19.72
Korea, Republic of	0.296	9.77	
Kyrgyz Republic	0.323	7.28	21.81
Lao People's Democratic Republic	0.318	7.34	43.96
Latvia	0.349	10.26	0.00
Lesotho	0.511	39.80	43.41
Liberia	0.370	12.81	83.65
Lithuania	0.350	10.29	0.43
Luxembourg	0.297	6.80	
Macedonia, FYR[a]	0.380	12.36	0.47
Madagascar	0.445	15.85	67.83
Malawi	0.378	10.82	73.86
Malaysia	0.371	10.97	0.54
Mali	0.380	11.19	51.43
Mauritania	0.382	11.64	21.16
Mexico	0.465	20.96	0.65
Moldova	0.347	9.45	8.14
Mongolia	0.324	8.68	22.38
Morocco	0.395	12.49	2.50
Mozambique	0.452	18.49	74.69
Namibia	0.609	49.54	49.14

Table 1   (Continued)

	Gini coefficient	10/10 ratio	Headcount poverty rate (%)
Nepal	0.454	14.75	80.19 (rural) 51.06 (urban)
Netherlands	0.303	9.20	
New Zealand	0.361	12.64	
Nicaragua	0.504	30.98	15.81
Niger	0.424	15.31	65.88
Nigeria	0.419	16.29	64.41
Norway	0.268	6.13	
Pakistan	0.303	6.73	22.59
Panama	0.532	49.92	9.48
Papua New Guinea	0.492	21.51	35.82
Paraguay	0.513	38.83	6.45
Peru	0.481	26.12	7.94
Philippines	0.430	14.07	22.62
Poland	0.341	8.98	0.10
Portugal	0.363	9.67	
Romania	0.308	7.58	0.75
Russian Federation	0.367	11.03	0.16
Rwanda	0.450	16.88	76.56
Senegal	0.383	11.87	33.50
Sierra Leone	0.414	12.76	53.37
Singapore	0.423	17.26	
Slovak Republic	0.253	6.81	0.26
Slovenia	0.304	7.29	0.00
South Africa	0.563	35.10	26.2
Spain	0.339	10.38	
Sri Lanka	0.394	11.65	13.95
St. Lucia	0.413	17.65	20.93
Suriname	0.512	40.40	15.54
Swaziland	0.488	22.42	62.85
Sweden	0.268	6.20	
Switzerland	0.326	8.47	
Tajikistan	0.328	8.22	21.49
Tanzania	0.339	8.86	88.52
Thailand	0.412	13.07	0.40
Timor-Leste	0.385	10.84	52.94
Togo	0.337	8.28	38.68
Trinidad and Tobago	0.393	14.44	4.16
Tunisia	0.398	13.34	2.55
Turkey	0.420	17.38	2.72
Turkmenistan	0.397	12.91	24.82
Uganda	0.414	13.15	51.53
Ukraine	0.277	5.96	0.10
United Kingdom	0.368	14.23	
United States	0.392	16.84	
Uruguay	0.412	16.20	0.02 (urban)
Uzbekistan	0.356	10.34	46.28
Venezuela	0.423	18.78	3.53
Vietnam	0.369	9.68	21.45
Yemen	0.365	10.59	17.53
Zambia	0.493	29.47	64.29
World total	0.665	100.00	

Source: World Bank PovcalNet supplemented by other World Bank sources.

Note: All figures are the latest available as of January 2009. The headcount poverty ratio is calculated by the World Bank only for developing countries.

[a] FYR, Former Yugoslav Republic

Table 2 Measures of Inequality by Region

	Average intracountry Gini coefficient	Intraregional Gini coefficient
North America	0.355	0.388
Western Europe	0.305	0.321
Eastern Europe	0.333	0.426
Latin America and the Caribbean	0.490	0.534
Sub-Saharan Africa	0.441	0.612
East Asia	0.391	0.574
West Asia and North Africa	0.381	0.459
South Asia	0.376	0.351
World total	0.391	0.665

Source: Author's calculations based on data from World Bank PovcalNet supplemented by other World Bank sources.

Table 3 The Gap between North and South

	1820	1870	1913	1950	1960	1970	1980	1990	2000	2006
A. Average income as percentage of the North										
GDP per head, North	100	100	100	100	100	100	100	100	100	100
Eastern Europe	62	53	54	53	49	43	44	33	30	36
Russia/USSR	62	53	48	71	63	55	48	41	23	31
Latin America and Caribbean	63	38	48	62	50	40	41	30	30	30
Africa	38	28	20	22	17	13	12	9	8	8
East Asia (excluding Japan)	54	31	20	14	12	10	11	13	18	26
West Asia	55	42	33	44	40	40	41	29	29	31
South Asia	48	30	22	16	12	9	7	8	10	12
B. Concept 2 world Gini coefficient	0.155	0.313	0.438	0.537	0.530	0.553	0.556	0.561	0.54	0.498
C1. Concept 3 world Gini coefficient	0.500	0.560	0.610[a]	0.640	0.635	0.650	0.657	0.657[b]		
C2. Concept 3 world Gini coefficient										0.665

Source: Data for lines A and B come from the author's calculations based on Angus Maddison, "Statistics on World Population, GDP and Per Capita GDP, 1–2006 AD," updated March 2009, available at: http://www.ggdc.net/maddison; data for line C1 come from François Bourguignon and Christian Morrisson, "Inequality among World Citizens: 1820–1992," *American Economic Review* 92, no. 4 (2002): 727–744; data for line C2 come from World Bank PovcalNet supplemented by other World Bank sources (the source also used for Table 1).

Note: North means Western Europe, North America, and Japan. GDP, gross domestic product.

[a]1910.

[b]1992.

Case Study—Brazil

At 0.563, Brazil's Gini coefficient is the fifteenth highest in the world. The 10/10 ratio is the ninth highest at 40.59. An important determinant of inequality is a person's relation to the labor market. As in many developing countries, an unusually large percentage of the Brazilian population is unemployed. Reasons for this unemployment include individuals' being too young, too old, or disabled; living in the subsistence sector; or being active in the informal sector. A disproportionate number of those outside the labor market have very low incomes.

The range of wages and salaries is wide for those who are actually in the labor market. Many jobs pay poorly even though a national minimum wage has been instituted. Women, both in and outside the labor market, receive a lower income than men because of the kind of jobs they have or because of direct gender discrimination. Nationally, women's wages are 71 percent of men's.

Another cause of inequality is ethnicity. Of the poorest 10 percent of Brazilians, 24 percent are white and 76 percent nonwhite; of the richest 1 percent of the population, 88 percent are white and 12 percent nonwhite. In addition, Brazil is a vast territory with geographical differences in economic development almost as great as those in the world as a whole. In 2005, the most-developed state, São Paulo, had a GDP per capita of over $13,000 (in 2005 international dollars), while that of the least-developed state, Piauí, had less than $2,700. (This difference in GDPs is similar to that between Poland and Mongolia.) The Gini coefficient of distribution among states is 0.260, but among municipalities it is 0.410. The richest municipality has an income per head that is 240 times that of the poorest.

The Brazilian government produces a large amount of information about the country's inequalities. The information shows, for instance, that the progressively combined effect of job, gender, ethnicity, and place of residence can produce mounting degrees of inequality. The income of women is 52 percent that of men; of rural dwellers is 44 percent that of urban dwellers; of inhabitants of the poorest region (the North East) is 48 percent that of the richest region (the South); and of black people (corrected for education differences) is 71 percent that of whites.

Despite these multiple examples of inequities, income inequality in Brazil, unlike in the majority of countries in recent years, has been declining. Although still high, the Gini coefficient has fallen steadily since its peak of 0.630 in 1989. In 2007, it was down to 0.563. The share of the national income taken by the bottom 50 percent of the population grew from 9.79 in 2002 to 12.24 percent in 2005, while in the same period the share of the top 10 percent fell from 49.47 to 46.31 percent (another example of Palma's law at work). The ratio of the family income of the top 10 percent to that of the bottom 40 percent fell from 23.4 in 1996 to 18.2 in 2006. The headcount rate of poverty fell from a peak of 17.7 percent in 1988 to 10.4 percent in 2003 and then to 5.2 percent in 2007.

So Brazil's poor are seemingly a little better off, absolutely and relatively, than they were a decade ago. This does not mean, however, that Brazil has discovered the secret of pro-poor growth; this rapid growth has occurred in only a very few years. Over the last thirty years Brazil's growth in GDP per capita has been, on average, 0.6 percent a year. Ten percent of the improvement in the situation of the poor was due to wage and job improvements. The rest is attributable to an expansion in the coverage of government social programs such as pensions (over 76 percent of the population is over sixty years old, and 85 percent of those over sixty-five receive some social security payment; the life expectancy is still only seventy-two) and, in particular, the Family grant, which provides financial aid to nearly 10 million families.

Brazil is an example of what has been called "pro-poor stagnation." The country, at least for a time, has done what all experts tend to say is virtually impossible—it has redistributed income when the country's total income is not rising quickly.

Case Study—China

At the time of the 1949 revolution, China was already considered one of the most equal (and poorest) countries in the world; in the next three decades, the revolutionary government preached and, to some extent, practiced egalitarianism. But in 1978, under the leadership of Deng Xiaoping, a series of profound economic changes started to bring China into the market system and the world economy, resulting in probably the greatest period of economic growth ever known. From 1980 to 2007, China's income per head rose from 525 to 5,046 international dollars, an annual rate of growth of 8.4 percent per year. China has become the world's second largest economy, and its total national income is likely to overtake that of the United States by the early 2020s.

Such an enormous change has, of course, had implications for both international and national inequality. This huge poor country has become much richer, which has helped reduce China's inequality in relationship to the rest of the world. But, inside the country, inequalities of many kinds have remained and, in some cases, have even grown. Among the most important of these is the inequality between men and women. Patterns of disease, selective abortions, and government restrictions allowing couples to have only one child have led to a large excess of males in the younger age groups.

Also important in China is inequality between rural and urban populations. Statistics clearly show that this gap has grown during the last three decades of rapid growth in spite of vast migration from rural to urban areas. This can be seen as the classic rise in inequality predicted by Kuznets, the first phase of the Kuznets curve, but China as yet shows no signs of moving to the second phase of the Kuznets curve, when inequality declines.

Writers on Chinese inequality also emphasize the growth in inequality between the coastal and inland provinces. A disproportionate amount of the new development has taken place in the coastal provinces, where foreign investment arrives and the big export industries are located. The provincial national product per capita ranges from that of Shanghai, a coastal province, which is about at the level of Hungary, to Guizhou, an interior province, whose income per head approximates that of Mauritania. The spatial interprovincial Gini coefficient, however, is only 0.269, certainly higher than before 1978 but much less than the interregional Gini for Brazil (0.410).

When these inequalities are added to those produced by differences in education, skills, and wages, the overall result is strongly rising inequality in the population as a whole. The Gini coefficient for China rose from less than 0.300 (a relatively low level by international standards) in the early 1980s to about 0.450 (a middle to high level) in the mid-2000s. Brazil has experienced pro-poor stagnation, but China has seen three decades of pro-rich growth. Neither of them, however, has developed a pro-poor growth strategy so important to analysts in the income inequality debate.

Biographical Sketches

Anthony Atkinson is a British economist and statistician at Oxford University who has brought greater rigor to the study and measurement of inequality.

Barbara Bergmann has made substantial contributions to research in the area of gender inequalities in income and earnings. Her research into the economic impact of gender roles on economic outcomes helped lay the foundations for subsequent work in the field. She is professor emerita at American University and the University of Maryland.

William Darity has examined inequalities in the distribution of income and earnings across different racial and ethnic groups. He has written extensively on racial inequalities in the United States, and he has also produced comparative studies of racial and ethnic inequalities in different countries.

James K. Galbraith has studied patterns of wage inequality as an important determinant of income inequality more generally. Not only has Galbraith analyzed the institutional factors behind shifts in wage inequality, he has also compiled a substantial database on U.S. wage differentials and global inequality.

Corrado Gini was an Italian statistician who in 1912 devised the indicator of inequality, which now bears his name, that is still most widely used. His idea was an algebraic version of the geometrical Lorenz curve devised in 1905 by the U.S. economist Max O. Lorenz.

Branko Milanovic is an economist working at the World Bank on questions of inequality. He has written articles and books on the relationship among intercountry, intracountry, and global inequality.

John Rawls was a political philosopher who wrote extensively on economic justice. He emphasized the need to address individual liberty and material well-being. He argued that a criterion for a just income distribution was the distribution people would freely choose if they were ignorant of what their future socioeconomic position in society would be.

Directory

Economic Policy Institute, 1333 H Street, NW, Suite 300, East Tower, Washington, D.C. 20005-4707. Telephone: (202) 775-8810; email: epi@epi.org; Web: http://www.epi.org.
Economic and economic policy research institute specializing in questions of concern to labor.

International Labour Organisation (ILO), Route des Morillons 4, 1211 Geneva 22, Switzerland. Telephone: (41) 22 799 6111; email: ilo@ilo.org; Web: http://www.ilo.org.
UN agency responsible for global human and labor rights.

International Monetary Fund (IMF), 700 19th Street, NW, Washington, D.C. 20431. Telephone: (202) 623-7000; email: publicaffairs@imf.org; Web: http://www.imf.org.
Global financial institution focusing on international financial stability.

Luxembourg Income Study and Luxembourg Wealth Study, 44 rue Emile Mark, P.O. Box 48, Differdange L-4501, Luxembourg. Telephone: (352) 58 58 55 518; email: caroline@lissy.ceps.lu; Web: http://www.lisproject.org.
Research organization that collects and analyzes income and wealth survey data.

Oxfam, Oxfam International Secretariat, 266 Banbury Road, Suite 20, Oxford OX2 7DL, United Kingdom. Telephone: (44) 1865 31 39 39; email: information@oxfaminternational.org; Web: http://www.oxfam.org.
Confederation of organizations specializing in global poverty.

Political Economy Research Institute, Department of Economics, University of Massachusetts, Amherst, Mass. 01003. Telephone: (413) 545-6355; Web: http://www.umass.edu/peri.
Research institute specializing in globalization, development, and labor markets.

Society for International Development, Via Panisperna 207, 00184 Rome, Italy. Telephone: (39) 06 487 2172; email: info@sidint.org; Web: http://www.sidint.org.
Nongovernmental organization (NGO) working on issues of sustainable development and poverty elimination.

United Nations Development Programme (UNDP), One United Nations Plaza, New York, N.Y. 10017. Telephone: (212) 906-5295; email: aboutundp@undp.org; Web: http://www.undp.org.
Agency responsible for human development and poverty programs.

University of Texas Inequality Project, c/o James Galbraith, LBJ School of Public Affairs, University of Texas, Austin, Tex. 78713-8925. Telephone: (512) 471-1244; email: galbraith@mail.utexas.edu; Web: http://utip.gov.utexas.edu.
Research institute specializing in measuring and explaining changes in inequality.

World Bank, 1818 H Street, NW, Washington, D.C. 20433. Telephone: (202) 477-1234; email: askus@worldbank.org; Web: http://www.worldbank.org.
Global financial institution specializing in development loans and research.

World Institute for Development Economics Research (WIDER), Katajano-kanlaituri 6 B FI-00160, Helsinki, Finland. Telephone: (358) 9 6159911; email: wider@wider.unu.edu; Web: http://www.wider.unu.edu.
Division of the United Nations University responsible for development and inequality research.

Further Research

Books

Atkinson, Anthony B., and François Bourguignon, eds. *Handbook of Income Distribution*. Amsterdam: Elsevier Science, 2000.

Atkinson, Anthony B., and T. Piketty, eds. *Top Incomes over the 20th Century: A Contrast between Continental European and English-Speaking Countries*. Oxford: Oxford University Press, 2007.

Bowles, Samuel, and Herbert Gintis. *Recasting Egalitarianism*. Ed. Eric Olin Wright. New York and London: Verso, 1998.

Callinicos, Alex. *Equality*. Cambridge, UK: Polity Press, 2000.

Davies, James B., ed. *Personal Wealth from a Global Perspective*. Oxford: Oxford University Press/UNU-WIDER, 2008.

Firebaugh, Glenn. *The New Geography of Global Income Inequality*. Cambridge, Mass.: Harvard University Press, 2003.

Folbre, Nancy. *The Invisible Heart: Economics and Family Values*. New York: New Press, 2001.

Galbraith, James K. *Created Unequal: The Crisis in American Pay*. New York: Free Press, 1998.

Glyn, Andrew, and David Miliband, eds. *Paying for Inequality*. London: Rivers Oram, 1994.

Green, Philip. *Equality and Democracy*. New York: New Press, 1998.

Irvin, George. *Super Rich: The Rise of Inequality in Britain and the United States*. Cambridge, UK: Polity Press, 2008.

Kawachi, Ichiro, Bruce P. Kennedy, and Richard G. Wilkinson. *Income Inequality and Health: The Society and Population Health Reader*. New York: New Press, 1999.

Milanovic, Branko. *Worlds Apart: Measuring International and Global Inequality*. Princeton, N.J.: Princeton University Press, 2005.

Phelps Brown, Henry. *The Inequality of Pay*. Oxford: Oxford University Press, 1977.

Pogge, Thomas. *World Poverty and Human Rights: Cosmopolitan Responsibilities and Reforms*. Cambridge, UK: Polity Press, 2002.

Rawls, John. *A Theory of Justice*. Cambridge, Mass.: Belknap, 1971.

Salverda, Wiemer, Brian Nolan, and Timothy M. Smeeding. *The Oxford Handbook of Economic Inequality*. Oxford: Oxford University Press, 2009.

Sen, Amartya. *Development as Freedom*. New York: Anchor Books, 1999.

Singer, Peter. *The Life You Can Save: Acting Now to End World Poverty*. London: Pan Macmillan (Picador), 2009.

Wan, Guanghua. *Inequality and Growth in Modern China*. Oxford: Oxford University Press and UNU-WIDER, 2008.

Articles and Reports

Ahuja, V., et al. "Everybody's Miracle?: Revisiting Poverty and Inequality in East Asia." Washington, D.C.: World Bank, 1997.

Alesina, Alberto, and Roberto Perotti. "Income Distribution, Political Instability, and Investment." *European Economic Review* 40 (1996): 1203–1228.

Alesina, Alberto, and Dani Rodrik. "Distributive Politics and Economic Growth." *Quarterly Journal of Economics* 109 (1994): 465–490.

Barro, Robert J. "Inequality and Growth in a Panel of Countries." *Journal of Economic Growth* 5, no. 1 (2000): 5–22.

Bernanke, Ben, and Mark Gertler. "Financial Fragility and Economic Performance." *Quarterly Journal of Economics* 105 (1990): 88–114.

Bourguignon, François, and Christian Morrisson. "Inequality among World Citizens: 1820–1992." *American Economic Review* 92, no. 4 (2002): 727–744.

Chotikapanich, Duangkamon, and D. S. Prasada Rao. "Inequality in Asia, 1975–1990: A Decomposition Analysis." *Asia Pacific Journal of Economics and Business* 2 (1998): 63–78.

Cornia, Giovanni Andrea, and Julius Court. "Inequality, Growth and Poverty in the Era of Liberalization and Globalization." UNU-WIDER Policy Brief no. 4. UNU-WIDER, Helsinki, 2001.

Council of Economic Advisers. *Changing America: Indicators of Social and Economic Well-Being by Race and Hispanic Origin.* Washington, D.C.: President's Initiative on Race, 1998. Available at: http://usinfo.state.gov/journals/itsv/0699/ijse/capop.htm.

Davies, James B., et al. "Estimating the Level and Distribution of Global Household Wealth." UNU-WIDER Research Paper no. 2007/77. UNU-WIDER, Helsinki, 2007.

Duflo, Easter. "Child Health and Household Resources in South Africa: Evidence from the Old Age Pension Program." *American Economic Review* 90 (2000): 15–62.

Galor, Oded, and Joseph Zeira. "Income Distribution and Macroeconomics." *Review of Economic Studies* 60 (1993): 35–52.

Glaeser, Edward L. "Inequality." NBER Working Paper no. 11511. National Bureau of Economic Research, Cambridge, Mass., 2005.

Gottschalk, P., and T. M. Smeeding. "Empirical Evidence on Income Inequality in Industrial Countries." In *Handbook of Income Distribution,* ed. Anthony B. Atkinson and François Bourguignon, 261–307. Amsterdam: Elsevier Science, 2000.

Harsanyi, John C. "Cardinal Utility in Welfare Economics and in the Theory of Risk-Taking." *Journal of Political Economy* 61 (1953): 434–435.

International Labour Organisation. *World of Work Report 2008: Income Inequalities in the Age of Financial Globalization.* Geneva: ILO, 2008.

Kanbur, Ravi. "Income Distribution and Development." In *Handbook of Income Distribution,* ed. Anthony B. Atkinson and François Bourguignon, 791–841. Amsterdam: Elsevier Science, 2000.

Kristov, Lorenzo, Peter Lindert, and Robert McClelland. "Pressure Groups and Redistribution." *Journal of Public Economics* 48 (1992): 135–163.

Kuznets, Simon. "Economic Growth and Income Inequality." *American Economic Review* 45 (1955): 1–28.

Lindert, P. H. "Three Centuries of Inequality in Britain and America." In *Handbook of Income Distribution,* ed. Anthony B. Atkinson and François Bourguignon, 167–216. Amsterdam: Elsevier Science, 2000.

Maddison, Angus. "Statistics on World Population, GDP and Per Capita GDP, 1–2006 AD." Updated March 2009. Available at: http://www.ggdc.net/maddison.

Milanovic, Branko, Peter H. Lindert, and Jeffrey G. Williamson. "Measuring Ancient Inequality." NBER Working Paper no. 13550. National Bureau of Economic Research, Cambridge, Mass., 2007.

Morrison, Christian. "Historical Perspectives on Income Distribution: The Case of Europe." In *Handbook of Income Distribution,* ed. Anthony B. Atkinson and François Bourguignon, 217–260. Amsterdam: Elsevier Science, 2000.

Neri, Marcelo. "Pro-Poor Growth: The Brazilian Paradox." UNDP/Getulio Vargas Foundation, Rio de Janeiro, 2006.

Organisation for Economic Cooperation and Development. *Growing Unequal: Income Distribution and Poverty in OECD Countries.* Paris: OECD, 2008.

Persson, Torsten, and Guido Tabellini. "Is Inequality Harmful for Growth?" *American Economic Review* 84 (1994): 600–621.

Pogge, Thomas. "The First UN Millennium Development Goal: A Cause for Celebration?" *Journal of Human Development* 5, no. 3 (2004): 377–397. Available at: http://www.globalpolicy.org/socecon/develop/2003/pogge.pdf.

Pollin, Robert. "Can Domestic Expansionary Policy Succeed in a Globally Integrated Environment?: An Examination of Alternatives." In *Globalization and Progressive Economic Policy,* ed. D. Baker, G. Esptein, and Robert Pollin, 433–460. Cambridge, UK: Cambridge University Press, 1998.

Roemer, John. "The 2006 World Development Report: Equity and Development (review essay)." *Journal of Economic Inequality* 4, no. 2 (2006): 233–244.

Rueda, David, and Jonas Pontusson. "Wage Inequality and Varieties of Capitalism." *World Politics* 52 (2000): 350–383.

Svensson, Jakob. "Investment, Property Rights, and Political Instability: Theory and Evidence." *European Economic Review* 42 (1998): 1317–1341.

United Nations Department of Economic and Social Affairs. *The Inequality Predicament: Report on the World Social Situation 2005.* New York: United Nations, 2005.

United Nations Development Programme. *Human Development Report 2007/2008: Fighting Climate Change: Human Solidarity in a Divided World.* New York: UNDP, 2008.

U.S. Department of the Census. "The Changing Shape of the Nation's Income Distribution, 1947–1998." Current Population Reports no. P60-204. Washington, D.C., June 2000.

———. "Money Income in the United States." Current Population Report no. P60-209. Washington, D.C., September 2000.

Wolff, Edward. "Recent Trends in the Size Distribution of Household Wealth." *Journal of Economic Perspectives* 12 (1998): 131–150.

Wood, Adrian. "Wage Inequality in Developing Countries: The Latin American Challenge to East Asian Conventional Wisdom." *World Bank Economic Review* 11 (January 1997): 33–57.

World Bank. *World Development Indicators 2008.* Washington D.C.: World Bank, 2008.

———. *World Development Report 2009: Reshaping Economic Geography.* Washington, D.C.: World Bank, 2008.

Web Sites

Brazilian Institute of Geography and Statistics (IBGE)
http://www.ibge.gov.br/english

Center for International Comparisons at the University of Pennsylvania
http://pwt.econ.upenn.edu

Luxembourg Income Study (LIS) and Luxembourg Wealth Study
http://www.lisproject.org

United Nations University—WIDER
http://www.wider.unu.edu

University of Texas Inequality Project
http://utip.gov.utexas.edu

U.S. Bureau of Labor Statistics (links to international statistical agencies)
http://www.bls.gov/bls/other.htm

U.S. Department of the Census
http://www.census.gov

WIDER World Income Inequality Database
http://www.wider.unu.edu/research/Database/en_GB/database

World Bank International Comparison Program
http://web.worldbank.org/WBSITE/EXTERNAL/DATASTATISTICS/ICPEXT/
0,,menuPK:1973757~pagePK:62002243~piPK:62002387~theSitePK:270065,00.html

World Bank PovcalNet
http://web.worldbank.org/WBSITE/EXTERNAL/EXTDEC/EXTRESEARCH/
EXTPROGRAMS/EXTPOVRES/EXTPOVCALNET/0,,contentMDK:2186710
1~pagePK:64168427~piPK:64168435~theSitePK:5280443,00.html

World Bank Poverty and Inequality
http://econ.worldbank.org/WBSITE/EXTERNAL/EXTDEC/
EXTRESEARCH/EXTPROGRAMS/EXTPOVRES/0,,menuPK:477905~page
PK:64168176~piPK:64168140~theSitePK:477894,00.html

Document

1. We the Peoples: The Role of the United Nations in the 21st Century

Kofi A. Annan, report of the UN secretary-general to the Millennium Assembly, September 2000

The full report is available at http://www.un.org/millennium/sg/report.

Extract

III. Freedom from Want

While more of us enjoy better standards of living than ever before, many others remain desperately poor. Nearly half the world's population still has to make do on less than $2 per day. Approximately 1.2 billion people—500 million in South Asia and 300 million in Africa—struggle on less than $1. . . . People living in Africa south of the Sahara are almost as poor today as they were 20 years ago. With that kind of deprivation comes pain, powerlessness, despair and lack of fundamental freedom—all of which, in turn, perpetuate poverty. Of a total world [labor] force of some 3 billion, 140 million workers are out of work altogether, and a quarter to a third are underemployed.

The persistence of income inequality over the past decade is also troubling. Globally, the 1 billion people living in developed countries earn 60 percent of the world's income, while the 3.5 billion people in low-income countries earn less than 20 percent.

Many countries have experienced growing internal inequality, including some of those in transition from communism. In the developing world, income gaps are most pronounced in Latin America, followed closely by sub-Saharan Africa.

Extreme poverty is an affront to our common humanity. It also makes many other problems worse. For example, poor countries—especially those with significant inequality between ethnic and religious communities—are far more likely to be embroiled in conflicts than rich ones. Most of these conflicts are internal, but they almost invariably create problems for [neighbors] or generate a need for humanitarian assistance.

Moreover, poor countries often lack the capacity and resources to implement environmentally sound policies. This undermines the sustainability of their people's meager existence, and compounds the effects of their poverty.

Unless we redouble and concert our efforts, poverty and inequality may get worse still. World population recently reached 6 billion. It took only 12 years to add the last billion, the shortest such span in history. By 2025, we can expect a further 2 billion—almost all in developing countries, and most of them in the poorest. . . . We must act now.

I call on the international community at the highest level—the [h]eads of [s]tate and [g]overnment convened at the Millennium Summit—to adopt the target of halving the proportion of people living in extreme poverty, and so lifting more than 1 billion people out of it, by 2015. I further urge that no effort be spared to reach this target by that date in every region, and in every country.

History will judge political leaders in the developing countries by what they did to eradicate the extreme poverty of their people—by whether they enabled their people to board the train of a transforming global economy, and made sure that everyone had at least standing room, if not a comfortable seat. By the same token, history will judge the rest of us by what we did to help the world's poor board that train in good order. . . .

INTERNATIONAL FINANCE

Clint Peinhardt

International finance is one of the most discussed and debated elements of globalization. Cross-border financial flows channel monetary savings from one country to another; that money can be used for immediate consumption, or it can be invested. Historically, the world has witnessed dramatic fluctuation in cross-border financial flows, and those flows have alternately been seen as the bane or boon of participation in the world economy. Which are they? How do countries benefit or suffer from international finance? How much leverage do country-level governments have over international financial flows? Despite the seeming newness of financial globalization, its current manifestation is neither the first nor the last such episode of the rise and fall of international finance.

Historical Background and Development

Senders and receivers of international financial flows can be either public or private. Throughout much of history, international finance came mostly from private sources and was closely tied to cross-border trade—credit was extended to a merchant to buy goods in one place, sell them in another, and pay back the credit with proceeds from the trade transaction. The origin of modern banks can be traced to the fifteenth-century credit needs of Italian merchants engaged in long-distance trade, but this was not a large part of economic activity at the time; few economies historically depended much on international trade, so financial flows rarely had a large impact on economic stability. Starting in the mid-1800s, however, international finance began to break its link with trade and began to facilitate cross-border ownership of assets. Supported by the classical gold standard, in which each country's currency was fixed in its value to gold, this first era of economic globalization (roughly 1870–1914) clearly witnessed not only large flows of trade in goods and people but also large financial flows. The United Kingdom became the world's largest net creditor and sent as much as half of its domestic savings overseas, much of it to Argentina, Australia, and the United States. British investors were well informed

146

about events in the recipient countries, and this first era of globalization looked in many ways remarkably similar to our own.

World War I brought that economic integration crashing to a halt as widespread conflict eroded the confidence necessary for investors to lend overseas. Even after the war ended, efforts to resurrect the prewar gold standard were unsuccessful, due at least in part to the newfound political strength of workers, who were unwilling to continue to bear the brunt of the domestic economic adjustments necessary to adjust to international financial imbalances. In many countries, newly enfranchised workers organized through the labor movement and made unemployment a key consideration for policymakers (see LABOR AND EMPLOYMENT). Attempts to restore the old system, which did not allow countries much latitude in manipulating unemployment, continued through 1925, but between the two wars, capital flows did not return to their prewar levels and states exerted their newfound ability to control the international transactions of both individuals and firms. World War II saw a further dampening of international economic relations, including finance.

After World War II, countries coordinated on a new international system of exchange rates that served as the foundation for the eventual postwar recovery of international finance. The Bretton Woods system used the U.S. dollar as the international currency; all other currencies were allowed to fluctuate in a narrow band around a fixed value to the dollar, which was in turn fixed to gold. This provided enough stability in international trade credit to undergird a postwar recovery of international trade. Unlike under the classical gold standard, however, countries placed strict controls on the movement of international finance, which returned to its close connection to international trade.

The Bretton Woods system worked so well that by the 1960s international trade was flourishing, and it became more difficult to control capital flows unrelated to trade. As the Bretton Woods system increased the number of dollars circulating outside the United States, new capital markets grew outside the control of the domestic regulators. These Eurodollar markets helped to undermine the role assigned to the dollar because the amount of Eurodollars—effectively any deposits of U.S. dollars outside of the U.S. domestic market—exceeded the amount of reserve gold in the United States, and the system collapsed by 1973. With the end of the Bretton Woods system, countries no longer needed the extensive system of capital controls they had maintained in the postwar years, and by the end of the 1970s, most of the world's developed economies had adopted policies of free capital mobility. The real growth in contemporary international capital markets dates to this change, and although the developing world moved more slowly in removing the controls on capital movements, many developing countries began to do so toward the end of the 1980s.

Current Status

Research

Financial transfers across borders from private entities can take several forms. Flows from one public entity to another are called official development assistance

(ODA) (see DEVELOPMENT AID); public entities can also receive private loans or issue bonds to private holders. Flows from one private entity to another can be portfolio investments, such as stocks, bonds, or bank loans, or foreign direct investment (FDI), in which a firm in one country takes a significant ownership stake in a firm in another country. The relative importance of each of these flows has varied over time, as has countries' ability to control them. Since the early 1990s, the growth of private flows has outpaced almost all other global trends, including trade and economic growth (see map, p. 153). As capital flows outgrew not only the abilities of individual countries to control them but also the international institutions meant to prop up the international economy, new challenges have emerged in dealing with the potential side effects, such as volatility and crisis.

In neoclassical economic theory, perfect markets should transfer savings to their most productive use, and economists have long expected capital to flow from rich countries to poorer countries, where it should be more productive. However, Robert Lucas (1990) famously pointed out that finance does not flow to the developing world and that, instead, most financial flows are from rich countries to other rich countries. Although this pattern of financial flows makes sense for investors who want to diversify their savings portfolios to minimize risk, the amount of cross-border investment is less than many economists expect. Investors seem to favor their domestic markets with a home bias, and domestic savings and investing rates are more highly correlated than neoclassical theory predicts.

Although the field of international financial research is quite broad, policy-oriented research has centered around two topics: the growth effects of financial flows and the relationship between international finance and crises. Despite expectations that international capital flows should help countries grow faster, the evidence on the relationship between capital market policies that welcome foreign investment and economic growth is decidedly mixed. Some recent research suggests that a positive relationship exists and that more (financially) open countries grow faster, but the more dominant conclusion is that the relationship is not robust. In fact, countries that depend more on marshalling domestic savings seem to grow faster. One explanation for the lack of relationship between openness and growth is that many developing countries simply do not have a large capacity to absorb foreign investment flows and that those flows that come in can have detrimental effects. For example, massive financial inflows can cause a country's currency to increase in value, which makes exports more expensive and can undermine export competitiveness, or they can lead to asset booms, which can end in banking crises. If capital inflows lead to such pernicious outcomes, their role in stimulating economic growth may be much more ambiguous than the scholarly and policy communities have historically appreciated.

A key focus of the current research on growth and international financial flows is on domestic institutions that both help attract international investment flows and help harness their benefits better for domestic purposes. Secure domestic property rights are thought to be a key factor in attracting international financial flows, and in turn, those financial flows may indirectly help to improve other domestic policies, such as laws on corporate governance to protect shareholders, and financial development as domestic banks learn to compete with their foreign counterparts. The major outstanding questions here are of cause and effect and timing: When do countries benefit from improving domestic institutions, and when should they focus on opening different domestic markets to international finance?

Another key question of recent research concerns the relationship between international financial flows and crises. Clearly, in the post–Bretton Woods period, a large crisis has affected multiple countries every few years. An incomplete list includes the 1982 debt crisis in the developing world; the 1992 European exchange rate mechanism crisis; the 1994 tequila crisis in Mexico; the 1997 Asian financial crisis in Southeast Asia, Russia, and Brazil; the 2001 Argentine crisis; and the current worldwide crisis that started in the U.S. housing market in 2007. Such crises seem to be a regular feature of economic globalization, and certainly the 1997 Asian financial crisis and the global recession that started in 2007 demonstrate that trade and financial integration contribute to the contagion of crisis across countries. An important but unresolved question concerns whether countries can protect themselves by implementing capital controls during crises. In some cases, capital controls have created a temporary wedge between domestic economies and international finance (see Case Study—Malaysia's Capital Controls during the 2007 Asian Financial Crisis), but they are unlikely to remain effective over time, and if enacted before a crisis begins, they may actually exacerbate the probability of a crisis.

The current crisis started in the U.S. housing market and quickly affected not just U.S. banks but many international institutions as well due to the integration of the financial markets. It has provoked comparisons with the Great Depression of the 1930s because this is the first time since then that a banking crisis began in a rich country and spread throughout much of the rest of the world. Worse in terms of their domestic impact are twin crises, such as those experienced by the Asian countries in 1997, in which countries simultaneously experience both banking and exchange rate crises. Few predictions seem viable in the current climate, but one certainty is a future wave of research on the current crisis, especially its patterns of transmission, a reanalysis of the costs and benefits of policies of openness toward international finance, and international cooperation on financial regulations.

Policies and Programs

From a narrowly economic perspective, no optimal policy choice toward international finance exists for most countries. International financial policies are more complicated and less well understood for both policymakers and the public at large than are choices regarding international trade. Policymakers may choose financial policies with fewer political constraints than when making decisions about trade; at the same time, they may face dire consequences if policies fail to achieve desired goals. For example, Domingo Cavallo, recognized as the architect of the Argentinean exchange rate system, is reviled by many of his countrymen due to the collapse of that system in 2001–2002.

Key to understanding the set of potential policy choices are the inter-relationships among several economic policy variables. In particular, the Mundell-Fleming framework from open-economy macroeconomics suggests that countries can use only two of the following three policies: (1) autonomous monetary policy, (2) fixed exchange rates, and (3) openness to international finance. *Autonomous monetary policy* means that the central government can change the money supply to stimulate or dampen economic activity, which is useful to manipulate price changes and/or unemployment. *Fixed exchange rates* mean that a country's central bank establishes a target value of the domestic currency, which must be maintained by intervening in currency markets. In the alternative to fixed exchange rates—floating exchange rates—central banks give up trying to have a par value for the currency and to let markets alone decide the exchange rate. Stable exchange rates are important for importers and exporters, and volatility in the value of a country's currency undermines cross-border exchange. *Openness to international finance* means that the government must remove policy restrictions that limit the ability of private individuals and firms to move money across borders.

Throughout history, different political and economic situations have led governments to make different choices about these three policies. Under the nineteenth-century classical gold standard, countries chose fixed exchange rates and openness toward foreign capital while limiting their ability to use domestic monetary policy. Under the Bretton Woods system, countries chose fixed exchange rates and autonomous monetary policy, but were then required to limit international capital movement to preserve the other policies. That was feasible given the strong economic involvement of national governments, many of which at that time possessed technocratic bureaucracies capable of effective regulation of the financial sector, and the very limited international integration that existed after World War II. However, thanks to the postwar growth of international trade, as well as technological developments in finance and communications, capital controls became less effective, and fixed exchange rates more difficult to maintain in the face of tremendous market forces that could create self-fulfilling currency crises.

Since 1973, the larger and more developed world economies have allowed their exchange rates to float—to be determined primarily by the supply and demand for their currency. In turn, they retain both openness toward foreign capital and an autonomous monetary policy. Some smaller trade-dependent economies have chosen exchange rate stability over autonomous monetary policy and, at one extreme, give up national currencies entirely, as have some Latin American countries in adopting the U.S. dollar or the EU members of the eurozone. Economists tend to expect countries to converge around either purely floating or purely fixed exchange rates given greater capital mobility, but in reality many countries maintain hybrid systems, allowing exchange rates to fluctuate within some range before intervening. Few states in either situation have been able to exercise widespread control of international finance, but one of the biggest debates in the academic literature concerns the efficacy of capital controls, the policies by which governments can hinder or perhaps even stop international finance.

In the late 1990s, the International Monetary Fund (IMF) debated a change to its charter that would allow it to impose capital account liberalization—the removal of controls on international financial transactions—on countries as a condition for loans. The 1997 Asian financial crisis put an end to the discussion, and the organization's advice regarding financial openness is now much more circumscribed. Few policy recommendations achieve any sort of consensus, but most analysts now agree that trade liberalization should precede financial liberalization and that other institutional reforms, such as balancing government receipts and expenditures and strengthening domestic regulatory authorities, are necessary in between. In addition, even the staunchest advocates of capital controls must admit that they are not always effective, and rather than insulating countries from the perils of financial volatility, they may actually play a role in speculative attacks on a country's currency. Given the right policy mix and bureaucratic capabilities, countries may be able to use capital controls to prevent international finance from entering or (less effectively) leaving, but their efficacy varies considerably and governments must be quite vigilant to adapt the controls to maintain their desired effects over time.

Because developed countries seem to benefit the most from financial integration, they are generally expected to allow most international financial transactions, and the Organisation for Economic Cooperation and Development (OECD), a group of thirty of the world's most developed economies, has pushed its members toward financial openness for some time. Even most OECD countries, however, reserve the right to oppose foreign investments in certain strategic sectors. The interagency Committee on Foreign Investment in the United States (CFIUS), for example, reviews all transactions that could result in a foreign entity's controlling a domestic firm with national security implications and has the ability to prevent such transactions. Rather than reviewing each transaction, other countries place limits on potential foreign ownership in particular industries. Concern over such foreign control has grown since many of the countries affected by the Asian financial crisis responded to it with enormous increases in holdings of foreign reserves, which in some cases funded sovereign wealth funds, that is, government-controlled investment entities. Although developing countries are now cautioned against opening too quickly to international finance, being too integrated into the global economy is hardly the problem for most developing countries, most of which receive very little international finance.

International institutions that existed under Bretton Woods continue to play important, although changed, roles in managing the current international financial system. The 2007 U.S. housing crisis, which burgeoned into a worldwide recession, has exposed just how inadequate those institutions have become. The IMF's total accessible resources at the beginning of the crisis hovered near $200 billion and were dwarfed by the reserve holdings of individual countries, especially China. The April 2009 summit of the G-20 countries increased IMF resources by $750 billion, and this may be a prelude to structural reforms in the organization. Less progress at the summit was made in refocusing capital market regulations, and in fact the crisis has put pressure on banks, especially those that receive public rescue funds, to lend domestically rather than internationally. As such, we are likely to witness some retrenchment in international financial flows and the reassertion of domestic markets and domestic regulators over capital markets.

Regional Summaries

The Americas

Few regions have experienced the volatility of Latin America in terms of international finance, and research has shown that the capital flows into Latin America are particularly driven by relative returns with the United States. Periods of low interest rates in the United States tend to fuel investment booms in Latin America, and some crises can be traced to a reversal of those conditions. Argentina's massive default on foreign obligations in 2001, however, was more directly attributable to the Brazilian decision to devalue its currency, which was in turn heavily influenced by investors' skepticism about emerging markets following the 1997 Asian financial crisis. Argentina's inability to follow suit made its exports less competitive and provoked the speculation that ultimately resulted in the crisis. Perhaps as a result of Latin America's experience with sudden stops and reversals of investment flows, a populist leftist revolt against international finance has emerged in countries such as Venezuela, Bolivia, and Ecuador. Likewise, Argentina has continued to remain outside international financial markets after its crisis; its inability to tap foreign credit markets led to the recent nationalization of private pensions. Other Latin American countries, such as Brazil, Chile, and Peru, remain more optimistic about the benefits from capital market integration and have in recent years shaped economic policy to become more integrated into global financial markets.

Europe

The most dramatic move toward fixed exchange rates and unlimited financial openness since the end of Bretton Woods occurred with the birth of the euro, introduced in eleven countries in 1999 and, as of 2009, used as a sole currency by sixteen of the twenty-seven EU members. Each country that joins the eurozone gives up its own currency as well as its central bank's authority to change interest rates and allows the free movement of capital across eurozone countries. However, several countries that initially benefited from historically low interest rates since joining the eurozone, such as Ireland and Greece, are now suffering severe economic contractions and could potentially default on foreign obligations. Eastern European countries have been particularly hard hit by the worldwide financial crisis that started in 2007, as has Iceland, whose domestic banking sector has entirely collapsed under the weight of toxic foreign assets.

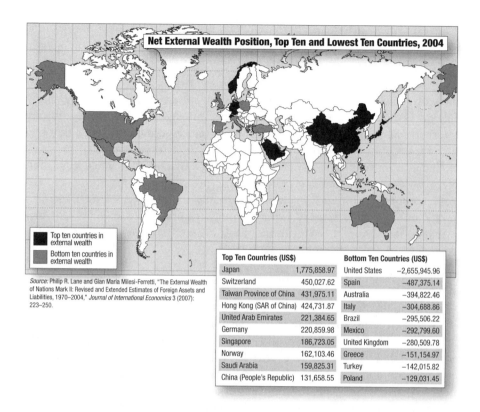

Net External Wealth Position, Top Ten and Lowest Ten Countries, 2004

Top ten countries in external wealth

Bottom ten countries in external wealth

Source: Philip R. Lane and Gian Maria Milesi-Ferretti, "The External Wealth of Nations Mark II: Revised and Extended Estimates of Foreign Assets and Liabilities, 1970–2004," *Journal of International Economics* 3 (2007): 223–250.

Top Ten Countries (US$)		Bottom Ten Countries (US$)	
Japan	1,775,858.97	United States	−2,655,945.96
Switzerland	450,027.62	Spain	−487,375.14
Taiwan Province of China	431,975.11	Australia	−394,822.46
Hong Kong (SAR of China)	424,731.87	Italy	−304,688.86
United Arab Emirates	221,384.65	Brazil	−295,506.22
Germany	220,859.98	Mexico	−292,799.60
Singapore	186,723.05	United Kingdom	−280,509.78
Norway	162,103.46	Greece	−151,154.97
Saudi Arabia	159,825.31	Turkey	−142,015.82
China (People's Republic)	131,658.55	Poland	−129,031.45

North Africa and the Middle East

Large oil exporters have frequently been a significant source of international capital flows. In fact, Middle Eastern countries played a large role in the 1982 debt crisis: when Western banks were inundated with oil-producer savings, they made higher-risk loans to many sovereign governments in the developing world. The more recent high oil prices of 2008 fueled domestic inflation in the oil exporters, as well as Western countries' worries about the growing potential of Middle Eastern governments to take over Western companies. A key story for the Middle East is the emergence in recent years of Dubai as a regional financial center.

Sub-Saharan Africa

Largely ignored by international finance, sub-Saharan Africa has little integration into the global financial system. Its avoidance of the current crisis is largely seen as an unexpected by-product of this economic isolation. Some countries, such as Angola and Chad, witnessed dramatic FDI growth over the last decade, and now have greater accumulations of FDI stock than foreign debt, which could be an encouraging sign of beneficial economic integration if that investment occurs in industries that transfer technology and skills to the local economy.

Central and South Asia

The countries of South Asia demonstrate great variation in their participation in international finance. Pakistan receives four times as much FDI as portfolio investment, but it attracts both. India, by far the largest economy in the region, has experienced both rapid economic growth and even more rapid growth in foreign investment, especially portfolio investments. India's openness toward international finance began in 1992 and has increased incrementally, although many transactions are still controlled. For example, many financial firms are excluded from trading in the forward exchange market, which allows participants to lock in an exchange rate at some prespecified future time, and the government caps foreign investment in many industries. Despite increasing capital inflows, India actually exported much capital in recent years, due primarily to the Central Bank of India's accumulation of large reserves of foreign currency.

Pacific Rim

East Asia and China have produced the most dramatic success stories regarding the role of international finance in development, as well as one of the largest crises. First the Asian tigers (South Korea, Hong Kong, Singapore, and Taiwan) and then China have used an export-led model of economic development to achieve stunning rates of growth, attributable partly to external sources of finance but ultimately due to high rates of domestic savings. China's enormous FDI inflows, mostly from other Asian countries, especially Hong Kong, South Korea, and Japan, have helped to generate a prolonged wave of economic growth that has lifted hundreds of millions of people out of poverty. China received very little foreign investment as late as the 1980s, yet it recently surpassed the United States as the greatest recipient of FDI. In some ways, this is surprising because China has relatively weak domestic institutions. Part of its FDI success has to be attributed to a very gradual liberalization; the country still retains many capital controls, and even restrictions on foreign investment have been removed slowly.

China remained relatively unscathed by the Asian financial crisis in 1997, but other Pacific Rim countries were not so fortunate. Even so, the most affected countries (for example, Indonesia, South Korea, and Thailand) maintained the openness of, or further opened, their economies to international finance.

Data

Table 1   Assets, Liabilities, and Net External Wealth, 2004 (US$)

Country	Total assets	Total liabilities	Net external position	GDP
Albania	1,914.29	3,120.48	−1,206.19	7,512.56
Algeria	48,791.61	29,477.43	19,314.18	81,463.25
Angola	7,921.46	27,114.67	−19,193.21	19,534.68
Argentina	133,936.98	206,315.61	−72,378.64	151,935.16
Armenia	1,025.38	2,664.03	−1,638.64	3,545.56
Australia	504,301.68	899,124.14	−394,822.46	617,607.31
Austria	544,222.01	594,537.58	−50,315.58	289,716.56
Azerbaijan	5,128.79	14,395.38	−9,266.59	8,540.22
Bahrain	107,267.66	98,732.86	8,534.80	10,754.29
Bangladesh	5,912.43	22,943.49	−17,031.07	56,154.75
Belarus	2,219.97	6,695.17	−4,475.20	22,754.35
Belgium	1,496,834.46	1,387,974.45	108,860.01	352,000.24
Benin	1,220.57	2,533.51	−1,312.94	3,564.93
Bolivia	3,325.35	12,481.69	−9,156.34	9,360.54
Bosnia and Herzegovina	5,814.66	6,813.90	−999.24	8,261.90
Botswana	9,552.85	2,747.31	6,805.54	9,125.29
Brazil	169,826.58	465,332.80	−295,506.22	599,731.91
Brunei Darussalam	42,430.07	7,967.39	34,462.68	5,692.25
Bulgaria	14,923.48	26,275.72	−11,352.25	23,773.47
Burkina Faso	1,106.51	2,080.58	−974.08	5,110.14
Cambodia	3,273.59	5,379.57	−2,105.98	4,879.34
Cameroon	2,406.48	8,118.45	−5,711.97	14,431.11
Canada	986,941.43	1,111,476.06	−124,534.62	995,833.35
Chad	493.37	4,898.58	−4,405.21	4,219.90
Chile	75,628.45	110,713.08	−35,084.63	93,650.52
China, People's Republic of	913,518.20	781,859.66	131,658.55	1,649,386.63
Colombia	34,204.66	67,297.91	−33,093.25	95,188.38
Congo, Democratic Republic of	1,602.67	10,643.08	−9,040.41	5,680.53
Congo, Republic of	558.91	8,041.29	−7,482.38	3,570.73
Costa Rica	4,074.32	12,725.51	−8,651.19	18,511.34
Côte d'Ivoire	7,210.07	19,046.10	−11,836.03	15,494.93
Croatia	20,531.43	41,905.00	−21,373.57	33,202.73
Cyprus	39,183.30	37,211.18	1,972.12	14,886.43
Czech Republic	68,447.05	105,523.41	−37,076.36	107,014.89
Denmark	473,345.64	503,500.15	−30,154.51	242,344.16
Dominican Republic	5,960.37	17,118.84	−11,158.47	19,444.76
Ecuador	4,317.21	29,765.31	−25,448.10	29,881.00
Egypt	44,329.83	58,791.14	−14,461.30	75,680.53
El Salvador	4,784.95	13,461.03	−8,676.09	13,842.26
Equatorial Guinea	386.98	4,338.19	−3,951.21	2,618.35
Estonia	8,686.49	20,097.78	−11,411.29	11,447.24
Ethiopia	3,606.48	8,755.16	−5,148.68	8,004.69
Euro Area	11,897,391.39	12,803,523.43	−906,132.04	9,397,694.01
Fiji	971.06	1,371.30	−400.24	2,281.79
Finland	363,857.18	386,407.34	−22,550.16	186,174.85
France	4,332,467.12	4,223,599.68	108,867.44	2,046,636.56
Gabon	1,647.22	4,831.26	−3,184.04	7,276.18
Georgia	775.95	4,164.10	−3,388.15	4,453.43
Germany	4,586,085.37	4,365,225.39	220,859.98	2,744,270.69

Table 1 (Continued)

Country	Total assets	Total liabilities	Net external position	GDP
Ghana	3,548.67	11,625.61	−8,076.93	8,832.72
Greece	137,092.63	288,247.60	−151,154.97	205,493.31
Guatemala	6,519.15	10,295.07	−3,775.93	26,117.94
Guinea	630.87	3,791.59	−3,160.71	3,916.90
Haiti	379.17	1,573.21	−1,194.04	2,956.80
Honduras	4,741.10	8,559.97	−3,818.87	7,427.46
Hong Kong (SAR of China)	1,376,289.98	951,558.11	424,731.87	164,553.53
Hungary	41,795.02	138,061.65	−96,266.63	99,347.37
Iceland	18,264.52	29,652.23	−11,387.71	12,258.24
India	154,887.66	226,868.17	−71,980.51	661,045.86
Indonesia	54,642.04	172,158.27	−117,516.23	225,185.25
Iran	68,815.10	20,825.29	47,989.82	168,970.89
Ireland	1,691,671.44	1,727,539.17	−35,867.74	181,869.29
Israel	109,469.51	134,972.60	−25,503.09	116,343.86
Italy	1,772,341.38	2,077,030.24	−304,688.86	1,680,111.73
Jamaica	6,394.88	12,607.54	−6,212.66	8,592.40
Japan	4,158,365.44	2,382,506.46	1,775,858.97	4,672,591.53
Jordan	8,864.19	11,611.05	−2,746.86	10,971.83
Kazakhstan	22,607.30	47,591.22	−24,983.92	40,753.68
Kenya	3,178.06	8,031.76	−4,853.71	15,614.63
Korea, South	358,263.58	385,710.46	−27,446.88	681,468.61
Kuwait	138,850.15	13,089.19	125,760.95	51,803.70
Kyrgyz Republic	1,052.83	2,822.42	−1,769.59	2,167.28
Lao People's Democratic Republic	497.26	3,649.85	−3,152.59	2,433.59
Latvia	9,229.20	16,737.59	−7,508.39	13,657.07
Lebanon	26,814.11	47,473.97	−20,659.86	19,513.10
Libya	73,976.70	7,571.06	66,405.64	29,027.30
Lithuania	7,331.59	15,956.69	−8,625.09	22,170.64
Luxembourg	3,299,476.51	3,261,696.38	37,780.12	31,782.90
Macedonia	1,929.44	3,548.00	−1,618.56	4,728.91
Madagascar	1,240.59	5,222.94	−3,982.34	4,359.43
Malawi	356.53	3,517.68	−3,161.15	1,765.50
Malaysia	130,743.20	133,147.79	−2,404.59	117,776.32
Mali	1,366.53	4,418.64	−3,052.11	4,936.78
Malta	22,905.38	21,296.67	1,608.71	5,389.05
Mauritius	3,265.92	2,035.01	1,230.91	5,901.93
Mexico	135,885.40	428,685.00	−292,799.60	676,497.31
Moldova	1,097.53	2,661.94	−1,564.41	2,582.13
Morocco	25,985.36	39,916.49	−13,931.13	49,816.44
Mozambique	2,247.86	6,619.28	−4,371.42	6,085.77
Myanmar	1,015.39	11,436.81	−10,421.42	7,838.78
Namibia	6,343.73	3,409.15	2,934.59	4,623.60
Nepal	2,290.17	3,605.21	−1,315.03	6,311.42
Netherlands	2,326,517.66	2,360,174.69	−33,657.03	577,985.40
New Zealand	64,930.93	154,015.30	−89,084.37	96,969.50
Nicaragua	1,263.30	5,891.50	−4,628.20	4,432.35
Niger	394.22	2,544.41	−2,150.19	2,736.34
Nigeria	34,274.76	64,561.35	−30,286.60	71,326.04
Norway	514,682.25	352,578.79	162,103.46	250,444.08
Oman	9,630.09	7,961.50	1,668.59	24,593.24
Pakistan	17,190.92	46,913.38	−29,722.46	81,759.50
Panama	16,023.21	28,666.74	−12,643.53	13,793.50
Papua New Guinea	1,621.21	5,096.54	−3,475.32	3,953.92
Paraguay	2,642.81	4,450.72	−1,807.91	6,994.74

Table 1 (Continued)

Country	Total assets	Total liabilities	Net external position	GDP
Peru	20,741.44	56,742.90	−36,001.46	67,856.68
Philippines	33,463.47	83,407.05	−49,943.58	85,136.11
Poland	76,651.55	205,683.00	−129,031.45	242,226.27
Portugal	294,424.84	410,906.98	−116,482.14	167,236.45
Qatar	82,356.72	20,461.15	61,895.56	28,451.37
Romania	21,731.06	46,583.70	−24,852.64	71,322.88
Russia	389,494.41	386,725.24	2,769.17	582,730.92
Rwanda	725.59	2,016.94	−1,291.35	1,834.72
Saudi Arabia	222,208.41	62,383.09	159,825.31	248,812.56
Senegal	3,055.28	5,764.45	−2,709.17	7,626.56
Singapore	639,846.51	453,123.45	186,723.05	106,822.49
Slovak Republic	24,443.98	39,873.79	−15,429.81	41,091.42
Slovenia	21,781.68	27,679.53	−5,897.85	32,794.49
South Africa	138,644.41	149,502.13	−10,857.72	212,898.34
Spain	1,245,715.48	1,733,090.62	−487,375.14	992,992.23
Sri Lanka	4,649.12	15,882.39	−11,233.27	20,133.00
Sudan	3,420.08	24,049.22	−20,629.14	21,269.91
Swaziland	1,891.40	1,539.72	351.68	2,360.88
Sweden	739,713.00	772,717.47	−33,004.47	346,531.23
Switzerland	1,963,375.84	1,513,348.22	450,027.62	344,000.92
Syria	20,963.54	33,721.23	−12,757.70	23,744.89
Taiwan (province of China)	631,260.97	199,285.86	431,975.11	305,201.79
Tajikistan	326.53	1,319.29	−992.76	2,073.22
Tanzania	4,032.92	10,598.34	−6,565.42	10,831.17
Thailand	73,554.09	121,234.61	−47,680.52	163,491.50
Togo	802.34	2,667.26	−1,864.92	2,032.05
Trinidad and Tobago	6,919.46	15,598.39	−8,678.93	12,542.43
Tunisia	7,232.61	38,406.76	−31,174.14	28,567.57
Turkey	84,900.33	226,916.15	−142,015.82	300,086.84
Turkmenistan	4,491.22	2,781.30	1,709.91	12,207.69
Uganda	2,454.10	6,448.40	−3,994.30	6,792.26
Ukraine	28,183.56	40,156.31	−11,972.75	65,039.11
United Arab Emirates	241,085.45	19,700.80	221,384.65	95,721.02
United Kingdom	7,596,963.93	7,877,473.71	−280,509.78	2,125,508.98
United States	9,859,082.04	12,515,028.00	−2,655,945.96	11,733,475.00
Uruguay	15,852.10	18,628.63	−2,776.53	12,044.00
Uzbekistan	3,278.61	6,067.50	−2,788.89	9,720.34
Venezuela	96,082.97	78,057.77	18,025.20	107,487.49
Vietnam	11,130.97	37,484.11	−26,353.14	43,890.75
Yemen	11,597.28	6,441.65	5,155.62	12,903.25
Yugoslavia (Serbia and Montenegro)	4,302.00	19,355.36	−15,053.36	24,133.13
Zambia	1,154.14	7,265.49	−6,111.34	5,409.10
Zimbabwe	534.78	5,579.33	−5,044.55	8,304.75

Source: Philip R. Lane and Gian Maria Milesi-Ferretti, "The External Wealth of Nations Mark II: Revised and Extended Estimates of Foreign Assets and Liabilities, 1970–2004," *Journal of International Economics* 3 (2007): 223–250.

Note: Total assets include all foreign assets owned by public and private entities from the country in question, including portfolio investment (stocks and bonds), foreign direct investment, loans, deposits, trade credits, financial derivatives, and reserve holdings. Total liabilities include all domestic assets owned by foreign entities. Net external wealth is calculated by subtracting total liabilities from total assets. All figures have been converted to U.S. dollars using end-of-year exchange rates. For more information, see Lane and Milesi-Ferretti (2007). Data are Lane and Milesi-Ferretti's estimates and are not official or International Monetary Fund (IMF) data. Data for Benin, Equatorial Guinea, Fiji, Haiti, Malawi, Niger, and Zimbabwe are from 2003. GDP, gross domestic product; SAR, special administrative region.

Case Study—Malaysia's Capital Controls during the 1997 Asian Financial Crisis

Perhaps the most critical case in ending the IMF's attempt to include financial openness in its mission was the use of capital controls by Malaysia toward the end of the Asian financial crisis. While its neighbors Korea and Thailand accepted large (at the time) IMF bailouts, promised to end crony capitalism, and maintained financial openness, Malaysia went in the opposite direction, refusing the IMF policy recommendations and attempting to reduce the impact of international finance on its economy.

From December 1997, Anwar Ibrahim, Malaysia's finance minister, responded to the crisis with policy reforms that mirrored those of neighbors who had accepted IMF aid, with the accompanying reform requirements. By the end of August 1998, offshore currency traders, primarily in Singapore, were making large speculative trades based on the possibility that the ringgit, Malaysia's currency, would lose value. To prevent such speculation from actually causing the devaluation of the ringgit, on September 1, 1998, Prime Minister Mahathir bin Mohamad announced the implementation of controls on offshore currency trades and draconian restrictions on currency exchange with the ringgit. Interestingly, the controls were designed not to impact FDI, which was viewed as having important positive effects such as technology transfer on the Malaysian economy. By February 1999, Mahathir's government reoriented the controls from an outright ban on many international financial transactions to a tax-based system of controls, and the economy never experienced a full-fledged currency crisis.

Analysis of the Malaysian case has been a key component in the postcrisis debate about the utility of capital controls. Some economists, such as Dani Rodrik and Ethan Kaplan, argued that Malaysia's unorthodox use of controls had in fact helped it to recover faster than Korea and Thailand. Their analysis is predicated on the assumption that Malaysia in September of 1998 was comparable to Korea and Thailand at the time when they accepted their IMF rescue packages, which was several months earlier. Critics of this approach argued that Malaysia had actually reached the nadir of the crisis around the time controls were implemented and that its recovery was related more to sound economic fundamentals than to the controls' effectiveness at insulating the domestic economy. Michael Hutchison (2003) and Simon Johnson, Kalpana Kochhar, Todd Mitton, and Natalia Tamirisa (2007) made good arguments that politically connected firms benefited disproportionately from the controls and that ultimately Mahathir's implementation of capital controls was aimed more at restoring his political authority and undermining his chief rival and champion of economic reform—Finance Minister Anwar Ibrahim—than at trying to insulate the economy from international finance.

The Malaysian case shows the difficulty of evaluating the effects of capital controls. Because the controls were implemented temporarily by an effective bureaucracy, the issue is not the effectiveness of the controls. Indeed, most analysts expected the controls to have an effect on international financial flows.

The difficulty lies in evaluating what would have happened in Malaysia without the controls, and although we can make direct comparisons to Malaysia's neighbors, an IMF rescue package could have changed the situation dramatically. Accompanied by demands for policy change (not just toward financial openness but also fiscal and monetary reforms), IMF involvement might have resulted in an entirely different political equilibrium, in which Mahathir lost power just as his counterpart in Indonesia, Suharto, did. Thus, in many ways, controls were used just as much for their political value as for their economic effects.

Biographical Sketches

Barry Eichengreen uses his expertise on the history of the international financial system to explain inadequacies of the current system. His book on the demise of the nineteenth-century gold standard, *Golden Fetters: The Gold Standard and the Great Depression,* is the classic on the subject; his more recent work covers a wider range of subject matter, from the relationship of globalization and democracy to the likelihood of international crises.

Robert Mundell won the 1999 Nobel Prize in Economics for his work on open economy macroeconomics. His pioneering work on economic policy under different exchange rate regimes led to a better understanding of the linkages among different macroeconomic policies, particularly how international capital flows can undermine intended policy effects. His work on optimum currency areas, helping to determine how widely a currency can efficiently be used, was also very influential in economic analyses of the eurozone both before and after its creation.

Raghuram Rajan is an economist at University of Chicago Graduate School of Business as well as adviser to the Indian government. Prior to returning to academia, Rajan was the youngest ever director of research at the International Monetary Fund, 2003–2006. His best-known work is probably his co-authored book *Saving Capitalism from the Capitalists,* and he received the 2003 Fischer Black Prize, awarded to young economists who have already made a great impact in the field of the study of finance.

Dani Rodrik, a Harvard University economist who is originally from Turkey, has frequently taken contrarian positions toward conventional wisdom in economics, especially international finance. Most recently, in a *Financial Times* editorial written with Arvind Subramanian, he argued that the overall volume of international financial flows needs to be reduced to curb its contribution to the cycle of international crises. His book *Has Globalization Gone Too Far?* is a good introduction to many of the debates discussed in this chapter.

James Tobin won the Nobel Prize in Economics in 1981 and is most renowned outside economics for his advocacy of a tax on international financial flows to reduce their volatility. This much-discussed "Tobin tax" is a popular policy recommendation, but it is difficult to implement in practice. His research also focused on the different types of investment and on the relationship between investor preferences and different forms of assets (bonds and equity as opposed to cash, for example).

Directory

Bank of International Settlements, Centralbahnplatz 2, CH-4002 Basel, Switzerland. Telephone: (41) 61 280 8080; email: email@bis.org; Web: http://www.bis.org.
Intergovernmental organization dedicated to central bank cooperation on regulation of private banks.

Committee on Foreign Investment in the United States, Department of the Treasury, 1500 Pennsylvania Avenue NW, Room 5221, Washington, D.C. 20220. Telephone: (202) 622-1860; email: CFIUS@do.treas.gov; Web: http://www.ustreas .gov/offices/international-affairs/cfius.
Agency of the U.S. government charged with reviewing all foreign acquisitions of domestic firms.

Institute of International Finance, 1333 H Street NW, Suite 800E, Washington, D.C. 20005-4770. Telephone (202) 857-3600; email: info@iif.com; Web: http:// www.iif.com.
Nongovernmental organization formed by the world's largest banks after the 1982 debt crisis.

International Finance Corporation, 2121 Pennsylvania Avenue NW, Washington, D.C. 20433. Telephone: (202) 473-1000; email: via Web site; Web: http://www .ifc.org.
A part of the World Bank, charged with mobilizing international finance for development.

International Monetary Fund (IMF), 700 19th Street NW, Washington, D.C. 20431. Telephone: (202) 623-7000; email: webmaster@imf.org; Web: http://www.imf.org.
Primary intergovernmental organization for international policy coordination, particularly focused on exchange rate management.

South Centre, CP 228, 1211 Geneva 19, Switzerland. Telephone: (41) 220791 8050; email: south@southcentre.org; Web: http://www.southcentre.org.
Intergovernmental organization and think tank with only developing countries as members.

United Nations Committee on Trade and Investment, Palais des Nations, 8-14, Avenue de la Paix, 1211 Geneva 10, Switzerland. Telephone: (41) 22 917 1234; email: info@unctad.org; Web: http://www.unctad.org.
UN agency focused on development issues in economic globalization, especially FDI.

Further Research

Books

Abdelal, Rawi. *Capital Rules: The Construction of Global Finance.* Cambridge, Mass.: Harvard University Press, 2007.

Edwards, Sebastian. *Capital Controls and Capital Flows in Emerging Economies: Policies, Practices, and Consequences.* National Bureau of Economic Research conference report. Chicago: University of Chicago Press, 2007.

Eichengreen, Barry. *Capital Flows and Crises.* Cambridge, Mass.: MIT Press, 2003.

———. *Globalizing Capital: A History of the International Monetary System.* Princeton, N.J.: Princeton University Press, 1996.

Ferguson, Niall. *The Ascent of Money: A Financial History of the World.* New York: Penguin Putnam, 2008.

Helleiner, Eric. *States and the Reemergence of Global Finance: From Bretton Woods to the 1990s.* Ithaca, N.Y.: Cornell University Press, 1994.

O'Rourke, Kevin H., and Jeffrey G. Williamson. *Globalization and History the Evolution of a Nineteenth-Century Atlantic Economy.* Cambridge, Mass.: MIT Press, 1999.

Obstfeld, Maurice, and Alan M. Taylor. *Global Capital Markets: Integration, Crisis, and Growth.* Cambridge, UK: Cambridge University Press, 2004.

Rajan, Raghuram G., and Luigi Zingales. *Saving Capitalism from the Capitalists: Unleashing the Power of Financial Markets to Create Wealth and Spread Opportunity.* New York: Crown Business, 2003.

Rodrik, Dani. *One Economics, Many Recipes: Globalization, Institutions, and Economic Growth.* Princeton, N.J.: Princeton University Press, 2007.

Simmons, Beth A. *Who Adjusts?: Domestic Sources of Foreign Economic Policy during the Interwar Years.* Princeton Studies in International History and Politics. Princeton, N.J.: Princeton University Press, 1994.

Sobel, Andrew. *Domestic Choices, International Markets: Dismantling National Barriers and Liberalizing Securities Markets.* Ann Arbor.: University of Michigan Press, 1994.

Wolf, Martin. *Fixing Global Finance.* Baltimore, Md.: Johns Hopkins University Press, 2008.

Articles and Reports

Bhagwati, Jagdish N. "The Capital Myth: The Difference between Trade in Widgets and Dollars." *Foreign Affairs* 77, no. 3 (May–June 1998): 7–12.

Calvo, Guillermo A., Leonardo Leiderman, and Carmen Reinhart. "Inflows of Capital to Developing Countries in the 1990s." *Journal of Economic Perspectives* 10, no. 2 (1996): 123–139.

Edwards, Sebastian. "How Effective Are Capital Controls?" *Journal of Economic Perspectives* 13, no. 4 (1999): 65–84.

Eichengreen, Barry, and David Leblang. "Capital Account Liberalization and Growth: Was Mr. Mahathir Right?" *International Journal of Finance and Economics* 8 (2003): 205–224.

Goodman, John B., and Louis W. Pauly. "The Obsolescence of Capital Controls?: Economic Management in an Age of Global Markets." *World Politics* 46, no. 1 (1993): 50–82.

Haggard, Stephan, and Sylvia Maxfield. "The Political Economy of Financial Liberalization in the Developing World." *International Organization* 50, no. 1 (1996): 35–68.

Hutchison, Michael M. "A Cure Worse than the Disease?: Currency Crises and the Output Costs of IMF-supported Programs." In *Managing Currency Crises in Emerging Markets,* ed. M. Dooley and Jeffrey A. Frankel. Chicago: University of Chicago Press, 2003.

Johnson, Simon, Kalpana Kochhar, Todd Mitton, and Natalia Tamirisa. "Malaysian Capital Controls: Macroeconomics and Institutions." In *Capital Controls and Capital Flows in Emerging Economies: Policies, Practices, and Consequences,* ed. Sebastian Edwards. Chicago: University of Chicago Press, 2007.

Kose, M. Ayhan, Eswar Prasad, Kenneth Rogoff, and Shang-Jin Wei. "Financial Globalization: Beyond the Blame Game." *Finance and Development* 44, no. 1 (2007). Available at: http://www.imf.org/external/pubs/ft/fandd/2007/03/kose.htm.

Lucas, Robert E. "Why Doesn't Capital Flow from Rich to Poor Countries?" *American Economic Review* 80, no. 2 (1990): 92–96.

Lukauskas, Arvid, and Susan Minushkin. "Explaining Styles of Financial Market Opening in Chile, Mexico, South Korea, and Turkey." *International Studies Quarterly* 44 (2000): 695–723.

Obstfeld, Maurice. "The Global Capital Market: Benefactor or Menace?" *Journal of Economic Perspectives* 12, no. 4 (1998): 9–30.

Quinn, Dennis, and Marie Toyoda. "Does Capital Account Liberalization Lead to Growth?" *Review of Financial Studies* 21, no. 3 (2008): 1403–1449.

Rodrik, Dani. "Who Needs Capital-Account Convertibility?" In *Should the IMF Pursue Capital Account Convertibility?,* ed. Peter Kenen. Princeton, N.J.: Princeton University Press, 1998. Available at: http://ksghome.harvard.edu/~drodrik/papers.html.

Rodrik, Dani, and E. Kaplan. "Did the Malaysian Capital Controls Work?" In *Preventing Currency Crises in Emerging Markets,* ed. Sebastian Edwards and Jeffrey A. Frankel. Chicago: University of Chicago Press, 2002.

Rogoff, Kenneth S. "Rethinking Capital Controls: When Should We Keep an Open Mind?" *Finance and Development* 39, no. 4 (2002). Available at: http://imf.org/external/pubs/ft/fandd/2002/12/rogoff.htm.

Simmons, Beth, and Zachary Elkins. "The Globalization of Liberalization: Policy Diffusion in the International Political Economy." *American Political Science Review* 98, no. 1 (2004): 171–190.

Stiglitz, Joseph. "Capital-Market Liberalization, Globalization and the IMF." *Oxford Review of Economic Policy* 20, no. 1 (2004): 57–71.

Summers, Lawrence H. "International Financial Crises: Causes, Prevention, and Cures." *American Economic Review* 90, no. 2 (2000): 1–16.

UN Conference on Trade and Development (UNCTAD). *World Investment Report.* UNCTAD, Geneva, annual, 1991–2008. Available at: http://www.unctad.org/Templates/Page.asp?intItemID=1485&lang=1.

World Bank. *World Economic Outlook.* International Monetary Fund, Washington, D.C., 1993–2009. Available at: http://www.imf.org/external/ns/cs.aspx?id=29.

Web Sites

The Economist
http://www.economist.com

Financial Times
http://www.ft.com

Foreign Policy **Magazine**
http://www.foreignpolicy.com

KOF Index of Globalization
http://globalization.kof.ethz.ch

Peterson Institute for International Economics
http://www.iie.com

RGE Monitor
http://www.rgemonitor.com

Document

1. Interim Committee Statement on Liberalization of Capital Movements under an Amendment of the IMF's Articles, as Adopted, Hong Kong SAR

International Monetary Fund, September 21, 1997

The full text is available at http://www.imf.org/external/np/sec/pr/1997/pr9744.htm.

Extract

1. It is time to add a new chapter to the Bretton Woods agreement. Private capital flows have become much more important to the international monetary system, and an increasingly open and liberal system has proved to be highly beneficial to the world economy. By facilitating the flow of savings to their most productive uses, capital movements increase investment, growth, and prosperity. Provided it is introduced in an orderly manner, and backed both by adequate national policies and a solid multilateral system for surveillance and financial support, the liberalization of capital flows is an essential element of an efficient international monetary system in this age of globalization. The IMF's central role in the international monetary system, and its near universal membership, make it uniquely placed to help this process. The Committee sees the IMF's proposed new mandate as bold in its vision, but requiring cautious implementation.

2. International capital flows are highly sensitive to, among other things, the stability of the international monetary system, the quality of macroeconomic policies, and the soundness of domestic financial systems. The recent turmoil in financial markets has demonstrated again the importance of underpinning liberalization with a broad range of structural measures, especially in the monetary and financial sector, and within the framework of a solid mix of macroeconomic and exchange rate policies. Particular importance will need to be attached to establishing an environment conducive to the efficient use of capital and to building sound financial systems solid enough to cope with fluctuations in capital flows. This phased but comprehensive approach will tailor capital account liberalization to the circumstances of individual countries, thereby maximizing the chances of success, not only for each country but also for the international monetary system.

3. These efforts should lead to the establishment of a multilateral and nondiscriminatory system to promote the liberalization of capital movements. The IMF will have the task of assisting in the establishment of such a system and stands ready to support members' efforts in this regard. Its role is also key to the adoption of policies that would facilitate properly sequenced liberalization and reduce the likelihood of financial and balance of payments crises.

4. In light of the foregoing, the Committee invites the Executive Board to complete its work on a proposed amendment of the Fund's Articles that would make the liberalization of capital movements one of the purposes of the Fund and extend, as needed, the Fund's jurisdiction through the establishment of carefully defined and uniformly applied obligations regarding the liberalization of such movements. Safeguards and transitional arrangements are necessary for the success of this major endeavor. Flexible approval policies will have to be adopted. In both the preparation of an amendment to the IMF's Articles and its implementation, the members' obligations under other

international agreements will be respected. In pursuing this work, the Committee expects the IMF and other institutions to cooperate closely.

5. Sound liberalization and expanded access to capital markets should reduce the frequency of recourse to Fund resources and other exceptional financing. Nevertheless, the Committee recognizes that, in some circumstances, there could be a large need for financing from the Fund and other sources. The Fund will continue to play a critical role in helping to mobilize financial support for members' adjustment programs. In such endeavors, the Fund will continue its central catalytic role while limiting moral hazard.

6. In view of the importance of moving decisively toward this new worldwide regime of liberalized capital movements, and welcoming the very broad consensus of the membership on these basic guidelines, the Committee invites the Executive Board to give high priority to the completion of the required amendment of the Fund's Articles of Agreement.

LABOR AND EMPLOYMENT

Scott B. Martin

Most people work locally, but today employment is increasingly affected by global economic processes. Greatly increased cross-border flows of trade and investment—economic globalization—have had a considerable impact on the quantity and quality of work, the nature of working conditions, and the collective rights of workers. This increased global interaction also leaves local labor markets open to the shocks of international economic downturns. This reality of globalization is starkly apparent in the current economic crisis, which began with the bursting of the bubble in the U.S. housing market in 2007. The crisis started to affect labor markets around the world in the second half of 2008, and by the end of the first quarter of 2009, unemployment in most major economies (and many smaller ones) has risen drastically.

With many of the world's wage workers left exposed to the wrenching economic downturns of 2008 and 2009, the relationship between globalization and world labor is thrown into stark relief. Given the complexity of this relationship, scholars, policymakers, and advocates concerned with labor and employment issues disagree on whether the developments associated with economic globalization are more positive or negative and on appropriate programs and policies to respond to them. Particular areas of contention are growing income inequality and low wage growth, employment generation, job security, social safety nets for the unemployed, and international labor rights in the context of multinational corporations and international economic agreements.

Historical Background and Development

Policies and norms governing conditions of work and employment have emerged and evolved over time in response to changing technological circumstances and shifting international economic and political conditions.

This chapter has been updated for this edition by the staff of MTM Publishing.

International and national initiatives and debates have continually shaped one another. The Industrial Revolution brought masses of impoverished laborers together in often highly unsafe and exploitative conditions in the first workshops and factories. While transforming Europe and the United States in the mid- to late nineteenth century, the revolution also generated national and international reform movements and the first workers' organizations. The International Workingmen's Association (First International), which lasted from 1864 to 1870, and the subsequent Second International, which was founded in the late 1880s and lasted through World War I, voiced revolutionary socialist demands and promoted international working-class solidarity.

The first national labor federations, or centrals, were formed in Europe in the latter decades of the nineteenth century. Also, the first national laws regulating conditions of work emerged during this period in the industrializing countries of Europe and in the United States, focusing on limiting child labor, women's labor, and hours of work; creating a weekly day of rest and limiting night work; and regulating dangerous occupations. The right to form trade unions and engage in strikes, however, was not formally established and was mostly restricted in practice. Based on the earlier work of European industrialists interested in promoting intergovernmental cooperation on labor laws, and responding to growing pressure from an emerging working class, the first international labor treaties—regulating working hours for women and children and night work by children—were drafted on the eve of World War I. They were not adopted or ratified, however, because of the war.

The momentum for the adoption of international labor norms survived the war, as the International Labour Organisation (ILO) was founded in 1919, in large part through the efforts of trade unions from the Allied powers to include an international labor charter in the Treaty of Versailles, which officially concluded World War I. A tripartite commission of government, union, and employer representatives established nine principles to guide the new organization, including the right of association, equal pay for equal work, an eight-hour workday (or forty-eight-hour workweek), the abolition of child labor, and equitable economic treatment of immigrant labor. Between the two world wars, the ILO functioned as an autonomous part of the League of Nations, the short-lived predecessor to the United Nations. With the end of World War II and the creation of the United Nations, the ILO became in 1946 the first of the specialized UN agencies, with specific responsibilities in the areas of labor and social policy, such as employment conditions, labor relations, social security, and vocational training. The ILO has continued to be organized under the principle of tripartism, with equal representation for member governments and national trade union and employer organizations.

On the national front, the interwar and immediate post–World War II periods were marked by considerable trade union activism and political and social conflict over the role of workers in society, particularly in the industrialized countries of the West but also in some of the industrializing countries of the Southern Hemisphere. The central place of labor in modernizing economies was recognized in an expanding network of labor laws improving working conditions and guaranteeing trade union and bargaining rights, as well as in newly created or expanded social benefits in the areas of retirement pensions, health care, education, and housing. U.S. examples are the Wagner Act of the mid-1930s, which guaranteed the right to organize and strike, and New Deal social legislation, both of the Roosevelt era. Meanwhile in socialist countries, such as the Soviet Union and China, social rights were formally guaranteed and benefits were expanded, but labor rights to freedom of association and political rights to free speech and assembly were sharply curtailed.

Although the workings of the ILO were at times stymied by a relatively small budget and staff and by cold war rivalries, the organization nevertheless remained at the center of international efforts to regulate conditions of work and employment in the post–World War II decades. In recent years, the end of the cold war, the burgeoning debate about the social impact of globalization, and the high profile of the ILO's leadership have focused renewed attention on the organization's role. Its official functions include not only setting international norms but also engaging in international technical cooperation with governments, unions, and employers, as well as promoting public education and conducting research. Nearly all nation-states are ILO members. Core international labor standards have been negotiated in a series of international conventions subject to ratification by member states and binding on ratifying countries (see Table 1; Documents 1 and 2). These agreements cover basic principles, such as the abolition of forced labor, freedom of association of workers through trade unions, rights to collective bargaining, antidiscrimination, and limits on child labor. Although the number of countries ratifying these conventions has steadily grown since their adoption, the United States has refused to ratify some of the major ILO instruments, including, for instance, the convention on freedom of association and the right to organize, and the convention on the right to collective bargaining. The United Nations, in addition to sponsoring ILO conventions, adopted the Universal Declaration of Human Rights in 1948; Article 20 of the declaration protects "the right to freedom of peaceful assembly and association" and establishes that "no one may be compelled to belong to any association."

Current Status

Research and policy efforts relating to global and comparative employment and labor trends are complicated by the complex difficult-to-measure connections between global processes and national and local employment patterns, as well as the unusual joining of new and old forms of work that globalization has wrought. For instance, in developing countries, historic problems of grinding poverty and income inequality persist, reflected in phenomena such as gender, ethnic, and racial discrimination in pay and employment and in children being sent to work to support impoverished families. Yet these problems take on a new cast under globalization. For example, studies show that an increasing share of the large segment of the workforce who have long eked out a living in the informal sector (the unregulated, sometimes underground economy that comprises a major portion of the working poor) now participates directly or indirectly in globalized economic activities. Women are disproportionately represented in the informal sector, particularly as declining family incomes and (in some cases) shifting cultural values lead them to enter the workforce as part of household survival strategies (see Table 2; see also WOMEN). Thus, for instance, street vendors may sell imported consumer goods, and industrial home workers and laborers, usually female, in clandestine workshops and factories may stitch together pieces of garments or make ceramics that are then sold internationally, often under name brand labels. Such low-skilled laborers are just as engaged in the globalizing economy as the workers in the high-tech sectors of the information economy who are often more commonly associated in the media with globalization.

Research

The most direct and immediate impact of global integration on labor and employment has been the enormous growth in the 1980s and 1990s of transnational corporations (TNCs), foreign direct investment (FDI), and complex international networks of production and trade centering on transnational firms. In the 2000s, this growth in TNCs continued unabated. As measured by and reported in 2008 by the United Nations Conference on Trade and Development (UNCTAD) *World Investment Report,* approximately 79,000 parent firms operated some 795,000 affiliates in almost every sector and country, compared to 63,000 parent firms and 690,000 foreign affiliates in 2000. Through direct investment, these companies route flows of money across national boundaries to establish offices and factories and managerial control of overseas employees. Examples of such companies are McDonald's, Shell Oil, and Volkswagen.

Direct investment by TNCs has become more diverse in terms of the location and nature of jobs it supports, but it remains concentrated in the developed economies (including those of North America, Western Europe, and Japan) making up approximately 70 percent of all such investment worldwide in 2008, according to the 2008 *World Investment Report*. This concentration means, for instance, that an increasing number of U.S. jobs depend directly or indirectly on investment in the United States by non-American firms. Yet FDI and related employment grew fastest in the 1980s and 1990s in developing and transitional economies, especially those of Brazil, China, Mexico, and Singapore. These increases continued into the 2000s. In 2007, FDI investment in developing and transition economies grew at the highest rate ever, charting an increase of 25 percent over 2006. Although the economic crisis that began in 2007, considered by many observers to be the worst since the Great Depression in the 1930s, is expected to slow investment in FDI, such investment in developing and transition economies will likely be less severely affected than in other countries.

The effect of international trade on employment has also grown dramatically since the middle of the twentieth century (see WORLD TRADE). Except for a dip in the 1970s and 1980s, when the rate slowed to less than 4 percent, the rate of increase in world trade, according to the World Trade Organization (WTO)'s "International Trade Statistics 2008," has been over 6 percent from the 1950s onward, rising to over 8 percent in the 1960s. The years 2008 and 2009, of course, are a different story because the worldwide recession has taken its toll. A WTO press release issued on March 23, 2009, predicted a 9 percent contraction in exports in 2009, the biggest downturn since World War II.

Although employment in many locations does not always correlate positively with growth in world trade, employment in many areas has benefited from rising world trade in the post–World War II era. Even in the United States—which, because of the sheer size of its domestic market, has tended to be internally oriented economically—more than 12 million jobs in the early 2000s depended on exports. In smaller national economies, such as those of Western Europe and East and Southeast Asia, a much higher percentage of jobs are trade related. One downside of this trend is that slumps in export markets are quickly felt at home. The current downturn is the starkest example of this. The United States alone experienced close to a 40 percent increase in its unemployment rate between 2008 and February of 2009, and other high-income countries, such as Sweden, Canada, and Australia, all experienced increases of their unemployment rates between 20 and 30 percent (see map, p. 176). And the worldwide increase in unemployment, as projected in the ILO "Global Employment Trends Update, May 2009" (GET 5/09), could range from 29 million in the ILO's best-case scenario to 59 million in its worst-case scenario.

International portfolio investment—purchases of stocks and other private financial instruments that do not usually imply direct managerial control over workers by the purchaser—has grown a great deal in scale but has also been subject to dramatic fluctuations in recent decades. By nature, these investments are more liquid than are direct investment monies, which are tied up in physical assets. From 1989 to 1996, during the boom in emerging markets, such short-term, sometimes speculative flows from wealthy to developing countries grew tenfold (1,000 percent). New jobs were thus indirectly generated in the process because firms had greater financing to initiate new activities or expand older ones. Portfolio investment flows then declined 70 percent during 1997–1999, when a financial crisis struck Asia and moved on to Russia and parts of Latin America. This downturn had a major negative effect on employment, working conditions, and job security in the countries affected. And from 2001 to 2007, global stocks of portfolio investment, according to the International Monetary Fund (IMF) Coordinated Portfolio Investment Survey (CPIS) Data, increased threefold. After the effects of the worldwide recession began to be felt in 2008, growth in portfolio investment froze up. This contraction, along with the slowdown in world trade and the reduction in FDI, has affected employment worldwide.

Research data aside, a virulent debate about globalization's impact on workers is a mainstay of contemporary public discourse. Complex trade-offs among competing goals and different social groups are a frequent theme. UNCTAD—a traditional critic of TNCs—has documented that they generally provide better pay and benefits, more training, greater job security, and more stimulus for innovation by local business partners than do domestically owned firms. This is because they are generally larger and more competitive firms that place a premium on the stability provided by more institutionalized human resources practices. This does not, however, always extend to cultivating working relations with unions because transnational subsidiaries adapt closely to national regulatory frameworks. In many countries, particularly in the developing world, formal and informal restrictions exist on independent union organization and labor-management collective bargaining over the terms of employment. Moreover, TNCs are capital intensive, so they tend to generate fewer jobs per unit of investment or output. Furthermore, human resource advantages do not always hold true for export-oriented affiliates in such lower-end industries as apparel, toys, some consumer electronics, and industries in tax-favorable export processing zones (EPZs) in regions of developing nations, such as those in southern China and northern Mexico. In EPZs, pay, working conditions, and job security are notoriously poor; freedom of association is seldom respected; and the primary workers are typically young women and other recent arrivals from the countryside, where material conditions are even more dire than in the new manufacturing centers.

Mainstream economists recognize international trade's aggregate benefits of promoting growth in world output and living standards and of providing benefits to consumers through lower trade barriers. Even these economists, however, agree that definite distributional effects on employment are apparent—workers in export-oriented industries and regions gain, while those in import-sensitive areas lose, at least in the short term. Certain industries—such as the textile, shoe, and garment sectors in the United States and other developed countries—are particularly sensitive to import competition, due, in part, to their labor-intensity, smaller firm size, and slimmer profit margins. Displaced workers may or may not regain secure employment at similar wages in another firm or industry in the medium to long term; their fate depends on their age, skills, and the availability of government assistance. In the meantime, their families and communities may endure great hardship.

Mainstream economists also argue that in the long term technology, not trade, determines the demand for and price of labor. Critics, however, point to evidence that technological change interacts in complex ways with openness to trade, producing a growing skills gap in which less-educated and less-skilled workers increasingly fall behind the rest as their employability and wages decline. Competition with lower-wage competitors overseas helps spur firms to invest in labor-saving technology (such as automation and robotics); even well-trained industrial workers from many developing and transitional economies, however, can suffer greatly in the face of lower wages and more efficient production from overseas.

By this same line of reasoning, one of the effects of the globalization of production and of trade has been to shift the bargaining power dramatically from labor to capital—firms can increasingly make credible threats to move production overseas, away from union pressure. The evidence for this weakening of trade unionism is broad (see Table 3). The ILO found in its "World of Work Report 2008" that union density declined since the late 1980s in almost all of the fifty-one countries it surveyed. The U.S. Bureau of Labor Statistics (BLS) reported, in an article by Dutch labor sociologist Jelle Visser, over a 20-point loss in union density in Australia, New Zealand, and Austria.

Another alleged impact of increased global integration and related portfolio capital flows is growing pressure on the ability of national governments to finance welfare states. Pension programs, health care, education, housing, and other social benefits have been part of an implicit social contract with citizens since the Great Depression and World War II in wealthy countries and on a smaller scale in many transitional and some developing countries. Capital assets, the argument goes, will move to those geographical locations where they earn the highest return (and suffer the least taxation), whereas labor is by nature limited in its mobility; hence, contemporary tax burdens will increasingly fall on wage earners whom states can more easily reach through, say, income or sales taxes. With more of the tax burden shifted to workers, political support for welfare state programs, particularly those seen as benefiting only certain groups in society, erodes. Skeptics find this argument faulty, arguing that even under such constraints nation-states make different political choices about maintaining strong welfare states (as in France, Germany, and Scandinavia) or reducing them substantially (as in Great Britain and the United States).

Whatever the effects of globalization on labor, work, and social safety nets, the persistence of the problem of the working poor draws more and more attention from analysts, particularly at the ILO, which focuses much of its research on the working poor. In its January 2007 "Global Employment Trends Brief" (GET 1/07), the ILO cited an overall reduction in the percentage of working poor in the previous ten years. However, the current recession will either halt or reverse this progress. In its GET 5/09 report, the ILO projects—in its best-case scenario for 2009—a virtual standstill in the fight to reduce the ranks of the working poor, but in its worst-case scenario, an additional 233 million will be added to the ranks, amounting to 28.2 percent of the world's workers.

Policies and Programs

We can identify, roughly speaking, three general approaches to policies regarding labor and employment issues in a globalizing economy. First, the mainstream perspective is strongly pro-market, pushing for labor market flexibility and less intrusive government policies. It rejects any linkage between labor rights and international trade and investment agreements and advocates a deepening of globalization. Second, the reformist perspective calls for more active domestic and international measures to regulate global integration to cushion its social impact and give a voice to organizations that speak for workers. Third, the antiglobalization perspective advocates a radical rollback or halt to continuing global integration and the domestic and international policies that foster it. Critiques of unfettered globalization from the last two perspectives, as well as signs of a mounting social gap between winners and losers of globalization within and across countries, have motivated subtle but important shifts in mainstream positions in recent years.

Flexible labor markets has been the term used by mainstream policymakers and analysts for the type of reforms they advocate. They call for private transactions and decisions to dictate the terms of wages, skill formation, and the hiring and dismissal of workers. Such reforms seek to make it easier for employers to fire workers for economic motives, decentralize labor-management negotiations to the firm level, pressure unions not to strike, foster part-time and temporary work contracts, and reduce minimum wages and their role in wage setting in the broader economy.

Labor market flexibility has also been seen as a key ingredient of a larger package of broad economic reforms, sometimes referred to as the Washington Consensus, embodying greater economic openness, less government spending and intervention, and increasing privatization. Many developing and transitional economies have adopted some or all of these reforms because of pressures from the World Bank and the IMF, both of which are heavily influenced by the United States, and because of changing economic doctrines among governing elites (see DEVELOPMENT AID and INCOME INEQUALITY). Many Western European nations (with their strong welfare states and significant labor movements) as well as Japan (with its corporate-centered system of lifetime employment in large companies) have pursued labor market reforms only selectively or timidly, even while generally moving toward more market- and outward-oriented macroeconomic policies.

The 1990s brought alarming and growing signs, however, that Washington Consensus reforms, even though they restored some growth and healthy government finances in many countries, were leaving many citizens behind in transitional and developing economies. Creditor countries and international financial institutions, although not abandoning market-oriented macroeconomic and labor market policies, responded in part by pushing for more active pro-poor policies. They advocated targeted spending on at-risk groups (such as women and the rural poor), generating income through microentrepreneurship, and strengthening the property rights of poor people over productive assets (such as their residences, often lacking title), among other measures. Somewhat at odds with these new policies was a heightened focus on the need to restructure social security systems in response to growing pressures on government budgets from aging workforces. Among the proposed changes were such measures as limiting benefits, increasing retirement ages, and privatizing pensions. These new policy orientations are still decidedly pro-market.

On the employment front, lending policies began to focus on measures that would foster human capital, the stock of abilities and skills of the population, through reform and expansion of basic education, vocational training, and school-to-work transitions. On the financial front, limited initiatives exist to forgive the debt of a few highly indebted developing countries that are instituting rigorous market reforms, as well as some initial efforts to rethink the policies and roles of the World Bank and IMF in light of growing criticism from many quarters.

Reformists and antiglobalists raise strong practical and philosophical objections to the mainstream policy agenda for employment and labor reform. Reformists, however, sometimes agree with specific new pro-poor initiatives. They generally believe that countries can and should balance high levels of social protection and strong labor rights with efficiency, innovation, and quality, while antiglobalists fundamentally question the social efficacy of the market system. Whereas mainstream analysts insist that income testing or work requirements for particular social benefits are necessary to promote personal responsibility, their reformist and antiglobalists critics view such measures as punitive procedures that blame individuals for systemic socioeconomic problems, such as the growing scarcity of well-paying work for less-educated people in wealthy countries. Reformists and antiglobalists regard radical efforts to overhaul social security systems through privatization as undermining the principle of intergenerational solidarity—today's workers pay taxes to support yesterday's workers who are now retired—and creating a danger of widening inequalities. They also express skepticism about whether the best-conceived pro-poor policies can deal with the structural inequalities generated by market-oriented developed and unregulated global integration.

The Decent Work movement, championed by the ILO, sprang from similar lines of critique. The movement promotes the establishment of a minimum set of standards for working conditions across the globe. In recognition of its ninetieth anniversary, the ILO noted in an April 20, 2009, press release that

> [t]he contemporary expression of the ILO's historic mission is embodied in the concept of Decent Work, defined as opportunities for all women and men to obtain productive work in conditions of freedom, equity, security and human dignity. . . . It is centred on employment and enterprise, rights at work, social protection and social dialogue. This is the basis for a balanced approach to action that responds both to people's enduring need for decent work and to the imperative of productive growth and sustainable development.

A cornerstone of the ILO's efforts to reduce working poverty, the Decent Work model has been the focus of other high-profile organizations, such as Realising Rights: The Ethical Globalisation Initiative, founded in October 2002 by Mary Robinson, former president of Ireland and UN High Commissioner for Human Rights. Supporters of the Decent Work movement also gain impetus from the UN Millennium Development Goals (MDGs), which include achieving decent work for all, including women and young people, while halving poverty by 2015 (from 1990).

Two other broad areas of international activism and proposed reforms have emerged loosely from the reformist and antiglobalist perspectives. One is the effort to promote responsible labor (and other social) practices by globally active corporations through consumer-focused campaigns. Examples are the "clean clothes" movement in Europe and the burgeoning antisweatshop movement in the United States; fair trade initiatives (see WORLD TRADE) to promote sales by small-scale, developing-country producers (for instance, in the coffee sector) that do not pass through powerful TNC intermediaries; and campaigns for socially responsible investing that take into account corporations' labor and other practices in choosing stocks. These efforts, in turn, have spurred initiatives by individual companies to improve their images through voluntary codes of conduct—called corporate social responsibility—as well as initiatives by governments, international organizations, and unionists and other advocates to create industrywide codes, such as the Fair Labor Association in the U.S. apparel industry.

Corporations have also responded to or contributed to intergovernmental and governmental initiatives that seek to elaborate acceptable labor practices, such as the ILO's 1996 Tripartite Declaration on Multinational Enterprises and Social Policy, which calls for respect for worker rights of association and bargaining, and the Organisation for Economic Cooperation and Development's (OECD) 2000 revised Guidelines for Multinational Enterprises, which call for consultation with worker representatives and governments in cases of mass layoffs and facility closures. The 2009 negotiations regarding the fate of the U.S. auto-industry companies General Motors and Chrysler, even though undertaken in the midst of a massive economic crisis, are a high-profile example of such tripartite discussions. Moreover, activist campaigns around the issue of child labor in export manufacturing, particularly in South Asia, helped give impetus to the 1999 adoption by the ILO of the Convention concerning the Prohibition and Immediate Action for the Elimination of Worst Forms of Child Labour.

Many trade unionists and antisweatshop activists criticize such efforts as well intentioned but limited only to the most egregious abuses, such as unsafe work environments, forced overtime, and gender discrimination. These efforts fall short on two counts: the independence and rigor of the outside monitoring of corporate labor practices can be limited, and some voluntary codes and admonitions omit the core labor right of freedom of association and avoid such economic issues as payment of "living wages." Loftier labor standards are set by initiatives such as the Worker Rights Consortium in the United States, and in a different way, by company framework agreements between international trade unions and a dozen or so European-based TNCs.

Another related area of activism and debate concerns efforts to rewrite the rules of major institutions of global and regional economic integration. Calls for the explicit linkage of labor (and other social) standards to international trade and investment agreements have grown in the past decade and have had some effect in shaping the debate. Under a European Union directive, large European transnational companies have recently implemented work councils that represent all the firms' workers regardless of national boundaries. In 1993, Canada, Mexico, and the United States negotiated side agreements to the North American Free Trade Agreement (NAFTA) to promote the enforcement of domestic environmental and labor laws (see Case Study—North American Free Trade Agreement: Free Trade with Mexico and the Uncertain Effects on U.S. Labor and Employment). U.S. proposals made later in the decade for a WTO working group to study labor standards and trade, in large part a response to pressure from unionists and other labor advocates, continue to be rejected by other WTO member states, particularly the developing countries, which fear that they are a protectionist attempt to keep their cheaper goods out of rich markets. Labor standards are one of the several issues causing problems in the advancement of new international and regional trade agreements.

In the United States, advocates' efforts to pressure for labor issues in the formulation of trade policy have had mixed results. Connecting labor rights to access by developing countries to the U.S. market is typically invoked only selectively and on the basis of broader diplomatic and political considerations. Only countries with poor relations with the United States tend to be singled out. Although a bilateral free-trade agreement (FTA) reached with Jordan in 2000 and ratified in 2001 was seen as a pioneering achievement because it explicitly incorporated core labor standards as the basis for greater bilateral market access, the agreement may not live up to the standards written into it. For instance, complaints in 2006 about labor conditions in Jordanian enterprises located in Jordanian export zones have left observers dismayed about the FTA's efficacy. Furthermore, the advocacy labor standards enacted in the U.S.-Jordanian FTA were not reproduced in later trade agreements initiated by the George W. Bush administration. A bilateral FTA with Peru, for instance, ratified by Congress in 2007, left critics concerned about its effects on issues such as child labor, and the FTAs with Chile and Singapore (both ratified in 2004), according to the Labor Advisory Committee (whose function by law is to advise the president and Congress on proposed FTAs), would undermine workers' rights, protections for guestworkers, and domestic labor markets.

Other efforts are in the works to improve labor and employment conditions. Initiatives for trade union revitalization include merging competing unions into larger entities, involving national confederations of unions in national negotiations, and reaching out to previously underrepresented segments of the workforce. Gauging the success of such efforts, however, is premature. Another strand of activity combines development research and policy as exemplified by the ILO International Institute for Labour Studies. This effort focuses on policies and strategies that play on the tendency of particular economic activities to cluster in specific geographical locations but to be linked to global production, trading, and sales networks. Local policymakers, unions, industry associations, and activists from nongovernmental organizations (NGOs) are urged to foster development alliances that can upgrade the position of localities and regions within global industries, moving them into higher-value-added activities with more stable long-term growth. Such an upgrade would generate more and better employment, improved working conditions, and an expanded tax base.

Regional Summaries

Employment and labor trends exhibit some common tendencies in relation to globalization but with significant differences from region to region. And the effects of the economic recession begun in 2007 have affected employment in all regions, although to varying degrees.

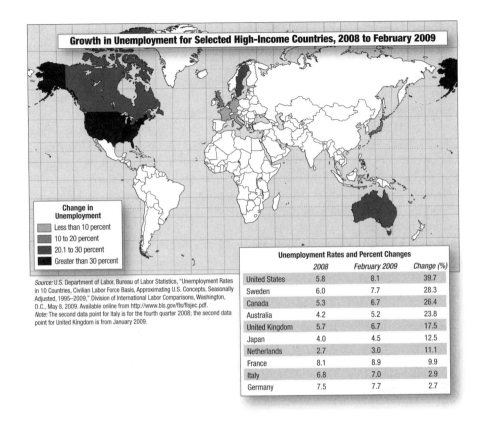

Growth in Unemployment for Selected High-Income Countries, 2008 to February 2009

Change in Unemployment
- Less than 10 percent
- 10 to 20 percent
- 20.1 to 30 percent
- Greater than 30 percent

Source: U.S. Department of Labor, Bureau of Labor Statistics, "Unemployment Rates in 10 Countries, Civilian Labor Force Basis, Approximating U.S. Concepts, Seasonally Adjusted, 1995–2009," Division of International Labor Comparisons, Washington, D.C., May 8, 2009. Available online from http://www.bls.gov/fls/flsjec.pdf.
Note: The second data point for Italy is for the fourth quarter 2008; the second data point for United Kingdom is from January 2009.

Unemployment Rates and Percent Changes			
	2008	February 2009	Change (%)
United States	5.8	8.1	39.7
Sweden	6.0	7.7	28.3
Canada	5.3	6.7	26.4
Australia	4.2	5.2	23.8
United Kingdom	5.7	6.7	17.5
Japan	4.0	4.5	12.5
Netherlands	2.7	3.0	11.1
France	8.1	8.9	9.9
Italy	6.8	7.0	2.9
Germany	7.5	7.7	2.7

The information and data in these regional summaries come from various sources, including the ILO GET reports; the 2006 report by Jelle Visser, "Union Membership Statistics in 24 Countries"; data prepared by the BLS on May 8, 2009, on unemployment rates in 10 countries; the BLS table "Unemployment Rates in 10 Countries, Civilian Labor Force Basis, Approximating U.S. Concepts, Seasonally Adjusted, 1995–2009" (on the BLS Web site); and the International Labour Office online database, LABORSTA Internet.

North America

Although the United States and Canada share a partnership (along with Mexico) in the NAFTA, their employment and work culture diverge considerably. The United States stands out not just from Canada but from many other industrialized countries in the world in the extent of the flexibility of its labor markets, which are built on the ease with which employers can hire and fire workers; comparatively weak unemployment and other benefits and an employer-based health-care system that together strongly discourage long periods of unemployment; and restrictions on labor organizing. Whereas other nations have lower union membership rates (see Table 3), the U.S. union density rate, reported in Visser's article, was only 12.4 percent, compared to the very high levels in the Scandinavian countries (the highest being Sweden at 78 percent). Even though the United States (due in part to its flexible labor markets) was considered a job-creating machine during the boom years of the 1990s and again during 2003–early 2007, the quality of these jobs and the effect of employment growth on overall well-being are in question. Critics point to the stubbornly high levels of working poor, particularly among blacks and Latinos, people in the inner cities, and female-headed households; the hollowing out of the manufacturing-based middle class; the highest rates of inequality of wealth and income among industrialized countries; and the eroding inflation-adjusted minimum wages and income for workers.

Just to the north, Canada has a markedly different institutional and cultural mind-set. Canada has much lower poverty rates; considerably higher rates of union density (28.4 percent), although lower than much of Europe; and a much more extensive welfare state, including universal health care. Efforts to pare back state social spending, however, have gained ground in recent years.

The decline in the trade unionism is one trait shared by both the United States and Canada (and mirrored across much of the world). Union density dropped by 11 points from 1970 to 2003 in the United States and by 6.5 points in Canada.

The recent worldwide economic crisis has seriously affected both the United States and Canada. The BLS May 8 data show unemployment increasing in the United States from an overall 2008 level of 5.8 percent to a March 2009 level of 8.5 percent. The figures for Canada are a bit less severe: 5.3 percent in 2008 and 6.9 percent in March 2009.

Latin America

The phenomenon of jobless growth is a problem for Latin America. Although the region experienced upsurges in annual GDP growth rates in 1990–1997, employment grew at only 2.2 percent, 0.7 points less than it had during the previous decade, according to Barbara Stallings and Wilson Peres in *Growth, Employment and Equity*. Job creation showed a slight improvement in the mid-2000s (after the downturn of the worldwide economy following the September 2001 terrorist attacks): in 2004–2006, as the region's economic output increased by over 4 percent per year, small upticks in labor market performance were felt, including a fractional drop in the unemployment rate from 8.1 to 8.0 percent. The slowness of the economies in Latin America, however, to reap fuller benefits from the growth in the mid-2000s is due largely to the ongoing implementation of more flexible labor markets. Combined with increased competition for domestic firms from imports and increased pressure for them to cut costs to be competitive in export markets, this trend encouraged employment shedding through restructuring in the privatized and tradable goods sectors and in the state bureaucracy, long-time bastions of union strength. The layoffs resulted, in turn, in a general decline in union density rates. Two other factors also probably help explain the region's disappointing employment picture: (1) weaknesses in human capital formation in terms of basic education and vocational training and (2) competition policies to promote adjustment by domestic firms plus greater labor market flexibility in ease of hiring and firing.

One recent positive outcome in Latin America is the improvement in women's employment prospects. Women's participation in the labor market grew from 41.5 percent in 1996 to 47 percent in 2006. Nevertheless, women still participate in the informal sector to a disproportionate degree, and a female unemployment rate of over 10 percent in 2006 reveals a gap of 2 percent in opportunities for women in the labor market.

The effects of the current economic downturn have begun to be felt across the region. The ILO, in its GET 5/09 update, projects that the economic output of some of the major countries of the region—including Argentina, Brazil, Venezuela, and Mexico—will contract; Mexico alone is expected to lose 3.7 percent of its productive output in 2009. This regional downturn will affect many sectors, particularly tourism and related activities in the Caribbean and commodity-related industries in South American countries.

Europe

Europe has a diverse set of employment and labor trajectories as a result of national differences in the levels of development and economic integration. Albeit with considerable national variations, European Union member states from northern, Western, and to some extent southern Europe have the world's most developed welfare states, the most institutionalized systems of union rights and collective bargaining, and the most tightly regulated labor markets. Persistently high unemployment levels have been a major issue since the early 1990s, and in 2003, the unemployment rate for major European economies was at 7.9 percent. In 2006, despite four years of sustained economic growth, unemployment in many of the region's economies—such as the Czech Republic, France, Germany, Italy, and Poland—remained higher than 7.5 percent. Slow economic growth, high wages and high payroll taxes to fund social programs, and increased competition from lower-cost manufacturers in Asia are among the causes widely cited for European unemployment. The implementation of the labor market "flexibilization" urged by conservative observers is controversial, particularly since the two countries that have pursued it most forcefully since the 1980s—Spain and the United Kingdom—have suffered on the unemployment front as well.

Most countries on the continent have resisted reforms in protective labor laws. In lieu of flexible labor reforms, these countries have variously tinkered with strengthening active labor market policies, such as retraining and job-search assistance, and existing bargaining mechanisms. Union density rates in the major economies of Europe vary to a wide degree, although they are high compared to industrial economies in the rest of the world. In the European Union as a whole, the percentage of union membership among workers was

26.3 percent in 2002, with the Scandinavian countries at the high end of the range (and Sweden the highest, with 78 percent) and France at an anomalous low of 8.3 (explained, perhaps, by the extensive guarantees of benefits and rights given to French workers through legal protections instituted by the government).

The Russian Federation, the countries of Eastern and central Europe, and the Baltic countries have suffered the social dislocations of "marketization" and integration into the global capitalist economy following the collapse of the Soviet Union in 1991. The Balkan states have also suffered economically from interethnic strife. Some countries clearly fared better than others in attracting foreign investment, creating market institutions, and stabilizing democratic structures, which are necessary (if not essential) conditions for retaining and creating jobs. After the increases in unemployment and poverty resulting from the tumultuous changes, labor market indicators had begun to stabilize by the mid-2000s. In the ten-year period ending in 2006, unemployment dropped from 9.7 to 9.3 percent, still well above the average in the European Union and Western Europe as a whole. In the face of persistently high unemployment, the generally well-educated workforce has opted for outward migration, resulting in a brain drain that many observers fear will limit future economic growth.

The current economic downturn has hit labor markets in Western Europe hard. In the first quarter of 2009, in Spain alone, the number of unemployed increased by over 800,000, and in Sweden the unemployment rate has grown in three short months from 6.5 to 7.9 percent. In central and Eastern Europe and the European republics of the former Soviet Union, the effects were as drastic, if not more so. In the Russian Federation, whose economy was especially buffeted by the downturns in world oil markets, the unemployment rate rose from 5.3 in September 2008 to 8.5 percent in February 2009. In its GET 5/09 update, the ILO projected a worst-case scenario for 2009 of a possible 35 percent increase in unemployment.

North Africa and the Middle East

Unemployment rates for the economies in North Africa and the Middle East are the highest in the world, representing a long-standing trend in the region. According to the ILO 1/07 GET brief, the region's unemployment rate was 12.2 percent, virtually unchanged from its 12.1 percent rate in 1993. This high rate, however, masks a considerable range, with Kuwait consistently recording some of the lowest rates and Algeria, along with the West Bank and the Gaza Strip, recording some of the highest. Not only is unemployment high, but labor force participation in 2006 was the lowest of any region in the world—53.9 percent of the country's total working-age population is employed, with women disproportionately represented in that share. Indeed, women are largely shut out of the labor market; only 30 percent of working-age women are employed.

In the Gulf States, such as Saudi Arabia and the United Arab Emirates, guestworkers have been a major presence in the labor force. Facing rising unemployment, governments in the this area have undertaken plans to create opportunities for their native populations, such as Saudi Arabia's Five-Year Development Plan, 2000–2004, which had as its goal the creation of 817,000 jobs for Saudis by 2005. As the working-age populations in the region are expected to increase substantially in the future, such Arabization of the workforce will become more important.

Given its reliance on the worldwide oil market, demand for which is affected by declining economies across the world, the region will not be immune from the employment effects of the current downturn, despite the fact that it has long been considered relatively insulated due to its oil wealth. The ILO projects an increase of 25 percent in unemployment in its worst-case scenario and an increase of 13 percent in its best-case scenario.

Sub-Saharan Africa

Although economic indicators have been stabilizing and even improving in sub-Saharan Africa as the gains in human development efforts (including increasing literacy and decreasing infant mortality) and peace agreements in many of the region's troubled areas produce economic dividends, the gains have not yet translated into consistent or comprehensive improvements in employment and working conditions. In the ten-year period 1996–2006, according to the ILO 1/07 GET brief, nineteen of the forty-two countries for which data were available showed annual increases in total economic output of over 4 percent per year, and eleven of those countries showed increases of 2–4 percent. Despite these growth rates, a reliance on extractive industries, on subsistence or smallholder agriculture, and on informal-sector livelihoods limits the progress of workers in the region. These factors, along with limitations on educational opportunities, bind the region to low levels of worker productivity.

This underperformance in terms of productivity is one of the main factors in the extent of working poverty in the region. According to the ILO GET 5/09 projections of the effects of the current economic downturn on the region, the number of working poor will increase, reversing the positive trends established earlier in the decade. Ironically, however, the fact that workers in many countries of the region rely on subsistence agriculture and informal domestically oriented economic activity will keep the region somewhat cushioned from the effects of the current economic crisis. That said, some of the more outward-looking economies, including South Africa and Botswana, could experience negative economic growth and related increases in unemployment. Another aspect of the current globalized downturn will affect the region: developed economies outside the region that experience economic contraction may reduce their commitments to official development assistance (ODA) and other forms of aid supporting initiatives that target education, technology, and other factors geared toward enhancing productivity. Such reductions in aid may indeed hobble the efforts of many countries in the region to improve their human and workforce development.

Asia

Economic trends across Asia and the Pacific have been uneven on a country-by-country basis despite the economic dynamism seen in much of the region as a result of global and intraregional integration. Several countries experienced the downside of global integration in the financial crises in the late 1990s, which were followed by a global economic slowdown that eroded demand for the region's exports and left employment security and creation at risk.

That said, the economies in East Asia, according to the ILO 1/07 GET brief, experienced growth rates of 8 percent or higher in 2002–2006. China leads the way as it continues its rapid process of capitalist reform and industrialization, which is built to a significant degree on direct investment from Japan and other Asian economies. Its average annual growth rate alone in this period was over 10 percent. Employment and incomes have been rapidly rising for many Chinese, but this trend is accompanied by large social dislocations and creeping social inequalities. India, just behind China in terms of total population, has opened up to large-scale foreign investment and moved to become more active as an exporter. It has led the other economies in South Asia, which experienced annual growth rates of 8.2 percent in 2005 and 7.9 percent in 2006.

Despite the high growth rates in China and, to a lesser extent, India, working poverty in the region is high. In South Asia alone, even though overall unemployment is relatively low, the working poor (mostly involved in the informal sector) account for approximately 40 percent of the total employed population.

The current global crisis is having its effects on the region, with East Asia, according to the ILO GET 5/09 update, facing a likely drop in GDP growth rates from 7.4 percent in 2008 to 4.0 percent in 2009. South Asia will probably experience similar reductions in economic output, from 7.0 percent to 4.3 percent. Southeast Asia's economic output is expected to contract by 0.7 percent in 2009, with Singapore's portion alone expected to contract by 10 percent. This downturn will have huge effects on unemployment. The ILO projects that unemployment will increase by 2.9 million workers in East Asia alone, resulting in a rise in the unemployment rate from 4.3 percent in 2008 to 5.8 percent in 2009, under the ILO worst-case scenario. Due to China's massive stimulus package, the East Asia numbers, however, are hard to predict. The ILO projects a more modest effect on both South Asia and Southeast Asia's unemployment. In the worst-case scenario, South Asia's unemployment rate will rise from 5.0 in 2008 to 5.6 percent in 2009, and Southeast Asia's unemployment will rise from 5.4 to 6.2 percent.

Pacific Rim

The major economies of the Pacific Rim—Australia, Japan, New Zealand, and South Korea—have increased their global economic ties since the 1980s, particularly through increased trade and investment links with Asia.

Australia's economic growth rate of 2.9 percent annually in the 1980s and 1990s outpaced population growth, even with substantial influxes of immigrants from Asia and increases in the labor force. This translated into solid gains in GDP per capita, which slowly converted into significant gains on the employment front, including a considerable reduction in unemployment. According to the ILO's LABORSTA database, Australia's unemployment rate dropped from a high of 10. 5 percent in 1992 to 4.4 percent in 2007. New Zealand dropped from a high of 10.9 percent in 1991 to a low of 3.6 percent in 2007.

Japan in this period charted a considerably different course. In the early to mid-1990s, a banking crisis, based on a boom-bust cycle in the real estate market, hit the country. The full effects of the crisis hit consumers and workers in 1997. Japan's traditionally very low unemployment rate—below 3 percent in the 1980s—hit 4.8 percent by the end of the 1990s. Aggravated in turn by the banking and currency crisis that hit its Southeast Asian trading and investment partners in 1997 (a crisis caused to some degree by Japan's own troubles and responses to it), Japan's economy continued to suffer. By 2003, unemployment had reached a peak of 5.3 percent, according to BLS May 8 report. And the shock of the current recession has forced unemployment back up; by March 2009, the BLS estimated Japan's unemployment rate to be close to 5 percent. Throughout these crises, however, the rates of unemployment have been low compared to other industrialized countries, reflecting a tradition of highly loyal employer-employee relationships and, at the highest corporate levels, honored de facto lifetime employment. Evidence (more anecdotal than statistical) points to the weakening of those lifelong employment assurances in Japan.

Union density varies across the major economies of the Pacific Rim. In the mid-1980s, the density of union membership was in the 40 percent range, moderately high by the standards of industrialized countries, but it had fallen by roughly half in New Zealand and by 30 percent in Australia by the mid-1990s, according to *World Labour Report, 1997–98*. This reflected a heavy loss of manufacturing jobs because of trade liberalization, declining competitiveness, and weak government support for the retention of such industries. By the early 2000s, according to Jelle Visser, union density had dropped to 23 percent in Australia and 22 percent in New Zealand. South Korea's rate has dropped only a small amount, from historically low levels of 12.6 percent in 1970 to 11.2 percent in 2003.

The effects of the current global economic crisis are quite strong throughout the region. Unemployment rates in Australia, for instance, rose from an overall 2008 level of 4.2 percent to 5.7 percent in March 2009, and in Japan, unemployment rose from 4 percent in 2008 to 4.9 percent in March 2009.

Data

Table 1   Ratification of the Core Labor Rights Conventions as of 2008

Convention title and number	Year adopted	Number of countries ratified, 2001	Number of countries ratified, 2008
Forced or Compulsory Labor (29)	1930	158[a]	173[a]
Freedom of Association and Protection of the Right to Organise (87)	1948	137	149
Right to Organise and Collective Bargaining (98)	1949	149	159
Equal Remuneration for Work of Equal Value (100)	1951	153	166
Discrimination in Employment and Occupation (111)	1958	151	168
Minimum Age for Employment (138)	1973	111	153
Elimination of the Worst Forms of Child Labour (182)	1999	93[a]	169[a]

Source: International Labour Organisation, "International Labour Standards," available at: http://webfusion.ilo.org/public/db/standards/normes/appl/index.cfm?lang=EN (accessed June 2009).

[a]Ratified by the United States.

Table 2   Female Participation in Workforce: Adult Female Employment to Population Ratios, 1998–2008 (%)

Region	1998	2000	2002	2004	2006	2008[a]
World total	51.9	52.2	52.4	52.5	53.1	53.1
Developed economies and European Union	48.3	49.0	48.9	49.4	50.3	50.4
Central and Southeastern Europe[b] and CIS	49.0	48.3	49.8	49.7	50.1	51.0
East Asia	70.0	70.	70.2	70.0	69.9	69.3
Southeast Asia and the Pacific	59.9	59.8	59.1	58.7	58.4	58.7
South Asia	36.7	36.8	36.9	36.5	37.7	37.6
Latin America and the Caribbean	44.2	46.2	48.0	49.9	51.9	52.6
Middle East	20.5	21.6	21.9	23.3	24.0	24.7
North Africa	22.6	23.1	23.3	25.0	26.3	27.0
Sub-Saharan Africa	60.8	60.4	60.9	61.5	62.3	62.9

Source: International Labour Office, *Global Employment Trends for Women* (Geneva: International Labour Organization, 2009), 38, available at: http://www.ilo.org/wcmsp5/groups/public/---dgreports/---dcomm/documents/publication/wcms_103456.pdf.

Note: CIS, Commonwealth of Independent States.

[a]Preliminary data.

[b]Non-EU countries.

Table 3 Trade Union Density in Selected Industrialized Countries as a Share of Employed Wage and Salary Workers

Country	Year	Density (%)	Change since 1970 (percentage points)
North America			
United States	2003	12.4	−11.1
Canada	2003	28.4	−6.5
Western Europe			
European Union	2002	26.3	−11.5
Germany	2003	22.6	−9.5
France	2003	8.3	−13.4
Italy	2003	33.7	−3.3
United Kingdom	2003	29.3	−15.5
Ireland	2003	35.3	−17.9
Finland	2003	74.1	22.8
Sweden	2003	78.0	10.3
Norway	2003	55.3	− 3.5
Denmark	2003	70.4	10.1
Netherlands	2003	22.3	−14.2
Belgium	2002	55.4	13.3
Spain	2003	16.3	3.4
Switzerland	2001	17.8	−11.2
Austria	2002	35.4	−27.3
Central and Eastern Europe			
Hungary	2001	19.9	−43.6[a]
Czech Republic	2001	27.0	−19.3[a]
Slovak Republic	2001	36.1	−21.2[a]
Poland	2001	14.7	−18.2[a]
Pacific Rim			
Australia	2003	22.9	−27.3
New Zealand	2002	22.1	−33.1
Japan	2003	19.7	−15.4
South Korea	2003	11.2	−1.5

Source: Jelle Visser, "Union Membership Statistics in 24 Countries," *Monthly Labor Review* 129, no. 1 (2006): 38–49, available at: http://www.bls.gov/opub/mlr/2006/01/art3full.pdf.

[a]Change since 1990.

Case Study— North American Free Trade Agreement: Free Trade with Mexico and the Uncertain Effects on U.S. Labor and Employment

In 1992, the governments of Canada, Mexico, and the United States entered into the NAFTA, eliminating most trade barriers among them and creating the world's largest free-trade area. Proponents argued that it would expand prosperity and employment in all three countries. Labor, consumer, and environmental advocates criticized the agreement on the grounds that it covered only trade and investment, ignoring such issues as labor rights, environmental protection, and democracy and human rights in Mexico. To ensure congressional approval of the agreement, the incoming administration of Bill Clinton nego-tiated labor and environmental side agreements to the basic text in 1993. The North American Agreement on Labor Cooperation (NAALC), the labor side agreement, was criticized at the time as lacking enforcement capacity in the form of trade sanctions, but it was nonetheless novel in establishing a formal link between a wide variety of labor rights, including for migrant laborers, and trade and in committing the three member nations to respect existing domes-tic labor rights.

As the agreement neared its ten-year anniversary, many studies of its effects were undertaken. The Congressional Research Service (CRS) Report for Congress, "NAFTA at Ten: Lessons from Recent Studies" (issued February 13, 2004), however, states that most of these studies found "NAFTA's effect on the U.S. and Mexican economies to be modest at most." The report describes a score of problems relating to measuring benefits that can be unequivocally ascribed to the agreement. Even in the area of increased trade and investment across the U.S.-Mexican border, the exact effects are hard to ascertain. Between 1994 and 2003, U.S. exports to Mexico rose by 91 percent and U.S. imports from Mexico surged by 179 percent; however, the report concludes, these increases began prior to the enactment of the agreement. The Congressional Budget Office (CBO) study, one of the four analyzed by the CRS report, found that 85 percent of the growth in U.S. exports and 91 percent of the growth in U.S. imports would have occurred despite NAFTA's implementation.

The effect of NAFTA on employment is perhaps the most hotly contested issue in the NAFTA debate, a debate revisited with great publicity during the 2008 presidential campaign in the United States. Again, however, the accumu-lated evidence is still unclear. The 2004 CRS report credited little if any of the changes in aggregate levels of U.S. or Mexican employment to the agreement. One of the studies that the CRS analyzed, conducted by the Carnegie Endow-ment for International Peace, suggested that, if certain assumptions were changed, NAFTA may have resulted in a net increase in U.S. employment of 270,000 jobs, a very small increase by any accounting.

Not surprisingly, representatives of the trade union constituency, including the American Federation of Labor–Congress of Industrial Organizations (AFL-CIO), and pro-worker think tanks and globalization watchdog groups, including the Economic Policy Institute and Global Trade Watch (part of Public Citizen), have cited negative effects on U.S. employment. For instance, "NAFTA at Year Twelve" testimony submitted on September 11, 2006, by AFL-CIO Policy Director Thea M. Lee to the U.S. Senate Subcommittee on Trade pronounced NAFTA a failure on not just employment but increased trade. Citing ballooning trade deficits with Mexico (which the CBO study says cannot be affirmatively attributed to NAFTA) and job losses in the half-million range (a number certified by the U.S. Labor Department in 2002), Lee pro-claims NAFTA's promise for win-win outcomes to be a failure. Perhaps the most damning trend that Lee pointed out is the continuing diminishment of the power of U.S. labor, including the concentration of consultancy functions relating to the evaluation of NAFTA and other potential FTAs in the hands of governments and corporations.

The conflicting rhetoric on its own is confusing and the political context is highly charged, but that the true effects of NAFTA, at least in its early stages, are so hard to establish makes the case for the agreement hard to make. Especially as the United States attempts to establish FTAs with other countries, this difficulty will plague both proponents and critics of such trade liberalization efforts for the foreseeable future.

Biographical Sketches

Jagdish Bhagwati is a professor of economics at Columbia University who has written widely in defense of multilateral free trade unencumbered by formal labor rights and other social linkages, stressing in particular trade's benefits for developing countries but also defending their right to regulate capital flows for national development. He has been a special adviser to the United Nations on globalization and an external adviser to the WTO.

Juan Somavia is secretary-general of the ILO. He has raised the ILO's profile, criticizing those who "see workers' rights as an obstacle to growth" and insisting that such rights are "essential to making the global economy work for everyone." Particular initiatives have been the establishment of the ILO's World Commission on the Social Dimension of Globalization in 2002 and the implementation of the ILO's Decent Work agenda, enshrined in the ILO's 2008 adoption of the Declaration on Social Justice for a Fair Globalization.

Lori Wallach is the director of Global Trade Watch, a division of the Washington-based group Public Citizen. She has been a leading articulator of domestic and international opposition to trade agreements lacking social protection for workers and the environment. Wallach has also lobbied intensely to prevent U.S. presidents from gaining fast-track authority that would enable them to negotiate international trade agreements not subject to congressional amendment and considered only on an up-or-down basis.

Directory

American Federation of Labor–Congress of Industrial Organizations (AFL-CIO), 815 16th Street NW, Washington, D.C. 20006. Telephone: (202) 637-5000; Web: http://www.aflcio.org/.
Umbrella organization of U.S. unions.

Fair Labor Association, 1707 L Street NW, Suite 200, Washington, D.C. 20036. Telephone: (202) 898-1000; email: info@fairlabor.org; Web: http://www.fairlabor.org. *Organization that administers an industrywide conduct and monitoring system for the apparel industry.*

Institute of Development Studies, University of Sussex, Brighton BN1 9RE, United Kingdom. Telephone: (44) 127 360 6261; email: ids@ids.ac.uk; Web: http://www.ids.ac.uk.
Leading international center for academic research on Third World economic and social development.

International Confederation of Free Trade Unions, 5 Boulevard Roi Albert II, Bte 1, 1210 Brussels, Belgium. Telephone: (32) 2 224 0211; email: internetpo@icftu .org; Web: http://www.icftu.org.
International grouping of 221 national trade union confederations and other union organizations from 148 countries representing 155 million workers.

International Organisation of Employers, 26 Chemin de Joinville, 1216 Cointrin/ Geneva, Switzerland. Telephone: (41) 22 929 0000; email: ioe@ioe-emp.org; Web: http://www.ioe-emp.org.
Confederation of 132 national employer organizations in 129 countries.

Office of the United States Trade Representative, 600 17th Street NW, Washington, D.C. 20508. Telephone: (202) 395-3230; email: contactustr@ustr.gov; Web: http://www.ustr.gov.
Executive branch agency charged with negotiating international trade agreements.

Organisation of Economic Cooperation and Development (OECD), Directorate for Education, Employment, Labour and Social Affairs, 2 Rue André Pascal, F-75775 Paris Cedex 16, France. Telephone: (331) 4524 8200; email: els.contact@ oecd.org; Web: http://www.oecd.org.
International organization of the leading industrialized nations.

Realizing Rights, 271 Madison Avenue, Suite 1007, New York, N.Y. 10016. Telephone: (212) 895-8080; email: info@eginitiative.org; Web: http://www.realizingrights.org.
Worldwide NGO advocating the centrality of human rights and the needs for the world's poorest and most vulnerable in global governance and policymaking.

School of Industrial and Labor Relations, Cornell University, Ives Hall, Ithaca, N.Y. 14853. Web: http://www.ilr.cornell.edu.
Center for research, education, and outreach on issues of employment relations and human resources.

Worker Rights Consortium, 5 Thomas Circle NW, 5th Floor, Washington, D.C. 20005. Telephone: (202) 387-4884; email: wrc@workersrights.org; Web: http://www .workersrights.org.
Organization formed by university antisweatshop activists and administrators to promote worker rights.

World Trade Organization (WTO), Centre William Rappard, Rue de Lausanne 154, CH-1211 Geneva 21, Switzerland. Telephone (41) 22 739 51 11; email: enquiries@ wto.org; Web: http://www.wto.org.
Organization dealing with the rules of trade among nations.

Further Research

Books

Bhagwati, Jagdish N. *A Stream of Windows: Unsettling Reflections on Trade, Immigration, and Democracy.* Cambridge, Mass.: MIT Press, 1998.

Candland, Christopher, and Rudra Sil, eds. *The Politics of Labor in a Global Age: Continuity and Change in Late-Industrializing and Post-Socialist Economies.* Oxford and New York: Oxford University Press, 2001.

Held, David, et al. *Global Transformations: Politics, Economics, and Culture.* Stanford: Stanford University Press, 1999.

International Labour Office. *International Labour Standards: A Workers' Education Manual.* 4th ed. Geneva: International Labour Organisation, 1998.

Pollin, Robert, et al. *A Measure of Fairness: The Economics of Living Wages and Minimum Wages in the United States.* Ithaca, N.Y.: ILR Press, 2008.

Rodrik, Dani. *Has Globalization Gone Too Far?* Washington, D.C.: Institute for International Economics, 1997.

Ross, Andrew, ed. *No Sweat: Fashion, Free Trade and the Rights of Garment Workers.* New York: Verso, 1997.

Sassen, Saskia. *Globalization and Its Discontents.* New York: New Press, 1998.

Stallings, Barbara, and Wilson Peres. *Growth, Employment, and Equity: The Impact of the Economic Reforms in Latin America and the Caribbean.* Washington, D.C.: United Nations Economic Commission for Latin America and the Caribbean and Brookings Institution Press, 2000.

Articles and Reports

Compa, Lance. "The Multilateral Agreement on Investment and International Labor Rights: A Failed Connection." *Cornell International Law Journal* no. 10 (1998).

Evans, Peter. "Fighting Marginalization with Transnational Networks: Counter-Hegemonic Globalization." *Contemporary Sociology: A Journal of Reviews* 29, no. 1 (January 2000): 230–241.

"The Face of Globalism: A Special Report on Globalization and Its Critics." *American Prospect* 12, no. 2 (2001), insert.

Featherstone, Liza, and Doug Henwood. "Clothes Encounters: Activists and Economists Clash over Sweatshops." *Lingua Franca* 11, no. 2 (2001): 27–33.

Gereffi, Gary, Ronie Garcia-Johnson, and Erika Sasser. "The NGO-Industrial Complex." *Foreign Policy* 125 (July–August 2001): 56–66.

"Global Capitalism: Can It Be Made to Work Better?" *Business Week,* November 6, 2000, 72–99.

Hornbeck, J. F. "NAFTA at Ten: Lessons from Recent Studies." Congressional Research Service Report for Congress. February 13, 2004. Available at: http://fpc.state.gov/documents/organization/34486.pdf.

Human Rights Watch. "Trading Away Rights: The Unfulfilled Promise of NAFTA's Labor Side Agreement." April 2001. Available at: http://www.hrw.org/reports/2001/nafta.

———. "Unfair Advantage: Workers' Freedom of Association in the United States under International Human Rights Standards." August 2000. Available at: http://www.hrw.org/reports/2000/uslabor.

International Labour Office. "Global Employment Trends." International Labour Organisation, Geneva, 1990–2008.

———. "World Employment Report." International Labour Organisation, Geneva, 2003–2009.

———. "World Labour Report." International Labour Organisation, Geneva, 1990–2000.

International Labor Organisation. "ILO Says Job Losses Are Increasing Due to Economic Crisis." ILO Press Release, May 28, 2009, ILO/09/31. Available at:

http://www.ilo.org/global/About_the_ILO/Media_and_public_information/ Press_releases/lang—en/WCMS_106525/index.htm.

———."ILO Warns of Cuts in Real Wages for Millions of Workers in 2009—Declines Follow Decade in Which Wages Failed to Keep Pace with Economic Growth." ILO Press Release, November 25, 2008, ILO/08/55. Available at: http://www.ilo.org/ global/About_the_ILO/Media_and_public_information/Press_releases/lang— en/WCMS_100783/index.htm.

International Monetary Fund. "Investment Portfolio: Coordinated Portfolio Investment Survey (CPIS) Data, Global Tables." Available at: http://www.imf.org/external/np/ sta/pi/global.htm.

Labor Advisory Committee (LAC) for Trade Negotiations and Trade Policy. "Report to the President, the Congress and the United States Trade Representative on the U.S.-Chile and U.S.-Singapore Free Trade Agreements." February 28, 2003. Available at: http://www.citizenstrade.org/pdf/chile_sing_lac.pdf.

Lee, Thea M. "NAFTA at Year Twelve." Submitted testimony of Thea M. Lee, policy director American Federation of Labor and Congress of Industrial Organizations, to the Subcommittee on Trade of the United States Senate Committee on Finance. September 11, 2006. Available at: http://www.aflcio.org/issues/jobseconomy/ globaleconomy/upload/LeeTestimony2006-0911.pdf.

NAFTA Free Trade Commission. "NAFTA at Seven: Building on a North American Partnership." Joint statement. January 2001. Available at: http://www.ustr.gov/ about-us/press-office/press-releases/archives/2001/july/joint-statement-nafta- free-trade-commission.

Portes, Alejandro. "The Informal Economy and Its Paradoxes." In *The Handbook of Economic Sociology,* ed. Neil Smelser and Richard Swedberg, 426–449. Princeton, N.J.: Princeton University Press, 1994.

Public Citizen Global Trade Watch. "Down on the Farm: NAFTA's Seven-Years War on Farmers and Ranchers in the U.S., Canada and Mexico." June 2001. Available at: http://www.citizen.org/publications/release.cfm?ID=6788.

———. "NAFTA Trade Adjustment Assistance." July 2001. Available at: http://www .citizen.org/trade/nafta/index.cfm.

Tilly, Charles, et al. "Scholarly Debate: Globalization Threatens Labor's Rights." *International Journal of Working Class History* 47 (spring 1995): 1–55.

Trubeck, David M., and Jeffrey S. Rothstein. "Transnational Regimes and Advocacy in Industrial Relations: A 'Cure' for Globalization?" Working Paper Series on Political Economy of Legal Change no. 4. University of Wisconsin, Global Studies Program, Madison, 1998.

United Nations Conference on Trade and Development (UNCTAD). *World Investment Report.* New York and Geneva: UNCTAD, 1990–2008.

United Nations Development Programme (UNDP). *Human Development Report.* New York and Geneva: UNDP, 1990–2008.

Visser, Jelle. "Union Membership Statistics in 24 Countries." *Monthly Labor Review* 129, no. 1 (2006): 38–49. Available at: http://www.bls.gov/opub/mlr/2006/01/art3full.pdf.

World Bank. *World Development Report.* New York and Washington, D.C.: Oxford University Press, 1990–2008.

World Trade Organization. "Statistics: International Trade Statistics 2008, Charts." Available at: http://www.wto.org/english/res_e/statis_e/its2008_e/its08_toc_e.htm.

———. "World Trade 2008, Prospects for 2009: WTO Sees 9% Global Trade Decline in 2009 as Recession Strikes." 2009 Press Releases, PRESS/554. March 23, 2009. Available at: http://www.wto.org/english/news_e/pres09_e/pr554_e.htm.

Web Sites

Academic Consortium on International Trade
http://www.spp.umich.edu/rsie/acit

Brookings Institution
http://www.brookings.edu

Economic Policy Institute
http://epinet.org

The Economist
http://www.economist.com

The Economist Intelligence Unit
http://www.eiu.com

European Trade Union Confederation
http://www.etuc.org

International Forum on Globalization
http://www.ifg.org

LABORSTA Internet (International Labour Office's online database)
http://laborsta.ilo.org

U.S. Department of Labor, Bureau of Labor Statistics
http://www.bls.gov/home.htm

Documents

1. Convention Concerning Freedom of Association and Protection of the Right to Organise

International Labour Organization, Convention 87, General Conference of the ILO, San Francisco, 1948

The full text is available at http://www.ilo.org/ilolex/cgi-lex/convde.pl?C087.

Extracts

Article 1

Each Member of the International Labour Organi[z]ation for which this Convention is in force undertakes to give effect to the following provisions.

Article 2

Workers and employers, without distinction whatsoever, shall have the right to establish and, subject only to the rules of the organisation concerned, to join organisations of their own choosing without previous authorisation.

Article 3

1. Workers' and employers' organisations shall have the right to draw up their constitutions and rules, to elect their representatives in full freedom, to organise their administration and activities and to formulate their programmes.

2. The public authorities shall refrain from any interference which would restrict this right or impede the lawful exercise thereof.

Article 4

Workers' and employers' organisations shall not be liable to be dissolved or suspended by administrative authority.

Article 5

Workers' and employers' organisations shall have the right to establish and join federations and confederations and any such organisation, federation or confederation shall have the right to affiliate with international organisations of workers and employers.

2. Convention Concerning the Prohibition and Immediate Action for the Elimination of the Worst Forms of Child Labour

International Labour Organization, Convention 182, ILO General Conference, Geneva, 17 June 1999

The full text is available at http://www.ilo.org/public/english/standards/relm/ilc/ilc87/com-chic.htm.

Extracts

Considering that the effective elimination of the worst forms of child labour requires immediate and comprehensive action, taking into account the importance of free basic education and the need to remove the children concerned from all such work and to provide for their rehabilitation and social integration while addressing the needs of their families, and. . . .

Recognizing that child labour is to a great extent caused by poverty and that the long-term solution lies in sustained economic growth leading to social progress, in particular poverty alleviation and universal education. . . .

Article 1

Each Member which ratifies this Convention shall take immediate and effective measures to secure the prohibition and elimination of the worst forms of child labour as a matter of urgency.

Article 2

For the purposes of this Convention, the term *child* shall apply to all persons under the age of 18.

Article 3

For the purposes of this Convention, the term *the worst forms of child labour* comprises:

(a) all forms of slavery or practices similar to slavery, such as the sale and trafficking of children, debt bondage and serfdom and forced or compulsory labour, including forced or compulsory recruitment of children for use in armed conflict;

(b) the use, procuring or offering of a child for prostitution, for the production of pornography or for pornographic performances;

(c) the use, procuring or offering of a child for illicit activities, in particular for the production and trafficking of drugs as defined in the relevant international treaties;

(d) work which, by its nature or the circumstances in which it is carried out, is likely to harm the health, safety or morals of children.

Article 4

1. The types of work referred to under Article 3(d) shall be determined by national laws or regulations or by the competent authority, after consultation with the organizations of employers and workers concerned, taking into consideration relevant international standards, in particular Paragraphs 3 and 4 of the Worst Forms of Child Labour Recommendation, 1999. . . .

Article 5

Each Member shall, after consultation with employers' and workers' organizations, establish or designate appropriate mechanisms to monitor the implementation of the provisions giving effect to this Convention.

Article 6

1. Each Member shall design and implement programmes of action to eliminate as a priority the worst forms of child labour.

2. Each Member shall, taking into account the importance of education in eliminating child labour, take effective and time-bound measures to:

(a) prevent the engagement of children in the worst forms of child labour;

(b) provide the necessary and appropriate direct assistance for the removal of children from the worst forms of child labour and for their rehabilitation and social integration;

(c) ensure access to free basic education, and, wherever possible and appropriate, vocational training, for all children removed from the worst forms of child labour;

(d) identify and reach out to children at special risk; and

(e) take account of the special situation of girls. . . .

WORLD TRADE

Kar-yiu Wong

Post–World War II world trade has been characterized by high growth rates that are well above those of the world economy. The increase in the movement of goods and services across national borders brought countries closer together, making them more dependent on one another, and affected domestic resource allocation, income distribution, economic growth, and societal welfare. Nevertheless, different people are affected by foreign trade in different ways, and some feel that foreign trade improves their well-being, while others do not. Thus, economists and government policy planners have attempted to address fundamental questions about the welfare impacts of international trade: Is foreign trade beneficial to society? How does it affect diverse groups of people differently? Should the government allow more trade or restrict trade? What are the policy options for the government, and how does the government rank various policies in different circumstances? This chapter analyzes fundamental features of world trade and examines answers to these questions.

Historical Background and Development

The mercantilists offered some of the earliest views on international trade in various writings between 1500 and 1750. They argued that the wealth of a nation is determined by the amount of precious metals (such as gold and silver) that a nation holds and that, for an open economy, one of the best ways to accumulate precious metals is through trade surpluses. Thus, a government, which hopes to help its nation accumulate wealth, should have the responsibility of encouraging the export of domestic products but discouraging the import of foreign products. Because the sum of all the trade surpluses and deficits of all nations is always equal to zero, the mercantilist argument implies that, if some nations are successful in getting a trade surplus, other nations must be experiencing trade deficits. If the governments of all countries try to accumulate wealth, avoiding importing foreign commodities as much as possible, the world trade volume (the sum of the values of imports and exports) will unavoidably shrink to very low levels.

Adam Smith (1723–1790), one of the founders of what became known as the classical school of economics, strongly criticized the mercantilist idea. In his famous book *An Inquiry into the Nature and Causes of the Wealth of Nations* (often referred to as simply *The Wealth of Nations*), he provided an alternative view about the nature and impact of foreign trade. Using simple examples and hypothetical numbers, he showed that free trade would benefit all trading countries. According to Smith, a country gains from trade not because it has accumulated additional precious metals but because trade allows countries to specialize in the production of the goods in which they have an absolute advantage. With such specialization and exchanges of commodities, countries can consume baskets of commodities that were not feasible before trade. In Smith's theories, a country has an absolute advantage in a commodity if it is technologically more efficient in producing the commodity, that is, if it requires fewer workers to produce one unit of the commodity, than another country.

David Ricardo, another classical economist, extended Smith's theory with the concept of comparative advantage—a country has a comparative advantage in a commodity if it is relatively more efficient in producing that commodity (with less labor input) than in producing another commodity. If countries trade the goods in which they have a comparative advantage, then both countries can make better use of their own resources and technologies, and both can gain (or at least not lose). Ricardo's theory, ultimately, is more useful than Smith's because the latter is not applicable when a country has no absolute advantage while Ricardo's theory applies to all cases.

The work of Smith and Ricardo has had enormous impact on trade theory and government policy formulation. Eli F. Heckscher (1879–1952) and Bertil Ohlin (1899–1979) proposed that a country's trade patterns (that is, which commodities it exports and which commodities it imports) can be explained in terms of the endowments of labor and capital in the country. Their work is summarized by the Heckscher-Ohlin theorem, which says that a capital-abundant (or labor-abundant) country will export a capital-intensive (or labor-intensive) commodity. Their work initiated a new way of looking at world trade and led to the development of a new theoretical framework, commonly called the neoclassical framework. Economists such as Jagdish Bhagwati, Ronald Jones, Murray Kemp, Wilfred Ethier, and Alan Deardorff have analyzed various properties and implications of this framework.

Within the neoclassical framework, some of the classical results were extended. For example, contemporary economists such as Paul Samuelson, Murray Kemp, Henry Wan, and Avinash Dixit showed that free trade is good for a country. (See the three propositions in the Research section.) The framework has also been used to examine the impact of trade on income distribution and to explain why trade liberalization receives different degrees of support from different constituencies in a country (see INCOME INEQUALITY).

The neoclassical framework was later modified by various economists to reflect more features of the real world. For example, the assumption of perfect competition was dropped to examine phenomena such as monopoly and oligopoly. Once some of the prerequisites of the framework have been eliminated, the proposition that free trade must benefit a country may no longer be true. Contemporary economists, including Harry G. Johnson (1923–1979), Jagdish Bhagwati, T. N. Srinivasan, and others, have analyzed these distortions (the term of art applied to situations in which neoclassical assumptions about an economy are not met) and the impact of policies in the presence of such distortions in an economy.

Trade theorists not only analyze trade issues related to a country and recommend policies but also focus on international trade orders. They look into possible methods of allowing countries to conduct international trade activities in more harmonious and beneficial ways. After World War II, for instance, international trade agreements and organizations were instituted. Over the past six decades, these organizations have implemented trade procedures and systems that aim to promote freer movements of products, services, and factors of production such as capital and workers across borders.

More recently, the idea of fair trade has been suggested as an alternative to, or an addition to, free trade. Although the meaning of *fair trade* may vary from one observer to another, the movement attempts to go beyond what markets can do. According to the Fair Trade Federation, fair trade is a system of exchange that seeks to create greater equity and partnership in the international trading system by:

- Creating opportunities for economically and socially marginalized producers
- Developing transparent and accountable relationships
- Building capacity
- Promoting fair trade
- Paying promptly and fairly
- Supporting safe and empowering working conditions
- Ensuring the rights of children
- Cultivating environmental stewardship
- Respecting cultural identity

The fair trade movement currently concentrates mainly on specific agricultural products, such as coffee and tea, and on handcrafted products and clothing.

Current Status

How does international trade affect the economic welfare of an economy or the world? This is one of the fundamental questions of international trade theory, one that is clearly critical to any analysis of trade policies.

Foreign trade can take many forms: exchanges in goods (so called merchandise trade), exchanges in services (such as tourism), movements of factors of production (for example, physical capital and workers), movements of financial assets (for example, financial capital and currencies), and even exchanges in different assets (for example, goods for services). Among these, merchandise trade (the focus of this chapter) is probably the most important form of trade, and it has received the most attention of government planners, economists, and the media. Moreover, the statistical data about merchandise trade, compared to data from other forms of trade, are the most comprehensive and reliable, and they take the least time to become available to the media and the public.

Research

In the current literature on international trade, three major propositions concerning the impacts of free trade on the economic welfare of countries have been established:

1. Free trade is better than no trade for an economy.
2. Free trade is the best policy for the world.
3. Free trade is the best policy for a small, open economy.

The meaning of these propositions, along with their implications, is clear. When a country permits free trade with other countries, domestic firms that are able to produce a product with lower costs than the foreign firms must pay will be able to compete in foreign markets and thus export their products. On the other hand, consumers will choose to buy (import) products from the foreign firms that are able to produce the products at lower costs than local firms must pay. These conditions show Smith's principle of absolute advantage and Ricardo's principle of comparative advantage at work—consumers will be able to buy goods from the places that have lower production costs and are therefore able to enjoy more goods. Countries can also benefit on the production side; they can produce more of the products that local firms are better at producing and less of the products that foreign firms are better in producing. The change in production levels of different products, and the associated allocation of resources, is called specialization in production. Through imports and exports, countries share the fruits of specialization in production, and thus all gain.

If free trade is good for an individual country, as proposition 1 suggests, it must be good for the world as a whole (proposition 2), and any attempt by a government to restrict trade will hurt the economic welfare of the world. The logic behind this is simple. The world as a whole is a closed economy. If restricting the movements of products within an economy by a single government does not make sense, restricting the movements of products in the world does not make any sense either.

Proposition 3 states that, for a simple open economy that has no monopoly power in the world markets, free trade is the best policy. This policy allows the economy to make the best use of world prices when taking them as given, based on the conditions of the world markets. It also rules out the use of taxes, subsidies, and quotas imposed on the flows of goods and services to improve the economic welfare of such an economy.

Although on paper these three propositions are logical and intuitive, in the real world many governments follow policies that contradict them. Much contemporary research in trade theory examines this paradox and analyzes the question: Why is trade not as free as the theory suggests? Clearly trade theorists do not argue for free trade under all circumstances, and they are careful to assert that the validity of the three free-trade propositions depends on certain assumptions, such as perfect competition. Perfect competition in an industry requires that all firms and consumers be small enough not to exert influence on the market price (that is, they are all price-takers). However, many industries exist in which the number of firms is limited and each firm is big enough to affect the market price by altering the quantity of the output it supplies to the market; examples of such industries are computers, cameras, television and radio stations, television and radio sets, cars, and aircraft. A firm that can effectively influence the market price is said to have monopoly power, and such a firm, for the sake of its own profit, has an incentive to control its output so that the market price increases. As a result, a firm with monopoly power tends to underproduce (produce too little compared to a competitive firm) and overcharge (set the price too high). Thus, economists argue, in the presence of monopoly power a firm will choose a suboptimal output level that maximizes its own profit while paying much less attention to the welfare of the society. Sometimes having a large number of producers in an industry may not be enough to guarantee that the firms' profit-maximizing objective coincides with the government's goal of maximizing the society's welfare. For example, in some industries, firms try their best to differentiate their products from the products of other firms so that each of them is able to maintain a certain monopoly power. (Economists call this type of market structure monopolistic competition; examples of monopolistic competition include soft drinks, toothpaste, and food.) Because of the tendency to underproduce and overcharge in the presence of monopoly power, the market outcome without any government intervention generally is not desirable from the society's point of view. In the presence of foreign trade, when monopoly power exists (in the local market, in the market of its trading partners, or externally in the world market), the government may have to consider appropriate policies to mitigate the effects of these distortions.

Policies and Programs

In the real world, direct trade interventions such as import and export taxes/subsidies (subsidies can be considered negative taxes) and quantitative restrictions (such as quotas on the import of certain commodities) are common in many countries and industries. Many domestic noneconomic policies also have a significant impact on foreign trade; for example, health requirements or environmental regulations can affect the trade levels of some products (see INTERNATIONAL FINANCE).

Although trade economists fully recognize that free trade is not always the optimal policy for a government, they are generally skeptical about the use of trade restrictions and government intervention. Even so, national governments use many arguments to justify the use of trade restrictions or other interventions. Some of these arguments come from economic theory, but others are based on nontrade or noneconomic objectives such as employment, environment, labor standards, and health. An evaluation of some of the cases in which government intervention has been suggested follows.

External Monopoly Power. In world markets, size does matter. Large economies, because they have large volumes of exports and imports, are able to influence world prices by changing their trade volumes. This means that large economies have external monopoly power.

Consider a large economy characterized by perfect competition. Based on the arguments presented here, free trade can bring an improvement in welfare. The question is: Can the economy exploit its external monopoly power and improve its welfare further? The answer is yes. To see why and how, recognize that, even though the economy may have perfect competition in local industries, it has monopoly power in the world markets. In other words, in world markets it is like a monopolist in an industry. Thus, it can behave like a monopolist to improve its welfare by underproducing (that is, exporting less and importing less) and overcharging (affecting the world prices in its own favor). Further, a large economy has the incentive to use trade taxes (for instance, a tariff) to limit the volume of trade. This incentive to impose trade taxes thus creates a gap between what some economies want and what is good for the world economy.

Trade War. The use of a tariff to exploit a large economy's external monopoly appears to be a powerful argument for trade restriction. However, two implications of this argument could lead to a lose–lose situation for the economy that imposes the tariff, as well as for other economies: (1) large economies in the world have an incentive to restrict trade (as mentioned previously), and (2) a tariff imposed by the large economy actually hurts other economies (that is, free trade by all economies is the best policy for the world). So, when an economy imposes a tariff, other economies want to retaliate with their own tariffs (or at least they have an incentive to do so), potentially resulting in a trade war.

A trade war is one of the least desirable outcomes for trade regulators, one in which some or even all economies lose. In the history of world trade, trade wars were not uncommon, but most of them were small-scale and affected only a small number of countries. The last big trade war involving a large number of countries occurred during the Great Depression. In 1930, shortly after the Great Depression began, the U.S. Congress passed the Smoot-Hawley Tariff Act, raising nearly nine hundred American import duties. This protectionist act led to retaliation from many countries, causing world trade to drop dramatically from US$4.9 billion in January 1930 to US$1.8 billion in January 1933. As a result, many (or even all) countries were hurt by the substantial decrease in export demands. In addition, many economists have argued that this trade war was a major reason why the world's recovery from the Great Depression took so long. In fact, this historical example has been cited as a cautionary tale as policymakers across the globe struggle to respond to the current worldwide economic recession and financial crisis (rooted in the 2007–2008 collapse of the U.S. housing and mortgage market).

Political Economy. Because trade policies are usually determined in a political process, political factors nearly always affect policy choices and decisions. In democratic societies, in which citizens have the right to express their policy preferences and in which government officials and representatives are elected (and subject to reelection), political factors can play an important role in the process of determining trade policies. And in such societies, the political spectrum of influence usually is different from the economic spectrum. Very often the political spectrum is biased toward those who prefer less trade. For developed countries, such as the United States, that import labor-intensive products (such as textiles, clothing, and shoes) from developing countries, the antitrade faction includes most labor unions, while the pro-trade faction primarily includes consumers and the owners of capital. Both groups have incentives to exert political pressure on the government to try to get the trade policy they want. The antitrade group is usually more concentrated and organized (labor unions) with fewer people (workers) and faces damages from higher levels of trade that are more direct and immediate (loss of jobs). The pro-trade group, on the other hand, consists of more people (consumers), is less concentrated and organized (consumer groups usually being weak), and faces less direct and severe damages should trade be restricted (rise of prices of imported products). Thus, the pro-trade group is usually less politically powerful than the antitrade group and often loses out. In fact, the antitrade lobbies often argue effectively that increased trade will threaten jobs, an argument that is frequently hard to counter. This has happened repeatedly in countries, including those of the European Union, where trade unions have political power in certain industries—transportation, for one—in which work shutdowns can seriously affect the daily economic life of the country (see LABOR AND EMPLOYMENT).

However, the calculus of pro- and antitrade factions in free democratic societies is complicated by other factors. For example, constituencies other than the general electorate, such as those that help to finance electoral campaigns, are in a position to pressure policymakers. Often donors who contribute to the electoral success of lawmakers and other policymakers are connected to corporations, which, in economic parlance, are the owners of capital. Many corporations have an interest in regulations that enhance free markets. This special interest can offer a counterbalance to the antitrade approach of trade unions and the like.

Imperfect Competition and Strategic Trade Policies. Industries under imperfect competition are common. In such industries, a limited number of large firms, each with monopoly power, exists. For example, consider airplane manufacturing and the specific case of Boeing in the United States and Airbus in Europe. Each of them is a monopoly in its own domestic market if trade is not allowed. When trade exists, they compete in world markets. In such a situation, governments often respond with strategic trade policies, that is, policies (such as subsidizing the production and export of a domestic firm's goods) that help domestic firms at the expense of the foreign firms. In the Boeing-Airbus case, both the U.S. government and the European governments accuse one another of subsidizing its own firm. Such policies take into consideration the strategic interactions between firms that have monopoly power in the markets. If such a policy is to be implemented correctly, a government has to be familiar with how the firms compete. If the right policy is chosen, not only the profit of the domestic firm but also domestic economic welfare will be improved. Trade theorists, however, are skeptical about the usefulness of strategic trade policies for several reasons. On the practical side, the development of a successful strategic trade policy requires a lot of information. However, much of the information required is firm specific. In other words, a firm possesses information such as the product's cost structure and the way it competes with rivals, but such information is not available to the public and the firm does not have an incentive to share the pertinent information with the government. In fact, it may, instead, supply misleading or wrong information to the government to draw more public subsidies. On the political side, when they know that the government is considering using subsidies to improve welfare, firms spend resources on lobbying for subsidies. The complexity of the situation is compounded when several industries vie for government subsidies. When this occurs, resources are wasted on lobbying and the winner of the lobbying competition may be the industry that has the strongest political backing, not necessarily the one that will bring the biggest economic benefit to the society.

Noneconomic Objectives. Some arguments for trade restrictions are based on noneconomic objectives, ones that are not directly related to the improvement of economic welfare of the economy. Examples of domestic noneconomic objectives include increasing employment, maintaining the production levels of certain strategic industries, and protecting an infant industry; examples of foreign noneconomic objectives include a variety of internationally accepted standards, such as the protection of environment, the prohibition of child labor, and the improvement of human rights in another country.

Trade restrictions often are used to achieve these objectives. For example, in the presence of import competition, with unemployment rising in a domestic industry, foreign competition is often blamed for domestic production problems and so a trade restriction (such as a tariff or a quota) may be suggested to protect domestic employment. After all, the foreign producers are not politically represented, so no one will speak for them when a protective measure is suggested. Prominent examples of this type of protective regulation include the U.S. Smoot-Hawley Trade Act in 1930 and the voluntary restraint on Japanese cars exported to the United States in the 1980s. Similarly, during the global financial crisis that took hold in 2008, policymakers in many countries, including the United States, faced political pressure to institute protective policies to bolster suffering domestic industries and employment; many policymakers—including U.S. president Barack Obama and German chancellor Angela Merkel—cautioned against such protectionism.

However, economists usually are cautious about the use of trade policies to achieve noneconomic goals and often suggest that trade restrictions are not the best policy for achieving particular objectives. For example, if a government's objective is to improve the employment level in an industry in the presence of import competition, an employment subsidy, which directly subsidizes the employment of workers, is better than a tariff because it does not create any unnecessary disturbance to the local economy (such as a higher price for the imported commodity). To take another example, a trade sanction used to pressure a targeted country to adopt a particular policy, such as environmental protection, may not work if a direct link between the sanction and the objective is not clear or if the sanction does not result in substantial damage to the targeted country. An alternative approach is to push for effective international agreements relating to noneconomic objectives—such as limitations on greenhouse gas emissions or support of human rights—that a country, due to its international and diplomatic relationships, is pressured to follow.

Thus economists, although recognizing the need for government interventions in some cases, usually are cautious about using them. Even if the right policy is chosen, the right information is available, and not too many resources are wasted in lobbying, economists first ask: Can the structure and features of the economy be improved so that government interventions are not necessary?

Regional Summaries

Although practically all countries in the world are open economies, not every country is equally trade oriented. Some countries may be able to generate larger volumes of trade than others (see map, p. 202). Many factors determine what volume of trade each country is able to generate: technologies; tastes; endowments of resources; domestic government policies; distances between its borders and its major trading partners; and even noneconomic factors such as political, historical, social, cultural, and legal institutions and traditions. A summary of the importance of trade in various regions in the world is given next. The data are taken from International Monetary Fund, "Direction of Trade Statistics," February 2009.

North America

This region consists of three countries, the United States, Canada, and Mexico (which is treated here as a North American country because it is part of the North American Free Trade Agreement [NAFTA]). The United States is not only the biggest economy in the world but also the biggest trader in terms of both export and import levels. In 2007, it sold US$1,163 billion worth of products to the rest of the world and purchased foreign goods worth US$2,017 billion, much more than the corresponding numbers of any other country. Canada and Mexico are also big traders, selling US$421 billion and US$272 billion of products, respectively, and buying US$418 billion and US$310 billion of goods, respectively. They are also the major trading partners of the United States.

The United States has huge deficits in its merchandise trade accounts (that is, it imports more than it exports). For example, in 2007, it recorded a huge merchandise trade deficit of US$855 billion, which was bigger than the level of exports and imports of nearly all other countries, except Germany and China. The merchandise trade deficits of the United States, which has worried many policymakers and has been used as an argument for protectionist measures aimed at limiting imports and/or promoting exports, were mainly financed by the surpluses of other trade accounts: trade in services, the current account (including the income earned by American firms investing abroad), and the capital

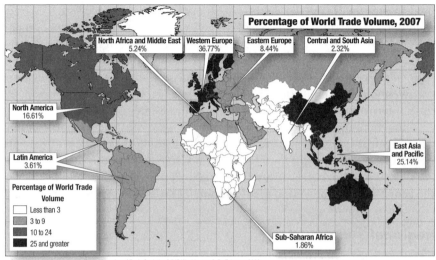

Source: International Monetary Fund, "Direction of Trade Statistics," IMF, Washington, D.C., February 2009.
Note: Volume of trade equals the sum of exports and imports.

account (the net inflow of foreign capital). Other countries' willingness to hold the U.S. dollars also helped finance part of the U.S. merchandise trade deficit.

South and Central America

Brazil is the biggest country—and the biggest trader—in this region. In 2007, its trade volume was US$290 billion, more than twice of that of the second-ranked country, Venezuela (US$133 billion). Chile and Argentina also had high volumes of trade with the rest of the world, selling and buying goods worth US$111 billion and US$97 billion, respectively.

In general, South American countries have small volumes of trade. This is due, in part, to the fact that they are relatively far away from many other countries and that most of the countries traditionally have adopted import-substitution policies geared toward developing their domestic industries. The Central American countries are small; their volumes of foreign trade are commensurately small as well.

Western Europe

Western Europe generates the biggest share of the volume of world trade. In 2007, it accounted for 36.8 percent of the world's volume of trade. This is mainly due to the formation of the European Union, within which products, capital, and workers are free to move. The biggest three traders in this region were Germany (with a trade volume of US$2,378 billion), France (US$1,172 billion), and the United Kingdom (US$1,065 billion). Interestingly, most of the countries in this region are trade dependent; that is, they rely heavily on trading with other countries for essential products.

Even though Western European countries have large foreign trade volumes and more or less similar trade policies, they differ greatly in terms of their trade balances. For example, in 2007 Germany had a trade surplus of US$266 billion, while France and the United Kingdom experienced trade deficits of US$68 billion and US$183 billion, respectively. The difference in the trade performance of these countries is just one example of how heterogeneous these Western European countries are. They have a wide range of tastes, technologies, factor endowments (the indigenous human and natural resources available for production), and government fiscal and monetary policies, which also affect their capital accounts.

Eastern Europe and the Transition Economies

This region consists mainly of the former socialist countries in Europe, including Russia. They are transition economies in that they are moving from an economic system characterized by government command and control to economies more dependent on market mechanisms. Turkey is also included here due to its geographical location (Turkey is in both Europe and in Asia).

The economies of these countries are less developed, and they do not trade significantly with the rest of the world. Despite the size of this region and the number of nations within it, the area generated only about 8.4 percent of the world trade in 2007. Russia is the biggest country in size and production level, and it is also the biggest trading country in this region. Its trade volume in 2007 was US$552 billion, much more than that of the second-ranked country, Poland (US$307 billion). The next three countries in terms of trade volumes are Turkey (US$277 billion), the Czech Republic (US$241 billion), and Hungary (US$191 billion).

Middle East and North Africa

The biggest trading countries in this region are Saudi Arabia (US$289 billion in 2007) and the United Arab Emirates (US$272 billion), both of which are important petroleum-exporting countries. The next most important trading country in this region is Israel, with a trading volume in 2007 of US$111 billion. Israel is not a petroleum-exporting country, but it is the region's most advanced country in terms of the diversity and viability of its international trade profile. Other countries in the region have much smaller trade volumes; for example, in 2007, the sum of the trade volumes of the next three countries was only a little more than that of Saudi Arabia: Iran (US$138 billion), Algeria (US$90 billion), and Egypt (US$74 billion).

Saudi Arabia, the United Arab Emirates, Qatar, Iran, Iraq, Kuwait, Libya, and Algeria are members of Organization of the Petroleum Exporting Countries (OPEC). (Other members of OPEC are Angola, Ecuador, Nigeria, and Venezuela. Indonesia withdrew from OPEC in 2008, after it became a net importer of oil.) Petroleum is the most important export product of these countries, and thus their ability to earn foreign reserves depends very much on the world's demand for petroleum, which in turn is closely linked to the economic conditions in the world.

Sub-Saharan Africa

With the exception of South Africa and Nigeria, the countries in this region do not engage greatly in foreign trade. In 2007, the trade volume of South

Africa was US$158 billion and that of Nigeria was US$100 billion. The trade volumes of all the other sub-Saharan African countries were much less than either South Africa or Nigeria.

South Africa is the most economically developed nation in this region so its relatively high trade volume is not surprising. Nigeria is a member of OPEC and depends on the export of petroleum as a source of its foreign reserves. All the other sub-Saharan countries are less developed and smaller. Furthermore, serious domestic economic and political problems and a severe lack of efficiency in their financial systems and transportation infrastructure present major roadblocks to the development of international trade.

Central and South Asia

Like sub-Saharan Africa, foreign trade is not important for most countries in central and South Asia. Some countries—such as Mongolia, Nepal and Bhutan—are geographically isolated; other countries—such as Afghanistan—have severe domestic problems that hamper their ability to focus on economic development, let alone international trade. Many countries in this region lack the transportation infrastructure and financial systems necessary to support large-scale trade activities.

India and Pakistan are the exceptions. These countries have the biggest economies and are the major trading nations in this region. In 2007, India (the second most populous country in the world) had a trade volume of US$403 billion, which was more than that of all other countries in the region combined.

Asia Pacific

Despite the differences among them in terms of the sizes of their economies, forms of government, and even culture and history, economies in this region engage actively and widely in international trade.

The biggest trader in this region, by far, is China, with a trade volume of US$2,714 billion in 2007. This was twice of that of the second most active trading country, Japan, which had a trade volume of US$1,336 billion. In fact, China is both the biggest exporter (US$1,218 billion in 2007) and importer (US$956 billion) in this region.

Hong Kong, Singapore, Taiwan, and South Korea, four of the region's newly industrialized economies, are touted for their high rates of growth and aggressiveness in promoting foreign exports. Other Asian economies, including Malaysia, Thailand, Indonesia, and the Philippines, have generally been following similar paths in promoting trade and growth. Australia, the region's major economy in the Southern Hemisphere, is more self-dependent, with smaller trade volumes, and is an important trading partner of New Zealand.

Most economies in this region are members of Asia-Pacific Economic Cooperation (APEC; the United States, Canada, Mexico, Chile, Peru, and Russia are also members). This organization was established in 1989 with the purpose of promoting trade opportunities and economic cooperation among its members. Foreign trade is expected to continue to be an important growth factor for these economies.

Data

Table 1 Trade of Selected Countries, 2007 (billions of U.S. dollars)

Country	Exports	Imports	Balance	Volume
Algeria	56.50	33.29	23.21	89.79
Argentina	54.81	42.35	12.46	97.16
Australia	141.45	173.54	−32.09	314.99
Austria	163.76	163.24	0.52	327.00
Belgium	432.26	413.58	18.68	845.84
Brazil	157.09	132.67	24.42	289.76
Canada	420.84	418.03	2.81	838.87
Chile	67.50	43.80	23.70	111.30
China (mainland)	1,218.13	956.26	261.87	2,174.39
Colombia	29.99	32.90	−2.91	62.89
Czech Republic	122.74	118.46	4.28	241.20
Denmark	102.79	98.65	4.14	201.44
DRC	1.93	3.04	−1.11	4.97
Egypt	23.86	50.50	−26.64	74.36
Finland	90.08	81.76	8.32	171.84
France	551.85	620.14	−68.29	1,171.99
Georgia	1.53	5.32	−3.79	6.85
Germany	1,322.02	1,055.83	266.19	2,377.85
Guatemala	7.05	12.84	−5.79	19.89
Hong Kong, China	344.74	368.22	−23.48	712.96
Hungary	95.55	95.72	−0.17	191.27
India	153.12	249.58	−96.46	402.70
Indonesia	114.10	74.47	39.63	188.57
Iran	80.95	56.68	24.27	137.63
Ireland	121.49	83.83	37.66	205.32
Israel	54.05	56.60	−2.55	110.65
Italy	492.00	504.83	−12.83	996.83
Japan	714.25	621.87	92.38	1,336.12
Korea	371.45	356.85	14.60	728.30
Malaysia	176.21	146.98	29.23	323.19
Mexico	271.87	310.14	−38.27	582.01
Netherlands	551.64	493.30	58.34	1,044.94
Nigeria	60.22	39.40	20.82	99.62
Norway	136.38	80.28	56.10	216.66
Philippines	50.46	55.51	−5.05	105.97
Poland	140.41	166.14	−25.73	306.55
Portugal	51.52	78.32	−26.80	129.84
Russia	352.37	199.44	152.93	551.81
Saudi Arabia	198.24	91.15	107.09	289.39
Singapore	299.17	263.33	35.84	562.50
South Africa	63.48	94.13	−30.65	157.61
Spain	252.06	389.62	−137.56	641.68
Sweden	169.25	151.53	17.72	320.78
Switzerland	171.80	160.96	10.84	332.76
Tajikistan	1.47	2.54	−1.07	4.01
Thailand	152.46	141.35	11.11	293.81
Turkey	107.11	169.99	−62.88	277.10
Uganda	0.85	2.84	−1.99	3.69
United Arab Emirates	125.70	146.05	−20.35	271.75
United Kingdom	441.19	624.13	−182.94	1,065.32
United States	1,162.60	2,017.38	−854.78	3,179.98
Venezuela	87.27	46.10	41.17	133.37

Source: International Monetary Fund, "Direction of Trade Statistics," IMF, Washington, D.C., February 2009.

Note: DRC, Democratic Republic of Congo

Table 2 Trade of Various Regions, 2007

Region	Exports (billions of U.S. dollars)	Imports (billions of U.S. dollars)	Balance (billions of U.S. dollars)	Volume	
				Billions of U.S. dollars	Percentage
North America	1,855.31	2,745.55	−890.24	4,600.86	16.61
South and Central America	521.06	479.53	41.53	1,000.59	3.61
Western Europe	5,111.74	5,072.38	39.36	10,184.12	36.77
Eastern Europe	1,110.88	1,226.37	−115.49	2,337.25	8.44
Middle East and North Africa	806.09	645.55	160.54	1,451.64	5.24
Sub-Saharan Africa	245.59	268.99	−23.40	514.58	1.86
Central and South Asia	254.32	388.15	−133.83	642.47	2.32
Asia Pacific	3,683.66	3,278.84	404.82	6,962.50	25.14
World total	13,588.65	14,105.36	−516.71	27,694.01	100.00

Source: International Monetary Fund, "Direction of Trade Statistics," IMF, Washington, D.C., February 2009.

Case Study—The General Agreement on Tariffs and Trade and World Trade Organization

At the end of World War II, many countries gathered together with the objective of formulating a new international trade order. In 1947, the General Agreement on Tariffs and Trade (GATT) was established (and signed by twenty-three countries on January 1, 1948) with the purpose of reducing trade barriers among countries. Under the GATT, member countries engage in multilateral negotiations about reducing trade restrictions. Since 1947, the GATT has conducted eight rounds of trade talks among member countries. The two more successful rounds were the Kennedy Round (1962–1967), after which the member countries' tariff rates on manufactured products were reduced by an average of 35 percent, and the Tokyo Round (1974–1979), after which the average tariff rate on manufacturing products in the United States dropped to 4.3 percent, in Canada to 5.2 percent, in France to 6.0 percent, in Japan to 2.9 percent, in the United Kingdom to 5.2 percent, and in West Germany to 6.3 percent.

In 1986, the GATT initiated a new round of multilateral trade talks, referred to as the Uruguay Round. The main objective was to ease the restrictions on trade in services and agricultural products. This quickly ran into resistance from many countries, especially from many European countries over the proposed reduction in subsidies on agricultural products. After the first deadline was extended at the end of 1990, an agreement was finally reached by 117 countries just before the second deadline on December 15, 1993. It took effect on January 1, 1995.

One of the provisions of the Uruguay Round agreement was to replace the GATT with a new trade organization, the World Trade Organization (WTO). The WTO was charged with the responsibility of supervising the implementation of the Uruguay Round agreement and of conducting new multilateral trade liberalization talks that would cover more goods and services than the GATT did.

In arranging multilateral trade liberalization, the GATT and WTO have a unique role. Many countries, because they choose their policies independently, might be inclined to engage in trade wars; the GATT and WTO as transnational treaty-making institutions (see TRANSNATIONAL GOVERNANCE) can mitigate these tendencies. They provide the needed coordination of policies, enforce trade liberalization mechanisms, and supervise agreements signed by the member countries.

The WTO and efforts to strengthen its global reach, however, have come under a great deal of criticism in recent years. As large companies gain access to more and more markets through increased trade liberalization, the power that these large companies possess increases. This increased corporate power can make the noneconomic objectives recognized by many nations and worldwide institutions, such as environmental protection and fair labor standards, harder to implement. Companies, whose primary objectives are increasing profits, often resist incorporating noneconomic goals into their strategies because such goals often have a negative impact on short-term profits.

Perhaps the most controversial feature of the WTO is its ability to settle trade disputes between member countries. Critics argue that countries lose sovereignty when they allow the WTO to evaluate and adjudicate the validity of their trade, and sometimes even domestic, policies. This potential loss of sovereignty to the WTO is complicated by the perception that the WTO is not a truly fair and representative worldwide organization but, instead, one ruled by the few large economies of the world. The most extreme criticism, perhaps, is that, due to the political pressure that large corporations often exert on their governments' trade representatives, the decisions of the WTO are in danger of being made not by objective economic judges but by parties interested in promoting their own economic welfare over the welfare of the world.

Biographical Sketches

Jagdish Bhagwati, Columbia University, is one of most influential trade theorists in current times. He has made important contributions to the theory of distortions, trade policy analysis, economic welfare, immigration, and the relation between political economy and trade policies. In 1971, he founded the *Journal of International Economics,* the most influential journal in the field. He later founded *Economics and Politics,* a journal with a focus on the relationship between economics and political science. Recently, he has focused more on policy-oriented issues and has served as economic policy adviser to the director-general of GATT, special adviser to the UN on globalization, and external adviser to the WTO.

Elhanan Helpman, Tel Aviv University, Israel, was one of the main contributors to the new theory of international trade that emphasizes imperfect competition. In a paper published in 1981, he showed how intraindustry trade (the simultaneous export and import of similar products, such as cars) and interindustry trade (the export and import of different products, such as exporting aircrafts and importing shoes) can be analyzed together in a single framework. His authoritative survey on the theory of international trade with imperfect competition in 1984 was widely accepted. His research later turned to growth and trade and to the political economy of trade policies.

Ronald Winthrop Jones, University of Rochester, is one of the main contributors to the development of the neoclassical framework. He has written many papers about the features of international trade and its impact on resource allocation, income distribution, and economic growth. His well-known paper, published in the 1956–1957 issue of the *Review of Economic Studies* soon after he completed his doctorate at the Massachusetts Institute of Technology (MIT), derived many new features and properties of the Heckscher-Ohlin theorem and the neoclassical framework. In the following years, he extended his research to international factor movement, externality, trade in intermediate inputs, and fragmentation of production and trade.

Murray C. Kemp, Macquarie University, Australia, has made significant contributions to trade theory, welfare economics, the theory of externality, and international capital movement. His 1962 paper, published in *Economic Journal* (with another paper on the same topic by Paul Samuelson), ignited enormous interest in issues related to the welfare effects of foreign trade. In 1966, he published a paper that is considered one of the first to extend the traditional framework of international trade to cover international capital movement. In 1976, he published a very influential paper (with Henry Wan Jr., Cornell University) showing that any new customs union can improve the economic welfare of the world (or, at least, that no country will be hurt).

Paul Krugman is an important figure in the new theory of international trade. His 1979 paper in the *Journal of International Economics* shows some of the important features of monopolistic competition and intraindustry trade in differentiated products. He has also contributed to the areas of exchange rates and target zones, currency crises, and economic geography. In 1991, he received the John Bates Clark medal from the American Economic Association; this award is given once every two years to "that American economist under forty who is adjudged to have made a significant contribution to economic thought and knowledge." In 2008, he received the Nobel Prize in Economic Sciences "for his analysis of trade patterns and location of economic activity."

Bertil Ohlin extended Eli F. Heckscher's ideas about the causes of foreign trade and developed a new theory of international trade, later called the Heckscher-Ohlin theorem. This theory, which says that a capital-abundant country exports the capital-intensive commodity and imports the labor-intensive commodity, marked a significant departure from the classical theory in that it considered two factors of production (such as labor and capital). In 1979, Ohlin and James Meade were awarded the Nobel Prize in Economic Sciences for their work on international trade theory.

David Ricardo became an economic theorist after successful work in securities and real estate. He was one of the most vocal opponents of protective measures in England, including the Corn Laws, which restricted the importation of grain into England. His book, *The Principles of Political Economy and Taxation,* is an elaboration and extension of Adam Smith's work. It also offers an innovative development of the classical theory. His theory of comparative advantage laid the foundation for the modern theory of the patterns of trade.

Paul Anthony Samuelson, a member of the economics faculty of Massachusetts Institute of Technology, has written many influential articles in fields such as international trade, consumer theory, welfare economics, capital theory, dynamics, mathematical economics, public finance, and macroeconomics. In the theory of international trade, his contributions include factor price equalization, social welfare and social utility, gains from trade, and the Stolper-Samuelson theorem. He was awarded the Nobel Prize in Economic Sciences in 1970 "for the scientific work through which he has developed static and dynamic economic theory and actively contributed to raising the level of analysis in economic science."

Directory

Asia-Pacific Economic Cooperation (APEC), 438 Alexandra Road, #14-00, Alexandra Point, Singapore 119958. Telephone: +65 276-1880; email: info@mail .apecsec.org.sg; Web: http://www.apecsec.org.sg.
Primary regional vehicle for promoting open trade and practical economic cooperation, with the goal of advancing Asia-Pacific economic dynamism and sense of community.

Association of Southeast Asian Nations (ASEAN), ASEAN Secretariat, 70A Jalan Sisingamangaraja, Jakarta 12110, Indonesia. Telephone: (6221) 7262991; email: public@aseansec.org; Web: http://www.aseansec.org.
Regional organization aiming to accelerate economic growth, social progress, and cultural development and to promote peace, stability, and active collaboration and mutual assistance on matters of common interest in Southeast Asia.

Fair Trade Federation (FTF), 1612 K Street NW, Suite 600, Washington, D.C. 20006. Telephone: (202) 872-5329; email: info@FairTradeFederation.org; Web: http://www.fairtradefederation.com.
Association of fair-trade wholesalers, retailers, and producers committed to providing fair wages and good employment opportunities to economically disadvantaged artisans and farmers worldwide.

International Monetary Fund (IMF), 700 19th Street NW, Washington, D.C. 20431. Telephone: (202) 623-7000; email: publicaffairs@imf.org; Web: http://www .imf.org.
International organization established to promote international monetary cooperation, to foster economic growth and high levels of employment, and to provide temporary financial assistance to countries to help ease balance-of-payments adjustment.

Organisation for Economic Cooperation and Development (OECD), 2, Rue André Pascal, F-75775 Paris, Cedex 16, France. Telephone: +33 1 45 24 82 00; Web: http://www.oecd.org.
Organization promoting economic cooperation and development among its member countries (thirty members in 2009) and other countries; also plays a prominent role in fostering good governance in public service and corporate activity.

World Bank, 1818 H Street NW, Washington, D.C. 20433. Telephone: (202) 473-1000; Web: http://www.worldbank.org.
Vital source of financial and technical assistance to developing countries around the world (185 member countries); the World Bank is made up of two institutions: the International Bank for Reconstruction and Development (IBRD), which aims to reduce poverty in middle-income and

credit-worthy poorer countries, and the International Development Association, which helps the world's poorest countries.

World Trade Organization (WTO), Rue de Lausanne 154, CH-1211 Geneva 21, Switzerland. Telephone: +41 22 739 51 11; email: enquiries@wto.org; Web: http://www.wto.org.

International organization dealing with the rules of trade between nations and helping the producers of goods and services, exporters, and importers conduct their business.

Further Research

Books

Appleyard, Dennis R., and Alfred J. Field. *International Economics.* Boston: Irwin/McGraw-Hill, 2001.

Bhagwati, Jagdish N. *Protectionism.* Cambridge, Mass.: MIT Press, 1988.

———. *A Stream of Windows.* Cambridge, Mass.: MIT Press, 1998.

Bhagwati, Jagdish N., Arvind Panagariya, and T. N. Srinivasan. *Lectures on International Trade.* Cambridge, Mass.: MIT Press, 1998.

Caves, Richard E., Jeffrey A. Frankel, and Ronald W. Jones. *World Trade and Payments: An Introduction.* New York: Harper Collins College, 1993.

Ethier, Wilfred J. *Modern International Economics.* New York: W. W. Norton, 1995.

Krueger, Anne O., ed. *The WTO as an International Organization.* Chicago: University of Chicago Press, 1998.

Krugman, Paul. *Pop Internationalism.* Cambridge, Mass.: MIT Press, 1998.

Krugman Paul, and Maurice Obstfeld. *International Economics: Theory and Policy.* Reading, Mass.: Addison-Wesley, 2000.

Roberts, Russell. *The Choice: A Fable of Free Trade and Protectionism.* Upper Saddle River, N.J.: Prentice Hall, 2001.

Rodrik, Dani. *Has Globalization Gone Too Far?* Washington, D.C.: Institute for International Economics, 1997.

Schott, Jeffrey J., ed. *The Uruguay Round: An Assessment.* Washington, D.C.: Institute for International Economics, 1994.

———, ed. *The World Trading System: Challenges Ahead.* Washington, D.C.: Institute for International Economics, 1996.

Whalley, John, and Colleen Hamilton. *The Trading System after the Uruguay Round.* Washington, D.C.: Institute for International Economics, 1996.

Wong, Kar-yiu. *International Trade in Goods and Factor Mobility.* Cambridge, Mass.: MIT Press, 1995.

Articles and Reports

Bhagwati, Jagdish N. "The Generalized Theory of Distortions and Welfare," in *Trade, Balance of Payments, and Growth: Papers in International Economics in Honor of Charles P. Kindleberger,* ed. Jagdish N. Bhagwati, Ronald W. Jones, Robert A. Mundell, and Jaroslav Vanek, 69–90. Amsterdam: North Holland Company, 1971.

Bhagwati, Jagdish N., and T. N. Srinivasan. "Optimal Intervention to Achieve Non-Economic Objectives." *Review of Economic Studies* 36 (1969): 27–38.

Brander, James A., and Paul R. Krugman. "A 'Reciprocal Dumping' Model of International Trade." *Journal of International Economics* 15 (1983): 313–323.

Brander, James A., and Barbara J. Spencer. "Export Subsidies and International Market Share Rivalry." *Journal of International Economics* 18 (1985): 83–100.

Eaton, Jonathan, and Gene M. Grossman. "Optimal Trade and Industrial Policy under Oligopoly." *Quarterly Journal of Economics* 101 (1986): 383–406.

Grossman, Gene M. "Strategic Export Promotion: A Critique." in *Strategic Trade Policy and the New International Economics,* ed. Paul R. Krugman, 47–68. Cambridge, Mass.: MIT Press, 1986.

Kemp, Murray C., and Henry Y. Wan Jr. "An Elementary Proposition Concerning the Formation of Customs Unions." *Journal of International Economics* 6 (1976): 95–97.

Samuelson, Paul A. "The Gains from International Trade Once Again." *Economic Journal* 72 (1962): 820–829.

Wong, Kar-yiu. "Welfare Comparison of Trade Situations." *Journal of International Economics* 30 (1991): 49–68.

Web Sites

Fair Trade Federation (FTF)
http://www.fairtradefederation.com

World Bank
http://www.worldbank.org

World Trade Organization
http://www.wto.org

Document

1. North America Free Trade Agreement

The full text is available at http://www.sice.oas.org/trade/nafta/CHAP-01.ASP.

Extract

Article 102

1. The objectives of this Agreement, as elaborated more specifically through its principles and rules, including national treatment, most-favored-nation treatment and transparency, are to:

(a) eliminate barriers to trade in, and facilitate the cross-border movement of, goods and services between the territories of the Parties;

(b) promote conditions of fair competition in the free trade area;

(c) increase substantially investment opportunities in the territories of the Parties;

(d) provide adequate and effective protection and enforcement of intellectual property rights in each Party's territory;

(e) create effective procedures for the implementation and application of this Agreement, for its joint administration and for the resolution of disputes; and

(f) establish a framework for further trilateral, regional and multilateral cooperation to expand and enhance the benefits of this Agreement.

PART III

Environment

BIODIVERSITY

Tim Allman

Biodiversity, a contraction of the term *biological diversity,* refers to the variety observed within the biosphere, or living world. This richness and variety of life are perhaps Earth's greatest wonder and one of its most important resources because human survival completely depends on the effective functioning of global biological systems. Most of Earth's diversity remains undiscovered, as science has classified only a small portion of the large number of species estimated to exist.

The study of biodiversity has been divided into three categories: genetic, species, and ecosystem. Genetic diversity is the inheritable variation that derives ultimately from variations in DNA sequence; species diversity characterizes the variety of different species observed in an area; and ecosystem diversity is the patterns of variation seen in ecosystems. Biodiversity in all these categories is declining ever more rapidly due to habitat destruction and other human activities. For example, eminent biologist Edward O. Wilson has predicted that half the planet's species face extinction in the next one hundred years if current trends continue. With global biodiversity under such overwhelming attack, the struggle to conserve it becomes all the more urgent.

Historical Background and Development

Given that many early societies exhibited an interest in and affinity with nature and its diversity, it seems quite probable that human societies have long sought to classify to some degree the species that they have encountered. Such cultural analyses of diversity are invariably related to the importance of the various species to the society. In a classic study, the eminent German biologist Ernst Mayr visited the remote Arfak mountains of New Guinea in 1928 and noted that the indigenous inhabitants gave names to 136 species of birds, many of which they depend on for food. Interestingly, these 136 correspond almost exactly to the species recognized by Western taxonomy, the science of the classification of organisms. However, the New Guineans had little interest in certain other groups; for instance, they did not distinguish among any of the numerous species of ants by which they are surrounded.

Recorded attempts at taxonomic classification began with the ancient civilizations of Europe and Asia, with philosophers from Greece, Rome, and Arabia proposing basic schemes. The classification and compilation of species inventories have been a theme of various scientific inquiries ever since, but studies of biological diversity really began in earnest in eighteenth-century Europe as scientific exploration, specimen collection, and classification came into vogue. The outstanding figure of this period was Carolus Linnaeus, who established the foundations for the binomial system of scientific naming of organisms that is still used today and who is thus considered the father of modern taxonomy. A century later, studies of the natural world were advanced sufficiently for Charles Darwin to develop his theory of evolution. This theory revolutionized the biological sciences by providing a coherent mechanism for explaining the staggering variety of life on Earth and provided the theoretical foundation for modern studies of the living world.

The modern conservation movement began to coalesce in the late nineteenth century as a reaction to the damage to natural landscapes by industrialization, urban growth, and resource extraction. This period saw the establishment of the world's first national parks, such as Yellowstone in 1872, Royal (in Australia) in 1879, and Banff (in Canada) in 1885.

Although scientific understanding of biology and ecology developed greatly throughout the twentieth century, biodiversity is a relatively new field of study; the term itself was coined in 1985. The concept of biodiversity had begun gaining currency against a background of increasing concern about the environment in many parts of the world two decades before the term was coined. This concern was reflected by the signing of such important agreements as the 1963 Convention on International Trade in Endangered Species (CITES), the 1972 World Heritage Convention, the 1983 Convention on Migratory Species, and the 1971 Ramsar Convention on Wetlands.

Research and policy focused specifically on biodiversity, and its conservation came to the fore only in the 1990s. Such initiatives were given great impetus by the Earth Summit held in Rio de Janeiro in 1992 and the resulting Convention on Biological Diversity, which came into force in December 1993. Recognition of the threats to global biodiversity and their possible repercussions helped create a general consensus about the urgency of the problem, often with scientists at the forefront of this concern; biologists Jared Diamond and Robert May, writing for the scientific journal *Nature* in 1985, memorably dubbed conservation biology a "discipline with a time limit." The critical question for the future is whether sufficient time, financial support, and political will exist to fight biodiversity decline at local, national, and international levels.

Current Status

There is no single, universally applicable unit of measure for biodiversity, only the requirement that the parameters used be appropriate to the situation. Biodiversity, however, is most often studied and described by scientists and policymakers at the species level. In particular, species richness—the number of species in an area or community, ideally relative to the total number of individuals of each species present—is a widely used measure of diversity.

Research

However biodiversity is characterized and despite differing estimates of its degree, it is clear that human activity threatens and reduces biodiversity in numerous ways. Today, habitat destruction is the primary driver of biodiversity decline in almost every area of the world, with overexploitation, introduction of alien species, and pollution also contributing (see POLLUTION and DEFORESTATION). In addition, impacts on biodiversity are likely to become increasingly dominated by climate change resulting from global warming, which is expected to have dramatic effects on species and ecosystems everywhere (see CLIMATE CHANGE).

The depletion of biodiversity has reached an alarming rate. Although quantifying extinction rates involves many assumptions, the California Academy of Sciences estimates that some 10,000 species become extinct every year. This is 1,000 times the background extinction rate indicated in fossil records. Most biologists now agree that the biosphere is facing an extinction crisis; indeed, it is widely accepted that we are experiencing a sixth mass extinction period in the history of life on Earth, the greatest upheaval in the living world since the extinction event that wiped out the dinosaurs at the end of the Mesozoic Era, some 65 million years ago.

The current mass extinction is unique for having been precipitated by human activities. Biologist E. O. Wilson has suggested that the human effects on the development of life are now so profound that the Earth may be considered to be leaving the Cenozoic Era (the period dominated by mammals, which followed the Mesozoic) and entering what he calls the Eremozoic Era, the age of loneliness.

Living on a severely biologically impoverished planet will present humanity with problems far beyond loneliness, however. Healthy natural systems provide us with ecosystem services—essential attributes such as food, fuel, water, fiber, medicine, recycling of nutrients, purification of air and water, and pollination of crops. In 1997, economists writing in *Nature* estimated the total monetary value to humanity of the Earth's ecosystem services at $33 trillion or more per year, almost twice the global gross domestic product (GDP). But, given their crucial importance for life on Earth, global ecosystems can justifiably be considered as priceless. Vital ecosystem services are damaged by biodiversity decline, with potentially catastrophic consequences for human societies.

Clearly, the need for ongoing accurate biodiversity research is urgent if ways to tackle the biodiversity crisis are to be found. The field is complex and broad, and it tends to rely on three scientific disciplines: genetics, taxonomy, and ecology. Each discipline approaches the analysis of diversity at a different level of organization, but they are all intimately related. For example, the geneticist studying DNA variation in a population of organisms might provide the taxonomist with knowledge that enables a revised classification of organisms to be made; this, in turn, could improve the ecologist's understanding of the ecosystem of which the organisms are a part.

Most research focuses on the estimation of the diversity that exists in an area or community and on the scientific assessment of which components of this diversity are of most significance to overall biodiversity, especially with regard to prioritizing conservation efforts. Objective comparisons of biodiversity are often difficult to make, however, and tackling these questions for even a small wildlife reserve is a considerable task. The work required on a global scale is extremely daunting.

Global estimates of biodiversity are often done by extrapolating from samples of smaller systems. Given the complexity of the project, species richness is the best measure of diversity because it is relatively simple to measure in most situations and easily compared between ecosystems (see Table 1). It is no surprise that estimates of the number of species on Earth differ greatly, ranging from 4 million to 100 million according to the assumptions made; remarkably, we have a better idea of the number of stars in the galaxy than of the number of species on our own planet. The International Union for the Conservation of Nature (IUCN) quotes a working estimate of between 8 and 14 million species in its "Review of the 2008 Red List of Threatened Species." However, only a small portion has been studied; the IUCN states that only about 1.8 million species are currently known to science and that the ecology of only a small portion of these has been studied in any detail. Around half of known species—950,000—are insects. Higher plants (seed plants and ferns) constitute the next largest group, with around 285,000 species.

It is certain that the discovery and classification of the majority of species will not keep pace with extinction rates. The scale of the task is too immense, and there are not enough taxonomic researchers, especially those specializing in poorly understood groups of organisms. Efforts are being made, however, to assist and coordinate taxonomic research. The most notable of these projects is the Catalog of Life, a joint project of two agencies, Species 2000 and the Integrated Taxonomic Information System (ITIS), both of which are themselves collaborative organizations involving many scientific bodies from all over the world. The Catalog of Life aims to establish an authoritative standardized index of all currently identified species, which can be accessed via the Internet. It is estimated that just over 60 percent of all known species are cataloged in existing databases, but the Catalog of Life aims to index all known species by 2011.

It is also important for scientists to understand how specific changes in biological diversity affect the functioning of ecosystems. For instance, it is generally accepted that more diverse communities are more productive. That is, they produce more organic matter, such as plant growth, in a given time and are more robust than less diverse ones, being better able to withstand disturbances. It is also generally agreed that more diverse ecosystems tend to be more resilient in the face of environmental change. Other research has attempted to explain the various interrelationships between geographical factors and biodiversity, the best known of which is the general increase in diversity in the latitudes approaching the equator. Exploring patterns such as these in more detail can lead to better understanding of the effects of conservation practices.

One attempt to highlight those areas most in need of conservation action is by designating biodiversity hotspots, a concept originated by British scientist Norman Myers. This analysis identifies areas that have very high biodiversity indicators (such as high levels of endemism, the occurrence of organisms that are unique to a particular area) and also a high risk of habitat destruction and, thus, are most in need of protection. Similarly, the Global 200 project of the World Wide Fund for Nature identifies two hundred regions of natural habitat with the most biodiversity significance. Of course, like all assessments of biodiversity, such classifications will always involve simplifications and subjective assumptions or judgments and, thus, attract debate; for example, the concept of biodiversity hotspots has been criticized for relying too heavily on endemic plants (those unique to an area) as a diversity indicator. Nonetheless, such analyses can play a useful role in conservation efforts.

Another important research project is the IUCN's "Red List," the world's most comprehensive inventory of the conservation status of the world's plant and animal species. The extinction risk of thousands of species and subspecies is assessed, and threatened species are then categorized in the list as vulnerable, endangered, or critically endangered. This informs policymakers about which species are most in need of conservation action and documents the urgency and scale of the extinction threat; for example, the 2008 list reported that nearly one-third of the world's remaining amphibian species were threatened (see Table 3).

Policies and Programs

The decline in biodiversity was one of the issues that dominated the 1992 Earth Summit (formally known as the United Nations Conference on Environment and Development). At the conference, 168 countries signed the Convention on Biological Diversity, the first global agreement on biodiversity conservation (see Document 1). The convention has three objectives: the conservation of biodiversity, the sustainable use of biodiversity's components, and the equitable sharing of genetic resources. A key challenge for its signatories is achieving a balance between the first two objectives. This means conserving biodiversity and all its components—such biological resources as species and habitats—while allowing sustainable human exploitation of these resources. The third objective also applies to human use of a component of diversity—genetic variation. In this respect, the convention aims to ensure that genetic resources (for example, wild plants whose genes may be of use to biotechnologists in the development of new drugs) provide as wide a benefit to humanity as possible.

Many policy approaches to biodiversity conservation tend to be utilitarian; that is, they seek to protect diversity because of its actual and potential value to humanity and the biosphere and, therefore, aim primarily to protect the most "valuable" elements of biodiversity. Although this pragmatic resource-value approach is necessary because of the scale of the problem and limits on time and resources, many groups involved in conservation programs point out that placing value on diversity will always be subjective and argue that biodiversity should deserve protection in its own right. Indeed, the Convention on Biological Diversity affirms the intrinsic value of biodiversity in its first line of text. Furthermore, because of the sheer complexity of the living world, even the most utilitarian-minded analysts would agree that any loss to biodiversity might have serious, unpredictable, and irreversible effects.

There are two broad approaches to biodiversity conservation: ex situ and in situ. Ex situ, or off-site, conservation measures focus on individual species and include the use of zoos, seed banks, and DNA storage facilities to preserve species. Because of the expense and effort required for ex situ conservation, especially for animals, such measures are generally limited to particularly rare, valued, or threatened species. A notable ex situ project with a comprehensive focus is the Svalbard Global Seed Vault, a secure underground storage facility in the Arctic permafrost. This aims to back up the work of seed banks around the world by storing the seeds of crop plant varieties, thus maintaining a reservoir of genetic diversity even in the face of catastrophic events.

In situ, or on-site, conservation aims to conserve biodiversity in its natural environment. This is the preferred approach and involves programs for the establishment of protected areas such as wildlife reserves and the legal protection of endangered species (see Table 2; map, p. 222). It is generally accepted that the most effective in situ paradigm is the ecosystem approach; this is favored by the Convention on Biological Diversity, which endorsed it at a 2000 meeting and defined it as "a strategy for the integrated management of land, water and living resources that promotes conservation and sustainable use in an equitable way." The crucial advantage of the ecosystem approach is its focus on integration; by recognizing that healthy ecosystems cannot exist in isolation from other factors (geographical, hydrological, social, and cultural), it aims to address conservation problems in a more holistic way. The challenge of translating this approach into success is now a major concern of many biodiversity policies.

The Convention on Biological Diversity has provided the policy framework for numerous projects relating to the full scope of its aims by national governments and international organizations. The convention is legally binding, and countries that ratify it are obliged to implement it (see TRANSNATIONAL GOVERNANCE). The vast majority of the world's nations—191 countries—were party to the convention by 2008. Although the convention has a scientific advisory body and a permanent secretariat, its ultimate authority derives from decisions made at the Conference of the Parties (COP) sessions, which are meetings of the signatory states.

COP sessions have approved important initiatives for achieving the objectives of the convention. Some of these initiatives are classed as thematic programs, such as studying inland waters, forests, mountains, and agricultural lands. Other initiatives are broader and are classed as cross-cutting issues, such as the analyses of invasive species and the effects of tourism on biodiversity. Also,

COP2 called for the periodic production of Global Biodiversity Outlook (GBO) reports that, in effect, stand as status reports on the progress made in achieving the aims of the biodiversity convention. The first GBO was published in November 2001 and the second in March 2006 (see Document 2).

One of the most significant policy goals to emerge from the COP sessions is called the 2010 Biodiversity Target; in 2002, COP6 resolved "to achieve by 2010 a significant reduction of the current rate of biodiversity loss at the global, regional and national level as a contribution to poverty alleviation and to the benefit of all life on earth." This is an ambitious and hugely challenging target; GBO2 admitted in 2006 that "unprecedented additional efforts" were required at all levels if this target is to be met.

As with all international agreements, the success of the Convention on Biological Diversity depends mainly on actions taken by the signatory countries. Among the commitments under the convention, governments are required to draft National Biodiversity Strategies and Action Plans (NBSAPs) and to integrate these into broader national plans for the environment and development. These plans vary, but they tend to be based on surveys of existing biodiversity resources coupled with evaluations of their importance and vulnerability. This permits governments to set targets for the conservation and sustainable use of local biodiversity and to craft strategies for meeting them. Other governmental obligations under the convention include the prevention of the spread of invasive species, restoration of degraded ecosystems, and promotion of public participation in conservation measures. Each government is required to submit a report at COP meetings describing what it has done in fulfillment of its treaty obligations. These reports are another important means by which the progress toward the convention's objectives can be judged.

The Convention on Biological Diversity has produced a specific subsidiary agreement, the Cartagena Protocol on Biosafety, which deals with issues in the field of biotechnology. Advances in the biotech industry have led to the increasing introduction of living modified organisms (LMOs), also called genetically modified organisms (GMOs), as foodstuffs, pharmaceuticals, and other products. There are concerns about LMOs because the creation of organisms with entirely novel genetic combinations may pose unknown risks to the genetic diversity of wild populations of similar organisms. Such concerns led to the negotiation of the protocol, which was adopted in January 2000. The Cartagena Protocol on Biosafety allows countries to restrict imports of agricultural products that contain LMOs and requires commodities containing LMOs to be labeled as such before export. The protocol also establishes mechanisms facilitating the exchange of information on LMOs and assisting countries in the implementation of the protocol.

Regional Summaries

Biodiversity tends to be greatest in the equatorial regions, although numerous other factors of geography and climate also exert influences. Many different

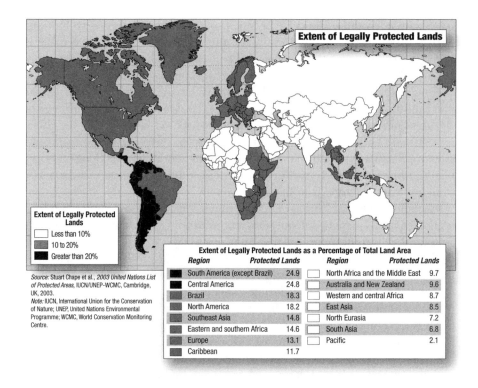

Extent of Legally Protected Lands

Extent of Legally Protected Lands

- Less than 10%
- 10 to 20%
- Greater than 20%

Source: Stuart Chape et al., *2003 United Nations List of Protected Areas*, IUCN/UNEP-WCMC, Cambridge, UK, 2003.
Note: IUCN, International Union for the Conservation of Nature; UNEP, United Nations Environmental Programme; WCMC, World Conservation Monitoring Centre.

Extent of Legally Protected Lands as a Percentage of Total Land Area

Region	Protected Lands	Region	Protected Lands
South America (except Brazil)	24.9	North Africa and the Middle East	9.7
Central America	24.8	Australia and New Zealand	9.6
Brazil	18.3	Western and central Africa	8.7
North America	18.2	East Asia	8.5
Southeast Asia	14.8	North Eurasia	7.2
Eastern and southern Africa	14.6	South Asia	6.8
Europe	13.1	Pacific	2.1
Caribbean	11.7		

types of ecosystems occur across the globe, and pressures on the living world, and hence priorities for conservation, vary from region to region. Unfortunately, the same underlying theme prevails everywhere—there is no region where biodiversity is not in general decline. The story is much the same in the deep oceans, which cover the majority of the planet, with the collapse of wild fish stocks highlighting the serious damage to marine ecosystems; the United Nations Food and Agriculture Organization reported in 2005 that around three-quarters of fish stocks are being harvested at or above their ecological capacity.

North America

The United States and Canada have per capita consumption rates of energy and resources that are among the highest in the world, creating enormous pressure on natural resources across the region (and, indeed, contributing disproportionately to pressures globally). A wide and important range of species and habitats is nonetheless found across this vast area, with Canada possessing one-quarter of the world's wetlands and one-quarter of its ancient forest. This is despite high rates of habitat depletion. For example, Canada has drained 65 percent of its coastal marshes, and the United States has destroyed half of its original wetlands. Biodiversity is in decline throughout North America; 660 species of higher plants in Canada are at some degree of risk according to "Wild Species 2005: The General Status of Species in Canada"; in addition, the U.S. Fish and Wildlife Service estimated in November 2008 that 746 plant species are endangered or threatened in the United States. The U.S. Geological Survey reported in 2008 that nearly 40 percent of fish species in North American streams, rivers, and lakes are now imperiled, and the National Audubon Society reported that a quarter of U.S. bird species are at risk of extinction. The main causes of such alarming declines are intensive agriculture, development, resource extraction, and clearance of old-growth forest. The introduction of exotic species has also affected biodiversity. According to a 2004 study from Cornell University, there are approximately 50,000 foreign species in the United States, which together cause environmental damage and losses estimated at almost $120 billion per year; furthermore, 42 percent of the species on the Threatened or Endangered Species lists are at risk primarily because of alien or invasive species.

Marine ecosystems in the area are also being degraded; pollution from agriculture, industry, and sewage is affecting areas such as the Florida Keys and the Gulf of Mexico, with the latter now displaying a dead zone where oxygen levels in the water are too low to support fish. Overfishing is a problem in many coastal waters, and some very important fish stocks, such as the cod fisheries of the Grand Banks (off Newfoundland, Canada) have collapsed and not recovered.

Policy initiatives to conserve biodiversity are generally well developed in North America; Yellowstone National Park, founded in 1872 and located mostly in Wyoming, is generally reckoned to have been the world's first national park. Some 11 percent of the North American land area is now legally protected. However, there have been land-use controversies in some protected areas, such as proposed oil drilling in the Arctic National Wildlife Refuge in Alaska. The United States remains one of the very few signatory nations not to have ratified the Convention on Biological Diversity, casting a shadow over the prospects for long-term biodiversity conservation in the region.

Latin America and the Caribbean

Latin America is exceptionally biologically rich. It includes five of the world's ten most biodiverse countries (Brazil, Colombia, Peru, Mexico, and Ecuador) as well as the single most biodiverse area in the world—the tropical Andes. Latin America is home to approximately 27 percent of the world's mammals, 34 percent of its plants, 37 percent of its reptiles, 43 percent of its birds, and 47 percent of its amphibians. The region has the highest diversity of plants on Earth. The World Wide Fund for Nature estimated that 80,000 species are found in the Amazon rainforest alone; yet the ecology of Latin America is still relatively poorly studied, especially in the tropical zones.

Habitat destruction across the region is the primary threat to biodiversity, with agricultural conversion, resource extraction, and infrastructure construction the main causes. The rapid depletion of the region's tropical forests is well known as a serious global problem, but other habitats are also declining. Caribbean coral reefs are suffering from the effects of coastal development, pollution, overfishing, and rising sea temperatures, and mangrove forests are being cleared for agriculture, shrimp farming, and development. Ecuador has lost over two-thirds of its original mangroves, according to the International Mangrove Network. Species across the region are at risk; the IUCN's "2008 Red List" cites 738 species nearing extinction in Brazil, 897 in Mexico, and 2,208 in Ecuador. Because of gaps in ecological knowledge about the region, such figures probably understate the true scale of the problem.

Countries throughout the region have responded to biodiversity depletion by establishing protected areas; approximately 20 percent of the region is thus designated, more than in any other region. One of the most high-profile conservation projects in Latin America is the Mesoamerican Biological Corridor, a network of protected areas linking southern Mexico to Panama. Such conservation measures will need to be very robust if they are to help ease the continuing pressures on Latin American biodiversity, especially forest loss.

Europe (including the Russian Federation)

Europe, the region with the longest history of industrialization, has suffered a lengthy decline in biodiversity, which greatly accelerated during the last century. Biodiversity is under strain from infrastructure development, forestry, agriculture, air and water pollution, wetland drainage, and the impact of introduced species. Large areas of wild land are rare, especially in the west of the region; due to the relatively small size and high population densities of most European countries, ecosystems tend to suffer from fragmentation, being split into smaller sections by developments such as highways or by farmland, further stressing wildlife. The European Environment Agency reports that butterfly populations in the region have declined by around 30 percent in the last twenty years. Species biodiversity is threatened everywhere; for instance, Spain risks losing 19 percent of its amphibians, 20 percent of its mammals and 27 percent of its reptiles, according to the IUCN. Marine ecosystems are also under stress, with the North Sea in serious trouble, mostly due to overfishing; the 2006 GBO reported that the number of large fish in the North Atlantic has declined by two-thirds in the last fifty years.

Europe has a relatively strong and popular green movement, and an awareness of Europe's declining biodiversity is well established among the public and policymakers. Protected areas have been increasing in size and number since the middle of the twentieth century, and they now cover around 9 percent of Europe's land area. Twelve national parks have been designated in England and Wales since 1949, for instance, with one more currently in the process of being created. Nonetheless, biodiversity seems likely to continue to decline across the region, with an important test being the ability of conservation measures to protect the relatively undeveloped habitats of Eastern Europe from the pressures of rapid economic expansion.

North Africa and the Middle East

This predominantly arid or subarid region is home to a variety of wildlife, including many rare species and a notably high proportion of endemic plants.

The coastal and freshwater zones are especially important, with more than 1,200 species of fish and 200 species of crab in the Arabian and Red seas. The Mediterranean coastal fringe of North Africa is also an important center of biodiversity in the region. Habitats, and therefore species, face an intimidating suite of pressures; overgrazing, desertification, oil drilling, deforestation, drainage, water pollution and soil salinization, unsustainable hunting and fishing, military action, and urban development all take a toll. The Arabian Oryx became extinct in the wild in 1972 because of overhunting across the Middle East; it was reintroduced to Oman (from captive stock) in 1982, but it still suffers from poaching and remains among the most threatened of animals in the world. Degradation due to these pressures seems likely to grow as the human population increases and development spreads. Protected areas cover some 10 percent of the region, but this is not enough to reverse these trends.

Sub-Saharan Africa

Sub-Saharan Africa possesses a vast richness of habitats and species, with notable concentrations of biodiversity in the equatorial zone, on the southern cape, and on the island of Madagascar (which has a very high proportion of endemic species). The most extensive habitat type in Africa is savannah (a tropical grassland with scattered trees), which covers almost half the land area of the continent. The savannah supports the world's largest concentration of large mammals, including iconic animals such as elephant, lion, giraffe, zebra, and a host of other species from other groups. Biodiversity is in decline across the continent; for example, South Africa's Department of Environmental Affairs and Tourism states that half the country's original wetlands have been destroyed. Deforestation, wetland drainage, desertification, mining, water scarcity, urbanization, and agriculture all contribute to habitat loss and biodiversity decline. Violent conflicts also play a significant role, as does, increasingly, the hunting of bushmeat (see Case Study—Primate Conservation and Bushmeat in the Congo Basin).

Although around 11 percent of the continent is protected for conservation, intense competition for land use outside (and sometimes within) protected areas means that the rates of species decline are likely to increase. As the human population grows rapidly and the great majority remains poor, it is difficult to see how the pressures on biodiversity can fail to increase dramatically.

Asia

Asia encompasses an enormous variety of habitat types, has climate zones ranging from equatorial to subarctic, and contains the world's highest mountain system, the world's second largest rainforest complex, and over half of the world's coral reefs. There are concentrations of extremely high biodiversity, with some of the most biodiverse nations on Earth (such as Indonesia, China, Malaysia, and India) in this region. The region is also the world's most densely populated and most rapidly developing, so biodiversity is under ever-increasing stress. For example, Indonesia has a greater variety of mammals than any other country on Earth, but the IUCN "2008 Red List" classed over one-quarter of these at risk of extinction. The IUCN also warned that, in Asia as a whole, 79 percent of monkeys and other primates face extinction. Deforestation, urbanization, agricultural expansion, mining, and pollution have all taken their toll. Wildlife also suffers directly from uncontrolled harvesting, hunting, and fishing.

Asia also displays a great richness of marine and coastal habitats, with very significant areas of coral reefs, mangroves, and seagrass beds. The greatest concentration of marine biodiversity in the world is found here—the Coral Triangle, which includes ocean areas around Indonesia, Malaysia, Papua New Guinea, Philippines, Solomon Islands, and Timor-Leste. Covering an area of 1.4 billion acres (570 million hectares) and hosting over six hundred reef-building coral species—75 percent of all those known to science—and over 3,000 species of reef fish, the Coral Triangle is a special priority for conservation. Nonetheless, it is not immune from the problems facing marine habitats all over the region, such as overfishing, pollution, sedimentation, and mangrove clearance for aquaculture.

Inadequate data collection in many parts of Asia means that the true extent of the decline in most species remains uncertain. Conservation problems are compounded by the patchy effectiveness of the protected areas across the region, which cover some 8 percent of the region's land area. For example, the Tanjung Puting reserve in Indonesia has suffered badly from illegal logging and poaching, and associated allegations of corruption have been made against the ranger staff. It seems that biodiversity conservation is likely to be a low priority in this poor region as its population and economies continue to grow rapidly, increasing pressure on scarce land.

The Pacific

The main feature of biodiversity in this area is the extraordinarily high levels of endemism. Around 80 percent of Australia's plants and animals are endemic, according to the Australian Museum; every native amphibian, reptile, and mammal in New Zealand is endemic; and many of the other islands in this region also feature very high endemism. The rich biological resources of this region are declining; in the two centuries since European colonization of Australia, 11 out of the country's 142 marsupial species disappeared—the worst mammal extinction in modern times. The IUCN "2008 Red List" detailed fifty-seven more as threatened with extinction. The introduction of many species has been particularly devastating to biodiversity in the region. In New Zealand, for example, stoats, weasels, and ferrets were introduced in the nineteenth century to control rabbits (themselves a problematic introduced species), but these species have preyed on and seriously reduced the native bird populations. Other pressures on biodiversity in the region include vegetation clearance (mainly for agriculture), wetland drainage, pollution, and soil salinization. Protected areas cover some 8 percent of Australia and 25 percent of New Zealand; most of the Pacific islands tend to have a smaller proportion of their land protected.

Rich marine life in all parts of Oceania, including the valuable coral reef systems, is being depleted by commercial overfishing and pollution. The largest coral reef system in the world, the Great Barrier Reef, is showing signs of degradation despite being protected by a marine park. Climate change is especially significant in Oceania; rising sea levels directly imperil many of the smaller island nations in the region, and warmer seas impact marine biodiversity.

Data

Table 1 Species Richness of Animals and Vascular Plants for Selected Countries

Country	Vascular plants	Birds	Mammals
Algeria	3,164	372	100
Australia	15,638	851	376
Brazil	56,215	1,712	578
Canada	3,270	472	211
China	32,200	1,221	502
Colombia	51,220	1,821	467
DRC	11,007	1,148	430
Ecuador	19,362	1,515	341
France	4,630	517	148
Honduras	5,680	699	201
India	18,664	1,180	422
Indonesia	29,375	1,604	667
Jamaica	3,308	298	35
Libya	1,825	326	87
Malaysia	15,500	746	337
Mexico	26,071	1,026	544
New Zealand	2,382	351	73
Oman	1,204	483	74
Papua New Guinea	11,544	720	260
Russian Federation	11,400	645	296
Saudi Arabia	2,028	433	94
South Africa	23,420	829	320
Sweden	1,750	457	85
Tanzania	10,008	1,056	375
United Kingdom	1,623	557	103
United States	19,473	888	468

Source: World Resources Institute (WRI), "EarthTrends: Environmental Information," World Resources Institute, Washington, D.C., 2007, available at http://earthtrends.wri.org. (Original data supplied to WRI by UNEP/WCMC, 2004.)

Note: DRC, Democratic Republic of Congo.

Table 2   Extent of the Protection of the World's Major Terrestrial Biomes

Biome name	Protected areas			Biome protected (%)	
	Area (km^2)	Number	Extent (km^2)	2003	1997
Tropical humid forests	10,513,210	3,422	2,450,344	23.31	8.77
Subtropical/temperate rainforests/woodlands	3,930,979	6,196	665,174	16.92	10.29
Temperate needle-leaf forests/woodlands	15,682,817	13,297	1,350,221	8.61	5.72
Tropical dry forests/woodlands	17,312,538	5,746	2,210,563	12.77	7.07
Temperate broad-leaf forests	11,216,659	35,735	856,502	7.64	3.60
Evergreen sclerophyllous forests	3,757,144	5,334	399,587	10.64	4.39
Warm deserts/semi-deserts	24,279,843	2,008	2,492,377	10.27	4.83
Cold-winter deserts	9,250,252	1,235	704,037	7.61	5.90
Tundra communities	22,017,390	405	2,606,041	11.84	8.38
Tropical grasslands/savannahs	4,264,832	318	654,310	15.34	7.42
Temperate grasslands	8,976,591	3,533	411,839	4.59	0.98
Mixed mountain systems	10,633,145	9,345	1,735,828	16.32	9.10
Mixed island systems	3,252,563	3,425	967,129	29.73	16.32
Lake systems	517,695	261	7,989	1.54	1.12
Total	145,605,658	90,260	17,511,941	12.03	6.52

Source : Stuart Chape et al., *United Nations List of Protected Areas* (Cambridge, UK : IUCN/WCMC, 2003).

Table 3   Threatened Species in Selected Animal Groups

Class	Threatened status					Total threatened
	EX	EW	CR	EN	VU	
Mammals	76	2	188	448	505	1,141
Birds	134	4	190	361	671	1,222
Reptiles	21	1	86	134	203	423
Amphibians	38	1	475	755	675	1,905
Crustaceans	7	1	84	127	395	606
Insects	60	1	70	132	424	626
Bivalves	31	0	52	28	15	95
Gastropods	257	14	216	196	471	883

Source: International Union for the Conservation of Nature, "2008 IUCN Red List of Threatened Species," IUCN, Gland, Switzerland, and Cambridge, UK, 2008.

Notes: EX, extinct; EW, extinct in the wild (known only in captivity); CR, critically endangered (extremely high risk of extinction in the wild); EN, endangered (very high risk of extinction in the wild); VU, vulnerable (high risk of extinction in the wild).

Case Study—Primate Conservation and Bushmeat in the Congo Basin

The Congo Basin of west central Africa holds a very important block of tropical rainforest covering nearly 500 million acres (200 million hectares) and spread over six countries: Cameroon, Central African Republic, Congo, Democratic Republic of Congo (DRC), Equatorial Guinea, and Gabon. These forests are well known for their wildlife diversity, with primates such as chimpanzees and gorillas—humankind's closest evolutionary relatives—among the most celebrated residents of the forests. The main threat to biodiversity in the region is deforestation, but humans' hunting for food (bushmeat) is increasingly threatening the survival of larger animals, in general, and primates, in particular.

There is a long tradition of hunting within the Congo Basin, with hunted forest meat an important food source, meeting between 30 and 80 percent of the dietary protein needs of rural dwellers in central Africa. Hunted animals also meet cultural and nonfood needs. However, the scale of hunting has rocketed in recent decades, with noticeable effects on wildlife. For example, the IUCN stated that the population of Lowland Gorilla (*Gorilla gorilla*) fell by 56 percent between 1983 and 2000 in Gabon, mostly attributed to hunting; because Gabon has the lowest density of human habitation in the Congo Basin, other countries are presumed to have experienced rates of loss even greater than this. The Lowland Gorilla is now classed as Critically Endangered in the IUCN "2008 Red List." Similar patterns have been observed with other primates, with an estimated 7 million Red Colobus Monkeys (*Piliocolobus* species) taken from the Congo Basin for food every year, for instance.

The bushmeat trade is of high economic importance in the region, with sales both within forest communities at local markets and, increasingly, exported to urban centers and sometimes abroad. There is a growing market for bushmeat in the rapidly expanding cities, with a growing number of commercial hunters serving this market, often via illegal hunting. An important additional factor driving the huge increase in hunting is the logging industry, which has opened up large areas of previously poorly accessible land by construction of roads, thus facilitating access into the forest for hunters and providing routes for the transport of carcasses to cities; in fact, logging trucks have been used for the direct transport of bushmeat carcasses in many areas. Also, camps set up by corporations undertaking logging, mining, or drilling operations in the forest to accommodate their workers increase the local demand for wild meat. Political instability and lawlessness have exacerbated primate decline in the area, especially because of increased hunting after influxes of combatants or refugees into remote areas.

Unfortunately, legislative protection of endangered species in the region has often proved ineffective, and protected areas in the Congo Basin have failed to maintain safe primate populations even within their borders. Surveys within Salonga National Park in the DRC between 2003 and 2006 found evidence that Bonobo Chimpanzees (*Pan paniscus*) were being regularly poached in many parts of the park.

Hunting for bushmeat is now so extensive that it may finally drive the threatened primates in the Congo Basin to extinction. Large apes are particularly vulnerable due to their slow reproduction rate, which means that their populations recover slowly from depletion. Human populations in the forest also face a precarious future as the wild animal populations decline; the explosion of commercial hunting, much of which is for export to urban centers, means that, as bushmeat resources are exhausted, forest-dwellers face a loss both of their main protein supply and of an important source of basic income.

Solving the bushmeat crisis will be a very difficult and complex task. Because of the ingrained importance of bushmeat to the people of the Congo Basin and the lack of effective enforcement measures in much of the area, a total ban on the bushmeat trade—advocated by some conservationists—is unlikely to be achieved. A more integrated approach, involving a combination of regulation, education, protection of local land rights, and poverty alleviation, would be more likely to succeed. As with many examples of ecological degradation, social, political, and economic factors must be crucial components in any attempt to prevent the bushmeat trade from wiping out threatened primate species in this troubled and poor region.

Biographical Sketches

Gonzalo Castro leads the biodiversity team of the World Bank's Environment Department, which has funded in full or in part numerous biodiversity projects in a variety of countries. He is a Peruvian biologist and former assistant professor of biology at Universidad Peruana Cayetano Heredia in Lima.

Tom E. Lovejoy is president of the Heinz Center for Science, Economics and the Environment. His previous posts include chief biodiversity adviser for the World Bank, senior adviser to the president of the United Nations Foundation, assistant secretary and counselor to the secretary at the Smithsonian Institution, and science adviser to the U.S. secretary of the Interior. Lovejoy is a very influential thinker on biodiversity issues and has initiated important policy concepts such as debt-for-nature swaps.

Jeffrey A. McNeely is chief scientist of the International Union for the Conservation of Nature. McNeely has done important work on the effectiveness of protected areas, notably in his capacity as the secretary-general of the 1992 World Congress on National Parks and Protected Areas.

Norman Myers has greatly developed awareness of important environmental problems such as tropical deforestation, the extinction crisis, and environmental refugees and has developed the concept of the biodiversity hotspot. He is visiting professor at several universities, including Oxford, Stanford, and Harvard, and he has advised numerous bodies on environmental policy.

Vandana Shiva is a writer, activist, and policy advocate and founder of the Research Foundation for Science, Technology, and Ecology. Shiva is well known for her work on biodiversity in relation to agriculture, and she is a fierce critic of the role of the biotech industry in agriculture.

Edward O. Wilson is perhaps the world's most eminent conservation biologist and is one of the most influential scientists working on biodiversity. His specialism is ant taxonomy, but he has also contributed landmark research in the fields of sociobiology, island biogeography, and evolution. He is a prolific author, having won Pulitzer Prizes for two of his books, and has done much to increase understanding of the biodiversity crisis. He is professor emeritus at Harvard University, where he has spent nearly all his long academic career.

Hamdallah Zedan is executive director of the Secretariat of the Convention on Biological Diversity, which is responsible for organizing meetings (especially Conference of the Parties sessions), drafting reports, and other roles important to the implementation of the convention. Zedan is an Egyptian microbiologist who previously worked for the United Nations Environment Programme's biodiversity unit.

Directory

Conservation International, 2011 Crystal Drive, Suite 500, Arlington, Va. 22202. Telephone: (703) 341-2400; Web: http://www.conservation.org.
Organization working to conserve global biodiversity in tandem with human well-being.

Friends of the Earth International, P.O. Box 19199, 1000 GD Amsterdam, Netherlands. Telephone: (31) 20 622 1369; email: foei@foei.org; Web: http://www.foei.org.
World's largest federation of environmental groups; its campaigns include biodiversity.

International Union for Conservation of Nature (IUCN), Rue Mauverney 28, Gland 1196, Switzerland. Telephone: (41) 22 999-0000; email: webmaster@iucn.org; Web: http://www.iucn.org.
Global partnership of government agencies and scientists aiming to conserve the diversity of nature.

International Union of Biological Sciences, Bat 442 Universite Paris–Sud 11, 91 405 Orsay cedex, France. Telephone: (33) 16 915 5027; email: secretariat@iubs.org; Web: http://www.iubs.org.
Organization promoting and facilitating the study of biological sciences.

National Audubon Society, 225 Varick Street, 7th Floor, New York, N.Y. 10014. Telephone: (212) 979-3000; email: education@audubon.org; Web: http://www.audubon.org.
Organization dedicated to conserving and restoring natural ecosystems.

Natural Resources Defense Council, 40 West 20th Street, New York, N.Y. 10011. Telephone: (212) 727-2700; email: nrdcinfo@nrdc.org; Web: http://www.nrdc.org.
Group campaigning for the protection of wildlife and wild places.

Nature Serve, 1101 Wilson Boulevard, 15th Floor, Arlington, Va. 22209. Telephone: (703) 908-1800; Web: http://www.natureserve.org.
Nonprofit organization providing research to support effective conservation action.

Sierra Club, 85 Second Street, 2nd Floor, San Francisco, Calif. 94105. Telephone: 415-977-5500; email: information@sierraclub.org; Web: http://www.sierraclub.org.

The oldest and largest grassroots environmental organization in the United States working to protect wild places.

Society for Ecological Restoration International, 285 W 18th Street, Suite 1, Tucson, Ariz. 85701. Telephone: (520) 622-5485; Web: http://www.ser.org.
Nonprofit network of ecological restoration projects and practitioners.

United Nations Environment Programme (UNEP), United Nations Avenue, Gigiri, P.O. Box 30552, 00100 Nairobi, Kenya. Telephone: (254-20) 762 1234; email: unepinfo@unep.org; Web: http://www.unep/org.
Agency tackling a range of environmental issues on an international basis.

Wilderness Society, 1615 M Street NW, Washington, D.C. 20036. Telephone: 1-800-THE-WILD; Web: http://wilderness.org.
Organization working to protect U.S. wilderness areas, mainly by pressing for the designation of protected lands.

World Conservation Monitoring Centre, 219 Huntingdon Road, Cambridge CB3 0DL, United Kingdom. Telephone: (44) 1223 277314; email: info@unep-wcmc .org; Web: http://www.unep-wcmc.org.
UNEP body aiming to provide authoritative information to inform conservation policy and action.

World Resources Institute, 10 G Street NE, Suite 800, Washington, D.C. 20002. Telephone: (202) 729-7600; Web: http://www.wri.org.
Think tank aiming to place environmental issues on the international agenda and influence societal change.

World Wide Fund for Nature (WWF; formerly World Wildlife Fund), 1250 24th Street NW, Washington, D.C., 20090-7180. Telephone: (202) 293-4800; Web: http://www.worldwildlife.org.
U.S. office of the world's largest privately supported conservation body.

Further Research

Books

Broswimmer, Franz. *Ecocide: A Short History of the Mass Extinction of Species.* London: Pluto, 2002.

Chivian, Eric, and Aaron Bernstein, eds. *Sustaining Life: How Human Health Depends on Biodiversity.* Oxford and New York: Oxford University Press, 2008.

Eldredge, Niles. *Life in the Balance: Humanity and the Biodiversity Crisis.* Princeton, N.J.: Princeton University Press, 1998.

Gaston, Kevin J., and John I. Spicer. *Biodiversity: An Introduction.* 2nd ed. Oxford: Blackwell, 2003.

Groombridge, Brian, and Martin D. Jenkins. *World Atlas of Biodiversity: Earth's Living Resources in the 21st Century.* Berkeley, Calif.: University of California Press, 2002.

Kushwar, Ram Bir Singh, and Vijay Kumar. *Economics of Protected Areas and Its Effects on Biodiversity.* New Delhi: APH, 2001.

Lovejoy, Thomas E., and Lee Hannah, eds. *Climate Change and Biodiversity.* New Haven, Conn.: Yale University Press, 2005.

Meyer, Stephen M. *The End of the Wild*. Cambridge, Mass: MIT Press/Boston Review, 2006.

Spicer, John I. *Biodiversity: A Beginners Guide*. Oxford: Oneworld, 2006.

Wilson, Edward O. *The Diversity of Life*. Rev. ed. London and New York: Penguin, 2001.

———. *The Future of Life*. New York: Knopf, 2002.

World Resources Institute. *EarthTrends: Environmental Information*. Washington, D.C.: World Resources Institute, 2007. Available at http://earthtrends.wri.org.

Articles and Reports

Allsopp, Michelle, et al. *Oceans in Peril: Protecting Marine Biodiversity*. Washington, D.C.: Worldwatch Institute, 2007.

Constanza, R., et al. "The Value of the World's Ecosystem Services and Natural Capital." *Nature* 387 (1997): 253–260.

Hanski, Ilkka, and Otso Ovaskainen. "Extinction Debt at Extinction Threshold." *Conservation Biology* 16, no. 2 (2002): 666–673.

Hearn, Josephine. "Unfair Game." *Scientific American* 284 (June 2001): 15–16.

International Union for the Conservation of Nature. "The Review of the 2008 Red List of Threatened Species." IUCN, Gland, Switzerland, 2008.

Kareiva, Peter, and Michelle Marvier. "Conserving Biodiversity Coldspots: Recent Calls to Direct Conservation Funding to the World's Biodiversity Hotspots May Be Bad Investment Advice." *American Scientist* 91 (2003): 344–349.

MacKenzie, Deborah. "Sick to Death." *New Scientist* 2250 (2000): 32–35.

Myers, Norman. "Biodiversity Hotspots Revisited." *Bioscience* 53, no. 10 (2003): 916–917.

Purvis, Andy, and Andy Hector. "Getting the Measure of Biodiversity." *Nature* 405 (2000): 212.

Schrope, Mark. "Mission Implausible: Extreme Schemes to Save the Reefs." *New Scientist* 2678 (October 15, 2008): 28–31.

Staedter, Tracy. "Brazilian Trees May Harbor Millions of Unidentified Species of Bacteria." *Scientific American* (June 2006). Available at http://www.scientificamerican.com/article.cfm?id=brazilian-trees-may-harbo.

World Resources Institute. "Millennium Ecosystem Assessment—Ecosystems and Human Well-Being: Biodiversity Synthesis." WRI, Washington, D.C., 2005.

World Wide Fund for Nature. "Living Planet Report." WWF International, Gland, Switzerland, 2008.

Worm, Boris, et al. "Impacts of Biodiversity Loss on Ocean Ecosystem Services." *Science* 314, no. 5800 (2006): 787–790.

Web Sites

Animal Info
http://www.animalinfo.org

Australian Museum Online, Fact Sheets
http://www.amonline.net.au/factsheets

Biodiversity and Biological Diversity Web Server
http://biodiversity.uno.edu

Biodiversity Counts, American Museum of Natural History
http://www.amnh.org/education/resources/biocounts

Biodiversity Hotspots
http://www.biodiversityhotspots.org

Biodiversity WorldMap, Natural History Museum (UK)
http://www.nhm.ac.uk/research-curation/research/projects/worldmap

California Academy of Sciences
http://www.calacademy.org

Catalogue of Life
http://www.catalogueoflife.org/search.php

Center for Applied Biodiversity Science
http://science.conservation.org/portal/server.pt

Convention on Biological Diversity
http://www.cbd.int

Convention on International Trade in Endangered Species of Wild Fauna and Flora
http://www.cites.org

Convention on Migratory Species of Wild Animals
http://www.cms.int

DIVERSITAS International Programme of Biodiversity Science
http://www.diversitas-international.org

Earthwatch Institute
http://www.earthwatch.org

EUNIS Biodiversity Database (for Europe)
http://eunis.eea.europa.eu

Global Biodiversity Information Facility
http://www.gbif.org

Integrated Taxonomic Information System (ITIS)
http://www.itis.gov

IUCN Red List of Threatened Species
http://www.iucnredlist.org

Mangrove Action Project
http://www.mangroveactionproject.org

Mangrove.org
http://www.mangrove.org

Mass Extinction Information Portal
http://www.well.com/~davidu/extinction.html

Mass Extinction Memorial Observatory
http://memoproject.org

Millennium Ecosystem Assessment
http://www.millenniumassessment.org/en/Index.aspx

North American Wildlife
http://www.wildlifenorthamerica.com

Ocean Biogeographic Information System
http://www.iobis.org

Plant Talk
http://www.plant-talk.org

Reefbase
http://www.reefbase.org

Smithsonian Tropical Research Institute
http://www.stri.org

Society for Conservation Biology
http://www.conbio.org

Species 2000
http://www.sp2000.org

Species Alliance
http://www.speciesalliance.org/index.php

UK Agricultural Biodiversity Coalition
http://ukabc.org

UK Biodiversity Action Plan
http://www.ukbap.org.uk

USDA National Invasive Species Information Center
http://www.invasivespeciesinfo.gov

U.S. Fish and Wildlife Service
http://www.fws.gov

Wild World Terrestrial Ecoregions of the World
http://www.nationalgeographic.com/wildworld/terrestrial.html

World Atlas of Biodiversity
http://stort.unep-wcmc.org/imaps/gb2002/book/viewer.htm

World Atlas of Seagrasses
http://www.unep-wcmc.org/marine/seagrassatlas/index.htm

World Biodiversity Database
http://nlbif.eti.uva.nl/bis/index.php

World Conference on Marine Biodiversity
http://www.marbef.org/worldconference

World Data Center for Biodiversity and Ecology
http://wdc.nbii.gov/portal/server.pt

World Land Trust
http://www.worldlandtrust.org

WWF Global 200 Ecoregions
http://www.worldwildlife.org/wildplaces/about.cfm

Documents

1. Convention on Biological Diversity

United Nations, Conference on Environment and Development, Rio de Janeiro, June 1992

The full text is available at http://www.cbd.int/convention/convention.shtml.

Extracts

Article 1. Objectives

The objectives of this Convention, to be pursued in accordance with its relevant provisions, are the conservation of biological diversity, the sustainable use of its components and the fair and equitable sharing of the benefits arising out of the utilization of genetic resources, including by appropriate access to genetic resources and by appropriate transfer of relevant technologies, taking into account all rights over those resources and to technologies, and by appropriate funding. . . .

Article 6. General Measures for Conservation and Sustainable Use

Each Contracting Party shall, in accordance with its particular conditions and capabilities:

(a) Develop national strategies, plans or programmes for the conservation and sustainable use of biological diversity or adapt for this purpose existing strategies, plans or programmes which shall reflect, inter alia, the measures set out in this Convention relevant to the Contracting Party concerned; and

(b) Integrate, as far as possible and as appropriate, the conservation and sustainable use of biological diversity into relevant sectoral or cross-sectoral plans, programmes and policies.

Article 7. Identification and Monitoring

Each Contracting Party shall, as far as possible and as appropriate, in particular for the purposes of Articles 8 to 10:

(a) Identify components of biological diversity important for its conservation and sustainable use having regard to the indicative list of categories set down in Annex I;

(b) Monitor, through sampling and other techniques, the components of biological diversity identified pursuant to subparagraph (a) above, paying particular attention to those requiring urgent conservation measures and those which offer the greatest potential for sustainable use;

(c) Identify processes and categories of activities which have or are likely to have significant adverse impacts on the conservation and sustainable use of biological diversity, and monitor their effects through sampling and other techniques; and

(d) Maintain and organize, by any mechanism data, derived from identification and monitoring activities pursuant to subparagraphs (a), (b) and (c) above.

Article 8. In-situ Conservation

Each Contracting Party shall, as far as possible and as appropriate:

(a) Establish a system of protected areas or areas where special measures need to be taken to conserve biological diversity;

(b) Develop, where necessary, guidelines for the selection, establishment and management of protected areas or areas where special measures need to be taken to conserve biological diversity;

(c) Regulate or manage biological resources important for the conservation of biological diversity whether within or outside protected areas, with a view to ensuring their conservation and sustainable use;

(d) Promote the protection of ecosystems, natural habitats and the maintenance of viable populations of species in natural surroundings;

(e) Promote environmentally sound and sustainable development in areas adjacent to protected areas with a view to furthering protection of these areas;

(f) Rehabilitate and restore degraded ecosystems and promote the recovery of threatened species, inter alia, through the development and implementation of plans or other management strategies;

(g) Establish or maintain means to regulate, manage or control the risks associated with the use and release of living modified organisms resulting from biotechnology which are likely to have adverse environmental impacts that could affect the conservation and sustainable use of biological diversity, taking also into account the risks to human health;

(h) Prevent the introduction of, control or eradicate those alien species which threaten ecosystems, habitats or species;

(i) Endeavour to provide the conditions needed for compatibility between present uses and the conservation of biological diversity and the sustainable use of its components;

(j) Subject to its national legislation, respect, preserve and maintain knowledge, innovations and practices of indigenous and local communities embodying traditional lifestyles relevant for the conservation and sustainable use of biological diversity and promote their wider application with the approval and involvement of the holders of such knowledge, innovations and practices and encourage the equitable sharing of the benefits arising from the utilization of such knowledge, innovations and practices;

(k) Develop or maintain necessary legislation and/or other regulatory provisions for the protection of threatened species and populations;

(l) Where a significant adverse effect on biological diversity has been determined pursuant to Article 7, regulate or manage the relevant processes and categories of activities; and

(m) Cooperate in providing financial and other support for in-situ conservation outlined in subparagraphs (a) to (l) above, particularly to developing countries.

Article 9. Ex-situ Conservation

Each Contracting Party shall, as far as possible and as appropriate, and predominantly for the purpose of complementing in-situ measures:

(a) Adopt measures for the ex-situ conservation of components of biological diversity, preferably in the country of origin of such components;

(b) Establish and maintain facilities for ex-situ conservation of and research on plants, animals and micro-organisms, preferably in the country of origin of genetic resources;

(c) Adopt measures for the recovery and rehabilitation of threatened species and for their reintroduction into their natural habitats under appropriate conditions;

(d) Regulate and manage collection of biological resources from natural habitats for ex-situ conservation purposes so as not to threaten ecosystems and in-situ populations of species, except where special temporary ex-situ measures are required under subparagraph (c) above; and

(e) Cooperate in providing financial and other support for ex-situ conservation outlined in subparagraphs (a) to (d) above and in the establishment and maintenance of ex-situ conservation facilities in developing countries.

Article 10. Sustainable Use of Components of Biological Diversity

Each Contracting Party shall, as far as possible and as appropriate:

(a) Integrate consideration of the conservation and sustainable use of biological resources into national decision-making;

(b) Adopt measures relating to the use of biological resources to avoid or minimize adverse impacts on biological diversity;

(c) Protect and encourage customary use of biological resources in accordance with traditional cultural practices that are compatible with conservation or sustainable use requirements;

(d) Support local populations to develop and implement remedial action in degraded areas where biological diversity has been reduced; and

(e) Encourage cooperation between its governmental authorities and its private sector in developing methods for sustainable use of biological resources.

2. Summary of the Second Edition of the Global Biodiversity Outlook

The full text is available at http://www.cbd.int/gbo2.

Extract

1. Biological diversity, or biodiversity, is the term given to the variety of life on Earth. It is the combination of life forms and their interactions with one another, and with the physical environment that has made Earth habitable for humans. Ecosystems provide the basic necessities of life, offer protection from natural disasters and disease, and are the foundation for human culture. The Millennium Ecosystem Assessment—a scientific undertaking involving over 1300 experts working in 95 countries—recently confirmed the overwhelming contributions made by natural ecosystems to human life and well-being. Yet even as we begin to better understand what is at stake, genes, species and habitats are rapidly being lost.

2. Concern over the loss of biodiversity and the recognition of its important role in supporting human life motivated the creation, in 1992, of the Convention on Biological

Diversity, a legally binding global treaty. The Convention encompasses three equally important and complementary objectives: the conservation of biodiversity, the sustainable use of its components, and the fair and equitable sharing of benefits arising out of the utilization of genetic resources. Participation in the Convention is nearly universal, a sign that our global society is well aware of the need to work together to ensure the survival of life on Earth.

3. In 2002, the Conference of the Parties of the Convention adopted a Strategic Plan, with the mission "to achieve, by 2010, a significant reduction of the current rate of biodiversity loss at the global, regional and national level, as a contribution to poverty alleviation and to the benefit of all life on Earth." This 2010 target was subsequently endorsed by the Heads of State and Government at the World Summit on Sustainable Development in Johannesburg, South Africa. Recently, world leaders meeting at the 2005 World Summit of the United Nations reiterated their commitment to meeting the 2010 target.

4. In order to assess progress towards the 2010 biodiversity target, the Conference of the Parties has established supporting goals and targets and identified indicators for evaluating biodiversity status and trends. The second edition of the Global Biodiversity Outlook makes use of these indicators and targets to describe current trends in biodiversity and prospects for achieving the 2010 target.

5. The services provided by healthy, biodiverse ecosystems are the foundation for human well-being. However, out of the 24 ecosystem services recently assessed by the Millennium Ecosystem Assessment, 15 are in decline. These include the provision of fresh water, marine fishery production, the number and quality of places of spiritual and religious value, the ability of the atmosphere to cleanse itself of pollutants, natural hazard regulation, pollination, and the capacity of agricultural ecosystems to provide pest control.

6. Biodiversity loss disrupts ecosystem functions, making ecosystems more vulnerable to shocks and disturbances, less resilient, and less able to supply humans with needed services. The damage to coastal communities from floods and storms, for example, can increase dramatically where protective wetland habitats have been lost or degraded.

7. The consequences of biodiversity loss and ecosystem disruption are often harshest for the rural poor, who depend most immediately upon local ecosystem services for their livelihoods and who are often the least able to access or afford substitutes when these become degraded. In fact, the Millennium Ecosystem Assessment has confirmed that biodiversity loss poses a significant barrier to meeting the needs of the world's poorest, as set out in the United Nations Millennium Development Goals.

8. Garnering the political will to halt ecosystem degradation will depend on clearly demonstrating to policy makers and society at large the full contribution made by ecosystems to poverty alleviation efforts and to national economic growth more generally.

9. Apart from nature's immediate usefulness to humankind, many would argue that every life form has an intrinsic right to exist, and deserves protection. We must also recognize the right of future generations to inherit, as we have, a planet thriving with life, and that continues to afford opportunities to reap the economic, cultural and spiritual benefits of nature.

DEFORESTATION

Tim Allman

Forests are estimated to have covered up to 50 percent of Earth's land surface in the preagricultural period. Today, according to the UN Food and Agriculture Organization (FAO) "State of the World's Forests Report" (SOFO 2007), they cover about 30 percent of the land. Deforestation continues, mainly in the tropics, at alarmingly rapid rates, and even where forest areas are slowly increasing in extent, their quality is generally declining. Reversing these trends to protect and restore the planet's forests is essential for the long-term survival of natural systems and human societies.

Historical Background and Development

Throughout history, humans have exploited forests for wood and other products or cleared them to use the land for farming or other purposes. The potentially disastrous effects of deforestation are not modern phenomena, as the collapse of Mayan civilization around 800 AD suggests. This complex society, centered in the forests of what is now Guatemala, had been established for centuries. Its decline in less than a century, thought to be largely due to the overexploitation of the forests of the region, is often cited as an example of the consequences of rapid development outstripping the carrying capacity of the local environment.

Recognition of the importance of forests as a resource has been a theme of all human societies, although earlier measures to protect forests were generally intended to preserve them for specific uses rather than for the forests' sake. For example, the primary objective of the strict forest laws of the English medieval period was the preservation of hunting rights for the king and nobility.

Deforestation reached new highs during the twentieth century, but only in the latter part of the century has serious attention been drawn to the global scale of the problem. The general burst of concern about environmental issues that characterized the 1970s and 1980s in developed countries was expressed in Europe by interest in the damage done to forests by air pollution and acid rain (see POLLUTION). The plight of the world's tropical forests, however, seems to have made even more of an impact on public consciousness. Images from

National Aeronautics and Space Administration (NASA) Landsat satellites first became available in the 1970s, providing striking illustrations of the scale of forest destruction. This revelation coincided with a surge of forest clearance in Latin America, mainly for cattle ranching and logging.

A consensus among the public, scientists, and policymakers about the urgency of rain forest conservation formed in developed nations during the 1980s and 1990s. The problem was, however, viewed differently in developing nations, many of which expressed resentment that developed countries, having already cleared the majority of their forests and reaping the development benefits from it, were placing pressure on poorer countries not to follow the same pattern. This polarization hampered efforts to tackle tropical deforestation.

In 1983 the first UN-sponsored International Tropical Timber Agreement (ITTA) attempted to regulate trade between producer and consumer nations. Two years later a collaboration among the World Resources Institute (WRI), the World Bank, the United Nations Development Programme (UNDP), and the FAO produced the Tropical Forestry Action Plan (TFAP), a framework within which individual countries could adopt strategies, formulated as national forestry action plans, to attract foreign aid and investment. The ITTA and TFAP attracted criticism and were judged to be of limited effectiveness. The TFAP, in particular, was condemned by nongovernmental organizations (NGOs), some claiming that tropical deforestation could actually increase in some countries as a result of its influence by, for example, funding new roads that would open new timber areas to harvesting. The 1980s, in general, were marked by controversies such as these, and little progress was made in tackling deforestation even as the issue reached its highest profile to date.

The 1992 United Nations Conference on Environment and Development—known as the Earth Summit—in Rio de Janeiro brought the debate into global focus, and a number of new initiatives followed, most of which were aimed at addressing the polarization between developed and developing nations. The profile and activities of NGOs and citizen groups in the deforestation debate has risen in subsequent years, with more collaborative projects involving NGOs, intergovernmental bodies such as the FAO, and scientific institutions. Despite increasing efforts to reverse deforestation, the world's forest cover continues to shrink every year. Many have accepted that the solutions to global deforestation lie well beyond the scope of simple forestry or conservation measures; rather, the state of the forests is inextricably linked to fundamental issues of political and economic organization.

Current Status

Human activities have affected the composition and extent of forests throughout history, but without a doubt, forests have been damaged and cleared at ever-increasing rates as human societies have expanded and technology has advanced. Forest destruction has accelerated dramatically in the last two hundred years, mainly due to agricultural expansion, timber extraction, and economic development. The last fifty years have seen the greatest reduction in global forest extent, and even now, as forests are at last expanding in some areas of the world, less forest remains on Earth than at any time in recorded history.

Research

Forests perform a number of essential roles in the functioning of natural systems. They play a key role in rainfall cycles, consolidate soils, reduce erosion, and represent vital reservoirs of biodiversity (see BIODIVERSITY). Their absorption of carbon dioxide from the atmosphere is a crucial aspect of the global carbon cycle; hence, the loss of forests exacerbates the problem of global warming (see CLIMATE CHANGE). Scientific bodies such as the Intergovernmental Panel on Climate Change and the Global Canopy Programme attribute about 20 percent of total global carbon emissions to forest clearance.

Humans rely heavily on forest timber for construction materials, fuel, and paper (the last of which demands around 40 percent of the world's industrial timber harvest). Forests also supply such products as fruits and nuts, medicines and drugs, oils and resins, and various other natural chemicals. Nonwood forest products number at least 150 and are of significance in international trade, according to the International Tropical Timber Organization. Furthermore, forests represent direct shelter and subsistence and help people around the world maintain their cultural identity. The vast majority of these people live in developing countries, where deforestation is generally at its greatest. The drastic decline of Earth's forests, in quantity and quality, is therefore a serious global issue.

The starting point for an analysis of the extent of deforestation is the estimation of the forest cover of the studied area at a point in time and its subsequent change (see Table 1). This requires crafting definitions of *forest* and *deforestation,* which is not as straightforward as might be expected. The FAO regards a forested area as one with a minimum tree canopy cover of 10 percent and without predominantly agricultural or urban use. This 10 percent criterion is one of the most widely used benchmarks, although it is arguably an overly generous definition. The criterion is also a very poor indicator of forest quality, failing to distinguish between natural primary forests and plantations. Other bodies have defined actual types of forest in more detail; for example, the World Conservation Monitoring Centre (WCMC) recognizes twenty-six categories of forest.

Definitions of *deforestation* follow on from definitions of *forest.* Thus, the FAO, whose quantification of global deforestation remains the most widely used, considers deforestation to be long-term reduction of canopy cover to below the 10 percent threshold involving conversion to other land uses (that is, excluding the felling of forests that will be replanted or allowed to regenerate). Again, the 10 percent criterion is convenient, but alone it offers only a partial analysis because it neglects reductions in forest cover—for example, from 80 to 20 percent coverage—that may greatly affect biodiversity or the carbon cycle and other systems. Moreover, forests can become ecologically damaged without the reduction of canopy cover. The FAO definition has therefore been criticized by various NGOs and academic commentators, who claim that FAO figures paint an overly optimistic picture of the state of the world's forests.

However *deforestation* is defined, measuring it relies on a variety of methods. Data on deforestation are available from ecological field surveys, project reports from government departments and NGOs, and such corporate bodies as timber companies. This type of data tends to give only a patchy picture of deforestation and is often restricted in its geographical scope. The FAO compiles information obtained from governments to help develop global deforestation statistics, which are used as the raw data for the FAO's global Forest Resources Assessments (FRAs), the most recent of which was produced in 2005. However, this process is complicated by gaps and interpretive inconsistencies in the data supplied by various governments.

Remote sensing, the scanning of Earth's surface from satellites or aircraft, has proved extremely valuable in studying deforestation. Aerial photography can provide adequate localized information, but satellite data are necessary for large-scale surveys. Various types of systems are used, employing a range of electromagnetic bands to suit the variety of information to be gathered. For example, the use of radar allows penetration through clouds and smoke. A number of satellite mapping projects have been undertaken, notably NASA's Landsat Pathfinder survey and the EU TREES project, both of which concentrate on tropical regions. Such projects tend to use geographical information system (GIS) computer technology to collate satellite data and draft maps.

Comparing satellite surveys to corresponding ground data gives the best overall estimate of forest cover and its changes. The FAO recognizes this and has carried out independent remote-sensing surveys to feed into its influential FRA reports and complement information received from governments. FRA 2005 was unable to include such a survey due to lack of resources, but a more ambitious remote-sensing analysis will be included in the forthcoming 2010 assessment.

The FAO estimates that the world's total forest cover decreased by 3 percent between 1990 and 2005, representing a 0.2 percent net decline every year— this is around 17 million acres (7 million hectares) per year, approximately equivalent to an area the size of Panama. Significantly, this statistic represents the overall balance between forest loss and increase; in fact, about 32 million acres (13 million hectares) of global forest are destroyed every year—nearly twice as much as is regenerated or planted. Moreover, the global balance between loss and gain is geographically uneven; forest cover increased in almost all developed countries from 1990 to 2005, while most developing countries displayed greater reductions in cover, particularly in tropical rain forests, than the overall global rate.

Deforestation also disproportionately affects primary forests, those consisting of native species, with no clearly visible indications of human activities or significant disturbance to ecological processes. (Terms such as *frontier, old-growth, native,* and *intact* are also used to describe such forests, although precise definitions vary.) FRA 2005 stated that primary forests make up 36 percent of the planet's total and that about 15 million acres (6 million hectares) are lost every year. This means that nearly half of the annual forest destruction occurs in the most ecologically valuable third of the world's forest area.

Despite the simplifications and assumptions inherent in the FRA study (as in all estimates of deforestation), the general picture is all too clear—deforestation continues (see map, p. 247). It is especially drastic in the tropics, which include the most environmentally significant forest areas on Earth.

Studying the causes of deforestation is vital to developing policies to address the problem. In this regard, researchers have identified two sets of factors. Proximate factors are those that immediately affect land use, such as agricultural clearance, logging, uncontrolled burning, infrastructure expansion, and fuel-wood cutting. Behind these are underlying, driving factors, which include overconsumption of resources, national fiscal policies and debt burdens, population pressures, and poverty. For example, a major proximate cause of rain forest clearance in the tropics of central Africa and the Amazon Basin is the practice of uncontrolled shifting cultivation, in which farmers clear a small plot of forest to grow crops. After a few years, the farmer moves on to clear new ground, leaving the old plot to regrow. On a small scale, this is a traditional and sustainable land use, provided that the land is farmed for only a few years and is subsequently allowed to regenerate for a sufficiently long period. Large numbers of inexperienced farmers, however, exploit this system inappropriately and degrade the forest. In this example, the underlying factors are the displacement of the urban and rural poor on to "new" forest lands, itself linked to a large number of global political pressures. The interplay of land uses is also relevant; thus, commercial logging encourages the encroachment by farmers on forest land by providing road access. As with most environmental and social problems, attempting to analyze the causes of deforestation is a complex and politically charged exercise.

Policies and Programs

Although the scale of global deforestation began to trigger serious concern in the 1970s, with particular attention paid to the plight of tropical rain forests, this concern took some time to crystallize into international policy initiatives. Most current programs have built on the foundations laid at the UN Earth Summit in 1992. The conference launched a (nonbinding) statement, "Forest Principles," outlining a model for sustainable management and conservation practices.

Since the Rio summit, a number of attempts have been made to formulate international strategies and policies to tackle deforestation, but no binding mandatory agreement has been reached. The third ITTA was negotiated in 2006 (see Document 1). This introduced criteria for sustainable forestry into the tropical timber trade, with a continuing objective of ensuring all timber exports from the tropics are from sustainable sources. The ITTA has been useful in providing a framework for the reform of the trade, but the goal of an entirely sustainable international timber trade remains unrealized (see Table 3).

An international policy consensus on tackling deforestation thus remains elusive. The main drivers of the quest for consensus have been various United Nations processes: the Intergovernmental Panel on Forests (IPF) in 1995–1997 and the Intergovernmental Forum on Forests (IFF) in 1997–2000. The ultimate goal of these was a legally binding treaty on forests; instead, the process resulted in a set of recommendations and expectations, not requirements enforced by treaty obligations. The problem of conflicting interests among the parties involved has been pivotal. This is illustrated by tensions at the broadest level—developing countries are under great pressure to exploit their natural resources to fuel their development aspirations through agricultural expansion and infrastructure improvement, but developed countries are pressing for tropical forest conservation while not restricting their own high-rate use of such forest resources as timber and paper. The independent World Commission on Forests and Sustainable Development (WCFSD) has considered the potential for resolving such conflicts. The WCFSD, established by a group of world leaders in 1995, issued its summary report in 1999 linking forest degradation and poverty and proposing "global, national and local level arrangements to involve people in all decisions concerning their forests."

The quest for an international legal framework on forests continued with the founding of the United Nations Forum on Forests (UNFF) in 2000. This has built on the work of the IPF and IFF processes and the UNFF agreed on a set of shared "Global Objectives on Forests" in 2006. After years of negotiations, a non–legally binding instrument on all types of forests was adopted by the UN General Council in 2007. This remains the current international framework for addressing global deforestation.

The UN Framework Convention on Climate Change (UNFCCC) now also specifically addresses deforestation. At a 2007 conference in Bali, Indonesia, an agreement was reached to include forest conservation in the UNFCCC process. This will be done via a program called Reducing Emissions from Deforestation and Degradation (REDD), which will involve a system of "carbon-trading" financial incentives for forest preservation (see CLIMATE CHANGE). However, REDD is not universally welcomed and is potentially very complex to implement.

In the absence of binding global agreements, various bodies have established their own ambitious programs. These tend to involve partnerships among various local, national, or international bodies and the sponsorship of local projects and case studies to illustrate and advance program objectives. High-profile examples include the Forest Alliance of the World Bank and World Wide Fund for Nature (WWF), the Global Forest Watch project of the WRI, and the Forest Conservation Program of International Union for the Conservation of Nature (IUCN). Some interesting work is being done. For example, Rainforest Concern, an NGO, has an ongoing project in the Choco-Andean corridor in Ecuador. This has involved a multitude of approaches, including the purchase of land and creation of reserves, support of indigenous groups in safeguarding their land, carefully managed ecotourism, and assistance for small-scale sustainable forest product-based livelihoods. Partnerships with local NGOs and communities have been created to facilitate these activities and will, hopefully, persist, thus conserving the forest in the longer term.

Another notable program is that of the Forest Stewardship Council (FSC), perhaps the most prominent effort at influencing the commercial timber industry to adopt sustainable practices. The FSC is a NGO that has developed procedures by which timber can be traced from forest to shop and is certified as being produced according to the FSC principles of sustainable forestry. Forty-six countries had FSC national certification initiatives in 2008. The FSC has been criticized, however, for allowing its certification standards to become more lax in order to expand the scheme and for, in some cases, awarding certification inappropriately to projects with poor environmental credentials.

The long-term success of any program tackling deforestation will depend mainly on how well it confronts the underlying causes of forest loss. Because many of these causes are rooted in complex social and political issues and often involve conflicts of interest among various parties, successful programs need to be ambitious and to look beyond the forest at the broader picture. Unfortunately, few signs of a global consensus on measures to address such underlying factors as inequality of resource consumption and inequality of income are apparent.

Regional Summaries

Deforestation has occurred in all regions of the world—but to different extents and at different rates. Various types of human activity—agricultural and industrial development, commercial exploitation, and use of wood for fuel—are the primary causes of deforestation worldwide. Climate changes also seem likely to adversely affect forests across the globe; for example, evidence exists that drier conditions are making tropical forests more vulnerable to damage by fire.

North America

According to FRA 2005, around one-third of Canada and the United States is forested, representing 17 percent of the world's total forest cover. The net forest area has remained fairly constant in recent years, displaying a slight increase since 1990 as, especially in the United States, planting and regrowth have outstripped removal. However, the U.S. Forest Service predicts that this trend will gradually reverse over the next half century, mostly due to increasing urbanization. The ecological quality of North American forests is declining, largely due to overexploitation and inappropriate management by the forestry industry, although important areas of primary forest persist. Industrial pollution has damaged forests in some areas, such as in the mountains of the northeastern United States. The forestry industry is technologically advanced, and employment in this increasingly mechanized U.S. industry has fallen over the last two decades. Consumption of paper products and timber is high and increasing, although much of this demand must be satisfied from overseas; in the last fifteen years, the United States has moved from being a net exporter of forest products to a net importer. The pressure on North American forests is likely to continue due to the rising demand for forest products, development, and increasing recreational demands.

Latin America

Almost a quarter of the world's forests are in the Caribbean and Central and South America. FRA 2005 recorded this as the region bearing the highest

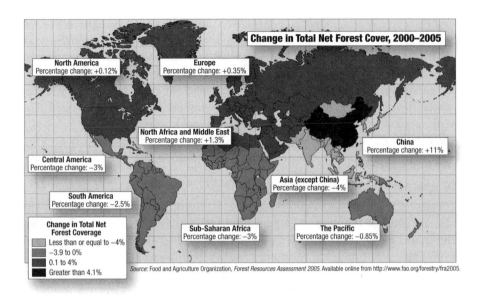

Change in Total Net Forest Cover, 2000–2005

North America
Percentage change: +0.12%

Europe
Percentage change: +0.35%

North Africa and Middle East
Percentage change: +1.3%

China
Percentage change: +11%

Central America
Percentage change: −3%

Asia (except China)
Percentage change: −4%

South America
Percentage change: −2.5%

Change in Total Net
Forest Coverage
- Less than or equal to −4%
- −3.9 to 0%
- 0.1 to 4%
- Greater than 4.1%

Sub-Saharan Africa
Percentage change: −3%

The Pacific
Percentage change: −0.85%

Source: Food and Agriculture Organization, *Forest Resources Assessment 2005*. Available online from http://www.fao.org/forestry/fra2005.

proportion of forested land, with almost half of Central and South America plus Mexico under forest. Nearly all this forest is in the tropical zone. The Amazon has the largest stretch of intact forest in the world; its rain forests are among the most ecologically diverse ecosystems on Earth and are of global significance as a carbon sink for removing carbon dioxide from the atmosphere. The region's impressive and important forest area declined by over 2.5 percent between 2000 and 2005—alarmingly, this rate of loss, equal to 0.5 percent each year, has accelerated since the 1990s. Agricultural expansion, especially cattle ranching, is by far the most important cause of Amazonian deforestation, but logging, development, fires, and extraction of oil and minerals also contribute. Nevertheless, the worst deforestation rates are seen in the much smaller area of Central America, with 3 percent lost each year in Honduras, for example.

Europe (including the Russian Federation)

Most of Europe's original extensive forest cover was cleared centuries ago, particularly in the west. The existing forests of Europe have generally been significantly altered by human activity, although in the east and the far north some significant blocks of indigenous boreal forest persist. According to the United Nations Environment Programme (UNEP) fourth Global Environmental Outlook report (GEO-4), 73 percent of forests are managed primarily for production in Europe, a larger proportion than in any other region. In recent decades, plantings and regeneration have increased the extent of European forests, so that some 44 percent of the region was forested in 2005. The Russian Federation is particularly important because it has the largest forest area of any country on Earth, with 20 percent of the world's forests in its territory.

Forest cover seems likely to continue to slowly increase throughout Europe, although in many cases the new plantings are of low wildlife value. Forest quality has declined in recent decades due mainly to air pollution; around 60 percent of the forests of Western and central Europe are believed to be damaged to some degree. The Chernobyl nuclear disaster of 1986 was also significant, contaminating some 17.3 million acres (7 million hectares) of forested land with radioactivity. As air pollution is reduced and mitigation measures develop, the health of European forests should gradually improve; the relatively progressive forestry institutions and policies of the region should assist.

North Africa and the Middle East

North Africa and the Middle East have a long history of deforestation, and climatic and soil conditions are generally not ideal for tree regrowth. These are the most sparsely forested of the world's regions, and the extent of natural forest is extremely limited in most countries. According to FRA 2005, Lebanon's forest cover of 13 percent represents the largest proportion of forest area of any country in the region. The region remains heavily dependent on imported wood products. Pressures on forests include overgrazing, fire, exploitation for fuelwood, agricultural expansion, and development. Nonetheless, the forest extent is stable or increasing throughout nearly all the Middle East and North Africa. Afforestation schemes in some countries have shown impressive results; for example, Syria's forests expanded by nearly 7 percent between 2000 and 2005.

Sub-Saharan Africa

Nearly 16 percent of the world's forests are found in sub-Saharan Africa, according to FRA 2005. They are distributed unevenly; the Democratic Republic of Congo (DRC) alone has 330 million acres (133.6 million hectares) of forest, some 21 percent of the region's total, which includes rain forest areas of global ecological importance. Forests across the continent are under pressure from agricultural expansion, logging, overgrazing, development, drought, uncontrolled burning, and firewood harvesting. Sub-Saharan Africa as a region is suffering very rapid deforestation, having lost an estimated 3 percent between 2000 and 2005. Forests are falling in almost every country in the region, with some countries displaying particularly dramatic losses. For instance, FRA 2005 showed that Burundi, devastated by civil war, lost over a quarter of its forest in just five years. Positive moves include increased designation of protected forest areas across Africa and the establishment of plantations and agroforestry schemes in parts of the region, but these are failing to balance the pace of deforestation. The future for African forests remains bleak because expanding populations, continuing poverty and debt burden, rapid urbanization, and political conflict seem certain to continue to exert severe pressure on the land.

Asia

Central, South, and East Asia contain large tracts of forests, including the world's second largest rain forest system, most of which is found in Malaysia, Indonesia, and other parts of Southeast Asia. FRA 2005 reported very high deforestation rates in most Asian countries, with the biggest losses in the important rain forest areas of the southeast; Indonesia, for instance, destroyed a tenth of its forest during 2000–2005. The primary causes of such losses are agricultural expansion and logging. The United Nations Economic and Social Commission for Asia and the Pacific recognizes Asia as the most populous and rapidly developing part of the world, with 60 percent of the global population. This will evidently continue to put pressure on forests.

Large-scale clearance in favor of oil palm plantations is a major driver of deforestation in the tropical part of the region (see Case Study—Oil Palm versus Forest in Indonesia). These are planted to supply an expanding global market for foodstuffs and, increasingly, for biofuels. Logging—both legal and illegal—is the other main cause of deforestation. Asia dominates the international market in tropical timber, with the International Timber Trade Organisation listing Malaysia as the world's largest exporter of tropical logs in 2007. Forest loss can also be attributed to development and infrastructure expansion, mining, fuelwood collection, and fire. Millions of hectares of Southeast Asian forests burned in the unusually dry period of 1997, with much of this burning thought to have been deliberate clearance.

Although nearly every Asian country reports net forest losses, afforestation projects have also been implemented in many countries, often due to the expansion of commercial plantations. China is exceptional here, having increased its forest cover from 12 percent in the 1980s to 21 percent by 2005. This is one of the most impressive afforestation rates in the world, and the rate of planting was greater in 2000–2005 than in the previous decade. Thus, Asia as a whole has actually displayed a net increase in forest area in 2000–2005 because China's efforts have helped to offset the losses seen elsewhere (in terms of forest area but not in terms of biodiversity).

The Pacific

In the Pacific region, forests have generally declined in extent and continue to do so. Australia, by far the largest land mass in the area, has lost about a third of its forest since the European incursion two hundred years ago, according to its government's "State of the Forests" report. Nonetheless, it remains the country with the sixth largest forest area in the world. Many of the smaller islands that make up most of the nations in this area have also suffered significant losses of original forest cover and are still deforesting. A loss of 8.5 percent in 2000–2005 in the Solomon Islands was reported in FRA 2005, for example. Unfortunately, many small island nations were unable to report accurately to the FAO due to a lack of data, but the picture is likely to be one of net loss for most. Commercial logging, agriculture, and development are some of the main pressures on the forests of Oceania, and many ecologically rich coastal mangrove forests have been cleared for aquaculture, such as shrimp farming. Plantation schemes have been implemented in New Zealand and Australia, mostly for timber and pulp production, although the Australian forest industry has been criticized for continuing to log in old-growth forest.

Data

Table 1 Total Forest Cover in Selected Countries, 2005

Country	Forest area (1,000 ha)	Land area (%)	Forest cover change, 2000–2005 (%)
Algeria	2,227	1.0	+6.0
Argentina	33,021	12.1	−2.0
Australia	163,678	21.3	−0.5
Brazil	477,698	57.2	−3.0
Canada	310,134	33.6	n.s.
China	197,290	21.2	+11.0
Colombia	60,728	58.5	−0.5
DRC	133,610	58.9	−1.0
Egypt	67	0.1	+13.0
France	15,554	28.3	+1.5
Georgia	2,760	39.7	n.s.
Germany	11,076	31.7	n.s.
Guatemala	3,938	36.3	−6.5
India	67,701	22.8	n.s.
Indonesia	88,495	48.8	−10.0
Israel	171	8.3	+4.0
Japan	24,868	68.2	n.s.
Russian Federation	808,790	47.9	n.s.
Saudi Arabia	2,728	1.3	n.s.
Spain	17,915	35.9	+8.5
Sweden	27,528	66.9	n.s.
Switzerland	1,221	30.9	+2.0
Tajikistan	410	2.9	n.s.
Thailand	14,520	28.4	−2.0
Turkey	10,175	13.2	+1.0
Uganda	3,627	18.4	−11.0
United Kingdom	2,845	11.8	+2.0
United States	303,089	33.1	+0.5
World total	3,952,025	30.3	−0.9

Source: UN Food and Agriculture Organization, "Global Tables," Forest Resources Assessment, 2005, available at http://www.fao.org/forestry/fra2005/en/.

Notes: DRC, Democratic Republic of Congo; n.s.. not significant.

Table 2 Total Area of Original, Current, and Frontier Forest

Region	Original forest (1,000 km²)	Remaining forest (1,000 km²)	Remaining forest, as a percentage of original forest	Frontier forest (1,000 km²)	Frontier forest, as a percentage of original forest	Frontier forest, as a percentage of remaining forest
Africa	6,799	2,302	34	527	8	23
Asia	15,132	4,275	28	844	6	20
Central America	1,779	970	55	172	10	18
Europe[a]	16,449	9,604	58	3,462	21	36
North America	10,877	8,483	78	3,737	34	44
Pacific[b]	1,431	929	65	319	22	34
South America	9,736	6,800	70	4,439	46	65
Total	62,203	33,363	54	13,501	22	40

Source: Dirk Bryant et al., *The Last Frontier Forests: Ecosystems and Economies on the Edge* (Washington, D.C.: World Resources Institute, 1997).

Notes: *Frontier forest* refers to large tracts of relatively undisturbed forest. *Remaining forest* consists of frontier and nonfrontier forest.

[a]Includes Russia.

[b]Australia, New Zealand, and Papua New Guinea.

Table 3 Value of Trade in Tropical Timber by International Tropical Timber Organization Producer Regions, 2006

Region	Product	Imports Value ($1,000)	Imports Unit value (dollars per m³)	Exports Value ($1,000)	Exports Unit value (dollars per m³)
Africa	Logs	84	1,417	776,903	228
	Sawn	330	79	832,736	487
	Veneer	300	728	292,241	806
	Ply	489	552	81,914	474
Asia and Pacific	Logs	987,406	288	1,321,026	143
	Sawn	715,508	420	1,578,249	217
	Veneer	37,426	712	184,735	395
	Ply	51,688	311	3,507,357	436
Latin America and Caribbean	Logs	6,792	308	45,425	109
	Sawn	43,791	275	749,654	377
	Veneer	27,787	1,374	81,802	435
	Ply	122,226	594	253,294	362
Producers' total	Logs	994,282	288	2,143,354	164
	Sawn	759,628	407	3,160,639	288
	Veneer	65,512	895	558,777	549
	Ply	174,403	468	3,842,565	431
World total		12,023,456		11,256,491	

Source: International Tropical Timber Organization, "Annual Review and Assessment of the World Timber Situation, 2007," available at http://www.itto.or.jp/live/Live_Server/400/E_AR_07.pdf.

Case Study—Oil Palm versus Forest in Indonesia

The African oil palm, *Eleais guineensis,* bears fruit that yields a valuable vegetable oil; it is one of the most productive oil plants in cultivation. It was established in Southeast Asia as a commercial crop by the start of the twentieth century; now, some one hundred years later, this palm tree is a dominant factor in the deforestation crisis affecting the region.

Indonesia has recently expanded its oil palm plantations at a phenomenal rate of around 2.5 million acres (approximately 1 million hectares) per year, thus overtaking Malaysia as the world's leading producer of palm oil in 2007. Now, Indonesia is estimated to have nearly 17 million acres (7 million hectares) used for cultivating the palm.

This remarkable plantation expansion has been driven by rocketing global demand for palm oil; Indonesia alone exported 17 million tons in 2007. It is now the world's leading edible oil, used in a wide range of food products and also in nonfood products such as cosmetics. In addition, biofuel production is becoming an increasingly important use of palm oil; the oil is currently the highest yielding source for biodiesel manufacture, and it is very versatile, being easily blended with petroleum-based diesel. A very strong impetus exists to reduce fossil fuel use resulting both from concerns about climate change and from increasing economic and geopolitical problems with the petroleum oil supply. Responding to this impetus, Indonesia has a target of planting an additional 10 million acres (4 million hectares) of oil palm dedicated to biodiesel production by 2015.

Meanwhile, Indonesia has suffered an alarming reduction in forest cover, with around 22 million acres (9 million hectares) lost in 2000–2005, some 10 percent of its total forest area; globally, only Brazil lost more forest area in this period. The rise of oil palm plantations and fall of the forests are not coincidental; scientists from Princeton University have estimated that over half of Indonesia's palm plantations have been established at the direct expense of forest, and the UNEP acknowledges oil palm plantations as the primary cause of the country's permanent rain forest loss.

In addition to the direct replacement of forests by oil palm plantations, a number of other concerns about oil palm plantations have been expressed: uncontrolled spreading of fires set for clearing forest land, land seizures from indigenous groups and small farmers (and associated human rights abuses), threats to endangered species such as the orangutan, and chemical pollution from plantation management. Palm oil has become very controversial, especially because demand continues to increase—global production is projected to double by 2020.

Clearly, tackling the oil palm issue is key if Indonesia is to have a chance of halting the destruction of its valuable rain forests. The most high-profile attempt to regulate the palm oil industry was the establishment of the Roundtable on Sustainable Palm Oil (RSPO) in 2004. This is an association, created by organizations in the industry, that aims to promote the growth and use of sustainable palm oil through cooperation within the supply chain and with industry stakeholders. It has proven successful in capturing an important slice of the global market, with 40 percent of global trade controlled by RSPO members. Certification by RSPO requires that producers satisfy eight principles with thirty-nine criteria, including environmental responsibility and conservation of natural resources and biodiversity.

However, Indonesian deforestation has continued since the inception of the RSPO; no Indonesian palm plantation has yet obtained full official RSPO certification, and claims have been made that some producers continue to clear primary rain forest, using RSPO membership as a smokescreen for their bad practices. The huge scale and remoteness of many growing areas, plus alleged corruption and malpractice, often make certification of dubious value.

Nonetheless, the RSPO remains the preferred vehicle for the attempted reform of the industry. This has often not worked in the forest's favor. The Indonesian Palm Oil Producers Association (GAPKI) announced a moratorium on planting on cleared forest land in 2008, but this highly promising move was overturned later in the year, with GAPKI stating a preference to continue working toward compliance with RSPO standards instead. Certainly, unless RSPO certification can become more effective, it will not stop deforestation.

Indeed, in a country with an expanding population, a goal of rapid development, and persistent widespread poverty, restricting palm oil production in the face of the ever-increasing world demand will never be an easy choice. Indonesian economists have called palm oil "liquid gold," and as long as burgeoning global markets for food and fuel drive this "gold rush," the forests are likely to continue to suffer.

Biographical Sketches

Jeff Burley was director of the Oxford Forestry Institute, United Kingdom, until 2002. He was formerly president of the International Union of Forestry Research Organizations, with whom he established a task force on sustainable forest management. His field of expertise is forest genetics, and he has also advised on forestry programs in a number of developing countries. Current projects include the commercial development of plantations as a carbon sink.

Andre Giacini de Freitas is executive director of the FSC, which works to promote and certify responsible forest management worldwide. A forester by training, he previously managed Brazilian NGO Imaflora and has worked with Brazilian banks to develop their social and environmental policies.

Jan Heino is assistant director-general and head of forestry at the UN FAO. Before this appointment, he was director-general of Finland's state forestry enterprise and was elected the first chairman of the European State Forests Association (EUSTAFOR) when it was founded in 2006. He has also previously chaired the FAO Committee on Forestry.

Wangari Maathai is an environmental activist and founder of the Green Belt Movement, a grassroots women-led initiative that has planted over 40 million trees in Kenya. She has been a supporter of many land restoration projects, has inspired similar Green Belt schemes in other African nations, and has been elected to the Kenyan parliament. In 2004, she was awarded the Nobel Peace Prize, the first African woman to be thus honored.

Frances Seymour is the director of the Center for International Forestry Research (CIFOR), one of the world's leading forest research organizations. She has worked on sustainable development issues for most of her career, notably with the World Wide Fund for Nature and the World Resources Institute. Forestry issues in Indonesia are a particular interest of hers.

Directory

Center for International Forestry Research (CIFOR), P.O. Box 0113 BOCBD, Bogor 16000, Indonesia. Telephone: (62) 251 8622 622; email: cifor@cgiar.org; Web: http://www.cifor.cgiar.org.
International research institution committed to the conservation of forests and their communities.

Coalition for Rainforest Nations, 2852 Broadway, New York, N.Y. 10025. Telephone: (212) 854-8181; email: info@rainforestcoalition.org; Web: http://www.rainforestcoalition.org.
Diplomatic alliance of southern nations seeking to improve rain forest stewardship.

Food and Agriculture Organization (FAO), Viale delle Terme di Caracalla, 00153 Rome, Italy. Telephone: (39) 06 57051; email: fao-hq@fao.org; Web: http://www.fao.org.
Lead UN agency for forestry, agriculture, fisheries, and rural development, aiming to eliminate hunger.

Forestry Stewardship Council (FSC), Charles de Gaulle Str. 5, 53113 Bonn, Germany. Telephone: (49) 228 367 660; email: communications@fsc.org; Web: http://www.fsc.org.
Nonprofit organization promoting and certifying the sustainable use of forests for commercial purposes.

Forests Monitor, 69a Lensfield Road, Cambridge CB2 1EN, United Kingdom. Telephone: (44) 1223 360975; email: mail@forestsmonitor.org; Web: http://www.forestsmonitor.org.
NGO researching timber companies and supporting citizen campaign groups.

Friends of the Earth International, P.O. Box 19199, 1000 GD Amsterdam, Netherlands. Telephone: (31) 20 622 1369; email: foei@foei.org; Web: http://www.foei.org.
World's largest federation of environmental groups; its campaigns include deforestation.

Global Canopy Programme, John Krebs Field Station, Wytham, Oxford OX2 8QJ, United Kingdom. Telephone: (44) 1865 724333; Web: http://globalcanopy.org.
Multinational alliance of scientific institutions undertaking research on forest canopies.

Greenpeace International, Ottho Heldringstraat 5, 1066 AZ Amsterdam, Netherlands. Telephone: (31) 20 718 2000; email: supporter.services@int.greenpeace.org; Web: http://www.greenpeace.org/international.
Independent multinational environmental activist organization.

International Tropical Timber Organization, International Organizations Center, 5th Floor, Pacifico-Yokohama 1-1-1, Minato-Mirai, Nishi-ku, Yokohama 220-0012, Japan. Telephone: (81) 45 223 1110; email: itto@itto.or.jp; Web: http://www.itto.or.jp.

Intergovernmental organization providing a platform for policy cooperation on the tropical timber economy, aiming for sustainable management.

Rainforest Action Network, 221 Pine Street, 5th Floor, San Francisco, Calif. 94104. Telephone: (415) 398-4404; email: answers@ran.org; Web: http://ran.org.
Group campaigning to preserve tropical rain forests and their inhabitants through education, lobbying, and direct action.

Society of American Foresters, 5400 Grosvenor Lane, Bethesda, Md. 20814-2198. Telephone: (301) 897-8720; email: safweb@safnet.org; Web: http://www.safnet.org.
Professional forestry organization in the United States.

Taiga Rescue Network, Box 4625, Asogatan 115, SE-11691, Stockholm, Sweden. Telephone: (46) 8559 22858; email: enquiries@taigarescue.org; Web: http://www.taigarescue.org.
Network of groups campaigning for the protection of boreal (northern) forests.

Temperate Forest Foundation, 10200 SW Greenburg Road, Suite 400, Portland, Ore. 97223. Telephone: (503) 445-9472; email: office@forestinfo.org; Web: http://www.forestinfo.org.
Scientific charity for the analysis of and public education about forestry and environmental issues.

United Nations Environment Programme (UNEP), United Nations Avenue, Gigiri, P.O. Box 30552, 00100 Nairobi, Kenya. Telephone: (254-20) 762 1234; email: unepinfo@unep.org; Web: http://www.unep.org.
Agency tackling a range of environmental issues on an international basis.

U.S. Forest Service, 1400 Independence Avenue, Washington, D.C. 20250-0003. Telephone: (800) 832-1355; email: webmaster@fs.fed.us; Web: http://www.fs.fed.us.
U.S. government agency responsible for forestry in the United States.

World Rainforest Movement, Maldonado 1858, Montevideo 11200, Uruguay. Telephone: (598) 2413 2989; email: wrm@wrm-org.uy; Web: http://www.wrm-org.uy.
International network of citizens groups involved in defending rain forests.

World Resources Institute (WRI), 10 G Street NE, Suite 800, Washington, D.C. 20002. Telephone: (202) 729-7600; email: front@wri.org; Web: http://www.wri.org/forests.
Environmental think tank disseminating knowledge about environmental research and issues to encourage public action.

World Wide Fund for Nature (WWF; formerly World Wildlife Fund), 1250 24th Street NW, Washington D.C. 20090-7180. Telephone: (202) 293-4800; Web: http://www.worldwildlife.org.
U.S. office of the world's largest multinational conservation body.

Further Research

Books

Andersen, Lykke E., et al. *The Dynamics of Deforestation and Economic Growth in the Brazilian Amazon.* Cambridge, UK: Cambridge University Press, 2002.

Barraclough, Solon, and Krishna B. Ghimire. *Agricultural Expansion and Tropical Deforestation: International Trade, Poverty and Land Use.* London: Earthscan, 2001.

Burley, Jeffery, Julian Evans, and John Yongquist, eds. *Encyclopedia of Forest Sciences.* Oxford: Elsevier, 2004.

Carrere, Ricardo, and Larry Lohmann. *Pulping the South: Industrial Tree Plantations and the World Paper Economy.* London: Zed Books, 1996.

Chew, Sing. *World Ecological Degradation, Accumulation, Urbanization and Deforestation, 3000BC–AD2000.* Lanham, Md.: AltaMira Press, 2001.

Colchester, Marcus, and Larry Lohmann, eds. *The Struggle for Land and the Fate of the Forest.* London: Zed Books, 1993.

Dudley, Nigel, Jean-Paul Jeanrenaud, and Francis Sullivan. *Bad Harvest?: The Timber Trade and the Degradation of the World's Forests.* London: Earthscan, 1995.

Fairhead, James, and Melissa Leach. *Reframing Deforestation: Global Analysis and Local Realities, Studies in West Africa.* London: Routledge, 1998.

Gibson, Clark, Margaret McKean, and Elinor Ostrom, eds. *People and Forests: Communities, Institutions and Governance.* Cambridge, Mass.: MIT Press, 2000.

Grainger, Alan. *Controlling Tropical Deforestation.* London: Earthscan, 1993.

Haggith, Mandy. *Paper Trails: From Trees to Trash—the True Cost of Paper.* London: Virgin/Random House, 2008.

Huxley, Peter. *Tropical Agroforestry.* Oxford: Blackwell Science, 1999.

Jensen, Derrick, and George Draffan. *Strangely Like War: The Global Assault on Forests.* White River Junction, Vt.: Chelsea Green, 2003.

Kuchli, Christian. *Stories of Regeneration.* London: Earthscan, 1997.

Spray, Sharon, and Matthew Moran, eds. *Tropical Deforestation: Exploring Environmental Challenges.* Lanham, Md.: Rowman & Littlefield, 2006.

Whitmore, Timothy. *An Introduction to Tropical Rain Forests.* Oxford: Oxford University Press, 1998.

Williams, Michael. *Deforesting the Earth: From Prehistory to Global Crisis.* Chicago: University of Chicago Press, 2003.

Articles and Reports

Biello, David. "Fragmentation Quickly Destabilizes Amazon Rain Forest." *Scientific American* (November 27, 2006). Available at http://www.scientificamerican.com/article.cfm?id=fragmentation-quickly-d.

Bowles, Ian A., et al. "Logging and Tropical Forest Conservation." *Science* 280 (1998): 1899.

Bryant, Dirk, et al. *The Last Frontier Forests: Ecosystems and Economies on the Edge.* Washington, D.C.: World Resources Institute, 1997.

Butler, Rhett A., and William F. Laurance. "New Strategies for Conserving Tropical Forests." *Trends in Ecology & Evolution* 23, no. 9 (2008): 469–472.

Carrere, Ricardo. "The Bitter Fruit of Oil Palm: Dispossession and Deforestation." World Rainforest Movement, Montevideo, Uruguay, 2001.

Food and Agriculture Organization. "Forests and Energy: Key Issues." FAO, Rome, 2008.

———. "The State of the World's Forests." FAO, Rome, 2007.

Geist, Helmut J., and Eric F. Lambin. "Proximate Causes and Underlying Driving Forces of Tropical Deforestation." *Bioscience* 52, no. 2 (2002): 143.

Greenpeace. "Roadmap to Recovery: The World's Last Intact Forest Landscapes." Greenpeace International, Amsterdam, 2006.

Gullison, Raymond E., et al. "Tropical Forests and Climate Policy." *Science* 316 (2007): 985.

Hellier, Chris. "Stemming the Tide." *Geographical* (June 1999): 42.

Intergovernmental Panel on Climate Change. "Land Use, Land-Use Change and Forestry." IPCC, Geneva, 2000.

Kemper, Steve. "Tree Thieves." *Ecologist* (September 2008): 36.

Krishnaswarmy, Ajit, and Arthur Hanson, eds. "Our Forest, Our Future: Summary Report." World Commission on Forests and Sustainable Development, Winnipeg, Canada, 1999.

Laschefski, Klemens, and Nicole Freris. "Saving the Wood from the Trees." *Ecologist* (July–August 2001): 40.

Laurance, William. "Switch to Corn Promotes Amazon Deforestation." *Science* 318 (2007): 1721.

Luyssaert, Sebastiaan, et al. "Old-Growth Forests as Global Carbon Sinks." *Nature* 455 (2008): 213–215.

Mayell, Hilary. "Study Links Logging with Severity of Forest Fires." *National Geographic News,* December 3, 2001. Available at http://news.nationalgeographic.com/news/2001/12/1203_loggingfires.htm.

Menotti, Victor. "Forest Destruction and Globalisation." *Ecologist* (May–June 1999): 180.

Web Sites

Agroforestry Research Trust
http://www.agroforestry.co.uk

Biofuelwatch
http://www.biofuelwatch.org.uk

Deforestation Watch
http://deforestationwatch.org

Environmental Paper Network
http://www.environmentalpaper.org

Food for All
http://www.foodforall.org

Forest Protection Portal
http://forests.org

Forest Resources Assessment, 2005
http://www.fao.org/forestry/fra2005/en

FSC Watch
http://www.fsc-watch.org

Global Forest Watch
http://www.globalforestwatch.org

Greenpeace World Intact Forest Landscapes
http://www.intactforests.org

International Forest Industries
http://www.internationalforestindustries.com

International Tree Foundation
http://www.internationaltreefoundation.org

Mongabay
http://www.mongabay.com

New Forests Project
http://www.newforestsproject.org

Rainforest Animals
http://www.rainforestanimals.net

Rainforest Concern
http://www.rainforestconcern.org

Timber Trade Federation
http://www.ttf.co.uk

Trees for Life
http://www.treesforlife.org.uk

Tropical Forest Group
http://www.tropicalforestgroup.org

UN Billion Tree Campaign
http://www.unep.org/billiontreecampaign

Virtual Library of Forestry
http://www.metla.fi/info/vlib/Forestry/delicious.htm

World Agroforestry Center
http://www.worldagroforestry.org

Documents

1. International Tropical Timber Agreement 2006

International Tropical Timber Organization, Yokohama, Japan

The full text is available at http://untreaty.un.org/English/notpubl/XIX_46_english.pdf.

Extract

Article 1

OBJECTIVES

The objectives of the International Tropical Timber Agreement, 2006 (hereinafter referred to as "this Agreement") are to promote the expansion and diversification of international trade in tropical timber from sustainably managed and legally harvested forests and to promote the sustainable management of tropical timber producing forests by:

(a) Providing an effective framework for consultation, international cooperation and policy development among all members with regard to all relevant aspects of the world timber economy;

(b) Providing a forum for consultation to promote non-discriminatory timber trade practices;

(c) Contributing to sustainable development and to poverty alleviation;

(d) Enhancing the capacity of members to implement strategies for achieving exports of tropical timber and timber products from sustainably managed sources;

(e) Promoting improved understanding of the structural conditions in international markets, including long-term trends in consumption and production, factors affecting market access, consumer preferences and prices, and conditions leading to prices which reflect the costs of sustainable forest management;

(f) Promoting and supporting research and development with a view to improving forest management and efficiency of wood utilization and the competitiveness of wood products relative to other materials, as well as increasing the capacity to conserve and enhance other forest values in timber producing tropical forests;

(g) Developing and contributing towards mechanisms for the provision of new and additional financial resources with a view to promoting the adequacy and pre-dictability of funding and expertise needed to enhance the capacity of producer members to attain the objectives of this Agreement;

(h) Improving market intelligence and encouraging information sharing on the international timber market with a view to ensuring greater transparency and better information on markets and market trends, including the gathering, compilation and dissemination of trade related data, including data related to species being traded;

(i) Promoting increased and further processing of tropical timber from sustainable sources in producer member countries, with a view to promoting their industrialization and thereby increasing their employment opportunities and export earnings;

(j) Encouraging members to support and develop tropical timber reforestation, as well as rehabilitation and restoration of degraded forest land, with due regard for the interests of local communities dependent on forest resources;

(k) Improving marketing and distribution of tropical timber and timber product exports from sustainably managed and legally harvested sources and which are legally traded, including promoting consumer awareness;

(l) Strengthening the capacity of members for the collection, processing and dissemination of statistics on their trade in timber and information on the sustainable management of their tropical forests;

(m) Encouraging members to develop national policies aimed at sustainable utilization and conservation of timber producing forests, and maintaining ecological balance, in the context of the tropical timber trade;

(n) Strengthening the capacity of members to improve forest law enforcement and governance, and address illegal logging and related trade in tropical timber;

(o) Encouraging information sharing for a better understanding of voluntary mechanisms such as, inter alia, certification, to promote sustainable management of tropical forests, and assisting members with their efforts in this area;

(p) Promoting access to, and transfer of, technologies and technical cooperation to implement the objectives of this Agreement, including on concessional and preferential terms and conditions, as mutually agreed;

(q) Promoting better understanding of the contribution of non-timber forest products and environmental services to the sustainable management of tropical forests with the aim of enhancing the capacity of members to develop strategies to strengthen such contributions in the context of sustainable forest management, and cooperating with relevant institutions and processes to this end;

(r) Encouraging members to recognize the role of forest-dependent indigenous and local communities in achieving sustainable forest management and develop strategies to enhance the capacity of these communities to sustainably manage tropical timber producing forests; and

(s) Identifying and addressing relevant new and emerging issues.

2. Non-legally Binding Instrument on All Types of Forests

United Nations Forum on Forests, New York, 2006

The full document is available at http://www.un.org/esa/forests/pdf/session_documents/ unff7/UNFF7_NLBI_draft.pdf.

Extract

7. To achieve the purpose of this instrument, Member States should:

(a) Make concerted efforts to secure sustained high-level political commitment to strengthen the means of implementation for sustainable forest management, including financial resources, to provide support, in particular for developing countries as well as countries with economies in transition, as well as to mobilize and provide significantly increased new and additional financial resources from private, public, domestic and international sources to and within developing countries as well as countries with economies in transition;

(b) Reverse the decline in official development assistance for sustainable forest management and mobilize significantly increased new and additional financial resources from all sources for the implementation of sustainable forest management;

(c) Take action to raise the priority of sustainable forest management in national development plans and other plans including poverty reduction strategies in order to facilitate increased allocation of official development assistance and financial resources from other sources for sustainable forest management;

(d) Develop and establish positive incentives, in particular for developing countries as well as countries with economies in transition, to reduce the loss of forests, to promote reforestation, afforestation, and rehabilitation of degraded forests, to implement sustainable forest management and to increase the area of protected forests;

(e) Support the efforts of countries, particularly in developing countries as well as countries with economies in transition, to develop and implement economically, socially and environmentally sound measures that act as incentives for the sustainable management of forests;

(f) Strengthen the capacity of countries, in particular developing countries, to significantly increase the production of forest products from sustainably managed forests;

(g) Enhance bilateral, regional and international cooperation, with a view to promoting international trade in forest products from sustainably managed forests harvested according to domestic legislation;

(h) Enhance bilateral, regional and international cooperation to address illicit international trafficking in forest products through the promotion of forest law enforcement and good governance at all levels;

(i) Strengthen, through enhanced bilateral, regional and international cooperation, the capacity of countries to effectively combat illicit international trafficking in forest products, including timber, wildlife and other forest biological resources;

(j) Strengthen the capacity of countries to address forest-related illegal practices according to domestic legislation, including wildlife poaching, through enhanced public awareness, education, institutional capacity-building, technological transfer and technical cooperation, law enforcement and information networks;

(k) Enhance and facilitate access to, and transfer of, appropriate, environmentally sound and innovative technologies and corresponding know how relevant to sustainable forest management and to efficient value added processing of forest products, in particular to developing countries for the benefit of local and indigenous communities;

(l) Strengthen mechanisms that enhance sharing among countries, and use of, best practices in sustainable forest management, including through freeware-based information and communication technologies;

(m) Strengthen national and local capacity in keeping with their conditions for the development and adaptation of forest-related technologies, including technologies for the use of fuelwood;

(n) Promote international technical and scientific cooperation, including South-South cooperation and triangular cooperation in the field of sustainable forest management, through the appropriate international, regional and national institutions and processes;

(o) Enhance the research and scientific forest-related capacities of developing countries as well as countries with economies in transition, particularly the capacity of research organizations to generate and access forest-related data and information, and promote and support integrated and interdisciplinary research on forest-related issues, and disseminate research results;

(p) Strengthen forestry research and development in all regions, particularly in developing countries as well as countries with economies in transition, through relevant organizations, institutions and centres of excellence, as well as through global, regional and subregional networks;

(q) Strengthen cooperation and partnerships at the regional and subregional levels to promote sustainable forest management;

(r) As members of the governing bodies of the organisations that form the Collaborative Partnership on Forests, help ensure that the forest-related priorities and programmes of members of the Collaborative Partnership on Forests are integrated and mutually supportive, consistent with their mandates, taking into account relevant policy recommendations of the United Nations Forum on Forests;

(s) Support the efforts of the CPF to develop and implement joint initiatives.

ENERGY

Richard B. Norgaard

Energy is integral to human well-being, but it is also central to global political and environmental problems. Energy heats and lights dwellings, fuels the transportation of people and products, powers industry, and fertilizes modern agriculture. Yet the combustion of fossil fuels is also the major driver of global warming. The mining, transport, and conversion of fossil fuels degrade land and air. Agricultural fertilizers run off into, and unnaturally enrich, rivers, lakes, and seas. The major consuming nations depend on the Middle East, a politically unstable region, for their oil. While many people equate ever-increasing energy use with the progress of humankind and its conquering nature, others are actively seeking ways to continue improving human well-being while using less energy and more environmentally sensitive sources of energy.

Historical Background and Development

Life evolved on Earth some 3 billion years ago. As plants captured energy from the sun through photosynthesis, life flourished, building organic matter from carbon in the atmosphere and increasing the air's oxygen content, making the globe suitable for animal life. Through various geological processes, some organic matter became fossil fuels—coal, tar sands, oil shale, conventional oil, and natural gas.

People evolved on Earth a mere 3 million years ago. For all but the last two hundred years of human history, people have used energy from the sun, mostly via the biosphere. Plants photosynthesize the sun's energy to combine carbon from the air and water with minerals from the soil, and humans exploited this process by turning the plants into food; fuel for cooking; fodder for livestock used for food, plowing, and transport; and materials for homes. The wind, generated by the differential warming of Earth's surface by the sun, powered sailboats and mills for grinding grain. Waterwheels tapped into the hydrologic cycle, which is also driven by the sun.

Beginning about two centuries ago, people began to switch from using the renewable energy sources produced currently or recently from the sun's energy to exploiting past flows of the sun's energy stored in the form of fossil hydrocarbons. Europeans, starting with the British, tapped into coal after their forests were too depleted to provide adequate fuel. Later, Americans developed petroleum resources. Initially, fossil fuels were inconvenient compared to wood, but they eventually proved superior because of the far higher amount of energy they produced per kilogram. This very recent energy transition vastly accelerated and transformed economic activity, redefined the nature of economic and political power, improved food supplies through the mechanization of agriculture and the application of synthetic fertilizers, facilitated population growth in the developing world, and improved material well-being overall. Tapping into fossil fuels, however, also produced most of the environmental problems of today: air, soil, and water pollution; congestion and urban sprawl; and the expansion of human activity into fragile ecosystems and the related loss of biodiversity. Burning fossil fuels is also rapidly reversing the Earth's biogeochemical development by releasing the carbon accumulated in fossil fuels back into the atmosphere as carbon dioxide, causing global warming and threatening human well-being and all life over the long term (see Document 1; see also BIODIVERSITY, CLIMATE CHANGE, and POLLUTION).

Current Status

Current research, policies, and programs in the energy field are now beginning to facilitate a transition to renewable energy sources and increased efficiency in energy use to reduce harmful environmental impacts, including the emission of the greenhouse gases that drive global warming. These research and policy efforts are being undertaken by universities, private enterprise, government agencies, and international governmental organizations. How the transition away from fossil fuels will work out in the end is unclear, but some endeavors to promote the transition will surely prove less successful than others.

Research

Early in the third millennium, energy use worldwide surpassed the equivalent of 10 billion metric tons of oil, or about 1.6 tons per capita, according to the *World Energy Assessment, Overview: 2004 Update.* Fossil fuels, which are used mostly in the industrialized world, accounted for almost 79 percent of all energy consumed; hydropower, nuclear power, and modern technologies for using geothermal, wind, and biomass energy were also important, amounting to a little more than 5 percent of all energy consumed; and wood and other forms of biomass played a critical role in cooking and heating in the nonindustrialized world and provided nearly 9 percent of the total energy used (see Table 1). Supplies of coal are fairly well distributed geographically, but most of the world's oil reserves are concentrated in the Middle East. Because most oil is consumed in Europe, Japan, the United States, and, increasingly, China but the oil resources are concentrated in the Middle East, oil is the most important item in world trade (see WORLD TRADE).

As dependence on fossil fuels increased during the twentieth century, many observers became concerned that available supplies might be rapidly depleted. Numerous studies comparing existing reserves to consumption levels indicate that coal is relatively abundant but that oil and gas supplies are limited to a few decades. Because reserves are defined as deposits with an existing mine or well, a more realistic picture is provided by comparing resources that are thought to exist (rather than known reserves) to projected increases in demand. Such a comparison suggests that about a century of oil supplies exists, two centuries of natural gas, and ten centuries of coal (see Table 1). Burning all this fossil fuel using current technology, however, would release vast amounts of carbon dioxide into the atmosphere and cause excessive global warming. According to the Millennium Ecosystem Assessment's 2005 report *Ecosystems and Human Well-Being,* fossil fuel combustion must be capped and then brought below existing levels over the next few decades to avoid the dangerous disruption of the climate system and ecosystem services.

Access to energy, which is highly unequal between rich countries and poor countries, is another serious issue that raises economic, social, and political concerns. According to the World Resources Institute (WRI) *World Resources, 2000–2001* report, at the turn of the millennium the United States consumed the equivalent of nearly 9 tons of energy per capita, while at that time Vietnam consumed less than 0.2 tons per capita. Whereas energy use in the developing world has increased dramatically and is beginning to level off in the developed world, inequalities of access to energy remain a critical roadblock to an international agreement on mitigating climate change.

Apart from concerns arising from climate change, the role of energy in international trade carries its own set of concerns. Energy prices, especially petroleum, are very sensitive to changes in supply and demand—or expectations of changes—resulting in highly fluctuating payments for energy between buying and selling regions. The subsequent economic instabilities can be severe, as seen in the rise of oil prices to a peak in summer 2008, only to be followed by a drastic downturn at the end of 2008 and the beginning of 2009 as the world began to suffer the shocks of an international economic downturn.

Policies and Programs

Augmenting the supply of energy to match rising demand has been a key theme of developing countries and development agencies (see DEVELOPMENT AID). The World Bank, other multilateral development agencies, and private banks from the industrialized countries dedicate a significant portion of their loan portfolios to financing the construction of large dams for hydropower production, the construction of electricity transmission systems, and the development of other aspects of the energy sectors of developing countries. Nongovernmental organizations (NGOs) have taken the lead in the development and transfer of technologies using renewable energy resources, including improved stoves to reduce indoor pollution and the use of small hydro facilities, photovoltaic panels, and wind turbines for generating electricity for villages beyond transmission grids.

Access to energy in developing countries has historically been facilitated by subsidies that made energy available at below-market prices. Energy subsidies, which reduce the costs of purchasing energy, were seen as a way to promote the development of industry and commerce as well as a way to assist the poorest households. Low prices promoted greater use of energy, but not necessarily more rapid development, and the low prices could only be maintained by collecting taxes elsewhere in the economy to offset the subsidies. For countries with petroleum resources, revenues from the export of oil have played a controversial role, sometimes promoting economic development but also typically resulting in greater disparities in income and political power because small segments of the population or foreign entities control the energy assets.

Since the 1990s, international financial and development agencies have encouraged developing countries to restructure their energy sectors to raise prices to world levels. State-owned electricity companies that historically charged low rates have been privatized in many developing countries, driving electricity prices up and leading to consumer protests. Gasoline is now being sold at world market prices rather than those reflecting the local cost of production. Thus, most domestic energy prices reflect changing global balances in supply and demand.

Like developing countries, the United States long subsidized the production of fossil fuels through tax advantages provided largely during the mining, or extraction, phase. Many of these subsidies were phased out after the energy crises of the 1970s, but some remain. European nations, in contrast, tax fossil fuels and subsidize renewable sources of energy to a greater extent than does the United States. Germany, for example, aggressively invested in wind and other renewable energy technologies for producing electricity, increasing capacity tenfold between 1995 and 2005, while the U.S. renewable electricity capacity increased only 50 percent. Over the next decade, Germany will produce a significant portion of its electricity through renewable energy sources. Other European nations are also moving steadily toward renewable energy. France is highly dependent on nuclear power and is content with how it is managing the risks associated with it, but many European nations prohibit the building of additional nuclear power plants and plan to phase out existing ones. Western Europe is also actively assisting Eastern European nations to replace or improve their aging Soviet-era nuclear power plants and is pressuring the United States to move away from fossil fuels and toward renewable sources of energy to ameliorate climate change.

The developed nations are taking the lead in efforts to ensure the availability of energy for the future, although the developed nations are also still consuming the vast majority of energy resources. Research to reduce the costs of drilling for oil and gas and of mining for coal, as well as to reduce the environmental damage of these activities, is largely being undertaken by private firms based in the industrialized countries. Such research does help lower the cost of developing fossil fuel from existing and new resources for future use. It can also facilitate access to lower-quality petroleum resources outside the Middle East and thereby limit the economic vulnerability of oil-importing nations to the political instabilities in that region.

The promise of reducing the environmental impact of fossil energy use is being realized through research on pollution control technologies and through pollution control policies. Sulfur and soot emissions from the burning of coal are being reduced through better power plant design and, in some cases, through processes that clean the coal before it is burned. Research is also under way to develop technologies to decarbonize fossil fuels. Decarbonization reduces the proportion of carbon to hydrogen, making petroleum more like natural gas and reducing natural gas to hydrogen, thereby reducing the local environmental impact of combustion. It is proving more difficult than expected to develop the technologies and infrastructure to remove carbon after combustion in power plants and sequester it in natural gas or petroleum fields so that it is not released into the atmosphere, but researchers are still hopeful. This technological path is likely to play some role in ameliorating global warming and, at the same time, to support the continued use of fossil fuels for transportation where alternative fuels are not likely to be sufficient. It will also sustain the economic structure and political power of the energy industry.

Brazil integrated ethanol from sugarcane into its transportation fuels after the energy crisis of the 1970s. The production of biofuels, typically biodiesel from rapeseed in Europe and ethanol from corn in the United States, increased dramatically after the turn of the century, encouraged by favorable subsidies and then by rising energy prices. From 2005 into 2007, many viewed biofuels as an excellent energy alternative, especially for transport. One of the major advantages, it was argued, was that plants absorbed carbon dioxide from the atmosphere as they grew and then released it as the biofuels underwent combustion, making them "climate neutral." By 2008, researchers had documented that most biofuels also contributed to climate change through fertilizer use and the expansion of agriculture into new areas, including tropical forests. At the same time, the production of biofuels added to a world food crisis set off by the combination of a rising demand for meat (which requires the production of 10 calories of grains for every calorie of beef, for example), higher production costs due to raising energy prices, and bad weather. In short, just as we finally were acknowledging how energy is related to the climate system, we also learned how it is related to food production and the well-being of the world's poor. While there is hope for biofuel production from the breakdown of cellulose through new genetic technologies, the idea that biofuels are an easy answer to climate change dissipated as fast as it arose.

The production of electricity from nuclear energy has been plagued by high costs, safety concerns, and problems associated with the long-term management of radioactive waste. Nuclear energy's future remains cloudy. On the one hand, nuclear power advocates argue that the production of electricity through nuclear energy does not directly produce greenhouse gases, although there are some produced indirectly in plant construction and in the mining, processing, and management of nuclear fuels. Advocates also argue that the new generation of nuclear technologies is less expensive and safer. Detractors, on the other hand, argue that the problem of long-term waste storage—finding safe and convenient ways and acceptable places to store the dangerous by-products of nuclear power processes—must be resolved before new plants are constructed. Many are also concerned that a well-planned terrorist attack on a nuclear plant might result in the release of radioactive materials that could cause a large number of deaths and contaminate wide areas for years.

Market approaches to reaching environmental goals continue to be advocated. Sulfur emissions from electricity generated from coal are being controlled in the United States through least-cost policies that fix the amount of sulfur that can be emitted from all power plants but allow emissions permits to be traded. Power plants that can reduce sulfur emissions for the least cost therefore are able to sell permits to those plants that would otherwise have to reduce their emissions at considerably higher costs. It is likely that global greenhouse gas emissions will be limited at least cost through a system whereby carbon emission permits are assigned to each nation. States that can control their emissions or sequester carbon relatively cheaply will be able to sell some of their permits to nations that can do so only at excessively higher cost.

To reach the specified goals of electricity production from renewable resources at least cost, many U.S. states have adopted tradable obligation programs, known as renewables portfolio standards, that are comparable to tradable pollution permit programs. Producers of electricity from renewable sources sell electricity to the power grid—the high-voltage, long-distance transmission lines that deliver electricity from power plants to local distribution systems— and sell renewable energy credits to wholesale or retail distributors of electricity. Distributors of electricity compete to purchase credits, and each distributor must hold a number of credits in proportion to its total electricity sales. European nations encourage the use of renewables in electricity production through feed-in tariffs that tailor the subsidy to the additional costs of feeding in particular sources of renewable energy. The transition to renewable energy also means that electricity transmission systems must be extended to areas especially suitable for wind, biomass, or solar generation.

As nations shift to new energy technologies, new infrastructure is necessary. In particular, transmission grids established for the distribution of electricity from large power plants need to be adapted to gather electricity, for example, from widely distributed wind-generation sites.

Now that we better understand the linkages among energy, climate, land use, agricultural production and food, and social well-being, it is becoming increasingly difficult to sort out what is energy research from what is not. Nevertheless, although the bulk of energy research still seems to be directed toward enhancing the recovery of fossil fuels and capturing their carbon dioxide, research effort on reducing the costs of renewable energy is becoming significant again after a long period of neglect. One estimate puts renewable energy research worldwide as high as $16 billion.

Because energy is so important, energy systems have long been a target of terrorists (see TERRORISM). Electricity grids in developing countries have been shut down by explosives detonated at the base of transmission towers. Nuclear power plants and petroleum refineries in the industrialized world are considered likely targets. The future of fossil fuel decarbonization and centralized hydrogen production for fuel cells is also darkened by concerns over terrorism. The more cost-effective facilities will probably be large and, therefore, inviting targets. Hence, the threat of terrorism complements other arguments for the decentralization of energy facilities. Decentralization favors renewable energy technologies that tend to comprise large numbers of relatively small units, even small units on consumers' sites. Electricity can also be produced using small-scale natural gas–fired generators located close to their markets.

Regional Summaries

Energy use varies widely across regions (and among countries within regions) due to differences in the levels of economic development and availability of particular forms of energy (see map, p. 269). Asia and the Pacific islands, Europe, and North America are energy-importing regions, while the others are energy-exporting regions, with the Middle East and North Africa being the most significant. Although income inequalities among nations are increasing slowly, disparities between the rich and poor within nations have widened the gap in energy use between the richest people and the poorest people overall (see INCOME INEQUALITY). Except as otherwise noted, the information presented in these regional summaries is based on data from Table 2 and its sources.

North America

North America, a net exporter of energy for the first half of the twentieth century, has in recent years imported about two-thirds of the petroleum it uses, according to the U.S. Department of Energy's Energy Information Administration. What additional petroleum resources remain in North America are largely in the Arctic regions of the continent and offshore. Further petroleum extraction and development of abundant coal resources are advocated to increase energy independence, but at the same time these measures are strongly opposed by environmentalists. Energy use based on gross domestic product (GDP) is higher than in Western Europe due to policies that have subsidized energy consumption and facilitated the use of cars rather than public transit and due to the greater distances between cities. Not only is the number of automobiles per thousand people notably higher in North America, but the cars are notably larger and fuel efficiency is lower. For these reasons, emissions of carbon dioxide per capita are extremely high in the region.

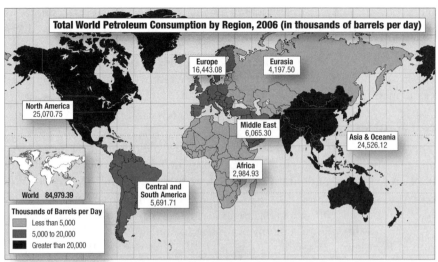

Total World Petroleum Consumption by Region, 2006 (in thousands of barrels per day)

Europe
16,443.08

Eurasia
4,197.50

North America
25,070.75

Middle East
6,065.30

Asia & Oceania
24,526.12

Africa
2,984.93

World   84,979.39

Central and
South America
5,691.71

Thousands of Barrels per Day
Less than 5,000
5,000 to 20,000
Greater than 20,000

Source: Energy Information Administration, "World Petroleum Consumption (Thousand Barrels per Day), 1980–2006," *International Energy Annual 2006*, 2008. Available online from http://www.eia.doe.gov/iea/wec.html.

Latin America

Latin America is a net exporter of energy, with nearly all of it traded to North America. The number of energy-exporting countries, however, is small: Ecuador, Mexico, and Venezuela. Venezuela, a major exporter since the 1950s, has lived off its oil earnings and has only just begun to use its oil-export revenues for internal development. All Latin American countries have some hydropower and wood energy resources, but those without significant quantities of oil have sacrificed trade earnings to import additional energy to promote development. High oil prices during the 1970s and early 1980s, however, drove these countries deeply into debt, drastically slowing and at times reversing development during the 1980s and into the 1990s. Periodic economic crises since the 1990s have been confounded with energy problems, especially during periods of high energy prices.

Europe

The eastern and western parts of Europe differ widely in economic output and energy use. Western Europe, which imports most of the fossil fuels it uses, has long sought energy efficiency through high taxes. (Charging elevated taxes on the purchase of energy creates incentives for consumers to conserve energy.) According to a 1998 LTI-Research Group report, several key European countries are moving aggressively toward renewable energy for electricity production. For these reasons, per capita fossil fuel use and emissions of carbon dioxide are considerably less than half that of North Americans, who have a comparable standard of living. The Soviet Union's economy was run on extremely inefficient energy technologies, and the new economies of the former republics have still not attained the same levels of production as under the old economy, making it difficult to invest in energy-efficient technologies. Taken together, the former Soviet republics are net exporters of energy; that is, they export more than they import. Russia has tremendous amounts of coal and natural gas, as well as considerable quantities of petroleum. Its per capita energy use, however, is comparable to that of Western Europe, even though per capita income is about one-tenth as high.

North Africa and the Middle East

The nations with the greatest reserves of petroleum are in North Africa and the Middle East. Much of these nations' income, accumulated wealth, and hence distribution of political power is directly related to oil. Multinational oil companies, many of them based in the West, and the oil-consuming nations have collaborated in the establishment and maintenance of authoritarian governments in this region. The oil-producing countries founded the Organization of Petroleum Exporting Countries (OPEC) in the 1950s, and by the late 1960s, OPEC had begun to limit the amount of oil exported in order to raise prices. Some governments have broken from and are hostile to Western development and policy in the region. The states that have not broken with the West are in some instances balancing their dependence on the West against popular animosity toward the ideas, attitudes, and lifestyles of Western nations and of the authoritarian regimes themselves. Indeed, financial resources derived indirectly from petroleum exports are in some instances financing activities against the West.

Sub-Saharan Africa

Sub-Saharan Africa includes many of the poorest countries of the world and has the lowest energy consumption of any region. The exception is South Africa, parts of which are very well developed and have relatively high rates of energy consumption. Sub-Saharan Africa's population density is relatively low, which, when combined with the low level of development, means that only those people who live in major cities have access to electricity from a grid. The reliability of the grids, however, is notoriously low. Transportation infrastructures in the region are also poorly developed. One contradictory outcome of the poor energy and transportation infrastructures and greater distances that need to be traveled is that high-tech solar photovoltaic panels and air travel play a relatively greater role in the region than in many other developing areas, although only the relatively rich can afford to take advantage of them.

Asia and the Pacific

Asia is home to more than half the world's population and some of the richest and poorest nations. Asia is a net importer of energy, but energy policies vary widely from country to country. India, which has a very low per capita income, consumes less than half a ton of energy (measured in oil equivalent per capita). It imports 12 percent of its total energy but considerably more than half of its petroleum. Japan and South Korea, with very high per capita incomes, consume about 4 tons of oil equivalent per capita and import more than 80 percent of their energy. Energy consumption per capita in the very poor countries of Bangladesh and Vietnam is approximately 0.01 of Japan's. Controversies have arisen over the Three Gorges Dam project in China (see FRESHWATER) and over the Narmada project in India because, in each case, the reservoirs of the hydropower dams will flood areas in which millions of people live.

Australia and New Zealand are two well-developed economies with small populations. They use large quantities of fossil fuels per capita and have proportionately high carbon dioxide emissions. Australia is a significant producer of coal, most of which it exports. Although New Zealand has well-developed hydropower resources, neither it nor Australia has made much effort to shift from fossil fuels to renewable resources. In addition, neither country has nuclear power.

Data

Table 1 Approximate Worldwide Primary Energy Consumption, Developed Reserves, and Estimated Resources, 2010

Resource	Primary energy (billion tons of oil equivalent)	Portion of world resources (%)	Existing reserves at current consumption levels (years)	Estimated resources at current consumption levels (years)	Estimated resources with exponential growth in consumption (years)
Fossil fuels (total)	8.8	78.6			
Oil	3.7	33.0	40	~200	95
Natural gas	2.4	21.5	60	~400	230
Coal	2.7	24.1	450	~1,500	1,000
Renewables (total)	1.8	16.1			
Large hydro	0.2	1.8		Renewable	
Traditional biomass	1.0	8.9		Renewable	
"New" renewables[a]	0.6	5.4		Renewable	
Nuclear[b]	0.6	5.4	50	> 300[c]	n/a
Total (fossil fuels + renewables + nuclear)	11.2	100.0			

Sources: Adapted from United Nations Development Programme, United Nations Department of Economic and Social Affairs, and World Energy Council, *World Energy Assessment, 2000: Energy and the Challenge of Sustainability* (New York: UNDP, 2000), and updated based on United Nations Development Programme, United Nations Department of Economic and Social Affairs, and World Energy Council, *World Energy Assessment, Overview: 2004 Update* (New York: UNDP, 2004); Renewables Energy Policy Network, *Renewables 2007 Global Status Report* (Paris: REN21 Secretariat, and Washington, D.C.: Worldwatch Institute), copyright © 2008 Deutsche Gesellschaft für Technische Zusammenarbeit (GTZ) GmbH.

Notes: n/a, not available.

[a]Includes modern biomass, small hydropower, geothermal energy, wind energy, solar energy, and marine energy.

[b]Converted from electricity produced to fuels consumed, assuming 33 percent thermal efficiency of power plants.

[c]Based on a once-through uranium fuel cycle, excluding thorium and low-concentration uranium from seawater. The uranium resource base is effectively sixty times larger if fast breeder reactors are used.

Table 2   Projected Energy and Economic Statistics by Major Region, 2010

Region	Population (millions)	GDP (billions of US$)[a]	Energy consumption (million metric tons oil equivalent)	Carbon emissions from energy consumption (million metric tons carbon)	Energy consumption per capita (metric tons of oil equivalent)	Energy consumption per GDP (metric tons per billion dollars)	Carbon emissions from energy consumption (metric tons per capita)
Asia							
Japan and South Korea	177	6,309	834	539	4.7	0.13	3.0
China	1,355	2,872	2,082	1,949	1.5	0.72	1.4
India	1,183	911	459	385	0.4	0.50	0.3
Other Asia[b]	1,079	2,565	935	721	0.9	0.36	0.7
North America[c]	344	13,735	3,074	2,059	8.9	0.22	6.0
Europe (OECD)	543	10,755	2,119	1,348	3.9	0.20	2.5
Eurasia[d]	338	931	1,378	920	4.1	1.48	2.7
Middle East	216	965	663	481	3.1	0.69	2.2
Africa	1,007	960	426	342	0.4	0.44	0.3
Central and South America	599	2,853	907	515	1.5	0.32	0.9
World total	6,841	42,856	12,877	9,259	1.9	0.30	1.4

Source: U.S. Energy Information Administration, *International Energy Outlook 2007,* App. A, Tables A1, A4, A10, A14.

Notes: GDP, gross domestic product; OECD, Organisation for Economic Cooperation and Development.

[a]Based on 2000 market exchange rates. Using purchasing power parity substantially increases the sizes of the economies of China and the former Soviet Union, but it substantially reduces the sizes of the economies of Japan and South Korea.

[b]Includes South Asia except India, Southeast Asia, Australia, New Zealand, and Pacific islands. Because this category aggregates countries with extremely different characteristics, it is best thought of as a residual.

[c]United States and Canada.

[d]Includes former Soviet Union and non-OECD Europe.

Case Study—Brazil

Brazil is a lower-middle-income developing nation of many very poor people, a few very rich people, and a now-expanding lower middle class. Heavily dependent on imported oil in the 1970s, Brazil responded to the energy crisis of that era by substituting domestically produced ethanol for imported petroleum. Over the past decade, petroleum discovery and production have made Brazil nearly energy independent, and new discoveries promise to make Brazil an oil exporter. Part of Brazil's evolving energy story entails its continued advance in production and use of domestically produced biofuels. Indeed, while other countries have begun to realize that biofuels are neither as inexpensive nor environmentally advantageous as initially thought, Brazil continues to expand production. Initially the emphasis was on using sugarcane to produce ethanol. Alcohol substitutes for lead and other performance enhancers in gasoline. Now most automobiles being purchased can run on alcohol alone. Other crops, including oil-producing crops such as soybeans (for biodiesel), are being used as the industry continues to expand. With over three decades of experience, Brazil has become a biofuels exporter and technological leader, strengths that have attracted the interest of U.S. and European developers of biofuels.

Brazil's approach to biofuels is by no means an ideal model for reducing greenhouse gases and avoiding dependence on Middle Eastern oil producers. Biofuel production and rising agricultural prices generally have driven an expansion of agricultural land under cultivation. The already weak policies meant to reduce tropical deforestation in the Brazilian Amazon have been completely overpowered by agricultural expansion. Environmental Minister Marina O. da Silva, born and raised in the Amazon herself, resigned in protest over the onslaught on the jungle. In the south and along the coasts of Brazil, where most of the sugarcane has been grown for centuries, accusations abound that ethanol production sustains colonial slavery-like labor conditions and impedes real economic development.

Biographical Sketches

Steven Chu is secretary of the Department of Energy under President Barack Obama. He is a Nobel Laureate in Physics, a former Stanford University professor, and, driven by concern with climate change, an advocate for the transition toward energy efficiency and renewable energy in the United States.

José Goldemberg is a physicist and former rector of the University of São Paulo. He served as Brazilian secretary of science and technology from 1992 to 1996. He has campaigned against nuclear power and for the development of renewable energy sources and has been a scientific leader of numerous international energy and climate change assessments.

John P. Holdren is science adviser to President Barack Obama. He trained in physics at the Massachusetts Institute of Technology and earned a doctorate at Stanford University; he was formerly a professor at the University of California, Berkeley, and is currently a professor at Harvard University. His research has focused on the causes and consequences of global environmental change, the analysis of energy technologies and policies, ways to reduce the dangers from nuclear weapons and materials, and science and technology policy.

Amory Lovins is an activist inventor and the author of numerous books on energy. He has worked to promote the development of a super-energy-efficient "hyper-car." Lovins is also the co-founder of the Rocky Mountain Institute, an organization that researches energy efficiency, renewable energy, and corporate incentives to be environmentally responsible.

Eric Martinot is a leading analyst of and advocate for the rapid expansion of renewable energy worldwide. He is the lead author of the *Renewables 2007 Global Status Report* and has worked with the Global Environmental Facility at the World Bank, Worldwatch Institute, Tsinghua University in Beijing, and other institutions. He holds a doctorate in energy and resources from the University of California, Berkeley.

Directory

American Petroleum Institute, 1220 L Street NW, Washington, D.C. 20005-4070. Telephone: (202) 682-8000; email: pr@api.org; Web: http://www.api.org.
Organization that collects information for the petroleum industry and represents its interests to the U.S. government.

Greenpeace International, 176 Keizersgracht, 1016 Amsterdam, Netherlands. Telephone: (31) 20 523 6222; email: greenpeace.usa@wdc.greenpeace.org; Web: http://www.greenpeace.org.
Membership organization that aims to raise awareness about environmental degradation.

Institute for Energy and Environmental Research, 6935 Laurel Avenue, Suite 204, Takoma Park, Md. 20912. Telephone: (301) 270-5500; email: ieer@ieer.org; Web: http://www.ieer.org.
Nongovernmental research institute promoting the democratization of science with a strong research program on nuclear waste.

International Association of Oil and Gas Producers, 25/28 Old Burlington Street, London W1S 3AN, United Kingdom. Telephone: (44) 20 7292 0600; email: llewellyn@ogp.org.uk; Web: http://www.ogp.org.uk.
Organization that represents the perspective of producers of oil and gas to international agencies.

Sustainable Energy and Economy Network (SEEN), 1112 16th Street NW, Suite 600, Washington, D.C. 20036. Telephone: (202) 234-9382; email: nmartinez@seen.org; Web: http://www.seen.org.
A project of the Institute for Policy Studies in Washington, D.C., and the Transnational Institute in Amsterdam focusing on energy, climate change, environmental justice, gender equity, and economic issues, particularly as these play out in North-South relations.

World Coal Institute, Cambridge House, 180 Upper Richmond Road, Putney, London SW15 2SH, United Kingdom. Telephone: (44) 20 8246 6611; email: info@wci-coal.com; Web: http://www.wci-coal.com
Organization that represents the perspective of the coal industry at international venues.

World Resources Institute (WRI), 10 G Street NE, Suite 800, Washington, D.C. 20002. Telephone: (202) 729-7600; email: front@wri.org; Web: http://www.wri.org.
NGO that researches and disseminates information on resources and the environment.

Further Research

Books

Andrews-Speed, Philip. *The Strategic Implications of China's Energy Needs.* Oxford: Oxford University Press, 2002.

Baev, Pavel. *Russian Energy Policy and Military Power: Putin's Quest for Greatness.* London: Routledge, 2008.

Cipti, Ben. *The Energy Construct: Achieving a Clean, Domestic, and Economical Energy Future.* Charleston, S.C.: Booksurge, 2007.

Deffeyes, Kenneth F. *Hubbert's Peak: The Impending World Oil Shortage.* Princeton, N.J.: Princeton University Press, 2001.

Hakes, Jay E. *A Declaration of Independence: How Freedom from Foreign Oil Can Improve National Security, Our Economy, and Our Environment.* Hoboken, N.J.: Wiley and Sons, 2008.

Kalicki, Jan H., and David L. Goldwyn, eds. *Energy and Security: Toward a New Foreign Policy Strategy.* Baltimore: Woodrow Wilson Center and Johns Hopkins University Press, 2005.

Schneider, Stephen H., and Randi Londer. *The Coevolution of Climate and Life.* San Francisco: Sierra Club Books, 1984.

Smil, Vaclav. *Energy at the Crossroad: Global Perspectives and Uncertainties.* Cambridge, Mass.: MIT Press, 2003.

Articles and Reports

InterAcademyCouncil. *Lighting the Way: Toward a Sustainable Energy Future.* Amsterdam: InterAcademyCouncil, 2007.

Millennium Ecosystem Assessment. *Ecosystems and Human Well-Being.* Washington, D.C.: Island Press, 2005.

National Academy of Sciences. *America's Energy Future: Technology Opportunities, Risks, and Tradeoffs.* Washington, D.C.: National Academy Press, 2009.

Renewable Energy Policy Network for the 21st Century. "Renewables 2007 Global Status Report." REN21 Secretariat, Paris, and Worldwatch Institute, Washington, D.C., 2008.

Srinivasan, Utthara, et al. "The Debt of Nations and the Distribution of Ecological Impacts from Human Activities." *Proceedings of the National Academy of Sciences* 105, no. 5 (2008): 1768–1773.

Web Sites

Energy Information Administration, U.S. Department of Energy
http://www.eia.doe.gov

International Energy Agency
http://www.iea.org

World Energy Assessment
http://www.undp.org/seed/eap/activities/wea

World Energy Council
http://www.worldenergy.org

Document

1. Energy and Climate Change

Dr. Steven Chu, secretary of energy under President Barack Obama, address before the American Academy of Sciences held at the University of California, Berkeley, November 20, 2007

Bulletin of the American Academy, *winter 2008. The full text is available at http://www .amacad.org/publications/bulletin/winter2008/energy.pdf.*

Extracts

Let me discuss some predicted effects of climate change. People are forecasting many events, including a dramatic increase in species extinction, a rise in sea level, increased damage from floods, storms, and wildfires, and so on. There is mounting evidence that many of these predictions are beginning to happen, and in many cases, faster than what was predicted in the 1980s. . . .

The United States is the leader in both wealth and energy consumption per capita, but our energy consumption per unit of wealth (measured as the GDP per capita) is leveling off. There are several reasons: increased energy efficiency, and a shift from a heavy industry-based economy to a service based economy. The more relevant issue is not energy consumption *per se,* but the amount of greenhouse gases one emits while using the energy. I believe that it is possible to continue to consume large amounts of energy that have led to our prosperity while dramatically decreasing the production of CO_2. The governor of California, Arnold Schwarzenegger, has set a target of reducing the state's carbon emissions by a factor of five by mid-century. Others think that dropping by a factor of ten may be needed to stabilize the carbon in the atmosphere and allow the rest of the world's population, which will peak at approximately 9 to 10 billion people, to enjoy the same standard of living as the United States. . . .

The developed countries, and especially the United States, must dramatically reduce their carbon emissions. A dual strategy is needed: 1) We need to maximize energy efficiency and decrease energy use. Increasing the efficient use of energy will remain the lowest hanging fruit among the set of solutions for the next several decades. 2) We have to develop new sources of clean, carbon-neutral sources of energy. . . .

Climate change is the biggest common problem we are facing today, and free markets will never respond to this problem. Ultimately, international agreements between governments have to intervene with a combination of regulations and fiscal incentives. . . .

Increasing the geothermal generation of energy should also be considered. Geothermal energy is actually a very clean form of fission energy, since the heat deep inside the Earth is generated by naturally occurring radioactive decay. A good geothermal energy source has a combination of hot, porous rock and a supply of replenishable water. Anywhere around the world, if one goes down into the earth, you automatically get heat. Water is needed to extract the heat in surrounding rock and transport this energy to the surface where it can be used. . . .

Wind is also a very good source of renewable energy. In terms of cost, it is within 20 percent of being competitive with fossil fuel. Currently, the biggest windmills have a generating capacity of 3 million watts per windmill, with the wingspan of a 747 airplane. Even larger, 5 MW windmills are on the drawing board, with wingspans of 126 meters. The bigger the windmills get, the more efficient they become, and because they stand higher off the ground, they can intercept more wind energy. I asked a senior engineer at GE how big he thought they could get. He answered, "5 MW is about as big as they can get. Any bigger, and we can't ship the blades. They cannot make turns on conventional railroad tracks and highways." . . .

Returning to the growing of plants for bio-fuels, plants that are better than corn? The answer is definitely "yes." As an example, consider the grass *Miscanthus.* This plant is perennial, and hence no tillage is needed for 10 years or more. As a perennial, it can be harvested annually, and like a weed whose roots are left in the ground, *Miscanthus* will grow back with a vengeance the following year. This plant is expected to produce ten times the amount of ethanol per acre as compared to corn, and without the heavy energy and water inputs that corn demands....

What do we want to do with this investment? We want to develop better plants and develop better methods of breaking down the woody ligno-cellulose material into material that can be converted into a biofuel. In the BP-funded project, we also want to look at the socioeconomic and environmental impacts of biofuels. The deployment of any new technology often is accompanied by unintended consequences, and it is important to try to anticipate and minimize (and ideally to avoid) harmful consequences. Biofuel production must be accomplished in an economically competitive and environmentally friendly way....

In the end, we need to seek transportation energy solutions that are not based on nature. Because of the limits on production of fuel using arable land, we need to develop an artificial photosynthetic system that will split water into oxygen and hydrogen, and to extract carbon dioxide out of the atmosphere and reduce it to carbon monoxide. These are the first three ingredients that are needed to construct hydrocarbon fuel....

At his Nobel banquet in 1950, William Faulkner said, "I believe that man will not merely endure: he will prevail. He is immortal, not because he alone among creatures has an inexhaustible voice, but because he has a soul, a spirit, capable of compassion and sacrifice and endurance." With these virtues, we can and will prevail over this great energy challenge.

FRESHWATER

Melanie Jarman

Water is what most distinguishes Earth from other planets, yet only 1 percent of the water that covers nearly three-fourths of Earth's surface is usable freshwater. Water may be the ultimate renewable resource, but in many parts of the world the demand now exceeds the supply. According to the United Nations "2006 Human Development Report" (HDR), 1.2 billion people do not have access to safe water and 2.6 billion do not have access to sanitation (the systems involved in effective sewage treatment). The report said, "Water, the stuff of life and a basic human right, is at the heart of a daily crisis faced by countless millions of the world's most vulnerable people—a crisis that threatens life and destroys livelihoods on a devastating scale." The report argued that poverty, power, and inequality are at the heart of the problem.

Historical Background and Development

Disputes over the world's water resources may seem a recent phenomenon, but according to water expert Peter Gleick, they date back to at least the sixteenth century. In one of the earliest recorded conflicts involving water, Leonardo da Vinci and Machiavelli devised a plan to divert Italy's Arno River during a conflict between Pisa and Florence in 1503. Water has figured in many conflicts since then, including the 1980–1988 Iran-Iraq War, the 1991 Persian Gulf War, and the 1999 Kosovo conflict.

Numerous initiatives have been launched to address water problems beyond the nation-state level. The 1971 Ramsar Convention on Wetlands has been an important instrument in protecting wetlands throughout the world. Another major initiative was the International Drinking Water Supply and Sanitation Decade, which began in 1980. Although the campaign successfully drew

This chapter is based on the original, written by Chris Woodford, that appeared in the first edition of *World at Risk*.

attention to water and sanitation problems, some 1.3 billion people were still without safe water, and 1.9 billion were without adequate sanitation by the decade's end. In 1992, freshwater resources featured prominently at the Earth Summit held in Rio de Janeiro. A chapter of the Agenda 21 agreement to curtail environmental damage was signed at the meeting; the agreement was based largely on the Dublin Statement on freshwater management that had been accepted at the groundbreaking International Conference on Water and the Environment earlier that year (see Document 1). In December 2000, the European Union signed the Water Framework Directive, an important piece of legislation heralding a new age of integrated water management. In 2001, the World Health Organization (WHO) called for the recognition of access to safe water and adequate sanitation as basic human rights.

Global efforts to secure water resources have sometimes taken their cue from local campaigns. International Rivers, an influential California-based nongovernmental organization (NGO) formed in 1985 as the International Rivers Network, has made its name by fighting destructive dams across the world. Its long-running campaigns have included supporting the local efforts of the group Narmada Bachao Andolan (NBA) in fighting the proposed Sardar Sarovar dam in India's Narmada Valley. The struggle of the NBA, which included mass protests by tens of thousands of people in the 1980s and a near-fatal twenty-two-day hunger strike by celebrated activist Medha Patkar in 1991, helped to highlight problems with dams across the world. Campaigns such as this prompted the World Bank to reevaluate its role in controversial development projects; the bank withdrew entirely from the Sardar Sarovar project in 1993. The campaign also led, ultimately, to the major study by the World Commission on Dams on the impact of large dams, released in November 2000.

For all the progress the world has made toward safer and more secure water resources, difficulties remain. Many nations seem increasingly prone to floods, droughts, and other natural disasters. In 2000, Kenya experienced its worst flooding in forty years, but in 2001, East Africa experienced its worst drought in living memory, with Kenya, ironically, the hardest hit. In Asia in 2007, floods across India, Pakistan, Bangladesh, and Nepal left 1,400 dead and displaced 31 million people. Some areas received 30–50 percent of their annual rainfall in just thirty days. Water crises and the global hydrological cycle are further complicated by other problems such as climate change and increasingly regular El Niño events. In a statement quoted by the Agence France-Presse news agency in 2003, the World Water Council described the increasing sea and atmosphere temperatures as "calamitous for traditional rainfall patterns."

Current Status

A variety of problems contribute to the world's water crisis, and numerous policies and programs have been proposed to address it. According to the United Nations, in the twentieth century, the use of water grew at more than twice the rate of population growth. The UN estimates that by 2025 about two-thirds of the world's population will live in areas facing moderate to severe water stress.

Research

The 2006 HDR said that every person should have access to at least 20 liters of water per day. On average, people in Europe use more than 200 liters a day and people in the United States use more than 400 liters a day. While a person in the United Kingdom or United States sends an average 50 liters down the drain each day simply by flushing their toilet, many poor people survive on less than 5 liters of contaminated water per day. This level of inequality occurs within nations as well as between nations. In high-income areas of cities in Asia, Latin America, and sub-Saharan Africa, people have access to several hundred liters of water per day delivered into their homes, while slum dwellers and poor households in rural areas of the same countries have access to far less than the recommended 20 liters. The poorest people not only have access to less water, and to less clean water, but they also tend to pay higher prices. HDR research found that poor people living in slums often pay five to ten times more per liter of water than wealthy people living in the same city.

Technologies for moving water to human settlements and irrigating crops were pioneered by the ancient Sumerians and contributed to a key stage in the advancement of civilization. Six thousand years later, the United Nations billed 2008 as an International Year of Sanitation, stating that 2.6 billion people—over 40 percent of the world's population—still did not have access to basic sanitation. In a 1997 report for the United Nations International Children's Emergency Fund (UNICEF), development expert Akhtar Hameed Khan said, "when you have a medieval level of sanitation, you have a medieval level of disease, and no country can advance without a healthy population."

Worldwide, 88 percent of cases of diarrhea (including those caused by cholera, typhoid, and dysentery) are attributable to unsafe water, inadequate sanitation, or insufficient hygiene (see HEALTH). These cases result in 1.5 million deaths each year, most being the deaths of children. A total of 860,000 deaths per year in children under five years of age are caused directly and indirectly by malnutrition induced by unsafe water, inadequate sanitation, and insufficient hygiene. The WHO has suggested that almost one-tenth of the global disease burden could be prevented by improving water supply, sanitation, hygiene, and management of water resources.

The problem of an adequate and clean supply of water is compounded by a progressive decline in the quality of the world's freshwater and the quantity of available freshwater. The World Wide Fund for Nature (WWF; formerly the World Wildlife Fund) reports on its Web site that more than half of global wetlands have been destroyed in the last century. WWF's index of freshwater species populations has also declined significantly since 1970. Water tables, water levels in underground aquifers, and water flows in major rivers are falling all over the world. The mismanagement of land and water resources in river basins is substantially to blame for the displacement of 25 million environmental refugees, who in 1998 exceeded the world's 21 million war refugees for the first time.

Rising human populations and degraded freshwater are still only part of the problem. In 2000, irrigation accounted for about 70 percent of global water use, whereas industry accounted for 20 percent and municipalities for only about 10 percent. Per capita demand for water continues to rise in many countries, mostly for irrigation and industrial uses. Forty percent of the world's food comes from irrigated lands; agriculture is by far the biggest user of water worldwide. According to the World Commission on Water, the freshwater crisis is a major impediment to achieving global food security. Tearfund predicts that the global agricultural demand for water will increase by 50 percent by 2025, forcing developing nations to make difficult choices between supplying water to human settlements or to crops—that is, between having enough food or having enough water. Industrialization is also driving huge increases in the demand for water. According to the United Nations World Water Assessment Programme, the annual water volume used by industry will rise from 752 cubic kilometers per year in 1995 to an estimated 1,170 cubic kilometers per year in 2025.

If every country had complete control over its own water, guaranteeing adequate and safe supplies would be easier. Some nations share their water supplies with others, so their fates are necessarily intertwined. In the Middle East, for example, considerable tension results from the way four major waterways—the Nile, Tigris, Euphrates, and the Jordan rivers—are shared between nations. For example, Egypt is 97 percent dependent on the Nile for its freshwater and Ethiopia, upstream, controls 86 percent of the river's flow. In sub-Saharan Africa, Namibia's plans to divert flows from the Okavanga River for irrigation prompted an outcry in neighboring Botswana, whose wildlife-rich Okavanga Delta, a major source of tourist income, is fed from the same source. Diplomats, including Ismail Serageldin, World Commission on Water chairman, and Boutros Boutros-Ghali, former UN secretary-general, have repeatedly suggested that wars may be fought over water in the twenty-first century, just as, according to many analysts, the 1991 Persian Gulf War was fought over oil in the twentieth century.

Attempts to engineer solutions to the water problem have been a mixed blessing. On the one hand, without large-scale irrigation schemes, reservoirs, and dams, Earth could not support the population that it currently does and many more people would be suffering the effects of water scarcity. Yet the very solutions to some of Earth's water problems are the direct cause of other, sometimes related problems. The world's 45,000-plus large dams, for example, have provided economic benefits, flood control, and a means of storing water for times of need; they also generate approximately one-fifth of the world's total electricity. Yet large dams have also ravaged ecosystems, fragmented rivers, and displaced millions of people. According to the World Commission on Dams, 40–80 million people have been displaced by dams and their reservoirs. The commission's groundbreaking 2000 report, *Dams and Development: A New Framework for Decision-Making,* confirmed the positive and negative effects of constructing large dams and raised questions about the future of some of the 1,000-plus dams that were then being planned or under construction.

Water also plays a key role in gender and family issues in many developing nations. In some parts of Sierra Leone, for example, nine-year-old girls spend as much as six hours a day on water-related activities, such as fetching and carrying. Women and young girls experience a double disadvantage because they are the ones who sacrifice their time and their education to collect water. Women are also overwhelmingly responsible for hygiene and sanitation. Health, gender, family, education, and poverty issues are inextricably intertwined with access to clean water and sanitation.

The water crisis compounds other pressing issues and is compounded, in turn, by other global concerns. As already noted, global warming is predicted to drastically change the pattern of precipitation over much of the planet, increasing the severity of droughts and floods, particularly in nations already facing water scarcity (see CLIMATE CHANGE).

Policies and Programs

According to the World Commission on Water, the starting point for solving the water crisis is integrated water resource management, an internationally accepted methodology based on sustaining the global ecosystem on which all water resources depend and on planning the use of water and land holistically across river basins, even where national borders divide them (see Document 2). This approach provides the foundation for Agenda 21 and the European Union Water Framework Directive. It also underpins the promotion of international cooperation on sustainable water management through an initiative called the Global Water Partnership. Encouraging signs have appeared that water-scarce nations see cooperation of this kind as a more productive route to solving their problems than confrontation. The United Nations is using integrated water resource management to help eight African nations resolve conflicting needs concerning the use of the Zambesi River and to help Angola, Botswana, and Namibia share the Okavanga. The countries that share the Nile are now working together under the umbrella of the Nile Basin Initiative.

Starting from the assumption that freshwater is not in short supply on Earth, another solution to the water crisis is to conserve and make better use of the water that is available. What that means, however, varies from country to country. According to Peter Gleick, up to 30 percent of the municipal water supply in developed nations is lost through leakage or poorly maintained systems. In developing nations, where irrigation accounts for up to 90 percent of water use, hose pipes or sprinklers can waste up to 50 percent of the water that flows through them due to evaporation and runoff. Low-tech drip irrigation systems that supply water underground directly to plant roots reduce water use by up to 70 percent and improve yields by up to 90 percent. The World Commission on Water's vision for 2025 is based on "more crop per drop," with a 40 percent increase in agricultural production achieved through only a 9 percent increase in irrigation.

The systematic degradation of freshwater habitats is less of a water problem than an issue that needs to be addressed as part of a more general approach to conserving and protecting the world's fragile ecosystems (see POLLUTION). Unlike other types of habitat destruction—the loss of coral reefs or tropical rain forests—the loss of freshwater habitats affects human needs more immediately. Various international conventions exist to preserve the world's freshwater habitats; the most important are the Ramsar Convention on Wetlands (1971), the Convention on the Protection and Use of Transboundary Watercourses and International Lakes (1992), and, within Europe, the European Union Habitats Directive (1992). Fortunately, degradation is not an irreversible process. Community groups play an important role in river and wetland restoration around the world, notably in the United States, where numerous alliances have been formed to protect and restore inland waters within state boundaries and, more appropriately, across entire river basins.

Protecting freshwater habitats also necessarily implies a rethinking of large-scale construction works, such as hydroelectric dams, whose reservoirs can destroy vast areas of valuable habitat (and create other problems, such as disrupting the transport of sediments or the flow of fish along rivers). Although large dams may bring social, economic, and environmental benefits such as improving water supplies for a community, providing reliable electricity, or reducing dependence on fossil fuels, they also carry social, economic, and environmental costs such as displacing many people, diverting money from low-tech development projects, destroying freshwater habitats, or emitting greenhouse gases. By balancing the economic, social, and environmental benefits against the costs of dams, the World Commission on Dams report, *Dams and Development,* was widely regarded as a milestone in the promotion and development of less-destructive projects.

Good management, better conservation, and halting the degradation of freshwater habitats are grounded in the principle of sustainable development. Other equally valid ways of viewing and attempting to solve the water crisis are also available. Water is essential to life, and, as previously noted, the lack of clean water and adequate sanitation is a key factor in high infant mortality rates. The WHO has repeatedly called for access to water to be recognized as a human right. In 2001, Gro Harlem Brundtland, then the director-general of the WHO, said, "Access to safe water is a universal need and indeed considered a basic human right." Although not explicitly recognized in the 1948 Universal Declaration of Human Rights, the right to water is implicitly recognized as part of the right to life, health, food, and an adequate standard of living. A human rights approach to the water crisis views the provision of water and sanitation as an obligation, not a charitable act, which must be respected and protected by national governments. Although viewing water as a basic human right is an important step forward, the history of human rights suggests that this is far from enough to guarantee water safety for everyone.

Economists may view the problem in terms of supply, demand, and pricing issues. Thus, if the demand for water exceeds the supply over much of the planet, economists might argue that water is underpriced virtually everywhere. The Dublin Statement recognized that "water has an economic value in all its competing uses and should be recognized as an economic good." In principle, addressing the water crisis then becomes an economic matter of making users pay the full cost of the water they use, called full-cost pricing. This was one of the World Commission on Water's strongest recommendations; Daniel C. Sikazwe and Maria Gemma reported the commission's reasoning in "World Water Forum Whets Interest," stating that "without full-cost pricing, the present vicious cycle of waste, inefficiency, and lack of service for the poor will continue." Unfortunately, the cost of water in poor countries and communities, where people have the least ability to pay for clean water and sanitation, is usually much greater than in rich countries and communities. For example, where no household connections have been laid, water may be bought from vendors so that the cost is higher than that of a piped supply. The costs do not end there—fuel may be needed to boil the water to make sure it is safe to drink.

For agencies working directly with people in developing nations who lack access to clean water and sanitation, theoretical discussions of the water crisis are less immediately important than pragmatic, technological solutions—installing an efficient water pump in a village is often a more direct benefit than talking about water pricing, sustainable development, or human rights. From the early irrigation schemes of the Sumerians to the elaborate hydroelectric dams funded by the World Bank, technology has always played a key role in water management and supply.

Today a considerable emphasis has developed on what *Small Is Beautiful* writer E. Fritz Schumacher calls intermediate technology—small-scale, affordable technologies appropriate to the lives of the people involved. These include efficient solar-powered water pumps, fog collectors (huge plastic sheets draped like fences over hillsides that catch fog and turn it into drinking water), simple techniques for purifying rainwater supplies through chlorination, and drip-feed irrigation systems to reduce water loss by evaporation. More elaborate technological solutions continue to be proposed—including desalination (turning saltwater into freshwater), dragging freshwater by sea in large plastic bags from areas of plenty to areas of need, and towing icebergs—but they currently provide only a tiny amount of the world's usable freshwater.

Regional Summaries

Stresses on the world's water vary dramatically from region to region. Water supplies are relatively plentiful in parts of northern Europe, the former Soviet Union, Central America, and West Africa. Elsewhere, notably in North Africa, the Middle East, and the western states of the United States, stresses on water are considerable.

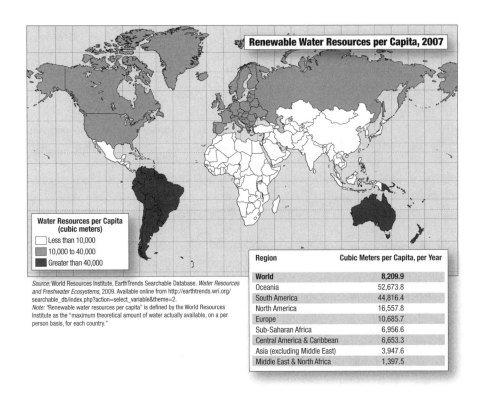

Renewable Water Resources per Capita, 2007

Water Resources per Capita (cubic meters)
- Less than 10,000
- 10,000 to 40,000
- Greater than 40,000

Source: World Resources Institute, EarthTrends Searchable Database. *Water Resources and Freshwater Ecosystems*, 2009. Available online from http://earthtrends.wri.org/searchable_db/index.php?action=select_variable&theme=2.
Note: "Renewable water resources per capita" is defined by the World Resources Institute as the "maximum theoretical amount of water actually available, on a per person basis, for each country."

Region	Cubic Meters per Capita, per Year
World	8,209.9
Oceania	52,673.8
South America	44,816.4
North America	16,557.8
Europe	10,685.7
Sub-Saharan Africa	6,956.6
Central America & Caribbean	6,653.3
Asia (excluding Middle East)	3,947.6
Middle East & North Africa	1,397.5

North America

Dramatic increases in irrigation, power generation, and industrialization in the United States have led to its having one of the highest annual per capita water use rates in the world (see Table 1). Although North America has plentiful freshwater, it is very unequally distributed. The western and midwestern states of the United States are the most water stressed and are among the regions of the world that are expected to become chronically short of water in the first few decades of the twenty-first century. According to a 2008 report on the Circle of Blue Web site, Lake Mead and Lake Powell, the two largest reservoirs in the southwestern United States, are forecast to become "dead pool" mud puddles in this time scale. The same report said that the largest U.S. underground reservoir, the Ogallala Aquifer, is being depleted at a rate of 12 billion cubic meters per year.

Declining water levels also affect North America. As reported by the Circle of Blue Web site, scientists have predicted that by approximately 2040 water levels in Lake Erie, which supplies drinking water to more than 11 million people, could fall by 3–6 feet. In an attempt to curb the draws on the Great Lakes and protect water resources in North America, eight U.S. states and two Canadian provinces have proposed a Great Lakes Compact.

Freshwater ecology in North America has been degraded as a result of habitat loss, introduction of non-native species, and climate change. In 2008, the ScienceDaily Web site reported that nearly 40 percent of the region's fish species were in jeopardy—an increase of 92 percent since 1989.

Latin America

With plentiful supplies of surface water from rivers, Latin America is one of the least water-stressed regions on Earth. Water availability, however, is quite different from access to clean water and adequate sanitation. A 2004 estimate from the WHO and UNICEF suggested that in Latin America and the Caribbean 34 million people in rural areas and 17 million people in urban areas did not have access to an improved drinking-water source. Increases in irrigation, urbanization, and industrialization have sometimes led to localized water supply problems because groundwater supplies are being pumped at rates exceeding their natural rate of regeneration or are being polluted through such activities as mining (see POLLUTION). A 2006 report by Inter Press Service and the International Federation of Environmental Journalists stated that in Brazil the amount of chemicals required to make water drinkable increased by 51 percent between 2001 and 2006. Maintaining clean and affordable supplies of water to increasingly urban areas is one of the region's key challenges for the future.

In the Caribbean, as the population increases, the demand for housing does as well. New housing developments, in turn, put pressure on already fragile mountain and coastal ecosystems.

Europe and Central Asia

Although most Europeans enjoy adequate supplies of clean water, the stress on river basins varies dramatically across the region. In northern countries and parts of the Russian Federation, water is relatively plentiful, although even in the United Kingdom, for example, hot summers cause restrictions on water use. In the hottest part of the region, the Mediterranean, water availability per capita is considerably scarcer due to the high degree of irrigated agriculture and the increasing demands of tourism. In addition, drought is a problem. The National Aeronautics and Space Administration (NASA) Earth Observatory found that between November 2004 and March 2005, Spain experienced its driest winter since records began in 1943 and Portugal experienced its worst drought in twenty-five years.

According to the European Environment Agency, since World War II water consumption in Western Europe has increased almost fivefold. In Eastern Europe, economic restructuring led to a temporary drop in water consumption during the 1990s, but increasing standards of living and urbanization have contributed to an increase in water use. In Central Asia, where more than 90 percent of water is used for agriculture, inefficient irrigation wastes vast amounts of water in an area where it should be in abundance. Habitat protection remains a major problem throughout Europe. According to the WWF, more than 60 percent of the region's wetlands were destroyed in the twentieth century.

North Africa and the Middle East

The most water-stressed region in the world is North Africa and the Middle East. Water availability per person is around 1,200 cubic meters per person per year (compared with a worldwide average of about 7,000), and per capita water availability is expected to halve by 2050 according to the World Bank Web site. The World Bank also noted that 85 percent of the region's water is used for agriculture. Much of the water supply comes from fossil aquifers, groundwater reserves from a once-wetter climate that receive very little resupply from the region's slight rainfall. Thus, aquifer depletion is a serious problem for the region.

Sixty percent of the region's water flows across international borders, and the sharing of this resource has led to tensions. Former UN secretary-general Boutros Boutros-Ghali's infamous statement that "The next war in the Middle East will be fought over water, not politics" reflects his experience as Egypt's foreign minister. According to Peter Gleick, water played a role in Middle Eastern conflicts on approximately twenty occasions during the twentieth century.

Sub-Saharan Africa

Sub-Saharan Africa has relatively abundant freshwater resources in numerous rivers and lakes. Forty-two percent of the region's people, however, lack access to a piped water supply, and only around 37 percent have access to improved sanitation, according to the World Bank. Wide variations in water availability across the region are complicated by poor management practices, frequent droughts, and the increasing effects of climate change. By 2025, twenty-five African nations and 16 percent of Africans (230 million people) are expected to experience water scarcity, and another 32 percent (460 million people) will experience water stress, based on figures from the United Nations Environment Programme (UNEP). Although agriculture is still by far the biggest use of water—accounting for 88 percent of consumption for Africa, including North Africa—industrialization, urbanization, increasing population, and pollution all present challenges for the future.

Asia and the Pacific

According to the World Bank Web site, South Asia's renewable freshwater resources are about 1,200 cubic meters per capita. For East Asia and the Pacific, according to the World Bank, the average per capita water availability is currently about 5,000 cubic meters, which is moderate by world standards. However, the World Bank also pointed out that much of East Asia and Pacific is using water at unsustainable rates, causing groundwater depletion and the drying up of rivers. Other regional water-related issues identified by the World Banks include overexploited aquifers, shrinking glaciers, soil erosion, and pollution.

Access to safe drinking water and lack of sanitation are other major problems. Opening the first Asia-Pacific Water Summit, in Japan in 2007, the

Japanese prime minister stated that one out of five people in the region did not have access to safe drinking water, that half the region's population did not have adequate sanitation, and that the region has accounted for 80 percent of the deaths worldwide caused by water-related disasters.

Data

Table 1 Freshwater Resources and Withdrawals in Selected Countries

Country	Annual renewable water resources (km³/year)[a]	Year of estimate	Total freshwater withdrawal (km³/year)	Per capita freshwater withdrawal (m³/year) [b]	Year of estimate
Algeria	14.3	1997	6.07	185	2000
Argentina	814.0	2000	29.19	753	2000
Australia	398.0	1995	24.06	1,193	2000
Brazil	8,233.0	2000	59.30	318	2000
Canada	3,300.0	1985	44.72	1,386	1996
China	2,829.6	1999	549.76	415	2000
Colombia	2,132.0	2000	10.71	235	2000
Congo, Republic of	832.0	1987	0.36	6	2000
Egypt	86.8	1997	68.30	923	2000
France	189.0	2005	33.16	548	2000
Georgia	63.3	1997	3.61	808	2000
Germany	188.0	2005	38.01	460	2001
Guatemala	111.3	2000	2.01	160	2000
India	1,907.8	1999	645.84	585	2000
Indonesia	2,838.0	1999	82.78	372	2000
Israel	1.7	2001	2.05	305	2000
Japan	430.0	1999	88.43	690	2000
Russian Federation	4,498.0	1997	76.68	535	2000
Saudi Arabia	2.4	1997	17.32	705	2000
Spain	111.1	2005	37.22	864	2002
Sweden	179.0	2005	2.68	296	2002
Switzerland	53.3	2005	2.52	348	2002
Tajikistan	99.7	1997	11.96	1,837	2000
Thailand	409.9	1999	82.75	1,288	2000
Turkey	234.0	2003	39.78	544	2001
Uganda	66.0	1970	0.30	10	2002
United Kingdom	160.6	2005	11.75	197	1994
United States	3,069.0	1985	477.00	1,600	2000

Source: Pacific Institute, "World Data from The World's Water," Table 1 Total Renewable Freshwater Supply by Country (2006 Update) and Table 2 Freshwater Withdrawal by Country and Sector (2006 Update), available at http://www.worldwater.org/data.html.

Notes: The data come from a wide variety of sources and are collected using a wide variety of approaches, with few formal standards. They do not include the use of rainfall in agriculture.

[a]Total natural renewable surface water and groundwater. Data typically include flows from other countries. Flows to other countries have not been subtracted from these values.

[b]National population estimates are from approximately the year of withdrawal.

Table 2   Drinking Water and Sanitation Coverage in Selected Regions, 2004

Region	Population (thousands)	Improved drinking water coverage (%)	Improved sanitation coverage (%)
North Africa	152,085	91	77
Sub-Saharan Africa	734,641	56	37
Latin America and the Caribbean	553,725	92	77
East Asia	1,388,052	78	45
South Asia	1,528,108	85	38
Southeast Asia	548,525	82	67
Western Asia	194,170	91	84

Source: World Health Organization and UNICEF, "Meeting the MDG Drinking Water and Sanitation Target: The Urban and Rural Challenge of the Decade." WHO and UNICEF, New York, 2006.

Case Study—Water Security in the Middle East

Water security is defined by the United Nations Development Programme (UNDP) "Human Development" Web site as maintaining water resources such that "every person has reliable access to enough safe water at an affordable price to lead a healthy, dignified and productive life" while also sustaining ecosystems that provide and depend on water. Lack of a clean and safe water supply limits the potential for human development. This contributes to political instability within nations and, where water resources are shared across boundaries, between nations.

Water is an important security issue in the Middle East; too little water is available to meet each country's internal needs, let alone to meet the needs laid out under transboundary agreements. The late King Hussein of Jordan suggested, as have other leaders in the region, that conflicts over water rights could bring the nations of the region to war.

One key water source in the region is the Jordan River system/basin, which is fed mainly by the Dan, Banias, and Hasbani streams. The Dan Stream is situated in Israel. The Banias Stream originates in Syria, but has been under Israeli control since 1967. The main source for the Hasbani is in Lebanon. The Yarmouk is the most significant tributary for the lower part of the Jordan River, and it forms the border between Jordan and Syria. Further downstream, it forms the border between Jordan and Israel shortly before it joins the Lower Jordan River. The Lower Jordan River then forms the border between Jordan and Israel and between Jordan and the Palestinian West Bank. Israel, Jordan, and Syria divert 95 percent of the water that is supposed to feed the Lower Jordan, and, as a result, the river has almost completely dried up. The Dead Sea, historically fed by the Lower Jordan River, has already shrunk by one-third in the past fifty years.

In 1994, Jordan and Israel signed a peace treaty containing the mutual recognition of their "rightful allocations" to water from the Jordan River and the

Yarmouk River. Described as one of the most creative and innovative treaties concerning water rights on record, the agreement included a requirement for Israel to store water for later transfer to Jordan. In 1999, a severe drought led Israel to indicate that it was unable to meet its water delivery schedule to Jordan, raising the possibility that it would not transfer the water allocation. Tensions mounted, and Jordan threatened to take action against Israel. In more recent years, Jordan has accused Syria of diverting excessive amounts from the Yarmouk, causing Jordan to be unable to meet its water transfer commitment to Israel.

Another issue contributing to water tensions in the Middle East is climate change, considered by the UNDP to be a transformative factor in worldwide global water insecurity. Climate change is predicted to bring more extreme weather to the region alongside decreased precipitation and increased evapotranspiration, making the fulfillment of Israel's and Jordan's water-sharing obligations increasingly difficult. Reduced precipitation in the Jordan Valley will also make maintaining its current agricultural practices difficult for Israel. Rising sea levels brought about by climate change will put the Coastal Aquifer at risk. This aquifer is the only drinking water source for 1.5 million Palestinians in Gaza, and it supports agricultural productivity there. The Coastal Aquifer is already overexploited and in some areas is experiencing salinity levels well above WHO standards.

A 2007 report by Friends of the Earth Middle East, *Climate Change: A New Threat to Middle East Security,* suggested that the existence of water-sharing agreements may help avoid future conflict because a forum and framework are already in place for dealing with water issues. However, the report warned that such agreements could be jeopardized if policies are not put in place to limit political instability brought about by water issues. These include policies to diversify incomes away from water-dependent activities such as agriculture, and policies to help mitigate and adapt to climate change.

Case Study—Agriculture and Water Use in California

California is one of the most productive agricultural regions in the world, with its agricultural sector producing $35 billion in goods and services in 2005. At California's agricultural heart is the Sacramento–San Joaquin Delta, an inland river delta and estuary. Almost half the water used for agriculture in California comes from rivers that once flowed into the delta, and more than 50 percent of Californians rely on water conveyed through the delta for at least some of their water supply. Yet the delta is an ecosystem in crisis—water quality is declining, fish populations are declining, decades of neglect combined with earthquakes have increased the risk of levee failure, and climate instability is bringing changes in the frequency and intensity of floods and droughts. A task force that looked at sustainability issues for the area found that too much water is being exported from the delta. Much of this is due to agriculture, which accounts for about 80 percent of delta water consumption. Agriculture is already feeling the impact of problems in the delta's water supply—pumping restrictions and water shortages from drought led to farm losses estimated to be as high as $245 million as of mid-summer 2008. The 2008 U.S.-based Pacific Institute report, *More with Less: Agricultural Water Conservation and Efficiency in California,* summed up the situation: "Actions are needed to both ensure a sustainable agricultural sector and to reduce the water required for it."

The 2008 report suggested four scenarios that could contribute to an agricultural sector that was more sustainable in its use of water: (1) shifting a small amount of lower-value water-intensive crops to higher-value water-efficient crops; (2) using irrigation scheduling information to help farmers irrigate more precisely and apply enough water to meet crop requirements at the right time; (3) applying advanced management methods that save water, such as varying irrigation levels; and (4) shifting some crops irrigated using flood irrigation to sprinkler and drip systems. The Pacific Institute report suggested that water savings made through these methods could be just as effective as savings made through new centralized water storage and infrastructure—and are often far less expensive. It compared the savings using "dam equivalents." The institute report suggested that, assuming that a dam yields 174,000 acre-feet of "new" water, the efficiency scenarios could save as much water as would be provided by three to twenty dams of this size.

To implement improved water use, the Pacific Institute report suggested a number of policy changes, including better combined land and water planning—for example, encouraging the protection of prime agricultural land from urban and suburban development and ensuring that all new developments have an adequate water supply for at least one hundred years. The report also suggested shifting subsidies from low-value water-intensive crops (such as hay and pastureland) to higher-value less-water-intensive crops (such as vegetables) and developing new legal mechanisms so that municipal water agencies or state or local wildlife agencies could invest in farmers' irrigation systems in exchange for some portion of the water conserved. According to the Pacific Institute, "Our report provides a new vision for California's future—one in which a profitable and sustainable agricultural sector thrives, while water withdrawals are significantly reduced."

Biographical Sketches

Mahmoud Abu Zeid, as president of the World Water Council, has played an important role in framing international solutions to the world's water crisis through such initiatives as the World Water Forum and the World Commission on Water for the 21st Century. As Egypt's minister of water resources and irrigation, Abu Zeid promoted integrated water resource management as a means of easing Egypt's water problems and tensions in the Middle East.

Asit K. Biswas has served as an adviser to seventeen governments and numerous international organizations, including UN agencies, the World Bank, and the Asian Development Bank. In 1994, Biswas was awarded the International Water Resources Association's prestigious Crystal Drop Award for "outstanding lifetime achievements in water management." He has published 56 books and more than 550 papers.

John Briscoe is a former chief of the World Bank Water and Sanitation Division. As the World Bank's senior adviser on water resources, he represented it on major international commissions and committees, including the World Commission on Dams and the Global Water Partnership. Formerly a professional water engineer, Briscoe has published numerous papers on the world's water crisis, notably from an economic perspective.

Malin Falkenmark is emeritus professor of applied hydrology at the Natural Science Research Council in Stockholm. As a hydrologist, Falkenmark brought a new clarity to the world's water crisis in 1989 by comparing water availability in different nations using such defined terms as *water stress* and *water scarcity*. She is better known for developing the concept of green water, the water needed for plant growth, which is not generally accounted for in water statistics. Falkenmark has also made distinguished contributions to international water policy through the International Hydrological Programme, the 1992 International Conference on Water and the Environment in Dublin, and numerous other initiatives.

Peter H. Gleick is president of the Pacific Institute for Studies in Development, Environment, and Security in Oakland, California, and one of the world's leading experts on freshwater and the impact of climate change on the world's water resources. He is the author of many publications on the subject, including *The World's Water,* a biennial report on the state of the world's freshwater resources.

Sandra Postel is director of the Global Water Policy Project in Amherst, Massachusetts, and a leading international authority on global water problems. In 2002, Postel was named one of the Scientific American 50 by *Scientific American* magazine, an award recognizing contributions to science and technology. The author of numerous scholarly articles, she is perhaps best known for a number of popular books and articles championing the need for the more efficient use of water, particularly in regard to irrigation, including *The Last Oasis* (1992) and *Pillar of Sand: Can the Irrigation Miracle Last?* (1999).

Ismail Serageldin is a former vice president of the World Bank and has most recently served as chairman of the World Commission on Water in the 21st Century. He was instrumental in delivering its groundbreaking report *A Water Secure World: Vision for Water, Life, and the Environment* (2000). Serageldin is also a former chairman of the Global Water Partnership.

Directory

Global Water Policy Project, 434 W Highway 6, Los Lunas, N.M. 87031. Telephone: (505) 565-1498; email (director): info@globalwaterpolicy.org; Web: http://www.globalwaterpolicy.org.
Research and policy think tank specializing in global water strategy.

International Commission on Irrigation and Drainage, 48 Nyaya Marg, Chanakyapuri, New Delhi 110021, India. Telephone: (91) 11 6116837; email: icid@icid.org; Web: http://www.icid.org.
Organization dedicated to improving the world food supply through better water and land management.

International Rivers, 1847 Berkeley Way, Berkeley, Calif. 94703. Telephone: (510) 848-1155; email: info@internationalrivers.org; Web: http://www.internationalrivers .org.
Organization campaigning against the negative environmental and human rights impacts of dams.

International Water Management Institute, 127, Sunil Mawatha, Pelwatte, Battaramulla, Sri Lanka. Telephone: (94) 11 2880000; email: iwmi@cgiar.org; Web: http://www.iwmi.cgiar.org.
Organization that fosters and supports sustainable use of irrigation for agriculture.

Pacific Institute for Studies in Development, Environment, and Security, 654 13th Street, Preservation Park, Oakland, Calif. 94612. Telephone: (510) 251-1600; email: info@pacinst.org; Web: http://www.pacinst.org.
Academic institution researching a variety of global issues.

Practical Action, The Schumacher Centre for Technology and Development, Bourton-on-Dunsmore, Rugby CV23 9QZ, United Kingdom. Telephone: (44) 1926 634400; email: practicalaction@practicalaction.org.uk; Web: http://www.practical action.org.
Organization working to assist developing countries using appropriate technologies.

Stockholm International Water Institute, Drottninggatan 33 SE - 111 51, Stockholm, Sweden. Telephone: (46) 8 522 13960; email: siwi@siwi.org; Web: http://www.siwi.org.
International institution that promotes research and understanding into global water issues.

Tearfund, 100 Church Road, Teddington, Middlesex TW11 8QE, United Kingdom. Telephone: (44) 845 355 8355; email: enquiry@tearfund.org; Web: http://www .tearfund.org.
Christian charity focusing on poverty relief in developing countries.

United States Society on Dams, 1616 17th Street, Suite 483, Denver, Colo. 80202. Telephone: (303) 628-5430; email: stephens@ussdams.org; Web: http://www.ussdams .org.
Organization concerned with dam issues.

WaterAid, 47-49 Durham Street, 2nd floor, London, SE11 5JD, United Kingdom. Telephone: (44) 845 6000 433; email: via Web site; Web: http://www.wateraid.org.uk.
Organization using water industry expertise to relieve water problems in developing countries.

World Bank, Water and Sanitation Division, 1818 H Street NW, Washington, D.C. 20433. Telephone: (202) 473-1000; email: via Web site; Web: http://www.worldbank .org/watsan.
International organization aiming to relieve poverty by financing development projects.

World Health Organization (WHO), 20 Avenue Appia, 1211 Geneva 27, Switzerland. Telephone (41) 227 912 111; email: info@who.int; Web: http://www .who.int.
UN organization advocating health for all people.

World Water Council, Espace Gaymard, 2-4 place d'Arvieux, 13002 Marseille, France. Telephone: (33) 491 99 41 00. email: via Web site; Web: http://www.world watercouncil.org.

International think tank on global water policy; responsible for the work of the World Commission on Water for the 21st Century.

WWF Living Waters Campaign, World Wide Fund for Nature (WWF), c/o Avenue du Mont-Blanc, 27 1196 Gland, Switzerland. Telephone: (41) 22 364 91 11; email: via Web site; Web: http://www.panda.org/about_wwf/what_we_do/freshwater/index .cfm.
Organization campaigning for freshwater protection and restoration.

Further Research

Books

Clarke, Robin. and Jannet King. *The Atlas of Water: Mapping the Global Crisis in Graphic Facts and Figures.* London: Earthscan, 2004.

De Villiers, Marq. *Water: The Fate of Our Most Precious Resource.* New York: Mariner Books, 2001.

————. *Water Wars: Is the World's Water Running Out?* London: Weidenfeld, 1999.

Gleick, Peter, ed. *The World's Water.* Oxford and New York: Oxford University Press, 1993.

————. *The World's Water, 2000–2001: The Biennial Report on Freshwater Resources.* Washington, D.C.: Island Press, 2000.

McCully, Patrick. *Silenced Rivers: The Ecology and Politics of Large Dams.* Berkeley, Calif.: International Rivers Network, 1996.

Pearce, Fred. *When the Rivers Run Dry: What Happens When Our Water Runs Out.* London: Eden Project Books, 2006.

Postel, Sandra. *Last Oasis: Facing Water Scarcity.* New York: W. W. Norton, 1992.

————. *Pillar of Sand: Can the Irrigation Miracle Last?* New York: W. W. Norton, 1999.

Articles and Reports

Berman, Ilan, and Paul Michael Wihbey. "The New Water Politics of the Middle East." *Strategic Review* (summer 1999). Available at http://www.iasps.org/strategic/water .htm.

Bromberg, Gidon, et al. *Climate Change: A New Threat to Middle East Security.* Friends of the Earth Middle East, 2007. Available at www.foeme.org/index_images/ dinamicas/publications/pub178_1.pdf.

Christian-Smith, Juliet, et al. *More with Less: Agricultural Water Conservation and Efficiency in California.* Oakland, Calif.: Pacific Institute, 2008. Available at http://www .pacinst.org/reports/more_with_less_delta/index.htm.

Cosgrove, William J., and Frank R. Rijsberman. *Making Water Everybody's Business.* World Water Council. London: Earthscan, 2000.

Gleick, Peter. "Making Every Drop Count." *Scientific American* (February 2001): 28–33.

Khan, Akhtar Hameed. "The Sanitation Gap: Development's Deadly Menace." UNICEF. Available at http://www.unicef.org/pon97/water1.htm.

Population Information Program, Johns Hopkins School of Public Health. *Solutions for a Water-Short World: Population Reports* 26, no. 1 (September 1998).

Postel, Sandra. "Growing More Food with Less Water." *Scientific American,* (February 2001): 45–51.

———. "Redesigning Irrigated Agriculture." In *State of the World, 2000,* ed. Lester R. Brown et al. London: Earthscan, 2000.

Postel, Sandra, Gretchen Daily, and Paul Ehrlich. "Human Appropriation of Renewable Fresh Water." *Science* 271 (1996): 785–788.

Pruss-Ustun, A., et al. "Safer Water, Better Health: Costs, Benefits and Sustainability of Interventions to Protect and Promote Health." World Health Organization, Geneva, 2008. Available at http://whqlibdoc.who.int/publications/2008/9789241596435_eng.pdf.

Robbins, Elaine. "Water, Water Everywhere: Innovation and Cooperation Are Helping Slake the World's Growing Thirst." *E Magazine* (September–October 1998).

Seckler, David, et al. *World Water Demand and Supply, 1990 to 2025: Scenarios and Issues.* Colombo, Sri Lanka: International Water Management Institute, 1998.

Shiklomanov, Igor. "Appraisal and Assessment of World Water Resources." *Water International* 25, no. 1 (March 2000): 11–32.

Sikazwe, Daniel C., and Maria Gemma B. "World Water Forum Whets Interest." *New Agriculturalist Online.* Available at http://www.new-agri.co.uk/00-3/develop/dev05.html.

Tearfund. *Running on Empty: A Call for Action to Combat the Crisis of Global Water Shortages.* London: Tearfund, 2001.

United Nations Development Programme. "Human Development Report, 2006." Available at http://hdr.undp.org/en/reports/global/hdr2006.

United Nations Environment Programme. *Global Environmental Outlook, 2000.* London: Earthscan, 2000. Available at http://www.grida.no/geo2000/english/index.htm.

World Commission on Dams. *Dams and Development: A New Framework for Decision-Making.* London: Earthscan, 2000.

World Commission on Water for the 21st Century. *A Water Secure World: Vision for Water, Life, and the Environment.* Cairo: World Water Council, 2000.

Web Sites

Global Environmental Outlook, 2000 (GEO-2000)
http://www.grida.no/geo2000/english/index.htm

Global Water Partnership
http://www.gwpforum.org

International Rivers Network, China Campaign, Three Gorges
http://internationalrivers.org/en/china/three-gorges-dam

International Water Law Project
http://www.internationalwaterlaw.org/index.html

Nile Basin Initiative
http://www.nilebasin.org

Nile River Dispute: Case Study
http://www.american.edu/projects/mandala/TED/ice/NILE.HTM

UK Rivers Network
http://www.ukrivers.net/index.html

UN Water for Life Decade
http://www.un.org/waterforlifedecade/index.html

World Heath Organization—Water
http://www.who.int/topics/water/en/

World Water Council
http://www.worldwatercouncil.org/index.php?id=192

World Water Day
http://www.worldwaterday.org

The World's Water
http://www.worldwater.org

WWF—UK Freshwater (World Wide Fund for Nature)
http://www.wwf.org.uk/researcher/issues/freshwater/index.asp

Documents

1. The Dublin Statement on Water and Sustainable Development

International Conference on Water and the Environment, 1992

*The full text is available at http://www.wmo.ch/pages/prog/hwrp/documents/english/icwedece
.html.*

Extracts

Guiding Principles

Concerted action is needed to reverse the present trends of overconsumption, pollution, and rising threats from drought and floods. The Conference Report sets out
recommendations for action at local, national and international levels, based on four
guiding principles.

Principle No. 1 Fresh water is a finite and vulnerable resource, essential to sustain life,
development and the environment

Since water sustains life, effective management of water resources demands a holistic
approach, linking social and economic development with protection of natural ecosystems. Effective management links land and water uses across the whole of a catchment
area or groundwater aquifer.

Principle No. 2 Water development and management should be based on a participatory approach, involving users, planners and policy-makers at all levels

The participatory approach involves raising awareness of the importance of water
among policy-makers and the general public. It means that decisions are taken at the
lowest appropriate level, with full public consultation and involvement of users in the
planning and implementation of water projects.

Principle No. 3 Women play a central part in the provision, management and safeguarding of water

This pivotal role of women as providers and users of water and guardians of the
living environment has seldom been reflected in institutional arrangements for the

development and management of water resources. Acceptance and implementation of this principle requires positive policies to address women's specific needs and to equip and empower women to participate at all levels in water resources programmes, including decision-making and implementation, in ways defined by them.

Principle No. 4 Water has an economic value in all its competing uses and should be recognized as an economic good

Within this principle, it is vital to recognize first the basic right of all human beings to have access to clean water and sanitation at an affordable price. Past failure to recognize the economic value of water has led to wasteful and environmentally damaging uses of the resource. Managing water as an economic good is an important way of achieving efficient and equitable use, and of encouraging conservation and protection of water resources.

2. A Water Secure World: Vision for Water, Life, and the Environment

World Commission on Water for the 21st Century, 2000

The full text is available at http://worldwaterforum5.0rg/fileadmin/wwc/Library/Publications_ and_reports/Visions/CommissionReport.pdf.

Extracts

Water is life. Every human being, now and in the future, should have access to safe water for drinking, appropriate sanitation, and enough food and energy at reasonable cost. Providing adequate water to meet these basic needs must be done in an equitable manner that works in harmony with nature. For water is the basis for all living ecosystems and habitats and part of an immutable hydrological cycle that must be respected if the development of human activity and well being is to be sustainable.

We are not achieving these goals today, and we are on a path leading to crisis and to future problems for a large part of humanity and many parts of the planet's ecosystems. Business as usual leads us on an unsustainable and inequitable path.

Achieving these goals requires drastic changes in the manner in which water is managed.

A holistic, systemic approach relying on integrated water resource management must replace the current fragmentation in managing water.

There are those who see water only by use: water for municipalities, for industry, for irrigation, for the environment, as if the last were a competing use, not an inherent part of maintaining the entire ecological system on which all water services depend. Or those who look at political and administrative boundaries as the basis of decision-making when these seldom conform to the catchment and basin areas that nature prescribes as the management units for water. . . .

But it is as much by activities on land that we affect the quality and availability of useable freshwater as by the direct withdrawals that humans make. A holistic approach means taking these issues into account—and linking the quality and quantity aspects of water management. Water is affected by everything, and water affects everything and everyone. . . .

No more business as usual

Considerable progress has been made in many countries, and yet at a macro level the arithmetic of water still does not add up. In the next two decades it is estimated that water use by humans will increase by about 40%, and that 17% more water will be needed to grow food for a growing population. In addition, the water demands for industry and energy will increase rapidly. And we know that aquatic ecosystems throughout the world have been degraded and will need greater protection and that water quality is deteriorating in poor countries. In short, with current institutional arrangements and current technologies, the arithmetic of water simply does not add up. Rapid and imaginative institutional and technological innovation is required. "Business as usual" will not do. With the commitment of all, however, the problems can be overcome. A water-secure world is possible, but we must change the way we manage water, starting now!

CLIMATE CHANGE

Melanie Jarman

C limate change is perhaps the ultimate global problem. It is caused by everyone, affects everyone, and requires the cooperation of everyone for its solution. Mounting evidence suggests that a warming world is already contributing to major problems, from refugee crises prompted by rising sea levels to famines caused by desertification. Yet national leaders have found reaching agreements on how to tackle this global challenge remarkably difficult.

Historical Background and Development

Global warming is a deceptively simple problem. Greenhouse gases—notably carbon dioxide (CO_2), methane, water vapor, nitrous oxide, ozone, and chlorofluorocarbons—trap heat in Earth's atmosphere in much the same way that glass traps heat inside a greenhouse. This natural effect keeps the planet around 86 degrees Fahrenheit (30 degrees Celsius), which is warmer than it would be otherwise. The amount of greenhouse gases in the atmosphere, however, has been on the rise since the Industrial Revolution and is causing a rise in average temperatures.

Although concern about climate change is widely considered a contemporary preoccupation, the science of global warming dates back to the nineteenth century. In 1827, French mathematician Jean-Baptiste Fourier noted the similarity between the warming of Earth's atmosphere and the workings of a greenhouse. Some thirty years later, Irish physicist John Tyndall showed how carbon dioxide and water vapor trap heat in Earth's atmosphere and proposed that ice ages—the flip side of global warming—might be caused by a reduction in atmospheric carbon dioxide.

The modern science of global warming was born in 1896, when Swedish chemist Svante Arrhenius calculated that a doubling of atmospheric carbon dioxide could increase Earth's temperature by around 5–6 degrees Celsius,

---

This chapter is based on the original, written by Chris Woodford, that appeared in the first edition of *World at Risk*.

which is roughly the estimate produced by the United Nations Intergovernmental Panel on Climate Change (IPCC) in the late twentieth century. Arrhenius's prediction might have remained a purely theoretical concern without the later work of Charles Keeling. Starting in 1958, Keeling made regular measurements of atmospheric carbon dioxide at the Mauna Loa observatory on Hawaii, demonstrating the trend of increasing amounts of carbon dioxide, a pattern that is confirmed by measurements of carbon dioxide in Antarctic ice cores. Since 1998, Keeling's measurements have been supplemented by a network of carbon dioxide–monitoring towers around the world.

International concern about rising levels of carbon dioxide was a major theme of the first World Climate Conference, held in 1979 and sponsored by the United Nations World Meteorology Organization (WMO), where delegates called on nations to anticipate and avert changes in climate caused by humans. A wake-up call came in 1988 when one of the world's leading climate modelers, NASA's James Hansen, told Congress that strong evidence for global warming exists and argued that they and other leaders could no longer afford to procrastinate. That same year, with considerable uncertainty about the science of climate change prevailing, the United Nations Environment Programme (UNEP) and the WMO established the IPCC to formulate an international scientific consensus on the subject.

Four IPCC assessments, released in 1990, 1995, 2001, and 2007, noted with increasing conviction that global warming is a real phenomenon, that it is caused by human activities, and that drastic action is required to prevent damaging climate change. The IPCC's work is not the only indication of a mounting scientific consensus. In 2008, the national science academies of Brazil, Canada, China, France, Germany, Italy, India, Japan, Mexico, Russia, South Africa, the United Kingdom, and the United States issued the "Joint Science Academies' Statement," which declared "that climate change is happening and that anthropogenic warming is influencing many physical and biological systems." They called for measures to speed up the transition to a low-carbon society.

Popular concern about global warming has been helped by an apparent increase in the severity of weather and the frequency of extreme weather events. For example, NASA scientists found that 2007 tied with 1998 for Earth's second warmest year in a century, and the eight warmest years on record have all occurred since 1998, and the fourteenth warmest years have all occurred since 1990. Scientists also have discovered other phenomena that may point to a warming world, notably a change in monsoon seasons and rapid glacier melt all around the globe. Note that catastrophic floods, droughts, and other disasters have been a regular feature of Earth's history. Although Earth's climate is highly variable and events of this kind could simply be coincidental, increasingly unpredictable weather and the relative increase in the speed of melting polar ice are key predictors of climate models and may be warning signs of the climate reaching a tipping point into dramatic and irreversible change.

Increasing consensus in climate science has not been mirrored by an increase in agreement about how the international community should respond to the threat. Nevertheless, most nations have supported what environmentalists term the precautionary principle, which states that attention should be paid to potential threats and preventive measures should be planned even when scientific evidence is not entirely conclusive. In June 1993, one year after the acceptance of the UN Framework Convention on Climate Change (UNFCCC) in Rio de Janeiro at the Earth Summit, 166 nations had signed the convention, the central objective of which was the "stabilization of greenhouse gas concentrations in the atmosphere at a level that would prevent dangerous anthropogenic [human-caused] interference with the climate system" (see Document 1). The convention officially went into effect March 21, 1994. Efforts to turn the convention into practical action, however, have proved more problematic.

The Kyoto Protocol to the United Nations Framework Convention on Climate Change extended the UNFCCC with, in part, a commitment by developed nations to cut greenhouse emissions, but it has led a troubled existence since it was agreed to in December 1997. In March 2001, amid fierce international criticism, President George W. Bush put the future of the protocol in doubt by withdrawing U.S. participation. Because the United States is the largest producer of greenhouse gases per capita, its participation in significantly reducing emissions is essential (see Table 2). Since 1997, China has come close to overtaking the United States as the world's biggest producer of carbon dioxide. With an increase of over 100 percent in carbon dioxide emissions from 1990 to 2004, China's participation is also essential (see Table 1; map, p. 307). This suggests that, to be effective, any agreement must be truly global.

Current Status

Most climatologists believe that since the Industrial Revolution the large-scale burning of fossil fuels—particularly coal, natural gas, and oil—has produced a heightened artificial greenhouse effect that has increased the concentration of atmospheric carbon dioxide from a preindustrial level of 280 parts per million per volume (ppmv) to 379 ppmv in 2005, the highest level in the last 650,000 years. Computer models suggest that the level of carbon dioxide will at least double during the twenty-first century, producing an estimated rise in the average global surface temperature of between 1.1 and 6.4 degrees Celsius and drastic changes in the global climate, including changes in patterns of rainfall and drought, changes in cyclone activity, and an increased likelihood of dangerously rising sea levels.

Research

Although systemic measurements of carbon dioxide have been made only since 1958, climate scientists can measure the composition of the atmosphere in much earlier periods using ice cores, ice samples that may be more than 2.5 kilometers (1 mile) long. These samples, extracted in thin borehole pipes and carefully stored in refrigerated warehouses, contain air bubbles that effectively preserve "memories" of earlier climates, thus allowing the chemical composition of air from earlier historical periods to be analyzed. Ice cores can contain data that cover many hundreds of years. To study the climate of the past million years, scientists examine ocean sediments.

The IPCC has the job of formulating the increasing volume of climate change research data into a form accessible to policymakers and the public so that it can be used to devise policies and programs. This collective of scientists and policy advisers has delivered increasingly pessimistic assessments summarizing the science behind and the likely effects of climate change.

The IPCC's fourth assessment—*Climate Change, 2007*—notes, "Most of the observed increase in global average temperatures since the mid-20th century is very likely due to the observed increase in anthropogenic greenhouse gas concentrations." It goes on to state that "anthropogenic carbon dioxide emissions will continue to contribute to warming and sea level rise for more than a millennium." Part of the report, published in November 2007, also notes that "those in the weakest economic position are often the most vulnerable to climate change."

In quantitative terms, the IPCC's findings seem more dramatic. Similar to the NASA findings already noted, the IPCC found that the period 1995–2006 was the warmest period on record since 1850. It found that, since 1978, average annual extent of the Arctic sea ice shrunk by 2.7 percent per decade, with larger decreases of 7.4 percent per decade measured during the summer seasons (see Case Study—A Melting Arctic). Episodes of El Niño—the reversal of climate conditions in the Pacific that can disrupt much of the world's weather— have become more intense and longer lasting and occur more often than they did a century ago. In Asia and Africa, droughts now occur more regularly and are more severe.

According to the IPCC, these changes strongly correlate with human activities such as fossil fuel burning and deforestation. Global greenhouse gas emissions from human activities have increased since the beginning of industrialization, with a more recent increase of 70 percent between 1970 and 2004. The IPCC underlines how extraordinary this change is in Earth's history. Research using ice cores found that in 2005 the atmospheric concentration of carbon dioxide, the most important anthropogenic greenhouse gas, "exceeds by far the natural range over the last 650,000 years."

The scientific consensus regarding climate change sometimes has appeared fragile and strained, with a relatively small number of skeptical scientists attracting what IPCC scientists perceive to be disproportionate media coverage with their dissenting view that global warming is simply an artifact of incomplete computer modeling. By definition, computer models must be incomplete; models of global warming are imperfect because the computational complexity of modeling the world's climate exceeds the power of even the fastest supercomputers unless a number of simplifying assumptions are made. Skeptics are concerned that these assumptions may not be justified or that the equations on which climate models are based do not accurately predict what happens in nature. Leading U.S. climate scientists Thomas Karl and Kevin Trenberth have argued that not enough data are available to feed into the computer models because the world's climate is not currently monitored in sufficient detail.

However, climate knowledge, climate data, and climate modeling are all improving over time as more resources are directed toward them.

Climate models give skeptics particular cause for concern because the projections they make—accurate or not—are used by environmental groups to argue for such changes in policy as major reductions in energy and automobile use, which, the skeptics argue, would drastically affect economic competitiveness. The environmentalists counter that the skeptics are simply mouthpieces for industrial vested interests, notably fossil fuel and automobile manufacturers. In the popular media, and perhaps in society as a whole, a perception still exists that global warming is an unresolved issue with environmentalists on one side; skeptics, who may or may not be linked to industrial interests, on the other; and climate scientists with imperfect computer models struggling to resolve the issue somewhere in between. Yet the scientific consensus that global warming is a real phenomenon has become increasingly robust during the IPCC's existence. Supporters of the IPCC note that its reports are a peer-reviewed international collaboration. The fourth IPCC assessment, for example, included the input of more than 2,500 scientific experts from around the world. In 2007, the IPCC, along with former U.S. vice president Al Gore (a long-standing advocate for controlling fossil fuel–related climate change), was awarded the Nobel Peace Prize for "efforts to build up and disseminate greater knowledge about man-made climate change, and to lay the foundations for the measures that are needed to counteract such change." The previous year, 2006, Al Gore's documentary film, *An Inconvenient Truth,* was viewed widely in the United States and other Western countries, helping to increase the coverage of global warming in the popular media and to further public awareness of the potential dangers of unchecked climate change.

Disagreements over the science aside, attention is increasingly focused on global warming's likely effect on humans (see Table 3). Two-thirds of the world's 6 billion people live within 37 miles (60 kilometers) of a coast. A projected rise in sea level of up to 59 centimeters within a century is expected to prove disastrous for low-lying nations such as Bangladesh and islands and atolls around the world. (The IPCC states the difficulty of estimating an upper limit for sea-level rise due to the limited understanding of some of the effects that drive it. Indeed, a presentation to a European Geosciences Union conference in 2008 forecast a rise in sea levels three times higher than that predicted by the IPCC.) Access to freshwater is expected to become one of the most pressing environmental problems of the twenty-first century as encroaching seas threaten groundwater supplies in coastal areas and as global warming increases the severity of droughts and floods. A 2000 report by the World Commission on Water for the 21st Century noted that more than half the world's river systems were already overexploited and polluted and concluded that drastic changes were needed in order to halt growing water shortages and environmental degradation (see FRESHWATER).

Changes in water availability necessarily will affect agriculture and food production. And, although climate change may improve productivity in some regions, for example, in the temperate wheat-growing areas of China, its overall impact will be detrimental. A 2008 study in the journal *Science* by David Lobell and colleagues suggested that climate change could lead to southern Africa's losing more than 30 percent of its production of maize (a staple crop) by 2030, while South Asia could lose more than 10 percent of its regional staple crops. The study's co-author Marshall Burke said, "For poor farmers on the margin of survival, these losses could really be crushing." Human health could suffer through increased heat stress and greater transmission of diseases through the spread of such pests as mosquitoes (see HEALTH). The geographical reach of malaria, for example, is predicted to increase from 45 to 65 percent of the world's population by the end of the twenty-first century. IPCC co-chair James McCarthy summed up the view of many when he delivered the group's third report, *Climate Change 2001*: "Most of the earth's people will be on the losing side."

With the effects of climate change uncertain, attaching a financial cost to them might seem impossible. Yet Sir Nicholas Stern, former World Bank chief economist, found that the cost of greenhouse gas emissions rising to dangerous levels will be at least 5 percent of global gross domestic product (GDP) and possibly more than 20 percent. His 2006 report said that the world needs to spend 1 percent of its wealth to limit these emissions. In 2008, he revised this figure to 2 percent, noting that climate change is advancing more quickly than previously thought. Even though this is a significant amount of money, the alternative—doing nothing—will cost even more.

Policies and Programs

That world leaders have reached any agreement at all on international policies to combat global warming, given the uncertainties in long-range computer climate models and the guarded wording of IPCC reports, is perhaps surprising. Yet, within a year of the acceptance of the UNFCCC at the Earth Summit in 1992, 166 countries had agreed to sign the convention.

Detailed agreements about how to accomplish the goals of the convention were left to subsequent meetings of the signatory states, or Conferences of the Parties (COPs). In the most important of these, COP3, held in Kyoto, Japan, in November 1997, 150 nations agreed to the Kyoto Protocol, which set legally binding targets for limits on the emission of greenhouse gases. These ranged from cuts of around 7 percent (for the United States) and 8 percent (for Europe) to allowable increases of 8 percent (for Australia) and 10 percent (for Iceland). Developing countries refused to accept and were exempted from specific cuts. The United States, despite being a signatory, refused to ratify the treaty until it included "meaningful participation" by developing countries.

Later COP sessions ran into difficulties over this issue, which is viewed more and more as a problem because the developing countries that are traditionally low emitters and thus have contributed little to the problem historically—including India, China, Brazil, and South Africa—are on course to become the leading contributors to global emissions in the next two decades. These countries maintain that they need to continue to increase their energy use, and so continue to increase their emissions, to support their development. Yet the more-industrialized countries, which are due to remain the highest greenhouse gas emitters on a per capita basis, are reluctant to make the dramatic cuts needed to allow for this.

COP sessions also have run into difficulties over differing interpretations of how emissions cuts could be achieved, particularly the use of flexibility mechanisms. These include emissions-trading schemes, such as the Clean Development Mechanism (CDM; in which countries with high greenhouse emissions can buy permits to emit from countries with lower emissions) and Joint Implementation (in which developed countries might offset their emissions by investing in projects in other countries). The use of these flexibility mechanisms means that the market for trading in carbon emissions has grown significantly during the time of the Kyoto initiative, despite criticisms that carbon-accounting methods are not robust enough to support such markets due to difficulties in verifying emissions reductions.

At times, political wrangling has meant that the whole Kyoto initiative seems to be on the brink of collapse, particularly since the United States, historically the world's highest emitter, withdrew its support in 2001. However, the overwhelming majority of countries seem determined to achieve a global agreement of some kind on greenhouse emissions.

Programs for addressing climate change fall into two main categories: mitigation (reducing the effects) and adaptation (adjusting to the effects). Mitigation programs involve cutting emissions either directly, with changes in energy use, or indirectly through, for example, the Kyoto emissions-trading mechanisms. Changes in energy use can include energy efficiency and conservation measures, moving away from the use of fossil fuels (oil, coal, and gas) that produce large amounts of carbon dioxide per unit of energy, eliminating subsidies and tax concessions that favor the use of fossil fuels, and promoting the use of renewable energy technologies (such as solar and wind power) that produce less carbon dioxide (see ENERGY). The strongest form of mitigation, proposed by some environmental groups, is simply to leave large amounts of fossil fuels underground.

Adaptation, the second category, is pragmatic; it assumes that humans can and must adapt to climate change. The world's poorer countries have called for more funding and support for adaptation because they have begun to experience the impacts of climate change yet have fewer resources and so less capacity to make adaptive changes. In response, some climate scientists already have shifted the emphasis of their work toward helping these countries plan ahead so that their people can adapt to a warming world. Adaptation may be of limited use, however, for the people of small island states and low-lying coastal areas, who could lose their homelands entirely if the forecasts of rises in sea level prove to be accurate.

Meanwhile, scientists continue to highlight the need for more powerful supercomputers that can run more detailed climate models. They also highlight the time scale in which information needs to be acted on. James Hansen of NASA's Goddard Institute for Space Studies was quoted by *CBS Evening News* (September 14, 2006) as saying, "I think we have a very brief window of opportunity to deal with climate change . . . no longer than a decade at the most."

Regional Summaries

Although global warming is very much a long-term problem for Earth and its people, significant climate changes are already occurring in every region of the planet.

North America

Canada and the United States are two of the world's largest emitters of greenhouse gases per capita. At climate negotiations, they are part of an informal grouping called JUSCANZ (Japan, the United States, Canada, Australia, and New Zealand) that is notably hostile to the deep emissions cuts proposed by Europe. Some scientists believe that record heat waves in Florida, New York, and Texas during the late 1990s and the habitat and beach loss due to sea-level rises in the Chesapeake Bay, Hawaii, and New Jersey were early warnings of more drastic effects of climate change in the future. Weather has intensified in North America, with record precipitation in California, Texas, and Washington state in 1998 and record droughts and forest fires in Florida, Louisiana, Mexico, and Texas that same year. In 2007, a record spring heat wave followed by a record summer heat wave across the western United States left firefighters anxious over the lethal combination of high temperatures and thousands of acres of tinder-dry brush and parkland. In that same year, U.S. weather stations recorded that 263 all-time high temperature records were broken or tied. The 2007 IPCC assessment said that moderate climate change may initially bring increased crop yields but that this will vary among regions, with major challenges projected for crops near the warm end of their suitable range or that depend on heavily used water resources.

Latin America

Brazil and Argentina, large developing nations, have played a key role in climate negotiations, although they have been exempt from (and hostile to) the binding emissions cuts proposed by the Kyoto Protocol. Argentina, whose representative Raul Estrada chaired the Kyoto negotiations, later said that Argentina would work toward voluntary emissions cuts. As middle-income countries undergoing rapid industrialization, Brazil and Mexico both have played host to a significant number of the Kyoto Protocol's CDM projects.

The possible effects of global warming are evident in Peru, which already experiences extreme climate variations during El Niño events. Coral bleaching, in which corals die and turn white in high-temperature ocean water as they expel the algae that keep them alive, is widespread in areas of the Caribbean; off Bermuda, Mexico, and Panama; and in the Florida keys. In Mexico and Central America, outbreaks of dengue fever—an infectious and painful tropical disease carried by mosquitoes—at higher altitudes than previously reported are consistent with global warming projections. Future effects of global warming are expected to include declining crop yields, the loss of deciduous tropical forests, the increasing prevalence of new diseases, and the significant loss of biodiversity through species extinction in many areas of tropical Latin America.

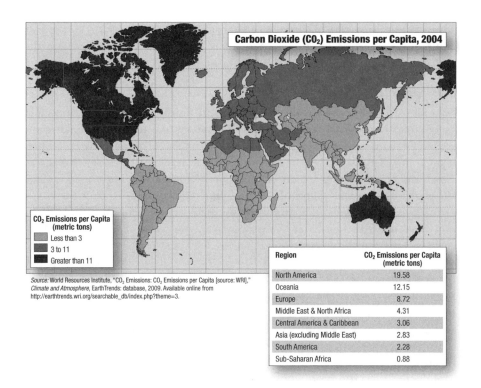

Carbon Dioxide (CO₂) Emissions per Capita, 2004

CO₂ Emissions per Capita
(metric tons)
- Less than 3
- 3 to 11
- Greater than 11

Source: World Resources Institute, "CO₂ Emissions: CO₂ Emissions per Capita [source: WRI]," Climate and Atmosphere, EarthTrends: database, 2009. Available online from http://earthtrends.wri.org/searchable_db/index.php?theme=3.

Region	CO₂ Emissions per Capita (metric tons)
North America	19.58
Oceania	12.15
Europe	8.72
Middle East & North Africa	4.31
Central America & Caribbean	3.06
Asia (excluding Middle East)	2.83
South America	2.28
Sub-Saharan Africa	0.88

Europe

The European Union, described by climate campaigner Jeremy Leggett (quoted in a 2008 article in *Journal of Global Ethics* written by Paul G. Harris) as "the most progressive force at the climate negotiations," has taken the lead in implementing cuts in greenhouse gases. Europe, however, is already experiencing early indications of global warming. Devastating floods in England in the early 2000s and intense fires and droughts in Mediterranean countries are both consistent with IPCC projections. In 2005, the worst drought in Spain since records began saw the loss of half the cereal crop in some areas. Some species, including alpine plants in Austria, birds in Britain, and mollusks in Germany, already have shifted their habitats to higher latitudes or altitudes that have warmed in recent years. Future possible effects include increased river flooding, loss of permafrost (a permanently frozen layer of soil), the melting glaciers (in the north), and the appearance of diseases never before seen in the region, such as malaria.

North Africa and the Middle East

The Organization of Petroleum Exporting Countries (OPEC) has frequently been accused of trying to frustrate climate negotiations that could spell a decline in the use of fossil fuels, yet North Africa and the Middle East, home to most OPEC nations, are no less subject to climate change than any other region. Coral bleaching has been reported in the Persian Gulf, and a rare cyclone spun up in the Middle East in 2007, hitting Oman and Iran. Looking ahead, research by the UNEP suggests that a 50-centimeter rise in sea level could displace nearly 2–4 million Egyptians by 2050. Water shortages are also expected to be a key source of tension in the region.

Sub-Saharan Africa

Sub-Saharan Africa, the world's poorest region, produces the lowest amount of greenhouse emissions, mainly from the basic survival activities of cooking and keeping warm, yet they are among the most likely to be affected by climate change and the least well equipped to respond to it. The nations of sub-Saharan Africa generally have opposed emissions cuts for developing countries, and although they remain skeptical of flexibility mechanisms—seeing them as a means by which developed nations can escape cuts in greenhouse emissions— they have tended to embrace the proposed CDM projects and the export of clean technologies from developed nations. Early indications of global warming include the retreat of Kenya's Mount Lewis Glacier by more than 800 meters between 1893 and 2004. Malaria, already one of the region's biggest killers, has spread as predicted by climate models—the Inter Press Service reported in 2008 that malaria had appeared in the highland areas of East Africa, where it was previously unheard of. The rising sea level is already causing the loss of coastal areas in Senegal. Bleak predictions for the region include more desertification and drought, increasing stress on water resources, and a significant decrease in crop production. In its 2007 report, the IPCC suggested that the cost of adaptation for Africa could amount to at least 5–10 percent of GDP.

Asia

Asia—with the world's densest population and most rapidly industrializing nations—might be regarded as the front line in the war against climate change. China has come close to overtaking the United States as the world's leading greenhouse gas polluter because economic development prompts it to burn increasing amounts of its vast coal reserves. If China is excluded from the statistics, Asia has relatively little greenhouse emissions. Asia, however, may be among the areas worst affected by climate change.

Early signs of global warming in the region include coral bleaching in the Indian Ocean and glacial retreat in the Himalayas and the Tien Shan Mountains of China. Extensive melting of glaciers in the Himalayas would cause devastating floods and water shortages for more than 500 million people. By the 2050s, freshwater availability in central, South, East, and Southeast Asia is projected to decrease. Heavily populated mega-delta areas will be especially affected by global warming due to their high exposure to rises in sea level, storm surges, and river flooding. In fact, a sea-level rise of 1 meter will displace approximately 7 million people from low-lying areas of Bangladesh.

The Pacific

The Pacific region includes the large developed nation of Australia plus many microstates on low-lying islands and atolls that are particularly vulnerable to

rising sea levels. Australia and New Zealand are part of the JUSCANZ grouping that is hostile to emissions cuts. Many Pacific islands support a different
grouping, the Alliance of Small Island States (AOSIS), a collective of low-lying
nations that argues powerfully that climate change threatens their very existence. Evidence of climate change includes widespread coral bleaching
throughout the region, a rise in sea level and coastal erosion in Fiji and Western
Samoa, and the extended geographical reach of malaria in Indonesia. The Great
Barrier Reef, which is economically important to Australia, is particularly vulnerable to climate change. Agricultural and forestry production in parts of
Australia may also decline due to increased drought and fire.

Data

**Table 1   Total and Per Capita Carbon Dioxide Emissions in
Selected Countries, 1990 and 2004**

Country	Total (million metric tons)		Per capita (metric tons)	
	1990	2004	1990	2004
Algeria	77.0	193.9	3.0	5.5
Argentina	109.7	141.7	3.4	3.7
Australia	278.5	326.6	16.3	16.2
Brazil	209.5	331.6	1.4	1.8
Canada	415.8	639.0	15.0	20.0
China	2,398.9	5,007.1	2.1	3.8
Colombia	58.0	53.6	1.6	1.2
Congo, Republic of	4.0	2.1	0.1	n/a
Egypt	75.4	158.1	1.5	2.3
France	363.8	373.5	6.4	6.0
Georgia	15.1	3.9	2.8	0.8
Germany	980.4	808.3	12.3	9.8
Guatemala	5.1	12.2	0.6	1.0
India	681.7	1,342.1	0.8	1.2
Indonesia	213.8	378.0	1.2	1.7
Israel	33.1	71.2	6.9	10.4
Japan	1,070.7	1,257.2	8.7	9.9
Russian Federation	1,984.1	1,524.1	13.4	10.6
Saudi Arabia	254.8	308.2	15.9	13.6
Spain	212.1	330.3	5.5	7.6
Sweden	49.5	53.0	5.8	5.9
Switzerland	42.7	40.4	6.2	5.4
Tajikistan	20.6	5.0	3.7	0.8
Thailand	95.7	267.9	1.7	4.2
Turkey	146.2	226.0	2.6	3.2
Uganda	0.8	1.8	n/a	0.1
United Kingdom	579.4	586.9	10.0	9.8
United States	4,818.3	6,045.8	19.3	20.6

Source: United Nations Development Programme, *Human Development Report 2007/2008* (Brasilia: UNDP,
2007), Table 24.

Note: n/a, not available.

Table 2   Recent Trends in Greenhouse Gas Production in the United States

	1995	2000	2001	2002	2003	2004	2005	2006	Growth rate (%)[a]
GDP[b]	113	138	139	141	145	150	155	159	3.0
Electricity consumption	112	127	125	128	129	131	134	135	1.9
Fossil fuel consumption	107	117	115	116	116	119	119	117	1.0
Energy consumption[c]	108	116	112	115	115	118	118	117	1.0
Population	107	113	114	115	116	117	118	119	1.1
Greenhouse gas emissions[d]	106	114	113	114	114	115	116	115	0.9

Sources: U.S. Environmental Protection Agency, "Inventory of U.S. Greenhouse Gas Emissions and Sinks, 1990–2006," EPA #430-R-08-005, Washington, D.C., April 2008; population figures from U.S. Census Bureau, 2007, http://www.census.gov/popest/estimates.html

Notes: Index: 1990 = 100. The index is the base year against which all other years are compared. GDP, gross domestic product.

[a]Average annual growth rate.

[b]GDP in chained 2000 dollars.

[c]Energy content-weighted values.

[d]Weighted to take account of the different global warming potentials of different greenhouse gases.

Table 3   Selected Predicted Impacts of Different Rises in Sea Level on Ecosystems

Sea-level rise above 1961–1990 average (cm)	Year	Matching temperature range increase (°C)[a]	Impacts to ecosystems	Regions affected
3–14	2025	0.4–1.1	Loss of coastal wetlands; shoreline erosion; saltwater intrusion into coastal aquifers	Global
30	Any	Any	57% of sandy beaches eroded	Asia
45	Any	Any	Mangroves cannot survive 45-cm sea-level rise	Asia
100	Any	Any	90% of sandy beaches eroded	Asia
300–500	2300	3	With a 3°C temperature increase, this sea-level rise will occur without the melting of the Greenland and West Arctic ice sheets.	Global
300–500	2300	3	Widespread loss of coastal and deltaic areas including Bangladesh, Nile, Yangtze, and Mekong	Global

Source: Hans-Joachim Schellnhuber et al., eds., Avoiding Dangerous Climate Change (Cambridge, UK: Cambridge University Press, 2006). Reprinted with permission.

Note: IPCC, Intergovernmental Panel on Climate Change.

[a]Volume assuming upper range of IPCC temperature matches upper range of IPCC sea-level rise.

Case Study—Climate Change and Poverty in Uganda

In 2008, the development agency Oxfam produced a report examining the impacts of global warming on agriculture, pastoralism, health, and water and, consequently, on poverty in Uganda. People in Uganda, whose contribution to global warming has been miniscule, are feeling the impacts of climate change first and worst. On the one hand, rainfall has become more erratic during the rainy season, bringing drought and reductions in crop yields and plant varieties; on the other hand, the rainfall, especially the later rains toward the end of the year, comes in more intense and destructive downpours, bringing floods, landslides, and soil erosion. In the future, climate scientists say that one of the most likely effects of climate change will be more rain. If Uganda becomes wetter, floods will become more likely, a product not only of higher rainfall and run-off but also of land use changes, such as the draining of swamps and, in cities, blocked drains.

Global warming is exacerbating existing problems and challenges, including deforestation, soil degradation, declining fish stocks, poverty, and ill health. Food security in Uganda is also affected negatively. The main impacts are lower yields of staple foods such as beans, cassava, maize, and matoke; a reduction in traditional varieties of crops; and more crop diseases.

The government of Uganda is planning programs to help it adapt to climate change and is seeking help from an international fund created to finance national adaptation programs of action (NAPAs) in poorer countries. Uganda needs nearly $40 million to implement immediate and urgent adaptation measures. However, the international fund, which relies solely on voluntary contributions from rich nations, holds only a fraction of the funds needed. According to a 2008 Oxfam report, "Turning Up the Heat: Climate Change and Poverty in Uganda," some $2 billion will be needed by all developing countries to fund their NAPAs alone, and far, far more will be needed for all eventual adaptation needs. In 2008, the NAPAs fund consisted of only $92 million. To address Uganda's needs alone, the country would need almost half of that.

Moreover, global warming affects Uganda's own ability to raise funds. For example, a rise in temperature of 2 degrees Celsius may wipe out most of Uganda's coffee production, on which some 5 million people rely directly or indirectly and which earns the country several hundred million dollars per year. And signs of trouble with Uganda's coffee crops are already apparent. Too much rain has reduced flowering, which in turn reduces production. It also hinders farmers' ability to dry the beans properly, so the quality is also compromised. In addition, too much rain increases diseases, pests, and mold, which affect both production and quality. Small-scale farmers produce almost all of Uganda's coffee, so many are affected. One farmer said, "Last year alone we lost 40 percent of our production. As a result, people struggle for everything."

Case Study—A Melting Arctic

In the Arctic, average temperatures are rising at a greater rate than in the rest of the world. The warming expected to take place during the twenty-first century is expected to an even greater extent here, with average annual temperatures projected to rise by 3–7 degrees Celsius. Already, the region's plants, animals, and people live in some of the most extreme conditions on the planet. Arctic animals such as polar bears, which rely on the presence of sea ice, will increasingly struggle to survive. Changes to vegetation will affect the animals that feed on them and will affect the predators and human communities that depend on these animals. Coastal communities will face increasing exposure to storms, and thawing ground will threaten infrastructure.

The Arctic is particularly important because changes in this region impact areas far beyond its boundaries. The melting Greenland ice sheet contributes to sea-level rise, a phenomenon also affected by melting Arctic glaciers. In general, the world's glaciers are melting at record rates, with the average rate of melting and thinning more than doubling between 2004–2005 and 2005–2006. Millions of people depend on glaciers as natural water-storage facilities for drinking water, agriculture, industry, and power generation. Current trends in glacial melt suggest that the Ganga, Indus, Brahmaputra, and other rivers in the northern Indian plain may become seasonal, with negative implications for poverty and local economies.

It is worth noting that not all the world's glaciers are thinning: climate change models predict some increase in precipitation, with increased moisture evaporating from lower latitudes transported to higher latitudes, thereby increasing the depth of some parts of existing glaciers. In the Arctic, however, a melting ice sheet will undermine the region's role as a feedback mechanism in global climate; this is because the Arctic is not just affected by temperature changes—it helps adjust global temperature in the first place. Ice sheets help to cool the planet, reflecting away the sun's light and heat. As the snow and ice melt, the amount of the sun's energy reflected back into space decreases, leading to a more intense surface warming. In turn, this leads to the increased melting of the Arctic permafrost, the permanently frozen subsoil that acts as a sink for greenhouse gases, including methane and carbon dioxide. Melting permafrost, and the resulting increase in greenhouse gas emissions, itself provides a powerful positive feedback to global warming, accelerating it and itself being accelerated by the process.

A melting Arctic brings easier access to the region's many resources, including minerals, oil, and gas. The U.S. Geological Survey estimates that the Arctic has as much as 25 percent of the world's undiscovered oil and gas, and Moscow reportedly sees the potential of minerals in its slice of the Arctic sector as approaching $2 trillion. The governments that form the Arctic Council—Canada, Denmark, Finland, Iceland, Norway, the Russian Federation, Sweden, and the United States—are paying increasing attention to the issue of sovereignty in this region that is priceless in so many ways.

Biographical Sketches

Bert Bolin is a distinguished Swedish meteorologist who conducted pioneering research into the carbon cycle and later became the first chairman of the IPCC in

1988. Bolin is credited with steering the IPCC on a prudent middle course of scientific consensus, between exaggerated environmental claims, on the one hand, and the vested interests of the fossil fuel lobby, on the other.

Al Gore is a former vice president of the United States. He is a cofounder and chairman of Generation Investment Management, a firm focusing on a new approach to sustainable investing. Gore is the author of *An Inconvenient Truth,* a best-selling book on the threat of and solutions to global warming, and the subject of the award-winning film of the same title. Gore was a joint recipient of the 2007 Nobel Peace Prize.

James Hansen is the director of the NASA Goddard Institute for Space Studies in New York City and an influential researcher into the mechanisms of climate change. Hansen's testimony to Congress in 1988 is widely considered a defining moment in waking the world to global warming. In August 2000, Hansen and his colleagues argued controversially that controlling carbon dioxide emissions is less important than reducing the emissions of other greenhouse gases, which, they said, have produced most of Earth's recent warming.

Sir John Houghton is an eminent British meteorologist and government adviser on environmental issues. As chair and later co-chair of the Scientific Assessment Working Group of the IPCC, he has steered the world's scientists toward a consensus on global warming. Houghton has contributed greatly to public understanding of the issue through many scientific publications, including *Global Warming: The Complete Briefing.*

Jeremy Leggett is a British academic, environmental campaigner, and solar energy entrepreneur. His career reflects, in miniature, the revolution he has been trying to bring about in world energy consumption. Originally a lecturer in geology and a consultant to the oil industry, he became Greenpeace's director of climate science in 1990. A prominent figure at climate negotiations, Leggett also has popularized the issue of climate change through the best-selling books *Global Warming: The Greenpeace Report* (1990) and *The Carbon War* (2000). Now a fellow of Oxford University, Leggett also runs a solar energy company called Solar Century.

Richard Lindzen is Alfred P. Sloan Professor of Meteorology at the Massachusetts Institute of Technology. As a distinguished meteorologist and climate scientist, Lindzen is the most articulate and highly respected of the climate skeptics. His views are summarized in an article he contributed in 1992 to the Cato Institute's *Regulation,* in which he states that "as a scientist, I can find no substantive basis for the warming scenarios being popularly described . . . [and] there would be little difficulty adapting to such warming if it were to occur."

Mohan Munasinghe is vice-chairman of the IPCC and professor of environmental management at the University of Colombo, Sri Lanka. An environmental adviser to the World Bank and the President's Council on Environmental Quality in the United States, Munasinghe has explored the economics of climate change extensively in numerous books and papers. His concept of sustainomics attempts to unite and trade off social, economic, and environmental concerns as a means of addressing climate change. Munasinghe shared the 2007 Nobel Peace Prize with IPCC colleagues and Al Gore for their efforts to build up and disseminate greater knowledge about climate change and to lay the foundations for the measures that are needed to counteract such change.

Directory

Environmental Defense, 257 Park Avenue South, New York, N.Y. 10010. Telephone: (800) 684-3322; Web: http://www.edf.org/page.cfm?tagID=65.
Environmental organization.

European Commission Environment Directorate, European Commission Environment DG, B—1049 Brussels, Belgium. Telephone: (32) 22958463; Web: http://europa.eu.int/comm/environment/climat/home_en.htm.
EU body responsible for promoting environmental issues on behalf of member states.

Greenpeace USA, 702 H Street NW, Suite 300, Washington, D.C. 20001. Telephone: (202) 462-1177; email: info@wdc.greenpeace.org; Web: http://www.greenpeace.org/~climate.
Environmental organization.

Hadley Centre for Climate Prediction and Research, Met Office, FitzRoy Road, Exeter, Devon, EX1 3PB, United Kingdom. Telephone: (44) 1392 885680; email: enquiries@metoffice.gov.uk; Web: http://www.metoffice.gov.uk/research/hadleycentre.
Part of the UK Meteorological Office responsible for developing climate models.

Harvard Environmental School Center for Health and the Global Environment, Harvard Medical School, 401 Park Drive, 2nd Floor East, Boston, Mass. 02215. Telephone: (617) 384-8530; email: chge@hms.harvard.edu; Web: http://chge.med.harvard.edu/index.html.
Provides education and conducts research into health aspects of climate change.

Intergovernmental Panel on Climate Change (IPCC), IPCC Secretariat, c/o World Meteorological Organization, 7bis Avenue de la Paix, P.O. Box 2300, 1211 Geneva 2, Switzerland. Telephone: (41) 22 730 8208; email: IPCC-Sec@wmo.int; Web: http://www.ipcc.ch.
UN agency responsible for climate change issues.

NASA Goddard Institute for Space Studies, 2880 Broadway, New York, N.Y. 10025. Telephone: (212) 678-5500; email: info@giss.nasa.gov; Web: http://www.giss.nasa.gov.
Division of NASA responsible in part for climate modeling and research.

Pew Center on Global Climate Change, 2101 Wilson Boulevard, Suite 550, Arlington, Va. 22201. Telephone: (703) 516-4146; email: info@pewclimate.org; Web: http://www.pewclimate.org.
Organization providing information about climate change policy.

Sierra Club, 85 Second Street, 2nd Floor, San Francisco, Calif. 94105-3441. Telephone: (415) 977-5500; email: information@sierraclub.org; Web: http://www.sierraclub.org/globalwarming.
Environmental organization.

Union of Concerned Scientists, 2 Brattle Square, Cambridge, Mass. 02238-9105. Telephone: (617) 547-5552; Web: http://www.ucsusa.org.
Organization presenting public and ethical concerns about scientific issues.

United Nations Environment Programme (UNEP), United Nations Avenue, Gigiri, P.O. Box 30552, 00100 Nairobi, Kenya. Telephone: (254-20) 7621234; email: unepinfo@unep.org; Web: http://www.unep.org.
Agency responsible for environmental issues of international importance.

University of East Anglia Climatic Research Unit, University of East Anglia, Norwich NR4 7TJ, United Kingdom. Telephone: (44) 16 03 592722; email: cru@uea. ac.uk; Web: http://www.cru.uea.ac.uk.
Scientific institution specializing in global climate research.

U.S. Environmental Protection Agency (EPA), Ariel Rios Building, 1200 Pennsylvania Avenue NW, Washington, D.C. 20460. Telephone: (202) 260-2090; Web: http://www.epa.gov/climatechange.
U.S. government agency responsible for environmental issues.

Further Research

Books

Arctic Climate Impact Assessment. *Impacts of a Warming Arctic. Overview Report.* Cambridge, UK: Cambridge University Press, 2004.

Drake, Frances. *Global Warming: The Science of Climate Change.* London: Arnold, and New York: Oxford University Press, 2000.

Gelbspan, Ross. *The Heat Is On: The Climate Crisis, the Cover-up, the Prescription.* New York: Perseus Books, 1998.

Gore, Al. *Earth in the Balance.* New York: Houghton Mifflin, 1992.

———. *An Inconvenient Truth: The Planetary Emergency of Global Warming and What We Can Do about It.* Emmaus, Pa.: Rodale Press, 2006.

Harvey, Danny. *Global Warming: The Hard Science.* Harlow, England and New York: Prentice Hall, 2000.

Hayes, Peter, and Kirk Smith, eds. *The Global Greenhouse Regime: Who Pays?* London: Earthscan and United Nations University Press, 1993.

Houghton, John. *Global Warming: The Complete Briefing.* New York and Cambridge, UK: Cambridge University Press, 1997.

Jepma, Catrinus, and Mohan Munasinghe. *Climate Change Policy: Facts, Issues, and Analysis.* New York and Cambridge, UK: Cambridge University Press, 1998.

Leggett, Jeremy. *The Carbon War.* New York and London: Penguin, 2000.

———, ed. *Global Warming: The Greenpeace Report.* New York and Oxford: Oxford University Press, 1990.

Mendlesohn, Robert. *The Impact of Climate Change on the United States.* New York: Cambridge University Press, 1999.

O'Riordan, Timothy, and Jill Jäger. *Politics of Climate Change: A European Perspective.* London: Routledge, 1996.

Simms, Andrew. *Ecological Debt: The Health of the Planet and the Wealth of Nations.* London: Pluto Press, 2005.

Articles and Reports

Adger, W. Neil, et al. "New Indicators of Vulnerability and Adaptive Capacity." Research Technical Report 7, Tyndall Centre for Climate Change, University of East Anglia, Norwich, UK, 2004. Available at http://www.tyndall.ac.uk.

Asian Development Bank. *Environmental Management of the Republic of Maldives: An Overview.* Manila, Philippines: Asian Development Bank, 1999.

Baer, Paul, with Michael Mastrandrea. "High Stakes: Designing Emissions Pathways to Reduce the Risk of Dangerous Climate Change." Institute for Public Policy Research, London, 2006.

Boehmer-Christiansen, Sonja. "Global Climate Protection Policy: The Limits of Scientific Advice." *Global Environmental Change* 4, no. 2 (1994): 140–159.

Brown, Kathryn. "Taking Global Warming to the People." *Science* 283, no. 5407 (1999): 1440–1441.

Calvin, William H. "The Great Climate Flip-Flop." *Atlantic Monthly,* January 1998, 47. Available at http://www.theatlantic.com/issues/98jan/climate.htm.

Gelbspan, Ross, et al. *E Magazine* Special Issue on Global Warming (September–October 2000). Available at http://www.emagazine.com/september-october_2000/0900feat1.html.

Gibson, Margie, and Sallie B. Schullinger. "Answers from the Ice Edge: The Consequences of Climate Change on Life in the Bering and Chukchi Seas." Greenpeace, 1998. Available at http://www.greenpeace.org/~climate/arctic/reports/testimonies.pdf.

"Glaciers Are Melting Faster than Expected, UN Reports." *ScienceDaily,* March 18, 2008. Available at http://www.sciencedaily.com/releases/2008/03/080317154235.htm.

Hodges, Glenn. "The New Cold War: Stalking Climate Change by Sub." *National Geographic* (March 2000): 30–41.

Hoegh-Guldberg, Ove. "Climate Change, Coral Bleaching, and the Future of the World's Coral Reefs." Greenpeace USA, July 6, 1999. Available at http://www.greenpeaceusa.org/media/publications/coral_bleaching.pdf.

Huq, Saleemul. "Adaptation to Climate Change: A Paper for the International Climate Change Taskforce." Institute for Public Policy Research, London, 2005.

"Joint Science Academies' Statement: Climate Change Adaptation and the Transition to a Low Carbon Society." National Science Academies. June 2008. Available at http://www.nationalacademies.org/includes/climatechangestatement.pdf.

Jones, Philip, and Tom Wigley. "Global Warming Trends." *Scientific American* 263 (August 1990): 66–73.

Karl, Thomas, and Kevin Trenberth. "The Human Impact on Climate." *Scientific American* 281 (December 1999): 62–68.

Kerr, Richard. "Will the Arctic Ocean Lose All Its Ice?" *Science* 286 (1999): 1828.

Lazaroff, Cat. "Global Warming Portends Water, Power Shortages in American West." Environment News Service, February 2, 2001. Available at http://www.ens.lycos.com/ens/feb2001/2001L-02-02-06.html.

———. "Melting Arctic Permafrost May Accelerate Global Warming." Environmental News Service, February 7, 2001. Available at http://ens-news.com/ens/feb2001/2001L-02-07-06.html.

Ledley, Tamara, et al. "Climate Change and Greenhouse Gases." *EOS* 80 (1999): 453–454, 457–458. Available at http://www.agu.org/eos_elec/99148e.html.

Lindzen, Richard S. "Global Warming: The Origin and Nature of the Alleged Scientific Consensus." *Regulation* 15, no. 2 (1992): 87–98. Available at http://www.cato.org/pubs/regulation/reg15n2g.html.

Lobell, David, et al. "Prioritizing Climate Change Adaptation Needs for Food Security in 2030." *Science* 319 (2008): 607–610.

Magrath, John. "Turning Up the Heat: Climate Change and Poverty in Uganda." Oxfam GB, London, 2008. Available at http://publications.oxfam.org.uk/oxfam/display.asp?K=9781848140394&TAG=&CID=.

"Many Coral Reefs Nearly Dead." *Popular Science,* October 24, 2000.

McCarthy, James J., et al., eds. *Climate Change 2001: Impacts, Adaptation, and Vulnerability.* Cambridge and New York: Cambridge University Press, 2001.

National Resources Defense Council, "Polar Thaw: Global Warming in the Arctic and Antarctic." 1999. Photographs by Gary Braasch. Available at http://www.nrdc.org/globalWarming/polar/polarinx.asp.

Niel, Laurenz. "Ocean Warming, Pollution Causing Death of Coral Reefs." *UniSci: Daily University Science News,* November 29, 2000. Available at http://unisci.com/stories/20004/1129002.htm.

Pomerance, Rafe. "Coral Bleaching, Coral Mortality, and Global Climate Change." Report for U.S. Coral Reef Task Force, March 5, 1999. Available at http://www.state.gov/www/global/global_issues/coral_reefs/990305_coralreef_rpt.html.

Schellnhuber, Hans-Joachim, et al., eds. *Avoiding Dangerous Climate Change.* Cambridge, UK: Cambridge University Press, 2006.

Schneider, Stephen H. "Climate Modeling." *Scientific American* 256 (May 1987): 72–80.

———. "The Changing Climate." *Scientific American* 258 (September 1989): 38.

Simms, Andrew, with Hannah Reid. *Africa: Up in Smoke?: The Second Report from the Working Group on Climate Change and Development.* New Economics Foundation, London, June 2005.

Socolovsky, Jerome. "Island Nations Desperate for Action." *Popular Science* (November 17, 2000).

United Nations Environment Programme. "Impact of Climate Change to Cost the World $US 300 Billion a Year." Press release, 3 February 2001. Available at http://www.unep.org/Documents/Default.asp?DocumentID=192&ArticleID=2758.

Watson, R. T., M. C. Zinyowera, and R. H. Moss, eds. *The Regional Impacts of Climate Change: An Assessment of Vulnerability.* New York: Cambridge University Press, 1998.

White, Robert M. "The Great Climate Debate." *Scientific American* 263 (July 1990): 18–25.

World Water Vision Commission Report. "The Water Crisis: Where We Are Today and How We Got There, November 1999." Available at http://watervision.cdinet.com/pdfs/commission/cchpt2.pdf.

Web Sites

Global Warning, Early Warning Signs
http://www.climatehotmap.org

An Inconvenient Truth
http://www.climatecrisis.net

IPCC Data Distribution Center
http://ipcc-ddc.cru.uea.ac.uk

NASA Goddard Institute for Space Studies
http://www.giss.nasa.gov

Pew Center on Global Climate Change, Global Warming Basics
http://www.pewclimate.org/global-warming-basics

Tiempo Climate Cyberlibrary
http://www.tiempocyberclimate.org

UK Meteorological Office, Hadley Centre
http://www.metoffice.gov.uk/research/hadleycentre

UK Rivers Network, Finding Out about Climate Change and Global Warming: Student Research Resources
http://www.ukrivers.net/climate.html

United Nations Environment Programme, Climate Change Information Kit
http://www.unep.org/Themes/climatechange/PDF/infokit2003-E.pdf

U.S. National Climatic Data Center
http://www.ncdc.noaa.gov/oa/ncdc.html

U.S. National Oceanic and Atmospheric Administration (NOAA), Global Monitoring Division
http://www.esrl.noaa.gov/gmd

We Can Solve It
http://www.wecansolveit.org

World Meteorological Organization
http://www.wmo.int/pages/index_en.html

Documents

1. United Nations Framework Convention on Climate Change

Entered into force March 21, 1994

The full text is available at http://unfccc.int/essential_background/convention/background/items/2853.php.

Extracts

Article 2: Objective

The ultimate objective of this Convention and any related legal instruments that the Conference of the Parties may adopt is to achieve, in accordance with the relevant provisions of the Convention, stabilization of greenhouse gas concentrations in the atmosphere at a level that would prevent dangerous anthropogenic interference with the climate system. Such a level should be achieved within a time-frame sufficient to allow ecosystems to adapt naturally to climate change, to ensure that food production is not threatened and to enable economic development to proceed in a sustainable manner.

Article 3: Principles

1. The Parties should protect the climate system for the benefit of present and future generations of humankind, on the basis of equity and in accordance with their common but differentiated responsibilities and respective capabilities. Accordingly, the

developed country Parties should take the lead in combating climate change and the adverse effects thereof.

3. The Parties should take precautionary measures to anticipate, prevent or minimize the causes of climate change and mitigate its adverse effects. Where there are threats of serious or irreversible damage, lack of full scientific certainty should not be used as a reason for postponing such measures, taking into account that policies and measures to deal with climate change should be cost-effective so as to ensure global benefits at the lowest possible cost. To achieve this, such policies and measures should take into account different socio-economic contexts, be comprehensive, cover all relevant sources, sinks and reservoirs of greenhouse gases and adaptation, and comprise all economic sectors. Efforts to address climate change may be carried out cooperatively by interested Parties.

Article 4: Commitments

1. All Parties, taking into account their common but differentiated responsibilities and their specific national and regional development priorities, objectives and circumstances, shall:

(a) Develop, periodically update, publish and make available to the Conference of the Parties, in accordance with Article 12, national inventories of anthropogenic emissions. . . .

(b) Formulate, implement, publish and regularly update national and, where appropriate, regional programmes containing measures to mitigate climate change by addressing anthropogenic emissions . . . and measures to facilitate adequate adaptation to climate change;

(c) Promote and cooperate in the development, application and diffusion, including transfer, of technologies, practices and processes that control, reduce or prevent anthropogenic emissions of greenhouse gases not controlled by the Montreal Protocol in all relevant sectors, including the energy, transport, industry, agriculture, forestry and waste management sectors;

(d) Promote sustainable management, and promote and cooperate in the conservation and enhancement, as appropriate, of sinks and reservoirs of all greenhouse gases not controlled by the Montreal Protocol including biomass, forests and oceans as well as other terrestrial, coastal and marine ecosystems;

(e) Cooperate in preparing for adaptation to the impacts of climate change; develop and elaborate appropriate and integrated plans for coastal zone management, water resources and agriculture, and for the protection and rehabilitation of areas, particularly in Africa, affected by drought and desertification, as well as floods;

(f) Take climate change considerations into account, to the extent feasible, in their relevant social, economic and environmental policies and actions. . . .

(g) Promote and cooperate in scientific, technological, technical, socio-economic and other research, systematic observation and development of data archives related to the climate system and intended to further the understanding and to reduce or eliminate the remaining uncertainties regarding the causes, effects, magnitude and timing of climate change and the economic and social consequences of various response strategies;

(h) Promote and cooperate in the full, open and prompt exchange of relevant scientific, technological, technical, socioeconomic and legal information related to the climate system and climate change, and to the economic and social consequences of various response strategies;

(i) Promote and cooperate in education, training and public awareness related to climate change and encourage the widest participation in this process, including that of non-governmental organizations.

2. Climate Change 2007: Fourth Assessment Synthesis Report, Summary for Policymakers

Intergovernmental Panel on Climate Change, November 2007

The full text is available at http://www.ipcc.ch/pdf/assessment-report/ar4/syr/ar4_syr_spm.pdf.

Extract

Summary Points

- Warming of the climate system is unequivocal, as is now evident from observations of increases in global average air and ocean temperatures, widespread melting of snow and ice and rising global average sea level
- Observational evidence from all continents and most oceans shows that many natural systems are being affected by regional climate changes, particularly temperature increases.
- There is *medium confidence* that other effects of regional climate change on natural and human environments are emerging, although many are difficult to discern due to adaptation and non-climatic drivers.
- Global greenhouse gas emissions due to human activities have grown since pre-industrial times, with an increase of 70 percent between 1970 and 2004.
- Global atmospheric concentrations of CO_2, methane (CH_4) and nitrous oxide (N_2O) have increased markedly as a result of human activities since 1750 and now far exceed pre-industrial values determined from ice cores spanning many thousands of years.
- Most of the observed increase in global average temperatures since the mid-20th century is *very likely* due to the observed increase in anthropogenic greenhouse gas concentrations. It is *likely* that there has been significant anthropogenic warming over the past 50 years averaged over each continent (except Antarctica).
- Altered frequencies and intensities of extreme weather, together with sea level rise, are expected to have mostly adverse effects on natural and human systems.
- There is high confidence that neither adaptation nor mitigation alone can avoid all climate change impacts; however, they can complement each other and together can significantly reduce the risks of climate change.

POLLUTION

Melanie Jarman

Pollution respects no geographical boundaries. The U.S. Environmental Protection Agency (EPA), according to the *New York Times,* has asserted that, on some days, almost 25 percent of the particulate matter in the Los Angeles sky can be traced to China. Similarly, toxic chemicals thought to have originated in Europe and North America have been found in the tissue of polar bears in remote parts of the Arctic. Incidents such as these highlight the transboundary nature of pollution, an often global problem that requires local and global solutions.

Historical Background and Development

Although pollution is considered to be a particularly modern phenomenon, the problem actually dates back several thousand years, to when people first began to live in cities. The world's first landfill is believed to have been constructed in Knossos, Crete, circa 3000 BC, and in Athens circa 500 BC municipal waste, by decree, was to be transported to a landfill 1 mile beyond the city gates. Yet the true beginning of the modern age of pollution was the Industrial Revolution, which began in Britain in the eighteenth century and later spread to continental Europe and North America. As coal-fired industry marched on, cities and towns were choked with smoke, and poor sanitation and polluted water supplies led to severe health problems. England passed a law as early as 1297 requiring households to keep the front of their homes free of refuse, and its Public Health Acts of 1848 and 1875 were among the world's first major pieces of antipollution legislation, introducing, among other things, methodical sewage treatment and the concept of "smokeless zones" to reduce pollution in urban areas.

Increasing awareness of the causes and effects of pollution prompted a progressive cleanup by many industrial nations during the twentieth century, not least because of a number of serious (and often fatal) incidents. For example, people became acutely aware of the need to tackle air pollution after severe

This chapter is based on the original, written by Chris Woodford, that appeared in the first edition of *World at Risk.*

cases of smog in Donora, Pennsylvania, in 1948 (when 20 people died and nearly 6,000 others became ill), in London in 1952 (when an estimated 4,000 people died), and in New York in 1963 and 1966 (when 405 and 168 people died, respectively). Indeed, the 1952 episode in London led directly to England's 1956 Clean Air Act. Pollution proved much harder to tackle, however, where the effects were more widely distanced from the cause. Such was the problem with Minamata disease, a degenerative and often fatal type of mercury poisoning that became epidemic in Minamata Bay, Japan, in the 1950s after a chemical factory discharged mercury into the bay. Although the factory had opened in 1938, the ecological changes were noted only in 1950 and the effects on humans only in 1953. Yet not until 1968 was Minamata disease linked to the chemical factory, by which time 2,000 people had been poisoned from eating contaminated fish. Forty-three people subsequently died, and more than seven hundred people were left disabled.

Rachel Carson's crusade against toxic pesticides and insecticides in *Silent Spring* is another example of how long it can take for society to address the effects of pollution even after the source has been identified. Although declining bird populations had been noted since the late 1950s and Carson's book was published in 1962, the production of dichlorodiphenyltrichloroethane (DDT), one of the chemicals whose misuse she highlighted, did not cease in the United States until 1971. Attempts by Sandra Steingraber and others to link environmental chemicals to such health problems as cancer, leading to the successful curbing of other toxic pollutants, may take even longer. Even establishing a causal link between a particular type of pollution and its effects may not be enough to prompt a cleanup. The method by which coal-fired power plants produce acid rain—rain that turns into acid after passing through oxides of nitrogen and sulfur contained in air pollution—was established in the 1960s, yet acidification remains a major problem in New York's Adirondack Mountains, downwind of power plants in the Midwest. The number of acidified lakes in the Adirondacks is expected to double by 2040.

No shortage of environmental legislation has been apparent in recent decades. Notable attempts to tackle marine pollution include the 1972 Convention on the Prevention of Marine Pollution by Dumping of Wastes and Other Matter (also called the London Dumping Convention, and updated in 1996) and the 1978 International Convention for the Prevention of Pollution from Ships (MARPOL). Other international initiatives include the 1979 Geneva Convention on Long-Range Transboundary Air Pollution, which entered into force in 1983; the 1987 Montreal Protocol on Substances That Deplete the Ozone Layer; the 1989 Basel Convention on Hazardous Waste (which has been updated to include electronic waste); and the 1982 Convention on the Law of the Sea.

Clearly, many global problems will one day be solved. For example, doctors may find a vaccine for human immunodeficiency virus (HIV)/acquired immunodeficiency syndrome (AIDS), and world leaders may be forced to agree to measures for tackling climate change. Pollution, however, is a more diffuse problem that will probably always affect humankind, not least because human ingenuity is constantly introducing new forms of pollution. Weapons that use depleted uranium, a very dense by-product of nuclear power that can penetrate armor plating, are just one example. These weapons, first deployed in the 1991 Persian Gulf War, attracted much more attention following their use in the 1999 Kosovo bombing campaign, when North Atlantic Treaty Organization (NATO) was estimated to have fired more than 30,000 depleted uranium shells. Concerns were later expressed by the World Health Organization (WHO) and the United Nations that civilian populations might be exposed to the effects of the uranium for years to come. Decades of progress in fighting pollution through technological improvements, international legislation, and growing environmental consciousness can be undermined in a matter of days or weeks by actions such as these.

Current Status

More than four decades have passed since the world's attention was focused on the problems of the polluted environment described in Carson's groundbreaking *Silent Spring*. Since its publication, more has been discovered about the causes and effects of pollution, and considerable effort has been devoted to preventing pollution through regulation, economic instruments, and technological solutions.

Research

Views have sometimes differed sharply on exactly what constitutes pollution, but the generally accepted definition is the introduction into the natural and human environment of harmful substances and organisms that do not belong there. In Carson's mind, no doubt existed about the effects of chemical pesticides and insecticides: "As crude a weapon as the cave man's club, the chemical barrage has been hurled against the fabric of life." In response, chemical companies vigorously defended the value of their products in fighting pests and diseases, increasing crop yields, and helping to combat such problems as world hunger.

Yet since the appearance of *Silent Spring*, and partly thanks to Carson's wake-up call, some of yesterday's champion chemicals have become today's toxics (see Table 2). Numerous pesticides and insecticides widely used in Carson's time are now banned in many countries and generally referred to as persistent organic pollutants (POPs). Among them are aldrin, chlordane, DDT, dieldrin, endrin, heptachlor, hexachlorobenzene, polychlorinated biphenyls (PCBs), and toxaphene. Not only do these chemicals not readily biodegrade, they systematically bioaccumulate—that is, they become more and more concentrated in organisms higher up the food chain—presenting a greater danger to humans than their ordinary concentration in the environment might suggest. Such heavy metals as lead, cadmium, and mercury have similarly fallen into disfavor. Lead, until recently a major gasoline additive, has been banned as an additive in many countries after several studies confirmed a correlation between high lead levels in the environment and reductions in childhood IQ.

According to the World Resources Institute (WRI), lead poisoning is the most preventable condition related to environmental toxicity. PCBs, once widely used to make electronic equipment, have also attracted criticism. A number of studies found significant traces of PCBs in fish, birds, and mammals in remote parts of the Arctic, thousands of miles from their presumed places of origin. Chlorofluorocarbons (CFCs), once described as "miracle compounds" because of their numerous industrial uses, are now known to destroy Earth's ozone layer, although they are not actually toxins per se.

Potentially harmful substances are still routinely discharged into the environment in large quantities. Calculating the amount of waste being generated is a problem because definitions and surveying methods employed by countries vary considerably. However, the Basel Convention estimated that the amount of hazardous waste (harmful by-products of industrial processes that often form the source of environmental pollution) and other waste generated for 2000 and 2001 was 351 million tons (318 million tonnes) and 373 million tons (338 millions tonnes), respectively.

Everyday human exposure to toxics can be high for other reasons as well. In 1980, Wayne Ott and Lance Wallace of the EPA began a major study of the exposure to environmental toxins of 3,000 carefully chosen human subjects. Their surprising discovery was that many citizens suffer greatest chemical exposure not through industrial pollution, which accounts for only around 3 percent of total exposure, but from a variety of sources *inside* their homes, such as household cleaning products, paints, tobacco smoke, and dust. A 1999 study by environmental engineers at the University of Texas confirmed the dangers of volatile organic compounds (VOCs), carbon-based chemicals that evaporate at low temperatures, originally in tap water and turned into potentially harmful indoor air pollution when boiled off by dishwashers and showers.

Not all forms of pollution are easily recognizable as such. Fertilizers have played a major role in increasing world food production. More than 50 percent of all nitrogen fertilizer use took place in the two decades from 1985 to 2005. A United Nations Environmental Programme (UNEP) report, *Global Environment Outlook 2000,*" suggested that "We are fertilizing the Earth on a global scale and in a largely uncontrolled experiment" (see map, p. 330). The consequences include nitrogen-contaminated water supplies; acid rain; photochemical smog; and harmful algal blooms, of which the red tides in coastal areas are the most familiar example. One of the most spectacular worldwide demonstrations of algal blooms is the dead zone in the Gulf of Mexico. Each summer, where the nutrient-rich Mississippi and Atchafalaya rivers empty into the gulf, a massive algal growth is induced that causes oxygen levels to drop to just 2 parts per million, a level so low that the water can no longer support marine life. The dead zone varies in size. In 2008, it covered 7,800 square miles, an area roughly the size of Connecticut and Delaware together.

Chemicals, natural and otherwise, are only one form of pollution. A less obvious form involves the introduction of living organisms into ecosystems where they do not naturally occur. The coastal waters of numerous countries have been affected by these alien species. The Mediterranean Sea, for example, has been swamped by a "killer algae," *Caulerpa taxifolia*. On the French Côte d'Azur, it spread from an area of just 1.2 square yards (1 square meter) in 1984 to around 15,000 acres (6,000 hectares) in 1999. An eradication program was swiftly launched in California after the same alga was found there in 2000. In 2005, the Global Invasive Species Programme was given responsibility for coordinating a global invasive alien species indicator, working toward the 2010 Biodiversity Target under the Convention on Biological Diversity.

Recent concern over the introduction of genetically modified organisms (GMOs) into the environment is the flip side of the same coin. While proponents argue that genetic engineering overcomes the inherent drawbacks of a system of natural selection that can no longer keep pace with human needs, opponents counter that GMOs are effectively a form of alien species pollution with the potential to decimate natural ecosystems.

Introducing "unnatural" substances and organisms into the environment is the cause of pollution, and the effects are water and air pollution on a global and local scale. The pollution of freshwater sources compounds the wider problem of meeting the world's growing demand for water (see FRESHWATER). Since 1900, half of the world's wetlands, the principal source of renewable freshwater, have been lost, according to publicity for World Water Day 2009, a project presented by UN-Water and coordinated by the United Nations Educational, Scientific, and Cultural Organization (UNESCO). Many rivers flow through more than one nation, so transboundary water pollution is an international issue. World Water Day 2009 stated that nearly 40 percent of the world's population lives in river and lake basins shared by two or more countries. It also stated that the world's 263 international river basins and transboundary aquifer systems include the territory of 145 countries; 158 of these 263 have no cooperative management framework in place.

Inland waterways are often used as high-speed drains or sewers and ultimately pollute the oceans. In 2009, the project Partnerships in Environmental Management for the Seas of East Asia stated that over 80 percent of all marine pollution in the East Asian region originated from land-based sources, with discharge of industrial wastes resulting in toxic accumulations in the marine food chain.

Sewage, persistent organic pollutants, PCBs, fertilizers, and alien species also find their way into the oceans eventually. Stricken oil tankers may provide the most spectacular incidents of marine pollution, yet the publicity they receive contrasts markedly with the scale of the global problem they pose compared to, for example, sewage discharges, which are the priority issue for most coastal regions.

Once pollution is in the ocean, it becomes a transboundary issue. The Sellafield nuclear plant on Britain's northwest coast reprocesses waste nuclear fuel from around the world, arguably therefore making the world a cleaner place. The plant, however, discharges radioactive effluent into the Irish Sea that is then carried by ocean currents to Ireland, Scandinavia, and farther afield. In 2007, the Irish media outlet RTE News reported that Ireland's minister for the environment said that his government would be opposed to any further construction at the plant and that it would be better if all operations at the plant were to cease.

Much ocean pollution causes concern because of its long-lasting nature. Nuclear waste, POPs, and PCBs all fall into this category. So too does plastic waste, which, being light, buoyant, and generally nonbiodegradable, can be considered a perfectly designed form of transboundary ocean pollution. Plastic waste has now been carried by the seas to all corners of the globe. It is estimated to kill at least 1 million seabirds per year and around 100,000 seals and cetaceans; one-fourth of the world's seabirds are thought to have traces of ingested plastic in their systems. Some of the ocean's pollution—a majority of its mercury and cadmium, for example—derives from air pollution via atmospheric deposition. The Joint Group of Experts on the Scientific Aspects of Marine Environmental Protection (GESAMP) reported that most nitrogen entering the oceans on the east coast of the United States originates from cities and power plants in the Midwest, some 600 miles (1,000 kilometers) away (see Document 1).

Smokestacks belching into the sky and car exhaust polluting the streets also make air pollution a local problem. Notoriously air-polluted cities, such as Athens, Beijing, Delhi, Los Angeles, Mexico City, Paris, and Rome, make their own air pollution. In 2007, the UN estimated the costs of urban air pollution in developing countries as upward of 5 percent of gross domestic product (GDP). Yet even in developed countries, such as the United States, air pollution remains a major problem. The American Lung Association reported that in 2007 over 100 million U.S. citizens lived in counties that did not meet EPA standards for at least one air pollutant. Air pollution is also a transboundary issue. One of the most spectacular examples occurred following substantial forest fires that burned on the Indonesian islands of East Kalimantan and Sumatra in 1997 and 1998, spreading dense smoke over six neighboring countries and ultimately reaching as far south as Darwin, Australia. According to the UNEP, 70 million people were affected by the fires, which cost Southeast Asia an estimated $1.4 billion. All told, air pollution is one of the world's biggest killers. According to WHO estimates, air pollution causes approximately 2 million deaths every year, with more than half the health burden from air pollution borne by people in developing countries. Poor indoor air quality, largely from biomass and coal fuels in badly ventilated homes, may pose a health risk to over half the world's population. In particular, this affects women and children, who spend the most time in the home.

Policies and Programs

Pollution can be viewed from a variety of perspectives and solved in as many different ways. From an environmentalist point of view, pollution is an inherently bad thing—toxic chemicals and wastes that do not occur naturally in the environment should not be introduced by humans or industrial processes in the first place. Pollution can also be seen as a technical problem requiring engineering solutions, such as catalytic converters or electrostatic scrubbers to prevent it from entering the environment. (Wayne Ott and John Roberts reported that simply wiping your feet on a doormat reduces lead pollution on household carpets by a factor of six, a very effective, low-tech solution.) From an economic perspective, pollution is arguably a necessary by-product of industrial development. No one pollutes the environment intentionally, but greater economic incentives to pollute exist than not to; pumping chemical waste untreated into rivers or seas is generally cheaper than cleaning it up. In *Through Green-Colored Glasses,* Oxford University economist Wilfred Beckerman argued that economic growth is an absolute prerequisite for tackling environmental and social problems and that the "small is beautiful" approach of environmentalists, which seeks to limit problems such as pollution by limiting growth, is really a case of "small is stupid." Finally, because pollution is often a transboundary, global issue, it can be viewed as a diplomatic problem whose solution lies in international antipollution laws and agreements motivated as much by the need to maintain good international relations as by the desire to preserve the environment. Inevitably, these perspectives are oversimplifications, and solutions advocated by various groups often combine approaches from different perspectives.

Many environmentalists, for example, believe in the "polluter pays" principle, an economic solution that seeks to reduce pollution by levying its costs on the people who cause it. Other solutions advocated by environmentalists may include imposing a public relations cost on polluters through the publication of a register of who pollutes, where, and how much. Generally, solutions to pollution combine environmental, economic, technological, and legislative or regulatory factors.

From a global perspective, pollution has traditionally been assumed to be a necessary consequence of industrialization. Developing nations are not only condemned to repeat the grossly polluted past of such nations as the United Kingdom and the United States, but they will be unable to address the problem until they reach a comparable level of affluence. Yet *Greening Industry,* a major report published by the World Bank in 1999, questioned this assumption, citing studies from a variety of developing nations, including China, India, and Brazil: "These experiences have persuaded us that the conventional wisdom is wrong: Economic development and industrial pollution are not immutably linked. We are convinced that developing countries can build on the new model to reduce industrial pollution significantly, even if they grow rapidly during the coming decade."

Greening Industry confirmed that communities, markets, and governments can act together to help poorer nations take a cleaner path toward development. For example, the Indonesian government's Program for Pollution Control, Evaluation and Rating (PROPER) program published information about how factories pollute the environment so that communities and markets could put pressure on companies to clean up. That developing nations could become "pollution havens" for waste exported by developed countries has long been a concern because of developing nations' lower labor costs, less stringent environmental legislation, lower environmental awareness, and need to earn foreign currency. Prior Informed Consent (PIC), a system operated by the UN Food and Agriculture Organization (FAO) and UNEP, aims to reduce this dangerous trade by providing developing nations with more information about the potentially damaging effects of waste that might be exported to them.

Both local and national initiatives are essential for tackling pollution problems. Global initiatives have proved essential in addressing transboundary pollution. A number of international agreements have targeted specific forms of pollution, including the London Dumping Convention; MARPOL; the Geneva Convention on Long-Range Transboundary Air Pollution; and the 1990 International Convention on Oil Pollution Preparedness, Response and Cooperation. One of the most successful global initiatives for tackling pollution has been the Montreal Protocol to cut worldwide production of CFCs that deplete the ozone layer. Now generally heralded as a model of how international environmental legislation can be swiftly and effectively implemented, the protocol cut global CFC consumption from 1.2 million tons (1.1 million tonnes) in 1986 to 121,000 tons (110,000 tonnes) in 1996, according to the UNEP. Yet the protocol has not been completely successful. This is because the hydrochlorofluorocarbons (HCFCs) and hydrofluorocarbons (HFCs) that have been used as an alternative to CFCs have contributed to another problem—climate change. On a molecule-for-molecule basis, these compounds are a far more potent greenhouse gases than carbon dioxide. The Montreal Protocol could therefore be even more effective as environmental legislation if it had some link to the Kyoto Protocol and the international policy process on climate change.

Several key components to policies and programs aim to control pollution. Information and education feature in most of them. Disseminating information about the established risks of using and disposing of chemicals in the environment is essential. One problem, however, is that the long-term risk of using some chemicals is unknown, especially if they cause genetic mutations, which may not appear in the current generation. Another problem is the difficulty of proving without long-term large-scale epidemiological studies that chemicals in the environment cause particular health problems, especially when transboundary pollution is involved. This last problem has proved a major stumbling block for environmental lawyers keen to seek compensation for communities affected by pollution.

Apart from information about pollution, most programs aim to put information about specific polluters into the hands of the communities that are most affected by them. Typically this means establishing registers of which companies are discharging what, where, when, and in how great a quantity and instituting freedom of information laws that allow ordinary people to inspect these registers. As the World Bank's *Greening Industry* argued in the context of cutting pollution in developing nations, "Armed with good information, poor citizens can work with environmental agencies and elect political leaders willing to pressure factories to curb emissions, as regions and countries make the transition to greener industry."

In successful pollution programs, economic instruments also feature strongly. The idea of a global commons that can be freely polluted at no charge is replaced by the "polluter pays" principle, in which factories are charged for polluting (either fined directly or indirectly through bad publicity and community or shareholder action) or are given incentives not to pollute. Equally, purist environmentalists are sometimes obliged to accept that in the case of pollution control, industry can justify investments only in what is sometimes called the best-practicable environmental option—that is, the most cost-effective solution. Finally, programs to address local pollution problems also need to bear in mind such broader problems as the risk of forcing polluting factories to move to less-regulated nations and the illegal trafficking in chemicals banned in certain nations (see Document 2).

Regional Summaries

Because of the transboundary nature of pollution, few places on Earth have escaped its effects. Developed nations generally pollute less than they used to, and developing nations are trying to follow cleaner paths to development, although not always successfully.

North America

The United States and Canada enjoy relatively high-quality water supplies, yet water pollution problems persist in both countries. A 2006 report by the U.S. Public Interest Research Group (U.S. PIRG) found that for the period July 2003–December 2004 more than 62 percent of industrial and municipal facilities across the United States discharged more pollution into waterways than their Clean Water Act permits allowed. U.S. PIRG claimed that more than 40 percent of U.S. waterways were unsafe for swimming and fishing.

The Great Lakes, bordering the United States and Canada, and supporting agriculture and supplying water to millions of people, have been described by the organization Environment Canada as a "chemical hot spot," with over 360 chemical compounds identified there. These include alkylated lead, benzo(a) pyrene, DDT, mercury, and mirex. Many of these are persistent toxic chemicals that are potentially dangerous to humans and are already destructive to the aquatic ecosystems. Various species of fish in the Great Lakes now suffer from tumors and lesions, and their reproductive capacities are decreasing.

Long-range air pollution has been a major problem in the northeastern United States and southeastern Canada, with thousands of lakes and inland waters contaminated by acid rain from power plants and industries in the Midwest. Despite substantial reductions in emissions during the 1980s and 1990s, many lakes remain too acidic to support fish. In Toronto, smog-related illnesses are estimated to kill three hundred people a year, according to the city's environment task force. For the United States, the American Lung Association's 2008 annual report on air pollution—the State of the Air report—found that one in six people in the United States lives in an area with unhealthy year-round levels of particle pollution and one in ten people lives in an area with unhealthy levels of three types of pollution: ozone, short-term particle pollution, and year-round particle pollution.

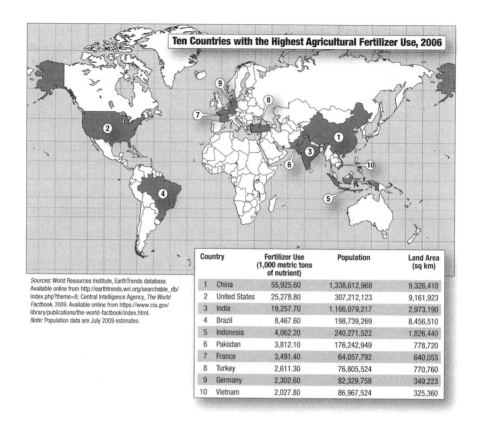

Ten Countries with the Highest Agricultural Fertilizer Use, 2006

Sources: World Resources Institute, EarthTrends database. Available online from http://earthtrends.wri.org/searchable_db/index.php?theme=8; Central Intelligence Agency, *The World Factbook,* 2009. Available online from https://www.cia.gov/library/publications/the-world-factbook/index.html. *Note:* Population data are July 2009 estimates.

	Country	Fertilizer Use (1,000 metric tons of nutrient)	Population	Land Area (sq km)
1	China	55,925.60	1,338,612,968	9,326,410
2	United States	25,278.80	307,212,123	9,161,923
3	India	19,257.70	1,166,079,217	2,973,190
4	Brazil	8,467.60	198,739,269	8,456,510
5	Indonesia	4,062.20	240,271,522	1,826,440
6	Pakistan	3,812.10	176,242,949	778,720
7	France	3,491.40	64,057,792	640,053
8	Turkey	2,611.30	76,805,524	770,760
9	Germany	2,302.60	82,329,758	349,223
10	Vietnam	2,027.80	86,967,524	325,360

Latin America

Latin America's abundant water resources have been compromised by pollution in industrializing areas. One of the key industries blamed for water pollution is mining. Honduran Catholic bishop Luis Alfonso Santos, an activist in the civil society movement against the presence of transnational mining companies in the region, was quoted by Inter Press Service News (September 9, 2006) as saying that mining generates problems like "cancer, pollution in the rivers, and [spontaneous] abortions."

Pollution from oil drilling is also an issue. In 2007, the Achuar tribe from the Peruvian Amazon filed a lawsuit against Occidental Petroleum Corporation accusing the company of causing environmental damage by dumping toxic oil by-products in watersheds used by the Achuar people. The oil company Chevron has also been sued over allegations that Texaco, which merged with Chevron in 2001, dumped toxic waste that polluted the Amazon.

Air pollution problems in the region have been made worse by smoke produced by slash-and-burn deforestation.

Europe and Central Asia

In 2007, the European Environment Agency (EEA) published its fourth assessment of environmental challenges faced in the region, measured against objectives of a European Union environment program and an environment strategy for countries of Eastern Europe, the Caucasus region, and central Asia. This assessment found that most air pollutants had increased in Eastern Europe and central Asia as a result of economic recovery, increases in transport, and the ineffectiveness of air pollution protection policies. The assessment stated that the health impact of air pollution includes a reduction by almost one year of average life expectancy in Western and central Europe.

Air pollutants also contribute to the acidification of forests and water ecosystems, and to the eutrophication of soils and waters. Eutrophication is a problem for all enclosed seas and sheltered marine waters in the region. Reducing diffuse nutrient sources, particularly from agriculture, remains a major challenge and, according to the EEA's fourth assessment ("Europe's Environment," 2007), "requires increased action."

For the European Union, new policies addressing the management of chemicals includes the legislation on registration, evaluation, and authorization of chemicals (REACH), which entered into force in 2007. REACH requires the manufacturers or importers of substances to register them with a central European Chemicals Agency.

North Africa and the Middle East

Water quality is a major issue for the region. A 2007 World Bank report, *Making the Most of Scarcity: Accountability for Better Water Management Results in the Middle East and North Africa,* estimated that water-related environmental problems cost many countries in the region between 0.5 and 2.5 percent of GDP per year. These problems include the fact that large parts of the region are supplied by shallow fossil aquifers. The excessive extraction of water has caused a drop in water tables and has led to such pollution problems as the inundation of some coastal agricultural areas with saltwater from the sea. Coastal pollution, indeed, is an ever-increasing problem in the region, with threats including the transportation of oil through the Indian Ocean and the Red Sea.

The World Bank Web site noted pollution-related health problems in the region, particularly in urban and industrial centers. The causes identified by the World Bank include open municipal waste dumps, the use of leaded gasoline in an aging and poorly maintained vehicle fleet, the inefficient use of fossil fuels for power generation, and particulate and sulfur-oxide emissions from industry.

Pollution issues came under the spotlight at the first Arab Regional Conference on the Inspection and Enforcement of Environmental Regulations, held in Jordan in 2007. This conference initiated a regional network and looked at the development of relevant legislation.

Sub-Saharan Africa

Air pollution is currently less of a problem in most African states than in such rapidly developing nations as India. However, emissions from thermal power stations are increasing, as are emissions from vehicles, partly due to an increase in urban populations. Heavy dependence on coal-fired power plants accounts for most air pollution, with mining making a major contribution. South Africa produces around two-thirds of all sulfur emissions in the region. Biomass provides 80 percent of energy in sub-Saharan Africa. Reliance on biomass for cooking is a major factor in the high incidence of respiratory diseases in the region.

Water pollution problems in Africa stem from eutrophication, industrial and wastewater discharges into inland waterways and the sea, and the spread of invasive alien plants. The water hyacinth (*Eichhornia crassipes*) has contaminated some of the continent's major waterways, including Lake Victoria and the Nile, where it disrupts power generation, fishing, and water supplies. Lake Victoria has also been contaminated by the Nile perch (*Lates niloticus*), which has killed off more than five hundred native fish species. Pollution from oil leaks and oil spills is a problem in oil-rich areas such as the Niger Delta.

Africa also has pollution problems from waste originating elsewhere (see Case Study—Electronic Waste). In 2006, 10 people were killed by noxious fumes and more than 70,000 needed medical treatment after toxic waste was dumped on open sites in Côte d'Ivoire. In a speech delivered at the opening of the Eighth Conference of the Parties to the Basel Convention on November 27, 2006, Achim Steiner, the executive director of the UNEP, described the incident as indicative of the challenge facing African nations, saying, "I sincerely hope that the tragedy in Côte d'Ivoire and the challenges of e-waste will serve as a wake up call to the Parties of the Basel Convention and other related treaties."

Asia and the Pacific

Asia and the Pacific islands suffer considerably from pollution. The region's two great industrializing nations, China and India, both rely heavily on cheap and abundant coal for electricity generation, contributing to substantial sulfur dioxide and greenhouse gas emissions. Sulfur dioxide emissions rose four times faster in Asia than in any other region between 1980 and 1996. A 2007 report by China's State Environmental Protection Administration (SEPA) found that about 60 percent of Chinese cities suffered from air pollution, with thirty-nine cities classified as suffering severe air pollution. Seven of these were in Shanxi Province, the country's largest coal supplier, and seven were in Liaoning Province, a base for heavy industries.

The WHO has suggested that air pollution in major Southeast Asian and Chinese cities contributes to the deaths of about 500,000 people each year. Air pollution is not just a problem for urban and industrialized areas, however. In 2005, drifting smoke from purposely set forest fires in Indonesia caused Malaysia to declare a state of emergency in one region. Hospitals reported a 150 percent increase in breathing problems, and seven people who had a history of respiratory problems reportedly died.

The biggest potential for marine pollution in the region comes from the high concentration of large cities along coastlines, which were predicted to house nearly half the world's total population by early in the twenty-first century. Coastal development has led to a variety of problems, notably the discharge of industrial waste and untreated sewage directly into the sea (damaging fisheries and causing red tides) and such related problems as the destruction of mangrove swamps and other important habitats.

Data

Table 1   Pollutants Emitted by Countries That Have Signed the 1979 Convention on Long-Range Transboundary Air Pollution

Country	Sulfur dioxide (1,000 metric tons)		Nitrogen oxides (1,000 metric tons)		Carbon monoxide (1,000 metric tons)	
	1995	2000	1995	2000	1995	2000
Armenia	15.3	13.9	18.2	34.1	83.0	165.3
Austria	212.0	196.0	202.0	211.6	856.8	712.4
Belarus	378.9	223.5	252.5	254.2	958.9	718.2
Belgium	1,799.7	1,279.2	371.4	623.2	1484.2	1,148.8
Bosnia-Herzegovina	109.9	353.0	25.5	110.0	402.6	1,166.9
Bulgaria	1,637.0	1,513.0	195.0	221.6	499.5	625.1
Canada	2,760.5	2,953.9	3,748.5	2,446.6	52,488.0	12,050.5
Croatia	81.6	115.3	76	102	518	597.9
Czech Republic	1,420.2	1,420.2	270.7	328.9	1,178.9	1,061.1
Denmark	173.5	138.6	223	284.1	730.5	400.3
Finland	331.2	294.1	207.6	531	902.1	654.9
France	1,468.4	1,285.6	1,482.7	1,518.4	8,200.8	4,580.4
Germany	3,604.2	2,402.1	2,001.2	2,013	3,214.9	6,032.0
Greece	740.5	814.9	327.8	611.2	1,525.7	985.6
Hungary	995	744.7	222.1	223.8	1,344.7	982.2
Iceland	9.4	9.6	8.5	13.8	43.1	102.2
Ireland	89.9	78.5	122.3	135.3	514.6	351.6
Italy	1,963.3	1,541.9	1,533.1	1,447	7,918.6	4,752.6
Latvia	80.3	25.4	49.6	48.6	200.1	407.3
Lithuania	111.9	89.9	81.5	90.7	487.1	634.8
Macedonia	93.9	74.3	33.6	36.3	248.1	216.5
Moldova	49.8	13.6	55.2	38.6	215.5	224.6
Netherlands	527	994.5	450.3	1,219.3	1,585.5	1,096.8
Norway	420.9	642.6	1,57.9	241.6	1,182	1,642.9
Poland	4,022.7	3,809	1,135.3	1,098.7	5,342.7	3,855.6
Portugal	192.1	202.4	282	284	2013	566.1
Romania	1,050.1	895.9	371.5	343.5	1,395	2,070.3
Russian Federation	9,772.7	9,792.9	5,148.1	5,805.7	18,967.1	27,893.6
Slovakia	469.7	370.9	155.7	152	580.9	486.0
Slovenia	89.8	87.4	62.3	64.4	481.8	360.0
Spain	1,544	2,112.6	1,204.2	2,754.1	4,932.9	2,610.1
Sweden	293.9	335.6	234	288.1	1259.6	715.5
Switzerland	93.7	78.9	124.5	123.3	825.3	649.1
Turkey	1,771.3	2,074.7	784.9	986	4,465.3	3,826.8
Ukraine	2,581.4	1,544.7	2,411.9	1,853.6	16,206.9	13,276.0
United Kingdom	2,953.9	1,621.6	2,220.1	2,054.8	8,604.9	4,400.1
United States	18,142.2	17,866	18,051.2	19,388.4	90,245.5	77,706.7

Source: World Resources Institute, EarthTrends database, available at http://www.wri.org/ (accessed March 12, 2009).

Table 2   Chemicals Widely Distributed in the Environment and Reported to Have Reproductive- and Endocrine-Disrupting Effects

Fungicides	Herbicides	Industrial chemicals	Insecticides	Metals	Nematocides
Benomyl	2,4-D	Dioxin (2,3,7,8-TCDD)	α-HCH	Mercury	Aldicarb
HCB	2,4,5-T		β-HCH	Cadmium	DBCP
Mancozeb	Alachlor	PBBs	Carbaryl	Lead	
Maneb	Amitrole	PCBs	Chlordanes		
Metiram-complex	Atrazine	PCP	Dicofol		
	Metribuzin	Alkylphenols	Dieldrin		
TBT	Nitrofen	Phthalates	DDT + metabolites		
Zineb	Trifluralin	Styrenes	Endosulfan		
Ziram			Heptachlor		
			Methomyl		
			Methoxychlor		
			Mirex		
			Parathion		
			Synthetic pyrethroids		
			Toxaphene		

Source: Joint Group of Experts on the Scientific Aspects of Marine Environment Protection (GESAMP) and the Advisory Committee on Protection of the Sea, *Protecting the Oceans from Land-Based Activities* (Nairobi: United Nations Environment Programme, 2001).

Notes: 2,4,5-T, 2,4,5-trichlorophenoxyacetic acid; 2,4-D, 2,4-dichlorophenoxyacetic acid; 2,3,7,8-TCDD, 2,3,7,8-tetrachlorodibenzo-p-dioxin; DBCP, dibromochloropropane; DDT, dichlorodiphenyltrichloroethane; HCB, hexachlorobenzene; HCH, hexachlorocyclohexane; PBBs, polybrominated biphenyls; PCBs, polychlorinated biphenyls; PCP, pentachlorophenol; TBT, tributyltin.

Table 3   Examples of Introduced (Alien) Species Causing Water Pollution since the 1980s

Species	Origin	Area affected
Comb jellyfish (Ctenophora)		
Mnemiopsis leidyi American comb jellyfish	North America	Black and Azov Seas
Crabs (Decapoda)		
Charybdis helleri Indo-Pacific swimming crab	Mediterranean Sea	Colombia, Cuba, United States, and Venezuela
Dinoflagellates		
Gymnodinium catenatum Chain-forming dinoflagellate	Japan	Australia
Mussels and clams (Bivalvia)		
Ensis americanus American razor clam	North America	Western and northern Europe
Musculista senhousia Japanese mussel	Japan	New Zealand
Dreissena polymorpha Zebra mussel	Black Sea	Eastern North America and the Great Lakes
Polychaete worms (Annelida)		
Marenzilleria viridis Spionid tubeworm	North America	Western and northern Europe
Seastars (Asteroidea)		
Asterias amurensis North Pacific seastar	Japan	Australia

Source: Joint Group of Experts on the Scientific Aspects of Marine Environment Protection (GESAMP) and the Advisory Committee on Protection of the Sea, *Protecting the Oceans from Land-Based Activities* (Nairobi: United Nations Environment Programme, 2001).

Case Study—The River That Runs Red

In 2008, the *International Herald Tribune* reported that a branch of the Yangtze River in China had turned "red and foamy." The provincial authorities did not elaborate on the source of the pollution in the Han River, but tests showed that the polluted waters contained high levels of ammonia, nitrogen, and permanganate, a chemical used in metal cleaning, tanning, and bleaching. Water supplies to as many as 200,000 people were cut, and water was diverted from a nearby lake to dilute the pollution.

The Yangtze is one of the world's greatest rivers, with a catchment area that covers one-fifth of China's land area. Its river basin accounts for 40 percent of China's freshwater resources, more than 70 percent of its rice production, 50 percent of its grain, more than 70 percent of its fishery production, and 40 percent of its GDP. The Yangtze river basin is also important in terms of biodiversity. It is home to a number of endangered species and is the sole habitat of the critically endangered Chinese Paddlefish, the endangered Finless Porpoise, and the (now believed to be extinct) Chinese River Dolphin.

In addition to being one of the world's greatest rivers, the Yangtze is also one of the most polluted. This is largely due to China's rapid large-scale industrial and domestic development and to agricultural runoff. Approximately 42 percent of China's annual sewage discharge and 45 percent of its annual industrial discharge run into the Yangtze. The conversion of the river's floodplains to agriculture has reduced the river basin's ability to detoxify pollutants, with devastating results. Cadmium levels in water used in agricultural irrigation have been found to be 160 times greater than the relevant water standards, and hair tests from affected populations revealed levels of cadmium only slightly lower than the threshold concentration that causes itai-itai disease in humans. Pollution in the Yangtze has been described by local experts as "cancerous."

The pollution has been aggravated by the building of the Three Gorges Dam, the main wall of which was completed in 2006. This dam holds back the flow of the river's water and sediment. The 2007 World Wide Fund for Nature (WWF; formerly the World Wildlife Fund) report, *World's Top Ten Rivers at Risk,* drew attention to the way in which dam construction made the problems of water pollution worse. Highlighting that construction for the dam never included a budget to clean towns of toxic waste before submerging them, the report said, "In Wanxian, Wan County, the Three Gorges Dam submerges part of the sewer system and waste water treatment plant as well as dumpsites along the river. Garbage heaps, boat effluent, pig and animal waste, factories, hospitals, and mines containing hazardous and possibly radioactive waste on the bottom of the reservoir are creating serious pollution."

The WWF is supporting Chinese government steps toward an integrated basin management plan to help stem the threat of pollution in the Yangtze. This will include protecting watersheds and wetlands from deforestation and conversion to other uses. As stated in the WWF report, "Integrated river basin management (IRBM) is vital to enable communities to restore the natural capacity of their watershed to 'treat' pollution." The organization describes IRBM as "a tool communities can use to balance development and conservation needs, such as whether to construct dams or diversions, which severely affect quality of water in a basin."

Case Study—Electronic Waste

The fastest growing type of manufacturing waste in the world is waste from discarded electronic goods, known as e-waste. In 2002, the UNEP estimated that up to 55 million tons (50 million tonnes) of e-waste is generated annually. As technology gets updated and the cost of replacing computers, mobile phones, and other gadgets decreases, more and more of this type of waste must be disposed of.

E-waste is generally shipped to Asia, Eastern Europe, and Africa, where whole communities, including children, may scavenge metals, glass, and plastic from equipment such as old computers. The Basel Action Network estimates that each computer yields about $6 worth of material. Along with this $6 comes significant pollution. For example, the plastic on electrical cords is burned to expose the copper wires. But this burning also releases dioxins and other toxic gases into the air. Other toxic waste from computers includes lead (from cathode ray tubes and solders), cadmium (from circuit boards and semiconductors), and mercury (from switches and housing), which leach into the soil.

A study by the Basel Action Network concluded that a minimum of 100,000 computers per month were entering the Nigerian port of Lagos alone. "If these were good quality, second hand, pieces of equipment this would perhaps be a positive trade of importance for development," said the UNEP's Achim Steiner in his November 11, 2006, speech at the Eighth Conference of the Basel Convention. "But local experts estimate that between a quarter to 75 per cent of these items, including old TVs, [computer central processing units] and phones, are defunct—in other words e-waste."

Parties to the Basel Convention on the Control of Transboundary Movements of Hazardous Wastes and Their Disposal have tightened controls on e-waste, and the European Union has attempted to address the issue through the 2003 Directive on Waste Electrical and Electronic Equipment. Still, the implementation of such controls remains difficult. In some cases, countries dealing with e-waste lack the infrastructure and regulatory and technical capacities necessary to ensure safe disposal. China, for example, has banned the importation of e-waste, although a significant volume still enters the country illegally. In other cases, the exporting countries need to take more responsibility. A 2008 report from the U.S. Government Accounting Office (GAO) found forty-three U.S. companies willing to export nonworking cathode-ray-tube monitors to foreign countries in direct opposition to U.S. regulations. Some of these companies had promoted themselves publicly as environmentally responsible companies, with at least three holding Earth Day electronics recycling events that year. "This GAO report brings us one step closer to developing a national solution for electronic waste," said Representative Mike Thompson (D-Calif.; as reported in the Basel Action Network news, September 17, 2008). "We can't just pretend that when this waste is shipped overseas it's not our problem anymore. We need to treat e-waste as a hazardous material, and create anti-dumping legislation."

Biographical Sketches

Shakeb Afsah is senior policy adviser for the U.S.-Asia Environmental Program. He was one of the architects of the Indonesian PROPER and previously worked as an environmental economist at the World Bank, where he collaborated with national governments on environmental monitoring programs. Afsah has also worked in rainforest conservation and on research projects in a number of developing countries.

Wilfred Beckerman is emeritus fellow of economics, Balliol College, Oxford University and formerly a member of the Royal Commission on Environmental Pollution. He is a leading skeptic of environmentalism, arguing that economic growth and wealth creation are the only credible methods of solving social and environmental problems, especially those facing developing nations.

F. Sherwood Rowland and **Mario Molina** published a groundbreaking scientific paper in *Nature* on June 28, 1974, explaining how CFCs were rapaciously destroying the ozone layer. Rowland is a professor of chemistry at the University of California, Irvine, and Molina, once Rowland's student, is now a professor of chemistry at the Massachusetts Institute of Technology. Their findings were initially greeted with skepticism but later accepted when a hole in the ozone layer was discovered in 1985. Ten years later, they were awarded the 1995 Nobel Prize in Chemistry for their work.

Sandra Steingraber came to prominence in 1997 with the publication of *Living Downstream: An Ecologist Looks at Cancer and the Environment*. Combining a scientific argument that toxins in the environment cause cancer with a poignant and poetic account of her own battles against the disease, Steingraber's book made her the natural successor to Rachel Carson and earned her numerous plaudits. She also served on the Bill Clinton administration's National Action Plan for breast cancer.

David Wheeler is a former lead economist in the Environment Unit of the World Bank Development Research Group. He has spent much of his life researching and formulating policy on pollution control in developing countries and has worked with pollution control agencies in Brazil, China, Colombia, India, Indonesia, Mexico, and the Philippines. He has published widely on environmental and development issues.

Directory

American Lung Association, 61 Broadway 6th Floor, New York, N.Y. 10006. Telephone: (212) 315-8700; email: info@lungusa.org; Web: http://www.lungusa.org.
Organization concerned with issues related to lung disease, including environmental pollution.

Environmental Defense, Environmental Health Program, 257 Park Avenue South, New York, N.Y. 10010. Telephone: (800) 684-3322; email: via Web site; Web: http://www.edf.org/home.cfm.
Environmental organization dedicated to research and policy solutions on a wide range of environmental concerns.

Friends of the Earth USA, 1717 Massachusetts Avenue, Suite 600, Washington, D.C. 20036. Telephone: (877) 843-8687; email: via Web site; Web: http://www.foe.org.
Network devoted to promoting the health and diversity of Earth by championing environmental issues.

National Pollution Prevention Roundtable, 11 Dupont Circle NW, Suite 201, Washington, D.C. 20036. Telephone: (202) 299-9701; email: staff@p2.org; Web: http://www.p2.org.
Forum for discussing pollution prevention by bringing together leading pollution experts.

United Nations Economic Commission for Europe (UNECE), Information Service, Palais des Nations, CH-1211 Geneva 27, Switzerland. Telephone: (41) 229 171 234; email: info.ece@unece.org; Web: http://www.unece.org/env/lrtap.

Agency responsible for administering the 1979 Convention on Long-Range Transboundary Air Pollution.

United Nations Environment Programme (UNEP), Secretariat of the Basel Convention, Geneva Executive Center, 13-15 Chemin des Anemones, CH-1219 Chatelaine, Switzerland. Telephone: (41) 229 178 218; Web: http://www.basel.int.
Agency responsible for administering the Basel Convention, which calls for monitoring the transboundary movement and disposal of hazardous wastes.

U.S. Environmental Protection Agency (EPA), 1200 Pennsylvania Avenue NW, Washington, D.C. 20460. Telephone: (202) 272-0167; email: via Web site; Web: http://www.epa.gov.
U.S. government agency responsible for assessing environmental issues.

World Bank, Environment Program, 1818 H Street NW, Washington, D.C. 20433. Telephone: (202) 473-1000; email: via Web site; Web: http://www.worldbank.org/environment.
International organization aiming to relieve poverty by financing development projects.

World Health Organization (WHO), 20 Avenue Appia, 1211 Geneva 27, Switzerland. Telephone: (41) 22 791 2111; email: info@who.int; Web: http://www.who.int.
UN agency responsible for drawing attention to health problems and promoting health programs around the world.

Further Research

Books

Alloway, B. J., and D. C. Ayres. *Chemical Principles of Environmental Pollution.* London and New York: Blackie/Chapman and Hall, 1997.

Beckerman, Wilfred. *Through Green-Colored Glasses: Environmentalism Reconsidered.* Washington, D.C.: Cato Institute, 1996.

Carson, Rachel. *Silent Spring.* New York: Houghton-Mifflin, 1962.

Farmer, Andrew. *Managing Environmental Pollution.* London and New York: Routledge, 1997.

Gourlay, K. A. *Poisoners of the Seas.* London: Zed Books, 1980.

———. *World of Waste.* London: Zed Books, 1992.

Steingraber, Sandra. *Living Downstream: An Ecologist Looks at Cancer and the Environment.* London: Virago, 1999.

Articles and Reports

"Alien Species Cost US $123 Billion a Year." Environment News Service. January 24, 1999. Available at http://news.bio-medicine.org/biology-news-2/Alien-Species-Cost-U-S—-24123-Billion-A-Year-13585-1.

Borgese, Elisabeth. "The Law of the Sea." *Scientific American* 248 (March 1983): 28–35.

Deere-Jones, Tim. "Back to the Land: The Sea-to-Land Transfer of Radioactive Pollution." *Ecologist* 21 (January–February 1991): 18–23.

Gumbel, Andrew. "Closing Surf City." *E Magazine* (January–February 2000). Available at http://www.emagazine.com/january-february_2000/0100ib_surfcity.html.

Joint Group of Experts on the Scientific Aspects of Marine Environmental Protection (GESAMP). *The State of the Marine Environment.* Oxford and New York: Blackwell, 1990.

Joint Group of Experts on the Scientific Aspects of Marine Environmental Protection (GESAMP) and the Advisory Committee on Protection of the Sea. *Protecting the Oceans from Land-Based Activities.* Nairobi: United Nations Environment Programme, 2001.

Malakoff, David. "Death by Suffocation in the Gulf of Mexico." *Science* 281, no. 5374 (1998): 190–192.

"Mercury Pollution Threatens Siberia and the Arctic Ocean." *Earth Island Journal* 14, no. 1 (1998–1999). Available at https://www.earthislandprojects.org/eijournal/winter99/wn_winter99merc.html.

Ott, Wayne, and John Roberts. "Everyday Exposure to Toxic Pollutants." *Scientific American* 278 (February 1998): 86–91.

Ryan, Heather E. "Sandra Steingraber: Living Downstream and Fighting Back." *E Magazine* (November–December 1999). Available at http://www.emagazine.com/november-december_1999/1199conversations.html.

Scheierling, Susanne M. "Overcoming Agricultural Water Pollution in the European Union." *Finance and Development* 33, no. 3 (September 1996). Available at http://www.worldbank.org/fandd/english/0996/articles/0100996.htm.

United Nations Environment Programme GEO Team. *Global Environment Outlook 2000.* Nairobi: UNEP, 1999.

Wong, C. M., et al. "World's Top Ten Rivers at Risk." WWF International Report, 2007. Available at http://assets.panda.org/downloads/worldstop10riversatriskfinalmarch13.pdf.

World Bank. *Greening Industry: New Roles for Communities, Markets, and Governments.* World Bank Policy Research Report. New York: Oxford University Press, 1999.

Web Sites

UK Rivers Network
http://www.ukrivers.net/pollution.html

United Nations Environment Programme, Global Environment Outlook
http://www.unep.org/geo

U.S. Fish and Wildlife Service, Environmental Contaminants Program
http://contaminants.fws.gov/Issues/EndocrineDisruptors.cfm

World Resources Institute
http://www.wri.org

World Wide Fund for Nature (WWF; formerly the World Wildlife Fund)
http://www.worldwildlife.org

Documents

1. Protecting the Oceans from Land-Based Activities

Joint Group of Experts on the Scientific Aspects of Marine Environmental Protection (GESAMP) and the Advisory Committee on Protection of the Sea, 2001

The full text is available at http://gesamp.imo.org.

Extracts

Executive Summary

Environmental processes are complex in nature. Interactions occur both within the biosphere and the abiotic environment and between them. Consequently, environmental problems are inextricably linked to, or influenced by, one another and do not recognize political boundaries. This is particularly the case for the problems of the marine environment. They cannot be remedied without taking into account the ecological interdependence of the oceans, the coastal areas and the freshwater systems associated with them.

Environmental processes and ecological systems are strongly influenced by social and economic systems and, in turn, influence them. A high proportion of the world's population lives in coastal areas, and many more of its people derive benefit from the use of marine and coastal resources, from employment linked with coastal and maritime activities, and from coastal recreational opportunities. However, population pressure, consumption patterns, and increasing demands for space and resources—combined with poor economic performance and the impoverishment of a large part of the global population—undermine the sustainable use of oceans and coastal areas, and of their resources.

Globally, both the environmental problems of the oceans and coastal areas, and their causes, have remained largely unchanged for several decades. Although some notable successes in addressing problems caused by some forms of marine pollution and in improving the quality of certain coastal areas have occurred, on a global scale marine environmental degradation has continued and in many places even intensified.

Persistent Problems

Marine pollution stemming from land-based sources and activities has previously been of predominant concern. However, improved appreciation of the scale of other forms of damage and threats to the marine and coastal environment has resulted in a more balanced perspective. Today, aside from the impacts expected in the long-term from global climate change, the following are considered to be the most serious problems affecting the quality and uses of the marine and coastal environment:

- alteration and destruction of habitats and ecosystems;
- effects of sewage on human health;
- widespread and increased eutrophication;
- decline of fish stocks and other renewable resources; and
- changes in sediment flows due to hydrological changes.

2. Agenda 21

Declaration on Environment and Development, Rio de Janeiro, June 3–14, 1992

The full text is available at http://www.unep.org.

Extract

Chapter 19 Environmentally Sound Management of Toxic Chemicals including Prevention of Illegal International Traffic in Toxic and Dangerous Products

INTRODUCTION

19.1. A substantial use of chemicals is essential to meet the social and economic goals of the world community and today's best practice demonstrates that they can be used widely in a cost-effective manner and with a high degree of safety. However, a great deal remains to be done to ensure the environmentally sound management of toxic chemicals, within the principles of sustainable development and improved quality of life for humankind. Two of the major problems, particularly in developing countries, are (a) lack of sufficient scientific information for the assessment of risks entailed by the use of a great number of chemicals, and (b) lack of resources for assessment of chemicals for which data are at hand.

19.2. Gross chemical contamination, with grave damage to human health, genetic structures and reproductive outcomes, and the environment, has in recent times been continuing within some of the world's most important industrial areas. Restoration will require major investment and development of new techniques. The long-range effects of pollution, extending even to the fundamental chemical and physical processes of the Earth's atmosphere and climate, are becoming understood only recently and the importance of those effects is becoming recognized only recently as well.

19.3. A considerable number of international bodies are involved in work on chemical safety. In many countries work programmes for the promotion of chemical safety are in place. Such work has international implications, as chemical risks do not respect national boundaries. However, a significant strengthening of both national and international efforts is needed to achieve an environmentally sound management of chemicals.

19.4. Six programme areas are proposed:

(a) Expanding and accelerating international assessment of chemical risks;

(b) Harmonization of classification and labeling of chemicals;

(c) Information exchange on toxic chemicals and chemical risks;

(d) Establishment of risk reduction programmes;

(e) Strengthening of national capabilities and capacities for management of chemicals;

(f) Prevention of illegal international traffic in toxic and dangerous products.

PART IV

Education, Health, and Welfare

AIDS

Ulla Larsen

According to recent estimates by the Joint United Nations Programme on HIV/AIDS (UNAIDS) and the World Health Organization (WHO), in 2007 as many as 2.5 million people became infected with human immunodeficiency virus (HIV), which causes acquired immunodeficiency syndrome (AIDS). More than 25 million people have died of AIDS since the first cases were reported in 1981, and according to UNAIDS and WHO, 33.2 million people were estimated to be living with HIV at the end of 2007.

HIV attacks the immune system and makes those people carrying it susceptible to diseases they would ordinarily ward off. People living with AIDS suffer immensely. AIDS-related deaths leave behind thousands of orphans every year, and the epidemic threatens the economic development of many nations. AIDS is more prevalent in some areas of the world than others, but no one is immune to HIV infection. Without international cooperation to stem rising infection rates and develop a vaccine, AIDS will continue to spread its devastation globally.

Historical Background and Development

The origins of HIV are unclear, although many scientists believe that it originated in Africa. Two theories regarding the source of the epidemic are widely accepted. The first is that HIV has existed for the past one hundred years in small isolated human populations and that it was introduced into the broader population in the 1970s as these isolated communities came into more frequent contact with outsiders. The second theory is that HIV originated in animals and crossed into the human population sometime during the last forty or fifty years, perhaps through contact with animal blood while hunting or slaughtering. The virus is believed to have spread to other continents through infected tourists, migratory workers, and military personnel.

On June 5, 1981, the U.S. Centers for Disease Control and Prevention (CDC) reported the deaths of five young men due to *Pneumocystis carinii* pneumonia,

This chapter is based on the original, written by Tamara Schuyler, that appeared in the first edition of *World at Risk*.

a disease that is rarely fatal. In July 1981, the CDC reported a similarly unusual incident—twenty-six young men had been diagnosed with Kaposi's sarcoma, a cancer normally found among older men. These two groups of men were later assumed to have died of the disease that became known as AIDS. Earlier, in December 1977, a Danish physician who had worked in Zaire died of *Pneumocystis carinii* pneumonia. She is assumed to have been infected with HIV and to have died of AIDS.

In 1982, the newly recognized disease was officially designated AIDS, and the discovery was made that the disease-causing virus could be transmitted through infected blood and blood products, through sexual intercourse, and from mother to child (MTCT). By 1983, health-care officials saw that clearly an AIDS epidemic had erupted in Africa, fueled almost exclusively by heterosexual transmission; by 1984, every region in the world had reported cases of AIDS. Epidemic proportions were not reached in other parts of the world until later in the decade. In the United States, despite an exponentially increasing number of AIDS deaths in the early 1980s, only in 1986, when Surgeon General C. Everett Koop issued a report on the epidemic, did the public became widely aware of it. By the late 1980s, around the globe, the epidemic was raging in high-risk populations—intravenous drug users, men who have sex with men, and commercial sex workers—and was beginning to take hold among other populations.

In January 1983, a team of researchers led by Luc Montagnier of the Pasteur Institute in Paris isolated the virus presumed to be responsible for suppressing the immune system of AIDS patients. They named the virus lymphoadenopathy-associated virus (LAV) because they had isolated it in a patient with lymphoadenopathy, or swollen lymph glands. In 1984, Robert Gallo of the National Cancer Institute in the United States and a team of scientists also isolated a virus associated with AIDS, which they named third human T-cell lymphotropic virus (HTLV III). By 1985, the scientific community had agreed on the name human immunodeficiency virus for the virus that causes AIDS.

AIDS is not a single disease but a condition consisting of a compromised immune system weakened by HIV plus the illnesses and diseases resulting from it. Once inside the body, HIV multiplies and attacks the immune system's T-cells, also known as CD4. The onset of opportunistic illnesses usually takes years. Early in the epidemic, the characteristics of the disease made it difficult to define, and several distinct definitions were adopted through the 1980s. This affected the early surveillance and treatment of patients as well as incidence reporting. In 1993, when the current definition of AIDS was adopted—infection with HIV plus a CD4 count below 200, the presence of one or more opportunistic infections, or both—the reported incidence went up worldwide due to the increased number of people whose condition fit the new definition. The Harvard Global AIDS Policy Coalition estimated in 1992 that the global incidence of the disease had been about 100,000 in 1981 and that by 1992 it had reached 12.9 million. At the end of 2007, authorities estimated that 33.2 million people were living with HIV and 2.5 million of these people were children (see Table 1; map, p. 352). As many as 2.5 million became infected in 2007.

In March 1985, the first test was introduced in the United States for detecting HIV. Infection was confirmed by the presence of HIV antibodies in the blood (antibodies are made by the immune system to help protect the body from foreign invaders, such as viruses). The new test enabled scientists to check frozen blood samples from people who had died prior to 1981 from conditions similar to those of recognized AIDS patients. Researchers also detected antibodies to HIV in blood samples that had been collected in 1959 in Central Africa and in the blood of an American man who had died in 1969. Hospital records also indicated a possible AIDS death in the United States in 1952 and one in 1959 based on symptoms of the disease.

Two major events in the history of AIDS occurred in 1987. The first was the formation of numerous organizations to address the accelerating epidemic: the WHO Special Programme on AIDS (later the Global Programme on AIDS), the International Council of AIDS Service Organizations, and the Global Network of People Living with AIDS. The second event was the approval by the U.S. Food and Drug Administration of the first drug for combating AIDS, Zidovudine (AZT). Two years later, doctors and scientists reported that strains of HIV had become resistant to AZT.

By the late 1980s, it was clear that the AIDS epidemic in Africa was unprecedented in its rate of spread; it was also evident that its effects were likely going to be worse than anticipated earlier in terms of people's health and well-being and in terms of economics. As AIDS cases continued to climb everywhere, observers recognized that the epidemic had become a global crisis (see Table 3). Strategies for education, prevention, care, treatment, and counseling were initiated in many regions of the world, but most developing nations—where the epidemic hit the hardest—did not have the resources to implement far-reaching policies. However, some success had been achieved. The AVERT Web site reported, for instance, that the prevalence of HIV declined in Uganda from 1992 to 2000 and stabilized in 2001–2005. Although a slight increase in HIV from 2006 has occurred, Uganda has made progress. Also, other developing countries have shown signs of a decline in the incidence of HIV since the mid 2000s; however, whether this is the beginning of a long-term trend is uncertain.

In 1994, AZT was first used in the United States to reduce the risk of transmission of HIV from mother to infant. Triple antiretroviral drug therapy, which keeps HIV in check, was approved in 1996 in the United States. In the late 1990s and early 2000s, drug efficacy improved, as reflected by increased tolerability of the drugs, decreased drug regiment complexity, and longer survival of HIV-infected individuals following the drug regiments. However, the drugs were so expensive that they were effectively unavailable to most people in developing nations and even to some people in developed countries as well. The prohibitive cost led activists around the world to begin demanding that pharmaceutical companies lower the cost of the drugs in poor countries. In 1997, South Africa altered its patent laws to allow the importation and manufacture of generic forms of patented drugs. This move started an ongoing battle between leading pharmaceutical companies, which sought to prevent the copying of their patented products, and the governments of some developing nations (as well as activists), which sought to provide affordable treatment to their AIDS-ravaged populations. The UN General Assembly in the 2006 Political Declaration called on all nations to work toward universal access to HIV prevention, treatment, care, and drug supply by 2010. Even if drugs were made easily available to poor countries, in many cases their health-care systems would not be capable of effectively distributing them.

Current Status

No cure or vaccination for AIDS exists. The HIV virus can be present in the blood, semen, vaginal secretions, and breast milk of an infected person and can therefore be transmitted through sexual contact, through direct contact with blood (for example, through blood transfusions or pricks from needles containing contaminated blood or the reuse or sharing of needles), and through childbirth and breast-feeding. Drug regimens are available that fight the effects of HIV and prolong the lives of HIV-positive people for years, but as already noted, the drugs are expensive and consequently available primarily to people in developed countries. Highly active antiretroviral therapy (HAART) is provided at no cost to selected populations in developing countries by agencies, such as the United Nations Development Programme (UNDP). Many people believe that the only hope for a global solution to the AIDS pandemic is a vaccine against HIV. Numerous researchers are currently working to develop one.

Research

Four main avenues of research related to the global AIDS epidemic are currently being pursued: vaccines and other therapeutic forms of prevention; drug treatment; reduction of MTCT; and sociological studies related to behavioral prevention of the disease, care of the victims and survivors, and the economic impact of the epidemic. A variety of groups are involved in this research: national and international government-sponsored research institutions, private research agencies, and nonprofit organizations.

The effort to develop a vaccine against HIV is guided by the International AIDS Vaccine Initiative (IAVI), a nonprofit scientific organization. IAVI testified on June 25, 2005, at the U.S. Senate Foreign Relations Committee hearing on AIDS vaccines. Seth Berkley, IAVI president and chief executive officer, called for expanded AIDS treatment in countries hardest hit by the disease: "The focus on the short-term emergency is critical, but without better tools we will not be able to end this terrible epidemic. And that must be our goal: to have an effective long-term strategy, including an AIDS vaccine."

One of the challenges faced by scientists working toward a vaccine is the absence of an appropriate animal model on which to experiment. Since HIV does not affect animals in the same way that it affects humans, most of the work has to be done on humans, which raises difficult ethical questions, such as whether experimenting on people without knowing the potential risks is justified. Another challenge is the existence of various strains of HIV, so scientists are fairly certain that a vaccine that is effective against the predominant strain in one region of the world will not necessarily be effective in other regions. Another difficulty is that scientists do not know what type of vaccine is most likely to be successful. A vaccine that would completely prevent infection is the most desirable option, but less desirable possibilities include vaccines for people who are already infected, such as vaccines that reduce the chance of transmission or that stop or delay progression of the disease. The latter type of vaccine might turn out to be more easily and quickly developed. Scientists and health-care officials are conflicted about how best to distribute research resources among the various vaccine-development ideas.

Even if an effective vaccine is developed, delivering it will be difficult. In addition to the challenges related to the enormous cost of manufacture and delivery, other potential roadblocks exist, such as deciding whom to target for vaccination first and how to reach high-risk groups. In 2008, about twenty HIV vaccines were in phase I, II, or III trials. Global HIV Vaccine Enterprise executive director Alan Bernstein summarized vaccine-related activities at the XVII International AIDS Conference and reiterated the need for a comprehensive prevention strategy that includes a safe and effective vaccine.

Another important area of research involves microbicides, substances that can be applied to the body in the form of a cream or gel to prevent infections. In the case of HIV, researchers hope to develop a microbicide that can be applied vaginally to help prevent infection with HIV and other sexually transmitted microorganisms. Some microbicides being studied have blocked HIV infection in the laboratory, and others have prevented disease-causing organisms from sticking to the outer layer of the reproductive tract (thus preventing infection). A large number of microbicides have been tested on animals, have been proven safe, and are currently being tested on humans. Microbicides have been hailed as a potential HIV-prevention breakthrough because they might offer a way for women to protect themselves against infection. Many women in developing countries—where, according to UNAIDS, 95 percent of new HIV infections occur—are not in control of decisions concerning abstinence, monogamy, and condom use. For these women, microbicides might offer a method of protection against HIV infection.

Numerous research universities and other institutions are researching more effective drug treatments and drug combinations to combat HIV. The treatment that is currently accepted as the most effective, called HAART, involves taking daily doses of a combination of drugs. The precise combination differs from patient to patient, depending on which drugs he or she has taken in the past and which have proven effective. The drugs work by inhibiting the ability of HIV to attack the immune system. This combination therapy has been shown to be effective at all stages of infection. Some people, however, cannot tolerate the side effects of HAART, such as redistributed body fat, increased cholesterol, and altered metabolisms. Other people show no benefit, for reasons that are not yet understood.

The AVERT Web site reported that in 2007 over 350,000 children under age fifteen became infected with HIV, mainly through MTCT. About 90 percent of these MTCT infections occurred in Africa, where AIDS is beginning to reverse decades of steady progress in child survival. MTCT can occur before, during, or after birth. Research has shown that the risk of MTCT can be significantly reduced by improved postpartum care, HIV testing and counseling, antiretroviral drug treatment, and avoidance of breast-feeding. A meta-analysis of clinical trials conducted in 1999–2007 in sub-Saharan Africa concluded that antiviral drugs are efficacious in decreasing MTCT and well tolerated.

Sociological investigations related to HIV/AIDS span a broad range of topics. The disease affects individuals, families, communities, and entire countries in various manners and with varying urgencies. Numerous organizations have researched the most promising responses that groups and governments can undertake in the face of the AIDS crisis. One major finding across a range of studies concerns the substantial material needs of people infected with HIV and their families and communities. Recommended responses to these needs include providing resources for children orphaned by AIDS, providing economic relief to families and communities affected by AIDS, increasing access to health-care services, and increasing literacy and educational access (thus increasing potential access to more lucrative employment). Research has also revealed the need for improved and increased counseling services within communities affected by HIV.

Policies and Programs

International efforts to combat HIV/AIDS are focused on implementing expanded prevention, care, and counseling services, increasing drug availability, gathering more extensive surveillance data, collecting nationally representative survey data, and researching vaccines and other biomedical vehicles to fight the disease.

The illnesses and deaths caused by AIDS threaten the gains in socioeconomic development made by third-world nations over the past few decades, especially nations in sub-Saharan Africa. Authorities have recorded negative trends in mortality rates, life expectancy, literacy, poverty levels, gross national product (GNP), and gender inequity. HIV/AIDS has also increased the incidence of other infectious disease, such as tuberculosis, which places a double burden on already fragile health-care systems (see HEALTH). Increasingly, policies are addressing the developmental burden that HIV/AIDS places on national economies and ultimately on the global economy. The UNDP provides guidance and development services to developing countries to combat the harmful effects of HIV/AIDS on their economies. This policy has resulted in practical gains that can be seen, for example, in UNDP-supported studies and surveys as well as its financial support for providing HAART. Ajay Mahal and colleagues reported in their 2008 article, "Assessing the Economic Impact of HIV/AIDS on Nigerian Households: A Propensity Score Matching Approach," in the journal *AIDS*, that private health-care costs and income lost per HIV-positive person were approximately 56 percent of the annual income per capita in affected households. The largest single cost, representing 54 percent of the total economic burden of HIV, was for out-of-pocket expenses for health care.

In 2001, UN secretary-general Kofi Annan began a campaign to mobilize a worldwide political commitment to fighting HIV/AIDS. Annan set forth five priorities: preventing the further spread of HIV/AIDS; reducing transmission of HIV from mother to child; providing care and treatment to all; pursuing scientific breakthroughs; and protecting those people made most vulnerable by the disease's impact, such as orphans. Annan also identified the factors crucial for meeting these goals: leadership and commitment, particularly from national officials; engagement of local communities; empowerment of women; strengthening of public health-care systems; and commitment of more money. The need for more money led Annan to propose the formation of a Global Fund to fight HIV/AIDS, tuberculosis, and malaria. He called on all sectors—governments, nongovernmental organizations, corporations, foundations, and the United Nations—to rise to the challenges posed by HIV/AIDS. As of 2008, the Global Fund has committed US$11.3 billion in 136 countries to support aggressive interventions against all three diseases.

Annan's mobilization campaign culminated in a UN General Assembly Special Session on HIV/AIDS held in 2001. At this meeting, all nations were encouraged to work on defeating the epidemic. The session resulted in the adoption of a formal Declaration of Commitment on HIV/AIDS by the heads of participating governments (see Document 1). In 2008, a UN General Assembly convened to review progress achieved in realizing the previous declarations (see Document 2).

The 2008 meeting resulted in a number of recommendations. Noting that many parts of the world will not have universal access to HIV prevention, treatment, care, and support by 2010, the meeting recommended that efforts be redoubled to expedite progress. Also, UNAIDS should strengthen its technical support to help facilitate essential HIV services, which should be integrated with other health services. Countries should promote gender equity and women's empowerment, and donors should recognize such efforts. The lack of monetary resources was recognized, and donor countries were urged to devote 0.7 percent of their gross domestic product (GDP) for development assistance. The epidemic is multigenerational and the ability to sustain efforts was s concern. Also, further mobilization of leadership was called for to ensure that the recent momentum is maintained.

Regional Summaries

Every country has citizens and residents living with HIV/AIDS, but the face of the epidemic varies from region to region. Its variables include the primary mode of transmission, the availability of drug treatments and care, and the effects on the community and economy.

North America

The AIDS epidemic in North America has thus far taken its largest toll on gay and bisexual men, African Americans, and intravenous drug users. The disease spread rapidly through these populations in the 1980s, leading their communities to initiate prevention strategies, including safe-sex education and

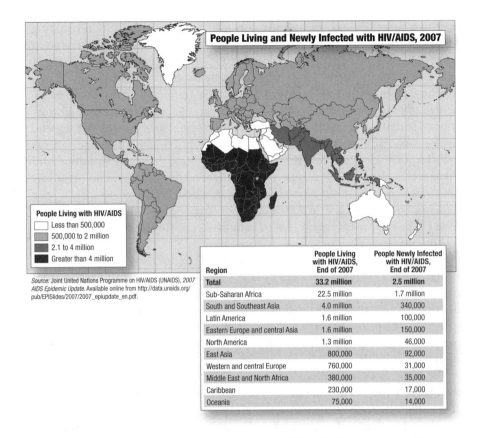

People Living and Newly Infected with HIV/AIDS, 2007

People Living with HIV/AIDS
- Less than 500,000
- 500,000 to 2 million
- 2.1 to 4 million
- Greater than 4 million

Source: Joint United Nations Programme on HIV/AIDS (UNAIDS), *2007 AIDS Epidemic Update.* Available online from http://data.unaids.org/pub/EPISlides/2007/2007_epiupdate_en.pdf.

Region	People Living with HIV/AIDS, End of 2007	People Newly Infected with HIV/AIDS, End of 2007
Total	**33.2 million**	**2.5 million**
Sub-Saharan Africa	22.5 million	1.7 million
South and Southeast Asia	4.0 million	340,000
Latin America	1.6 million	100,000
Eastern Europe and central Asia	1.6 million	150,000
North America	1.3 million	46,000
East Asia	800,000	92,000
Western and central Europe	760,000	31,000
Middle East and North Africa	380,000	35,000
Caribbean	230,000	17,000
Oceania	75,000	14,000

needle-exchange programs. In some areas of North America, notably those with large numbers of gay men, such as New York and San Francisco, high-profile education campaigns had been launched by the mid-1980s. The reported level of unprotected sex among gay men fell during the decade, and although the number of HIV-infected members of this population rose during that time, health officials estimated that the infection rate would have been much worse without concerted prevention efforts. The number of gay and bisexual men in the United States with HIV leveled off in the early 1990s, rose in the late 1990s, and has been rather stable in the 2000s. In 2006, reports from the CDC confirmed that the impact of HIV was greatest among gay and bisexual men of all races. Men who had sex with men accounted for 53 percent of those with new HIV infections (28,700) in 2006.

Prevention strategies targeting intravenous drug users, such as needle-exchange programs and nonintravenous alternative drug maintenance, are expensive and controversial, and their implementation has been difficult for supporters to maintain. Education in prevention is less successful among drug users than among the general population because users are difficult to locate and educate openly and because most addicts have difficulty simply stopping taking drugs. HIV infection rates among intravenous drug users in the United States have risen steadily since the beginning of the epidemic, and in 2006 as many as 12 percent (6,600) of new HIV infections occurred in this population.

AIDS drugs are very accessible in the United States. Consequently, AIDS patients there tend to live longer and remain healthier than those in other parts of the world, for example, sub-Saharan Africa. A stall in the effectiveness of prevention efforts in the late 1990s was thought to be mainly due to the success of medical breakthroughs. With new treatments, AIDS patients were not dying as quickly or in the same numbers as they had been at the beginning of the epidemic, thus reducing fears among people in high-risk groups about contracting the disease.

The CDC estimated an incidence of 56,300 HIV infections in the United States in 2006. This number increased from the previously reported incidence of 40,000 cases. However, the CDC deemed that the HIV incidence had been roughly stable since the late 1990s and that the higher number was largely due to a new laboratory technique and a national surveillance system. Heterosexuals accounted for 31 percent (16,800) of all new HIV infections in 2006. According to the UNAIDS "Epidemic Update, December 2007," women constituted more than one-quarter of all new HIV-positive diagnoses in 2005; among these women, intravenous drug use and heterosexual intercourse were the primary modes of transmission. Further, this report noted that the African American population has been hit disproportionately hard—blacks constituted 48 percent of AIDS cases, but made up only 13 percent of the population in 2005.

In Canada, the number of HIV-positive tests increased from 2000 to 2006 following a steady decline after 1995. Women accounted for one-quarter of the adult HIV diagnoses since 2000. This proportion is more than double the percentage (12 percent) in 1985–1997. Simultaneously, the number of people diagnosed with AIDS declined yearly since 1983. Again, the percentage of women has risen; women accounted for 7 percent of AIDS cases reported in 1979–1994, but in 2005, that proportion was 23 percent. The proportion of white people with AIDS declined from 91 percent in 1988 to 62 percent in 2005. Over the same period, steep increases in the percentages of aboriginals and black people with the disease were observed.

Latin America

In Latin America, the AIDS epidemic varies greatly from country to country. The Caribbean, where the majority of HIV transmissions are heterosexual, is the second most heavily affected area of the world (after sub-Saharan Africa), with an estimated prevalence of 1.1 percent. According to the AVERT Web site, in 2007 about 20,000 people were newly HIV infected and an estimated 230,000 people were living with HIV and AIDS in the Caribbean. The number of people living with HIV/AIDS was 120,000 in Haiti, 62,000 in the Dominican Republic, and 27,000 in Jamaica, or 2.2, 1.1, and 1.6 percent, respectively, of adults ages fifteen to forty-nine. In 2006, access to antiretroviral therapy was provided to everybody in need in Cuba; similarly, the Bahamas and Barbados were able to reach almost everybody in need. However, in Trinidad and Tobago, the supply of the drug covered less than half of the demand, and the supply was even lower in Haiti and the Dominican Republic. It is believed that the Caribbean epidemic is fueled by the fact that people there typically begin sexual activity at relatively younger ages and frequently change sexual partners. Coupled with the poverty in much of the region, these facts make the HIV epidemic difficult to manage there.

In Central and South America, the HIV epidemic is generally stable, although it is most prevalent in the countries bordering the Caribbean and in Brazil. HIV transmission occurs especially in high-risk populations, such as men who have sex with men and intravenous drug users. In 2007, UNAIDS/WHO estimated that 1.7 million people lived with HIV in Latin America compared to 1.4 million in 2001. With few countries reporting these statistics, the prevalence of HIV peaked in the capital cities of Bolivia and Guyana in 2007 and 2006 among men who have sex with men at 21.5 and 21.3 percent, respectively. The prevalence in the capital cities of Paraguay and Argentina was 9.1 (in 2006) and 6.7 percent (in 2007), respectively.

Brazil faces a growing AIDS epidemic among heterosexuals in addition to already experiencing high rates of infection among men who have sex with men and intravenous drug users. In 2007, about 0.6 percent of people ages fifteen to forty-nine are estimated to live with HIV, and the prevalence has been stable the last ten years. Further, among fifteen- to twenty-four-year-olds, the prevalence was 1.0 percent among men and 0.6 percent among women. The Brazilian government mandates that antiretroviral drug treatment be provided to all people with HIV; the estimated antiretroviral therapy coverage was 80 percent in 2007. The government has also funded significant education and prevention efforts, which probably were largely responsible for the adoption of safer sex practices by young people. The estimated number of deaths from AIDS declined during the late 1990s and early 2000s. However, the number of AIDS deaths has increased since 2004; from 9,400 in 2001, it increased to 15,000 in 2007.

Europe and the Former Soviet Union

The pictures of HIV/AIDS in Europe and in the countries of the former Soviet Union are very different. Many AIDS patients in Europe, as in North America, have access to and use antiretroviral drugs, and many countries launched education, prevention, and surveillance programs early in the epidemic. EuroHIV (a WHO and UNAIDS collaborating center) was formed in 1984 to collect, analyze, and distribute information on the size, location, and nature of the epidemic in participating countries. The fifty-three countries of the WHO European Region report data to EuroHIV that are then used to guide prevention and treatment policies.

As of December 2006, according to the AVERT Web site, Europe had 327,068 reported AIDS diagnoses, and the former Soviet states had the largest number of new HIV infections in the European region. At the end of 2007, the prevalence of HIV varied from 1 percent in parts of the former Soviet Union to less than 0.1 percent in parts of central Europe. For example, in Slovenia in 2007, thirty-six HIV diagnoses were reported and the rate of HIV infections was 17.8 per million. HIV infections through heterosexual contact have increased throughout the region, and women account for a rising number of infections. In Western Europe, more than half the new infections are probably acquired through heterosexual contact, one-third through men having sex with men, and the rest through intravenous drug use. Women accounted for 35 percent of all new infections. The incidence of HIV has grown, and the total for 2006 was deemed twice as high as in 1999. Central Europe has been relatively spared from the HIV epidemic, with adult prevalence rates around 0.1 percent or less. However, this region has the largest proportion of pediatric AIDS cases. HIV/AIDS is probably underreported in Eastern Europe. The number of HIV/AIDS cases has gone up—the incidence increased from 1,781 in 2002 to 6,208 in 2006.

North Africa and the Middle East

Data about HIV/AIDS remain limited in this region. Using the available data, UNAIDS and WHO estimated that in 2007 35,000 people acquired HIV, HIV prevalence was 380,000, and 25,000 people died from AIDS-related illnesses. HIV infection is highest in urban areas and among men. Throughout the region, unprotected paid sex is an important factor in the epidemic. Further, intravenous drug use plays a role in some countries, such as Iran, Libya, and Tunisia.

Sub-Saharan Africa

The countries of sub-Saharan Africa have suffered the most from the global AIDS epidemic. According to the UNAIDS and WHO "07 AIDS Epidemic Update," in 2007 1.7 million people in the region became infected with HIV, 22.5 million people were living with HIV/AIDS by the year's end, and the adult prevalence was 5.0 percent; in 2001, 2.2 million people became infected with HIV, 20.9 million people were living with HIV/AIDS, and the adult prevalence was 5.8 percent. Thus, the incidence of HIV declined in sub-Saharan Africa during the 2000s, but the number of people who died due to AIDS increased from 1.4 million in 2001 to 1.6 million in 2007.

More than three-quarters of AIDS deaths globally in 2007 occurred in sub-Saharan Africa. The AIDS epidemic presents countries south of the Sahara with enormous challenges. In addition to the loss of life, perhaps the most important concern is the long-range effect on their economies. Many countries of the region face a tremendous loss of economic viability, along with correlative damage to the social infrastructure and safety nets as the epidemic ravages vast portions of their populations. The prevalence of HIV varies substantially from region to region and from country to country, but women have suffered from more HIV infections than men. UNAIDS and WHO estimated, based on population-based surveys, that in 2007 more than one-quarter of the population in Botswana and Swaziland was infected with HIV, while less than 1 percent was HIV-positive in Senegal and Niger.

In 2007, southern Africa accounted for almost one-third of new HIV infections globally, with the national adult HIV prevalence exceeding 15 percent in eight countries (Botswana, Lesotho, Mozambique, Namibia, South Africa, Swaziland, Zambia, and Zimbabwe). However, the epidemic has declined slightly in some areas, and it appears to have plateaued in numerous countries. In Zimbabwe, UNAIDS and WHO reported, based on population-based surveys, an HIV prevalence trend of 33.7, 24.6, and 20.1 percent in 2001, 2003, and 2005, respectively. The decline—which occurred mainly in urban areas—is largely explained by both men and women having fewer sexual partners and the deaths of some people who were HIV-positive.

In East Africa, where the epidemic has always been less severe than in southern Africa, evidence also exists of a slight decline in HIV. In 2007, about 7 percent were HIV-positive in Kenya, Tanzania, and Uganda, and the percentage was lower in many countries. Changes in the behavior and the deaths of some people who were HIV-positive are considered the main factors leading to lower levels of HIV prevalence. In West and Central Africa, adult HIV prevalence has remained stable, and signs of a slight decline in selected areas have been reported. In fact, the prevalence rate is below 2 percent in numerous West African countries, while it was about 6 percent in Cameroon and the Central African Republic. Unprotected paid sex is an important factor in the transmission of HIV, especially in West Africa, but inadequate HIV surveillance and population-based data hamper accurate assessments.

At least three issues are in need of immediate and ongoing attention in sub-Saharan Africa. First, large populations of HIV-infected patients and their families need better access to health care and financial support. Second, the rate of new infections needs to be stemmed further, by undertaking additional large-scale prevention education. Third, more mechanisms must be provided to help communities cope with the effects of AIDS deaths, including an increasing number of orphans and other survivors and the damage to economic development.

Because the antiretroviral drugs that can prolong the lives of AIDS patients are too expensive for most Africans, the increase in HIV/AIDS is likely to continue for several years. Efforts by some drug companies to give countries discounts have not made the drugs affordable to the majority of African AIDS sufferers. The provision of free drugs to everybody in need by the UNDP is eagerly awaited in this region.

The HIV/AIDS epidemic in sub-Saharan Africa is so acute that it affects every level of society. Households have to cope financially and emotionally with the sickness and death of family members. Communities and surviving family members, who are often poor, are faced with the responsibility of caring for the thousands of children orphaned by AIDS every year, and national economies are becoming burdened by the toll that HIV/AIDS takes on business and on economic and social development. Policies to address these problems are beginning to take shape as the epidemic places increasing pressures on already strained economic and social infrastructures.

Asia and the Pacific

In Asia and the Pacific, the prevalence of HIV varies widely across countries, with the highest prevalence in Southeast Asia. Overall in Asia in 2007, according to the UNAIDS/WHO "07 AIDS Epidemic Update," the estimated prevalence was 4.9 million, the incidence of new infection was 440,000, and about 300,000 died from AIDS-related illnesses.

The "07 AIDS Epidemic Update" also reports that studies concerning China have found a HIV prevalence, among men who have sex with men, of 1.5 percent in Shanghai, 1.7 percent in the south, and 3.1–4.6 percent in Beijing. The overlap in populations that engage in intravenous drug use and sex work is an important factor in China. Almost half of people living with HIV are thought to have been infected through drug use and a similar proportion to have been infected during unprotected sex.

In India in 2006, the prevalence of HIV was about 2.5 million. An improved surveillance system and better methodology led to downward revisions of previous estimates. The prevalence of HIV varies substantially among states and regions in India. The majority of HIV-positive people in India live in the south. Based on a 2007 national population-based survey, the prevalence of HIV was 0.07 percent in Uttar Pradesh, 0.34 percent in Tamil Nadu, 0.62 percent in Maharashtra, 0.69 percent in Karnataka, 0.97 percent in Andhra Pradesh, and 1.13 percent in Manipur. In all other states taken together, the prevalence was 0.13 percent.

In 2005, in Cambodia, Myanmar, and Thailand, the countries with the highest prevalence of HIV in the region, the prevalence of HIV declined. In Thailand, the pattern of HIV transmission changed over time, with HIV transmission increasingly happening in people once considered at low risk, such as young people. During the same time, HIV rates ranged from 30 to 50 percent among drug users and high rates of HIV prevailed among men who have sex with men.

The Pacific region has relatively low levels of HIV/AIDS. In 2007, the prevalence was 0.4 percent, up from 0.2 percent in 2001. In Australia, the number of people living with HIV increased from 14,000 in 2001 to 18,000 in 2007, and in New Zealand, the number increased from 1,200 in 2001 to 1,400. These numbers are a minor fraction of the numbers of HIV-positive people in sub-Saharan Africa or Latin America. Nevertheless, some evidence exists that rates of infection are on the rise in Australia and New Zealand, where unsafe sex and intravenous drug use are the primary causes of the upsurge.

Data

Table 1   Snapshot of AIDS Worldwide, 2007

	Adults	Children under 15 years
AIDS deaths	1,700,000	330,000
Number of people living with HIV	30,800,000	2,500,000
Women	15,400,000	
Number of people newly infected with HIV	2,100,000	420,000

Source: Joint United Nations Programme on HIV/AIDS and World Health Organization, "07 AIDS Epidemic Update, December 2007," UNAIDS and WHO, Geneva, 2007.

Notes: AIDS, acquired immunodeficiency syndrome; HIV, human immunodeficiency virus.

Table 2   Regional HIV/AIDS Statistics and Features, 2007

Region	Start of epidemic	Main modes of transmission for adults	People living with HIV/AIDS	People newly infected with HIV	Adult prevalence rate (%)[a]	Deaths due to AIDS
Sub-Saharan Africa	Late 1970s–early 1980s	H	22,500,000	1,700,000	5.00	1,600,000
North Africa and the Middle East	Early 1980s	H, IDU	380,000	35,000	0.30	25,000
South and Southeast Asia	Early 1980s	H, IDU	4,000,000	340,000	0.30	270,000
East Asia	Early 1980s	IDU, H, MSM	800,000	92,000	0.10	32,000
Oceania	Early 1980s	IDU, H, MSM	75,000	14,000	0.40	1,200
Latin America	Late 1970s–early 1980s	MSM, H, IDU	1,600,000	100,000	0.50	58,000
Caribbean	Late 1970s–early 1980s	H, MSM	230,000	17,000	1.00	11,000
Eastern Europe and central Asia	Early 1980s	IDU	1,600,000	150,000	0.90	55,000
Western and central Europe	Late 1970s–early 1980s	IDU, MSM	760,000	31,000	0.30	12,000
North America	Late 1970s–early 1980s	H, IDU, MSM	1,300,000	46,000	0.60	21,000
World			33,200,000	2,500,000	0.80	2,100,000

Source: Joint United Nations Programme on HIV/AIDS and World Health Organization, "07 AIDS Epidemic Update, December 2007" UNAIDS and WHO, Geneva, 2007.

Notes: AIDS, acquired immunodeficiency syndrome; H, heterosexual transmission; HIV, human immunodeficiency virus; IDU, transmission through injection-drug use; MSM, sexual transmission among men who have sex with men.

[a]Proportion of adults (15–49 years of age) living with HIV/AIDS in 2007, using 2007 population numbers.

Table 3 Estimated Adults and Children Living with HIV/AIDS and Female and Male HIV Prevalence Rates for Selected Countries, 2007

Country	Adults living with HIV/AIDS[a]	Children living with HIV/AIDS[b]	Prevalence among young females (%)[c]		Prevalence among young males (%)[c]	
			Low	High	Low	High
Algeria	21,000	n/a	< 0.1	0.2	< 0.1	0.3
Argentina	120,000	n/a	0.2	0.4	0.3	0.9
Australia	18,000	n/a	< 0.1	0.1	0.1	0.4
Brazil	710,000	n/a	0.3	0.9	0.6	1.5
Canada	73,000	n/a	0.1	0.4	0.2	0.7
China	690,000	n/a	< 0.1	0.2	< 0.1	0.2
DRC	730,000	6,600	1.3	3.3	0.03	1.1
Egypt	9,000	n/a	n/a	< 0.1	n/a	< 0.1
France	140,000	n/a	0.1	0.5	0.2	0.8
Georgia	2700	n/a	< 0.1	0.2	< 0.1	0.4
Germany	52,000	n/a	< 0.1	0.2	< 0.1	0.2
Guatemala	53,000	n/a	0.6	2.4	n/a	< 0.1
India	2,300,000	n/a	< 0.1	0.5	< 0.1	< 0.5
Indonesia	270,000	n/a	< 0.1	0.2	0.01	0.5
Israel	4,900	n/a	< 0.1	0.02	n/a	0.1
Japan	9,600	n/a	n/a	< 0.1	n/a	< 0.1
Russian Federation	940,000	5,200	0.3	1.0	0.6	2.3
Saudi Arabia	n/a	n/a	n/a	n/a	n/a	n/a
Spain	140,000	n/a	< 0.1	0.4	0.2	1.1
Sweden	6,200	n/a	< 0.1	0.2	< 0.1	0.2
Switzerland	25,000	n/a	0.2	1.0	0.1	0.9
Tajikistan	10,000	< 100	< 0.1	0.4	0.2	1.2
Thailand	600,000	14,000	0.4	2.0	0.5	2.1
Turkey	n/a	n/a	n/a	n/a	n/a	n/a
Uganda	810,000	130,000	2.7	5.2	0.6	1.9
United Kingdom	77,000	n/a	< 0.1	0.3	0.1	0.6
United States	1,100,000	n/a	0.1	0.6	0.3	1.3

Source: Joint United Nations Programme on HIV/AIDS and World Health Organization, "2008 Report on the Global AIDS Epidemic," available at http://data.unaids.org/pub/GlobalReport/2008/jc1510_2008_global_report_pp211_234_en.pdf.

Notes: AIDS, acquired immunodeficiency syndrome; DRC, Democratic Republic of Congo; HIV, human immunodeficiency virus; n/a, not available.

[a]Ages 15 plus.

[b]Ages 0–14.

[c]Ages 15–24.

Case Study—HIV/AIDS in Uganda

Uganda is representative of sub-Saharan African countries in that a large number of its people are HIV-positive. In the 2000s, over 5 percent of Ugandans were living with HIV/AIDS. Uganda, however, is unique in having successfully reduced HIV infection rates throughout the 1990s. Uganda's policies serve as a model for countries prepared to aggressively address the AIDS epidemic within their borders.

Uganda was among the first countries to experience an alarming spread of HIV during the early 1980s, and in the late 1980s it had one of the highest rates of infection in the world. Around 1990, the Ugandan government organized an AIDS prevention campaign involving governmental institutions and nongovernmental organizations. Officials invited leaders from traditional, religious, and educational communities to raise the awareness of the threat of AIDS and to carry out prevention initiatives. As in the rest of Africa, the primary mode of HIV transmission in Uganda is (and has always been) unprotected sexual intercourse between men and women. Therefore, programs to reduce infection rates focused largely on educating people about safer sexual behavior, such as delaying the onset of sexual activity, having fewer sexual partners, and using condoms (the ABC approach: abstinence, be faithful, and condoms). Information was disseminated via newspapers, radio, posters, and theater. Counselors were trained to help families who were living with HIV/AIDS, and HIV-testing services became more widely available.

The numbers suggest that these policies were crucial factors in reducing the incidence of HIV/AIDS in Uganda during the 1990s. In addition, the national blood supply of Uganda has been screened for HIV since the late 1980s. Because Uganda's AIDS epidemic has been among the most systematically documented in Africa, statistics are readily available. For instance, in 1989 and 1995, Ugandan government officials carried out surveys in the large cities of Kampala and Jinja, asking people to report anonymously on various aspects of their sexual behavior. According to a 1997 report of the survey's results in "Change in Sexual Behaviour and Decline in HIV Infection among Young Pregnant Women in Urban Uganda," published in *AIDS,* Godwil Asiimwe-Okiror and a team of analysts found that, during the six-year period covered, among people ages fifteen to twenty-four, a two-year delay in the start of sexual activity had evolved and that the frequency of men indulging in casual sex dropped by 9 percent. In addition, officials reported that men used condoms 40 percent more often in 1995 than in 1989 and that women experienced the use of condoms 30 percent more often.

The Ugandan government's prevention initiatives continued throughout the 1990s with high levels of funding from both the government and international donors, such as the World Bank. The prevalence of HIV infection fell from an estimated peak of around 15 percent in 1991 to around 5 percent in 2001. The decline in HIV is attributed to a decline in the incidence of new HIV infections and to the deaths of many people infected with HIV during the 1990s. (Individuals infected with HIV in Africa are estimated to live nine to ten years after infection, a trend enforced by the unavailability of antiretroviral drugs).

The prevalence of HIV stabilized during the early 2000s at 5–7 percent, although anecdotal indications show an increase in HIV prevalence and incidence the last few years. The Uganda HIV and AIDS Sero-Behavioural Survey, 2004–2005, a nationally representative, population-based survey, found a HIV prevalence of 6.4 percent for people ages fifteen to forty-nine. HIV rates increased gradually from ages fifteen to nineteen to ages thirty to thirty-four and declined at older ages. As many as 7.5 percent of women and 5.0 percent of men had HIV, and the HIV rates were 10.1 and 5.7 percent in urban and rural areas, respectively. The prevalence of HIV varied significantly by marital status. Almost one-third of widowed men and women had HIV, compared to 6 percent among individuals in a union. Finally, as many as 20.7 percent of all children in Uganda were orphans and vulnerable children, almost 15 percent of children had lost one or both parents, and 3 percent had lost both (many of these adults had died from AIDS).

Other problems typical of underdeveloped sub-Saharan countries—including women's limited access to contraception and low funding for health services and education—exacerbate the AIDS-related problems these countries face. In addition, poverty, illiteracy, and poor overall health are rampant, particularly among women. The U.S. Census Bureau estimated that in 2005 the life expectancy in sub-Saharan Africa was 50.9 and 54.0 without AIDS and 44.7 and 45.7 with AIDS for men and women, respectively. The increase in mortality and decline in life expectancy from HIV/AIDS have caused psychological and social stress as well as economic strain. Based on economic modeling of HIV/AIDS in Uganda, Wolfgang Hladik and colleagues in their 2008 article, "The Estimated Burden of HIV/AIDS in Uganda, 2005–2010," published in *AIDS,* concluded that more effective prevention programs are needed. Traditional herbal medicines are widely used, but their effectiveness is not well known and interactions between antiretroviral drugs and traditional herbal medicines need to be further examined.

In addition, labor shortages have left agricultural land uncultivated, and land still in use is being employed increasingly for subsistence crops rather than cash crops. The economic injuries that AIDS has inflicted on Uganda exemplify the effects of AIDS on all sub-Saharan African countries with a high incidence of the disease.

In Uganda, antiretroviral drugs have been available for free since 2004, and some researchers think that the availability of drugs has resulted in complacency or "treatment optimism." Furthermore, starting in the early 2000s, Uganda has gradually changed its prevention policy from the ABC approach to abstinence-only programs, and comprehensive sex education and condom promotion programs are no longer widespread. To provide direction on HIV policies, a national response was developed in 2007. It aimed at reducing the incidence of HIV by 40 percent by 2012; improving the quality of life of people with HIV by mitigating the health effects of HIV; reducing the social, cultural, and economic effects of HIV at individual, household, and community levels; and expanding services. Several campaigns have focused on awareness and on the behavior gaps and have addressed behavior change. The Global Fund, UNAIDS, other UN agencies, the Clinton Foundation, and the World Bank, among others, have given funds to combat the AIDS epidemic in Uganda.

Biographical Sketches

Françoise Barre-Sinoussi received the 2008 Nobel Prize together with Luc Montagnier and Harald zur Hausen. Today, Barre-Sinoussi is the director of the Regulation of Retroviral Infections Unit at the Pasteur Institute in Paris. Her work is focused on retroviruses. She has initiated multiple collaborations with developing countries, and she has furthered the areas of prevention, clinical care, and treatment.

Harley Henriques do Nascimento is an influential AIDS activist working to prevent the spread of AIDS in low-income areas of Brazil. In the late 1980s, do Nascimento founded the Grupo de Apoio à Prevenção á AIDS (GAPA-Bahia; Support Group for the Prevention of AIDS in Bahia), a nonprofit organization that works with community volunteers to provide AIDS prevention and caregiving services, public policy guidance, and education programs aimed at reducing human rights violations and discrimination against people with HIV. Do Nascimento's work has served as a model for volunteer recruitment strategies, and he has received humanitarian awards for his role in jump-starting Brazil's response to the AIDS epidemic.

Robert Gallo is the director of the Institute of Human Virology and professor of medicine, microbiology, and immunology at the School of Medicine, University of Maryland, Baltimore. Gallo, a pioneer in the study of human retroviruses, is credited with much of the science that made the discovery of the HIV virus—and its role in causing AIDS—possible. Gallo also led the team that developed the first HIV antibody test, which was approved in 1985, and performed crucial research that led to the development of drugs to fight HIV and treat AIDS.

David Ho is scientific director and chief executive director of the Aaron Diamond AIDS Research Center in New York and professor and physician at Rockefeller University. Working on the front lines of HIV/AIDS research, Ho was instrumental in the development of the life-saving triple antiretroviral drug therapy, called the AIDS cocktail, introduced in the United States in 1996. Currently, Ho is pursuing multiple vaccine strategies.

Luc Montagnier received the Nobel Prize for Medicine in 2008, together with Françoise Barre-Sinoussi, for isolating and describing the virus that was later called HIV (along with Harald zur Hausen for his work on cervical cancer). In 1983, at the time of this discovery, Luc Montagnier worked at the Pasteur Institute in Paris. In the subsequent years, a public dispute emerged between Montagnier and Robert Gallo over the discovery of HIV, with each claiming that the other had misused viral samples, but eventually they agreed to share credit. However, in 1991, further studies documented that Montagnier was indeed the main person behind the discovery. In 2002, they co-wrote a paper in *Science,* in which they acknowledged the pivotal roles that each had played in the discovery of HIV. In 1993, Montagnier co-founded the World Foundation for AIDS Research and Prevention in Paris, a global network of HIV/

AIDS research institutions. Today, he is its director and his work focuses on the design of an HIV vaccine and making drug treatments available to AIDS sufferers who do not have sufficient funds to purchase them.

Peter Piot was executive director of the UNAIDS up to the end of 2008, and he is undersecretary-general of the United Nations. Before creating UNAIDS in 1995, Piot worked as a scientific researcher and professor at various institutes in Africa, Europe, and the United States. Piot's research has focused on AIDS and on women's health in the developing world. He is credited as a co-discoverer of the Ebola virus.

Directory

European Centre for the Epidemiological Monitoring of AIDS (EuroHIV), National Electronic Library of Infection, City eHealth Research Centre, City University Northampton Square, London EC1V0HB. Telephone: 44(0) 207 040 8391; email: contact@neil.org.uk; Web: http://www.eurohiv.org.
Organization performing HIV/AIDS surveillance in Europe.

Family Health International, HIV/AIDS Department, P.O. Bo 13950, Research Triangle Park, N.C. 27709; 2101 Wilson Boulevard, Suite 700, Arlington, Va. 22201. Telephone: (919) 544-7040; email: services@fhi.org; Web: http://www.fhi.org.
Organization aimed at providing health prevention and care services globally.

Global Network of People Living with HIV/AIDS (GNP+), P.O. Box 11726, 1001 GS Amsterdam, Netherlands. Telephone: (31) 20 423 4114; email: infognp@gnpplus.net; Web: http://www.gnpplus.net.
Organization working to improve the quality of life of people living with HIV/AIDS.

International AIDS Society-USA, 425 California Street, Suite 1450, San Francisco, Calif. 94104-2120. Telephone: (415) 544-9400; email: info2009@iasusa.org; Web: http://www.iasusa.org/contact/index.html.
Professional society of scientists and health-care workers engaged in HIV/AIDS prevention, control, and care.

International AIDS Vaccine Initiative, 110 William Street, Floor 27, New York, N.Y. 10038-3901. Telephone: (212) 847-1111; email: info@iavi.org; Web: http://www.iavi.org.
Organization working to speed the development and distribution of AIDS vaccines.

International Council of AIDS Service Organizations, 65 Wellesley Street East, Suit 403, Toronto, Ontario M4Y 1G7, Canada. Telephone: (416) 921-0018; email: icaso@icaso.org; Web: http://www.icaso.org.
Organization mobilizing and supporting diverse organizations to build an effective response to HIV and AIDS.

Joint United Nations Programme on HIV/AIDS (UNAIDS), 20 Avenue Appia, 1211 Geneva 27, Switzerland. Telephone: (41) 22 791 3666; email: unaids@unaids.org; Web: http://www.unaids.org.
Agency advocating worldwide action against HIV/AIDS.

National AIDS Trust, New City Cloisters, 196 Old Street, London EC1V 9FR, United Kingdom. Telephone: (44) 020 7814 6767; email: info@nat.org.uk; Web: http://www.nat.org.uk.
Organization promoting HIV/AIDS education, prevention, and patient treatment and care; focusing on early diagnosis, equity of care, and eradication of any HIV-related stigma.

U.S. Centers for Disease Control and Prevention (CDC), 1600 Clifton Road, Atlanta, Ga. 30333. Telephone: (800) 232-4636; email: go to http://www.cdc.gov/netinfo.htm; Web: http://www.cdc.gov.
U.S. government agency for protecting public health and safety.

World Health Organization (WHO), 20 Avenue Appia, CH-1211 Geneva 27, Switzerland. Telephone: (41) 22 791 2111; email: info@who.int; Web: http://www.who.int.
UN agency advocating health for all people.

Further Research

Books

Alexander, Ivy L., ed. *AIDS sourcebook.* 4th ed. Detroit, Mich.: Omnigraphics, 2008.

Aloo, Jeniffer. *HIV & AIDS: My Story, Rejected but Not Forsaken.* Nairobi: Uzima, 2007.

Bauer, Henry H. *The Origin, Persistence and Failings of HIV/AIDS Theory.* Jefferson, N.C.: McFarland & Co., 2007.

Chalmers, James. *Legal Responses to HIV and AIDS.* Portland, Ore.: Hart, 2008.

Gorgens-Albino, Marelize, et al., eds. *The Africa Multi-Country AIDS Program, 2000–2006: Results of the World Bank's Response to a Development Crisis.* Washington, D.C.: World Bank, 2007.

Finkel, Madelon Lubin. *Truth, Lies, and Public Health: How We Are Affected When Science and Politics Collide.* Westport, Conn.: Praeger, 2007.

International Labour Office. *HIV/AIDS and the World of Work.* 1st ed. Paris: International Labour Office, 2008.

Landowe, Janet V., ed. *Health Care Spending: Upward Bound.* New York: Nova Science Publishers, 2008.

Mukudi, Edith, Stephen Commins, and Azeb Tadesse, eds. *HIV/AIDS in Africa: Challenges and Impact.* Trenton, N.J.: Africa World Press, 2008.

Seckinelgin, Hakan. *International Politics of HIV/Aids: Global Disease—Local Pain.* New York: Routledge, 2008.

Seeger, Matthew W., Timothy L. Sellnow, and Robert L. Ulmer, eds. *Crisis Communication and the Public Health.* Cresskill, N.J.: Hampton Press, 2008.

Wallace, Robert B., and Neal Kothatsu, eds. *Maxcy-Rosenau-Last Public Health and Preventive Medicine.* 15th ed. New York: McGraw-Hill Medical, 2008.

Articles and Reports

Beegle, Kathleen, Joachim De Weerdt, and Stefan Dercon. "The Intergenerational Impact of the African Orphans Crisis: A Cohort Study from an HIV/AIDS Affected Area." *International Journal of Epidemiology* 38, no. 2 (2009): 561–568.

Carrel, Margaret, and Stuart Rennie. "Demographic and Health Surveillance: Longitudinal Ethical Considerations." *Bulletin of the World Health Organization* 86, no. 8 (2008): 612–616.

Elliott, Julian H., et al. "Rational Use of Antiretroviral Therapy in Low-Income and Middle-Income Countries: Optimizing Regimen Sequencing and Switching." *AIDS* 22, no. 16 (2008): 2053–2067.

Elliott, Richard, et al. "Harm Reduction, HIV/AIDS, and the Human Rights Challenge to Global Drug Control Policy [Review]." *Health Human Rights* 8, no. 2 (2005): 104–138.

Gonzalez, Adam, et al. "Size Matters: Community Size, HIV Stigma, and Gender Differences." *AIDS and Behavior,* September 25, 2008. [Epub ahead of print.]

Heymann, S. Jody, Shelley Clark, and Timothy F. Brewer. "Moving from Preventing HIV/AIDS in Its Infancy to Preventing Family Illness and Death (PFID)." *International Journal of Infectious Diseases* 12, no. 2 (2008): 117–119.

Joint United Nations Programme on HIV/AIDS (UNAIDS). "07 AIDS Epidemic Update." 2007. Available at http://www.unaids.org/en/KnowledgeCentre/HIV Data/EpiUpdate/EpiUpdArchive/2007/default.asp.

———. "08 AIDS Epidemic Update." 2008. Available at http://www.unaids.org/en/ KnowledgeCentre/HIVData/default.asp.

———. "The Global Coalition on Women and AIDS." Web site. http://womenandaids .unaids.org.

Mahajan, Anish P., et al. "Stigma in the HIV/AIDS Epidemic: A Review of the Literature and Recommendations for the Way Forward [Review]." *AIDS* 22, Suppl. 2 (2008): S67–S79.

Mahal, Ajay, et al. "Assessing the Economic Impact of HIV/AIDS on Nigerian Households: A Propensity Score Matching Approach." *AIDS* 22, Suppl. 1 (2008): S95–S101.

Maplanka, Charlotte. "AIDS: Is There an Answer to the Global Pandemic?: The Immune System in HIV Infection and Control [Review]." *Viral Immunology* 20, no. 3 (2007): 331–342.

Merson, Michael H., et al. "The History and Challenge of HIV Prevention." *Lancet* 372, no. 9637 (2008): 475–488.

Moss, Kellie. "International HIV/AIDS, Tuberculosis, and Malaria: Key Changes to U.S. Programs and Funding. Foreign Affairs, Defense, and Trade Division." Congressional Research Service, 2008. Available at http://assets.opencrs.com/rpts/RL 34569_20080714.pdf.

Reid, Alasdair, et al. "Towards Universal Access to HIV Prevention, Treatment, Care, and Support: The Role of Tuberculosis/HIV Collaboration [Review]." *Lancet Infectious Diseases* 6, no. 8 (2006): 483–495.

Salomon, Joshua A., and Daniel R. Hogan. "Evaluating the Impact of Antiretroviral Therapy on HIV Transmission." *AIDS* 22, Suppl. 1 (2008): S149–S159.

Shannon, Kate, et al. "Reconsidering the Impact of Conflict on HIV Infection among Women in the Era of Antiretroviral Treatment Scale-Up in Sub-Saharan Africa: A Gender Lens." *AIDS* 22, no. 14 (2008): 1705–1707.

Szekeres, Greg. "The Next 5 Years of Global HIV/AIDS Policy: Critical Gaps and Strategies for Effective Responses." *AIDS* 22, Suppl. 2 (2008): S9–S17.

United Nations Development Fund for Women (UNIFEM). Web Portal: Gender and HIV/AIDS. http://www.genderandaids.org.

United Nations Development Programme (UNDP). "Human Development Report 2007/2008." Available at http://hdr.undp.org/en/media/HDR_20072008_EN_ Complete.pdf.

Walker, Bruce D., and Dennis R. Burton. "Toward an AIDS Vaccine [Review]." *Science* 320, no. 5877 (2008): 760–764.

White, Richard G., et al. "Male Circumcision for HIV Prevention in Sub-Saharan Africa: Who, What and When?" *AIDS* 22, no. 14 (2008): 1841–1850.

Web Sites

ACT UP: AIDS Coalition to Unleash Power
http://www.actupny.org

AIDS in Africa
http://www.aidsandafrica.com

AIDS Prevention and Vaccine Research Site (*Science*)
http://AIDScience.com

AIDS Vaccine Advocacy Coalition
http://www.avac.org

allAfrica.com
http://allafrica.com

AVERT: AVERTing HIV and AIDS (AVERT is an international HIV and AIDS charity aimed at combating HIV/AIDS)
http://www.avert.org/worldstats.htm

Family Health International
http://www.fhi.org/en/HIVAIDS/index.html

HIV/AIDS Fact Sheets, Centers for Disease Control and Prevention
http://www.cdc.gov/hiv/pubs/facts.htm

HIV InSite
http://hivinsite.ucsf.edu/InSite

International AIDS Economic Network
http://www.iaen.org

International AIDS Vaccine Initiative (IAVI)
http://www.iavi.org

JAMA HIV/AIDS Information Center (*Journal of the American Medical Association*)
http://www.medicalonline.com.au/medical/professional/aids/hivhome.htm

Population Council, Research That Makes a Difference
http://www.popcouncil.org/hivaids

UNAIDS Uniting the World against AIDS
http://search.unaids.org/Results.aspx?q=hiv%2Faids&x=0&y=0&o=html&d=en&1=en&s=false

UN General Assembly Special Session on HIV/AIDS
http://www.ua2010.org/en/UNGASS

World Health Organization
http://www.who.int/topics/hiv_aids/en/index.html

Documents

1. Declaration of Commitment on HIV/AIDS: Global Crisis-Global Action

Joint United Nations Programme on HIV/AIDS, Special Session on HIV/AIDS, New York, 2001

The full text is available at http://www.un.org/ga/aids/coverage/FinalDeclarationHIVAIDS.html.

Extracts

1. We, Heads of State and Government and Representatives of States and Governments, assembled at the United Nations, from 25 to 27 June 2001, for the twenty-sixth special session of the General Assembly convened in accordance with resolution 55/13, as a matter of urgency, to review and address the problem of HIV/AIDS in all its aspects as well as to secure a global commitment to enhancing coordination and intensification of national, regional and international efforts to combat it in a comprehensive manner;

2. Deeply concerned that the global HIV/AIDS epidemic, through its devastating scale and impact, constitutes a global emergency and one of the most formidable challenges to human life and dignity, as well as to the effective enjoyment of human rights, which undermines social and economic development throughout the world and affects all levels of society—national, community, family and individual;

3. Noting with profound concern, that by the end of the year 2000, 36.1 million people worldwide were living with HIV/AIDS, 90 percent in developing countries and 75 percent in sub-Saharan Africa;

4. Noting with grave concern that all people, rich and poor, without distinction of age, gender or race are affected by the HIV/AIDS epidemic, further noting that people in developing countries are the most affected and that women, young adults and children, in particular girls, are the most vulnerable;

5. Concerned also that the continuing spread of HIV/AIDS will constitute a serious obstacle to the realization of the global development goals we adopted at the Millennium Summit; . . .

36. Solemnly declare our commitment to address the HIV/AIDS crisis by taking action as follows, taking into account the diverse situations and circumstances in different regions and countries throughout the world;

Leadership

Strong leadership at all levels of society is essential for the effective response to the epidemic

Leadership by Governments in combating HIV/AIDS is essential and their efforts should be complemented by the full and active participation of civil society, the business community and the private sector

Leadership involves personal commitment and concrete actions

2. Statement from the Joint United Nations Programme on HIV/AIDS, Special Session on HIV/AIDS, New York, 2008

From the 2008 high-level meeting on the comprehensive review of the progress achieved in realizing the Declaration of Commitment on HIV/AIDS and the Political Declaration on HIV/AIDS

The full text is available at http://data.unaids.org/pub/BaseDocument/2008/20080703_pgasummary_a62895_en.pdf.

Extracts

1. The 2008 high-level meeting on HIV/AIDS was convened to review progress achieved in realizing the 2001 Declaration of Commitment on HIV/AIDS and the 2006 Political Declaration on HIV/AIDS (General Assembly resolution 60/262, annex). Millennium Development Goal 6 commits the world to halt and reverse the global AIDS epidemic by 2015. Building on the time-bound targets established in the 2001 Declaration of Commitment on HIV/AIDS (General Assembly resolution S-26/2), the 2006 Political Declaration called on all countries to work towards universal access to HIV prevention, treatment, care and support by 2010.

Review of progress and challenges

11. The Executive Director of UNAIDS, Peter Piot, noted that despite recent progress in almost every region, at the current pace, we will not achieve universal access in most low- and middle-income countries by 2010. AIDS is the leading cause of death in Africa and the seventh highest cause of mortality worldwide. He noted that unless efforts to prevent new HIV infections are strengthened, treatment queues will lengthen, dooming efforts to achieve universal access to antiretroviral therapy. Dr. Piot said that the AIDS response must move to a new phase, which involves both an immediate response and the development of a longer-term strategy.

In particular, he cautioned against complacency resulting from recent successes in the response to the epidemic. In addition to strengthened HIV prevention, he said that key steps are needed with respect to treatment, including strengthening health systems, improving the affordability of medications, investing in new drugs for the future, and integrating HIV prevention and treatment in tuberculosis, maternal and child health, and sexual and reproductive health programmes. He stressed that long-term success in the AIDS response requires improved HIV prevention for young people, effective action to address gender inequality and other human rights violations, and substantial increases in funding.

Towards universal access

43. *Accelerating progress towards universal access.* The push towards universal access to HIV prevention, treatment, care and support by 2010 represents an important step on the road to achievement of the Millennium Development Goals by 2015. Although some countries reported having achieved some of their universal targets, most have indicated that they do not have the human and financial resources to achieve these targets by 2010. Efforts should be redoubled to expedite progress in moving towards universal access and should recognize civil society as an essential partner in this regard. UNAIDS should continue monitoring progress of national AIDS responses.

HEALTH

David E. Bloom,
David Canning, and Jennifer O'Brien

The 1978 Alma-Ata Declaration, signed by representatives of the International Conference on Primary Health Care, defined *health* as "a state of complete physical, mental, and social well-being, and not merely the absence of disease or infirmity." The signatories aimed to achieve world health for all by the year 2000. Despite significant improvements since the declaration, massive disparities are apparent between the health status of people who live in rich countries and those who live in poor countries. In the latter, public health-care systems may be inadequate and underfunded, and private health care may be absent or unaffordable. In addition, some members of society tend to be more vulnerable to disease than others: the poor, those living in isolated rural areas, the elderly, infants and children, and women. Poor health, in turn, affects a country's economic development by, for instance, reducing the productivity of its workforce. Yet, in terms of health-care costs, prevention of disease is cheaper than providing a cure. The increased attention given by many countries to solving health problems is a response to the recognition of the wide-ranging effects of poor health.

Historical Background and Development

Babylonian King Hammurabi's code of laws, written nearly 4,000 years ago, provides one of the earliest known cases of state intervention in health. Echoes of its sliding scale of physicians' fees, in which payment is determined by how much the patient can afford, can be found in many modern national health systems. Its code of conduct for physicians presages today's strict regulation of the medical profession. Recognition of the importance of health to society since Hammurabi's time has been erratic, however. Although the Romans built hospitals for their soldiers and slaves and introduced public sanitation measures, states did not make consistent efforts to improve the health of their people until much later.

In the middle ages, people's lives were dominated by the fear of illness and death. The practice of medicine, such as it was, relied heavily on the ancient studies of Galen, Avicenna, and Hippocrates, whose *Airs, Waters and Places,* published in 400 BC, was the first known work to discuss the impact of environmental factors on disease. More than 1,000 years later, physicians still had made no progress in combating the myriad epidemics that killed vast swaths of population at increasingly frequent intervals. Such treatments as bloodletting had no positive impact on a patient's well-being beyond the psychological effect of having been treated. Trust in the medical profession was low, and people often turned instead to other forms of healing. Traveling vendors toured fourteenth-century England selling "wonder cures" to unsuspecting patients. Religious sects looked after the sick with faith healing, and many patients took matters into their own hands, ordering their physicians to bleed them despite the physician's advice to the contrary. Sickness was widely regarded as a message from God. Preachers persuaded their congregations that illness and early death were punishments from above or warnings to people to mend their evil ways. A wayward lifestyle, many thought, would inevitably lead to some degree of physical discomfort—if not as a divine punishment then as a result of evil spirits or witches' spells.

Although the low standing of doctors forced most people to take individual responsibility for their own health, efforts were emerging in some parts of the world to provide for those who could not look after themselves. By the eleventh century, all major Muslim towns had hospitals, which were set up to care for the poor and travelers. Christian hospitals and almshouses also began to have an impact on health care. Asian children had been inoculated against smallpox for many centuries before the practice became common in Europe in the eighteenth century and before vaccination became an important tool of public health.

The Black Death—the plague that wiped out perhaps one-fourth of the population of Europe from the fourteenth to the sixteenth centuries—provided the first major impetus for states to become involved in protecting health. In the fifteenth century, Italian doctors implemented a system to quarantine the plague; York, England, and other cities were closed off to prevent the plague from entering. Hospitals were built not only to look after the poor but also to cordon off those with the plague from the rest of society. Hospitals also enabled physicians to better observe the symptoms of the disease and to track its progress. This greater knowledge eventually enabled more systematic responses to disease to evolve, which had the collateral effect of raising physicians' standing with their patients.

The Industrial Revolution provided the next great impetus to widespread health improvements. Mass labor was essential to the efficient functioning of industry, and as workers fell ill or became the victims of industrial accidents, their employers came to a greater realization of the benefits of a healthy populace. Many employers took steps to improve workers' health via workplace medical insurance schemes or donations to hospital charities. Simultaneously, as increased wealth and productivity gave people more leisure time, their attentions turned to "luxuries," such as health. Demand for health care therefore grew.

The 1848 Public Health Act in England, which created a General Board of Health to deal with public health problems, was the natural result of the increasing importance given to health. The expansion of medical knowledge that was propelled by these major societal changes made possible Louis Pasteur's late-nineteenth-century discovery that germs were responsible for infectious disease. The Germ Theory (as it was called) facilitated other major breakthroughs, such as the discovery of the tubercle bacillus, the bacterium responsible for tuberculosis, and, in 1928, the discovery of penicillin. These developments meant that medicine could break from the methods of the ancients and focus on destroying the microorganisms that caused people to die. Physicians, who now possessed great stores of knowledge, were looked on with a new respect. Public health administration, whose initial rumblings had facilitated the dramatic advances of science, now had a solid base from which to attack infectious disease.

In "The Untilled Field of Public Health," a 1920 article published in *Modern Medicine,* Charles-Edward A. Winslow, one of the founders of modern public health in the United States, defined *public health* as "the science and art of preventing disease" and promoting health through community efforts and organization. The development of social machinery, he added, should "enable every citizen to realize his birthright of health and longevity." Public health, which is grounded not just in medicine but also in a variety of sciences ranging from epidemiology (the study of disease in populations) to economics, encompasses a wide range of efforts directed toward protecting the health of entire populations. It also aims to link health to government and public policy, viewing health not in isolation but as part of a broad effort to improve quality of life.

Systems such as Britain's National Health Service, established in 1948 to provide free health care to all who need it, and the World Health Organization (WHO), set up in 1946 by the United Nations, were the culmination of the progress achieved in health provision. The WHO's successful global effort to eradicate smallpox in 1979 is the clearest evidence yet of the potential of public health systems.

Current Status

Although the world as a whole has seen significant health improvements, the situation varies dramatically from country to country and region to region. Some areas have even seen a decline in overall health status.

Research

Researchers look at changes in populations' health status using a number of indicators. One common indicator of overall health is life expectancy (how long a child born in a particular year is likely to live). For example, based on the UN "World Population Prospects 2006," between 1975 and 2005 life expectancy rose in 178 of the 195 countries for which data are available. A child born in Japan in 2008 can look forward to 82.6 years of life; this contrasts dramatically with the nineteen countries where children can expect less than 50 years of life and with Swaziland, where life expectancy is less than 40 years (see map, p. 377). Other indicators of a population's health status are the mortality rates (the proportion of a population that dies in a given time period), morbidity rates (the proportion of a population that is ill in a given time period), proportions of children vaccinated, and expenditures on health (see Tables 1 and 2). According to a 2006 World Bank report, *Health Financing Revisited,* global spending on health has risen, accounting for approximately 10 percent of the world's gross domestic product (GDP) in 2002—but, again, this figure hides large disparities between countries and regions.

Some countries that had seen previous improvements in their health status are now experiencing declines. For example, according to the UN "World Population Prospects 2006," life expectancies in some of the republics of the former Soviet Union have been declining since the 1960s. In another example, human immunodeficiency virus (HIV)/acquired immunodeficiency syndrome (AIDS) is having a devastating social and economic effect in many sub-Saharan African countries (see AIDS). In South Africa alone, life expectancy has returned to its 1960 level. Instances such as these are drawing increased attention to public health measures. After a period of neglect, governments are refocusing attention on other infectious diseases, such as tuberculosis, which is staging a comeback in many parts of the industrial world.

According to research on the global burden of disease, two types of disease account for a majority of all deaths globally: chronic diseases (conditions that can render people disabled or in pain for years) and "lifestyle" diseases (conditions that arise as countries become wealthier, for example, when people switch from their previous healthier diets to a diet higher in fat) (see Table 3). Accidents and violence are also claiming more lives. By 2020, traffic accidents, suicide, violence, and war could rival infectious disease as sources of premature mortality worldwide.

The Alma-Ata Declaration provides three justifications for devoting resources to health—health is a basic human right, it is a vital social goal, and it is an essential ingredient for developing strong economies (see Document 1). Improved health leads to social and economic development, improves people's quality of life, and creates conditions that are more conducive to world peace. By declaring health to be a fundamental human right, the declaration asserts that people are entitled to a certain quality of life; that is, they are entitled to be well, not just to have access to remedies when they are sick. Governments, working as appropriate with the world community, are primarily responsible for fulfilling this entitlement. By signing a declaration that declares health to be a fundamental human right, governments implicitly recognize that health, like security, freedom of speech, and freedom of thought, is something that the state owes its citizens.

Despite the failure of the Alma-Ata Declaration to meet its goal of health for all by 2000, this rights-based approach to health has several practical implications. First, it emphasizes the need for ongoing global action on health because human rights can be enforced only in the presence of a global framework (see TRANSNATIONAL GOVERNANCE). As Gro Harlem Brundtland, former director-general (1998–2003) of the WHO, suggested in the "World Health Report, 1999," the main reason for the failure of the Alma-Ata Declaration to meet its goal of health for all by 2000 was the lack of global leadership and advocacy. Second, a rights-based approach underscores the need for democracies that can be held responsible for safeguarding their people's rights. According to Amartya Sen's *Development as Freedom,* political freedoms are essential for ensuring that people can protect their quality of life, while large-scale systematic abuse of human rights invariably results in social breakdowns and "new wars." Third, the rights-based approach underscores the importance of empowerment at the grassroots level. For instance, the rapid spread of HIV/AIDS in many societies has been caused, in part, by young women's lack of control over sexual relations. Attempts to curb the spread of HIV/AIDS must therefore include a focus on extending women's rights and enforcing those rights.

In line with the Alma-Ata Declaration viewing improved health as a vital, worldwide, social goal, recent research has looked at the social determinants of health. In 2005, the WHO assembled a Commission on the Social Determinants of Health. Its findings confirmed that levels of health are related to people's social environment as well as to how rich or poor the society is in which they live. For example, in sub-Saharan Africa, roughly 85 percent of the workforce lives on $2 or less per day; this is four times the percentage of people in the Middle East who live on $2 or less per day. Although social and economic inequality can affect health through such factors as lack of access to opportunities, lack of control, feelings of hopelessness, and chronic stress, the reverse is also true. Poor health contributes to these social factors, creating a situation in which people become trapped in a cycle of social exclusion.

Sen, in *Development as Freedom,* stressed, however, that a country does not have to be rich for its population to be healthy and that economic development alone is not sufficient for people's health status to improve. Although richer countries do tend to have healthier populations, the correlation is not automatic; instead, it depends on such factors as how the society deploys its resources and how much control citizens have over their lives. In addition, sectors unrelated to health care contribute to improvements in health, including agriculture, education, and communications.

The social implications of health may also affect international relations. As noted, researchers have observed a link between health and political stability and also between health and war. Wars not only kill soldiers and civilians, but they also destroy infrastructure and social structures, which can lead to outbreaks of disease. Again, the reverse may also be true—the prevalence of disease and poor health can lead to conflict and war. Combatants in many modern conflicts are drawn from the socially excluded. Poor health and nutrition, according to a 2008 study by Per Pinstrup-Andersen and Satoru Shimokawa, may have a greater role in inducing armed conflict than GDP per capita and GDP growth.

Research increasingly supports the Alma-Ata Declaration's assertion that a healthy population is a cornerstone of a strong and growing economy. The traditional view that wealth leads to health is complementary to, and does not contradict, this new research because health and wealth can be mutually reinforcing. Although a broad correlation between per capita GDP and life expectancy exists, researchers have been unable to fully demonstrate a causal link (in either direction) between wealth and health. For example, research conducted by David Bloom and David Canning in 2000 shows that little evidence supports a hypothesis that periods of rapid health improvement follow periods of high income growth. According to the WHO's "World Health Report, 1999," other factors, such as access to health-care technology, are more important than income growth for improving health outcomes. In the same vein, Arjumand Siddiqi and Clyde Hertzman argued in a 2007 article comparing Canada and the United States that greater economic prosperity and health-care spending do not necessarily lead to better health outcomes. Regarding a potential causal link from health to wealth, Bloom and Canning contended that countries with educated healthy populations are better positioned to prosper economically, but convincing causal inferences are difficult to make.

In the end, of course, research alone is insufficient for improving global health. The results of research must be applied. After all, the development of new antibiotics and vaccines against infectious diseases cannot be considered a major success if people in poor countries cannot afford to buy them, and investigation into how new or emerging diseases spread is not helpful if people are unaware of the actions they can take to protect themselves. Investing in research is one thing, but deploying that knowledge to create change is what counts.

Policies and Programs

The remarkable health gains of the early twentieth century resulted in some complacency toward disease in the late twentieth century. Many assumed that diseases such as tuberculosis would continue retreating as health standards steadily increased, but that assumption has been shaken. The fact that health outcomes are declining for many people has become a political issue and has alarmed policymakers. In 2000, the United Nations Security Council debated the impact of AIDS on peace and security in Africa; this was the first time in fifty years that a health issue had been considered a security issue. Later that year, the G-8 (a group of eight of the major industrialized nations) pledged to cut deaths from tuberculosis by 50 percent by 2010 and the number of young people contracting HIV by 25 percent. The final declaration of the UN Millennium Summit committed heads of state and governments to reducing maternal mortality by 75 percent; lowering mortality among children under five by 67 percent; and reversing the spread of AIDS, malaria, and other major diseases by 2015.

Programs to control malaria, a disease that, according to WHO's "World Health Report, 2002," kills at least 1 million people per year, are not new, but the most recent programmatic efforts for its containment include a collaborative approach that unites the resources and expertise of the United Nations International Children's Emergency Fund (UNICEF), the United Nations Development Programme (UNDP), the WHO, the World Bank, and a multitude of local and international partners. The WHO's Roll Back Malaria program is two-pronged, attempting to control malaria and improve health services. According to a 1998 WHO press release, the goals of the program are to:

> strengthen health systems to ensure better delivery of health care, especially at the district and community levels; ensure the proper and expanded use of insecticide-treated mosquito nets; ensure adequate access to basic healthcare and training of healthcare workers; encourage the development of simpler and more effective means of administering medicines, such as training of village health workers, mothers and drug peddlers on early and appropriate treatment of malaria, especially for children; encourage the development of more effective and new anti-malaria drugs and vaccines.

Another major programmatic effort—primary health care—began with Alma-Ata. The primary health-care approach, the focus of WHO's "World Health Report, 2008," includes a core set of services, as spelled out in paragraph 3 of the declaration:

> education concerning prevailing health problems and the methods of preventing and controlling them; promotion of food supply and proper nutrition; an adequate supply of safe water and basic sanitation; maternal and child health care, including family planning; immunization against the major infectious diseases; prevention and control of locally endemic diseases; appropriate treatment of common disease and injuries; and provision of essential drugs.

This basic package changed health programming from one focused solely on medical treatment to one focused on the provision of largely prevention-based basic medical and public health measures. These services target the interventions that have proved to have the greatest impact on the long-term health of a population as a whole, such as maternal health care and immunizations for pregnant women and children.

The World Bank's *World Development Report, 1993: Investing in Health* was another pioneering step; it was the first publication to present a complete, coherent case for applying rational decision making in the allocation of resources in the health sector. The report concluded that world spending on health had been misallocated, inefficient, and substantially directed toward the affluent rather than the poor. It identifies five policy areas as particularly important for low-income countries: improving primary education, especially for girls; investing in highly cost-effective public health activities, such as immunization programs; investing in health-care infrastructure at the district level to deliver a range of basic clinical services; reducing waste, especially through more effective use of pharmaceuticals; and decentralizing health systems to permit communities to have greater control over health expenditures.

When making decisions on the rational use of funds for the organization and provision of health services, policymakers and service providers can choose from various types of interventions. The primary health-care approach initially promoted by the Alma-Ata Declaration demonstrates what is considered the basic package of primary health-care services. The *World Development Report, 1993* expanded this core package to include education—and not necessarily only health education. The introduction of nonhealth interventions and their potential effect on a population's health status are important to consider when planning for health. Essentially, policymakers have access to three different approaches to producing or protecting good health. The first delivers medical interventions, such as vaccines, drugs, and primary health care. The second delivers nonmedical health interventions, such as training for medical personnel and more effective systems for procuring, storing, and developing pharmaceuticals and equipment. The third uses nonhealth interventions, such as better basic education. Each country needs to make its own decisions about relative investments in each of these areas.

Regional Summaries

Health conditions vary greatly across the world, and income is closely entwined with health. The poorest countries tend to suffer most from infectious diseases, while economic development tends to bring chronic and lifestyle-related diseases to the fore.

The Americas

The UN "World Population Prospects 2006" reports a life expectancy for North America of 78.5 for a child born in 2008 and a life expectancy for Latin America and the Caribbean of 73.3. The report estimates an infant mortality rate (IMR) of seven deaths per 1,000 live births for North America, which contrasts with the IMR of twenty-two deaths per 1,000 live births for Latin America and North Korea. Due to differences in income, however, North America faces different health concerns and challenges than Latin American and the Caribbean.

The WHO "World Health Report, 2002" estimated that the leading cause of death in the Americas was cardiovascular disease, accounting for 33 percent of all deaths, with cancer as the second leading cause at 19 percent. In North America, according to studies by the Pan American Health Organization (PAHO), heart disease and cancer are also the leading causes of poor health. Diabetes and other diseases of the circulatory system are on the rise, due, in large part, to obesity and sedentary lifestyles.

PAHO also reported that this is in contrast to the significantly higher rates of communicable and infectious diseases prevalent in Central and South America. Mortality rates from diarrhea and respiratory disease, although dropping in most countries, remain high in Central America and the Andean region, particularly among children under five. Several departments of the WHO are

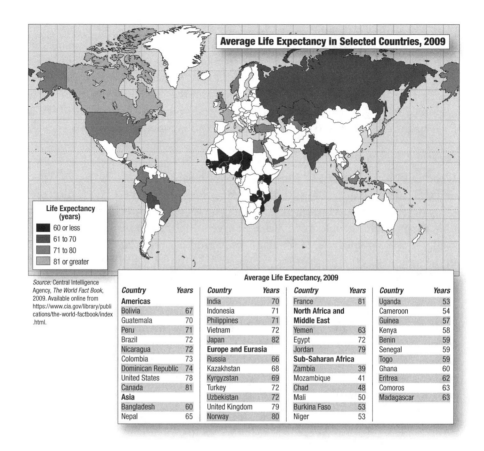

Average Life Expectancy in Selected Countries, 2009

Life Expectancy (years)
- 60 or less
- 61 to 70
- 71 to 80
- 81 or greater

Source: Central Intelligence Agency, The World Fact Book, 2009. Available online from https://www.cia.gov/library/publications/the-world-factbook/index.html.

Average Life Expectancy, 2009

Country	Years	Country	Years	Country	Years	Country	Years
Americas		India	70	France	81	Uganda	53
Bolivia	67	Indonesia	71	**North Africa and**		Cameroon	54
Guatemala	70	Philippines	71	**Middle East**		Guinea	57
Peru	71	Vietnam	72	Yemen	63	Kenya	58
Brazil	72	Japan	82	Egypt	72	Benin	59
Nicaragua	72	**Europe and Eurasia**		Jordan	79	Senegal	59
Colombia	73	Russia	66	**Sub-Saharan Africa**		Togo	59
Dominican Republic	74	Kazakhstan	68	Zambia	39	Ghana	60
United States	78	Kyrgyzstan	69	Mozambique	41	Eritrea	62
Canada	81	Turkey	72	Chad	48	Comoros	63
Asia		Uzbekistan	72	Mali	50	Madagascar	63
Bangladesh	60	United Kingdom	79	Burkina Faso	53		
Nepal	65	Norway	80	Niger	53		

using the Integrated Management of Childhood Illness approach to target this vulnerable age group.

Europe

According to the UN "World Population Prospects 2006," Europe has the world's second highest life expectancy (74.5 years) and second lowest IMR (8.0 deaths per 1,000 live births). Although these may be indicators of relatively good health, a significant health divide can be seen in Europe, generally between the eastern and western parts of the region (life expectancy is 68.6 and 79.9, respectively). This divide steadily increased during the 1990s. Eastern Europe now faces a variety of local health crises, including an AIDS epidemic.

According to WHO's "World Health Report, 2002," health risks facing Western Europeans are usually noncommunicable diseases, with cardiovascular diseases accounting for more than half of all deaths. Cancer is responsible for about 19 percent of deaths, and external causes of death, such as accidents, suicide, and homicide, account for approximately 8 percent.

Many countries in the east and southeast have seen civil unrest, political conflict, wars, and economic collapse in the last decade. As a result, the quality of health care and health services has dropped significantly, resulting in the reemergence of many diseases previously thought to have been eradicated, including tuberculosis, as well as a rise in many other communicable diseases associated with poverty. The spread of HIV/AIDS has caused a major health crisis, particularly in the Russian Federation and the Ukraine—these countries account for roughly 90 percent of the 1.5 million people living with HIV in Eastern Europe and the Commonwealth of Independent States (CIS).

North Africa and the Middle East

Although North Africa and the Middle East have a relatively high life expectancy (71.8 years) according to the U.S. Census Bureau, the IMR is also high (32.3 deaths per 1,000 live births). Problems with infant and child health reflect underlying health problems that the relatively high life expectancy somewhat masks. For example, the percentage of children under age five who were underweight in 2005, according to the UN "Human Development Report, 2007/2008," is 11 percent in Iran and 10 percent in Algeria and Morocco; the percentage of infants with low birth weight is 7 percent in Iran and Algeria and 15 percent in Morocco.

Plagued by war and civil unrest, North Africa and the Middle East have become a top priority for international health organizations. Iran and Iraq have both suffered through war and armed conflict in recent decades, resulting in populations with limited access to well-functioning health-care systems. The situation is worst perhaps in Afghanistan, where the health-care system is practically nonexistent and the shortage of health workers is severe. According to a WHO report from 2005, these dire conditions have boosted the maternal mortality rate in Afghanistan to the third highest in the world, at 1,800 per 100,000 live births.

Sub-Saharan Africa

According to the U.S. Census Bureau, sub-Saharan Africa has both the lowest life expectancy and the highest IMR on the planet. This troubling situation is associated with the severe poverty endemic to the region. According to the World Bank "World Development Indicators, 2008," the ten poorest countries, as measured by national income per capita, are in sub-Saharan Africa.

The WHO "Global Burden of Disease, 2002" estimates that the leading cause of death in the region is HIV/AIDS—19.2 percent of all deaths—making sub-Saharan Africa the worst affected region in the world. According to the UNAIDS "2008 AIDS Epidemic Update," sub-Saharan Africa bears 67.5 percent of the global burden of HIV. In eight countries of southern Africa, more than 15 percent of adults test positive for HIV. Prevention efforts in some areas have slowed the transmission of HIV and therefore the spread of AIDS.

Another major health problem in sub-Saharan Africa is malaria. The spread of the disease occurs under natural as well as human-made conditions, and it is especially prevalent in poor rural areas with little access to health care and health services. Malaria makes its greatest impact on children in sub-Saharan African, who, according to a 2007 WHO fact sheet, suffer higher mortality from the disease than any other group. Children in rural areas of the region, where health care is particularly limited, are especially at risk.

Asia and the Pacific

Asia and the Pacific are divided by the WHO into two areas: the South-East Asian countries (Bangladesh, Bhutan, India, Indonesia, Maldives, Myanmar, Nepal, North Korea, Sri Lanka, Thailand, and Timor-Leste) and the Western Pacific countries (China, Japan, and the rest of the countries of East Asia and the Pacific).

South-East Asia has experienced a decrease in IMRs in recent years and an increase in life expectancy. Nevertheless, some countries, such as India and Bangladesh, still have a relatively low life expectancy compared with the countries of Europe and the Americas. The health conditions of South-East Asia represent contradictions resulting from a gradual increase in economic status. The region is experiencing an increase in diseases typical of more developed countries, such as cardiovascular disease and cancer, but it still faces the challenges typical of less-developed countries, such as a variety of infectious diseases. Nevertheless, much progress has been made; polio, for instance, has been nearly eradicated. AIDS is also a major concern for South-East Asia, with India, Myanmar, and Thailand experiencing 95 percent of the AIDS problem in the area in 2005.

The Western Pacific displays some similarities to South-East Asia in that it experiences health conditions typical of more-developed countries as well as of less-developed countries. Heart disease and cancer accounted for 70 percent of deaths in 2005. Dengue fever, which had been on a brief decline following the 1998 epidemic, has begun to rise due to the increase of the urban mosquito population. Life expectancy and IMRs span a broad range and mostly reflect the wide variations in socioeconomic conditions across the area. For instance, according to the UN "World Population Prospects," Australia and Singapore have a life expectancy of 81 and 80 years, respectively, compared with 64 and 71 years for Laos and Indonesia, respectively.

Data

Beginning in 2002, the WHO prepared updated projections of future trends for mortality and burden through 2030 using methods similar to those used in the original Global Burden of Disease study. A set of relatively simple models were used to project future health trends under various scenarios, based largely on projections of economic and social development, and using the historically observed relationships of these with cause-specific mortality rates. The data inputs for the projections and models have been updated to take into account (1) the greater number of countries reporting death registration data to the WHO, particularly from developing regions; (2) other recently developed projection models on HIV/AIDS and other conditions, where appropriate; and (3) smoking epidemics.

Table 1   Infant Mortality Rate and Childhood Vaccination Coverage in Selected Countries

Country	Year of survey	Infant mortality rate (infant deaths per 1,000 live births)[a]	Children fully vaccinated (%)[b]
Sub-Saharan Africa			
Burkina Faso	2003	81.4	43.9
Cameroon	2004	74.1	48.2
Chad	2004	101.7	11.3
Congo, Republic of	2005	75.5	52.1
Eritrea	2002	47.7	75.9
Ethiopia	2005	77.0	20.4
Ghana	2003	64.3	69.4
Guinea	2005	91.4	37.2
Kenya	2003	77.2	51.8
Lesotho	2004	91.0	67.8
Madagascar	2003–2004	57.8	52.9
Malawi	2004	76.1	64.4
Mozambique	2003	100.7	63.3
Niger	2006	81.4	29.0
Nigeria	2003	100.0	12.9
Rwanda	2005	86.1	75.2
Senegal	2005	61.1	58.7
Tanzania	2004	68.0	71.1
Uganda	2006	71.1	8.1
Zambia	2001–2002	95.0	70.0
Zimbabwe	2005–2006	59.9	52.6
North Africa, West Asia, and Europe			
Armenia	2005	25.6	16.5
Egypt	2005	33.2	81.1
Jordan	2002	22.1	27.9
Moldova, Republic of	2005	12.8	37.0
Morocco	2003–2004	40.4	89.1
South and Southeast Asia			
Bangladesh	2004	65.2	73.1
Cambodia	2005	65.6	66.6
Indonesia	2002–2003	34.7	51.4
Philippines	2003	28.7	69.8
Vietnam	2002	18.2	66.7
Latin America and the Caribbean			
Bolivia	2003	53.6	50.4
Colombia	2005	18.7	58.1
Dominican Republic	2002	31.3	34.9
Honduras	2005	23.4	74.9

Source: Macro International Inc., "MEASURE DHS STATcompiler," 2008, available at http://www.measuredhs .com (accessed August 18, 2008).

[a]Infant mortality (five-year rates): Infant mortality rates by five-year periods preceding the survey (excludes month of interview from analysis).

[b]Vaccination data refer to children under twelve or twenty-three months, as appropriate. See the MEASURE DHS STATcompiler for detail.

Table 2   Health Expenditures per Capita in Selected Countries, 2004 (PPP/US$)

Country	Per capita expenditure
Europe and Eurasia	
Kazakhstan	264
Kyrgyzstan	102
Uzbekistan	160
Latin America	
Bolivia	186
Brazil	1520
Colombia	570
Dominican Republic	377
Guatemala	256
Nicaragua	231
Peru	235
South and Southeast Asia	
Bangladesh	64
Indonesia	118
Nepal	71
Philippines	203
Vietnam	184
Sub-Saharan Africa	
Benin	40
Burkina Faso	77
Chad	42
Ghana	95
Guinea	96
Kenya	86
Madagascar	29
Mali	54
Mozambique	42
Niger	26
Senegal	3.5
Tanzania	2.3
Togo	63
Uganda	135
Zambia	63

Source: United Nations Development Programme, "UNDP Human Development Report 2007/2008," UNDP, New York, 2007.

Note: Per capita expenditure is calculated in terms of purchasing price parity (PPP).

Table 3   Ten Leading Causes of Death Worldwide, 2005

Diseases or injury	Deaths (millions)	Percentage of total deaths
Coronary heart disease	7.2	12.2
Stroke and other cerebrovascular diseases	5.7	9.7
Lower respiratory infections	4.2	7.1
Chronic obstructive pulmonary disease	3.0	5.1
Diarrhoeal diseases	2.2	3.7
HIV/AIDS	2.0	3.5
Tuberculosis	1.5	2.5
Trachea, bronchus, lung cancers	1.3	2.3
Road traffic accidents	1.3	2.2
Prematurity and low birth weight	1.2	2.0

Source: World Health Organization. *The Global Burden of Disease: 2004 Update.* Geneva: World Health Organization, 2008, available at http://www.who.int/healthinfo/global_burden_disease/GBD_report_2004 update_part2.pdf.

Case Study—The Value of Vaccination

Immunization, although a recent champion of the public health community, has been a practice in the Chinese and Indian civilizations since 200 BC. It was later made popular in early-eighteenth-century Europe through the writings of Lady Mary Montague and in the 1790s was then introduced to the United States by Edward Jenner.

Some two hundred years later, vaccination became a valuable tool in the effort to eradicate smallpox, and the year 1973 signaled a major milestone in this crusade—smallpox had been restricted to just five countries in Asia and Africa. Riding on this success, and making use of its existing infrastructure, in 1974 the WHO founded the Expanded Program on Immunization (EPI). The EPI continued to combat smallpox (which was officially eradicated in 1979), but also included additional vaccines in its portfolio, including bacilli Calmette-Guerin (BCG) vaccine; diphtheria-tetanus-pertussis (DTP) vaccine; measles vaccine; the oral polio vaccine (OPV); and, for pregnant women in select areas, tetanus toxoid (TT) vaccine to prevent maternal and neonatal tetanus.

The success of the EPI can be measured, in part, by the remarkable reductions in child morbidity and mortality. According to the UN "World Population Prospects 2006," during the period 1975–2005 IMRs declined from 90 deaths per 1,000 live births to 49 deaths per 1,000 live births, a 46 percent decline. Declines in IMRs are essential to the success of the Millennium Development Goals (MDGs), laid out in 1990. In particular, the attainment of the fourth MDG (MDG4), which calls for a two-thirds reduction in under-five mortality by 2015, is especially dependent on high coverage rates of childhood immunizations.

The twenty-first century has seen the dawn of a new generation of vaccines that target some of today's biggest threats to child, adolescent, and elderly populations. Among new childhood vaccines are those against pneumococcal disease, meningitis, and rotavirus (a virus causing diarrhea); new vaccines for adolescent and elderly populations include those against the human papillomavirus (HPV) and the herpes zoster virus (HZV), respectively. Compared to the vaccines offered by EPI, these new vaccines are significantly more expensive, and their hefty price tag have many policymakers questioning the adoption of what was once considered an unquestionable tool in fighting infectious disease.

Analyses have been performed to gauge the effectiveness of these new, more costly vaccines in an attempt to justify their cost. This exercise has actually spawned research into how to properly evaluate vaccines. Historically, calculations have relied on cost-effectiveness analysis (CEA), but according to research published by Bloom and Canning in 2005, CEA is too narrow a tool to account for all the benefits of immunization. Rather, a proper accounting of the benefits of vaccination requires that we take into consideration a series of benefits, including the gains in productivity and cognitive performance that can result from healthier children who, for example, miss school less frequently than children who are suffering from vaccine-preventable disease. To sufficiently capture these benefits, economists must use cost-benefit analysis (CBA), the same instrument used to evaluate investments in education—arguably the most powerful tool of development.

In the context of today's HIV/AIDS epidemic, the benefits attributed to childhood vaccination are potentially larger, considering the deleterious link between HIV and other infectious diseases. All children are more susceptible to infectious disease due to their nascent immune systems, but children born HIV-positive are severely immunocompromised and are therefore at an even greater risk of developing and dying from infectious diseases. Moreover, children who are HIV-affected (that is, who are HIV-negative but who live in close proximity to HIV-positive people) are also at an increased risk for contracting infectious disease. The threshold for developing infectious disease is lower among people who are HIV-positive, which increases the probability that a nearby child will be exposed to a disease carrier. For example, cases of pneumococcal disease, for which a newly licensed vaccine is available, have risen dramatically since the start of the HIV epidemic, increasing fortyfold in parts of Africa.

Thus, the field of public health stands at a crossroads with respect to vaccination. Adopting new vaccines will help to continue past success in reducing child death, which makes MDG4 more attainable, especially at a time when HIV has provided some inertia to this trend. However, the costs of these new vaccines are high, and for many national health budgets, finding the funds to finance them is a great challenge. Yet the results of CBA, which to date have shown that the returns to investments in vaccination are at least as strong as those in education, should encourage national and international leaders to strongly consider the cost of *not* investing in vaccination.

Biographical Sketches

Gro Harlem Brundtland is a former director-general of the WHO (1998–2003). She was a pioneer in recognizing the effect of the environment on economic development and public health, as well as solidifying the concept of sustainable development as a policy platform for countries around the world. Brundtland now serves as a special envoy on climate change for UN secretary-general Ban Ki-Moon.

Chris Elias is the president of the Program for Appropriate Technology and Health (PATH), an international nonprofit organization. PATH has made vast advances in the field of global public health by adapting existing medical knowledge and tools to specific financial and cultural situations. Such technologies include the SoloShot, a syringe that automatically disables after a single use to prevent accidental transmission of diseases from needle-sharing. Elias is particularly recognized for his work in reproductive health in South Asia, including his role in the expansion of contraceptive choice and the development of vaginal microbicides.

Roger Glass is the director of the National Institutes of Health (NIH) Fogarty International Center and works to advance the NIH mission through international partnerships. Glass's research has focused on the prevention of gastroenteritis from rotaviruses and noroviruses, with a particular focus on the epidemiology of the rotavirus in South Asia. He has also maintained field studies in India, Bangladesh, Brazil, Mexico, Israel, Russia, Vietnam, China, and elsewhere.

Joel Lamstein is the CEO and co-founder of John Snow, Inc. (JSI), a leading public health consulting firm. JSI is dedicated to collaborating with local partners around the world to build local capacity and sustainable public health. Lamstein is also the CEO of World Education, an organization founded to meet the unique needs of the educationally disadvantaged. In his spare time, Lamstein is on the faculty at the Harvard School of Public Health and teaches organizational strategy, nonprofit management, international development, and strategic management.

Joy Phumaphi is a former minister of health in Botswana and a former assistant director-general of the WHO Family and Community Health Program. She is currently the vice president of the Human Development Network at the World Bank. Phumaphi is globally acclaimed for conceptualizing HIV/AIDS not only as a health issue but also as a challenge with political and development consequences for nations and psychological implications for individuals.

Srinath Reddy is the president of the Public Health Foundation of India and formerly headed the Department of Cardiology at the All India Institute of Medical Sciences (AIIMS). Reddy is a specialist in clinical management, clinical preventive services, health services research, and surveillance for chronic conditions in general. He especially focuses on cardiovascular diseases, diabetes, and hypertension.

Allan Rosenfield is dean emeritus of the Mailman School of Public Health at Columbia University. Rosenfield is an obstetrician gynecologist and is known for his work on women's reproductive health and human rights. Of particular note is Rosenfield's early identification of the ethical challenges associated with decreasing the transmission of HIV to newborns by treating mothers with antiretroviral drugs before delivery without consideration for the ongoing care and treatment of mothers.

Directory

Bill and Melinda Gates Foundation, P.O. Box 23350, Seattle, Wash. 98102. Telephone: (206) 709-3140; email: info@gatesfoundation.org; Web: http://www .gatesfoundation.org.
Foundation that promotes global health equity.

Joint United Nations Programme on HIV/AIDS (UNAIDS), 20 Avenue Appia, 1211 Geneva 27, Switzerland. Telephone: (41) 22 791 3666; email: unaids@unaids.org; Web: http://www.unaids.org.
Agency advocating worldwide action against HIV/AIDS.

Pan American Health Organization, 525 23rd Street NW, Washington, D.C. 20037. Telephone: (202) 974-3000; Web: http://www.paho.org.
The WHO regional office for the Americas.

Rockefeller Foundation, 420 Fifth Avenue, New York, N.Y. 10018-2702. Telephone: (212) 869-8500; Web: http://www.rockfound.org.
Foundation dedicated to environmentally sustainable development, with recent work focusing on combating the spread of HIV/AIDS.

United Nations International Children's Emergency Fund (UNICEF), 3 United Nations Plaza, New York, N.Y. 10017. Telephone: (212) 326-7000; email: unicef@unicef.org; Web: http://www.unicef.org.
Agency working to resolve problems related to the poverty and rights of children around the world.

United Nations Population Fund (UNFPA), 220 East 42nd Street, 18th Floor, New York, N.Y. 10017. Telephone: (212) 297-5020; Web: http://www.unfpa.org.
Multilateral funding agency for population and development.

U.S. Agency for International Development (USAID), Family Planning Programs, 1300 Pennsylvania Avenue NW, Washington, D.C. 20523-1000. Telephone: (202) 712-4810; email: pinquiries@usaid.gov; Web: http://www.usaid.gov/our_work/ global_health/pop/index.html.
U.S. government agency for international assistance, including administering family planning programs.

World Bank, 1818 H Street NW, Washington, D.C. 20433. Telephone: (202) 477-1234; Web: http://www.worldbank.org.
International organization dedicated to the eradication of poverty worldwide.

World Health Organization (WHO), 20 Avenue Appia, 1211 Geneva 27, Switzerland. Telephone: (41) 22 791 2111; email: info@who.int; Web: http://www.who.int.
UN organization dedicated to improving health worldwide.

Further Research

Books

Bloom, David E., Patricia H. Craig, and Pia N. Malaney. *Quality of Life in Rural Asia.* New York: Oxford University Press, 2001.

Jamison, Dean T., et al., eds. *Disease Control Priorities in Developing Countries.* New York: Oxford University Press, 1993.

McNeill, William H. *Plagues and Peoples.* New York: Monticello Editions, 1976.

Merson, Michael H., Robert E. Black, and Anne J. Mills, eds. *International Public Health.* Gaithersburg, Md.: Aspen, 2001.

Murray, Christopher J. L., and Alan D. Lopez, eds. *The Global Burden of Disease: A Comprehensive Assessment of Mortality and Disability from Diseases, Injuries, and Risk Factors in 1990 and Projected to 2020.* Cambridge, Mass.: Harvard School of Public Health, on behalf of the World Health Organization, 1996.

Porter, Roy. *Disease, Medicine and Society in England, 1550–1860.* Cambridge, UK: Cambridge University Press, 1993.

Savedoff, William D., and T. Paul Schultz. *Wealth from Health: Linking Social Investments to Earnings in Latin America.* Washington, D.C.: Inter-American Development Bank, 2000.

Sen, Amartya. *Development as Freedom.* Oxford: Oxford University Press, 1999.

Articles and Reports

Bloom, David E., and David Canning. "The Health and Wealth of Nations." *Science* 287 (2000): 1207–1208.

Doyle, Michael. "Kant, Liberal Legacies, and Foreign Affairs: Part 1." *Philosophy and Public Affairs* 12 (1983): 213–215.

Easterlin, Richard A. "How Beneficent Is the Market?: A Look at the Modern History of Mortality." *European Review of Economic History* 3 (1999): 257–294.

Gwatkin, Davidson R., et al. "Socio-Economic Differences in Health, Nutrition, and Population." World Bank, Washington, D.C., 2007.

Joint United Nations Programme on HIV/AIDS (UNAIDS). "2007 AIDS Epidemic Update." United Nations, Geneva, 2007.

———. "2008 Report on the Global AIDS Epidemic." United Nations, Geneva, 2007.

Macro International Inc. "MEASURE DHS STATcompiler." 2008. Available at http://www.measuredhs.com (accessed August 18, 2008).

Mann, Jonathan M., et al. "Health and Human Rights." *Health and Human Rights* 1, no. 1 (1994): 6–23.

Mathers, Colin D. and Dejan Loncar. "Projections of Global Mortality and Burden of Disease from 2002 to 2030." *PLoS Med* 3(11): e442. doi:10.1371/journal.pmed.0030442.

Pinstrup-Anderson, Per, and Satoru Shimokawa. "Do Poverty and Poor Health and Nutrition Increase the Risk of Armed Conflict Onset?" *Food Policy* 33, no. 6 (2008): 513–520.

Siddiqi, Arjumand and Clyde Hertzman. "Towards an Epidemiological Understanding of the Effects of Long-term Institutional Changes on Population Health: A Case Study of Canada versus the USA." *Social Science & Medicine* 64 no. 3 (2007): 89-603

Thomason, Jane A. "Health Sector Reform in Developing Countries: A Reality Check." Available at http://www.desentralisasi-kesehatan.net/id/moduldhs/artikel/18.HEALTH%20SECTOR%20REFORM%20ARTIKEL.pdf.

United Nations. "The Millennium Development Goals Report, 2007." United Nations, New York, 2007.

United Nations Development Programme (UNDP). "Human Development Report, 2007/2008." UNDP, New York, 2007.

United Nations Population Division. "World Population Prospects." UN Population Division, New York, 2007.

U.S. Census Bureau. "International Data Base." Washington, D.C., 2008. Available at http://www.census.gov/ipc/www/idb.

Wilkinson, Richard G. "The Impact of Inequality." *Social Research* 73, no. 2 (2006): 711–732.

Winslow, Charles-Edward A. "The Untilled Field of Public Health." *Modern Medicine* 2 (1920): 183–191.

World Bank. "Assessing Aid: What Works, What Doesn't, and Why." World Bank, Washington, D.C., 1998.

———. "A Practitioner's Guide: Health Financing Revisited." World Bank, Washington, D.C., 2006.

———. "World Development Indicators, 2008." World Bank, Washington, D.C., 2008.

———. *World Development Report, 1993: Investing in Health.* New York: Oxford University Press, 1993.

———. *World Development Report, 2001: Mental Health.* New York: Oxford University Press, 2001.

World Health Organization (WHO). "Closing the Gap in a Generation: Health Equity through Action on the Social Determinants of Health." WHO Commission on the Social Determinants of Health, Geneva, 2008. Available at http://www.who.int/social_determinants/final_report/en/index.html.

———. "Health Topics: Dengue and Dengue Hemorrhagic Fever." WHO Regional Office for the Western Pacific, Geneva, 2008. Available at http://www.wpro.who.int/health_topics/dengue (accessed August 22, 2008).

———. "Malaria Fact Sheet No. 94." WHO, Geneva, May 2007.

———. "Maternal Mortality in 2005." WHO, Geneva, 2007.

———. "Projections of Mortality and Burden of Disease, 2004." WHO, Geneva, November 2004.

———. "Projections of Mortality and Burden of Disease, 2006." WHO, Geneva, December 2006.

———. "World Health Report, 1999." WHO, Geneva, 1999.

———. "World Health Report, 2000." WHO, Geneva, 2000.

———. "World Health Report, 2001." WHO, Geneva, 2001.

———. "World Health Report, 2002." WHO, Geneva, 2002.

———. "World Health Report, 2006." WHO, Geneva, 2006.

———. "World Health Statistics, 2008." WHO, Geneva, 2008.

Web Sites

Global Burden of Disease, 2000
http://www.who.int/healthinfo/bodestimates/en/index.html

United Nations, Electronic Library, Population Division of the Department of Economic and Social Affairs
http://www.un.org/popin/infoserv.htm

World Health Report
http://www.who.int/whr

Document

1. Alma–Ata Declaration

International Conference on Primary Health Care, Alma–Ata, Soviet Union, September 6–12, 1978

The full text is available at http://www.who.int/hpr/NPH/docs/declaration_almaata.pdf.

Extract

Declaration

I

The Conference strongly reaffirms that health, which is a state of complete physical, mental and social well-being, and not merely the absence of disease or infirmity, is a fundamental human right and that the attainment of the highest possible level of health is a most important world-wide social goal whose realization requires the action of many other social and economic sectors in addition to the health sector.

II

The existing gross inequality in the health status of the people particularly between developed and developing countries as well as within countries is politically, socially and economically unacceptable and is, therefore, of common concern to all countries.

III

Economic and social development, based on a New International Economic Order, is of basic importance to the fullest attainment of health for all and to the reduction of the gap between the health status of the developing and developed countries. The promotion and protection of the health of the people is essential to sustained economic and social development and contributes to a better quality of life and to world peace. . . .

VI

Primary health care is essential health care based on practical, scientifically sound and socially acceptable methods and technology made universally accessible to individuals and families in the community through their full participation and at a cost that the community and country can afford to maintain at every stage of their development in the spirit of self-reliance and self-determination. . . .

VII

Primary health care:

1. reflects and evolves from the economic conditions and sociocultural and political characteristics of the country and its communities and is based on the application of the relevant results of social, biomedical and health services research and public health experience;

2. addresses the main health problems in the community, providing promotive, preventive, curative and rehabilitative services accordingly;

3. includes at least: education concerning prevailing health problems and the methods of preventing and controlling them; promotion of food supply and proper nutrition; an adequate supply of safe water and basic sanitation; maternal and child health care, including family planning; immunization against the major infectious

diseases; prevention and control of locally endemic diseases; appropriate treatment of common diseases and injuries; and provision of essential drugs;

4. involves, in addition to the health sector, all related sectors and aspects of national and community development, in particular agriculture, animal husbandry, food, industry, education, housing, public works, communications and other sectors; and demands the coordinated efforts of all those sectors;

5. requires and promotes maximum community and individual self-reliance and participation in the planning, organization, operation and control of primary health care, making fullest use of local, national and other available resources; and to this end develops through appropriate education the ability of communities to participate;

6. should be sustained by integrated, functional and mutually supportive referral systems, leading to the progressive improvement of comprehensive health care for all, and giving priority to those most in need;

7. relies, at local and referral levels, on health workers, including physicians, nurses, midwives, auxiliaries and community workers as applicable, as well as traditional practitioners as needed, suitably trained socially and technically to work as a health team and to respond to the expressed health needs of the community.

VIII

All governments should formulate national policies, strategies and plans of action to launch and sustain primary health care as part of a comprehensive national health system and in coordination with other sectors. To this end, it will be necessary to exercise political will, to mobilize the country's resources and to use available external resources rationally.

IX

All countries should cooperate in a spirit of partnership and service to ensure primary health care for all people since the attainment of health by people in any one country directly concerns and benefits every other country. In this context the joint WHO/ UNICEF report on primary health care constitutes a solid basis for the further development and operation of primary health care throughout the world.

X

An acceptable level of health for all the people of the world by the year 2000 can be attained through a fuller and better use of the world's resources, a considerable part of which is now spent on armaments and military conflicts. A genuine policy of independence, peace, détente and disarmament could and should release additional resources that could well be devoted to peaceful aims and in particular to the acceleration of social and economic development of which primary health care, as an essential part, should be allotted its proper share.

HUNGER AND FOOD SECURITY

Suresh C. Babu

As a result of chronic food insecurity and the added burden of high food prices, which have vastly increased since 2003, more than 963 million people do not have adequate food to eat on a daily basis. Most of these people live in South Asia or sub-Saharan Africa. One of the major causes of food insecurity and hunger is the abject poverty afflicting the more than 1 million people who earn less than $1 per day. Other causes of food insecurity include high food prices, highly skewed income distributions, and a lack of productive resources for the poor. With so many technological advances in agricultural and life sciences, including the development of biotechnology and information and communication technology, why does such a large population remain vulnerable to hunger and food insecurity? What technological, institutional, and policy innovations are needed to reduce the level of hunger and malnutrition? What set of trade and marketing policies are needed to improve food access and availability? What safety nets should be in place to protect the poor and hungry from the vagaries of food prices?

These questions cover the scope and complexity of the problems surrounding hunger and food security and illustrate that no single answer to the issues arising from world hunger exists.

Historical Background and Development

Famines have been a regular part of human history. The last major famine in the West was the Irish potato famine of the 1840s, resulting from a failure of the potato crop due to blight disease. The great Bengal famine of the 1940s, the Chinese famine of the 1950s, the Bangladesh famine of the 1970s, and the Horn of Africa famine in the 1970s and 1980s killed millions of people. Between 1983 and 1985, some 8 million people in Ethiopia were affected by drought that led to famine. An estimated 1 million of them died, along with a large number of livestock. Famine and faminelike conditions continue to threaten several developing countries and regions.

Although famine prevention, food insecurity, and hunger are seemingly at the top of the current global development agenda, the first warning of the impact of population growth on food security was issued more than two hundred years ago. In 1798, Thomas Robert Malthus, a population scientist, predicted that population growth would outstrip food production. But not until the 1960s, when the world population started to grow at an unprecedented rate of 2 percent per year, did Malthus's predictions generated renewed concern among policymakers.

The United Nations Food and Agriculture Organization (FAO) was founded in October 1945 and charged with the mission to improve the food and agricultural situation at the global level. In 1960, the FAO launched the Freedom from Hunger Campaign. During the 1960 U.S. presidential campaign, candidates Vice President Richard Nixon and Sen. John Kennedy announced support for a multilateral food distribution system. In January 1961, President Kennedy established the Food for Peace office in the White House and appointed George McGovern as its first director. Also in 1961, an FAO conference passed a resolution establishing the World Food Programme (WFP) to oversee the use of surplus food in developed countries for emergency and development activities.

The South Asian countries, particularly India, faced a major food crisis in the early 1960s and led a "ship to mouth" existence. India imported 10 million tons of food under Public Law 480 during 1965 and 1966. By 1970, through expanded use of high-yielding seeds, India and Pakistan increased their food production multifold, resulting in what is now called the Green Revolution. Between 1971 and 1975, Ethiopia experienced a major famine due to drought; an estimated 250,000 people died. Bangladesh faced a major famine in 1974. That year, the first World Food Conference was held in Rome. The concept of food security originated at this conference, and delegates recognized the need for improved food policies. As a result, the International Food Policy Research Institute (IFPRI) was established in 1975 to identify sustainable policy options for reducing hunger and food insecurity. The FAO established the Global Information and Early Warning System to forewarn the global community of impending food shortages.

Three major events in the early 1990s—the United Nations International Children's Emergency Fund (UNICEF) Children's Summit (1990), the Conference on Environment and Development (1992), and the International Conference on Nutrition (ICN) (1992)—addressed hunger and endorsed recommendations and targets for its reduction and elimination. In 1993, the World Bank organized the Conference on Overcoming Global Hunger, held in Washington, D.C. This conference highlighted the strong link between hunger and poverty alleviation. In 1994, the International Conference on Population and Development, organized by the United Nations Population Fund (UNFPA) and held in Cairo, identified high fertility rates and growing population as the major causes of increasing poverty and natural resource degradation in developing countries. Global Vision, a program to reduce food insecurity through the sustainable use of natural resources, was launched in 1995 by the IFPRI. The 2020 Vision Conference, organized by the IFPRI and held in October 1995, identified several key challenges, including overcoming complacency, lack of commitment, and political apathy to eradicate poverty and hunger and to protect the natural resource base.

In 1994, the conclusion of the Uruguay Round of the General Agreement on Tariffs and Trade (GATT) and the creation of the World Trade Organization (WTO) provided opportunities to review food trade and food aid in a liberalized global economy. The 1995 UN World Summit on Social Development, held in Copenhagen, Denmark, and the Fourth World Conference on Women, held in Beijing, China, also in 1995, focused on food security and hunger issues as key development concerns. The FAO organized the World Food Summit in 1996 in Rome. The Rome Declaration, agreed to by 186 countries, pledged to achieve food security for all and to eradicate hunger in all countries, with an immediate view to reducing the number of undernourished people by half by 2015.

By 2000, policymakers could see that the World Food Summit's goal of halving food insecurity would not be achieved. In 2001, the IFPRI organized a major campaign to revitalize the efforts of the international community to place food security and hunger problems at the top of the development agenda. A 2020 Vision Conference held in Bonn, Germany, in 2001 helped to reestablish the commitment of donors to world food security. The FAO also organized a World Food Summit in 2002 to revisit the goal set in 1996 and to identify new opportunities for the future. The summit called for an international alliance to speed up the progress of eradicating hunger and to meet the goals originally set in 1996.

Since 2005, prices of food commodities on the global level have been on the rise, creating another food crisis. By April 2008, the prices of maize, wheat, and rice—staple foods for most of the human population—increased by 164 percent, 187 percent, and 437 percent, respectively, above their levels in 2001. In June 2008, the FAO convened a Global Food Security Summit to address this issue, which resulted in donor pledges to support the recovery of countries suffering from food crisis. The G-8 (Canada, France, Germany, Italy, Japan, Russia, the United Kingdom, and the United States) leaders also made a special statement on various strategies to improve global food security in their meeting in July 2008 in Hokkaido, Japan. As of December 2008, the estimated number of hungry people on Earth stood at 963 million.

Current Status

As multifaceted as the problem of hunger is, fundamental and seemingly simple questions—for instance, "What is hunger?"— must be addressed to explore the issue fully. Research geared toward understanding the nature and causes of food insecurity and hunger is the starting point from which broad-based and effective policies and programs can be developed.

Research

The current research on food security and hunger issues revolves around two major areas: quantifying and predicting food insecure and hungry populations, and identifying the causes of food insecurity to design and assess policy and program solutions to reduce food insecurity and hunger.

Quantifying and Predicting Food Insecurity and Hunger. Currently an estimated 963 million people are food insecure. This figure is based on the FAO's measure of chronic food insecurity, which represents the number of people in each country who consume too few calories to meet their minimum dietary energy requirements. This measurement is based on three factors: per capita energy supply available in a country, distribution of energy consumption among the country's population, and the minimum per capita daily energy requirement. This measure of the food insecure is used as a benchmark for comparing changes in levels of hunger over time as well as across nations and regions. Although this approach has been criticized, the FAO's figures are widely used and extensively relied on by national planners and policymakers.

Quantifying the number of hungry people in the world includes more than measuring those not receiving daily minimum dietary requirements. The Global Hunger Index (GHI) developed by the IFPRI is a multidimensional approach to measuring hunger and malnutrition. The index combines undernourishment of the population, the prevalence of underweight children under five years of age, and the mortality rate of children under five years of age. Combining these three indicators captures various aspects of hunger beyond food security, including the physiological vulnerability of children and adults and the lack of nutrients in early childhood that creates a high risk of illness and death in children. Table 1 presents the GHI for the 120 countries in 2008 for which GHI data was available. The 2008 GHI indicates that slow progress has been made since 1990 in reducing food insecurity. South Asia and sub-Saharan Africa particularly remain highly vulnerable to hunger. Countries such as the Democratic Republic of Congo, Eritrea, Burundi, Niger, and Sierra Leone are at the bottom of the list, meaning they experience the greatest amount of hunger.

In general, countries where poverty is highly prevalent are also affected by the problem of hunger. The IFPRI reports of Klaus von Grebmer and colleagues recommend that reducing a population's vulnerability to hunger needs to go beyond food aid for poor people. Increasing investment for agricultural production, particularly among small landholders; scaling up social protection programs to provide health and education; reforming the world food trade system by reducing protectionist approaches and high levels of subsidies in developed countries; and better data collecting and monitoring of the food and nutrition situation will help to formulate better policies for reducing hunger in severely affected countries.

A fundamental question that confronts food security planners and policymakers is whether the World Food Summit's goal of reducing the number of food insecure by half by 2015 can be achieved. According to analysis by Ben Senauer and Mona Sur, information on the factors underlying food security measurements indicate that this goal will not be met in 2015 or even by 2025 as long as the current trend in economic and population growth continues.

What is needed to achieve food for all by at least 2050? First, the world's poor, who are most vulnerable to food insecurity and hunger, must share in the broad benefits of economic growth. Second, the policies and programs of developing countries should address the basic needs of the poorest segments of society (see DEVELOPMENT AID and INCOME INEQUALITY). Third, investments in human capital—including universal primary education, health care, and productive activities for the poor—must be made to attain sustainable food security and the eradication of hunger. Fourth, programs and policies that increase the access of the poor to food by reducing prices are essential. Investment in agricultural research and development will play a crucial role in the quantity, quality, and affordability of food for the poor. Finally, protecting the poor and the vulnerable from periodic economic shocks that increase food prices is needed through appropriately designed and well-targeted safety-net programs. Designing appropriate programs and policies will require a better understanding of the causes of food insecurity and hunger and of the options and strategies needed to improve the food security of the poor.

A Conceptual Framework for Understanding the Causes of Food Insecurity and Hunger. A complex set of factors determines food security and hunger outcomes. The conceptual framework in Figure 1 identifies the causes of food and nutrition security and the food policy and program linkages to them. It also identifies the points of entry for direct and indirect food security and nutrition programs and policy interventions as well as the human capacity gaps for analysis and evaluation of food and nutrition policies and programs. This framework attempts to encompass the life-cycle approach to food security and nutrition, given the role of nutrition in the human life cycle. In addition, it includes the cause of food and nutrition security at the macro and micro levels. Achieving food security at the macro level requires economic growth that provides for poverty alleviation and increased equity in the distribution of income. For example, in a predominantly agrarian economy, economic growth is driven by increases in agricultural productivity and, therefore, depends on the availability of natural resources, agricultural technology, and human resources. These are depicted as potential resources at the bottom of Figure 1.

Technology and natural resources are necessary to generate dynamic agricultural growth, but they are not sufficient by themselves. Also needed are policies that appropriately price resources and allocate them efficiently and that stabilize investment in human and natural resources through political and legal institutions. These factors affect the underlying causes of nutrition security: food security, care, and health. Attaining food security is one of the key determinants of the nutritional status of individuals. According to the World Bank, food security is attained when all people have physical and economic access to sufficient food, at all times, to meet their dietary needs for a productive and healthy life. Although this definition is applied at the national, subnational, and household levels, it is more meaningful at the household level. Resources for

Figure 1 A Policy-Focused Conceptual Framework for Analyzing Food and Nutrition Security

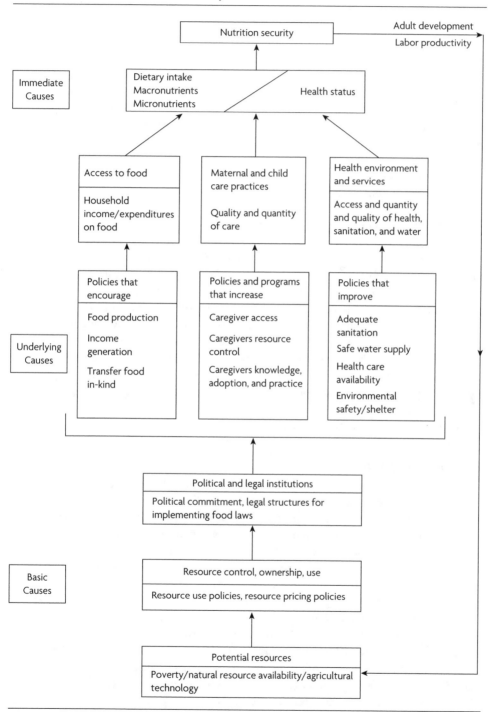

Source: Adapted from L. Smith and L. Haddad, *Explaining Child Malnutrition in Developing Countries: A Cross-Country Analysis* (Washington, D.C.: International Food Policy Research Institute, 1999).

achieving food security are influenced by policies and programs that increase food production, provide income for food purchases, and establish the in-kind transfers of food through formal or informal support mechanisms.

In the "World Declaration on Nutrition," adopted at the 1992 International Conference on Nutrition, *care* was defined as the provision by households and communities of "time, attention, and support to meet the physical, mental, and social needs of children and other vulnerable groups." Resources for the provision of care depend on policies and programs that increase caregivers' access to income; strengthen their control of income use; and improve their knowledge, adoption, and practice of care. Child feeding, health-seeking behavior, and caring for and supporting mothers during pregnancy and breast-feeding are examples of caring practices. Resources for health can be improved through policies and programs that increase the availability of safe water, sanitation, health care, and environmental safety.

Food security that ensures a nutritionally adequate diet at all times, plus a care and health environment that ensures the biological use of food, determines the nutrition security of individuals. Thus, the components of nutrition security are dietary intake of macronutrients (energy, protein, and fat) and micronutrients (iodine, vitamin A, iron, zinc, and folate) and health status. Adequate nutrition security for children results in the development of healthy adolescents and adults and contributes to the quality of human capital. Healthy female adults with continuous nutrition security during pregnancy contribute to fewer incidences of low-birth-weight babies, thereby minimizing the probability of the infants becoming malnourished. In the case of adults, improved nutrition security in terms of timely nutrient intakes increases labor productivity (given opportunities for productive employment), thus resulting in reduced poverty. Lower poverty, in turn, increases the potential resources available for attaining nutrition security (see HEALTH).

Policies and Programs

Many developing countries, particularly in sub-Saharan Africa, continue to experience slow and stagnant economic growth. This trend, combined with frequent natural disasters, has resulted in chronic food shortages. Food security remains a development problem even in regions and among groups of households that have shown considerable progress in combating poverty. A number of programs and policies designed to improve food and nutrition security have been implemented in these countries.

Trade and Macroeconomic Policies. Macroeconomic stability is undeniably a necessary condition for sustained economic growth. Conversely, macroeconomic imbalances invariably lead to rapid inflation, real exchange rate appreciation, and chronic balance-of-payment difficulties. In addition, globalization brings countries closer and enables better trading opportunities. In their 2008 book, *Globalization of Food and Agriculture and the Poor,* Joachim von Braun and Eugenio Diaz-Bonilla recommended global trade policy reforms in the interest of achieving food security for all, including reduced protectionism and the reduction of high-level subsidies in developed countries. Policies that encourage the generation of foreign exchange by focusing on a country's comparative advantage can help in achieving food security. The choice between increasing the food supply through domestic food production and food import, however, should depend on the food supply in the world or regional markets, the cost of foreign exchange, and the comparative advantage of the country in international trade (see WORLD TRADE).

Social Protection for Food Security. Social protection programs include health, life, and asset insurance; income transfers in the form of food, cash, vouchers, and subsidies; and services such as maternal and child health and nutrition programs. According to research conducted by Michelle Adato and John Hoddinott, social protection policies and programs can protect people against food-related risk and vulnerability and support those who suffer from chronic hunger and malnutrition. The successful implementation of large-scale programs in Ethiopia and South Africa indicate that even poorer countries can use these types of policies to reach out to millions of hungry people.

Food-for-work programs that provide access to food for drought-affected households during periods of distress have not been effective in improving the nutritional status of the vulnerable groups. Poor targeting and high levels of leakage—pilfering of food from distribution centers that is then made available to consumers—have plagued food-transfer programs. Targeted interventions are more effective in transferring income to the poor than are universal subsidies provided through public food distribution programs. Studies that have evaluated targeted intervention programs indicate that poor households change the quantity and quality of their food intake when they face changes in income and the price of rice; therefore, targeting the poor by the use of poor-quality rice, also known as self-targeting of commodities (because only the desperate will participate in the intervention program), is one way to reduce the cost involved in universal subsidies. Foods that are less preferred to staple foods are also useful as a self-targeting tool. Geographical targeting of nutritionally vulnerable households in urban areas is the most widely used approach for increasing the cost-effectiveness of nutrition interventions. In the wake of high food prices in 2008, Joachim von Braun and his colleagues called for scaling up social protection policies in developing countries. They argued that, where food markets do not function well, providing food is a better option than cash.

Food Price Stabilization. Stabilization of food prices continues to be an important element of food policy in many developing countries. Domestic food price stabilization has found a central place in the management of the food economy because of uncertainties in food production resulting from dependency on rainfall and international trade. Food economist Peter Timmer has determined that food price stabilization policies are designed to meet one or more of the following objectives:

- Maintain food prices low enough to be affordable to most consumers
- Maintain food prices high enough to meet production objectives
- Provide stability of price levels to protect the poor from price shocks

- Keep domestic prices close enough to world market prices to reduce distortions and illegal trade
- Allow enough seasonal fluctuations to permit the domestic private sector to profitably operate in the market

The stabilization of food prices, if accompanied by the provision of necessary investment in rural infrastructure and agricultural research, could contribute to macroeconomic stability and accelerated economic growth. Price stabilization can be cost-effective if it goes hand in hand with building an active and competitive private sector. The role of price stabilization agencies must be constantly modified to meet the changing role of food grains in the economy and to adjust to evolving domestic private marketing systems. In the event of high food prices, having mechanisms in place that will calm the markets is important. Overregulation, however, is not an answer to the speculative behavior of the producers and marketing agents. Reducing speculation without curtailing the effectiveness of markets requires effective market monitoring and modest grain reserves at the local, regional, and global levels.

Emergency and Humanitarian Food Assistance. In 2007, US$3 billion were spent on food aid by WFP alone to provide 86 million people with 3.3 million tons of food. The provision of food commodities to developing countries from donor countries in the form of food aid has been a major method of international assistance in improving food security. Food aid is usually classified according to three categories: program food aid, project food aid, and emergency food aid. Program food aid is used to generate local currency by selling surplus food in the recipient country's market. The funds generated through the local market operations are used for implementing development interventions. Project food aid provides food for programs specifically designed to help vulnerable groups in a recipient country to improve their food security. Targeted supplementary feeding programs and food-for-work programs in developing countries typify project food aid. Emergency food aid is the provision of food directly to the victims of human-made or natural disasters, including refugees and internally displaced persons.

Regional Summaries

Food insecurity and hunger affect populations in every country. These problems are chronic in many developing regions (see map, p. 399). This section focuses on the regions where the intensity of food insecurity is severe and needs the immediate attention of the global community. Even though the developed regions of North America and Europe continue to have pockets of hunger, the magnitude of their food problems are miniscule compared to the looming nature of food insecurity in Latin America, North Africa and the Middle East, sub-Saharan Africa, and Asia.

Latin America

Latin American countries have been most successful in reducing hunger in the last two decades. They rapidly expanded food and agricultural production in the

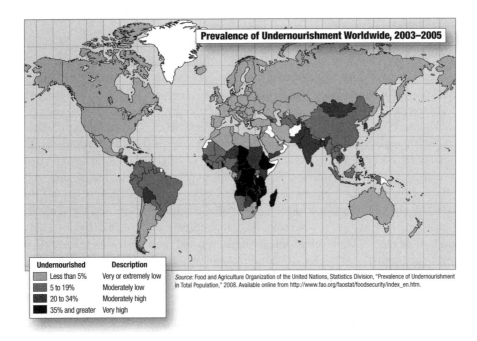

Prevalence of Undernourishment Worldwide, 2003–2005

Undernourished	Description
Less than 5%	Very or extremely low
5 to 19%	Moderately low
20 to 34%	Moderately high
35% and greater	Very high

Source: Food and Agriculture Organization of the United Nations, Statistics Division, "Prevalence of Undernourishment in Total Population," 2008. Available online from http://www.fao.org/faostat/foodsecurity/index_en.htm.

1990s, primarily through policies that resulted in macroeconomic expansion in the 1960s and 1970s. In the 1980s, this expansion was temporarily interrupted—unsustainable macroeconomic policies resulted in an economic crisis that affected the food and agricultural sectors. This led to reductions in agricultural research investments and negative growth in food production in the 1980s. But the 1990s recovery, indeed, translated into increased food production for many countries in the region. In fact, according to the FAO, ten out of twelve countries in South America are likely to achieve the target of reducing hunger levels by half by 2015. However, Central American countries such as El Salvador, Guatemala, Haiti, and Panama continue to face challenges in reducing hunger. With 50 percent of the population suffering from chronic hunger, the April 2008 riots in Haiti over high food prices were a reminder that food insecurity and hunger can be a major destabilizing force for a country's progress.

North Africa and the Near East

Among developing countries, North African and Near East countries exhibit the lowest levels of hunger and food insecurity. However, because of low rainfall, this area faces severe challenges in expanding food and agricultural production. Due to conflicts in Afghanistan and Iraq, food insecurity in the Near East region doubled to 28 million people from 2003 to 2005. One in three people in Yemen suffers from chronic hunger. The number of food insecure people is likely to be the same in twenty-five years because the region has a limited resource base of arable land and water, low and erratic rainfall and frequent droughts, and low productivity growth. Past policies have encouraged the misuse of land and natural resources. In addition, skewed land distribution and insecure property rights have been important constraints on food and agricultural production (see FRESHWATER).

Sub-Saharan Africa

The population in sub-Saharan Africa increased by 200 million since the early 1980s. With a current population of 700 million and modest growth in its agriculture sector, food insecurity and hunger remain a formidable challenge. Several factors condition the poor performance of the region in meeting its food needs. Poor resource endowment—such as poor land quality; large land-locked and inaccessible areas; endemic livestock diseases; and human diseases, including malaria and human immunodeficiency virus (HIV)/acquired immunodeficiency syndrome (AIDS) (see AIDS)—reduces the food production potential of many countries. Years of colonial exploitation have negatively affected the development of agriculture. A poor policy environment and the lack of supporting institutions have consistently undermined agricultural development and food production. Recent studies show that in 2008 some 312 million of the 700 million people living in sub-Saharan Africa were food insecure. Sub-Saharan Africa is the only region where the number of the food insecure and hungry is projected to increase.

Africa's food problem will not be solved by expanding the amount of land used for food production. Yields of food crops are indeed low and must grow at higher rates, but this is only one area that needs attention. Subsistence farmers must be encouraged to move toward market-oriented commercial food production, and the ongoing degradation and desertification that has devastated Africa's agricultural lands must be reversed with proper investment in soil and water management technologies. The policies of the 1980s and 1990s have not been helpful in reducing food insecurity and hunger. Renewed investment in agricultural research and extension, along with institutional and market reforms, will be necessary to meet the future food and nutritional needs of sub-Saharan Africa (see Case Study—Reviving African Agriculture for Food Security).

Asia and the Pacific

According to the FAO in 2008, the progress in reducing the prevalence of hunger has been modest in Asia, with hunger dropping from 20 percent in 1996 to 16 percent in 2005. Asia is home to the largest number of hungry people, 542 million, which accounts for nearly two-thirds of the world's hunger-stricken population. China and India together are home to 42 percent of the world's chronically hungry people. The level of hunger in South Asia has decreased from 25 percent in the 1990–1992 period to 21 percent in the 2003–2005 period, a slow progress. Although the income levels of people in South Asia have been increasing, a large share of the population is still unable to get adequate levels of nutrition due to a slowdown in the growth rates of food production and the widening inequalities among the rich and the poor.

Although increased agricultural productivity through Green Revolution technologies has increased national food availability, high levels of food insecurity in South Asia still exist. This situation points to the challenge of increasing the entitlements of resource-poor households to meet their food needs. This challenge will require increasing the income of poor households through labor-intensive agricultural production activities. Appropriate research that improves the productivity of crops that poor households cultivate and consume will provide a direct method of reducing poverty and food insecurity.

Data

Table 1   The Global Hunger Index by Country, 1990 and 2008

Country	1990	2008
Mauritius	6.1	5.0
Jamaica	8.0	5.1
Moldova	n/a	5.4
Cuba	7.3	5.5
Peru	19.5	5.6
Trinidad and Tobago	8.0	5.9
Algeria	7.4	6.0
Albania	10.5	6.3
Turkmenistan	n/a	6.4
El Salvador	9.7	6.5
Malaysia	9.5	6.5
Morocco	7.7	6.5
Colombia	9.6	6.7
South Africa	7.4	6.9
China	11.6	7.1
Fiji	12.7	7.3
Suriname	10.7	7.5
Gabon	11.3	7.6
Venezuela	8.3	7.7
Paraguay	8.3	7.9
Guyana	14.6	8.6
Panama	10.1	8.9
Thailand	18.4	9.9
Armenia	n/a	10.2
Azerbaijan	n/a	10.4
Uzbekistan	n/a	11.2
Indonesia	16.0	11.3
Honduras	16.1	11.4
Bolivia	16.5	11.7
Dominican Republic	14.0	12.0
Mongolia	18.9	12.1
Vietnam	23.9	12.6
Nicaragua	16.4	12.8
Ghana	24.4	13.9
Philippines	18.9	14.0
Lesotho	14.2	14.3
Namibia	21.4	14.3
Guatemala	16.1	14.6
Myanmar*	18.7	15.0
Sri Lanka	19.1	15.0
Benin	22.8	15.1
Côte d'Ivoire	19.4	15.3
Senegal	22.1	15.4
Uganda	19.9	17.1
Gambia	18.4	17.3
Mauritania	n/a	17.6
Swaziland	13.4	17.7

Table 1 (Continued)

Country	1990	2008
Botswana	16.7	17.9
Togo	23.0	18.2
Nigeria	23.7	18.4
Timor-Leste	n/a	18.4
Korea, People's Democratic Republic of*	13.1	18.8
Congo, Republic of	26.2	19.1
Kenya	23.5	19.9
Sudan*	24.5	20.5
Lao People's Democratic Republic	28.1	20.6
Nepal	27.6	20.6
Djibouti	n/a	20.9
Guinea	29.3	20.9
Pakistan	25.3	21.7
Malawi	32.2	21.8
Rwanda	28.3	22.3
Cambodia	32.4	23.2
Burkina Faso	25.1	23.5
India	32.5	23.7
Zimbabwe	20.2	23.8
Tanzania	26.1	24.2
Haiti	35.9	24.3
Bangladesh	32.3	25.2
Tajikistan	n/a	25.9
Mozambique	40.9	26.3
Mali	29.6	26.9
Guinea-Bissau	23.0	27.5
Central African Republic	32.0	28.0
Madagascar	29.1	28.8
Comoros	26.4	29.1
Zambia	29.1	29.2
Angola	39.8	29.5
Yemen	30.7	29.8
Chad	37.5	29.9
Ethiopia	44.0	31.0
Liberia	27.3	31.8
Sierra Leone	32.4	32.2
Niger	38.0	32.4
Burundi	32.6	38.3
Eritrea	n/a	39.0
Congo, Democratic Republic of	25.5	42.7
Argentina	< 5.0	< 5.0
Belarus	n/a	< 5.0
Bosnia and Herzegovina	n/a	< 5.0
Brazil	7.8	< 5.0
Bulgaria	n/a	< 5.0
Chile	< 5.0	< 5.0
Costa Rica	< 5.0	< 5.0
Croatia	n/a	< 5.0
Ecuador	6.8	< 5.0
Egypt	8.6	< 5.0
Estonia	n/a	< 5.0
Iran	8.3	< 5.0
Jordan	< 5.0	< 5.0
Kazakhstan	n/a	< 5.0

Table 1 (Continued)

Country	1990	2008
Kuwait	12.6	< 5.0
Kyrgyz Republic	n/a	< 5.0
Latvia	n/a	< 5.0
Lebanon	5.1	< 5.0
Libya*	n/a	< 5.0
Lithuania	n/a	< 5.0
Macedonia	n/a	< 5.0
Mexico	8.1	< 5.0
Romania	< 5.0	< 5.0
Russian Federation	n/a	< 5.0
Saudi Arabia	6.9	< 5.0
Serbia and Montenegro	n/a	< 5.0
Slovak Republic	n/a	< 5.0
Syria	9.6	< 5.0
Tunisia	< 5.0	< 5.0
Turkey	6.2	< 5.0
Ukraine	n/a	< 5.0
Uruguay	5.2	< 5.0

Source: Klaus von Grebmer et al., "The Challenge of Hunger 2008," *Global Hunger Index* (Bonn: Welthungerhilfe; Washington, D.C.: International Food Policy Research Institute; and Dublin: Concern Worldwide, 2008).

Note: Countries with a Global Hunger Index (GHI) of less than 5 are not included in the ranking. Differences in the GHI of these countries are minimal, and for some countries (marked with an asterisk), the underlying data are unreliable. Countries with identical 2008 GHI are ranked equally. n/a, not available.

Table 2 Prevalence of Undernourishment in Developing Regions

Region	Number of undernourished, 2003–2005 (millions)	Proportion of undernourished compared to total population (%)		
		1990–1992	1995–1997	2003–2005
Caribbean	7.6	26	28	23
North and Central America	8.8	8	8	6
South America	28.8	12	10	8
Near East	28.4	7	11	11
North Africa	4.6	n/a	n/a	n/a
Central Africa	53.3	34	51	57
East Africa	86.0	45	44	35
Southern Africa	36.8	45	43	37
West Africa	36.0	20	16	14
East Asia	131.8	15	12	10
South Asia	313.6	25	22	21
Southeast Asia	86.9	24	18	16
Developing world total	832.2	20	18	16

Source: Food and Agriculture Organization, *High Food Prices and Food Security Threats and Opportunities: The State of Food Insecurity in the World, 2008* (Rome: FAO, 2008).

Note: n/a, not available.

Case Study—Food Prices and Financial Crisis

Since 2003, after more than one hundred years of decline in real food prices (until around 2000), world market food prices have steadily risen. Prices increased by about 25 percent between 2003 and 2006 and by about 57 percent between March 2007 and March 2008 according to the FAO in 2008. Although food prices showed a slight decline during the latter part of 2008, the dramatic increase in the world food prices up until April 2008 (for example, rice, a commodity eaten by a majority of the Asian population, reached a 437 percent increase from its 2001 price) drew the attention of the development community to the plight of poor consumers in developing countries and to the need for reviving food systems to avoid such dramatic volatility in price levels.

Increased food prices have also resulted in reduced access to food for millions of people whose purchasing power was already at a low level. A key result of high food prices is the increase in the rate of general inflation that reduces the ability of households to purchase food and other essential commodities. Due to this erosion of purchasing power, poor and middle-income households spend a major portion of their income on food, with little left for health and education. According to the World Bank, food price increases are likely to add 1.5 million more children to the existing 45 percent of Indian children who are already malnourished.

Studies conducted by the FAO, IFPRI, and other organizations suggest several major contributing factors in this dramatic rise in food prices. Both supply and demand have played a role. The demand for food is on the rise partly due to an increase in the income levels of many of the developing economies of the world. Demand levels have exceeded supply levels, resulting in a gradual decrease in the availability of surplus food in several countries and in the reduction of food stocks kept by developing countries.

Other factors have added to the problem. Several droughts in key food-producing countries, particularly in Australia, have resulted in reduced harvests. These droughts, combined with low levels of food stocks, resulted in a sharp decline in the food supply and a dramatic increase in food prices. In addition, since 2004, the prices of fossil fuels have been increasing. Fossil fuels contribute in a major way to the cost of production and transportation of food commodities, further adding to the increase of food prices. In response to the increasing cost of fossil fuels, developed countries have invested in the production of cereal-based biofuels, which has resulted in the diversion of food crops and land to biofuel production, reducing the supply of food in the global market (see ENERGY and Case Study—Biofuels and Food Security).

The sharp price increases for food starting in 2003 pushed several million people back into poverty and food insecurity. This food price increase is estimated to have resulted in about a 4.5 percent increase in poverty among developing countries. Until that time, efforts to reduce poverty had resulted in an annual percentage reduction in poverty at the rate of 0.7 percent per year since 1984, highlighting, by comparison, the significance of the increase in poverty at the beginning of the twenty-first century.

Countries have reacted with different policies to protect their populations in the light of high food prices. While some of these policy responses have been beneficial, others have triggered further increases in food prices. In Asia, for example, Bangladesh has reduced taxes on food grains while arranging to sell its rice stock at subsidized prices in urban areas along with restricting food exports. China, which is the largest producer and consumer of food grains in Asia, has introduced a series of quotas and restrictions on grain exports. It also introduced production support programs by increasing the minimum purchase price of wheat and rice and providing agricultural input subsidies. India has banned rice exports of nonbasmati varieties and, to increase the food supply to the country, has authorized duty-free imports of rice. Other initiatives include a release of 650,000 tons of rice to the local markets to be sold at subsidized prices in Thailand and a reduction in the export of rice to Vietnam from 4.5 million tons in 2007 to 3.5 million tons in March 2008. According to the FAO in 2008, measures such as export bans have helped protect the local population from being severely affected by food price increases, but at the same time have contributed to the further destabilization of price levels at the international level, particularly in countries that are traditional exporters of rice such as Thailand and Vietnam.

Among the twenty African countries that have taken proactive measures to address rising food prices, about sixteen of them resorted to reduced taxes on food grains; six of them have taken measures to increase the supply of food using their own stocks; seven countries have used price controls including consumer subsidies; and Ethiopia, Niger, Sudan, and Tanzania have restricted exports of food grains, according to the World Bank in 2008.

Although food prices started to decline in the latter part of 2008, coordinated effort is still needed to ease the burden of high food prices on the poor and hungry and to enable the agricultural sector to respond to the opportunities of higher prices. Without such efforts, achieving long-term food security will remain a challenge. Promoting pro-poor agriculture growth by investing in the smallholder agriculture sector, reducing market volatility by investing in appropriate market institutions and infrastructure for transportation of food commodities, and implementing appropriate social protection policies and programs to protect the poor and vulnerable would in the short run help alleviate the impact of high food prices and the economic slowdown resulting from global financial crisis.

Case Study—Biofuels and Food Security

Increases in oil and energy prices between 2002 and 2008 have encouraged both developed and developing countries to invest in producing substitutes for petroleum products such as gasoline and diesel. The increased investment in the production of biofuels and biodiesel has further contributed to increases in food-grain prices at the global level. For example, along with the recent droughts in major cereal-producing countries and the continued reduction in cereal stocks in several cereal exporters, the increased demand for biofuel crops has resulted in higher worldwide prices of maize, which rose by 54 percent between 2004 and 2006; of wheat, which rose by 34 percent; and of soybean oil, which rose by 71 percent. The increase in food-grain prices created by biofuel demand can have a significant impact on the food security of the poor and the vulnerable in developing countries. The food security of poor farmers who depend on their land for producing food for their own consumption, but who are also net buyers of food, will further be affected by increased demand for biofuel crops. However, increased demand for biofuel crops can result in increased income for farmers who grow these crops (including maize, soybeans, wheat, and cassava) and have surplus to sell locally and internationally.

Such opportunities for growing biofuel crops are curtailed by the trade and subsidy policies of developed countries, which are also investing in biofuel crops and directing cereal production to feed into biofuel production. The biofuel policies of developed countries—undertaken to speed the development of an alternative to petroleum-based energy sources—directly violate the efforts of the WTO Doha Round Negotiations that aim at reducing domestic subsidies and expanding the market access of developing countries to the developed-country market.

The policy package being implemented by developing countries includes the diversion of a growing share of feed grains, oil seeds, and other crops to the production of biofuel crops. For example, the United States, which is a reliable supplier of export grains, diverted more than 30 percent of its maize production in 2007 to biofuel production, a share likely to increase to 50 percent by 2015. Developed countries have also been subsidizing the production of biofuels to encourage production increases. The United States has spent US$6 billion in support of biofuel production, while the European Union spent US$4.8 billion. Other countries, such as Brazil, which has been investing in biofuel production for the past twenty years, also subsidize their farmers, both directly and indirectly, to use sugarcane for the production of biofuels. In addition to the subsidy and support of the biofuel industry, the mandatory blending requirements of the United States (which require 36 billion gallons of biofuels in 2022) and EU regulations (that target 5.7 percent of liquid motor fuel to come from biofuels by the year 2010) increase the pressure on the use of feedstocks for biofuels as well.

Through tariffs, both Europe and the United States have protected their biofuel industry. For example, the United States has imposed a tariff of 54 cents per gallon on imported ethanol. Such protection from competition reduces the opportunity for developing countries to supply ethanol to the developed country market. The United States and European Union have also provided subsidies for distribution, transportation, and storage of ethanol-based production and have invested substantial amounts of resources for research to develop second-generation cellulose biofuels. These developments indicate that, even if the biofuel sector in developing countries grows, competing in the international markets for biofuels will be difficult. Recent work by the IFPRI indicates that, due to the high share of food expenditure and low share of energy expenditure in developing countries (for example, Ethiopia spends 70 percent on food and 10 percent on energy, Bangladesh spends 66 percent on food and 9 percent on energy, and Tajikistan spends 71 percent on food and 5 percent on energy), the real commodity prices of food could increase 25–60 percent under a large expansion of biofuel production. Such an increase could result in low levels of calorie availability and a significant decrease in nutritional intake for the food-insecure population.

While developed countries have encouraged biofuel production through trade restrictions and subsidies, countries without resources to develop a biofuel sector may end up importing both food and oil with disastrous consequences. To reduce the possibility of such consequences making biofuel policies more market-oriented through an open-trade approach is important. Developing markets for biofuels produced in developing countries and allowing international free trade can benefit these producers. Countries such as India and China are also investing a large amount of resources to develop their biofuel sectors. For example, the government of India has invested in growing the biodiesel crop *Jatropha curais* on degraded and marginal lands, which could potentially increase the income of the rural population as well as reduce the cost of fuel for India. However, technological and structural issues of production remain challenging. Unless developing countries invest in research and development of biofuels that are appropriate for their environment, the contribution of the biofuel boom to local food security and income will remain questionable.

Case Study—Reviving African Agriculture for Food Security

The African continent has been chronically affected by a series of famines and food shortages since the 1960s. Only 5 percent of the continent's arable land is irrigated, while the rest of the land depends on annual rainfall for crop production. The size of arable land holdings is also small, with most farms having fewer than 2.5 acres for cultivation. The yield levels of major staple food crops are low, even by developing-country standards, hovering around 1.0–1.5 tons per hectare.

Several attempts have been made to revamp the agricultural sector, but considerable further development is needed. Agricultural research systems have been weak, with a limited capacity to conduct smallholder-oriented research. Higher education systems in Africa do not produce an adequate number of quality graduates who can contribute to agricultural development. Due to the structural adjustment policies of the World Bank in the 1980s and 1990s, agricultural extension systems have collapsed and technologies that have been developed by researchers remain unimplemented.

The lack of market development is a major hindrance. Weak road and communication infrastructures and a poor network for selling farm inputs and buying crop outputs limit the capacity for farmers to earn an adequate living, even in situations that have shown promise. For example, in the early 2000s, the Ethiopian strategy of giving credits to farmers in the form of fertilizers and high-yielding varieties of maize did increase the production of maize in various parts of the country. Yet such an increase could not be translated into an improved food security for the country or welfare for the producers due to a poor marketing infrastructure. The surplus maize produced in local areas reduced the prices of maize locally, leaving most farmers worse off in terms of income. However, when smallholder farmers become connected to high-value agriculture supply chains—such as Ethiopia's cut-flower industry, Kenya's vegetable production for export, and Mali's mango farmers' connection to European markets—positive agricultural development and income growth can occur.

Technological interventions that enhance yields and productivity offer another means of agricultural development. In fact, massive subsidies to farmers to encourage them to use fertilizers and high-yielding seeds have shown that, if disseminated properly, the technologies available to farmers can increase the productivity of smallholder agriculture. For example, since 2006 the high level of subsidies for smallholder farmers in Malawi, in the form of small packages of fertilizer and high-yielding hybrid maize seeds, has resulted in surplus food production to the point where Malawi was able to export maize. Such large subsidies, however, cannot be sustained over the long term.

Sustainable approaches to productivity increases have to come from increasing the ability of rural systems to identify problems and develop ways to solve them. Institutional reforms are also needed at the national level to effectively address the productivity challenges of farmers. At the regional level, agricultural research forums, such as the Forum for Agricultural Research in Africa (FARA), have been working to organize Africa-wide programs to address ecological-specific problems. Yet, such attempts can be effective only if they are adopted by the countries.

At the continental level, the New Partnership for Africa Development (NEPAD) has mobilized a Comprehensive African Agricultural Development Program (CAADP) to encourage African governments to invest 10 percent of their annual budget in agriculture, which could result in a future 6 percent growth in the agriculture sector. Although such approaches are laudable, the capacity to implement them at the country level still remains a challenge.

To address wide-ranging problems faced by the smallholder sector, the Bill and Melinda Gates Foundation and the Rockefeller Foundation have put together a program to reduce poverty and food insecurity among smallholder farmers in Africa. Formed in 2006 with a grant of US$330 million and called the Alliance for a Green Revolution in Africa (AGRA), the program is led by former UN Secretary-General Kofi Annan. AGRA addresses the challenges faced by smallholder farmers in terms of accessing inputs such as seeds and fertilizers and creating a network of partners who can develop innovations for addressing the smallholder sector. The goal of these efforts is to increase the productivity of smallholder farmers in order to achieve food security. Clearly, however, unless long-term investments are made in developing human and institutional capacity, any amount of external aid will not be able to address the problem.

Biographical Sketches

Jacques Diouf is the director-general of FAO. Since 1963, he has held positions in national and international agricultural institutions, as director of the European Office and the Agricultural Program of the Marketing Board (Paris/Dakar); executive secretary of the African Groundnut Council in Nigeria; executive secretary of the West Africa Rice Development Association in Liberia; and adviser to the president and regional director of the International Development Research Center, Ottawa (Canada). He was the secretary of state for science and technology in the cabinet of the Senegalese government, member of the Senegalese Parliament, and an ambassador for the permanent mission of the Republic of Senegal to the United Nations. He also served as secretary-general and special adviser to the governor of the Central Bank for West African States, Dakar.

Monty Jones, a leader in African agricultural research started his career in 1975 at the West Africa Rice Development Agency (WARDA) in its Mangrove Swamp Rice Research Project in Rokupr, Sierra Leone. At that time, West African farmers grew an indigenous rice species, *Oryza glaberrima,* with great difficulties, obtaining lower yields compared to its Asian counterpart *Oryza sativa.* Jones brought the good traits of these varieties together to increase the yields of African rice farmers, resulting in the New Rice for Africa (NERICA) variety. For this breakthrough, he received the World Food Prize in 2004. In 2002, he was appointed the executive secretary of the FARA, where he oversees advocacy and coordination efforts in support of regional research.

Per Pinstrup-Andersen is the J. Thomas Clark Professor of Entrepreneurship and the H. E. Babcock Professor of Food, Nutrition and Public Policy at Cornell University. He was director-general of the International Food Policy Research Institute in the mid-1990s, a time when international commitment and aid to agricultural development and reduction of food insecurity were at their lowest levels. In response, he organized IFPRI's researchers to alleviate apathy to and complacency toward global poverty and hunger. Pinstrup-Andersen has been the driving force behind the 2020 Vision initiative to assist world leaders in focusing on food security and hunger in the twenty-first century. He is the recipient of the 2001 World Food Prize for his efforts to enable the governments of several developing countries to transform their food policies.

Nevin S. Scrimshaw is an authority on international nutrition and senior adviser to the World Hunger Programme of the United Nations University in Japan. As the founding director of the Institute of Nutrition for Central America and Panama in the 1950s, Scrimshaw studied kwashiorkar, a deadly protein-deficiency disease, and developed cost-effective foods to alleviate it. Scrimshaw also addressed an iodine-deficiency disorder that results in mental retardation, deafness, and dwarfism in newborns and developed a method of salt iodization. In 1975, Scrimshaw initiated and directed the World Hunger Programme and trained more than five hundred scientists from developing countries to address food and nutrition problems. He was awarded the Alan Shawn Feinstein Hunger Merit Award and the World Food Prize in 1991 for his lifelong dedication to alleviating hunger and malnutrition in developing countries.

Joachim von Braun has been the director general of the IFPRI since 2002, overseeing the Institute's efforts to provide research-based sustainable solutions for ending hunger and malnutrition. Under his leadership, IFPRI has continued to grow in food policy–related strategy and governance, technology policy, markets, and health nutrition policy and has significantly expanded its teams in Africa, Asia, and Latin America. From 2000 to 2003, von Braun was president of the International Association of Agricultural Economists (IAAE). He has published research on international development topics; policy issues relating to trade, aid, famine, health, and nutrition; and a wide range of other agricultural economics research.

Directory

Bread for the World, 50 F Street NW, Suite 500, Washington, D.C. 20001. Telephone: (202) 639-9400 or 1-800-82-BREAD; email: bread@bread.org; Web: http://www.bread.org.
Organization mobilizing resources and support for reducing food insecurity and malnutrition in developing countries, primarily by sensitizing policymakers in the U.S. government.

Consultative Group on International Agriculture Research, World Bank, MSN G6-601, 1818 H Street NW, Washington, D.C. 20433. Telephone: (202) 473-8951; email: cgiar@cgiar.org; Web: http://www.cgiar.org.
Consortium of sixteen international agricultural research centers addressing global food security and hunger through scientific research and capacity strengthening.

Food and Agriculture Organization (FAO), Viale delle Terme di Caracalla, 00100 Rome, Italy. Telephone: (39) 06 5705 1; email: FAO-HQ@fao.org; Web: http://www.fao.org.
UN agency devoted to alleviating poverty and hunger through food security.

Food First, Institute for Food and Development Policy, 398 60th Street, Oakland, Calif. 94618. Telephone: (510) 654-4400; email: foodfirst@foodfirst.org; Web: http://www.foodfirst.org.
Development organization promoting alternative solutions for the food security problems of developing countries.

Institute of Development Studies, University of Sussex, Brighton BN1 9RE, United Kingdom. Telephone: (44) 0 1273 606261; email: ids@ids.ac.uk; Web: http://www.ids.ac.uk/ids.
Center that conducts research on food security issues in developing countries.

International Food Policy Research Institute, 2033 K Street NW, Washington, D.C. 20006-1002. Telephone: (202) 862-5600; email: ifpri@cgiar.org; Web: http://www.ifpri.org.
Policy research and outreach institution identifying sustainable options for reducing food insecurity, poverty, and natural resource degradation.

Sasakawa Peace Foundation, Nippon Foundation Building, 4th Floor, 1-2-2, Akasaka, Minato-ku, Tokyo, Japan. Telephone: (81) 3 6229 5400; email: spfpr@spf.or.jp; Web: http://www.spf.org.
Organization working to emulate the Asian success in food production in Africa through various field-based projects.

World Food Programme, Via C. G. Viola 68, Parco dei Medici, 00148 Rome, Italy. Telephone: (39) 6 65131; email: wfpinfo@wfp.org; Web: http://www.wfp.org.
UN organization serving the food insecure in developing countries.

Further Research

Books

Association for Strengthening Agricultural Research in East and Central Africa (ASARECA). *Emerging Technologies to Benefit Farmers in Sub-Saharan Africa and South Asia*. Washington, D.C.: National Academies Press, 2008. Available at: http://www.nap.edu/catalog.php?record_id=12455#toc.

Conroy, A. C., et al. *Poverty, AIDS and Hunger: Breaking the Poverty Trap in Malawi*. New York: Palgrave Macmillan, 2008.

Devereux, S., B. Vaitla, and S. H. Swan. *Seasons of Hunger: Fighting Cycles of Starvation among the World's Rural Poor*. London: Pluto Press, 2008.

Guha-Khasnobis, B., S. S. Acharya, and B. Davis. *Food Security: Indicators, Measurement, and the Impact of Trade Openness*. New York: Oxford University Press, 2007.

National Research Council. *Food Insecurity and Hunger in the United States: An Assessment of the Measure*. Panel to Review U.S. Department of Agriculture's Measurement of Food Insecurity and Hunger, National Research Council of the National Academies. Washington, D.C.: National Academies Press, 2006.

Sanchez, P., et al. *Halving Hunger: It Can Be Done*. UN Millennium Project, UNDP. London: Earthscan, 2005.

Sridhar, Devi. *The Battle Against Hunger: Choice, Circumstance, and the World Bank*. New York: Oxford University Press, 2008.

Swaminathan, M. S. *Towards Hunger Free India: From Vision to Action*. Chennai, India: East West Books Madras, 2006.

Swan, S. H., and B. Vaitla. *Hunger Watch Report 2007–08: The Justice of Eating*. Action Against Hunger. London: Pluto Press, 2007.

United Nations World Food Program. *Hunger and Health*. World Hunger Series 2007. London: Earthscan, 2007. Available at: http://www.earthscan.co.uk/?tabid=1498 (accessed December 15, 2008).

von Braun, J., and E. Diaz-Bonilla, eds. *Globalization of Food and Agriculture and the Poor*. New Delhi: Oxford University Press, 2008.

Articles and Reports

Adato, M., and J. Hoddinott. "Social Protection: Opportunities for Africa." IFPRI Policy Brief no. 5. International Food Policy Research Institute, Washington, D.C., 2008.

Adoho, Franck, et al. "Food Price Crisis in Africa." *World Bank Research Digest* 3, no. 1 (2008). Available at: http://econ.worldbank.org/WBSITE/EXTERNAL/EXTDEC/0,,contentMDK:22.

Al Jazeera English News. "Bangladesh Hit by Food Price Riots." Available at: http://english.aljazeera.net/News/aspx/print.htm (accessed June 2, 2008).

Asenso-Okyere, K., and S. Babu. "Technological Tools to Address the Food Crises." *Perspectives in Agriculture, Veterinary Science, Nutrition, and Natural Resources* 3 (December 2008): 1–11.

Asenso-Okyere, K., K. E. Davis, and D. Aredo. "Advancing Agriculture in Developing Countries through Knowledge and Innovation (Synopsis of an International Conference)." International Food Policy Research Institute, Washington D.C., 2008. Available at: http://www.ifpri.org/events/conferences/2008/20080407.asp.

Babu, S. C., P. Anandajayasekeram, and M. Rukuni. "Challenges Facing African Agriculture." In *Impact of Science on African Agriculture and Food Security,* ed. P. Anandajayasekeram et al. Cambridge, Mass.: CABI, 2007.

Baltzer, K., H. Hansen, and K. M. Lind. "A Note on the Causes and Consequences of the Rapidly Increasing International Food Prices." Institute of Food and Resource Economics, University of Copenhagen, 2008.

Benson, Todd, et al. "Global Food Crises: Monitoring and Assessing Impact to Inform Policy Responses." Food Policy Report. International Food Policy Research Institute, Washington, D.C., 2008.

Coulombe, H., and Q. Wodon. "Assessing the Geographic Impact of Higher Food Prices in Guinea." Policy Research Working Paper no. 4743. World Bank, Washington, D.C., 2008.

Dorosh, Paul. "Trade, Public Stocks and Food Price Stabilization: Policy Implications from Country Experiences in South Asia and Sub-Saharan Africa." Presentation at the IFPRI Brown Bag Lunch Seminar, Washington, D.C., June 12, 2008.

International Conference on Nutrition. "World Declaration on Nutrition," December 1992. Available at: http://www.fao.org/docrep/u9920t/u9920t0a.htm.

International Food Policy Research Institute (IFPRI). "Best-Bet Investments in Agricultural Research." IFPRI Forum. IFPRI, Washington, D.C., October 2008.

International Herald Tribune. "UN: High Commodity Prices from Biofuel Demand Could Last a Decade," July 5, 2007. Available at: http://www.iht.com/bin/print.php?id=6486774 (accessed August 20, 2007).

Joseph, H., and Q. Wodon. "Assessing the Potential Impact on Poverty of Rising Cereal Prices: The Case of Mali." Policy Research Working Paper no. 4744. World Bank, Washington, D.C., 2008.

Mitchell, D. "A Note on Rising Food Prices." Policy Research Working Paper no. 4682. World Bank Development Prospects Group, Washington, D.C., July 2008.

Quisumbing, A., R. Meinzen-Dick, and L. Bassett. "Helping Women Respond to the Global Food Price Crisis." IFPRI Policy Brief no. 7. International Food Policy Research Institute, Washington, D.C., 2008.

Rhoads, James. "Biodiesel and India's Rural Economy (case study 7–8)." In *Food Policy for Developing Countries: Case Studies,* ed. Per Pinstrup-Andersen and Fuzhi Cheng. Ithaca, N.Y.: Cornell University Division of Nutritional Sciences, 2007. Available at: http://cip.cornell.edu/dns/gfs/1200428188.

Rosegrant, M. W. "Outlooks and Global Change: New Developments and Ways Forward." Presentation, 2007 Internal Program Review. International Food Policy Research Institute, Washington, D.C., 2008.

Surowiecki, J. "The Perils of Efficiency." *New Yorker,* November 24, 2008. Available at: http://www.newyorker.com/talk/financial/2008/11/24/081124ta_talk_surowiecki?printable (accessed December 3, 2008).

Technical Center for Agricultural and Rural Cooperation (CTA). "Rising Food Prices: An Opportunity for Change?" Brussels Rural Development Briefing Session no. 7, 2008.

United Kingdom Food Group. "More Aid for African Agriculture: Policy Implications for Small-Scale Farmers." August 28, 2008. Available at: http://www.ukfg.org.uk/more-aid-for-african-agriculture.php (accessed December 10, 2008).

United Nations Food and Agriculture Organization (FAO). "Bioenergy Policy, Markets and Trade and Food Security." Technical Background Document from the Expert Consultation held on February 18–20, 2008. FAO, Rome, 2008.

———. "High Food Prices and Food Security: Threats and Opportunities." In *The State of Food Insecurity in the World 2008*. Rome: FAO, 2008.

———. "Number of Hungry People Rises to 963 million." Press release. December 9, 2008. Available at: http://www.fao.org/news/story/en/item/8836/icode (accessed December 11, 2008).

———. "Undernourishment around the World." In *The State of Food Insecurity in the World 2008*. Rome: FAO, 2008.

United Nations Office for the Coordination of Humanitarian Affairs. "Sri Lanka: Food Insecurity a Growing Problem." IRIN Print Report. 2008. Available at: http://www.irinnews.org/Report.aspx?ReportId=77678 (accessed June 2, 2008).

———. "Sri Lanka: High Prices and Food Shortages Taking Toll." IRIN Print Report. 2008. Available at: http://www.irinnews.org/PrintReport.aspx?ReportId=77985 (accessed June 2, 2008).

von Braun, J. "Food and Financial Crises: Implications for Agriculture and the Poor." Brief prepared for the CGIAR Annual General Meeting. Mozambique. International Food Policy Research Institute, Washington, D.C., December 2008.

———. "High Food Prices: The Proposed Policy Actions." Keynote address to the ECOSOC special meeting The Global Food Crisis, United Nations Headquarters, New York, May 20, 2008.

———. "Rising Food Prices: What Should be Done?" IFPRI Policy Brief. International Food Policy Research Institute, Washington, D.C., 2008.

von Braun, J., et al. "International Agricultural Research for Food Security, Poverty Reduction, and the Environment: What to Expect from Scaling Up CGIAR Investments and 'Best Bet' Programs." IFPRI Issue Brief no. 53. International Food Policy Research Institute, Washington, D.C., 2008.

von Braun, J., J. Sheeran, and N. Ngongi. "Global Food Prices." In *2007–2008 IFPRI Annual Report*. Washington, D.C.: Graphic Communications, 2008.

von Grebmer, K., et al. "The Challenge of Hunger 2008." In *Global Hunger Index*. Bonn: Welthungerhilfe; Washington, D.C.: International Food Policy Research Institute; and Dublin: Concern Worldwide, 2008.

Wodon, Q., et al. "Potential Impact of Higher Food Prices on Poverty: Summary Estimates for a Dozen West and Central African Countries." Policy Research Working Paper no. 4745. World Bank, Washington, D.C., 2008.

Wodon, Q., C. Tsimpo, and H. Coulombe. "Assessing the Potential Impact on Poverty of Rising Cereal Prices: The Case of Ghana." Policy Research Working Paper no. 4740. World Bank, Washington, D.C., 2008.

Wodon, Q., and H. Zaman. "Rising Food Prices in Sub-Saharan Africa: Poverty Impact and Policy Responses." Policy Research Working Paper no. 4738. World Bank, Washington, D.C., 2008.

World Bank. "Rising Oil, Food Prices Hurting Pakistan's Poor." May 30, 2008. Available at: http://www.worldbank.org.pk/WBSITE/EXTERNAL/COUNTRIES/SOUTHASIAEXT/PAKISTANEXTN/0,,contentMDK:21784810~menuPK:293071~pagePK:2865066~piPK:2865079~theSitePK:293052,00.html (accessed June 3, 2008).

———. "World Bank Calls for Urgent Action on Food in Advance of Development Aid Talks in Ghana." August 31, 2008. Available at: http://web.worldbank.org/WBSITE/EXTERNAL/TOPICS/EXTHEALTHNUTRITIONANDPOPULATION/EXTNUTRITION/0,,contentMDK:21886394~menuPK:282580~pagePK:64020865~piPK:149114~theSitePK:282575,00.html (accessed September 3, 2008).

Web Sites

African Union
www.africa-union.org

Asian Development Bank
http://www.adb.org/Food-Crisis/default.asp

BBC (British Broadcasting Corporation)
http://news.bbc.co.uk/2/hi/in_depth/world/2008/costoffood/default.stm

Consultative Group on International Agricultural Research (CGIAR): Battling Rising Food Prices with Productivity-Boosting Science, May 2008
http://www.cgiar.org/pdf/news_foodcrisis_what_ICRISAT_thinks.pdf

Consultative Group on International Agricultural Research (CGIAR): Understanding and Containing Global Food Price Inflation, May 2008
http://www.cgiar.org/monthlystory/may2008.html

***Financial Times* Portal on Global Food Crisis**
http://www.ft.com/foodprices

Food and Agriculture Organization of the United Nations: FAO Initiative on Soaring Food Prices
http://www.fao.org/isfp/isfp-home/en

Food and Agriculture Organization of the United Nations: Food World Situation
http://www.fao.org/worldfoodsituation/en

IFAD Portal: Rising Food Prices
http://www.ifad.org/operations/food

International Centre for Trade and Sustainable Development (ICTSD)
http://ictsd.net

International Food Policy Research Institute (IFPRI): Food Prices Crisis Portal
http://www.ifpri.org/themes/foodprices/foodprices.asp

International Monetary Fund: Responding to the Food and Fuel Price Surge Portal
http://www.imf.org/external/np/exr/foodfuel/index.htm

Organisation for Economic Cooperation and Development (OECD): Agriculture and Fisheries
http://www.oecd.org/topic/0,3373,en_2649_37401_1_1_1_1_37401,00.html

Overseas Development Initiative (ODI): Food portal
http://www.odi.org.uk/themes/food/index.asp

Reliefweb: Global Food Crisis
http://www.reliefweb.int/rw/rwb.nsf/GlobalFoodCrisis?Readform

United Nations: UN High-Level Task Force on the Global Food Security Crisis
http://www.un.org/issues/food/taskforce

World Bank: Food Crisis Portal
http://www.worldbank.org/html/extdr/foodprices

World Food Programme
http://www.wfp.org

Document

1. G8 Leaders Statement on Global Food Security

G8 Summit, Hokkaido Toyako, July 8, 2008

The full text is available at http://www.mofa.go.jp/policy/economy/summit/2008/doc/doc080709_04_en.html.

Extract

1. We are deeply concerned that the steep rise in global food prices coupled with availability problems in a number of developing countries is threatening global food security. The negative impacts of this recent trend could push millions more back into poverty, rolling back progress made towards achieving the Millennium Development Goals. We have taken additional steps to assist those suffering from food insecurity or hunger, and today renew our commitment to address this multifaceted and structural crisis.

2. We are determined to take all possible measures in a coordinated manner, and since January 2008 have committed, for short, medium and long-term purposes, over US$ 10 billion to support food aid, nutrition interventions, social protection activities and measures to increase agricultural output in affected countries. In the short-term, we are addressing urgent needs of the most vulnerable people. In this regard, we welcome the contributions which others have made to address the global food crisis. We call on other donors to participate along with us in making commitments, including through the World Food Programme (WFP), to meet remaining immediate humanitarian needs and to provide access to seeds and fertilizers for the upcoming planting season. We will also look for opportunities to help build up local agriculture by promoting local purchase of food aid. We underline the importance of strengthening the effective, timely and needs-based delivery of food assistance and increasing agricultural productivity.

3. Responding effectively to this crisis requires leadership, ambition and an appropriate scale of resources. The international community needs a fully coordinated response and a comprehensive strategy to tackle this issue in an integrated fashion from short to medium and long-term. We welcome in this regard the outcomes of relevant international fora including the Food and Agriculture Organization (FAO) High-Level Conference on World Food Security in Rome and the Tokyo International Conference for African Development (TICAD) IV in Yokohama. We commend the leadership of the United Nations (UN) and Bretton Woods institutions in convening the High Level Task Force on the Global Food Crisis to establish the "Comprehensive Framework for Action," and urge the relevant stakeholders to swiftly implement plans to achieve prompt delivery for countries in need.

4. To coordinate and implement this effectively, we will work with the international community in forming a global partnership on agriculture and food, involving all relevant actors, including developing country governments, the private sector, civil

society, donors, and international institutions. This partnership, strengthening and building on existing UN and other international institutions, could provide efficient and effective support for country-led processes and institutions and for local leadership, draw on the expertise in existing international organizations and, in particular, ensure monitoring and assessment on progress. The UN should facilitate and provide coordination. As part of this partnership, a global network of high-level experts on food and agriculture would provide science-based analysis, and highlight needs and future risks.

5. We are committed to thorough reform of the FAO to enhance its effectiveness in helping to ensure food security for all. In this context, we expect the next FAO extraordinary conference to provide effective follow-up to the Rome Food Summit and outline concrete steps to enhance the effectiveness of the FAO.

6. Food security also requires a robust world market and trade system for food and agriculture. Rising food prices are adding inflationary pressures and generating macroeconomic imbalances especially for some low-income countries. In this regard, we will work toward the urgent and successful conclusion of an ambitious, comprehensive and balanced Doha Round. It is also imperative to remove export restrictions and expedite the current negotiation at the World Trade Organization (WTO) aimed at introducing stricter disciplines on these trade actions which prolong and aggravate the situation, and hinder humanitarian purchases of food commodities. Furthermore, we continue to promote the development of open and efficient agricultural and food markets, and support monitoring of the functioning of such markets by relevant agencies, with a view to minimizing the volatility of food prices and preempting future crises. We also call for countries with sufficient food stocks to make available a part of their surplus for countries in need, in times of significantly increasing prices and in a way not to distort trade. We will explore options on a coordinated approach on stock management, including the pros and cons of building a "virtual" internationally coordinated reserve system for humanitarian purposes.

7. We fully recognize the need for a wide range of mid- to long-term measures to tackle the issue of food security and poverty, inter alia, the importance of stimulating world food production and increasing investment in agriculture. To this end, we will:

(a) reverse the overall decline of aid and investment in the agricultural sector, and to achieve significant increases in support of developing country initiatives, including—in Africa—through full and effective implementation of the Comprehensive Africa Agricultural Development Programme (CAADP);

(b) support CAADP's goal of 6.2% annual growth in agricultural productivity, and work toward the goal of doubling production of key food staples in African countries meeting CAADP criteria in five to ten years in a sustainable manner, with particular emphases on fostering smallholder agriculture and inclusive rural growth;

(c) promote agricultural research and development, and the training of a new generation of developing country scientists and experts focusing on the dissemination of improved, locally adapted and sustainable farming technologies, in particular via the Consultative Group on International Agricultural Research (CGIAR), and through partnerships such as the Alliance for a Green Revolution in Africa (AGRA);

(d) support improvement of infrastructure, including irrigation, transportation, supply chain, storage and distribution systems and quality control;

(e) assist in the development of food security early warning systems;

(f) encourage the efforts of international financial institutions including regional development banks and the International Fund for Agricultural Development (IFAD); in this regard, we particularly welcome the World Bank's recent announcement of a new US$ 1.2 billion rapid financing facility to address immediate needs, and the work of the International Monetary Fund (IMF) to address the needs of food-importing countries facing balance of payments difficulties, including through the Poverty Reduction and Growth Facility and the review of the Exogenous Shocks Facility;

(g) accelerate research and development and increase access to new agricultural technologies to boost agricultural production; we will promote science-based risk analysis including on the contribution of seed varieties developed through biotechnology;

(h) support country-led development strategies in adapting to the impact of climate change, combating desertification, and promoting conservation and sustainable use of biological diversity, while intensifying our efforts to address climate change;

(i) ensure the compatibility of policies for the sustainable production and use of biofuels with food security and accelerate development and commercialization of sustainable second-generation biofuels from non-food plant materials and inedible biomass; in this regard, we will work together with other relevant stakeholders to develop science-based benchmarks and indicators for biofuel production and use;

(j) promote good governance in developing countries with particular emphasis on their food security and market policies; and

(k) mainstream food security objectives into the development policies of donors and recipient countries, reaffirming our common commitment to the principles of the Paris Declaration on Aid Effectiveness.

8. We have tasked a G8 Experts Group to monitor the implementation of our commitments, and identify other ways in which the G8 can support the work of the High Level Task Force on the Global Food Crisis and work with other interested parties for the next UN General Assembly to realize the global partnership.

9. We also ask our ministers of agriculture to hold a meeting to contribute to developing sound proposals on global food security.

10. We will review the progress on this issue at our next Summit.

LITERACY AND EDUCATIONAL ACCESS

Ulla Larsen

Universal primary education by 2015 is one of the United Nations Millennium Development Goals (MDGs). Globally, enrollment in schools has increased. For example, the number of children of primary school age who did not attend school fell from 103 million in 1993 to 73 million in 2006. However, many people still have limited reading and writing abilities, and the United Nations Educational, Scientific and Cultural Organization (UNESCO) estimated that 774 million of the world's adult people were illiterate—about one-fifth of the world's adult population—in 2005–2007. Nearly two-thirds of these adults were women. A main source of illiteracy is the lack of primary education, even though the United Nations declared education to be a fundamental human right in 1948. Literacy empowers people personally, and having a literate population is important to a country economically, making UNESCO's commitment to worldwide literacy a powerful tool for individual and national development.

Historical Background and Development

The ancient Greek and Roman civilizations are examples of early societies that developed systems of writing, but the general populations of these societies were probably not literate. Although village schools existed, they seem to have been limited in number, and no true network of schools for the masses existed in either society. The Protestant Reformation played a large role in promoting mass literacy. Priests in the Catholic Church at the time read and wrote Latin rather than the local languages (vernaculars). The Church, in fact, was against mass literacy because it was linked to heresy; if a people read the scriptures for themselves, they might form an opinion that opposed the teachings of the Church. Martin Luther, leader of the Reformation, published the *Small Catechism,* which became basic reading for his followers. The first mass literacy

---

This chapter is based on the original, written by Anya Hogoboom, that appeared in the first edition of *World at Risk.*

campaign took place in Sweden in the seventeenth century as an effort to increase Bible reading and study.

Note that functional literacy has not always been the goal of primary education. In France, reading skills were taught three hundred years before writing was an instructional concern because a population that is able to read is relatively nonthreatening but people with the ability to write may challenge established norms and the parties in power. Although many European countries passed legislation that addressed universal primary education in the eighteenth century, in most cases it took around one hundred years for this goal to be seriously pursued. Prior to 1800, countries in northern and western Europe had generally literate societies with respect to the ability to read. The countries in the southern and eastern areas of the continent had significantly fewer literate people and communities.

General education came of age in Europe during the nineteenth century. Although all European countries made gains in the 1800s, at the century's end the literacy rate in Hungary, Italy, Russia, and Spain lagged far behind the rest of the continent. In the early twentieth century, wide differences remained in the literacy rates among different areas of many nations. According to *The Rise of Mass Literacy,* in 1911 Piedmont, an urbanized region in the industrialized north of Italy, had an illiteracy rate of 11 percent, compared to 70 percent in Calabria, a rural area in the far south of the country.

Sub-Saharan African countries colonized by the British began to see the benefits associated with literacy in the nineteenth century. The demand for printed material in many British-occupied African countries rose during this period. Actual literacy campaigns in these countries, however, did not begin until some years after their independence.

Japan stands out as a non-Western country that addressed education and literacy in the nineteenth century. By 1910, Japan had achieved a 90 percent enrollment of children in its six-year schooling system. The achievement of mass literacy in Japan is thought to be due to the primary education system.

Access to basic education became a fundamental human right in 1948 through its inclusion in the UN Universal Declaration of Human Rights as Article 26, which guarantees the right to free primary education (see HUMAN RIGHTS). Since then, literacy and educational access have been of prime concern to the United Nations. UNESCO was established in 1945 to foster world peace through educational and cultural exchanges and programs. From 1969 to 1974, UNESCO oversaw the Experimental World Literacy Program (EWLP) with funding from the United Nations Development Programme (UNDP). This was the first major mass literacy campaign on an international scale, and although the EWLP had no stated aim of world literacy, it was harshly criticized in the press for failing to end illiteracy. More recently, 1990 was declared the International Year of Literacy. As a consequence of UNESCO's efforts during the latter part of the twentieth century, developing countries have benefited from numerous literacy and educational programs. The United Nations General Assembly proclaimed 2003–2012 to be the United Nations Literacy Decade. It reaffirmed that literacy for all was at the heart of the notion of basic education for all and that creating literate environments was essential to eradicating poverty, achieving gender equity, and ensuring sustainable development.

Current Status

The question of what constitutes literacy poses a major difficulty for researchers and workers in the field as well as for government and international policymakers. Should being able to read and write in one's native language or dialect be considered sufficient, or should one also be able to read and write in the official language designated by government? Further, different governments use different criteria for determining literacy, from being able to write one's name to being able to read and write in any situation needed in society. UNESCO and others often use the term *functional literacy* for the last definition. This definition allows for differences between communities—for example, the functional level of literacy in industrialized nations is higher than in developing countries—making an international literacy standard difficult. Therefore, comparisons and statistics should be viewed with these words of caution in mind. Increasingly, literacy and illiteracy are not seen as static states but, instead, as two ends of a continuum, and researchers are beginning to speak in terms of degrees of literacy rather than literacy versus illiteracy.

Research

Literacy and basic education are often blurred, so in the literature and research on literacy differentiating what is specifically a benefit or effect of literacy from what is a general benefit or effect of basic education can be difficult. Basic education can mean primary schooling, or it can mean nonformal education, such as adult literacy programs. Schooling is considered formal education. Often, people (and organizations) speak of literacy as though it were the sole end and measure of basic education. But, of course, other aspects of basic education are also important; for example, numeracy, the basic awareness and use of mathematics, has begun to gain attention in the research on literacy and in nonformal basic education programs.

According to the UNESCO Institute for Statistics Data Centre, in 2005–2007 developing countries had 765 million illiterate people and developed countries had 8 million. This illustrates that literacy is strongly tied to financial constraints (see Table 2). Developing countries have less money to spend on primary education (see map, p. 425), and many families in developing countries cannot afford school supplies and such basic items as shoes. They therefore do not send their children to school (see INCOME INEQUALITY).

UNESCO measures a country's primary school enrollment ratio in two ways. The gross enrollment ratio is measured by dividing the total number of students enrolled in primary school, which includes late enrollments and retentions (that is, students who have been held back to repeat a grade), by the number of children of primary school age; gross enrollment ratios can therefore be more than 100 percent. The net enrollment is calculated by dividing the number of students enrolled in primary school who are the official age for first grade by the number of children in the age group that officially corresponds to primary school. According to UNESCO's "Education for All Global Monitoring Report 2008: Education for All by 2015: Will We Make it?" the global net enrollment ratio rose from 83 to 87 percent between 1999 and 2005 and participation levels increased most rapidly in sub-Saharan Africa (23 percent) and South and West Asia (11 percent). Collectively, developed countries had a gross enrollment ratio of 101 percent in 2005. Developing countries, by contrast, had a gross enrollment ratio of 114 percent. Gross and net enrollment ratios vary significantly by country (see Table 3). In developing countries not only do a smaller percentage of children attend school than in developed countries but a wider gap also is apparent between gross and net enrollments, reflecting a larger number of students who are not age-appropriate for the first grade.

Globally, a gender gap exists in education and in literacy. Proportionally, more boys than girls attend primary school, and more men than women are literate. This has been overwhelmingly true historically and is due to traditions that keep girls and women at home with little or no access to education. The gender gap has all but disappeared in developed countries and has narrowed in the developing countries. Other literacy gaps include the social gap (people in higher social classes tend to have better access to education and higher literacy rates than people in lower classes) and the rural-urban gap (urban areas often have literacy rates that are significantly higher than rural areas). The second gap reflects the fact that schools and programs accessible to higher concentrations of people are easier to set up.

As we can see, literacy and education are not isolated issues. They are linked to poverty, employment, health, fertility rates, and infant mortality, among other factors. For instance, a strong link has been found between parental education and child health. Although both parents' level of education corresponds to better health in their children, the mother's has the greater impact. The reason for this is unclear, but Shireen Jejeebhoy's explanation of the correlation between women's education and children's health is that education makes women more autonomous, thereby giving them greater control over health decisions regarding their children. In keeping with Jejeebhoy's analysis, some have suggested that the reason this correlation does not hold as strongly in sub-Saharan Africa is because women there have a higher degree of autonomy regardless of their level of education. Even a small amount of education can make a positive difference in the health of offspring and in the lowering of fertility rates and infant mortality rates (see HEALTH).

Macro- and micro-rationales can be advanced for fostering literacy. On the macro level, the expectation is that increased literacy will help the economic development of a nation because of the increased potential for meaningful employment and for productivity gains (see LABOR AND EMPLOYMENT). In fact, one school of thought claims that the economic situation in a country cannot improve unless higher literacy rates are attained. Educated and literate workers are able to perform more work that requires advanced skills, enabling a country to produce more. Doubts exists, however, regarding this correlation between literacy and economic growth because, for example, if a newly literate person takes the job of a less literate person, nothing has been altered except for the people directly involved. In short, having more literate people does not automatically create more work requiring advanced skills. The micro-effects of literacy are clearer. Literacy often leads to increased social status and respect from peers. Also, the ability to perform such functions as reading medicine bottles and writing checks increases a person's ability to function successfully in daily life.

Primary education is one of the main routes to literacy. Much of the literacy rate increase in some countries, such as Mexico in recent years, is due to the increase in primary school attendance rather than to nonformal programs. Just because a person has attended school does not, however, mean that he or she is literate. Many countries have problems with high dropout rates; that is, many children are leaving school before literacy has been attained or at least before a high level of literacy has been reached. UNESCO reports that Burkina Faso, Djibouti, Central African Republic, Eritrea, Liberia, and Niger had more than 40 percent of primary school–age children out of school in 2006. Literacy is not a static state; it needs to be used and reinforced to be retained or improved. Therefore, children who drop out of school with only a basic level of literacy are less likely to become functionally literate adults.

Literacy statistics are often based on the number of years of schooling received. For example, in gathering literacy statistics, many countries assume that a person who has attended school for at least four or five years is literate; four or five years are generally considered the minimum number of years necessary for literacy to be achieved. This is not an absolute correlation, however, because some people attain literacy in less time, while others need more time. In countries with high retention rates, if children only go to school for a few years they are potentially not completing enough schooling to acquire literacy. For example, in South American countries, children go to school for a regional average of five years; however, because of the high retention rates, fewer than five grades are completed by the average child. (Schooling that does not result in literacy is called wastage.) Therefore, literacy statistics based on the number of years of schooling are not necessarily accurate.

Although the acquisition of literacy is generally thought to be empowering, it can also be a tool of oppression. Many countries with low literacy rates have multiple languages within their borders. This is particularly true of sub-Saharan African nations and the Pacific islands. National literacy campaigns tend to focus on only one language. Thus, a person's native language may be devalued, and the individual may be forced to adopt the national language chosen by the ruling party. National literacy campaigns highlighting a particular language can, however, also serve to bring about a sense of national unity.

Policies and Programs

UNESCO is the premier international organization concerned with promoting basic education and achieving literacy worldwide. It advocates a two-pronged approach to raising literacy rates: providing quality education to all children and providing literacy classes for adults. UNESCO has pursued these goals largely through its Education for All (EFA) initiative. This project, through which a large number of countries are now committed to providing primary education to all school-age children and resources for adult education, was launched at the World Conference on Education for All in Jomtien, Thailand, in March 1990, in conjunction with the UN-declared International Year of Literacy. The conference was attended by representatives from 155 governments. The result of the conference was a World Declaration on Education for All calling for a rise in global literacy rates and a broadening of education parameters to encompass all basic learning functions, such as oral expression and problem solving (see Document 1).

Following up on the world declaration, a major evaluation of basic education in more than 180 countries was undertaken in 1998. The general opinion was that governments had not lived up to the promises they committed themselves to in Jomtien. A renewed effort is now taking place to fulfill the EFA goals. A framework for action was adopted at the World Education Forum in Dakar, Senegal, in April 2000 (see Document 2). The agreement was approved by 181 nations, thus committing their governments to achieving the goals set forth by 2015. The targets include expanding primary education to all children (with special emphasis on bridging the education gap for girls, ethnic minorities, and the disadvantaged) and bringing about a 50 percent improvement in the literacy rate of adults (see Table 4). The main responsibility for meeting these goals rests with national governments.

A variety of literacy campaigns are being initiated by governments and nongovernmental organizations. These programs take many different approaches. The government of India oversees a national literacy program of community-based projects. Literacy programs targeting the family have been developed in many countries. Some of these programs emphasize strengthening childhood education by helping parents learn how to facilitate their children's learning, whereas others focus on illiterate or barely literate parents. Programs in some countries tie literacy to other issues. For example, in Nepal family literacy, microfinance, and health-promoting programs are combined.

Many adult literacy programs are administered by nongovernmental organizations (while national governments tend to invest in primary schooling). Programs for illiterate adults are changing in important ways. In contrast to the traditional thinking that illiterate adults also lack such skills as critical thinking and problem solving and that they are "blank pages," many programs now take into consideration the skills that illiterate adults already possess as well as the topics they find valuable. Many argue that adults' interest will be held only by literacy programs that address topics that are immediately relevant to their everyday lives.

In ongoing monitoring of the EFA initiative conducted by UNESCO (and published yearly in *Education for All Global Monitoring Reports*), UNESCO concluded in its 2007 report *Education for All by 2015—Will We Make It?* that progress has been made, although it has been uneven. Access to and participation in primary education have increased since Dakar, and most regions are close to having universal primary education. However, inequalities remain between urban and rural areas, between rich and poor households, and among ethnic groups. Gender disparities persist in many countries, especially at the secondary or higher levels of education, and the rate of adult illiteracy has changed little. Further, acute shortages of teachers are common, especially in sub-Saharan Africa and in South and West Asia (see Table 5). Throughout the review, the importance of equity and equality was emphasized and encouraged.

Regional Summaries

North America

Canada and the United States had literacy rates of 99 percent in 2007, as reported by the UNESCO Institution for Statistics. In 2006, the gross enrollment rate was 98.2 percent in primary, 93.9 percent in secondary, and 81.8 percent in tertiary education in the United States. The ratio of girls to boys was 1 in primary and secondary education, while the gender gap was 28.0 percent in tertiary education (girls having gross enrollment rates of 96.1 percent versus 68.1 percent among boys). In 2004, in Canada, the respective rates were 99.7, 117.3, and 62.4, and the gender gap was 0.6 for primary, 3.0 for secondary, and 19.0 for tertiary education (girls having gross enrollment rates of 72.1 percent versus 53.1 percent among boys in tertiary education).

The United States and Canada have very high attendance in their systems of free compulsory education, yet problems of functional illiteracy persist. Functional illiteracy is now recognized as a problem because the demand for unskilled labor has diminished due to continuing automation, which leaves many functional illiterates without a job. According to the U.S. National Assessment of Adult Literacy Survey from 2003, fewer adults tested as having "Below Basic" literacy skills (no more than the most simple and concrete literacy skills) and fewer adults tested as having "Proficient" literacy skills (able to perform complex and challenging literacy activities) in 2003 than in 1992 (the previous comparable survey was conducted in 1992), suggesting that literacy skills were becoming more uniform. The group "Below Basic" numbered 14 percent (30 million) of adults sixteen years of age and older, and nonwhites were overrepresented in this group—39 percent were Hispanic and 20 percent were black. A pressing issue regarding the education of ethnic minorities is whether their native language or dialects should be incorporated into the curricula.

In Canada, a significant increase in education is apparent from the 1991 census to the 2001 census. For example, 37 percent had less than a high school education in 1991 compared to 29 percent in 2001, while 20 percent finished university in 2001 compared to 15 percent in 1991. Canadian literacy surveys have found that the lowest levels of literacy correspond with low educational attainment. The 2000 Programme for International Student Assessment showed that students in urban areas outperformed students in rural areas and that the difference was significant in Newfoundland, Labrador, Prince Edward Island, and New Brunswick.

Latin America and the Caribbean

According to the MDGs, between 1995 and 2004, 38 million adults in Latin America and the Caribbean lacked basic literacy skills, as reported by the UNESCO Institute for Statistics. The average adult literacy rate stood at 90 percent in the decade 1995–2004; some areas of the region had much lower

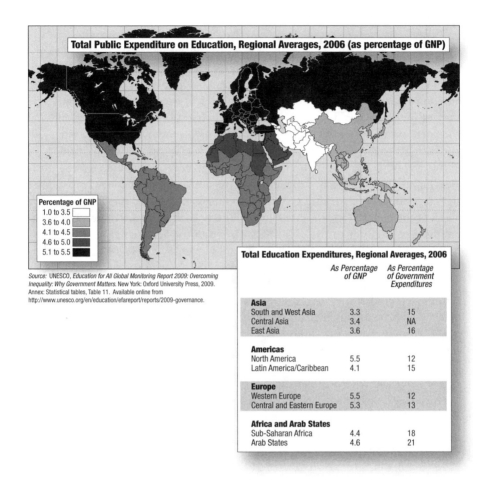

Total Public Expenditure on Education, Regional Averages, 2006 (as percentage of GNP)

Percentage of GNP
- 1.0 to 3.5
- 3.6 to 4.0
- 4.1 to 4.5
- 4.6 to 5.0
- 5.1 to 5.5

Source: UNESCO, *Education for All Global Monitoring Report 2009: Overcoming Inequality: Why Government Matters.* New York: Oxford University Press, 2009. Annex: Statistical tables, Table 11. Available online from http://www.unesco.org/en/education/efareport/reports/2009-governance.

Total Education Expenditures, Regional Averages, 2006

	As Percentage of GNP	As Percentage of Government Expenditures
Asia		
South and West Asia	3.3	15
Central Asia	3.4	NA
East Asia	3.6	16
Americas		
North America	5.5	12
Latin America/Caribbean	4.1	15
Europe		
Western Europe	5.5	12
Central and Eastern Europe	5.3	13
Africa and Arab States		
Sub-Saharan Africa	4.4	18
Arab States	4.6	21

rates. According to the UNESCO Institute for Statistics, Latin America and the Caribbean had net enrollment rates in 2002 of 92 percent for primary education and 74 percent for secondary education; the net enrollment rates for secondary education was 71 percent for men and 78 percent for women. Most countries have succeeded in expanding their primary education systems, and according to UNESCO's assessment, the region is making steady progress toward universal primary education. As a result, illiteracy rates in Latin America and the Caribbean are dropping. Brazil, for instance, has seen impressive increases in its literacy rate, largely due to improvements in its education system. According to Brazil's "Education for All Monitoring Report 2005," in 1990, 81 percent of children were in school compared to 96 percent in 2005. Literacy rates are lowest among native populations. Bolivia and Peru have particularly high populations of Indians and the illiteracy percentages were 86 in 1980 and 95 in 2002 in Bolivia and 91 in 1980 and 97 in 2004 in Peru. A large percentage of South American children enter primary school, but many drop out before basic literacy is achieved. A substantial variability in the level of literacy exists across countries and within countries, although some countries, such as Argentina, have achieved 99 percent literacy.

Europe

Because mass literacy has been part of Western European society for more than a century, residual illiteracy is considered shameful. Based on international standards of literacy, the illiteracy rate is about 1 percent. In industrial countries, however, functional literacy involves more skills than in developing countries because the level of literacy needed for day-to-day living, transportation, employment, and commercial transactions is much higher. Although most European countries do not have a literacy gender gap, they do have a social gap. Some countries have instigated positive discrimination policies to try to compensate for social inequalities. France and Portugal, for example, have similar programs in which poorer areas receive extra financial and human resources and are encouraged to take the needs of the children in their area into account when planning their educational programs. According to the UNESCO Institute for Statistics figures for 2004, Europe had net enrollment ratios of 96.7 for primary and 90.4 for secondary education, while the gross enrollment ratio was 59.4 for tertiary education.

With the end of the cold war, the education systems of central and Eastern Europe required some overhauling, such as updating teaching methods and materials. The governments, however, have lacked the resources to make many of the needed changes because recovery from the economic downturn in the early and mid-1990s has been slow. On a positive note, the illiteracy rate is generally low in these areas. In 2000–2004, 2–3 percent were illiterate in the region, except in Turkey, where 13 percent were illiterate. Central and Eastern European countries are able to provide (near-) universal primary education, but the *Education for All Global Monitoring Report 2007* reported varying trends in national spending on education. For example, the percentages of national spending in the Czech Republic, Hungary, and Poland increased from 4.1, 5.0, and 4.8 in 1999 to 4.8, 6.3, and 6.6 in 2004, respectively, but the trend declined in other countries, such as in Turkey from 4.0 to 3.8 and in Belarus from 6.0 to 5.8. The Romany (Gypsy) population remains one of the most disadvantaged groups in terms of achieved education. Traditionally, the Romany home-schooled their children and have shown resistance to participating in public education systems. The Romany live throughout Europe, with a concentration in Eastern Europe, where 6 million Gypsies reside in a marginalized condition. This marginalization of the Gypsies has educational, political, and economic overtones.

North Africa and the Middle East

According to the *Education for All Global Monitoring Report 2007,* the gross enrollment ratios for the total population in North Africa and the Middle East were 93 percent for primary education in 2004 and 32 percent for secondary education in 2002; the gross enrollment ratios for men were 98 (primary education) and 38 percent (secondary education) compared to 88 and 22 percent for women. The gross enrollment ratios varied substantially across countries, from 39 percent in Djibouti to 60 percent in Sudan to above 100 percent in several countries, such as Algeria and the Syrian Arab Republic. The female primary gross enrollment ratio in Egypt rose from 97 to 102 percent between 2000 and 2007, and the female secondary gross enrollment ratio rose from 82 to 85 percent between 2000 and 2005, according to the UNESCO Institute for Statistics.

The illiteracy rate in North Africa and the Middle East, according to the *Education for All Global Monitoring Report 2007,* was 66 percent in 2000–2004—the second worst in the world, following sub-Saharan Africa. One serious impediment to higher literacy in this region is that the official language of all of these countries, Modern Standard Arabic (or *Fusha*), is no one's native language and is difficult to learn. This, however, is the language that is used in all official documents, as well as in literature and in the media. In addition, the gender gap remains a serious problem. Egypt and Tunisia, for example, share a high female illiteracy rate (71 and 69 percent of all illiterate people, respectively, according to 2006 data from the UNESCO Institute for Statistics), in part due to cultural values and traditions that discriminate against women. The regional literacy rates are 72.5 percent for the total population, 82.4 percent for males, and 62.2 percent for females. Enrollment rates for girls have improved.

Sub-Saharan Africa

The UNESCO Institute for Statistics reported that 45 million school-age children did not attend school in sub-Saharan Africa in 2001–2002, a large percentage of the global estimate of 115 million. The region accounted for 47 percent of the world's out-of-school children, and 54 percent of these children were girls. Adult literacy varies substantially from country to country, and the MEASURE Demographic and Health Surveys conducted within the last five years show that literacy is as high as 85 percent in Zimbabwe and 79 percent in Lesotho in southern Africa and as low as 13 percent in Niger and 18 percent in Burkina Faso in West Africa. Women have particularly low literacy rates—7.5 percent of girls in Niger and 11.9 percent of girls in Burkina Faso are literate, compared to 20.9 and 24.3 percent of boys, respectively, illustrating the gender gap in literacy. With respect to gender differences in education, as many as 73 percent of boys and 67 percent of girls of relevant ages are enrolled in primary education in sub-Saharan Africa. The UNESCO Institution for Statistics's data show that, although primary school attendance was up globally in the early 2000s, it fell in some African counties, including Botswana and Lesotho, largely due to civil unrest and the HIV/AIDS epidemic. Many sub-Saharan countries have a high retention rate and the majority of countries have less than 50 percent of students completing primary education. According to *The Untapped Opportunity: How Public-Private Partnerships Can Advance Education for All,* sustainable development is unlikely to be achieved unless adequate learning attainments are achieved at the secondary and higher education levels. Furthermore, it has been noted that no country has reached universal primary education without having at least a 35 percent secondary education enrollment.

Most countries have large discrepancies between rural and urban education, especially at higher levels of schooling. For example, according to the MEASURE Demographic and Health Surveys, the gaps between urban and rural areas in Tanzania were 7.7 percent for primary education and 17.9 percent for secondary (and above) education for women, respectively, and −10.7 percent for primary education and 21.1 percent for secondary (and above) education for men, respectively. (The negative indicator for men at the primary level means that more men had primary education in rural areas in Tanzania.)

West, Central, and South Asia

According to the UNESCO Institute for Statistics data for 2008, the primary gross enrollment ratio for West, Central, and South Asia ranged from 84 to 126 percent. Large regional as well as gender gaps are evident—the primary gross enrollment ratio for males ranged from 94 to 129 percent, compared to 73 to 132 percent for females. The fast-growing populations of many countries in this region have strained educational funding.

The UNESCO Institute for Statistics reported that this region had one of the lowest levels of literacy in the world, although literacy has been increasing. South Asia (as measured by the MDGs) had adult literacy percentages of 47.5, 58.9, and 64.3 in the periods 1985–1994, 1995–2004, and 2005–2007, respectively, and western Asia had literacy percentages of 75.6, 82.2, and 83.8 for these periods. In India, the trend was 40.8, 48.2, and 61.0 percent in 1981, 1991, and 2001, respectively, with men having higher literacy than women. The gender gap, however, has begun to narrow in the last couple of years, and in 2007, 76.9 percent of men and 54.5 percent of women were literate. According to the 2005 Global Education Monitoring Report, 34 percent of the world's illiterate population lived in India. Adult illiteracy in India continues to be a struggle despite multiple national campaigns in the latter half of the twentieth century and the beginning of the twenty-first century.

A large rural-urban education gap exists in the region. The Indian National Family Health Survey in 2005–2006 shows that education varies markedly between urban and rural areas. In urban areas, 22 percent of the population has no education compared to 50 percent in rural areas; in urban areas, 24 percent of the population has twelve or more years of education compared to 6 percent in rural areas. Adults who become literate often slip back into illiteracy because of the absence of support systems for neoliterates. For this reason, and because many children complete primary school without having reached sustainable levels of literacy, wastage is high in this region.

East Asia and the Pacific

Primary school attendance has made general gains in East Asia and the Pacific over the last couple of decades, and primary education is almost universal. In 2004, the primary net enrollment ratio was 98 percent and the gross enrollment ratio was 111, according to the UNESCO Institute for Statistics. Intraregional variations exist, however. The net enrollment was over 99 percent in Japan and New Zealand, and only 90 in Cambodia. Literacy is generally high—over 90 percent—but exceptions exist, and as few as 57.8 percent were literate in Papua New Guinea in 2007. For many people in the South Pacific, literacy remains unincorporated into their daily lives, and personal reading is regarded as antisocial. In China, the literacy rate increased from 91 percent in 2001 to 93 percent in 2007, and the gross enrollment ratio went up from 67 in 2001 to 69 in 2007.

Many countries in East Asia and the Pacific have rapidly increasing populations and therefore need to continually expand their primary education systems.

The populations in many Pacific nations—Indonesia, for example—are spread unevenly across small islands, presenting further challenges. The countries in this region tend to be culturally diverse, so large numbers of people use a language other than the official language or languages. Australia and New Zealand, with high levels of education of the white population, have increased efforts to focus on the schooling needs of the indigenous populations of Aborigines and Maori, respectively.

Data

Table 1 Literate Populations Ages Fifteen and Over, 2005–2007 (%)

Region	Males	Females
World	88.4	79.3
Developing countries	85.5	73.5
Countries in transition	99.6	99.1
Developed countries	99.3	98.9
Arab states	82.4	62.2
East Asia and the Pacific	96.0	90.6
Latin America	92.5	91.1
Caribbean	72.7	76.5
East Asia	96.1	90.6
South and West Asia	74.6	53.5
Sub-Saharan Africa	71.0	53.7

Source: United Nations Educational, Scientific and Cultural Organization (UNESCO), "Regional Literacy Rates for Youths (15–24) and Adults (15+)," available at: http://stats.uis.unesco.org/unesco/TableViewer/tableView .aspx?ReportId=201.

Note: Regions are EDUCATION FOR ALL groupings; UNESCO uses a slightly different grouping.

Table 2 Illiterate Populations Ages Fifteen and Over, 2005–2007 (millions)

Region	Males	Females
World	278.0	497.0
Developing countries	274.0	491.0
Countries in transition	0.4	1.0
Developed countries	3.0	5.0
Arab states	19.0	39.0
East Asia and the Pacific	33.0	77.0
Latin America	14.0	18.0
Caribbean	1.0	1.0
East Asia	32.0	76.0
South and West Asia	144.0	250.0
Sub-Saharan Africa	57.0	94.0

Source: United Nations Educational, Scientific and Cultural Organization (UNESCO), "Regional Literacy Rates for Youths (15–24) and Adults (15+)," available at: http://stats.uis.unesco.org/unesco/TableViewer/tableView.aspx? ReportId=201.

Note: Regions are EDUCATION FOR ALL groupings; UNESCO uses a slightly different grouping.

Table 3 Duration, Population, and Enrollment Ratios for Primary Education in Selected Countries, 2006

Country	Duration (years)[a] Compulsory education	Duration (years)[a] Primary education	School-age population (thousands)[b]	Gross enrollment ratio (%)[c] Total	Gross enrollment ratio (%)[c] Male	Gross enrollment ratio (%)[c] Female	Net enrollment ratio (%)[d] Total	Net enrollment ratio (%)[d] Male	Net enrollment ratio (%)[d] Female
Algeria	9	6	3,720	110	114	106	94	96	94
Argentina[e]	10	6	4,119	112	113	112	99	99	98
Australia	11	7	1,849	105	105	105	96	96	97
Brazil	8	4	13,751	137	141	133	94	93	95
Canada[f]	11	6	2,324	100	100	99	n/a	n/a	n/a
China	9	5	97,931	111	112	111	n/a	n/a	n/a
Colombia	10	5	4,568	116	117	115	88	89	88
DRC	10	6	573	108	113	102	55	58	52
Egypt	8	5	9,466	103	107	100	94	96	92
France	11	5	3,690	110	110	109	99	98	99
Georgia	9	6	341	96	94	97	89	88	91
Germany	13	4	3,224	103	103	103	98	98	98
Guatemala	9	6	2,117	114	118	109	94	96	92
India	9	5	124,357	112	114	109	89	90	87
Indonesia	9	6	25,394	114	116	112	96	97	94
Israel	11	6	730	110	109	111	97	96	94
Japan	10	6	7,231	100	100	100	100	100	100
Russian Federation	10	4	5,381	96	96	96	91	91	91
Saudi Arabia	6	6	3,220	n/a	n/a	n/a	n/a	n/a	n/a
Spain	11	6	2,388	105	106	104	100	100	99
Sweden	10	6	656	96	96	95	95	95	95
Switzerland	9	6	531	97	98	97	89	89	89
Tajikistan	9	4	686	100	103	98	97	99	95
Thailand	9	6	5,417	108	108	108	94	94	94
Turkey	9	6	8,438	94	96	92	91	93	89
Uganda	7	7	6,309	117	116	117	n/a	n/a	n/a
United Kingdom	12	6	4,293	105	105	106	98	98	99
United States	12	6	24,767	98	98	99	92	94	95

Source: United Nations Educational, Scientific and Cultural Organization (UNESCO), "UNESCO Institute for Statistics Data Centre," available at: http://stats.uis.unesco.org/unesco/TableViewer/document.aspx?ReportId=143&IF_Language=eng.

Note: DRC, Democratic Republic of Congo; n/a, not available.

[a]Duration of compulsory education is the number of years of compulsory education, according to the regulations of each country. Duration of primary education is the number of grades (years) in primary education, according to the education system of each country in 2006.

[b]School-age population is the population of the age group that officially corresponds to primary schooling.

[c]Gross enrollment ratio is the total enrollment in primary education, regardless of age, divided by the population of the age group that officially corresponds to primary schooling.

[d]Net enrollment ratio includes only the enrollment of the age group corresponding to the official age range for primary education, divided by the population of school-age children.

[e]Gross enrollment and net enrollment for Argentina are from 2005.

[f]Gross enrollment and net enrollment for Canada are from 2004.

Table 4   Estimated Adult Illiteracy in Countries with More than 10 Million Illiterate Adults, 1970 and 2006

| Country | 1970 | | | | 2006 | | | |
| | Number of illiterate adults (millions) | Adult illiteracy rate (%) | | | Number of illiterate adults (millions) | Adult illiteracy rate (%) | | |
		Total	Male	Female		Total	Male	Female
China	244	49	34	64	73	7	4	10
India	221	67	53	81	270	35	24	47
Indonesia	30	44	32	56	14	9	5	13
Pakistan	28	79	68	91	47	46	32	60
Bangladesh	28	76	65	88	48	47	42	53
Nigeria	22	80	69	90	23	29	21	37
Brazil	18	32	28	36	14	10	11	10
Egypt	14	69	54	83	14	29	17	40
Ethiopia[a]	14	87	81	94	27	n/a	50	77

Source: Data for 1970 from United Nations Educational, Scientific and Cultural Organization (UNESCO), *World Education Report, 2000: The Right to Education. Towards Education for All throughout Life* (Paris: UNESCO, 2000), 38, Fig. 2.4, available at: http://openurl.ingenta.com/content?genre=article&issn=0738-0593&volume=21&issue=5&spage=472&epage=473. Data for 2006 from UNESCO, "UNESCO Institute for Statistics Data Centre," available at: http://stats.uis.unesco.org/unesco/TableViewer/document.aspx?ReportId=143&IF_Language=eng.

Note: n/a, not available.

[a]Data for Ethiopia are from 1970 and 2004.

Table 5   Regional Pupil–Teacher Ratio in Primary Education, 2006

Arab states	22
Central and Eastern Europe	18
Central Asia	19
East Asia and the Pacific	20
Latin America and the Caribbean	23
North America and the Western Europe	14
South and West Asia[a]	39
Sub-Saharan Africa	45

Source: United Nations Educational, Scientific and Cultural Organization, UNESCO Institute for Statistics, Available at: http://stats.uis.unesco.org/unesco/TableViewer/tableView.aspx?ReportId=196.

[a]The figure for South and West Asia is from 2004.

Case Study—Literacy Efforts in Rural Nepal

South Asia has one of the highest illiteracy rates in the world. From 1981 to 1992, the rural areas along the Seti River in western Nepal were the focus of a successful literacy campaign. Subsequently, numerous literacy campaigns have been implemented, such as the PACT Nepal Women's Empowerment Project and WELNepal. Among South Asian nations, Nepal has one of the highest prevalences of adult illiteracy. In 2008, more than 7 million people ages fifteen and above were illiterate, and as many as 67 percent of adult illiterates were women, according to UNESCO. Similarly, Nepal has a high gender gap in literacy, with a literacy rate of 69.2 percent for men compared to 42.0 percent for women, again based on UNESCO figures for 2008. This gap is due in part to families' relying on the work that girls perform at home, which leaves little time for school attendance, and in part to social and legal discrimination against women.

The UNESCO-supervised Seti Project (officially called Education for Rural Development in the Seti Zone) grew out of the national Equal Access of Girls to Education program, which began in Nepal in 1970. Girls who participated in the Seti Project had the highest rates of academic success and achievement. Based on the results of the effort, another national program, the Basic and Primary Education Project (BPEP), was developed. The BPEP is a larger-scale attempt to repeat the success of the Seti Project.

The PACT Nepal Women's Empowerment Project is combating female illiteracy and poverty by combining literacy training with microfinance, empowering women with knowledge and economic opportunities. The vast majority of clients have passed a literacy test and saved money via microfinance.

The program WELNepal was started in 2007. It offers basic and more advanced literacy classes, agricultural courses, lectures on oncology, and it has built a number of libraries. It aims to extend its services to include income-generating programs and to fund the education of some of the women students' daughters.

One of the aspects that made these programs successful was their practical instructions, which related directly to the participants' daily lives. The programs focused on issues of health and hygiene and taught literacy while conveying information on these issues to young girls and women. These programs are also thought to have been effective because of their multifaceted approach, including improving school conditions, supplying materials for literacy training and postliteracy support, short- and long-term teacher training, agricultural training, and microfinances.

Case Study—Literacy Options in Norway

Norway has a largely heterogeneous population of around 4.7 million people. Numerous dialects of Norwegian are spoken nationwide. The Sami (Laplanders) are a significant minority in the northern part of the country as well as in the north of Sweden, Finland, and the northwest section of the Russian Federation. Three Sami languages exist; they are not mutually understandable.

Norway also has other ethnic minorities, largely due to refugee immigration. The country thus faces difficult education issues and is noteworthy for its response to them.

Most governments provide literacy instruction only in the official language of the country, so Norway is distinguished in its efforts in this area. In the 1850s, a Norwegian language based on the dialects of the country was formed. This stood in contrast to the official written language of the time, Danish; Norway had been under Danish rule for some four hundred years. Written Danish in Norway has been influenced by spoken Norwegian and is called *Bokmål* (book language). The language created to reflect Norwegian dialects was given the name *Nynorsk* (New Norwegian). In the late 1800s, *Nynorsk* was given equal legal status with *Bokmål,* so children could then be taught in either language. This is the situation today, but whether a child is taught primarily in one language rather than the other often depends on the preferences of local government. In addition, in the 1960s Sami began to be used in Sami district schools, and now all Sami children in Norway can receive their first ten years of education in Sami. More recently, all children were given the right to receive literacy instruction in their native language. In practice, many linguistic minorities receive their initial literacy instruction either solely in their native language or in their native language and either *Nynorsk* or *Bokmål.* Norway's success with this approach is evident in its 99 percent literacy rate. However, the Organisation for Economic Cooperation and Development (OECD) reported in 2006, based on a literacy survey, that as many as 30 percent of adult Norwegians, or about 900,000 people, have dysfunctional literacy skills, as defined by international standards. That is, a large number of people have minimal reading and writing skills and hence impaired functional abilities.

A substantial body of research shows that acquiring literacy in a second language is more difficult than attaining it in one's native language because the learner is learning literacy and the language at the same time. Therefore, programs that provide literacy instruction in a child's native language, such as those used in Norway, are instrumental in helping children acquire literacy and also preserve their cultural roots.

Biographical Sketches

Paulo Freire is an adult educator who established national adult literacy programs in Brazil and later in Chile, where he was forced into exile in 1964. In the 1970s, Freire worked to establish adult literacy programs in newly independent nations, including Guinea-Bissau and Tanzania. He feels that illiteracy was closely related to oppression and worked to liberate people through raising literacy levels. He has published more than twenty-five works on literacy, his most famous being *Pedagogy of the Oppressed* (1970).

Nancy Hornberger is a professor at the University of Pennsylvania who is concerned with minority education and literacy programs as they pertain to indigenous populations and immigrants. She uses an approach that combines methods and perspectives from anthropology, linguistics, sociolinguistics, and policy studies. Her research focuses on South America, especially Peru and Bolivia, and the United States, where she has studied Cambodian and Puerto Rican populations in Philadelphia. She also studies minority language groups in other parts of the world. In the 1990s, Hornberger served as a consultant to the United Nations on education programs in El Salvador and Bolivia.

Shoichi Noma is a publisher who has worked to make books available in developing countries and to promote reading there. He is the president of a publishing company in Japan, and he established the Noma Prize, which is awarded each year to the writer of an outstanding (children's or academic) book published in Africa.

Nelly Stromquist is a professor of comparative and international education at the University of Southern California and a former president of the Comparative and International Education Society. A Fulbright New Century Scholar during 2005–2006, her research focus is gender inequality in education as applied through programs and policies, especially in Latin America and West Africa. Her research also includes the social and practical obstacles women face in becoming literate. She is the author of numerous articles and several books. Among her most recent books are *Feminist Organizations and Social Transformation in Latin America* (2006) and *Education in a Globalized World: The Connectivity of Economic Power, Technology, and Knowledge* (2002).

Daniel Wagner is a professor at the University of Pennsylvania School of Education who also serves as the director of the National Center on Adult Literacy, the International Literacy Institute, and the Penn Global Development Institute. He has published many articles on children and adult literacy acquisition. He is the co-editor of *Pro-Equity Approaches to Monitoring and Evaluation: Gender, Marginalized Groups and Special Needs Populations* (2007).

Directory

Dhaka Ahsania Mission, Road #12, House #19 (New), Dhanmondi R/A, Dhaka-1209, Bangladesh; Telephone: 8115909, 8119521-22; email: dambgd@bdonline.com; Web: http://www.ahsania.org.
Organization headquartered in Bangladesh and dedicated to economic development through education.

Global Campaign for Education, c/o Education International, 5 Boulevard Roi Albert II, 8th Floor, 1210 Brussels, Belgium. Telephone: (32) 2 224 06 11; email: global .edu.campaign@ei-ie.org; Web: http://global.campaignforeducation.org.
Organization that promotes education as a basic human right and mobilizes public pressure on governments and the international community to provide free, compulsory public education and take action against poverty.

International Association for the Evaluation of Educational Achievement, Herengracht 487, 1017 Amsterdam, Netherlands. Telephone: (31) 20 625 3625; email: department@iea.nl; Web: http://www.iea.nl.
Independent international cooperative of research centers concerned with the educational policies and practices of its members.

International Bureau of Education, P.O. Box 199, 1211 Geneva 20, Switzerland. Telephone: (41) 22 917 78 00; Web: http://www.ibe.unesco.org.
UNESCO affiliate that observes and assists education efforts worldwide.

International Literacy Institute (ILI), National Center on Adult Literacy (NCAL), University of Pennsylvania, Graduate School of Education, 3910 Chestnut Street,

Philadelphia, Pa. 19104-3111. Telephone: (215) 898-2100; email: boyle@literacy. upenn.edu; Web: http://www.literacy.org.
A collaboration of UNESCO and the University of Pennsylvania Graduate School of Education; involved in education research and development around the world.

International Reading Association, 800 Barksdale Road, P.O. Box 8139, Newark, Del. 19714-8139. Telephone: (302) 731-1600; email: pubinfo@reading.org; Web: http://www.reading.org.
Organization promoting high levels of literacy and quality literacy instruction.

National Center for Family Literacy, 325 West Main Street, Suite 200, Louisville, Ky. 40202-4251. Telephone: (502) 584-1133; email: ncfl@famlit.org; Web: http://www.famlit.org.
Organization supporting family literacy in the United States.

United Nations Educational, Scientific and Cultural Organization (UNESCO), 7 Place de Fontenoy, 75352 Paris, France. Telephone: (33) 1 45 68 10 00; email: bpi@unesco.org; Web: http://www.unesco.org.
Agency promoting justice and peace in the world through international collaboration in the scientific, educational, and cultural arenas.

United Nations International Children's Emergency Fund (UNICEF), UNICEF House, 3 United Nations Plaza, New York, N.Y. 10017. Telephone: (212) 326-7000; email: unicef@unicef.org; Web: http://www.unicef.org.
Agency concerned with the welfare of the world's children.

World Education, 44 Farnsworth Street, Boston, Mass. 02210. Telephone: (617) 482-9485; fax: (617) 482-0617; email: wei@worlded.org; Web: http://www.worlded.org.
Organization committed to helping the poor through education development.

Further Research

Books

Aronowitz, Stanley. *Against Schooling: For an Education that Matters.* Boulder, Colo.: Boulder Paradigm Publishers, 2008.

Cossa, José Augusto. *Power, Politics, and Higher Education in Southern Africa: International Regimes, Local Governments, and Educational Autonomy.* Amherst, Mass.: Cambria Press, 2008.

Fresch, Mary Jo, ed. *An Essential History of Current Reading Practices.* Newark, N.J.: International Reading Association, 2008.

Jones, Ken, et al. *Schooling in Western Europe: The New Order and Its Adversaries.* New York: Palgrave Macmillan, 2008.

Kabeer, Naila, and Agneta Stark, with Edda Magnus, eds. *Global Perspectives on Gender Equality: Reversing the Gaze.* New York: Routledge, 2008.

Kress, Gunther. *Literacy in the New Media Age.* London: Routledge, 2003.

Lind, Agneta. *Literacy for All: Making a Difference.* Paris: UNESCO, 2008.

Manjeet, Bhatia, et al., eds. *Gender Concerns in South Asia: Some Perspectives.* Jaipur, India: Rawat Publications, 2008.

Ofori-Attah, Kwabena Dei. *Going to School in the Middle East and North Africa.* Westport, Conn.: Greenwood Press, 2008.

Reese, William J., and John L. Rury, eds. *Rethinking the History of American Education*. New York: Palgrave Macmillan, 2008.

Tompkins, Gail. *50 Literacy Strategies: Step-by-Step*. Upper Saddle River, N.J.: Prentice Hall, 2008.

———. *Literacy for the 21st Century*. Upper Saddle River, N.J.: Pearson, 2006.

Wagner, Daniel A., et al., eds. *Monitoring and Evaluation of ICT in Education Projects: A Handbook for Developing Countries*. Washington, D.C.: World Bank/InfoDev, 2007.

Yi, Lin. *Cultural Exclusion in China: State Education, Social Mobility and Cultural Difference*. New York: Routledge, 2008.

Articles and Reports

Ahmed, Akhter U., and Mary Arends-Kuenning. "Do Crowded Classrooms Crowd Out Learning?: Evidence from the Food for Education Program in Bangladesh." *World Development* 34 (2006): 665–684.

Ainsworth, Martha, and Deon Filmer. "Inequalities in Children's Schooling: AIDS, Orphanhood, Poverty, and Gender." *World Development* 34 (2006): 1099–1128.

Altbach, Philip G., and Patti McGill Peterson. "America in the World: Higher Education and the Global Marketplace." *International Perspectives on Education and Society* 9 (2008): 313–335.

Bona, Xavier. "On Global Absences: Reflections on the Failings in the Education and Poverty Relationship in Latin America." *International Journal of Educational Development* 27 (2007): 86–100.

Bennell, Paul. "Hitting the Target: Doubling Primary School Enrollments in Sub-Saharan Africa by 2015." *World Development* 30 (2002): 1179–1194.

Bruneforth, Michael, Albert Motivans, and Zhang Yanhong. "Investing in the Future: Financing Education in Latin America and the Caribbean." UNESCO Institute for Statistics, Montreal, 2004.

Brunswic, Étienne, and Jean Valérien. "Multigrade Schools: Improving Access in Rural Africa?" Fundamentals of Educational Planning no. 76. UNESCO, 2004. Available at: http://publishing.unesco.org/details.aspx?Code_Livre=4285.

Chapman, David W., et al. "The Search for Quality: A Five Country Study of National Strategies to Improve Educational Quality in Central Asia." *International Journal of Educational Development* 25 (2005): 514–530.

Clements, Michael A. "The Long Walk to School: International Education Goals in Historical Perspective." Center for Global Development, Washington, D.C., 2004. Available at: http://papers.ssrn.com/s013/papers.cfm?abstract_id=1112670.

Cusso, Roser, and Sabrina D'Amico. "From Development Comparatism to Globalization Comparativism: Towards More Normative International Education Statistics." *Comparative Education* 41, no. 2 (2005): 199–216.

García, Francisco J. Lozano, Kathleen Kevany, and Donald Huisingh. "Sustainability in Higher Education: What Is Happening?" *Journal of Cleaner Production* 14 (2006): 757–760.

Ingram, George, et al. "The Untapped Opportunity: How Public-Private Partnerships Can Advance Education for All." Education Policy and Data Center, Washington, D.C., 2006. Available at: http://www.epdc.org/static/UntappedOpportunity.pdf.

Jansen, Jonathan D. "Targeting Education: The Politics of Performance and the Prospects of 'Education For All.'" *International Journal of Educational Development* 25 (2005): 368–380.

Lemke, Mariann, et al. "Highlights from the 2003 International Adult Literacy and Lifeskills Survey." IES National Center for Education, Washington, D.C., 2005. Available at: http://nces.ed.gov/pubs2005/2005117.pdf.

Magno, Cathryn, and Iveta Silova. "Teaching in Transition: Examining School-Based Gender Inequities in Central/Southeastern Europe and the Former Soviet Union." *International Journal of Educational Development* 27 (2007): 647–660.

Maldonado, Jorge H., and Claudio González-Vega. "Impact of Microfinance on Schooling: Evidence from Poor Rural Households in Bolivia." *World Development* 36 (2008): 2440–2455.

Mundy, Karen. "Education for All: Paradoxes and Prospects of a Global Promise." *International Perspectives on Education and Society* 8 (2007): 1–30.

RA Malatest & Associates Ltd. "Best Practices in Increasing Aboriginal Postsecondary Enrollment Rates." Prepared for the Council of Ministers of Education, Canada. 2002. Available at: http://www.cmec.ca/postsec/malatest.en.pdf.

Rao, Nitya, and Anna Robinson-Pant. "Gender Equality in Adult Education." *International Journal of Educational Development* 26 (2006): 135–139.

Robinson, Clinton. "Promoting Literacy: What Is the Record of Education for All?" *International Journal of Educational Development* 25 (2005): 436–444.

Stromquist, Nelly P. "Women's Rights to Adult Education as a Means to Citizenship." *International Journal of Educational Development* 26 (2006): 140–152.

Semali, Ladislaus M. "Challenges of Rebuilding Education in Crisis: Access to Universal Primary Education in Africa." *International Perspectives on Education and Society* 8 (2007): 395–425.

Sundaram, Aparna, and Reeve Vanneman. "Gender Differentials in Literacy in India: The Intriguing Relationship with Women's Labor Force Participation." *World Development* 36 (2008): 128–143.

United Nations Educational, Scientific and Cultural Organization (UNESCO). "The Dakar Framework for Action: Education for All. Meeting Our Collective Commitments." World Education Forum, Dakar, Senegal, April 26–28, 2000. Available at: http://www.unesco.org/education/efa/ed_for_all/dakfram_eng .shtml.

———. *Education for All Global Monitoring Report 2002: Education for All—Is the World on Track?* Oxford: Oxford University Press, 2002. Available at: http://www.unesco .org/education/efa/monitoring/monitoring_2002.shtml.

———. *Education for All Global Monitoring Report 2003/4: Gender and Education for All: the Leap to Equality.* Oxford: Oxford University Press, 2003. Available at: http:// portal.unesco.org/education/en/ev.php-URL_ID=23023&URL_DO=DO_ TOPIC&URL_SECTION=201.html.

———. *Education for All Global Monitoring Report 2005: Education for All—the Quality Imperative.* Oxford: Oxford University Press, 2004. Available at: http://portal .unesco.org/education/en/ev.php-URL_ID=35939&URL_DO=DO_TOPIC &URL_SECTION=201.html.

———. *Education for All Global Monitoring Report 2006: Education for All—Literacy for Life.* Oxford: Oxford University Press, 2005. Available at: http://portal.unesco.org/ education/en/ev.php-URL_ID=43283&URL_DO=DO_TOPIC&URL_ SECTION=201.html.

———. *Education for All Global Monitoring Report 2007: Strong Foundations: Early Childhood Care and Education.* Oxford: Oxford University Press, 2006. Available at:

http://portal.unesco.org/education/en/ev.php-URL_ID=50643&URL_DO=DO_TOPIC&URL_SECTION=201.html.

———. *Education for All Global Monitoring Report 2008: Education for All by 2015—Will We Make It?* Oxford: Oxford University Press, 2007. Available at: http://www.unesco.org/education/gmr2008/press/Full-report.pdf.

———. "The Plurality of Literacy and Its Implications for Policies and Programs: Position Paper." UNESCO, Paris, 2004.

UNESCO Institute for Statistics. "International Literacy Statistics: A Review of Concepts, Methodology and Current Data." UNESCO, Montreal, 2008. Available at: http://www.uis.unesco.org/template/pdf/Literacy/LiteracyReport2008.pdf.

Urquiola, Miguel, and Valentina Calderón. "Apples and Oranges: Educational Enrollment and Attainment across Countries in Latin America and the Caribbean." *International Journal of Educational Development* 26, no. 6 (2006): 572–590.

Wagner, Daniel A., and Robert B. Kozma. "New Technologies for Literacy and Adult Education: A Global Perspective." Education on the Move Series. UNESCO, Paris, 2005.

Wolhuter, CC. "Education for All in Sub-Saharan Africa: Prospects and Challenges." *International Perspectives on Education and Society* 8 (2007): 337–362.

Web Sites

International Literacy Explorer
http://www.literacy.org/Projects/explorer/sitemap.html

Seti Project, Nepal, Young Girls' and Women's Literacy through Basic Skills Education
http://www.literacy.org/Projects/explorer/seti_act.html

SIL International
http://www.sil.org

UNESCO, Education for All
http://portal.unesco.org/education/en/ev.php-URL_ID=46881&URL_DO=DO_TOPIC&URL_SECTION=201.html

UNESCO in Nepal
http://portal.unesco.org/geography/en/ev.php-URL_ID=6054&URL_DO=DO_TOPIC&URL_SECTION=201.html

UNESCO Institute for Statistics
http://www.uis.unesco.org

United Nations Literacy Decade
http://www.unesco.org/education/litdecade

Documents

1. World Declaration on Education for All: Meeting Basic Learning Needs

World Conference on Education for All: Meeting Basic Learning Needs, Jomtien, Thailand, March 5–9, 1990

The full text is available at http://www2.unesco.org/wef/en-conf/Jomtien%20Declaration%20eng.shtm.

Extracts

EDUCATION FOR ALL: THE PURPOSE

Article I Meeting Basic Learning Needs

1. Every person—child, youth and adult—shall be able to benefit from educational opportunities designed to meet their basic learning needs. These needs comprise both essential learning tools (such as literacy, oral expression, numeracy, and problem solving) and the basic learning content (such as knowledge, skills, values, and attitudes) required by human beings to be able to survive, to develop their full capacities, to live and work in dignity, to participate fully in development, to improve the quality of their lives, to make informed decisions, and to continue learning. The scope of basic learning needs and how they should be met varies with individual countries and cultures, and inevitably, changes with the passage of time.

2. The satisfaction of these needs empowers individuals in any society and confers upon them a responsibility to respect and build upon their collective cultural, linguistic and spiritual heritage, to promote the education of others, to further the cause of social justice, to achieve environmental protection, to be tolerant towards social, political and religious systems which differ from their own, ensuring that commonly accepted humanistic values and human rights are upheld, and to work for international peace and solidarity in an interdependent world.

3. Another and no less fundamental aim of educational development is the transmission and enrichment of common cultural and moral values. It is in these values that the individual and society find their identity and worth.

4. Basic education is more than an end in itself. It is the foundation for lifelong learning and human development on which countries may build, systematically, further levels and types of education and training.

EDUCATION FOR ALL: AN EXPANDED VISION AND A RENEWED COMMITMENT

Article II Shaping the Vision

To serve the basic learning needs of all requires more than a recommitment to basic education as it now exists. What is needed is an "expanded vision" that surpasses present resource levels, institutional structures, curricula, and conventional delivery systems while building on the best in current practices. New possibilities exist today which result from the convergence of the increase in information and the unprecedented capacity to communicate. We must seize them with creativity and a determination for increased effectiveness. As elaborated in Articles III–VII, the expanded vision encompasses:

> Universalizing access and promoting equity;
>
> Focusing on learning;
>
> Broadening the means and scope of basic education;
>
> Enhancing the environment for learning;
>
> Strengthening partnerships.

The realization of an enormous potential for human progress and empowerment is contingent upon whether people can be enabled to acquire the education and the start needed to tap into the ever-expanding pool of relevant knowledge and the new means for sharing this knowledge. . . .

Article IX Mobilizing Resources

1. If the basic learning needs of all are to be met through a much broader scope of action than in the past, it will be essential to mobilize existing and new financial and human resources, public, private and voluntary. All of society has a contribution to make, recognizing that time, energy and funding directed to basic education are perhaps the most profound investment in people and in the future of a country which can be made.

2. Enlarged public-sector support means drawing on the resources of all the government agencies responsible for human development, through increased absolute and proportional allocations to basic education services with the clear recognition of competing claims on national resources of which education is an important one, but not the only one. Serious attention to improving the efficiency of existing educational resources and programmes will not only produce more, it can also be expected to attract new resources. The urgent task of meeting basic learning needs may require a reallocation between sectors, as, for example, a transfer from military to educational expenditure. Above all, special protection for basic education will be required in countries undergoing structural adjustment and facing severe external debt burdens. Today, more than ever, education must be seen as a fundamental dimension of any social, cultural, and economic design.

2. Dakar Framework for Action: Education for All. Meeting Our Collective Commitments

World Education Forum, Dakar, Senegal, April 26–28, 2000

The full text is available at http://www2.unesco.org/wef/en-conf/dakframeng.shtm.

Extract

2. The Dakar Framework is a collective commitment to action. Governments have an obligation to ensure that EFA goals and targets are reached and sustained. This is a responsibility that will be met most effectively through broad-based partnerships within countries, supported by cooperation with regional and international agencies and institutions. . . .

7. We hereby collectively commit ourselves to the attainment of the following goals:

   (i) expanding and improving comprehensive early childhood care and education, especially for the most vulnerable and disadvantaged children;

   (ii) ensuring that by 2015 all children, particularly girls, children in difficult circumstances and those belonging to ethnic minorities, have access to and complete free and compulsory primary education of good quality;

   (iii) ensuring that the learning needs of all young people and adults are met through equitable access to appropriate learning and life skills programmes;

   (iv) achieving a 50 per cent improvement in levels of adult literacy by 2015, especially for women, and equitable access to basic and continuing education for all adults;

   (v) eliminating gender disparities in primary and secondary education by 2005, and achieving gender equality in education by 2015, with a focus on ensuring girls' full and equal access to and achievement in basic education of good quality;

   (vi) improving all aspects of the quality of education and ensuring excellence of all so that recognized and measurable learning outcomes are achieved by all, especially in literacy, numeracy and essential life skills.

8. To achieve these goals, we the governments, organizations, agencies, groups and associations represented at the World Education Forum pledge ourselves to:

   (i)   mobilize strong national and international political commitment for education for all, develop national action plans and enhance significantly investment in basic education;

   (ii)   promote EFA policies within a sustainable and well-integrated sector framework clearly linked to poverty elimination and development strategies;

   (iii)   ensure the engagement and participation of civil society in the formulation, implementation and monitoring of strategies for educational development;

   (iv)   develop responsive, participatory and accountable systems of educational governance and management;

   (v)   meet the needs of education systems affected by conflict, national calamities and instability and conduct educational programmes in ways that promote mutual understanding, peace and tolerance, and help to prevent violence and conflict;

   (vi)   implement integrated strategies for gender equality in education which recognize the need for changes in attitudes, values and practices;

   (vii)   implement as a matter of urgency education programmes and actions to combat the HIV/AIDS pandemic;

   (viii) create safe, healthy, inclusive and equitably resourced educational environments conducive to excellence in learning with clearly defined levels of achievement for all;

   (ix)   enhance the status, morale and professionalism of teachers;

   (x)   harness new information and communication technologies to help achieve EFA goals;

   (xi)   systematically monitor progress towards EFA goals and strategies at the national, regional and international levels; and

   (xii)   build on existing mechanisms to accelerate progress towards education for all.

WOMEN

Aili Tripp

Since the United Nations held the first international conference on women in Mexico City in 1975, important steps have been taken toward furthering gender equality, with women making gains in education, health care, employment, and other areas. The global gender gap has closed, to 96 percent in health and 92 percent in education, according to a 2007 study by the World Economic Forum. But the gender gap is still significant in the area of economic rights, where it has narrowed to only 57 percent, and in political participation, where the gap is the largest at 14 percent. Women still are underrepresented in nearly all national legislative bodies, holding an average of 17.7 percent of lower house parliamentary seats worldwide.

However, today, a general consensus is evident within the international community regarding women's rights—according to a 2008 World Public Opinion poll, an overwhelming majority of people around the world agree that for "women to have full equality of rights compared to men" is important. Strong support has also emerged for the ideas that government has the responsibility to prevent gender-based discrimination and to take steps to eliminate discrimination and that the UN should further the rights of women. In spite of this consensus, many challenges remain.

Historical Background and Development

The first advocates of women's rights in Europe, especially in the area of education, emerged in the seventeenth century. Women generally were not the beneficiaries of the social, political, and economic rights that accompanied the eighteenth-century Enlightenment, despite its democratic ideals and emphasis on individual rights. Thus, women such as Mary Wollstonecraft, author of *A Vindication of the Rights of Woman* (1792), began advocating for educational and political equality with men.

The first major international struggle in defense of women's rights was over the right to vote, which started in Europe and spread around the world, in part as a consequence of colonization. New Zealand was the first country to grant women the right to vote (1893), Finland was the first country in Europe

(1906), Canada was the first country in North America (1918), Ecuador the first country in Latin America (1928), Sri Lanka the first country in Asia (1931), and Senegal the first country in Africa (1945). Women in the United States gained the right to vote in 1920. During the period of decolonization following World War II, a large number of newly independent nations institutionalized universal suffrage.

As increasing numbers of women joined the workforce in the industrially developed countries, they confronted new forms of discrimination. In the United States and parts of Europe, the changing labor market, the phenomenon of more women attaining higher levels of education, changes in expectations regarding marriage, and the introduction of birth control pills were all driving forces in the 1960s and 1970s in what became known as the women's liberation movement. The movement quickly took on international dimensions as women began to resist discrimination and demand equality in political, economic, social, religious, educational, and other institutions. National, regional, and international women's organizations focused on such issues as abortion, sexual harassment, violence against women, lack of political representation, migration, sex trafficking and coerced prostitution, lack of access to credit, land and property rights, lack of legal rights, and many other concerns that had not been on the agenda prior to the 1970s. In international forums, women leaders sought to frame women's rights as human rights, bringing greater recognition to women's demands for equality and opposition to discrimination. Women's organizations worked through the United Nations to encourage governments to commit to advancing women's status with international conventions and agreements such as the Convention on the Elimination of All Forms of Discrimination Against Women (CEDAW) (see Document 1).

Current Status

Women's status is influenced by a combination of factors, including cultural and religious beliefs, access to education, and economic and political opportunities and conditions. Women's movements, both local and global, have played important roles in advancing women's position in society. An examination of current research along with the current policies and programs shows that progress as well as setbacks have been made in improving the lives of women worldwide.

Research

During the last decade, considerable progress was made in improving women's status, but not surprisingly, current research tends to focus on the enormous hurdles that still must be scaled, especially in low-income countries, which usually rank low on the Human Development Index (HDI) and the Gender-Related Development Index (GDI) (see Table 1; map, p. 451). The HDI is based on a combination of three indicators: life expectancy at birth; education; and standard of living, as measured by real per capita gross domestic product (GDP). The GDI measures the same elements as the HDI, but accounts for disparities between men and women. Another tool for evaluating women's status is the Gender Empowerment Measure, which examines whether women and men are able to participate actively in economic and political life and take part in decision making. Women's status is reflected in the effect of various societal factors on their lives, including politics, economic activity, health and reproductive rights, violence and other forms of abuse, and education.

Politics. Female representation in national legislatures provides a useful glimpse into how countries compare in their commitment and openness to women in prominent law-making positions. Since the 1960s, a gradual increase worldwide has been seen in the level of female representation in national legislatures, with a jump, according to Inter-Parliamentary Union data, from roughly 5 percent of women-held seats in 1960 to 17.7 percent in 2008 (see Table 2). Some of biggest gains have been in Africa, whereas Eastern European countries and those of the former Soviet Union experienced sharp decreases with the demise of communism at the end of the 1980s. Only the Nordic countries consistently have been able to maintain female representation rates above 30 percent. About 14 out of 188 countries have more than one-third female representation. Rwanda has the highest levels of female representation, with women constituting 56 percent of its parliament. One of the most important developments since 2000 has been the increased use of legislative quotas to increase the number of women in national and subnational legislatures. Today over one hundred countries have adopted some form of quota, either in the form of reserved seats or compulsory quotas mandated by the constitution or by legislation, or quotas adopted by parties themselves on a voluntary basis.

Economic Activity. Policymakers are increasingly aware that such key economic indicators as GDP, which measures the value of economic output produced within a country, do not account for women's unpaid labor in the home and in their communities (see LABOR AND EMPLOYMENT). This includes taking care of the family, volunteer work, subsistence agricultural labor, and self-employment or contracted labor in informal markets, which involve small or microscale enterprises that tend to be untaxed and unlicensed and are prevalent in many developing countries. Were such labor accounted for, economic reform and welfare and labor policies would be structured to respond not only to the demands of the market but also to the needs and priorities of those people involved in unpaid labor, informal labor markets, and other forms of "hidden" labor. In India, for example, 94 percent of working women belong to the informal sector, working in their homes rolling cigarettes and producing foodstuffs, garments, lace, and footwear, according to the Self-Employed Women's Association. Also included among this group are weavers, potters, patch workers, incense makers, and spinners. Waste-paper collectors recycle and sell their finds. Some are service workers; others are agricultural workers.

New understandings of women's labor are reconfiguring the way many policymakers think about the market as well as notions of value, efficiency, and productivity. Debates focus on how best to account for women's labor in the home. Some would like to adopt a market cost, output-based evaluation scheme to measure how much would be earned if all the services performed inside the home were sold on the market. A second approach, similar to the first, suggests measuring women's work by replacement, that is, by determining how much would be paid to have someone come in to perform household jobs. A third approach involves opportunity cost; here one determines how much a person could earn in a job outside the home if he or she were not doing housework full time. Still others argue that community work and household work have an intrinsic value of their own that cannot and should not be captured by a value for exchange because the very act of quantification diminishes its value; one cannot put a price tag on nurturing and loving one's children.

Globalization has opened opportunities for some women, but it also has posed new challenges as financial crises in several regions, caused in part by the increasing global nature of economic activity, have forced women to serve as the primary safety net for their households. Globalization has increased women's share of paid employment in industries and services since the mid-1980s in most parts of the world, resulting in the phenomenon called the feminization of labor. According to the International Labour Organisation (ILO) report "Global Trends for Women 2008," the numbers of employed women increased by 200 million since 1997, reaching 1.2 billion in 2007, compared with 1.8 billion men. The service sector has overtaken agriculture as the main source of employment for women globally in this same period, with over one-third of women engaged in agricultural production and close to one-half (46 percent) employed in the service sector. Despite this trend, the terms and conditions of employment remain generally poorer for women than for men. In part, because of these contradictory consequences of globalization, scholars have adopted competing evaluations of globalization. One group touts the benefits of transnational capital flows and the expansion of global markets for women, while another group criticizes the inequality and job insecurity for women created by the new world order.

The increased flexibility of labor has resulted in changes in employment for both men and women. For women, in particular, it has resulted in the rise of informal economic activities, subcontracting between formal and informal enterprises, and part-time or home-based work. State regulation of labor standards have been loosened or lifted globally. The deregulation of labor markets, fragmentation of production processes, and creation of export-processing zones in developing countries have resulted in new demands for low-paid female workers, especially in the clothing and electronics industries. Trade liberalization has resulted in the creation of nontraditional exports, such as the production and sale of flowers, spices, birds, and tobacco, especially in Africa. These high-value export products have resulted in the employment of large numbers of women in low-paid seasonal jobs.

Health and Reproductive Rights. Women worldwide are healthier than ever, as demonstrated by the rise in their life expectancy rates (see HEALTH). Drinking water is safer, sanitation is better, many infectious diseases have been virtually eradicated, nutrition has improved, and medical care and family planning services are more accessible. Nevertheless, according to the United Nations Development Programme (UNDP) "Human Development Report, 2007/2008," the average life expectancy of women in twelve of the world's poorest nations remains below age fifty. The World Health Organization (WHO) 2005 "World Health Report" puts maternal mortality rates at 400 maternal deaths per 100,000 live births. These rates are unevenly distributed, with maternal mortality rates of 830 per 100,000 births in Africa and 24 per 100,000 births in Europe. Infections, blood loss, and unsafe abortions account for the majority of maternal deaths, many of which would be preventable with proper prenatal care and skilled health personnel attending births.

Even though only 10 percent of the world's population lives in Africa, an overwhelming 68 percent of all adult HIV/AIDS cases and 90 percent of all children infected with HIV/AIDS live on the continent (see AIDS). According to the Joint United Nations Programme on HIV/AIDS (UNAIDS), in countries worldwide where HIV is transmitted primarily through heterosexual relations, women make up 57 percent of all adults living with HIV, while young women make up three-quarters of those aged fifteen to twenty-four living with HIV in Africa. These higher prevalence rates result in part from physiological factors, but they are also the result of social and cultural factors that make women's insisting on safe sex practices difficult. Women also may have less access to public health information and services.

Fertility rates are decreasing worldwide, contributing to slower population growth rates (see POPULATION). Sub-Saharan Africa has not, however, experienced this decline, and in some African countries fertility rates have actually risen. Africa also leads the world in births by teenagers. According to the UNDP "Human Development Report, 2007/2008," in highly developed countries the average fertility rate is 1.8 children per woman, while in least-developed countries the average fertility rate is 6.0 children. The decline in fertility rates is the result of successful family planning programs, female education, and expanded job opportunities. Family planning allows women to space out or limit the number of children they have, improving the health of the mother and the children. The WHO 2005 figures estimate that, out of approximately 211 million pregnancies, about 46 million are terminated each year by induced abortion and that of these only 60 percent are carried out under safe conditions.

Violence and Other Forms of Abuse. Although violence against women increasingly has been acknowledged in legislative measures prohibiting it, violence against wives and marital rape are still acceptable in many, if not most countries. In the United States, the Violence Against Women Act, which declared domestic violence a federal crime, was not passed until 1994. Generally, in a global context, few rapes are reported, even fewer are prosecuted and the perpetrators convicted, and sentences remain light. Mass rape and torture of women and girls also have been used as weapons of war in international and civil conflict, as witnessed in the former Yugoslavia in the 1990s and Darfur,

Sudan, in the 2000s. The trafficking of women and girls for purposes of forced labor, prostitution, and slavery continues unabated. The U.S. State Department estimates that more than 1 million women and children are trafficked internationally each year and that about 50,000 women and children are brought into the United States under false pretenses or voluntarily, only to find themselves working in sweatshops or in the sex industry (see HUMAN TRAFFICKING).

Education. Literacy rates are rising worldwide, and they are rising faster for women than men (see LITERACY AND EDUCATIONAL ACCESS). Girls' enrollment in primary school is increasing; the percentage of girls in primary school rose in developing countries from 92 percent in 1990 to 96 percent in 2000 (and from a male-female ratio of 0.87 in 1990 to 0.92 in 2000). According to a 2008 United Nations Educational, Scientific, and Cultural Organization (UNESCO) report, about 63 percent of countries have attained gender parity at the primary level of education. The highest gains have been made in sub-Saharan Africa in this period (38 percent) and, to a lesser extent, in South and West Asia (19 percent) and the Arab states (17 percent). Only 37 percent of countries have achieved similar parity at the secondary level; however, interestingly, 60 percent of countries today have more women than men enrolled at the tertiary level. Educating women has multiple benefits. It helps women in their pursuit of a livelihood and has implications for the nutrition, health, and well-being of the entire household. It improves women's bargaining power in the home by giving them more knowledge, confidence, and leverage to defend their interests vis-à-vis their husbands and other family members concerning decisions affecting the family's future, including child birth.

Policies and Programs

In 1975, the United Nations held the First World Conference on Women in Mexico City, and the UN Commission on the Status of Women declared 1975 International Women's Year, followed by the UN Decade of Women (1976–1985), which culminated in the Third World Conference on Women in 1985 (in Nairobi). In 1995, the Fourth World Conference on Women was held (in Beijing). These conferences helped galvanize the international women's movement and assisted women throughout the world in making strides toward gender parity. Several international conventions, treaties, and platforms of action are testaments of these gains and of ongoing challenges as their implementation, monitoring, and enforcement remain problematic.

Convention on the Elimination of All Forms of Discrimination Against Women. After thirty years of work by the UN Commission on the Status of Women, CEDAW was adopted by the General Assembly in 1979 and entered into force on September 3, 1981. As of June 2009, more than 90 percent of all UN members—or 185 countries—had ratified the treaty, which commits them to take steps to end discrimination against women and incorporate the principle of gender equality into their legal systems. The convention also commits governments to establishing public institutions and adopting other measures to protect women against discrimination, exploitation, and trafficking. The convention guarantees women equal opportunities in public life, politics, education, health, and economic activities. CEDAW also addresses the influences of culture and tradition in shaping family roles and women's opportunities more generally. It is the only human rights treaty to affirm the reproductive rights of women—women's role in procreation should not be used against them as a basis for discrimination. Moreover, states are obligated to include family planning advice through their education systems, to provide women with the information to make informed decisions regarding family planning, and to allow women the right to decide freely on the number and spacing of their children. CEDAW also allows women the right to choose their nationality and that of their children.

Millennium Development Goals. In September 2000, world leaders agreed on the Millennium Declaration, which identifies eight Millennium Development Goals (MDGs) and pledges that all 191 UN member states will reach these goals by 2015. The third goal (MDG3) is to "promote gender equality and empower women." In addition, all the other goals have gender implications, including the goals of eradicating extreme poverty and hunger; achieving universal primary education; reducing child mortality; improving maternal health; combating HIV/AIDS, malaria, and other diseases; ensuring environmental sustainability; and developing a global partnership for development. These goals are linked to targets and indicators. For the goal of promoting gender equality and empowering women, the key goal is to eliminate gender disparities in primary and secondary education by 2015 at the latest. The indicators include the ratio of girls to boys in primary, secondary, and tertiary education; the ratio of literate females to males for fifteen- to twenty-four-year-olds; the share of women in wage employment in the nonagricultural sector; and the proportion of seats held by women in national parliament. Although significant progress has been made in many areas such as education—where the gender parity index in primary education has reached 95 percent or higher in six of ten world regions—high fuel and food prices along with the global economic crisis threaten to undercut these gains.

Protocol to Prevent, Suppress and Punish Trafficking in Persons, Especially Women and Children. This protocol, opened for signature in December 2000, supplements the UN Convention against Transnational Organized Crime. Trafficking includes the recruitment, transportation, transfer, holding, and receipt of people through coercion, abduction, fraud, or deception. It also refers to the abuse of power to exploit someone through prostitution, sexual exploitation, forced labor, slavery, servitude, or other such means (see HUMAN TRAFFICKING). The protocol contains strong law enforcement provisions against the trafficking of individuals, but much to the dismay of women's and human rights organizations, it does not contain equally strong protections for the people trafficked. This means that governments are not obligated to pay for any services (for example, health care) rendered the victim, although they may do so voluntarily.

The Inter-Parliamentary Union Plan of Action. The Inter-Parliamentary Union (IPU) is the organization of national parliaments. Prior to the 1995 UN Beijing conference, the IPU determined that, because men dominated political and parliamentary life in all countries, it would advocate temporary affirmative action measures, under the assumption that when parity was reached the measures would be abolished. Quota systems, the IPU's 1994 Plan of Action states, should promote a situation in which neither gender occupies a disproportionate number of seats relative to its percentage in the population. In the 1990s, new efforts to introduce quotas to improve women's legislative representation were especially notable in Latin America and Africa, and after 2000 they spread to the Middle East.

The Beijing Declaration and Platform for Action. This plan, which emerged out of the Fourth World Conference on Women, obligates governments to work toward gender parity, fight discrimination, and enhance the status of women in the following areas: poverty, education, health, the economy, human rights, the media, armed conflict, environment, political representation, violence against women, and the welfare of girls (see Document 2). It also discusses institutional mechanisms for the advancement of women, such as legislative quotas, changes in laws, and policies to address gender imbalances. The Beijing Declaration helped step up ways to promote "gender mainstreaming," eliminating gender discrimination and establishing gender equality at all stages of policy making. Gender mainstreaming has been implemented increasingly in not only national government bodies, such as ministries, but also into the practices of international bodies such as the UNDP, World Bank, and European Union.

UN Security Council Resolution 1325. This resolution, passed on October 31, 2000, calls for states to include women in peace negotiations and give them roles in peacekeeping missions around the world. It also requires protection for women and girls against sexual assault in civil conflicts and heightened efforts to place women in decision-making positions in international institutions. Prior to the passage of this resolution, women had been active in informal peace initiatives in civil conflicts in Bosnia, Burundi, Colombia, Guatemala, Israel, Northern Ireland, and Rwanda. In these countries, they had formed coalitions of women's organizations "across enemy lines" that focused on practical concerns, such as education and housing. Since the resolution was passed, however, women generally have been left out of formal peacekeeping and peacebuilding efforts, as was evident in the aftermath of the U.S. bombing of Afghanistan.

Gender Budgets. After the 1995 women's conference in Beijing, many countries adopted women's budgets patterned along the lines of South Africa's 1994 budget exercise and the budgets of federal and state governments in Australia (see INTERNATIONAL FINANCE). By 2000, gender-sensitive budget initiatives had been adopted in thirty-eight countries, with the largest number of these countries in Africa. Gender budget initiatives are generally coordinated by the finance ministries and involve collaboration among nongovernmental organizations (NGOs) and legislatures. They involve an analysis of existing budgets to determine the differential gender impact on women, men, girls, and boys, with the intention of making recommendations for future budgets to improve the way in which funds are allocated.

Many of the instruments discussed here and the policies flowing from them represent a shift in accepted norms and goals regarding gender equity. In spite of some gains, such as the adoption of gender budgets and the passage of international treaties pertaining to women's rights, the actual implementation of these policies, treaties, and programs is not always realized due to a lack of resources allocated to carry out the policy, a lack of commitment to following through, and a lack of accountability and oversight. Gender-related policies have not always translated into major transformations if success or failure is judged by the continuing absence of women in key leadership positions within economic, political, military and peacekeeping, religious, and other powerful societal institutions. At the same time, some of the most important changes are being advanced through women's national and local grassroots organizations that are addressing problems of literacy, access to credit, legal aid, violence against women, and many other such concerns.

Regional Summaries

North America

In the United States, women's status slowly has been improving through the passage of legislation at the federal and state levels. The Equal Pay Act of 1963; Title VII of the Civil Rights Act of 1964; and Title IX, the Educational Amendments of 1972 are examples of landmark legislation affecting women's status. The Family and Medical Leave Act, which was signed into law in 1993, permits any employee who has worked for at least one year to take up to twelve weeks of unpaid leave a year to look after a newborn, an adopted child, or other family members in need of care. In 2008, the U.S. House of Representatives passed the Paycheck Fairness Act that amended the Equal Pay Act by strengthening the penalties for equal pay violations. It was seen as an important step toward reducing the 23 percent pay differential between women and men.

By 1993, almost twenty-seven states had legislation barring an abusive spouse or partner from the home. In 1994, the Violence Against Women Act declared domestic violence a federal crime; it was reauthorized in 2006. Still, about 1,400 women die every year as a result of domestic violence, while 132,000 women report they have been victims of rape or attempted rape annually. Many states have begun adopting legislation that would lift the privilege of spousal immunity, which permits one spouse to forgo testifying against the other. Such new laws would allow prosecutors to call on abused wives to testify against their husbands.

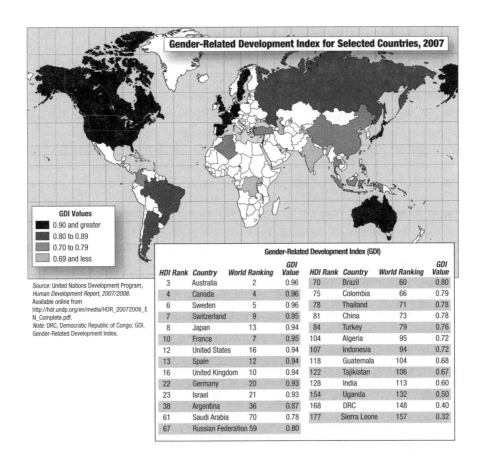

Gender-Related Development Index for Selected Countries, 2007

GDI Values
- 0.90 and greater
- 0.80 to 0.89
- 0.70 to 0.79
- 0.69 and less

Source: United Nations Development Program, Human Development Report, 2007/2008. Available online from http://hdr.undp.org/en/media/HDR_20072008_EN_Complete.pdf.
Note: DRC, Democratic Republic of Congo; GDI, Gender-Related Development Index.

Gender-Related Development Index (GDI)

HDI Rank	Country	World Ranking	GDI Value	HDI Rank	Country	World Ranking	GDI Value
3	Australia	2	0.96	70	Brazil	60	0.80
4	Canada	4	0.96	75	Colombia	66	0.79
6	Sweden	5	0.96	78	Thailand	71	0.78
7	Switzerland	9	0.95	81	China	73	0.78
8	Japan	13	0.94	84	Turkey	79	0.76
10	France	7	0.95	104	Algeria	95	0.72
12	United States	16	0.94	107	Indonesia	94	0.72
13	Spain	12	0.94	118	Guatemala	104	0.68
16	United Kingdom	10	0.94	122	Tajikistan	106	0.67
22	Germany	20	0.93	128	India	113	0.60
23	Israel	21	0.93	154	Uganda	132	0.50
38	Argentina	36	0.87	168	DRC	148	0.40
61	Saudi Arabia	70	0.78	177	Sierra Leone	157	0.32
67	Russian Federation	59	0.80				

Women still are not close to parity with men in key areas of political and economic life. According to 2008 IPU statistics, women account for only 16.8 percent of the seats in Congress. Representative Nancy Pelosi (D-Calif.), however, became the first female Speaker of the House in 2007. Democratic presidential candidate Sen. Hillary Rodham Clinton (D-N.Y.) won more primaries and delegates than any other woman in U.S. history until she conceded victory to Sen. Barack Obama (D-Ill.) in a historic and close presidential nomination race in 2008. Following his victory in the 2008 presidential election, Obama appointed Clinton secretary of state.

In 2007, women made up 46 percent of the workforce, according to the U.S. Bureau of Labor Statistics "Employment and Earnings" reports, but in traditionally male-dominated fields they lagged far behind. For instance, in 2007 only 15 percent of clergy were women, 25 percent were architects, and 10 percent were engineers. Three-quarters of low-income workers have no paid sick leave, and over 19 million women are uninsured. Women tend to delay or be less likely than men to seek medical care under such circumstances.

Women in Canada have had a slight edge over women in the United States in terms of political representation. Canadians elected their first female prime minister in 1993, and today women constitute 34.4 percent of the Senate and

21.3 percent of the House of Commons. Yet Canada's labor market is highly segregated by gender, and women's earnings are on average about 64 percent of men's, according to the UNDP "Human Development Report, 2007/2008." According to the report, Canadian women are among the healthiest in the world, with a life expectancy of over eighty-two years. Naomi Neft and Ann Levine reported in *Where Women Stand: An International Report on the Status of Women in 140 Countries, 1997–1998* that, in terms of social welfare provisions, Canadian women fare better, with seventeen weeks of maternity leave for full-time workers and 60 percent of the mother's salary paid by unemployment insurance for up to fifteen weeks.

Latin America

In Latin America, women constitute one-third of the labor force and their numbers have been growing: about 33 million women entered the job market between 1990 and 2004. Women make up more than half of the university students in many countries (with a 1.17 female-to-male ratio). Nevertheless, women's salaries trail those of men by 20–30 percent, and they are prevented from increased participation. Women today hold roughly 18.4 percent of legislative seats, a large increase from an average of 2 percent in 1970, based on UNDP "Human Development Report, 2007/2008" data. Many of the changes in female representation are the result of pressure from women's movements for the adoption of national laws requiring parties to increase female candidacies. Women also have been visible in the executive, with Chile electing its first woman president in 2006 and Argentina electing its second woman president in 2007. Women's movements succeeded in having governments create state agencies that address women's concerns, change discriminatory laws, and adopt policies to improve women's lives in general. Brazil, for example, passed a legal code in August 2001 that makes women equal to men. It abolishes the concept of paternal power, which had allowed Brazilian fathers to unilaterally make all decisions on behalf of their families. The new code requires husbands and wives to divide authority, and single mothers can now be regarded as heads of households. In spite of such progressive legislation, frequently these laws are poorly implemented due to lack of funding and weak enforcement mechanisms.

Women are still often prohibited from certain categories of employment. In some countries, sex crimes can only be committed against a woman deemed "honest." Abortion is considered a crime in all Latin American countries, with the exception of Cuba, Chile, El Salvador, and the Dominican Republic. This has led to millions of women seeking clandestine abortions at enormous risk to their health and lives. Domestic violence remains one of the largest problems, with approximately 50 percent of women admitting to suffering from violence in the home. In the 1990s, thirty-two Latin American and Caribbean countries passed legislation declaring domestic violence a crime and implementing policy measures for enforcement, following Brazil's adoption of such policies in 1985. Hundreds of police stations staffed by women and for women in need of assistance were formed throughout the region. These have been important in dealing with cases of rape and domestic violence.

Europe and the Former Soviet Union

The biggest changes in women's status in the 1990s were experienced by women in Eastern Europe and the former Soviet republics as a result of economic and political reforms. The fall of communist governments left women without the safety net of social security provisions, low-cost child care, job security, and relatively high levels of political representation. According to UNICEF's "Women in Transition," by the end of the 1990s Russia had one of the largest gender gaps in wages, and by 2007 women were earning about 62 percent of what men earned. In Georgia, women earned slightly over one-third the wages that men did. Overall in Eastern Europe and the former Soviet Union, the ratio of female-to-male earnings was 60 percent. Prior to the 1990s, Soviet women had enjoyed job security and one of the highest rates of labor-force participation in the world. By the end of the 1990s, female and male unemployment was on the rise in all the former Soviet republics. By the mid-2000s, the numbers had improved again in some countries. The percentage of economically active women was 40 percent in the Russian Federation in 1998; by 2006 it had reached 49 percent, according to the ILO. Similarly, in the Ukraine the numbers of economically active women increased from 41 percent in 1999 to 58 percent in 2003.

A consequence of women's unemployment and lack of job security in the former Soviet Union and Eastern Europe is the growing problem of sex trafficking. Criminal groups lure young women with the promise of working as waitresses and barmaids overseas and then confiscate their passports, sometimes raping and beating them into submission, and forcing them to work as prostitutes. The number of women trafficked from Ukraine, Russia, and other former Soviet republics was among the highest in the world, matching or even surpassing the number of Asian and Latin American women being trafficked.

Economic uncertainty also has contributed to precipitous drops in birth and marriage rates throughout the former Soviet Union. According to the "Human Development Reports," the fertility rates dropped by 40 percent between 1970–1975 and 2000–2005 to a rate of 1.5 percent in central and Eastern Europe and the Commonwealth of Independent States (CIS). In Estonia, Latvia, and Lithuania, marriage rates similarly dropped by 52 percent during the same period.

Changes in women's political status were also stark. In the 1990s, Eastern Europe and the former republics of the Soviet Union experienced the sharpest drops in female legislative representation in the world as the quotas that had guaranteed women seats in parliament were eliminated. According to IPU statistics, the percentage of seats occupied by women in the legislature dropped in the region from a high of 31 percent in 1980 to 9 percent in 1990, before rising slightly to 15 percent by 2008. In contrast, the Nordic countries experienced an increase in women's representation from 32 percent in 1990 to 41.4 percent in 2008, reflecting the overall improvement of the status of women in this part of Europe. Rates of female representation for the rest of Europe rose as women increased their number of seats from 11 percent in 1990, to 18 percent in 2000, and to 19 percent by 2008.

North Africa and the Middle East

Considerable variation exists in the rights enjoyed by women in the Middle East. Tunisian women, for example, have made great strides in key areas. According to the UNDP "Human Development Report, 2007/2008," the ratio of female to male students stood at 1.01 at the primary school level, 1.09 at the secondary level, and 1.40 at the tertiary level. Women are well represented in the professions as magistrates, lawyers, journalists, and professors. Tunisia has outlawed polygamy, and women can retain custody of their children in divorce. Women can obtain an abortion on request and have access to medical services and contraception, which accounts in part for Tunisia's low fertility rate.

Similar gains for women are evident in other parts of the Middle East. Women outnumber men in university enrollments in thirteen Middle Eastern states, with three times as many women as men in universities in United Arab Emirates and Qatar. Maternity leave benefits in many Middle Eastern countries are comparable to those in Europe and superior to those in the United States (where women get twelve weeks with no pay). Most women in the Middle East enjoy paid maternity leave. Women in Algeria have fourteen weeks leave, in Mauritania fourteen weeks, and in Morocco twelve weeks—with 100 percent of their wages paid by social security. According to the UN Statistics Division, maternal mortality rates in Kuwait, Qatar, and the United Arab Emirates are comparable to European rates, and in Iran and Jordan they are much lower than the average rates of states in Africa, Asia, and Latin America.

Many of the gains of the women's and feminists movements in the Middle East, especially in the areas of education and employment, came increasingly under threat in the 1990s as a result of the rise of Islamic fundamentalism. In some countries, Islamists colluded with or succeeded in pressuring the state to curtail women's rights. National and international women's organizations, including, for example, Women Living Under Muslim Laws, have been calling for reforms in marriage, family, and personal conduct codes, have resisted limits on women's employment, and have opposed domestic violence and female genital cutting.

Women's organizations also have targeted the practice of honor killings, in which a woman, who is seen as the property of her husband, can be murdered by a family member with impunity if she "dishonors" the family by disobeying her husband or is thought to have committed a number of other acts considered dishonorable. Women can be murdered for being seen with a male nonfamily member without the permission of a male of the family or for marrying outside her faith. If a girl is sexually molested by a family member and becomes pregnant, she can be killed by the family. Young women who are raped may be killed.

Honor killings are also practiced in countries outside the region, including in Bangladesh, Brazil, Ecuador, India, and Pakistan. The United Nations Population Fund (UNFPA) estimated in 2000 that as many as 5,000 women and girls were murdered each year in honor killings around the world. Such killings are legally sanctioned in Jordan, Morocco, and Syria, and evidence of the practice also exists in Egypt and Israel. Women's organizations have been especially active in resisting honor killings in Jordan and are working to have them outlawed.

The representation of women in parliaments within the Middle East is increasing in some countries, often as a result of the introduction of electoral quotas for women. In the United Arab Emirates 23 percent of the representatives in its legislature are women, in Tunisia 23 percent, and in Iraq 26 percent. In Bahrain's upper house, 25 percent are women, and in Oman's upper house, 20 percent are. These changes represent an opening to women more generally within society

Sub-Saharan Africa

Since the 1990s, women have become active in African politics in new and unexpected ways. Africa has some of the highest rates of female legislative representation in the world, and women have moved into political leadership roles—including Liberia's Ellen Johnson-Sirleaf, Africa's first elected woman president—in ways not seen before. Through grassroots activism, the advancement of women's rights and gender equity has accompanied this increase of women in prominent positions. Women also are taking their land and inheritance claims to court on a scale not seen in the past and are challenging laws and constitutions that do not uphold gender equality (see Case Study—The New Face of Power in Africa: Women and Politics).

Central and South Asia

In South Asia, the women's movement has focused on, among other things, issues such as economic empowerment through organizations such as the Self-Employed Women's Association in India and the Grameen Bank in Bangladesh (see DEVELOPMENT AID). Such organizations have successfully linked economic empowerment to social empowerment issues, including access to health care, literacy, housing, and opposition to domestic violence. Women's organizations also have focused on rising prices, the link between alcohol and greater incidence of domestic violence, unfair housing practices, discrimination in employment, violence against women in general, and inadequate health care.

Female infanticide has been a major concern of the women's movement. In countries where sons are generally preferred to daughters—such as Bangladesh, India, and Pakistan (as well as Brunei and China)—the sex ratio is skewed, with men outnumbering women. This is related to the nutritional and medical neglect of girls and, in some cases, to female infanticide and feticide (abortion after the sex of the fetus has been determined). The actual number of aborted female fetuses has been widely debated. *The Lancet,* a British medical journal, estimated in 2006 that up to 10 million female fetuses may have been aborted in India in the previous two decades. The courts outlawed the practice in 2001, leading the Indian Medical Association to claim that the number of abortions due to gender selection have subsequently declined. Honor killings are also sanctioned in some parts of this region. More than a 1,200 women had been victims of honor killings in Pakistan yearly, and as a result, the legislature banned the practice in 2005. In India, women's organizations also have worked to eradicate "dowry deaths," the murder of young brides whose husbands or in-laws have not delivered adequate dowries. *Sati,* which has been outlawed since 1829, is the old custom in which a widow is burned alive on her husband's funeral pyre as a sign of devotion. Although widow immolation is rare (about forty cases since Indian independence in 1947), with the rise of Hindu fundamentalism in the 1980s the practice has changed in one significant respect—the women who have committed *sati* are now glorified, with countless people visiting shrines built for them. Roop Kanwar's self-immolation in 1987 has been particularly glorified.

East and Southeast Asia

The women's movement in East and Southeast Asia has focused on issues ranging from the low wages and working conditions of women in factories to prostitution, sex tourism, and sex trafficking. Another issue of concern has been the migration of women to the Middle East and other parts of Asia and Europe, primarily as domestic and sex workers. More than 8 million Filipinos work overseas, half of them women. These women often suffer poor working conditions, sexual harassment, and physical abuse.

Although women have benefited monetarily from the new employment generated by globalization, they receive lower wages than men, are discriminated against when trying to access higher-paying jobs, suffer greater job insecurity, and have found that they can be replaced when pregnant. They may not enjoy the privilege of being able to organize into unions or have proper representation in the workplace. Cheap labor by women often has been used as an excuse for not providing adequate social services in many countries because their wages are seen as a source of compensation.

After the 1980s, women were having fewer children and living longer, leading to substantial increases in the numbers of women seeking employment. By 2005, 48 percent of women were represented in the labor force, especially in the service sector and in part-time labor, according to the UNDPs "Human Development Report, 2007/2008." Nevertheless, they are paid only 45 percent of what men earn, despite doing similar jobs and putting in long work hours. As women grow older, the gap in pay increases. Moreover, part-time workers do not have benefits, paid vacation, or bonuses.

Data

Table 1   Gender–Related Development Index, 2007–2008

HDI rank	Country	Ratio of estimated female to male earned income	Adult literacy (%)[a]		Life expectancy at birth (years)	
			Female	Male	Female	Male
3	Australia	0.70	99.0	99.0	83.3	78.5
4	Canada	0.64	99.0	99.0	82.6	77.9
6	Sweden	0.81	99.0	99.0	82.7	78.3
7	Switzerland	0.63	99.0	99.0	83.7	78.5
8	Japan	0.45	99.0	99.0	85.7	78.7
10	France	0.64	99.0	99.0	83.7	76.6
12	United States	0.63	99.0	99.0	80.4	75.2
13	Spain	0.50	99.0	99.0	83.8	77.2
16	United Kingdom	0.66	99.0	99.0	81.3	76.7
22	Germany	0.58	99.0	99.0	81.8	76.2
23	Israel	0.65	97.7	97.7	82.3	78.1
38	Argentina	0.54	97.2	97.2	78.6	71.0
61	Saudi Arabia	0.16	76.3	87.5	74.6	70.3
67	Russian Federation	0.62	99.2	99.7	72.1	58.6
70	Brazil	0.58	88.8	88.4	75.5	68.1
75	Colombia	0.63	92.9	92.8	76.0	68.7
78	Thailand	0.62	90.5	94.9	74.5	65.0
81	China	0.64	86.5	95.1	74.3	71.0
84	Turkey	0.35	79.6	95.3	73.9	69.0
96	Georgia	0.33	n/a	n/a	74.5	66.7
104	Algeria	0.34	60.1	79.6	73.0	68.2
107	Indonesia	0.46	86.8	94.0	71.6	67.8
112	Egypt	0.23	59.4	83.0	68.5	59.4
118	Guatemala	0.32	63.3	75.4	73.2	66.2
122	Tajikistan	0.57	99.2	99.7	69.0	63.8
128	India	0.31	47.8	73.4	63.5	62.3
154	Uganda	0.70	57.7	76.8	50.2	49.1
168	DRC	0.52	54.1	80.9	47.1	44.4

Source: United Nations Development Programme (UNDP), *Human Development Report, 2007–2008,* available at: http://hdr.undp.org/en/media/HDR_20072008_EN_Complete.pdf, pp. 326–329.

Note: DRC, Democratic Republic of Congo; HDI, Human Development Index; n/a, not available.

[a]Ages fifteen and older.

Table 2 **Women in the National Legislatures of Selected Countries, as of March 31, 2008 (%)**

Country	Lower or single house	Upper house or senate
Algeria	7.7	2.9
Argentina	40.0	38.9
Australia	26.7	35.5
Brazil	9.0	12.3
Canada	21.3	34.4
China	21.3	—
Colombia	8.4	11.8
Congo	8.4	4.6
Egypt	1.8	6.8
France	18.2	18.2
Georgia	9.4	—
Germany	31.6	21.7
Guatemala	12.0	—
India	9.1	9.9
Indonesia	11.6	—
Israel	14.2	—
Japan	9.4	18.2
Jordan	6.4	12.7
Russian Federation	14.0	4.7
Spain	36.3	30.3
Sweden	47.0	—
Switzerland	28.5	21.7
Tajikistan	17.5	23.5
Thailand	11.7	16.0
Turkey	9.1	—
Uganda	30.7	—
United Kingdom	19.5	19.7
United States	16.8	16.0

Source: Inter-Parliamentary Union, "Women in National Parliaments," available at: http://www.ipu.org/wmn-e/classif.htm.

Note: —, not applicable.

Case Study—The New Face of Power in Africa: Women and Politics

One of the most interesting changes in Africa since the early 1990s has been the rise of women political leaders. Rwanda has the highest rate of representation for women in the world, with 56 percent of its parliamentary seats held by women. Angola follows with 37 percent. Women in Burundi, Mozambique, Namibia, Uganda, and South Africa claim around 30 percent of their country's parliamentary seats. The dramatic increases in the rates of female legislative representation are the result, in part, of three strategies involving quotas: (1) the introduction of quotas in the form of reserved seats (a legal or constitutional mandate that a percentage of seats be set aside so that only women can compete for them), (2) compulsory quotas (a legal or constitutional requirement that all parties adopt quotas for women), and (3) voluntary quotas (in which political parties themselves create a mechanism to boost the number of female candidates by placing a certain percentage of women high or by alternating men and women zebra style on the party list).

Women's new political engagement has been evident in other levels of government as well. Liberia's Ellen Johnson-Sirleaf became the first elected woman president in Africa in 2005. Women are running for the presidency in African countries in unprecedented numbers. Specioza Wandera Kazibwe served as vice president of Uganda for a decade (1994–2003). Six female prime ministers have held office in African countries since the mid-1990s. At the regional level, Gertrude Mongella of Tanzania became the first president of the Pan-African Parliament of the African Union, and half the parliamentarians are women. In countries such as Namibia and Uganda, women have a significant presence in local government. Women are forming and leading political parties on a scale not evident prior to the 1990s.

Women's new engagement with politics in Africa is manifested in many other ways as well. Women's movements have sought constitutional reforms that include gender equity and antidiscrimination clauses. They have pushed for new legislation to expand women's rights, especially in the area of family law, land rights, and violence against women. Women are for the first time making bids to participate in an official capacity in national-level peace talks in countries where conflicts have come to an end.

Many of these changes are the result, in part, of activism by a new generation of women's organizations that emerged and grew exponentially after the mid-1980s in Africa. They are significantly different from earlier associations in their goals, mobilization, and relation to the state. Women are taking their claims to land and inheritance to court on a scale not seen in the past and are challenging laws and constitutions that do not uphold gender equality. The changes are also a product of changing international and regional norms that have resulted from pressure from international women's movements. They are, in addition, influenced by regional and subregional organizations such as the African Union and Southern African Development Community. Donor pressures and access to new resources also have contributed to women's new political empowerment, as have opportunities brought about by the end of major conflicts in Africa since the 1990s.

(This summary is based on Aili Tripp, Isabel Casimiro, Joy Kwesiga, and Alice Mungwa, *African Women's Movements: Transforming Political Landscapes*, Cambridge University Press, 2008.)

Biographical Sketches

Flora Brovina is a pediatrician, journalist, and leading activist for the human rights of ethnic Albanian women in Kosovo. As the founder and president of the Albanian Women's League of Kosovo, she became known for her efforts to promote interethnic tolerance and understanding between ethnic groups in Kosovo. During the war between Serbia and Kosovo in 1998, Brovina established the Center for the Rehabilitation of Women and Children to provide assistance to those who had fled war-torn areas of Kosovo.

Shirin Ebadi won the Nobel Peace Prize in 2003 for her work in the area of democracy and human rights, becoming the first Iranian and the first Muslim woman to receive this honor. As a lawyer, she has defended many dissidents and Iran's Bahai community. She was a judge, but was ousted from her bench after the Islamic Revolution. Ebadi then fought for the right to practice law as a private attorney while writing scholarly articles and books, including her memoir *Iran Awakening.*

Asma Jahangir has been a leading advocate for women's and human rights in Pakistan for more than two decades. Jahangir and her sister, Hina Jilani, established the first all-women's law firm in Pakistan; founded the Women's Action Forum, an interest group for women's rights; and set up AGHS Legal Aid, the first free legal aid center in Pakistan. Jahangir became a founding member of the Human Rights Commission of Pakistan. As a lawyer before the supreme court of Pakistan, Jahangir has drawn attention to victims of domestic and fundamentalist violence and female victims of so-called honor killings.

Wangari Maathai won the Nobel Peace Prize in 2004 "for her contribution to sustainable development, democracy and peace." Maathai is an internationally recognized environmentalist who founded the Green Belt Movement (GBM) in Kenya, one of the most successful grassroots efforts combining community development with environmental protection. In recent years, Maathai has focused on the human rights situation in Kenya and has been a fierce advocate of a democratic multiethnic Kenya.

Nawal el Saadawi is a novelist, psychiatrist, and women's rights activist, who is best known for *Hidden Face of Eve* (1977), which explores violence against women, female genital cutting, prostitution, sexual relationships, marriage, divorce, and Islamic fundamentalism. In 1982, she formed the Arab Women's Solidarity Association, the first legal, independent feminist group in Egypt. The organization was banned by the Egyptian government in 1991.

Directory

Association of Women in Development, Toronto Office, 215 Spadina Ave, Suite 150, Toronto Ontario M5T 2C7. Telephone: (416) 594 3773; Fax: (416) 594 0330; email: contact@awid.org; Web: http://www.awid.org.
International organization connecting, informing, and mobilizing thousands of people and organizations committed to achieving women's rights.

Development Alternatives with Women for a New Era, Dawn Secretariat, 44 Ekpo Abasi Street, Calabar, Cross River State, Nigeria. Telephone: (234) 87-230929; email: info@dawnnet.org; Web: http://www.dawnnet.org.
Network of women scholars and activists from the economic South who engage in feminist research and analysis of the global environment and are committed to working for economic justice, gender justice, and democracy.

Division for the Advancement of Women, United Nations, 2 UN Plaza, DC2-12th Floor, New York, N.Y. 10017. Fax: (212) 963-3463; email: daw@un.org; Web: http://www.un.org/womenwatch/daw.
Advocacy organization aimed at "the improvement of the status of women of the world, and the achievement of their equality with men—as equal actors, partners, and beneficiaries of sustainable development, human rights, peace and security."

Global Alliance Against Traffic in Women, International Secretariat, 191/41 Sivalai Condominium, Soi 33, Itsaraphap Rd, Bangkok-yai, Bangkok, Thailand 10600. Telephone: (662) 864 1427/8; email: gaatw@gaatw.org; Web: http://www.gaatw.net. *Alliance of over eighty NGOs from across the world that works against trafficking in women on a global scale.*

Global Fund for Women, 1375 Sutter Street, Suite 400, San Francisco, Calif. 94109. Telephone: (415) 202-7640; email: gfw@globalfundforwomen.org; Web: http://www .globalfundforwomen.org. *International network of women and men committed to a world of equality and social justice that advocates for and defends women's human rights by making grants to support women's groups around the world.*

International Center for Research on Women, 1120 20th Street NW, Suite 500 North, Washington, D.C. 20036. Telephone: (202) 797-0007; email: info@icrw.org; Web: http://www.icrw.org. *Organization working in the areas of poverty reduction and economic growth, HIV/AIDS, reproductive health and nutrition, social conflict, population and social transition, and policy and communications.*

International Research and Training Institute for the Advancement of Women, Cesar Nicolas Penson, Santo Domingo, Dominican Republic. Telephone: (809) 685-2111 ext. 235; Web: http://www.un-instraw.org. *UN institution devoted to research and training for the advancement of women.*

International Women's Tribune Centre, 777 United Nations Plaza, New York, N.Y. 10017. Telephone: (212) 687-8633; email: iwtc@iwtc.org; Web: http://www.iwtc .org. *Group dedicated to achieving women's full participation in shaping the development process through information dissemination, education, communication, networking, technical assistance, and training resources for women worldwide.*

Network of East-West Women, ul. Miszewskiego 17 p. 100, 80 - 239 Gdańsk, Poland. Telephone: (+48 58) 344 97 50; fax: (+48 58) 344 38 53; email: neww@ neww.org.pl; Web: http://www.neww.org. *International communication and resource network supporting dialogue, informational exchange, and activism among those concerned about the status of women in central and Eastern Europe, the newly independent states, and the Russian Federation.*

United Nations Development Fund for Women (UNIFEM), 304 East 45th Street, 15th Floor, New York, N.Y. 10017. Telephone: (212) 906-6400; Web: http:// www.unifem.org. *UN women's fund that provides financial and technical assistance to innovative programs and strategies to foster women's empowerment and gender equality.*

Women, Law and Development International, 1350 Connecticut Avenue NW, Suite 1100, Washington, D.C. 20036. Telephone: (202) 463-7477; email: wld@wld.org. *Human rights organization that holds forums for women leaders from around the world to articulate strategies for promoting and defending women's rights, initiates and carries out research, and assists in the launching of independent regional women's rights organizations.*

Women Living Under Muslim Laws, International Coordination Office, P.O. Box 28445, London N19 5NZ, United Kingdom. E-mail: wluml@wluml.org; Web: http://www.wluml.org.
International network that provides information, solidarity, and support for women whose lives are shaped, conditioned, or governed by laws and customs said to derive from Islam.

Women's Net, SANGONeT, 31 Quinn Street, Newtown, Johannesburg, South Africa. Telephone: (27) 11 429 0000/1; email: women@womensnet.org; Web: http://womensnet.org.za.
Networking support program enabling South African women to use the Internet to find the people, issues, resources, and tools for promoting women's social activism.

Women's World Banking, 8 West 40th Street, 9th Floor, New York, N.Y. 10018. Telephone: (212) 768-8513; email: wwb@swwb.org; Web: http://www.swwb.org.
Organization that helps affiliates provide responsive, efficient, and sustainable microfinance services.

World Association of Women Entrepreneurs, Organisation Seat, Forum Francophone des Affaires, 3 Place de la Coupole, BP98, Charenton 94223, Cedex, France. Email: worldpresident@fcem.ws; Web: http://www.fcem.org.
Association of women businessowners from more than thirty-five countries.

Further Research

Books

Burns, Nancy, Kay Lehman Schlozman, and Sidney Verba. *The Private Roots of Public Action: Gender, Equality, and Political Participation.* Cambridge, Mass.: Harvard University Press, 2001.

Cook, Rebecca J. *Human Rights of Women: National and International Perspectives.* Philadelphia: University of Pennsylvania Press, 1994.

Dahlerup, Drude, ed. *Women, Quotas and Politics.* London: Routledge, 2006.

Ehrenreich, Barbara, and Arlie Russell Hochschild, eds. *Global Woman: Nannies, Maids, and Sex Workers in the New Economy.* New York: Metropolitan Books, 2003.

Feree, Myra Marx, and Aili Mari Tripp, eds. *Global Feminism: Transnational Women's Activism, Organizing, and Human Rights.* New York: New York University Press, 2006.

Giles, Wenona, and Jennifer Hyndman, eds. *Sites of Violence: Gender and Conflict Zones.* Berkeley, Calif.: University of California Press, 2004.

James, Stanlie M., and Claire Robertson, eds. *Genital Cutting and Transnational Sisterhood: Disputing U.S. Polemics.* Champaign: University of Illinois Press, 2002.

Kabeer, Naila. *Reversed Realities: Gender Hierarchies in Development Thought.* London and New York: Verso, 1994.

Moghadam, Valentine. *Globalization and Social Movements: Islamism, Feminism, and the Global Justice Movement.* Lanham, Md.: Rowman & Littlefield, 2008.

Molyneux, Maxine, and Shahra Razavi. *Gender Justice, Development, and Rights.* Geneva: United Nations Research Institute for Social Development, 2003.

Neft, Naomi, and Ann D. Levine. *Where Women Stand: An International Report on the Status of Women in 140 Countries, 1997–1998.* New York: Random House, 1997.

Tripp, Aili, et al. *African Women's Movements: Transforming Political Landscapes.* New York: Cambridge University Press, 2008.

Waylen, Georgina. *Engendering Transitions: Women's Mobilization, Institutions and Gender Outcomes.* Oxford: Oxford University Press, 2007.

Articles and Reports

Hausmann, Ricardo, Laura D. Tyson, and Saadia Zahidi. "The World Gender Gap 2008." Geneva: World Economic, 2007. Available at: http://www.weforum.org/en/initiatives/gcp/Gender%20Gap/index.htm.

International Labour Organisation. "Global Employment Trends for Women 2008." ILO/08/6. Available at: http://www.ilo.org/global/About_the_ILO/Media_and_public_information/Press_releases/lang—en/WCMS_091102/index.htm.

United Nations. "The Millennium Development Goals Report 2008." Available at: http://mdgs.un.org/unsd/mdg/default.aspx.

United Nations Development Fund for Women (UNIFEM). "Progress of the World's Women 2008/2009: Who Answers to Women?" Available at: http://www.unifem.org/progress/2008.

United Nations Development Programme (UNDP). "Human Development Report, 2007/2008." Available at: http://hdr.undp.org/en/reports/global.

World Health Organization (WHO). "Gender, Women and Health." Available at: http://www.who.int/gender/documents/en.

Web Sites

Convention on the Elimination of All Forms of Discrimination Against Women
http://www.un.org/womenwatch/daw/cedaw

Inter-Parliamentary Union, Women in National Parliaments
http://www.ipu.org/wmn-e/world.htm

Progress of the World's Women, 2008/2009
http://www.unifem.org/progress/2008

United Nations Development Fund for Women
http://www.unifem.org

WomanStats Project
http://www.womanstats.org

Women Watch (United Nations Inter-agency Network on Women and Gender Inequality)
http://www.un.org/womenwatch

World Bank Gender Statistics
http://genderstats.worldbank.org

Documents

1. Convention on the Elimination of All Forms of Discrimination Against Women (CEDAW)

United Nations General Assembly, September 3, 1981; as of June 2009, ratified by 185 countries

The full text is available at http://www.un.org/womenwatch/daw/cedaw/cedaw.htm.

Extract

The States Parties to the present Convention . . . have agreed on the following:

PART I

Article 1

For the purposes of the present Convention, the term "discrimination against women" shall mean any distinction, exclusion or restriction made on the basis of sex which has the effect or purpose of impairing or nullifying the recognition, enjoyment or exercise by women irrespective of their marital status, on a basis of equality of men and women, of human rights and fundamental freedoms in the political, economic, social, cultural, civil or any other field.

Article 2

States Parties condemn discrimination against women in all its forms, agree to pursue by all appropriate means and without delay a policy of eliminating discrimination against women and, to this end, undertake:

(a) To embody the principle of the equality of men and women in their national constitutions or other appropriate legislation if not yet incorporated therein and to ensure, through law and other appropriate means, the practical realization of this principle;

(b) To adopt appropriate legislative and other measures, including sanctions where appropriate, prohibiting all discrimination against women;

(c) To establish legal protection of the rights of women on an equal basis with men and to ensure through competent national tribunals and other public institutions the effective protection of women against any act of discrimination;

(d) To refrain from engaging in any act or practice of discrimination against women and to ensure that public authorities and institutions shall act in conformity with this obligation;

(e) To take all appropriate measures to eliminate discrimination against women by any person, organization or enterprise;

(f) To take all appropriate measures, including legislation, to modify or abolish existing laws, regulations, customs and practices which constitute discrimination against women;

(g) To repeal all national penal provisions which constitute discrimination against women.

Article 3

States Parties shall take in all fields, in particular in the political, social, economic and cultural fields, all appropriate measures, including legislation, to ensure the full development and advancement of women, for the purpose of guaranteeing them the exercise and enjoyment of human rights and fundamental freedoms on a basis of equality with men.

Article 4

1. Adoption by States Parties of temporary special measures aimed at accelerating de facto equality between men and women shall not be considered discrimination as defined in the present Convention, but shall in no way entail as a consequence the maintenance of unequal or separate standards; these measures shall be discontinued when the objectives of equality of opportunity and treatment have been achieved.

2. Adoption by States Parties of special measures, including those measures contained in the present Convention, aimed at protecting maternity shall not be considered discriminatory.

Article 5

States Parties shall take all appropriate measures:

(a) To modify the social and cultural patterns of conduct of men and women, with a view to achieving the elimination of prejudices and customary and all other practices which are based on the idea of the inferiority or the superiority of either of the sexes or on stereotyped roles for men and women;

(b) To ensure that family education includes a proper understanding of maternity as a social function and the recognition of the common responsibility of men and women in the upbringing and development of their children, it being understood that the interest of the children is the primordial consideration in all cases.

Article 6

States Parties shall take all appropriate measures, including legislation, to suppress all forms of traffic in women and exploitation of prostitution of women.

IN WITNESS WHEREOF the undersigned, duly authorized, have signed the present Convention.

2. Platform of Action Mission Statement

Fourth World Conference on Women, Beijing, 1995

The full text is available at http://www.un.org/womenwatch/daw/beijing/platform/plat1.htm.

Extract

Mission Statement

1. The Platform for Action is an agenda for women's empowerment. It aims at accelerating the implementation of the Nairobi Forward-looking Strategies for the Advancement of Women and at removing all the obstacles to women's active participation in all spheres of public and private life through a full and equal share in economic, social, cultural and political decision-making. This means that the principle of shared power and responsibility should be established between women and men at home, in the workplace and in the wider national and international communities. Equality between women and men is a matter of human rights and a condition for social justice and is also a necessary and fundamental prerequisite for equality, development and peace. A transformed partnership based on equality between women and men is a condition for people-centered sustainable development. A sustained and long-term commitment is essential, so that women and men can work together for themselves, for their children and for society to meet the challenges of the twenty-first century.

2. The Platform of Action Mission Statement reaffirms the fundamental principle set forth in the Vienna Declaration and Programme of Action, adopted by the World Conference on Human Rights, that the human rights of women and of the girl child are an inalienable, integral and indivisible part of universal human rights. As an agenda for action, the Platform seeks to promote and protect the full enjoyment of all human rights and the fundamental freedoms of all women throughout their life cycle.

3. The Platform of Action Mission Statement emphasizes that women share common concerns that can be addressed only by working together and in partnership with men towards the common goal of gender equality around the world. It respects and values the full diversity of women's situations and conditions and recognizes that some women face particular barriers to their empowerment.

4. The Platform for Action requires immediate and concerted action by all to create a peaceful, just and humane world based on human rights and fundamental freedoms, including the principle of equality for all people of all ages and from all walks of life, and to this end, recognizes that broad-based and sustained economic growth in the context of sustainable development is necessary to sustain social development and social justice.

5. The success of the Platform of Action Mission Statement will require a strong commitment on the part of Governments, international organizations and institutions at all levels. It will also require adequate mobilization of resources at the national and international levels as well as new and additional resources to the developing countries from all available funding mechanisms, including multilateral, bilateral and private sources for the advancement of women; financial resources to strengthen the capacity of national, subregional, regional and international institutions; a commitment to equal rights, equal responsibilities and equal opportunities and to the equal participation of women and men in all national, regional and international bodies and policy-making processes; and the establishment or strengthening of mechanisms at all levels for accountability to the world's women.

PART V

Politics and Governance

HUMAN RIGHTS

Daan Bronkhorst

The concept of human rights is arguably the most widely endorsed element of international law and the most widely shared ideal of the international community. The liberties and freedoms encompassed by this concept can extend beyond the simple, or foundational, civil rights—such as the rights to life, free speech, and assembly—to definitions that include the rights to an education and employment. The broader conception of human rights is not shared by all observers and analysts. Nevertheless, the consensus against blatant human rights abuses has been an invaluable tool in helping to stop, curtail, or at the very least acknowledge some of the worst instances of human inhumanity to humans.

Historical Background and Development

The history of human rights incorporates Western and non-Western philosophies and traditions. Most of the concepts that have gradually been integrated into modern international law, starting with the United Nations 1948 Universal Declaration of Human Rights (UDHR) (see Document 1), are phrased in a terminology stemming from the European Enlightenment, the broad philosophical movement that addressed, among other ideas, the rationality of government. Among the movement's propositions was the idea that the general will of the people should form the basis of a social contract between citizens and government.

Basic principles of decent human social behavior can be found throughout the world's religions and traditions. An elaborate comparative study of these was made during the preparation of the UDHR. According to that study and to later research, in early Mesopotamian and Greek philosophy and in Buddhist, Confucian, Christian, Hindu, Islamic, and Jewish texts one can find the concepts human dignity, fair treatment, protection against arbitrary violence by authorities, redress of injustices, protection of women and children, rights accorded to foreigners, and more.

No author as yet has published a definitive history of human rights, but stages of its development have been traced. The first stage established the innate dignity of the human being, an idea that may date back 5,000 years. The Sumerian Gilgamesh Epic contains the notion of humans having rights to security, freedom of opinion, and free will, even vis-à-vis the gods. Around 1751 BC, the Babylonian king Hammurabi had his code of laws engraved in stone. Although Hammurabi's laws were harsh, they carried the promise of protecting the weak and prohibiting arbitrary decisions by authorities. Classical Athens of the sixth to fourth centuries BC is often regarded as the zenith of the concepts of traditional human dignity. Circa 590 BC, the Athenian reformer Solon established new laws to alleviate poverty and give large groups of male and free citizens a vote in the government and in court decisions. Yet some of the most prominent Greek philosophers were highly discriminatory, authoritarian, and antidemocratic in their thinking. Plato sketched a utopian society in which only those of "merit"— a very small proportion of the population—were allowed to rule and live as free citizens. Slaves were generally excluded from the attribution of human dignity, even by such humane philosophers as Aristotle.

Following the principle of inherent human dignity, the idea of natural law evolved from Stoic philosophy around 300 BC. The presumption of eternal natural principles of law gave rise to varying degrees of awareness that people should be considered equals, whatever their origin, station, or class. One of the most compelling figures of this school is the philosopher Panaetius, who in the second century BC. developed the idea that "barbarians" (foreigners) were equal to Romans and that even slaves should be treated on an equal basis with free citizens.

The concept of human rights developed further in the late eighteenth century when intellectual and popular movements prompted governments to abolish slavery, protect minimum rights to a livelihood for workers, and set women on equal footing with men. This was partly the result of the Enlightenment but also of the French and American revolutions, on which the British writer Thomas Paine put his mark with *The Rights of Man*. Paine justified these movements by citing human rights as the guiding principle of the American colonists' claim to independence and the French desire for parliamentary democracy.

The modern evolution of human rights found expression in international human rights law during the twentieth century, particularly in the aftermath of World War II, of which UN conventions form the core. Major regional conventions were the European Convention for the Protection of Human Rights and Fundamental Freedoms (1950), the American Convention on Human Rights (1969), and the African Charter on Human and People's Rights (1981). The significance of these conventions is strengthened by a wide range of commissions, rapporteurs, and institutions responsible for their implementation. No accepted human rights charter has been adopted yet in the Arab world.

The world's primary human rights institution is the United Nations Human Rights Council (formerly the Commission on Human Rights), which meets regularly in Geneva and discusses violations in particular countries and dozens of themes, including torture, arbitrary detention, extrajudicial executions, disappearances, threats to indigenous peoples, and the rights of women.

Current Status

The concept of human rights is simultaneously clear-cut on fundamental rights and ambiguous regarding the appropriate scope of additional guarantees. Foundational human rights preclude many forms of violations, such as discrimination, torture, genocide, political imprisonment, and extrajudicial killings (see map, p. 477; see also GENOCIDE and INTERNATIONAL CRIMINAL JUSTICE). However, what the sphere of human rights should include remains an ongoing debate. For example, are the claims of nations and peoples, such as the desire for political autonomy among ethnic Serbs in Bosnia, the Native Americans in Canada, and the Kurds in Turkey, covered by the umbrella of human rights? Should drinkable water or a clean environment be a human right to? Should euthanasia or abortion be defended or restricted in terms of human rights? Such debates do not necessarily point to a weakness in the concept of human rights but indicate that international support for human rights encourages a natural tendency to incorporate ever more guarantees as rights to secure legitimacy for given causes, groups, and interests.

Research

Part of the complexity of the concept human rights derives from the use of the term in three different categories. First, the concept of human rights is a tenet in international law that encapsulates more than a hundred different principles (see Table 1). These include various subcategories such as integrity rights (such as those that protect life, body, and mind), political rights (such as those that grant participation in government), social and economic rights (such as the rights to work, housing, and food), and cultural rights (such as copyright and the right to academic freedom). A less-established category of collective rights also exists, which includes the rights of peoples and nations to self-determination, to the use of their own natural resources, and to their development as a group. Some experts feel that this last category is too distant from the older, individual-oriented human rights concept to be included under the human rights umbrella.

Second, human rights are used in monitoring and corrective campaigns as a tool of denunciation and in the political sphere by governments and, in particular, nongovernmental organizations (NGOs) to put pressure on governments or to legitimate various forms of humanitarian or armed intervention. Denunciation campaigns can be honest and appropriate, but they can also be biased. For example, NGOs have extensively documented political imprisonment, torture, use of the death penalty, and other violations in the People's Republic of China. U.S. and other governments have voiced support for human rights improvements in China, but these governments may well have ulterior motives. For instance, they can use the proposition that Chinese workers are oppressed to ban imports from China and thus protect their own business interests (see Case Study—Human Rights and the Business Community in China).

Third, human rights are an ideological appeal to empathy, solidarity, and human dignity. From the perspective of many activists and thinkers, human rights have taken over the role previously played by religions and traditions. Buddhism, Christianity, Islam, Judaism, and other religions each lay claim to particular concepts of human dignity and to their own moral precepts. These various belief systems, however, do not satisfy the large portion of the world's population that desires a universal moral system. Human rights ideals may fulfill such a desire. They have a worldwide appeal that is strongly rooted in universal concerns for justice and law. Human rights, however, lack much of what religions have to offer. They do not proffer pronouncements on love or hate, compassion or vengeance, hope or remorse, or transcendent values and life after death. Clearly, the human rights ideal has limitations as an ultimate moral standard.

The literature on human rights is vast. Particularly in recent years, official, nongovernmental, and academic human rights research has shown impressive growth. Academic institutions worldwide produce thousands of reports on countries and issues annually, as well as a multitude of policy papers and official statements.

Major NGOs, such as Amnesty International and Human Rights Watch, have also been instrumental in analyzing human rights under the conditions of war, especially in the distinction they draw between "killings in war," as in encounters between armed groups, and "extrajudicial killings." Killings in war can only be justified within the context of international humanitarian law, that is, when they occur during encounters between warring armed factions. Extrajudicial killings are arbitrary killings of unarmed people (civilians) in war, as well as killings of civilians in situations outside war. Examples of these kinds of killings are the murdering of ethnic group members by the military (sometimes to the extent of genocide), the killing of suspects by police, and the targeting of community leaders by death squads. That the overwhelming majority of those killed in recent wars by military or other official forces have been victims of extrajudicial killings is generally assumed. Governments, however, often attempt to portray such killings as a justified means of military or law enforcement.

Journalists also publish field reports that constitute human rights denunciations. For instance, American journalist Seymour Hersh gained worldwide recognition in 1969 for exposing the My Lai massacre and its coverup during the Vietnam War. His 2004 reporting on the U.S. military's mistreatment of detainees at Abu Ghraib prison in Iraq galvanized international public opinion regarding the necessity of addressing human rights violations committed by Western allies in the "war on terror."

A growing number of academics now study the context of human rights violations. In 2003, Samantha Power published a Pulitzer Prize–winning book analyzing the persistent failure of the United States and other governments to respond effectively to genocides ranging from the Armenian massacres in 1915 to the Rwandan genocide in 1994. In 2006, Belgian-born expert Marie Dembour published a commentary on the European Convention that is simultaneously a theoretical analysis of the concept of human rights. She describes four human rights schools, which conceive of these rights as given (natural school), agreed on (deliberative school), fought for (protest school), and talked about (discourse school).

At the United Nations, the Human Rights Council has commissioned over thirty-five special rapporteurs, representatives, and experts on a variety of issues, such as food, indigenous peoples, torture, migrants, violence against women, and child prostitution. In 2000, Pakistani lawyer Hina Jilani was chosen to be the special rapporteur on human rights defenders. In 2001, in her first report, Jilani described dozens of cases of individuals who had been persecuted for their work in local human rights organizations. Many became prisoners of conscience, individuals detained solely for expressing their opinion. Others were held in administrative detention, that is, detained without trial. She appealed to governments to urge the protection of these individuals. In her 2008 annual report, Jilani described dealing with the cases of 835 defenders in 76 countries and visiting Indonesia, Serbia, Kosovo, and Macedonia.

Policies and Programs

The roles of international law and monitoring and corrective campaigns in the development of human rights policy are essential (see INTERNATIONAL LAW). Intergovernmental organizations, in particular the United Nations, have adopted an array of conventions and declarations aimed at developing a body of international law on human rights issues. Their basis is in the UDHR, which is simply a statement of principles and, therefore, cannot be legally enforced. The declaration has, however, led to a formulation of special legal instruments, called covenants, that become legally binding when a country ratifies them. Five such instruments constitute the core of present-day binding human rights law.

The International Covenant on Civil and Political Rights (1966) and the International Covenant on Economic, Social and Cultural Rights (1966) derive nearly all their articles from the UDHR. However, the principles of the UDHR are elaborated in much more detail in the covenants. For example, Article 3 of the UDHR states that "Everyone has the right to life, liberty and the security of the person." Article 6 of the Covenant on Civil and Political Rights has six paragraphs on the right to life, dealing with genocide, the death penalty, and pardons.

The First Optional Protocol (1966) is an annex convention to the International Covenant on Civil and Political Rights; an optional protocol is one that the states party to a convention can opt to include in their ratification. The First Optional Protocol recognizes the right of an individual within the jurisdiction of a state party to the protocol to file a complaint with the Human Rights Committee, the UN body that supervises the observance of the convention. By ratifying the Second Optional Protocol (1989), states agree to abolish the death penalty.

The Convention against Torture and Other Cruel, Inhuman or Degrading Treatment or Punishment (1984) (see Document 2) defines the crime of torture and the related abuses of "cruel, inhuman and degrading treatment" as acts that cause serious physical and mental suffering and that are committed or condoned by state functionaries or a state. It further describes the purposes of torture, which include obtaining information or a confession and punishing or intimidating a person. Most conspicuous among its many provisions is the article stating that torturers should be brought before a court or extradited when they are found within a nation's jurisdiction.

In these five instruments, as well as others of more limited importance, human rights are clearly and strictly defined, fostering their inclusion in the domestic law and jurisprudence of ratifying nations. In some countries, national law is automatically overridden by international conventions that the government ratifies. Increasingly, judges on domestic courts are referring to international conventions and common international law in rulings on discrimination, women's rights, freedom of opinion, asylum policies, and other issues. For example, in deciding on asylum cases, judges in European Union countries have not only referred to international conventions but also to nonbinding principles of the UDHR, such as those that guarantee the "right to enjoy asylum."

Yet the ratification of conventions is not an adequate reflection of the actual observance of human rights (see Table 2). For example, Colombia has ratified all major UN human rights conventions, but since the 1990s its government has been among the worst violators of human rights in Latin America, according to groups such as Amnesty International. Conversely Bhutan, which has not ratified most conventions, was relatively free of serious violations. In many cases, however, international instruments have proven highly effective. For example, on the basis of the Convention against Torture, General Augusto Pinochet was arrested in London in 1998 for his responsibility in the torture of civilians while he was Chilean head of state from 1974 to 1990. (He was returned for medical reasons in 2000, and died in 2006.) The Spanish judge who had ordered Pinochet's arrest, Baltasar Garzón, in 2003 jailed a former Argentinean naval officer who was extradited from Mexico to Spain for torture charges relating to the years of Argentina's military dictatorship.

The monitoring and corrective role of human rights has proved significant in the effort against violations, in particular in the work of international and national NGOs. Arguably, the most important of these is Amnesty International, the only organization that systematically monitors human rights violations in all countries. Its work focuses on prisoners of conscience; fair trials for political prisoners (even if they may have used violence); and the abolition of torture, capital punishment, extrajudicial executions, and disappearances. In recent years, the organization has also taken on issues such as violence against women, the rights and dignity of those trapped in poverty, and the regulation of the global arms trade. Its campaign methods include writing letters to authorities, lobbying at national and international levels, publicity, awareness campaigns, human rights, and education.

Human Rights Watch monitors a large selection of countries, often with a focus on relations with the United States. It claims to have successfully campaigned for an international coalition to press for the adoption of a treaty banning the use of child soldiers, the international campaign to ban land mines, the call for an international war crimes tribunal for former Yugoslavia and Rwanda, and the just punishment of former heads of state and other authorities involved in genocide, war crimes, and crimes against humanity.

Other organizations publish on a case-by-case basis. These organizations do not deal with all or most countries of the world systematically but publish reports and advise governments according to their specific research capacities and country expertise. For example, the U.S.-based Human Rights First (formerly the Lawyers Committee for International Human Rights) has initiated programs on human rights defenders, the status and rights of refugees, fact-finding by local human rights groups, and the human rights responsibilities of the U.S. business community. It has also engaged in rigorous efforts to monitor and evaluate human rights issues relating to the U.S.-led "war on terror."

The research and appeals of such organizations often have been followed up by governments and intergovernmental organizations. For example, the work of most monitors, or rapporteurs, assembled by the UN Human Rights Council is based almost entirely on nongovernmental input, and the U.S. State Department issues reports on human rights that are heavily dependent on the same nongovernmental sources.

A significant recent development has been the application of monitoring and corrective human rights practice in formal governmental and judicial initiatives of redress. One example is the globalization of adjudication through the use of international tribunals and the establishment of a permanent International Criminal Court. Another example is the prosecution of foreign perpetrators on the basis of universal jurisdiction, of which the arrest of Pinochet in London was a groundbreaking case (see INTERNATIONAL CRIMINAL JUSTICE).

So far, the results of such international administrations of justice have been minimal, but the international judicial system is expected to grow rapidly. Another example of the system's use is the plethora of truth commissions and official inquiries concerning gross human rights violations. These commissions have been lauded as an effective tool for dealing with human rights in a transition to the rule of law, that is, for states emerging from civil war or recovering from a period of dictatorship. The process was used more or less successfully in Argentina, Chile, Germany, South Africa, Guatemala, Peru, Morocco, East Timor, Liberia, and Sierra Leone. In many cases, however, their results have been disappointing or even nonexistent. Many truth commissions have also exacerbated demands for real justice to be meted out in court rulings. For example, the UN-sponsored truth commission in El Salvador in 1992 provided little more than a summary of cases and the names of some of those responsible for violations. The publication of the report was followed almost immediately by a general amnesty releasing all the responsible individuals from any sort of punishment. In late 2005, after Morocco's official truth commission's report was published, the Moroccan Association for Human Rights published a list of alleged torturers it thinks should face trial. Although the commission mentioned a total of 322 victims of state violence, the group stated that many more had been killed in protests in 1965 and 1981.

For many people, the ideological appeal of human rights is such that these rights should be regarded as the ultimate standard of ethics and justice, a substitute for the wide variation in religious and political values. This trend toward universalism has been attacked by some governments, most prominently by

China and Iran, but NGOs and independent actors in those countries, including dissidents, political reformists, lawyers, journalists, and human rights activists, generally subscribe to it. Despite such advocacy, clearly human rights are, for now, far from capable of addressing the many aspects of morality because they do not sufficiently touch on the human emotions and everyday values that are often appealed to by religion or popular ideology.

Two trends in the conceptualization of human rights are distinguishable. One trend proposes the inclusion of certain rights and values that currently are excluded in the human rights concept, such as the aspirations and needs of groups and peoples. This entails the risk of eroding the practical application of human rights. If human rights are considered too extensive with the addition of collective rights, governments may be less willing to listen seriously to the complaints of NGOs. The other trend is to restrict human rights mainly to the "classical" rights of individual integrity and personal liberty. Other claims would be relegated to debates about social, economic, and cultural development, where progress is being achieved by negotiation, increasing opportunities, and technical and intellectual advancements rather than by reference to well-defined rights.

The right to work is an instructive example. Employment involves the participation of employers, employees, and government. Businesses must be profitable for employment to be sustainable. In turn, sustainable employment depends on investment, economic conditions, the labor pool, worker skills, the market, and much more. The employment contract implied in the right to work establishes that employers offer opportunities and that employees offer good work. Stating that a right to work exists may not mean very much if the implementation of that right depends on so many factors and so many parties. However, the human rights perspective requires that available work is accessible without discrimination.

Regional Summaries

The following information has been gathered from reports by Amnesty International and Human Rights Watch.

The Americas

In virtually all countries of the American continents, the human rights situation has improved considerably since the 1980s. Argentina, Brazil, Chile, El Salvador, Guatemala, Honduras, Paraguay, Peru, and Suriname have made efforts to expose past abuses through truth commissions and trials. Few individuals, however, have been prosecuted for gross human rights violations. Cuba has remained the only one-party state in the region, with decreasing numbers of political prisoners. Serious violations have continued to occur in a number of countries. In Colombia, for instance, military, paramilitary, and armed opposition groups kill thousands of people annually. Human rights defenders are systematically harassed on occasion in most Latin American countries. Governments resort to repressive law enforcement to deal with the consequences of state neglect, discrimination,

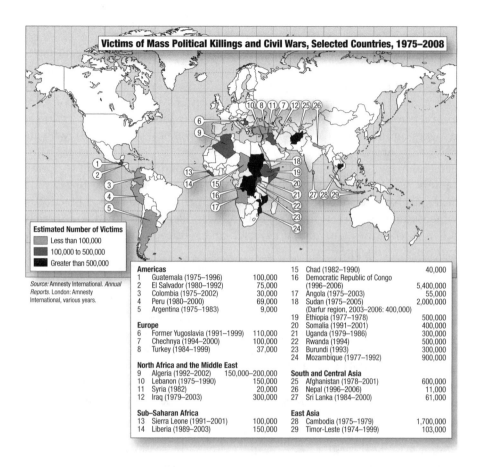

Victims of Mass Political Killings and Civil Wars, Selected Countries, 1975–2008

Source: Amnesty International. *Annual Reports*. London: Amnesty International, various years.

Estimated Number of Victims
- Less than 100,000
- 100,000 to 500,000
- Greater than 500,000

Americas

1	Guatemala (1975–1996)	100,000
2	El Salvador (1980–1992)	75,000
3	Colombia (1975–2002)	30,000
4	Peru (1980–2000)	69,000
5	Argentina (1975–1983)	9,000

Europe

6	Former Yugoslavia (1991–1999)	110,000
7	Chechnya (1994–2000)	100,000
8	Turkey (1984–1999)	37,000

North Africa and the Middle East

9	Algeria (1992–2002)	150,000–200,000
10	Lebanon (1975–1990)	150,000
11	Syria (1982)	20,000
12	Iraq (1979–2003)	300,000

Sub–Saharan Africa

13	Sierra Leone (1991–2001)	100,000
14	Liberia (1989–2003)	150,000
15	Chad (1982–1990)	40,000
16	Democratic Republic of Congo (1996–2006)	5,400,000
17	Angola (1975–2003)	55,000
18	Sudan (1975–2005) (Darfur region, 2003–2006: 400,000)	2,000,000
19	Ethiopia (1977–1978)	500,000
20	Somalia (1991–2001)	400,000
21	Uganda (1979–1986)	300,000
22	Rwanda (1994)	500,000
23	Burundi (1993)	300,000
24	Mozambique (1977–1992)	900,000

South and Central Asia

25	Afghanistan (1978–2001)	600,000
26	Nepal (1996–2006)	11,000
27	Sri Lanka (1984–2000)	61,000

East Asia

28	Cambodia (1975–1979)	1,700,000
29	Timor-Leste (1974–1999)	103,000

and social exclusion. One consequence is violence in overcrowded prisons. In Brazil, El Salvador, Guatemala, Haiti, Honduras, Jamaica, and other countries, youth and armed criminal gangs pose a serious threat.

In the United States, the application of the death penalty is decreasing significantly, due to changing public opinion and, in some cases, to DNA-based forensic investigation that have absolved death-row convicts. Violence during arrest and detention, which disproportionally affects ethnic minorities, is increasingly being exposed. In the waging of the U.S.-led "war on terror," thousands of detainees were held in U.S. custody without charge or trial in Iraq, Afghanistan, and Guantánamo Bay, a practice that the U.S. Congress—despite considerable opposition to the policy from within—has yet to invalidate. However, several court proceedings in the United States have thrown the U.S. detainee policy into question, including a June 2006 U.S. Supreme Court ruling that the military commissions established by the George W. Bush administration to try suspected terrorists were unnecessary, not authorized by federal law, and outside the standards of the Geneva Conventions. Since the inauguration of Barack Obama in 2009, the entire military commission system relating to the detainees held as a result of the U.S. "war on terror" has been called into question and put under review.

Europe

In Western Europe, the human rights situation is, generally speaking, in compliance with international norms. Incidental reports from France, Germany, Italy, and the United Kingdom have been filed concerning mistreatment by police, mostly of foreigners and ethnic minorities. More systematic concerns exist regarding the treatment of asylum seekers (people seeking protection as refugees on the basis of a well-founded fear of political persecution), who are being discouraged from seeking refuge in this part of the world and are hampered in many ways, including by the degrading conditions found in reception centers (see REFUGEES AND FORCED MIGRANTS). Quite a few European governments have been complicit in the U.S. program of renditions, a practice in which numerous terrorism suspects have been illegally detained and secretly flown to countries where they have suffered mistreatment, including torture and enforced disappearance.

In most of the formerly communist countries of Eastern Europe, the situation has significantly improved since the 1980s. In the Russian Federation, however, federal security forces have killed thousands of people in Chechnya—according to some reports as many as 100,000—since the mid-1990s in the name of counterterrorism. In Belarus, hundreds of people have been detained for peaceful opposition activities. The death penalty is applied secretly in both Belarus and Uzbekistan. Torture and other abuses, often race-related and frequently used to extract confessions, are reported from some other countries, including Russia, Turkey, and Uzbekistan, where failures to conduct impartial investigations perpetuate an entrenched culture of impunity. The gradual unification of Europe, in particular through the European Union, has clearly had a positive effect on the observance of human rights because integration has provided an incentive for closer adherence to the rule of law in European countries.

North Africa and the Middle East

The human rights situation in North Africa and the Middle East leaves much to be desired, although an improvement, seen in the release of political prisoners and the suppression of torture, has been reported in Morocco and Syria. However, arrests continue on a wide scale throughout the region. Egypt has detained thousands of people without charge or trial for alleged membership in Islamist groups. The Palestinian Authority has also arrested hundreds of people and has also suppressed dissidents. Israel annually arrests thousands of Palestinians for political reasons, and Israeli forces also have killed an estimated 20,000 Palestinians during security operations in the areas under Israeli occupation since the 1990s.

Since the 1990s, as many as 2 million lives may have been lost in intrastate and interstate wars in the Arab world. The government of Algeria has taken steps toward abolishing the death penalty; however, it has not taken steps to address its culture of impunity, which protects members of armed groups and government security forces who killed on a large scale during the conflict of the 1990s, a conflict estimated to have claimed 200,000 lives. Iraq had one of the world's worst human rights records up to 2003, with the systematic torture and secret execution of hundreds of people each year. Thereafter, the U.S.-led allied occupation and internal strife there may have claimed over 150,000 lives as of 2008. Iran executes people for a wide range of crimes, including prostitution and "acts of treason," and it severely restricts freedom of expression, although a gradual loosening of such restrictions was witnessed during the 1990s.

The major obstacle for human rights in North Africa and the Middle East is the absence of democratic institutions, including free elections, independent political parties, autonomous judicial systems, civil society, and independent NGOs, and of an awareness regarding human rights. Only Israel can be labeled as a functioning democracy. Democratization in other countries has been a slow process or has been thwarted by civil strife, war, and, most of all, by strong traditions of autocratic rule and entrenched elite interests.

Sub-Saharan Africa

The states of sub-Saharan Africa exhibit wide variations in their observance of human rights. On the one hand, Benin, Botswana, and Mali generally succeed in maintaining the principles and practices of the rule of law. South Africa, even given its history of systematic discrimination against its nonwhite population, has made progress since apartheid's abolition in the early 1990s. On the other hand, the continent was the scene of some of the worst atrocities of the 1980s and 1990s. The 1994 genocide in Rwanda claimed an estimated half a million lives. Since 1983, the civil war in Sudan claimed over 2 million lives up to 2003; thereafter, in Darfur some 300,000 people have died and 2.5 million have been internally displaced. Innumerable people were killed in armed conflicts or under oppressive conditions in Angola, Liberia, Sierra Leone, Somalia, and Zimbabwe. In the Democratic Republic of Congo, in a war that has raged since the mid-1990s, the UN estimates that 5.4 million people have perished.

Regional organizations, including the African Union (originally the Organization of African Unity) and the Economic Community of West African States (ECOWAS), have hardly been able to make a difference. Wherever they have tried to intervene, as in the wars in Liberia and Sierra Leone, the situation has improved, although only after massive backlash. Although various African scholars and politicians assert that violations of the right to life are directly connected to violations of economic and social rights, in reality no direct correlation between the level of development and the application of the rule of law exists in African countries. For example, a very poor country such as Mali has progressed in the protection of civil and political rights. Kenya, on the other hand, with a per capita income nearly three times that of Mali, still shows persistent patterns of extrajudicial killings, torture, political imprisonment, and press censorship. True civil society has not yet developed in most African states, due to the lack of education, shortage of democratic safeguards, economic vulnerability, poverty, international intervention or neglect, and other factors.

Central and South Asia

Central and South Asia contain some small countries with a fair or reasonable human rights situation, such as Bhutan and Singapore, although the latter is a record-holder in capital punishment per capita. The "war on terror" has resulted in thousands of deaths and enforced disappearances, particularly in Afghanistan and Pakistan. In Afghanistan, international military forces have caused the deaths of hundreds of civilians, sometimes in indiscriminate aerial bombardments. Between local warring parties, many thousands have been killed in roughly equal numbers by government-allied forces and insurgent groups. Thousands of lawyers, journalists, and human rights activists were arrested in Pakistan in 2007. That year, at least 135 people were executed and many more were sentenced to death.

India, although the world's largest functioning democracy, is the scene of continuous political violence in the states of Assam, Punjab, Jammu, and Kashmir. Myanmar (Burma) is practically unique in its widespread use of slavery, whereby members of ethnic minorities are forced to work for the military government. The human rights and refugee situations in Cambodia, Laos, Thailand, and Vietnam are still affected by the aftermath of the wars of the 1970s and the devastation wrought by ultra-right and communist regimes. Since 2006, armed conflicts have killed thousands and have displaced 300,000 people in Sri Lanka. In the same period, a significant improvement in the situation in Nepal has been observed.

East Asia and the Pacific

China has world-record figures for judicial executions—possibly over 50,000 in the years 2000–2007—and in its administrative detention of an estimated 500,000 people. It has also detained some 2,000 prisoners of conscience. Freedom of expression has improved somewhat with increasing standards of living, but the formation of independent political parties and NGOs still is fiercely repressed.

Indonesia shows patterns of free press and politics, which exist alongside wholesale arbitrary violence by security forces that has claimed the lives of thousands in Aceh. Widespread violence by security forces has also been observed in Papua New Guinea and East Timor (Timor-Leste). Political killings in the Philippines have created widespread fear among human rights defenders wanting to speak out against unlawful killings and the lack of investigations into them. The main human rights concern in Australia is the arbitrary detention of asylum seekers and boat people.

Regional economic cooperation in the Pacific is increasing, but opinions about human rights principles and politics may be more diverse here than in any other region of the world. Asia is the only continent that has not yet produced a regional human rights convention or a strong intergovernmental body for political deliberation.

Data

Table 1 International Human Rights Norms

Everyone has the right to:		
General and integrity rights	Freedom rights	Participation rights
Enjoyment of all rights	Liberty and security of the person	Vote and be elected
Equal protection by the law	Freedom of thought, conscience,	in secret ballot
Equality before the law	and religion[a]	Equal suffrage
Recognition as a person before	Freedom to manifest religion	Take part in the
the law[a]	Freedom to adopt religion	conduct of public
Life[a]	Freedom to seek and impart	affairs
Integrity of the person	information	Access public service
Protection of privacy, home, and	Peaceful assembly and association	Enjoy one's own
correspondence	Freedom from coercion in	culture
Protection of honor and	membership associations	Individual petition
reputation	Freedom from slavery and servitude[a]	and complaints
Freedom from torture and cruel	Free consent in marriage	Nationality
treatment[a]	Liberty to ensure religious education	
Commutation of the death penalty	Liberty to choose schools	
Freedom from discrimination	Freedom to deny consent in medical	
Freedom from national, racial, and	and scientific experiments	
religious hatred	Freedom of expression	
Freedom from war propaganda	Freedom of the press	
	Liberty of movement within one's	
	own country	
Rights of those charged or detained	Rights of categories of persons	Rights of aliens and refugees
Effective remedies	Equal rights for men and women	Leave and enter
Freedom from arbitrary arrest	Not be sentenced to death if under	one's own country
Prompt informing of charges	eighteen years of age	Seek and enjoy
Fair and public hearing by an	Not be sentenced to death if over	asylum
independent and impartial	seventy years of age[b]	Protection from
tribunal	Not be sentenced to death if	*refoulement*[c]
Presumption of innocence until	pregnant	Protection against
proven guilty	Special care for mothers and	collective
Adequate time and facilities for	children	expulsion of
preparation of one's defense	Protection of children from harmful	aliens[b]
Trial without undue delay	work	Protection and
Legal assistance of one's own	Protection of the family	support of
choosing	Equal rights within marriage	migrants
Legal assistance, if necessary		Family reunion of
without payment		migrants
Examination of witnesses		
Free assistance of an interpreter		
Not be compelled to confess guilt		
Review of one's sentence by a		
higher tribunal		
Not be tried again for the same		
offense		
Not be held guilty for an offense		
that was not criminal at the time[a]		
Compensation after a miscarriage		
of law		
Not be imprisoned for failing to		
fulfill a contractual obligation[a]		

Table 1 (Continued)

Social and economic rights	Cultural rights	Collective rights
Fair standard of living	Copyright	International peace and
Free choice of employment	Rectification	security
Full employment	Speak one's own language	Economic, social, and
Protection against unemployment	Carry one's own name	cultural development
Social security	Develop one's personality	Self-determination of
Freedom of trade unions	Freedom of scientific research	peoples
Collective bargaining	Share in scientific progress	Use of natural resources
Freedom to strike		by peoples
Safe labor conditions		Liberation from
Rest and holidays		colonization and
Equal payment for man and		oppression
woman		An environment beneficial
Fair payment		to development[d]
Property		Cultures, languages, and
Food		religions of minorities[d]
Housing		
Education		
Public health services		

Source: Daan Bronkhorst, *Encyclopedie van de menselijkheid* [Encyclopedia of Humanity] (Breda, Netherlands: De Geus, 2007).

Note: These rights and norms are recognized in key human rights documents and conventions, including the Universal Declaration of Human Rights (1948), the Convention on the Prevention and Punishment of the Crime of Genocide (1948), the Convention Relating to the Status of Refugees (1951), and the five conventions detailed in Table 2.

[a]A "non-derogatory right" (under the International Convention on Civil and Political Rights) that cannot be suspended, even in emergency situations.

[b]Only in the Inter-American Convention on Human Rights.

[c]*Refoulement* is to be returned to a country where one fears persecution.

[d]Only in the African Charter of Human Rights.

Table 2   Human Rights Ratings and Ratifications of Conventions

Country	Human rights ratings[a]	Ratifications[b]
Afghanistan	E	1, 2, 5
Albania	C	1, 2, 3, 4, 5
Algeria	E	1, 2, 3, 5
Andorra	B	2, 3, 5
Angola	E	1, 2, 3
Antigua and Barbuda	B	5
Argentina	B	1, 2, 3, 5
Armenia	C	1, 2, 3, 5
Australia	A	1, 2, 3, 4, 5
Austria	A	1, 2, 3, 4, 5
Azerbaijan	C	1, 2, 3, 4, 5
Bahamas	B	—
Bahrain	C	1, 2, 5
Bangladesh	C	1, 2, 5
Barbados	B	1, 2, 3
Belarus	D	1, 2, 3, 5
Belgium	A	1, 2, 3, 4, 5
Belize	B	2, 5

Table 2 (Continued)

Country	Human rights ratings[a]	Ratifications[b]
Benin	C	1, 2, 3, 5
Bhutan	C	—
Bolivia	C	1, 2, 3, 5
Bosnia-Herzegovina	C	1, 2, 3, 4, 5
Botswana	B	2, 5
Brazil	C	1, 2, 5
Brunei	C	—
Bulgaria	C	1, 2, 3, 4, 5
Burkina Faso	C	1, 2, 3, 5
Burundi	E	1, 2, 5
Cambodia	D	1, 2, 5
Cameroon	D	1, 2, 3, 5
Canada	A	1, 2, 3, 4, 5
Cape Verde	B	1, 2, 3, 4, 5
Central African Republic	D	1, 2, 3
Chad	E	1, 2, 3, 5
Chile	B	1, 2, 3, 5
China	D	1, 5
Colombia	D	1, 2, 3, 4, 5
Comoros	C	—
Congo, Democratic Republic of	E	1, 2, 3, 5
Congo, Republic of the	D	1, 2, 3, 5
Costa Rica	B	1, 2, 3, 4, 5
Côte d'Ivoire	D	1, 2, 3, 5
Croatia	C	1, 2, 3, 4, 5
Cuba	D	5
Cyprus	A	1, 2, 3, 4, 5
Czech Republic	B	1, 2, 3, 4, 5
Denmark	A	1, 2, 3, 4, 5
Djibouti	C	1, 2, 3, 4
Dominica	B	1, 2
Dominican Republic	C	1, 2, 3
Ecuador	C	1, 2, 3, 4, 5
Egypt	D	1, 2, 5
El Salvador	C	1, 2, 3, 5
Equatorial Guinea	D	1, 2, 3, 5
Eritrea	E	1, 2
Estonia	A	1, 2, 3, 4, 5
Ethiopia	E	1, 2, 5
Fiji	C	—
Finland	A	1, 2, 3, 4, 5
France	B	1, 2, 3, 4, 5
Gabon	C	1, 2, 5
Gambia	D	1, 2, 3
Georgia	D	1, 2, 3, 4, 5
Germany	A	1, 2, 3, 4, 5
Ghana	B	1, 2, 3, 5
Greece	C	1, 2, 3, 4, 5
Grenada	B	1, 2
Guatemala	C	1, 2, 3, 5
Guinea	D	1, 2, 3, 5
Guinea-Bissau	C	1
Guyana	C	1, 2, 3, 5

Table 2 (Continued)

Country	Human rights ratings[a]	Ratifications[b]
Haiti	D	2, 3
Honduras	C	1, 2, 5
Hungary	B	1, 2, 3, 4, 5
Iceland	A	1, 2, 3, 4, 5
India	C	1, 2
Indonesia	D	1, 2, 5
Iran	E	1, 2
Iraq	E	1, 2
Ireland	A	1, 2, 3, 4, 5
Israel	C	1, 2, 5
Italy	B	1, 2, 3, 4, 5
Jamaica	C	1, 2, 3
Jordan	D	1, 2, 5
Kazakhstan	D	1, 5
Kenya	D	1, 2, 5
Kiribati	B	—
Korea, Democratic People's Republic of	E	1, 2
Korea, Republic of	C	1, 2, 3, 5
Kuwait	C	1, 2, 5
Kyrgyzstan	C	1, 2, 3, 5
Lao People's Democratic Republic	C	1
Latvia	B	1, 2, 3, 5
Lebanon	D	1, 2, 5
Lesotho	C	1, 2, 3, 5
Liberia	D	1, 2, 4, 5
Libya	D	1, 2, 3, 5
Liechtenstein	A	1, 2, 3, 4, 5
Lithuania	A	1, 2, 3, 4, 5
Luxembourg	A	1, 2, 3, 4, 5
Macedonia	C	1, 2, 3, 4, 5
Madagascar	C	1, 2, 3, 5
Malawi	D	1, 2, 3, 5
Malaysia	C	—
Maldives	C	1, 2, 3, 5
Mali	C	1, 2, 5
Malta	A	1, 2, 3, 4, 5
Mauritania	D	1
Mauritius	B	1, 2, 3, 5
Mauru	B	—
Mexico	C	1, 2, 3, 4, 5
Micronesia	B	—
Moldova	C	1, 2, 4, 5
Monaco	A	1, 2, 4, 5
Mongolia	B	1, 2, 3
Montenegro	B	1, 2
Morocco	C	1, 2, 5
Mozambique	C	2, 4, 5
Myanmar	E	—
Namibia	C	1, 2, 3, 4, 5
Nepal	E	1, 2, 3, 4, 5
Netherlands	A	1, 2, 3, 4, 5
New Zealand	A	1, 2, 3, 4, 5
Nicaragua	C	1, 2, 3

Table 2 (Continued)

Country	Human rights ratings[a]	Ratifications[b]
Niger	C	1, 2, 3, 5
Nigeria	D	1, 2, 5
Norway	A	1, 2, 3, 4, 5
Oman	C	—
Pakistan	E	—
Palau	A	—
Palestinian Authority	D	—
Panama	C	1, 2, 3, 4, 5
Papua New Guinea	C	—
Paraguay	C	1, 2, 3, 5
Peru	C	1, 2, 3, 5
Philippines	D	1, 2, 3, 5
Poland	B	1, 2, 3, 5
Portugal	A	1, 2, 3, 4, 5
Qatar	C	5
Romania	B	1, 2, 3, 4, 5
Russian Federation	D	1, 2, 3, 5
Rwanda	E	1, 2
Samoa	B	—
San Marino	A	1, 2, 3, 4, 5
São Tomé and Principe	B	—
Saudi Arabia	D	5
Senegal	C	1, 2, 3, 5
Serbia	C	1, 2, 3, 4, 5
Seychelles	B	1, 2, 3, 4, 5
Sierra Leone	E	1, 2, 3
Singapore	C	—
Slovak Republic	B	1, 2, 3, 4, 5
Slovenia	B	1, 2, 3, 4, 5
Solomon Islands	B	1
Somalia	E	1, 2, 3, 5
South Africa	C	2, 3, 4, 5
Spain	A	1, 2, 3, 4, 5
Sri Lanka	D	1, 2, 3, 5
St. Christopher and Nevis	B	—
St. Lucia	B	—
St. Vincent and the Grenadines	B	1, 2, 3, 5
Sudan	E	1, 2
Suriname	C	1, 2, 3
Swaziland	C	1, 2
Sweden	A	1, 2, 3, 4, 5
Switzerland	A	1, 2, 4, 5
Syria	E	1, 2, 5
Taiwan	B	—
Tajikistan	D	1, 2, 3, 5
Tanzania	D	1, 2
Thailand	C	1, 2, 5
Timor-Leste	D	1, 2, 4, 5
Togo	C	1, 2, 3, 5
Trinidad and Tobago	C	1, 2, 3
Tunisia	D	1, 2
Turkey	C	1, 2, 3, 4, 5
Turkmenistan	D	1, 2, 3, 4, 5

Table 2 (Continued)

Country	Human rights ratings[a]	Ratifications[b]
Tuvalu	B	—
Uganda	D	1, 2, 3, 5
Ukraine	C	1, 2, 3, 4, 5
United Arab Emirates	C	—
United Kingdom	A	1, 2, 4, 5
United States	B	2, 5
Uruguay	B	1, 2, 3, 4, 5
Uzbekistan	D	1, 2, 3, 5
Vanuatu	B	—
Vatican	B	—
Venezuela	D	1, 2, 3, 4, 5
Vietnam	D	1, 2
Yemen	E	1, 2, 5
Zambia	C	1, 2, 3, 5
Zimbabwe	E	1, 2

Source: Human rights ratings from Daan Bronkhorst, *Encyclopedie van de menselijkheid* [Encyclopedia of Humanity] (Breda, Netherlands: De Geus, 2007). Ratifications from Netherlands Institute of Human Rights, Utrecht School of Law, available at: http://sim.law.uu.nl/SIM/Library/RATIF.nsf/Country?OpenView.

[a]Human rights ratings, A to E: Human rights situation, rated generally good (A) to very bad (E). The list, roughly reflecting the period 2003–2007, is a combination of rankings and reports provided by Amnesty International, Human Rights Watch, *The Guardian*, *The Economist*, Freedom House, Reporters without Borders, UN Development Program Index of Human Development, Transparency International, World Bank "Ease of Doing Business Rank," and International Crisis Group.

[b]Ratification of UN Human Rights Conventions as of May 2008: —, no ratifications; 1, International Covenant on Economic, Social and Cultural Rights (157 states); 2, International Covenant on Civil and Political Rights (160 states); 3, First Optional Protocol to the International Covenant on Civil and Political Rights (right to individual petition by citizens) (112 states); 4, Second Optional Protocol to the International Covenant on Civil and Political Rights (abolition of the death penalty) (64 states); 5, Convention Against Torture and Other Cruel, Inhuman or Degrading Treatment or Punishment (145 states).

Case Study—Human Rights and the Business Community in China

The norms for the protection of workers and their rights have been elaborated in some two hundred conventions of the International Labour Organisation (ILO). They deal with child labor, forced labor, fair wages, safe labor conditions, discrimination against women, holidays and rest periods, and other issues. In the mid-1970s, various international statements of principles were drafted especially for the business community. Among these is the ILO's Tripartite Declaration of Principles Concerning Multinational Enterprises and Social Policy (adopted in 1977, and repeatedly amended and revised), concerning employment, working conditions, and training.

In 1989, six years after the People's Republic of China's first delegation attended an ILO annual conference, the Chinese spokesperson dismissed the possibility of being able to apply all ILO conventions and recommendations in China because of his country's size and lack of official mandate. In fact, two laws passed by the Chinese government, the Trade Union Law (1992) and the

Labor Law (1995), both violate core ILO principles. The right to strike is not recognized.

China still has not ratified many ILO conventions, including the Freedom of Association and Protection of the Right to Organize Convention, the Right to Organize and Collective Bargaining Convention, the Forced Labour Convention, and the Abolition of Forced Labour Convention. In the 1990s, complaints backed by the International Transport Workers Federation and the International Confederation of Free Trade Unions referred to the Chinese government's denial of the right to freedom of association, the ill-treatment of Chinese crewmen at sea, the detention of labor activists, and impediments to collective bargaining.

The Chinese government insists that international labor standards and ILO requirements are unfair. At a 1997 ILO conference, Labor Minister Li Boyong argued, "For developing countries which constitute the overwhelming majority in the membership, the existing labour standards, taken as a whole, do have the defect of being excessive in number and in criteria." As reported in "China and the ILO, Part 1" (published by Hong Kong's independent *China Labour Bulletin*), he went on to say that developing countries' inability to live up to these standards "is not because of the lack of political will, but rather as a result of their limited capabilities." This prompted the *China Labour Bulletin* to comment in the report that "it appears that the irony of a representative of a 'workers' state' arguing for diminishing labor standards while attending an international labor conference was lost on Mr. Li."

The work-injury insurance system covers only 37 million of the country's 200 million industrial workers. Many former employees of state-owned enterprises lost their pensions when their companies were privatized or went bankrupt. Millions of citizens who have left the countryside to seek work in cities face serious problems. Without official residence permits, these migrant workers lack access to basic services and are vulnerable to police abuse. More than 5 million children (under the age of sixteen) work in export-serving industries in China. Often, workers are deprived of their right to rest during long hours of enforced overtime. The 1996 Labour Law stipulates a maximum of 36 hours of monthly overtime, but this standard is often violated. Employers ignore the minimum wage requirements and fail to implement required health and safety measures.

Workers are limited in their capacity to seek redress by the government's ban on independent trade unions. The only union permitted is the government-controlled All China Federation of Trade Unions (ACFTU). Of the 100–150 million rural migrants who work in the cities, a total of 14 million, the ACFTU claimed, had joined the union as of 2006. However, most migrants working in low-value-added jobs in the manufacturing and service sectors are not represented. Workers repeatedly take to the streets, and some have gone to prison. The rural labor force, consisting of approximately 540 million people, has no union or similar organization.

When producing in China, or exporting from China, foreign companies may be confronted with forced prison labor. Prison camps are often concealed behind a façade of commercial factories, masked by a company name. Moreover, most camps have two names: an enterprise name and an internal administrative name. In these prison camps, the circumstances and conditions of work are extremely exploitative.

Since the late 1990s, NGOs for human rights and labor rights have pressed the international business community to help promote basic human rights in China. One approach is the application of an international standard called SA8000—an "auditable standard for third-party verification" of labor practices published by the U.S.-based Social Accountability International. The standard is based on core ILO conventions that guarantee protection from discrimination, protection from forced and bonded labor, freedom of association, the right to collective bargaining, minimum age requirements, occupational safety and health, fair wages, and decent working hours. After China hosted the 2008 Summer Olympics, trade and investment in China by the international business community were expected to greatly increase; however, the worldwide economic crisis that began in 2007–2008 makes a conclusion concerning increased trade and investment in China resulting from the Olympics difficult to ascertain. Along with the promotion of objectively monitored standards, such contacts can have a significant impact on China's human rights performance if transnational companies make a collective stand, either on the basis of voluntary principles or under obligation by binding international standards.

Biographical Sketches

Louise Arbour was the UN high commissioner for human rights from 2004 to 2008. Among many other remarkable stands, during the 2006 Israel-Lebanon conflict she stated that "those in positions of command and control" could be subject to "personal criminal responsibility" for their actions in the conflict. Previously, she had served on the Supreme Court of Canada and as prosecutor for the International Tribunals for former Yugoslavia and for Rwanda. She indicted President Slobodan Milošević for war crimes, the first time a serving head of state had been brought before an international court. She has been awarded honorary doctorates by twenty-seven universities.

Aung San Suu Kyi is the leader of the opposition Burmese party that won an overwhelming victory in the national elections held in 1990. The military junta annulled the results and placed Suu Kyi under house arrest, a situation that has continued for eighteen years with short periods of release. The daughter of Aung San, who led Burma (now Myanmar) to independence, Suu Kyi became an outspoken critic of the ruling junta. Her popularity among the Burmese has grown to enormous proportions. In 1991, she won the Nobel Peace Prize for her efforts to bring democracy to Burma. Under house arrest, she has on occasion been allowed to meet political allies, as in 2004 and 2007.

Baltasar Garzón is one of Spain's six investigating judges, assigned to gather evidence and evaluate whether cases should be brought to trial. Garzón's most prominent case thus far has been the international warrant he issued against General Augusto Pinochet, the former head of Chile, for genocide, hostage taking, and conspiracy to commit murder. As a result of the warrant, Pinochet was detained for seventeen months in London before being released on medical grounds.

Dele Olojede is a Nigerian journalist, the first African-born winner of the Pulitzer Prize in 2005 for his reporting on Rwanda, ten years after the 1994 genocide. In 1984, he joined *Newswatch,* a Nigerian news magazine whose editor was killed by a mail bomb in 1986. Olojede publicly accused Nigeria's military leader of being responsible. After moving to the United States, he wrote on domestic issues and was sent as a correspondent to China. In 1994, he was covering the South African general elections; he later said he might have helped the situation in Rwanda if he had gone there instead. He moved to South Africa in 2006.

Jose Zalaquett is a Chilean human rights lawyer. After the military coup that ousted the government on September 11, 1973, he joined Comité Pro Paz, a church-based human rights organization. He was imprisoned from 1975 to 1976 and then went into exile until 1986. He was chairperson of Amnesty International from 1979 to 1982. In 1990, he was asked by Chile's president to put together a National Truth and Reconciliation Commission and proceeded to serve as a commission member. In 1999–2000, he joined the "dialogue panel" between the armed forces and human rights defenders. He was a member and chairman of the Inter-American Commission on Human Rights from 2000 to 2005.

Directory

Amnesty International, International Secretariat, 1 Easton Street, London WC1X 8DJ, United Kingdom. Telephone: (44) 207 413 5500; email: aimember@aiusa.org; Web: http://www.amnesty.org.
Organization that systematically monitors human rights violations worldwide.

Freedom House, 120 Wall Street, 26th Floor, New York, N.Y. 10005. Telephone: (212) 514-8040; email: info@freedomhouse.org; Web: http://www.freedomhouse.org.
Organization that publishes reports on press freedom and civil liberties worldwide.

Human Rights First (formerly the Lawyers Committee for International Human Rights), 333 Seventh Avenue, 13th Floor, New York, N.Y. 10001-5108. Telephone: (212) 845–5200; email: MinteerK@humanrightsfirst.org; Web: http://www.human rightsfirst.org.
Organization that works to advance universal rights and freedoms through the defense of and advocacy for at-risk individuals and groups, and through media campaigns and direct action aimed at top-level policymakers.

Human Rights Internet, 1 Nicholas Street, Suite 301, Ottawa, ON K1N 7B7, Canada. Telephone: (613) 789-7407; email: info@hri.ca; Web: http://www.hri.ca.
Organization that documents the activities of human rights groups.

Human Rights Watch, 350 Fifth Avenue, 34th Floor, New York, N.Y. 10118-3299. Telephone: (212) 736-1300; email: hrwnyc@hrw.org; Web: http://www.hrw.org.
Organization that reports on human rights violations in many countries and on a large array of worldwide human rights themes.

International Commission of Jurists, P.O. Box 91, 33 rue des Bains, 1211 Geneva 8, Switzerland. Telephone: (41) 22 9793800; email: info@icj.org; Web: http://www.icj.org.
An independent group that is particularly strong on the inclusion of human rights law in domestic law; has national sections and affiliated legal organizations around the world.

International Crisis Group, 420 Lexington Avenue, Suite 2640, New York, N.Y. 10170. Telephone: (212) 813–0820; email: via Web site; Web: http://www.crisisgroup.org.
Nongovernmental organization working to prevent and resolve deadly conflict.

International Gay and Lesbian Human Rights Commission, 80 Maiden Lane, Suite 1505, New York, N.Y. 10038. Telephone (212) 268-8040; email: iglhrc@iglhrc .org; Web: http://www.iglhrc.org.
Group that works to protect and advance human rights of all individuals and communities subject to discrimination on the basis of sexual orientation, gender identity, or HIV status.

International League for Human Rights, 352 Seventh Avenue, Suite 1234, New York, N.Y. 10001. Telephone: (212) 661-0480; email: info@ilhr.org; Web: http:// www.ilhr.org.
The oldest general human rights organization, established in 1942; particularly defends human rights advocates.

Minority Rights Group International, 54 Commercial Street, London E1 6LT, United Kingdom. Telephone: (44) 20 7422 42003; email: minority.rights@mrgmail .org; Web: http://www.minorityrights.org.
Organization that documents human rights violations that affect ethnic and other minorities worldwide.

Office of the United Nations High Commissioner for Human Rights, Palais Wilson, 52 rue des Pâquis, CH-1201 Geneva, Switzerland. Telephone: (41) 22 917 9000; email: infodesk @ohchr.org; Web: http://www.ohchr.org.
Office in charge of UN policymaking efforts relating to human rights protection around the world.

U.S. State Department, Public Communication Division, Bureau of Public Affairs, Room 5827, 2201 C Street NW, Washington, D.C. 20520-6810. Telephone: (202) 647-6575; email: AskPublicAffairs@state.gov; Web: http://www.state.gov.
U.S. government agency responsible for foreign policy; tracks human rights worldwide and its Web site has extensive annual reports on an array of human rights issues in most countries.

Further Research

Books

Alston, Philip, and Ryan Goodman. *International Human Rights in Context: Law, Politics, Morals.* 3d ed. Oxford: Oxford University Press, 2007.

Bales, Kevin. *Disposable People: New Slavery in the Global Economy.* Rev. ed. Berkeley: University of California Press, 2004.

Dembour, Marie-Bénédicte. *Who Believes in Human Rights?: Reflections on the European Convention.* Cambridge, UK: Cambridge University Press, 2006.

Donnelly, Jack. *Universal Human Rights in Theory and Practice.* Rev. ed. Ithaca, N.Y.: Cornell University Press, 2002.

Forsythe, David, et al., eds. *Encyclopedia of Human Rights.* Oxford: Oxford University Press, 2008.

Hayner, Priscilla. *Unspeakable Truths: Confronting State Terror and Atrocity. How Truth Commissions around the World Are Challenging the Past and Shaping the Future.* New York: Routledge, 2001.

Hersh, Seymour. *Chain of Command: The Road from 9/11 to Abu Ghraib.* New York: HarperCollins, 2004.

Jones, Adam. *Genocide: A Comprehensive Introduction.* New York: Routledge, 2006.

Lauren Gordon, Paul. *The Evolution of International Human Rights: Visions Seen.* Rev. ed. Philadelphia: University of Pennsylvania Press, 2003.

McGregor Burns, James, and Steward Burns. *A People's Charter: The Pursuit of Rights in America.* New York: Knopf, 1991.

Osse, Anneke. *Understanding Policing: A Resource for Human Rights Activists.* Amsterdam: Amnesty International, 2007. Available at: http://www.amnesty.nl/documenten/phrp/Understanding%20policing%20Part%201.pdf.

Perry, Michael. *Toward a Theory of Human Rights: Religion, Law, Courts.* Rev. ed. Cambridge, UK: Cambridge University Press, 2008.

Poole, Hilary, ed. *Human Rights: The Essential Reference.* Phoenix, Ariz.: Oryx Press, 1999.

Power, Samantha. *A Problem from Hell: America and the Age of Genocide.* Rev. ed. New York: Perennial, 2007.

Rejali, Darius. *Torture and Democracy.* Princeton, N.J.: Princeton University Press, 2007.

Robertson, Geoffrey. *Crimes against Humanity: The Struggle for Global Justice.* Rev. ed. New York: New Press, 2007.

Schultz, William, ed. *The Phenomenon of Torture: Readings and Commentary.* Philadelphia: University of Pennsylvania Press, 2007.

Sheen, Juliet, ed. *Freedom of Religion and Belief: A World Report.* New York: Taylor & Francis, 2007.

Shelton, Dinah. *Remedies in International Human Rights Law.* Oxford: Oxford University Press, 2005.

Articles and Reports

Amnesty International. *Annual Reports.* New York, 1990–2008.

———. "Facts and Figures on the Death Penalty." Available at: http://www.web.amnesty.org.

———. "When in China: Encounters with Human Rights." September 2006. Available at: http://www.amnesty.nl/documenten/diversen/When%20in%20China%20(september%202006).pdf.

"China and the ILO, Part 1." *China Labour Bulletin* no. 58 (January–February 2001). Available at: http://iso.china-labour.org.hk/iso/article.adp?article_id=1166#note9.

Human Rights Watch. *World Report.* New York, various years. Available at: http://www.hrw.org.

Jilani, Hina. "Promotion and Protection of Human Rights: Human Rights Defenders." Office of the High Commissioner for Human Rights, Geneva. 2006. Available at: www2.0hchr.org/english/issues/defenders/docs.

Web Sites

Amnesty International Web Site Against the Death Penalty
http://www.amnestyusa.org/our-priorities/death-penalty

Derechos
http://www.derechos.org

International Covenant on Civil and Political Rights
http://www.unhchr.ch/html/menu3/b/a_ccpr

International Covenant on Economic, Social and Cultural Rights
http://www.unhchr.ch/html/menu3/b/a_cescr.htm

Social Accountability International
http://www.sa-intl.org

Documents

1. Universal Declaration of Human Rights

United Nations General Assembly, December 10, 1948

The full text is available at http://www.un.org/Overview/rights.html.

Extracts

Preamble

Whereas recognition of the inherent dignity and of the equal and inalienable rights of all members of the human family is the foundation of freedom, justice and peace in the world,

Whereas disregard and contempt for human rights have resulted in barbarous acts which have outraged the conscience of mankind, and the advent of a world in which human beings shall enjoy freedom of speech and belief and freedom from fear and want has been proclaimed as the highest aspiration of the common people,

Whereas it is essential, if man is not to be compelled to have recourse, as a last resort, to rebellion against tyranny and oppression, that human rights should be protected by the rule of law,

Whereas it is essential to promote the development of friendly relations between nations,

Whereas the peoples of the United Nations have in the Charter reaffirmed their faith in fundamental human rights, in the dignity and worth of the human person and in the equal rights of men and women and have determined to promote social progress and better standards of life in larger freedom,

Whereas Member States have pledged themselves to achieve, in co-operation with the United Nations, the promotion of universal respect for and observance of human rights and fundamental freedoms,

Whereas a common understanding of these rights and freedoms is of the greatest importance for the full realization of this pledge,

Now, Therefore,

THE GENERAL ASSEMBLY

proclaims

THIS UNIVERSAL DECLARATION OF HUMAN RIGHTS as a common standard of achievement for all peoples and all nations, to the end that every individual and every organ of society, keeping this Declaration constantly in mind, shall strive by teaching and education to promote respect for these rights and freedoms and by progressive measures, national and international, to secure their universal and effective recognition and observance, both among the peoples of Member States themselves and among the peoples of territories under their jurisdiction. . . .

Article 2

Everyone is entitled to all the rights and freedoms set forth in this Declaration, without distinction of any kind, such as race, colour, sex, language, religion, political or other opinion, national or social origin, property, birth or other status. . . .

Article 15

(1) Everyone has the right to a nationality.

(2) No one shall arbitrarily be deprived of his nationality nor denied the right to change his nationality.

Article 17

(1) Everyone has the right to own property alone as well as in association with others.

(2) No one shall be arbitrarily deprived of his property.

Article 18

Everyone has the right to freedom of thought, conscience and religion; this right includes freedom to change his religion or belief, and freedom, either alone or in community with others and in public or private, to manifest his religion or belief in teaching, practice, worship and observance.

Article 27

(1) Everyone has the right freely to participate in the cultural life of the community, to enjoy the arts and to share in scientific advancement and its benefits.

(2) Everyone has the right to the protection of the moral and material interests resulting from any scientific, literary or artistic production of which he is the author.

2. Convention against Torture and Other Cruel, Inhuman or Degrading Treatment or Punishment

United Nations General Assembly, December 10, 1984

The full text is available at http://www.unhchr.ch/html/menu3/b/h_cat39.

Extract

PART I

Article 1

1. For the purposes of this Convention, the term "torture" means any act by which severe pain or suffering, whether physical or mental, is intentionally inflicted on a person for such purposes as obtaining from him or a third person information or a confession, punishing him for an act he or a third person has committed or is suspected of having committed, or intimidating or coercing him or a third person, or for any reason based on discrimination of any kind, when such pain or suffering is inflicted by or at the instigation of or with the consent or acquiescence of a public official or other person acting in an official capacity. It does not include pain or suffering arising only from, inherent in or incidental to lawful sanctions.

2. This article is without prejudice to any international instrument or national legislation which does or may contain provisions of wider application.

Article 2

1. Each State Party shall take effective legislative, administrative, judicial or other measures to prevent acts of torture in any territory under its jurisdiction.

2. No exceptional circumstances whatsoever, whether a state of war or a threat of war, internal political instability or any other public emergency, may be invoked as a justification of torture.

3. An order from a superior officer or a public authority may not be invoked as a justification of torture.

Article 3

1. No State Party shall expel, return ("refouler") or extradite a person to another State where there are substantial grounds for believing that he would be in danger of being subjected to torture.

2. For the purpose of determining whether there are such grounds, the competent authorities shall take into account all relevant considerations including, where applicable, the existence in the State concerned of a consistent pattern of gross, flagrant or mass violations of human rights.

Article 4

1. Each State Party shall ensure that all acts of torture are offences under its criminal law. The same shall apply to an attempt to commit torture and to an act by any person which constitutes complicity or participation in torture.

INTERNATIONAL LAW

Bruce Cronin

International law is the body of legal rules, customs, and norms that regulate activities carried on beyond the borders of individual states, primarily those between governments. For hundreds of years, its principles have provided a mechanism for political leaders to define and evaluate acceptable state behavior and determine when a political actor violates the commonly agreed-on rules of coexistence. International law developed gradually over several centuries and is derived from a highly diverse collection of lawmaking treaties, customary practices, and judicial opinions that states accept as binding obligations. Although the scope of international law's jurisdiction is limited, it covers a wide range of practices, including the use of force, the behavior of military combatants, the distribution and use of territory and waterways, and diplomatic interaction. All countries are legally bound to adhere to its principles as a condition of their participation in the international community.

Historical Background and Development

International law evolved with the development of the nation-state system during the sixteenth and seventeenth centuries. The nation-state system consists of sovereign countries throughout the world that carry on formal political and diplomatic relations with one another. Drawing from Roman and medieval legal traditions, international law was originally based on a view that all sovereigns were subject to a natural law that consisted of universal principles of right and wrong. Over time, philosophers, political leaders, and legal scholars began to move away from natural law doctrines and toward a positivist approach that saw international law as the product of human will grounded in voluntary consent. Legalists began to examine the behavior of states and tried to determine from it which practices had become accepted as obligations in the international community. From this, they developed a set of legal principles that came to be known as customary law, which was considered to be binding on all states specifically because it reflected a set of consistent practices that states had viewed as obligatory over a long period of time. For example, the tenet that all ships have a right to free navigation on the high seas derives from the fact that countries had long espoused and accepted this principle as a legal obligation in international relations.

As the nation-state system expanded, political leaders gradually realized that they needed a more formal set of rules to regulate their relations and a stable environment for trading, resolving disputes, and minimizing suffering. Yet they had to confront a tension between increasing international obligations and their desire to assert their independence and autonomy. This created problems in the development of a coherent *law of nations,* another term for international law used in this period. States are legally sovereign entities and are therefore not subject to legal sanction by a higher authority. They jealously guard their sovereignty and are reluctant to submit to external, or international, judgment.

On this basis, political realists long argued that international law is not in fact law but, rather, positive morality that states follow only when doing so is in their interest. Given what political scientist and diplomat George Kennan describes in *American Diplomacy* as "chaotic and dangerous aspirations of governments" coupled with the lack of a central authority to protect individual states, governments can ultimately rely only on their own resources to promote their interests. States do not "obey" international law because no law exists to obey. Rather, strong states follow the rules when it is convenient, and weak ones follow them when they are forced to. For these reasons, studies by realist legal scholars and political scientists have tended to focus on the role of the great powers in making and enforcing the rules of order.

This bleak view remained dominant until the twentieth century. After World War I, many political leaders and transnational nongovernmental organizations (NGOs) began to explore the possibility of creating a stronger system of international law through the establishment of international organizations, such as the League of Nations. Article 12 of the League Covenant, which is legally considered a treaty, prohibited states from using force until a determination was made by a court of arbitration. This was strengthened in 1929, when Belgium, Czechoslovakia, France, Germany, Great Britain, Italy, Japan, Poland, and the United States signed the Treaty for the Renunciation of War, also known as the Kellogg-Briand Pact, in an ambitious attempt to make warfare illegal (see Table 1). NGOs, such as the International Law Society, and international institutions, such as the Permanent Court of International Justice, supported these efforts and tried to reorganize international relations as a society of states based on the rule of law.

Ultimately, a variety of factors, including trade conflicts and economic depression, undermined these efforts. In addition, because the main point of the League of Nations was to prevent aggression, the fact that it was unable to stop German and Italian aggression in the 1930s essentially meant its functional end. This problem was intensified by the failure of two great powers—the United States and the Soviet Union—to join the league. Therefore, although the Treaty for the Renunciation of War technically remained in effect, it had no effective force. Following World War II and the onset of the cold war, efforts to expand international law became subordinate to power politics and, outside of Western Europe, was no longer considered to be a major factor in international relations.

At the same time, the success of Western European integration and the rise of economic interdependence among the industrialized states convinced many government officials and leaders within NGOs to initiate new efforts toward greater international cooperation and legalization. Moreover, the creation and expansion of the United Nations spurred a proliferation of new lawmaking treaties. Thus, during the cold war the number and strength of international organizations and multilateral agreements grew significantly, at least in the West (see TRANSNATIONAL GOVERNANCE). The most comprehensive agreement on the treatment of prisoners of war was concluded in Geneva in 1949 (see Document 1). Accompanying this expansion of intergovernmental organizations was an increase in the influence of transnational NGOs, such as Greenpeace and Amnesty International. Such groups sought to expand the scope of international law by promoting greater legal commitments to human rights and environmental protection.

All this activity led to the ascendancy of the institutionalist and internationalist approaches to the study and practice of international law during the 1980s. Specifically, an increasing number of scholars and political leaders began to explore the various conditions that lead states to cooperate with one another toward the attainment of common goals. In developing this approach, internationalists argued that states formed a type of international community in which they were bound by a common set of rules in their relations with one another.

The end of the cold war in 1989–1991 brought a new optimism among academics and policymakers that international law and organizations could play an increasingly important role in regulating the relations of states. The ensuing consensus on the basic principles of international order raised expectations unseen since the end of World War I. The rapid spread of nationalist, ethnic, and religious conflict and civil war in Africa, Eastern Europe, and the Middle East has since dampened this optimism; however, international law has continued to assume an important place in international relations at the beginning of the twenty-first century. In fact, contemporary challenges have actually driven states to develop new legal principles that could address such thorny issues as terrorism; global warming; genocide; and the proliferation of biological, chemical, and nuclear weapons.

Current Status

According to legal scholar John Austin, law consists of a command issued by a sovereign power and backed by a sanction. Unlike most national legal systems, international law operates within a global environment that lacks a central government with the authority to enact legislation, adjudicate disputes, and punish transgressors. As a result, international law is highly decentralized. Its main functions are not primarily provided by global legal institutions but by individual states that often must interpret and enforce the rules themselves. When conflicts over interpretation arise, they are usually addressed through political and diplomatic means rather than legal ones.

This situation is complicated by the fact that political leaders are wary of making commitments to follow general principles that would apply in unforeseen future circumstances—the very essence of a legal obligation. States jealously guard their sovereignty and will not easily cede their authority to a higher power, be it a legal norm or global institution. For these reasons, a long-standing debate continues among legal scholars and political leaders over the degree to which international law can be considered law in the traditional sense. Indeed, many researchers ask why nations obey international law at all.

Research

Despite these roadblocks, international law has expanded in the range of issues that fall within its jurisdiction and the number of institutions that administer it. Increased economic integration, or globalization, and the dramatic spread of democratization have led to a rising demand for more precise and binding commitments by states. The degree to which international law may be assuming a greater role in regulating relations among states is thus of great concern to legal scholars, political scientists, and officials from international institutions and NGOs. Current research and policy analysis are primarily concerned with two questions: (1) To what degree has the legal authority of international organizations increased over that of individual states, and (2) how are changing international norms increasing the range of issues that fall within the scope of international law?

There is little doubt that a dramatic increase has been seen in the use of legal mechanisms to solve the problems of collective action. Between 1899 and 1950, for example, states signed approximately forty legally binding multilateral treaties and conventions. From 1951 to 2007, this figure is closer to two hundred. Moreover, these agreements expanded from the traditional focus on diplomatic relations and conduct during war to include trade, arms control, limitations on the use of force, human rights, and the environment (see Table 2). In addition, the development and expansion of international institutions such as the European Union, the United Nations, the World Trade Organization (WTO), and the International Criminal Court has greatly accelerated the ability of the international community to create new legal obligations and implement existing ones. Legal scholars such as José Alvarez specifically argue that international organizations have increasingly become the primary mechanism for creating new international law that binds states in a wider variety of issue areas. Similarly, Oscar Schachter and Frederic Kirgis have documented the dramatic increase in what they term lawmaking treaties, which some scholars find to be akin to international legislation. Some of the most ambitious attempts to expand international law into the areas of the environment, intellectual property, organized crime, terrorism, arms control, and human rights have emanated from United Nations conferences in the form of lawmaking treaties (for example, the widely used Vienna Convention on Diplomatic Relations).

Other researchers have focused on the role of institutions such as the International Criminal Court (ICC) and the United Nations Security Council in further legalizing international relations. The ICC holds individual government officials accountable for violating international law in the areas of genocide, war crimes, and crimes against humanity, while in limited cases the UN Security Council has acted almost like a legislature by developing new legal obligations in such areas as international terrorism and the proliferation of weapons of mass destruction.

Recent scholarship has also explored the degree to which changing international norms have led to an expansion in both the scope and intrusiveness of international law. Specifically, legal research has focused on the regulation of behavior that states have traditionally considered to fall within the sovereign prerogatives of national governments. This has been particularly notable in the areas of human rights (see Case Study—Human Rights and International Law) and the acquisition of weapons of mass destruction by states.

Policies and Programs

Creating new international law is a slow, usually politically contentious process. Typically, governments are wary of accepting new obligations that could limit their flexibility in promoting their foreign policy interests in unforeseen circumstances. Moreover, because many states are involved in negotiating new multilateral treaties, the text of an international legal instrument must incorporate a wide range of individual state interests and concerns, many of which may contradict one another.

For this reason, international law has traditionally focused primarily on broad issues of coexistence, such as diplomatic relations, behavior in wartime, the use of such common-pool resources as the high seas, and the rights and duties of states. Yet, as the need for greater interstate cooperation has increased, states have pursued more efficient mechanisms for expanding the range of issues that fall within the body of international law. Efforts to expand the scope of international law and strengthen the world's legal institutions have thus been initiated by a variety of international institutions and NGOs. The most active is the International Law Commission, which was established by the United Nations General Assembly in 1947 to promote the development and codification of international law. Although the founding members of the United Nations were overwhelmingly opposed to granting the organization legislative power to enact binding rules of international law, they strongly supported giving the General Assembly the more limited powers of study and recommendation. As a result, the commission has been the central player in conducting research and drafting recommendations on strengthening international law in select issue areas, such as state responsibility, unilateral acts of states, diplomatic protection, jurisdiction with regard to crimes committed outside national territory, and defining aggression.

The International Law Commission examines existing law to determine its adequacy in addressing specific issues in international relations and then submits detailed reports to the General Assembly. Sometimes the commission will propose a specific treaty or convention for consideration by the UN membership. These reports often lead to General Assembly resolutions, and sometimes they become the basis for organizing international conferences where proposed treaties are negotiated. For example, the commission was the driving force in developing such landmark treaties as the Vienna Convention on Diplomatic Relations (completed in 1961 and ratified by 174 countries). In doing so, the convention took a hodgepodge of customary law that had developed over hundreds of years and organized it into a coherent treaty defining the various types of diplomats, stipulating their rights and duties, providing for their immunities, and articulating a precise set of rules for the conduct of diplomatic relations.

Although the General Assembly lacks the legal authority to create new international law, it often acts as a vehicle for drafting legally binding treaties and conventions. Some of the most ambitious attempts to expand international law into the areas of the environment, intellectual property, organized crime, terrorism, arms control, and human rights have emanated from UN agencies. For example, the 1996 United Nations Diplomatic Conference on an International Total Ban on Anti-Personnel Land Mines produced a legally binding convention outlawing the use of land mines. Each signatory state must adhere to the convention after ratifying it (usually through some form of domestic legislation) and officially informs the UN secretary-general of its ratification. The convention is binding only on those states that have ratified it. Participating governments can be held accountable for complying with its provisions by their own national courts and (if they voluntarily agree) by the International Court of Justice. As of 2009, 156 nations had ratified (or otherwise approved of) the land mine convention; China, Russia, and the United States have refused to sign. Similarly, the 1992 United Nations Framework Convention on Climate Change led to the approval of the Kyoto Protocol, a legally binding agreement on reducing ozone depletion to which 179 countries have signed on as of 2009 (see CLIMATE CHANGE).

Not all General Assembly efforts have been successful. For example, the Conference on the Illicit Trade in Small Arms and Lights Weapons failed to produce an anticipated treaty banning international trade in small weapons. The limits of international law undoubtedly will be seriously tested by its effectiveness in helping states cope with international terrorism (see Table 3). In particular, states and international organizations will probably assess the effectiveness of existing international legal instruments relating to terrorism, such as the International Convention for the Suppression of Terrorist Bombings (see Case Study—Terrorism and International Law).

Perhaps the most ambitious attempt to expand the scope of international law is in the area of human rights (see HUMAN RIGHTS). Traditionally, international law has been restricted to regulating the relations *between* states, not *within* them, such as through the Vienna Convention on Diplomatic Relations and the Declaration on Rights and Duties of States, also known as the Montevideo Convention (see Document 2). With support from such NGOs as Amnesty International and Human Rights First (formerly the Lawyers Committee for Human Rights), regional and international organizations have begun to work toward making human rights treaties a key part of international law. Although this has been a slow and uneven process, the United Nations and regional organizations have developed several legally binding conventions, including the Covenant on Civil and Political Rights and the Covenant on Social and Economic Rights, which put into a legal framework many of the nonbinding principles enshrined in the Universal Declaration of Human Rights passed by the General Assembly in 1948. At the regional level, such organizations as the European Union, the Organization of American States, and the Organization of African Unity each have legally binding charters and conventions that provide for the protection of human rights. Although the mechanisms for implementing these guarantees vary widely, from simple standard setting to coercive enforcement, in all cases the signatories accept them as legal obligations.

Another expanding area of international law involves the environment. Although progress has been slow, states have approved the Basel Convention (which regulates the movement of hazardous waste from developed to developing states) and the Convention on Biological Diversity (which seeks to maintain maximum diversity of Earth's species and the equitable distribution of genetic resources). The most contentious, and certainly the most significant, work has been done on the issue of global warming. In 1985, the Vienna Convention for the Protection of the Ozone Layer was approved by more than one hundred states. This was soon updated by the 1987 Montreal Protocol. Following this, the U.N. Framework Convention on Climate Change was passed in 1992 and was then updated by the Kyoto Protocol in 1997. Currently, an intensive effort by states to move even further in this area is underway, although it has been hampered by the refusal of the United States to sign on to the Kyoto Protocol and its principles, especially its approach to reducing worldwide greenhouse emissions, which exempts developing countries from reductions.

In addition to expanding law into new areas, international and regional organizations have worked to strengthen transnational adjudication mechanisms through the creation of international courts and tribunals. The UN-sponsored International Court of Justice, created in 1945, has had a limited mandate and thus cannot act as a world court. During the 1990s, however, the United Nations created new mechanisms for holding individuals and political leaders responsible for violations of international law. Specifically, the UN Security Council established several ad hoc tribunals to try both civilian and military leaders who committed crimes against humanity and war crimes in the Balkans and Sierra Leone and committed genocide in Rwanda (see GENOCIDE, INTERNATIONAL CRIMINAL JUSTICE, and WAR CRIMES). In 1998, 120 countries approved the Rome Statute of the ICC, a multilateral treaty establishing for the first time in modern history an international tribunal with the authority to try individuals accused of committing genocide, crimes against humanity, and grave breaches of the laws of war. The treaty went into force in 2002, and as of 2008, 106 countries agreed to participate in the court system. Under the treaty, the ICC can exercise jurisdiction in any case where (1) the person accused of committing a crime is a national of a treaty signatory, (2) the alleged crime was committed on the territory of a signatory, or (3) it is referred to the ICC by the UN Security Council. The effectiveness of the court is hampered, however, by the refusal of the United States and China (among others) to participate.

In addition to the international courts and tribunals that have been established by the United Nations, a number of treaties provide for adjudication in specific areas of international law. For example, as part of the 1994 WTO agreement, all member states are required to submit to the authority of the organization's Dispute Settlement Body in all matters within the jurisdiction of the WTO. Similarly, under the various treaties of the European Union, all members are subject to decisions issued by the European Court of Justice and, under the European Convention for the Protection of Human Rights and Fundamental Freedoms, the European Court of Human Rights. Unlike the jurisdiction of most international courts, in EU courts individuals and private organizations have legal standing along with states. Signatories to the American Convention on Human Rights, drafted by the Organization of American States and signed by twenty-six of its member countries, are under the limited jurisdiction of the Inter-American Court of Human Rights. However, despite these advancements in international adjudication, most issues of international law are addressed not by transnational courts but by national ones.

Regional Summaries

The expansion of international law and the growth of international organizations have been uneven around the world. Although virtually all states are members of the United Nations and signatories to the most important diplomatic agreements, the level of legalization varies widely from region to region. International law tends to be strongest where regional arrangements as defined by the UN Charter are present. According to Chapter VIII, "regional arrangements or agencies" that address matters relating to the maintenance of international peace and security are permitted, but all regional organizations must gain approval from the Security Council before undertaking any enforcement action. These regional arrangements are strengthened by the fact that their charters tend to be legal documents imposing domestic obligations on its members (see map, p. 503).

The Americas

International law has long played a role in relations among states in the Americas, but it has also been hampered by the great disparity in power and wealth between North America and South America. In addition, the role of law was restrained by the rise of authoritarian governments in South America during the 1960s and 1970s. By the late 1980s, however, several factors increased the role of international law in the Americas. First, virtually all the authoritarian regimes in Latin America either resigned or were overthrown and were replaced by democratic governments. This turn of events, coupled with the end of the cold war, made states more likely to implement human rights agreements. Second, the conclusion of the North American Free Trade Agreement (NAFTA) in 1994 created a new transnational legal system in the areas of trade and investment. Although at present NAFTA is restricted to Canada, Mexico, and the United States, the Central America Free Trade Agreement (CAFTA)

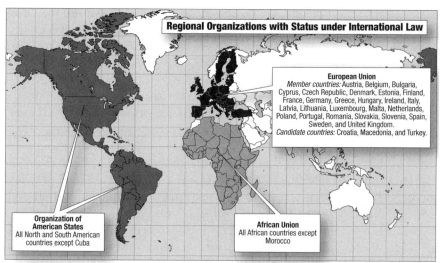

Source: Organization of American States, *OAS Member States*, 2009. Available online from http://www.oas.org. African Union, *Member States*, 2009. Available online from http://www.africa-union.org. European Union, "European Union: Delegation of the European Commission to the USA," 2009. Available online from http://www.eurunion.org.

has expanded the trade zone to include Costa Rica, El Salvador, Guatemala, Honduras, Nicaragua, and the Dominican Republic.

All states of the Americas except Cuba are members of the Organization of American States. Although dominated by the United States, the organization's charter nevertheless guarantees sovereign equality among its members and parallels many of the provisions of the UN Charter in addressing nearly all facets of economic and political life in the region. Although this has not led to the development of a regional legal system, it has facilitated the conclusion of the legally binding American Convention on Human Rights and the creation of the Inter-American Court of Human Rights. Both institutions impose a weak set of obligations on their members, although the treaty and the court have grown stronger in recent years. Two additional regional bodies are the Organization of Central American States, which resolves disputes between its member states, and the Andean Court of Justice, which was created by the 1969 Treaty of Bogotá (commonly known as the Andean Pact) and whose judgments are directly enforceable in the national courts of member states.

Europe

Europe has the most developed international legal system in the history of the nation-state system. The twenty-five-member European Union is the closest that the world has come to a transnational government. Although the union was originally formed as a common economic market, it gradually evolved into a complex organization with the authority to set policies and create laws binding on member states. European law is superior to state law in the areas of its jurisdiction, which have moved far beyond economic activity to include immigration, social policy, labor relations, human rights, and local governance. The laws and regulations passed by the various EU legal bodies have direct effect, meaning that they are binding not only on the member states but also on individuals and organizations within these states. The European Court of Justice and the European Court of Human Rights have compulsory jurisdiction over EU states and can order them to change their laws to conform to EU policy. Efforts to create a more comprehensive European constitution have been slowed by the refusal of several states—most recently Ireland in June 2008—to approve the text.

In addition to the EU network, several other structures impart quasi-legal obligations. The Council of Europe, established in 1949, is an intergovernmental organization comprising states committed to democratic governance, human rights, and the rule of law. Toward this end the council developed two human rights treaties, the European Convention for the Protection of Human Rights and Fundamental Freedoms and the European Social Charter, both of which are legally binding on their signatories. The former is enforced by the European Court of Human Rights. The North Atlantic Treaty Organization (NATO)—the world's largest military alliance, which includes members outside of Europe, including the United States—was formed through treaty, thereby imposing legal obligations on its members. By definition, however, military treaties are exclusive—that is, only certain countries can sign—and they are binding only in regard to military matters. Thus, military alliances are not considered in discussions of international law. Nevertheless, NATO has worked with the United Nations and the Organization for Security and Cooperation in Europe (OSCE) to undertake military enforcement missions, such as those conducted in Bosnia and Kosovo in the 1990s. The legality of the missions in the Balkans is questionable because, technically, NATO has no legal status in international law and only the United Nations or a regional arrangement is permitted to engage in military action (aside from immediate self-defense). The fifty-five-member OSCE includes, despite its name, all states "from Vancouver to Vladivostok," covering Canada, the United States, the states of Europe, and most of the former Soviet republics. The OSCE lacks international legal standing and in fact was not created through a treaty. It is, nonetheless, recognized by the United Nations as a Chapter VIII regional arrangement and thus has the authority to carry out various peacekeeping and peacemaking missions.

Middle East and North Africa

Efforts to create regional security and economic organizations in the Middle East have been stymied by inter-Arab rivalries, the Arab-Israeli conflict, and the cold war. The two most ambitious efforts—the United Arab Republic and the Arab Cooperation Council—were short-lived attempts at forging closer cooperation among states in North Africa and the Middle East. The Cooperation Council for the Arab States of the Gulf (also known as the Gulf Cooperation Council) has successfully forged closer cooperation among most of the Persian Gulf states (Iran and Iraq are excluded).

Africa

African states, many of which are politically, economically, and militarily weak, benefit from international law inasmuch as it places legal constraints on stronger powers from intervening in their internal affairs. Among the most basic principles in international law are the legal equality of states and the right of all states to territorial integrity and nonintervention. Thus, weak states benefit from international law because, in its absence, strong states have no legal limits. At the same time, the principles of sovereignty and nonintervention have also served to protect highly abusive governments from international scrutiny. Thus, the United Nations and its stronger member states, who failed to intervene and stop the genocide in Rwanda in 1994, have hesitated to become involved in ending the genocide in the Sudan from 2003 until the present. They have also wavered on what to do regarding the Robert Mugabe regime's illegal electoral abuses in Zimbabwe in 2008. Most recently, the African states have been badly divided over the degree to which they should become involved in the domestic conflict in Zimbabwe, particularly President Mugabe's campaigns of repression and intimidation.

At the same time, the African states have taken steps to provide regional solutions to problems on the continent. In 1963, the Organization of African Unity (OAU) was formed, and all independent states on the continent became members. Its primary purpose was to promote self-government and social progress throughout Africa. The OAU Charter committed members to pursue the "peaceful settlement of disputes" and the renunciation of all "subversive activities." To this end, the organization established a commission to mediate disputes among its members. As a legal organization, the OAU was weak and has imposed few legal obligations on its members. Moreover, it lacked the resources and cohesion to stabilize the continent during its turbulent periods of civil war.

Recognizing the need for at least some oversight, African governments concluded the 1986 Ganjul Charter on Human Rights, which offers minimal protection for individuals. Yet the charter tends to focus more on responsibilities of individual citizens to their governments than it does on their rights as we have come to understand them. The African Commission on Human Rights, which was created by the charter, has the power to investigate, report, and make recommendations, but it has no enforcement authority. At the same time, African states took another step toward creating stronger legal ties within the continent in 2002 when they formed the African Union (AU) as a successor to the African Economic Community (AEC) and the OAU. The main purpose of the AU is to accelerate the political and socioeconomic integration of the continent; to promote and defend African common positions on issues of interest to the continent and its peoples; to achieve peace and security in Africa; and to promote democratic institutions, good governance, and human rights. Most recently, the AU has become an important institution providing peacekeeping in such volatile areas as Sudan and Somalia.

Asia and the Pacific

As in Africa, regional international law in Asia is weak. The two regional organizations—the Association of Southeast Asian Nations (ASEAN) and the Asia-Pacific Economic Cooperation forum (APEC)—help to facilitate economic cooperation, but they impose few legal obligations on their members. Although most Asian states have signed various international human rights treaties, unlike Africa, the Americas, and Europe, they have no human rights charter of their own. Moreover, the states of the region lack a security organization other than memberships in the United Nations. Part of this is due to the heavy influence of the United States in the region. During the cold war, the United States signed a number of security agreements (allowing for the basing of American troops) with Japan, South Korea, and the Philippines. As a result, Asia remains divided into sectarian blocs, particularly now that China has emerged as both a global and regional power challenging American hegemony. Consensus on security and human rights issues is, therefore, difficult to achieve among states in the region. Moreover, because Asia encompasses more than half of the world's population and 30 percent of Earth's landmass, it is perhaps too diverse to be represented by any one particular organization.

Data

Table 1 Treaties and Conventions Promoting Human Rights

Treaty or convention	Year signed
Convention on the Prevention and Punishment of the Crime of Genocide	1948
International Convention on the Elimination of All Forms of Racial Discrimination	1965
International Covenant on Civil and Political Rights	1966
International Covenant on Economic, Social and Cultural Rights	1966
Optional Protocol to the International Covenant on Civil and Political Rights	1966
Convention on the Elimination of All Forms of Discrimination Against Women	1979
Convention Against Torture and Other Cruel, Inhuman or Degrading Treatment or Punishment	1985
Convention on the Rights of the Child	1989
Second Optional Protocol to the International Covenant on Civil and Political Rights	1989
International Convention on the Protection of the Rights of All Migrant Workers and Members of Their Families	1990
Optional Protocol to the Convention on the Elimination of Discrimination Against Women	1999
Optional protocol to the Convention on the Rights of the Child on the Involvement of Children in Armed Conflict	2000
Optional Protocol to the Convention on the Rights of the Child on the Sale of Children, Child Prostitution and Child Pornography	2000
Optional Protocol to the Convention against Torture and Other Cruel, Inhuman or Degrading Treatment or Punishment	2002
Convention on the Rights of Persons with Disabilities	2006
International Convention for the Protection of All Persons from Enforced Disappearance	2007
Optional Protocol to the Convention on the Rights of Persons with Disabilities	2008

Note to all tables: The execution of a treaty involves three processes. First, it is signed by the heads of state from the countries that negotiated the treaty. These are the original signers, or parties, to the agreement, but other countries can later join by "acceding." Second, the treaty needs to be ratified by each country. The ratification process differs significantly from country to country. (The United States requires a two-thirds vote of the Senate.) Third, once a specified number of countries has ratified the treaty—the number is contained within the treaty—it is considered "in force" and becomes legally binding on those countries that have ratified it. Since 1945, a fourth step has been in place—registering the treaty with the secretary-general of the United Nations. This last step is required by the UN Charter, which is itself a legally binding treaty.

Table 2 Multilateral Treaties and Conventions by Issue Area

Treaty or convention	Number
Maritime and coastal	52
Human rights	41
Environment[a]	36
Trade and commercial relations	32
Rules of warfare	22
Atmosphere and space	17
Cultural protection	12
Control on weapons	11
Diplomatic relations	4

Source: Database of the Multilaterals Project, Edwin Ginn Library, Fletcher School of Diplomacy, Tufts University, available at: http://fletcher.tufts.edu/multilaterals.

[a]Excluding those that specifically address the atmosphere and space.

Table 3 Multilateral Treaties and Conventions on Terrorism

Treaty or convention	Year signed
Tokyo Convention on Offenses and Certain Other Acts Committed on Board Aircraft	1963
Hague Convention on the Suppression of Unlawful Seizure of Aircraft	1970
Montreal Convention for the Suppression of Unlawful Acts Against the Safety of Civil Aviation	1971
Convention on the Prevention and Punishment of Crimes Against Internationally Protected Persons [diplomats]	1973
Convention Against the Taking of Hostages	1979
Convention for the Suppression of Unlawful Acts Against the Safety of Maritime Navigation Located on the Continental Shelf	1988
Convention for the Suppression of Unlawful Acts Against the Safety of Civil Aviation	1988
Convention on the Marking of Plastic Explosives for the Purposes of Detection	1991
International Convention for the Suppression of Terrorist Bombings	1998
Convention for the Suppression of the Financing of Terrorism	(not yet in force)
International Convention for the Suppression of Acts of Nuclear Terrorism	2005

Source: United Nations Treaty Series [database], available at: http://untreaty.un.org/English/treaty.asp (by subscription) or at United Nations depository libraries.

Case Study—Terrorism and International Law

The use of political violence by nonstate actors is not a new phenomenon. Since the beginning of the nation-state system, pirates, secessionists, insurgents, guerrilla armies, private militias, revolutionary organizations, and death squads have all waged campaigns of violence against established authorities and sovereign states. Such campaigns have included attacks on both military and civilian targets, and have been directed at both people and property. When such violence is politically motivated and designed to spread fear and intimidation in either a population or a political authority, most scholars and political leaders consider it to be terrorism.

Although most of the perpetrators of such acts have tended to be private (nongovernmental) organizations, states have long been complicit in terrorism. Throughout the cold war, for example, both the United States and Soviet Union provided financing, training, armaments, and political cover to rebels and militias committing terrorist campaigns against the other's allies. Currently, governments supporting opposing sides in civil conflicts in the Middle East and Africa continue to back organizations that use terrorism as a political tactic. Traditionally, a state's attitude toward the use of terrorism has not been based on principle but, rather, has depended on the identity of the perpetrator and target.

At the same time, a consensus among government leaders and diplomats is growing that the use of terrorism is an illegitimate practice, particularly when perpetrated by nonstate actors. Indeed, the widespread use of terrorism in Europe, Latin America, and the Middle East over the past quarter century has motivated many political leaders to pursue legal avenues to curtail this use of political violence. The attacks on the World Trade Center and Pentagon on September 11, 2001, spurred many of these efforts along, particularly among the great powers in the United Nations Security Council.

The use of political violence to spread terror, particularly when targeting civilians, has long been a violation of diplomatic protocol. Under customary international law, states are required to ensure that conditions in their territory do not "menace international peace" and are obliged to prevent activities in their territory that are calculated to produce civil strife in the territory of another state. Legal and political analysts interpret this to mean that governments cannot allow private organizations to use their territory to plan or launch terrorist attacks against other countries. In addition, currently almost a dozen multilateral treaties and conventions are aimed at stopping the spread of terrorist violence around the world (see Table 3). Most of the treaties address specific types of activities such as hijacking and hostage-taking; however, states have begun to develop a more comprehensive approach to preventing the spread of international terrorism.

Since 1996, the United Nations has attempted to develop a more wide-ranging treaty to address the issue. Currently, states are negotiating a Comprehensive Convention on International Terrorism, which would obligate all parties to cooperate in the prevention and punishment of all acts of terrorism. Progress on completing the draft convention has been hampered by disagreements surrounding the legal definition of *terrorism,* the effect of the convention on national liberation movements, and the activities of states' military forces in the exercise of their official duties.

At the same time, the United Nations Security Council has exercised its mandatory powers by passing Resolutions 1368 and 1373 in response to the terrorist attacks in the United States on September 11, 2001, both of which have been described by legal analysts as the equivalent of international legislation. Resolution 1368 labels all terrorist acts as "threats to international peace and security," thereby giving the Security Council virtually unlimited authority under the UN Charter to take any action it deems appropriate in combating terrorism, regardless of existing treaties. More significantly, Resolution 1373 directs all states to criminalize assistance for terrorist activities, deny financial support and safe haven to terrorists, and share information about groups planning terrorist attacks. Because this resolution has general applicability (rather than referring to a specific incident), it currently provides the most comprehensive legal obligation on terrorism to date.

Case Study—Human Rights and International Law

Traditionally the jurisdiction of international law had been limited to regulating relations between states, not within them. Although states have long been concerned about the political and social environment within their neighbors when such conditions could potentially threaten their own security, they have tended to view the relationship between governments and their populations as a strictly domestic concern. This began to change at the end of World War II as former resistance leaders, NGOs, and allied governments sought to provide a minimal level of legal protection for individuals living within the jurisdiction of sovereign governments. Over the past half century, the resulting human rights movement has had a significant impact on changing the nature of international law.

International human rights law has evolved slowly over the past few decades. The key principles for all human rights law can be found in the 1948 Universal Declaration of Human Rights. The declaration enumerates a comprehensive set of rights that are enjoyed by all individuals regardless of where they live. At the same time, as a United Nations General Assembly Resolution, it is not legally binding on governments, although it does have strong moral and political force. The two most important legally binding agreements are the Covenant on Civil and Political Rights and the Covenant on Social and Economic Rights; 160 states are parties to the former and 158 to the latter. In addition to these broad-based documents, dozens of other treaties address more specific issues, such as the rights of women, the rights of children, the protection of refugees, and the illegality of racial discrimination. Moreover, several comprehensive regional human rights agreements, such as the European Convention on Human Rights and Fundamental Freedoms, have been made.

The main problem with international human rights law is the lack of adequate enforcement mechanisms. In most cases, the treaties are self-enforcing, meaning that individual states must determine for themselves when violations have occurred and decide what remedies should be applied. The two main human rights bodies—the Human Rights Committee (which monitors compliance with the Covenant on Civil and Political Rights) and the Human Rights Council (the primary UN body responsible for the protection and promotion of Human Rights)—have very limited authority and have done little to stop flagrant human rights abuses. Still, at least twelve different official human rights bodies, most affiliated with the United Nations, have been charged with monitoring and implementing the various agreements. The most influential of these is the office of the UN High Commissioner on Human

Rights, a position that carries with it a fair amount of independence and political clout. Probably the most important body for enforcing human rights law is the ICC, which is empowered to prosecute and try individuals—public officials, military officers, or other authorities—for genocide, crimes against humanity, and war crimes.

Perhaps the most significant international law in the area of human rights involves the most egregious practices: genocide, torture, and crimes against humanity. The 1948 Convention on the Prevention and Punishment of the Crime of Genocide defines *genocide* as any attempt to destroy in whole or in part a national, ethnic, religious, or racial group. It not only designates genocide as illegal under international law, but it also requires the 137 signatory states to intervene actively to stop its practice in all cases where genocide occurs. The Convention Against Torture and Other Cruel, Inhuman or Degrading Treatment or Punishment (which has 145 signatory states as of 2008) requires states to take effective measures to prevent torture within their borders and forbids governments from sending people back to their home country if they might be tortured. The Committee Against Torture, a UN-affiliated body, is charged with implementing the convention. *Crimes against humanity* is defined as inhuman acts that are committed as part of a widespread or systematic attack directed against a civilian population in pursuit of a state goal. Although no specific treaty outlaws this practice, the Nuremberg Principles (adopted by the United Nations after the post–World War II Nuremberg trials) and the charter of the ICC designate these as criminal acts under international law.

Biographical Sketches

José Alvarez is a professor of international law and diplomacy at Columbia University Law School, the executive director of the Center on Global Legal Problems, and president of the American Society of International Law. He was previously an adviser with the Office of the Legal Adviser of the U.S. Department of State, where he worked on cases before the Iran-U.S. Claims Tribunal, served on the negotiation teams for bilateral investment treaties and the Canada-U.S. Free Trade Agreement, and was legal adviser to the administration of justice program in Latin America coordinated by the Agency of International Development. His book *International Organizations as Law-Makers* is considered by many scholars to be among the best in the field.

Abram and **Antonia Chayes** have produced a vast body of scholarship on the architecture of international organizations and patterns of treaty compliance in the areas of arms control and the environment. Abram was a legal adviser to the U.S. State Department, and Antonia was an undersecretary of the U.S. Air Force. The Chayes, paving the way for development of the international process school of international law, argue that states comply with international law as part of a general diplomatic process through which they conduct their international relations. To understand compliance, then, is to understand how and why states interact with one another.

Thomas Franck is a professor of international law at New York University. He is one of the foremost proponents of new thinking in international law. Franck's theories focus on how international law has been transformed since World War II and, more recently, since the end of the cold war. His influential *Power of Legitimacy among Nations* established a new school of thought in international law, arguing that compliance is not based on state self-interest but on a widespread acceptance of the law's legitimacy in international affairs.

Louis Henkin is professor emeritus at the Columbia University School of Law, former president of the American Society of International Law, and one of the foremost scholars on international law. His co-authored *International Law: Cases and Materials* is a standard in most law schools. A passionate advocate for the rule of law in international relations, he helped to keep the field alive when many had abandoned it during the cold war. His most influential work, *How Nations Behave,* was the first authoritative book to argue that "almost all nations observe almost all principles of international law and almost all of their obligations almost all of the time."

Ian Johnstone is associate professor of international law at the Fletcher School of Law and Diplomacy, Tufts University. He has served in the Office of the United Nations Secretary-General as well as that organization's Department of Peace-keeping Operations and Office of Legal Affairs. Johnstone's work on the legal aspects of the United Nations Security Council and on the role of interpretive communities (organizations of recognized political leaders that other states believe have the authority and competence to make judgments concerning legal obligation) make him one of America's most prominent contemporary international law scholars.

Anne-Marie Slaughter is a professor at Harvard University and one of the few international law scholars bridging the disciplinary divide between political science and international law. Slaughter combines Kantian philosophy, which bases legal principles on moral imperative, with practical politics. Her chief contribution to the development of international law theory is the provocative thesis that liberal states act according to the rule of law in their relations with one another but operate according to the rule of power politics when dealing with nonliberal states. Such behavior has obvious implications for the future of international law in a rapidly democratizing world.

Directory

American Society of International Law, 2223 Massachusetts Avenue NW, Washington, D.C. 20008. Telephone: (202) 939-6000; email: mclincy@asil.org; Web: http://www.asil.org.
Private organization that educates and engages the public in international law.

Amnesty International, 322 8th Avenue, New York, N.Y. 10001. Telephone: (212) 807-8400; email: admin-us@aiusa.org; Web: http://www.amnestyusa.org.
Advocacy and research nongovernmental organization that deals with human rights and the application of international standards of behavior regarding nations' relationship with their citizens.

Center for Human Rights and Humanitarian Law, American University, Washington College of Law, 4801 Massachusetts Avenue NW, Washington, D.C. 20016. Telephone: (202) 274-4000; email: humlaw@wcl.american.edu; Web: http://www.wcl.american.edu/humright/center.
Research organization dealing with human rights and humanitarian law.

Center for International Environmental Law, 1367 Connecticut Avenue NW, Suite 300, Washington, D.C. 20036. Telephone: (202) 785-8700; email: info@ciel.org; Web: http://www.ciel.org.
Nongovernmental organization that works to increase compliance with international environmental law.

Court of Justice of the European Communities, Palais de la Cour de Justice, Boulevard Konrad Adenauer, 2925 Kirchberg, Luxembourg. Telephone: (352) 4303 3367; email: info@curia.eu.int; Web: http://curia.europa.eu/en/transitpage.htm.
Court for members of the European Union.

European Court of Human Rights, Council of Europe, 67075 Strasbourg, France. Telephone: (33) 03 88 41 20 18; email: Webmaster@echr.coe.int; Web: http://www.echr.coe.int.
Court adjudicating issues related to the European Convention on Human Rights.

Inter-American Court of Human Rights, P.O. Box 6906-1000, San José, Costa Rica. Telephone: (506) 234 0581; email: corteidh@sol.racsa.co.cr; Web: http://www.corteidh.or.cr.
Agency of the Organization of American States that deals with human rights issues and cases of its member states.

International Court of Justice, Peace Palace, 2517 KJ The Hague, Netherlands. Telephone: (31) 0 70 302 2323; email: information@icj-cij.org; Web: http://www.icj-cij.org.
UN agency that settles legal disputes between states according to international law and advises recognized international agencies on legal questions.

International Criminal Court (ICC), P.O. Box 19519, 2500 CM, The Hague, Netherlands. Email: otp.informationdesk@icc-cpi.int; Web: http://www.icc-cpi.int/home.html&1=en.
A treaty-based permanent court that tries individuals accused of committing genocide, crimes against humanity, or grave breaches of the laws of war.

International Law Association, Charles Clore House, 17 Russell Square, London WC1B 5DR, United Kingdom. Telephone: (44) 20 7323 2978; email: info@ila-hq.org; Web: http://www.ila-hq.org.
Private organization promoting the study of international law.

International Law Commission, Secretary of the International Law Commission, Room S3460A, United Nations Plaza, New York, N.Y. 10017. Email: ilcweb@un.org; Web: http://www.un.org/law/ilc.
United Nations agency that promotes the development and codification of international law.

International Law Institute, 1615 New Hampshire Avenue NW, Washington, D.C. 20009. Telephone: (202) 483-3036; email: training@ili.org; Web: http://www.ili.org.
Educational organization that sponsors training sessions and conferences on international law.

International Law Students Association, 1615 New Hampshire Avenue NW, Washington, D.C. 20009. Telephone: (202) 299-9101; email: ilsa@iamdigex.net; Web: http://www.ilsa.org.
Private organization for students studying international law.

Permanent Court of Arbitration, International Bureau, Peace Palace, 2 Carne-gieplein, 2517 KJ The Hague, Netherlands. Telephone: (31) 0 70 302 4165; email: bureau@pca-cpa.org; Web: http://www.pca-cpa.org.
International organization that settles disputes between states on a voluntary basis.

Project on International Courts and Tribunals, Center on International Cooperation, New York University, 418 Lafayette Street, Suite 543, New York, N.Y. 10003. Telephone: (212) 998-3680; email: cr28@acf2.nyu.edu; Web: http://www.pict-pcti.org. *Private advocacy organization that addresses legal, institutional, and financial issues arising from the proliferation of international courts and tribunals.*

United Nations Commission on International Trade Law, Vienna International Centre, P.O. Box 500, 1400 Vienna, Austria. Telephone: (43) 1 26060 4061; email: uncitral@uncitral.org; Web: http://www.uncitral.org.
Agency dealing with international law relating to trade.

World Trade Organization (WTO), Centre William Rappard, 154 Rue de Lausanne, 1211 Geneva 21, Switzerland. Telephone: (41) 22 739 51 11; email: enquiries@wto.org; Web: http://www.wto.org/.
Organization that imposes binding obligations on members in all areas of international trade.

Further Research

Books

Alvarez, José. *International Organizations as Law-Makers.* Oxford: Oxford University Press, 2006.

Cassese, Antonio. *International Law.* Oxford: Clarendon Press, 2005.

———. *Self-Determination of Peoples: A Legal Reprisal.* Cambridge, UK: Cambridge University Press, 1995.

Charlesworth, Hilary, Richard Falk, and Burns Weston. *International Law and World Order.* St. Paul, Minn.: West Group, 1997.

Chayes, Abram, and Antonia Handler Chayes. *The New Sovereignty: Compliance with International Regulatory Agreements.* Cambridge, Mass.: Harvard University Press, 1995.

Franck, Thomas. *Fairness in International Law and Institutions.* Oxford: Clarendon Press, 1995.

———. *The Power of Legitimacy among Nations.* New York: Oxford University Press, 1990.

Ginsburgs, George. *From Soviet to Russian International Law: Studies in Continuity and Change.* The Hague: Martinus Nijhoff, 1998.

Goldsmith, Jack, and Eric Posner. *The Limits of International Law.* Oxford: Oxford University Press, 2006.

Gray, Christine. *International Law and the Use of Force.* Oxford: Oxford University Press, 2004.

Henkin, Louis. *International Law: Politics and Values.* The Hague: Martinus Nijhoff, 1995.

Janis, Mark, and John Noyes. *Cases and Commentary on International Law.* St. Paul, Minn.: West Group, 1997.

Joyner, Christopher, ed. *The United Nations and International Law.* Cambridge, UK: Cambridge University Press, 1997.

Kennan, George. *American Diplomacy.* Chicago: University of Chicago Press, 1984.

Ku, Charlotte, and Paul Diehl, eds. *International Law: Classic and Contemporary Readings.* Boulder, Colo.: Lynne Rienner, 2003.

Malanczuk, Peter. *Akehurst's Modern Introduction to International Law.* New York: Routledge, 1997.

Martin, Francisco Forrest, et al. *International Human Rights and Humanitarian Law: Treaties, Cases, and Analysis.* Cambridge, UK: Cambridge University Press, 2006.

Schachter, Oscar. *International Law in Theory and Practice.* The Hague: Kluwer Academic, 1999.

Scott, Shirley. *International Law in World Politics.* Boulder, Colo.: Lynne Rienner, 2004.

White, N. D. *Keeping the Peace: The United Nations and the Maintenance of International Peace and Security.* Manchester, UK: Manchester University Press, 1997.

Articles and Reports

Arend, Anthony Clark. "Do Legal Rules Matter?: International Law and International Politics." *Virginia Journal of International Law* 38 (1998): 125–140.

Guzman, Andrew T. "A Compliance-Based Theory of International Law." *California Law Review* 90, no. 6 (2002): 1823–1888.

International Law Commission. *Report on the Work of the Fifty-fifth Session.* United Nations General Assembly, Official Records, Fifty-Fifth Session, Suppl. 10 (A/55/10).

Johnstone, Ian. "Security Council Deliberations: The Power of the Better Argument." *European Journal of International Law* 14, no. 3 (2003): 437–480.

———. "Treaty Interpretation: The Authority of Interpretive Communities." *Michigan Journal of International Law* 12 (1991): 391–419.

Keohane, Robert. "International Relations and International Law: Two Optics." *Harvard International Law Journal* 38 (1997): 487–502.

Koh, Harold Hongju. "Why Do Nations Obey International Law?" *Yale Law Journal* 106, no. 8 (1997): 2599–2659.

Lobel, Jules, and Michael Ratner. "Bypassing the Security Council: Ambiguous Authorizations to Use Force, Ceasefires, and the Iraqi Inspection Regime." *American Journal of International Law* 93 (1999): 124–154.

Nowak, Manfred. "What Practices Constitute Torture?: US and UN Standards." *Human Rights Quarterly* 28, no. 4 (2006): 809–841.

Robinson, Darryl. "Defining Crimes against Humanity at the Rome Conference." *American Journal of International Law* 93, no. 1 (1999): 43–58.

van Schaack, Beth, "The Crime of Political Genocide: Repairing the Genocide Convention's Blind Spot." *Yale Law Journal* 106, no. 7 (1997): 2259–2291.

Web Sites

Draft Comprehensive Convention Against International Terrorism
http://www.ilsa.org/jessup/jessup08/basicmats/unterrorism.pdf

International Law Commission
http://www.un.org/law/ilc

International Law Links, E. B. Williams Law Library, Georgetown University
http://www.11.georgetown.edu/intl/intl.html

International Law Research on the Web
http://lic.law.ufl.edu/~willipam/intlweb.htm

International Law Resources, Westminster Law Library, University of Denver
http://law.du.edu/index.php/library/research/web-research-links/international-and-foreign-resources

Legal Research on International Law Issues Using the Internet
http://www.lib.uchicago.edu/~llou/forintlaw.html

Multilaterals Project, The Fletcher School, Tufts University
http://fletcher.tufts.edu/multi/multilaterals.html

Statute of the International Court of Justice
http://www.icj-cij.org/documents/index.php?p1=4&p2=2&p3=0

Treaties, U.S. State Department
http://www.state.gov/www/global/legal_affairs/tifindex.html

United Nations Charter
http://www.un.org/aboutun/charter

United Nations International Law
http://www.un.org/law

Documents

1. Geneva Convention Relative to the Treatment of Prisoners of War

Conference for the Establishment of International Conventions for the Protection of Victims of War, Geneva, August 12, 1949

The full text is available at http://fletcher.tufts.edu/multi/texts/BH240.txt.

Extracts

Article 3

In the case of armed conflict not of an international character occurring in the territory of one of the High Contracting Parties, each Party to the conflict shall be bound to apply, as a minimum, the following provisions:

(1) Persons taking no active part in the hostilities, including members of armed forces who have laid down their arms and those placed hors de combat by sickness, wounds, detention, or any other cause, shall in all circumstances be treated humanely, without any adverse distinction founded on race, colour, religion or faith, sex, birth or wealth, or any other similar criteria.

To this end the following acts are and shall remain prohibited at any time and in any place whatsoever with respect to the above-mentioned persons:

(a) violence to life and person, in particular murder of all kinds, mutilation, cruel treatment and torture;

(b) taking of hostages;

(c) outrages upon personal dignity, in particular, humiliating and degrading treatment;

(d) the passing of sentences and the carrying out of executions without previous judgment pronounced by a regularly constituted court affording all the judicial guarantees which are recognized as indispensable by civilized peoples.

(2) The wounded and sick shall be collected and cared for. . . .

Article 13

Prisoners of war must at all times be humanely treated. Any unlawful act or omission by the Detaining Power causing death or seriously endangering the health of a prisoner of war in its custody is prohibited, and will be regarded as a serious breach of the present Convention. In particular, no prisoner of war may be subjected to physical mutilation or to medical or scientific experiments of any kind which are not justified by the medical, dental or hospital treatment of the prisoner concerned and carried out in his interest.

Likewise, prisoners of war must at all times be protected, particularly against acts of violence or intimidation and against insults and public curiosity.

Measures of reprisal against prisoners of war are prohibited.

2. Convention on Rights and Duties of States (Montevideo Convention)

Montevideo, December 26, 1933

The full text is available at http://avalon.law.yale.edu/20th_century/intam03.asp.

Extracts

Article 3

The political existence of the state is independent of recognition by the other states. Even before recognition the state has the right to defend its integrity and independence, to provide for its conservation and prosperity, and consequently to organize itself as it sees fit, to legislate upon its interests, administer its services, and to define the jurisdiction and competence of its courts.

The exercise of these rights has no other limitation than the exercise of the rights of other states according to international law.

Article 4

States are juridically equal, enjoy the same rights, and have equal capacity in their exercise. The rights of each one do not depend upon the power which it possesses to assure its exercise, but upon the simple fact of its existence as a person under international law. . . .

Article 8

No state has the right to intervene in the internal or external affairs of another.

Article 9

The jurisdiction of states within the limits of national territory applies to all the inhabitants.

Nationals and foreigners are under the same protection of the law and the national authorities and the foreigners may not claim rights other or more extensive than those of the nationals. . . .

Article 11

The contracting states definitely establish as the rule of their conduct the precise obligation not to recognize territorial acquisitions or special advantages which have been obtained by force whether this consists in the employment of arms, in threatening diplomatic representations, or in any other effective coercive measure. The territory of a state is inviolable and may not be the object of military occupation nor of other measures of force imposed by another state directly or indirectly or for any motive whatever even temporarily.

INTERNATIONAL CRIMINAL JUSTICE

Eric Stover

Behind much of the savagery of modern history lies impunity. Tyrants commit atrocities, including genocide and crimes against humanity, when they calculate that they can get away with them. But, as we move into the new millennium, the international community has demonstrated a renewed commitment to the pursuit of international criminal justice. More than 145 countries have signed the Rome Statute of the International Criminal Court (ICC), and as of July 18, 2008, 108 countries had ratified it (see map, p. 527; Document 1). At the end of 2007, two ad hoc international criminal tribunals sat in judgment for war crimes and genocides committed in Rwanda and the former Yugoslavia (see GENOCIDE and WAR CRIMES). Meanwhile, hybrid tribunals, courts comprising international and national judges and staff, have pursued justice for international crimes in Cambodia, Sierra Leone, East Timor (Timor-Leste), Kosovo, Bosnia-Herzegovina, and Lebanon. Domestic courts have also applied the concept of universal jurisdiction to try suspected war criminals whose alleged crimes were committed outside the boundaries of the prosecuting state. In June 2001, a Belgian court convicted and sentenced two Rwandan women, both Roman Catholic nuns, to up to fifteen years in prison for their complicity in the 1994 Rwandan genocide. In 1998, a Spanish court tried unsuccessfully to extradite General Augusto Pinochet from Great Britain to stand trial for human rights violations allegedly committed in Chile in the 1970s while he was head of state. A Senegalese court in 2006 agreed to prosecute Hisséne Habré, the former Chadian dictator, for thousands of political killings, systematic torture, and ethnic cleansing during his rule. At issue concerning the growing emphasis on international justice is whether such attempts at universal legal accountability will help make the twenty-first century less bloody than the twentieth.

Historical Background and Development

The first international trial for war crimes took place in Breisach, Germany, in 1474, when twenty-seven judges of the Holy Roman Empire ruled that Peter von Hagenbach had violated the "laws of God and man" by allowing his troops to rape, murder, and pillage. The court sentenced him to death. Von Hagenbach's conviction underscored one of the defining ideas of civilized society since antiquity—even in war, unnecessary suffering inflicted on civilians is strictly forbidden. Not until the nineteenth century, however, were formal international agreements embodying this principle accepted and ratified by governments.

The codification of the laws of war date back to the mid-1800s, when several countries established internal codes of conduct. U.S. President Abraham Lincoln, for example, authorized the War Department to promulgate guidelines—the Lieber Code—consisting of 159 articles, to govern the conduct of the army during the Civil War. The first international agreement on the laws of war, the Convention for the Amelioration of the Condition of the Wounded in Armies in the Field, was signed by twelve European governments in Geneva in 1864. Thirty-five years later, in 1899, the Convention with Respect to the Laws and the Customs of War on Land was adopted at The Hague, codifying generally accepted principles of customary international law that promulgated, among other things, the protection of civilians and civilian institutions, such as hospitals and churches.

The world's second attempt at prosecuting war crimes followed World War I, but the effort was abandoned because the Allies feared that the search for justice would look like the victors' revenge and shatter Germany's chances of making an orderly postwar transition to democracy. On November 20, 1945, a little more than six months after the end of World War II, the trial of the Major War Criminals of the European Axis before the International Military Tribunal, now known as the Nuremberg trials, took place (see Document 2 and WAR CRIMES). Among the twenty-two high-ranking Nazis who stood trial were Hitler's successor, Hermann Goering; deputy Rudolf Hess; and foreign policy adviser Joachim von Ribbentrop. Allied armies were instrumental in capturing suspects and retrieving evidence from buildings previously under the control of the Nazi regime. Three defendants were acquitted, seven were sentenced to ten years to life, and twelve were sentenced to hang.

In Tokyo between May and November 1946, the International Military Tribunal for the Far East prosecuted twenty-eight Japanese military and civilian leaders for war crimes. The tribunal's charter was influenced by the Nuremberg trials, but significant differences affected the outcomes in Tokyo. For instance, while the judges of the Nuremberg tribunal were from the four major Allied powers, judges from thirteen nations sat on the Far East tribunal, resulting in less than unanimous decisions concerning sentencing and other matters.

In the wake of World War II, one might think that nations would have had an interest in suppressing massive violations of human rights because of their possible threat to world peace. In a world largely divided into communist and noncommunist camps, however, the Chinese, Soviet, and U.S. governments, claiming national and regional security interests, promoted and maintained authoritarian governments no matter how abusive they were of their citizens. Only in 1991 did the idea of punishing war criminals resurface.

After Iraq's invasion of Kuwait, U.S. President George Bush and British Prime Minister Margaret Thatcher called for a UN tribunal to try Iraqi leader

Saddam Hussein and Iraqi military officers for crimes committed during the invasion, but the political will of the European and U.S. leaders soon faded. During the 1980s, the West had provided massive aid to Hussein, whose government had served as a counterweight to the anti-Western Islamic republic of Iran. While supplying Iraq with financial assistance and weaponry, the West had turned a blind eye to the generally repressive nature of Hussein's government, in addition to such extraordinary acts as the use of chemical weapons against Kurdish citizens. For some Western leaders, the idea that this hypocrisy would surface in an international trial was reason enough to dampen their pursuit of the Iraqi leader. Close to thirty years later, in 2003, Hussein's regime was eliminated in the U.S.-led Iraq War, and Hussein himself was tried and executed in 2006 for genocide, crimes against humanity, and war crimes in a process that, in its best assessment, can be characterized as seriously flawed.

A half century after the Nuremberg and Tokyo trials, the United Nations breathed new life into the pursuit of international criminal justice when it created the International Criminal Tribunal for the Former Yugoslavia at The Hague in May 1993 to investigate alleged war crimes committed during the wars there following the disintegration of the Yugoslav state. After a Hutu-led slaughter in Rwanda claimed the lives of hundreds of thousands of people between April and July 1994, the UN Security Council established the International Criminal Tribunal for Rwanda in Arusha, Tanzania, in November 1994 to prosecute war crimes and acts of genocide.

These ad hoc UN tribunals emerged in far less propitious circumstances than their predecessors following World War II. The Yugoslav and Rwandan tribunals, in contrast to those following World War II, do not have political or military authority over the territory in which the alleged war crimes were committed, and they do not have police powers to arrest suspects. Instead, they have had to rely on the goodwill of national governments, UN member states, and regional organizations, such as the North Atlantic Treaty Organization (NATO), to locate and arrest suspected war criminals. Governments, with a few exceptions, initially hindered the tribunal's investigative work by failing to provide adequate funding and intelligence information. They were also unwilling to risk the safety of their troops by removing land mines and guarding suspected mass gravesites, let alone arrest indicted war criminals. Some of these problems—inherent in the ad hoc status of these tribunals—were addressed on November 25, 1992, when the UN General Assembly adopted a resolution calling on the International Law Commission to draft a statute for a permanent international criminal court.

Current Status

International criminal tribunals derive their authority from the notion that certain crimes—genocide, crimes against humanity, and war crimes—concern the entire international community and consequently should be subject to universal jurisdiction. Inherent in the notion of relinquishing sovereignty to an international criminal court is the conviction that certain crimes are so abominable that they violate not only the individual victims but also all of humanity. These crimes are defined under international law as deportation, extermination, enslavement, mass murder, and other inhumane acts committed against any civilian population, before or during a war, or persecutions on political, racial, or religious grounds. Those who commit such crimes are to be considered *hostis humani generis* (enemies of all humankind) over which all governments shall have jurisdiction.

International criminal justice has at least three distinct levels or applications. On the international level, the ICC (which came into being on July 1, 2002) and ad hoc tribunals convened under the authority of the UN Security Council will pursue war criminals across borders. In bilateral situations, extradition procedures can be invoked when alleged perpetrators travel or live abroad; extradition provisions in international criminal law treaties and the growing authority of the principle of universal jurisdiction allow states to apprehend and try individuals suspected of serious international crimes. Finally, foreign courts may also obtain civil jurisdiction over defendants charged with international crimes when lawyers for the victims file for damages. In the United States, for instance, the Alien Tort Claims Act and Torture Victim Protection Act allow civil damage suits against foreign defendants for torture, summary execution, and other "torts in violation of the law of nations."

Research

The ICC and the Yugoslav and Rwanda tribunals have spawned a growing body of research and debate among legal scholars, political theorists, and social scientists about the efficacy of international criminal tribunals and their objectives. So-called realists, such as Henry Kissinger, former U.S. secretary of state, oppose such courts because they believe that governments, and by extension diplomats, might be shackled by the overextension of international law. They have long regarded the pursuit of international justice as a potentially dangerous extravagance that could threaten peace and international stability and jeopardize U.S. national security interests. Realists fear that, as the international community turns increasingly to international criminal courts to solve what are inherently issues of state politics and diplomacy, as Kissinger states in "The Pitfalls of Universal Jurisdiction: Risking Judicial Tyranny," it runs the "risk of substituting the tyranny of judges for that of governments." From the realist perspective, war crimes tribunals are nothing more than the crude application of state power, something the victors who decisively win a war inflict on the defeated.

Proponents of international criminal courts argue that without justice no enduring peace can be achieved following conflict. They consider the tribunals for Rwanda and the former Yugoslavia, in the words of human rights activist Aryeh Neier in *War Crimes: Brutality, Genocide, Terror, and the Struggle for Justice,* "the most dramatic innovations in international law to protect human rights in half a century." Justice and international order, Neier argues in the same work, are best served through "the disclosure and acknowledgment of abuses, the purging of those responsible from public office, and the prosecution and punishment of those who commit crimes against humanity." The Yugoslav tribunal, in its 1994 annual report, stated that its work is essential to peace and security in the former Yugoslavia: "[I]t would be wrong to assume that the Tribunal is based on the old maxim *fiat justitia et pereat mundus* (let justice be done, even if the world were to perish). The Tribunal is, rather, based on the maxim propounded by German philosopher Georg Hegel in 1821: *fiat justitia ne pereat mundus* 'let justice be done lest the world should perish.'"

Liberal law theorists and human rights activists argue that justice, like the pursuit of rights, is a universal historic practice that exists above politics (see HUMAN RIGHTS). Thus, justice can moderate desires for revenge and foster respect for democratic institutions by demonstrating that no individual—from foot soldier to high government official—is above the law. Insofar as legal proceedings confer legitimacy on otherwise contestable facts, trials make it more difficult for individuals and societies to take refuge in denial and avoid the truth. Criminal trials, even of a few arch-criminals, followed by convictions and appropriate punishment, constitute an acknowledgment of the suffering inflicted on the victims. Some liberal legal theorists, including Mark Osiel, view trials as a moral pedagogy. They contend that international tribunals, through their ability to distinguish between proper and improper conduct, can help postwar societies foster tolerance and reconciliation, forge a shared truth of past events, and reshape national identities.

The Nuremberg trials introduced the concept that individuals—and not society as a whole—should be held accountable for crimes committed in war. Thus, one function of an international postwar trial of government leaders is to differentiate between the criminal leaders of a nation and their deceived populations. "Crimes against international law," the Nuremberg tribunal stated in its judgment, "are committed by men, not by abstract entities, and only by punishing individuals who commit such crimes can the provision of international law be enforced." For public attitudes to shift in postwar societies, writes political scientist Gary Jonathan Bass in *Stay the Hand of Vengeance: The Politics of War Crimes Tribunals,* "criminal leaders must be tried—their aura of mystery shattered by showing their weaknesses and stupidities, and their prestige deflated by the humiliation of standing in the dock." Bass warns, however, that tribunal justice "is inevitably symbolic: a few war criminals stand for a much larger group of guilty individuals. Thus, what is billed as individual justice actually becomes a de facto way of exonerating many of the guilty."

Some social scientists take issue with the sweeping claims—or what historian Michael Ignatief calls articles of faith—made by international lawyers and human rights activists about the virtues of international criminal justice. They contend that such high-flown rhetoric fails to recognize that courts, like all institutions, exist because of, and not in spite of, politics. People and entire communities can interpret a tribunal's decisions, procedures (modes and manner of investigation, selection of cases, timing of trials, and types and severity of punishments), and even its very existence in a variety of ways. Even the idea that war crimes tribunals will individualize guilt is fraught with ambiguity, especially in the wake of a genocide such as in Rwanda, where so many people planned and carried out the killing and where so much of the violence was localized, pitting community against community, neighbor against neighbor.

The reality is that ad hoc international tribunals have limited mandates and resources, restricted powers of subpoena, and no authority to make arrests. With such limitations, they can never come close to meting out justice to all war criminals. The logic of law, as the social critic Hannah Arendt warns, can never make sense of the logic of atrocity or how it is interpreted by survivors and perpetrators. The picture that emerges from strictly legal interpretations of wartime atrocities, especially when they are committed by all sides to a conflict, often can be skewed. While victims and their communities may feel some measure of vindication from international trials, the communities from which the perpetrators came may feel as if they have been made the scapegoats.

"[A]lthough most people have a sense that prosecuting war criminals is a morally good thing to do," writes Bass in *Stay the Hand of Vengeance,* "there is no reliable proof that so doing will always have good results." In fact, very little research exists on the role, good or bad, that international justice plays in communities torn asunder by genocide and ethnic violence. Without systematic empirical studies of the effects that international criminal courts have had on postwar communities, says Bass, "we are left with only our scruples and our hunches."

In 2004, researchers from the University of California, Berkeley, in collaboration with universities and research institutes in Rwanda and the former Yugoslavia, published in two books—*My Neighbor, My Enemy: Justice and Community in the Aftermath of Mass Atrocity* and *The Witnesses: War Crimes and the Promise of Justice in The Hague*—the findings of a four-year study examining how communities in these countries perceived and interpreted the work of the international war crimes tribunals. What they learned was threefold. First, no direct link existed between the criminal trials and reconciliation, although this possibly could change over time. In fact, criminal trials—especially those of local perpetrators—often appeared to divide small multienthic communities by causing further suspicion and fear.

Second, the relationship of trauma to a desire for trials of suspected war criminals was not clear-cut. It was colored by previous relationships with members of the opposing group, the types of trials that were contemplated, and other social factors. This finding calls into question claims that trials have some therapeutic value and can provide a sense of closure for those most traumatized by war and mass atrocity. Indeed, many traumatized people simply found following the progress of trials too painful.

Third, for the survivors of ethnic war and genocide, the idea of justice emcompassed more than criminal trials and the *ex cathedra* pronouncement of foreign judges in The Hague and Arusha. It meant returning stolen property; locating and identifying the bodies of the missing; capturing and trying all the war criminals, from the commonplace killers in their communities all the way up to the nationalistic idealogues who had poisoned their neighbors with ethnic hatred; securing reparations and apologies; and helping those traumatized by atrocities to recover. It also meant creating the circumstances for individuals to lead lives devoid of fear, secure meaningful jobs, and provide their children with good schools and teachers. In other words, international criminal justice alone cannot suture the lesions of individual and collective trauma. "It requires," as Kristen Campbell suggests in "The Trauma of Justice," "a fundamental change to the social order which made possible the original trauma of crimes against humanity. In this sense, justice remains the event yet to happen."

Policies and Programs

The establishment of the ICC was, in the words delivered by UN Secretary-General Kofi Annan at the ceremony celebrating the adoption of the court, "a giant step forward in the march towards universal human rights and the rule of law." The treaty establishing the court was agreed to in Rome on July 17, 1998, with 120 nations voting in favor, 7 voting against, and 21 abstaining (see Document 1). The court came into being on July 1, 2002 (the date its founding treaty, the Rome Statute of the International Criminal Court, entered into force), and it can prosecute only crimes committed on or after that date.

The ICC—headquartered at The Hague—will prosecute individuals for war crimes, crimes against humanity, and genocide, including crimes committed in international and local armed conflicts. The court can exercise jurisdiction only in cases where the accused is a national of a state party, the alleged crime took place on the territory of a state party, or a situation is referred to the court by the United Nations Security Council. The court is designed to complement existing national judicial systems; it can exercise its jurisdiction only when national courts are unwilling or unable to investigate or prosecute such crimes. By 2008, the court had opened investigations into four situations—northern Uganda, the Democratic Republic of the Congo (DRC), the Central African Republic, and the region of Darfur in Sudan—and had issued public arrest warrants for twelve people, of whom six remain free, two have died, and four are in custody awaiting trial. The ICC is sometimes referred to as the world court, but it should not be confused with the International Court of Justice, also known as the World Court and located in The Hague, which is the UN organ that settles disputes between nations.

As a permanent entity, the ICC's supporters argue, the body's very existence stands as a deterrent, sending a strong warning to would-be perpetrators. It also encourages states to investigate and prosecute egregious crimes committed in their territories or by their nationals because, if they do not, the ICC will exercise its jurisdiction. Consistent with international human rights standards, the ICC has no competence to impose a death penalty. It can impose lengthy terms of imprisonment, including life, if justified by the gravity of the case. The court may, in addition, order a fine or forfeiture of proceeds, property, or assets derived from the crimes committed. Some aspects of the court are groundbreaking in terms of international law, including the recognition of sexual violence as a crime against humanity (which was first recognized by the tribunal for the former Yugoslavia), special services to victims and witnesses, and the court's independence from the UN Security Council. Some of the key legal principles governing the ICC include:

- All individuals have the right to a fair trial, and all individuals are innocent until proven guilty; the burden of proof lies with the prosecution, and guilt must be proven beyond a reasonable doubt.
- The intent to commit a crime must be proven.
- Individuals cannot be tried twice for the same alleged offense.
- Alleged crimes that occurred before the court takes effect cannot be tried.
- The court cannot try anyone who committed the alleged offense while under age eighteen.
- No statute of limitations is in effect for the crimes covered by the court.
- An accused person has certain rights on arrest, such as the right to legal advice, the right to remain silent, and freedom from coercion or degrading punishment.
- Accused individuals cannot use "I was following orders" as a defense, except in the rarest of circumstances.
- Convicted individuals have the right to a review of their sentence after serving two-thirds of it.
- The court can try any person regardless of his or her official status or any immunity from prosecution he or she may ordinarily enjoy because of that status.

The ICC's creation is fraught with controversy. Several states, including China, India, and the United States, are critical of the court and have not joined. The United States is opposed to the court, arguing that it challenges national judicial sovereignty and that U.S. armed forces personnel may face politically motivated trials. Proponents of the ICC counter that checks and balances are built into the process. Still, some U.S. legislators introduced a bill that would withdraw military assistance from states that ratify the ICC treaty. Other countries are opposed to the treaty establishing the ICC because some of its provisions conflict with their constitutions. Most notably, heads of state are not immune from prosecution by the ICC. Other issues with the ICC treaty that may have constitutional implications for countries include the absence of a statute of limitations and the right to a trial by jury, as well as extradition requirements.

For the ICC to operate effectively and provide for fair trials, it must be able to secure the cooperation of its state parties in surrendering suspects and in procuring the witnesses and evidence necessary for a successful investigation and prosecution. Thus, many states willing to cooperate with the ICC have begun altering or modifying their national laws and regulations. First, states need to ensure that they have effective provisions for the extradition of individuals indicted by the ICC. Second, the ICC requires access to prosecution and defense witnesses. Securing unwilling witnesses could prove extremely difficult for the court and for the country where the potential witness resides if neither the witness nor the state wants the witness to testify. Third, like domestic courts, the ICC needs to have access to documentary evidence if it is to be fair to victims and defendants alike. Article 93 of the Rome Statute states that the court can request certain documentary evidence from governments; however, it has no effective enforcement options if states refuse to cooperate.

States and their citizens can turn to other international and domestic mechanisms to hold human rights violators and war criminals accountable for their crimes. Depending on the prevailing political conditions, they can pursue human rights abusers residing in their own countries through the establishment of truth commissions or through domestic or regional courts. Victims whose human rights have been violated in another country can use extradition agreements to have offenders transferred to a national court. If an alleged offender travels to certain countries, such as the United States, victims residing there can file for civil damages for their suffering.

With the creation of the ICC, many international and national human rights organizations have established programs to better educate the public about the spectrum of accountability mechanisms, including trials, truth and reconciliation commissions, and traditional justice ceremonies, that can be implemented to deal with past crimes. Since 2001, for instance, the New York–based International Center for Transitional Justice has assisted countries pursuing accountability for past mass atrocities or human rights abuses. The center works in societies emerging from repressive rule or armed conflict, as well as in established democracies where historical injustices or systemic abuses remain unresolved.

Regional Summaries

Numerous countries are struggling to come to terms with the past in the wake of communal violence, genocide, or prolonged civil war. Some of these countries have brought human rights offenders to trial, while others have formed local or UN-led truth and reconciliation commissions to investigate and expose patterns of atrocity, lines of responsibility, and complicity.

North America

The United States has in its history incidents of crimes against humanity, of which the most significant—slavery and massacres of Native Americans—ended in the nineteenth century. Many have argued, and continue to argue, that the U.S. bombing of Hiroshima and Nagasaki on August 6 and 9, 1945, respectively, was a war crime and a crime against humanity. While military targets were no doubt destroyed, nonmilitary targets suffered the overwhelming brunt of the bombs, which killed more than 200,000 civilians.

More recently, in the 1990s, the United States and Canada played key roles in the creation of the ad hoc International Criminal Tribunals for the Former Yugoslavia and for Rwanda, but they took divergent paths on the creation of the ICC. The Canadian government has signed and ratified the Rome Statute establishing the court, and a Canadian, Philippe Kirsch, chaired the Preparatory Committee for the ICC, which had overall responsibility for thrashing out issues involving the jurisdiction and operations of the institution, and later was appointed president of the ICC in 2003. His fellow judges elected him to a further three-year term in March 2006.

Although the Bill Clinton administration initially supported the establishment of a permanent war crimes tribunal, in an about-face the United States

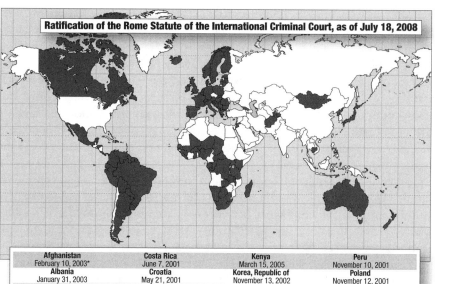

Ratification of the Rome Statute of the International Criminal Court, as of July 18, 2008

Afghanistan February 10, 2003*	**Costa Rica** June 7, 2001	**Kenya** March 15, 2005	**Peru** November 10, 2001
Albania January 31, 2003	**Croatia** May 21, 2001	**Korea, Republic of** November 13, 2002	**Poland** November 12, 2001
Andorra April 30, 2001	**Cyprus** March 7, 2002	**Latvia** June 28, 2002	**Portugal** February 5, 2002
Antigua & Barbuda June 18, 2001	**Denmark** June 21, 2001	**Lesotho** September 6, 2000	**Romania** April 11, 2002
Argentina February 8, 2001	**Djibouti** November 5, 2002	**Liberia** September 22, 2004	**Samoa** September 16, 2002
Australia July 1, 2002	**Dominica** February 12, 2001*	**Liechtenstein** October 2, 2001	**San Marino** May 13, 1999
Austria December 28, 2000	**Dominican Republic** May 12, 2005	**Lithuania** May 12, 2003	**Senegal** February 2, 1999
Barbados December 10, 2002	**Ecuador** February 5, 2002	**Luxembourg** September 8, 2000	**Serbia** September 6, 2001
Belgium June 28, 2000	**Estonia** January 30, 2002	**Macedonia, FYR** March 6, 2002	**Sierra Leone** September 15, 2000
Belize April 5, 2000	**Fiji** November 29, 1999	**Madagascar** March 14, 2008	**Slovakia** April 11, 2002
Benin January 22, 2002	**Finland** December 29, 2000	**Malawi** September 19, 2002	**Slovenia** December 31, 2001
Bolivia June 27, 2002	**France** June 9, 2000	**Mali** August 16, 2000	**South Africa** November 27, 2000
Bosnia-Herzegovina April 11, 2002	**Gabon** September 20, 2000	**Malta** November 29, 2002	**Spain** October 24, 2000
Botswana September 8, 2000	**Gambia** June 28, 2002	**Marshall Islands** December 7, 2000	**St. Kitts & Nevis** August 22, 2006*
Brazil June 20, 2002	**Georgia** September 5, 2003	**Mauritius** March 5, 2002	**St. Vincent & Grenadines** December 3, 2002*
Bulgaria April 11, 2002	**Germany** December 11, 2000	**Mexico** October 28, 2005	**Suriname** July 15, 2008*
Burkina Faso April 16, 2004	**Ghana** December 20, 1999	**Mongolia** April 11, 2002	**Sweden** June 28, 2001
Burundi September 21, 2004	**Greece** May 15, 2002	**Montenegro** October 23, 2006	**Switzerland** October 12, 2001
Cambodia April 11, 2002	**Guinea** July 14, 2003	**Namibia** June 25, 2002	**Tajikistan** May 5, 2000
Canada July 7, 2000	**Guyana** September 24, 2004	**Nauru** November 12, 2001	**Tanzania** August 20, 2002
Central African Republic October 3, 2001	**Honduras** July 1, 2002	**Netherlands** July 17, 2001	**Timor Leste** September 6, 2002*
Chad November 1, 2006	**Hungary** November 30, 2001	**New Zealand** September 7, 2000	**Trinidad & Tobago** April 6, 1999
Colombia August 5, 2002	**Iceland** May 25, 2000	**Niger** April 11, 2002	**Uganda** June 14, 2002
Comoros August 18, 2006	**Ireland** April 11, 2002	**Nigeria** September 27, 2001	**United Kingdom** October 4, 2001
Congo, Democratic Republic of April 11, 2002	**Italy** July 26, 1999	**Norway** February 16, 2000	**Uruguay** June 28, 2002
Congo, Republic of May 3, 2004	**Japan** July 17, 2007*	**Panama** March 21, 2002	**Venezuela** June 7, 2000
Cook Islands July 18, 2008*	**Jordan** April 11, 2002	**Paraguay** May 14, 2001	**Zambia** November 13, 2002

Source: Coalition for the International Criminal Court, "Ratification and Implementation > Ratification of the Rome Statute > World Signatures and Ratifications," 2008. Available online from http://www.iccnow.org/?mod=romesignatures.

Note: An asterisk indicates accession, that is, approval of the treaty by states that were not official signatories during the initial signing period.

became one of only seven countries to vote against the Rome Statute in 1998. Some of the strongest opposition to the ICC has come from military officials, who couch their public objections in terms of sovereignty, claiming that the court would infringe on U.S. jurisdiction. Many observers interpret this argument, however, as the military's desire for a guarantee that no American will ever be prosecuted by the court. The government's official stance is that the statute puts U.S. military personnel at risk of frivolous prosecution and hinders the president's ability to deploy armed forces. On December 31, 2000, the deadline for signing the Rome Statute, outgoing president Bill Clinton put his signature on the document.

In May 2002, President George W. Bush "unsigned" the document, renouncing the U.S. government's obligations under the Rome treaty. After that, the Bush administration somewhat played down its resistance to the ICC. The United States, in effect, supported using the ICC to prosecute atrocities in Darfur, as evidenced by the fact that it abstained from a vote on the 2005 UN Security Council Resolution 1593, which referred the situation in Darfur to the ICC. The ICC continues to be the subject of intense debate within the United States, and the U.S. position will likely be revisited, at least to a certain extent, by the current president and Congress.

Latin America

By the mid-1980s, as the cold war began to thaw, entrenched authoritarian regimes in Latin America began to relinquish power to elected civilian governments. Most of these new governments emerged after years of repressive military and sometimes civilian rule, under which systematic violations of human rights took place. In Brazil, the military thwarted any possibility of trials for such violations by passing de facto amnesties absolving themselves of past crimes. The fledgling civilian governments of Bolivia, Chile, Ecuador, El Salvador, Guatemala, and Uruguay, where the military retains substantial power, set up truth commissions to expose state abuses by gathering victims' testimonies, holding public hearings, and issuing reports of their findings. Argentina is the only country that has pursued trials of past military leaders in addition to a truth commission process. Chile, Guatemala, and Honduras also have held trials—although only a few and with limited success—of past human rights offenders.

Perhaps the most well-publicized case in the region involves former Chilean dictator General Augusto Pinochet. Human rights activists praised Pinochet's arrest in London on October 16, 1998, in response to an extradition request by Spanish magistrate Baltasar Garzón, who had indicted the former military ruler for human rights abuses committed in Chile in the 1970s. A year later, a British magistrate ordered Pinochet's extradition to Spain, but in early 2000, the British government released the general because of his declining health and allowed him to return to Chile.

Earlier attempts had been made to bring Pinochet to justice. Since 1989, a Chilean judge had been trying to prosecute Pinochet on charges that he covered up the killings of political opponents by a death squad shortly after he seized power in 1973. However, a court ruling in 2002 acknowledged that Pinochet had vascular dementia and prevented the case from going to trial. Chile's courts reversed the ruling of dementia in 2004, declaring him fit for trial. Several other cases of human rights abuses were progressing through the court system when Pinochet died at the age of ninety-one on December 10, 2006.

Europe

Ironically, the most significant event in Europe that led to greater universal accountability for wartime atrocities took place largely because UN member states feared taking definitive military action to stop a bloody war. Thus, on February 22, 1993, as ethnic cleansing raged in Bosnia, the UN Security Council in Resolution 808 voted unanimously to establish an ad hoc international criminal tribunal to prosecute "persons responsible for serious violations of international humanitarian law committed in the territory of the former Yugoslavia since 1991." To date, forty-three people, including former Yugoslav president Slobodan Milošević, have been in the custody of the tribunal awaiting trial or serving sentences. (Milošević died while he was in custody in 2006.) Two of the court's major indictees—former Bosnian Serb president Radovan Karadžić and his top military commander, General Ratko Mladić—were charged for their role in the bombardment of civilians in Sarajevo, where approximately 10,000 people died during the three-and-a-half year siege, and for the massacre of 7,000 Muslim men and boys during the fall of Srebrenica in July 1995. Karadžić was arrested in 2008, but as of June 2009, Mladić remains in hiding. Among the offenses listed in the indictment is the most heinous of all state-sponsored crimes—genocide. By characterizing the widespread killing of Bosnian Muslims as an act of genocide, the tribunal asserted that the two Bosnian Serb leaders were not engaged merely in a quest for territory but also in a quest to destroy—or at least eliminate—a large proportion of the Muslim population of Bosnia.

The tribunal's work has introduced a new dimension into global affairs. The tribunal, once an institution openly scorned or ignored by world leaders, now commands not only the attention of many political and national security thinkers but also their respect. As former chief prosecutor Louise Arbour said in a press conference (reported by UN Wire), "[W]e have moved international criminal justice. . . to a point of no return."

North Africa and the Middle East

The most significant, although controversial, application of international criminal justice to violations of human rights and international humanitarian law in this region has been the trials in Iraq of Saddam Hussein and other high officials of his government after the U.S. and Allied forces swept into Baghdad in April 2003. On December 10, 2003, a few days before images of Saddam Hussein's capture were broadcast worldwide, L. Paul Bremer, a career diplomat in the U.S. Department of State and the chief administrator for the Coalition Provisional Authority, the body initially set up to oversee the transition from Hussein's rule, issued a decree creating the Iraqi Special Tribunal for Crimes

Against Humanity. The tribunal, later renamed the Iraqi High Tribunal, serves to prosecute Iraqi nationals or residents of Iraq accused of genocide, crimes against humanity, and war crimes. Politically, Iraqi insurgents and much of the surrounding Arab region viewed the new tribunal, although Iraqi-led, as the illegitimate and politicized weapon of the U.S. aggressor, an argument expertly wielded by Hussein and other defendants in the tribunal's first trial. Human Rights Watch and other international human rights organizations called the tribunal fundamentally flawed and warned that it would inherently be vulnerable to political manipulation. By September 2007, the tribunal had completed two trials, *al-Dujail* and *al-Anfal,* and had begun a third trial involving crimes committed during the 1991 uprising of Iraq Kurds against the government of Saddam Hussein. Tribunal officials have announced that a total of fourteen trials will be convened.

The first trial involved charges of crimes against humanity related to the aftermath of a failed July 1982 assassination attempt against Saddam Hussein in the Shiite town of al-Dujail. The *al-Dujail* trial ran from October 19, 2005, to December 26, 2006, when final judgments were handed down. The ruling found Hussein and his six co-defendants guilty of a series of crimes, including crimes against humanity, willful killing, torture, and arbitrary detention. Hussein was executed four days later, and three other high-ranking officials were executed in the following weeks. After its sensationalistic details emerged, Hussein's public hanging was greatly criticized for being mishandled and inflammatory. As one of Hussein's executioners, face covered in a balaclava, tightened a noose around Hussein's neck, a group of onlookers began shouting insults. One man chanted a Shiite version of a Muslim prayer, clearly a sectarian barb aimed at Hussein, a Sunni. Later that day, an illegally recorded video of the execution was aired repeatedly on Iraqi television. And, as numerous journalists reported, the video's strong sectarian overtones worried many Iraqis—Sunnis and Shiites alike—who feared it would only fan the violence raging around them. Equally disturbing, they said, was the feeling of déjà vu that the execution evoked. During Hussein's thirty-five-year reign, prisoners—many of whom had been executed at the same gallows—were also regularly taunted and mistreated in their last hours.

Unlike the *al-Dujail* trial, which concerned crimes committed in a single town, the *al-Anfal* trial involved massive crimes, including the alleged gassing, imprisonment, execution, and displacement of over 100,000 Kurds during the eight-phase al-Anfal military campaign of 1988. When the *al-Anfal* trial opened in August 2006, Hussein, his cousin Ali Hassan Al-Majid, and five security officials were accused of genocide, crimes against humanity, and war crimes. But after Hussein's execution, public interest in the continuing trial of the remaining six accused declined dramatically among all groups except the Kurds. Indeed, for much of the second half of the trial at most one visitor was present in the observation chamber—an Iraqi observer for an international organization. Final verdicts were handed down in August 2007. Three defendants were given multiple death sentences. Two other defendants were given life imprisonment, and the charges against the sixth were dropped for lack of evidence.

Another application of international criminal justice in the Middle East involves the February 2005 assassination of Rafik Hariri, the former prime minister of Lebanon. In April 2005, the UN Security Council, condemning the attack in which Hariri was killed as a terrorist act and a potential threat to regional and international security, established the International Independent Investigation Commission (IIIC) to help Lebanon investigate the circumstances surrounding the Hariri attack. In March of the following year, the Security Council also began negotiations with the Lebanese authorities to set up a Special Tribunal for Lebanon to investigate not just the Hariri assassination, in which over twenty other people were killed, but also other suspected terrorist attacks committed between October 2004 and December 2006. At issue is whether the Hariri attack—and other attacks in this period—constitute a broad-based policy to target civilians due to their political connections and activities. The fate of the tribunal, which began its work in March 2009, is complicated by the instability of the political situation in Lebanon. On top of that, regional and international politics complicate the tribunal's potential success, given that much of the early evidence points to Syria's involvement in the Hariri attack. In addition, the hybrid nature of the tribunal, which is governed by Lebanese law in an international UN-sponsored context to take place in The Hague, adds to the complexity of the challenges faced by the IIIC investigations, and the work of the Special Tribunal.

Sub-Saharan Africa

The ICC has focused its first four investigations on suspected war criminals from four sub-Saharan countries. These four trials all involve alleged war crimes committed during civil wars in Uganda, DRC, Central African Republic, and Sudan, and as of fall 2008, they are all at various stages in their prosecution (see Case Study—The First Trials of the International Criminal Court).

The Special Court for Sierra Leone (SCSL) was established in 2002 by the Sierra Leonean government and the United Nations. According to the official Web site of the SCSL, it is a hybrid court, consisting of national and international officials, that "try those who bear the greatest responsibility for serious violations of international humanitarian law and Sierra Leonean law committed in the territory of Sierra Leone since 30 November 1996." Thirteen people have been indicted so far, and ten are facing trial. One of these is Charles Taylor, the former president of Liberia, who is charged with crimes against humanity and war crimes for his involvement with rebel groups who fought for control over Sierra Leone during the ten-year civil war in Sierra Leone that began in 1991. Although the SCSL resides in Freetown, the capital of Sierra Leone, it has relocated the trial to the facilities of the ICC for security reasons. This is the first time that an African president has been tried before an international court.

Since 1994, the International Criminal Tribunal for Rwanda in Arusha, Tanzania, has been investigating and prosecuting people responsible for the 1994 genocide that largely destroyed Rwanda. The potential defendants can be divided into three groups. The first consists of the leaders who ordered the genocide—close associates of the late president Juvénal Habyarimana, military and militia leaders, mayors, and officials of Radio de Milles Colines. The second group, numbering in the tens of thousands, consists of lower-level municipal and administrative officials who were not part of the core group of instigators but who used their authority to order mass killings. Many of these potential defendants are now held in jails throughout Rwanda and are being tried by national courts. The third group comprises people who were caught up in the fighting or were forced to kill or be killed. Many of them will be tried under a traditional form of justice, *gacaca,* predating the arrival of Europeans in Africa. Under *gacaca,* judges chosen from the community accompany the accused to crime scenes in the hope that the guilty will confess and ask forgiveness. Those who insist on their innocence and are found not guilty will be allowed to return to the community; those who profess innocence but are found guilty face life imprisonment or the death penalty. So far, the Arusha tribunal has secured the arrest of seventy-four people, of which thirty-five have been tried. Of these, Jean-Paul Akayesu, the former district mayor of Taba in central Rwanda, has received the severest sentence—three life sentences for genocide and crimes against humanity plus eighty years for other violations that included torture and rape (see Case Study—The Trial of Jean-Paul Akayesu).

Ethiopia continues to use its own courts to pursue people who committed crimes under the Mengistu Haile Mariam regime that controlled the state from 1974 to 1991. On December 12, 2006, an Ethiopian Court found the former Ethiopian leader Mengistu guilty of genocide *in absentia* for his role in the killing of nearly 2,000 people during the Red Terror of 1977–1978. The evidence against him included signed execution orders, videos of torture sessions, and personal testimonies. He was sentenced to life in prison in January 2007. Amnesty International estimates that a total of half a million people were killed during the Red Terror. Over one hundred former Ethiopian officials were accused of genocide during the trials, but only thirty-six of them were present in the court. Following an appeal in May 2008, Mengistu was sentenced to death *in absentia* by Ethiopia's High Court, overturning his previous sentence of life imprisonment. The Zimbabwean government has said that Mengistu still enjoys asylum in Zimbabwe and will not be extradited.

Mozambique declined to pursue trials or a truth commission process following the conclusion of its sixteen-year civil war, which ended in a peace agreement in 1992. Ten days after the signing of the accord, the parliament declared a general amnesty for "crimes against the state." At various times in their troubled pasts, Zimbabwe (1985), Chad (1990), South Africa (1994), Sierra Leone (1999), and Nigeria (1999) have formed national truth commissions (with decidedly mixed results) in an effort to come to terms with the past and promote reconciliation.

Asia and the Pacific

Cambodia's Constitutional Council approved legislation in August 2001 to establish a special court to try former Khmer Rouge leaders for crimes against humanity, clearing a hurdle in the effort to prosecute for some of the worst human rights atrocities in Asia since World II. The legislation established a hybrid tribunal comprising foreign and local judges to try the surviving Khmer Rouge leaders, who are blamed for the deaths of an estimated 1.7–2 million people—roughly 20 percent of Cambodia's population—in the late 1970s (see GENOCIDE). In May 2006, Cambodia's highest judicial body approved thirty Cambodian and UN judges to preside over the court. The tribunal began its first hearing in February 2008. The case involves Khang Khek Ieu, also known as "Duch," for his alleged role in the torture and murder of an estimated 16,000 people, of whom only 7 or 10 are known to have survived, at the Toul Sleng prison in Phnom Penh. Khang Khek Ieu has admitted guilt but contends that everything he did was under the orders of others. Four other suspects—Nuon Chea, Ieng Sary, Ieng Thirith, and Khieu Smphan—have also been apprehended and will be brought to trial by the end of 2009.

On May 20, 2005, the Special Panels of the Dili District Court, also called the East Timor Tribunal, completed more than four years of trials arising from crimes committed during the 1999 violence following the referendum in which East Timorese voted overwhelmingly for independence from Indonesia. A hybrid international–East Timorese tribunal that was created in 2000 by the United Nations Transitional Administration in East Timor (Timor-Leste), and the judicial body completed fifty-five trials, most involving relatively low-level defendants. In the course of these trials, eighty-four individuals were convicted and three were acquitted. Legal scholar David Cohen, in his report *Indifference and Accountability: The United Nations and the Politics of International Justice,* makes a highly critical examination of the functioning of the court. He notes that a significant number of cases where the rights of the accused appear to have been compromised, including being convicted of crimes not charged in the indictment and against which they had no opportunity to defend themselves. "At the root of all the problems of the process," he writes, "was the failure by the United Nations to ensure proper leadership, a clear mandate, political will, and clear 'ownership' of the process from the very beginning."

Case Study—The Trial of Jean-Paul Akayesu

On September 2, 1998, the International Criminal Tribunal for Rwanda found Jean-Paul Akayesu, the former district mayor of the Taba commune in central Rwanda, guilty on nine of fifteen counts of genocide, direct and public incitement to commit genocide, and crimes against humanity. A month later, Judge Laity Dama of Senegal sentenced the former mayor to three life sentences. The 294-page judgment made Akayesu the first person to be found guilty of genocide by an international tribunal. His case also represented the first conviction in which rape—one of the most ancient of war crimes—was held by a court of law to be an act of genocide and a crime against humanity.

Akayesu was arrested in Zambia on October 10, 1995, and handed over to the Arusha tribunal. His detention came not at the behest of the tribunal but because his name appeared on a list of suspected war criminals wanted by the Rwandan government. Under the tribunal's rules, prosecutors had ninety days to decide whether to file charges. From the start, they sought to organize their case around the charge of mass murder, linking the defendant to the more than 2,000 deaths in Taba. The tribunal investigators, mostly male, often unconsciously failed to ask about rape or did not consider it important enough to ask about. Women from Taba did not volunteer that they had been raped. Therefore, that the first indictment lodged against Akayesu on February 26, 1996, made no mention of rape is not surprising.

The Akayesu indictment caused a furor in feminist and human rights circles, as Elizabeth Neuffer notes in *The Key to My Neighbor's House: Searching for Justice in Bosnia and Rwanda*. Human Rights Watch, in a 1996 report based on its own investigations in Rwanda, concluded that rape had been widespread in the Taba commune. The first mention of rape in the Akayesu trial surfaced unexpectedly in January 1997, when a protected witness on the stand described Akayesu's role in various murders. During her testimony, she mentioned that her six-year-old daughter had been raped by three members of the Interahamwe, the Hutu militia group responsible for much of the death and destruction in Rwanda. Two months later, another protected witness testified that Hutu military and militia had raped women at Taba's Bureau Communale. Astounded that the prosecution had not pursued these allegations, Judge Navanethem Pillay, a respected women's advocate who had served on South Africa's Truth and Reconciliation Commission, and Swedish judge Lennert Aspegren peppered the witness with questions to determine the mayor's responsibility for the rapes.

When the court reconvened months later, the prosecutor announced that he wanted to amend the indictment against Akayesu to include three additional charges of rape and sexual violence. The judges agreed. In ensuing months, more than a dozen women from Taba came forward to describe the rapes and other crimes that they had witnessed or suffered at the hands of the Interahamwe. Their testimony proved that Akayesu had not only ordered that the Tutsi residents of Taba give themselves up and go to the Bureau Communale, but that he had also been present on the second day of the rapes there.

In February 2001, judges at the International Criminal Tribunal for the Former Yugoslavia referred to the precedent set in the Akayesu judgment when issuing their verdict against three Bosnian Serb commanders found guilty of raping Bosnian Muslim women and girls, some as young as twelve and fifteen years old, in the town of Foca in eastern Bosnia. Two of the accused were also found guilty of sexual enslavement—a crime against humanity—by holding women and girls captive in de facto detention centers near Foca. Forced prostitution, although common in the Far East during World War II, was never prosecuted in the international tribunals following that war. The Akayesu and Foca judgments are historic developments in international criminal law and should encourage individual nations to treat sexual violence more seriously.

Case Study—The First Trials of the International Criminal Court

Starting in December 2003, the Office of the Prosecutor of the ICC, as the international community's newly commissioned body charged with prosecuting international criminal justice, launched its first four investigations, all taking aim at war crimes committed during civil wars in Africa. The Ugandan government, in December 2003, referred to the prosecutor the situation concerning the Lord's Resistance Army (LRA), a spiritualist rebel group with no clear political agenda that has waged war against the Uganda People's Army since the late 1980s. Known for its extreme brutality, the LRA has killed and mutilated countless civilians and abducted tens of thousands of adults and children to serve as soldiers, porters, and sexual partners for its commanders. In October 2005, the court unsealed arrest warrants and indictments against LRA leader Joseph Kony and four of his rebel commanders, two of whom have since died. Kony has repeatedly demanded immunity from ICC prosecution in return for an end to the insurgency. The Ugandan government has proposed establishing a national criminal tribunal that meets international standards, thereby allowing the ICC warrants to be set aside.

In March 2004, the government of the DRC referred to the prosecutor "the situation of crimes" in its country. A year later, Thomas Lubanga, former leader of the Union of Congolese Patriots militia in Ituri, was arrested and charged, according to the official ICC Web page for the DRC case, with allegedly "conscripting and enlisting children under the age of fifteen years. . . and using them to participate actively in hostilities." His trial commenced in June 2008. Two more suspects, Germain Katanga and Mathieu Ngudjolo Chui, were subsequently surrendered to the court by the Congolese authorities. Both men were charged with six counts of war crimes and three counts of crimes against humanity, relating to an attack on the village of Bogoro in 2003, in which at least two hundred civilians were killed and women and girls were sexually enslaved.

In May 2007, two-and-a-half years after the government of the Central African Republic referred the situation in its country to the ICC, the prosecutor opened an investigation into allegations of killing and rape in 2002 and 2003, a period of intense fighting between the government and rebel forces. On May 23, 2008, the court unsealed an arrest warrant for Jean-Pierre Bember, a former vice president of the DRC, charging him with war crimes and crimes against humanity. He was arrested near Brussels the following day.

As of July 2008, the court has issued arrest warrants against three Sudanese war crimes suspects: Omar al-Bashir, the Sudanese president; Ahmad Muhammad Harun, the Sudanese humanitarian affairs minister; and Ali Kushayb, Janjaweed militia leader. However, Sudan says that the ICC has no jurisdiction over this matter and refuses to hand over the men. The United Nations Security Council referred "the situation prevailing in Darfur" to the prosecutor on March 31, 2005.

Although these four trials have not all been completed, the fact that the aggrieved parties have an international venue in which to seek justice for war crimes is clearly a step forward. In addition, the four trials reflect the difficulty of prosecuting international criminal justice through the ICC, which operates under the mandate of an international treaty but must seek justice within the context of individual states' political environments, with all the complexity that context implies.

Biographical Sketches

Louise Arbour is a judge on the Ontario Court of Appeals and a former criminal law professor who replaced Richard Goldstone as chief prosecutor of the International Criminal Tribunals for the Former Yugoslavia and for Rwanda in 1996. She introduced the practice of secret indictments, which resulted in more suspected war criminals turning themselves in to the Yugoslav tribunal. She served as the United Nations High Commissioner for Human Rights from 2004 to 2008.

Richard J. Goldstone has been a justice of the Constitutional Court of South Africa since 1994 and has served as chairperson of the Commission of Inquiry Regarding the Prevention of Public Violence and Intimidation in South Africa. He was appointed chief prosecutor of the International Criminal Tribunals for the Former Yugoslavia and for Rwanda in 1994. In *For Humanity: Reflections of a War Crimes Investigator,* Goldstone provides an intimate account of his progression from a young activist opposing South Africa's racial policies to the world's first independent war crimes prosecutor.

Gabrielle Kirk McDonald began her career as a civil rights lawyer in 1966 with the National Association for the Advancement of Colored People (NAACP). In 1979, she became the first African American to be appointed a federal court judge in Houston, Texas. In 1993, the UN General Assembly appointed her as a judge on the International Criminal Tribunal for the Former Yugoslavia. From 1997 to 2000, she served as the tribunal president.

Louis Moreno-Ocampo is a 1978 graduate of University of Buenos Aires Law School who rose to prominence as the assistant prosecutor of the National Tribunal on the Disappearance of Persons, which tried nine leading figures, including three former heads of state, of the military dictatorship that ruled Argentina from 1976 to 1983. He was elected unopposed to the position of prosecutor of the International Criminal Tribunal in 2003 by a ballot of more than seventy countries and sworn in on June 16, 2003.

Aryeh Neier is a human rights activist and writer who fled Nazi Germany as a child. He is an ardent supporter of international justice and, as director of Human Rights Watch in the early 1990s, played a key role in garnering support among American and European diplomats for the creation of the International Criminal Tribunals for the Former Yugoslavia and for Rwanda. He is currently president of the Soros Foundation and its Open Society Institute.

Navanethem Pillay was a defense attorney for members of the African National Congress until 1995, when she was elected judge of the International Criminal Tribunal for Rwanda. In 1999, she was elected tribunal president. Pillay was instrumental in prompting tribunal prosecutors to investigate widespread reports of rape during the 1994 genocide in Rwanda.

Directory

Amnesty International, 99-119 Rosebery Avenue, London EC1R 4RE, United Kingdom. Telephone: (44) 207 814 6200; email: info@amnesty.org.uk; Web: http://www.amnesty.org.

Organization working to promote the human rights enshrined in the Universal Declaration of Human Rights and other international standards.

Coalition for International Justice, 740 Fifteenth Street NW, 8th Floor, Washington, D.C. 20005-1009. Telephone: (202) 505-2100; email: coalition@cij.org.
Organization working to support the war crimes tribunals for Rwanda and the former Yugoslavia.

Crimes of War, 1325 G Street NW, Suite 730, Washington, D.C. 20005. Email: office@crimesofwar.org; Web: http://www.crimesofwar.org.
Collaboration of journalists, lawyers, and scholars raising awareness of the laws of war and the human consequences when armed conflict becomes entrenched.

Human Rights Watch, 350 Fifth Avenue, 34th Floor, New York, N.Y. 10118-3299. Telephone: (212) 290-4700; email: hrwnyc@hrw.org; Web: http://www.hrw.org.
Organization dedicated to protecting the human rights of people around the world.

Institute for War and Peace Reporting, Lancaster House, 33 Islington High Street, London N1 9LH, United Kingdom. Telephone: (44) 2 07 713 7130; email: info@iwpr.net; Web: http://www.iwpr.net.
Educational charity that supports democratization and development in crisis zones throughout the world.

International Center for Transitional Justice, 5 Hanover Square, Floor 24, New York, N.Y. 10004. Telephone: (917) 637-3800; email: info@ictj.org; Web: http://www .ictj.org.
Organization dedicated to promoting transitional justice worldwide; a permanent, treaty-bound international court that prosecutes individuals for genocide, crimes against humanity, and war crimes.

International Criminal Court (ICC), Maanweg 174, 2516 AB, The Hague, Netherlands. Telephone: (31) 70-515-8515; email: info@icc-cpi.int; Web: http://www .icc-cpi.int.
An independent, permanent court that tries people accused of the most serious crimes of international concern: genocide, crimes against humanity, and war crimes.

International Criminal Tribunal for the Former Yugoslavia, 1 Churchillplein, 2501 EW, The Hague, Netherlands. Telephone: (31) 0 70 512 8656; Web: http:// www.un.org/icty.
UN-sanctioned tribunal to prosecute people responsible for serious violations of international humanitarian law committed in the former Yugoslavia.

International Criminal Tribunal for Rwanda, Arusha International Conference Centre, P.O. Box 6016, Arusha, Tanzania. Telephone: Arusha (255) 27 250 4369 or 4372, New York (212) 963-2850; Web: http://www.ictr.org.
UN-sanctioned tribunal to prosecute people responsible for genocide and other serious violations of international humanitarian law committed in the territory of Rwanda between January 1 and December 31, 1994.

International Crisis Group, 400 Madison Avenue, Suite 11C, New York, N.Y. 10017. Telephone: (212) 813-0820; email: icgny@crisisweb.org, Web: http://www .crisisgroup.org/home/index.cfm.
Organization committed to strengthening the capacity of the international community to anticipate, understand, and act to prevent and contain conflict.

Office of the United Nations High Commissioner for Human Rights, 8-14 Avenue de la Paix, 1211 Geneva 10, Switzerland. Telephone: (41) 22 917 9000; email: webadmin.hchr@unoq.ch; Web: http://www.ohchr.org.
UN office that oversees the work of several agencies promoting and protecting human rights and fundamental freedoms.

South Asian Human Rights Documentation Centre, B-6/6 Safdariang Enclave Extension, New Delhi 110029, India. Telephone: (91) 11 619 1120; email: hrdc_online@hotmail.com; Web: http://www.hrdc.net/sahrdc.
Network of individuals across South Asia working to investigate, document, and disseminate information about a wide range of human rights issues.

United States Institute of Peace, 1200 17th Street NW, Suite 200, Washington, D.C. 20036-3011. Telephone: (202) 429-3828; email: usip_requests@usip.org; Web: http://www.usip.org.
Independent, nonpartisan federal institution created and funded by Congress to strengthen the U.S. capacity to promote the peaceful resolution of international conflict.

Further Research

Books

Arendt, Hannah. *Eichman in Jerusalem: A Report on the Banality of Evil.* Middlesex, UK: Penguin, 1964.

Ball, Howard. *Prosecuting War Crimes and Genocide: The Twentieth-Century Experience.* Lawrence: University Press of Kansas, 1999.

Bass, Gary Jonathan. *Stay the Hand of Vengeance: The Politics of War Crimes Tribunals.* Princeton, N.J.: Princeton University Press, 2000.

Bassiouni, M. Cherif, and Peter Manikas. *The Law of the International Criminal Tribunal for the Former Yugoslavia.* Irvington-on-Hudson, N.Y.: Transnational Publishers, 1996.

Chang, Iris. *The Rape of Nanking: The Forgotten Holocaust of World War II.* New York: Basic Books, 1997.

Goldstone, Richard J. *For Humanity: Reflections of a War Crimes Investigator.* New Haven, Conn.: Yale University Press, 2000.

Gutman, Roy, and David Rieff, eds. *Crimes of War: What the Public Must Know.* New York: Norton, 2007.

Hayner, Priscilla B. *Unspeakable Truths: Confronting State Terror and Atrocity.* New York: Routledge, 2001.

Hersh, Seymour M. *Chain of Command: The Road from 9/11 to Abu Ghraib.* New York: HarperCollins, 2004.

Kritz, Neil J. *Transitional Justice: How Emerging Democracies Reckon with Former Regimes.* Washington, D.C.: United States Institute of Peace Press, 1995.

Minnow, Martha. *Between Vengeance and Forgiveness: Facing History and Genocide and Mass Violence.* Boston: Beacon Press, 1998.

Neier, Aryeh. *War Crimes: Brutality, Genocide, Terror, and the Struggle for Justice.* New York: Times Books, 1998.

Neuffer, Elizabeth. *The Key to My Neighbor's House: Searching for Justice in Bosnia and Rwanda.* New York: Picador, 2001.

Osiel, Mark. *Mass Atrocity, Collective Memory, and the Law.* New Brunswick, N.J.: Transaction Publishers, 1997.

Peskin, Victor. *International Justice in Rwanda and the Balkans: Virtual Trials and Rwanda and the Balkans.* Cambridge, UK: Cambridge University Press, 2008.

Roht-Arriaza, Naomi, and Javier Mariezurrena, eds. *Transitional Justice in the 21st Century: Beyond Truth vs. Justice.* Cambridge, UK: Cambridge University Press, 2006.

Stover, Eric. *The Witnesses: War Crimes and the Promise of Justice in The Hague.* Philadelphia: University of Pennsylvania Press, 2005.

Stover, Eric, and Gilles Peress. *The Graves: Srebrenica and Vukovar.* Zurich: Scalo, 1998.

Stover, Eric, and Harvey M. Weinstein, eds. *My Neighbor, My Enemy: Justice and Community in the Aftermath of Mass Atrocity.* Cambridge, UK: Cambridge University Press, 2004.

Tanaka, Yuki. *Japanese War Crimes in World War II.* Boulder, Colo.: Westview Press, 1996.

Taylor, Telford. *The Anatomy of the Nuremberg Trials.* New York: Knopf, 1992.

———. *Nuremberg and Vietnam: An American Tragedy.* New York: New York Times, 1970.

Totani, Yuma. *The Tokyo War Crimes Trial: The Pursuit of Justice in the Wake of World War II.* Cambridge, Mass.: Harvard University Press, 2008.

Articles and Reports

Akhavan, Payam. "Justice in The Hague, Peace in the Former Yugoslavia?: A Commentary on the United Nations War Crimes Tribunal." *Human Rights Quarterly* 20, no. 4 (1998): 737–816.

Alvarez, Jose E. "Lessons from the Akayesu Judgment." *IlSA Journal of International and Comparative Law* 5, no. 2 (1999): 359–370.

Cohen, David. "Beyond Nuremberg: Individual Responsibility for War Crimes." In *Human Rights in Political Transitions: Gettysburg to Bosnia,* ed. Carla Hesse and Robert Post. New York: Zone Books, 1999.

———. *Indifference and Accountability: The United Nations and the Politics of International Justice in East Timor.* Honolulu: East-West Center, 2006.

Crawford, James. "First Report on State Responsibility." Report of the International Law Commission, Fifth Session. Available at: http://www.un.org/law/ilc/sessions/50/english/n9812606.pdf.

Farer, Tom J. "Restraining the Barbarians: Can International Criminal Law Help?" *Human Rights Quarterly* 22, no. 1 (2000): 90–117.

Fletcher, Laurel E., and Harvey M. Weinstein. "Violence and Social Repair: Rethinking the Contribution of Justice to Reconciliation." *Human Rights Quarterly* 24, no. 3 (2002): 573–639.

Human Rights Watch. "Justice in the Balance: Recommendations for an Independent and Effective International Criminal Court." June 1998. Available at: http://www.hrw.org/reports98/icc.

———. "Milosevic in The Hague." August 2001. Available at: http://www.hrw.org/legacy/campaigns/Serbia.

Human Rights Watch and the Fédération Internationale des Ligues des Droits de l'Homme. "Shattered Lives: Sexual Violence during the Rwandan Genocide and Its Aftermath." September 1, 1996. Available at: http://www.hrw.org/reports/1996/Rwanda.htm.

International Center for Transitional Justice. *Handbook for Reparations.* Oxford: Oxford University Press, 2006.

Katz Cogan, Jacob. "The Problem of Obtaining Evidence for International Criminal Courts." *Human Rights Quarterly* 22, no. 2 (2000): 404–427.

Kissinger, Henry A. "The Pitfalls of Universal Jurisdiction: Risking Judicial Tyranny." *Foreign Affairs* 80, no. 4 (2001): 86–96.

Klarin, Miko. "The Tribunal's Four Battles." *Journal of International Criminal Justice* 2 (2004): 546–557.

Neier, Aryeh. "What Should Be Done about the Guilty?" *New York Review of Books,* February 1, 1990, 32–35.

Orentlicher, Diane F. "Settling Accounts: The Duty to Prosecute Human Rights Violations of a Prior Regime." *Yale Law Journal* 100 (1991): 2538–2618.

Osiel, Mark J. "Why Prosecute?: Critics of Punishment for Mass Atrocity." *Human Rights Quarterly* 22, no. 1 (2000): 118–147.

Phuong Pham et al. *When the War Ends: A Population-Based Survey on Attitudes about Peace, Justice, and Social Reconstruction in Northern Uganda.* Berkeley, Calif.: Human Rights Center and International Center for Transitional Justice, 2007.

Roht-Arriaza, Naomi. "Institutions of International Justice." *Journal of International Affairs* 52, no. 2 (1999): 474–491.

Saliba, Issam Michael. "International Tribunals, National Crimes and the Hariri Assassination: A Novel Development in International Law." June 6, 2007. Law Library of Congress (Library of Congress). Available at: http://www.lcweb.loc.gov/law/help/hariri/hariri.pdf.

Stover, Eric. "Dreamtime of Vengeance in Kosovo." Crimes of War Project, August 2001. Available at: http://www.crimesofwar.org/tribun-mag/mag_stover.html.

Trueheart, Charles. "A New Kind of Justice." *Atlantic Monthly,* April 2000, 80–90.

Ya Libnan. "Lebanon's Special Tribunal to Begin Work Early 2009." August 1, 2008. Available at: http://yalibnan.com/site/archives/2008/08/lebanons_specia.php.

Web Sites

Akayesu Judgment and Sentence, International Criminal Tribunal for Rwanda
http://www.ictr.org/english/cases/akayesu/judgement.htm

International Center for Transitional Justice
http://www.ictj.org/en/index.html

Milosevic Hearing and Trial Transcripts, British Broadcasting Corporation
http://news.bbc.co.uk/2/hi/europe/1419971.stm

Milosevic Indictment, International Criminal Tribunal for the Former Yugoslavia
http://www.un.org/icty/indictment/english/mil-ii990524e.htm

Rome Statute of the International Criminal Court
http://untreaty.un.org/cod/icc/index.html

Documents

1. Rome Statute of the International Criminal Court

United Nations Diplomatic Conference of Plenipotentiary on the Establishment of an International Criminal Court, Rome, July 17, 1998

The full text is available at http://untreaty.un.org/ilc/texts/instruments/english/conventions/7_4_1998.pdf.

Extract

Preamble

The States Parties to this Statute,

Conscious that all peoples are united by common bonds, their cultures pieced together in a shared heritage, and concerned that this delicate mosaic may be shattered at any time,

Mindful that during this century millions of children, women and men have been victims of unimaginable atrocities that deeply shock the conscience of humanity,

Recognizing that such grave crimes threaten the peace, security and well-being of the world,

Affirming that the most serious crimes of concern to the international community as a whole must not go unpunished and that their effective prosecution must be ensured by taking measures at the national level and by enhancing international cooperation,

Determined to put an end to impunity for the perpetrators of these crimes and thus to contribute to the prevention of such crimes,

Recalling that it is the duty of every State to exercise its criminal jurisdiction over those responsible for international crimes,

Reaffirming the Purposes and Principles of the Charter of the United Nations, and in particular that all States shall refrain from the threat or use of force against the territorial integrity or political independence of any State, or in any other manner inconsistent with the Purposes of the United Nations,

Emphasizing in this connection that nothing in this Statute shall be taken as authorizing any State Party to intervene in an armed conflict or in the internal affairs of any State,

Determined to these ends and for the sake of present and future generations, to establish an independent permanent International Criminal Court in relationship with the United Nations system, with jurisdiction over the most serious crimes of concern to the international community as a whole,

Emphasizing that the International Criminal Court established under this Statute shall be complementary to national criminal jurisdictions,

Resolved to guarantee lasting respect for and the enforcement of international justice.

2. Principles of International Law Recognized in the Charter of the Nuremberg Tribunal and in the Judgment of the Tribunal

International Law Commission of the United Nations, 1950

The full text is available at http://untreaty.un.org/ilc/texts/instruments/english/draft%20 articles/7_1_1950.pdf.

Extract

Principle I

Any person who commits an act which constitutes a crime under international law is responsible therefor and liable to punishment.

Principle II

The fact that internal law does not impose a penalty for an act which constitutes a crime under international law does not relieve the person who committed the act from responsibility under international law.

Principle III

The fact that a person who committed an act which constitutes a crime under international law acted as Head of State or responsible Government official does not relieve him from responsibility under international law.

Principle IV

The fact that a person acted pursuant to order of his Government or of a superior does not relieve him from responsibility under international law, provided a moral choice was in fact possible to him.

Principle V

Any person charged with a crime under international law has the right to a fair trial on the facts and law.

Principle VI

The crimes hereinafter set out are punishable as crimes under international law:

(a) Crimes against peace

    i. Planning, preparation, initiation or waging of a war of aggression or a war in violation of international treaties, agreements or assurances;

    ii. Participation in a common plan or conspiracy for the accomplishment of any of the acts mentioned under (i).

(b) War crimes

    Violations of the laws or customs of war which include, but are not limited to, murder, ill-treatment or deportation to slave-labor or for any other purpose of civilian population of or in occupied territory; murder or ill treatment of prisoners of war, of persons on the seas, killing of hostages, plunder of public or private property, wanton destruction of cities, towns, or villages, or devastation not justified by military necessity.

(c) Crimes against humanity

    Murder, extermination, enslavement, deportation and other inhuman acts done against any civilian population, or persecutions on political, racial or religious grounds, when such acts are done or such persecutions are carried on in execution of or in connection with any crime against peace or any war crime.

Principle VII

Complicity in the commission of a crime against peace, a war crime, or a crime against humanity as set forth in Principle VI is a crime under international law.

TRANSNATIONAL GOVERNANCE

Daan Bronkhorst

Transnational governance is an umbrella term for organizations and structures that have transnational significance for policies, law, conflict resolution, and social issues. It relates to the management of global processes in the absence of global government. Strong governance is seen in binding agreements, such as those of United Nations conventions, regional treaties, and the International Criminal Court. Weaker forms of governance, which are based on voluntary participation but may adopt a binding nature over the years, grow from networks of states, intergovernmental organizations, and nongovernmental organizations (NGOs). These "soft" forms set standards and rules for human rights, the environment, social justice, and corporate responsibility. The issues that come under the auspices of such governance are as diverse as sport rules, exchanges among museums, standardized postage, and the prohibition of the trade in diamonds from areas of armed conflict.

Historical Background and Development

The present-day practice of state sovereignty is very strong, even though it has been weakened by many international agreements and institutions. Paradoxically, transnational governance is a rather recent phenomenon because historically people would generally feel less committed to a national sovereignty above a regional, local, or religious one. Yet in another sense more transnational governance existed historically through the large empires and the colonial regimes. Many of today's transnational governance patterns reflect historical power blocks and borders.

The Achaemenid Persian Empire (550–330 BC) was the largest empire of the ancient world. It was most widespread in its early phase, under Darius and Xerxes. The latter was defeated by Athens in the Battle of Salamis (480), an event that changed the course of history—it established a pattern of independent cities and small states in the Western world, against the power of huge monolithic empires. China's sphere of influence nowadays reflects the Tang dynasty (~600–900), which united an area not equaled since, with large inroads into territory that later became Southeast Asia and the Islamic Arab world.

The Holy Roman Empire was a union of territories in Europe from Otto I, its first emperor, in 962 until the abdication of Francis II in 1806. At its peak, the empire covered the whole or parts of what now are Germany, Italy, France, Austria, Switzerland, Belgium, the Netherlands, Luxembourg, the Czech Republic, Slovenia, and Poland (but not Rome itself). The number of territories rose to three hundred at the time of the Peace of Westphalia (1648), many of minute size. Governance in the empire lay with the Reichstag, the legislative body that was superior to the emperor.

Colonialism had a strong worldwide presence from the sixteenth century onward. The late eighteenth and early nineteenth centuries brought decolonization, first in the Americas. Britain, France and the Netherlands, however, strengthened their colonial rule in Africa and South and Southeast Asia. Germany took much of East Africa. Italy occupied Eritrea, Somalia, and Libya, and later invaded Abyssinia. Present-day organizations such as the British Commonwealth and La Francophonie, as well as the routes of development aid, migration, and diplomacy, show persistent traces of the colonial past.

Transnational governance, in the modern sense of the word, has precedents in peace treaties such as those of Westphalia (1648), Utrecht (1713), Paris (1815), and Versailles (1919). The body of international law, however, has seriously developed only since the end of World War II in 1945, even though it was envisaged in earlier periods, notably by the seventeenth-century Dutch legal philosopher Hugo Grotius, who expounded his thesis of a common law for all nations. In the twentieth century, some major initiatives of transnational governance have been the League of Nations; the Permanent Court of International Justice; the Permanent Court of Arbitration; the Nuremberg and Tokyo trials; the United Nations; regional bodies including those of the Americas, Europe, and Africa; financial and economic institutions such as International Monetary Fund (IMF), World Bank, and World Trade Organization (WTO); and ad hoc international tribunals and the International Criminal Court.

Utopian concepts and movements have been common throughout modern history. They include the one described in *Utopia* (1516) by Thomas Moore and the negative utopia in *Brave New World* (1932) by Aldous Huxley. Important, often devastating utopian versions of the praxis of communism, fascism, and Maoism have also been proposed. In addition, some argue that a strong United Nations should be leading to world government. Less utopian are the advocates of global movements, such as for human rights, protection of the environment, and corporate responsibility; these movements have had an extensive impact on international and national policies. The new international information and communication order, proposed by the UN from the late 1970s, was another ideal that looked quite utopian at the time but that gained concrete form in the globalization of the Internet from the mid-1990s.

Current Status

Over 10,000 international governance bodies exist today. Among them are the International Chamber of Commerce; the network of central bankers; bodies such as the United Nations Educational, Scientific, and Cultural Organization (UNESCO), with a presence in over 190 countries; the Universal Postal Union and the International Organization of Supreme Audit Institutions, both in some 190 countries; the Roman Catholic Church, the largest organized world religion; conservation agencies such as the World Wide Fund for Nature (WWF); and action groups, including OneWorld, Oxfam, Rainforest Action Network, Greenpeace, and Amnesty International. Less formally organized, but important, international networks are those of universities, law firms, and sport federations. Some media have a transnational reach, such as the *Financial Times, International Herald Tribune, Newsweek,* and *The Economist.* Some international governance organizations run the globalized world's daily life, for example, the aviation union International Air Transport Association (IATA), the International Organization for Standardization (ISO), and the International Accounting Standards Board (IASB). Crucial for specific sectors are, for instance, the International Egg Commission, the Confederation of International Soft Drinks Associations, and the International Cremation Federation. The most influential transnational organization may be the WTO, and the most well-known and popular work of any transnational organization may be that of the International Olympic Committee.

Research

International academic thinking about transnational governance shows much variation, often reflecting underlying paradigms of political philosophy. One idealist view is that the world should strive for true global government, all the covenants and agreements being building blocks of that system. Another view, often called realist, is that states should continue to be the crucial elements of world order because, in part, they are a way to siphon off aggression and feed pride and identity. A liberal view proffers a world with a minimum of (international) governance and a maximum span of freedom to behave and move around the world as we please, with NGOs representing the critical voices. Marxist thinkers, and many of the conservation movements and social-consciousness groups, agree on advocating a transnational governance that strictly regulates business so as to ward off destruction, pollution, and gross social injustice.

The academic literature on transnational governance is immensely varied because forms of transnational governance have spread to virtually all domains of human activity. Some of the major issues of current academic debate have been:

- The growing global free market: To what extent should it be allowed to interfere with national policies and the protection of interests?
- The globalization of democracy: Should a particular form of government be standardized in strict rules and conditions, or should ample national and local variation be allowed?
- The position of transnational business: What are the demands and limits of corporate responsibility?
- The human rights framework: Is progress toward the development of a truly universal set of principles and practices apparent?

- The global environment: Who is responsible for safeguarding an environment that benefits both the world now and future generations?
- The position of NGOs: Should they gradually be bound to uniform standards and accountability, or even certification?

Among individual researchers, Marie-Laure Djelic and Kerstin Sahlin-Andersson gained prominence with the collection of articles they edited in 2006. The book's authors show that national regimes, which have long held sway over most arenas of political, economic, and social life, are being supplemented and challenged by the rise of a multitude of transnational institutions. NGOs, central bankers, multinational corporations, and others are developing a host of new international modes of regulation and governance. Rule-making has exploded everywhere. World-level organizations increasingly reorder traditional regulatory patterns.

International journalist Thomas Friedman argues in *Hot, Flat, and Crowded* (2008) that in the convergence of hot (global warming), flat (globalization) and crowded (population growth), the indispensable green revolution would be the largest innovation project in history. All nations are challenged by five major problems: growing demand, massive transfer of wealth, climate change, poverty, and accelerating loss of biodiversity.

German political philosopher Hans Kochler has, since the 1970s, been promoting the idea of a "dialogue of civilizations." In his thinking, human rights are the basis of the validity of international law. He questions the representative paradigm of democracy in international relations. World order, including the role and philosophical foundations of civilizations and their dialog, is founded on dialectic relationships between power and law. On this basis, he has suggested UN reforms and a comprehensive system of international criminal justice.

Joseph Nye, a prominent U.S. philosopher embraced by the administration of U.S. president Barack Obama, developed the concepts of asymmetrical and complex interdependence, and a focus on the civilian instruments of diplomacy, foreign aid, civic action, and economic reconstruction and development. He pioneered the notions of "soft power" and "smart power." While traditional international power relations have been generally based on coercion or payment, an alternative form of power is to attract and coopt adversaries so that they will want what you want. This approach, he argues, has huge benefits in saving money and lives.

Policies and Programs

Much of the fundamental debate on policies and programs pivots on Max Weber's distinction (in *Politics as a Vocation*, 1918) between the "ethics of principles" and "ethics of responsibility." Sources of moral and legal fundamentals are needed, such as those embedded in international law conventions and humanitarian convictions and are spread mainly by NGOs in the fields of human rights, environment, social justice, and progress. But the responsibility for developing actual policies demands negotiations about when and how to act, which is the remit of governments, military coalitions, interest groups, and others. In such policies, it is not so much the fundamentals that are at stake (most prominently, freedom) but the weighting of their relative pertinence. Free market or freedom from want? Free speech or freedom from discrimination? Free trade, also in weapons, or freedom from fear?

A number of factors restrict and define the parameters of the huge variety of initiatives. First, *transnational* is not the same as *global*. Transnational governance is a reflection of the diversity of power, in that some regions and countries are much more influential than others. These more influential countries are also the main venues of transnational technology, such as in weapons, engineering, science, conservation, and the Internet. Second, transnational governance may be "governance without government," but governments are indispensable for its realization. Governments have always engaged in transnational governance (trade, diplomacy, and military coalitions) and cannot do without it. What is called the increasing "scriptedness" of states is the reason why we now speak of failed states, but unfortunately some of the most damaging states were not failed at all (for example North Korea and Iraq under Saddam Hussein). The states that most jeopardize international relations and security are not so much the failed states but those that detract from international governance. Third, much of transnational governance is based on "soft" law but moves into the direction of hard law. Agreements tend to gradually attain the status of binding conventions or law, such as can be seen in EU regulations. Meanwhile, where "soft" law has become so global and so dominant, especially when flowing from the United States and Europe, it may in many cases be no less effective than hard law. Fourth, transnational governance has all the benefits and risks of an "old boys network." On the one hand, much of the dynamics is the same as that of governments: power struggle, alliances, elite adherence, and position over money. But in other aspects, transnational governance is quite different: groups and members can freely opt out, staff can leave and go to work in another field, and organizing is largely built on networks.

In a summary of such defining factors, social scientists Sebastian Botzem and Sigrid Quack (in their 2006 article in *Transnational Governance: Institutional Dynamics of Regulation*) present the maturing of the International Accounting Standards Committee, created in 1973 by nine countries, as a prototype for transnational governance. They observe:

> Standardization activities moved out of one area and into another. Actors were coming and going. Intergovernmental actors were pushed aside by professions, but with the shift towards capital market efficiency they came back again in their function as financial market regulators. Governments shifted from professional to market logic. The boundaries of the field were stretched in this or that direction depending on the evolution of interests and power interactions.

This description fits many other bodies of governance very aptly.

Among the major programs and international initiatives that are intended to foster transnational governance are:

- Trade, development and financial agreements, more specifically the regimes of the WTO, IMF, and World Bank
- International conventions and declarations on human rights, humanitarian law, refugee law, labor rights, and international criminal law
- Institutions to control war, major armed conflicts, the spread of weapons and international crime, and institutions that engage in the "responsibility to protect" endangered populations
- Globalizing initiatives in ethics, as related to, for instance, the biosphere, the technology of human biology, and the responsibility of the media
- International programs for education as a means to enhance civil society and world citizenship in balancing the demands of business, technology, cultural expression, and personal self-realization
- Programs for the conservation of nature and cultural heritage
- Programs fostering the cooperation of NGOs and business in recreation, tourism, the Olympics, international sports associations, and the like

The most obvious and direct manifestations of transnational governance are the various intergovernmental bodies that exist to structure the international relations of nations in both the political and economic arenas on a worldwide basis. The most prominent of these is the UN, which was founded in 1945 after World War II. In a way, it replaced the League of Nations, which was established after World War I under the auspices of U.S. president Woodrow Wilson. Ironically, the United States never joined the League because the U.S. Senate failed to ratify the treaty of which the league was a part, due largely to Republican opposition. The UN now counts 193 member states. These include virtually all recognized independent states in the world; the last states to join included North Korea in 1991, Switzerland in 2002, and Montenegro in 2006. Taiwan (Republic of China) is not a member, and the Holy See (Vatican) has observer status.

The UN budget is funded by its member states. Its major contributors are the United States (over 20 percent), Japan, Germany, the United Kingdom, and France; together, these five countries donate about 60 percent of the budget. The UN organization spans a wealth of administrative bodies. Central are the General Assembly, where each member state has one vote, and the Security Council, whose five permanent (China, France, Russia, the United Kingdom, and the United States) and ten alternating members decide on urgent issues of peace and security (see map, p. 551). The Economic and Social Council debates and decides on economic, social, development, and human rights issues that are then brought to the General Assembly for final approval. The UN's daily management rests with the Secretariat and the secretary-general.

Most of the UN subsidiary organs are quasi-independent. The Food and Agriculture Organization (FAO) leads international efforts to defeat hunger. Its Special Program for Food Security has the aim of halving the number of hungry (presently some 850 million) by 2015, as part of the Millennium Development Goals (MDGs). UNESCO has programs that cover education, the natural sciences, the social and human sciences, culture, and communication and information. Its projects focus on areas such as literacy, teacher training, the promotion of independent media, cultural history, and international cooperation in science. The UN International Children's Emergency Fund (UNICEF) provides long-term humanitarian and developmental assistance to children and mothers in developing countries. The organization also has a high profile in refugee assistance. The UN Development Fund for Women (UNIFEM), established in 1976 (much later than most UN bodies), promotes women's rights, political participation, and economic security. The UN Development Programme (UNDP) issues the annual Human Development Index (HDI), a comparative measure ranking countries by life expectancy, literacy, educational attainment, and gross domestic product (GDP) per capita. The WHO, Joint United Nations Programme on HIV/AIDS (UNAIDS), and the Global Fund to Fight AIDS, Tuberculosis and Malaria are the foremost international agents for remedying diseases. The UN Population Fund provides reproductive services, for which it has come under scrutiny and criticism by the George W. Bush administration in the United States and by the Vatican.

The UN struggles with the limitation of its effectiveness. The Security Council, charged to take action on urgent security issues, is often hindered from taking bold action in the face of conflicts between and within member states. UN peacekeeping deployments often are dwarfed by the armed conflicts they are charged to oversee. National sovereignty is both fundamental and obstructive to the UN because the state-level representation in this organization precludes identification with the plight of nations that are threatened within those states. In 2006, the concept Responsibility to Protect (R2P), initiated by Canada in 2001, was adopted by the UN Security Council as a basis for humanitarian intervention to stop genocide, war crimes, ethnic cleansing, and crimes against humanity (see GENOCIDE). R2P rules that if a state is unwilling or unable to carry out its responsibility, the international community must intervene by peaceful means, such as dialog, or with military force as a last resort. If implemented, R2P would come close to making the UN a body of transnational *government* rather than governance.

Although many observers question its efficacy, UNESCO's World Heritage program, begun in 1972, has adopted sites for the "protection of the world cultural and natural heritage," with the goals of encouraging the participation of the local population and international cooperation in conservation and encouraging states to establish management plans and set up reporting systems for the preservation of these sites. As of 2008, 878 sites were listed: 678 cultural, 174 natural, and 26 mixed properties, in 145 nations. The greatest number, 43 sites, is in Italy. The worldwide list includes Australia's Great Barrier Reef, Austria's Historic Centre of the City of Salzburg, Belgium's Grand-Place in Brussels, Bolivia's City of Potosí, Brazil's Jesuit Missions of the Guaranis, Cambodia's Angkor, and the Central African Republic's Manovo-Gounda National Park.

The IMF and World Bank Group are independent agencies within the UN framework. The IMF oversees the global financial system, attempts to stabilize international exchange rates, and offers loans to member states. The World Bank provides financial and technical assistance to developing countries to reduce poverty. Both organizations are criticized for adhering to free-market reform policies. Both organizations, however, remain popular with governments, both rich and poor, because they are a last resort for monetary security and basic development. In 2005, the IMF implemented a huge debt-relief program for the world's poorest countries (see DEVELOPMENT AID and INTERNATIONAL FINANCE).

Secretary-General Kofi Annan started a reform of the UN organization in 1997. The proposals included changing the five-state permanent membership of the Security Council (established in 1945) so as to reflect how the world has changed since 1945, but this did not materialize. The reform compromise resulted in, among other things, a Peacebuilding Commission, a Human Rights Council, major investments in the realization of the MDGs, and the adoption of the R2P (see HUMAN RIGHTS and PEACEMAKING AND PEACEBUILDING).

Another global intergovernmental organization is the G-20, which gathers finance ministers and central bank governors from twenty economies (the nineteen largest national economies plus the European Union). One of the most powerful, and perhaps most controversial, international governing bodies is the WTO, which came into being in 1995, succeeding the 1947 General Agreement on Tariffs and Trade (GATT). It has 153 members, representing more than 95 percent of total world trade. It deals with the rules of trade between nations, is responsible for negotiating and implementing new trade agreements, and is in charge of policing member countries' adherence. WTO rules are based on the principles of nondiscrimination (what applies to one country applies to all), reciprocity (agreements are favorable to all parties), and transparency (maximum openness on trade regulation). Rules are made binding by tariff commitments; in case of disagreement between member states, a WTO dispute settlement procedure can be called on. However, in specific circumstances governments may restrict or intervene in trade. The WTO has received a great deal of criticism; detractors argue that its tariff barriers favor rich countries and big companies, that the regulatory framework it imposes disregards labor rights, and that it is lacking in democratic transparency. The WTO responds that it has established a level of security and rule-enforced negotiations that is crucial for more marginal nations in the world economic system.

The International Red Cross and Red Crescent Movement is an international humanitarian movement with some 100 million volunteers worldwide. Founded in 1863, its twenty-five-member committee now has authority under international humanitarian law to protect the life and dignity of the victims of international and internal armed conflicts. In many countries, national chapters are tightly linked to the health-care system by providing emergency medical services.

Regional Summaries

By definition, many transnational organizations are transregional as well. They are among the most well-known organizations; however, in many areas regional organizations have so far proven more effective.

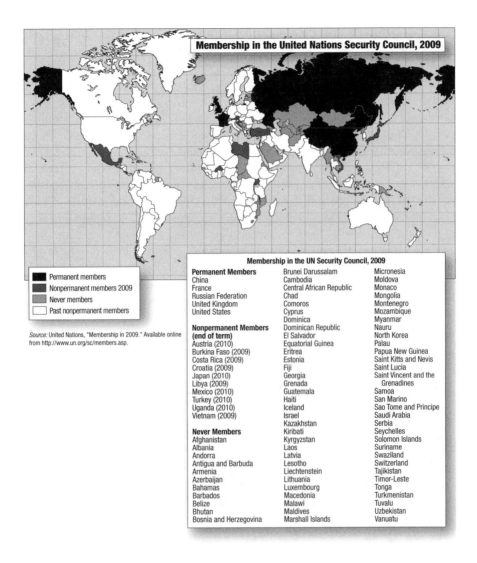

Membership in the United Nations Security Council, 2009

Source: United Nations, "Membership in 2009." Available online from http://www.un.org/sc/members.asp.

- Permanent members
- Nonpermanent members 2009
- Never members
- Past nonpermanent members

Membership in the UN Security Council, 2009

Permanent Members
China
France
Russian Federation
United Kingdom
United States

Nonpermanent Members (end of term)
Austria (2010)
Burkina Faso (2009)
Costa Rica (2009)
Croatia (2009)
Japan (2010)
Libya (2009)
Mexico (2010)
Turkey (2010)
Uganda (2010)
Vietnam (2009)

Never Members
Afghanistan
Albania
Andorra
Antigua and Barbuda
Armenia
Azerbaijan
Bahamas
Barbados
Belize
Bhutan
Bosnia and Herzegovina

Brunei Darussalam
Cambodia
Central African Republic
Chad
Comoros
Cyprus
Dominica
Dominican Republic
El Salvador
Equatorial Guinea
Eritrea
Estonia
Fiji
Georgia
Grenada
Guatemala
Haiti
Iceland
Israel
Kazakhstan
Kiribati
Kyrgyzstan
Laos
Latvia
Lesotho
Liechtenstein
Lithuania
Luxembourg
Macedonia
Malawi
Maldives
Marshall Islands

Micronesia
Moldova
Monaco
Mongolia
Montenegro
Mozambique
Myanmar
Nauru
North Korea
Palau
Papua New Guinea
Saint Kitts and Nevis
Saint Lucia
Saint Vincent and the Grenadines
Samoa
San Marino
Sao Tome and Principe
Saudi Arabia
Serbia
Seychelles
Solomon Islands
Suriname
Swaziland
Switzerland
Tajikistan
Timor-Leste
Tonga
Turkmenistan
Tuvalu
Uzbekistan
Vanuatu

The Americas

In the United States and Canada, civil governance has always been strong in associations of churches, antidiscrimination groups, the civil rights movement, and voluntary organizations. But as to truly international organizing and mobilizing for development, trade union freedom, the environment, and the like, this region has often proved weaker than Europe.

The Organization of American States (OAS) is the intergovernmental organization of the thirty-five independent states of the Americas. Established in 1948, it is the world's oldest regional organization. Its historic steps have included the creation of the Inter-American Commission on Human Rights (1959), the American Convention on Human Rights (1969), and the Inter-American Court of Human Rights (1979). The North American Free Trade

Agreement (NAFTA) is a trilateral trade bloc in North America created by the governments of the United States, Canada, and Mexico; it is the largest trade bloc in the world.

Of the organizations that link this region to other parts of the world, the North Atlantic Treaty Organization (NATO) and the Organisation for Economic Cooperation and Development (OECD) are perhaps the most important. NATO is a military alliance established in 1949, which now counts twenty-six member states in North America and Europe. It constitutes a system of collective defense whereby member states agree to mutual defense in response to an attack by any external party. The combined military spending of all NATO members constitutes over 70 percent of the world's defense spending. The OECD gathers thirty high-income states that accept the principles of representative democracy and free-market economy. It originated in 1948 as an organization to help administer the Marshall Plan for the reconstruction of Europe after World War II.

The countries of Latin America historically have strong intraregional ties because of its common languages (Spanish and Portuguese, which are linguistically very close). Also, nongovernmental organizing in Latin America began early in the history of the postcolonial continent. Many of the links with Europe go through Spain and Portugal, while relations with North America have varied considerably. For instance, at the 2009 OAS meeting in Trinidad and Tobago, the outright hostility toward the United States from left-wing leaders, such as those of Cuba and Venezuela, showed signs of ebbing, due directly to the change in presidential leadership from George W. Bush to Barack Obama, whose commitment to a more open diplomacy was apparent at the meeting. Latin American governments and individuals were active in the formative years of the UN and throughout the UN's establishment of its human rights and development initiatives. In particular, they have lobbied for placing socioeconomic and civil rights on an equal footing.

Mercosur (Mercado Común del Sur) is an agreement among Argentina, Brazil, Paraguay, and Uruguay founded in 1991. Its purpose is to promote free trade and the fluid movement of goods, people, and currency. Discussions have been underway for the inclusion of Venezuela. The Union of South American Nations (USAN), founded in 2008, is modeled on the European Union. It integrates two existing economic unions: Mercosur and the Andean Community (Bolivia, Colombia, Ecuador, and Peru). The Association of Caribbean States (ACS) comprises twenty-five states; its effectiveness so far has been limited.

Europe

Europe shows strong transnational cooperation, in particular among Western European states; it also has strong networks of NGOs. The NGO concept originated in Europe in the late eighteenth century in movements opposing the slave trade, torture, and religious oppression. By virtue of its colonial, commercial, religious, and cultural past, Western and central Europe have historically had more ties with other regions than any other continental group.

Transnational governance is also more relevant in this region than anywhere else because so many states (over fifty), languages, and political traditions exist in an area less than half the size of North America.

The Council of Europe, founded in 1949, has forty-seven member states, with a Committee of Ministers, a Parliamentary Assembly, and a European Court of Human Rights. The Commonwealth of Independent States (CIS) is a regional organization of former Soviet republics. CIS participates in UN peacekeeping forces and discourages its members from joining the European Union. For a discussion of the European Union and European Parliament, see Case Study—The European Union.

North Africa and the Middle East

The two factors that might have united this region—religion and oil—have proved to be the most divisive. Islam, which unites hundreds of millions in the region on the basis of the Quran, has produced denominations and groups that are often mutually competitive or hostile. Oil production has led to a multitude of strains, despite the existence of the Organization of Petroleum Exporting Countries (OPEC), which includes the six major oil-producing countries in the region. Political repression hampers all NGO development, and legal bodies are heavily dominated (and divided) by political-religious creeds.

The Arab League, formed in 1945, is the organization of Arab states in Southwest Asia and North and Northeast Africa. The league currently has twenty-two members. It has served as a forum for settling disputes among Arabs, promoting economic integration in shaping school curricula, advancing the role of women, promoting child welfare, and preserving Arab cultural heritage. The league's accomplishments have not equaled those of the European and American intergovernmental organizations.

Sub-Saharan Africa

Since the movements for independence from European rule begun in the 1960s, the region has had few effective lines of communications both within the continent and with the rest of the world. The African Union (AU) is a federation of all of Africa's states except Morocco; it was formed in 2001 as a successor to the Organization of African Unity (established in 1963). The AU has often shown limited effectiveness in protecting populations and in peacekeeping, and it has shied away from many of the major conflict areas on the continent. However, its Peace and Security Council, established in 2004, has been more actively involved in helping solve crises as in Darfur, Somalia, Côte d'Ivoire, and Comoros.

The Economic Community of West African States (ECOWAS), founded in 1975 to promote economic integration, is a regional group of fifteen West African countries. After minimal progress toward its economic goals, its treaty was revised in 1993 to make the collaboration less ambitious, less strict, and more adaptive to actual developments. In 2005, ECOWAS, the UN, and the

United States agreed that West African nations should form the vanguard of a stabilization force in Liberia.

Asia and the Pacific

No functioning overall international body of governance exists in this area. The two most populous countries in the world, China and India, show considerable variation in their approach to international and national governance. The Chinese government is reluctant to join international governance, as witnessed for example in its independent way of handling development aid, without tying it to conditions of human rights and democracy. China does, however, put a stamp on selected UN debates, such as on armed intervention. No truly independent domestic NGOs exist, and many international NGOs are not allowed to operate in China. On the other hand, India, which is not a permanent member of the UN Security Council, is eager to join international partnerships. It also has a strong civil society, with a great number of domestic and internationally liaised NGOs.

The Association of Southeast Asian Nations (ASEAN) is an economic organization of ten countries in Southeast Asia, formed in 1967. Its aims include the acceleration of economic growth, social progress, cultural development, the protection of the peace and stability of the region, and peaceful mediation. The Shanghai Cooperation Organization (SCO) is an intergovernmental mutual-security organization founded in 2001 by China, Kazakhstan, Kyrgyzstan, Russia, Tajikistan, and Uzbekistan. The SCO is primarily focused on protection from threats of terrorism, separatism, and extremism. All SCO members except China are also members of the Eurasian Economic Community. The Commonwealth of Nations, better known as the British Commonwealth, is wider than the continent but comprises mainly Asian member states. It is an intergovernmental organization of fifty-three independent states, most of them formerly parts of the British Empire. It works for democracy, human rights, good governance, the rule of law, and free trade.

In 2003, the Australian Senate proposed the creation of the Pacific Union (as a further development of the Pacific Islands Forum) through which a political and economic intergovernmental community would be developed, although as of June 2009 the union had not yet been established. The Pacific Plan (2005) of the Pacific Islands Forum was initiated by Australia, the Federated States of Micronesia, New Zealand, Papua New Guinea, and other islands of the region. Central to the plan are four pillars: economic growth, sustainable development, good governance, and security. As a "living document," the plan now forms the basis of ongoing regional cooperation and integration efforts.

Data

Table 1   Membership of Fifteen Intergovernmental Organizations, 2009

Country	Organization
Afghanistan	UN
Albania	UN, WTO, CoE, NATO
Algeria	UN, AU, AL
Andorra	UN, CoE
Angola	UN, WTO, AU
Antigua and Barbuda	UN, WTO, OAS, BC
Argentina	UN, WTO, G-20, OAS, USAN
Armenia	UN, WTO, CoE, CIS
Australia	UN, WTO, OECD, BC, G-20
Austria	UN, WTO, OECD, EU, CoE
Azerbaijan	UN, CoE, CIS
Bahama	UN, OAS, BC
Bahrain	UN, WTO, AL
Bangladesh	UN, WTO, BC
Barbados	UN, WTO, OAS, BC
Belarus	UN, CIS
Belgium	UN, WTO, OECD, EU, CoE, NATO
Belize	UN, WTO, OAS, BC
Benin	UN, WTO, AU, ECOWAS
Bhutan	UN
Bolivia	UN, WTO, OAS, USAN
Bosnia and Herzegovina	UN, CoE
Botswana	UN, WTO, AU, BC
Brazil	UN, WTO, G-20, OAS, USAN
Brunei	UN, WTO
Bulgaria	UN, WTO, EU, CoE, NATO
Burkina Faso	UN, WTO, AU, ECOWAS
Burundi	UN, WTO, AU
Cambodia	UN, WTO, ASEAN
Cameroon	UN, WTO, AU, ECOWAS, BC
Canada	UN, WTO, G-20, OECD, OAS, BC
Cape Verde	UN, WTO, AU, ECOWAS
Central African Republic	UN, WTO, AU,
Chad	UN, WTO, AU, ECOWAS
Chile	UN, WTO, OAS, USAN
China	UN, WTO, G-20
Colombia	UN, WTO, OAS, USAN
Comoros	UN, AU, AL
Congo, Democratic Republic of	UN, WTO, AU
Congo, Republic of	UN, WTO, AU
Costa Rica	UN, WTO, OAS
Côte d'Ivoire	UN, WTO, AU, ECOWAS
Croatia	UN, WTO, CoE, NATO
Cuba	UN, WTO, OAS#
Cyprus	UN, WTO, EU, CoE, BC
Czech Republic	UN, WTO, OECD, EU, CoE, NATO
Denmark	UN, WTO, OECD, EU, CoE, NATO
Djibouti	UN, WTO, AU, AL
Dominica	UN, WTO, OAS, BC
Dominican Republic	UN, WTO, OAS

Table 1 (Continued)

Country	Organization
Ecuador	UN, WTO, OAS, USAN
Egypt	UN, WTO, AU, AL
El Salvador	UN, WTO, OAS
Equatorial Guinea	UN, AU
Eritrea	UN, AU
Estonia	UN, WTO, EU, CoE, NATO
Ethiopia	UN, WTO, AU
Fiji	UN, WTO, BC#
Finland	UN, WTO, OECD, EU, CoE
France	UN, WTO, G-20, OECD, EU, CoE, NATO
Gabon	UN, WTO, AU
Gambia	UN, WTO, AU, ECOWAS, BC
Georgia	UN, WTO, CoE, CIS
Germany	UN, WTO, G-20, OECD, EU, CoE, NATO
Ghana	UN, WTO, AU, ECOWAS
Greece	UN, WTO, OECD, EU, CoE, NATO, BC
Grenada	UN, WTO, OAS, BC
Guatemala	UN, WTO, OAS
Guinea	UN, WTO, AU#, ECOWAS
Guinea-Bissau	UN, WTO, AU, ECOWAS
Guyana	UN, WTO, OAS, USAN, BC
Haiti	UN, WTO, OAS
Honduras	UN, WTO, OAS
Hong Kong	WTO
Hungary	UN, WTO, OECD, EU, CoE, NATO
Iceland	UN, WTO, OECD, EU, CoE, NATO
India	UN, WTO, G-20, BC
Indonesia	UN, WTO, G-20, ASEAN
Iran	UN
Iraq	UN, AL
Ireland	UN, WTO, OECD, EU, CoE
Israel	UN, WTO
Italy	UN, WTO, G-20, OECD, EU, CoE, NATO
Jamaica	UN, WTO, OAS, BC
Japan	UN, WTO, G-20, OECD, ASEAN#, NATO
Jordan	UN, WTO, AL
Kazakhstan	UN, CIS
Kenya	UN, WTO, AU, BC
Kiribati	UN, BC
Korea, Democratic People's Republic of	UN
Korea, Republic of	UN, WTO, G-20, OECD
Kuwait	UN, WTO, AL
Kyrgyzstan	UN, WTO, CIS
Lao People's Democratic Republic	UN, ASEAN
Latvia	UN, WTO, EU, CoE, NATO
Lebanon	UN, AL
Lesotho	UN, WTO, AU, BC
Liberia	UN, AU, ECOWAS
Libya	UN, WTO, AU, AL
Liechtenstein	UN, WTO, CoE
Lithuania	UN, WTO, EU, CoE, NATO
Luxembourg	UN, WTO, OECD, EU, CoE, NATO
Macau	WTO

Table 1 (Continued)

Country	Organization
Macedonia	UN, WTO, CoE
Madagascar	UN, WTO, AU#,
Malawi	UN, WTO, AU, BC
Malaysia	UN, WTO, ASEAN, BC
Maldives	UN, WTO, AU, BC
Mali	UN, WTO, AU, ECOWAS
Malta	UN, WTO, EU, CoE, BC
Marshall Islands	UN
Mauritania	UN, WTO, AU#, AL
Mauritius	UN, WTO, AU, BC
Mexico	UN, WTO, G-20, OECD, OAS
Micronesia	UN
Moldova	UN, WTO, CoE, CIS
Monaco	UN, CoE
Mongolia	UN, WTO
Montenegro	UN, CoE
Morocco	UN, WTO, AL
Mozambique	UN, WTO, AU, BC
Myanmar (Burma)	UN, WTO, ASEAN
Namibia	UN, WTO, AU, BC
Nauru	UN, BC
Nepal	UN, WTO
Netherlands	UN, WTO, OECD, EU, CoE, NATO
New Zealand	UN, WTO, OECD, BC
Nicaragua	UN, WTO, OAS
Niger	UN, WTO, AU, ECOWAS
Nigeria	UN, WTO, AU, ECOWAS, BC
Norway	UN, WTO, OECD, CoE, NATO
Oman	UN, WTO, AL
Pakistan	UN, WTO, BC
Palau	UN
Palestinian Authority	AL
Panama	UN, WTO, OAS
Papua New Guinea	UN, WTO, BC
Paraguay	UN, WTO, OAS, USAN
Peru	UN, WTO, OAS, USAN
Philippines	UN, WTO, ASEAN
Poland	UN, WTO, OECD, EU, CoE, NATO
Portugal	UN, WTO, OECD, EU, CoE, NATO
Qatar	UN, WTO, AL
Romania	UN, WTO, EU, CoE, NATO
Russia	UN, WTO, G-20, CoE, CIS
Rwanda	UN, WTO, AU
St. Kitts and Nevis	UN, WTO, OAS, BC
St. Lucia	UN, WTO, OAS, BC
St. Vincent and the Grenadines	UN, WTO, OAS, BC
Samoa	UN, BC
San Marino	UN, CoE
São Tome and Principe	UN, AU
Saudi Arabia	UN, WTO, G-20, AL
Senegal	UN, WTO, AU, ECOWAS
Serbia	UN, CoE
Seychelles	UN, AU, BC

Table 1 (Continued)

Country	Organization
Sierra Leone	UN, WTO, AU, ECOWAS, BC
Singapore	UN, WTO, ASEAN, BC
Slovakia	UN, WTO, OECD, EU, CoE, NATO
Slovenia	UN, WTO, EU, CoE, NATO
Solomon Islands	UN, WTO, BC
Somalia	UN, AU, AL
South Africa	UN, WTO, G-20, AU, BC
Spain	UN, WTO, OECD, EU, CoE, NATO
Sri Lanka	UN, WTO, BC
Sudan	UN, AU, AL
Suriname	UN, WTO, OAS, USAN,
Swaziland	UN, WTO, AU, ECOWAS, BC
Sweden	UN, WTO, OECD, EU, CoE
Switzerland	UN, WTO, OECD, CoE
Syria	UN, AL
Taiwan	WTO
Tajikistan	UN, CIS
Tanzania	UN, WTO, AU, BC
Thailand	UN, WTO, ASEAN
Timor Leste	UN
Togo	UN, WTO, AU, ECOWAS
Tonga	UN, WTO, BC
Trinidad and Tobago	UN, WTO, OAS, BC
Tunisia	UN, WTO, AU, AL
Turkey	UN, WTO, G-20, OECD, CoE, NATO
Turkmenistan	UN, CIS
Tuvalu	UN, BC
Uganda	UN, WTO, AU, BC
Ukraine	UN, WTO,
United Arab Emirates	UN, WTO, AL
United Kingdom	UN, WTO, G-20, OECD, EU, CoE, NATO, BC
United States	UN, WTO, G-20, OECD, OAS, NATO
Uruguay	UN, WTO, OAS, USAN
Uzbekistan	UN, CIS
Vanuatu	UN, BC
Venezuela	UN, WTO, OAS, USAN
Vietnam	UN, WTO, ASEAN
Western Sahara	AU
Yemen	UN, AL
Zambia	UN, WTO, AU, BC
Zimbabwe	UN, WTO, AU

Source: Data from the Web sites of the listed intergovernmental organizations.

Note: #, suspended as of early 2009. The G-20 is a group of nineteen major national economies (Argentina, Australia, Brazil, Canada, China, France, Germany, India, Indonesia, Italy, Japan, Mexico, Russia, Saudi Arabia, South Africa, South Korea, Turkey, the United Kingdom, and the United States) plus the European Union. AL, Arab League; ASEAN, Association of Southeast Asian Nations; AU, African Union; BC, (British) Commonwealth of Nations; CIS, Commonwealth of Independent States; CoE, Council of Europe; ECOWAS, Economic Community of West African States; EU, European Union; G-20, Group of 20; NATO, North Atlantic Treaty Organization; OAS, Organization of American States; OECD, Organisation for Economic Co-operation and Development; UN, United Nations; USAN, Union of South American Nations; WTO, World Trade Organization (includes the European Union).

Case Study—The European Union

The formative stages of European integration, which resulted in the European Union (EU), were the treaties of Paris (1951), Rome (1957), and Maastricht (1992). The EU now has twenty-seven member countries, a total population of some 500 million, a GDP (corrected for purchasing power) of over $15 trillion (about 30 percent of gross world product), and a per capita annual income of just over $30,000. By all accounts, it is a rich region. It is also labeled by some experts as the most complex organization in the world. The union has both intergovernmental and supranational characteristics. Some decisions are based on agreement among all the member states. But once adopted, such decisions become supranational law and do not need unanimity among all national governments or the agreement of new member states. The EU presidency rotates every six months among all the members in a kind of alphabetical order. For example, the Czech Republic and Sweden preside in 2009, and Belgium and Spain in 2010.

Among the EU bodies are the European Commission, a group of executives for policies and programs; the European Parliament, with 785 members and national representation proportional to the population size of the member states elected for five-year terms; the Council of the European Union, where the heads of state and government meet; the European Court of Justice; and the European Central Bank. An added complication is that another European organization, the Council of Europe, exists that is quite similar. It also has an executive body, a council of ministers, a parliament (the Parliamentary Assembly) and a court (the European Court of Human Rights). The EU headquarters are in Brussels, Belgium, but the European Parliament convenes both in Brussels and, for one week per month, in Strasbourg, France; the EU Court is in Luxembourg. The Council of Europe's parliament and its European Court of Human Rights also meet in Strasbourg.

The EU has various levels of transnational governance. The organization promotes a single market and a standardized system of laws. In principle, freedom of movement of individuals and goods is allowed within the union, but often this is subject to special temporary clauses. For its wide array of policies, the EU has devised a system of three pillars: (1) agriculture and other economic issues, (2) the Common Foreign and Security Policy, and (3) the police and judiciary. The EU issues regulations, which are binding and override domestic laws, and directives, which require certain results without stipulating how they should be achieved. Directives cover a wide range of issues: antidiscrimination; intellectual property; nature conservation; and also specifications on pharmaceuticals, food supplements, and batteries. All these provisions are subject to varying procedures that emanate from the EU Commission and Parliament, making EU governance extremely complex. When the European Constitution was voted on in 2005, most of the electorate in a number of countries apparently did not realize that the document included thousands of pages of management rules, processes, and clauses. (A majority of the French and Dutch voted against the constitution, so it did not pass.)

For those living in the territory of the EU, the benefits of the organization are considerable. The (near) single market generates economic development. Countries such as Spain, Portugal, and Ireland have seen spectacular economic progress after joining the EU. The conditions required of the member states greatly reduced corruption, particularly for new members. Other benefits include the legal protections and positive action for minorities and the economically less developed areas of the EU, the spread of the euro (the common currency), and the exchange of university and college students.

Among the weaknesses of the EU is the lack of incentive for members to cooperate in military action and armed humanitarian intervention. The EU was conspicuously hesitant, or absent, in the heat of the war in the former Yugoslavia. According to widespread popular feeling, the EU also has a tendency to overregulate; for example, it has regulations on the size and shape of bananas. Further, the EU is an enormous bloc that sets many restrictions on immigration, even though immigrants are deemed to be a necessary part of the economy of many EU countries. The EU apparatus makes it hard for asylum seekers to seek refuge in any European country.

The irony of the EU, which, according to objective standards, can be considered possibly the best example of efficient cooperation between states, is that it is not popular. While on one continent citizens mostly experience a sense of pride to be in the United States of America under one elected president, on another continent many citizens of individual countries in the EU rebel against its centralized authority; in fact, many are leery of, or even scared by, the very thought of a United States of Europe.

Biographical Sketches

Hugo de Groot was a jurist born in 1583 in the Dutch Republic. In his work, he defended such principles as the sea is international territory, in war the principles of natural law are binding on all nations, and rules for a "just" war exist. His distinction of *ius ad bellum* (right to engage in war) and the *ius in bello* (justice in the conduct of war) are still used today.

Gro Brundtland, a former prime minister of Norway, served as director of the WHO and special envoy on climate change for the United Nations. In 2007, she was one of the founding members of The Elders, a group of world leaders who address global issues, which also includes Nelson Mandela, Kofi Annan, Jimmy Carter, Mary Robinson, and Muhammad Yunus and has South African archbishop Desmond Tutu as chair.

Mohamed El Baradei is director general of the International Atomic Energy Agency (IAEA). El Baradei and the IAEA were jointly awarded the 2005 Nobel Peace Prize. He is both lauded and criticized for his position that Iran's nuclear potential demands dialog, not threats.

Ban Ki Moon is secretary-general of the United Nations; his term began in 2007 when he succeeded Kofi Annan. Before this, he was foreign minister of South Korea. Although he is generally considered to be more of a bureaucrat than a visionary, he has taken some important steps on such issues as global warming, the war in Darfur, and the armed intervention in Afghanistan.

Franklin Delano Roosevelt was the only U.S. president to have served more than two terms (from 1933 to 1945). During the Great Depression, he created the New Deal to provide economic relief, recovery, and reform. In January 1941, in his Four Freedoms speech, he listed as fundamental freedom of expression, freedom of religion, freedom from want, and freedom from fear. These were adapted into the Charter of the United Nations.

Joseph Stiglitz is an American economist and former vice president of the World Bank. He criticizes the management of globalization by institutions such as IMF and World Bank, which often do not seriously foster development. He founded the Initiative for Policy Dialogue (IPD), a think tank on international development. He sees successful development as conditional on people's having essential information, adequate markets, and open institutions.

Directory

Centre for Global Governance, Houghton Street, London, WC2A 2AE, United Kingdom. Telephone: +44 20 7955 7434; email: f.c.holland@lse.ac.uk; Web: http://www.lse.ac.uk/depts/global.
International research institution focusing on research and analysis concerning global governance; based at the London School of Economics.

Centre for International Governance Innovation, 57 Erb Street W., Waterloo, Ont., Canada N2L 6C2. Telephone: +1 519 885 2444; email: via Web site; Web: http://www.cigionline.org.
Nonpartisan think tank that conducts research, issues publications, and makes policy recommendations.

Global Governance Project, Institute for Environmental Studies, Vrije Universiteit Amsterdam, De Boelelaan 1087, 1081 HV Amsterdam, Netherlands. Email: hilko.blok @ivm.vu.nl; Web: http://www.glogov.org.
Research group consisting of twelve European institutions and focusing on advancing the knowledge and understanding of the mechanisms of global governance, including new actors and institutions involved in it.

Institute for Research and Debate on Governance, 38 Rue Saint-Sabin, 75011 Paris, France. Telephone: 33 1 43 14 75 86; email: martin.vielajus@institut-gouvernance .org; Web: www.institut-gouvernance.org/index_en.html.
Multidisciplinary think tank bringing a range of actors—academic, policy and national administrative personnel, civil society groups, and traditional and religious leaders—together to address issues relating to good governance at all levels.

United Nations Institute for Training and Research, Palais des Nations, CH-1211 Geneva 10, Switzerland. Telephone: +41 22 917 8400; email: info@unitar.org; Web: http://www.unitar.org/home.
UN center of expertise with a large array of international academic and institutional partners.

United Nations Intellectual History Project, City University of New York, 365 Fifth Avenue, Suite 5203, New York, N.Y. 10016-4309. Telephone: (212) 817 1920; email: unhistory@gc.cuny.edu; Web: http://www.unhistory.org.
Research program of books and oral histories related to the origins and evolution of economic and social ideas within the world organization and their impact on international thinking and action.

Uppsala University Department of Peace and Conflict Research, Box 514, SE 751 20 Uppsala, Sweden. Telephone: +46 18 471 0000; email: info@pcr.uu.se; Web: http://www.pcr.uu.se.
Located at one of the oldest universities with global study programs, the department offers courses and academic expertise.

Further Research

Books

Dilling, Olaf, Martin Herberg, and Gerd Winter, eds. *Responsible Business: Self-Governance and Law in Transnational Economic Transactions.* London: Hart Publishing, 2008.

Dingwerth, Klaus. *The New Transnationalism: Transnational Governance and Democratic Legitimacy.* London: Palgrave Macmillan, 2007.

Djelic, Marie-Laure, and Kerstin Sahlin-Andersson, eds. *Transnational Governance: Institutional Dynamics of Regulation.* Cambridge, UK: Cambridge University Press, 2006.

Friedman, Thomas. *Hot, Flat and Crowded: Why We Need a Green Revolution—and How It Can Renew America.* New York: Farrar, Straus and Giroux, 2005.

Garrett, Laurie, et al. *Global Governance and Transnational Issues.* New York: Norton, 2002.

Gawin, Dariusz, and Piotr Glinski, eds. *Civil Society in the Making.* Warsaw: IFiS Publishers, 2006.

Graz, Jean-Christophe, and Andreas Nölke, eds. *Transnational Private Governance and Its Limits.* London: Routledge, 2008.

Grotius, Hugo. *The Laws of War and Peace.* 1625. Whitefish, Mont.: Kessinger, 2004.

Karns, Margaret P., and Karen A. Mingst. *International Organizations: The Politics and Processes of Global Governance.* Boulder, Colo.: Lynne Rienner, 2004.

Köchler, Hans. *Democracy and the International Rule of Law.* Vienna/New York: Springer, 1995.

Nye, Joseph. *The Powers to Lead.* New York: Oxford University Press, 2008.

Overbeek, Henk, Bastiaan van Apeldoorn, and Andreas Nölke, eds. *The Transnational Politics of Corporate Governance Regulation.* Abingdon, UK: Routledge, 2007.

Peterson, John, and Michael Shackleton, eds. *The Institutions of the European Union.* 2d ed. Oxford: Oxford University Press, 2006.

Rifkin, Jeremy. *The European Dream: How Europe's Vision of the Future Is Quietly Eclipsing the American Dream.* Los Angeles: Tarcher, 2004.

Tarrow, Sidney. *The New Transnational Activism.* New York: Cambridge University Press, 2005.

Ward, Thomas, ed. *Development, Social Justice, and Civil Society: An Introduction to the Political Economy of NGOs.* London: Paragon House, 2005.

Weiss, Thomas G., and Sam Daws, eds. *The Oxford Handbook on the United Nations.* New York: Oxford University Press, 2007.

Weiss, Thomas G., and Ramesh Thakur, eds. *Global Governance and the UN: An Unfinished Journey.* Bloomington: Indiana University Press, forthcoming.

Zeitlin, J., and O. Pochet, eds. *The Open Method of Co-ordination in Action: The European Employment and Social Inclusion Strategies.* Brussels: Peter Lang, 2005.

Articles and Reports

Bohman, James. "Constitution Making and Democratic Innovation: The European Union and Transnational Governance." *European Journal of Political Theory* 3, no. 3 (2004): 315–337.

Brown, L. David, and Vanessa Timmer. "Civil Society Actors as Catalysts for Transnational Social Learning." *Voluntas, International Journal of Voluntary and Nonprofit Organizations* 17, no. 1 (2006): 1–16.

Eriksen, Erik Oddvar, and John Erik Fossum. "Europe at a Crossroads: Government or Transnational Governance?" ARENA Working Paper no. 02/35. Available at: http://www.arena.uio.no/publications/wp02_35.htm.

Nickel, Rainer. "Participatory Transnational Governance." European University Institute Department of Law Working Paper LAW No. 2005/20. Available at: http://www.iue.it/PUB/LawWPs/law2005-20.pdf.

"Roundtable—A Multiplicity of Actors and Transnational Governance." Free Library. Available at: http://www.thefreelibrary.com/Roundtable+-+a+multiplicity+of+actors+and+transnational+governance.-a0177100801.

Sandholtz, Wayne, and Alec Stone Sweet. "Law, Politics, and International Governance." In *The Politics of International Law,* ed. Christian Reus-Smit, 238–271. Cambridge, UK: Cambridge University Press, 2004. Available at: http://works.bepress.com/cgi/viewcontent.cgi?article=1018&context=alec_stone_sweet.

Web Sites

African Union
http://www.africa-union.org

Association of Southeast Asian Nations
http://www.aseansec.org

The Elders
http://www.theelders.org

European Parliament
http://www.europarl.europa.eu

European Union
http://europa.eu

G-20
http://www.g20.org

International Chamber of Commerce
http://www.iccwbo.org

International Committee of the Red Cross
http://www.icrc.org/eng

League of Arab States
http://www.arableagueonline.org/las/index.jsp

Millennium Development Goals
http://www.undp.org/mdg/basics.shtml

Organization of American States
http://www.oas.org

United Nations
http://www.un.org/english

World Trade Organization
http://www.wto.org

World Wide Fund for Nature (WWF; formerly the World Wildlife Fund)
http://www.worldwildlife.org

Document

1. Preamble to the United Nations Charter, and Excerpts from Chapter IV: The General Assembly and Chapter V: The Security Council

The full text is available at http://www.un.org/en/documents/charter/index.shtml

Extracts

Preamble

WE THE PEOPLES OF THE UNITED NATIONS DETERMINED

- to save succeeding generations from the scourge of war, which twice in our lifetime has brought untold sorrow to mankind, and
- to reaffirm faith in fundamental human rights, in the dignity and worth of the human person, in the equal rights of men and women and of nations large and small, and
- to establish conditions under which justice and respect for the obligations arising from treaties and other sources of international law can be maintained, and
- to promote social progress and better standards of life in larger freedom,

AND FOR THESE ENDS

- to practice tolerance and live together in peace with one another as good neighbours, and
- to unite our strength to maintain international peace and security, and
- to ensure, by the acceptance of principles and the institution of methods, that armed force shall not be used, save in the common interest, and
- to employ international machinery for the promotion of the economic and social advancement of all peoples,

HAVE RESOLVED TO COMBINE OUR EFFORTS TO ACCOMPLISH THESE AIMS

Accordingly, our respective Governments, through representatives assembled in the city of San Francisco, who have exhibited their full powers found to be in good and due form, have agreed to the present Charter of the United Nations and do hereby establish an international organization to be known as the United Nations.

Chapter IV: The General Assembly

COMPOSITION

Article 9

1. The General Assembly shall consist of all the Members of the United Nations.

2. Each Member shall have not more than five representatives in the General Assembly.

FUNCTIONS and POWERS

Article 10

The General Assembly may discuss any questions or any matters within the scope of the present Charter or relating to the powers and functions of any organs provided for in the present Charter, and, except as provided in Article 12, may make recommendations to the Members of the United Nations or to the Security Council or to both on any such questions or matters.

Article 11

1. The General Assembly may consider the general principles of co-operation in the maintenance of international peace and security, including the principles governing disarmament and the regulation of armaments, and may make recommendations with regard to such principles to the Members or to the Security Council or to both.

2. The General Assembly may discuss any questions relating to the maintenance of international peace and security brought before it by any Member of the United Nations, or by the Security Council, or by a state which is not a Member of the United Nations in accordance with Article 35, paragraph 2, and, except as provided in Article 12, may make recommendations with regard to any such questions to the state or states concerned or to the Security Council or to both. Any such question on which action is necessary shall be referred to the Security Council by the General Assembly either before or after discussion.

3. The General Assembly may call the attention of the Security Council to situations which are likely to endanger international peace and security.

4. The powers of the General Assembly set forth in this Article shall not limit the general scope of Article 10.

Article 12

1. While the Security Council is exercising in respect of any dispute or situation the functions assigned to it in the present Charter, the General Assembly shall not make any recommendation with regard to that dispute or situation unless the Security Council so requests.

2. The Secretary-General, with the consent of the Security Council, shall notify the General Assembly at each session of any matters relative to the maintenance of international peace and security which are being dealt with by the Security Council and shall similarly notify the General Assembly, or the Members of the United Nations if the General Assembly is not in session, immediately the Security Council ceases to deal with such matters. . . .

Chapter V: The Security Council

COMPOSITION

Article 23

1. The Security Council shall consist of fifteen Members of the United Nations. The Republic of China, France, the Union of Soviet Socialist Republics, the United Kingdom of Great Britain and Northern Ireland, and the United States of America shall be permanent members of the Security Council. The General Assembly shall elect ten other Members of the United Nations to be non-permanent members of the Security Council, due regard being specially paid, in the first instance to the contribution of Members of the United Nations to the maintenance of international peace and security and to the other purposes of the Organization, and also to equitable geographical distribution.

2. The non-permanent members of the Security Council shall be elected for a term of two years. In the first election of the non-permanent members after the increase of the membership of the Security Council from eleven to fifteen, two of the four additional members shall be chosen for a term of one year. A retiring member shall not be eligible for immediate re-election.

3. Each member of the Security Council shall have one representative.

FUNCTIONS and POWERS

Article 24

1. In order to ensure prompt and effective action by the United Nations, its Members confer on the Security Council primary responsibility for the maintenance of international peace and security, and agree that in carrying out its duties under this responsibility the Security Council acts on their behalf.

2. In discharging these duties the Security Council shall act in accordance with the Purposes and Principles of the United Nations. The specific powers granted to the Security Council for the discharge of these duties are laid down in Chapters VI, VII, VIII, and XII.

3. The Security Council shall submit annual and, when necessary, special reports to the General Assembly for its consideration.

Article 25

The Members of the United Nations agree to accept and carry out the decisions of the Security Council in accordance with the present Charter.

Article 26

In order to promote the establishment and maintenance of international peace and security with the least diversion for armaments of the world's human and economic resources, the Security Council shall be responsible for formulating, with the assistance of the Military Staff Committee referred to in Article 47, plans to be submitted to the Members of the United Nations for the establishment of a system for the regulation of armaments.

VOTING

Article 27

1. Each member of the Security Council shall have one vote.

2. Decisions of the Security Council on procedural matters shall be made by an affirmative vote of nine members.

3. Decisions of the Security Council on all other matters shall be made by an affirmative vote of nine members including the concurring votes of the permanent members; provided that, in decisions under Chapter VI, and under paragraph 3 of Article 52, a party to a dispute shall abstain from voting.

PROCEDURE

Article 28

1. The Security Council shall be so organized as to be able to function continuously. Each member of the Security Council shall for this purpose be represented at all times at the seat of the Organization.

2. The Security Council shall hold periodic meetings at which each of its members may, if it so desires, be represented by a member of the government or by some other specially designated representative.

3. The Security Council may hold meetings at such places other than the seat of the Organization as in its judgment will best facilitate its work.

Article 29

The Security Council may establish such subsidiary organs as it deems necessary for the performance of its functions.

Article 30

The Security Council shall adopt its own rules of procedure, including the method of selecting its President.

Article 31

Any Member of the United Nations which is not a member of the Security Council may participate, without vote, in the discussion of any question brought before the Security Council whenever the latter considers that the interests of that Member are specially affected.

WAR CRIMES

Timothy L. H. McCormack

Whether killings and rapes in Darfur, attacks on civilians in Iraq, or the use of child soldiers in Africa, daily atrocities committed by the armed forces in ongoing conflicts today confirm a widespread view that war is by nature inhumane and uncontrollable and that war is no place for law. Despite this view, the notion of imposing constraints on the waging of war has existed in every legal, cultural, and religious tradition throughout the history of warfare. The existence of normative legal standards is a fundamental basis for the objective evaluation of human behavior and for the possibility of future trials of the people responsible for atrocities. Further, the principle of individual criminal liability for violations of international law in times of war has been extended to additional categories of international crime, including crimes against humanity and genocide, committed within or beyond the confines of warfare.

Since the early 1990s, a proliferation of new international criminal courts and tribunals have been set up to try those alleged to have committed war crimes, crimes against humanity, and acts of genocide. War crimes trials are now occurring at a greater rate than at any time since the end of World War II, and these trials are accompanied by a growing global expectation that those responsible for atrocities should not escape justice but should be brought to trial. Recent media coverage of the capture of Radovan Karadjic and his transfer to The Hague, for example, is evidence of this growing expectation. Intriguingly, however, countries choosing to establish their own domestic war crimes trial processes are expected to do so fairly. For instance, the U.S. Military Commission process established at Guantánamo Bay, Cuba, to prosecute enemy combatants in the U.S. "war on terror" has been subject to intense international criticism because of its fundamental lack of fair-trial guarantees.

Historical Background and Development

The contemporary international law of armed conflict is sometimes simplistically assumed to have originated in the medieval codes of chivalry for dueling, which had strict limitations on the circumstances and the manner in which opponents could be struck. Western history does include notions of human dignity and respect for the military opposition, and some excellent research by Theodor Meron has analyzed some of these notions in Shakespeare's literature, notably in *Henry V,* which reflects the ideology and practice of warfare between France and England at that time. Constraints on the waging of war, however, are not confined to Western culture, and they certainly predate medieval times. The earliest extant writings on the conduct of war are by the Chinese warrior Sun Tzu and date to the sixth century BC. In *The Art of War,* Sun Tzu exhorts constraint by combatants in the treatment of civilian populations and prisoners captured by opposing forces. Similarly, the texts of all the major religious traditions and the historical records of all the major civilizations reflect two related concepts: the conduct of war is subject to limitations, and the actions of individuals in excess of those limitations are subject to legal sanction.

By the middle of the nineteenth century, a number of countries had developed military codes of conduct. In the United States, for example, President Abraham Lincoln promulgated the Lieber Code—named after its author, the Harvard jurist Francis Lieber—to apply to government forces during the Civil War. The impetus for an international agreement on constraints on the waging of war is inextricably linked to the formation of the International Committee of the Red Cross (ICRC). In 1859, Henri Dunant, a Swiss merchant banker, happened across the aftermath of the Battle of Solferino, part of the French campaign to help liberate Italy from Austro-Hungarian occupation. One day of fighting had left 40,000 men dead and an additional 40,000 to subsequently die from their wounds in the ensuing weeks. Dunant was appalled that so many wounded had been left on the battlefield without medical treatment, food, or blankets. After rallying the citizens of the nearby village of Castiglione to attend to as many of the wounded as possible, Dunant wrote about his observations and experiences in *Un Souvenir de Solferino* and distributed copies throughout Europe to support his call for the establishment of an independent, impartial, humanitarian relief organization to provide assistance to victims of war. His vision was realized in 1863 with the establishment of the ICRC.

In 1864, the ICRC's inaugural year, the international community of states adopted the first multilateral treaty on the conduct of war—the Convention for the Amelioration of the Condition of the Wounded in Armies in the Field. This convention was followed in 1868 by the St. Petersburg Declaration banning the use of exploding bullets and by a succession of treaties and declarations emanating from the two international peace conferences held at The Hague in 1899 and 1907. By the outbreak of World War I, an identifiable international law of war was well established (see INTERNATIONAL LAW). Each of the peace treaties imposed on the defeated Central Powers of World War I contained clauses for the establishment of Allied tribunals for the prosecution of alleged war criminals. Although these tribunals failed to materialize for political reasons, the principle of holding individuals accountable for alleged violations of the international law of war was established. Germany and Turkey conducted trials of their own nationals under the watchful eye of Allied observers.

Although the international law of war was bolstered during the interwar years—notably by the adoption of the 1925 Geneva Protocol prohibiting chemical and biological warfare and the 1929 Geneva Convention Relative to the Treatment of Prisoners of War—the experiences of World War II proved to be the single most significant catalyst for its further development. First, in relation to the development of the law itself, the unprecedented level of civilian casualties and the devastation caused by the war prompted a fundamental review of existing law. The four Geneva Conventions of 1949, which have come to represent the cornerstones of the contemporary international law of war, are the direct result of this review. Second, the ruthless attempt by the Nazis to destroy Europe's Jewish population by implementing their "final solution" and the extent of the aggressive wars of invasion and brutal occupations by the Nazis in Europe and the Japanese in the Pacific Theater of World War II so shocked the world that international trials for war crimes and crimes against humanity were demanded. The conduct of the trials by the Nuremberg and Tokyo tribunals established the precedent of individual accountability for violations of international criminal law. The current momentum for international criminal justice would not exist without the precedent of the post–World War II trials for war crimes (see GENOCIDE).

The promise of Nuremberg and Tokyo for the establishment of an effective international criminal law regime has taken decades to begin to materialize. In the meantime, international criminal law has continued to develop and has been occasionally enforced at the national level. Several states have conducted trials for alleged war crimes and crimes against humanity pursuant to domestic criminal law. The Israeli trial of Adolf Eichmann and the U.S. court-martial of Lieutenant William Calley remain the exemplars of different kinds of national war crimes trials.

Adolf Eichmann was a senior Nazi leader who headed up the Jewish Office of the Gestapo and who was responsible for implementing the "final solution." The Israeli court trying Eichmann relied on the principle of universality as well as the fact that his victims were primarily Jewish as the dual bases of jurisdiction in the case. The District Court of Jerusalem convicted Eichmann of offenses under Israel's Nazis and Nazi Collaborators (Punishment) Law and sentenced him to death. The Eichmann trial remains the leading precedent for trying non-nationals for war crimes and crimes against humanity on the basis of universal jurisdiction.

The trial of Lieutenant William Calley for his involvement in the massacre of 504 unarmed civilians in the South Vietnamese hamlet of My Lai remains a leading example of the domestic trial of a member of a country's own military forces. This particular case attracted intense media scrutiny because, according to Leslie Green in *Superior Orders in National and International Law,* although the United States prosecuted a number of other servicemen for various offenses in the conduct of the Vietnam War, "all the crimes alleged to have been committed in Vietnam pale into insignificance when compared with the extent of the killings perpetrated at My Lai."

Calley was convicted in 1972 by court-martial of three counts of premeditated murder and one count of assault with intent to commit murder. He was sentenced to hard labor for the term of his natural life, dismissed from military service, and stripped of all pay and allowances. Although painful for the U.S. Army to face the reality of the My Lai atrocities perpetrated by its members, the court-martial and appeal process adduced and tested the available evidence, Calley was convicted and sentenced accordingly, the story of the massacre was faithfully recorded in the official reports series of the judgments of the U.S. Army Court of Military Review, and the lessons from the incident can be used repeatedly in the training of soldiers in the United States and elsewhere.

With the more recent establishment of the ad hoc International Criminal Tribunals for the Former Yugoslavia and for Rwanda, as well as the entry into force of the Rome Statute for the International Criminal Court (ICC), the development of international criminal law has experienced a reawakening that is beginning to express itself in an increased commitment to trials at the national and international levels (see map, p. 578).

Current Status

Much of the current research on the law on war crimes focuses on the purpose of war crimes trials, the efficacy of these trials, and alternative approaches to justice (including truth commissions and civil action for monetary compensation); the scope of the application of the law and the problems associated with the strict legal criteria for applying its rules; and the development of the law itself, such as exposing gaps in it, pushing for new developments, or clarifying the content of specific rules, particularly as they relate to more effective enforcement of the law. Major policies and programs include education and training in the law of armed conflict to increase understanding of and respect for the law, along with criminal tribunals themselves, both in international and national jurisdictions. In addition, institution building in international criminal law appears to have inspired some states to take a more proactive approach to the prosecution of international crimes under their domestic legal systems. A number of programs also exist for the collection and preservation of evidence for future trials of alleged war criminals as well as for the identification of war crimes suspects and the monitoring of their whereabouts.

Research

The international law of armed conflict, also known as international humanitarian law, regulates conduct in two distinct categories. The first deals with minimum standards of protection for victims of armed conflict: wounded combatants, prisoners of war, and civilians. The principal legal instruments covering this category are the four Geneva Conventions of 1949 (see Document 1) and the bulk of the provisions of the two Additional Protocols of 1977 (see Documents 2 and 3). The second category of the law regulates the means and methods of warfare, including, for example, prohibitions on certain categories of weapons, rules about targeting, the protection of cultural property, the protection of civilian populations, and a prohibition on using starvation as a tactic. The principal legal instruments covering this category of rules emanate from the 1899 and 1907 international peace conferences at The Hague, some provisions of Additional Protocol I of 1977, and a succession of arms control and disarmament treaties.

The existence of war is a necessary precondition for the commission of a war crime. This may seem obvious, but in a strict legal sense this requirement can prove to be problematic. A substantial amount of research has been done on the issue of how to determine the precise nature of any specific conflict. The term *state of war* has a strict legal meaning, describing a situation in which a formal declaration of war between two or more sovereign nation-states has been made. Because most conflicts do not involve formal declarations of war, the preferred legal approach is to require the existence of an armed conflict. The Geneva Conventions of 1949, for example, apply to armed conflicts between two or more states irrespective of a formal declaration of war by any of the parties to the conflict. Although the term *war crime* has remained in use (preferred over a much clumsier term, such as *armed conflict crime*), the term *law of war* has been replaced by *law of armed conflict* to label the body of rules that govern the conduct of war, the violation of which constitutes a war crime. The ICRC and the academic community use the alternative *international humanitarian law* to emphasize the motivation behind the law, which is to alleviate the suffering of people affected by conflict.

The question of the existence of an armed conflict, however, is still not as straightforward as might be expected. International humanitarian law distinguishes between *international armed conflicts* and *noninternational armed conflicts*. The bulk of the provisions in the Geneva Conventions apply only to international armed conflicts, which the conventions define as armed conflict between two or more nation-states. Currently, only a small number of armed conflicts in the world fall clearly within this definition. These include the conflict between Ethiopia and Eritrea over their land border and between India and Pakistan over Kashmir. The overwhelming majority of the world's conflicts do not meet this definition of *international armed conflict* because they are waged within the territory of a single state, sometimes between the government and rebel forces and on other occasions between rival rebel forces. Such conflicts include those in Algeria, Colombia, Liberia, Mozambique, Myanmar, the Philippines, Sierra Leone, the Solomon Islands, Somalia, Sri Lanka, and Sudan. Also, the conflicts between insurgencies and the Afghani and Iraqi governments—both supported by U.S.-led coalitions—fall into this category; they are not considered international armed conflicts within the definition of that term in the Geneva Conventions.

A more complex example, one that brings the analysis of war crimes into new territory, is the U.S.-led "global war on terror." The George W. Bush administration argued that its armed conflict with Al Qaeda was neither an international armed conflict (Al Qaeda is not a sovereign independent nation state) nor a noninternational armed conflict (the war against Al Qaeda is not limited to the physical territory of one state, but will be pursued wherever Al Qaeda is present) but an "armed conflict of an international character," falling in a gap in the law between the two recognized forms of armed conflict. The rationale for the administration's argument seemed to be prompted by a desire to deny legal rights to detained Al Qaeda fighters. However, in 2006, the U.S. Supreme Court rejected that argument in *Hamdan v. Rumsfeld* (548 U.S. 547). In its decision, the court decided that no gap in the law exists. Instead, the judges found that *minimum* legal rights apply to combatants in any armed conflict, including to Al Qaeda fighters.

Some disparity exists between the list of acts considered war crimes in international armed conflicts and those that are criminalized in noninternational armed conflicts. The difficulties inherent in characterizing a particular conflict at a particular time can be seen in the decisions of the International Criminal Tribunal for the Former Yugoslavia, particularly the tribunal's examination of the Bosnian conflict in determining whether the Serbian government's support for the Bosnian Serb militias, which were operating in Bosnia-Herzegovina, rendered the conflict international (see INTERNATIONAL CRIMINAL JUSTICE).

A number of scholars have criticized the overemphasis on the characterization of conflicts at the expense, on occasion, of punishment for particular conduct. Steven Ratner has exposed many of the inconsistencies and disparities in the distinction between types of conflicts, which he describes as "the schizophrenias of international criminal law" (a phrase he used as the title of a 1998 article in the *Texas International Law Journal*). Imagine the perception of injustice when two victims suffer the same atrocity but only one experience is considered a war crime because one victim suffered in the context of an international armed conflict while the other victim suffered the same fate in the context of a noninternational armed conflict. Although the definition of *war crimes* in Article 8 of the 1998 Rome Statute for the ICC redresses the disparity of coverage between international and noninternational armed conflicts more extensively than any other international instrument to date, the statute still maintains the distinction and, with it, a lingering unequal level of regulation between the two types of armed conflict.

The distinction between international and noninternational armed conflicts is not the only sticking point regarding the determination of the existence of an armed conflict. Some situations of internal strife, widespread rioting, and civil disturbance may involve the use of armed force, but may not necessarily reach a threshold of violence between rival forces high enough to constitute an armed conflict. The precise threshold for a situation to be considered an armed conflict is not always easy to identify, and often some ambiguity is present in the characterization of the situation for the purposes of identifying the applicable international legal standards. For example, despite the volatility and violence in Aceh, in Ambon, in Kalimantan, in Irian Jaya, and on Java, the Indonesian government argues that none of these situations represents an armed conflict. All of them involve armed clashes, rioting, and violence, but are more appropriately regulated by the more general international human rights law—which does not limit itself to armed conflict—than by international humanitarian law (see HUMAN RIGHTS).

In addition to issues about the scope of application of international humanitarian law, extensive recent research has focused on the development of the content of the law. Given the modalities of many contemporary conflicts, the precise demarcation between entitlement to civilian protection and forfeiture of that protection has come under increasing scrutiny. The law traditionally grants protective status (that is, immunity from military attack) to all civilians. This noncombatant immunity is forfeited whenever a civilian "takes a direct part in hostilities"; so a civilian who takes a weapon and fires at the enemy is unquestionably taking a direct part in hostilities and so can legitimately be targeted. However, the increasing use of civilian contractors to undertake military support roles has introduced some uncertainties into the clear identification of the demarcation. The ICRC has completed a four-year study of this complex issue, but at the time of this writing, the final report of the study is yet to be released.

Scholars such as Helen Durham, Kelly Dawn Askin, Christine Chinkin, and Judith Gardam have also exposed the past lack of willingness to prosecute sexual offenses as war crimes. Other scholars, including Cherif Bassiouni and Jordan Paust, have argued that rape and sexual violence have been recognized as war crimes for more than a hundred years. The paucity of trials for such offenses, however, despite the longevity of the prohibitions, only reinforces feminist arguments about a tendency to overlook—or at least not take sufficiently seriously—gender-specific atrocities in postconflict trials. Chinkin and Gardam have called for a new protocol to the Geneva Conventions focusing exclusively on increased protection for women in armed conflict. Critics of such a new protocol argue that the existing law is adequate to cover these concerns and provides sufficient protection to women; the real problem is a lack of observance of the existing law and a lack of systematic enforcement when the law is violated. Irrespective of this debate, the definitions of *war crimes* and *crimes against humanity* in the Rome Statute include a more extensive list of sexual offenses than any previous international legal instrument, a development that is directly attributable to the successful efforts of feminist scholars and activists. The brutality of sexual atrocities in the Balkans in the early 1990s, particularly the establishment of Serb rape camps for the forcible impregnation of Muslim women to produce ethnic Serb offspring, led to overwhelming support for the arguments of women's groups in the course of negotiations on the Rome Statute.

Arms control and disarmament are aspects of the legal regulation of war that everyone agrees require the almost constant negotiation of new treaties. Technological developments ensure that international humanitarian law will almost always be engaged in catching up because new categories of weapons will require new conventions. The first clear exception to this trend occurred in 1995–1996, with the adoption of an international agreement to ban blinding laser weapons before the technology had been deployed on the battlefield. The conclusion of negotiations for prohibitions on chemical weapons and antipersonnel land mines were much more protracted and followed decades of devastation caused by both categories of weapons. The most recent arms control treaty to be negotiated involves a prohibition on cluster munitions. The motivation for the negotiation of this new treaty has been the deleterious impact on the civilian population where clusters have been used in residential or agricultural areas and the deaths and serious physical injuries caused by submunitions that explode after hostilities have ceased.

Policies and Programs

The Geneva Conventions of 1949 explicitly acknowledge that if war breaks out, a much greater chance of respecting the law of armed conflict exists if the combatants specifically, as well as civilian populations generally, know the law beforehand. Consequently, the ICRC has a program for disseminating such information. ICRC delegates, many of them former military officers, are currently involved in training programs and seminars with national militaries and representatives from national Red Cross and Red Crescent societies around the world. Organizations such as the Asia Pacific Centre for Military Law (a collaborative initiative of the Melbourne Law School and the Australian Defence Force Legal Service) in Australia and the International Institute for International Humanitarian Law in Sanremo, Italy, regularly run training programs for military officers around the world in an attempt to raise the level of understanding of and respect for the laws of armed conflict.

Unfortunately, when war does break out international humanitarian law is all too often disregarded. Even though uncertainties exist in the law, the overwhelming majority of atrocities perpetrated in the course of armed conflict represent clear violations of well-established legal rules. Why then do so few of the people responsible for war crimes come to trial? States cannot claim a lack of legal capacity, or jurisdiction, to explain their failure to prosecute. Under international law, states can try alleged war crimes on any of the following bases:

- Territory—the acts occurred on the physical territory of the prosecuting state.
- Nationality—the acts were perpetrated outside the prosecuting state's territory but by a national (a citizen or otherwise legal resident) of the prosecuting state.
- Passive personality—the acts occurred outside the territory of the prosecuting state and were perpetrated by a non-national, but the victims of the acts were nationals of the prosecuting state.
- Universality—the acts were committed outside the territory of the prosecuting state and were perpetrated by a non-national against non-nationals of the prosecuting state, but because the acts constitute crimes against the whole of humanity, any state is free to prosecute them.

Universal jurisdiction, the most extensive of these standards, is the basis on which Spain requested the extradition from the United Kingdom of Augusto Pinochet in 1998 for alleged acts of torture committed in Chile and also the basis on which the House of Lords twice agreed that the charges against Pinochet constituted "extraditable offences." That is, they were offenses for which Pinochet could have been tried in British courts if the charges had been brought against him there. Many people were surprised that Pinochet, as a former head of state, could be tried in foreign courts for acts allegedly committed in his own country against his own nationals, but the reality is that the principle of universal jurisdiction for the prosecution of war crimes has lain largely dormant since the adoption of the Geneva Conventions of 1949. The Pinochet case shows that the failure to try war crimes has nothing to do with a lack of legal capacity but with the lack of political will to investigate and to prosecute.

The experience of the Nuremberg and Tokyo tribunals raised global expectations that those responsible for attacking, invading, and occupying many countries in Europe and in the Asia Pacific region; for attempting to annihilate the Jews as well as other minority groups, including homosexuals, Jehovah's Witnesses, and the Romany (or Gypsies); and for failing to stop the brutal mistreatment of prisoners of war and of civilian populations in occupied countries would be brought to justice. Although only twenty-one Germans were tried at Nuremberg, thousands of others were tried either by Allied war crimes tribunals or under the domestic laws of a number of different states (see map, p. 578). The Federal Republic of Germany tried more than 90,000 defendants for involvement with the Nazis. Many other states tried former Nazis and collaborators on one of the four bases of jurisdiction. This experience was repeated regarding actions by the Japanese military in the Pacific Theater of the war. Only twenty-eight Japanese defendants were prosecuted in Tokyo, but literally thousands were prosecuted by national military tribunals. Australia, for example, prosecuted more than eight hundred Japanese defendants in over three hundred war crimes trials, all conducted under Australian domestic law.

Many of the trials of German defendants were facilitated by the contributions of historians and investigators and by the relentless pursuit of Nazi criminals by international organizations. The Simon Wiesenthal Center is one of the foremost organizations with a dedicated program for the pursuit of Nazi war criminals. A number of governments also maintain war crimes investigation units to minimize the opportunities for former war criminals to conceal their past and enjoy sanctuary in their post–World War II adopted countries. These various entities have made crucial contributions to the identification of witnesses, the preservation of evidence, and the maintenance of pressure on states to initiate proceedings. More than sixty years after the start of World War II, the number of Nazi officials still alive and in good health is steadily dwindling, and trials of them are few. The trials that have been held established important precedents in the countries that conducted them. A number of senior Nazi officials, however, have managed to successfully evade justice because of a lack of political will to institute proceedings against them.

Until recently, the willingness of some states to try former Nazis has not been matched by a commitment to try their own troops for serious breaches of discipline during deployment or to investigate alleged war criminals during conflicts since World War II. While, for example, U.S. military trials have been conducted against those allegedly responsible for war crimes in Abu Ghraib prison and in Haditha in Iraq, the criminal investigations in both situations have been criticized for failing to extend up the chain of command to include the prosecution of any relatively senior military (or political) officers. In these cases, the U.S. military justice system has been involved in these trials. In contrast, evidence suggests that the Sudanese military have been complicit in the Janjah-weed militia attacks in Darfur, and Khartoum shows no intention of bringing those responsible to account. Trials of senior officials from discredited political regimes seem to be the only situations, other than alleged atrocities from World War II, that have consistently resulted in national judicial proceedings. The Pinochet case, however, has revolutionized thinking about the possibilities of national trial processes. Suddenly, demands for the trials of the people responsible for atrocities wherever they occur are more relentless and vociferous than ever before.

That all nations of the world will demonstrate a new willingness to investigate and prosecute those responsible for war crimes, crimes against humanity, and genocide is naïve, but pressure is mounting on states to take more seriously their responsibilities for the enforcement of international criminal law. The new ICC will try individuals only if a state with a claim to jurisdiction (on the basis of the nationality of the accused or the territory of the alleged offense) is either "unwilling or genuinely unable" to do so itself. Perhaps the greatest contribution of the ICC—before it has undertaken even its first trial—is its role as a catalyst for states to use their own national criminal processes more extensively than in the past. Many states (including Australia, Canada, Germany, New Zealand, Norway, the United Kingdom, and South Africa) that are signatories to the Rome Statute have already implemented comprehensive domestic criminal legislation to cover all the crimes within the ICC's statute. The motivation may well be ignoble—to ensure the supremacy of national jurisdiction over that of the ICC—but if the consequence of this circumvention is that states take more seriously the national enforcement of international criminal law, the ICC will have made a profound contribution to the efficacy of the law. The Pinochet proceedings sent a clear message to Chile and to other states to take seriously the international crimes committed on their territories or by their nationals. For states to claim a commitment to the ideals of international criminal justice in the absence of a willingness to investigate and prosecute (or extradite) those suspected of committing war crimes or crimes against humanity in other conflicts will become more difficult.

Regional Summaries

North America

The United States prefers to deport alleged war criminals that have settled in the United States rather than to try them under U.S. law. In recent years, a number of former Nazis have been extradited from the United States to face trial in other countries. The United States has appointed an ambassador-at-large for war crimes and also has an extremely active Office of Special Investigations for War Crimes. U.S. service personnel alleged to have committed war crimes or crimes against humanity abroad are routinely tried by specially constituted military tribunals under U.S. law.

The military commissions at Guantánamo Bay, Cuba, where the United States military has detained "enemy combatants" captured or seized during its

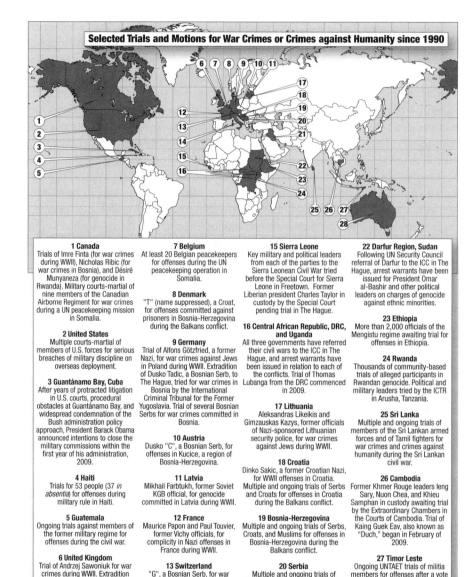

Selected Trials and Motions for War Crimes or Crimes against Humanity since 1990

1 Canada
Trials of Imre Finta (for war crimes during WWII), Nicholas Ribic (for war crimes in Bosnia), and Désiré Munyaneza (for genocide in Rwanda). Military courts-martial of nine members of the Canadian Airborne Regiment for war crimes during a UN peacekeeping mission in Somalia.

2 United States
Multiple courts-martial of members of U.S. forces for serious breaches of military discipline on overseas deployment.

3 Guantánamo Bay, Cuba
After years of protracted litigation in U.S. courts, procedural obstacles at Guantánamo Bay, and widespread condemnation of the Bush administration policy approach, President Barack Obama announced intentions to close the military commissions within the first year of his administration, 2009.

4 Haiti
Trials for 53 people (37 *in absentia*) for offenses during military rule in Haiti.

5 Guatemala
Ongoing trials against members of the former military regime for offenses during the civil war.

6 United Kingdom
Trial of Andrzej Sawoniuk for war crimes during WWII. Extradition proceedings against Augusto Pinochet for trial in Spain for acts of torture in Chile in the 1970s. Military courts-martial of U.K. army members for mistreatment of detainees in Iraq.

7 Belgium
At least 20 Belgian peacekeepers for offenses during the UN peacekeeping operation in Somalia.

8 Denmark
"T" (name suppressed), a Croat, for offenses committed against prisoners in Bosnia-Herzegovina during the Balkans conflict.

9 Germany
Trial of Alfons Götzfried, a former Nazi, for war crimes against Jews in Poland during WWII. Extradition of Dusko Tadic, a Bosnian Serb, to The Hague, tried for war crimes in Bosnia by the International Criminal Tribunal for the Former Yugoslavia. Trial of several Bosnian Serbs for war crimes committed in Bosnia.

10 Austria
Dusko "C", a Bosnian Serb, for offenses in Kucice, a region of Bosnia-Herzegovina.

11 Latvia
Mikhail Farbtukh, former Soviet KGB official, for genocide committed in Latvia during WWII.

12 France
Maurice Papon and Paul Touvier, former Vichy officials, for complicity in Nazi offenses in France during WWII.

13 Switzerland
"G", a Bosnian Serb, for war crimes committed against Bosnian Muslims in the Balkans conflict.

14 Italy
Trials of Erich Priebke, Max Josef Milde, and Michael Seifert for war crimes committed during WWII.

15 Sierra Leone
Key military and political leaders from each of the parties to the Sierra Leonean Civil War tried before the Special Court for Sierra Leone in Freetown. Former Liberian president Charles Taylor in custody by the Special Court pending trial in The Hague.

16 Central African Republic, DRC, and Uganda
All three governments have referred their civil wars to the ICC in The Hague, and arrest warrants have been issued in relation to each of the conflicts. Trial of Thomas Lubanga from the DRC commenced in 2009.

17 Lithuania
Aleksandras Likeikis and Gimzauskas Kazys, former officials of Nazi-sponsored Lithuanian security police, for war crimes against Jews during WWII.

18 Croatia
Dinko Sakic, a former Croatian Nazi, for WWII offenses in Croatia. Multiple and ongoing trials of Serbs and Croats for offenses in Croatia during the Balkans conflict.

19 Bosnia-Herzegovina
Multiple and ongoing trials of Serbs, Croats, and Muslims for offenses in Bosnia-Herzegovina during the Balkans conflict.

20 Serbia
Multiple and ongoing trials of Muslims and Serbs for offenses in Serbia during the Balkans conflict.

21 Iraq
Trial of Saddam Hussein and other political military leaders from his regime before the Iraqi Special Tribune.

22 Darfur Region, Sudan
Following UN Security Council referral of Darfur to the ICC in The Hague, arrest warrants have been issued for President Omar al-Bashir and other political leaders on charges of genocide against ethnic minorities.

23 Ethiopia
More than 2,000 officials of the Mengistu regime awaiting trial for offenses in Ethiopia.

24 Rwanda
Thousands of community-based trials of alleged participants in Rwandan genocide. Political and military leaders tried by the ICTR in Arusha, Tanzania.

25 Sri Lanka
Multiple and ongoing trials of members of the Sri Lankan armed forces and of Tamil fighters for war crimes and crimes against humanity during the Sri Lankan civil war.

26 Cambodia
Former Khmer Rouge leaders Ieng Sary, Nuon Chea, and Khieu Samphan in custody awaiting trial by the Extraordinary Chambers in the Courts of Cambodia. Trial of Kaing Guek Eav, also known as "Duch," began in February of 2009.

27 Timor Leste
Ongoing UNTAET trials of militia members for offenses after a vote for independence.

28 Australia
Ivan Polyukhovich, Mikael Berezowsky, and Heinrich Wagner, former Nazis, for WWII offenses in Europe.

Source: Timothy L.H. McCormack

Note: DRC, Democratic Republic of Congo; ICC, International Criminal Court; ICTR, International Criminal Tribunal for Rwanda; WWII, World War II.

prosecution of the "war on terror," have been subjected to sustained criticism for their lack of political independence and their use of offenses unknown in the laws of war. An example of this is the trial of the Australian David Hicks, the first detainee to be subjected to the military commission process in Guantánamo Bay. Hicks was captured by the Northern Alliance in Kandahar,

Afghanistan, late in 2001 after he had trained with and prepared himself to fight with Al Qaeda against the coalition forces, and he was subsequently transferred to Guantánamo. The charge leveled against David Hicks—that he took up arms against the United States and its allies—is not and never has been a war crime. The fact that the U.S. Military Commissions Act of 2006 labels this offence a "violation of the laws of war" does not alter its status in international law. The military commissions have also been criticized repeatedly for their failure to maintain the minimum standards of a fair trial that exist in U.S. domestic law and also in the U.S. military court-martial system; for example, due-process guarantees are lacking—in particular, evidence obtained both by torture and from hearsay can be admitted in trial proceedings. Critics have consistently observed that such evidence could not be admitted in trial proceedings before either U.S. civilian courts or U.S. military courts-martial.

Canada has passed extensive legislation on war crimes, crimes against humanity, and genocide. On the basis of these laws, Canada has instituted criminal proceedings against former Nazis and, more recently, against Nicholas Ribich, a Canadian national of Serb descent, who fought with the Bosnian Serb militias during the North Atlantic Treaty Organization (NATO) air strikes in 1995 in Bosnia-Herzegovina. In the mid-1990s, Canada also tried several members of its own military for offenses committed during their deployment to the UN peacekeeping operation in Somalia. Accepting that such breaches of military discipline had occurred was painful for Canadians, and the experience resulted in the disbanding of the Canadian Airborne Regiment, a unit with a previously proud and untarnished history.

Latin America

Much of Latin America has been subject to armed conflicts, military coups, dictatorships, and extensive human rights abuses. The most recent national trials for war crimes or crimes against humanity have occurred in Haiti. Following a transition from military to democratic civilian rule in 1995, trials were instituted for gross human rights violations, including torture, forced disappearances, and mass killings (although several of those trials have been conducted *in absentia,* with the convicted defendants not yet in custody to serve out their sentences).

Other states in the region that have also moved from military to civilian rule have adopted blanket amnesties for past wrongs as a means of focusing on the future. In Guatemala, for example, the Constitutional Court ruled in 2005 that a 1996 amnesty law applied to all offenses, including alleged massacres, and so terminated a major war crimes trial against sixteen senior military figures for an alleged atrocity committed during the civil war in that country.

In Chile, Augusto Pinochet was made a senator for life and granted amnesty for the many human rights atrocities committed during his rule in the 1970s. Spain's request for Pinochet's extradition from the United Kingdom to face trial placed a great deal of political pressure on Chile to revisit its commitment to amnesties for past international crimes. Although Chile reversed Pinochet's amnesty for life, the general died before he was brought to justice.

Argentina was, for many years after World War II, a haven for Nazis attempting to avoid justice. In recent years, it has been more willing to extradite these individuals, and a number have faced trial abroad as a consequence. Argentina's own national trials of some of its senior military officers for atrocities perpetrated throughout the *Guerra Sucia* (or Dirty War) set an important precedent in Latin America.

Europe

Trials of former Nazis and Nazi collaborators have been held recently in Croatia, France, Germany, and Italy, but it is unlikely that there will be many more such trials arising from the events of World War II. The number of perpetrators of wartime atrocities is dwindling rapidly. Latvia, for example, requested the extradition of Konrads Kalejs from Australia to face trial for involvement with the Nazis, but Kalejs died in Melbourne at the age of eighty-eight before extradition proceedings were completed. Hungary has requested extradition of Charles Zentai from Australia to face a charge of murder of a young Jewish boy in Budapest during World War II. Zentai is contesting the extradition proceedings and, because of his advanced age (eighty-six years at the time of writing), may also escape justice for his alleged crimes.

The Balkan states of Bosnia-Herzegovina, Croatia, and Serbia have conducted trials for war crimes and crimes against humanity committed during the conflicts that erupted during the breakup of Yugoslavia. The International Criminal Tribunal for the Former Yugoslavia at The Hague has been subjected to a completion strategy imposed by the UN Security Council. Under the strategy, the tribunal is precluded from issuing any new indictments and is required to complete all trials and appeals within the next few years. The arrest of Radovan Karadzic and his transfer to The Hague leaves only two indicted war criminals at large: the Bosnian Serb General Ratko Mladić and the Croatian Serb leader Goran Hadzić. The trials of any other suspected war criminals from the Balkans conflicts will have to occur in national courts and will probably continue for some years.

Other European states have tried suspected war criminals from contemporary conflicts when those suspects have attempted to immigrate without disclosing their wartime involvement in conflicts elsewhere (see IMMIGRATION). In addition, Belgium and Italy have tried members of their own military forces for offenses committed against civilians while on peacekeeping deployments in Somalia in 1992–1993.

The International Court of Justice in The Hague delivered an important decision in 2002 in favor of the Democratic Republic of the Congo (DRC; a Belgian colony from 1908 to 1960) against Belgium following the issuance of an arrest warrant in Belgium for the then-serving DRC foreign minister to face trial for various international crimes perpetrated in the DRC (see Case Study—Belgian Arrest Warrant Case).

Middle East

Israel has tried—in addition to Nazi Adolf Eichmann— John Demjanjuk in 1987 for alleged atrocities against Jews during World War II. The Demjanjuk trial was difficult for many Israelis, and the outcome was controversial because the accused was acquitted due to lack of witnesses able to positively identify him. Israel also tried Jewish collaborators—*kapos,* or concentration camp guards—in trials that fueled national feelings of anger and betrayal against those convicted.

One relatively recent controversy involved a decision by Belgium's highest court in 2003 that Ariel Sharon, then prime minister of Israel, could be the subject of an extradition request once his term as prime minister ended. Sharon was wanted for his alleged failure as then Israeli defense minister to prevent the Lebanese Christian Phalangist atrocities against Palestinians in the Beirut refugee camps of Sabra and Shatila in 1982 during Israel's occupation of the city. Following the court decision, the government of Belgium amended its war crimes legislation to require some connection between Belgium and the non-national subject of any arrest warrant (a requirement satisfied in relation to the arrest warrant for the DRC foreign minister because the DRC was a former colony of Belgium).

On March 29, 2006, the UN Security Council adopted Resolution 1664 authorizing the establishment of a special international criminal tribunal to try those allegedly responsible for the assassination of former Lebanese prime minister Rafik Hariri. At the time of this writing, the tribunal has yet to issue any arrest warrants in relation to the case and trial proceedings still seem unlikely for some time as the investigation continues.

In Baghdad, the Iraqi High Tribunal has been conducting trials since 2004 against Saddam Hussein and his senior officials for alleged crimes against humanity perpetrated during the former dictator's regime. The trial of Hussein himself has been heavily criticized by many professional legal associations and human rights organizations for alleged political interference by the Iraqi government in the judicial proceedings (one judge was removed from the case for allegedly treating Hussein with too much respect, for example) and for the lack of security for the defense lawyers involved in the trial (one lawyer was assassinated, and others were subjected to death threats and harassment throughout the course of the trial). The trial was also clouded by the perception that the overriding objective was to gain a quick conviction followed by Hussein's execution, which did occur in 2006.

Sub-Saharan Africa

No other region of the world is riddled with as many recent and ongoing war crimes and crimes against humanity as sub-Saharan Africa. From Liberia to Somalia and from the Darfur region of Sudan to Zimbabwe, many states have suffered atrocious international crimes. Many in the international humanitarian community have expressed profound discouragement at the developed world's demonstrated lack of commitment to assisting Africa because it deems the extent and intensity of the conflicts sweeping the continent too overwhelming.

Although Sudan is not a party to the Rome Statute for the ICC, the UN Security Council adopted resolution 1593 in 2006 to refer the situation in Darfur to the prosecutor of the ICC, Luis Moreno Ocampo. After conducting extensive investigations into the situation in Darfur, Ocampo issued indictments against two senior Sudanese government officials, including Ahmad Harun, the then foreign minister. More recently, Ocampo has increased political pressure on Khartoum by announcing his intention to seek judicial approval to issue an international arrest warrant for Omar al-Bashir, the president of Sudan. Ocampo alleges that the Sudanese government is responsible for a campaign of genocide, war crimes, and crimes against humanity on the indigenous ethnic minorities of the Darfur region. Ocampo's decision has been controversial because of delicate international negotiations for a peaceful settlement to the Darfur conflict, but Ocampo claims that he has evidence against al-Bashir and that his job as prosecutor is to act on that evidence.

Trials for war crimes and crimes against humanity have been conducted in a number of states, but significant challenges remain. Rwanda still holds tens of thousands of prisoners awaiting trial for suspected involvement in the genocide against the Tutsis in 1994. Ethiopia still holds more than 2,000 officials of the deposed Mengistu regime pending trial. In both cases, individual suspects have been imprisoned for years. In South Africa, discussion is ongoing about the extent to which amnesties ought to be granted to the perpetrators of apartheid-era atrocities, including those who confessed to their actions in testimony to the Truth and Reconciliation Commission that was established in 1995.

Sierra Leone requested assistance from the international community to prosecute atrocities committed throughout its civil war. The UN Security Council helped leaders of the country to establish the Special Court for Sierra Leone, a hybrid international/national tribunal with international and Sierra Leonean judges, prosecutors, defense lawyers, and registry officials and using a mixture of international and Sierra Leonean domestic criminal law. The Special Court has conducted its key trials of senior leaders of each of the parties to the civil war in Freetown, the capital; however, the trial of former Liberian leader Charles Taylor for his alleged involvement in the Sierra Leonean conflict is occurring in The Hague. Security concerns about conducting the trial in Freetown have resulted in an offer from the ICC in The Hague to make its courtroom facilities available to the Special Court to conduct the trial in the Netherlands.

The ICC is currently focused on Africa. In addition to the Darfur situation, three other African countries, all state parties to the court—the DRC, Central African Republic, and Uganda—have requested assistance from the ICC for the prosecution of international crimes occurring within their domestic territories. Ocampo has issued indictments for all three situations. Thomas Lubanga from the DRC has been in custody in The Hague awaiting trial since March 2006.

Asia and the Pacific

Despite the extensive post–World War II trials of Japanese defendants by the Tokyo Tribunal and by other Allied nations under domestic laws, Japan has never accepted full responsibility for its wartime atrocities. The "comfort women"—sex slaves for Japanese military officers—want monetary compensation and an apology for the war crimes perpetrated against them, but successive Japanese governments have refused to meet their demands.

After decades of impunity, former Cambodian ruler Pol Pot, just prior to his death, was finally subjected to a (limited) trial for crimes against humanity committed by the Khmer Rouge under his leadership in the late 1970s. The Cambodian government of Hun Sen finally relented in 2006 and agreed to the establishment of a hybrid national-international tribunal for the trial of other surviving leaders of the Khmer Rouge, the Extraordinary Criminal Chambers in the Courts of Cambodia. The chambers, as of August 2008, have issued their initial indictments but are yet to commence the first trial.

In Indonesia, the government wanted to avoid an internationalization of trials of military leaders and militia members for atrocities committed in East Timor in 1999 following the announcement of the overwhelming East Timorese vote for independence. Jakarta conducted a number of national trials that have been heavily criticized for political interference in the selection of those to be tried (and those protected from criminal justice) and for the leniency of the sentences handed down to those few actually convicted of war crimes. In Timor-Leste, by contrast, the United Nations Transitional Administration in East Timor established a Serious Crimes Unit that has already conducted some trials of East Timorese militia members for atrocities committed after the balloting. The Serious Crimes Unit has no independent capacity to secure the physical custody of any Indonesian nationals, and that Jakarta will allow the extradition of any Indonesian nationals for trial in Timor-Leste is unlikely.

After unsuccessfully instituting proceedings against three former Nazis in the early 1990s, Australia disbanded its Special Investigations Unit and decided not to pursue other identified war crimes suspects from World War II living there. Successive Australian governments have refused to respond in any meaningful way to allegations that war criminals from more recent conflicts are also living contentedly in Australia, free of any fear of prosecution. Exceptions to this hands-off policy are situations in which a foreign government has requested the extradition of particular alleged war criminals. At present, extradition proceedings are ongoing against Charles Zentai (Hungary) and Dragan Vasiljković (Croatia), but at the time of writing neither of those proceedings has concluded.

Case Study—Belgian Arrest Warrant Case

On April 11, 2000, a Belgian judge issued an international arrest warrant for Abdulaye Yerodia Ndombasi, the foreign minister of the DRC, to face trial in Belgium for alleged public speeches vilifying ethnic Tutsis in the DRC that allegedly resulted in the killing of several hundred Tutsis. Yerodia was charged pursuant to Belgium's criminal legislation implementing the Geneva Conventions of 1949 and their Additional Protocols of 1977. Following the precedent of the Israeli prosecution of Adolf Eichmann for international crimes committed outside Israel, the Belgian legislation extends universal jurisdiction to Belgian courts for alleged war crimes, crimes against humanity, and acts of genocide.

The DRC government was affronted by the Belgian intention to prosecute one of its senior ministers and so instituted legal proceedings against Belgium in the International Court of Justice. The essence of the DRC's claim was that

Belgium was in violation of the international rule extending absolute immunity for government officials in the domestic courts of a foreign country. The case raised some important issues as to the circumstances under which national courts are free to try foreign government officials for alleged war crimes.

The International Court of Justice delivered its judgment in the case in 2002, finding by majority against Belgium and in favor of the DRC. The court confirmed that senior ministers do in fact enjoy absolute immunity from prosecution in the national courts of foreign countries during the term of their incumbency and that they cannot be tried—even for the most serious international crimes.

The decision attracted widespread criticism, particularly because it came so soon after, and in apparent contradiction to, the dramatic extradition proceedings before successive benches of the House of Lords in London against Augusto Pinochet, former president of Chile. In fact, the majority judges of the International Court of Justice qualified their decision in two important ways, and these qualifications are the key to reconciling apparently conflicting developments in the national prosecution of war crimes. First, the judges in The Hague decided that absolute immunity from prosecution in foreign domestic courts does not apply to senior ministers *after* they have left office. Pinochet was, of course, long retired from the presidency when he was arrested in London. Second, heads of state and senior ministers do not enjoy absolute immunity from prosecution by *international* courts and tribunals. So, for example, the ICC can issue an arrest warrant against Omar al-Bashir, the current president of Sudan, but another country (Belgium, South Africa, or China) cannot while Bashir is still in office.

Biographical Sketches

Raoul Hilberg is a professor of political science at the University of Vermont and widely regarded as the world's leading historian on the Holocaust. His *Destruction of the European Jews* (1961) is considered one of the preeminent scholarly works on the Holocaust. Hilberg has appeared as an expert witness in numerous war crimes trials of former Nazis on the basis of his contribution to the scholarly literature.

Chea Leang is the Cambodian co-prosecutor (with Canadian Robert Petit) responsible for conducting the cases against former Khmer Rouge leaders brought to trial before the Extraordinary Chambers in the Courts of Cambodia. Leang trained as a prosecutor in former East Germany and now has the challenging task of prosecuting crimes against humanity perpetrated in Cambodia thirty years ago.

Theodor Meron was, for many years, the Charles Denison Professor of Law at New York University Law School and became a global authority on the laws of war and on international criminal law. He was appointed judge of the International Criminal Tribunal for the Former Yugoslavia in The Hague in 2001 and served as the tribunal's fourth president in 2003–2005.

Yuki Tanaka is a professor at the Hiroshima Peace Institute in Japan and a leading international scholar on Japanese war crimes during World War II. He has had a profound impact on the Japanese denial of wartime atrocities, and two of his books, *Hidden*

Horrors: Japanese War Crimes in World War II (1996) and *Japan's Comfort Women: Sexual Slavery and Prostitution during World War II and the U.S. Occupation* (2002), have become the seminal works in English on the subject.

Simon Wiesenthal was a Holocaust survivor who devoted his life to exposing Nazi perpetrators of atrocity. Wiesenthal was responsible for tracking down Adolph Eichmann in Argentina in the 1960s and, in so doing, facilitating the events that led to Eichmann's trial in Jerusalem.

Directory

Amnesty International, 99-119 Rosebery Avenue, London EC1R 4RE, United Kingdom. Telephone: (44) 207 814 6200; email: info@amnesty.org.uk; Web: http://www.amnesty.org.
Organization committed to individual accountability for the perpetration of international crime; promotes and monitors trials for alleged violations of international criminal law.

Asia Pacific Center for Military Law, Melbourne Law School, University of Melbourne, Victoria 3010, Australia. Telephone (61) 3 8344 4775; email: law-apcml@unimelb.edu.au; Web: www.apcml.org.
Research and training collaboration between academics and the military promoting understanding of and respect for the rule of law in militaries in the Asia Pacific region.

Asser Instituut, TMC Asser Instituut, 20-22 R J Schimmelpennicklaan, 2517 The Hague, Netherlands. Telephone: (31) 70 342 0300; email: tmc@asser.nl; Web: www.asser.nl.
Organization that publishes the Yearbook of International Humanitarian Law, *the only academic journal attempting to systematically gather information on the practice of states in relation to international humanitarian law.*

Crimes of War, American University, 4400 Massachusetts Avenue NW, Washington, D.C. 20016-8017. Email: office@crimesofwar.org; Web: www.crimesofwar.org.
A collaboration of journalists, lawyers, and scholars that seeks to raise awareness of the laws of war and the human consequences when armed conflict becomes entrenched.

Helsinki Foundation for Human Rights, 18 Bracka Street, Apt. 62, 00-028 Warsaw, Poland. Telephone: (48) 22 828 1008; email: hfhr@hfhrpol.waw.pl; Web: http://www.hfhrpol.waw.pl/index.php?lang=en.
Organization promoting education and research in human rights with national committees across Europe; monitors and reports on the human rights situations in countries where it has committees.

Human Rights Watch, 350 Fifth Avenue, 34th Floor, New York, N.Y. 10118-3299. Telephone: (212) 290-4700; email: hrwnyc@hrw.org; Web: http://www.hrw.org.
Organization dedicated to protecting the human rights of people around the world; reports on national developments in the pursuit of trials against alleged violators of international criminal law.

International Committee of the Red Cross (ICRC), 19 Avenue de la Paix, 1202 Geneva, Switzerland. Telephone: (41) 22 734 6001; email: webmaster.gva@icrc.org; Web: www.icrc.org.
Organization mandated by governments to provide independent, neutral, and impartial humanitarian assistance to victims of armed conflict wherever it occurs, known as the Guardian of the Geneva Conventions.

International Crisis Group, 149 Avenue Louise, Level 16, 1050 Brussels, Belgium. Telephone: (32) 2 502 9038; email: icgbrussels@crisisweb.org; Web: http://www .crisisgroup.org/home/index.cfm.
Private organization committed to strengthening the capacity of the international community to anticipate, understand, and act to prevent and contain conflict.

Simon Wiesenthal Center, 1 Mendele Street, Jerusalem 92147, Israel. Telephone: (972) 2 563 1273; email: information@wiesenthal.net; Web: http://www.wiesenthal .com/site/pp.asp?c=lsKWLbPJLnF&b=4441251.
Organization dedicated to preserving the history of the Holocaust.

Further Research

Books

Angers, Trent. *The Forgotten Hero of My Lai: The Hugh Thompson Story.* Lafayette, La.: Acadian House Publishing, 1999.

Arendt, Hannah. *Eichmann in Jerusalem: A Report on the Banality of Evil.* New York: Viking Press, 1964.

Askin, Kelly Dawn. *War Crimes against Women: Prosecution in International War Crimes Tribunals.* The Hague: Kluwer Law International, 1997.

Bass, Gary Jonathan. *Stay the Hand of Vengeance: The Politics of War Crimes Tribunals.* Princeton, N.J.: Princeton University Press, 2000.

Bassiouni, M. Cherif. *Crimes against Humanity in International Criminal Law.* 2d ed. The Hague: Kluwer Law International, 1999.

Best, Geoffery. *War and Law since 1945.* London: Clarendon Press, 1997.

Denma Translation Group, eds. *Sun Tzu—The Art of War: A New Translation.* Boston: Shambhala Publications, 2001.

Dunant, Henry. *A Memory of Solferino.* Geneva: International Committee of the Red Cross, 1987.

Durham, Helen, and Tracey Gurd, eds. *Listening to the Silences: Women and War.* Leiden: Martinus Nijhoff, 2005.

Ferencz, Benjamin B. *An International Criminal Court: A Step toward World Peace. A Documentary History and Analysis.* Vols. 1 and 2. New York: Oceana Publications, 1980.

Gardam, Judith G., and Michelle Jarvis. *Women, Armed Conflict and International Law.* The Hague: Kluwer Law International, 2001.

Goldstein, Joseph, Burke Marshall, and Jack Schwartz, eds. *The My Lai Massacre and Its Cover-Up: Beyond the Reach of Law?* New York: Free Press, 1976.

Green, Leslie C. *The Contemporary Law of Armed Conflict.* Manchester, UK: Manchester University Press, 1993.

———. *Superior Orders in National and International Law* Leidan: Sijthoff International Publishing, 1976.

Gutman, Roy, and David Rieff, eds. *Crimes of War: What the Public Must Know.* New York: Norton, 1999.

Hausner, Gideon. *Justice in Jerusalem.* London: Thomas Nelson and Sons, 1967.

Hersh, Seymour M. *My Lai 4: A Report on the Massacre and Its Aftermath.* New York: Random House, 1970.

McCormack, Timothy L. H., and David Blumenthal, eds. *The Legacy of Nuremberg: Civilising Influence or Institutionalised Vengeance?* Leiden: Martinus Nijhoff, 2008.

McCormack, Timothy L. H., and Gerry J. Simpson, eds. *The Law of War Crimes: National and International Approaches.* The Hague: Kluwer Law International, 1997.

Meron, Theodor. *War Crimes Law Comes of Age.* Oxford: Clarendon Press, 1998.

Papadatos, Peter. *The Eichmann Trial.* London: Stevens and Sons, 1964.

Peers, William R. *The My Lai Inquiry.* New York: Norton, 1979.

Pictet, Jean S. *Commentary on the Geneva Conventions of 1949.* Vols. 1–4. Geneva: International Committee of the Red Cross, 1952.

Ratner, Steven R., and Jason S. Abrams. *Accountability for Human Rights Atrocities in International Law: Beyond the Nuremberg Legacy.* 2d ed. Oxford: Oxford University Press, 2001.

Roberts, Adam, and Richard Guelff, eds. *Documents on the Laws of War.* 3d ed. Oxford: Oxford University Press, 2000.

Rogers, Anthony P. V. *Law on the Battlefield.* Manchester, UK: Manchester University Press, 1996.

Sandoz, Yves, Christophe Swinarski, and Bruno Zimmerman, eds. *Commentary on the Additional Protocols of 8 June 1977 to the Geneva Conventions of 1949.* Geneva: International Committee of the Red Cross and Martinus Nijhoff, 1987.

Sassòli, Marco, and Antoine A. Bouvier. *How Does Law Protect in War?: Cases, Documents and Teaching Materials on Contemporary Practice in International Humanitarian Law.* Geneva: International Committee of the Red Cross, 1999.

Schindler, Deitrich, and Jiří Toman, eds. *The Laws of Armed Conflicts: A Collection of Conventions, Resolutions and Other Documents.* 3d rev. ed. Dordrecht: Martinus Nijhoff, and Geneva: Henry Dunant Institute, 1988.

Simpson, Gerry. *Law, War and Crime: War Crimes Trials and the Reinvention of International Law.* Cambridge, UK: Polity Press 2007.

Tanaka, Yuki. *Hidden Horrors: Japanese War Crimes in World War II.* Boulder, Colo.: Westview Press, 1996.

———. *Japan's Comfort Women: Sexual Slavery and Prostitution during World War II and the U.S. Occupation.* London: Routledge, 2002.

Taylor, Telford. *Nuremberg and Vietnam: An American Tragedy.* Chicago: Quadrangle Books, 1970.

Woetzel, Robert K. *The Nuremberg Trials in International Law with a Postlude on the Eichmann Case.* New York: Frederick A. Praeger, 1962.

Articles and Reports

Chinkin, Christine. "Women: The Forgotten Victims of Armed Conflict?" In *The Changing Face of Conflict and the Efficacy of International Humanitarian Law,* ed. Helen Durham and Timothy L. H. McCormack. The Hague: Kluwer Law International, 1999.

Gardam, Judith. "Women and the Law of Armed Conflict: Why the Silence?" *International and Comparative Law Quarterly* 46 (1997): 55–80.

Greenwood, Christopher. "Historical Development and Legal Basis." In *The Handbook of Humanitarian Law in Armed Conflicts,* ed. Dieter Fleck. Oxford: Oxford University Press, 1995.

———. "International Humanitarian Law and the Laws of War: Report for the Centennial Commemoration of the First Hague Peace Conference 1899." In *The Centennial of the First International Peace Conference: Reports and Conclusions,* ed. Frits Kalshoven. The Hague: Kluwer Law International, 2000.

Lippman, Matthew. "War Crimes: The My Lai Massacre and the Vietnam War." *San Diego Justice Journal* 1 (1993): 295–364.

McCormack, Timothy L. H. "David Hicks and the Charade of Guantánamo Bay." *Melbourne Journal of International Law* 8 (2007): 273–291.

———. "Their Atrocities and Our Misdemeanours: The Reticence of States to Try Their Own Nationals for International Crimes." In *Justice for Crimes against Humanity,* ed. Mark Lattimer and Philippe Sands. Oxford: Hart Publishing, 2003.

Meron, Theodor. "Shakespeare's *Henry V* and the Law of War." *American Journal of International Law* 86, no. 1 (1992): 1–45.

Ratner, Steven. "The Schizophrenias of International Criminal Law." *Texas International Law Journal* 33 (1998): 237–256.

Schwarzenberger, Georg. "The Eichmann Judgment: An Essay in Censorial Jurisprudence." *Current Legal Problems* 15 (1962): 248–265.

Web Sites

Crimes of War
http://www.crimesofwar.org

Rome Statute of the International Criminal Court
http://untreaty.un.org/cod/icc/index.html

Simon Wiesenthal Center
http://www.wiesenthal.com/

Documents

1. The Geneva Conventions of 1949

Negotiated under the auspices of the International Committee of the Red Cross and opened for signature in Geneva on August 12, 1949

The full text of the four conventions is available at www.icrc.org/ihl.nsf/WebCONVFULL.

Extracts

Article 2

[Common to all four conventions: Geneva Convention (I) for the Amelioration of the Condition of the Wounded and Sick in Armed Forces in the Field; Geneva Convention (II) for the Amelioration of the Condition of Wounded, Sick and Shipwrecked Members of Armed Forces at Sea; Geneva Convention (III) Relative to the Treatment of Prisoners of War; and Geneva Convention (IV) Relative to the Protection of Civilian Persons in Time of War]

In addition to the provisions which shall be implemented in peace time, the present Convention shall apply to all cases of declared war or of any other armed conflict which may arise between two or more of the High Contracting Parties, even if the state of war is not recognized by one of them.

The Convention shall also apply to all cases of partial or total occupation of the territory of a High Contracting Party, even if the said occupation meets with no armed resistance. . . .

Article 3

[Common to all four conventions]

In the case of armed conflict not of an international character occurring in the territory of one of the High Contracting Parties, each party to the conflict shall be bound to apply, as a minimum, the following provisions:

(1) Persons taking no active part in the hostilities, including members of armed forces who have laid down their arms and those placed *hors de combat* by sickness, wounds, detention or any other cause, shall in all circumstances be treated humanely without any adverse distinction founded on race, colour, religion or faith, sex, birth or wealth, or any other similar criteria. To this end, the following acts are and shall remain prohibited at any time and in any place whatsoever with respect to the above-mentioned persons:

    (a) violence to life and person, in particular murder of all kinds, mutilation, cruel treatment and torture;

    (b) taking of hostages;

    (c) outrages upon personal dignity, in particular, humiliating and degrading treatment;

    (d) the passing of sentences and the carrying out of executions without previous judgment pronounced by a regularly constituted court affording all the judicial guarantees which are recognized as indispensable by civilized peoples.

(2) The wounded and sick shall be collected and cared for.

2. Protocol Additional to the Geneva Conventions of 12 August 1949 and Relating to the Protection of Victims of International Armed Conflict (Protocol I)

Negotiated under the auspices of the International Committee of the Red Cross and opened for signature in Geneva on June 8, 1977

The full text is available at www.icrc.org/ihl.nsf/WebCONVFULL.

Extract

Article 1 General Principles and Scope of Application

1. The High Contracting Parties undertake to respect and to ensure respect for this Protocol in all circumstances.

2. In cases not covered by this Protocol or by other international agreements, civilians and combatants remain under the protection and authority of the principles of international law derived from established custom, from the principles of humanity and from dictates of public conscience.

3. This Protocol, which supplements the Geneva Conventions of 12 August 1949 for the protection of war victims, shall apply in the situations referred to in Article 2 common to those Conventions.

4. The situations referred to in the preceding paragraph include armed conflicts in which peoples are fighting against colonial domination and alien occupation and against racist regimes in the exercise of their right of self-determination, as enshrined in the Charter of the United Nations and the Declaration on Principles of International Law concerning Friendly Relations and Co-operation among States in accordance with the Charter of the United Nations.

3. Protocol Additional to the Geneva Conventions of 12 August 1949 and Relating to the Victims of Non–International Armed Conflicts (Protocol II)

Negotiated under the auspices of the International Committee of the Red Cross and opened for signature in Geneva on June 8, 1977

The full text is available at www.icrc.org/ihl.nsf/WebCONVFULL.

Extract

Article 1 Material field of application

1. This Protocol, which develops and supplements Article 3 common to the Geneva Conventions of 12 August 1949 without modifying its existing conditions of application, shall apply to all armed conflicts which are not covered by Article I of the Protocol Additional to the Geneva Conventions of 12 August 1949, and relating to the Protection of Victims of International Armed Conflicts (Protocol I) and which take place in the territory of a High Contracting Party between its armed forces and dissident armed forces or other organized armed groups which, under responsible command, exercise such control over a part of its territory as to enable them to carry out sustained and concerted military operations and to implement this Protocol.

2. This Protocol shall not apply to situations of internal disturbances and tensions, such as riots, isolated acts of violence and other acts of a similar nature, as not being armed conflicts.

PART VI

Security

ARMS CONTROL

J. Peter Scoblic

Although the threat of nuclear war has greatly diminished since the end of the cold war, weapons of mass destruction (WMD)—that is, chemical, biological, and especially nuclear weapons—remain one of the chief security concerns of the international community. Many of the established nuclear powers have significantly reduced the quantity of atomic arms they possess, but they continue to upgrade their quality. In addition, a number of countries are—or are feared to be—developing chemical, biological, and nuclear weapons and the missiles to deliver them. The September 11, 2001, attacks on the United States and subsequent cases of anthrax also heightened concern about the possibility of terrorists acquiring and using WMD. International diplomacy has proven effective in reversing the superpowers' arms race and slowing the proliferation of these weapons, but serious challenges remain if the world is to avoid the devastating loss of life and property that the use of these weapons can cause.

Historical Background and Development

In 1945, the United States conducted the first test of a nuclear weapon, and a few months later it dropped two atomic bombs on Japan, killing approximately 100,000 people and changing the nature of warfare forever. The Soviet Union tested its first atomic weapon in 1949, and as the U.S.-Soviet geopolitical rivalry grew, an arms race ensued. Over the next two decades, both superpowers built weapons far more powerful than those used against Japan and developed ballistic missiles that could strike one another's homelands despite the thousands of miles between them. Indeed, the United States and the Soviet Union built enough weapons to ensure that a major nuclear conflict would destroy both sides, regardless of who struck first. This uncomfortable but perversely stable relationship became known as mutual assured destruction (MAD), and it deterred each side from attacking the other.

By the mid-1960s, Britain, China, and France had also conducted nuclear tests, and international concern about the uncontrolled spread of nuclear weapons led to the negotiation of the Treaty on the Non-Proliferation of Nuclear Weapons, commonly referred to as the Non-Proliferation Treaty

(NPT) (see Document 1). The treaty, signed by fifty-eight countries in 1968 and by many more in subsequent decades, allowed the five states that had already conducted nuclear tests to retain their weapons (although it committed them to eventual disarmament), but prohibited all others from developing them. In return, the states forswearing nuclear weapons were promised assistance in developing nuclear technology for peaceful purposes, such as energy production.

In the late 1960s, the United States and the Soviet Union began to discuss ways to stabilize their nuclear competition in the hope of lowering tensions and reducing the risk of nuclear war. In 1972, they signed the Anti-Ballistic Missile (ABM) Treaty, prohibiting most defenses against strategic ballistic missiles. The rationale behind the treaty was that if either side developed a defense that could counter its enemy's offensive missiles, its opponent would simply expand its offensive capacity, which in turn would spur better defenses, and so on. The pace of the arms race, already proceeding at a frightening clip, would increase. Just as important, the two countries feared that missile defense could undermine the stability of MAD by suggesting that, during a crisis, a decisive advantage might exist in launching first.

The United States and the Soviet Union also negotiated caps on the number of weapons that each could deploy, but even though they signed two agreements in the 1970s—SALT I and II (from the Strategic Arms Limitation Talks)—only in the mid-1980s did they agree to significant reductions. In 1987, the United States and the Soviet Union banned intermediate-range missiles through the Intermediate-Range Nuclear Forces (INF) Treaty. In 1991, with the cold war winding down and the Soviet Union disintegrating, the two nations signed the Strategic Arms Reduction Treaty (START I), obligating each side to reduce its strategic arsenal to 6,000 deployed nuclear warheads—nearly a 50 percent reduction for the United States and the Soviet Union. Two years later, they signed START II, obligating further reductions to 3,500 warheads apiece.

The atmosphere of cooperation that followed the end of the cold war also allowed the international community to intensify its nonproliferation efforts. In 1993, 130 nations signed the Chemical Weapons Convention outlawing chemical weapons and requiring states that had them to dismantle and dispose of them; as of 2008, 184 states had signed the treaty. In 1995, the NPT was extended indefinitely. Today, all but four nations (India, Israel, North Korea, and Pakistan) are parties to the treaty. In 1996, negotiators also concluded the Comprehensive Test Ban Treaty (CTBT), which bans all nuclear testing, with the objectives of preventing states without nuclear weapons from getting them and stopping nations with nuclear weapons from developing new types. A number of key countries, including the United States, have not ratified the treaty, so it has not yet taken effect. In addition, in 1997, President Bill Clinton and Russian president Boris Yeltsin agreed to a negotiating framework for a START III agreement, which would limit each country to 2,000–2,500 deployed strategic warheads and provide for warhead dismantlement, rendering the force reductions permanent.

The George W. Bush administration opposed traditional arms control, however, arguing that diplomatic and legal instruments are ineffective guarantors of U.S. security. It generally shunned treaties and diplomacy with states thought to be illicitly developing weapons, instead preferring unilateral action, including the use of force. Although it did negotiate reductions in the U.S. and Russian nuclear arsenals and did oversee the end of Libya's WMD programs, the Bush administration failed to prevent North Korea and Iran from accelerating their nuclear programs, and many experts fear the collapse of the nonproliferation regime. To strengthen it and to reduce the risk of both nuclear war and nuclear terrorism, leading American statesman have recently advocated recommitting the United States to the goal of nuclear disarmament and quickly taking dramatic steps toward that goal. And in his April 5, 2009, speech in Prague, President Barack Obama did just that, calling for a "world without nuclear weapons" and outlining interim steps toward that end.

Current Status

Arms control refers to the use of diplomatic and legal instruments to reduce military threats and is intended to complement the security provided by traditional military defenses. Although arms control measures have been applied to conventional weapons, such as tanks and ships, the term more frequently refers to the use of diplomacy to contain the threat from WMD, which is the focus here.

Since the advent of the nuclear age in 1945, the international community has used arms control for a variety of purposes: to stabilize, slow, and eventually reverse the nuclear arms race between the United States and the Soviet Union; to prevent the spread of nuclear weapons; to outlaw biological and chemical weapons; and to disarm nations of particular concern to global security. In the twenty-first century, arms control remains a useful tool for combating the remaining problems posed by nuclear, chemical, and biological weapons and missiles.

During the George W. Bush administration, little progress was made in expanding formal diplomatic arrangements. Instead, the administration pursued a variety of voluntary, ad hoc initiatives to stem the spread of WMD, and where proliferation had already occurred, it often preferred confrontation to negotiation. However, in its first months, the Barack Obama administration has reembraced arms control, engaging or attempting to engage states with nuclear programs, pledging to strengthen the international nonproliferation regime, and even promising to work toward a world free of nuclear weapons.

Research

Understanding which countries have which WMD and missiles is a difficult task because of the secrecy with which governments guard such programs. The most accessible data tend to come from unclassified U.S. government reports, but the information they provide is often vague, and as the faulty intelligence provided prior to the Iraq war shows, they must be treated with skepticism.

Equally essential is understanding which countries possess poorly guarded fissile material that could be stolen by terrorists and used to make a nuclear device.

Nuclear Weapons. The NPT, which has been signed by nearly every country in the world, gave only five states—Britain, China, France, the Soviet Union, and the United States—the legal right to possess nuclear weapons and required all others to refrain from developing them. As of 2009, the United States had fewer than 2,200 strategic nuclear warheads deployed; Russia had perhaps 3,000; and Britain, China, and France had a combined total of fewer than 1,000 (see map, p. 602). *Strategic warheads* refers to those with high explosive yields intended to be delivered against the homeland of an adversary. (Nuclear-armed nations may also possess tactical weapons, which generally have smaller yields and are intended for use on the battlefield, as if they were simply powerful conventional explosives.) *Deployed warheads* refers to those actually mounted on missiles or on bombers and ready for use. The United States and Russia also maintain warheads in a reserve stockpile, which can be put on missiles or bombers if needed.

India, Pakistan, and Israel also have nuclear weapons, but they have never been members of the NPT and are not legally recognized as nuclear weapon states. North Korea withdrew from the NPT in 2003 and tested one nuclear weapon in 2006 and another in 2009. Based on the amount of fissile material each of these countries is thought to have, Pakistan is believed capable of building up to sixty warheads, and India is thought to be capable of building between seventy-five and two hundred warheads. North Korea is thought capable of building eight to fifteen nuclear warheads. Israel, which has never publicly acknowledged its possession of nuclear weapons, is believed to have enough fissile material for seventy-five to two hundred warheads. However, it is not known how far these nations have progressed in weaponizing their nuclear material, for example, in making warheads small enough to mount on missiles.

In 2002, two secret Iranian nuclear facilities were discovered and the International Atomic Energy Agency (IAEA) subsequently found that Iran had been clandestinely trying to enrich uranium. (Enriched uranium can be used either to fuel a nuclear reactor or to build a nuclear warhead.) Despite efforts by France, Germany, and the United Kingdom to halt the program, as well as the implementation of UN Security Council sanctions, Iran's uranium-enrichment program continues, although it is not believed to be capable of producing enough material for a nuclear bomb until 2012 or 2015.

In addition, a number of countries—such as Algeria, Egypt, Saudi Arabia, and Syria—are developing nuclear energy programs or expanding existing ones. Because the technology and material used in such programs are helpful in building a nuclear weapon, enabling a country to develop nuclear arms in a relatively short time, these programs represent potential proliferation threats.

Biological and Chemical Weapons. The 1972 Biological Weapons Convention (BWC), which in 2008 had 155 parties, outlaws weapons that use microbial agents or toxins to cause harm, but the United States believes that six nations may, nevertheless, have biological weapons. An August 2005 State Department report judged that Russia, Iran, North Korea, Syria, and China maintain complete or partial offensive biological weapons programs. It also expressed concern that Cuba may have a biological weapons program. Libya is in the process of dismantling its biological weapons program.

The 1993 Chemical Weapons Convention banned weapons that use poisonous compounds to incapacitate or kill. Although chemical weapons are considered weapons of mass destruction, killing large numbers of people with them is far more difficult than with nuclear or biological weapons. India, Russia, South Korea, Libya, and the United States, as per their obligations under the convention, have formally admitted possessing chemical weapons and are in the process of destroying them. A number of other countries have declared facilities for producing chemical weapons and are either destroying them or converting them to peaceful uses.

Despite the prohibition on chemical weapons, a number of countries are believed to still be pursuing them. According to the U.S. Defense Department, North Korea has a considerable supply of chemical weapons. In 1998, Iran admitted that it once had a chemical weapons program, and the United States believes that Iran still has chemical weapons and continues to develop them. Syria is also believed to have a chemical arsenal.

Ballistic Missiles. Ballistic missiles are guided rockets that can deliver conventional, nuclear, chemical, or biological warheads from great distances. The type of warhead that can be delivered depends on the size of the missile and the weight of the warhead. Ballistic missiles themselves are not considered weapons of mass destruction, but their proliferation is considered almost as important because they allow countries to deliver such weapons from a great distance and with little possibility that the country being attacked will be able to defend itself. The United States has developed an advanced version of the Patriot antimissile system (used during the Persian Gulf War), which is capable of shooting down short-range missiles. However, neither the United States nor any other nation has a proven ability to defend itself against intercontinental ballistic missiles (ICBMs), which have ranges of more than 5,500 kilometers (3,300 miles) and travel much faster than short-range missiles. No international treaty regulates the proliferation of ballistic missiles, but in 1989 several industrialized nations with advanced missile capabilities agreed to restrict their exports of missiles and missile technology via the Missile Technology Control Regime (MTCR).

Only a handful of nations have missiles that can reach the United States. Approximately thirty-two nations have ballistic missiles that can travel farther than 100 kilometers (60 miles)—and twenty-six of these countries have ballistic missiles that can travel 300 kilometers (180 miles) or more (see Table 1)—but most of these countries have only short-range Scud missiles, low-grade weapons bought or inherited from the Soviet Union. (Iraq used these missiles during the Persian Gulf War.) Each of the five nuclear-weapon states deploys land-based ICBMs, submarine-launched ballistic missiles (SLBMs), or both. India, Iran, Israel, Pakistan, and North Korea have either produced or flight-tested a missile with a range greater than 1,000 kilometers (620 miles). Both India and Pakistan are aggressively developing ballistic missiles, with Russia providing assistance to India and with China providing assistance to Pakistan. Iran has tested a 1,300-kilometer ballistic missile and may have tested a ballistic missile with a range over 2,000 kilometers. It is actively pursuing longer-range missiles with the help of China, North Korea, and Russia. North Korea tested a missile with a range of 3,500 to 5,500 kilometers in 2006, although the missile failed 40 seconds after launch.

Terrorism and Weapons of Mass Destruction. Terrorists have attempted to acquire and/or use chemical, biological, and nuclear weapons. For example, in 1995 the group Aum Shinrikyo killed twelve people on the Tokyo subway using Sarin nerve gas. (Aum Shinrikyo had previously attempted nine biological weapons attacks, all of which failed.) Al Qaeda's leader Osama bin Laden has described obtaining nuclear weapons as a "religious duty," and senior Al Qaeda members have repeatedly affirmed their desire to kill 4 million Americans in retaliation for the deaths of Muslims—a feat only possible with nuclear weapons or a particularly effective pathogen. Al Qaeda has made numerous attempts to acquire components for nuclear arms.

Fortunately, although terrorists are capable of building a crude nuclear bomb on their own, without assistance they cannot produce the fissile material (either plutonium or highly enriched uranium) that forms the explosive core of an atomic weapon. For this reason, arms control experts are intent on securing fissile material worldwide.

The most likely source of such material is Russia, which has approximately 600 tons of weapons-usable nuclear material, some of it poorly guarded. Although a number of U.S. programs, collectively known as cooperative threat reduction efforts, have upgraded the security of this material, much of it remains unaccounted for and vulnerable to theft. Pakistan also possesses significant quantities of fissile material for both civilian and military use, which could be vulnerable to theft or diversion by Islamic radicals sympathetic to Al Qaeda. Pakistan also has an extremely poor proliferation record, although it has periodically cooperated with the United States to improve its nuclear safeguards. North Korea and Iran are also potential sources of fissile material.

In addition, terrorists could acquire nuclear material from the 135 research reactors around the world that use highly enriched uranium (HEU) for scientific purposes. These reactors—located in countries from the United States and Russia to Argentina, Bangladesh, Japan, and the Democratic Republic of Congo—are often poorly guarded. Some naval reactors also use HEU fuel, and a number of countries continue to stockpile plutonium for use in civilian reactors. Programs such as the Department of Energy's Global Threat Reduction Initiative are working to proliferation-proof many of these facilities, converting them to use low-enriched uranium, removing fissile material, and upgrading security measures—a process colloquially known as "global cleanout." These efforts are still in progress.

Policies and Programs

Despite the utility of arms control in helping to contain the superpowers' arms race and limit the spread of biological, chemical, and nuclear weapons, significant challenges and threats remain: the United States and Russia still deploy thousands of strategic warheads; China, Russia, India, and Pakistan are upgrading their nuclear arsenals; North Korea exploded a nuclear device in 2006 and has not yet denuclearized; and Iran continues to enrich uranium, possibly for use in a nuclear weapon. In addition, a number of countries are considering developing their own nuclear fuel cycle capabilities, a development that threatens the nonproliferation regime because the same technology used to produce fuel for nuclear power reactors can also be used to build nuclear bombs.

Diplomatic efforts to contain the spread of WMD have been hindered by recent U.S. skepticism toward arms control. When the George W. Bush administration took office in 2001, the international community hoped to strengthen the nonproliferation regime by bringing the CTBT into force and negotiating a fissile material cutoff treaty, which would outlaw the production of plutonium and enriched uranium for use in nuclear weapons. Arms control supporters at home and abroad also hoped that the United States and Russia would preserve the ABM Treaty and continue strategic arms reductions under the START process. On the subject of biological weapons, an international negotiating body had put forward a draft protocol to strengthen the BWC, which outlawed germ weapons but contained no enforcement provisions.

However, in 1999 the U.S. Senate rejected the CTBT, arguing that the treaty was unverifiable and would threaten the U.S. ability to maintain its nuclear stockpile; and after taking office in 2001, the Bush administration indicated that it would not press for another Senate vote. It also scuttled the draft protocol to the BWC; and, most notably, it pulled out of the ABM Treaty, arguing that the agreement was a relic of the cold war and would prevent the United States from defending itself against the emerging threat from rogue state missiles. Later, the Bush administration effectively halted negotiations on a fissile material cutoff treaty by insisting that such an agreement could not be verified, a position with which other states disagreed.

Instead, the Bush administration emphasized military and technological approaches to countering proliferation. For example, in the absence of the ABM Treaty, it pushed ahead with missile defenses, deploying more than two dozen interceptors in California and Alaska, although the system is still being tested. And it invaded Iraq to halt Saddam Hussein's alleged WMD programs, not trusting UN inspections to uncover and destroy any such efforts.

When it pursued diplomatic measures, it preferred agreements that were largely voluntary and therefore preserved U.S. freedom of action. For example, it established the Proliferation Security Initiative (PSI), a loose affiliation of countries that pledged to interdict transfers of WMD and WMD-related material, but the initiative was not legally binding and did not grant members any new authority to seize suspicious shipments. And although the Bush administration backed UN Security Council Resolution 1540, which required states to criminalize proliferation and adopt "appropriate effective" safeguards against the spread of WMD, that resolution did not specifically define what such safeguards entail. The Bush administration actually undermined the nonproliferation regime by offering to aid India's civilian nuclear program. One of the incentives for non–nuclear-weapon states to join the NPT was the promise of nuclear technology. By offering that assistance to a state that was not party to the treaty, the Bush administration removed one reason to adhere to the agreement. More problematically, it opened itself to charges of hypocrisy because, while providing nuclear technology to a state outside the treaty, it was simultaneously arguing that Iran, a party to the treaty, should be prevented from enriching uranium. To these criticisms, the Bush administration countered that India was a friendly democracy, while Iran was not. However, in international relations, "friendliness" is a relative term, and nonproliferation efforts are most effective when their strictures are universal—that is, when they focus on limiting the spread of weapons regardless of the nature of regimes seeking to acquire them.

Going forward, one of the key outstanding nonproliferation questions is how to prevent nuclear arms from spreading even as a growing number of states turn to nuclear power to fill some of their energy needs. Article IV of the NPT specifies the "inalienable right" of all countries to develop nuclear technology for peaceful purposes. Unfortunately, a country that develops uranium-enrichment and plutonium-reprocessing technologies for ostensibly peaceful purposes can use those capabilities to build nuclear weapons as well. North Korea, India, and Pakistan each began their nuclear programs this way, and U.S. officials believe that Iran is doing the same thing.

In 2004, the Bush administration called on members of the Nuclear Suppliers Group (NSG; a cartel of countries that possess nuclear technology and that attempts to restrict transfers of sensitive nuclear technology to countries that might put it to ill use) to refrain from transferring uranium-enrichment and plutonium-reprocessing technology to states that did not already have it. Two years later, the Bush administration proposed the Global Nuclear Energy Partnership, which it claimed would permit the spread of nuclear energy but minimize the risks of proliferation by encouraging states that did not have the ability to make fuel to get the enriched uranium and plutonium they needed from states that already had such technologies. However, domestic and international reaction to this approach has been mixed.

Believing that states develop their own enrichment and reprocessing capabilities in part so they will not be at the mercy of fuel-supplier states, the IAEA is considering how its members can ensure that states have access to reliable sources of nuclear fuel, for example, by establishing an international "fuel bank" that would sell nuclear fuel to a state that suddenly found itself unable to purchase fuel on the open market. The IAEA has also suggested establishing multilaterally operated nuclear fuel facilities that would provide a stable supply of fuel so that no one state could decide not to sell to another. All these plans, however, would formalize a two-tier system of supplier states and consumer states, a dichotomy to which many countries object. One radical solution to this problem would be to place all nuclear fuel facilities under international control. The United States actually suggested this immediately after World War II, but the proposal failed because of cold war tensions.

Regional Summaries

United States and Russia

Although separated by thousands of miles, the United States and the Soviet Union constituted the single most important "region" for arms control during the cold war. Today, the U.S.-Russian axis remains critical because these nations still possess the vast majority of the world's nuclear weapons and continue to wield significant international influence.

Despite rapid progress in the late 1980s and early 1990s with the INF Treaty and START I and START II, the future of coordinated reductions in U.S. and Russian nuclear weapons is uncertain. In 1997, Presidents Bill Clinton and Boris Yeltsin agreed to pursue a START III agreement that would further reduce the number of deployed nuclear weapons to 2,000–2,500 warheads each, but those talks accomplished little after the Clinton administration linked progress in the discussion to Russia's allowing limited missile defenses. The potential for progress was further diminished when the Russian legislation ratifying START II, which was not passed until April 2000, mandated that the treaty not legally take effect until the United States had approved a package of ABM Treaty–related agreements signed in 1997.

In 2001, the United States and Russia each announced its desire to cut its deployed strategic arsenal to between 1,700 and 2,200 warheads. The Bush administration wanted each country to make reciprocal, unilateral cuts, while the Russians insisted on a legally binding START-like treaty. The result was the Strategic Offensive Reductions Treaty (SORT), which is legally binding but allows significant flexibility, as the Bush administration preferred. It contains no verification provisions, no limits on nondeployed warheads, and no provisions for warhead dismantlement. In fact, it goes into effect on the same day it expires—December 31, 2012.

The United States and Russia could not reach an agreement on the ABM Treaty and missile defenses, so the United States pulled out of the agreement in 2002. Russia's response was initially muted, but grew increasingly aggressive. In 2007, Russia suspended its participation in the Conventional Armed Forces in Europe (CFE) Treaty, threatened to pull out of the INF Treaty, threatened to target missile defense sites in Poland and the Czech Republic with nuclear arms, and resumed long-range Russian strategic bomber patrols. These actions were motivated by Russia's disagreement with the United States over missile defense, as well as by its concerns about Chinese and Pakistani

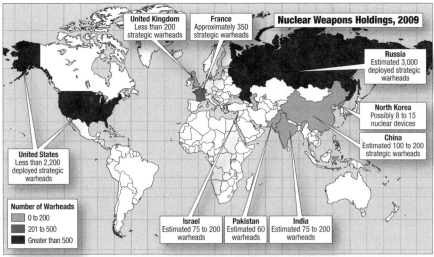

United Kingdom
Less than 200
strategic warheads

France
Approximately 350
strategic warheads

Nuclear Weapons Holdings, 2009

Russia
Estimated 3,000
deployed strategic
warheads

North Korea
Possibly 8 to 15
nuclear devices

China
Estimated 100 to 200
strategic warheads

United States
Less than 2,200
deployed strategic
warheads

Number of Warheads
0 to 200
201 to 500
Greater than 500

Israel
Estimated 75 to 200
warheads

Pakistan
Estimated 60
warheads

India
Estimated 75 to 200
warheads

Source: Arms Control Association, "Nuclear Weapons: Who Has What at a Glance," Washington, D.C. 2009. Available online from http://www.armscontrol.org/factsheets/Nuclearweaponswhohaswhat

intermediate-range ballistic missiles. Relations with the United States soured further after the military conflict between Russia and Georgia in August 2008.

The Obama administration has attempted to reset relations with Russia. In June 2009, the United States and Russia agreed to negotiate a follow-up agreement to START that would reduce the number of strategic warheads in each side's arsenal to between 1,500 and 1,675 and the number of missiles and bombers to between 500 and 1,100. Although such warhead cuts would be relatively modest, the treaty would preserve the verification procedures set out in START, which is set to expire in December 2009. The disagreement over missile defense remains, but the two countries continue to work together in other areas. Through cooperative threat reduction programs, the United States continues to help Russia downsize its vast nuclear weapons complex and secure its nuclear materials to prevent their theft by terrorists. The two countries have also worked together to some extent to counter the North Korean and Iranian nuclear programs.

The United States and Russia are also working to destroy their stockpiles of chemical weapons, which were outlawed by the Chemical Weapons Convention. At the time the convention was signed, the United States declared that it had approximately 30,000 tons of chemical agent, and Russia asserted that it had 40,000 tons. Neither country is expected to finish the destruction of its stockpiles until after 2012.

The United States and the Soviet Union both pledged to give up biological weapons when they signed the BWC in 1972, but the Soviets continued operating a clandestine germ warfare program. Although the Russians admitted the illegal program in 1992 and said it had been terminated, the United States believes it is still operating. Currently, the United States has several programs in place to employ former Soviet bioweapons scientists and secure former bioweapons facilities.

Europe

Although Britain and France are de jure nuclear weapon states and permanent members of the UN Security Council, Europe's role in proliferation and arms control was long subordinate to the superpower rivalry between the United States and the Soviet Union. Since the end of the cold war, however, Europe has taken a more active role in arms control, particularly in areas where the United States does not seem willing to lead.

For example, Britain, France, and Germany spearheaded negotiations with Iran over its nuclear program for several years when the United States indicated that it did not want to enter into talks. Europe also plays an important role in the dispute between the United States and Russia over U.S. missile defense plans, which include building antimissile sites in Poland and the Czech Republic. And in 2002, the G-8 nations (Canada, France, Germany, Italy, Japan, Russia, the United Kingdom, and the United States) committed to aiding U.S. cooperative threat reduction efforts by providing $10 billion over ten years to secure and destroy WMD-related material in the former Soviet Union.

European nations have also played a central role in trying to control the spread of biological weapons, taking the lead in international negotiations to strengthen the BWC. European nations have also been key participants in the Australia Group, an organization that seeks to regulate the export of chemical and biological agents, as well as dual-use equipment, to reduce the risks of proliferation.

North Africa and the Middle East

The Middle East is one of the most problematic areas for arms control and nonproliferation efforts because the United States believes that Iran is attempting to build nuclear weapons, an action that could provoke military strikes by Israel or the United States, or cause neighboring countries, such as Turkey, Egypt, Saudi Arabia, Syria, to develop nuclear arms in response. Efforts to prevent Arab states from acquiring WMD are complicated by the fact that Israel is a nuclear armed power that refuses to acknowledge its capability. Israel is thought to have developed a nuclear weapons capability several decades ago, with French assistance and U.S. consent. Israel has never officially acknowledged having nuclear weapons, saying only that it would not be the first to introduce nuclear weapons into the region.

During the 1990s, U.S. intelligence suspected Iran of having a nuclear weapons program, but according to the IAEA, the organization responsible for measuring compliance with the NPT, Iran was an NPT member in good standing. However, in 2002 and 2003 it was discovered that Iran had a secret uranium-enrichment program. The IAEA pressed Iran for full disclosure of its nuclear activities, but Iran continued to insist that its nuclear program was peaceful and that uranium enrichment was a right guaranteed under the NPT.

Britain, France, and Germany (a group informally called the EU-3) subsequently entered into talks with Iran to convince it to suspend its uranium-enrichment program in exchange for incentives. Until 2008, the United States declined to participate in the talks, instead pressing the IAEA to refer Iran to the United Nations Security Council. In 2006, the IAEA declared Iran in breach of its Safeguards Agreement and referred it to the United Nations Security Council, which imposed several rounds of targeted sanctions. Iran continues to expand and upgrade its uranium-enrichment program, although it will not be able to produce enough uranium for a nuclear bomb until 2012 or 2015.

The United States also believes that Iran has a substantial stockpile of chemical weapons, as well as the means to deliver them short distances. Because Iran is a member of the Chemical Weapons Convention, other signatories have the right to request an international inspection of Iran's facilities. The United States, despite its repeated accusations that Iran has violated the treaty, has never demanded an inspection.

By contrast, the decommissioning of Libya's WMD programs is one of the most successful recent arms control efforts. The international sanctions imposed on Libya after the 1988 bombing of Pan Am flight 103 crippled Libya's economy for much of the 1990s. In 1999, Libya's leader, Muammar Gaddafi, entered into talks with the United States and Britain aimed at resolving the impasse over prosecuting the Libyan officials involved in the attack. In August 2002, Gaddafi indicated that he was interested in giving up his chemical weapons programs in exchange for steps toward normalizing relations with the United States. After international authorities interdicted a ship filled with centrifuge components that A. Q. Khan's network was transferring to Libya, Gaddafi offered to give up his nuclear program as well in exchange for the lifting of U.S. sanctions. In December 2003, Libya officially renounced its WMD programs, promising to adhere to its commitments under the NPT and BWC, join the Chemical Weapons Convention, and adhere by the rules of the MTCR. Libya subsequently dismantled its nuclear program, although it has had procedural problems disposing of its chemical weapons. In 2006, the United States removed Libya from its list of state sponsors of terrorism and restored full diplomatic relations.

Until the U.S.-led invasion of Iraq in 2003, the United States was highly concerned about Iraq's suspected WMD and ballistic missile programs. As a result of Iraq's 1990 invasion of Kuwait and its subsequent defeat, the UN Security Council had placed Iraq under strict economic sanctions and mandated that it dismantle its nuclear program and destroy its chemical and biological weapons, as well as all missiles with a range greater than 150 kilometers. However, UN weapons inspectors were forced to leave Iraq in 1998, leaving the international community with little information about its weapons programs. This uncertainty, combined with other concerns in the aftermath of the September 11, 2001, attacks, convinced the Bush administration to pressure Iraq to re-admit inspectors in 2002 and, subsequently, to invade the country to destroy Saddam Hussein's suspected chemical and biological weapons and to prevent him from reconstituting a nuclear capability. However, in the aftermath of the invasion, the Iraq Survey Group found no stockpiles of unconventional arms and no nuclear program.

Northeast Asia

China first tested a nuclear weapon in 1964 and proceeded to develop a small nuclear arsenal as a way of putting itself on more equal footing with the United States and the Soviet Union during the cold war. Today, its arsenal remains small—the U.S. Defense Department estimates that China has only twenty or so nuclear-armed missiles capable of hitting the United States—but Beijing is modernizing its nuclear forces and developing more advanced missiles. The Defense Department has long contended that China is capable of rapidly expanding its ICBM arsenal.

For decades, China refused to participate in international arms control efforts. For example, even though the NPT allowed China to retain nuclear weapons, only in 1992 did China accede to the treaty. During the 1990s, however, China increased its participation, signing the Chemical Weapons Convention and the CTBT. China joined the NSG and applied to join the MTCR in 2004, but U.S. concerns about Chinese ballistic missile proliferation—especially shipments of missiles and missile components to Pakistan—prevented it from joining the MTCR.

China opposes the development of a U.S. missile defense because even a limited system could negate Beijing's minimal deterrent. It has also joined with Russia to call for a ban on the "weaponization" of space, and in 2007 it successfully test fired an antisatellite weapon, demonstrating that it can threaten U.S. orbital assets. U.S. policymakers and analysts disagree about how U.S. missile defense plans could affect China's arsenal, with some arguing that China is going to upgrade its nuclear weaponry regardless of U.S. activities and others arguing that missile defenses would prompt quantitative, as well as qualitative, improvements to China's nuclear armory. Some U.S. policymakers and analysts have also expressed concern that a Chinese nuclear buildup could encourage Japan and Taiwan to develop nuclear weapons of their own.

The other significant player in northeast Asia is North Korea, an impoverished, communist dictatorship that, despite its horrible economic situation, has devoted significant resources to developing WMD and the means of delivering them. Its nuclear weapons program was temporarily halted by a 1994 agreement with the United States, but that accord subsequently broke down and North Korea tested nuclear devices in 2006 and 2009 (see Case Study—North Korea's Nuclear Program). North Korea continues work on a ballistic missile program as well. In 1998, it raised international (particularly U.S.) concern by test-firing a Taepo Dong-1 intermediate-range ballistic missile over Japan, and in 2006 and 2009 it test-launched the 3,500- to 5,000-kilometer range Taepo Dong-2. North Korean missiles are of particular concern because the country has chemical, biological, and nuclear weapons, but none of the Taepo Dong tests was successful and it is highly unlikely that North Korea has developed a nuclear warhead capable of being delivered via ballistic missile. In addition, North Korea continues to sell ballistic missile technology to a number of countries, including Iran, Pakistan, Yemen, Syria, and Egypt.

South Asia

India exploded what it called a "peaceful nuclear device" in 1974. Although India never acknowledged having a nuclear weapons program, other nations thereafter assumed that India could build at least primitive nuclear arms. India's rival Pakistan is thought to have acquired a nuclear weapons capability in the mid-1980s, but it too kept quiet about its capabilities. The programs of these states remained below board until May 1998, when India conducted several nuclear tests to demonstrate its weapons capability. Days later, Pakistan reciprocated, and the South Asian nations' nuclear weapons capabilities came fully out of the closet. Immediately after the 1998 tests, India and Pakistan both announced a moratorium on further tests. Both have also indicated an interest in signing the CTBT, but they have not yet done so, and their weapons programs continue apace. Tensions eased somewhat in 2003, and the countries have since engaged in a number of confidence-building measures intended to reduce the risk of nuclear war: creating a hot-line between Delhi and Islamabad, signing an agreement on advance notification of ballistic missile tests, and resolving a number of border issues.

The United States imposed economic and military sanctions on India and Pakistan in 1998 in an attempt to roll back their nuclear programs, but the sanctions had little impact. Following the September 11, 2001, attacks on the United States, Washington quickly lifted most sanctions on both countries to secure their cooperation in the campaign against Afghanistan. According to the U.S. Defense Department, India and Pakistan are at an advanced stage of nuclear and missile development.

Pakistan's nuclear program is of particular concern because of the government's instability and its historical association with Islamic militants such as the Taliban. Although the weapons themselves are thought to be well-guarded, Pakistan's fissile material could be vulnerable to Al Qaeda sympathizers residing in the country's tribal areas. Pakistan has also been a major source of nuclear proliferation. In 2004, Pakistani nuclear scientist A. Q. Khan revealed that he had run a global nuclear technology smuggling ring, which proliferated to several countries including Libya and Iran. In response to international concerns, Pakistan placed Khan under house arrest, but the extent to which his network has been shut down remains unclear.

In 2005, President Bush broke with long-standing U.S. nonproliferation policy and offered India full-scale civilian nuclear cooperation with the United States, a benefit that is usually granted only to states that agree to forgo nuclear arms under the NPT. The U.S.-India nuclear deal would theoretically divide India's nuclear industry into civilian and military sectors, providing U.S. aid only to the civilian sector, but nearly all analysts believe that this would free up nuclear material for India to expand its weapons program. In addition to undermining the NPT, this could prompt Pakistan to augment its nuclear weapons program and further destabilize the region. Nevertheless, the Obama administration is working to implement the agreement.

Data

Table 1   Distribution of Ballistic Missiles with Ranges of 300 Kilometers or More

Country	System	Status	Range/payload	Source
Afghanistan	Scud-B	Unknown	300 km/1,000 kg	Soviet Union
Armenia	Scud-B	Operational	300 km/1,000 kg	Russia
Belarus	Scud-B	Operational	300 km/1,000 kg	Soviet Union
China	DF-3A	Operational	2,800 km/2,150 kg	Domestic/Russia
	DF-4	Operational	5,470+ km/2,200 kg	Domestic
	DF-5	Operational	12,000 km/3,200 kg	Domestic
	DF-5A	Operational	13,000 km/3,200 kg	Domestic
	DF-11	Operational	300 km/500 kg	Domestic
	DF-15	Operational	600 km/500 kg	Domestic
	DF-21	Operational	2,500 km/600 kg	Domestic
	DF-21A	Operational	1,770+ km/2,000 kg	Domestic
	DF-31	Operational	7,250+ km/700 kg	Domestic
	DF-31A	Development	11,270+ km/800 kg	Domestic
	Julang 1 (SLBM)	Operational	1,700+ km/600 kg	Domestic
	Julang 2 (SLBM)	Tested/ development	8,000 km/700 kg	Domestic
Egypt	Scud-B	Operational	300 km/1,000 kg	Soviet Union/ North Korea
	Project-T	Operational	450 km/985 kg	Domestic/ North Korea
	Scud-C	Operational	550 km/600 kg	Domestic/ North Korea
France	M4A/B (SLBM)	Operational	6,000 km/1,200 kg	Domestic
	M45 (SLBM)	Operational	6,000 km/1,000 kg	Domestic
	M51 (SLBM)	Tested/ development	8,000 km/1,380 kg	Domestic
Georgia	Scud-B	Operational	300 km/1,000 kg	Soviet Union
India	Prithvi-3	Development	350 km/500–1,000 kg	Soviet Union/ Domestic
	Sagarika (SLBM)	Development	250–350 km/500 kg	Domestic/Russia
	Agni-1	Development	700 km/1,000 kg	Domestic/ U.S./France
	Agni-1 variant	Tested/ development	1,000 km/1,000 kg	Domestic/ U.S./France
	Agni-2	Operational	2,000 km/1,000 kg	Domestic
	Agni-3	Operational	3,000 km/1,000? kg	Domestic/Russia
	Surya	Development	5,500+ km/2,000 kg	Domestic/Russia
Iran	Scud-B	Operational	300 km/1,000 kg	Domestic/ Libya/ North Korea
	Scud-C	Operational	550 km/600 kg	Domestic/ North Korea
	Shahab-3	Operational	1,300–2,000? km/750 kg	Domestic/ North Korea/ Russia

Table 1 (Continued)

Country	System	Status	Range/payload	Source
	Shahab-3 variant/Ghadr?	Tested/ development?	1,800 km/750 kg	Domestic/ North Korea/ Russia
	Shahab-4	Development?	2,000 km/1,000 kg	Domestic/ North Korea/ Russia
Israel	Jericho-1	Operational	500 km/750–1,000 kg	Domestic/France
	Jericho-2	Operational	1,500 km/1,000 kg	Domestic/France
	Jericho-3	Operational?	3,000–6,500 km/ 1,000 kg	Domestic
Kazakhstan	Scud-B	Operational	300 km/1,000 kg	Soviet Union
Libya	Scud-B	Operational	300 km/1,000 kg	Soviet Union
North Korea	Scud-B	Operational	300 km/1,000 kg	Soviet Union/Egypt?
	Scud-C variant	Operational	500 km/700 kg	Domestic
	No-Dong-1	Operational	1,300 km/ 700–1,000 kg	Domestic
	No-Dong-2	Tested/ development	1,500 km/770 kg	Domestic
	Taepo Dong-1	Tested/ development	2,000 km/1,000 kg	Domestic
	Taepo Dong-2	Tested/ development	3,500–5,500 km/1,000 kg	Domestic
	SS-N-6 variant	Development	2,500–4,000? km/680 kg	Domestic
Pakistan	Hatf-3 (Ghaznavi)	Operational	300 km/500 kg	Domestic/China
	Shaheen-1	Operational	750 km/500 kg	Domestic/China
	Ghauri-1	Operational	1,300 km/700 kg	Domestic/ North Korea
	Ghauri-2	Tested/ development	2,300 km/700 kg	Domestic/ North Korea
	Shaheen-2	Tested/ development	2,500 km/1,000 kg	Domestic/China
	Ghauri-3	Development	3,000 km/? kg[a]	Domestic/ North Korea
Russian Federation	Scud B	Operational	300 km/1,000 kg	Domestic
	SS-18	Operational	10,000 km/8,800 kg	Domestic
	SS-19	Operational	10,000 km/4,350 kg	Domestic
	SS-24 (silo, rail)	Operational	10,000 km/4,050 kg	Domestic
	SS-25	Operational	10,500 km/1,000 kg	Domestic
	SS-26	Operational	400 km/480 kg	Domestic
	SS-27 (silo, road mobile)	Operational	10,500 km/ 1,000–1,200 kg	Domestic
	SS-N-8 (SLBM)	Operational	8,000 km/1,100 kg	Domestic
	SS-N-18 (SLBM)	Operational	6,500 km/8,000 kg	Domestic
	SS-N-20 (SLBM)	Being retired	8,300 km/2,550 kg	Domestic
	SS-N-23 (SLBM)	Operational	8,000 km/2,800 kg	Domestic
	RSM-56	Tested/ development	10,000 km/ 1,000–2,000 kg	Domestic

Table 1   (Continued)

Country	System	Status	Range/payload	Source
Saudi Arabia	Dong Feng-3	Operational	2,600 km/2,150 kg	China
South Korea	ATACMS Block 1/A	Operational	300 km/560 kg	Domestic/ United States
Syria	Scud-B	Operational	300 km/1,000 kg	Domestic/ Soviet Union
	Scud-C	Operational	500 km/600–770 kg	Domestic/ North Korea
	Scud-D	Tested/ development	700 km/500 kg	Domestic/ North Korea
Taiwan	Tien Chi	Operational	300 km/500 kg	Domestic
Turkmenistan	Scud-B	Operational	300 km/1,000 kg	Soviet Union
Ukraine	Scud-B	Operational	300 km/1,000 kg	Soviet Union
United Arab Emirates	Scud-B	Operational	300 km/1,000 kg	Soviet Union
United Kingdom	D-5 Trident II (SLBM)	Operational	7,400 km/2,800 kg	United States
United States	ATACMS Block IA	Operational	300 km/160 kg	Domestic
	Minuteman III	Operational	9,650–13,000 km/1,150 kg	Domestic
	D-5 Trident II (SLBM)	Operational	7,400+ km/2,800 kg	Domestic
Vietnam	Scud-B	Operational	300 km/1,000 kg	Soviet Union
Yemen	Scud-B	Operational	300 km/1,000 kg	Soviet Union
	Scud variant	Operational	300–500 km/ 600–1,000 kg	North Korea

Source: Arms Control Association, 2007, http://www.armscontrol.org/factsheets/missiles.

Note: SLBM, submarine-launched ballistic missile.

[a]Value not available.

Case Study—North Korea's Nuclear Program

In December 1985, North Korea acceded to the NPT, which required it to forgo nuclear weapons but allowed it to maintain nuclear facilities for peaceful purposes, such as energy production. In 1992, inspectors from the IAEA became concerned that, despite its NPT commitments, North Korea might be illicitly producing weapons-grade plutonium. When Pyongyang refused to address their concerns, an international crisis erupted. Washington began high-level talks with the North Koreans, but little progress was made, and by the end of 1993, U.S. intelligence estimated that North Korea probably had separated enough plutonium from spent fuel produced by its nuclear complex at Yong-byon for one or two weapons.

As tensions escalated, former U.S. president Jimmy Carter traveled to Pyong-yang to discuss the situation with North Korean officials. Carter, whose trip was unofficial, persuaded the North Koreans to freeze their nuclear program in exchange for high-level talks with the United States. The Clinton adminis-tration agreed, and talks began that summer. On October 21, 1994, the United States and North Korea signed the Agreed Framework, which called for North Korea to freeze the operation and construction of (and to eventually dismantle) its nuclear reactors. Pyongyang also agreed to allow special IAEA inspections to verify its compliance. In return, an international consortium would be estab-lished to build North Korea two light-water reactors (nuclear reactors from which deriving weapons-usable fissile material is difficult). Until the light-water reactors were complete, North Korea would receive shipments of heavy fuel oil to meet its energy needs.

The implementation of the Agreed Framework encountered a number of obstacles, including delays in the construction of the light-water reactors and in the delivery of the heavy fuel oil shipments. A number of analysts and mem-bers of Congress criticized the Agreed Framework because it seemed to reward North Korea for violating its international commitments and because it pro-vided North Korea with nuclear technology (albeit proliferation-resistant technology) in the form of the light-water reactors. Nevertheless, the frame-work was widely considered one of the more successful arms control actions in the post–cold war era because it had convinced a reluctant state to freeze and dismantle its nuclear program.

The Bush administration initially signaled its intention to continue the Agreed Framework, but it soon called for "improved implementation" of the framework—suggesting that it wanted to alter the terms of the deal—and for 100 percent verification (even though absolute certainty in such an agreement is impossible to achieve). In 2002, the Bush administration labeled North Korea a member of the "axis of evil," along with Iran and Iraq. It also acquired new intelligence information that indicated North Korea had been attempting to purchase uranium-enrichment technology, which meant it was pursuing a uranium-based nuclear program in parallel to the plutonium-based program that it had frozen under the Agreed Framework.

In late 2002, the Bush administration confronted North Korean officials about the suspected uranium-enrichment program and cut off deliveries of heavy fuel oil. In response, North Korea declared the Agreed Framework dead, expelled the IAEA inspectors, pulled out of the NPT, and began reprocessing the spent fuel rods that had remained at Yongbyon since 1994. Focused on invading Iraq in spring 2003, the Bush administration argued that the situation in North Korea was not a crisis. Initially, it indicated that it would not hold direct talks with North Korea or provide any sort of incentives for the country to halt reprocessing. Instead, the Bush administration apparently hoped that North Korea would collapse without access to heavy fuel oil and energy. Even-tually, under pressure to do something about North Korea's nuclear program, the Bush administration agreed to join the six-party talks, which convened Russia, Japan, South Korea, China, the United States, and North Korea. These talks did not reach a breakthrough until 2005, when the Bush administration changed its policy and offered North Korea the outlines of a deal with terms similar to those contained in the Agreed Framework. However, North Korean recalcitrance and divisions within the Bush administration prevented further progress for several more years. In the meantime, North Korea reprocessed enough plutonium for eight to fifteen nuclear warheads and tested its first nuclear bomb.

Finally, in 2007 North Korea promised to dismantle all its nuclear facilities, and in return the United States promised to provide energy aid, remove North Korea from the list of state sponsors of terrorism, and lift sanctions under the Trading with the Enemy Act. North Korea began to disable its nuclear facilities, and the following year it submitted a declaration of its nuclear activities. However, in 2009, the talks stalled over verification disputes and ultimately broke down. North Korea, apparently destabilized by the illness of its leader, Kim Jong-Il, began launching ballistic missiles in defiance of UN resolutions, ejected IAEA monitors from its nuclear facilities, and tested a second nuclear device in May 2009. In response, the Obama administration, which has said it will return to the six-party talks if North Korea does, successfully lobbied for strong UN Security Council sanctions.

Biographical Sketches

John R. Bolton was undersecretary of state for arms control and international security from 2001 to 2005, heading U.S. nonproliferation efforts. He was U.S. ambassador to the United Nations from 2005 to 2006. He was a leading opponent of the ABM Treaty and helped shift U.S. emphasis from traditional arms control measures to voluntary approaches such as the PSI. In 2002, he expanded President Bush's original "axis of evil," accusing Libya, Cuba, and Syria of developing WMD.

Mohamed El Baradei has been the director general of the IAEA, which monitors compliance with the NPT, since 1997. He played a key role in pressing for more IAEA inspections of Iraq during the run-up to the U.S.-led invasion in 2003 and has since been a forceful advocate of suspending Iran's uranium enrichment program and producing a full accounting of the country's nuclear activities. His agency's findings have been central to the negotiations between Iran and the EU-3.

Robert McNamara was U.S. secretary of defense from 1961 to 1968. A key figure in the Kennedy and Johnson administrations, McNamara was one of the first U.S. policymakers to articulate the concept of MAD, which maintained that the strategic situation between the United States and the Soviet Union would remain stable as long as each had the ability to inflict unacceptable damage on the other in a nuclear conflict, regardless of who struck first.

Directory

Arms Control Association, 1313 L Street NW, Suite 130, Washington, D.C. 20005. Telephone: (202) 463-8270; email: aca@armscontrol.org; Web: http://www.arms control.org.

Nonpartisan organization that works to promote public understanding and support for effective arms control policies; publishes Arms Control Today.

Federation of American Scientists, 1725 DeSales Street NW, 6th Floor, Washington, D.C. 20036. Telephone: (202) 546-3300; email: fas@fas.org; Web: http://www.fas.org. *Research and advocacy group focusing on issues at the intersection of science and public policy, including nuclear and biological weapons.*

Henry L. Stimson Center, 1111 19th Street NW, 12th Floor, Washington, D.C. 20036. Telephone: (202) 223-5956; email: info@stimson.org; Web: http://www.stimson.org.
Think tank devoted to international security issues.

International Atomic Energy Agency (IAEA), P.O. Box 100, Wagramer Strasse 5, A-1400 Vienna, Austria. Telephone: (+431) 2600-0; email: Official.Mail@iaea.org; Web: http://www.iaea.org/worldatom.
UN-based agency supporting the peaceful use of nuclear technology; responsible for ensuring that states comply with the NPT.

James Martin Center for Nonproliferation Studies, Monterey Institute of International Studies, 460 Pierce Street, Monterey, Calif. 93940. Telephone: (831) 647-4154; email: cns@miis.edu; Web: http://www.cns.miis.edu.
Largest U.S. nongovernmental organization devoted to researching WMD and training new specialists in nonproliferation; publishes the Nonproliferation Review.

Missile Defense Agency, 7100 Defense Pentagon, Washington, D.C. 20330. Telephone: (703) 697-8997; email: mda.info@mda.mil; Web: http://www.mda.mil/mdalink/html/mdalink.html.
Central manager of the Defense Department's efforts to develop weapons systems to protect the United States and deployed U.S. forces from attack by ballistic missiles.

Natural Resources Defense Council, 40 West 20th Street, New York, N.Y. 10011. Telephone: (212) 727-2700; email: nrdcinfo@nrdc.org; Web: http://www.nrdc.org.
Environmental advocacy and research organization that seeks to reduce the threat from nuclear weapons.

Non-Proliferation Project, Carnegie Endowment for International Peace, 1779 Massachusetts Avenue NW, Washington, D.C. 20036. Telephone: (202) 483-7600; email: npp@ceip.org; Web: http://www.ceip.org/npp.
Project that produces a variety of materials addressing WMD.

Nuclear Threat Initiative, 1747 Pennsylvania Avenue NW, 7th Floor, Washington, D.C. 20006. Telephone: (202) 296-4810; email: contact@nti.org; Web: http://www.nti.org.
Foundation founded by media mogul Ted Turner and former U.S. senator Sam Nunn to support activities designed to reduce the threat from WMD.

Office of the Undersecretary of State for Arms Control and International Security, U.S. State Department, 2201 C Street NW, Washington, D.C. 20520. Telephone: (202) 647-1049; Web: http://www.state.gov/t.
Section of the State Department responsible for negotiating and implementing arms control agreements to which the United States is party.

Organization for the Prohibition of Chemical Weapons, Johan de Wittlaan 32, 2517 JR - The Hague, Netherlands. Telephone: (+31) 70 416 3300; email: media@opcw.org; Web: http://www.opcw.org.
International body responsible for ensuring the implementation of the Chemical Weapons Convention.

Stockholm International Peace Research Institute, Signalistgatan 9, SE-169 70 Solna, Sweden. Telephone: (+46) 8-655-97-00; email: sipri@sipri.org; Web: http://www.sipri.org.
Think tank addressing issues related to international peace and security.

Union of Concerned Scientists, 2 Brattle Square, Cambridge, Mass. 02238-9105. Telephone: (617) 547-5552; email: ucs@ucsusa.org; Web: http://www.ucsusa.org.
Organization that promotes environmental issues and addresses such nuclear weapons–related issues as missile defense and nuclear testing through its Global Security Program.

United Nations Department for Disarmament Affairs, Monitoring, Database and Information Branch, S-3151 United Nations, 1st Avenue at 46th Street, New York, N.Y. 10017. Email: ddaweb@un.org; Web: http://disarmament.un.org/dda.htm.
UN agency that analyzes global developments concerning disarmament, observes the implementation of existing arms control agreements, and assists with the negotiation of new ones.

Further Research

Books

Arms Control Association. *Arms Control and International Security: An Introduction.* Washington, D.C.: Arms Control Association, 1989.

Baucom, Donald R. *The Origins of SDI, 1944–1983.* Lawrence, Kans.: University Press of Kansas, 1992.

Bundy, McGeorge. *Danger and Survival: Choices about the Bomb in the First Fifty Years.* New York: Random House, 1988.

Bunn, George, and Christopher Chyba, eds. *U.S. Nuclear Weapons Policy: Confronting Today's Threats.* Washington, D.C.: Brookings Institution Press, 2006.

Butler, Richard. *The Greatest Threat: Iraq, Weapons of Mass Destruction, and the Growing Crisis in Global Security.* New York: Public Affairs, 2000.

Campbell, Kurt, Robert J. Einhorn, and Mitchell B. Reiss, eds. *The Nuclear Tipping Point: Why States Reconsider Their Nuclear Choices.* Washington, D.C.: Brookings Institution Press, 2004.

Cohen, Avner. *Israel and the Bomb.* New York: Columbia University Press, 1998.

Cirincione, Joseph, Jon B. Wolfsthal, and Miriam Rajkumar. *Deadly Arsenals: Nuclear, Biological and Chemical Threats.* 2nd ed. Washington, D.C.: Carnegie Endowment for International Peace, 2005.

FitzGerald, Frances. *Way Out There in the Blue: Reagan, Star Wars, and the End of the Cold War.* New York: Simon and Schuster, 2000.

Freedman, Lawrence. *The Evolution of Nuclear Strategy.* New York: St. Martin's Press, 1981.

Holloway, David. *Stalin and the Bomb: The Soviet Union and Atomic Energy, 1939–1956.* New Haven, Conn.: Yale University Press, 1994.

International Institute for Strategic Studies. *The Military Balance, 2008–2001.* London: Oxford University Press, 2008.

Kaplan, Fred. *The Wizards of Armageddon.* New York: Simon and Schuster, 1983.

Miller, Judith, Stephen Engelberg, and William Broad. *Germs: Biological Weapons and America's Secret War.* New York: Simon and Schuster, 2001.

National Academy of Sciences. *Nuclear Arms Control: Background and Issues.* Washington, D.C.: National Academy Press, 1985.

Perkovich, George, *India's Nuclear Bomb: The Impact on Global Proliferation.* Berkeley, Calif.: University of California Press, 1999.

Reiss, Mitchell. *Bridled Ambitions: Why Countries Constrain Their Nuclear Capabilities.* Washington, D.C.: Woodrow Wilson Center Press, 1995.

Rhodes, Richard. *The Making of the Atomic Bomb.* New York: Simon and Schuster, 1986.

Sagan, Scott D., and Kenneth N. Waltz. *The Spread of Nuclear Weapons: A Debate.* New York: W.W. Norton, 1997.

Schell, Jonathan. *The Seventh Decade: The New Shape of Nuclear Danger.* New York: Metropolitan Books, 2007.

Schwartz, Stephen, ed. *Atomic Audit: The Costs and Consequences of Nuclear Weapons since 1940.* Washington, D.C.: Brookings Institution Press, 1998.

Scoblic, J. Peter. *U.S. vs. Them: Conservatism in the Age of Nuclear Terror.* New York: Viking, 2008.

Sigal, Leon V. *Disarming Strangers.* Princeton, N.J.: Princeton University Press, 1997.

Smith, Gerard. *Doubletalk: The Story of SALT I.* Garden City, N.Y.: Doubleday and Company, 1980.

Stockholm International Peace Research Institute. *SIPRI Yearbook, 2008: Armaments, Disarmament, and International Security.* New York: Oxford University Press, 2008.

Talbott, Strobe. *Deadly Gambits: The Reagan Administration and the Stalemate in Nuclear Arms Control.* New York: Knopf, 1984.

Tucker, Jonathan B., ed. *Toxic Terror: Assessing Terrorist Use of Chemical and Biological Weapons.* Cambridge, Mass.: MIT Press, 1999.

Articles and Reports

Bunn, Matthew. "Securing the Bomb 2007." September 2007. Available at http://www.nti.org/e_research/securingthebomb07.pdf.

Director of National Intelligence. "Iran: Nuclear Intentions and Capabilities." November 2007. Available at http://www.dni.gov/press_releases/20071203_release.pdf.

International Security Advisory Board. "Report on Proliferation Implications of the Global Expansion of Civil Nuclear Power." Report to the State Department. April 2008. Available at http://www.state.gov/documents/organization/105587.pdf.

Iraq Survey Group. "Iraq Survey Group Final Report." September 2004. Available at http://www.globalsecurity.org/wmd/library/report/2004/isg-final-report.

Joseph, Robert G. "U.S. Strategy to Combat the Proliferation of Weapons of Mass Destruction." March 2006. Available at http://www.state.gov/t/us/rm/63877.htm.

"Key Judgments from October 2002 National Intelligence Estimate on Iraq's Weapons of Mass Destruction." Declassified July 2003. Available at http://www.fas.org/irp/cia/product/iraq-wmd.html.

Obama, Barack. "Remarks by President Barack Obama, Hradcany Square, Prague, Czech Republic, April 5, 2009." White House Office of the Press Secretary. Available at http://www.whitehouse.gov/the_press_office/Remarks-By-President-Barack-Obama-In-Prague-As-Delivered.

"Report of the Commission to Assess the Ballistic Missile Threat to the United States." The Rumsfeld Report. July 15, 1998. Available at http://www.house.gov/hasc/testimony/105thcongress/BMThreat.htm.

Shultz, George P., et al. "A World Free of Nuclear Weapons." *Wall Street Journal,* January 2007. Available at http://www.fcnl.org/issues/item.php?item_id=2252&issue_id=54.

U.S. Department of State. "Adherence to and Compliance with Arms Control, Nonproliferation, and Disarmament Agreements and Commitments." August 2005. Available at http://www.state.gov/t/vci/rls/rpt/51977.htm.

Web Sites

Arms Control Today
http://www.armscontrol.org/act

Bulletin of the Atomic Scientists
http://www.thebulletin.org

Nuclear Threat Initiative (NTI)
http://www.NTI.org

Nonproliferation Review
http://www.rienner.com/npr.htm

Documents

1. Treaty on the Non-Proliferation of Nuclear Weapons (Nuclear Non-Proliferation Treaty), July 1, 1968

The full text is available at http://www.state.gov/www/global/arms/treaties/npt1.html.

Extracts

The States concluding this Treaty, hereinafter referred to as the "Parties to the Treaty,"

Considering the devastation that would be visited upon all mankind by a nuclear war and the consequent need to make every effort to avert the danger of such a war and to take measures to safeguard the security of peoples,

Believing that the proliferation of nuclear weapons would seriously enhance the danger of nuclear war,

In conformity with resolutions of the United Nations General Assembly calling for the conclusion of an agreement on the prevention of wider dissemination of nuclear weapons,

Undertaking to cooperate in facilitating the application of International Atomic Energy Agency safeguards on peaceful nuclear activities, . . .

Have agreed as follows:

Article I

Each nuclear-weapon State Party to the Treaty undertakes not to transfer to any recipient whatsoever nuclear weapons or other nuclear explosive devices or control over such weapons or explosive devices directly, or indirectly; and not in any way to assist, encourage, or induce any non-nuclear weapon State to manufacture or otherwise acquire nuclear weapons or other nuclear explosive devices, or control over such weapons or explosive devices.

Article II

Each non-nuclear-weapon States Party to the Treaty undertakes not to receive the transfer from any transferor whatsoever of nuclear weapons or other nuclear explosive devices or of control over such weapons or explosive devices directly, or indirectly; not to manufacture or otherwise acquire nuclear weapons or other nuclear explosive devices; and not to seek or receive any assistance in the manufacture of nuclear weapons or other nuclear explosive devices.

Article III

1. Each non-nuclear-weapon State Party to the Treaty undertakes to accept safeguards, as set forth in an agreement to be negotiated and concluded with the International Atomic Energy Agency in accordance with the Statute of the International Atomic Energy Agency and the Agency's safeguards system, for the exclusive purpose of verification of the fulfillment of its obligations assumed under this Treaty with a view to preventing diversion of nuclear energy from peaceful uses to nuclear weapons or other nuclear explosive devices. Procedures for the safeguards required by this article shall be followed with respect to source or special fissionable material whether it is being produced, processed or used in any principal nuclear facility or is outside any such facility. The safeguards required by this article shall be applied to all source or special fissionable material in all peaceful nuclear activities within the territory of such State, under its jurisdiction, or carried out under its control anywhere.

2. Each State Party to the Treaty undertakes not to provide: (a) source or special fissionable material, or (b) equipment or material especially designed or prepared for the processing, use or production of special fissionable material, to any non-nuclear-weapon State for peaceful purposes, unless the source or special fissionable material shall be subject to the safeguards required by this article.

3. The safeguards required by this article shall be implemented in a manner designed to comply with article IV of this Treaty, and to avoid hampering the economic or technological development of the Parties or international cooperation in the field of peaceful nuclear activities, including the international exchange of nuclear material and equipment for the processing, use or production of nuclear material for peaceful purposes in accordance with the provisions of this article and the principle of safeguarding set forth in the Preamble of the Treaty.

4. Non-nuclear-weapon States Party to the Treaty shall conclude agreements with the International Atomic Energy Agency to meet the requirements of this article either individually or together with other States in accordance with the Statute of the International Atomic Energy Agency. Negotiation of such agreements shall commence within 180 days from the original entry into force of this Treaty. For States depositing their instruments of ratification or accession after the 180-day period, negotiation of

such agreements shall commence not later than the date of such deposit. Such agreements shall enter into force not later than eighteen months after the date of initiation of negotiations.

2. Treaty between the United States of America and the Russian Federation on Strategic Offensive Reductions (The Treaty of Moscow, or SORT), May 24, 2002

The document is available at http://www.state.gov/t/vci/trty/127129.htm#1.

Full Text of Treaty

The United States of America and the Russian Federation, hereinafter referred to as the Parties,

Embarking upon the path of new relations for a new century and committed to the goal of strengthening their relationship through cooperation and friendship,

Believing that new global challenges and threats require the building of a qualitatively new foundation for strategic relations between the Parties,

Desiring to establish a genuine partnership based on the principles of mutual security, cooperation, trust, openness, and predictability,

Committed to implementing significant reductions in strategic offensive arms,

Proceeding from the Joint Statements by the President of the United States of America and the President of the Russian Federation on Strategic Issues of July 22, 2001 in Genoa and on a New Relationship between the United States and Russia of November 13, 2001 in Washington,

Mindful of their obligations under the Treaty Between the United States of America and the Union of Soviet Socialists Republics on the Reduction and Limitation of Strategic Offensive Arms of July 31, 1991, hereinafter referred to as the START Treaty,

Mindful of their obligations under Article VI of the Treaty on the Non-Proliferation of Nuclear Weapons of July 1, 1968, and

Convinced that this Treaty will help to establish more favorable conditions for actively promoting security and cooperation, and enhancing international stability,

Have agreed as follows:

Article I

Each Party shall reduce and limit strategic nuclear warheads, as stated by the President of the United States of America on November 13, 2001 and as stated by the President of the Russian Federation on November 13, 2001 and December 13, 2001 respectively, so that by December 31, 2012 the aggregate number of such warheads does not exceed 1700-2200 for each Party. Each Party shall determine for itself the composition and structure of its strategic offensive arms, based on the established aggregate limit for the number of such warheads.

Article II

The Parties agree that the START Treaty remains in force in accordance with its terms.

Article III

For purposes of implementing this Treaty, the Parties shall hold meetings at least twice a year of a Bilateral Implementation Commission.

Article IV

1. This Treaty shall be subject to ratification in accordance with the constitutional procedures of each Party. This Treaty shall enter into force on the date of the exchange of instruments of ratification.

2. This Treaty shall remain in force until December 31, 2012 and may be extended by agreement of the Parties or superseded earlier by a subsequent agreement.

3. Each Party, in exercising its national sovereignty, may withdraw from this Treaty upon three months written notice to the other Party.

Article V

This Treaty shall be registered pursuant to Article 102 of the Charter of the United Nations.

Done at Moscow on May 24, 2002, in two copies, each in the English and Russian languages, both texts being equally authentic.

FOR THE UNITED STATES OF AMERICA George W. Bush

FOR THE RUSSIAN FEDERATION Vladimir V. Putin

DRUG TRAFFICKING

Mary Sisson

Drug trafficking is the illegal shipment and distribution of drugs. Although in some cases the drugs being trafficked are themselves legal (for example, a trafficker might illegally smuggle an otherwise legal prescription drug from one country to another), the vast majority of drugs trafficked are psychoactive substances that are used recreationally, such as marijuana, heroin, and cocaine. In addition to supplying dangerous and addictive substances to users, drug trafficking is dominated by violent criminal organizations that have significantly challenged governments in some areas for control.

Historical Background and Development

The use of psychoactive drugs dates back to ancient times. Certain plants create psychoactive effects when they are eaten or smoked, and humans throughout history and in different parts of the world have discovered and used these plants. There is archeological evidence that the opium poppy and the cannabis plant were being used more than 6,000 years ago, while the coca plant was being cultivated some 5,000 years ago. Large-scale trafficking in drugs is a modern phenomenon, however. For much of human history, psychoactive plants were mainly cultivated and consumed locally because they tended to lose potency during travel.

The exception to this rule was opium. By the end of the sixteenth century, European traders were shipping large quantities of opium grown in India to China. The demand for opium in East Asia began to increase rapidly in the seventeenth century, when the practice of smoking opium spread through the region. The increase in opium abuse and addiction led the emperor of China to ban its import and sale in 1729.

The result was an intense drug-trafficking effort by European traders, culminating in the Opium Wars of 1839–1842 and 1856–1860 between Great Britain and China. Great Britain, which by this point controlled India's lucrative opium farms, won the wars and forced China to legalize the opium trade. The result was a devastating increase in the number of opium addicts in China.

China was not the only country with a problem. The Western powers were also beginning to develop significant populations of addicts. In the nineteenth century, advances in chemistry allowed the purification of psychoactive compounds from plants, including cocaine from the coca leaf and morphine and heroin from the opium poppy. These compounds were highly concentrated and maintained their potency over time, making them ideal for shipping and processing. An entire industry of what were called patent medicines sprang up in the United States and Europe. Many of these medications contained cocaine or opiates, and cocaine was even used in soft drinks, such as the original Coca Cola. Cocaine and opiate addiction became increasingly common.

By the early twentieth century, public opinion had largely turned against narcotics, and governments were increasingly pressured to restrict or ban them. This change in attitudes, combined with the fact that the opium trade to China had become less lucrative to Great Britain as domestic growers competed with imports from India, resulted in the first international agreement to curtail the drug trade, issued in the report of the International Opium Commission, which met in Shanghai in 1909. That agreement, which over time expanded into the body of international drug-trafficking law that exists today, helped establish one of its basic principles: nations should refrain from exporting drugs into countries where their use is illegal.

Drug trafficking remained a persistent but relatively small-scale problem until the 1960s and 1970s, when drug use went through a period of greater acceptability, even stylishness and popularity, in the United States and Europe. New, synthetic drugs, such as amphetamines, were developed during the twentieth century and found users as well.

In response to this larger market, drug trafficking underwent a remarkable expansion in the 1970s and 1980s. Trafficking networks became increasingly well-funded and sophisticated, and drug traffickers have amassed incredible personal fortunes.

Current Status

The 1909 Shanghai agreement applied only to opium, but a series of international treaties have since been put into place that have greatly expanded the kinds of drugs under prohibition (see Document 1). Countries have agreed to ban the production, export, and use (except for medical and scientific purposes) of many drugs, including opiates, cocaine, cannabis, hallucinogens, and synthetic drugs.

Although under international law the legal trade in these drugs is profoundly restricted, large-scale drug trafficking is remarkably lucrative, and traffickers have not sat idly by as governments have tried to suppress their business. Drug traffickers often use bribery and intimidation to obtain cooperation from government and police officials, and in some parts of the world they have allied themselves with antigovernment groups and obtained effective control of significant territory.

Research

Because nearly every aspect of the drug trade, including production and consumption, is illegal, all statistics regarding drug trafficking should be regarded with skepticism. Typically researchers rely on measures of the legal response to the drug trade. For example, to determine where drugs are being consumed, researchers examine the number of users who seek help with their addiction. The volume of trafficking is typically determined by looking at the amount of drugs seized by law enforcement. These measures can be affected by factors that are unrelated to the drug trade itself, such as the availability of drug-treatment programs and the competence and honesty of local police. In addition, because local governments and law enforcement agencies are usually under pressure to show progress in suppressing drug trafficking, the statistics they produce can be unreliable.

Nonetheless, it is clear that drug trafficking is big business. Globally, some 1.6 million drug-seizure cases were reported in 2006, with the amount seized equivalent to 31 billion doses, according to the United Nations Office on Drugs and Crime "2008 World Drug Report" (see map, p. 626). Approximately 65 percent of the seizure cases involved cannabis, which includes marijuana (cannabis herb) and hashish (cannabis resin). Fourteen percent involved opiates, including opium, morphine, and heroin. Coca leaf products, such as cocaine, made up 9 percent of seizures, and the remaining 12 percent were synthetic drugs, such as amphetamines, methamphetamines, and ecstasy (MDMA; 3,4-methylenedioxymethamphetamine).

These different types of drugs are trafficked in different ways to different places, depending on a wide variety of factors. Some drugs, such as cocaine, are typically trafficked by large centralized criminal organizations that operate internationally and routinely cooperate with one another. Other drugs, such as marijuana, are just as frequently trafficked by small-scale producers who distribute only locally and do not communicate with one another at all. Heroin and cocaine are produced in only a small handful of countries and must be transported to markets worldwide; in contrast, cannabis is grown just about everywhere and synthetic drugs can be produced any place there is a lab, the expertise, and the necessary ingredients.

Drug trafficking is a truly global phenomenon, and no one nationality has a monopoly on it. But because the trade is illegal, drug traffickers are motivated to seek out couriers they can trust. As a result, trafficking is sometimes dominated by certain families or ethnic groups who typically have members both in the drug-producing countries and the countries where the drugs are consumed. This practice allows for a certain element of coercion. If the individuals selling drugs in a country with more functional law enforcement gets caught, they will be less likely to testify against the drug organization if they have relatives in a part of the world where the organization can easily retaliate against them.

Like any other trade, drug trafficking is an effort to connect producers with consumers. Drug consumers tend to be concentrated in wealthy regions, such as North America, Japan, and Western Europe. But such areas often tend to have robust law enforcement organizations, making drug production there more difficult. Drug production, in turn, tends to be concentrated in regions that are poor and where law enforcement is ineffective or corrupt—in particular, certain areas of South America, Southwest Asia, and Southeast Asia.

The distinction between drug-consuming and drug-producing areas is far from clear-cut, however. Sizable drug-production operations certainly exist in wealthy drug-consuming countries, such as the United States, Canada, and the Netherlands, and countries such as Colombia and Afghanistan that produce drugs or that are frequently used as trafficking routes often have high rates of drug use and addiction as well.

The routes used to traffic drugs can quickly change. That is because in their pure form, before they are diluted and sold to users, drugs are typically highly concentrated. As a result, a large number of doses can be transported in a relatively small package. Because they are not bulky, drugs can be shipped through the mail, hidden in cargo, smuggled in luggage, and even transported inside the bodies of people.

The main factor that determines which drug-trafficking route is followed is the efforts of law enforcement. For example, in the United States, the early 2000s saw an increasing number of small-scale domestic laboratories that produced and distributed methamphetamine, a powerful synthetic stimulant. In 2005, however, the United States adopted regulations that greatly restricted the availability of ephedrine and pseudoephedrine, chemicals used in cold medications that are also used to make methamphetamine.

Within months, methamphetamine production shifted to larger laboratories located in Mexico. New networks, dominated by Mexican criminal organizations, sprang up to smuggle the drug across the border and distribute it in the United States. The Mexican government quickly responded by restricting the imports of ephedrine and pseudoephedrine into Mexico. By 2007, according to the U.S. National Drug Intelligence Center, imports of methamphetamine from Mexico had declined and the cost of the drug in the United States had gone up. But by 2008, the price had stabilized, suggesting that domestic U.S. operations had found new sources of ephedrine and pseudoephedrine, and had increased production again.

Because effective law enforcement can complicate their business, drug traffickers tend to seek out areas where local governments are weak and local law enforcement officials corrupt. For example, 2006 saw a sharp increase in the amount of cocaine seized in West and central Africa, according to the "2008 World Drug Report." This increase is believed to be a result of cocaine traffickers finding it easier to ship drugs from South America to Europe through Africa, where customs inspections are apparently more lax, rather than sticking to established smuggling routes through North America or the Caribbean.

Policies and Programs

Although drug trafficking as an activity is distinct from drug production and drug consumption, traffickers can and do influence production and consumption, and they are influenced by them. As a result, policies attacking drug trafficking need to take drug consumption and production into account as well.

For example, drug trafficking exists because certain drugs are illegal. A seemingly simple solution to the violence and criminality of the drug trade would be to legalize all drugs. Although such legalization has its supporters, it has not been a widely adopted as a policy because of concerns that legalization would lead to the greater availability of drugs, resulting in increased consumption and even greater numbers of addicts.

Another reason to pay attention to production and consumption is that trafficking itself is very hard to stop. Although drug trafficking is illegal everywhere (and in some countries, such as Laos and Iran, the penalty for trafficking is execution), there is a tremendous amount of legitimate trade and tourism happening around the world, and drugs are easy to smuggle in along with ordinary goods. Although customs inspections and border checks can certainly have an effect, it is simply not realistic to expect them to filter out all the illegal drugs coming into a country without seriously damaging legitimate international commerce.

Production operations, on the other hand, tend to be harder to hide. Law enforcement agencies have focused a good deal of attention on suppressing drug production, mainly through programs that eradicate illicit crops such as opium poppies, coca plants, and cannabis. These programs can have unintended consequences, however. In North America, the eradication of outdoor cannabis plots has led growers to focus on cultivating even more potent strains of cannabis indoors. In addition, in many countries the farmers who grow these crops (as opposed to the traffickers who process and trade them) are quite poor, and eradication programs can lead to significant hardship for them.

Another strategy to inhibit drug production is to restrict access to the precursor chemicals (the chemicals used to manufacture the drugs). This strategy can be very effective in disrupting certain types of production. For example, restricting the sales of ephedrine and pseudoephedrine in the United States helped significantly reduce the number of small illegal laboratories synthesizing methamphetamine. These labs, which used toxic chemicals, posed serious health risks to the communities in which they were located.

But restricting the precursor chemicals rarely puts an end to trafficking. Indeed, it can lead to more extensive trafficking as drug-processing operations are moved away from the prime markets to countries with lax enforcement. In addition, as precursor chemicals have become more and more restricted, new trafficking networks specializing in their trade have emerged.

Another law enforcement strategy is to focus on the illicit profits that drug traffickers make. Strict laws against money laundering (the practice of taking money made illegally and making it appear as though it were the result of a legitimate business) can make it more difficult for drug traffickers to avoid imprisonment. Likewise, laws that impose harsh penalties on organized crime can help disrupt trafficking networks.

Nonetheless, a country with strict laws and effective law enforcement agencies can still have serious problems with drug trafficking if the countries that surround it lack strong laws and officials who are willing to enforce them. Drug trafficking is an international business, and traffickers gravitate to countries where they can do business with impunity.

International pressure has been brought to bear on countries with particularly lax banking laws to tighten their standards, but typically a country becomes a haven for drug trafficking because its government is weak. In countries such as Afghanistan, Colombia, and Myanmar, the government's control over drug-producing regions is tenuous at best. Drug-trafficking operations in many countries survive because officials are either bribed or intimidated by violence (see Case Study—Cocaine Trafficking in Colombia).

As a result, some argue that drug trafficking should not be approached simply as a law enforcement problem but, instead, as a problem of weak states. In this approach, the strength of a government must first be built up so that law enforcement and judicial officials can effectively address the problem of drug trafficking.

The United States has probably been the most ardent supporter of this approach. The country has provided funding, advice, and even military assistance to countries such as Mexico and Colombia to combat drug trafficking. Countries such as Colombia even extradite drug traffickers to the United States to face criminal prosecution, on the theory that traffickers will be less able to bribe or intimidate officials in the United States.

This approach is not without its critics; some regard the U.S. interest in how other governments are run as, at best, foreign meddling. Nonetheless, some aspects are less controversial. For example, increasing the pay of police officers and judges can make them less willing to accept bribes from drug traffickers. Likewise, providing police with adequate weaponry and equipment can make them less vulnerable to threats of violence.

Others argue that drug production and trafficking are mainly a problem of poverty. Farmers grow drug crops because they need to make a living, and couriers smuggle drugs because they lack economic alternatives. To this way of thinking, economic development, especially programs that provide substitute crops for farmers who grow drugs, would help reduce the supply.

However, although substitute-crop programs can certainly help ease the financial hardship caused by eradication, they can be difficult to effectively enact. A substitute crop may not be well suited to a particular climate, may not have an established market, or simply may not be as profitable for the farmer. If government control over a region is not secure, traffickers may punish farmers who stop growing drug crops.

Many drug-producing regions are remote, and traffickers are often willing to transport the drug crop out to market for the farmers, a service that the buyers of other crops typically do not provide. To help with this, roads have been built to these regions, but even though such roads help establish markets for legitimate crops, they have also been used to facilitate drug trafficking.

Needless to say, drug trafficking would not exist if there was no demand for drugs. Reducing consumption can reduce drug trafficking, and it also has benefits for public health because psychoactive drugs can be lethal in the short term and very detrimental to people's health in the long term.

It is possible to reduce the number of users, in particular the so-called casual drug users who use drugs infrequently and make no great effort to seek them out. Public awareness campaigns and media stories exposing the harm that drugs cause can dissuade people from trying them.

Reducing the demand for drugs can be tricky, however. Poorly designed drug-education programs aimed at youth can actually make them more likely to use drugs. People sometimes use drugs specifically because they are illegal— as an expression of rebellion or to indicate their membership in an "outlaw" culture. In such cases, public awareness campaigns and antidrug messages from authority figures can simply make drug use seem all the more enticing.

In addition, people who develop drug problems, such as addiction, are by definition unlikely to stop using, no matter how dire the consequences. Drug-treatment programs can help, although the relapse rates for some drugs are very high. A greater availability of such programs, especially in poor countries where health services are often unavailable, would probably help reduce the demand for drugs.

Regional Summaries

The Americas

The Americas are home to extensive, well-organized, and entrenched drug-trafficking networks dedicated to the processing and distribution of cocaine. Coca plants are grown almost exclusively in Colombia, Bolivia, and Peru, and cocaine's largest market is in North America. Cocaine traffickers use a variety of routes through Central America and the Caribbean to reach North America, but the majority of cocaine that reaches the United States travels through Mexico.

Although North Americans remain the primary consumer of cocaine, South Americans have increasingly been using the drug (Western Europe is also a growing market). In addition, coca cultivation and cocaine trafficking have had serious negative effects in Colombia, Peru, and Bolivia. Separatist guerrilla organizations such as the Revolutionary Armed Forces of Colombia (FARC; Fuerzas Armadas Revolucionarias de Colombia) and the Shining Path in Peru have funded themselves through drug operations. In addition, cocaine traffickers have amassed sufficient wealth and firepower to pose threats to the central governments on their own.

The Americas also have large networks dedicated to the trafficking of marijuana, or cannabis herb. Although marijuana is mostly trafficked locally, a significant quantity is trafficked from South America to the United States, mainly through Mexico, and a lesser quantity is trafficked from Canada into the United States. Marijuana grown in Canada and the United States is of

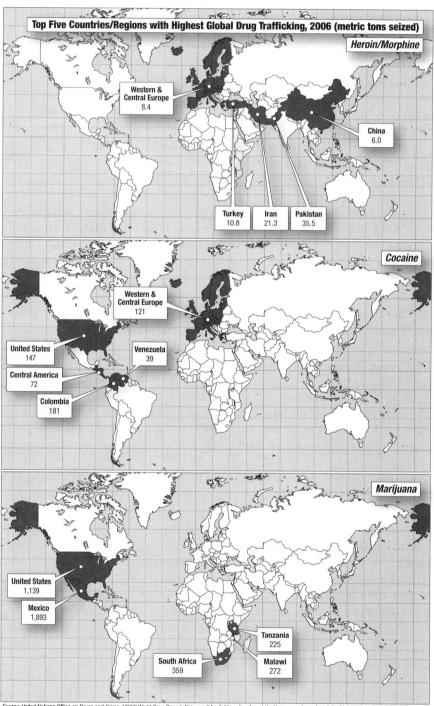

Top Five Countries/Regions with Highest Global Drug Trafficking, 2006 (metric tons seized)

Heroin/Morphine

Western & Central Europe
8.4

China
6.0

Turkey
10.8

Iran
21.3

Pakistan
35.5

Cocaine

Western & Central Europe
121

United States
147

Venezuela
39

Central America
72

Colombia
181

Marijuana

United States
1,139

Mexico
1,893

Tanzania
225

South Africa
359

Malawi
272

Source: United Nations Office on Drugs and Crime. "2008 World Drug Report: Seizures." Available online from http://www.unodc.org/unodc/en/data-and-analysis/WDR-2008.html.

particular concern because, thanks to campaigns in both countries to eradicate outdoor growing, the drug is usually grown indoors. Such marijuana tends to be extremely potent.

The United States is a significant market for methamphetamine, which is usually produced locally or trafficked from Mexico or, less commonly, Canada. North America is also a significant market for ecstasy. Previously, most ecstasy seized in North America was European in origin, but since 2003 production has shifted largely to U.S. and Canadian laboratories. Canadian ecstasy production has been dominated by Asian criminal gangs, and ecstasy from Canada has been trafficked to Hong Kong and Australia.

Mexico's role as a major drug-trafficking corridor into the United States has caused serious problems of government corruption and violence as criminal gangs fight one another for a share of the lucrative business. In response, in late 2006, Mexican president Felipe Calderon began sending army troops to areas plagued by drug violence.

The result has been a major outburst of fighting as well-armed drug traffickers battle army and police forces. In 2008 alone, more than 6,000 people were killed in drug-related violence in Mexico. Fighting near the border with the United States has sparked fears there that violence could spill over into U.S. territory. The Calderon administration has claimed that the violence simply proves that the drug cartels are under pressure, and it has asked the United States to support its efforts against trafficking with increased military aid, as well as to crack down on the smuggling of guns into Mexico from the United States.

Europe

Europe, in particular Western Europe, is a significant importer of illegal drugs. The vast majority of heroin production takes place in Afghanistan, and most of that heroin is, in turn, trafficked to Europe.

Afghani heroin travels into Europe via two routes. The Silk Route, which goes through Central Asia, serves the Russian, Nordic, and, to an extent, the Balkan markets. The Balkan Route, which has becoming increasingly important, passes through Turkey and the Balkan countries to markets in Western Europe.

Europe is also a major importer of marijuana. Marijuana grown in western and southern Africa is trafficked to Western and central Europe, while smaller trafficking operations ship marijuana from central Asia to Eastern Europe, in particular Russia. Western and central Europe is a major destination for trafficked hashish, which is most commonly smuggled into Europe via Spain.

Western Europe is also believed to be the largest market for cocaine outside the Americas. Cocaine, which is produced in South America, is most commonly smuggled into Europe through Spain or Portugal.

The global production and trafficking of amphetamines are concentrated in Europe, in particular Western and central Europe. These drugs are typically produced for local consumption, although they are also exported to the Middle East. The Netherlands and Belgium are centers of ecstasy production in Europe. Previously ecstasy was commonly trafficked from Europe to North America, but the rise of North American ecstasy laboratories has curtailed that trade.

North Africa and the Middle East

North Africa, in particular Morocco, remains an important producer of hashish, which is primarily trafficked to Western Europe. Since 2004, however, hashish production in Morocco has declined.

Nevertheless, hashish trafficking in the region has held its ground. Middle Eastern traffickers have increasingly turned to hashish produced in Afghanistan, which they import and then smuggle into Europe. In addition, trafficking networks have sprung up within the region as the local consumption of hashish has increased.

Amphetamine trafficking has become a serious problem over the past few years, with the amphetamine seizures in the region increasing rapidly since 2002. These amphetamines are mainly produced in Bulgaria and Turkey, and are trafficked primarily to Saudi Arabia.

Sub-Saharan Africa

Sub-Saharan Africa is a major producer of marijuana, both for domestic use and for export into Europe. The region is also becoming an increasingly important trafficking stop for a variety of other drugs, presumably because traffickers find local officials relatively easy to bribe or intimidate.

As a result, hashish from North Africa and Afghanistan is being trafficked through coastal African countries to markets in Canada. Cocaine from South America is increasingly passing through West and central Africa on its way to Western Europe. And methamphetamines have been seized in African countries in recent years.

As drug-trafficking routes through sub-Saharan Africa become better established, the local use of drugs such as hashish and cocaine is increasing. As a result, local trafficking networks for these drugs are also developing.

Central Asian and South Asia

South Asia was once the prime growing area for the opium poppy, but these days more than 90 percent of the world's heroin and morphine production takes place in Afghanistan. Heroin production in Afghanistan has been used to fund terrorist organizations such as Al Qaeda, and it is also a significant source of income for the Taliban and other extremist groups. It is believed that Afghani drug traffickers are becoming more sophisticated and doing more of the processing of the opium poppy into heroin themselves.

Afghanistan's neighbors, in particular Pakistan and Iran, are major centers for trafficking Afghani heroin abroad. In addition to the law enforcement challenge posed by the heroin trade, these countries also have high rates of opiate use and addiction. In addition, Afghanistan is a large and increasingly significant producer of hashish, much of which is trafficked through Pakistan on its way to markets abroad.

Pacific Rim

Southeast Asia has a long history of heroin production. Myanmar remains the world's second-largest producer of heroin, and Asia has high rates of opiate abuse. Nonetheless, heroin production in the region has tapered off since the mid-1990s. Southeast Asia once produced the majority of the world's heroin; now that dubious honor belongs to Afghanistan. Unfortunately, heroin production in the region is apparently being replaced by the production of methamphetamine. Myanmar has become a major producer of methamphetamine, and China is becoming an increasingly important producer and consumer of the drug.

Methamphetamine is trafficked to and through several Asian countries. Methamphetamine from Myanmar goes to China, Thailand, India, and Bangladesh, while China's methamphetamine goes to Hong Kong, Taiwan, Japan, Indonesia, Korea, and the Philippines. In some cases, the drug is consumed in those markets; in other cases, it is trafficked along to Australia, New Zealand, the United States, and Canada.

Data

Table 1   Drug-Producing Regions, 2007 (%)

Opium	
Afghanistan	92
Myanmar	5
Rest of world	2
Coca leaf	
Colombia	60
Peru	29
Bolivia	10
Marijuana[a]	
North America	31
South America	24
Africa	22
Asia	16
Europe	6
Oceania	1

Source: United Nations Office on Drugs and Crime, "2008 World Drug Report," available at http://www.unodc.org/unodc/en/data-and-analysis/WDR-2008.html.

Notes: Percentage of global yield.

[a]2006 data.

Table 2   Drug Seizure Distribution: Five Countries with the Largest Shares of Drug Seizures in 2006 (%)

Heroin/morphine	
Pakistan	34
Iran	20
Turkey	10
China	6
Afghanistan	5
Cocaine	
Colombia	26
United States	21
Spain	7
Venezuela	6
Panama	5
Marijuana	
Mexico	36
United States	22
South Africa	7
Malawi	5
Tanzania	4
Hashish	
Spain	45
Pakistan	11
Morocco	9
France	7
Iran	6
Amphetamines	
Saudi Arabia	28
China	14
United States	13
Myanmar	7
United Kingdom[a]	5

Source: United Nations Office on Drugs and Crime, "2008 World Drug Report," available at http://www.unodc.org/unodc/en/data-and-analysis/WDR-2008.html.

Notes: Percentages based on kilogram-equivalents seized worldwide.

[a]2005 data for England and Wales only.

Table 3   Drug Consumption: Primary Drugs of Abuse among People Treated for Drug Problems (%)

	Cannabis	Opiates	Cocaine	Amphetamines
Africa	63.6	15.7	9.6	5.2[a]
North America	35.3	9.8	31.2	10.7
South America	30.8	2.6	54.0	1.8
Asia	11.5	63.3	0.4	18.4
Eastern Europe	16.6	66.1	2.7	9.4
Western Europe	20.8	55.4	12.9	11.5

Source: United Nations Office on Drugs and Crime, "2008 World Drug Report," available at http://www.unodc.org/unodc/en/data-and-analysis/WDR-2008.html.

Notes: Percentages are the average of all countries in the region, taken from the most recent available reports.

[a]Includes all amphetamine-type stimulants.

Case Study—Cocaine Trafficking in Colombia

Cocaine, first synthesized from the coca leaf in the 1850s, was at first a legal substance, and the coca plant was cultivated all around the world. But cocaine's addictiveness and unpredictable effects in people caused a major scare in the late nineteenth and early twentieth centuries that eventually led to international agreements to prohibit the drug. Coca cultivation came to a halt, except in certain regions of South America where it had been grown for thousands of years. In the 1970s, however, a series of events conspired to bring cocaine back on to the world stage.

At that time, marijuana use had significantly increased in the United States. Much of that marijuana was imported from Mexico, but in 1975 Mexican officials enacted a major crackdown on the trade. With supplies from Mexico cut off and demand in the United States still high, traffickers from Colombia decided to step in. Law enforcement in Colombia was weak, and Colombian criminals were already experienced traffickers in emeralds and consumer goods. They began trafficking marijuana to the United States.

Soon, however, they switched to another drug—cocaine. Cocaine is less bulky than marijuana, making it easier to disguise and to transport. At that time, the U.S. Drug Enforcement Administration had decided to focus its efforts on heroin, so the cocaine trade was more or less tolerated (although this would soon change). Cocaine was phenomenally profitable for traffickers, selling in the United States for twenty or thirty times what it cost to produce.

In the 1970s and 1980s, the cocaine trade was dominated by the Medellin Cartel, a criminal organization based in the Colombian city of Medellin. Previously, cocaine had been smuggled into the United States via suitcase, but the Medellin Cartel used small planes to transport massive amounts of cocaine into the country, even purchasing acreage on a Bahamian island for use as a transport stop. By the 1980s, the cartel was taking in billions of dollars, and U.S. and Colombian officials started cracking down. The Colombian government signed an extradition treaty with the United States in 1981, threatening to send cartel leaders there to face justice. The cartel responded by engaging in a spiraling campaign of violence, assassinating officials, undertaking a bombing campaign, and declaring "total and absolute war" against the government in 1989.

The Colombian government finally won the war against the Medellin Cartel in the early 1990s, killing or arresting most of the cartel leaders. The Colombian government did so with military assistance from the United States, but it also received considerable help from a less-savory partner—the Cali Cartel. A rival cocaine-trafficking organization based in the city of Cali, the cartel dominated the cocaine trade during the early 1990s and is believed to have developed the cocaine market in Europe. The Cali Cartel tried to remain beneath the notice of law enforcement by eschewing violence against government officials and the general populace—although the cartel readily murdered rival traffickers and recalcitrant employees, as well as homeless people, prostitutes, and others living in the poorer neighborhoods of Cali who the cartel considered socially undesirable.

To ensure cooperation from officials, the Cali Cartel relied primarily on bribery. Allegations that the cartel gave millions of dollars to the 1994 campaign of Colombian president Ernesto Samper Pizano seriously damaged U.S.-Colombian relations and may have prompted the Samper administration's crackdown on the cartel. The Cali Cartel leaders were arrested in the mid-1990s, and some were eventually extradited to the United States.

The cartels were extremely violent. By the late 1980s, at the height of the Medellin Cartel's antigovernment campaign, the leading cause of death in Colombia was homicide. The cocaine trade also worsened other forms of violence in Colombia.

Since the 1960s, Colombia has been home to several left-wing guerrilla insurgencies, most notably the FARC. In response, a number of right-wing paramilitary groups have sprung up, notably the United Self-Defense Forces of Colombia (AUC; Autodefensas Unidas de Colombia). Such groups have attacked one another and slaughtered civilians. The cocaine trade created a source of funding that both groups use to finance their warfare. These groups "tax" drug traffickers operating in the areas they control and provide them with armed protection against law enforcement. An AUC leader claimed in 2000 that the group received 70 percent of its funding from cocaine, and law enforcement officials in other countries have arrested cocaine traffickers with extensive ties to FARC.

The money derived from cocaine trafficking has had a serious destabilizing effect in Colombia. At its height, the AUC is thought to have had some 20,000 fighters, while FARC's power grew to such an extent that in 1998 the Colombian government granted the group effective control over 16,200 square miles of territory.

Recent years have seen setbacks for both groups. The FARC has suffered a series of military defeats since 2002, and the AUC officially disbanded in 2006. The rates of violent crime in Colombia have fallen considerably. Nonetheless, the country remains the world's foremost producer of cocaine, and drug trafficking will doubtless present many more challenges to peace and the rule of law in Colombia in the years to come.

Biographical Sketches

Antonio Maria Costa is the executive director of the United Nations Office on Drugs and Crime, which helps countries fight drug trafficking and other illegal activities. Costa, who was appointed executive director in 2002, has a background in economic development and advocates programs that help growers of drugs switch to alternative crops. Costa has strongly criticized celebrities for glamorizing cocaine use while ignoring the damage that drug trafficking does to developing countries. More controversially, he has criticized efforts to decriminalize marijuana in Europe.

Pablo Escobar (1949–1993) was a founder of the Medellin cocaine cartel in Colombia. Escobar was a car thief and smuggler who in the 1970s branched out into the cocaine business. Escobar became fantastically wealthy, and he courted publicity, running for public office in the 1980s. He also began ordering the assassination of uncooperative Colombian officials, including a leading presidential candidate in 1989. Another botched assassination attempt that same year resulted in the bombing of an airplane and the death of all 107 people on board. Escobar surrendered to Colombian officials in 1991, escaped prison the next year, and was killed in 1993 in a gun battle with government troops.

Theodore Roosevelt (1858–1919) was president of the United States from 1901 to 1909. Roosevelt made his reputation as a reformer, and while president, he pushed through regulations to ensure the safety and purity of food and drugs. In the process, Roosevelt took on patent medicines, which sometimes contained opiates and cocaine. Roosevelt became convinced that such substances were dangerous, and his administration took the initiative to arrange the first meeting of the International Opium Commission in Shanghai in 1909, a meeting that resulted in the first international agreement to control the trade in narcotics.

Khun Sa (1934–2007) was a drug lord who dominated the opium trade in Southeast Asia for three decades. Khun Sa (born Chang Chi-fu) entered the opium trade in Myanmar in 1963. Following an imprisonment, he moved into Thailand in 1974 and consolidated his hold over the opium trade. During the 1970s and 1980s, Southeast Asia produced roughly 70 percent of the world's heroin. In 1996, Khun Sa surrendered to Myanmar authorities and lived under house arrest until his death in 2007. Opium production in Southeast Asia dwindled following his arrest.

Álvaro Uribe Vélez was elected president of Colombia in 2002 and reelected in 2006. Uribe's administration has arrested and extradited more drug traffickers to the United States than any other presidential administration. The benefits of this policy have been mixed. The rates of violent crime in Colombia have plummeted, but the impact on cocaine production is thought to have been minimal. In 2009, U.S. President George W. Bush awarded Uribe the Presidential Medal of Freedom, the highest civilian award in the United States.

Directory

Asia-Pacific Non-Government Organization on Drug and Substance Abuse Prevention, Room #510, 2nd Building, 5th Floor, 5 Din Daeng Road, Phyathai District, Bangkok 10400, Thailand. Telephone: + 662-6409340; email: aspacngo@ webmail.aspacngo.org; Web: http://www.aspacngo.org.
Organization dedicated to preventing drug abuse and trafficking in Southeast Asia.

Drug Policy Alliance Network, 70 West 36th Street, 16th Floor, New York, N.Y. 10018. Telephone: (212) 613-8020; email: nyc@drugpolicy.org; Web: http://www .drugpolicy.org/homepage.cfm.
Organization created to reform drug policies in the United States.

Drug Policy Information Clearinghouse, P.O. Box 6000, Rockville, Md. 20849-6000. Telephone: (800) 666–3332; email: via Web site; Web: http://www.white housedrugpolicy.gov/index.html.
Resource for data on drug policy that supports the U.S. White House Office of Drug Control Policy.

European Coalition for Just and Effective Drug Policies, Lange Lozanastraat 14 - 2018 Antwerpen, Belgium. Telephone: +32 (0)3 293 0886; email: office@encod .org; Web: http://www.encod.org/info/-English-en-.html.
Coalition of organizations seeking to reform drug policies in Europe.

European Monitoring Centre for Drugs and Drug Addiction, Rua da Cruz de Santa Apolónia 23-25, PT-1149-045 Lisbon, Portugal. Telephone: (351) 21 811 3000; email: info@emcdda.europa.eu; Web: http://www.emcdda.europa.eu/html.cfm/ index190EN.html.
EU center that collects data on illegal drugs.

International Narcotics Control Board, Vienna International Centre, Room E-1339, P.O. Box 500, A-1400 Vienna, Austria. Telephone: +(43) (1) 26060 - 0; email: secretariat@incb.org; Web: http://www.incb.org/incb/index.html.
UN organization that monitors the implementation of the UN drug control conventions.

International Narcotic Enforcement Officers Association, 112 State Street, Suite 1200, Albany, N.Y. 12207-2079. Telephone: (518) 463-6232; email: info@ineoa. org; Web: http://www.ineoa.org.
Organization representing the worldwide drug enforcement community.

National Drug Intelligence Center (NDIC), 319 Washington Street, 5th Floor, Johnstown, Pa. 15901-1622. Telephone: (814) 532-4601; email: NDIC.Contacts@ usdoj.gov; Web: http://www.usdoj.gov/ndic.
Part of the U.S. Department of Justice; provides drug-related intelligence to law enforcement.

National Institute on Drug Abuse, 6001 Executive Blvd., Room 5213, Bethesda, Md. 20892-9561. Telephone: (301) 443-1124; email: information@nida.nih.gov; Web: http://www.nida.nih.gov/index.html.
Part of the U.S. National Institutes of Health; studies drug abuse and addiction.

United Nations Office on Drugs and Crime, Vienna International Centre, P.O. Box 500, A 1400 Vienna, Austria. Telephone: + (43) (1) 26060; email: via Web site; Web site: http://www.unodc.org/unodc/index.html.
UN organization that tracks the production, use, and trafficking of illegal drugs.

U.S. Drug Enforcement Administration, Drug Enforcement Administration, Mailstop: AES, 8701 Morrissette Drive, Springfield, Va. 22152. Telephone: (202) 307-1000; email: via Web site; Web: http://www.usdoj.gov/dea/index.htm.
U.S. government agency that enforces drug policy.

Further Research

Books

Bergquist, Charles, et al., eds. *Violence in Colombia 1990–2000: Waging War and Negotiating Peace.* Wilmington, Del.: Scholarly Resources, 2001.

Bowden, Mark. *Killing Pablo: The Hunt for the World's Greatest Outlaw.* New York: Atlantic Monthly Press, 2001.

Chepesiuk, Ron. *The Bullet or the Bribe: Taking Down Colombia's Cali Drug Cartel.* Westport, Conn.: Praeger, 2003.

Courtwright, David T. *Forces of Habit: Drugs and the Making of the Modern World.* Cambridge, Mass.: Harvard University Press, 2001.

Davenport-Hines, Richard. *The Pursuit of Oblivion: A Global History of Narcotics.* New York: W. W. Norton & Co., 2002.

Escobar, Roberto. *The Accountant's Story: Inside the Violent World of the Medellin Cartel.* New York: Grand Central Publishing, 2009.

Hanes, W. Travis III, and Frank Sanello. *The Opium Wars: The Addiction of One Empire and the Corruption of Another.* Naperville, Ill.: Sourcebooks, 2002.

Hodgson, Barbara. *In the Arms of Morpheus: The Tragic History of Laudanum, Morphine, and Patent Medicines.* Buffalo, N.Y.: Firefly Books, 2001.

McCoy, Alfred W. *The Politics of Heroin: CIA Complicity in the Global Drug Trade, Afghanistan, Southeast Asia, Central America, Colombia.* 2nd rev. ed. Chicago: Lawrence Hill Books, 2003.

Peters, Gretchen. *Seeds of Terror: How Heroin Is Bankrolling the Taliban and Al Qaeda.* New York: Thomas Dunne Books, 2009.

Stares, Paul B. *Global Habit: The Drug Problem in a Borderless World.* Washington, D.C.: Brooking Institution, 1996.

Articles and Reports

Akyeampong, Emmanuel. "Diaspora and Drug Trafficking in West Africa: A Case Study of Ghana." *African Affairs* 104, no. 416 (2005): 429–447.

Clarke, Ryan. "Narcotics Trafficking in China: Size, Scale, Dynamic and Future Consequences." *Pacific Affairs* 81, no. 1 (2008): 73–93.

Desroches, Frederick. "Research on Upper Level Drug Trafficking: A Review." *Journal of Drug Issues* 37, no. 4 (2007): 827–844.

Emmers, Ralf. "International Regime-Building in ASEAN: Cooperation against the Illicit Trafficking and Abuse of Drugs." *Contemporary Southeast Asia: A Journal of International and Strategic Affairs* 29, no. 3 (2007): 506–525.

Dolan, Chris J. "United States' Narco-Terrorism Policy: A Contingency Approach to the Convergence of the Wars on Drugs and against Terrorism." *Review of Policy Research* 22, no. 4 (2005): 451–471.

European Monitoring Centre for Drugs and Drug Addiction. "State of the Drugs Problem in Europe: Annual Report 2008." November 6, 2008. Available at http://www.emcdda.europa.eu/publications/annual-report/2008.

Friesendorf, Cornelius. "Squeezing the Balloon?: United States Air Interdiction and the Restructuring of the South American Drug Industry in the 1990s." *Crime, Law & Social Change* 44, no. 1 (2005): 35–78.

International Narcotics Control Board. "2008 Report." February 19, 2009. Available at http://www.incb.org/incb/annual-report-2008.html.

Johnston, Lloyd D., et al. "Monitoring the Future: National Results on Adolescent Drug Use: Overview of Key Findings, 2008." December 11, 2008. Available at http://www.monitoringthefuture.org/pubs/monographs/overview2008.pdf.

Lubin, Nancy. "Who's Watching the Watchdogs?" *Journal of International Affairs* 56, no. 2 (2003): 43–56.

Payan, Tony. "The Drug War and the U.S.-Mexico Border: The State of Affairs." *South Atlantic Quarterly* 105, no. 4 (2006): 863–880.

Raisdana, Fariborz, and Ahman Gharavi Nakhjavani. "The Drug Market in Iran." *Annals of the American Academy of Political and Social Science* 582 (July 2002): 149–166.

United Nations Educational, Scientific and Cultural Organization. "Globalization, Drugs and Criminalization: Final Research Report on Brazil, China, India and Mexico." UNESCO, Paris, October 14, 2002.

United Nations Office on Drugs and Crime. "2008 World Drug Report." June 26, 2008. Available at http://www.unodc.org/unodc/en/data-and-analysis/WDR .html.

U.S. Department of State. "2009 International Narcotics Control Strategy Report." February 27, 2009. Available at http://www.state.gov/p/inl/rls/nrcrpt/2009.

U.S. National Drug Intelligence Center. "National Drug Threat Assessment 2009." December 2008. Available at http://www.usdoj.gov/ndic/pubs31/31379/index .htm.

———. "National Methamphetamine Threat Assessment 2009." December 2008. Available at http://www.usdoj.gov/ndic/topics/ndtas.htm.

Web Sites

Frontline: "Drug Wars"
http://www.pbs.org/wgbh/pages/frontline/shows/drugs

Interpol: Drugs
http://www.interpol.int/Public/Drugs/default.asp

Paris Pact Initiative
http://www.paris-pact.net

United Nations Office on Drugs and Crime: 100 Years of Drug Control
http://www.unodc.org/unodc/en/commissions/CND/one-hundred-years-of-drug-control.html

Document

1. The United Nations' Single Convention on Narcotic Drugs, 1961, as Amended by the 1972 Protocol Amending the Single Convention on Narcotic Drugs

The full document can be found at http://www.incb.org/pdf/e/conv/convention_1961_en.pdf.

Extracts

Preamble

The Parties,

Concerned with the health and welfare of mankind,

Recognizing that the medical use of narcotic drugs continues to be indispensable for the relief of pain and suffering and that adequate provision must be made to ensure the availability of narcotic drugs for such purposes,

Recognizing that addiction to narcotic drugs constitutes a serious evil for the individual and is fraught with social and economic danger to mankind,

Conscious of their duty to prevent and combat this evil,

Considering that effective measures against abuse of narcotic drugs require co-ordinated and universal action,

Understanding that such universal action calls for international co-operation guided by the same principles and aimed at common objectives,

Acknowledging the competence of the United Nations in the field of narcotics control and desirous that the international organs concerned should be within the framework of that Organization,

Desiring to conclude a generally acceptable international convention replacing existing treaties on narcotic drugs, limiting such drugs to medical and scientific use, and providing for continuous international co-operation and control for the achievement of such aims and objectives,

Hereby agree as follows. . . .

Article 4

GENERAL OBLIGATIONS

The parties shall take such legislative and administrative measures as may be necessary:

(a) To give effect to and carry out the provisions of this Convention within their own territories;

(b) To co-operate with other States in the execution of the provisions of this Convention; and

(c) Subject to the provisions of this Convention, to limit exclusively to medical and scientific purposes the production, manufacture, export, import, distribution of, trade in, use and possession of drugs.

ETHNIC AND REGIONAL CONFLICT

Murat Somer

E thnic and regional conflict threatens the stability of nation–states, which continue to be the key players in global economy and politics. Globalization affects ethnic and regional conflict in competing ways. On the one hand, it lessens the likelihood of such conflicts, first, by enabling people to interact and perhaps identify with others outside their ethnic group and regions and, second, by helping countries prosper and democratize through the international movement of ideas, commodities, capital, and labor. On the other hand, globalization may act as a catalyst for ethnic and regional conflict, first, by making politically or economically disadvantaged groups more aware of the world's inequalities and, second, by possibly weakening states (which often resolve or suppress ethnic and regional conflicts) before alternative international, supranational, and nongovernmental institutions have sufficiently developed to provide security and stability. These aspects of globalization, coupled with what seems to be the emergence of a multipolar or nonpolar world, in which no leading state is at the vanguard of international cooperation, are key concerns in efforts to understand and resolve ethnic and regional conflicts.

Historical Background and Development

Before nation–states first emerged in Western Europe in the seventeenth and eighteenth centuries, most of the world was a kaleidoscope of ethnic, religious, and linguistic communities loosely connected to one another by monarchies and empires. Ruling establishments cared little about their subjects' identities and concerned themselves only with military loyalty and taxation, which were typically extracted by local power holders. Rulers did not need to have the same ethnic identity or culture as their subjects; in a nondemocratic world, communication with their subjects was limited and their legitimacy did not necessarily derive from popular endorsement. Also, the borders between empires were not well defined because states had neither the resources nor sufficient interest to effectively control movements across borders.

The emergence of territorially defined nation-states led to administrative centralization, the homogenization of national cultures, and the forging of nations to which citizens were expected to be more loyal than to their tribes and clans, ethnic groups, and regions. This process went hand in hand with the transfer of power from religious authorities such as the pope (with nonterritorial authority) to secular rulers, as well as from monarchies to popular sovereignty. Rulers needed, and took advantage of, a popular base, that is, the endorsement of a "nation," to rule. The rise of nation-states also contributed to the economic development of many societies by fostering education and common legal and linguistic standards, which facilitated trade and cooperation among people of different ethnic and regional backgrounds. This process, however, was far from smooth and fair.

All ethnic and regional groups and cultures did not participate in the nation-building process on equal terms. Usually one group dominated the process and took the lion's share in controlling economic and political resources and in the determination of the national culture. Many local cultures and languages came to be overshadowed by the dominant group—Anglo-Saxon Protestants in the United States, for example, and the French in France—whose culture and language became the mainstream, often in reinvented and transformed forms. For example, in 1789, long before nation building homogenized France culturally and linguistically, French was only spoken by half of those who considered themselves French. The rest of the population spoke dozens of other languages and dialects.

Today, the damage that nationalism has wrought on cultural diversity is regretted, similar to the regret associated with industrialization's effects on the environment. Assimilation into mainstream culture was often achieved through pressure and manipulation. Members of some minorities, such as Native Americans in the United States, were practically barred from assimilation into the mainstream culture, ultimately leading their cultures into oblivion. Governments of countries such as Canada and Australia have apologized to their aboriginal people for such injustices. Indigenous peoples colonized by Europeans, as well as the Jewish and Roma minorities in pre–World War II Europe, suffered extermination at the hands of the dominant groups where nationalism coalesced with colonialism or fascism.

From the eighteenth through the twentieth century, nationalism spread from Western Europe to central and Eastern Europe, Asia, the Americas, the Middle East, and Africa. The creation of nation-states was especially painful in the areas of multiethnic and multicultural empires, such as those controlled by the Austro-Hungarians and the Ottomans, who had for centuries respected the autonomy and the coexistence of their ethnic and regional subjects. The territorial "unmixing" of these people in the early twentieth century in pursuit of homogeneous nation-states led to numerous fratricidal wars; suffering; and conflicts among ethnic and regional groups, imperial centers, and the emerging nation-states.

Another major wave of ethnic and regional conflict erupted in the aftermath of World War II, when numerous colonies in Africa and Asia gained their independence. Many of these new nations were subsequently divided into smaller entities. In 1947, for instance, British India's Muslims seceded to form Pakistan, and Bengali Muslims seceded from the latter to form Bangladesh in 1971. For a variety of reasons, in many of these new nations, ethnic and regional groups and tribes failed to achieve economic and political integration. Many of the inequalities created by colonialist powers carried over into the postindependence period, thus creating a foundation for ethnic and regional conflicts.

A rash of ethnic and regional conflicts broke out in formerly socialist states following the end of the cold war. Yugoslavia disintegrated through a tragic war during the 1990s, in which the greatest suffering was inflicted on the ethnically and religiously mixed Bosnians. Kosovo's semirecognized independence in 2008 was the latest stage of former Yugoslavia's disintegration (see Case Study—Kosovo, South Ossetia, and Abkhazia). Numerous ethnically heterogeneous new states were founded as a result of the Soviet Union's disintegration, and ethnic and regional groups such as the Ossetians in Georgia and the Russians in the Ukraine suddenly found that they had become minorities within the borders of the newly independent countries. Many of these groups mobilized to secure their position or to settle old accounts. Along with economic decline and political chaos, these ethno- and geopolitical transformations led to tensions, such as the ongoing conflict between the Russian government and Chechen separatists.

Reactions to past injustices gave rise to competing sentiments. Many people in Western societies began to see their societies no longer as melting pots into which minorities and newcomers were expected to assimilate. Instead, many began to imagine their nations as multicultural salad bowls, in which the diversity of ethnic communities and cultures is protected, and sometimes promoted, by national institutions.

New social norms and policies echoed this trend. For instance, terms such as *kaleidoscope* and *rainbow coalition* gained currency in descriptions of the ethnic composition of Western nations. Public interest grew in cultural heritage, in retrieving old ways, and reinventing ostensible traditions. These movements contrasted sharply with the attitude that had prevailed among nineteenth-century liberals and among Marxists, who underscored the importance of social cohesion based on modernization and cultural homogenization.

The changing attitudes and political trends in Western democracies affect the way people view and express themselves in the rest of the world and vice versa. Wherever people are troubled by ethnic divisions, they use, to differing degrees, such concepts as multiculturalism, diversity, and self-determination (all initially developed in the West) to conceptualize, justify, and promote their cause. Conversely, the pervasiveness of violent ethnic conflict in the developing world lures some Western observers into complacency about the relative peacefulness of ethnic relations in their own countries. Others, however, doubt that Western democracies are immune to ethnic disintegration.

Current Status

Along with the number of states, the frequency of violent ethnic and regional conflict steadily rose from the 1950s to a peak in the early 1990s, following the end of the cold war (see map, p. 648). Since that time, a slow decline has been evident (see Table 1), attributed largely to the proliferation of democratic regimes in the world. Although the biggest current threats to regional and international security seem to involve religious radicalism and terrorism, many of these conflicts themselves entail ethnic and regional dimensions, such as the divisions among the Shi'a, Sunni, and Kurds of Iraq. Terrorist groups flourish in regions where ethnic, regional, and religious conflicts have generated either oppressive states and popular resentment, as in many Middle Eastern and North African countries, or weak states, chaos, and widespread poverty as in Sudan and Afghanistan. At the same time, the terrorist attacks of September 11, 2001, and perceived social problems associated with the increased visibility of ethnic and cultural heterogeneity have fed anti-immigrant and antiminority sentiments, especially against Muslims, in Western countries.

Research

Current research on ethnic and regional conflict deals with questions of prevention, management, and reconstruction, which are all required to explain the nature of ethnic and regional identities and movements. To explore how to prevent conflicts, researchers analyze the nature of ethnic and regional identities, and the relationships between ethnic and regional conflict and economic and political development. Researchers investigate conflict management and postconflict restructuring by examining social and political institutions that can help reconcile ethnic and regional grievances and render the recurrence of conflict less likely. Hence, researchers and practitioners of conflict resolution are trying to develop blueprints and guidelines for policymakers (see PEACEMAKING AND PEACEBUILDING). A major area of investigation is the proper role of foreign intervention and of international and supranational organizations in preventing, managing, and rehabilitating conflicts.

Researchers find that both domestic and international factors influence the rise and fall of ethnic and regional movements. However, although international actors cannot by themselves create these conflicts, they play crucial roles wherever an actual or potential conflict already exists. These existing conflicts are mainly political, caused by the perennial questions: (1) Who will rule, and who will be ruled (relating to the geographical borders and ethnocultural identity of a government) and (2) for whom (relating to a government's relations with its own citizens and the outside world, and revolving around the question of in whose social and economic interests a government rules)? Although existing ethnic and cultural differences may contribute to these conflicts by becoming a medium for their expression, the differences and divisions often are as much by-products of the conflicts themselves as they are causes of them.

Cross-country studies conducted by researchers at the World Bank and by others reveal that ethnic and linguistic heterogeneity—measured in terms of ethnolinguistic fractionalization indices—is significantly correlated with low economic and political development. But ethnic and linguistic fractionalization does not automatically create conflict and underdevelopment, and vice versa. Many countries, such as Switzerland and the United States, have prospered and have developed successful democracies despite their considerable ethnic, cultural, and linguistic diversity. India, a low-income developing country and democracy, also has been able to manage existing interethnic and interregional conflicts relatively peacefully and has been able to sustain a working democracy despite its tremendous diversity and economic challenges.

Although democracies are not immune to ethnic and regional conflicts, mature democracies are much better able to manage them peacefully than autocracies and semidemocracies (that is, democracies that are not yet sufficiently mature and institutionalized). In fact, semidemocracies are the most vulnerable to violent conflict. Thus, most ethnic and regional conflicts are caused partly by, and contribute to, state failure. Take the ongoing bloody conflict in Sudan, which has cost the lives of more than 2.5 million people since the 1980s. The strife in the Sudan is the product of various complex ethnic, religious, and regional economic grievances; groups, mainly in the south and western (Darfur) regions of the country, rebelled against this social and economic marginalization, Islamization, and domination by the Arabs who control the Sudanese state. Sudan, stricken by the seeming intractable complexity of these divisive conflicts and accused of supporting an ongoing genocide in Darfur, is a striking example of a failed state—it cannot provide basic security, cannot guarantee basic human rights for much of its citizenry, and cannot claim legitimacy for major portions of its population. A complete collapse of the Sudanese state, however, could give rise to an even greater humanitarian disaster than has so far occurred.

Countries that successfully manage diversity show that there is no single way to do so. Switzerland recognized and institutionalized ethnic and linguistic differences by organizing the country administratively into cantons, each representing one of the constituent groups. The United States achieved intergroup coexistence and cooperation by cultivating the strong public consciousness of a common identity and by supporting a common language, English, although ethnic group members' cultural and linguistic needs are respected and accommodated whenever it is economically and politically feasible to do so. Countries such as Britain and Spain are becoming union states by devolving substantial administrative and legislative powers to regional nationalities such as the Scots and the Catalans while maintaining their external sovereignty vis-à-vis other states.

Identifying the causes of intergroup conflict across time and in different parts of the world is not easy. Ethnic identities are by no means well-defined categories. Max Weber, the renowned German sociologist and political economist, defined *ethnicity* as a subjective belief in common descent; no objective blood relationship is necessary. Ethnic group members may form a belief in

their common descent on the basis of various combinations of shared characteristics, such as race, religion, language or dialect, custom, occupation, or even
social class. Often, the dominant markers of membership are the characteristics
that visibly distinguish group members from neighboring groups. Similarly,
outsiders may ethnically label a group of people for a variety of reasons. The
outsiders' and insiders' categorizations need not coincide. In the United States,
for instance, outsiders may view all Spanish-speaking Americans as Hispanics,
although many people in this group may prefer to call themselves, say, Mexican
Americans or Guatemalan Americans, or simply Americans.

Although ethnic and cultural diversity has been part of society throughout
history, it has not always caused conflict. Ethnic or regional activists tend to
base their claims for resources in ancient disputes and enduring traditions, but
most current conflicts are actually rooted in modern disagreements. Many
neighboring groups have long histories of coexistence, intermingling, and
cooperation. Often, national or religious identities override ethnic or regional
identities. Social class divisions often crosscut and weaken ethnic and regional
divisions. Ethnic and regional divisions become the most polarizing when they
accumulate and overlap with other divisions, such as social class and religion.
In some cases, intergroup grievances have been created by invaders or outside
rulers who used ethnic classification as an easy means of categorizing and controlling people. Many times, colonial powers favored one group over others
and used the former as intermediaries to rule over the latter. Rwanda, where a
cycle of violence since the 1960s has cost the lives of more than a million
people, including those who died in the genocide of 1994, offers a good example. Relations between the Hutu and Tutsi, the country's two main ethnic
groups, were relatively stable and peaceful, and interethnic mixing was common until the Belgians colonized the country after World War I. The Belgian
administration sowed the seeds of future interethnic conflict by choosing to
rule through the Tutsi elite in exchange for economic and educational favors
for the members of that group. This turned the majority Hutus and minority
Tutsis against one another by creating a highly unequal relationship between
them. Over time, group boundaries were solidified and intergroup animosities
were cultivated, demonstrating how the nature of ethnic and regional group
relations can change in response to economic and political circumstances (see
GENOCIDE).

Once created, however, ethnic and regional group identity can prove quite
resilient to changing circumstances, and memories of past conflicts can resurface during contemporary conflicts even after long years of peace and cooperation. The primordialist perspective of conflict prevention focuses on the
psychological and historical aspects of ethnic and regional conflicts. For primordialists, ethnic identities are determined by birth and are rooted in the
human cognitive and psychological tendency to favor one's own group members. They assert that the family resemblance of ethnic group membership, that
is, the blood tie that is purported to exist among group members, makes intergroup relations more inflammatory and compromise less likely. Primordialists
generally are skeptical of nation-building practices that underestimate the zeal

of ethnic group members for cultural and political autonomy in multicultural societies. They are also generally against outside involvement in peacemaking in ethnic conflicts because they believe that foreign intervention has little to contribute to the resolution of age-old conflicts that are inherently complex.

Another perspective on conflict prevention, instrumentalism, highlights the importance of competition for resources and that current ethnic and regional identities are more the products of modern situations than circumstances in the distant past. Instrumentalists observe that previously insignificant ethnic categories become important when ethnic groups mobilize in pursuit of economic and political interests and in competition over scarce natural resources. Sometimes the geographical distribution of ethnic groups creates disadvantages for some groups, which then mobilize politically to improve their lot. In other situations, governments encourage ethnic interest groups to become politically active by tying government benefits to group membership or by failing to create equal opportunities for individuals regardless of ethnic descent. Thus, ethnic groups become vehicles for promoting economic and political ends, in the form of interest groups, political parties, or armed organizations or rebel groups. Accordingly, the key to preventing conflict is to remedy regional or ethnic-based advantages (or disadvantages) and to create equal opportunities for all individuals. Another point that instrumentalists emphasize is the role that elite interests and elite manipulation play in the creation of ethnic and regional conflict. For instance, in former Yugoslavia previous communist political elites incited interregional grievances and ethnonationalist sentiments to remain in power following the decline of socialism.

The constructivism perspective emphasizes the social processes through which ethnic, regional, and national identities are created. It points to the discourse of ethnic and national politics and maintains that competition over the use of names, images, and historical myths in the construction of identities is a source of conflict. For instance, Greeks object to Macedonians' naming their country *Macedonia* because they consider it part of the Greek national heritage. Constructivists encourage people to recognize the biases in their own ethnic and national self-images and to use inoffensive and conciliatory language to prevent conflict. At the same time, constructivists usually maintain that political and cultural institutions should explicitly recognize the multiethnic and multicultural composition of societies, enable people to express their ethnic and cultural identities, and accommodate identity needs in educational and cultural policies.

Policies and Programs

The way in which researchers address issues such as the modern or ancient origins of ethnic identities affects international public opinion and the actions that the international community takes regarding ethnic and regional conflicts. For example, insofar as Macedonian identity is ancient and nations are based in ethnic identities, the territory of ancient Macedonia becomes a contested area divided among three contemporary nation-states: Bulgaria, Greece, and Macedonia. Insofar as Macedonian identity today is a modern phenomenon that emerged as a consequence of Macedonia's status as a constituent republic within Yugoslavia, those parts of ancient Macedonia that are now part of Greece and Bulgaria become irrelevant to those interested in state building.

As the examples of Kosovo and Georgia reveal, the birth and evolution of nation-states are, to a considerable extent, an internationally determined phenomenon; nation-states need the recognition and support of other nation-states to legitimize their existence and to survive. For example, the establishment of the multiethnic state of Bosnia-Herzegovina, which consists of a Muslim-Croat federation and a Serbian republic, was preceded by a bloody ethnic conflict and the genocide of Muslims in the early 1990s. Many of its inhabitants, especially the Serbs, may prefer to have a state of their own. However, Bosnia-Herzegovina was established with the decisive involvement of the international community. To give another example, the Kurds, a large ethnic group in the Middle East whose members mostly live in Iran, Iraq, Syria, and Turkey, do not have a state in which they form the core, or titular, ethnic group. One of the primary reasons for this is that such an idea has been opposed by the states in the region, which view a Kurdish state as counter to their national interests. They argue that creating a state from an ethnic group that resides in four different national territories would destabilize the region. However, the claims of Iraqi Kurdish nationalists that they constitute an ancient ethnic group entitled to a nation-state (or an autonomous entity within the Iraqi state) have garnered more support after the Kurds helped the United States in the invasion of Iraq. Nevertheless, the prospects for a Kurdish state continue to be limited, mostly because Iraq's other groups do not want to give up their rights to oil resources in areas such as Kirkuk, a multiethnic province harboring Kurdish, Turkmen, and Arab communities.

In terms of policy, the best prospects for conflict prevention and postconflict rehabilitation lie in two areas. The first is successful international cooperation to create and promote democratic norms regarding the peaceful negotiation of group rights and administrative arrangements between nation-states and ethnic and regional groups. Such norms should discourage the use of state and nonstate violence and encourage the pursuit of democratic deliberation and consensus-building by all sides and should be impartially enforced by international actors.

The second is the proliferation and strengthening of such international organizations as the United Nations, whose body of covenants and declarations include important instruments of international law relating to the protection of ethnic groups (see Documents 1 and 2). Other international and supranational organizations include the Association of Southeast Asian Nations (ASEAN), the European Union (EU), the Organization for Security and Cooperation in Europe (OSCE), and the Southern Cone Common Market (Mercosur, Mercado Común del Sur). These organizations help resolve ethnic and regional conflicts in two major ways. First, they induce economic and political integration among the participating countries. This has the effect of taking the edge off many ethnic and regional conflicts by creating political and economic incentives. However, the timing and conditional provision of such

incentives are also crucial. Take, for example, the conflict in Cyprus, a strategically important eastern Mediterranean island that is de facto divided between
a Turkish Cypriot state in the north and a Greek Cypriot state in the south.
The UN-sponsored unification efforts gained momentum when the EU
announced in 2002 that a unified Cyprus could join the EU in 2004. This
decision and the pull of EU membership tilted the balance of opinion in favor
of unification for many Turkish Cypriots who hitherto had opposed unification because of their fear of domination by Greek Cypriots. The government
of mainland Turkey, which pursued EU membership itself and which therefore
was mindful of good relations with the EU, also endorsed the UN unification
plan. However, rather than making membership conditional on the acceptance
of unification by both communities, the EU declared that the Greek part of
the island would join the EU even if unification would fail to materialize.
Largely as a result, in twin referendums in April 2004, the UN unification plan
was endorsed by Turkish Cypriots but was rejected by Greek Cypriots. Greek
Cyprus joined the EU soon afterward while the EU took some steps to ease
the isolation of the Turkish Cypriots in the north. The EU thus failed to use its
power effectively to unify the island, and currently it is unclear whether or not
the island will ever become one state and what kind of a power-sharing can be
achieved between the two ethnic communities. Nevertheless, the lure of the
full participation of the whole island in the EU continues to be the key factor
motivating the continuing negotiations to unify it.

Second, international and supranational organizations help resolve ethnic
and regional conflicts through conflict-resolution mechanisms, and peacekeeping and postconflict missions. Having learned from past missions and mistakes
and the advancement of practical and scholarly knowledge on ethnic and
regional conflict, these organizations' contributions in this area have become
more sophisticated and constructive. Whereas in the past international involvement in such conflicts began only after confrontations had erupted and was
limited to peacekeeping missions, it is now more focused on conflict prevention, which entails intervention at an early stage. International and supranational organizations now have a large array of early warning systems in place.
Nevertheless, it is important to note that the effectiveness of these systems
depends on the ability to find common cause and the willingness of the international community to act. In Rwanda, Bosnia, and Sudan, for example, the
international community was widely criticized for delayed and improper or
insufficient action.

Another focus of international organizations is on postconflict reconstruction. In the aftermath of conflict, priority should be given to instituting
measures that will help prevent the recurrence of conflict (see PEACEMAKING
AND PEACEBUILDING). These include check-and-balance mechanisms, legal
and effective guarantees for the protection of human rights, and confidence-
building measures to reestablish trust between ethnic or regional groups (see
INTERNATIONAL CRIMINAL JUSTICE). International monitoring of and assistance in the implementation of peace accords and reconstruction efforts are

crucial. Prominent examples of ongoing missions and projects in this respect include:

- Bosnia and Herzegovina. In 2004, the North Atlantic Treaty Organization (NATO) handed over peacekeeping duties to the EU-led European Forces in Bosnia and Herzegovina (EUFOR). Also, an OSCE mission aims to develop inclusive political discourse and democratically accountable institutions that respect diversity, promote consensus, and respect the rule of law.
- Timor-Leste. A UN-mandated and Australian-led international peacekeeping force, the UN Integrated Mission in Timor-Leste (UNMIT), returned to Timor-Leste in 2006 when atrocities erupted after the earlier international peacekeeping force, the United Nations Mission of Support in East Timor (UNMISET), which was to help the Timorese authorities following the country's independence from Indonesia in 2002, left the country prematurely in 2005. The UNMIT's mandate is to review and reform the security sector; to strengthen the rule of law, economic, and social development; and to promote a culture of democratic governance.
- Kosovo. The NATO-led international Kosovo Force (KFOR) works to maintain law and order until the UN mission in Kosovo can assume peacekeeping responsibility. A parallel OSCE mission has the task of verifying compliance with UN Security Council decisions and supporting democratic institutions, human rights, good governance, and public safety and security.
- Macedonia. The OSCE Spillover Monitor Mission in Macedonia works to monitor the border with Yugoslavia and promote communication between ethnic Albanian and Slavic Macedonians.
- Darfur, Sudan. The joint African Union–United Nations Mission in Darfur (UNAMID) has as its core mandate the protection of civilians. It also has the task of contributing to the security for humanitarian assistance and of monitoring and verifying the implementation of peace agreements.

Regional Summaries

An imperfect yet often reliable predictor of the level of ethnic and regional conflict in a country is the region of the world in which the country is situated. Generally, a country's ability to manage such conflicts increases with economic and democratic development, and countries tend to be clustered with others that have similar levels of democracy and prosperity. Another geographical predictor of the location of conflict is contagion—peace as well as conflict tends to spread among neighboring countries. Presently, for instance, none of the prosperous democracies in Western Europe faces major armed insurgencies. Even though significant conflicts exist in France, Spain, Belgium, and Northern Ireland, the level of violence is incomparably less than in central and Southeast Asia. Similarly, the level of armed conflict in Latin America and the Caribbean significantly subsided during the 1990s, coinciding with the general trend toward democratization in the region. By contrast, Middle Eastern, Southeast Asian, and sub-Saharan African nations and the former republics of

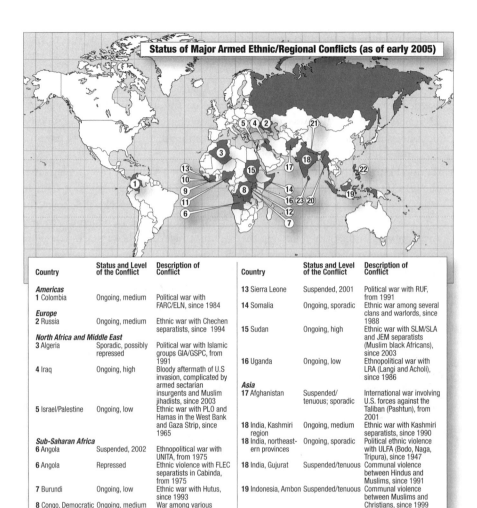

Status of Major Armed Ethnic/Regional Conflicts (as of early 2005)

Country	Status and Level of the Conflict	Description of Conflict	Country	Status and Level of the Conflict	Description of Conflict
Americas			13 Sierra Leone	Suspended, 2001	Political war with RUF, from 1991
1 Colombia	Ongoing, medium	Political war with FARC/ELN, since 1984	14 Somalia	Ongoing, sporadic	Ethnic war among several clans and warlords, since 1988
Europe					
2 Russia	Ongoing, medium	Ethnic war with Chechen separatists, since 1994	15 Sudan	Ongoing, high	Ethnic war with SLM/SLA and JEM separatists (Muslim black Africans), since 2003
North Africa and Middle East					
3 Algeria	Sporadic, possibly repressed	Political war with Islamic groups GIA/GSPC, from 1991			
4 Iraq	Ongoing, high	Bloody aftermath of U.S invasion, complicated by armed sectarian insurgents and Muslim jihadists, since 2003	16 Uganda	Ongoing, low	Ethnopolitical war with LRA (Langi and Acholi), since 1986
			Asia		
			17 Afghanistan	Suspended/ tenuous; sporadic	International war involving U.S. forces against the Taliban (Pashtun), from 2001
5 Israel/Palestine	Ongoing, low	Ethnic war with PLO and Hamas in the West Bank and Gaza Strip, since 1965	18 India, Kashmiri region	Ongoing, medium	Ethnic war with Kashmiri separatists, since 1990
Sub-Saharan Africa			18 India, northeast-ern provinces	Ongoing, sporadic	Political ethnic violence with ULFA (Bodo, Naga, Tripura), since 1947
6 Angola	Suspended, 2002	Ethnopolitical war with UNITA, from 1975			
6 Angola	Repressed	Ethnic violence with FLEC separatists in Cabinda, from 1975	18 India, Gujurat	Suspended/tenuous	Communal violence between Hindus and Muslims, since 1991
7 Burundi	Ongoing, low	Ethnic war with Hutus, since 1993	19 Indonesia, Ambon	Suspended/tenuous	Communal violence between Muslims and Christians, since 1999
8 Congo, Democratic Republic of	Ongoing, medium	War among various ethnic/regional factions, since 1996	19 Indonesia, Aceh	Ongoing, low	Ethnic war with GAM separatists (Acehnese), since 1997
9 Côte d'Ivoire	Ongoing, low	Ethnopolitical war with MPCI/MPJ/MPIGO (Muslims; non-Ivoirians), since 2002	20 Myanmar (Burma)	Ongoing, medium	Ethnic war with various non-Burmans, since 1948
10 Liberia	Suspended, 2003	Political war with LURD/MODEL, from 2000	21 Nepal	Ongoing, medium	Political war with UPF/CPN-M (communist Maoist groups), since 1996
11 Nigeria, delta state	Ongoing, sporadic	Communal violence between Itsekeri and Ikaw, since 1997			
11 Nigeria, northern Muslim states	Ongoing, low	Communal violence between Muslims and Christians, since 2001	22 Philippines	Ongoing, low	Ethnic war with MILF/Abu Sayyaf (Moros), since 1972
12 Rwanda	Repressed, 2001	Ethnic war with Hutus, from 1994	23 Sri Lanka	Suspended, tenuous	Ethnic war with LTTE separatists (Tamils), from 1983

Source: Monty G. Marshall and Ted Robert Gurr, *Peace and Conflict, 2005: A Global Survey of Armed Conflicts, Self-Determination Movements, and Democracy*. College Park, Md.: Center for International Development and Conflict Management, 2005. Available online from http://www.cidcm.umd.edu/publications/publication.asp?pubType=paper&id=15.
Notes: Some conflicts have escalated, ebbed, or otherwise changed substantially since this analysis was done. FARC/ELN, Revolutionary Armed Forces of Colombia (Fuerzas Armadas Revolucionarias de Colombia)/National Liberation Army (Ejército de Liberación Nacional); FLEC, Front for the Liberation of the Enclave of Cabinda (Frente para a Libertação do Enclave de Cabinda); GAM, Free Aceh Movement (Gerakan Aceh Merdeka); GIA/GSPC, Armed Islamic Group (Groupe Islamique Armé)/Salafist Group for Preaching and Combat (Groupe Salafiste pour la Prédication et le Combat); JEM, Justice and Equality Movement; LRA, Lord's Resistance Army; LTTE, Liberation Tigers of Tamil Eelam; LURD/MODEL, Liberians United for Reconciliation and Democracy/Movement for Democracy in Liberia; MILF, Moro Islamic Liberation Front; MPCI/MPJ/MPIGO, Patriotic Movement of Côte d'Ivoire (Mouvement Patriotique de Côte d'Ivoire) /Movement for Peace and Justice (Movement pour la Paix et la Justice)/Ivorian Popular Movement of the Great West (Movement Populaire Ivoirien du Grand Ouest); PLO, Palestinian Liberation Organization; RUF, Revolutionary United Front; SLM/SLA, Sudan Liberation Movement/Sudan Liberation Army; ULFA, United Liberation Front of Asom; UNITA, National Union for the Total Independence of Angola (União Nacional para a Independência Total de Angola); UPF/CPN-M, United People's Front/Communist Party of Nepal-Maoist.

the Soviet Union are much more likely to suffer from ethnic and regional conflicts.

North America

The most important sources of ethnic and religious conflict in the Americas have traditionally been the treatment of indigenous peoples and racial minorities and related regional inequalities. The exception is the separatist movement in Canada's Quebec province, where the majority of French speakers voted for secession in 1995. (The proposal was defeated largely by the votes of indigenous people and other minorities, who feared that their rights would not be respected in an independent Quebec.) It is not thought that the Québécois separatist sentiment will lead to violence because Canada, as a prosperous democracy, is committed to democratic processes of conflict resolution, multiculturalism, and multilingualism. The Canadian Parliament recognized the Québécois nation, and the government agreed that it would negotiate if the majority of the Québécois population voted for secession, although its Supreme Court also ruled that secession can only occur with the federal government's consent. In 1998, the Canadian government formally apologized to its indigenous people for its past policies of paternalism, discrimination, and assimilation. Although the United States has had numerous ethnic and regional conflicts, and current interethnic and interracial relations are worrisome, the country retains a high capacity to resolve group conflict before it becomes violent.

Latin America

The bulk of ethnic and regional minorities in Latin America consist of indigenous people and the descendants of African slaves. In countries such as Bolivia and Ecuador, members of indigenous populations have become important political actors, including Evo Morales, who was elected president of Bolivia in 2005. Also, indigenous groups were granted land and cultural rights in countries such as Colombia and Venezuela and were partially successful in gaining autonomy in Nicaragua. Nevertheless, social exclusion and regional poverty continue to be major problems.

Overall, ethnic and regional conflict in Latin America since the 1990s has been lessening, largely thanks to democratization. The case of Mexico is illustrative. In the 1990s, the government of Vicente Fox devoted considerable efforts to accommodate the Zapatistas, who had begun an armed uprising on January 1, 1994, the day the North American Free Trade Agreement (NAFTA) went into effect. The Zapatistas seek more autonomy and economic and cultural rights for the indigenous people living in the Chiapas region, where they are economically deprived and fear domination by other ethnic groups as well as by powerful landowners. The Zapatista rebels' denouncement of armed struggle in favor of an international media campaign had helped the Fox government gain power through promises of democratization. The Fox government returned the favor by letting the guerrillas address the national legislature at the end of a well-publicized two-week-long Zapatour trip to Mexico City.

Although the much-expected Indian Rights Bill was watered down in the Mexican assembly, its passage helped to reduce the conflict. In the long run, the course of this problem will be determined by the level of economic progress in Chiapas.

In an ongoing conflict in Colombia, the United Self-Defense Forces of Colombia (a pro-government paramilitary group), the Revolutionary Armed Forces of Colombia (FARC; Fuerzas Armadas Revolucionarias de Colombia), and the National Liberation Army continue to fight over control of the country's hinterland and profits from the lucrative drug trade. Political negotiations have produced little progress. In recent years, military firmness coupled with U.S. support and the prosecution of rebel and right-wing drug lords appears to have paid dividends for the government, and it appears to have gained the upper hand militarily. A final settlement, however, will probably involve amnesty for the rebels and the right to participate in the legitimate political system in return for their disarmament. The ongoing conflict frequently creates tensions between Colombia and its neighbors, Venezuela and Ecuador.

In Peru, a revolutionary movement of lowland indigenous people has been weakened and is now involved in militant, aggressive, yet unarmed politics. In Guatemala, an armed conflict pitting the Maya against government forces ended with a negotiated settlement in 1996. Other conflicts, notably those involving the indigenous people of Brazil and Chile, Tobagonians in Trinidad and Tobago, and Nevisians in St. Kitts-Nevis, continue as low-level strife that mostly play out within the context of militant but conventional politics.

Europe

Europe has been home to numerous movements of militant nationalism and bloody ethnic and regional conflict in the past. Western Europe, however, has mostly been able to manage such conflicts and to prevent related violence since World War II, thanks largely to economic prosperity, democracy, devolution to regional governments, and economic and political integration under the umbrella of the European Union and its predecessors. This is not to say that no significant ethnic or regional conflicts exist but, rather, that they are largely managed through negotiation and within the confines of democratic politics. Political crises and bickering between the Dutch-speaking Flemish and the French-speaking Walloon continue to threaten the unity of Belgium as a state. A violent ethnopolitical conflict in Northern Ireland between Catholics (many of whom favored unification with the Republic of Ireland in the south) and Protestants (many of whom wished to remain part of the United Kingdom) was settled in the aftermath of the 1998 Good Friday (Belfast) agreements. The accords stipulated demilitarization and institutional reforms, along with a power-sharing arrangement between the Catholics and Protestants; they also guaranteed that any future changes in the status of the Northern Ireland would occur only by mutual consent. Despite the settlement, remaining underlying tensions sometimes erupt, including such events as the killing of an off-duty constable by a member of a residual militant band of the Irish Republican Army in March 2009. Other conflicts in Western Europe include those in

France involving the Corsicans, in Spain involving the Basques and the Catalans, and in Italy involving the Germans of South Tyrol. The civil unrest that shook France in 2005 also had ethnic undertones because many of the immigrants who took part were Muslim immigrants from former French colonies in North Africa (see IMMIGRATION).

Violent conflict has occurred in Eastern Europe and Eurasia, where communist rule and Soviet domination ended in the late 1980s and 1990s. The most flagrant of these conflicts occurred in the Balkans among the heirs of former Yugoslavia. The containment of these conflicts in the 1990s benefited from two factors that are lacking in such places as Africa: (1) intense international involvement in conflict prevention and peacekeeping and (2) the positive influence of the prospects of integration with Europe. The most notable exception to this rule is the Chechen conflict in Russia.

Political chaos and conflict largely ended in Albania in 1997 when the country began to focus on integration with the rest of Europe. In Bosnia, the future of a fragile peace and multiethnic government, which were achieved with the 1996 Dayton Accords, depends on continuing international involvement and economic and political development in neighboring countries. Peace has largely been established in Croatia's Krajina region. Conflict between the ethnic Albanians and Serbs in Kosovo ended with Kosovo's declaration of independence, which in early 2009 remains contested in the international arena (see Case Study—Kosovo, South Ossetia, and Abkhazia). Montenegro, another constituent state of former Yugoslavia, became independent in 2007, ending the union of Serbia and Montenegro.

In the sphere of the former Soviet Union, Georgia remains torn in the face of the Russian-supported secession of Abkhazia and South Ossetia. The Trans-Dneister region in Moldova and the Armenian-occupied Nagorno-Karabakh region and its surroundings in Azerbaijan enjoy de facto self-rule but no recognition or permanent peace. Sporadic armed clashes have restarted in the latter. Armed conflict between Russian forces and Chechen rebels in Chechnya continues. In Turkey, armed clashes between the security forces and the Kurdish-separatist Kurdistan Workers' Party (PKK; Partiya Karkerên Kurdistan) began anew in 2004.

North Africa and the Middle East

Since the end of World War II, the Middle East and North Africa have been a hotbed of ethnic and regional conflict. For centuries, ethnic communities in this region have historically lived side by side relatively peacefully. To find the origins of ethnic and regional conflict here, we must look elsewhere—to insecure and oppressive states, ill-fated foreign interventions lured by the region's vast oil reserves, and economic straits that make unemployed youth turn to militant political and religious groups. Even the most important conflict in the region, the one between Israelis and Palestinians, was imported. The founding of Israel resulted when masses of Jews who were persecuted in Europe poured into Palestine in search of safe haven, displacing the Palestinian Arabs. Arguably, one reason that the United Nations recognized Israel, despite fierce opposition from the Arab world, was sympathy for the victims of the Holocaust (which took place in Europe, where anti-Semitism was much stronger than in the Middle East).

As in other regions of the world, ethnic and regional conflicts in North Africa and the Middle East have been decreasing since the early 1990s. In Algeria, which was the scene of a murderous civil war between the government and Islamist forces, large numbers of rebels have accepted the military regime's offer of a general amnesty, and violence has decreased significantly. In Egypt, Islamists, most notably the Gamaat-i Islamiyya, appear to have been repressed and forced underground. In Iraq, since the United States overthrew Saddam Hussein in 2003, sectarian violence between the Sunni and the Shi'a continue alongside U.S. and local efforts to build a viable state. In northern Iraq, Kurds, who were formerly persecuted by Hussein, enjoy de facto self-rule and relative peace. The conflict between Israelis and Palestinians continues to be the greatest potential source of instability in the region, with spillovers to Lebanon, Jordan, Syria, and other countries. Conflicts in the Middle East have a very high potential to damage economic growth and political stability on a global scale because of the importance of the region's energy resources and its cultural linkages to the rest of the world.

Sub-Saharan Africa

Sub-Saharan Africa is the epitome of ethnic and regional conflict. Economic and democratic development have not been successful in most countries in this part of the world; the relationship between underdevelopment and ethnic and regional conflict runs both ways. However, some sub-Saharan success stories exist. In 1994, South Africa was able to terminate the National Party regime based on apartheid (racial separation) and since then has taken major steps to face its past and establish interracial trust and peace. South Africa's positive steps appear to have influenced its neighbors. Botswana, Madagascar, and Namibia have been able to avoid conflict and spur economic and political development. Truth and reconciliation commissions were held in countries such as Sierra Leone. Angola ended its civil war in 2002 and reached a 2006 peace deal with separatists in the northern enclave of Cabinda. In 2007, power was transferred from one civilian government to another for the first time in postindependence Nigeria. If it is successful in its transition to democracy, Nigeria could trigger positive effects in neighboring West African states. This large and resourceful country is beset by numerous ethnic rivalries as well as regional and religious rifts between the north and the south.

Ethnic and regional conflicts with high potential for violence are ongoing in several countries, including Burundi, the Democratic Republic of Congo, Liberia, Somalia, and Sudan. Sudan reached a Comprehensive Peace Agreement with the rebels in the south and the Nuba, but an unresolved conflict with the rebels in the west has inflicted a human catastrophe of genocidal proportions on the black Muslims of Darfur.

Evidence in Africa as well as elsewhere in the world indicates that three factors can lead to improvements in ethnic and regional conflict: the establishment of stable and effective states and advancement toward democracy and economic growth, international involvement in conflict prevention and management, and economic and political cooperation among states and the emergence of new countries as positive role models. Because of sub-Saharan Africa's relatively insignificant role in the world economy, and because of its relative isolation from the rest of the world, conflicts here have a lower potential to affect conflicts in other parts of the world. At the same time, as the example of once-ignored Afghanistan has shown, thinking that ethnic and regional conflict in sub-Saharan Africa can forever be contained on the continent, and can therefore be ignored, would be a grave mistake.

Central and South Asia

Central and South Asia are prime candidates for international crises with the potential to cause major damage to global security and cooperation. The region is home to a host of countries that are unable to control their flourishing ethnic and religious movements as well as drug trafficking and corruption within their territories.

Afghanistan, ridden with interethnic rivalries, such as the one between the Tajiks and the Uzbeks, is a country currently in chaos and a major source of international terrorism and instability in the region—2008 was the most violent year in the country since the U.S. invasion in 2001. Developments in Afghanistan destabilize Pakistan, which has ethnic and cultural bonds with Afghanistan and was shaken by two Baluchi insurgencies in 1973–1977 and 2001–2006. If Pakistan further destabilizes, shielding India, Iran, Tajikistan, and Uzbekistan from the fallout will be difficult. They all have significant economic and ideological interests in and ethnic and religious ties with Pakistan and Afghanistan.

Pakistan and India have nuclear arms, and relations between them are already volatile, largely because of their conflict over Kashmir. This disputed area has been divided between the two countries by a "line of control" since 1972, and Kashmiri insurgents and their Pakistani supporters fight India for secession in the southern and southeastern parts of the area. India also has significant interests in neighboring Sri Lanka, where violent conflict has reignited between the majority Sinhala and minority Tamil communities after a cessation of hostilities in 2001.

Similarly, instability in central Asia would invite Russian involvement and, thus, affect democratic development there. Russia views this region as its periphery, and substantial numbers of ethnic Russians live in central Asian states. The United States also has significant interests in the region, and its relationship with Russia is still evolving.

As in the cases of the Middle East and sub-Saharan Africa, the best prospects for the prevention of ethnic and regional conflict in this region lie in economic and political development and in foreign assistance. For example, most countries in central Asia are ruled by authoritarian, yet insecure, states that possess important natural resources but are unable to exploit them because they do not have adequate access to Western markets. External assistance could focus on providing such access and in supporting democratic development. Regional cooperation among the central Asian states would also contribute to stability, but would require overcoming old rivalries and animosities, such as between Uzbekistan and Tajikistan. Almost all of the regimes in central Asia fear radical Islamic movements, but also use them as an excuse to oppress all opposition.

East Asia and the Pacific

The Pacific Rim is a mixture of relatively ethnically homogenous countries (China, Japan, and South Korea) and enormously heterogeneous countries (Indonesia and Papua New Guinea). It also contains both prosperous countries that have little prospect of ethnic and regional conflict, such as Japan, and countries that have a high potential for conflict, such as Indonesia. Because the region is evolving as an economic powerhouse, its stability is important. An armed regional conflict between China and Taiwan would be a threat to world peace. Especially during the cold war, the region experienced severe wars (for example, in Vietnam and Cambodia), but ethnic and regional conflicts have been declining since 1991. The Philippine government, for instance, has been able to contain a thirty-year rebellion by leftist insurgents. However, the likelihood of renewed conflict in the region exists. In particular, conflicts in South Asia could spread to the Pacific Rim, especially if they destabilized India. Indonesia's territorial integrity and stability are vulnerable to Muslim-Christian conflicts and separatist movements in Aceh and Irian Jaya, but recently Indonesia reached cease-fire agreements with the Acehnese and the Papuans in Irian Jaya. Other ongoing tensions in the region include Thailand's conflict with the Muslim Malay in the south, and Myanmar's conflicts with ethnic groups such as the Shan and the Karen.

With the exception of Australia, Japan, and New Zealand, the states in this region are developing nations. Some of them, such as South Korea, are already prosperous, but the rest are mostly middle- and low-income countries. Democratic development in this region has not, however, matched the level of economic development. Burgeoning regional and international organizations, such as the Asia-Pacific Economic Cooperation (APEC) forum and the ASEAN, tend to focus on economic cooperation but avoid political and security issues. To manage ethnic and regional conflicts the way Europe has, the countries of the Pacific Rim might be advised to expand their economic cooperation to democracy and human rights issues.

Finally, the greatest unknown in this region is China. China faces significant ethnic and regional conflicts with several groups in its sphere of influence, including the Muslim Uyghurs in the resource-rich Xinjiang region and the Tibetans. Its conflict with Taiwan, which occasionally flairs into tense standoffs, constitutes one of the most potent flashpoints in the region. If China can develop economically and democratize at the same time, this will generate very positive effects in the whole region.

Data

Table 1 Armed Conflicts for Self-Determination and Their Outcomes, Pre-1956–2004

Period	New armed conflicts	Ongoing conflicts at end of period	Conflicts contained	Conflicts settled or won
Pre-1956	4			
1956–1960	4	8		
1961–1965	5	12		1
1966–1970	5	15	2	
1971–1975	11	23		3
1976–1980	9	30	2	
1981–1985	6	35		1
1986–1990	10	40	2	3
1991–1995	17	39	9	9
1996–2000	5	32	6	6
2001–2004	6	25	8	5
Total	82		29	28

Source: Monty G. Marshall and Ted Robert Gurr, *Peace and Conflict, 2005: A Global Survey of Armed Conflicts, Self-Determination Movements, and Democracy* (College Park, Md.: Center for International Development and Conflict Management, 2005).

Table 2 Armed Self-Determination Conflicts by Region and Regime Type, 1955–2005

Region	Conflicts	Democracies	Anocracies[a]	Autocracies
Asia and the Pacific	39	15	6	7
Latin America and the Caribbean	1	21	1	1
North Africa and the Middle East	5	3	6	11
Former socialist bloc	14	18	4	5
North Atlantic	3	18	0	0
Sub-Saharan Africa	17	13	27	5
World total	79	88	44	29

Sources: Monty G. Marshall and Ted Robert Gurr, *Peace and Conflict, 2005: A Global Survey of Armed Conflicts, Self-Determination Movements, and Democracy* (College Park, Md.: Center for International Development and Conflict Management, 2005); Joseph Hewitt, Jonathan Wilkenfeld, and Ted Robert Gurr, *Peace and Conflict, 2008* (College Park, Md.: Center for International Development and Conflict Management, 2008).

[a]Anocracies are societies where central authority is weak or nonexistent.

Case Study—Kosovo, South Ossetia, and Abkhazia

In February 2008, Kosovar Albanians declared an independent state. Kosovo had been the site of an ethnic and regional conflict since the 1980s. On one side was the Serbian minority of Kosovo and Serbia, of which Kosovo was formally an autonomous province. The Serbs saw Kosovo as part of the Serbian historical homeland and internationally recognized territory. On the other side was Kosovo's Muslim Albanian majority, who deeply distrusted the Serbs and also saw Kosovo as their homeland. Serbia had tried to oppress the Albanians' aspirations for independence and their possible unification with the Albanians in Albania and Macedonia, often brutally. However, Serbia's efforts met with decreasing success, due largely to the increasing perception in the world of the Albanians as an ethnoreligious minority persecuted by a state—Serbia— associated with the ethnic cleansing in Bosnia-Herzegovina in the 1990s. Since the NATO air strikes in 1999 that followed Serbian offensives and forced the Serbs to yield control of the region, the Kosovar Albanians had effectively been ruling themselves with the support of a UN peace implementation force. The majority of Western democracies, that is, the members of NATO, EU, and Organisation for Economic Cooperation and Development (OECD), recognized Kosovo's declaration of independence when it was adopted by a Kosovar "self-government assembly" on February 17, 2008. Countries that had their own secessionist movements, such as China and Spain, withheld their recognition of Kosovo, and allies of Serbia, notably Russia, strongly opposed and condemned the declaration as an illegal and destabilizing move.

Five months after Kosovo's declaration of sovereignty, the Georgian government launched a violent military operation to assert its sovereignty in South Ossetia, which, Georgia feared, wanted to secede and unite with the Republic of North Ossetia-Alania in neighboring Russia. South Ossetia was formally part of Georgia's territory, but since the 1990s it had effectively been self-ruled by independence-minded Ossetians and controlled by Russian-dominated international peacekeeping forces. In response to Georgian self-assertiveness, Russia took the opportunity to crush the Georgian forces, invade part of Georgian territory, and recognize the independence of both South Ossetia and Abkhazia, another secessionist ethnic region of Georgia. This time, Russia was strongly criticized and opposed by the United States and other Western powers, which upheld Georgia's sovereignty and territorial integrity.

In many ways, these two examples exemplify the dilemmas posed by ethnic/ regional conflicts throughout the world, although most of them get much less international attention. And the way they are managed by the international community may significantly affect the future evolution of other existing and dormant conflicts. Will more countries recognize the independence of Kosovo, Abkhazia, and South Ossetia? Will ethnic/regional conflicts be intensified by secessionist movements encouraged by the developments in Kosovo and South Ossetia, or will they be suppressed by national governments and by international and supranational institutions concerned with their destabilizing effects? The long-term consequences of events in these two regions on world politics are unclear.

Biographical Sketches

Martti Ahtisaari is former president of Finland (1994–2000). Upon leaving office, he founded the Crisis Management Initiative and has taken on various tasks, including peace mediation and conflict resolution, facilitating the peace process between the government of Indonesia and the Free Aceh Movement in 2005, and acting as the special envoy of the secretary-general of the United Nations for the future status process for Kosovo between 2005 and 2008. Ahtisaari was the recipient of the Nobel Peace Prize in 2008.

Frederik Willem de Klerk was South African president from 1989 to 1994 and led his country from an apartheid state, and growing social unrest and international isolation, to official acceptance of racial integration, inclusive democracy, and international acceptance. With Nelson Mandela, whom de Klerk released from prison, he was awarded the Nobel Prize for Peace in 1993.

Ted Robert Gurr is Distinguished University Professor at the University of Maryland, College Park, and a leading expert on ethnic and regional conflict. He is best known for his empirical work on ethnopolitical conflict and for his policy-related work on conflict prevention and early warning systems. He co-founded the Minorities at Risk project, which is a major source of data for researchers, and his 1993 book by the same name has become an authoritative text for advanced students in peace studies. Gurr has been a senior consultant on the White House State Failure Task Force since 1994 and on the steering committee of the Conflict Early Warning Systems Research Program of the United Nations Educational, Scientific, and Cultural Organization (UNESCO) International Social Science Council.

Donald Horowitz is a professor of law and political science at Duke University and a leading expert on ethnic conflict in general and on constitutional engineering in divided societies in particular. His 1985 *Ethnic Groups in Conflict* has become a must-read for researchers with an interest in the subject. Horowitz's proposals have contributed to institution building in divided societies, including in Fiji, Nigeria, Northern Ireland, and Russia. In *The Deadly Ethnic Riot* (2001), he investigates the group dynamics of ethnic group violence.

Nelson Mandela is a political activist for black rights, statesman, and former president of South Africa (1994–1999). Mandela, who was jailed between 1964 and 1990, played a key role in the relatively peaceful death of apartheid in South Africa. Although he earlier had preached violent resistance, his relatively moderate stance and lack of vindictiveness contributed to the ruling South African whites' agreeing to share power with the blacks without a decisive and bloody military battle. As president, Mandela established the Truth and Reconciliation Commission to investigate past human rights abuses and helped the society to come to terms with its past. Together with Frederik Willem de Klerk, he was awarded the Nobel Prize for Peace in 1993.

Directory

Amnesty International, 322 8th Avenue, New York, N.Y. 10001. Telephone: (212) 807-8400; email: aimember@aiusa.org; Web: http://www.aiusa.org.
Nongovernmental organization that campaigns against human rights abuses and pressures governments and others to refrain from such activities.

Doctors Without Borders, 6 East 39th Street, 8th Floor, New York, N.Y. 10016. Telephone: (212) 679-6800; email: doctors@newyork.msf.org; Web: http://www.doctorswithoutborders.org.

Grassroots humanitarian aid organization that provides assistance to people caught in ethnic and regional conflicts.

Human Rights Watch, 350 Fifth Avenue, 34th Floor, New York, N.Y. 10118-3299. Telephone: (212) 290-4700; email: go to http://www.hrw.org/contact.html; Web: http://www.hrw.org.
Watchdog organization that reports and condemns human rights abuses and that pressures governments and others to refrain from such abuses.

Organization for Security and Cooperation in Europe (OSCE), OSCE Secretariat, Kärntner Ring 5-7, 4th Floor, 1010 Vienna, Austria. Telephone: (43) 1 14-36 180; email: info@osce.org; Web: http://www.osce.org.
Regional security organization heavily involved in postconflict reconstruction and in preventing and managing ethnic and regional conflicts in Europe and Eurasia.

United Nations, First Avenue at 46th Street, New York, N.Y. 10017. Telephone: (212) 963-4475; email: inquiries@un.org; Web (for peacekeeping operations): http://www. un.org/Depts/dpko/dpko/home_bottom.htm.
International organization that attempts to prevent ethnic and regional conflicts through negotiation and multilateral sanctions, and that maintain peace through multilateral operations.

United States Institute of Peace, 1200 17th Street NW, Suite 200, Washington, D.C. 20036-3011. Telephone: (202) 457-1700; email: usip_requests@usip.org; Web: http://www.usip.org.
An independent, nonpartisan federal institution that tries to strengthen the U.S. capacity to promote the peaceful resolution of international conflict, mainly through research and educational activities.

Further Research

Books

Brown, Michael E., et al. *Nationalism and Ethnic Conflict.* Cambridge, Mass.: MIT Press. 2001.

Brubaker, Rogers. *Ethnicity without Groups.* Cambridge, Mass.: Harvard University Press, 2006.

Cashmore, Ellis, et al. *Dictionary of Race and Ethnic Relations.* New York: Routledge, 1996.

Chirot, Daniel, and Clark McCauley. *Why Not Kill Them All?: The Logic and Prevention of Mass Political Murder.* Princeton, N.J.: Princeton University Press, 2006.

Esman, Milton J., and Ronald J. Herring. *Carrots, Sticks, and Ethnic Conflict: Rethinking Development Assistance.* Ann Arbor, Mich.: University of Michigan Press, 2001.

Guibernau, Montserrat, and John Hutchinson, eds. *Understanding Nationalism.* Malden, Mass.: Polity Press, 2001.

Gurr, Ted Robert. *Minorities at Risk: A Global View of Ethnopolitical Conflicts.* Washington, D.C.: United States Institute of Peace Press, 1993.

Horowitz, Donald L. *The Deadly Ethnic Riot.* Berkeley, Calif.: University of California Press, 2001.

———. *Ethnic Groups in Conflict.* Berkeley, Calif.: University of California Press, 1985.

Hutchinson, John, and Anthony D. Smith, eds. *Ethnicity.* New York: Oxford University Press, 1996.

Kalyvas, Stathis N. *The Logic of Violence in Civil War.* New York: Cambridge University Press, 2007.

Keating, Michael, and John McGarry, eds. *Minority Nationalism and the Changing International Order.* Oxford: Oxford University Press, 2001.

Kymlicka, Will, ed. *The Rights of Minority Cultures.* New York: Oxford University Press, 1995.

Laitin, David D. *Nations, States and Violence.* New York: Oxford University, 2007.

Lake, David A., and Donald Rothchild, eds. *The International Spread of Ethnic Conflict: Fear, Diffusion, and Escalation.* Princeton, N.J.: Princeton University Press, 1998.

Levinson, David. *Ethnic Groups Worldwide: A Ready Reference Book.* Phoenix, Ariz.: Oryx Press, 1998.

Marshall, Monty G., and Ted Robert Gurr. *Peace and Conflict, 2005: A Global Survey of Armed Conflicts, Self-Determination Movements, and Democracy.* College Park, Md.: Center for International Development and Conflict Management, 2005.

Wippman, David, ed. *International Law and Ethnic Conflict.* Ithaca, N.Y.: Cornell University Press, 1998.

Wolff, Stefan. *Ethnic Conflict: A Global Perspective.* Oxford: Oxford University Press, 2006.

Articles and Reports

Annan, Kofi. "Two Concepts of Sovereignty." *Economist,* September 16, 1999.

Easterly, William. "Polarized People." In *The Elusive Quest for Growth: Economists' Adventures and Misadventures in the Tropics.* Cambridge, Mass.: MIT Press, 2001.

Fearon, James D., and David D. Laitin. "Ethnicity, Insurgency, and Civil War." *American Political Science Review* 97, no. 1 (2003): 75–90.

———. "Violence and the Social Construction of Ethnic Identity." *International Organization* 54, no. 4 (2000): 845–877.

Horowitz, Donald L. "A Right to Secede?" In *Comparative Politics,* ed. Bernard E. Brown. Belmont, Calif.: Thomson-Wadsworth, 2006.

Web Sites

Ethnic and Racial Studies
http://www.tandf.co.uk/journals/routledge/01419870.html

Ethnic Conflict Research Digest
http://www.incore.ulst.ac.uk/ecrd/index.html

Ethnologue.com
http://www.ethnologue.com

Ethnopolitics
http://www.ethnopolitics.org

Journal of Conflict Resolution
http://www.uk.sagepub.com/journalsProdDesc.nav?prodId=Journa1200764&

Minorities at Risk Project
http://www.cidcm.umd.edu/mar

United Institute of Peace, Peacekeeping Web Links
http://www.usip.org/library/topics/peacekeeping.html

United Nations Human Rights: Office of the High Commissioner for Human Rights
http://www.ohchr.org/EN/Pages/WelcomePage.aspx

World Conference against Racism, Racial Discrimination, Xenophobia and Related Intolerance
http://www.unhchr.ch/html/racism

World Directory of Minorities and Indigenous Peoples
http://www.minorityrights.org/directory

Documents

1. Declaration on the Rights of Persons Belonging to National or Ethnic, Religious and Linguistic Minorities

United Nations General Assembly, Resolution 47/135, December 18, 1992

The full text is available at http://www.unhchr.ch/html/racism/minorpart1-1.doc.

Extracts

Article 1

1. States shall protect the existence and the national or ethnic, cultural, religious and linguistic identity of minorities within their respective territories and shall encourage conditions for the promotion of that identity.

2. States shall adopt appropriate legislative and other measures to achieve those ends.

Article 2

1. Persons belonging to national or ethnic, religious and linguistic minorities (hereinafter referred to as persons belonging to minorities) have the right to enjoy their own culture, to profess and practice their own religion, and to use their own language, in private and in public, freely and without interference or any form of discrimination.

2. Persons belonging to minorities have the right to participate effectively in cultural, religious, social, economic, and public life.

3. Persons belonging to minorities have the right to participate effectively in decisions on the national and, where appropriate, regional level concerning the minority to which they belong or the regions in which they live, in a manner not incompatible with national legislation.

4. Persons belonging to minorities have the right to establish and maintain their own associations.

5. Persons belonging to minorities have the right to establish and maintain, without any discrimination, free and peaceful contacts with other members of their group and with persons belonging to other minorities, as well as contacts across frontiers with citizens of other States to whom they are related by national or ethnic, religious or linguistic ties.

Article 3

1. Persons belonging to minorities may exercise their rights, including those set forth in the present Declaration, individually as well as in community with other members of their group, without any discrimination.

2. No disadvantage shall result for any person belonging to a minority as the consequence of the exercise or non-exercise of the rights set forth in the present Declaration.

Article 4

1. States shall take measures where required to ensure that persons belonging to minorities may exercise fully and effectively all their human rights and fundamental freedoms without any discrimination and in full equality before the law.

2. States shall take measures to create favourable conditions to enable persons belonging to minorities to express their characteristics and to develop their culture, language, religion, traditions and customs, except where specific practices are in violation of national law and contrary to international standards.

3. States should take appropriate measures so that, wherever possible, persons belonging to minorities may have adequate opportunities to learn their mother tongue or to have instruction in their mother tongue.

4. States should, where appropriate, take measures in the field of education, in order to encourage knowledge of the history, traditions, language and culture of the minorities existing within their territory. Persons belonging to minorities should have adequate opportunities to gain knowledge of the society as a whole.

5. States should consider appropriate measures so that persons belonging to minorities may participate fully in the economic progress and development in their country.

2. International Convention on the Elimination of All Forms of Racial Discrimination

United Nations General Assembly, Resolution 2106 (XX), December 21, 1965, entered into force January 4, 1969

The full text is available at http://www.unhchr.ch/html/menu3/b/d_icerd.htm.

Extracts

The States Parties to this Convention,

Considering that the Charter of the United Nations is based on the principles of the dignity and equality inherent in all human beings, and that all Member States have pledged themselves to take joint and separate action, in co-operation with the Organization, for the achievement of one of the purposes of the United Nations which is to promote and encourage universal respect for and observance of human rights and fundamental freedoms for all, without distinction as to race, sex, language or religion,

Considering that the Universal Declaration of Human Rights proclaims that all human beings are born free and equal in dignity and rights and that everyone is entitled to all the rights and freedoms set out therein, without distinction of any kind, in particular as to race, colour or national origin,

Considering that all human beings are equal before the law and are entitled to equal protection of the law against any discrimination and against any incitement to discrimination,

Considering that the United Nations has condemned colonialism and all practices of segregation and discrimination associated therewith, in whatever form and wherever they exist, and that the Declaration on the Granting of Independence to Colonial

Countries and Peoples of 14 December 1960 (General Assembly resolution 1514 (XV)) has affirmed and solemnly proclaimed the necessity of bringing them to a speedy and unconditional end,

Considering that the United Nations Declaration on the Elimination of All Forms of Racial Discrimination of 20 November 1963 (General Assembly resolution 1904 (XVIII)) solemnly affirms the necessity of speedily eliminating racial discrimination throughout the world in all its forms and manifestations and of securing understanding of and respect for the dignity of the human person,

Convinced that any doctrine of superiority based on racial differentiation is scientifically false, morally condemnable, socially unjust and dangerous, and that there is no justification for racial discrimination, in theory or in practice, anywhere,

Reaffirming that discrimination between human beings on the grounds of race, colour or ethnic origin is an obstacle to friendly and peaceful relations among nations and is capable of disturbing peace and security among peoples and the harmony of persons living side by side even within one and the same State,

Convinced that the existence of racial barriers is repugnant to the ideals of any human society,

Alarmed by manifestations of racial discrimination still in evidence in some areas of the world and by governmental policies based on racial superiority or hatred, such as policies of apartheid, segregation or separation,

Resolved to adopt all necessary measures for speedily eliminating racial discrimination in all its forms and manifestations, and to prevent and combat racist doctrines and practices in order to promote understanding between races and to build an international community free from all forms of racial segregation and racial discrimination,

Bearing in mind the Convention concerning Discrimination in Respect of Employment and Occupation adopted by the International Labour Organization in 1958, and the Convention against Discrimination in Education adopted by the United Nations Educational, Scientific and Cultural Organization in 1960,

Desiring to implement the principles embodied in the United Nations Declaration on the Elimination of All Forms of Racial Discrimination and to secure the earliest adoption of practical measures to that end.

GENOCIDE

Edward Kissi

Genocide is a twentieth-century term describing an ancient crime. In the minds of many people, genocide is any kind of morally objectionable killing of people. We could describe this view as the "popular-moral" discourse on genocide. The existence of this type of discourse—the use of the word *genocide* and the imagery of annihilation that it conjures to draw public attention to mass killing—should not obscure the actual meaning of *genocide* or the specific crime it describes. To scholars who study genocide, the word *genocide* means the intentional destruction, which includes killing, of particular groups of people by a perpetrator, often a state, and in recent years, by organized and armed nonstate groups or militias. We could describe this view as the "academic-legal" discourse on genocide. Genocide, thus, describes a specific crime against humanity, which must be understood within a historical and legal context. A great deal of effort has been made by the United Nations, individual states, and scholars to define *genocide* as a crime against humanity punishable under international law. Yet genocide persists in many forms, and the perpetrators often escape the grasp of the law in their own countries and internationally.

Historical Background and Development

The origin of the word *genocide* can be attributed to Raphael Lemkin (1900–1959). He coined the word from the Greek word *genos* ("race, nation or tribe") and the Latin word *cide* ("to kill"). As Lemkin later articulated in his book *Axis Rule in Occupied Europe, genocide* meant "a coordinated plan of different actions" undertaken by a state or government to destroy the "essential foundations of the life of an ethnic group" as part of completely annihilating the group. Thus, Lemkin's original idea of genocide emphasized the physical destruction of groups as well the deliberate destruction of the culture or identity (the essential foundations of the life) of the target group. Lemkin tried, but failed, in 1933 at the Fifth International Conference for the Unification of Criminal Law in Madrid, to convince the participants to declare the destruction of what he called "racial, religious or social collectivities" a crime under international law.

663

An aspect of what Lemkin characterized as genocide actually took place during the course of World War II in the deliberate and systematic attempt by Nazi Germany to exterminate European Jews in what is now called the Holocaust. After the war, with the images of the Holocaust still fresh in public memory and through Lemkin's lobbying efforts, the new postwar international body, the United Nations, passed a unanimous resolution on December 11, 1946, to label as a crime under international law the forms of killing that Lemkin had described as genocide. This nonbinding resolution pointed to the many instances in history in which racial, religious, political and other groups had been partially or totally killed by governments. The resolution condemned the crimes committed during World War II by the governments of Germany, Italy, and Japan in an effort to legitimize the Nuremberg trials (see INTERNATIONAL CRIMINAL JUSTICE and INTERNATIONAL LAW). Despite its nonbinding character, the resolution criminalized any form of killing of people because of their political beliefs.

However, the victorious Allied powers—Britain, France and the United States—wanted the protection of political groups to be stipulated in a UN-backed international law against genocide; such a stipulation would serve as a condemnation of the mass murder of communists and social democrats by the Nazi government. In the end, political groups were excluded from the eventual United Nations convention on genocide adopted in December 1948 due to politics. During the debate on the convention, delegates from Iran, Poland, and the Soviet Union opposed the inclusion of political groups; they argued that political groups have no stable, natural, or permanent characteristics as do racial and religious groups. On the other side, France and Haiti supported their inclusion. The French delegation pointed out that past genocides had been committed on racial and religious grounds and therefore it was likely that future genocides would be committed on political grounds. In hindsight, the delegation was correct in its arguments. Today, it is very likely that, in the name of national security and political stability, governments will convert particular ethnic, national, racial, and religious groups into "political enemies" or "terrorists" and target them for annihilation, thus disguising their intent to destroy these groups as such.

The U.S. delegation argued that the inclusion and protection of religious groups in an international law against genocide made the inclusion and protection of political groups necessary and consistent. The delegation had accurately noted that what bound religious and political groups together was their belief in a set of ideas. However, in the face of opposition from the Soviet Union, the U.S. delegation relented. Clearly, the Soviet delegation wanted to limit the meaning of *genocide* to the racial supremacy theories and imperialist ideologies that had characterized national socialism in Germany. The U.S. delegation's lack of conviction on this point highlighted, in part, its fear of Congress's reaction to an international treaty such as this. The Senate had previously rejected U.S. membership in the League of Nations after World War I, showing Congress's distrust of internationally binding agreements that might restrict U.S. sovereignty.

On December 9, 1948, the United Nations General Assembly adopted the Convention on the Prevention and Punishment of the Crime of Genocide (hereafter called the Genocide Convention), The broad scope of the Convention, which came into force on January 12, 1951, is consistent with Lemkin's original view of genocide (see Document 1). Although a product of ideological compromise, the Genocide Convention is, today, the only internationally accepted document that defines *genocide*.

Current Status

Despite nearly universal condemnation of genocide as a crime against humanity, there is a lack of unanimity on the policies or actions required to prevent or punish those who commit this grave crime against humanity.

Research

Research on genocide has progressed steadily since the academic study of the legal concept began in the 1970s with the examination of the Holocaust as a type of genocide. And since the 1990s, there have been some notable shifts in research and scholarship on genocide. There is a continuing movement away from specialization in the study of particular cases of genocide (the case study approach) to comparative studies of multiple cases of genocide (the comparative approach) that identify and analyze their similarities and differences. Legal scholar David Scheffer has called for a new terminology (atrocity crimes) and a new field of international law (atrocity laws) to allow scholars and the general public to use this common and easily understood term (*atrocity*) to describe a wide range of crimes that include genocide. His concept of atrocity crimes is the most recent and significant attempt to change the way scholars and analysts discuss genocide.

Despite this notable change in the academic discourse on genocide, the UN Genocide Convention continues to set the standards for the determination of genocide. Article 1 of the Genocide Convention declares that, whether it is committed in a time of war or peace, genocide "is a crime under international law" that all members of the United Nations should pledge to "prevent and punish." According to Article 2, "genocide means any of the following acts committed with intent to destroy, in whole or in part, a national, ethnical, racial or religious group, as such:" "killing members of the group," "causing serious bodily or mental harm to members of the group," "deliberately inflicting on the group conditions of life calculated to bring about its physical destruction in whole or in part," "imposing measures intended to prevent births within the group," and "forcibly transferring children of the group to another group."

The Genocide Convention continues to generate controversy. For example, the phrases *in whole* and *in part,* the word *intent* and groups declared "racial," "religious," "ethnical," and "national" are not clearly defined. The convention also fails to resolve the following questions: How many of the target group must be killed by the perpetrator for the group to be recognized in international law as a victim of genocide? Does the extermination of an ethnic group by members of the same group constitute genocide? What should be the standard of proof of intent to commit genocide? When is a group a group? These questions point to a key problem. If the success of prosecuting and punishing perpetrators of genocide depends on proving the intent of the perpetrator to destroy a type of target group identified in the genocide convention, then genocide may be a crime that is hard to prove and prosecute because few perpetrators of genocide reveal their reasons for targeting a group for extermination. And if genocide is hard to prove and also detect, it would be equally hard to make public policy aimed at preventing genocide or mobilizing the general public to stop genocide while it is occurring, either in wartime or peacetime. Scholars and other analysts who study genocide have provided some answers to these important questions and concerns. Many of them have called for a redefinition or rethinking of the concept of genocide in the light of recent mass murders.

Social scientists who study genocide fall into two overlapping categories. The first group includes those who seek a narrow or restrictive concept or definition of *genocide* out of concern that a broader concept might lead to frivolous use of the word. Those who seek a restrictive definition of *genocide,* such as sociologist and legal scholar Leo Kuper, historian Frank Chalk, and sociologists Kurt Jonassohn and Helen Fein, argue that *genocide* should not be a cliché or buzzword to be used recklessly in political and social activism to label every form of violence. To make it so would distort the meaning of *genocide* and minimize the gravity of acts that are truly genocidal in nature. The second group comprises scholars who seek a broad definition of *genocide* that makes any act that leads to the killing of human beings on a substantial scale an act of genocide. This group includes psychologist Israel Charny and political scientist Rudolph J. Rummell. They argue that every human life matters, and it would be morally absurd to exclude some instances of mass killing from recognition as genocide as if those human lives destroyed were undeserving of protection. Herein lies the outline of the characterization of the academic-legal versus popular-moral discourses on genocide.

For Leo Kuper, the search for an appropriate definition of *genocide* is less important than the establishment of a strong genocide-prevention mechanism in the form of an international court of justice to prosecute and punish the perpetrators of genocide. In *Genocide: Its Political Uses in the Twentieth Century,* Kuper focuses on the social conditions that produce genocide, arguing that societies with rigid ethnic hierarchies and in which minority groups are always viewed with suspicion have a greater capacity for mass violence (see ETHNIC AND REGIONAL CONFLICT). Under such social structures, the rise of minority groups to prominent economic, social, and political positions generates intense hatred of them by the majority and often-dominant ethnic group.

In the *History and Sociology of Genocide,* Frank Chalk and Kurt Jonassohn address the largest loopholes in the genocide convention, arguing that the United Nations made a mistake by excluding the protection of political groups—the key victims of state-organized genocide—from legal protection under the convention. Although Chalk and Jonassohn criticize the omission of these groups, they agree with the provision in the convention that, for any killing to be considered a genocide, it must be part of a deliberate attempt by a perpetrator to destroy a particular group of people, an action that the United Nations labels "acts committed with intent."

Chalk and Jonassohn see the intent of a perpetrator to destroy a group as an essential identifier of genocide; this view, also held by other analysts and observers, exclude cases in which genocide was the outcome of an action that was not originally intended to achieve that result. They criticize the failure of the framers of the Genocide Convention to draw a clear distinction (in the list of five actions that constitute genocide) between violence intended to destroy a group and nonviolent attacks on members of the group. Chalk and Jonassohn argue that violent acts intended to destroy a group, such as killing members of the group, should not be considered the same as nonlethal or nonviolent acts, such as transporting members of the group to another group that could ultimately cause the physical destruction of the group or alteration of aspects of its culture and identity, when destruction was not the original intent. For example, Chalk and Jonassohn exclude from their conception of genocide civilian deaths resulting from military actions, such as aerial bombardments of enemy territory in times of war, no matter how morally objectionable those actions are, including, for example, the U.S. bombing of Japan in 1945 with nuclear weapons. They argue that in war civilians are often considered combatants or part of the group or nation that is at war—that, in effect, civilians become collateral targets of military actions.

Chalk and Jonassohn have, therefore, proposed a research definition that classifies genocide according to the motives of the perpetrator: "a form of one-sided mass killing in which a state or other authority intends to destroy a group, as that group and membership in it are defined by the perpetrator." They argue that genocides have occurred throughout history and that in all cases the perpetrators have been states and governments, or armed groups working on their behalf, acting on the basis of one or more of four motives: to eliminate a real or potential threat; to spread terror among real or potential enemies; to acquire economic wealth; or to implement a belief, a theory, or an ideology. In all four categories, the killing must be one-sided to constitute genocide. One-sided mass killings are killings in which the victims lack the means to defend themselves against annihilation or in which they may possess the means but are still powerless to avert extermination because of the preponderant power of the perpetrator. Chalk and Jonassohn's definition of *mass killing* also includes killings in which all the members of a group are targeted for extermination even though the perpetrator does not succeed in eliminating the entire group.

A major contribution of Chalk's and Jonassohn's research definition of *genocide* is the view, as previously mentioned, that the perpetrator of genocide defines the characteristics of a target group. For example, it was the racist ideology of Nazi Germany that defined *Jewishness* in strict racial terms and that provided no room for escape. In Cambodia in 1975, it was the Pol Pot regime's revolutionary ideology of racial and ideological purity that turned a diverse group of humanity—educated people, traders, and urban dwellers—into "impure" Khmers to be destroyed. That is, the intellectuals, traders, and Western-educated Cambodians that the Khmer Rouge killed in Cambodia from 1975 to 1979 became a group because they were defined as such by the Pol Pot regime; their identity as a group was fabricated by the Khmer Rouge because the regime saw them as posing a threat to its revolutionary ideology. Thus, according to Chalk and Jonassohn, in situations of genocide, the perpetrator's ideology can convert particular ethnic, national, racial, and religious groups into political enemies or ideological opponents to be destroyed with impunity. This is one reason why Chalk and Jonassohn consider the exclusion of political groups from legal protection in the genocide convention as a mistake.

Political scientists Barbara Harff and Ted Robert Gurr have coined the term *politicide* to distinguish the deliberate destruction of political groups from intentional racial killings or genocide. As they admit in "Towards Empirical Theory of Genocides and Politicides," however, it is difficult to differentiate genocide from politicide because the racial or ethnic victims of genocide are often politically active and, therefore, targeted on grounds of their political beliefs as well.

Sociologist Helen Fein addresses the issue of proving intent in her research on genocide. Fein suggests that the intent of a perpetrator to destroy a group can be proven by establishing an identifiable pattern that ultimately leads to the destruction of a significant number of the victim group. She cites three patterns of purposeful actions for identifying an ongoing genocide: sustained attacks on a target group by an organized entity such as a state or armed political groups, selection of victims on the basis of their membership in a group, and persecution of the victims regardless of whether they resist or surrender.

Political scientist Robert Melson focuses his work on identifying contexts or situations that encourage genocide. Melson sees revolution and war as providing such situations and contexts. He argues in *Revolution and Genocide: On the Origins of the Armenian Genocide and the Holocaust* that it was extreme nationalist ideologies that led the Young Turks regime of the Ottoman Turkish Empire to kill 1.5 million Armenians during World War I and the Nazis to murder some 6 million Jews during World War II. In each of these cases, revolution and war provided the contexts for the extreme ideologies to be turned into instruments of genocide. Melson is careful to note, however, that not every revolution leads to genocide and not every genocide is the consequence of revolution and war.

A pertinent illustration of Melson's cautionary arguments can be found in Edward Kissi's 2006 *Revolution and Genocide in Ethiopia and Cambodia*. Kissi argues that, although genocide actually occurred in the course of Cambodia's social revolution, the specific crime did not occur in Ethiopia's revolution because the members of armed political groups were the main targets of organized and indiscriminate killing in a protracted power struggle in revolutionary Ethiopia. The Ethiopian government and antigovernment armed groups were responsible for the estimated 2 million deaths. Kissi does not see these deaths, despite their extent, as constituting an attempt on the part of the Ethiopian government or its armed opponents to destroy, in whole or in part, the ethnic groups from which the targeted political opponents came. In contrast, he contends that in Cambodia the Khmer Rouge carried out extensive genocide against ethnic and religious groups. He also argues that not regarding a particular form of violence as a genocide does not mean one condones murder. Rather, *genocide* risks losing its meaning if it becomes a generic word for any objectionable atrocity committed by individuals or governments and insurgent groups in power struggles and counterinsurgency actions, which may have nothing to do with an intention to destroy particular ethnic, racial, religious, or national groups.

A critical attempt to reconcile the competing popular-moral and academic-legal discourses on genocide has been made by legal scholar David Scheffer. In his 2006 article "Genocide and Atrocity Crimes," Scheffer suggests the use of a new term, *atrocity crimes,* to allow scholars, governments, and the general public to "identify precursors of genocide" without being constrained by the legal requirements that the Genocide Convention imposes on the description of a particular atrocity as a genocide. He describes atrocity crimes as "a grouping of crimes that includes genocide but is not confined to that particular crime." Scheffer's call for a terminology that everyone can agree on stems from what he calls the "confusion and garbled terminology" that scholars, governments, and activists reach for when describing what is taking place in an atrocity zone such as a domestic war or in a struggle for political power. The struggle among the United States, the United Nations, and scholars who study genocide over how to describe the atrocities in Sudan's Darfur region highlights Scheffer's frustration.

What is innovative about Scheffer's attempt to fundamentally shift thinking and research on genocide is that *atrocity crimes* provides an all-embracing and simplified term that governments and the general public can use to describe, condemn, and also mobilize a response to atrocities occurring in war zones when anyone is uncertain that an actual genocide is occurring in that conflict situation. The ongoing war in Darfur, Sudan, and the conflicting public and academic perspectives on the nature of the atrocities taking place there indicate that determining accurately what is actually happening in an armed conflict between government and insurgent groups is often difficult. The way Scheffer simplifies the debate on such a moral issue as saving and protecting lives in an atrocity zone represents the most compelling recent attempt to change the way analysts should discuss genocide.

Policies and Programs

Since 1990, humanitarian interventions and international criminal tribunals have become the most popular genocide-prevention policies and programs. Intervening to stop genocide before it occurs and prosecuting perpetrators of genocides that could not be prevented affirm the readiness, amid some occasional hesitation, of the world's family of nations to do something about this persistent problem. However, both options are fraught with legal and political complexities.

Examples of intervention since the mid-1990s are telling. In June 1999, the North Atlantic Treaty Organization (NATO) led an armed intervention to save ethnic Albanian Muslims in Kosovo after more than a hundred thousand of them had been killed by the Serbian government in a clear case of genocide against a religious group. However, such UN efforts were not reflected in the events in Rwanda earlier in the decade. In 1994, while armed groups from the Hutu ethnic group slaughtered some 800,000 Tutsi in Rwanda, with full U.S. and UN awareness of what was happening. The Bill Clinton administration (1992–2000) found reasons not to use the word *genocide* to describe what was clearly a planned extermination campaign. This hesitation arose from the U.S. concern that recognition of the Rwandan killings as genocide would impose a moral and legal obligation on the United States, under the UN Genocide Convention, to intervene.

That policy thinking had changed when the George W. Bush administration (2000–2008) took over from the Clinton administration. The Bush administration demonstrated that the U.S. government can use the word *genocide* to describe atrocities occurring in a given place, with or without investigation, and still not be morally or legally bound to intervene to stop it. Thus, on September 9, 2004, after nearly two months of a U.S. State Department–sponsored field investigation of what Scheffer would call atrocity crimes in Sudan's Darfur region, U.S. Secretary of State Colin Powell declared, in a statement to the U.S. Congress, that a "genocide" had taken place in Darfur. Powell based his conclusions on "consistent and widespread pattern of atrocities (killings, rapes, burning of villages)" carried out by Sudanese government forces and government-backed armed militia groups known as the Janjawid, against "non-Arab villagers" in Darfur.

The United Nations held a different view. From its separate field investigation of the crimes committed in Darfur (launched in 2004), the UN reported in January 2005 that the government of Sudan and its armed militia had committed crimes against humanity and not necessarily genocide. The UN's "Report of the International Commission of Inquiry on Darfur" concluded that "serious violations of international human rights and humanitarian law" in the form of "killings of civilians, torture, enforced disappearances, rape and other forms of sexual violence" had taken place in Darfur. The different terminologies that the UN and the United States used to describe the killing in Darfur highlight the problem that David Scheffer seeks to resolve in his call for a uniform terminology unimpeded by any form of wrangling over the legal determination of genocide. Scheffer's idea has yet to reshape the discourse on genocide or influence genocide-prevention policy.

In the aftermath of the Rwanda genocide, international criminal tribunals have become the most popular genocide-prevention policy, more often used than humanitarian military interventions (see INTERNATIONAL CRIMINAL JUSTICE and WAR CRIMES). The UN-sponsored International Criminal Tribunal for the Former Yugoslavia (ICTY), established in April 1993 and based in The Hague, has indicted key Bosnian Serb politicians such as Radovan Karadzic (who was arrested on July 21, 2008, living under the assumed name Dragan Dabic in a Belgrade suburb after fifteen years of eluding capture) and Ratko

Mladić for genocide against Bosnian Muslims. The ICTY also considers rape and other dehumanizing sexual offenses against women in wartime as crimes of genocide. This designation is a new and important development in the international policy on genocide prevention and one of the primary innovations of the tribunal. The International Criminal Tribunal for Rwanda, established by the United Nations in November 1994 and based in Arusha, Tanzania, has likewise set impressive precedents in the prosecution of genocide. As of October 2001, the tribunal had convicted six former Rwandan state officials of genocide, the first international tribunal since Nuremberg to do so. The convicted include former Rwandan prime minister Jean Kambanda, Jean Paul Akayesu, and Colonel Theoneste Bagosora, all former prominent government officials. There are also other military and political figures in custody awaiting trial. The Rwanda tribunal has been a testimony to the efficacy of international criminal tribunals as tools in punishing genocide and, therefore, reducing the possibility of future genocidal acts.

Progress in the institutionalization of international criminal tribunals occurred in June 1998. More than 160 countries met in Rome to discuss and adopt a treaty establishing the first permanent International Criminal Court (ICC) for prosecuting perpetrators of genocide, as well as war crimes and other crimes against humanity. On July 17, 1998, 120 countries approved the treaty and 26 countries signed it the following day. But the authority of the resulting ICC is compromised by legal limitations. The court can try only cases of genocide that the UN Security Council refers to it, which means that Security Council members can use their veto to protect the perpetrators of genocide in their own states or in states to which they are bound with a vital strategic interest. Furthermore, the court cannot try any perpetrator of genocide who is a citizen of a country that has not signed the treaty establishing the court. This is a serious flaw that allows some nations to put their citizens who perpetrate genocide beyond the jurisdiction of the court by their refusal to sign the treaty. Despite these limitations, the idea of a permanent ICC is important because it institutionalizes the principle of accountability. The ICC was used by the United Nations Security Council in reference to genocide when it referred the crimes in Darfur to the court on March 31, 2005. On July 14, 2008, Luis Moreno-Ocampo, the chief prosecutor of the ICC, issued an official indictment against Sudanese president Omar Hassan al-Bashir for culpability in genocide in Darfur.

Not everyone, however, believes that international tribunals have a positive effect on genocide prevention. The previous indictments and trials of Bosnian Serb and Rwandan politicians at the international tribunals did not deter Sudanese leaders from murderous behavior. So, while some analysts hailed the indictment of the Sudanese leader as a significant act in the history of international justice, others have dismissed it as a form of moral posturing and a meaningless indictment from an illegitimate court. To the extent that indictments lead to successful prosecutions or put pressure on leaders of states and militias committing or condoning genocide to change their behavior, these indictments serve a useful purpose. They can be seen as new and innovative tools in genocide prevention and prosecution policy.

Regional Summaries

R. J. Rummell has argued that almost 170 million people were shot, beaten, tortured, murdered, burned, buried alive, bombed, starved, or worked to death by states, governments, and armed political movements during the first eighty-eight years of the twentieth century. He adds that struggles for power, the absolute exercise of power, and ethnic conflicts led to the deaths of more than 203 million people in the twentieth century. Every region of the world has had its share of these incidents of genocide.

The Americas

It is difficult to know the exact number of the indigenous population that has been systematically wiped out by governments in North, Central, and South America. However, with the settlement of Europeans in the Americas in the nineteenth century and with the expansion of national borders and the pursuit of development by governments in the United States, Canada, Brazil, Mexico, Colombia, and Chile in the twentieth century, indigenous people (the American Indians or Native Americans) have paid dearly with their lives. The process of the destruction of the native population varied in time and place. The intentional state-organized extermination of Native Americans did not occur on any significant scale. A large number died from European infectious diseases after their encounter with European settlers. In Mexico, for instance, epidemic diseases, more than direct massacres, wiped out large numbers of the native people. But local and federal state authorities in the United States and Canada, for instance, also adopted policies that undermined what Lemkin calls the foundations of the livelihood of the native people. For example, according to some scholars, including Clinton F. Fink, during the California gold rush in the 1850s, entire groups of Native Americans were exterminated to gain control of their territory. This is an example of what Chalk and Jonassohn call genocide committed for the purpose of acquiring economic wealth. Also, by destroying the buffalo (a key source of food and survival for native people) and by putting Native Americans on marginal agricultural lands (reserves or reservations), the governments of Canada, the United States, and Brazil exposed these groups to famine, starvation, and disease. According to Chalk and Jonassohn, the failure to mitigate the adverse conditions on the reserves that killed native people and lowered their birthrates constituted deliberate neglect of the welfare of a group, betraying an intent to destroy them. The indigenous people of Colombia, Brazil, Chile, and Mexico, according to Ted Robert Gurr, Monty G. Marshall, and Deepa Khosla, are seriously at risk of becoming victims of state-sponsored genocide in the twenty-first century.

Europe

The major genocides of the twentieth century took place in Europe. Between 1915 and 1922, according to Richard G. Hovannisian's essay "The Historical Dimensions of the Armenian Question, 1878–1930," about 1.5 million Armenians in the Ottoman Empire were killed by the Young Turks revolutionary

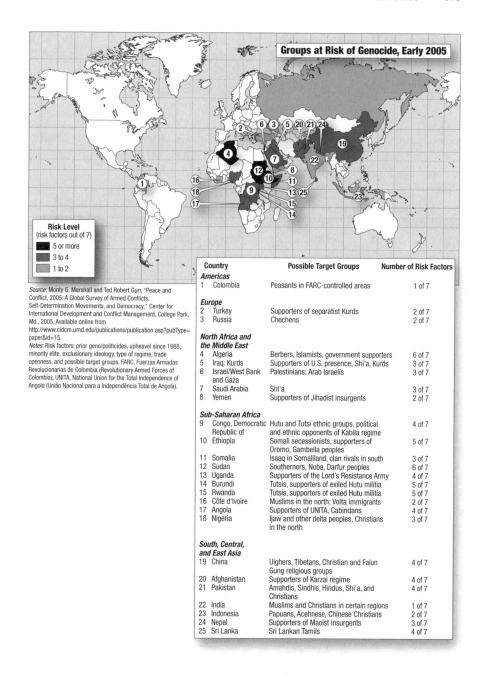

Groups at Risk of Genocide, Early 2005

Risk Level
(risk factors out of 7)

■	5 or more
■	3 to 4
■	1 to 2

Source: Monty G. Marshall and Ted Robert Gurr, "Peace and Conflict, 2005: A Global Survey of Armed Conflicts, Self-Determination Movements, and Democracy," Center for International Development and Conflict Management, College Park, Md., 2005. Available online from http://www.cidcm.umd.edu/publications/publication.asp?pubType=paper&id=15.

Notes: Risk factors: prior geno/politicides, upheaval since 1988, minority elite, exclusionary ideology, type of regime, trade openness, and possible target groups. FARC, Fuerzas Armadas Revolucionarias de Colombia (Revolutionary Armed Forces of Colombia); UNITA, National Union for the Total Independence of Angola (União Nacional para a Independência Total de Angola).

Country	Possible Target Groups	Number of Risk Factors
Americas		
1 Colombia	Peasants in FARC-controlled areas	1 of 7
Europe		
2 Turkey	Supporters of separatist Kurds	2 of 7
3 Russia	Chechens	2 of 7
North Africa and the Middle East		
4 Algeria	Berbers, Islamists, government supporters	6 of 7
5 Iraq: Kurds	Supporters of U.S. presence, Shi'a, Kurds	3 of 7
6 Israel/West Bank and Gaza	Palestinians; Arab Israelis	3 of 7
7 Saudi Arabia	Shi'a	3 of 7
8 Yemen	Supporters of Jihadist insurgents	2 of 7
Sub-Saharan Africa		
9 Congo, Democratic Republic of	Hutu and Tutsi ethnic groups, political and ethnic opponents of Kabila regime	4 of 7
10 Ethiopia	Somali secessionists, supporters of Oromo, Gambella peoples	5 of 7
11 Somalia	Isaaq in Somaliland, clan rivals in south	3 of 7
12 Sudan	Southerners, Nuba, Darfur peoples	6 of 7
13 Uganda	Supporters of the Lord's Resistance Army	4 of 7
14 Burundi	Tutsis, supporters of exiled Hutu militia	5 of 7
15 Rwanda	Tutsis, supporters of exiled Hutu militia	5 of 7
16 Côte d'Ivoire	Muslims in the north; Volta immigrants	2 of 7
17 Angola	Supporters of UNITA, Cabindans	4 of 7
18 Nigeria	Ijaw and other delta peoples, Christians in the north	3 of 7
South, Central, and East Asia		
19 China	Uighers, Tibetans, Christian and Falun Gung religious groups	4 of 7
20 Afghanistan	Supporters of Karzai regime	4 of 7
21 Pakistan	Amahdis, Sindhis, Hindus, Shi'a, and Christians	4 of 7
22 India	Muslims and Christians in certain regions	1 of 7
23 Indonesia	Papuans, Acehnese, Chinese Christians	2 of 7
24 Nepal	Supporters of Maoist insurgents	3 of 7
25 Sri Lanka	Sri Lankan Tamils	4 of 7

government. Conflict exists in present–day Turkey over the applicability of the use of the term *genocide* to the killings and persecutions of Turkish Armenians; nevertheless, many observers do consider the word to be an accurate description of the actions taken against the Armenian minority. In fact, according to many, this genocide by the Turkish regime supports Melson's view that war and revolution sometimes provide the conditions for genocide. From 1918 to 1921, about 100,000–250,000 Jews living in the Ukraine were killed by the

Ukrainian government. In 1932–1933, Josef Stalin used famine and starvation as weapons to kill about 38,000,000 Ukrainians. In 1939–1945, about 18 million people were killed by the Nazi government of Germany in Europe alone; of these 5–6 million were Jews, 3.3 million were Soviet prisoners of war, 2 million were Gypsies, 1 million were Serbs, and hundreds of thousands were Jehovah's Witnesses and handicapped people. In 1992, according to Thomas Cushman in his article "Critical Theory and the War in Croatia and Bosnia," Croat and Serbian nationalists annihilated about 200,000 Muslims in Bosnia. In 2001, according to Ted Robert Gurr, Monty G. Marshall, and Deepa Khosla in "Peace and Conflict 2001," the groups in Europe most seriously at risk of becoming the victims of state-organized genocide and politicide include the Kurds and Islamists in Turkey, Chechens in Russia, Serbs and Croats in Bosnia, Serbs in Croatia, Catholics in Northern Ireland, and Basques in Spain.

North Africa and the Middle East

According to "Peace and Conflict 2001," the groups most seriously at risk of becoming victims of genocide in North Africa and the Middle East include the Palestinians in the West Bank and Gaza, Saharawis in Morocco, and Kurds in Iran and Iraq. Since 1967, Israel's military has often targeted Palestinians in the West Bank and Gaza who seek the creation of a Palestinian state through militant politics and acts of terror against Israel. As Ted Gurr, Monty Marshall, and Deepa Khosla note, until all agreements between the Palestinian Authority and Israel have been implemented, conflict will progress and the Palestinians will be the more vulnerable group in any hostility. Since 1975, the Kingdom of Morocco has continued to stifle the determination of the Saharawi people to create their own independent state of Western Sahara. Their leaders have been the targets of systematic Moroccan state-organized killing, and many Saharawis have been displaced and annihilated. The Kurds have been the targets of state repression, discrimination, and killing in Iran and Iraq since 1979. Their persecution results from their quest for more rights and privileges as a minority group in both countries.

Sub-Saharan Africa

Africa south of the Sahara Desert is home to many countries and thousands of ethnic groups, and this part of Africa has experienced some of the most serious genocides of the twentieth century. From April to July 1994, 800,000 Tutsis (10 percent of the total population) were slaughtered by extremist Hutu militia in Rwanda (see Case Study—Comparing Sudan and Rwanda).

In the twenty-first century, the groups most seriously at risk of becoming victims of genocide in sub-Saharan Africa are the political opponents of the Robert Mugabe government in Zimbabwe; supporters of the Oromo and Somali secessionists in Ethiopia; Isaaq ethnic groups in Somalia; Nuba, Fur, Maasalit, and Zaghawa ethnic groups in Sudan; supporters of the Lord's Resistance Army, an armed political group opposed to the Museveni government in Uganda; Hutus in Burundi and supporters of exiled Hutu militants in Rwanda and Hutu; and Tutsis in the Democratic Republic of Congo.

Asia and the Pacific Rim

There are deep historical memories of genocide in Asia, and the continent's numerous minority groups are at greater risk of becoming victims of genocide in the twenty-first century. The groups most seriously at risk of becoming the victims of state-organized genocide are mainly in East, central, and South Asia. In China, the groups at risk include the Uighers and Tibetan ethnic groups, and the Christian and Falun Gung religious groups. In Afghanistan and Pakistan, the groups at risk are the Hazaris, Tajiks, Uzbecks, Sindhis, Hindus, Shi'a, and Christians. In India, Muslims and Assamese are greatly at risk of becoming victims of genocide. Australia's native people (the Aborigines) are the victims of a continuing genocide in the Pacific Rim; they have been forcibly removed from their settlements, assimilated into the dominant white Australian population, and subjected to birth-control injections to prevent births within the group.

Case Study—Comparing Sudan and Rwanda

The continuing debate over the nature of the crimes in Sudan's Darfur region since February 2003 is the best example of the collision of the popular-moral and academic-legal discourses on genocide. In early 2003, resentment over the Sudanese government's continued neglect of the economic and development needs of Darfur (in the western region of Sudan) led to the outbreak of an armed insurgency in the region. Since then, the government of Sudan and the insurgents in Darfur have fought a war of attrition that has killed thousands of people in the region.

Much public interest in Darfur, especially in the United States and most Western countries, has centered on one key question: Is genocide taking place in Darfur? However, as is often the case, the facts present a complex situation. In fact, anthropologist Gerard Prunier has described the Darfur situation (in his 2007 book) as an "ambiguous genocide." Prunier does not make the same judgment about what took place in Rwanda between April 6 and July 15, 1994, when about 800,000 Tutsis, and those Hutus who sympathized with them, were systematically sought out and killed by Hutu extremists wielding machetes and other deadly instruments. On Rwanda, Prunier shares the view of most scholars who study genocide—that what happened in that central African country in 1994 is a classic example of genocide.

What is unambiguous about organized violence in Sudan and Rwanda since the late 1990s is that it has resulted from domestic and regional wars waged by governments and insurgents. These wars on the African continent, fueled also by ecological disasters that threaten the existence of peoples who rely on the land for their livelihoods, are becoming common, deadly, and difficult to resolve. In these circumstances, clear lines among genocide, state terrorism, insurgent violence, and counterinsurgency have become very difficult to draw. Distinguishing between victims and perpetrators is equally difficult. Over the last thirty years, there has been a massive influx of small arms into many regions of Africa due to regional wars. One inescapable political reality has resulted—states no longer have a monopoly over violence. And violence has taken many extreme forms on the continent.

The 1994 genocide in Rwanda was triggered in part by a war in neighboring Uganda. Yoweri Museveni's National Resistance Army insurgency in Uganda against the Obote regime had served as a recruiting and training ground for aggrieved Tutsi refugees who had been driven out of Rwanda since the 1960s and had made Uganda and Tanzania their home. The end of the antigovernment insurgency in Uganda in the 1980s should have been followed by the confiscation of the arms that Tutsi recruits possessed, but that did not happen.

Some demobilized Tutsi fighters formed the Rwandan Patriotic Force (RPF) and sought to reproduce in Rwanda the successful Ugandan insurgency. The initial successes of the RPF over the Rwandan national army were astonishing for a guerrilla force operating from foreign bases. The consequent anger in Rwanda, especially among peasants who had been displaced by RPF war tactics, was frightening. Hutu extremists were outraged over the failure of the Rwandan army to repel the incursions of the guerrilla force. Hutus, who saw their power and dominance slipping away as a result of concessions made by the Juvénal Habyarimana government, which was under international pressure to form a government of national unity with the RPF, no longer saw the state as a guarantor of Hutu power. Nor did the RPF see the state as an impartial protector of Tutsi life and political interests. The majority of Rwanda's Hutu population saw the complete extermination of their Tutsi political competitors as the key to the permanent retention of power. Thus, armed Hutu paramilitary groups in Rwanda saw their fate and the state's as intertwined. War in that country indeed took a turn toward genocide—it became a conflict for ethnic self-preservation. After April 6, 1994, and following the death of Rwanda's president Juvénal Habyarimana, a Hutu (in a plane crash whose causes remain unknown), Hutu paramilitary groups such as the Akazu and Interahamwe, wielding machetes, sought out Tutsis and politically moderate Hutus and killed them in a murderous process aimed at destroying the Tutsi population of Rwanda as a group.

In Sudan, regional wars and domestic insurgency are also connected. What Gerard Prunier calls an "ambiguous genocide" and David Scheffer might characterize as atrocity crimes in Sudan have been fueled by neighboring wars in Chad and Ethiopia. In the 1980s, Libya's Muammar Gaddafi tried to create a belt of Islamic states across North and East Africa. Libya saw Chad—a religiously pluralistic state that was ideologically pro-Western and had a Christian leader, Hissien Habre—as a threat to Gaddafi's vision of a northeastern African region of Islamic states. Prior to February 2003, Gaddafi's solution to the Chad dilemma had been to arm rebels opposed to the Habre regime, who operated from Darfur, along the Sudan-Chad border. Libya flooded Darfur with weapons. Other non-African geopolitical actors such as France and the United States helped the Habre government with weapons as the Chadian government responded to Libya's geopolitical ambitions in the region. With that help, Habre's government armed pro-Chad and discontented Fur, Maasalit, and

Zaghawa rebels in Darfur to fight the pro-Gaddafi and anti-Habre insurgents in the Darfur region.

The Sudan government was initially too weak to intervene in these proxy conflicts in Darfur because of its own preoccupation with a protracted war with the Sudan Peoples Liberation Army (SPLA) in southern Sudan. The SPLA had sanctuary and logistical support from Ethiopia because the Sudanese government was giving similar aid and comfort to the Eritrean Peoples Liberation Front (EPLF), an armed insurgent group that was locked in a war of secession with the Mengistu regime in Ethiopia. As in Rwanda, the regional wars along Sudan's borders had deadly consequences. Large quantities of weapons were now available to ethnic groups in Darfur with long histories of low-intensity conflicts with one another over land, water, and grazing rights. Equally important, the availability of arms in the Darfur region strengthened the ability of the Fur, Maasalit, and Zaghawa groups in the region to contest the authority of the Sudanese state. These groups, who shared a distaste for Khartoum's unequal development policies, formed armed movements to reshape the relationship between Khartoum and Darfur.

As events in Rwanda and Sudan demonstrate, under the reality of insurgency, beleaguered states show a greater willingness to subcontract violence to militia or paramilitary groups. When the army of fighters in domestic insurgencies change, from poorly paid and less-motivated professional soldiers to destitute and angry youth, the wars that ensue are often waged without rules. In Darfur, the lure of loot and rape has become the appealing motives of combat in insurgent and counterinsurgency warfare.

While regional wars and the availability of weapons have bred insurgency, ecological distress has worsened the livelihoods of people and weakened confidence in the state as guarantor of group survival. Over the past two decades, irregular rainfall patterns, due to regional climate change; desertification; and the drying up of wells have affected the livelihoods of the pastoral communities in Darfur, driving many, if not most, residents of the region into destitution. Such entrenched poverty and the intensified anger in pastoral communities that goes along with it have also made it easier for the state to recruit aggrieved nomads, who have their own local scores to settle with their peasant neighbors, to conduct the state's counterinsurgency violence.

Indeed, competition over water resources and pasturelands have allowed the Janjawid, an armed militia group to which the Sudanese state has delegated its counterinsurgency warfare in Darfur, to kill thousands, rape women, and destroy property in the name of race, ethnicity, and religion. The Janjawid and the insurgents in Darfur have presented their conflict to the world as one between "White Sudanese" or "Arabs," who are "Muslim" and live closer to the Sahara and speak the language of the Koran (Arabic), and "Black Sudanese" or "Africans," who are "Christian" and live closer to the Sahel. Many Western analysts of Darfur have uncritically accepted this racial, ethnic, and religious explanation and have, mistakenly, described the atrocity crimes in Sudan as the product of a racial and religious conflict. What is unmistakable is that what has taken place in Darfur has generated a moral narrative. In that narrative, determining whether or not a particular mass killing is a genocide becomes a moral judgment that individuals make and not a scholarly verdict that experts render on the weight of the available evidence. Thus, in situations of genocide, social activism or the popular-moral discourse on genocide often supersedes the legal-academic discourse. Academic debates over whether the crimes committed in Darfur fit the legal definition of *genocide,* while human lives are being destroyed in daily atrocities, come across as a heartless academic exercise.

The debate over Darfur makes David Scheffer's case concerning atrocity zones more solidly; clearly, it is difficult to determine what actually happens in a civil war. Thus, an all-embracing terminology is needed that can be used when one is uncertain that an actual genocide is occurring in a domestic war. As the Sudan case demonstrates, as long as regional wars and access to weapons continue to breed insurgency, dredge up historical grievances, and trigger state counterinsurgency warfare, and as long as nature fuels or complicates these processes, understanding the link between ecology and warfare may be an essential step toward understanding or preventing many genocides.

Biographical Sketches

Frank Chalk served as president of the International Association of Genocide Scholars from 1999 to 2001. He is the co-author, with Kurt Jonassohn, of the acclaimed book *The History and Sociology of Genocide: Analyses and Case Studies,* which presents a broader definition of *genocide* (one that protects political groups) and identifies four types of genocide that have occurred from antiquity to the present. Chalk has lectured and presented papers on genocide at conferences and universities around the world and before the prosecution staff of the ICTY at The Hague.

Helen Fein is the executive director of the Institute for the Study of Genocide, New York, and a research associate of the Belfer Center at the Kennedy School of Government, Harvard University. Her research work on genocide is extensive and well respected. She coined the influential phrase "universe of moral obligation" to show why perpetrators of genocide kill with such impunity. As Fein suggests, perpetrators of genocide put the victims beyond their concept of moral obligation to protect the groups they kill.

Ted Gurr is Distinguished University Professor at the University of Maryland, College Park. He founded and directs the Minorities at Risk Project, which tracks the political status and activities of more than three hundred communal grounds around the globe. His work provides important data for analyzing the causes and management of ethnic and political rebellions in genocide studies.

Barbara Harff is professor of political science at the U.S. Naval Academy in Annapolis, Maryland, and a senior consultant to the White House–initiated Political Instability Task Force (originally called the State Failure Task Force). She has contributed to research and analysis on genocide by designing data-based analyses of the preconditions and accelerators of genocide and politicide for the U.S. Center for Early Warning Humanitarian Crisis. She has written extensively on the subject of genocide from a comparative perspective.

Kurt Jonassohn, retired professor of sociology, co-authored *The History and Sociology of Genocide* with Frank Chalk. He is also the co-director of the Montreal Institute for Genocide and Human Rights Studies at Concordia University in Montreal, Canada. His many articles and conference papers have influenced the study of genocide especially in the growing field of comparative genocide. His sociological approach to the study of genocide has helped scholars to determine intent from the extent of the actions of perpetrators.

Leo Kuper (1908–1994) is one of the pioneers of the academic study of genocide. Born in Johannesburg, South Africa, Kuper was an active member of the Liberal Party and practiced law there until the outbreak of World War II, in which he fought. In 1961 when he moved to the United States, he taught sociology at the University of California, Los Angeles. He was a founding member of the Council of Holocaust and Genocide. He won international acclaim for his important book *Genocide: Its Political Use in the Twentieth Century.*

Raphael Lemkin (1900–1959), coined the term *genocide* and is also the father of the study of genocide as an academic subject. Following the German invasion of Poland in September 1939, Lemkin (who was thirty-nine years old at the time) joined the Polish underground resistance. It was during his military service in World War II that he witnessed the annihilation of European Jews and other groups of people. He escaped in 1941 to the United States and spent the rest of life in scholarship and political activism until his death in 1959.

Robert Melson is a founder of the Association of Genocide Scholars. His work on the relationship between revolution and genocide is recognized as a ground-breaking approach to the study of genocide. It identifies revolutions that are launched to restructure nations and the identity and patriotism of their inhabitants as one of the contexts for defining who is a true member and patriot and thus should belong to the nation versus who is expendable. He has testified before the House Committee on International Operations and Human Rights concerning the Armenian genocide.

Directory

Cape Town Holocaust Center, Albow Centre, 88 Hatfield St. Gardens, Cape Town 8001, South Africa. Telephone: (21) 462-5553; email: admin@ctholocaust.co.za; Web: http://www.ctholocaust.co.za.
Organization that provides lectures, seminars, and films on the Holocaust and genocide.

Center for Holocaust and Genocide Studies (CHGS), Clark University, 950 Main Street, Worcester, Mass. 01610. Telephone: (508) 793-8897; email: chgs@clarku.edu; Web: http://www.clarku.edu/departments/holocaust.
Leading teaching and research center in the United States, providing undergraduate and graduate studies on the Holocaust and a broad range of interdisciplinary and comparative subjects relating to genocide in the non-Western world.

Genocide Watch, P.O. Box 809, Washington, D.C. 20044. Telephone: (703) 448-02222; email: genocidewatch@aol.com; Web: http://www.genocidewatch.org.
Organization that coordinates the international campaign to end genocide.

Institute for the Study of Genocide, John Jay College of Criminal Justice, 899 Tenth Avenue, 325 T, New York, N.Y. 10019. Telephone: (617) 354-2785; email: info@instituteforthestudyofgenocide.org; Web: http://www.instituteforthestudyofgenocide.org.
Organization that promotes and disseminates scholarship and analyses on the causes, consequences, and prevention of genocide.

International Center for Human Rights and Democratic Development (ICHRDD), 1001 de Maisonneuve Blvd. West, Suite 1100, Montreal, Quebec, Canada H2L 4P9. Telephone: (514) 283-6073; Web: http://www.ichrdd.ca.
Nonpartisan organization that encourages and supports universal values of human rights and promotes democratic institutions and practices around the world.

Montreal Institute for Genocide and Human Rights Studies (MIGS), Concordia University, 1455 de Maisonneuve Blvd. West, Montreal, Quebec, Canada H3G 1M8. Telephone: (514) 848-2404; Web: http://migs.concordia.ca.
Research institute for the comparative study of genocide and human rights.

Tokyo Holocaust Education Resource Center, 28-105 Daikyo-cho, Shinjuku-ku, Tokyo 160-0015, Japan. Telephone: (81) 3-5363-4808; email: holocaust@tokyo.email.ne.jp; Web: http://www.ne.jp/asahi/holocaust/tokyo.
Repository of important papers and videotapes on the Holocaust and genocide; also offers seminars for teachers and students.

Yad Vashem—the Holocaust Martyrs and Heroes' Remembrance Authority, P.O. Box 3477, Jerusalem, Israel 91034. Telephone: 972-2-644-3400; email: general.information@yadvashem.org.il; Web: http://www.yadvashem.org.il.
Renowned international repository of archival materials on the Holocaust.

Further Research

Books

Chalk, Frank, and Kurt Jonassohn. *The History and Sociology of Genocide: Analyses and Case Studies.* New Haven: Yale University Press, 1990.

Chandler, David P. *The Tragedy of Cambodian History: Politics, War, and Revolution since 1945.* New Haven, Conn.: Yale University Press, 1991.

Chorbajian, Levon, and George Shirinian. *Studies in Comparative Genocide.* New York: St. Martin's Press, 1999.

Dadrian, Vahakn. *The History of the Armenian Genocide: Ethnic Conflict from the Balkans to Anatolia to the Caucasus.* Providence, R.I.: Berghahn Books, 1995.

Dawit Wolde Giorgis. *Red Tears: War, Famine and Revolution in Ethiopia.* Trenton, N.J.: Red Sea Press, 1989.

De Nike, Howard J., John Quigley, and Kenneth J. Robinson. *Genocide in Cambodia: Documents from the Trial of Pol Pot and Ieng Sary.* Philadelphia: University of Pennsylvania Press, 2000.

Fein, Helen. *Genocide: A Sociological Perspective.* New York: Sage Publications, 1990.

Hovannisian, Richard G., ed. *The Armenian Genocide: History, Politics, Ethics.* New York: St. Martin's Press, 1992.

Kiernan, Ben. *The Pol Pot Regime: Race, Power, and Genocide in Cambodia under the Khmer Rouge, 1975–79.* New Haven, Conn.: Yale University Press, 1996.

Kissi, Edward. *Revolution and Genocide in Ethiopia and Cambodia.* Lanham, Md.: Lexington Books, 2006.

Kuper, Leo. *Genocide: Its Political Use in the Twentieth Century.* New Haven, Conn.: Yale University Press, 1981.

Riemer, Neal, ed. *Protection against Genocide: Mission Impossible?* Westport, Conn.: Praeger, 2000.

Melson, Robert. *Revolution and Genocide: On the Origins of the Armenian Genocide and the Holocaust.* Chicago: University of Chicago Press, 1992.

Prunier, Gerard. *Darfur: The Ambiguous Genocide.* Rev. ed. Ithaca, N.Y.: Cornell University Press, 2007.

———. *The Rwanda Crisis: History of a Genocide.* New York: Columbia University Press, 1995.

Rosenbaum, Alan S., ed. *Is the Holocaust Unique?: Perspectives on Comparative Genocide.* 2nd ed. Boulder, Colo.: Westview Press, 2001.

Rummell. R. J. *Statistics of Democide: Genocide and Mass Murder since 1900.* New Brunswick, N.J.: Transaction Press, 1999.

Vickery, Michael. *Cambodia, 1975–82.* Boston: South Bend Press, 1984.

Articles and Reports

Australian Government. "Bringing Them Home: Report of the National Inquiry into the Separation of Aboriginal and Torres Strait Islander Children from their Families." Human Rights and Equal Opportunity Commission, Sydney, 1997.

Burkhalter, Holly J. "The Question of Genocide: The Clinton Administration and Rwanda." *World Policy Journal* 11 (winter 1995): 44–54.

Charny, Israel W. "Innocent Denials of Known Genocides: A Further Contribution to a Psychology of Denial of Genocide." *Human Rights Review* 1, no. 3 (2000): 15–39.

———. "Towards a Generic Definition of Genocide." In *Genocide: Conceptual and Historical Dimensions,* ed. George Andreopoulos, 64–94. Philadelphia: University of Pennsylvania Press, 1997.

Cushman, Thomas. "Critical Theory and the War in Croatia and Bosnia." Donald W. Treadgold Papers in Russian, East European and Central Asian Studies, no. 13. Seattle, Wash.: Henry M. Jackson School of International Studies, University of Washington, 1992.

Fink, Clinton F. "Denials of the Genocide of Native Americans." In *Encyclopedia of Genocide,* ed. Israel W. Charny, Vol. 2, 166. Santa Barbara, Calif.: ABC-CLIO, 1999.

Gurr, Ted Robert, Monty G. Marshall, and Deepa Khosla. "Peace and Conflict 2001: A Global Survey of Armed Conflicts, Self-Determination Movements, and Democracy." Center for International Development and Conflict Management, University of Maryland, 2001.

Harff, Barbara, and Ted Robert Gurr. "Genocide and Politicide in Global Perspective: The Historical Record and Future Risks." In *Just War and Genocide: A Symposium,* ed. Stan Windass. Foundation for International Security. London: Macmillan, 2001.

———. "Systematic Early Warning of Humanitarian Emergencies." *Journal of Peace Research* 35, no. 5 (1998): 551–579.

———. "Towards Empirical Theory of Genocides and Politicides: Identification and Measurement of Cases since 1945." *International Studies Quarterly* 32 (1988): 359–371.

Heuveline, Patrick. "Between One and Three Million: Toward the Demographic Reconstruction of a Decade of Cambodian History (1970–1980)." *Population Studies* 52 (1998): 49–65.

Hinton, Alexander. "A Head for an Eye: Revenge, Culture, and the Cambodian Genocide." Paper presented at the meeting of the Association of Genocide Scholars, Montreal, 1997.

Hovannisian, Richard G. "The Historical Dimensions of the Armenian Question, 1878–1930." In *The History and Sociology of Genocide: Analyses and Case Studies,* ed. Frank Chalk, 250–262. New Haven: Yale University Press, 1990.

Krieger, David. "International Criminal Court for Genocide and Major Human Rights Violations." In *Encyclopedia of Genocide,* ed. Israel W. Charny, Vol. 2, 364. Santa Barbara, Calif.: ABC-CLIO, 1999.

Mirkov, Damir. "The Historical Link between the Ustasha Genocide and the Croato-Serb Civil War." *Journal of Genocide Research* 2, no. 3 (2000): 363–373.

Rummell, R. J. "The New Concept of Democide." In *Encyclopedia of Genocide,* ed. Israel W. Charny, Vol. 1, 18–19. Santa Barbara, Calif.: ABC-CLIO, 1999.

———. "Power Kills, Absolute Power Kills Absolutely." In *Encyclopedia of Genocide,* ed. Israel W. Charny, Vol. 1, 28–29. Santa Barbara, Calif.: ABC-CLIO, 1999.

Scheffer, David. "Genocide and Atrocity Crimes." *Genocide Studies and Prevention* 1, no. 3 (2006): 229–250.

Smith, David N. "The Psycho-Cultural Roots of Genocide: Legitimacy and Crisis in Rwanda." *American Psychologist* 53, no. 7 (1998): 743–753.

Smith, Roger W. "Genocide and Denial: The Armenian Case and Its Implications." *Armenian Review* 42, no. 1 (1989): 1–38.

Stanton, Gregory H. "The Seven Stages of Genocide." Genocide Studies Program Working Paper no. GS 01. Yale Center for International and Area Studies, New Haven, Conn., 1998.

Totten, Samuel. "The US Investigation into the Darfur Crisis and the US Government's Determination of Genocide." *Genocide Studies and Prevention* 1, no. 1 (2006): 57–77.

United Nations. "Report of the International Commission of Inquiry on Darfur to the United Nations Secretary-General." Available at http://www.un.org/News/dh/sudan/com_inq_darfur.pdf.

United Nations Environmental Program. "Sudan: Post-Conflict Environmental Assessment." UNEP, Nairobi, 2007.

United Nations International Criminal Tribunal for the Former Yugoslavia, "Indictment: Karadzic & Mladic." Press and Information Office, The Hague, November 16, 1995.

Van Schaack, Beth. "The Crime of Political Genocide: Repairing the Genocide Convention's Blind Spot." *Yale Law Journal* 106 (May 1997): 202–230.

Web Sites

The Armenian National Institute
http://www.armenian-genocide.org

The Dith Pran Holocaust Awareness Project, Inc.
http://www.DithPran.org

Genocide Studies Program
http://www.yale.edu/gsp

***Frontline:* "The Triumph of Evil"**
http://www.pbs.org/wgbh/pages/frontline/shows/evil

Documents

1. Convention on the Prevention and Punishment of the Crime of Genocide

The full text is available at http://www.unhchr.ch/html/menu3/b/p_genoci.htm.

Extracts

Approved and Proposed for Signature and Ratification or accession by General Assembly Resolution 260 A (III) of 9 December 1948 entry into force 12 January 1951 in accordance with article XIII

The Contracting Parties,

Having considered the declaration made by the General Assembly of the United Nations in its resolution 96 (1) dated 11 December 1946 that genocide is a crime under international law, contrary to the spirit and aims of the United Nations and condemned by the civilized world,

Recognizing that at all periods of history genocide has inflicted great losses on humanity, and

Being convinced that, in order to liberate mankind from such an odious scourge, international cooperation is required,

Hereby agree as hereinafter provided:

Article 1

The Contracting Parties confirm that genocide, whether committed in time of peace or in time of war, is a crime under international law which they undertake to prevent and punish.

Article 2

In the present Convention, genocide means any of the following acts committed with intent to destroy, in whole or in part, a national, ethnical, racial or religious group, as such:

(a)   Killing members of the group;

(b)   Causing serious bodily or mental harm to members of the group;

(c)   Deliberately inflicting on the group conditions of life calculated to bring about its physical destruction in whole or in part;

(d)   Imposing measures intended to prevent births within the group;

(e)   Forcibly transferring children of the group to another group.

Article 3

The following acts shall be punishable

(a)   Genocide;

(b)   Conspiracy to commit genocide;

(c)   Direct and public incitement to commit genocide;

(d)   Attempt to commit genocide;

(e)   Complicity in genocide.

2. Penal Code of the Empire of Ethiopia: Proclamation No. 158 of 1957

The full text is available at http://www.preventgenocide.org/law/domestic/ethiopia.htm.

Extract

Title II OFFENCES AGAINST THE LAW OF NATIONS

CHAPTER 1.—FUNDAMENTAL OFFENCES

Art. 281.—Genocide; Crimes against Humanity

Whosoever, with intent to destroy, in whole or in part, a national, ethnic, racial, religious or political group, organizes, orders or engages in, be it in time of war or in time of peace:

(a) killing, bodily harm or serious injury to the physical or mental health of members of the group, in any way whatsoever; or

(b) measures to prevent the propagation or continued survival of its members or their progeny; or

(c) the compulsory movement or dispersion of peoples or children, or their placing under living conditions calculated to result in their death or disappearance, is punishable with rigorous imprisonment from five years to life, or, in cases of exceptional gravity, with death.

HUMAN TRAFFICKING

Rachel Shigekane

uman trafficking is a modern term that describes a practice rooted in ancient history. Facilitating the movement of people and then forcing them to work has occurred throughout recorded history and into modern times. What has changed over time are who conducts the trafficking, who the victims of trafficking are, how trafficking occurs, what repercussions traffickers may face if caught, and what relief and protections victims can count on. Today, all countries have outlawed slavery, and many countries have outlawed human trafficking. Yet both practices flourish in our global economy.

Historical Background and Development

Modern trafficking in humans has its roots in chattel slavery and other forms of forced labor, including indentured servitude and debt bondage. Chattel slavery refers to situations where humans are legally bought, sold, and held as property to perform labor. Indentured servitude occurs when a person agrees to work for a specified time period in return for transport and boarding; debt bondage occurs when a person agrees to work to cancel a debt.

The Code of Hammurabi, established by King Hammurabi of Babylonia (who ruled 1792–1750 BC), contains some of the earliest references to slavery. Slavery is well documented in the Greek and Roman empires, where slaves were accumulated as a result of winning battles, with members of the vanquished being considered war booty, or the spoils of war, and being enslaved. The Romans spread the practice of chattel slavery throughout the Roman Empire.

Chattel slavery disappeared in regions of northern Europe during the Middle Ages and was replaced by serfdom, a system of enforced labor in the fields of powerful landowners in return for protection and the right to work on their leased fields. However, chattel slavery regained prominence in the sixteenth century as European explorers started plying the coasts of Africa and the Americas in search of riches. European powers worked cooperatively with newly emerging private companies (such as the Dutch West India Company) to create and rule colonial holdings. Colonies, such as those in the Americas, generated wealth through large-scale plantation agriculture and extractive industries. Both require cheap mass labor to reap maximum profits. This spurred the development of the trans-Atlantic slave trade in which European ships brought African slaves to the New World and then turned around and carried colonial-grown sugar, rice, cotton, tobacco, and other goods to European markets. From 1660 to 1867, a total of 10 million slaves left Africa bound for American colonies. While Spain and Portugal were initially the leaders in the slave trade, by the eighteenth century the British had overtaken them. Between 1700 and 1810, British traders brought some 3 million African slaves to the American colonies, according to Maggy Lee in *Human Trafficking* and John T. Picarelli in the article "Historical Approaches to the Trade in Human Beings." In 1807, Great Britain outlawed trading in slaves, and in 1834, it abolished slavery altogether. The United States outlawed slavery in 1865 with the ratification of the Thirteenth Amendment to the Constitution.

Indentured servitude was also used as a form of cheap labor. Indentured servants were mostly European migrants who agreed to work in the American colonies for a fixed duration in exchange for transport and housing. According to Lee and Picarelli, at least 50 percent of all white immigrants to the American colonies between 1633 and 1776 first arrived as indentured servants. Despite the abolition of slavery, the practice of indentured servitude persisted.

After 1870, laborers from European colonial holdings in Asia were targeted for indentured servitude to feed the appetite for cheap labor stoked by the American industrial revolution. Laborers, particularly from China and India, were heavily recruited, often through unscrupulous, coercive, and fraudulent means. From 1831 to 1920, approximately 380,651 Chinese and 552,605 Indians migrated as indentured servants to the Americas—a phenomenon dubbed the "yellow peril" or the "yellow slave trade," sparking acts of violence against Asians and leading to the passage of a series of severely restrictive U.S. immigration laws against Asians. Their labor contracts often contained provisions that allowed the employer to dock their pay and limit their work time accrued for even the smallest of infractions, practices that reduced the wages earned and extended the duration of the contract. Other contracts called for imprisonment if the terms were not met. The lack of government oversight of these dubious contracts enabled employers to easily manipulate their terms, leaving laborers with little recourse and turning them into little more than chattel slaves.

Modern trafficking is also influenced by the rise of the "white slave trade," an oblique reference to the growth of prostitution involving European and American women and girls at the turn of the twentieth century. (During this time, incidents of young girls being purchased or abducted were reported in Europe and United States with scant details, but this was enough to generate widespread panic and fear.) Concern about white slavery resulted in several international conventions: the 1910 White Slavery Convention, the 1919 Covenant of the League of Nations, the 1921 Convention for the Suppression of the Traffic of Women and Children, the 1933 Convention for the Suppression of the Traffic of Women of Full Age, and the 1949 Convention for the Suppression of the Traffic in Persons and of the Exploitation of the Prostitution of Others.

Current Status

The signing of the UN Protocol to Prevent, Suppress, and Punish Trafficking in Persons, Especially Women and Children (UN Trafficking Protocol) in 2000 marked a renewed international interest in combating and preventing human trafficking. The protocol, which supplemented the UN Convention Against Transnational Organized Crime, entered into force on December 25, 2003; it has 117 signatories as of 2008.

Many states followed suit, passing domestic legislation that criminalized trafficking and provided for some relief for the survivors of trafficking. The broad coalition of state governments, civil society organizations, nongovernmental organizations (NGOs), faith-based organizations, and scholars that played a role in the development of the UN Trafficking Protocol has helped to shape the current public policies, research questions, advocacy strategies, and service delivery approaches designed to eliminate trafficking and assist the survivors of trafficking.

Research

What do we mean by *human trafficking*? Although the term has been used for many years, it received its first international definition in the UN Trafficking Protocol (see Document 1). In lay terms, trafficking in persons has two components. The first component involves the facilitated movement or arranged migration of an individual, often across an international border through the use of deception, coercion, or force. The second involves subjecting the trafficked person to some form of involuntary servitude, slavery, or its modern variant, forced labor, once a destination is reached. *Forced labor* is defined, according to the Forced Labor Convention of the International Labour Organisation (ILO No. 29), as "work or service which is exacted from any persons under the menace of any penalty and for which the said person has not offered himself voluntarily."

What does human trafficking look like? Who is involved, and from what parts of the globe do they hail? Answering these questions is not easy given the clandestine nature of trafficking; the vulnerability of the survivors of trafficking, many of whom have migrated illegally and are fearful of cooperating with government officials; and the sometimes inconsistent tracking of cases and confusing definitions of *trafficking* employed by local authorities. For example, the 2003 U.S. Department of Justice Report to Congress estimates that 14,500–17,500 people are trafficked into the United States annually and that approximately 600,000–800,000 people are trafficked internationally. However, some experts have questioned the methodology used to arrive at these statistics.

The Global Programme Against Trafficking in Human Beings of the UN Office on Drugs and Crime has attempted to collect information on trafficking. Analyzing these data, as Kristina Kangaspunta did in her 2003 article "Mapping the Inhuman Trade: Preliminary Findings of the Database on Trafficking in Human Beings," reveals that the Russian Federation, Ukraine, and

Nigeria were most frequently cited as the countries of origin (the countries from which trafficked people originate) and that Asia, the Commonwealth of Independent States (CIS; which consists of eleven former Soviet republics: Armenia, Azerbaijan, Belarus, Georgia, Kazakhstan, Kyrgyzstan, Moldova, Russia, Tajikistan, Ukraine, and Uzbekistan), and Africa were the most common global regions of origin. The United States, several European Union countries, and Japan were most frequently mentioned as destination countries (countries to which people are trafficked). Countries in central and Eastern Europe and in East Asia were frequently identified as countries of transit (countries through which people are trafficked to reach destination countries). Where the gender of the victim could be identified, women were reported to be 83 percent and men 4 percent of the cases in the database. Children were 48 percent. Of the 3,671 cases analyzed, more than 80 percent involved trafficking for sexual exploitation and 19 percent for other types of forced labor.

Data collection and reporting on trafficking present researchers with difficult problems. Although the Global Programme data are valuable in analyzing trends, it is important to keep in mind that these data were collected only about trafficking cases that were criminally investigated and prosecuted by states and that they may not reflect broader trends in human trafficking. The Office of the Dutch National Rapporteur Against Trafficking in Human Beings estimates that only 5 percent of victims report their victimization or come to the attention of authorities. Other data sets exist. For instance, the International Organization for Migration (IOM) has systematically entered information on trafficking victims whom they have assisted into a database, using a standardized methodology. Analysts have written on the problems associated with human trafficking statistics, for example, Frank Laczko and Marco A. Gramegna in "Developing Better Indicators of Human Trafficking."

Who are the traffickers, and how is trafficking conducted? Some believe that trafficking is carried out by transnational organized crime syndicates, which use business models that place a value on high returns and relatively minimal exposure. Criminal syndicates are attracted to human trafficking because of the potentially high profits, low risk of detection, and relatively minor criminal penalties. These syndicates do not operate universally, but are highly influenced by regional and cultural differences. Louise Shelley has identified six business models in human trafficking. One model, which is found in former Soviet satellite countries, involves a highly segmented industry with short-term profits in which female trafficking victims are quickly sold to intermediaries who deliver them to brothels. In another model, employed by Chinese and Thai criminal organizations, the trafficking operation is highly integrated and tightly controlled, from recruitment through debt bondage to eventual assignment in a brothel, by a single entity to maximize long-term profits. Other scholars, including Maggy Lee, believe that the emphasis on the role of transnational organized crime syndicates is misplaced. They believe that trafficking is carried out by more nebulous and localized crime networks, short-lived "mom and pop"–type operations, opportunistic freelance criminals, and employers engaged in otherwise legitimate businesses.

A hotly contested issue among antitrafficking experts is the role of sex trafficking and prostitution in combating human trafficking. Some advocate for the criminalization of prostitution in order to reduce sex trafficking. Others believe that the effective way to address trafficking is to have access to the victims of sex trafficking and to provide them with a broad range of services; they argue that criminalizing prostitution serves only to drive sex-trafficking victims further underground and to make them shun assistance for fear of being arrested and deported. Still others express concern that the conflation of the terms *sex trafficking* and *prostitution* disregards a woman's agency, her right to freely choose her own occupation. Some nations, including the United States, have been criticized for focusing on the prosecution of sex-trafficking cases at the expense of other types of human trafficking. According to Grace Chang and Kathleen Kim, in 2005 over two-thirds of the trafficking cases prosecuted by the U.S. government involved sex trafficking, and at least one U.S.-based organization serving survivors of trafficking, the Coalition to Abolish Slavery and Trafficking (CAST) in Los Angeles, reported that 40 percent of those they served were domestic servants, 17 percent were factory/industrial workers, 17 percent were sex workers, 13 percent were restaurant workers, and 15 percent were in servile marriages.

Policies and Programs

The reasons that human trafficking occurs are complex and driven by conditions in both the countries of origin and countries of destination. In the countries of origin, armed conflict, natural disasters, lack of economic opportunity and education, discriminatory practices, and abusive family environments may cause people to become vulnerable to traffickers in their desperate attempts to flee. In the countries of destination, growing low-wage or service industries that are unregulated or poorly regulated combined with restrictive migration policies lead to trafficking. Although restrictive migration policies are intended to stem the flow of migrants, some scholars argue that, instead, such policies simply cause migrants to go underground—to seek to illegal and unsafe means for migration, including the use of smugglers and traffickers.

Trafficking can be analyzed equally as a labor, criminal, migration, development, or human rights issue. The human rights perspective, for instance, considers the liberty and security of the person to be a basic right, and a host of human rights instruments of international law enshrine this principle (see HUMAN RIGHTS and INTERNATIONAL LAW). Some countries, such as Canada, are moving toward addressing trafficking through a human rights framework, meaning that the human rights concerns of the survivors are prioritized in policies designed to reduce trafficking. However, the dominant paradigm to combat trafficking currently emphasizes the prosecution of traffickers, with less focus placed on relief for survivors of trafficking. This approach is modeled on the UN Trafficking Protocol, and states have struck different balances between these two policies—prosecution and survivor relief—in crafting domestic responses. Four key examples illustrating the basic variations in how individual states balance these two policies, are discussed next.

Thailand. Thailand is considered a source, destination, and transit country. Rural Thai women and girls are trafficked into urban centers, such as Bangkok and abroad; in addition, individuals from neighboring countries—Myanmar (Burma), Cambodia, Laos, China and Vietnam—may be trafficked into Thailand as agricultural, construction, factory, and sex workers. Others are trafficked through Thailand to Australia, Japan, Western Europe, and the United States. In November 2007, Thailand passed new comprehensive antitrafficking legislation that went into effect in June 2008. The new law criminalizes all forms of trafficking in persons. Previously, only sex trafficking had been criminalized and only women and children could be considered victims of trafficking in persons and were entitled to government relief assistance.

United States. The Trafficking Victims Protection Act of 2000 (the Trafficking Act) forms the framework for how trafficking is addressed in the United States. The Trafficking Act criminally punishes traffickers, provides federal assistance to certain survivors of trafficking, and monitors trafficking globally. Certain survivors of trafficking may be eligible for federal assistance for refugees, including health care; financial assistance; housing; access to food; and longer-term services such as job training, case management, support, and advocacy, which are often provided by NGOs under contract with the government. These programs, however, are available only to survivors of trafficking who are willing or able to participate in the criminal investigation and prosecution of the traffickers. Immigration relief in the form of a special visa, known as the "T Visa," which allows an undocumented survivor of trafficking to legalize his or her immigration status and remain legally in the United States, is also conditional on cooperation with a criminal investigation. Some antitrafficking experts have criticized the United States and other nations for such policies. These experts argue that making survivor relief conditional on cooperation with a criminal investigation and prosecution prioritizes law enforcement objectives over the care and rehabilitation of the survivors. The Trafficking Act also requires that the U.S. government engage in the global fight against human trafficking: it stipulates that the United States should support both global and domestic efforts to prevent and combat trafficking and should monitor and evaluate other states' efforts to combat trafficking in an annually published report.

Netherlands. According to the UN Office on Drugs and Crime, the Netherlands is among the top ten destination countries for trafficked people. The Netherlands criminalized sex trafficking shortly after ratifying the UN Trafficking Protocol by enacting Article 250a of Dutch Criminal Code. According to Monika Smit in "Trafficking in Women," because prostitution has been legalized in the Netherlands *sex trafficking* is carefully defined to be distinguishable from consensual prostitution as "holding human beings in prostitution or other forms of sexual exploitation by means of force, coercion or deception." Because brothels operate legally and under state regulation, if a brothel owner is found to be engaging in an illegal activity such as employing trafficked people, he or she may be subject to stiff fines or face the loss of his or her business license. Under state regulation, the risk of having to close down a brothel business may outweigh the potential profits to be made by engaging in sex trafficking. Thus, some argue that the legalization of the sex industry is the most effective way to eliminate sex trafficking.

Under the Dutch immigration regulation known as B-9, assistance to survivors of trafficking is limited to those who cooperate with the criminal investigation and prosecution of traffickers but only for the duration of the legal proceedings. During this time, a survivor is entitled to a temporary right of residence, shelter, medical aid, and psychological and legal assistance. Once the legal proceedings have terminated, a survivor of trafficking is expected to return to his or her country of origin or to apply for permanent residence on other grounds, including humanitarian reasons. Yet, admittedly, according to Smit, such permanent residence is rarely granted. In 2005, the enactment of Article 273a of the Dutch Criminal Code served to expand the definition of *trafficking* beyond sex trafficking to include other forms of severe labor exploitation and the induced removal of organs.

Italy. Italy is a frequent destination country for trafficked people. Article 18 of Legislative Decree 286/98 provides temporary, and sometimes permanent, residence and social support for the survivors of trafficking. The government directly provides and also contracts with NGOs to provide social assistance and integration programs that include access to housing, financial assistance, job training, and counseling., People who have completed the program and have been successfully integrated into Italian communities may be assisted in applying for extended or permanent residence. Only in 2003, however, did the Italian parliament pass domestic legislation criminalizing trafficking, Law 228/2003 (Measures Against Trafficking in Persons).

Unlike survivor assistance in the United States and the Netherlands, access to social services programs and immigration relief is not made conditional on cooperating with the criminal investigation and prosecution of traffickers. Several obstacles, however, operate to hinder the full realization of Article 18 of the law. According to Vanessa E. Munro, in some instances documents show that the government officials responsible for the implementation of Article 18 essentially require cooperation with law enforcement before granting victims access to survivor assistance and immigration relief. In addition, the passage of restrictive immigration laws has prevented some survivors of trafficking from taking advantage of Article 18 because they are subject to expedited removal before they can invoke their rights.

Regional Summaries

The Americas

The United States is one of the primary destination countries in the world and greatly influences the flow of human trafficking in the Americas.

Mexico, on its southern border, is a country of origin, destination, and transit. Mexico is the largest source of undocumented migrants to the United States, and the UN lists Mexico as the number one source of trafficked children to North America. Mexican nationals are trafficked into a number of unregulated or poorly regulated U.S. industries, including domestic service, agricultural work, and the sex industry. Traffickers transport people from other countries

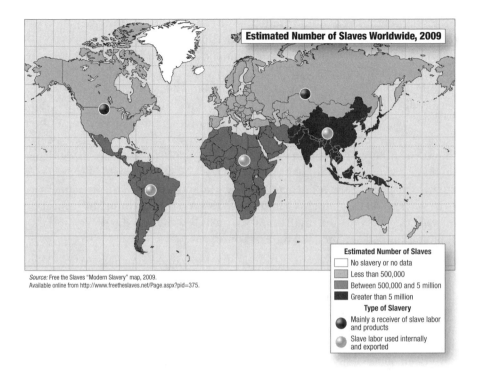

Estimated Number of Slaves Worldwide, 2009

Estimated Number of Slaves
☐ No slavery or no data
◻ Less than 500,000
▨ Between 500,000 and 5 million
■ Greater than 5 million

Type of Slavery
● Mainly a receiver of slave labor
  and products
◐ Slave labor used internally
  and exported

Source: Free the Slaves "Modern Slavery" map, 2009.
Available online from http://www.freetheslaves.net/Page.aspx?pid=375.

through Mexico and into the United States, believing that the U.S.-Mexican border is more porous than other points of entry. Mexican NGOs report assisting trafficked people from African and Asian countries who escaped their captors and had been seeking entry into the United States through Mexico. People are also trafficked to Mexico to work in transnational manufacturing or industrial plants, especially those found along the U.S.-Mexican border and, some believe, in the growing sex industry. Unfortunately, information on the Mexican government's antitrafficking activities is scarce.

Although Canada had been heavily involved in the negotiations leading up to the drafting and signing of the UN Trafficking Protocol, its domestic response to trafficking has been slow and fractured. Although statistics on trafficking in Canada are difficult to find, many see Canada as both a destination and transit country. Some research indicates that those who are not successful in applying for refugee status may become vulnerable to traffickers instead. To date, most Canadian antitrafficking efforts have focused on tougher immigration laws and increased border controls to identify "irregular migrants," but recent developments may indicate a shift to addressing trafficking through a human rights framework.

Trafficking for sexual exploitation is the most widespread and oppressive form of trafficking in Latin America and the Caribbean. The countries of origin include the Dominican Republic, El Salvador, Guatemala, Honduras, and Nicaragua, countries characterized by the lowest gross domestic product (GDP) figures and highest youth illiteracy rates. The countries of transit or destination include Mexico, Belize, Costa Rica, and Panama. Women are also trafficked to serve the sex industries in the United States, Western Europe, Japan, and other Asian countries.

Europe

Currently, the largest flows of trafficking take place within Europe. This marks a shift from previous decades when trafficked people originated primarily in Asia and Africa and were trafficked into Europe. This shift is due, in part, to the breakup of the Soviet Union, armed conflict in the Balkans, and the expanding borders of the European Union. Like elsewhere, trafficking flows in Europe follow common migration patterns, with trafficked people moving from Eastern and central Europe into Western Europe. People are trafficked into Western Europe to work in domestic service, agriculture, manufacturing, and the sex industry. Incidents of women being trafficked for sex from the former Soviet Union, including Russia, Ukraine, Moldova, and Belarus, to Western Europe and Israel are well documented.

In the Balkans, women and girls, in particular, are trafficked within the Balkan region or into the Balkans to feed the sex industry that had burgeoned with the increase of UN peacekeepers and other military personnel stationed there at end of the war. Amnesty International asserted that the sex industry in Kosovo had grown ten times since the early 1990s and that many of the women participating in it had been trafficked. People desperate to leave their war-torn homes in the Balkans may also have fallen victim to traffickers. In recent years, Turkey has become a hot spot for human trafficking due to its strategic location, large size, burgeoning economic development, and open visa system, which encourages tourism and creates an environment conducive to trafficking sex workers into the country.

North Africa and the Middle East

The Middle East accounts for more than 10 percent of the world's total migrants and the Arab Gulf states, rich from oil revenues, host the highest concentration of migrant workers in the world. This is a growing destination region for trafficked people for domestic service, the sex industry, the construction industry, and other types of labor. Recruitment agencies in African, Asian, and the Pacific Rim countries encourage women to migrate to the Middle East, particularly the Gulf states, where work is plentiful and wages are high. Some of these women find themselves held captive and subject to abusive conditions and treatment as domestics or sex workers. They may find themselves trapped in substandard living and working conditions that include excessive working hours, verbal and physical abuse, sexual harassment, and sexual attacks.

Women from the former Soviet Union, including Russia, Ukraine, and Moldova, are trafficked for the sex industry into Israel. A significant number of Russian migrants live in Israel, a few of whom are believed to be affiliated with Russian organized crime syndicates and may be responsible for running trafficking operations into Israel. Some trafficked women arrive in Egypt as tourists from Moscow and then are taken across the desert, a journey of several days, by Bedouins. Survivors of this trafficking route have recounted being raped and held in the desert for several months. Construction firms and other businesses have brought male laborers from China and Bulgaria into Israel to work under conditions equivalent to debt bondage or involuntary servitude.

Children are also trafficked to the Middle East. Instances of trafficked children, some as young as five or six years old, being forced to work as camel jockeys have been well-documented.

Sub-Saharan Africa

Although human trafficking afflicts almost all countries in sub-Saharan Africa, it is most widespread in West and central Africa with Ghana, Nigeria, and Senegal functioning as countries of origin, transit, and destination. Three main types of trafficking have been identified in the region: trafficking in children, primarily for farm labor and domestic work within the region; trafficking of women and young people for sexual exploitation, mainly to destinations outside the region (such as to western Europe); and trafficking in women for the sex industry in South Africa.

Trafficking in children occurs both from rural areas to urban centers and across borders, especially from Mali, Benin, Nigeria, Mauritania, Burkina Faso, Togo, and Ghana to cocoa farms in Côte d'Ivoire and to domestic and other labor markets in Gabon, Benin, Nigeria, and Niger. Most of these children are recruited through a network of agents to work as domestic servants or on plantations or commercial farms. Deepening rural poverty may force families to relinquish their children to traffickers, sometimes under the traffickers' pretense of providing them with an opportunity to secure good jobs and better lives. On other occasions, children have been sold by their parents or contracted to agents for work in exchange for cash. Poverty, lack of access to education, unemployment, and family disintegration and neglect (due to the ravages of HIV/AIDS) may make younger people more vulnerable to traffickers.

Central and South Asia

The largest number of children and women are trafficked within or from Asia, with a significant number of them originating in South Asia (India, Nepal, Pakistan, Bangladesh, Sri Lanka, Afghanistan, the Maldives, and Bhutan). In particular, some estimates show that, over the last thirty years, trafficking for sexual exploitation alone has victimized approximately 30 million Asian women and youth. While trafficking into many labor sectors exists in Asia, including trafficking into manufacturing/industrial factories, domestic service, and servile marriages, the sex industry is by far the largest sector into which women and girls are trafficked. In fact, the United Nations International Children's Emergency Fund (UNICEF) maintains that the numbers of women and youth being trafficked for sex in Asia represents nearly half the world total—with South Asia bearing the brunt. The increase in sex trafficking has caused grave public health consequences, increasing the spread of sexually transmitted diseases (including HIV/AIDS), the spread of pelvic inflammatory diseases, unwanted pregnancies, forced abortion, and mental and emotional health problems.

Since the 1990s, increasing numbers of women have chosen to migrate in search of greater stability and economic opportunities, creating a phenomenon known as the feminization of migration. This, in combination with the growth of the sex industry, has made more Asian women vulnerable to traffickers. For example, women fleeing poverty in India and Bangladesh or armed conflict in Afghanistan and Nepal may migrate under the false impression that they will be given educational and economic opportunities, only to be forced to work in the sex industry. Women are recruited by private employment agencies to work as domestics in more affluent Asian countries or in the Middle East; however, some of these women, having been deceived into migrating for supposedly legitimate work, are trafficked into positions of unwanted servitude including, in some cases, as sex workers. The continued existence of caste systems in some parts of Asia lead women of particular ethnic minority groups to flee their home countries, making them more at risk to trafficking (see WOMEN).

Pacific Rim

Although experts assert that trafficking in the Pacific Rim is increasing, the issue has not been widely studied. Countries such as Indonesia, the Philippines, Sri Lanka, and North Korea are identified as the countries of origin, while others such as Japan, South Korea, Australia, and New Zealand are the countries of destination. Trafficking occurs into, out of, and within China. Very little is known about trafficking in the Pacific islands.

The majority of female migrants are from the Philippines, Indonesia, and Sri Lanka. They are commonly trafficked for domestic service and the entertainment/sex industry. Many women and girls are trafficked for the sex industry to Japan and South Korea. Both countries offer an "entertainment visa" that can be manipulated by sex traffickers. A major trafficking route has been established from Southeast Asian countries, including Thailand and the Philippines, to Japan and South Korea.

In China, Chinese nationals are trafficked into the United States and Western Europe. In a well-documented case, approximately three hundred Chinese trafficking victims were discovered aboard the freighter *Golden Venture,* which ran aground off New York City in 1993. U.S. prosecutors believed that some owed as much as $25,000–30,000 to their traffickers and were most likely intended to work in brothels, sweatshops, and restaurants to pay off their debts. Those fleeing poverty and starvation in North Korea may be vulnerable to trafficking into northeastern China. Trafficked people within China are frequently forced into the sex industry, servile marriages, or bonded labor.

Data

Data Reported in the United Nations Office on Drugs and Crimes, "Trafficking in Persons: Global Patterns, April 2006" Report

Table 1 Global Patterns of Human Trafficking (%)

Trafficking victims	
Men	9
Women	77
Children	33
Boys	12
Girls	48
Purpose of trafficking	
Sexual exploitation	87
Forced labor	28

Source: United Nations Office on Drugs and Crime (UNODC), "Trafficking in Persons: Global Patterns, April 2006," Vienna, 33, Fig. 16.

Table 2 Countries of Origin, Transit, and Destination with Very High Incidence of Reporting

Origin countries	Transit countries	Destination countries
Albania	Albania	Belgium
Belarus	Bulgaria	Germany
Bulgaria	Hungary	Greece
China	Italy	Israel
Lithuania	Poland	Italy
Nigeria	Thailand	Japan
Moldova		Netherlands
Romania		Thailand
Russian Federation		Turkey
Thailand		United States
Ukraine		

Source: United Nations Office on Drugs and Crime (UNODC), "Trafficking in Persons: Global Patterns, April 2006," Vienna, 18–20.

Note to all tables: Although the data in Tables 1 and 2 are helpful in understanding the nature of human trafficking, they should be interpreted with a few limitations in mind. As the United Nations Office on Drugs and Crimes (UNODC) report itself acknowledges:

> The Report compiles and analyzes the work of sources reporting on human trafficking. The Report does not provide information regarding actual numbers of victims, nor does it provide statistics directly reflecting the severity of human trafficking around the globe. Rather than the actual occurrence of trafficking in persons, the Report reflects what is reported by inter-governmental, governmental and non-governmental sources.

It is important to keep in mind that the source institutions relied on in the report were heavily law enforcement entities. Twenty-seven percent of the source institutions were governments and national criminal justice organizations (police, intelligence agencies, public prosecution departments, and judicial branches), and another 32 percent were international organizations that included some law enforcement agencies such as Interpol. The data may largely reflect trends only among trafficking incidents that were criminally investigated, and almost all experts agree that the number of trafficking incidents that come to the attention of law enforcement is relatively small and not representative of the larger phenomenon.

Case Study—Trafficking Garment Workers to American Samoa

Kil Soo Lee, a Korean businessman, recruited over two hundred Chinese and Vietnamese women and men to work in his garment factory, Daewoosa Samoa, on the island of American Samoa from 1998 to 2000, when the factory was closed.

On many fronts, American Samoa is an ideal place to locate a business that depends on human trafficking. It is extremely remote and, although an American territory, exercises some self-governance. U.S. legislation designed to stimulate the local economy allows for minimum wages that are set lower than wages on the mainland United States; the garments are allowed to carry the "Made in the USA" label; and significantly, America Samoa is responsible for its own immigration laws, which favor employers. According to court records, a foreign worker's sponsor (usually an entity working closely with the employer, such as a recruitment agency in the country of origin) has "almost unlimited discretion" to revoke a worker's sponsorship. In addition, the Immigration Board has the power to deport a foreign worker in response to a request from a sponsor or employer who wishes to revoke his or her sponsorship or terminate employment. These provisions provided an employer, such as Lee, with considerable power over his or her foreign workers.

Government-affiliated "tour companies" that arrange work in foreign countries for Vietnamese nationals recruited over two hundred Vietnamese workers. According to court records, many Vietnamese workers took out loans to pay the large fees required for the opportunity to work abroad. The fees ranged from $3,000 to $7,600 to cover security deposits, the workers' airfares, government fees, and taxes. To pay these exorbitant fees, many families took out high-interest loans. One worker reported selling her home. Another survivor explained that her mother used the family home as collateral for a high-interest loan. As a result, entire families accrued heavy debts. Many of the workers expected to return to Vietnam after a few years wealthy enough to not only repay the family loans but to support themselves, their children, their parents, and their extended family. Lee also recruited Chinese workers during trips to China. Their numbers were far smaller; only about eighteen Chinese nationals were recruited.

The workers lived in large dormitory-style rooms with thirty-six people in each room. The rooms were overcrowded, and not enough beds were provided for all the workers, requiring some to double-up in single bunk beds. One to two showers and two to five toilets served each room. Workers complained that these were not well maintained and often did not function. The workers were fed primarily cabbage soup that was supplemented two to three times per week by chicken or another type of meat. No fresh vegetables or fruit was provided, prompting the workers to try to cultivate vegetable patches outside their rooms. Many of the workers complained of being hungry and weak. Lee charged the workers up to $200 per month for accommodations and food even during months when they were not being paid, resulting in the accrual of more debt for the workers.

The workers were paid irregularly and the availability of work was not consistent. The factory would be idle for weeks or months at a time due to delays in the shipments of materials and due to a lack of work contracts with clothing companies. Some workers tried to obtain private sewing business from locals to sustain themselves, but Lee prohibited the use of his sewing machines for private work. In response to these conditions, some Chinese workers sought legal advice from a local attorney, but Lee had these workers deported in retribution. On another occasion, a large group of Vietnamese workers staged a strike. The strike lasted for two days, during which time Lee withheld food, attempted to confiscate the workers' identity cards, and eventually called in the police and had some workers arrested. Those arrested were eventually deported. While in jail, one desperate worker threw a rock out the window with an "SOS" message wrapped around it, pleading for help from the Vietnamese embassy.

Lee used many methods to control the workers and compel them to remain at the factory. Many were under tremendous pressure to stay in order to pay off the family debts incurred in coming to American Samoa. Lee exploited this situation to his benefit. He confiscated many of the workers' passports and alien registration cards, which limited their ability to leave the compound and prevented them from escaping. He threatened workers with arrest and deportation, and used violence and threats of violence to control the workers. According to court records, one worker was struck in the face with a PVC pipe and lost her vision during an attack by Samoan managers and security agents at the garment factory.

With the help of local social service workers and church representatives, the remaining workers were freed. Eventually with help of a U.S.-based NGO, they resettled in the United States. Under the U.S. Trafficking Victims Protection Act, the workers agreed to assist criminal investigators and prosecutors and, in turn, received social services and legal help to apply for T-visas to stay in the United States. In February 2003, Lee was convicted of criminal charges of involuntary servitude, extortion, and money laundering. He was sentenced to a forty-year prison term in June 2005.

Biographical Sketches

Kevin Bales is co-founder and president of Free the Slaves, the U.S. counterpart of Anti-Slavery International, and a professor of sociology at Roehampton University in London. He is a leading expert on trafficking and the author of the influential book *Disposable People: New Slavery in the Global Economy* (1999).

Joy Ngozi Ezeilo Emekekwue was appointed the special rapporteur on trafficking for the UN Human Rights Council in June 2008. Emekekwue has extensive human rights experience in Nigeria, a significant country of origin for women trafficked to Europe and a destination country for men, women, and children trafficked from West Africa.

Anne Gallagher is the technical director of Asia Regional Trafficking in Persons Project, an Australian International Aid Agency (AusAID) project that works with the Association of Southeast Asian Nations (ASEAN) and national criminal justice agencies in Southeast Asia to strengthen their legal, technical, and institutional responses to human trafficking. Formerly, Gallagher worked with the Office of the UN High Commissioner for Human Rights from 1992 to 2002.

Sigma Huda, a UN special rapporteur on trafficking in persons, especially women and children, has advocated for women's rights at national and international levels. Huda is a founder of Bangladesh Women Lawyers Association and the Institute for Law and Development. Working with Bangladesh legal organizations, She has fought against the trafficking and sexual exploitation of women and girls from Bangladesh to India.

Ann Jordan directs the Initiative Against Trafficking in Persons for Global Rights. A lawyer, she organized Freedom Network (USA), whose members provide direct services and advocacy for trafficked people. She was a member of the Women's Caucus for Gender Justice in the International Criminal Court, and she formed the Human Rights Caucus to advocate for a human rights framework during negotiations for the UN Trafficking Protocol (2000).

Joyti Sanghera, an advocate for women, migrants, and other vulnerable groups for three decades, is deputy representative in Nepal of the UN High Commissioner for Human Rights (UNHCHR). Prior to this appointment, Sanghera was senior human rights adviser for the Office of the High Commissioner for Human Rights (OHCHR) in Sri Lanka, a trafficking and migration adviser at OHCHR Geneva, and a UNICEF senior adviser on trafficking and migration in South Asia.

Directory

Action for Reach Out (AFRO), P.O. Box 98108, T.S.T. Post Office, Tsim Sha Tsui, Kowloon, Hong Kong. Telephone: (852) 27701065; email: afro@afro.org.hk or afro@iohk.com; Web: http://hkaids.med.cuhk.edu.hk/reachout.
Organization fostering the self-representation of sex workers and providing direct services to women working in Hong Kong's commercial sex industry.

Anti-Slavery International, Thomas Clarkson House, The Stableyard, Broomgrove Road, London SW9 9TL, United Kingdom. Telephone: (44) 02075018920; email: info@antislavery.org; Web: http://www.antislavery.org.
World's oldest international human rights organization and the only charity in the United Kingdom to work exclusively against slavery and related abuses at the local, national, and international levels.

Asosiasi Tenaga Kerja Indonesia (ATKIHK; Association of Indonesian Migrant Workers in Hong Kong), c/o Asia Pacific Mission for Migrants (APMM) G/F, No. 2 Jordan Road, Kowloon, Hong Kong SAR. Telephone: (852) 23147316; email: atkihk_2000@yahoo.com.
Organization formed to assert and defend the rights and welfare of Indonesian migrant workers in Hong Kong.

Cambodia Prostitutes Union (CPU), c/o Cambodia Women's Development Agency (CWDA), P.O. Box 2334, Phnom Penh III, Cambodia. Telephone: 855 23 210 449; fax: 855 23 210 487; email: cwda@online.com.kh.
Organization, founded in 1998, focusing on empowering women working in the sex industry; reducing violence; and improving women's health, particularly in regards to HIV/AIDS

infection. It grew from an HIV prevention project of the Cambodian Women's Development Agency (CWDA).

Coalition Against Trafficking in Women-International, International Secretariat, Brussels, Belgium. Fax: (32) 23442003; email: brussels@catwinternational.org; Web: http://www.catwinternational.org.
International NGO promoting women's human rights by working to combat sexual exploitation.

Coalition to Abolish Slavery & Trafficking (CAST), 5042 Wilshire Blvd. #586, Los Angeles Calif. 90036. Telephone: (213) 365-1906; email: info@castla.org; Web: http://www.castla.org.
A human rights NGO that provides direct service to trafficked individuals and training and technical assistance to NGO and government personnel within the larger context of worker exploitation, transnational migration, and violence against women and children.

Free the Slaves, 514 10th Street NW 7th Floor, Washington, D.C. 20004. Telephone: (202) 638-1865; email: info@freetheslaves.net; Web: http://www.freetheslaves.net.
NGO formed in response to Kevin Bales's book Disposable People, *which combines research with grassroots movements, strategic thinking on leveraging power, and sharing the stories of slavery worldwide.*

Freedom Network. Web: http://www.freedomnetworkusa.org.
Coalition of twenty-five NGOs that provide services to and advocate for the rights of trafficking survivors in the United States.

Global Alliance Against Traffic in Women International Secretariat (GAATW), 191/41 Sivalai Condominium, Soi 33, Itsaraphap Rd, Bangkok-yai, Bangkok, Thailand 10600. Telephone: (66) 28641427/8; email: gaatw@gaatw.org; Web: http://www.gaatw.org.
Alliance of ninety-plus NGOs advocating for migrant workers and their families.

Human Trafficking.org, Academy for Educational Development, 1825 Connecticut Avenue NW, Washington, D.C. 20009. Telephone: (202) 884-8916; email: director@humantrafficking.org; Web: http://www.humantrafficking.org.
Web site providing country-specific information for governments and NGOs in East Asia and the Pacific to promote cooperation and information sharing on regional efforts to combat human trafficking.

International Labour Organisation, 4 Route des Morillons, CH-1211 Geneva 22, Switzerland. Telephone: (41) 0227996111; email: ilo@ilo.org; Web: http://www.ilo.org.
UN agency that seeks the promotion of social justice and internationally recognized human and labor rights.

International Organization for Migration (IOM), 17 Route des Morillons, CH-1211 Geneva 19, Switzerland. Telephone: (41) 0227179111; email: hq@iom.int; Web: http://www.iom.int.
Intergovernmental organization committed to the principle that humane and orderly migration benefits migrants and society.

La Strada International, De Wittenstraat 25, 1052 AK Amsterdam, Netherlands. Telephone: (31) 0206881414; email: info@lastradainternational.org; Web: http://lastradainternational.org.

Network of nine independent human rights NGOs in central and Eastern Europe working to prevent human trafficking; improve the position of women; and promote their universal rights, including the right to choose to emigrate and work abroad and to be protected from violence and abuse.

Legal Support for Children and Women (LSCW), #132E–F, Street 135, Phasar Doeum Thkov, Chamkarmorn, Phnom Penh, Cambodia. Telefax: (855) 23220626; email: info@lscw.org; Web: http://www.lscw.org.
Organization that promotes gender equality, protecting children and women from exploitation, increasing children's and women's awareness of their rights, and human rights.

Sex Workers' Network of Bangladesh (SWNOB). Email: swnob2002@yahoo .com.
Network linking sex-worker organizations in Bangladesh regarding the prevention of violence, child care and support for sex workers' children, health information, documentation of sex-worker issues, and income-generation strategies such as cooking and savings groups.

STV/Foundation Against Trafficking in Women, P.O. Box 1455, 3500 BL Utrecht, Netherlands. Telephone: (31) 30716044; email: fe@stv.vx.xs4all.nl; Web: http://www.bayswan.org/FoundTraf.html.
Advocacy organization that develops legislation, programming, and campaigns on behalf of trafficked individuals.

United Nations Global Initiative to Fight Human Trafficking (UN.GIFT), United Nations Office on Drugs and Crime, P.O. Box 500, 1400 Vienna, Austria. Telephone: (43) 1260600; email: UN.GIFT@unvienna.org; Web: http://www .ungift.org.
Global initiative to increase knowledge about and awareness of human trafficking, promote effective rights-based responses, build capacity of state and nonstate actors, and foster partnerships for joint action against human trafficking.

United Nations Inter–Agency Project on Human Trafficking, UNIAP Regional Management Office, United Nations Building, 7th Floor Block B, Rajdamnern Nok Ave., Bangkok 10200, Thailand. Telephone: (66) 22882213; Web: http://www .no-trafficking.org.
UN agency that facilitates coordinated response to human trafficking in the greater Mekong subregion and beyond.

U.S. Office to Monitor and Combat Trafficking in Persons, U.S. Department of State, 2201 C Street NW, Washington, D.C. 20520. Telephone: (202) 647-4000; Web: http://www.state.gov/g/tip.
U.S. government office that provides the tools to combat trafficking in persons and assists in the coordination of antitrafficking efforts both worldwide and domestically.

Women's Consortium of Nigeria (WOCON), 13 Okesuna Street, Off Igbosere Road, Lagos, Nigeria; P.O. Box 54627, Ikoyi, Lagos, Nigeria. Telephone: (234) 12635300; email: wocon95@yahoo.com; Web: http://www.wocononline.org.
NGO committed to enforcing women's rights and status in all aspects of development.

Further Research

Books

Bales, Kevin. *Disposable People.* Berkeley, Calif.: University of California Press, 1999.

———. *Ending Slavery: How We Free Today's Slaves.* Berkeley, Calif.: University of California Press, 2007.

Kempadoo, Kamala, ed. *Trafficking and Prostitution Reconsidered.* Boulder, Colo.: Paradigm Publishers, 2005.

Lee, Maggy, ed. *Human Trafficking.* Devon, UK: Willan Publishing, 2007.

van den Anker, Christien L., and Jeroen Doomernik, eds. *Trafficking and Women's Rights.* New York: Palgrave Macmillan, 2006.

Articles and Reports

Adepoju, Aderanti. "Review of Research and Data on Human Trafficking in Sub-Saharan Africa." *International Migration* 43, no. 1–2 (2005): 75–98.

Bureau of the Dutch National Rapporteur on Trafficking in Human Beings. *Trafficking in Human Beings: The Fifth Report by National Rapporteur on Trafficking in Human Beings.* The Hague, June 15, 2007.

Calandruccio, Giuseppe. "A Review of Recent Research on Human Trafficking in the Middle East." *International Migration* 43, no. 1–2 (2005): 267–299.

Chang, Grace, and Kathleen Kim. "Reconceptualizing Approaches to Human Trafficking: New Directions and Perspectives from the Field(s)." *Stanford Journal of Civil Rights & Civil Liberties* 3 (2007): 317–344.

Farquet, Romaine, Heikki Mattila, and Frank Laczko. "Human Trafficking: Bibliography by Region." *International Migration* 43, no. 1–2 (2005): 301–342.

Goodey, Jo. "Migration, Crime and Victimhood/Responses to Sex Trafficking in the EU." *Punishment & Society* 5, no. 4 (2003): 415–431.

Gozdziak, Elzbieta M., and Elizabeth A. Collett. "Research on Human Trafficking in North America: A Review of Literature." *International Migration* 43, no. 1–2 (2005): 99–128.

Huda, S. "Sex Trafficking in South Asia." *International Journal of Gynecology & Obstetrics* 94 (2006): 374–381.

Hughes, Donna M. "Best Practices to Address the Demand Side of Sex Trafficking." August 2004. Available at http://www.uri.edu/artsci/wms/hughes/demand_sex_trafficking.pdf.

Human Rights Center and Free the Slaves. *Hidden Slaves: Forced Labor in the United States.* University of California, Berkeley, September 2004. Available at http://digitalcommons.ilr.cornell.edu/cgi/viewcontent.cgi?article=1007&con.

Human Rights Watch. "Borderline Slavery: Child Trafficking in Togo." New York, April 1, 2003. Available at http://www.hrw.org/en/reports/2003/04/01/border line-slavery-0.

———. "Hidden in the Home: Abuse of Domestic Workers with Special Visas in the U.S." New York, June 1, 2001. Available at http://www.hrw.org/legacy/reports/2001/usadom/usadom0501.pdf.

———. "Hopes Betrayed: Trafficking of Women and Girls to Post-Conflict Bosnia and Herzegovina for Forced Prostitution." New York, November 26, 2002. Available at http://www.hrw.org/legacy/reports/2002/bosnia/Bosnia1102.pdf.

————. "Owed Justice: Thai Women Trafficked into Debt Bondage in Japan." New York, September 21, 2000. Available at http://www.hrw.org/en/reports/2000/09/21/owed-justice.

Initiative Against Trafficking in Persons. "Resources and Contacts on Human Trafficking." Global Rights, Washington, D.C., January 27, 2005. Available at http://www.globalrights.org/site/DocServer?docID=643.

International Labour Organisation. *The Mekong Challenge: 41 Brothels—Prostitution, Trafficking and Human Rights in Sihanouk Ville, Cambodia.* Geneva: ILO, 2008.

————. *The Mekong Challenge: Winding Roads—Young Migrants from Lao PDR and their Vulnerability to Human Trafficking.* Geneva: ILO, 2008.

Kangaspunta Kristina. "Mapping the Inhumane Trade: Preliminary Findings of the Database on Trafficking in Human Beings." *Forum on Crime and Society* 3, no. 1–2 (2003): 81–103.

Kelly, Liz Kelly. "'You Can Find Anything You Want': A Critical Reflection on Research on Trafficking in Persons within and into Europe." *International Migration* 43, no. 1–2 (2005): 235–265.

Laczko, Frank, and Marco A. Gramegna. "Developing Better Indicators of Human Trafficking." *Brown Journal of World Affairs* 10, no. 1 (2003): 179–194.

Langberg, Laura. "A Review of Recent OAS Research on Human Trafficking in the Latin American and Caribbean Region." *International Migration* 43, no. 1–2 (2005): 129–139.

Lee, June J. H. "Human Trafficking in East Asia: Current Trends, Data Collection, and Knowledge Gaps." *International Migration* 43, no. 1–2 (2005): 165–201.

Munro, Vanessa E. "Stopping Traffic?: A Comparative Study of Responses to Trafficking in Women for Prostitution." *British Journal of Criminology* 46 (2006): 318–333.

Oxman-Martinez, Jacqueline, Andrea Martinez, and Jill Hanley. "Human Trafficking: Canadian Government Policy and Practice." *Refuge* 19, no. 4 (2001): 14–23.

Picarelli, John. "Historical Approaches to the Trade in Human Beings." In *Human Trafficking,* edited by Maggy Lee. Devon, UK: Willan Publishing, 2007.

Piper, Nicole. "A Problem by a Different Name?: A Review of Research on Trafficking in South-East Asia and Oceania." *International Migration* 43, no. 1–2 (2005): 203–233.

Shelley, Louise. "Trafficking in Women: The Business Model Approach." *Brown Journal of World Affairs* 10, no. 1 (2003): 119–131.

Shigekane, Rachel. "Rehabilitation and Community Integration of Trafficking Survivors in the United States." *Human Rights Quarterly* 29 (2007): 112–136.

Smit, Monika. "Trafficking in Women: Dutch Country Report." Contribution at the NEWR workshop on trafficking in women, Amsterdam, April 25 and 26, 2003.

U.S. Department of State. "Trafficking in Persons Report 2008." Office to Monitor and Combat Trafficking in Persons, Washington, D.C., June 2008. Available at http://www.state.gov/g/tip/rls/tiprpt/2008.

Web Sites

Anti-Slavery International
http://www.antislavery.org

Human Trafficking.org
http://www.humantrafficking.org

United Nations Global Initiative to Fight Human Trafficking
http://www.ungift.org.

Document

1. UN Protocol to Prevent, Suppress, and Punish Trafficking in Persons, Especially Women and Children

Entered into force December 25, 2003

The full text can be found at www.uncjin.org/Documents/Conventions/dcatoc/final_documents_2/convention_%20traff_eng.pdf.

Extract

Article 3: Use of Terms

(a) "Trafficking in persons" shall mean the recruitment, transportation, transfer, harbouring or receipt of persons, by means of the threat or use of force or other forms of coercion, of abduction, of fraud, of deception, of the abuse of power or of a position of vulnerability or of the giving or receiving of payments or benefits to achieve the consent of a person having control over another person, for the purpose of exploitation. Exploitation shall include, at a minimum, the exploitation of prostitution of others or other forms of sexual exploitation, forced labour or services, slavery or practices similar to slavery, servitude or the removal of organs;

(b) The consent of a victim of trafficking in persons to the intended exploitation set forth in subparagraph (a) of this article shall be irrelevant where any of the means set forth in subparagraph (a) have been used;

(c) The recruitment, transportation, transfer, harbouring or receipt of a child for the purpose of exploitation shall be considered "trafficking in persons" even if this does not involve any of the means set forth in subparagraph (a) of this article;

(d) "Child shall mean any person under eighteen years of age.

PEACEMAKING AND PEACEBUILDING

Mary Hope Schwoebel and Erin McCandless

Peacekeeping, peacemaking, and peacebuilding are the three primary strategic approaches to achieving peace supported by the international community in countries and regions in conflict. These terms, popularized by UN Secretary-General Boutros Boutros-Ghali in the 1992 Agenda for Peace, provide the conceptual and practical basis for international, national, and local peace initiatives and conflict-resolution efforts. Although all three are useful in different contexts and are frequently used together, or sequentially, the trend toward a greater emphasis on peacebuilding reflects the nature of contemporary wars. Compared to conflicts in previous eras, today's wars are more violent and protracted; more destructive of social, political, and economic infrastructure; result in more civilian than combatant deaths; employ child soldiers and create child victims; and result in large population displacements, both within and across borders. Peacebuilding addresses these aspects of war, targeting the history and context of the conflict and supporting the structures that will catalyze and consolidate peace.

Historical Background and Development

Attempts to end war have traditionally been the domain of statesmen. The theory and practice of diplomacy has long been driven by political realism, a model that prioritizes the pursuit of national interests and the exercise of economic and military power. Deterrence (achieving security through the threat of force) and maintaining the balance of power through the formation of expedient alliances are the pillars of political realism. This was the dominant paradigm during the cold war era. Civil wars were considered nonthreatening to the world order and of little concern to anyone outside the states affected, given the overriding international principles of sovereignty and nonintervention across state borders (see INTERNATIONAL LAW).

During the current era, with the agenda notably defined by the "war on terror," proponents of political realism adhere to the goals of conflict management and security based on the assumption that conflicts can be resolved only through coercion and/or deterrence. This has led to a resurgence of the field of security studies, which often has reduced funding opportunities for peace and conflict studies, in both scholarly and practice-oriented pursuits. At the same time, however, intrastate conflicts are now recognized and acknowledged to be the dominant form of conflict and to pose a considerable threat to global security—an issue that practitioners and theorists in security studies have not historically paid attention to, given their interstate focus.

Theories of liberalism within international affairs, which grew from the field of international relations in the 1970s, paved the way for assumptions about the interdependence of states in the global system. This opened the door for a greater sense of responsibility on the part of the international community to become more involved in civil wars, particularly in cases involving large-scale abuses of human rights and humanitarian disasters.

Meanwhile, the field of peace and conflict studies was emerging to challenge traditional notions of diplomacy in the context of both interstate and intrastate conflicts and drawing from two intellectual and activist streams. Conflict resolution emerged from organizational theory and practice, from social psychology in general, and from human relations in particular. Conflict was perceived as a natural, even constructive force for positive social change. The focus was on identifying and developing the skills that would lead to win-win solutions, and a realization grew that the root causes of conflict needed to be analyzed and addressed—this became a pillar of the peacebuilding approach. Peace studies, the second stream, emerged from the cold war–era nuclear disarmament movement during the 1970s but rapidly expanded to embrace to the goals of global social justice, social inclusion, and political and economic equality. Johan Galtung eloquently articulated the underpinnings of peace studies by coining terms such as *structural violence, cultural violence, positive peace,* and *negative peace.* Positive peace, in particular, provided a vision for peacebuilding efforts, in going beyond simply the absence of violence, which characterizes negative peace, and leading toward a structural transformation of a social, political, and economic system so that it is capable of fostering justice and ensuring a peace that is self-sustaining (see ETHNIC AND REGIONAL CONFLICT).

Both these streams laid critical foundations for present-day notions of peacebuilding. In the 1990s, John Paul Lederach operationalized peacebuilding, developing models based on his experience as a conflict-resolution teacher, trainer, and practitioner. Contemporary conflicts necessitate transforming negative relationships and destructive systems into positive relationships and constructive systems that enable all groups and individuals to meet their non-negotiable needs. Peacebuilding, Lederach argues, is a holistic strategy that encompasses, generates, and sustains the full array of processes, approaches, and stages needed for this task. Over the last decade, the term has become increasingly popularized within the United Nations system and has been institutionalized through the UN Peacebuilding Commission.

Current Status

Peacemaking and peacebuilding are concepts gaining widespread understanding and use by the international community. Research in these areas is driven by practice and the changing nature of war. Since the early 1990s, the idea that violent conflicts can be managed through diplomatic processes alone has been discredited because all too often cease-fires and peace agreements were failing to achieve peace, in part because they were not addressing the root causes of conflicts. A large portion of conflicts relapse into conflict, and risks are particularly high five to ten years following an agreement. Often the violence that resurfaces can be even more devastating, as old and new issues comingle after the expectations for peace that were raised are dashed, leading to greater distrust, cynicism, and hopelessness. At the same time, root-cause analysis has its limits—although the root causes of conflicts may remain, the ways in which they resurface and play out changes, demanding dynamic and evolving responses. Even though research and international mechanisms are adapting to this greater awareness of the role of root causes in conflicts, the escalation of global threats such as organized crime and terrorism greatly challenge both the thinking and practice rooted in peace- rather than security-driven approaches.

Research

The changing nature of conflict and war has demanded new conceptual models of and practices regarding peacebuilding, which have found a receptive audience among diplomats, policymakers, and humanitarian and development workers. Research and practice are therefore very much intertwined. In fact, much of the theorizing about peacebuilding and peacemaking is turned inward on the very practitioners active in the field, including extensive study and analysis of what the international community—especially the United Nations—is doing in the peacebuilding and peacemaking arenas.

Peacebuilding focuses on the context of conflicts—both the institutions of peace and the attitudes, behaviors, capacities, circumstances, and interrelations of the people who are affected by war and who will build the peace—rather than military movements and issues that divide the parties and marginalize stakeholders who need to be at the center of the process. This holistic approach focuses on the multitude and, no doubt, majority of actors that have experienced war firsthand and on the structures and processes that are required to achieve and sustain a peace agreement.

Other principles of peacebuilding considered fundamental by practitioners include:

- The drivers of violent conflict are complex. Conflicts are never monocausal; they inevitably result from multiple causes that emanate broadly from psychosocial and relational issues (that is, they result from the attitudes that the parties hold about one another and the ways they behave toward one another) and they are structural (that is, they are based in economic and political realities).

- Multiple peacebuilding efforts do not simply add up to ensure a sustained peace, as the Local Capacities for Peace project has found. Strategic coordination and integration are essential, with attention to phasing and sequencing and to the unintended negative interactions and impacts of ongoing attempts to ensure peace and conflict sensitivity of programmatic and policy efforts.
- Conflict and peace develop and are sustained within particular cultures and societies. Therefore, drawing on cultural and social resources is necessary in the design and implementation of efforts.
- National ownership of peacebuilding efforts must be a key priority, although building national capacities to drive and sustain efforts is often needed where the massive "brain drain" that occurs in war severely undermines institutional capacities.
- The participation of communities in the design, implementation, and evaluation of efforts must ensure the local ownership and sustainability of efforts.
- Peacebuilding is undoubtedly a long-term effort, and thus international support must be premised on sustained engagement.
- The interplay among theory, research, and practice keeps the fields of peacemaking and peacebuilding relevant. Therefore, the development of policy must be informed by all of them.

An analysis of peacebuilding efforts since the 1990s illustrates that *peacebuilding* has come to refer to a vast array of activities, such as facilitation, communication and dialogue between communities, initiating reconciliation, assisting with the resettlement of ex-combatants and returning displaced populations, identifying common goals between communities, undertaking confidence-building measures, institutionalizing respect for human rights, promoting democratic pluralism and the rule of law, promoting diversity, psychological trauma healing, and strengthening state conflict resolution institutions and capacities. During this period, as the definition and reach of peacebuilding have expanded so widely, recognition has also grown that overlapping and at times conflicting projects and programs often do not create a sustainable peace. This has led to scholarship and, increasingly, program development designed to produce more integrated peacebuilding strategies.

While the focus of peacebuilding initiatives for intergovernmental institutions such as the United Nations and the World Bank is on postconflict stages, many theorists, practitioners, and policymakers view peacebuilding as an ongoing process to be undertaken during all phases of a conflict. Prevention of conflict is considered by many practitioners and theorists to be deeply intertwined with peacebuilding, and even the driving goal of peacebuilding efforts. According to some analysts concerned with international affairs and national sovereignty, however, this focus on prevention and the new forms of interventionism that preventive efforts (and even peacebuilding efforts more broadly) may require provides potential threats to national sovereignty. Nevertheless, conflict prevention remains a critically valued goal. Intervening before violent conflict erupts or escalates has been recognized to be a far less costly form of intervention in terms of loss of lives and infrastructrural and environmental destruction.

Peacekeeping and peacemaking play important complementary roles to peacebuilding. Researchers point to the necessity of peacekeeping in stopping violence long enough for the parties to agree to a cease-fire or to reach a peace agreement, in monitoring a cease-fire, and sometimes in overseeing disarmament. Peacekeepers also prevent the looting of humanitarian equipment and supplies. Debates continue about the appropriate roles for peacekeepers in conflicts and their relationships with other state and nonstate international and local actors. Scholarly debates have sought to assess the role and effectiveness of UN Integrated Peace Support Operations and the various strategies and challenges in sustaining peace, as well as the added value and comparative advantages of different actors in the peacebuilding process.

Efforts to evaluate peacebuilding have increased in recent years, building on trends within the humanitarian aid and development sectors to assess impacts. The assessments of larger international efforts to address national or international conflicts, such as in Kosovo, Afghanistan, and Iraq (often called peacebuilding enterprises or efforts) have deeply critiqued the strategies employed and the resulting impacts. The critiques have centered around the poor coordination and use of financial resources in a manner that does not sufficiently build national capacities and institutions; the pursuit of the national security interests of interveners over local needs; and the potential for the uncritical employment of liberal economic policies and practices to have adverse effects in vulnerable postconflict economies. Significantly, the practice of peacebuilding at this level is a highly complex endeavor, given the widely diverse contexts demanding attention, the vast array of needs to be measured against available resources, and the newness of the field. While scholarly analysis continues with a view to strengthening the practice of peacebuilding, another increasing focus is on assessing the ways that the causes of and risks involved in a conflict can be factored—recycled, in a way—into new policymaking and program development to ensure that each is conflict-sensitive.

Since the late 1990s, departments of conflict analysis and resolution, peace and conflict studies, and peace and justice studies have been established in colleges and universities throughout the United States and around the world. As of 2009, ninety-four graduate credential-granting peace studies, conflict resolution, and alternative dispute-resolution programs existed in American universities, awarding approximately 164 certificate and degree options, according to Brian D. Polkinghorn and colleagues. Simultaneously, international donors, intergovernmental organizations, and nongovernmental organizations (NGOs) have hired conflict-resolution and peacebuilding personnel, established conflict-resolution and peacebuilding divisions, and engaged in conflict resolution and peacebuilding.

Also, new subfields have emerged at the intersections of peace and conflict studies and other social science disciplines. Some of these new subfields include peacebuilding and development, peacebuilding and gender, peacebuilding and religion, peacebuilding and nonviolence, peacebuilding and education, and peacebuilding and the environment. Related to these interdisciplinary research interests are new approaches to policy and practice that involve "doing no harm"; employing peace- and conflict-sensitive analyses and practices; and mainstreaming peace efforts and conflict interventions into other domains, such as humanitarian assistance, development, governance, human rights, and disaster management.

Policies and Programs

Peacemaking and peacebuilding policies and programs are currently at the forefront of numerous governmental and intergovernmental agendas. Areas of consensus continue to emerge, such as the need for holistic, multilevel (vertical), and multisectoral (horizontal) approaches; the need for coordination among the various interveners; the need for consultation with the various stakeholders; and the need for activities that are appropriately timed and sequenced. However, challenges continue relating to the proliferation of governmental and nongovernmental policies and practices, both internal and external. The discussion here focuses on intergovernmental policies and programs.

United Nations. Collective global security is the organizing precept of the UN Charter. The end of the cold war presented new challenges for the United Nations, perhaps the greatest of which has been choices about when and where to intervene in violent conflicts in the face of dwindling resources. The UN secretary-general implements the peace and security mandates issued by the Security Council and the General Assembly and works with special representatives and envoys and other emissaries to fulfill them. At the same time, however, the United Nations can play a role only if the parties to a conflict agree that it should do so.

Since its creation, the United Nations has played a vital role in facilitating peace agreements and assisting in their implementation. But *postconflict peacebuilding* officially entered UN language only in 1992, when UN Secretary-General Boutros Boutros-Ghali's landmark *An Agenda for Peace* was published. The concept was linked to preventive diplomacy, peacemaking, and peacekeeping. This mandate was reaffirmed in the *Supplement to An Agenda for Peace,* published in 1995. That same year, the secretary-general established a UN interdepartmental Task Force to identify peacebuilding activities that could be undertaken by UN agencies, described in *An Inventory of Post-Conflict Peace-Building Activities,* published in 1996. The successive publications of *An Agenda for Development* (1994) and *An Agenda for Democracy* (1995), as well as the 1994 United Nations Development Programme (UNDP) report on human security, have contributed to a greater interaction between analysts who consider issues that traditionally fall under the security agenda and those who consider issues related to development, democratization, and human rights. The 2000 "Report of the Panel on United Nations Peace Operations" (known as the "Brahimi Report") further helped to bridge the divide between those within the UN who saw peacebuilding as primarily a political exercise and those who saw it as an economic one; it stated that "Effective peacebuidling is, in effect, a hybrid of political and development activities targeted at the sources of conflict." The work of the secretary-general's High Level Panel, which resulted in the report

"A More Secure World" (2004), as well as the secretary-general's report *In Larger Freedom* (2005), also contributed to greater consensus regarding the meaning and practice of peacebuilding.

These discussions and reports culminated in identical resolutions of the Security Council and the General Assembly in 2005, establishing a new United Nations architecture for peacebuilding focusing on the Peacebuilding Commission, Peacebuilding Fund, and Peacebuilding Support Office, together serving as a dedicated institutional mechanism to address the special needs and to assist countries in laying the foundations for sustainable peace and development.

Department of Political Affairs. The UN Department of Political Affairs (DPA) provides advice and support on all political matters to the UN secretary-general in that office's exercise of its global responsibilities under the UN Charter relating to the maintenance and restoration of peace and security. This involves monitoring and analyzing political developments and latent and manifest conflicts globally; recommending appropriate actions; and executing approved activities and policies to be carried out in the areas of preventive diplomacy, peacemaking, peacekeeping, and peacebuilding. Specific DPA activities include fact finding, mediation, and negotiation; undertaking goodwill and other missions, establishing partnerships with funds and programs as well as other agencies in the UN system, supporting Track II processes (involving civil society organizations, CSOs, or citizens' initiatives) where the United Nations is not able to play a direct role; assisting in elections (including providing technical help and support for national electoral institutions and processes); cooperating with regional organizations; and reaching out to CSOs and the media.

In the area of peacemaking, DPA has established the Mediation Support Unit (MSU), which serves as a central repository for peacemaking experience and acts as a clearing house for lessons learned and best practices. The MSU also coordinates training for mediators and provides them with advice on UN standards and operating procedures. DPA contributes to peacebuilding by providing strategic political analysis and valuable expertise gained through its participation in the design of peace agreements and in the management of postconflict peace operations.

Office for the Coordination of Humanitarian Affairs. The mission of the Office for the Coordination of Humanitarian Affairs (OCHA) is to mobilize and coordinate effective and principled humanitarian action in partnership with national and international actors to alleviate human suffering in disasters and emergencies, advocate for the rights of people in need, promote preparedness and prevention, and facilitate sustainable solutions. OCHA often has a presence in conflict settings before UN or regional peacekeeping or peacemaking efforts have been launched. As the coordinator of humanitarian aid for all UN agencies, and in theory, of all government organizations and NGOs, OCHA often becomes the primary link between political and military leaders of different parties to a conflict concerning the needs and interests of vulnerable civilian populations, including refugees and internally displaced persons (IDPs).

Department of Peacekeeping Operations, United Nations Agencies, and Integrated Missions. Peacekeeping operations are based on the principle that an impartial UN presence on the ground can ease tensions and facilitate the implementation of a peace agreement. In the past, such operations normally fell into two categories: (1) military-observer missions composed of relatively small numbers of unarmed officers charged with such tasks as monitoring cease-fires, verifying troop withdrawals, and patrolling borders or demilitarized zones and (2) peacekeeping forces composed of national contingents of troops from around the world deployed to carry out tasks similar to those of military observers and, often, to act as a buffer between hostile parties. In response to new contexts and situations, peacekeeping operations now increasingly fit into a third category—complex deployments composed of military personnel; civilian police; and other civilian personnel, such as human rights monitors, electoral experts and observers, deminers trained to identify and eliminate land mines, and specialists in civil affairs and communications. Together, these peacekeepers work alongside governments and CSOs to provide emergency relief, demobilize and reintegrate former fighters into society, clear mines, and organize and conduct elections. In multidimensional peacekeeping missions, the Department of Peacekeeping Operations (DPKO) is also involved in various peacebuilding activities: restoring a state's ability to ensure security and public order; strengthening rule of law and prospects for human rights; supporting the emergence of legitimate political institutions and participatory processes; and promoting social and economic recovery and development, including the return and resettlement of refugees and IDPs.

Peacekeeping or political (DPA-led) missions are often the most visible UN peace operations in conflict zones, but many other UN agencies and offices are usually present, have often been in the country long before a peacekeeping mission arrives, and stay long after a peacekeeping mission departs. These include the United Nations International Children's Emergency Fund (UNICEF), the Office of the UN High Commissioner for Human Rights (UNHCHR), Office of the UN High Commissioner for Refugees (UNHCR), and the World Food Programme (WFP), all of which work together with peacekeepers as one UN, making up an Integrated Mission, now increasingly referred to as Integrated Peace Support Operations. Often a special representative of the secretary-general is appointed to direct and coordinate the work of the peacekeeping operation and other UN bodies present, maintaining the political momentum toward peace. Although UN agencies each have explicit mandates in specific aspects of multidimensional peace operations, their activities often overlap with one another as well as with various external and internal actors in the overall peacebuilding, or "peace consolidation," process.

The Peacebuilding Commission. The new UN peacebuilding architecture comprises three central bodies and has recently adopted a "virtual" fourth pillar. The Peacebuilding Commission (PBC) is a thirty-one-member-state subsidiary advisory body of both the General Assembly and Security Council, which brings together all relevant actors (including international donors, the international financial institutions, national governments from focus countries, troop contributor countries, UN actors, and civil society representatives) to promote a common approach to helping a country emerge from conflict. It is mandated to:

- Propose integrated strategies for postconflict peacebuilding and recovery
- Marshal resources to help ensure predictable financing for early recovery activities and sustained financial investment over the medium to long term
- Extend the period of attention provided by the international community to post-conflict peacebuilding and recovery
- Develop best practices on issues that require extensive collaboration among political, security, humanitarian, and development actors

The Peacebuilding Fund (PBF) is a multiyear standing trust fund for post-conflict peacebuilding that provides catalytic support to countries emerging from conflict. Thus, it serves as a crucial bridge between conflict and recovery when other funding mechanisms may not yet be available.

The Peacebuilding Support Office (PBSO), part of the UN Secretariat, provides support to the work of the PBC in all its deliberations and manages the PBF. The PBSO assists the UN secretary-general to catalyze the wide range of capacities from within UN institutions and to partner with external actors in efforts to develop peacebuilding strategies, marshal resources, and enhance international coordination.

The fourth, virtual pillar was established in March 2008 to serve as a knowledge base for information, lessons learned, and best practices on peacebuilding, drawing on the range of capacities and experience in the UN system. The virtual pillar consists of several Web-based knowledge platforms and includes the UN Peacebuilding Community of Practice, the first UN-wide network linking UN peacebuilding practitioners around the world.

Governmental and Civil Society Organizations. Governments have their own policies and programs related to peacemaking and peacebuilding globally, regionally, or nationally. The United Kingdom's Department for International Development (DFID) addresses conflict through its Conflict and Humanitarian Affairs Department. The DFID attempts to address the underlying causes of conflict stemming from social inequality and poverty. It conducts conflict appraisals when preparing country assistance programs, into which it integrates conflict-reduction objectives that build the political and social means to enable the equitable representation of different interest groups, the promotion of human rights, and the resolution of disputes and grievances without recourse to violence.

In 1994, the U.S. Agency for International Development (USAID) established the Office for Transition Initiatives (OTI) to provide assistance in conflict-prone and postconflict settings for the types of activities outside the mandate of the Office for Foreign Disaster Assistance (OFDA), which provides short-term emergency assistance, and USAID's regular long-term development activities.

The OTI works with local partners to promote peaceful democratic change and to address the causes of conflict with fast, flexible, short-term assistance. The OTI has programs for reintegrating former combatants, demining, resettling refugees and IDPs, and establishing transparency and good governance. It also assists with civil society development, civilian-military relations, human rights, policy reform, conflict management, community relations, and reconciliation.

In 2004, the United States established the Office of the Coordinator for Reconstruction and Stabilization (CRS) within the Department of State to lead, coordinate, and institutionalize the U.S. government's civilian capacity to prevent conflict or to prepare for postconflict situations, and to help stabilize and reconstruct societies in transition from conflict or civil strife so they can reach a sustainable path toward peace, democracy, and a market economy. In 2002, USAID established the Office of Conflict Management and Mitigation (CMM) within the Bureau for Democracy, Conflict, and Humanitarian Assistance (DCHA). The purpose of the CMM is to prevent, mitigate, and manage the causes and consequences of violent conflict, instability, and extremism.

CSOs also engage in peacebuilding activities, such as training and education, dialog, citizen diplomacy, action research, nonviolent action, and peace advocacy. These groups, which include NGOs and community-based organizations (CBOs), also forge alliances with intergovernmental organizations, particularly in the areas of peacebuilding and development, as their critical role in envisioning, facilitating, and promoting innovative and participatory approaches from the grassroots to the global levels is increasingly recognized.

Regional Summaries

The Americas

The primary peacebuilding activities of the Organization of American States (OAS) are its postconflict demining program in Central America and the joint OAS-UN International Civil Mission in Haiti (MICIVIH). A commitment to human rights is realized through the Inter-American Court of Human Rights and the Inter-American Commission on Human Rights.

Over the years, the United Nations has had eight peace operations in five countries in the Americas; four of these were carried out in Haiti between September 1993 and March 2000. The conflict in Haiti has been largely resolved; however, the country continues to be plagued by extreme poverty and criminal violence. Other missions were deployed to the Dominican Republic, May 1965 to October 1966; Central America, November 1989 to January 1992; El Salvador, July 1991 to April 1995; and Guatemala, January 1997 to May 1997 (see Case Study—Interpeace in Guatemala). Most recently, countries in the region of concern to the international community include Haiti, Bolivia, Peru, Columbia, Venezuela, and Guyana. The issues of concern in these countries include narcotics trafficking, human trafficking, right-wing paramilitary groups, left-wing armed rebel groups, and the conduct of electoral processes.

United Nations Peacekeeping Operations, February 2009

MINUSTAH
United Nations Stabilization Mission in Haiti
Began June 2004
Military and police strength: 9,070
Civilian strength: 1,906
Fatalities: 43
Budget 07/08–06/09: $601,580,100 (gross)

UNMIK
United Nations Interim Administration Mission in Kosovo
Began June 1999
Military and police strength: 77
Civilian strength: 2,043
Fatalities: 54
Budget 07/08–06/09: $207,203,100 (gross)

UNOMIG
United Nations Observer Mission in Georgia
Began August 1993
Military and police strength: 145
Civilian strength: 312
Fatalities: 11
Budget 07/08–06/09: $36,084,000 (gross)

UNFICYP
United Nations Peacekeeping Force in Cyprus
Began March 1964
Military and police strength: 922
Civilian strength: 147
Fatalities: 179
Budget 07/08–06/09: $57,392,000 (gross) including voluntary contributions of one third from Cyprus and $6.5 million from Greece

UNTSO
United Nations Truce Supervision Organization
Began May 1948
Military and police strength: 151
Civilian strength: 220
Fatalities: 49
Budget 2008–2009: $66,217,000 (gross)

MINURSO
United National Mission for the Referendum in Western Sahara
Began April 1991
Military and police strength: 226
Civilian strength: 279
Fatalities: 15
Budget 07/08–06/09: $47,702,500 (gross)

MINURCAT
United Nations Mission in the Central African Republic and Chad
Began September 2007
Military and police strength: 317
Civilian strength: 646
Fatalities: 2
Budget 07/08–06/09: $315,083,400

UNMIL
United Nations Mission in Liberia
Began September 2003
Military and police strength: 11,471
Civilian strength: 1,687
Fatalities: 126
Budget 07/08–06/09: $631,689,100 (gross)

UNOCI
United Nations Operation in Côte d'Ivoire
Began April 2004
Military and police strength: 9,176
Civilian strength: 1,391
Fatalities: 55
Budget 07/08–06/09: $497,455,100 (gross)

MONUC
United Nations Organization Mission in the Democratic Republic of the Congo
Began November 1999
Military and police strength: 18,406
Civilian strength: 3,743
Fatalities: 143
Budget 07/08–06/09: $1,242,729,000 (gross)

UNIFIL
United Nations Interim Force in Lebanon
Began March 1978
Military and police strength: 12,542
Civilian strength: 961
Fatalities: 279
Budget 07/08–06/09: $680,932,600 (gross)

UNDOF
United Nations Disengagement Observer Force
Began June 1974
Military and police strength: 1,041
Civilian strength: 135
Fatalities: 43
Budget 07/08–06/09: $47,859,100 (gross)

UNMIS
United Nations Mission in the Sudan
Began March 2005
Military and police strength: 9,969
Civilian strength: 3,494
Fatalities: 44
Budget 07/08–06/09: $858,771,200 (gross)

UNAMID
African Union/United Nations Hybrid Operation in Darfur
Began July 2007
Military and police strength: 15,120
Civilian strength: 2,575
Fatalities: 30
Budget 07/08–06/09: $1,569,255,200

UNMOGIP
United Nations Military Observer Group in India and Pakistan
Began January 1949
Military and police strength: 43
Civilian strength: 71
Fatalities: 11
Budget 2008-2009: $16,957,100 (gross)

UNMIT
United Nations Integrated Mission in Timor-Leste
Began August 2006
Military and police strength: 1,611
Civilian strength: 1,376
Fatalities: 5
Budget 07/08–06/09: $180,841,100

Source: United Nations, Department of Public Information, *United Nations Peacekeeping Operations*, Background note: February 28, 2009. Available online from http://www.un.org/Depts/dpko/dpko/bnote.htm.
Note: "Military and police strength" data may include troops, military observers, and/or police; "Civilian strength" data may include international civilians, local civilians, and/or UN volunteers.

Europe

The fifty-six-nation Organization for Security and Cooperation in Europe (OSCE) is often held up as an infrastructural model for regional peace and security. During the cold war, the OSCE secured agreements for arms control, security, and human rights and assisted civil societies in Eastern and central Europe and the republics of the former Soviet Union in challenging their governments. Today, the OSCE's Conflict Prevention Center serves as the focal point for the organization's prevention and peacebuilding activities. The OSCE currently has missions and field activities in central, Eastern, and southeastern Europe and in the Caucasus and central Asia. The focus of these operations are democracy-building and human rights. Special envoys and observer missions are regularly sent to member states to work directly with governments and opposition groups dealing with minority rights and other internal conflicts.

For example, the OSCE Spillover Monitor Mission to Skopje is the organization's longest-serving field mission. It was established in September 1992 to help prevent tension from spreading and violent conflict from erupting in the former socialist Republic of Yugoslavia. Among the Mission to Skopje's activities are confidence-building interventions to help maintain stability and security in the country through proactive monitoring and reporting of situations affecting the political and security situation on the country, such as inter- and intra-ethnic disputes, ethnic polarization and cross-border problems. The Mission to Skopje is also engaged in media development, police development, public administration, and rule of law.

A new impetus to strengthen the European Union's conflict prevention and crisis management infrastructure resulted from Europe's failure to lead the crisis management operation in former Yugoslavia. A number of peacekeeping and humanitarian assistance exercises and operations are coordinated regionally under the direction of the North Atlantic Treaty Organization (NATO) Partnership for Peace (established in 1994) and its Euro-Atlantic Partnerships Council (established in 1997). The Partnership for Peace has established multinational peacekeeping battalions for deployment in UN and NATO peace missions. In addition, the EU has engaged in extraregional support in peacemaking and peacebuilding, for example, in Afghanistan and the Democratic Republic of Congo (DRC).

Africa

The United Nations has completed fifteen peace operations in eleven African countries. Africa has more institutions devoted to preventing and resolving conflicts than any other region, but a severe lack of financial capacity has hampered the effectiveness of these organizations. The African Union's (AU) peace infrastructure includes the Mechanism for Conflict Prevention, Management and Resolution; the Mechanism for Negotiation, Mediation and Conciliation; and the Peace Fund. The AU heads of state have committed to the implementation of the AU Early Warning System.

The Southern African Development Community (SADC) has an Organ on Politics, Defense, and Security committed to the peaceful settlement of disputes by negotiation, mediation, and arbitration. According to Article 4 of the SADC Treaty, military intervention "shall be decided upon only after all possible remedies have been exhausted in accordance with the AU and UN Charters."

Eastern and central Africa have been the sites of numerous peace initiatives since the first peacekeeping mission to the DRC. The Intergovernmental

Authority on Development (IGAD) was established in 1996 to unite East African states through a regional economic initiative. But IGAD has increasingly assumed roles in peacemaking and peacebuilding in the region. In 2002, IGAD established a conflict early warning and response mechanism (CEWARN) in recognition of the fact that timely interventions to prevent the escalation of conflicts are more effective and less costly in terms of human suffering and material damage than addressing conflicts after they have become full blown and violent. One of CEWARN's strengths is its capacity to link the official and unofficial sectors and the national and local levels to address conflicts that cross borders. For example much of its work has centered on insecure pastoralist areas—in the Karamoja region, on the borders of Sudan, Kenya, and Ethiopia; in the Somali regions on the borders between Kenya, Ethiopia, and Somalia; and in the border regions between Somalia, Ethiopia, and Djibouti—where intercommunal livestock raiding is a way of life but where conflicts have escalated due to the abundance of small arms flowing from the region's inter- and intrastate wars.

The Economic Community of West Africa States (ECOWAS) was formed in 1975 by sixteen West African states to coordinate the gradual economic and political integration of the region. ECOWAS adopted a nonaggression protocol in 1978 and a Mutual Assistance Protocol in 1981 and established the ECOWAS Monitoring Group (ECOMOG) to respond to the wars in Liberia and Sierra Leone in the early 1990s (see Case Study—Civil Society and the Peacebuilding Commission in Sierra Leone). ECOMOG has since also intervened elsewhere in the region.

The Caucasus and Central Asia

The former Soviet central Asian republics have been plagued by violence, political instability, and economic hardship since gaining independence from the former Soviet Union in 1991. Peacemaking efforts have been undertaken by the OSCE and the United Nations, through the bilateral and multilateral involvement of a number of states, and through civil society initiatives by international and local NGOs. Regardless, little progress has been made in the conflicts in Armenia, Azerbaijan, Nagorno-Karabakh, and Georgia-Abkhazia. Peacemaking and peacebuilding in parts of central Asia have been distorted by the U.S.-led "war on terror" in Afghanistan and its recruitment of Afghanistan's neighbors as members of the coalition in the "war on terror."

South Asia and Southeast Asia

The charter of South Asian Association for Regional Cooperation (SAARC) explicitly excludes intervention in bilateral conflicts in South Asia. Furthermore, India's regional dominance and the ongoing rivalry between India and Pakistan have limited the potential of SAARC to contribute to peacemaking and peacebuilding in general, and to ending the conflict in Kashmir, an area claimed by the governments of both India and Pakistan. SAARC has also limited the potential of external actors to play roles in interstate and intrastate conflicts in the region, including Kashmir, Pakistan and Sri Lanka. SAARC has, however, focused on regional efforts to combat terrorism.

The Association of Southeast Nations (ASEAN) has entered the peacemaking and peacebuilding arena through its monitoring of the cease-fire in Aceh, a Muslim region of the Indonesian island of Sumatra that has been the site of an independence movement (the agreement, following a tsunami in 2004, granted Aceh broader local autonomy) and through limited conflict-prevention initiatives in Cambodia and Burma. Through the Bali Concord II of 2003, ASEAN subscribed to the notion that regional peace and stability can be achieved and sustained through a democratic peace, in which members states agree that democratic governance is a goal toward which to work. The commitment to peacemaking and peacebuilding on the part of the parties to internal conflicts in Thailand, the Philippines, and Indonesia has been mixed.

Case Study—Civil Society and the Peacebuilding Commission in Sierra Leone

Case study contributed by Heather Sonner

The PBC selected Burundi and Sierra Leone as the first states whose conflicts it would address. In doing so, it hoped to identify "easy cases" in order to develop effective working methods and build credibility within the United Nations relatively quickly. Sierra Leone's progress in consolidating peace since the cessation of violence in 2002 may have assuaged concerns about a rapid return to conflict, but the existence of multiple strategies already in place presented a challenge to the PBC. The difficult exercise of learning by doing and the struggle to make a unique contribution to peace consolidation has defined the PBC process in Sierra Leone.

Following nearly a year of substantive and organizational negotiations, the PBC agreed to develop framework documents to guide its engagement with countries on its agenda. These documents outline key priorities in peacebuilding, challenges to the consolidation of peace and the roles of various actors in aiding the government to meet peacebuilding goals. The government in each country was asked to lead the process of identifying challenges and goals to ensure national ownership. The priority areas identified in the first outline of the framework were broadly defined and reflected well-known priorities (youth employment and empowerment, justice and security sector reform, democracy and good governance, capacity building, and regional dimensions).

The negotiations on the priorities and commitments of various stakeholders took place in Sierra Leone and at UN headquarters. During a series of PBC meetings to discuss key issues within priority areas, as well as through discussions in the joint steering committee in Freetown that included UN, partner, government, and civil society participants, obstacles to the implementation of existing strategies began to emerge; gaps in peacebuilding efforts and coordination issues remained more difficult to identify.

Some PBC members struggled to resolve the dilemma between a desire to undertake direct coordination and deliver tangible benefits to Sierra Leone and the limitations of an intergovernmental advisory body with no resources under its direct control (the PBF is managed by the secretary-general). Other members felt the PBC should focus its attention on mobilizing resources for existing priorities. Ultimately, during the first phase of engagement, the added value of the PBC proved to be primarily political and informal, rooted in the flexible working methods of the organization.

The PBC provided a unique forum for national civil society interests and groups to engage with government and other stakeholders on peacebuilding challenges. In one example, the role of CSOs shifted from challenging the government to deliver on commitments to partnering with the government to demand that the international community respond to locally identified priorities, notably the lack of development in the energy sector and the slow delivery of projects in this area by major donors. By working to hold international actors to account and strategically cooperating with their government, Sierra Leonean NGOs recognized an opportunity to enhance their role in a peacebuilding process based on genuine national ownership.

The role of the PBC during contested elections in 2007 is difficult to measure; however, the PBC's ability to bring international attention to the situation and its flexibility in requesting that the PBF meet the budgetary shortfall in the National Electoral Commission may have been invaluable to the peaceful change of government. While key bilateral donors were unable to release funds in advance of the election, the PBC, by framing the budgetary shortfall as a potential threat to peace and an important peacebuilding priority, was able to call on other actors to meet the challenge. At the PBC's urging, the PBF provided additional funding to pay poll workers and facilitate safe elections.

The PBC's formalized processes of developing a framework for peacebuilding and monitoring the progress in meeting key peacebuilding goals are the most visible aspects of this new UN body; however, early experiences suggest that informal political engagement between various stakeholders and the government through the PBC may prove to be its greatest added value to the consolidation of peace in countries on its agenda.

Case Study—Interpeace in Guatemala

Case study contributed by Bernardo Arevalo

Since 1999, Interpeace (formerly known as WSP International) has been implementing a series of initiatives in support of security-sector reform efforts following the end of a thirty-six-year internal armed conflict in Guatemala. Authoritarian notions and practices of state security have been two of the key factors leading to political conflict and widespread armed violence in Guatemalan history. The Peace Accords, therefore, clearly stated that the effective democratization of the institutional and legal security frameworks must be a key component in the overall effort to consolidate peace and prevent relapse into armed conflict. But institutional resistance to transformation within the armed forces and a huge perception gap between civilians and the military on their new roles after the signature of the Peace Accords threatened to derail the proposed transformations.

In efforts to advance the institutional transformation, local organizations attempted to address the gap between the military and civilians in a way that transformed collective attitudes and perceptions on security and provided more solid foundations for reform. These local Guatemala-based initiatives applied Interpeace's research-based inclusive dialog approach (which Interpeace uses for the development of local capacities for sustained peace) to questions of institutional reform and policy development. Relevant stakeholders—security-sector institutions, national political authorities, CSOs, and academic institutions—participated in processes that promoted a participatory analysis of the issues at stake and fostered consensus-based operational proposals on how to address the identified challenges.

These efforts began with the Policy for Democracy Project (POLSEDE; Hacia una Política de Seguridad para la Democracia) between 1999 and 2001 that focused on the demilitarization of state security institutions. Following POLSEDE, a new project in 2002–2003, Toward a Policy in Citizenship Security (POLSEC; Plataforma de Investigacicon y Diálogo Intersectorial para el Diseño de una Política de Seguridad Ciudadana), focused on the development of a new institutional framework for addressing public security issues. In 2003, a third project, Capacities of Civil Society on Security Issues (FOSS; Fortalecimiento de Organizaciones Sociales en Tema de Seguridad), was established to strengthen the technical capacities of NGOs involved in security issues and to develop an integrated strategy for constructive engagement with the national authorities; it was still ongoing as of spring 2009.

These efforts have had several concrete results:

- The consensual proposals that emerged from discussions on the role of the military in a democracy in POLSEC became official documents for the dialog process that led to a new White Paper on Defence Policy prepared by the government of Guatemala in 2002.
- The proposals on intelligence reform generated by POLSEDE and POLSEC formed the basis for draft legislation on the national intelligence framework and the creation of the General Directorate for Civilian Intelligence. These innovations are the basis for ongoing intelligence reform.
- The agreement signed between the National Congress and FOSS established a Liaison Office to enable the direct support by specialized NGOs and academic institutions in advising relevant congressional committees in the discussion and approval of different pieces of security legislation.

In addition to these tangible products, the accumulated experiences led to the development in the government and the society of a sense of ownership of the reform process, to technical capacities in security-sector issues, and to concrete tools for constructive engagement that enhanced possibilities for sustained impact. Specifically, these efforts:

- Facilitated the development of more knowledge and shared understandings among a diverse group of governmental officers, politicians, social activists, and academics

- Instilled skills and attitudes for dialog that are now used by the relevant stakeholders for sustained engagement, such as efforts to develop a National Security Policy in 2008–2009
- Led to the development of a policy community composed of a network of diverse stakeholders, underpinned by mechanisms for constructive engagement

These impacts not only provide more solid foundations for the effective post-conflict transformation of security frameworks in the country, but by doing so, they directly address one of the structural root causes of conflict and political violence throughout the country's history—the repressive nature of state security perceptions, institutions, and policies.

With the support of the Central American Integration Secretariat, Interpeace is currently applying the same approach in the development of a regional initiative that brings together national authorities and civil societies in Guatemala, El Salvador, and Honduras to better address the challenges of youth gangs from a multidisciplinary perspective and to transform the current, mostly repressive policies.

Biographical Sketches

Mohammed Abu-Nimer is professor at the American University School of International Service in International Peace and Conflict Resolution and is the founder and faculty director of the Peacebuilding and Development Institute. He is most well known for his work related to the Israeli-Palestinian conflict and for his work integrating Islamic and Western conflict resolution models among Muslim communities. He has authored and edited numerous books and articles in on these topics. He is the co-founder and co-executive editor, along with Erin McCandless, of the *Journal of Peacebuilding and Development*.

Edward Azar is a political scientist who has facilitated the understanding of protracted social conflicts in the third world that are rooted in identity, inequality, and the international development system. He has sought to shift international relations away from its superpower bias and toward a focus on the other two-thirds of the world. He has also championed the need for humanistic study in which security and stability are based on human dignity, quality of life, and genuine peace. He was active in efforts to resolve conflicts in the Middle East during the 1960s, 1970s, and 1980s.

Elise Bjorn-Hansen Boulding is a sociologist, professor, peace activist, researcher, writer, and speaker. She has served as the secretary-general of the International Peace Research Association and a board member for several leading peace institutions. Boulding is the author of nineteen books and hundreds of articles addressing critical peace and conflict issues, including democracy, development, and women in society. Boulding played a seminal role in conceiving and establishing the United States Institute of Peace. She was nominated for the 1990 Nobel Peace Prize.

John Burton is a leading pioneer in the field of conflict resolution. He catalyzed the shift in thinking about the causes of conflicts from positions and interests (international relations thinking) to frustrated needs. Burton's revolutionary theory posited that conflict results from the frustration by social institutions of the universal basic (nonnegotiable) human needs of individuals. If these needs are denied, people will rebel against the responsible institutions, even irrationally or against all odds. Burton also introduced the pluralist paradigm—the world society perspective, which emphasizes the values and relationships of multiple actors in the global system.

Samuel G. Doe is a Liberian scholar-practitioner who has worked in war-torn countries around the world on issues of peacemaking, conflict prevention, and reconciliation. He has contributed extensively to the design and development of conflict management and prevention tools that are used internationally. He founded the West Africa Network of Peacebuilding (WANEP), a subregional network of peacebuilding organizations focusing on capacity building, networking, and direct intervention in social and political conflicts in West Africa. The network also operates a regional early warning network. As of early 2008, WANEP had four hundred member organizations in sixteen West African countries, with offices operating in fourteen countries. He has also worked extensively with child soldiers and facilitated the development of a West African subregional movement of women in peacebuilding.

Johan Galtung is considered by many observers to be the "father of peace studies." In *Essays in Peace Research* (1975), Galtung put forth the tripartite classification of conflict-resolution strategies: peacekeeping, peacemaking, and peacebuilding. He has written more than fifty books and more than a thousand articles advancing the field of peace and conflict resolution. In 1959, he established the International Peace Research Institute in Oslo, Norway, the first peace research institute in the world, and served as its director for ten years. Galtung also founded the *Journal of Peace Research* and TRANSCEND: A Peace and Development Network, which he directs. In 1987, he was awarded the Alternative Nobel Peace Prize.

Rama Mani is an Indian national and the executive director and CEO of the International Centre for Ethnic Studies (ICES) in Sri Lanka. An established international peace practitioner and scholar, she teaches, publishes, and does policy work on issues of justice and human rights, conflict and peacebuilding, rule of law and the security sector, and the United Nations and terrorism. She was the senior strategy adviser to the Centre for Humanitarian Dialogue in Geneva from January to December 2002, addressing issues of humanitarian policy and conflict mediation. She also worked as Oxfam's Africa strategy manager from 1999 to 2001, based in Uganda, where she led a continent-wide campaign against humanitarian and development crises, war, and illicit economies in the African continent. Previously, as Oxfam's regional policy coordinator for the Horn of Africa, based in Ethiopia, she developed policies and programs addressing regional conflict, arms trade, and peacebuilding.

Oscar Arias Sanchez, president of Costa Rica 1986–1990, was again elected president in 2006. He was awarded the Nobel Peace Prize in 1987 for his peacemaking work during the war in Central America. He contributed the monetary portion of his prize to establish the Arias Foundation for Peace and Human Progress, founded in 1988 with the goal of promoting just and peaceful societies worldwide. For over a decade, he has continued to play an active role through the Arias Foundation in peace processes, democratization, and development in Central America and elsewhere.

Directory

Collaborative for Development Action, CDA Collaborative Learning Projects, 17 Dunster Street, Suite 202, Cambridge, Mass. 02138. Telephone: (617) 661-6310; Web: http://www.cdainc.com/cdawww/default.php.
Nonprofit organization committed to improving the effectiveness of international actors that provide humanitarian assistance, engage in peace practice, and are involved in supporting sustainable development.

Copenhagen Peace Research Institute, 18 Fredericiagade, 1310 Copenhagen, Denmark. Telephone: (45) 3 345 5050; email: bmoeller@copri.dk; Web: http://www.copri.dk.
Organization that promotes debate on issues related to peace and security studies through research, seminars, and publications.

European Platform for Conflict Prevention and Transformation, P.O. Box 14069, 3508 Utrecht, Netherlands. Telephone: (31) 30 253 7528; email: euconflict@euconflict.org; Web: http://www.euconflict.org.
Network of European NGOs involved in the prevention and resolution of violent conflicts.

Initiative on Conflict Resolution and Ethnicity (INCORE), University of Ulster, Magee Campus, Aberfoyle House, Northland Road, Londonderry BT48 7JA, Northern Ireland, United Kingdom. Telephone: (440) 28 713 75 500; email: secretary@incore.ulst.ac.uk; Web: http://www.incore.ulst.ac.uk.
Center for the study and resolution of conflict that combines research, training, and other activities to inform and influence national and international organizations working in the field of conflict resolution.

Institute for Security Studies, South Africa (ISS), P.O. Box 1787, Brooklyn Square, Tshwane (Pretoria), 0075, South Africa. Telephone: (27) 012 346 9500/2; Web: http://www.iss.co.za.
Regional research institute operating across sub-Saharan Africa; a leading African human security research institution guided by a broad approach to security that reflects the changing nature and origin of threats to human development.

International Centre for Ethnic Studies (ICES), 554/6A, Peraddeniya Road, Kandy, Sri Lanka. Telephone: (94) 081 223 4892; email: ices_cmb@sri.lanka.net; Web: http://www.icescolombo.org.
Leading South Asian think tank researching and publishing on violent conflict, governance, and development.

International Peace Institute, 777 United Nations Plaza, New York, N.Y. 10017-3521. Telephone: (212) 687-4300; email: ipi@ipinst.org; Web: http://www.ipacademy.org.
Independent institution founded to make a contribution to multilateral efforts to prevent and settle armed conflicts around the world.

International Peace Research Institute (PRIO), P.O. Box 9229, Grønland, NO-0134, Oslo, Norway. Telephone: (47) 22 54 77 00; email: info@prio.no; Web: http://www.prio.no.

Organization that focuses on conditions of war and peace, conflict resolution, peacebuilding and ethics, and norms and identities; publishes the Journal of Peace Research *and* Security Dialogue.

Stockholm International Peace Research Institute, 9 Signalisgatan, 169 70 Solna, Sweden. Telephone: (46) 8 655 97 00; email: sipri@sipri.se,; Web: http://www .sipri.se.
Organization researching questions of conflict and cooperation that are of importance for international peace and security.

TRANSCEND Research Institute (TRI), 7 rue du Crêt de la Neige, F-01210 Versonnex, France. Email: tri@transcend.org; Web: http://www.transcend.org/tri.
Organization dedicated to bringing about a more peaceful world by using action, education/training, dissemination of information, and research to handle conflicts with empathy, nonviolence, and creativity.

UN Peacebuilding Portal, 2 United Nations Plaza, Room. 1726, New York, N.Y. 10017. Telephone: (212) 963-8381; email: rosenblum-kumar@un.org; Web: http:// www.peacebuildingportal.org.
Web tool that supports multilateral collaboration and networking on conflict prevention and peacebuilding by offering local, national, and international stakeholders tools to strengthen their work with one another and the United Nations and to better respond to issues surrounding human security, peacebuilding, and conflict.

West Africa Network for Peacebuilding (WANEP), P.O. Box CT 4434, Cantonment-Accra, Ghana. Telephone: (233) 21 775 975/77; 775 981/89; email: wanep@wanep.org; Web: http://www.wanep.org.
Regional NGO network that aims to enable and facilitate the development of mechanisms for cooperation among civil society–based peacebuilding practitioners and organizations in West Africa by promoting cooperative responses to violent conflicts.

Further Research

Books

Abu-Nimer, Mohammed, ed. *Reconciliation, Justice and Co-Existence.* Lanham, Md.: Rowman and Littlefield, 2001.

Adebajo, Adekeye, and Helen Scanlon, eds. *A Dialogue of the Deaf: Essays on Africa and the United Nations.* Auckland Park, South Africa: Jacana Media, 2007.

Anderlini, Sanam Naraghi. *Women Building Peace: What They Do, Why It Matters.* Boulder, Colo.: Lynne Rienner, 2007.

Anderson, Mary B. *Do No Harm: How Aid Can Support Peace—Or War.* Boulder, Colo.: Lynne Rienner, 1999.

Ausburger, David. W. *Conflict Mediation across Cultures.* Louisville, Ky.: John Knox Press, 1992.

Avruch, Kevin. *Culture and Conflict Resolution.* Washington, D.C.: United States Institute for Peace, 1998.

Ballentine, Karen, and Jake Sharman. *The Political Economy of Armed Conflict: Beyond Greed and Grievance.* Boulder, Colo.: Lynne Rienner, 2003.

Curle, Adam. *Tools for Transformation.* London: Hawthorne Press, 1990.

Galtung, Johan. *Peace by Peaceful Means: Peace and Conflict, Development and Civilization.* London: Sage, 1996.

Gopin, Marc. *Between Eden and Armageddon: The Future of World Religions, Violence and Peacemaking.* Oxford: Oxford University Press, 2000.

Jeong, Howon. *Peacebuilding in Postconflict Societies: Strategy and Process.* Boulder, Colo.: Lynne Rienner, 2005.

Keating, Tom, and Andy Knight. *Building Sustainable Peace.* Edmonton, Canada: University of Alberta Press, and Tokyo: UN University Press, 2004.

Leatherman, Janie, et al. *Breaking Cycles of Violence: Conflict Prevention in Intrastate Crises.* West Hartford, Conn.: Kumarian Press, 1999.

McCandless, Erin, and Abdul Karim Bangura. *Peace Research for Africa: Critical Essays on Methodology,* ed. Mary E. King and Ebrima Sall. Addis Ababa/Geneva: University for Peace, Africa Programme, 2007.

Paris, Roland. *At War's End: Building Peace after Civil Conflict.* Cambridge, UK: Cambridge University Press, 2004.

Reychler, Luc, and Thania Paffenholz, eds. *Peacebuilding: A Field Guide.* Boulder, Colo.: Lynne Rienner, 2001.

Stedman, Stephen John, Donald Rothchild, and Elizabeth Cousens. *Ending Civil Wars: The Implementation of Peace Agreements.* Boulder, Colo.: Lynne Rienner, 2002.

Articles and Reports

Barbero, Christian, et al. *Conflict-Sensitive Approaches to Development, Humanitarian Assistance, and Peacebuilding: Tools for Peace and Conflict Impact Assessment.* Conflict Sensitivity.org, 2003. Available at http://www.conflictsensitivity.org/resource_pack.html.

Barnett, Michael, et al. "Peacebuilding: What Is in a Name?" *Global Governance* 13, no. 1 (January–March 2007): 35–58.

Center on International Cooperation. *Annual Review of Global Peace Operations.* Boulder, Colo.: Lynne Rienner, 2008.

Cutillo, Alberto. "International Assistance to Countries Emerging from Conflict: A Review of Fifteen Years of Interventions and the Future of Peacebuilding." International Peace Academy report. New York, February 2006.

Goodhand, Jonathan, and David Hulme. "From Wars to Complex Political Emergencies: Understanding Conflict and Peacebuilding in the New World Disorder." *Third World Quarterly* 20, no. 1 (1999): 13–26.

McCandless, Erin. "Lessons from Liberia: Integrated Approaches to Peacebuilding in Transitional Settings." Institute for Security Studies, Tshwane (Pretoria), South Africa, 2008. Available at http://www.issafrica.org/index.php?link_id=3&slink_id=5915&link_type=12&slink_type=12&tmpl_id=3.

Nathan, Laurie. "The Four Horsemen of the Apocalypse: The Structural Causes of Crisis and Violence in Africa." *Peace and Change* 25, no. 2 (2000): 188–207.

Polkinghorn, Brian D., Haleigh La Chance, and Robert La Chance. "Constructing a Baseline Understanding of Developmental Trends in Graduate Conflict Resolution Programs in the United States." In *Recent Developments in Conflict Resolution and Collaboration* (Research in Social Movements, Conflict and Change), ed. Rachel Fleishman, Rosemary O'Leary, and Catherine Gerard, Vol. 29, 233–265. Bingley, UK: Emerald Group Publishing, 2008.

Smith, Dan. "Towards a Strategic Framework for Peacebuilding: Getting Their Act Together. Overview Report of the Joint Utstein Study of Peacebuilding." Royal Norwegian Ministry of Foreign Affairs, Oslo, 2004.

Tschirgi, Neclâ. "Postconflict Peacebuilding Revisited: Achievements, Limitations, Challenges." International Peace Academy, New York, 2004.

United Nations. "A More Secure World: Our Shared Responsibility." Report of the Secretary-General's High-Level Panel on Threats, Challenges and Change. United Nations, New York, 2004. Available at http://www.wwan.cn/secureworld/report2 .pdf.

———. "Report of the Panel on UN Peace Operations." ("Brahimi Report.") A/55/305. United Nations, New York, August 21, 2000. Available at http://www .un.org/peace/reports/peace_operations/docs/full_report.htm.

UN General Assembly and Security Council. "Report of the Peacebuilding Commission on Its First Session." A/62/137–S/2007/458. United Nations, New York, June 2006–June 2007.

Web Sites

ACCORD Publications on Peace Agreements
http://www.c-r.org/our-work/accord

African Journal on Conflict Resolution
http://www.accord.org.za/publications/ajcr

Coexistence International
http://www.brandeis.edu/coexistence

Conflict Prevention Newsletter
http://www.conflict-prevention.net/page.php?id=54

Cooperation and Conflict
http://intl-cac.sagepub.com

International Crisis Group Reports
http://www.crisisgroup.org

International Journal of Peace Studies
http://www.gmu.edu/academic/ijps

International Journal on World Peace
http://www.pwpa.org/IJWP

JEMIE: Journal on Ethnopolitics and Minority Issues in Europe
http://www.ecmi.de/jemie

Journal of Conflict Resolution
http://jcr.sagepub.com

Journal of Peacebuilding and Development
http://www.journalpeacedev.org

Journal of Peace Research
http://jpr.sagepub.com

Online Journal of Peace and Conflict Resolution
http://www.trinstitute.org/ojpcr

Peace and Change: A Journal of Peace Research
http://www.wiley.com/bw/journal.asp?ref=0149-0508

Peace and Conflict Studies
http://www.gmu.edu/academic/pcs

Peace and Justice Studies Association
http://www.peacejusticestudies.org

The Peacebuilding Initiative
http://www.peacebuildinginitiative.org

Peace Research Abstracts Journal
http://www.ebscohost.com/thisTopic.php?marketID=4&topicID=954

Peace Review
http://www.usfca.edu/peacereview

Documents

1. An Agenda for Peace: Preventive Diplomacy, and Peace-Keeping

United Nations, report of the secretary-general, June 17, 1992

The full text is available at http://www.un.org/Docs/SG/agpeace.html.

Extract

15. . . . Our aims must be:

- To seek to identify at the earliest possible stage situations that could produce conflict, and to try through diplomacy to remove the sources of danger before violence results;
- Where conflict erupts, to engage in peacemaking aimed at resolving the issues that have led to conflict;
- Through peace-keeping, to work to preserve peace, however fragile, where fighting has been halted and to assist in implementing agreements achieved by the peacemakers;
- To stand ready to assist in peace-building in its differing contexts: rebuilding the institutions and infrastructures of nations torn by civil war and strife; and building bonds of peaceful mutual benefit among nations formerly at war;
- And in the largest sense, to address the deepest causes of conflict: economic despair, social injustice and political oppression. It is possible to discern an increasingly common moral perception that spans the world's nations and peoples, and which is finding expression in international laws, many owing their genesis to the work of this Organization.

16. This wider mission for the world Organization will demand the concerted attention and effort of individual States, of regional and non-governmental organizations and of all of the United Nations system, with each of the principal organs functioning in the balance and harmony that the Charter requires. The Security Council has been assigned by all Member States the primary responsibility for the maintenance of international peace and security under the Charter. In its broadest sense this responsibility must be shared by the General Assembly and by all the functional elements of the world Organization. Each has a special and indispensable role to play in an integrated

approach to human security. The Secretary-General's contribution rests on the pattern of trust and cooperation established between him and the deliberative organs of the United Nations.

17. The foundation-stone of this work is and must remain the State. Respect for its fundamental sovereignty and integrity are crucial to any common international progress. The time of absolute and exclusive sovereignty, however, has passed; its theory was never matched by reality. It is the task of leaders of States today to understand this and to find a balance between the needs of good internal governance and the requirements of an ever more interdependent world. Commerce, communications and environmental matters transcend administrative borders; but inside those borders is where individuals carry out the first order of their economic, politic al and social lives. The United Nations has not closed its door. Yet if every ethnic, religious or linguistic group claimed statehood, there would be no limit to fragmentation, and peace, security and economic well-being for all would become ever more difficult to achieve.

18. One requirement for solutions to these problems lies in commitment to human rights with a special sensitivity to those of minorities, whether ethnic, religious, social or linguistic. The League of Nations provided a machinery for the international protection of minorities. The General Assembly soon will have before it a declaration on the rights of minorities. That instrument, together with the increasingly effective machinery of the United Nations dealing with human rights, should enhance the situation of minorities as well as the stability of States.

19. Globalism and nationalism need not be viewed as opposing trends, doomed to spur each other on to extremes of reaction. The healthy globalization of contemporary life requires in the first instance solid identities and fundamental freedoms. The sovereignty, territorial integrity and independence of States within the established international system, and the principle of self-determination for peoples, both of great value and importance, must not be permitted to work against each other in the period ahead. Respect for democratic principles at all levels of social existence is crucial: in communities, within States and within the community of States. Our constant duty should be to maintain the integrity of each while finding a balanced design for all.

2. An Agenda for Development

United Nations, report of the secretary-general, May 6, 1994

The full text is available at http://www.un.org/Docs/SG/agdev.html.

Extract

22. Peace-building means action to identify and support structures which will tend to strengthen and solidify peace in order to avoid a relapse into conflict. As preventive diplomacy aims to prevent the outbreak of a conflict, peace-building starts during the course of a conflict to prevent its recurrence. Only sustained, cooperative work on the underlying economic, social, cultural and humanitarian problems can place an achieved peace on a durable foundation. Unless there is reconstruction and development in the aftermath of conflict, there can be little expectation that peace will endure.

23. Peace-building is a matter for countries at all stages of development. For countries emerging from conflict, peace-building offers the chance to establish new institutions, social, political and judicial, that can give impetus to development. Land reform and

other measures of social justice can be undertaken. Countries in transition can use peace-building measures as a chance to put their national systems on the path of sustainable development. Countries high on the scale of wealth and power must hasten the process of partial demobilization and defense conversion. Decisions made at this stage can have an immense impact on the course of their societies and the international community for future generations.

24. The most immediate task for peace-building is to alleviate the effects of war on the population. Food aid, support for health and hygiene systems, the clearance of mines and logistical support to essential organizations in the field represent the first peace-building task.

25. At this stage too, it is essential that efforts to address immediate needs are undertaken in ways that promote, rather than compromise, long-term development objectives. As food is provided there must be concentration on restoring food production capacities. In conjunction with the delivery of relief supplies, attention should be given to road construction, restoration and improvement of port facilities and establishment of regional stocks and distribution centres. . . .

29. As conflict typically takes a heavy toll on the mechanisms of governance, post-conflict efforts must pay special attention to their repair. Key institutions of civil society, judicial systems, for example, may need to be reinforced or even created anew. This means assistance for a variety of governmental activities, such as a fair system for generating public sector revenue, a legislative basis for the protection of human rights, and rules for the operation of private enterprise.

30. Pulling up the roots of conflict goes beyond immediate post-conflict requirements and the repair of war-torn societies. The underlying conditions that led to conflict must be addressed. As the causes of conflict are varied, so must be the means of addressing them. Peace-building means fostering a culture of peace. Land reform, water-sharing schemes, common economic enterprise zones, joint tourism projects and cultural exchanges can make a major difference. Restoring employment growth will be a strong inducement to the young to abandon the vocation of war.

TERRORISM

Ann E. Robertson

Nearly a decade has passed since the September 11, 2001, terrorist attacks on the United States. With over 3,000 fatalities, the incident remains the worst foreign assault on U.S. soil in history. In addition, the principal culprit, Osama bin Laden, remains at large, and the aftershocks of the attacks have affected U.S. foreign policy, military policy, justice, and law enforcement, as well as the daily lives of every citizen. At least initially, bin Laden achieved the goals shared by all terrorists—to terrify innocent bystanders and bring attention to his cause.

Bin Laden and his Al Qaeda organization remain one of the primary terrorist threats to U.S. security. After being driven from Afghanistan following the U.S. invasion in October 2001, the core of Al Qaeda's top leadership relocated to the Afghanistan-Pakistan border and has been slowly rebuilding and gaining affiliates, using Pakistan as an international hub. However, bin Laden is not the only terrorist threat. A small but active number of violent homegrown associations, such as environmental, animal-rights, and white supremacist groups still threaten the United States. Abroad, Spain's separatist Basque movement has revived, and Colombia's Fuerzas Armadas Revolucionarias de Colombia (FARC; Revolutionary Armed Forces of Colombia) continues to expand its narcotics trafficking activities. But even when terrorists can be identified, located, and intercepted, prosecution is difficult due to laws regarding national secrets and questionable interrogation techniques.

Historical Background and Development

Although a single definition of *terrorism* is hard to arrive at, and many opportunists throughout history have used this epistemological uncertainty to their advantage, a very basic working definition can be arrived at if we examine the various instances and strains of terrorism throughout history. Terrorism is a violent act designed to frighten citizens and force a government or a society to change a particular political, economic, or social policy. It is a tactic, not an

---

This chapter is based on the original, written by David Leheny, that appeared in the first edition of *World at Risk*.

ideology. Terrorism is and has often been the weapon of choice for individuals and movements that could not win a conventional war against their perceived enemy. Instead, they hope to frighten a population to the point of demanding a government concession.

Throughout the many examples in history, it is clear that terrorists need an audience to be fully effective; they need to maximize public knowledge of their act and the cause they advocate. Thus, they often select highly visible or symbolic targets. The Pentagon in 2001, the Murrah Federal Building in Oklahoma City in 1995, U.S. embassies in Kenya and Tanzania in 1998, and the *USS Cole* in 2000 were all attacked as symbols of U.S. imperialism. Although the terrorists who attacked the Israeli team at the 1972 Munich Olympics died in the subsequent rescue operation, they brought tremendous attention to their cause—Palestinian independence—which remains indelibly linked to images of the raid. Although most Americans say they oppose negotiating with terrorists, watching operatives hold a gun to the head of a hostage or dump the body of an elderly, wheelchair-bound U.S. citizen from a cruise ship, as happened in the 1985 terrorist takeover of the *Achille Lauro,* often changes their minds.

Terrorists may organize themselves into formal groups that operate for years, such as the Popular Front for the Liberation of Palestine, formed in 1967 in response to the Israeli takeover of the West Bank during the Six-Day War, or the Japanese Red Amy, active in the 1970s with the goal of overthrowing the Japanese monarchy and triggering a worldwide communist revolution. Or they may be loners, such as Timothy McVeigh, responsible for the 1995 bombing in Oklahoma City, or the suspected perpetrator of the anthrax mailings of 2001. States may sponsor terrorists by funding activities or allowing terrorist groups to operate freely on their territory. Al Qaeda operates as an umbrella organization, training operatives and supervising cells scattered across Africa, the Middle East, Europe, and other regions. Homegrown terrorist movements may try to affiliate with a larger, better-funded, and better-known group to maximize their impact, for example, the Algerian Salafist Group for Preaching and Combat and the Libyan Islamic Fighting Group when they allied themselves with Al Qaeda. Names can often be deceptive; a dozen or so like-minded terrorists may attach *army* to their group's name to appear more imposing. Finally, terrorists may be assigned to ad hoc groups organized for specific attacks, such as the September 11, 2001, attacks or the 1993 World Trade Center bombing. Advances in communications, especially the Internet and World Wide Web, have greatly facilitated communication among disparate terrorist groups, creating "virtual safe-havens," as well as raising the possibility of cyber attacks disrupting vital control systems at power plants, bank, hospitals, and other critical infrastructure.

Terrorism has a long and bloody history. Irish statesman Edmund Burke first used the term *terror* to describe Robespierre's witch hunt for alleged traitors following the French Revolution. Long before 1789, however, disaffected individuals often resorted to violence to make their point. The Zealots (66–73 AD) were Jewish terrorists trying to eject foreign settlers from the Holy Land; in India, the Thugs (600s–1200s) were Hindus who believed violence would please their god; and in Syria and Iran, the Assassins (1090–1275) sought to purify Islam by stabbing infidels.

The motives for terrorism have evolved over the years. For centuries religion was the primary organizing motive; then, terrorists of the eighteenth and nineteenth centuries organized around implementing or expanding the notion of equality. In Russia, for example, between 1878 and 1917, the group People's Will deployed violent tactics to overthrow the monarchy, calling their strategy "propaganda by deed." They preached tyrannicide to trigger a popular revolution and assassinated Tsar Alexander II in 1881 and Grand Duke Sergei Alexandrovich in 1905. Members of People's Will, like many terrorists seeking to liberate the oppressed and poor, often were well educated and from more prosperous families, a pattern repeated in the United States in the 1960s, when college students formed the Weather Underground and Symbionese Liberation Army to end capitalism, U.S. imperialism, and racial division.

Nationalism, self-determination, and anticolonialism dominated terrorist goals in the late nineteenth and early twentieth centuries. Groups were dissatisfied with the reconfiguration of international borders following the European revolutions of 1848 and the two world wars. Members of Black Hand assassinated the Austrian Arch Duke Franz Ferdinand and his wife in 1914 to protest Serbian oppression in Bosnia, an act that launched World War I. The establishment of Israel in 1948 led to numerous groups' seeking Palestinian liberation. African and Asian colonies seeking independence in the 1950s and 1960s produced groups such as the Algerian National Front, which targeted Europeans.

Nor was the United States free of nationalist violence. Puerto Rican nationalists fired bullets into the U.S. Capitol in 1954 and tried to assassinate President Harry Truman. Embracing a different take on nationalism, right-wing white supremacist and Christian identity groups, such as the Covenant, the Sword, and the Arm of the Lord and Aryan Nations, wanted to "purify" the United States by eliminating Jews, blacks, and evolutionists. For years, the legal community classified the Ku Klux Klan (KKK) a hate-crime group because their attacks seemed spontaneous and isolated. But because twenty-first-century terrorist groups, such as Al Qaeda, seek to exterminate a particular category of people, analysts are reconsidering the status of the KKK.

By the 1990s and the first years of the twenty-first century, the most visible and most lethal acts of terrorism were again connected to religion. Specifically, bin Laden and Al Qaeda sought to create a global Islamic state, which required the elimination of the main obstacle—the United States—and the destruction of governments in the Middle East that do not adhere to strict Islamic teaching. Bin Laden decreed that it was the duty of all Muslims to kill U.S. citizens in 1996. His declaration of war coincided with a surge in terrorist violence. Increasingly, terrorist acts were designed to maximize the body count; the degree of restraint that resulted from groups in the 1970s and 1980s prioritizing visibility over homicide faded. In the United States in the 1980s, for example, the Federal Bureau of Investigation (FBI) reported 267 terrorist events leading to 23 deaths; in the 1990s, there were 60 attacks and 182 deaths. Suicide bombers became increasingly common because of desperation on the part of many disaffected individuals, especially in the Middle East and South Asia. At the same time, they became more effective because, unlike timed explosives or bulky truck bombs, suicide bombers can make last-minute adjustments as they position themselves near their target; in doing so, they create more havoc and achieve higher body counts, garnering even wider publicity.

Current Status

Today there is no widely accepted definition of *terrorism,* which complicates efforts to prevent attacks and to prosecute perpetrators. Consequently, counterterrorism actions are handled piecemeal. Different agencies focus on different ideologies, geographical locales, and tactics.

Part of the problem in defining *terrorism* is perception. Terrorists commit violent acts against innocent targets to call attention to their cause, and some groups or states may support the same goal. There is, in fact, a very fine line between rebels and freedom fighters. Self-determination is a particularly difficult cause to condemn, especially in countries that emerged from colonialism. Furthermore, UN Resolution 1514, the 1960 Declaration on the Granting of Independence to Colonial Countries and Peoples, defines self-determination as a basic human right and legitimizes actions taken to achieve self-determination.

The more recent approach, however, has been to outlaw specific terrorist activities. The United Nations has passed over a dozen conventions against terrorist-type acts such as hijacking and taking hostages. In addition, UN Security Council Resolution 1373, on suppressing the financing of terrorist acts—passed just weeks after the September 2001 terrorist attacks in the United States—called on all states to ban terrorism and to coordinate efforts to combat terrorism in lawful ways that respect human rights. It also created a Counter-Terrorism Committee to monitor compliance.

Research

Scholars and policy analysts generally categorize terrorists by their ideology, tactics, and sponsors. The beliefs of terrorist groups run the full spectrum of political ideology. Left-wing groups oppose capitalism, while far-left groups, such as the Japanese Red Army and Peru's Tupac Amaru Revolutionary Movement, plan to institute a communist or socialist system that would eliminate most or all forms of private property. At the opposite end, right-wing groups tend to resist change, hail the importance of tradition for society, and favor a hierarchical society in which some groups, races, or religions have more privileges than others.

Terrorism tends to run in cycles. As previously discussed, after centuries of religious-based terrorism many movements of the nineteenth and twentieth centuries were based on rectifying social wrongs such as demanding national self-determination for repressed populations (Tamils, Algerians, and Palestinians), ending U.S. military activities (Baader Meinhof Gang and the Weather Underground), or introducing egalitarian societies (Symbionese Liberation

Army and Shining Path). The shift toward religious justifications in the 1990s was accompanied by higher body counts. Groups were no longer satisfied with drawing attention to their cause; rather, they were focused on eliminating the enemy. Internationally, the most prominent religious-based groups are Islamic fundamentalists, devotees who advocate strict adherence to the Koran, including governance based on Islamic law. In the United States, homegrown terrorists tend to be white Christian supremacists, who believe the federal government has been corrupted by Jews, African Americans, and Hispanics. Convinced of the validity of their cause, religious terrorists are often more willing to use suicide tactics, believing their sacrifice will be rewarded in the afterlife.

Terrorist tactics reveal the type of training as well as the mindset and educational level of the terrorist. The Zealots killed with daggers and the Assassins with swords; by the French Revolution, guns and bombs were becoming the weapons of choice. Little formal education is needed to aim, shoot, or detonate, which leads many lower-level operatives—such as suicide bombers—to be placed in the front lines of many terrorist activities. However, much greater skill—and sometimes a higher level of training—is needed to build high-yield explosives, to hijack airplanes, or to deploy weapons of mass destruction (WMD). Consequently terrorist leaders and top-level operatives tend to be well educated. Aum Shinrikyo, the cult that released sarin gas into the Japanese transit system in 1995, had numerous recruits with high-level science degrees.

The 2007 edition of the U.S. State Department "Country Reports on Terrorism" noted a shift in traditional terrorist tactics. In particular, Al Qaeda and its affiliates are evolving from expeditionary terrorism to guerrilla terrorism. Expeditionary terrorism uses recruits trained abroad for a specific attack, such as the attacks on U.S. embassies in Kenya and Tanzania and the attacks against the World Trade Center and the Pentagon on September 11. The commandos are then transported to the appropriate country to launch their attack, at considerable cost. Guerrilla terrorism, in contrast, is opportunistic, exploitive, and relatively cheap. Leaders recruit disaffected locals to carry out single, often highly visible attacks, such as the 2004 bombings in the Madrid commuter train system or the 2005 suicide bombings in the London Underground, which they then exploit for propaganda purposes. Furthermore, Al Qaeda actively seeks to create a cadre of disaffected angry youth. It manipulates existing economic or anti-immigrant grievances to undermine national governments and destabilize countries. Consequently, combating terrorism now requires anticipating which groups seem ripe for manipulation and recruitment by leaders of terrorist groups and trying to ameliorate the problems that the disenfranchisement of these groups creates—restive youth and immigrant communities must be viewed as potential targets of terrorist recruitment.

Policies and Programs

Historically, states have created antiterrorism policies in reaction to attacks. Countries that faced active terrorist groups in the 1970s and 1980s, such as the United Kingdom and Spain, have more developed legislation than countries that only recently have suffered attacks, such as the United States. The measures usually address the specific group's demands and tactics, making it difficult to generalize approaches and even definitions of terrorism. But whatever the threat, these policies seek to prevent future attacks, facilitate recovery from an attack, and prosecute the perpetrators.

The United States has traditionally used law enforcement, intelligence, and military resources to prevent terrorist attacks from occurring. Officials may stake out sites linked to suspects, monitor weapons purchases and financial transactions, and place wiretaps on telephone and computer equipment. The U.S. government regularly provides counterterrorism training and equipment to friendly governments abroad to create a global monitoring network.

Surveillance and vigilance successfully prevented a planned millennium attack on the United States. By monitoring activities of suspected terrorists, U.S. intelligence discovered plans to stage several attacks on New Year's Eve 1999, and Washington, D.C., put federal, state, and local officials on high alert. Then on December 14, 1999, a customs officer in Washington state thought a passenger on a ferry from British Columbia was acting oddly. When she went to investigate, 100 pounds of bomb-making equipment was discovered in his car; he had been trained by Al Qaeda to bomb Los Angeles International Airport on New Year's Eve.

Retaliatory military strikes are another option used to prevent an attack or send a warning not to try again. However, such strikes come with sizable risks: they can misidentify a perpetrator, they are often not effective in the face of the extreme militancy of some groups, and they can frequently trigger a chain of retaliation. For example, President Ronald Reagan ordered air strikes against Libya in 1986 after U.S. servicemen died when a bomb exploded in a German disco. Unfortunately, subsequent information revealed that German groups were actually responsible for the bombing, and Libya responded by destroying Pam Am Flight 103 in 1988. President Bill Clinton ordered surgical strikes against Al Qaeda sites following the 1998 attacks on U.S. embassies in Kenya and Tanzania, but the organization continued to function.

States need a unified strategy to counter all forms of terrorist threats. In the United States, the FBI was designated the lead investigative agency for terrorism in the 1970s because the number of domestic threats far outweighed the odds of foreign attacks on U.S. territory. There was no unified policy on international terrorism in those years; rather, the issue was categorized by country: the Irish Republic Army was assigned to the UK desk, for example, and the Palestine problem was assigned to the Middle East specialists. But as foreign-based threats increased in the 1990s and especially after the September 11, 2001, attacks, responsibility shifted to the Central Intelligence Agency (CIA), military, and National Security Agency (NSA). A new Department of Homeland Security was created, and related agencies were reorganized and placed under its supervision.

Governments also plan how to facilitate recovery efforts should an attack take place. Such preparations are prudent and cost effective because the same strategies and resources can be used to alleviate damage from natural disasters, such as hurricanes and tsunamis. National, state, and local governments must prepare evacuation plans and determine the optimal deployment of rescue personnel and equipment, ranging from blood to medications, blankets, and bathroom provisions. Officials also need to standardize communications and other protocols to maximize communication among first responders. The Israeli government requires all homes and public buildings be equipped with a bomb shelter and even provides each citizen with a gas mask, while the U.S. government has issued similar instructions for how to "shelter in place" should a disaster occur.

Prosecuting actual or potential terrorists raises a variety of issues related to privacy and procedure. Even when suspects can be identified, securing legal permission to monitor them to gain sufficient evidence for a conviction can be difficult, especially in democracies built on the rights of freedom of expression, personal privacy, and due process. Following the September 11, 2001, attacks the George W. Bush administration revised many of the procedures previously used for domestic terrorism cases, often provoking criticism.

The USA PATRIOT Act (Uniting and Strengthening America by Providing Appropriate Tools Required to Intercept and Obstruct Terrorism Act of 2001), enacted by Congress soon after the September 11 attacks, handed the Bush administration a new set of tools to combat terrorism, including domestic terrorism. The PATRIOT Act created a new legal category—domestic terrorism. Law enforcement and foreign intelligence tactics used to monitor foreign terrorists—investigating suspicious financial transactions, conducting physical searches, and monitoring communications—could now be used on U.S. soil against U.S. citizens. In addition, any person who "lends support" to a terrorist organization was now subject to the same laws as the terrorist operatives. Controversy erupted particularly over a provision that allowed the government to investigate business, school, telephone, library, employment, medical, and Internet records without probable cause and without notifying the suspect before the search.

A particularly serious point of controversy in U.S. terrorism policy following September 11 concerned terrorism-related surveillance, which is governed by the Foreign Intelligence Surveillance Act (FISA). This 1978 act established guidelines for securing a court order to wiretap a U.S. citizen suspected of involvement in foreign terrorist operations—permission to wiretap is granted to the FBI by Special Foreign Intelligence Surveillance Courts, which FISA mandated so that the government would not risk disclosing potentially classified evidence in a public court. The Bush administration eased the rules on obtaining a warrant in cases where it claimed national security outweighed the right to privacy. It also allowed the NSA to eavesdrop on communications within the United States; traditionally, NSA had focused on foreign communications, while the FBI handled the domestic side.

Prior to September 11, 2001, U.S. terrorism cases were adjudicated in U.S. criminal courts in a jurisdiction related to the target or site of a terrorist attack. Timothy McVeigh was tried in the U.S. District Court for Western Oklahoma, for example. Members of the Symbionese Liberation Army were tried in California, where they had planted bombs and robbed banks. In 1995, the U.S.

District Court for the Southern District of New York convicted ten men of trying to blow up the Lincoln Tunnel and other landmarks in New York City. But when President Bush labeled the campaign against Al Qaeda a "war on terror" in 2001, he called for prosecutions to be held under the standards of military law—most at the military base at Guantanamo Bay, Cuba—by specially created military commissions because of the danger of revealing intelligence sources and tactics in open court. Critics said the closed commissions violated the right of a defendants to face their accusers. Until June 2008, the U.S. government could hold terror suspects without charges indefinitely, and without formal charges or access to U.S. courts, they could not petition for their release. If a case were to come to trial, defendants often would not be able to see the evidence against them because the government believed it would reveal information pertaining to national security. Critics argued that this practice violated the constitutional right to a speedy trial and the prohibition against cruel punishment. Within the first days of his administration in 2009, President Barack Obama ordered the secret CIA prisons closed, declared that Guantanamo would close by early 2010, and suspended the military commission trial system.

Counterterrorism responses in other countries since 2001 have created controversy as well. German officials revived a terrorist profiling technique, used originally in the 1970s in pursuit of the terrorist group Baader-Meinhof, in order to identify "suspicious students" in Hamburg, where members of one of the cells that planned the September 11 attacks had once lived. The United Kingdom created a similar profile after explosions on July 7, 2005, ripped apart three London Underground trains and one bus. Based on the 7/7 bombers, London built a physical and psychological profile of a potential terrorist, which resulted in the police killing of an innocent man aboard an Underground train.

British officials also drew up new counterterrorism procedures in response to the 7/7 attacks. The government asked for the right to hold suspects for ninety days without charges, a provision reduced to twenty-eight days. In an interesting take on free speech and freedom of religion, another initiative made it a crime to "glorify" terrorism, following reports of people celebrating the 9/11 hijackers as "the Magnificent 19." Critics complained that the government took extreme measures not to make the new policies appear aimed at Muslims, in particular pointing to a law against incitement to religious hatred, designed to prevent Muslim-bashing.

Committing a terrorist act in the United States or against U.S. citizens is a capital offense, subject to the death penalty. McVeigh was executed by lethal injection in June 2001. But the possibility of a death sentence creates two problems. First, the majority of the countries in the world have either abolished the death penalty or not carried out a death sentence in decades. These states are reluctant to extradite accused criminals to the United States if they may be put to death, making it difficult for the U.S. to gain custody of foreign terrorist suspects. Second, suicide bombers, including the men responsible for the attacks on September 11, 2001, may actively be seeking martyrdom. This creates a catch-22, in which the accused may plead guilty because they want to die to augment the effect of their violent action and incite the admiration and enhanced dedication of their fellow terrorists.

International efforts to combat terrorism increased following September 11, 2001. For the first time in the organization's history, the North Atlantic Treaty Organization (NATO) invoked Article 5 of the Washington Treaty, which states that "an armed attack against one or more of the Allies in Europe or North America shall be considered an attack against them all." U.S. allies in NATO agreed to send troops to Afghanistan to destroy Al Qaeda, but most balked when the Bush administration expanded its "war on terror" to Iraq. The few countries that initially joined the United States in Iraq have since scaled back their involvement or recalled their troops completely (see Case Study—Al Qaeda and Transnational Terrorism).

Within two weeks of the September 11, 2001, attacks, the UN Security Council adopted Resolution 1373, which requires states to suppress terrorist financing, refrain from supporting terrorist groups, deny safe haven to terrorist groups, better enforce border controls, share information about terrorist activities, and cooperate in the prosecution of terrorist crimes. However, the resolution does not label specific groups as "terrorists"; in fact, it does not even clearly define *terrorism*—individual states are left to make their own judgments.

In June 2002, the European Union adopted a Framework Decision on Combating Terrorism that instructs member states to outlaw specific terrorist activities, such as attacking people or property; kidnapping; seizing aircraft; and manufacturing nuclear, biological, and chemical weapons. Members were to harmonize their laws related to terrorism to facilitate prosecution. In 2004, the EU and the United States issued a Declaration on Combating Terrorism, which led to a reevaluation and revamping of counterterrorism policy in all EU member states. The first wave of arrests under the new laws came to trial in 2006 and 2007, signaling a concerted effort to curb terrorism threats before attacks can take place. Moscow joined with the United States to announce a Global Initiative to Combat Nuclear Terrorism in 2006 and is active in efforts to improve the security of nuclear materials.

As discussed previously, U.S. international and bilateral cooperation has been constrained by Washington's refusal to renounce the death penalty. For example, Egypt and Italy refused to hand over the suspects in the hijacking of the *Achille Lauro.* Similarly, West Germany refused to extradite Mohammed Ali Hamadi, one of the suspects in the 1985 hijacking of TWA Flight 847. Wary of the U.S. death penalty, Bonn decided instead to try him in German courts for the murder of U.S. Navy diver Robert Stethem and sentenced him to life. When Hamadi was paroled in December 2005, Germany released him to Lebanon rather than the United States.

Regional Summaries

See the map (p. 739) for a list of major terrorist attacks in 2001–2009.

Major Terrorist Attacks, March 2000–March 2009

1 New York and Arlington, Virginia
September 11, 2001
Planes crashed into the World Trade Center and the Pentagon
Approximately 3,000 dead
Linked to Al Qaeda

2 Antrim, Northern Ireland
March 7, 2009
British soldiers stationed at the Massereene army base attacked in drive-by shooting
2 killed, 4 injured
The Real Irish Republican Army

3 London, England
July 7, 2005
Four coordinated suicide bombers set off bombs in three underground trains and one double-decker bus
52 killed, over 770 injured
Linked to Al Qaeda

4 Madrid, Spain
March 11, 2004
Coordinated set of ten explosions in four commuter trains during rush hour
191 killed, over 1,800 injured
Moroccan Islamic Combatant Group (linked to Al Qaeda)

4 Madrid, Spain
December 30, 2006
Bomb exploded in parking garage at the Madrid airport
2 killed
The Basque Fatherland and Liberty movement

5 Aleg, Mauritania
December 24, 2007
Gunmen shot French tourists on a picnic near Senegal border
4 killed, 1 injured
Al Qaeda in the Islamic Magreb

6 Moscow, Russia
October 23–26, 2002
Theater siege that held 800 people hostage
129 dead (police gassing of theater may have contributed to deaths)
Chechen rebels

7 Tel Aviv, Israel
June 1, 2001
Suicide bombing of a disco
19 killed, more than 70 injured
Islamic Jihad

8 Iraq
2003-ongoing
Iraq War is followed by instability leading to repeated terrorist attacks by a range of insurgent and Islamic groups throughout the country
Approximately 26,000 civilians dead
Various insurgent and Islamic extremist groups

9 Islamabad, Pakistan
September 20, 2008
Truck filled with explosives rammed into gates of the Islamabad Marriott Hotel
Over 50 people killed
Fedayeen Islam claimed responsibility

10 Chadisinghpoora Village, near Punjab, India
March 21, 2000
Massacre of Sikh residents prior to a visit by President Bill Clinton
At least 30 killed
Lashkar-e-Tayyiba, a Muslim separatist group in Kashmir, suspected

11 Aden, Yemen
October 12, 2000
Two suicide-bombers ran a barge of explosives into the *USS Cole*
17 killed, 47 injured
Linked to Al Qaeda

12 Somalia
October 2008
Somali-American Shirwa Ahmed, who was radicalized in his hometown of Minneapolis, Minnesota, involved in suicide bombing
At least 30 killed
Al Shabab

13 Mumbai, India
November 26–29, 2008
Insurgents attacked multiple sites through coordinated bombings and shootings
Over 170 killed
Leaders in New Delhi accused Pakistan-based Lashkar-i-Taiba, a group linked to Al Qaeda

14 Kuta, Bali
October 12, 2002
Militant Islamic group attacked a nightclub
202 killed
Jemaah Islamiah

15 Mindanao, Philippines
May 2001
Kidnapping of American and Filipino tourists from Palawan Island
20 hostages taken, at least 3 beheaded
Abu Sayyaf group

Source: Material has been taken from a variety of government, print, and Internet sources, although information on all of these attacks can be found on the Web site of the Office of the Coordinator for Counterterrorism, U.S. State Department, http://www.state.gov/s/ct.
Note: This accounting is in no way exhaustive because of the contested definitions of what is or is not a terrorist attack. Even so, this list provides a glimpse of the range of motives and techniques available to terrorists, as well as of the wide array of nations that have been affected by terrorist violence.

The Americas

The Western Hemisphere has few active Islamist groups; instead active terrorist groups are homegrown, with secular orientations. The most active terror groups in the United States are the Animal Liberation Front and the Earth Liberation Front, which focus on animal rights and environmental protection. Their numerous arson attacks have cost over $100 million in property damage. Right-wing xenophobic groups have begun to reawaken thanks to the anti-immigrant movement and faltering economy. The Southern Poverty Law

Center reports 926 active hate groups in 2008, up from 602 in 2000. As the debate over Hispanic immigration increased, hate crimes against Latinos rose 40 percent between 2003 and 2007. For many members of this movement, the election of President Barack Obama is merely another example of non-whites taking over the United States. Several white supremacists have been arrested for plotting to kill Obama, and he was burned in effigy in multiple incidents following the presidential election.

Left-wing groups are still active in South America. After a wave of arrests and prosecutions in the 1990s, the Marxist group Shining Path began to revive in Peru in the early 2000s. The Peruvian government has suspended civil liberties in five regions in an effort to maintain public order. In the late 2000s, the FARC and Ejército de Liberación Nacional (ELN; National Liberation Army) continued to carry out kidnappings and drug trafficking, while many members of the Autodefensas Unidas de Colombia (AUC; United Self-Defense Forces of Colombia) have accepted government amnesty offers. The rescue of several high-profile hostages, including the 2008 rescue of former presidential candidate Ingrid Betancourt, took away from the terrorist groups vital bargaining chips.

The tri-border area of South America continues to be a principal high-level concern for counterterrorism experts. A lawless unregulated zone at the intersection of Argentina, Brazil, and Paraguay, the tri-border area has been an income-generating haven for illegal groups. Islamist groups, including Al Qaeda, Hamas, and Hezbollah, are believed to use or have used the area. Numerous incidents of drug trafficking, gun running, money laundering, smuggling, and document fraud can be traced to this area.

Regional cooperation in the Western Hemisphere focuses on efforts to disrupt the ability of terrorist groups to raise funds and recruit new members. The multilateral Inter-American Committee Against Terrorism under the Organization of American States is the largest regional counterterrorism program in the world. The U.S. government is also providing bilateral cooperation to remediate specific law enforcement weaknesses. This includes sharing air passenger data with Mexico, providing training and equipment to improve local counterterrorism capacity, and identifying weaknesses in financial surveillance and port security.

Europe

Europe faces ongoing challenges from Al Qaeda–linked Islamist groups. Germany broke up a ring of ethnic Germans and Turks preparing for widespread car-bomb attacks in 2007; the men were allegedly linked to Islamic Jihad. French nationals have been targeted by Algerian Islamists from Al Qaeda in the Islamic Maghreb. Italy has broken up Al Qaeda recruiting cells on its territory, while Islamist and Kurdish groups use the country as a logistical and financial hub. Al Qaeda reportedly wants to recapture Spain's Andalusia region, part of the Arab empire in 700–1200. Recent attacks and attempted attacks in the United Kingdom have been traced to Al Qaeda and its affiliates in Pakistan, including the 2005 London transit bombings, the foiled August 2006 plot to blow up ten airplanes in flight, and an attempted car bombing at the Glasgow airport by individuals who had failed to detonate two bombs in central London the day before.

However, these countries also face threats to people and property from domestic groups, primarily those pursuing self-determination. These include Basques (Spain and France), Corsicans (France), and Irish (United Kingdom). The Euskadi Ta Askatasuna (ETA; Basque Fatherland and Liberty) movement declared a ceasefire with Spain in 2006, but still claimed credit for bombing a parking garage at the Madrid airport in late 2006. The ETA formally renounced the cease-fire a year later. Greece also contends with November 17 (possibly regrouped as Revolutionary Struggle), a Marxist group that targets NATO-related facilities and personnel in Greece, while Italy is still discovering plots by the leftist anti-NATO Red Brigades to attack political leaders. In the United Kingdom, the St. Andrews Accord of 2006 formally ended the conflict between London and Northern Ireland. Nevertheless, a few Irish militants refused to comply and continue to stage attacks, including killing two British soldiers stationed in Northern Ireland in March 2009. Turkey, in addition to Kurdish nationalists, also hosts the Marxist-Leninist Revolutionary People's Liberation Front and the Great Eastern Islamic Raiders Front.

Money laundering is a particular problem; Islamist groups and nationalist groups, including the Liberation Tigers of Tamil Eelam and the FARC, seek to raise money from sympathizers and expatriate communities across Europe. The EU's expanding visa-free travel region, the Schengen Zone, has facilitated all travel, including that of terrorists and aspiring terrorists.

France, Germany, and the Netherlands have recently introduced economic, cultural, and social programs specifically targeting at-risk groups most likely to be cultivated by terrorists. Efforts include after-school sports, language, and cultural programs to facilitate their integration. Germany has established a consultative Islam Conference, while the Netherlands offer Dutch-language instruction to local imams.

Middle East

The Middle East remains the most complicated and intertwined region concerning the development and the activities of terrorist organizations. Al Qaeda and its affiliates have established a presence in many countries in the Middle East, but the Palestinian problem involves a different set of organizations. The region is home to two U.S.-classified state sponsors of terrorism: Iran and Syria. Finally, the lawless atmosphere of postinvasion Iraq provided terrorist groups such as Abu Musab al-Zarqawi's Al Qaeda faction in Iraq with opportunities to attack. Al-Zarqawi's followers began kidnapping foreign nationals to protest the presence of the United States and its allies in Iraq. When their demands were not met, the militants beheaded their captives and videotaped the executions to later post on the Internet.

Since the state of Israel was established in 1948, Palestinian groups have contested Israel's right to exist and called for the return of Palestinian land and the creation of a new Palestinian homeland. Currently the two main militant advocates for the Palestinians and their cause are Hamas, located in the Gaza strip, and Hezbollah, based in Lebanon. The U.S. government classifies both as foreign terrorist organizations, even though both groups have gained a measure of legitimacy through electoral successes in their respective countries. Increasingly since 2003, Hamas has fired rockets from the Gaza strip into Israeli territory, hitting Israeli targets. Although the overall damage inflicted by Hamas has been low, Israel has responded with force, entering the area to round up members, occasionally closing transit points, and launching a full-scale air and ground attack on Gaza in December 2005 and January 2006. Hezbollah forces attacked a northern Israeli military patrol from southern Lebanon in July 2006, sparking a month-long conflict during which Israel invaded Lebanon, conducting bombing raids on Beirut's international airport and further north. Both Hamas and Hezbollah receive funding and weapons from Iran. Syria had effectively controlled Lebanon since the Lebanese Civil War, but after Lebanon's Prime Minister Rafik Hariri was assassinated in 2005 and the Cedar Revolution that followed his assassination, Damascus ostensibly bowed out of its position as strongman in the country. Further, Lebanon has not made any effort to prevent Hezbollah from operating on its territory; in fact, Hezbollah continues to augment its legitimacy as a successful player in Lebanon's fractious political landscape.

Israeli officials fear that Hamas and Hezbollah could be infiltrated by militant Islamists connected to Al Qaeda. Already Al Qaeda has absorbed Algerian and Libya Islamist groups.

Counterterrorism laws in the region vary widely. Egypt and Saudi Arabia repel terrorists with their vigilant intelligence and security forces, and Libya has become a model for cooperation with the United States; in contrast, Kuwait and Yemen often ignore domestic extremist elements and have lax terrorist-financing regulations.

The U.S. invasion of Iraq in 2003 and subsequent overthrow of Saddam Hussein triggered internal competition for power in that country and a lawlessness attractive to terrorists. The homegrown Ansar Al Islam eventually allied with Al Qaeda, while regional and intersectarian rivalries led to bombings and suicide attacks. As the country's new government began to stabilize, the various domestic factions, such as the Al Mahdi militia, began to cooperate in the eradication of Al Qaeda forces.

Former Soviet Union

The fifteen countries born from the collapse of the Soviet Union have followed different trajectories on many issues, and terrorism is no different. Estonia, Latvia, and Lithuania have joined both the European Union and NATO and sent token forces to both Afghanistan and Iraq in the aftermath of the 2001 terrorist attacks in the United States. They have joined EU conventions and counterterrorism efforts, particularly focusing on money laundering and drug trafficking.

The three Caucasus states, with lax border and financial controls, are conveniently located near Iran, a U.S.-classified state sponsor of terrorism. Armenia has improved its policies to reduce money laundering, but the continued corruption within the government makes it both attractive and vulnerable to potential weapons smugglers. Armenia is near to normalizing relations with Iran, which complicates its position on many counterterrorism issues. Azerbaijan already has cultural, historical, and diplomatic ties with Iran. Georgia's ongoing conflict with Russia over the separatist regions of Abkhazia and South Ossetia creates lawless conditions that encourage illegal trafficking in radioactive materials that terrorists could use to build nuclear weapons. Georgia sent troops to both Iraq and Afghanistan in the U.S. "war on terror."

Due to their extremely long and poorly guarded frontier, the five central Asian successor states have been directly affected by Islamist insurgents and the war in Afghanistan. After a protracted civil war, Tajikistan was unable to adequately defend its border with Afghanistan and turned to Russia for help. The Islamic Movement of Uzbekistan has expanded its original goal of overthrowing the government of Uzbekistan and establishing an Islamist state to a broader one that includes anti-Western attacks across the region. A breakaway faction, the Islamic Jihad Group, harbors similar ambitions. Active across the region, Hiz but-Tahrir is a nonmilitary religious organization that seeks to establish an Islamic caliphate spanning all central Asia. However, its anti-Western, anti-Semitic pronouncements could attract militant Islamic groups interested in an alliance. These groups are already active in Kazakhstan, Tajikistan, Uzbekistan, and possibly Kyrgyzstan and Turkmenistan.

Africa

Although Africa has had fewer terrorist attacks than other regions, the chaotic atmosphere in many countries make it an attractive safe haven for terrorist groups to train, smuggle contraband, raise funds, and recruit members. Somalia, in particular, is attractive to outlaw groups, not just terrorists but also pirates who brazenly operate in its territorial waters. The U.S. Department of State has also cited Burkina Faso, the Comoros, Mali, Senegal, Tanzania, and possibly Kenya as safe havens for terrorists.

Al Qaeda maintains a presence in Somalia, and in 2006, it merged with a local organization, the Salafist Group for Preaching and Combat, under the new name Al Qaeda in the Islamic Magreb (AQIM), focusing its activities on Algeria, Mali, Mauritania, Niger, and Chad. Al Qaeda has not sponsored any major attacks in Africa since the 1998 bombings of the U.S. embassies in Kenya and Tanzania; the organizers of those bombings have never been captured and are believed to be in the Comoros. AQIM, however, killed four French tourists and attacked a military checkpoint in Mauritania in December 2007.

Although there is evidence of an emerging "Taliban in Nigeria," the government in Abuja has concentrated on protecting Western business interests. The Movement for the Emancipation of the Niger Delta (MEND) has kidnapped foreign oil workers in Nigeria, demanding that Shell and other foreign oil companies go home and allow locals to benefit from the delta region's vast oil holdings.

The Africa Union (AU) and the Trans-Sahara Counterterrorism Partnership both seek multilateral solutions to terrorist operations while improvising domestic counterterrorism capabilities. They sponsor conferences and promote coordination; in addition, the AU established the African Center for Study and Research in Terrorism in 2004. However, African counterterrorism activities are severely handicapped by financial limitations; civil wars in the Democratic Republic of Congo, Somalia, and Sudan; and weak border controls. Libyan leader Muammar Gaddafi, a former sponsor of terrorism, became AU chairman in February 2009.

South Asia

Terrorism threats in South Asia run from Afghanistan to Sri Lanka, off the tip of the subcontinent. Although Islamist groups have been the most visible in recent years, self-determination conflicts dating from the end of World War II still cause considerable bloodshed. Maoist and agrarian insurgents further complicate the situation in these countries.

The fundamentalist hard-line Islamic Taliban regime in Afghanistan provided a safe haven for Osama bin Laden and Al Qaeda in the 1990s. Plans to attack the U.S. embassies in Kenya and Tanzania, the *USS Cole,* and the World Trade Center and Washington, D.C., landmarks were launched from Afghanistan. When this connection became clear, U.S. and NATO forces invaded Afghanistan in October 2001 to eradicate bin Laden. Although the Taliban were overthrown, its defeated members along with those of Al Qaeda fled to the Afghan border regions with Pakistan. Over time, both groups recovered in size and strength and began to challenge not only the Western-backed government in Kabul but also one another, the government in Islamabad, and other militants in northwestern Pakistan.

Islamabad also faced long-standing problems with India over the partition of the country in 1947, especially the disputed Kashmir region. There is a long history of skirmishes and the occasional large-scale attack between Indian and Pakistani forces in the region over the years, as well as numerous attacks by insurgents suspected to be surreptitiously funded by various governments. The United Liberation Front of Assam, which seeks an independent Assam state, operates out of Bangladesh. In June 2009 the Indian government banned the Maoist Communist Party of India, which seeks to eradicate poverty in the country, as do the agrarian Naxalites. The governments of India, Pakistan, and Bangladesh have all sought outside assistance to improve counterterrorism activities.

As Nepal transitions from a monarchy to a republic, numerous ethnic groups are pushing for autonomy or independence. The long-standing and violent Maoist Communist Party of Nepal briefly entered the transitional government, but continued to violate the fragile peace process. It was excluded from the new government and resumed its practice of terrorizing villages and extorting urban groups.

The Sri Lankan military defeated the Tamil Tiger separatist movement in 2009, but peace is not a given. The separatist conflict has halted several times only to later revive, as occurred following the 2002 cease-fire agreement. For nearly thirty years, the Liberation Tigers of Tamil Eelam carried out a bloody campaign targeting civilians, as well as government officials, usually with suicide bombers. The group, designated by the U.S. government as a foreign terrorist organization, has also been condemned for recruiting child soldiers and for forced conscription.

East Asia and Pacific

Although East Asia and the Pacific have few homegrown terrorist groups, the region provides many attractive opportunities for money laundering and smuggling that support terrorist activities. Domestic terrorist groups in the region have long targeted popular tourist sites, hoping to damage the economy in the process.

In October 2002, Jemaah Islamiah, a militant Islamic group, attacked a nightclub in Kuta on the Indonesian island of Bali, killing 202 people, primarily foreign tourists. The following year, foreign tourism to Indonesia dropped by 48 percent. The government subsequently launched a major crackdown on Jemaah Islamiah, raiding its hideouts and prosecuting its members.

The Philippines face a variety of terrorist threats. The main groups are Abu Sayyaf (a militant Islamic group seeking an independent Islamic state in Muslim-populated areas of the southern Philippines) and the Communist Party of the Philippines/New People's Army, as well as the Indonesian group Jemaah Islamiya.

The dispersed nature of the many archipelagos in the region has both hampered regional cooperation and created de facto safe havens, but Australia and Japan have been at the forefront of efforts to improve multilateral coordination. Australia sponsors numerous conferences, collaborative projects, and joint military maneuvers, while Japan has funded efforts to increase counterterrorism capacities. Drawing on the lessons of the 1995 Aum Shinrikyo sarin subway attack, Tokyo also continued to improve Japan's domestic response capabilities, especially those related to chemical and biological weapons. The government continues to monitor Aum Shinrikyo, now Aelph, and the perpetrators of the attack remain on death row.

The xenophobia and secrecy surrounding Burma (Myanmar) presumably make it an attractive safe haven. Cambodia, in contrast, has been enthusiastic in its alliance with the U.S. "war on terror," but does not have sufficient funds or personnel to make a significant contribution. It is working to create a legal foundation for its efforts. China's cross-border trade and cash-based economy encourages money laundering, but Beijing is working to crack down on these efforts. Although the government faces a genuine separatist movement in Xinjiang province, critics say terrorism charges are often invented as a pretext for repression.

Data

Table 1   Number of Terrorist Attacks Worldwide, 1982–2008

Year	Number
1982	500
1983	506
1984	565
1985	635
1986	612
1987	665
1988	605
1989	375
1990	437
1991	565
1992	363
1993	431
1994	332
1995	440
1996	296
1997	304
1998	274
1999	395
2000	426
2001	355
2002	205
2003	208
2004	651
2005	11,157
2006	14,545
2007	14,506
2008	11,770

Sources: U.S. Department of State, Office of the Coordinator for Counterterrorism, "Country Reports on Terrorism and Patterns of Global Terrorism," Washington, D.C., 1982–2003; U.S. Department of State, National Counterterrorism Center, Worldwide Incidents Tracking System, "NCTC Report on Terrorism," available at http://wits.nctc.gov/Reports.do.

Table 2   Terrorist Attacks by Region, 1998–2008

	1998	1999	2000	2001	2002	2003
Africa	21	53	55	33	6	6
Asia	49	72	98	68	101	80
Eurasia	14	35	31	3	8	2
Latin America	111	122	192	201	46	20
Middle East	31	26	20	29	35	67
North America	0	2	0	4	0	0
Western Europe	48	85	30	17	9	33
Total	274	395	426	355	205	208

Table 2 (Continued)

	2004	2005	2006	2007	2008
Africa		253	422	835	718
East Asia and Pacific		1,007	1,036	1,429	978
Europe and Eurasia		780	659	606	774
Near East		4,230	7,755	7,540	4,594
South Asia		3,974	3,654	3,607	4,354
Western Hemisphere		867	826	482	352
Total		11,111	14,352	14,499	11,770

Sources: U.S. Department of State, Office of the Coordinator for Counterterrorism, "Country Reports on Terrorism and Patterns of Global Terrorism," Washington, D.C., 1982–2003; U.S. Department of State, National Counterterrorism Center, Worldwide Incidents Tracking System, "NCTC Report on Terrorism," available at http://wits.nctc.gov/Reports.do.

Note to all tables: Statistics for terrorism are notoriously difficult to interpret. Because there is no one universal definition of *terrorism,* counts can be manipulated by categorizing some incidents as terrorism and others as not. It becomes particularly difficult in the years after the wars in Iraq and Afghanistan began because whether an incident is an act of terrorism or an act of war is subjective. Totals in the regional breakdown in Table 2 do not necessarily match the totals shown in Table 1 on page 746.

The big increase after 2004 shown in these tables resulted from a change in the methodology used by the U.S. State Department. The increase, in fact, prompted the State Department to initially omit the statistical portion of the report. That prompted an outcry, and the Department of State eventually released the numbers, but admitted that the data could be misleading. Newly released numbers for 2004 are not shown here.

Case Study—Al Qaeda and Transnational Terrorism

The U.S. and NATO invasion of Afghanistan in October 2001 overthrew the Taliban government, which had allowed Al Qaeda to operate within its borders for years. Osama bin Laden and his fighters fled to the Tora Bora caves along the mountainous Afghanistan–Pakistan border. In the ensuing years, the Taliban regrouped and began fighting its way back to Kabul, and Al Qaeda turned the border region into a hub of terrorist activity that threatened to destabilize Pakistan, India, and Afghanistan.

With poorly defined borders, inadequate border patrols, and a legacy of religious and ethnic tension, the region may surpass the Middle East as a breeding ground for terrorist activities. Weak political systems, regional warlords, difficult-to-identify operatives, and scant regional cooperation further complicate peace efforts.

Since 2006, while pursuing suspected terrorists, CIA drones have frequently crossed into Pakistani territory and fired missiles without permission from the Pakistani government. The air strikes have killed almost half of Al Qaeda's top leadership and Taliban commanders such as Mullah Abdul Karim but also many civilians. Washington justified its actions by accusing Islamabad of failing to protect its population by not working to halt such insurgencies or eradicate Taliban safe havens. At the same time, U.S. and NATO forces in Afghanistan are driving the Taliban deeper into Pakistani territory, where they have begun to attack NATO supply convoys headed for Afghanistan via the Khyber Pass. The fighters have recruited local Islamists into a Pakistani Taliban that cooperates with its Afghan counterpart. Afghan officials, in turn, have accused Pakistan's Inter-Service Intelligence Agency of aiding the Taliban in its campaign against Kabul. Starting in April 2009, however, the Pakistani military moved against the Taliban in the Swat Valley in western Pakistan, after the Taliban failed to live up to the terms of a peace deal granting it control of the region; as of August 2009, the military's success in truly defeating the Taliban in the area cannot be ascertained.

Increasingly attacks within Pakistan bear the hallmarks of Al Qaeda. On September 20, 2008, for example, a truck laden with explosives slammed into the gates of the Islamabad Marriott and detonated. As people fled the hotel, a second, more powerful explosion erupted, killing more than fifty people and destroying the landmark hotel popular with foreigners. Pakistani citizens blamed the government and its support for the U.S.-led war in Afghanistan. Although a new group, Fedayeen Islam, claimed responsibility, other Pakistanis accused their own intelligence services of facilitating the attack to destabilize an unpopular government.

Pakistan now faces the risk of a two-front war: with the Taliban in the north and with India in the south. Taliban insurgents seized part of Pakistan's North West Frontier Province and Federally Administered Tribal Areas, where they have carried out raids, bombed facilities, and kidnapped or killed officials. Peshawar has become a particularly dangerous city for foreigners, with U.S., Chinese, Afghan, and Iranian nationals targeted.

When insurgents attacked multiple sites in Mumbai, India, on November 26, 2008, Indian officials and citizens were quick to blame Pakistan. Leaders in New Delhi accused the Pakistan-based Lashkar-i-Taiba (Army of the Righteous) of staging the three-day assault that killed over 170 people. However, the attack may have been staged, or at least backed, by Al Qaeda to fuel the long-simmering tensions between India and Pakistan. For almost a decade, Lashkar-i-Taiba has fought Indian forces in the disputed Kashmir region, and in December 2001 members seized the Indian parliamentary building. As New Delhi and Islamabad traded accusations over the Mumbai attacks, both countries sent troops toward their shared border; Pakistan had to draw on its troops stationed along the Afghan border and send them south.

The developments around Pakistan mirror Al Qaeda tactics elsewhere—exploiting local fighters to further their own cause. The organization is swiftly expanding its global reach, as homegrown terrorist movements seek to join the better-known organization. Abu Musab al-Zarqawi's Ansar Al Islam in Iraq evolved into Al Qaeda in Iraq, Algeria's Salafist Group for Preaching and Combat became AQIM, and Libya's Islamic Fighting Group merged with Al Qaeda in late 2007. Germany, France, the Netherlands, and Saudi Arabia have begun educational programs to better integrate disaffected immigrant populations, with the goal of steering them away from radical forms of Islam and stemming Al Qaeda's continued expansion.

Biographical Sketches

Mia Bloom, author of *Dying to Kill: The Allure of Suicide Terror* (2005) examines the history of suicide terrorism and argues that the tactic often backfires because it inevitably generates a harsh response from the target population. The book includes a section on the increasing role of women as suicide bombers.

Richard Clarke was the first White House counterterrorism chief, serving during the Bill Clinton administration and in the early part of George W. Bush's term. In *Against All Enemies: Inside America's War on Terror* (2004), Clarke claims that the incoming Bush administration was not only ill-informed but uninterested in his warnings of the threat from Al Qaeda.

Bruce Hoffman is perhaps the most-often quoted expert on terrorism today. After leading the Center for the Study of Terrorism and Political Violence, based in Scotland, and the RAND think tank's program on terrorism, he joined Georgetown University in 2006. The original 1998 version of his best-known work, *Inside Terrorism,* was a standard text for students of terrorism because of its clear writing, thorough history of the causes of terrorism, and vivid descriptions of groups and incidents. The new edition has been updated to include the September 11, 2001, attacks.

Walter Laqueur, the preeminent U.S. historian of terrorism, has long called attention to the inherent problems related to defining the meaning of *terrorism*—not only the problem of finding a legal definition acceptable to all countries but the newer problem of political correctness and media outlets that do not want to use the inflammatory label *terrorist.* In his 2004 book *No End to War: Terrorism in the 21st Century* he warns that the escalating violence of terrorism in the twenty-first century will continue to produce higher and higher body counts.

Brigitte L. Nacos studies the nexus between terrorism and the media, and she led a landmark study focusing on the romanticized image of female terrorists in the media, illuminating and categorizing the most common stereotypes. She has published *Terrorism and the Media: From the Iran Hostage Crisis to the Oklahoma City Bombing* (1996), *Mass-Mediated Terrorism: The Central Role of the Media in Terrorism and Counterterrorism* (2002), and *Terrorism and Counterterrorism: Understanding Threats and Responses in the Post-9/11 World* (2005).

Marc Sageman, a professor of psychiatry and former CIA operative who worked along Afghanistan's border with Pakistan, provides a sociopsychological profile of terrorists, specifically members of Al Qaeda. In *Understanding Terror Networks* (2004), he shows that with Islamic fundamentalists terror networks often begin with ordinary friendships among alienated individuals. As friends discuss their grievances, their anger increases, eventually fueling them to action.

Michael Scheuer spent twenty-two years as a CIA analyst and created the unit responsible for tracking Osama bin Laden. His book *Imperial Hubris: Why the West Is Losing the War on Terror* (2007) criticizes the Bush administration's Iraq policy. The book was published anonymously, but it is believed to have had CIA authorization, making it an agency indictment of the White House. His latest book, *Marching Toward Hell: America and Islam after Iraq* (2008), appeared under his own name.

Jessica Eve Stern served as director for Russian, Ukrainian, and Eurasian Affairs at the National Security Council (1994–1995) and has frequently testified on the proliferation of WMD among terrorist groups. More recently, she has turned her attention to the link between religion and terrorism. In *Terror in the Name of God: Why Religious Militants Kill* (2003), she draws on interviews with numerous terrorists to explain how they reconcile murder and serving God. Unlike most studies of religion and terrorism, Stern moves beyond Islamic fundamentalism to include hard-line Israeli attacks and right-wing American movements.

Directory

Centre for the Study of Terrorism and Political Violence, School of International Relations, University of St. Andrews, New Arts Building, Library Park, The Scores, St. Andrews, Fife, KY16 9AX, United Kingdom. Telephone: +44 (0) 1334 462935; email: gm39@st-andrews.ac.uk; Web: http://www.st-and.ac.uk/academic/intrel/research/cstpv.
Independent research institution based at St. Andrews University that focuses on causes of terrorism, maintains a database of terrorist groups and incidents, and grants degrees in terrorism studies.

Combating Terrorism Center at West Point, Lincoln Hall, West Point, N.Y. 10996. Telephone: (845) 938-8495; email: james.taylor@usma.edu; Web: http://www.ctc.usma.edu.
Research and curriculum development center focusing on terrorism, counterterrorism, homeland security, and WMD.

Department of State, Office of the Coordinator for Counterterrorism, 2201 C Street NW, Washington, D.C. 20520. Web: http://www.state.gov/s/ct.
Central clearinghouse for U.S. information on terrorist activities; publishes annual "Country Reports on Terrorism" and maintains official lists of terrorist organizations and state sponsors of terrorism.

International Institute for Counter-Terrorism, Interdisciplinary Center Herzlia, P.O. Box 167, Herzlia, 46150, Israel. Telephone: 972-9-9527277; Web: http://www.ict.org.il.
Research institute and think tank dedicated to developing innovative public policy solutions to international terrorism.

National Consortium for the Study of Terrorism and Responses to Terrorism (START), 3300 Symons Hall, University of Maryland, College Park, Md. 20742. Telephone: (301) 405-6600; email: infostart@start.umd.edu; Web: www.start.umd.edu.
Organization sponsored by the Department of Homeland Security that aims to provide timely guidance on how to disrupt terrorist networks, reduce the incidence of terrorism, and enhance the resilience of U.S. society in the face of the terrorist threat; hosts the Global Terrorism Database.

Memorial Institute for the Prevention of Terrorism, P.O. Box 889, 621 North Robinson, 4th Floor, Oklahoma City, Okla. 73101. Telephone: 405-278-6300; email: webmaster@mipt.org; Web: http://www.mipt.org.
Nonprofit organization dedicated to preventing terrorism or mitigating its effects and especially focusing on improving the skills of first responders.

Terrorism Research Center, Va. Telephone: (877) 635-0816; email: TRC@terrorism. com; Web: http://www.terrorism.com.

Independent institute dedicated to research on terrorism, information warfare and security, critical infrastructure protection, homeland security, and other issues of low-intensity political violence and gray-area phenomena; Web site includes a continuously updated list of terrorist incidents.

Further Research

Books

Bloom, Mia. *Dying to Kill: The Allure of Suicide Terror.* New York: Columbia University Press, 2005.

Cassese, Antonio. *Terrorism, Politics and Law: The Achille Lauro Affair.* Princeton, N.J.: Princeton University Press, 1989.

Clarke, Richard A. *Against All Enemies: Inside America's War on Terror.* New York: Free Press, 2004.

Coll, Steve. *Ghost Wars: The Secret History of the CIA, Afghanistan and Bin Laden, from the Soviet Invasion to September 10, 2001.* New York: Penguin, 2004.

Gambetta, Diego, ed. *Making Sense of Suicide Missions.* New York: Oxford University Press, 2005.

Hoffman, Bruce. *Inside Terrorism.* 2nd ed. New York: Columbia University Press, 2006.

Jurgensmeyer, Mark. *Terror in the Mind of God: The Global Rise of Religious Violence.* 3rd ed. Los Angeles: University of California Press, 2003.

Laqueur, Walter. *No End to War: Terrorism in the 21st Century.* New York: Continuum, 2004.

Napoleoni, Loretta. *Terror Incorporated: Tracing the Dollars behind the Terror Networks.* New York: Seven Stories Press, 2005.

Pape, Robert A. *Dying to Win: The Strategic Logic of Suicide Terrorism.* New York: Random House, 2005.

Reich, Walter, ed. *Origins of Terrorism: Psychologies, Ideologies, Theologies, States of Mind.* Washington, D.C.: Woodrow Wilson Center Press, 1998.

Robertson, Ann E. *Terrorism and Global Security.* New York: Facts on File, 2007.

Sageman, Marc. *Understanding Terror Networks.* Philadelphia: University of Pennsylvania Press, 2004.

Scheuer, Michael. [Published anonymously.] *Imperial Hubris: Why the West Is Loosing the War on Terror.* Dulles, Va.: Potomac Books, 2007.

————. *Marching Toward Hell: America and Islam after Iraq.* New York: Free Press, 2008.

Stern, Jessica. *Terror in the Name of God: Why Religious Militants Kill.* New York: Harper Collins, 2003.

Articles and Reports

Doyle, Charles. "The USA Patriot Act: A Sketch." *CRS Report for Congress.* Congressional Research Service, 2002. Available at http://www.fas.org/irp/crs/RS21203.pdf.

————. "The USA Patriot Act Sunset: A Sketch." *CRS Report for Congress.* Congressional Research Service, 2004. Available at http://www.fas.org/irp/crs/RS21704.pdf.

Hassan, Nasra. "An Arsenal of Believers: Talking to the 'Human Bombs.'" *New Yorker,* November 19, 2001. Available at http://www.bintjbeil.com/articles/en/011119_hassan.html.

Krueger, Alan B., and Jitka Maleckova. "Does Poverty Cause Terrorism?: The Economics and Education of Suicide Bombers." *New Republic,* June 24, 2002, 27–33.

Laqueur, Walter. "We Can't Define 'Terrorism,' but We Can Fight It." *Wall Street Journal,* July 15, 2002, A12.

Long, David E. "Coming to Grips with Terrorism after 11 September." *Brown Journal of World Affairs* 8, no. 2 (2002): 37–42.

National Commission on Terrorist Attacks upon the United States. *The 9/11 Commission Report: Final Report of the National Commission on Terrorist Attacks upon the United States.* New York: W. W. Norton, 2004.

Pitcavage, Mark. "Every Man a King: The Rise and Fall of the Montana Freeman." *ADL Militia Watchdog* (1996). Available at http://www.adl.org/mwd/freemen.asp.

Rapoport, David C. "Fear and Trembling: Terrorism in Three Religious Traditions." *American Political Science Review* 78, no. 3 (1984): 658–677.

Saul, Ben. "Definition of 'Terrorism' in the UN Security Council: 1985–2004." *Chinese Journal of International Law* 4, no. 1 (2005): 141–166.

Southern Poverty Law Center. "The Rise and Decline of the 'Patriots.'" *Intelligence Report* (summer 2001). Available at http://www.splcenter.org/intel/intelreport/article.jsp?aid=195.

Web Sites

Anti-Defamation League
http://www.adl.org

Center for Defense Information
http://www.cdi.org

Constitutional Rights Foundation
http://www.crf-usa.org/terror/terrorism_links

Council on Foreign Relations
http://www.cfr.org/issue/135/terrorism.html

Federation of American Scientists Intelligence Resource Program
http://fas.org/irp/index.html

Global Security
http://www.globalsecurity.org

Global Terrorism Database
http://www.start.umd.edu/data/gtd

Jamestown Foundation
http://www.Jamestown.org

Knox Dudley Library, Naval Postgraduate School, U.S. Navy
http://library.nps.navy.mil/home/terrorism.htm

Library of Congress, September 11, 2001, Documentary Project
http://memory.loc.gov/ammem/collections/911_archive/index.html

National Counterterrorism Center
http://www.nctc.gov

RAND Corporation
http://www.rand.org/publications/electronic/terrorism.html

Rick A. Ross Institute for the Study of Destructive Cults, Controversial Groups, and Movements
http://www.rickross.com

September 11 News
http://www.september11news.com

Southern Poverty Law Center
http://www.splcenter.org/intel/intpro.jsp

Terrorism Files
http://www.terrorismfiles.org

Terrorism Research Center
http://www.terrorism.com

United States Institute of Peace
http://www.usip.org/library/topics/terrorism.html#docs

U.S. Department of State, Counterterrorism Office
http://www.state.gov/s/ct/rls/crt

Documents

1. Excerpt from Fact Sheet: Foreign Terrorist Organizations (FTOs)

U.S. Department of State, Office of Counterterrorism, April 8, 2008

The full text is available at http://2001-2009.state.gov/s/ct/rls/fs/08/103392.htm.

Extract

Foreign Terrorist Organizations (FTOs) are foreign organizations that are designated by the Secretary of State in accordance with section 219 of the Immigration and Nationality Act (INA), as amended. FTO designations play a critical role in our fight against terrorism and are an effective means of curtailing support for terrorist activities and pressuring groups to get out of the terrorism business. . . .

Identification

The Office of the Coordinator for Counterterrorism in the State Department (S/CT) continually monitors the activities of terrorist groups active around the world to identify potential targets for designation. When reviewing potential targets, S/CT looks not only at the actual terrorist attacks that a group has carried out, but also at whether the group has engaged in planning and preparations for possible future acts of terrorism or retains the capability and intent to carry out such acts.

Designation

Once a target is identified, S/CT prepares a detailed "administrative record," which is a compilation of information, typically including both classified and open sources information, demonstrating that the statutory criteria for designation have been satisfied. If the Secretary of State, in consultation with the Attorney General and the Secretary of the Treasury, decides to make the designation, Congress is notified of the Secretary's intent to designate the organization and given seven days to review the designation, as the INA requires. Upon the expiration of the seven-day waiting period and in the absence of Congressional action to block the designation, notice of the designation is published in the *Federal Register,* at which point the designation takes effect. By law an organization designated as an FTO may seek judicial review of the designation in the United States Court of Appeals for the District of Columbia Circuit not later than 30 days after the designation is published in the *Federal Register.*

Until recently the INA provided that FTOs must be redesignated every 2 years or the designation would lapse. Under the Intelligence Reform and Terrorism Prevention Act of 2004 (IRTPA), however, the redesignation requirement was replaced by certain review and revocation procedures. IRTPA provides that an FTO may file a petition for revocation 2 years after its designation date (or in the case of redesignated FTOs, its most recent redesignation date) or 2 years after the determination date on its most recent petition for revocation. In order to provide a basis for revocation, the petitioning FTO must provide evidence that the circumstances forming the basis for the designation are sufficiently different as to warrant revocation. If no such review has been conducted during a 5 year period with respect to a designation, then the Secretary of State is required to review the designation to determine whether revocation would be appropriate. In addition, the Secretary of State may at any time revoke a designation upon a finding that the circumstances forming the basis for the designation have changed in such a manner as to warrant revocation, or that the national security of the United States warrants a revocation. The same procedural requirements apply to revocations made by the Secretary of State as apply to designations. A designation may be revoked by an Act of Congress, or set aside by a Court order.

Legal Criteria for Designation under Section 219 of the INA as amended

1. It must be a *foreign organization.*

2. The organization must *engage in terrorist activity,* as defined in section 212 (a)(3) (B) of the INA (8 U.S.C. § 1182(a)(3)(B)), or *terrorism,* as defined in section 140(d)(2) of the Foreign Relations Authorization Act, Fiscal Years 1988 and 1989 (22 U.S.C. § 2656f(d)(2)), *or retain the capability and intent to engage in terrorist activity or terrorism.*

3. The organization's terrorist activity or terrorism must threaten the security of U.S. nationals *or* the national security (national defense, foreign relations, *or* the economic interests) of the United States.

Legal Ramifications of Designation

1. It is unlawful for a person in the United States or subject to the jurisdiction of the United States to knowingly provide "material support or resources" to a designated FTO. (The term "material support or resources" is defined in 18 U.S.C. § 2339A(b)(1) as "any property, tangible or intangible, or service, including currency

or monetary instruments or financial securities, financial services, lodging, training, expert advice or assistance, safehouses, false documentation or identification, communications equipment, facilities, weapons, lethal substances, explosives, personnel (1 or more individuals who maybe or include oneself), and transportation, except medicine or religious materials." 18 U.S.C. § 2339A(b)(2) provides that for these purposes "the term 'training' means instruction or teaching designed to impart a specific skill, as opposed to general knowledge." 18 U.S.C. § 2339A(b)(3) further provides that for these purposes "the term 'expert advice or assistance' means advice or assistance derived from scientific, technical or other specialized knowledge."

2. Representatives and members of a designated FTO, if they are aliens, are inadmissible to and, in certain circumstances, removable from the United States (see 8 U.S.C. §§ 1182 (a)(3)(B)(i)(IV)–(V), 1227 (a)(1)(A)).

3. Any U.S. financial institution that becomes aware that it has possession of or control over funds in which a designated FTO or its agent has an interest must retain possession of or control over the funds and report the funds to the Office of Foreign Assets Control of the U.S. Department of the Treasury.

2. Presidential Military Order on Detention, Treatment, and Trial of Certain Non-Citizens in the War Against Terrorism

White House Press Release, November 13, 2001

The full text is available from the American Presidency Project online at http://www.presidency .ucsb.edu/ws/?pid=63124.

Extracts

By the authority vested in me as President and as Commander in Chief of the Armed Forces of the United States by the Constitution and the laws of the United States of America, including the Authorization for Use of Military Force Joint Resolution (Public Law 107-40, 115 Stat. 224) and sections 821 and 836 of title 10, United States Code, it is hereby ordered as follows:

Section 1. Findings

(a) International terrorists, including members of al Qaida, have carried out attacks on United States diplomatic and military personnel and facilities abroad and on citizens and property within the United States on a scale that has created a state of armed conflict that requires the use of the United States Armed Forces.

(b) In light of grave acts of terrorism and threats of terrorism, including the terrorist attacks on September 11, 2001, on the headquarters of the United States Department of Defense in the national capital region, on the World Trade Center in New York, and on civilian aircraft such as in Pennsylvania, I proclaimed a national emergency on September 14, 2001 (Proc. 7463, Declaration of National Emergency by Reason of Certain Terrorist Attacks).

(c) Individuals acting alone and in concert involved in international terrorism possess both the capability and the intention to undertake further terrorist attacks against the United States that, if not detected and prevented, will cause mass deaths, mass injuries, and massive destruction of property, and may place at risk the continuity of the operations of the United States Government.

(d) The ability of the United States to protect the United States and its citizens, and to help its allies and other cooperating nations protect their nations and their citizens, from such further terrorist attacks depends in significant part upon using the United States Armed Forces to identify terrorists and those who support them, to disrupt their activities, and to eliminate their ability to conduct or support such attacks.

(e) To protect the United States and its citizens, and for the effective conduct of military operations and prevention of terrorist attacks, it is necessary for individuals subject to this order pursuant to section 2 hereof to be detained, and, when tried, to be tried for violations of the laws of war and other applicable laws by military tribunals.

(f) Given the danger to the safety of the United States and the nature of international terrorism, and to the extent provided by and under this order, I find consistent with section 836 of title 10, United States Code, that it is not practicable to apply in military commissions under this order the principles of law and the rules of evidence generally recognized in the trial of criminal cases in the United States district courts.

(g) Having fully considered the magnitude of the potential deaths, injuries, and property destruction that would result from potential acts of terrorism against the United States, and the probability that such acts will occur, I have determined that an extraordinary emergency exists for national defense purposes, that this emergency constitutes an urgent and compelling government interest, and that issuance of this order is necessary to meet the emergency.

Section 2. Definition and Policy

(a) The term "individual subject to this order" shall mean any individual who is not a United States citizen with respect to whom I determine from time to time in writing that:

(1) there is reason to believe that such individual, at the relevant times,

(i) is or was a member of the organization known as al Qaida; (ii) has engaged in, aided or abetted, or conspired to commit, acts of international terrorism, or acts in preparation therefor [sic], that have caused, threaten to cause, or have as their aim to cause, injury to or adverse effects on the United States, its citizens, national security, foreign policy, or economy; or (iii) has knowingly harbored one or more individuals described in subparagraphs (i) or (ii) of subsection 2(a)(1) of this order;

and

(2) it is in the interest of the United States that such individual be subject to this order.

(b) It is the policy of the United States that the Secretary of Defense shall take all necessary measures to ensure that any individual subject to this order is detained in accordance with section 3, and, if the individual is to be tried, that such individual is tried only in accordance with section 4.

(c) It is further the policy of the United States that any individual subject to this order who is not already under the control of the Secretary of Defense but who is under the control of any other officer or agent of the United States or any State shall, upon delivery of a copy of such written determination to such officer or agent, forthwith be placed under the control of the Secretary of Defense.

Section 3. Detention Authority of the Secretary of Defense

Any individual subject to this order shall be—

(a) detained at an appropriate location designated by the Secretary of Defense outside or within the United States;

(b) treated humanely, without any adverse distinction based on race, color, religion, gender, birth, wealth, or any similar criteria;

(c) afforded adequate food, drinking water, shelter, clothing, and medical treatment;

(d) allowed the free exercise of religion consistent with the requirements of such detention; and

(e) detained in accordance with such other conditions as the Secretary of Defense may prescribe.

Section 4. Authority of the Secretary of Defense Regarding Trials of Individuals Subject to this Order

(a) Any individual subject to this order shall, when tried, be tried by military commission for any and all offenses triable by military commission that such individual is alleged to have committed, and may be punished in accordance with the penalties provided under applicable law, including life imprisonment or death.

(b) As a military function and in light of the findings in section 1, including subsection (f) thereof, the Secretary of Defense shall issue such orders and regulations, including orders for the appointment of one or more military commissions, as may be necessary to carry out subsection (a) of this section.

(c) Orders and regulations issued under subsection (b) of this section shall include, but not be limited to, rules for the conduct of the proceedings of military commissions, including pretrial, trial, and post-trial procedures, modes of proof, issuance of process, and qualifications of attorneys, . . .

GEORGE W. BUSH

THE WHITE HOUSE

November 13, 2001

3. United Nations Security Council Press Release SC/7158

United Nations Security Council, September 28, 2001

The full text is available at http://www.un.org/News/Press/docs/2001/sc7158.doc.htm.

Extracts

Security Council

4385th Meeting (Night)

- SECURITY COUNCIL UNANIMOUSLY ADOPTS WIDE-RANGING ANTI-TERRORISM RESOLUTION;

- CALLS FOR SUPPRESSING FINANCING, IMPROVING INTERNA-
  TIONAL COOPERATION
- Resolution 1373 (2001) Also Creates Committee to Monitor Implementation

Reaffirming its unequivocal condemnation of the terrorist acts that took place in New York, Washington, D.C., and Pennsylvania on 11 September, the Security Council this evening unanimously adopted a wide-ranging, comprehensive resolution with steps and strategies to combat international terrorism.

By resolution 1373 (2001) the Council also established a Committee of the Council to monitor the resolution's implementation and called on all States to report on actions they had taken to that end no later than 90 days from today.

Under terms of the text, the Council decided that all States should prevent and suppress the financing of terrorism, as well as criminalize the wilful [sic] provision or collection of funds for such acts. The funds, financial assets and economic resources of those who commit or attempt to commit terrorist acts or participate in or facilitate the commission of terrorist acts and of persons and entities acting on behalf of terrorists should also be frozen without delay.

The Council also decided that States should prohibit their nationals or persons or entities in their territories from making funds, financial assets, economic resources, financial or other related services available to persons who commit or attempt to commit, facilitate or participate in the commission of terrorist acts. States should also refrain from providing any form of support to entities or persons involved in terrorist acts; take the necessary steps to prevent the commission of terrorist acts; deny safe haven to those who finance, plan, support, commit terrorist acts and provide safe havens as well.

By other terms, the Council decided that all States should prevent those who finance, plan, facilitate or commit terrorist acts from using their respective territories for those purposes against other countries and their citizens. States should also ensure that anyone who has participated in the financing, planning, preparation or perpetration of terrorist acts or in supporting terrorist acts is brought to justice. They should also ensure that terrorist acts are established as serious criminal offences in domestic laws and regulations and that the seriousness of such acts is duly reflected in sentences served.

By further terms, the Council decided that States should afford one another the greatest measure of assistance for criminal investigations or criminal proceedings relating to the financing or support of terrorist acts. States should also prevent the movement of terrorists or their groups by effective border controls as well.

Also by the text, the Council called on all States to intensify and accelerate the exchange of information regarding terrorist actions or movements; forged or falsified documents; traffic in arms and sensitive material; use of communications and technologies by terrorist groups; and the threat posed by the possession of weapons of mass destruction.

States were also called on to exchange information and cooperate to prevent and suppress terrorist acts and to take action against the perpetrators of such acts. States should become parties to, and fully implement as soon as possible, the relevant international conventions and protocols to combat terrorism.

By the text, before granting refugee status, all States should take appropriate measures to ensure that the asylum seekers had not planned, facilitated or participated in terrorist acts. Further, States should ensure that refugee status was not abused by the perpetrators, organizers or facilitators of terrorist acts, and that claims of political motivation were not recognized as grounds for refusing requests for the extradition of alleged terrorists.

The Council noted with concern the close connection between international terrorism and transnational organized crime, illicit drugs, money laundering and illegal movement of nuclear, chemical, biological and other deadly materials. In that regard, it emphasized the need to enhance the coordination of national, subregional, regional and international efforts to strengthen a global response to that threat to international security.

Reaffirming the need to combat by all means, in accordance with the Charter, threats to international peace and security caused by terrorist acts, the Council expressed its determination to take all necessary steps to fully implement the current resolution.

INDEX

Tables and figures are indicated by t and f after page numbers.